P E A C H P I T ' S **P A G E M A K E R 5** C O M P A N I O N

Robin Williams

with

Barbara Sikora *and*

Vicki Calkins

Peachpit Press
Berkeley ▾ California

What others have said about books by Robin Williams

The Little Mac Book

The Little Mac Book may well be the best book ever written about the Macintosh
—LAWRENCE I. CHARTERS, *RESOURCES*

If I had it to do over again, and I just bought a Macintosh, this book would be my most important purchase, next to the Mac itself.
—PHILIP C. RUSSELL, *MOUSE DROPPINGS*

I would suggest that Apple Computer purchase the rights to this book and package it, labeled "Open Me First," with every purchase of a new Mac.
—JIM CAREY, *THE MACPAC PRINTOUT*

Read it even if you never read a manual.
—LON POOLE, *MACWORLD MAGAZINE*

Simply one of the best books ever written on the basic elements of the Macintosh.
—BILL DRENNEN, *VMEG CONNECTION*

Read her first. There is no better introduction to the Mac than *The Little Mac Book.*
—BOB LEVITUS, *MACUSER MAGAZINE*

The Mac is not a typewriter

Buy this book, read it, follow its advice. Rarely have I been as impressed with a book as I am with this one.
—JERRY WHITING, *ALDUS MAGAZINE*

A great little book for novice and expert alike.
—*MACUSER MAGAZINE*

This book should be required reading for every newly-dubbed desktop publisher, regardless of hardware platform.
—C.J. METCHSKE, *FROM THE DESKTOP*

If you create pages on the Mac, you need this book!
—*BMUG NEWSLETTER*

The Mac is not a typewriter should be required reading for every writer and designer who uses the Mac. It covers everything you need to know to turn out professional-looking documents.
—*MACUSER MAGAZINE*

Wow! What a superlative book! This is the most useful Mac book I've come across in a long time.
—WILI SCHER-GRODNER, *MAC STREET JOURNAL*

PageMaker 4: An Easy Desk Reference

So what is the best PageMaker book? It's the best computer book on any subject, one that could close down Aldus tech support, and remove the need for PageMaker courses. It's *PageMaker 4: An Easy Desk Reference,* by Robin Williams.
—DAVID FIELD, *BOSTON COMPUTER SOCIETY*

This book is an incredible reference work. Aldus should include a coupon towards the purchase of this book with every program sold.
—JEAN MICKELSON, *MAD MAC NEWS*

What a great way to reference! I love it . . . so much clarity and accessibility. Above all, one must keep in mind that this is not an instructional manual; it is a reference manual that is interesting and alluring.
—*COLUMBIA APPLE PI*

. . . by the incomparable Robin Williams. This is undoubtedly the best $29.95 value on the computer bookshelf.
—HOWARD GOLDSTEIN, *MICRO PUBLISHING NEWS*

Tabs & Indents on the Mac

In a few concise pages, Williams reveals the mysteries . . . . Anyone who uses a Macintosh word processing application will benefit from the hands-on exercises and clear advice in *Tabs & Indents on the Macintosh.*
—SAM McMILLAN, *COMMUNICATION ARTS DESIGN ANNUAL*

Like all Robin Williams' books, this one is a pleasure to read. The text is friendly and addresses you like a person.
—PHIL RUSSELL, *MOUSE DROPPINGS*

Easy to use, and well-documented with screen shots. It is well worth the financial and time investment.
—DARRYL GORDON, *SAN DIEGO COMPUTER JOURNAL*

In the world of computer books, Robin Williams already occupies the pinnacle of excellence. This little 64-page book is her best effort yet. Get this book.
—ROGER LEVIT, *MACCOUNTRY NEWS*

Yes, yes, I know—how could a book on tabs and indents be fun? But it is.
—SHELLY FRIEDLAND, *MAC STREET JOURNAL*

Jargon, an informal dictionary of computer terms

It is *without exception* the best computer dictionary I have read—and I've read plenty.
—JEAN MICKELSON, *MAD MAC NEWS*

Jargon is definitely a book that should be parked near your computer and used as a handy reference.
—GEORGE PICKAVET, *MOUSE TIMES*

This is an attractive book, nicely designed and laid out, easy to look at as well as to read. It is, to coin some jargon, User Irresistible.
—CAMPUS-WIDE INFORMATION SYSTEM

If you're tired of colorless, conventional reference sources, *Jargon* is for you. *Jargon's* style is easily accessible, and its definitions are thorough and detailed.
—RUBIN RABINOVITZ, *PC MAGAZINE*

Finally! A computer dictionary that not only defines words but explains the concepts behind them.
—GEORGE PICKAVET, *MOUSE TIMES*

How to Boss Your Fonts Around

Robin Williams has done it again. Her latest book, *How to Boss Your Fonts Around,* is likely to become a new standard in the field.
—JIM ALLEY, *PRINT MAGAZINE*

There are bigger font books on the market, but none provides as much focused information as clearly as Robin's. Robin makes us a bold promise— "I guarantee *you* will be in total control of your fonts." And she delivers!
—RICK THRASHER, CMUG PRESIDENT

Robin has done it again. In her own inimitable style, she demystifies the arcane world of fonts. I recommend this book to anyone, whether you work with fonts daily or not.
—LEA BROMLEY, *ARIZONA MACINTOSH USERS GROUP*

Robin Williams has done it yet again— a fascinating and useful volume.
—*MUG ONE*, ONEONTA MAC USERS GROUP

The Non-Designer's Design Book

Just off the press, May, 1994!

Peachpit's PageMaker 5 Companion
Robin Williams, with Barbara Sikora and Vicki Calkins

Peachpit Press
2414 Sixth Street
Berkeley ▾ California ▾ 94710
510.548.4393
800.283.9444
510.548.5991 fax
Peachpit Press is a division of Addison-Wesley Publishing Company.

© 1994 by Robin Williams

Book Design: Robin Williams
Cover Design: Ted Mader +
  Associates (TMA)
Editor, Revised Edition: Vicki Calkins
Editor, First Edition: Mary Grady
Project Manager, Revised Edition:
Barbara Sikora

Proofreader: Alisandra Brewer
Indexers: Barbara Sikora and
  Mary Johnson
Imagesetting: Petaluma Imagesetting
Photography: Robin and hats and
  Vicki by Alan Bartl
  Barbara by Tom Bourret

Library of Congress Cataloging-in-Publication Data
Williams, Robin
    Peachpit's PageMaker 5 Companion: Macintosh ed. / Robin Williams
    with Barbara Sikora and Vicki Calkins
        p. cm.
    Includes index.
    1. PageMaker (computer file) 2. Desktop publishing. I. Calkins, Vicki. II. Sikora, Barbara.
III. Williams, Robin. PageMaker 4. IV. Title. V. Title: PageMaker four.
Z253.532.P33W55 1994
686.2'2544536—dc20   94-15142
                                           CIP

ISBN 1-56609-096-2   098765432

Printed on recycled paper

Printed and bound in the United States of America

Used with permission
etaoin shrdlu, by Herb Caen. First printed in the San Francisco Chronicle in 1979.

beginnings, by Carl Dair. From his most wonderful book, *Designing with Type*. Published by University of Toronto Press, 1967.

A quote from Sean Morrison in his great little book, *A Guide to Type Design*. Published by Prentice-Hall, Inc., 1986.

The cartoon, *Sally Forth*, by Greg Howard and Craig MacIntosh, reprinted with special permission of King Features Syndicate.

Articles designed by Harrah Argentine
etaoin shrdlu, by Herb Caen
beginnings, by Carl Dair
Herr Gutenberg, by Robin Williams
Mind your p's and q's, by Robin Williams

Article designed by Vicki Calkins
Signatures and Impositions, by Vicki Calkins

The quotes and sayings in the book are favorites of the authors collected over the years on yellowing scraps of paper or scribbled on the back of old notebooks. Some are from movies, some are from books, some are the favorite words of some of their favorite people. Exact wording and attribution was obtained from the original source or, when necessary, from standard anthologies of quotes including
The New Quotable Woman by Elaine Partnow, the Penguin Group, 1992
The Merriam-Webster Dictionary of Quotations, Merriam-Webster, Inc., 1992
The Oxford Dictionary of Modern Quotations by Tony Augarde, Oxford University Press, 1991

This book is dedicated, with so much love and respect,

To **Ryan,** who asked, "When you finish this book, are you going to spend time with us again?"

And to **Jimmy,** who mused, "I can't figure out whether you're diurnal or nocturnal; you work all day and you work all night."

And to **Scarlett,** who kept reminding me, "That's the way it is in Life, Mom."

—Robin Williams

To **John,** my musical husband, whose love, quick wit and wisdom, not to mention his afternoon lattés, can get me through anything.

And to **Gaia,** who, when everything is just a little too scattered, reminds me that the essence of life is order.

And to **Kiki,** who, when everything is just a little too orderly, reminds me that the spice of life is spontaneity.

—Barbara Sikora

To **Kent,** husband, wordsmith, and fellow adventurer, without whom I'd never be at the point of actually writing this part of the book and who is, even at this very moment, still stuffing words into my mouth.

And to **Gabriel,** the son who spoon-fed me the Mac back when the hot item was the Mac Plus.

And to **Tim:** only ducks go "quark…"

—Vicki Calkins

Overview of Contents

1   SECTION 1 ▾ **BEGINNING BASICS**

109   SECTION 2 ▾ **DRAWING TOOLS**

133   SECTION 3 ▾ **CONTROL PALETTE**

165   SECTION 4 ▾ **TEXT**

267   SECTION 5 ▾ **TEXT SPACING**

333   SECTION 6 ▾ **INDENTS & TABS**

361   SECTION 7 ▾ **RULES (LINES)**

381   SECTION 8 ▾ **STYLE SHEETS**

413   SECTION 9 ▾ **STORY EDITOR**

461   SECTION 10 ▾ **GRAPHICS**

531   SECTION 11 ▾ **LINKING TEXT & GRAPHICS**

563   SECTION 12 ▾ **LIBRARY PALETTE**

575   SECTION 13 ▾ **TEXT WRAP**

589   SECTION 14 ▾ **TEMPLATES**

601   SECTION 15 ▾ **BOOK PUBLICATIONS** *including Table of Contents and Indexing*

665   SECTION 16 ▾ **COLOR**

697   SECTION 17 ▾ **IMPORTING & EXPORTING**

717   SECTION 18 ▾ **SAVING & REVERTING**

727   SECTION 19 ▾ **PRINTING**

785   SECTION 20 ▾ **ADDITIONS**

813   SECTION 21 ▾ **SPECIAL TECHNIQUES**

839   SECTION 22 ▾ **HELP!!**

867   **APPENDICES**

909   **INDEX**

CONTENTS

XVII   **INTRODUCTION**

Don't read this book from
cover to cover!   *xvii*

1   SECTION 1 ▾ **BEGINNING BASICS**

A Few Definitions   2
Setting Defaults   3
     Scenario #1: Setting defaults   4
     Tasks   5
     List of defaults you can set   7
Page Setup   10
     The "Page setup" dialog boxes   11
     Tasks   12
Rulers & Ruler Guides   18
     The rulers and ruler guides   19
     Tasks   20
     Scenario #2: Aligning baselines   22
     Tasks   23
     Scenario #3: Using the zero point   28
Columns and Column Guides   29
     Tasks   30
Pages and Page Views   35
     Tasks   36
Master Pages   44
     Tasks   45

Multiple Publications   51
     Tasks   53
Selecting, Layering, and Moving   57
     Selecting   58
     Layering   59
     Moving objects   60
     Tasks   61
Preferences   67
     Tasks   69
     PANOSE Font Matching   77
     Tasks   80
Miscellaneous info and tasks   83
     Cut/Copy/Paste and the Clipboard   84
     Multiple paste   88
     Scrapbook   94
     Bounding box   98
     Overriding ruler measurements   101
     Numeric keypad   102
     Key Caps   104
     Find File   107
     Creating more window space   108

109   SECTION 2 ▾ **DRAWING TOOLS**

General: the drawing tools   109
Printer examples   112
Tasks   113
Lines: **tasks**   119
Rectangles and squares: **tasks**   120
Ovals and circles: **tasks**   122
Custom line dialog box   124
Fill and line dialog box   125
Tasks   126
Drawing tool defaults: **tasks**   129
Rotating tool   130
Tasks   131

133   SECTION 3 ▾ **CONTROL PALETTE**

The Control palettes   134
Control palette basics   136
Tasks   138
The object-view Control palette   142
Apply button   143
The Proxy   144
Tasks   146
Position and Sizing options   147
Scaling and Cropping options   148
Rotating and Skewing options   149
Reflecting options   150
Tasks   151
Keyboard shortcuts   159
Tasks   160
Scenario #4: Keyboarding the palette   164

165   SECTION 4 ▾ **TEXT**

Creating text directly on the page   165
Watch that insertion point!   167
Formatting the insertion point   168
Tasks   169
Placing text into PageMaker   171
The Options for placing text   172
The "Place" dialog box for text   173
Tasks   174
Placing other PageMaker files
    into PageMaker   181
The "Story Importer" dialog box   182
Tasks   183
Text flow   186
Tasks   188
Text blocks   192
Tasks   194
Additions for text   206
"Find overset text"   206
"Traverse text blocks"   206
"Display story info"   207
"Display text block info"   208
"Add cont'd line"   209
"Balance columns"   210
Tasks   211
Selecting and formatting text   216
Selecting text: character formatting
    vs. paragraph formatting   217
Tasks   218

The "Type specifications" dialog box 222
The character-view Control palette 223
Tasks 224
Alignment 234
Change the size and placement
of superscript and subscript 240
Rotating text 247
Tasks 248
Paragraphs 251
The "Paragraph specifications"
dialog box 252
The paragraph-view Control palette 253
Tasks 254
Paragraph dialog box "Options" 258
Widows and orphans 260
Line breaks 261
Scenario #5: Using the
line break feature 262
Special characters 263
Type specification defaults 265

267   SECTION 5 ▾ **TEXT SPACING**

What's the difference?
*(the difference between leading, paragraph
spacing, word spacing, letter spacing, auto
kerning, manual kerning, and tracking)* 268
Points and picas 268
Measurement system 268

The "Spacing attributes" dialog box 269
Leading 270
Auto leading 271
Auto leading applied 271
Fixed leading 271
Selecting text to change the leading 272
Slugs 273
The leading submenu 273
Leading methods 273
"Proportional" leading and examples 274
"Baseline" leading and examples 275
"Top of caps" leading and examples 276
Comparison of leading examples 277
Tasks 278
Paragraph spacing 285
An important note 286
Paragraph space examples 286
Use points to override the
measurement system 287
Scenario #6: Paragraph space
"before" and "after" 288
Tasks 289
Align to grid 291
Guidelines for aligning to grid 293
With "Snap to rulers" 293
With inline graphics 293
Tasks 294
Word spacing 295
Examples of word spacing 297
Tasks 298

Letter spacing   299
  Examples of letter spacing   301
  Tasks   302
Kerning   304
  Visually consistent   305
  Auto kerning pairs   305
  Manual kerning   305
  Tasks   306
  "Expert kerning" Addition   310
  Tasks   311
Tracking   313
  Examples of tracking   314
  Tasks   316
  "Edit tracks" Addition   317
  Tasks   318
Set width   321
  Examples of set width   321
  Tasks   322
Hard spaces (non-breaking)   323
  Tasks: creating hard spaces   324
Hyphenation   325
  The Hyphenation dialog boxes   325
  Manual only   326
  Discretionary hyphens   326
  Manual plus dictionary   326
  Manual plus algorithm   327
  Limit consecutive hyphens   327
  Hyphenation zone   327
  Adding words to the user dictionary   328
  Tasks   329

333   SECTION 6 ▾ **INDENTS & TABS**

If you have trouble with indents and tabs,
  review these principles   334
Tabs and the line break command   335
  Examples of.tab alignments   335
How tabs work   336
Defaults and miscellaneous info   337
Using the ruler   338
The Indents/tabs ruler   339
More on tabs   340
Indents   342
Examples of indents   342
  Scenario #7: Indents and tabs together—
    creating numbered paragraphs   343
  Scenario #8: Example of nested indents   344
  Tab tasks   345
  Indent tasks   354
  Miscellaneous tasks   359

361   SECTION 7 ▾ **RULES (LINES)**

The "Paragraph rules" dialog box   362
Notes about paragraph rules   364
Points and picas   364
How paragraph rules work   365
The "Paragraph rule options" dialog box   366
Baseline leading   367
Line styles and point sizes   367
  Tasks   368

381   SECTION 8 ▾ **STYLE SHEETS**

The "Define styles" dialog box   382
New, Edit, and Copy buttons   383
Based on   384
Next style   385
Formatting options   386
Overrides and imported styles   386
"List styles used" Addition   387
    Tasks   388
    Scenario #9: Using style sheets
      (the "create as you go" method)   410
    Scenario #10: Using style sheets
      (the "I know what I want" method)   411
    Wow   412

413   SECTION 9 ▾ **STORY EDITOR**

About the Story Editor   414
The Story Editor menu   416
Opening windows; editing: **Tasks**   417
"Find"   427
    Scenario #11: Using "Find…"   428
    Tasks   429
"Change"   434
    Scenario #12: Finding and
      changing text   435
    Tasks   436
Closing windows; placing text: **Tasks**   441
The spell checker   444

The user dictionary and
    other dictionaries   445
The Spelling window   446
    Tasks   448
The Dictionary Editor Utility   456
    Tasks   457

461   SECTION 10 ▾ **GRAPHICS**

The basics   462
Paint-type graphics   463
PICT graphics   464
TIFF graphics   465
EPS graphics   466
Photo CD images   467
Other graphic formats   467
Scanned images   468
    Line art scans   469
Halftones, grayscales . . .   470
. . . and scanning   471
    Halftone examples   472
    Rules of thumb for grayscale scans   473
The best way to save a graphic image
    for later placement into PageMaker   474
Include complete copy?   475
Update original copy   475
Paste and Paste special   476
Insert object and
    Publish and Subscribe   477

Independent *vs.* inline graphics   477
Independent graphics: **Tasks**   478
Image control   497
    Lightness and contrast settings   501
    Preset settings   502
    Tasks   503
Inline graphics   506
    What to expect   508
    Tasks   509
Additions for graphics   520
    "PS Group it"   521
    "PS Ungroup it"   523
    Tasks   524
    "Create keyline"   528
    "Acquire image"   529
    Tasks   530

531   Section 11 ▾ Linking Text & Graphics

About linking   532
Managing links   533
Updating links   534
Missing links   535
Printing   535
The "Links" dialog box   536
    Status chart and indicators   537
The "Link info" and "Link options"
    dialog boxes   539
    Tasks   540

Publish and Subscribe   553
    The "Subscriber options" dialog boxes   554
    Tasks   555
OLE: object-linking and -embedding   557
    Tasks   559
"Insert object"   561
    Tasks   562

563   Section 12 ▾ Library Palette

Library palette basics   564
The Library palette window   566
Palette preferences   567
Adding information to palette items   567
    Tasks   568
"Search library"   572
    Tasks   573

575   Section 13 ▾ Text Wrapping

The "Text wrap" dialog box   576
The "Text wrap" dialog box icons   577
Standoff   578
    Examples of text wrapping   579
    Tasks   580
    Scenario #13: Using text wrap
       on master pages   585

589 SECTION 14 ▾ **TEMPLATES**

Scenario #14: When, why, and how
  to create your own template   590
Tasks   591
"Open template" Addition   595
How to use the templates provided
  by PageMaker   497
What is a grid?   600

601 SECTION 15 ▾ **BOOK PUBLICATIONS**
(INCLUDING TABLE OF CONTENTS AND INDEXING)

The Book List   602
The "Book publication list" dialog box   603
Tasks   604
Table of Contents (TOC)   612
The process of creating a Table   613
The "Create table of contents"
  dialog box   615
Examples of Tables of Contents   616
Tasks   617
Indexing   623
The basic process   624
The "Add index entry" dialog box   625
Page range   626
The "Add index entry" dialog box
  for Cross-referencing   627
Options and methods   628

The "Select topic" and "Select cross-
  reference topic" dialog boxes   629
The "Show index" dialog box   630
Topic *vs.* entry   631
Import   631
Index prefix   631
Move-down button, Sort   632
Show index   633
Remove, Add, Accept, and Capitalize   633
Tasks   634
Formatting and placing
  the actual index   657
The "Index format" dialog box   658
Index format specifications   659
  Character codes   660
Tasks   661

665 SECTION 16 ▾ **COLOR**

The basics of color reproduction:
  one color   666
  multicolor, spot color   667
  four color, process color   670
Separations   668
Knockouts and traps   669
Color models: which one to use   671
RGB, HLS, CMYK   672
Color Libraries   673
Apple Color Wheel   674

The color Registration, the color Paper,
   and the fill Paper   675
The "Define colors" dialog box   676
The "Edit color" dialog boxes   677
The Color palette   678
Color defaults   679
   Tasks   680
Create a custom color library   693
The dialog box for printing color   694

697   SECTION 17 ▾ **IMPORTING & EXPORTING**

Import and export filters   698
The "Smart ASCII import filter"   700
   Tasks   701
Convert a 4.x Mac to 5.0 Mac   713
Open a PC PageMaker publication
   on the Mac   714

717   SECTION 18 ▾ **SAVING & REVERTING**

The "Save publication as" dialog box   718
   Tasks   719

727   SECTION 19 ▾ **PRINTING**

Printers: Laser printers, Quickdraw printers,
   and PostScript imagesetters   728
PPDs, LaserWriter 8, Print spoolers   729
Setting up a PostScript printer   730
Fonts: Bitmapped and outline   731
   Screen and printer   731
   Resident and downloadable   732
   TrueType   732
Downloading the downloadables   733
The "Print" dialog box
   "Document"   734
   "Paper"   738
   "Options"   742
   "Color"   746
Printing to a non-PostScript printer   749
   Tasks   750
Making a PostScript file   758
   Tasks   760
Using a service bureau   762
Troubleshooting   765
Additions for printing   767
   "Update PPD"   768
   Tasks   769
   "Display pub info"   770
   Tasks   771
   "Printer styles"   772
   Tasks   774
   "Build booklet"   779
   Tasks   782

785   SECTION 20 ▾ **ALDUS ADDITIONS**

Installing Additions	786
"Bullets and Numbering"	787
Tasks	789
"Drop cap"	792
Tasks	794
"Run script"	797
Tasks	798
"Running headers\footers"	801
Tasks	805
"Sort pages"	809
Tasks	811

813   SECTION 21 ▾ **SPECIAL TECHNIQUES**

List of special techniques in the book	814
Tasks	816

839   SECTION 22 ▾ **HELP!!**

Tasks	840

867   **APPENDICES**

Appendix A: Menus and their dialog boxes	
(cross-referenced)	867
A1: File menu	868
A2: Edit menu	870
A3: Utilities menu	871
A4: Story menu	872
A5: Layout menu	873
A6: Type menu	874
A7: Element menu	877
A8: Window menu	879
Appendix B: List of all tasks	880
Appendix C: Installing PageMaker	896
Setting up a	
PostScript printer	897
Running the 5.0a patch	899
Appendix D: Entry codes	900
Appendix E: Alternate characters	900
Appendix F: Accent marks	902
Appendix G: Zapf Dingbats chart	903
Appendix H: Symbols and cursors	904
Chart Keyboard shortcuts	905
Appendix I: Control palette	907
Appendix J: Third-party Additions	908
Tear out chart of keyboard shortcuts	

909   **INDEX**

Acknowledgments

I first want to thank **Mary Grady,** for the incredible amount of work she put into the first edition of this book. Mary tested, edited, copy-edited, and indexed each section, penciling in the thousands of cross-references along the way. Oh my gosh it was a lot of work. I thank you, Mary, for the strength and value you added to this book. And I thank you for your friendship.

Another great bundle of thanks to **Harrah Argentine,** who designed four of the almost-irrelevant articles included in this book. Harrah spent an enormous amount of time researching and illustrating images for the stories, and then designing the pages;

Olav Martin Kvern and **Steve Roth,** truly nice guys and authors of *Real World Page-Maker* for their willingness to share their expertise and their great tips; and thanks to Kimberly Scott, Dan Burke, Majorie Cerletti, and Ellen Geoghegan.

An enormous thank you to **Ted Nace,** publisher of Peachpit Press and almost wonderful person. The entire staff at Peachpit is an incredibly special group of people, and I feel very proud and lucky to be a Peachpit author.

We'd like to thank first and foremost **Robin Williams,** our teacher and mentor. As former students of Robin's, we thought we knew what we were getting into when we took on the awesome task of revising *PageMaker 4, An Easy Desk Reference.* We soon came to realize how deep and true her knowledge of PageMaker, typesetting, and design runs, and what huge boots we had to fill. As you can see, it took two of us to try to bring current the framework of information that she had so carefully crafted.

And how could we have gotten along without **Alisandra Brewer?** More than a proofreader, she proved to be a wealth of technical knowledge. Her suggestions for improving our info without becoming too "techy" were most welcome. Nothing escaped the prying eyes of APB!

And hugs and thanks to **Mary Johnson,** indexer extraordinaire, who somehow managed to squeeze the humongous job of indexing this monster in between the demands of an active graphic design business.

And to **Vicki Garwacki** who diligently test-ran all the Additions tasks.

And to the regulars on the **CompuServe Aldus Forum:** we bombarded you with tedious and seemingly trivial questions, and you answered every one of them;

And **Ellen Wixsted** at Aldus, we can't believe you answered every one of our phone calls;

And to **Janet Butcher,** for her expertise as a service bureau owner, and for her care in nursing all these pages out of the lino;

And to **Ted Nace, Rosyln Bullas,** and **Tom Serianni** of Peachpit Press, who were so patient with us as this edition got bigger and bigger and farther and farther behind deadline: now we know what Robin's raves are all about. She's right. The entire staff at Peachpit *is* an incredible group of people, and we feel very proud and lucky to have been included by them.

But, most of all, we'd like to acknowledge each other, for **nobody** knows the trouble we've seen :)

Including philosophical reflections,
the like not to be found in any
Ordinary manual.

Don't read this book from cover to cover!

This book is definitely not meant to be read from cover to cover. It would be stupid of me to write a software reference manual this large that had to be read from one end to the other because nobody would read it.

This book is not a tutorial. It does not take you through lesson plans to teach you how to use PageMaker. There are already good books like that. This is strictly a reference book. But an interesting reference book.

In the first part of each section, you'll find background information on one particular topic. For instance, in the Indents and Tabs section, there is information on the logic behind indents and tabs (yes, there really is logic), along with lots of examples and suggestions. Then each section breaks into a list of tasks: for instance, how to create a tab, move a tab, delete a tab, make tabs with leaders, etc. Every possible thing you could ever think of to do in PageMaker has a separate task with step-by-step directions for accomplishing that task.

So you can choose to read the preliminary information to understand the whole picture, or you can skip it and jump directly to the task you want to accomplish. Find the task you need by skimming through the appropriate section, looking it up in the index, or finding the exact reference number in the list of tasks in Appendix B. Or you *could,* of course, read from cover to cover.

I repeat myself a lot in this book. I tried never to assume that you previously read any other part of the book. Although everything is extensively cross-referenced, many times I repeat information so you don't have to waste time flipping to another section for important info.

I felt it was my obligation to make this book as useful as possible to you. Hopefully, between its two covers, you'll find all the information you need to keep you out of trouble.

Please note:

- Numbers in parentheses—like so: (3.102–3.107)—mean you will find relevant, interrelated information in those paragraphs. You don't *have to* read the relevant information; the references are just there for your convenience.

- A dotted line along the side of a column indicates that the info next to it is of particular importance or interest.

- A short quotation separate from the main body of information indicates an educative statement or comic relief.

- Here and there throughout the book are short articles of vaguely relevant interest, stories of Aldus Manutius, Johannes Gutenberg, or some historical curiosity relating to type and printing (like the story on the next page). These exist simply because this is my book and I wanted to put them in. The articles may make for interesting reading while you wait for your work to come out of the printer.

beginnings

The use of written or printed symbols as a basic element of design is not a discovery of our era; it is not even a result of the invention of movable type by Gutenberg. It reaches back into the dawn of civilization, to wherever and whenever man took up a tool and attempted to inscribe on a receptive surface a message to be preserved. It would seem that there was something of an instinctive urge in the dark recesses of the pre-civilized mind towards an orderliness and a pattern in the grouping of the symbols which were to convey this message.

As far back in the history of man's effort to write as you care to go, this innate sense of orderliness has dominated his graphic art. The clay tablets of Mesopotamia and the hieroglyphs of Egypt, the circular tables of Crete and the precise geometry of the Greek letters, the careful alignment of the flowing characters of the Chinese and the musical lilt of Persian script, the solemnity of the Roman inscriptions and the decorated pages of the Book of Kells—need one go on?—all these attest the desire of the hand that recorded to please the eye that would read. The forms of these patterns were many, and they arose out of the whole composite of the art and the culture from which they stemmed.

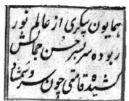

The invention of movable type did not change this urge towards the beautiful in graphic presentation; it simply provided the means, denied to the ancients, of reproducing the original work and so widening the public who would see and read. The early printers of Mainz and Basle and Venice were not indifferent to the obligation this freedom imposed on them, and so they sought, with meticulous care and craftsmanship, to make each letter, each line, each page as beautiful as they had been in the manuscripts which had sired the art of printing. The typecutter put all his skill and sense of form into the creation of beautiful individual letters; the typesetter sought to combine these characters into pages of dignity; and the pressman took painstaking care to reproduce the whole uniformly, with just the right amount of ink, so that none of this elegance might escape making its timeless imprint upon paper.

Each in his own time, often with crude tools poised against resisting surfaces, tried to make the written record the epitome of the art and culture of his own period. Bone against clay, chisel against stone, brush against silk, quill against parchment, lead against paper, each tool made its characteristic mark, and each surface received the impression in its characteristic way. The hand of the artist accepted his materials and made the most of them. The tradition is long and the urge is deep.

The speed of reproduction of the written word by machines in a modern printing plant would astound the ancients. But if they could see it, they might wonder why, with the labour of writing so eased by mechanical devices, we are not able to put even greater thought into the design of our printing.

No doubt these same ancients would also not understand the cost sheet we would show them; they would find the urgency of deadlines as an excuse for shoddiness incomprehensible; they would be bewildered by the complex relationships of individual specialists involved in doing the work they once did single-handed. And they would probably return to their primitive tools shaking their heads with awe at the accomplishments of twentieth-century printing technology, but yet distressed that all the art and loving care they had lavished on the written and printed word counted for so little. They might well conclude that, while we can produce more and faster, they could give a better product.

Carl Dair

DESIGNING WITH TYPE

Never bother to remember anything
you can look up in a book.

— *Albert Einstein*

1 ▾ BASICS

This section covers just the basics of working in PageMaker, with some of the basic Macintosh functions explained as well, as they are related to creating publications in PageMaker.

Although the rest of the book assumes you understand the features discussed here, you will always find cross-references directing you to the specific details that can be found in this section.

Remember, this book is not meant to be read from cover to cover (see the introduction on page xvii). If you are just beginning with PageMaker, you may want to skip the first segment on defaults and return to it later when the terms make more sense.

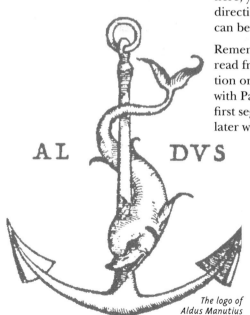

*The logo of
Aldus Manutius*

A Few Definitions 2
Setting Defaults 3
   Scenario #1: Setting defaults 4
Page Setup 10
   The "Page setup" dialog boxes 11
Rulers and Ruler Guides 18
   Scenario #2: Aligning baselines 22
   Scenario #3: Using the zero point 28
Columns and Column Guides 29
Pages and Page Views 35
Master Pages 44
Multiple publications 51
Selecting, Layering, and Moving 57
Preferences 67
PANOSE Font Matching 77
Miscellaneous 83
   **Cut, Copy, Paste, and the Clipboard,
      including power-pasting** 84
   Multiple paste 88
   Scrapbook 94
   **Using the bounding box,
      or drag-placing** 98
   Overriding ruler measurements 101
   Numeric keypad 102
   Key Caps 104
   Find File 107
   Creating more window space 108

A few definitions

1.1 Press

With the mouse, *pressing* is very different than *clicking*—a *click* is when you give a short tap on the button, while a *press* is when you *hold the button down.* They accomplish very different objectives.

1.2 Press-and-drag

Whenever you see the term *press-and-drag,* it means to *press* the mouse button down, *hold it down,* and *drag* the mouse across the table.

1.3 Keyboard *vs.* Keypad

When you read the word *keyboard,* it is referring to the normal keyboard you see in front of you with all the characters on it. The word *keypad* is referring to the numeric section on the right of the keyboard. The *keypad* looks like calculator keys.

1.4 Pasteboard

The *pasteboard* is the area in the window that is outside of the page outline. It acts just like a drafting table: a page you are working on in PageMaker is comparable to a paste-up board on your drafting table; as you change paste-up boards, your drafting table stays the same, right? Same with this pasteboard—anything you place on it at any time will still be there when you change pages. This comes in very handy. Also, you have more room than you see—choose "Show pasteboard" from the "View" submenu under the Layout menu and you will see the boundaries of the pasteboard that you have available to work within (see 1.110–1.121 for other view options).

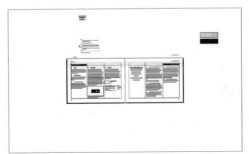

The outer border shown here appears in the "Show pasteboard" view, defining the limits of the pasteboard.

1.5 Handles

In an object-oriented program such as PageMaker, every object is a separate entity. Every object—text blocks, imported graphic files, clip art, PageMaker graphic shapes, lines—has its outer edges defined by *handles.* The handles appear on the object when you click on it with the pointer tool. *Once the handles are showing,* the object can then be manipulated (deleted, resized, copied, cut, transformed, etc.).

The eight handles that appear on a graphic image.

This text block has been selected with the pointer tool. Notice the four handles on the corners. Text blocks also have window shade loops, seen at the top and bottom. See 4.102–4.109.

The four handles and two loops that appear on a text block.

T ❖ Y ❖ P ❖ E

gives body and voice

to silent thought.

The speaking page

carries it

through the centuries.

Friedrich Schiller

❖

1.6   A **default** is a pre-set option that PageMaker automatically reverts to if nothing else is chosen. For instance, with the standard defaults, every time you begin a new text block the text comes up with Times, 12 point, auto leading, with no indent. When you draw a line, the pre-set option is 1 point. When you draw a box, the border is 1 point and the fill inside is None. You can adjust these so the pre-set options, or *defaults*, are exactly what *you* need to work with.

You can set two different sorts of defaults: *application* and *publication*.

1.7   **Application defaults.** You can change the defaults for the entire Page-Maker application so every time you open the program and create a *new* publication, it is already set to your specifications. This is very handy if you create a lot of one particular kind of publication, perhaps tabloid newsletters. See 1.11, Scenario #1.

1.8   **Application defaults** will not affect any publications you have already created. The application defaults *you* set will override the original PageMaker defaults (to restore the original ones, see 1.17).

1.9   **Publication defaults.** You can set the defaults for just the particular *publication* you are working on at the moment (1.16). These are temporary defaults that will *not* be carried over into the next publication you open or create, but they will be saved along with this one. You can change them over and over again, depending on what part of the project you are working on. See 1.11, Scenario #1. *Publication defaults override any application defaults.*

1.10   Be careful! It is possible to set reverse text or a reverse line as the default, so every time you type or draw a line or shape, it shows up invisible. It's also possible to set a default text wrap so every object you draw or paste forces the text away from itself (text wrapping is discussed in Section 13). *Whenever something happens over and over again, it is because there is a default somewhere.* Reset it.

1.11 Scenario #1: Setting defaults

The key to recognizing defaults and knowing when it is time for you to change them is this: if something occurs regularly, it is a default. If you want something different to occur regularly, it is time for you to change the defaults.

For instance, if a box fills itself with a solid shade every time you draw with the rectangle tool, there is a default; if you want to draw boxes with a 10% shade, change the default. If the insertion point jumps to the middle of the column every time you click the I-beam, there is a default of a center alignment; if you want a regular left alignment, change the default. If you get extra space between the paragraphs every time you hit a Return, there is a default. If the text appears in some strange font every time you type, there is a default.

Sometimes things change and you don't know why. I'll tell you why: it's because you are *accidentally changing the default*. **If there is nothing selected when you choose anything from the menu or any dialog box or palette, you are setting a default.** It happens all the time: we forget to select before we try to change something. Whenever we do that, we set a new publication default.

Let's say your department regularly produces tabloid publications—every morning you have to create a new publication and you change the Page Setup to your tabloid specs. Well, rather than reset the Page Setup and all the other specs each time you begin a new publication, you can set the **application defaults** to those specifications you regularly need; e.g., tabloid-sized paper, eight pages, one-inch margins all around, double-sided with facing pages, autoflow text, wrap all graphics with a 1-pica standoff, all boxes with a thin double border and a solid fill. Set up your style sheets (Section 8)—from which of course you may deviate on the various publications. Then, every morning when you begin a new publication, these specs are already set up!

This scenario gets more complex, but if you're ready for it, read on: Let's say you typically bring in your stories from a word processor, but you always type the heads directly into PageMaker because you want to override the columns. In your style sheet, before you open any publication, select the style Headline as an application default; whenever you start a new text block, you will automatically type in the Headline style.

Let's say you've created your publication, placed all your stories, positioned all your graphics, typed all the heads, and now you need to draw a series of 8-point lines. But remember, you previously set an application default to a thin double line. So now you can set a temporary (**publication**) default: with nothing on the page selected, choose the 8-point line. Now all your lines will automatically draw in 8 point.

You are ready to put captions under all the photos. You previously set your **application** default for text as Headline, so every time you start to type, the text shows up in the Headline font. But that's not what you want now! So override the application default with a **publication** default: with *nothing* selected, choose your Caption style from your style sheet (or choose *No Style* and select the font, size, and style from the menus); now everything you type will be in the Caption formatting, so you don't have to go back and change it after each time you type.

Next time you begin a *new* publication, you will again have the *application* defaults, but not these temporary ones you created in this publication.

If you want to do this: ▪	**Then follow these steps:** ▪	**Shortcuts ▾ Notes ▾ Hints** ▪
1.12 Launch the Pagemaker application  Aldus PageMaker 5.0	▪ Locate the folder "Aldus PageMaker 5.0." Double-click on it to open it. ▪ Double-click on the application icon.	▪ When you installed PageMaker, you chose where to store the "Aldus PageMaker 5.0" folder. If you customized the name of the folder, locate it by the name you gave it. ▪ This opens to the PageMaker desktop. From here you can set application defaults, and open new or existing files.
1.13 Set the **application** defaults (1.7–1.8) for the entire PageMaker program	▪ From the PageMaker desktop, *when you can see the PageMaker menu but no publication is open,* use the **pointer** to choose any menu item that is not gray, or change any item in any dialog box you can call up.	▪ Anything you change at this point will become an *application* default. ▪ The "Print" command is gray when no publication is open, so you cannot set application defaults for printing. ▫ The LaserWriter 8 set up (19.20), defines the PPD application default. ▫ You can create *publication* defaults for all of the print options, see 1.16.
1.14 Open a new publication	▪ Double-click on the "Aldus PageMaker 5.0" application icon. ▪ From the File menu, choose "New." ▪ Click OK to open a publication with the application default specifications, *or* ▪ Change the specifications in the "Page setup" dialog box (1.23), then click OK.	▪ The "Page setup" dialog box options are explained in 1.23–1.37. ▪ At any point you can come back to the "Page setup" dialog box and change a publication's specifications.

If you want to do this:	Then follow these steps:	Shortcuts ▾ Notes ▾ Hints

1.15 Open an existing PageMaker publication

Basics v.1

A publication icon looks like this. Note the turned down corner.

- If PageMaker is open, from the File menu, select "Open."
- In the "Open publication" dialog box, find the publication you want to open. Select it and click OK.
- If PageMaker is not open, at the Finder/Desktop, double-click on the publication icon, to launch PageMaker *and* open the publication.

- You can have more than one publication open at a time. PageMaker will open new or existing publications one on top of the other. You can easily switch between open publications and even view them all at once on screen (1.160).
- You can always double-click on a publication icon to open it, even if PageMaker is already open.

1.16 Set **publication** defaults for the current open publication

- Your publication must be open.
- Click once on the **pointer tool,** *even if the pointer tool is already selected.*
- Choose any menu item that is not gray, or change any item in any dialog box that you can call up.
- From the File menu, choose "Print." Set the options in the dialog box the way you want them. Hold down the Shift key and click the "Print" button.

- You can really click on *any* tool to ensure that nothing in the window is selected.
- Anything you change at this point will become a *publication* default.
- *Publication* defaults will override *application* defaults just for this publication.
- Print specs are saved as soon as you print a publication and save it. When you press the Shift key as you click the "Print" button, you save the specifications without having to print the publication.

1.17 Revert back to the original PageMaker defaults

PM5.0 Defaults

- At the Finder/Desktop (before starting or after quitting PageMaker), open your System Folder.
- In the System Folder, open the "Preferences" folder. In the "Preferences" folder find the document titled "PM5.0 Defaults."
- Throw that file in the trash.

- Really, this is OK! The "PM5.0 Defaults" file contains the *current* application defaults that you have set. When you restart PageMaker, the *original* application default settings built into the program will be returned. The "PM5.0 Defaults" file reappears in your System folder.

1.18 The Defaults

The following is a list of the specifications you can adjust—some items from the menu, some from the appropriate dialog box.

FILE MENU	YOU CAN SET:
Preferences	Measurement system
	Vertical ruler measure
	Whether to let you know if word spacing is too tight or too loose
	Whether to let you know if text lines are violating the paragraph "keeps" controls
	Screen resolution of detailed graphics
	Whether the guides are on the front layer or on the back layer
	Save option of Faster or Smaller
	Control palette nudge measurement system and amount; snap to constraints

Other: Autoflow display

Set maximum size of internal bitmap

Graphic alert above the size of your choice

Use typographer's quotes

Preserve line spacing or character shape in TrueType

Size of type to show as "greek" text in the smaller window views

What size and what font to show in the Story Editor and whether to display style names and non-printing characters

Map fonts: Font substitution options, default font for missing fonts

Page setup		Page type
		Page dimensions
		Orientation
		The page number to start numbering with
		The number of pages in the publication
		Whether the publication is single- or double-sided
		Whether to show facing pages for double-sided publications
		Margins
		Restart page numbering
		Target printer resolution
	Numbers:	Style of numbers for automatic page numbering
		Prefix to use for Table of Contents and Index
Print		Printer type

EDIT MENU	YOU CAN SET:
	Multiple paste options

—continued

Defaults   —continued

UTILITIES MENU	YOU CAN SET:
Aldus Additions	Bullet style in Bullets and numbering Addition
Create index	All options
Create TOC	All options

LAYOUT MENU	YOU CAN SET:
Rulers	To show or to hide
Snap to rulers	On or off
Zero lock	Locked or unlocked (*if Rulers is on*)
Guides	To show or to hide
Snap to guides	On or off (*if Guides is on*)
Lock guides	On or off (*if Guides is on*)
Scroll bars	To show or to hide (*including page icons*)
Column guides	Number of columns and space between (*if Guides is on*)
Autoflow	On or off

TYPE MENU	YOU CAN SET:
Font	Any font
Size	Any "graphic art" size listed
Leading	Any leading listed
Set width	Condensed (70%) to **Expanded** (130%) or anywhere between 5% and 250%
Track	Very loose letterspacing to very tight letterspacing
Type style	Any style listed
Type specs	Font
	Size
	Leading
	Set width
	Color
	Position: whether to set normal (hello), in superscript (hello), or in subscript (goodbye)
	Case: whether to set in ALL CAPS, lower case, or SMALL CAPS
	Track (any setting)
	Type style of your choice

Options:	Small cap size
	Super/subscript size
	Superscript position
	Subscript position
	Baseline shift
Paragraph	Indents
	Paragraph space (*the amount of leading before and/or after a Return*)
	Text alignment (*same as the Alignment command in the Type menu*)
	Dictionary
(Options)	"Keeps" controls
	Widow and orphan control
	Column and page break controls
	Inclusion of Table of Contents label
Rules:	Rules (lines) above and below paragraphs
	Grid size (*under Options…*)
	Grid alignment (*under Options…*)

Defaults *—continued*

		ELEMENT MENU	YOU CAN SET:	WINDOW MENU	YOU CAN SET:
Spacing:	Word spacing	**Line**	Any line or border	**Tool palette**	To show or to hide
	Letter spacing	**Fill**	Any fill or shade	**Style palette**	To show or to hide
	Pair kerning on or off; above the point size of your choice	**Fill and line**	Any fill or line, any color, overprint option, transparent line option	**Color palette**	To show or to hide
	Leading method			**Control palette**	To show or to hide
	Percentage of the point size for auto leading	**Text wrap**	Wrap option and standoff	**Library palette**	To show or to hide
Indents/Tabs	Left indent				
	Right indent	**Rounded corners**	Any corner		
	First-line indent	**Define colors**	Create or remove colors		
	Tabs		Text color		
Hyphenation	On or off	**Link options**	Options for updating and storing links for text and graphics		
	Manual with dictionary, or Manual with algorithm				
	Limit number of consecutive hyphens				
	Hyphenation zone				
Alignment	Any paragraph alignment				
Style	Which of the styles in the style sheet to type with				
Define styles	All parts of the style sheets can be changed				

GEOMETRY
can produce legible letters,

*but Art alone
makes them beautiful.*

Paul Standard

Page setup

1.19 Minimums and maximums:

Item	Minimum	Maximum
Page size	.5" x .5"	42 x 42 inches
No. pages	1	999
Numbering sequence	1	9999
Margins	0	Total not to exceed page size

1.21   In PageMaker when you choose to create a *New* publication, the first thing you see is the **"Page setup" dialog box,** (1.23) because in PageMaker you can have control over *everything*. This is the place to set up the size and number of your pages, the orientation of the screen, the number with which to begin paginating, the parameters of the outer margins, and the format of your automatic numbering.

1.22   At any point in the creation of your document you can come back to "Page setup" and change any of the specifications. Just remember, though, if you have several pages already created and you decide to change the size or the orientation of the page, the text and graphics already placed on the pages *will not* adapt themselves to the new specifications—they will sit very patiently right where you left them, and you will have to adjust them all manually.

1.20 **Page sizes** are as follows:

Letter size: 8.5 x 11 inches

Legal size: 8.5 x 14 inches

Tabloid size: 11 x 17 inches

A4:   8.268 x 11.693 inches

A3:   11.693 x 16.535 inches

A5:   5.827 x 8.268 inches

B5:   6.929 x 9.842 inches

Magazine: 8.375 x 10.875 inches

Magazine narrow: 8.125 x 10.875 inches

Magazine wide: 9 x 10.875 inches

Magazine broad: 10 x 12 inches

Compact disk: 4.722 x 4.75 inches

Letterhalf: 5.5 x 8.5 inches

Legalhalf: 7 x 8.5 inches

Custom size: Any size from the minimum to maximum (1.19)

1.23 **The "Page setup" dialog boxes** *(from the File menu, choose "Page setup…")*

This submenu contains pre-set page sizes; see 1.25; 1.26.

You can customize the size of any page; see 1.25; 1.26.

See 1.26; 1.27.

This is for automatic page numbering; see 1.30; 1.31.

See 1.34; 1.35

Check to override automatic page renumbering in Book lists; see 15.29.

This sets non-printing margin guidelines on the page; see 1.37.

Select the final output resolution so PageMaker can "magic-resize" graphics accordingly; see 10.20–10.22 and 10.141.

Hit Return to shortcut OK.

You can press Command Period.

See 1.28

See 1.36

Page setup

Page: **Letter**

Page dimensions: **8.5** by **11** inches

Orientation: ◉ **Tall**   ○ **Wide**

Start page #: **1**   Number of pages: **1**

Options: ☒ **Double-sided**   ☒ **Facing pages**
☐ **Restart page numbering**

Margin in inches: Inside **1**   Outside **0.75**
Top **0.75**   Bottom **0.75**

Target printer resolution: **300** ▷ dpi

OK
Cancel
Numbers…

1.24 *Click on the button "Numbers…" in the "Page setup" dialog box to get the "Page numbering" options. These options allow you to customize the automatic page numbering (1.32; 1.147a,b).*

When you are ready to create a table of contents or an index, you can use this option to customize the page numbers that appear within the table or the index; see 1.33.

See 1.32

Page numbering

Style: ◉ **Arabic numeral**   1, 2, 3, …
○ **Upper Roman**   I, II, III, …
○ **Lower Roman**   i, ii, iii, …
○ **Upper alphabetic**   A, B, C, … AA, BB, CC, …
○ **Lower alphabetic**   a, b, c, … aa, bb, cc, …

TOC and index prefix:

OK
Cancel

If you want to do this:	**Then follow these steps:**	**Shortcuts ▾ Notes ▾ Hints**
1.25 Change the page size	▪ From the File menu choose "Page setup." ▪ Press on the box next to "Page" to see the pop-up menu of sizes; select the size of your choice. Its measurements will appear in the "Page dimensions" boxes.	▪ The maximum page size is 42 x 42 inches. If you use a printer that cannot supply paper large enough to print your full page on one piece, you can **tile** when you print (19.75–19.78) and use the tiles to paste up. ▪ If the publication *page* size is smaller than the printer's *paper* size, your job will print centered on the paper. Choose to print Printer's marks (19.95) to show the outer dimensions of your publication page.
1.26 Create a custom page size	▪ From the File menu choose "Page setup." ▪ Press on the box next to "Page" to see the pop-up menu of sizes; select Custom. ▪ Type in the size of your choice in the boxes next to "Page dimensions" (the first box is the horizontal measurement; the second is the vertical measurement.)	▪ If you type the dimensions for a wide format (say, 10 x 7) but leave the orientation on "Tall," the orientation command will take precedence and you will get a 7 x 10 page.
1.27 Change the orientation	▪ From the File menu choose "Page setup." ▪ Choose "Tall" for a vertical format; choose "Wide" for a horizontal format.	▪ If you return to Page Setup later and switch orientations, all customized columns will recenter between the new margins.
1.28 Establish the number of pages	▪ From the File menu choose "Page setup." ▪ Type in the number of pages you want in the "# of pages:" box, up to 999.	▪ Obviously, don't put more pages in one publication than you can easily back up. ▪ After your publication is set up, you can add and remove pages through the Layout menu (1.127–1.128).

If you want to do this:	**Then follow these steps:**	**Shortcuts ▪ Notes ▪ Hints**
1.29 Add or delete pages	▪ You can add or delete pages from the Page Setup dialog box, but they will be added to, or deleted from, the end of the publication.	▪ You *can* add pages, or delete pages from, anywhere within your publication through the Layout menu (1.127–1.129).
1.30 Start numbering pages with a number other than 1 Start page #: 2	▪ From the File menu choose "Page setup." ▪ Type in the number you wish to begin the document with in the "Start page #" edit box.	▪ The page icons (1.32; 1.99) will reflect these numbers, as well as the automatic page-numbering feature (1.146–1.148). ▪ Standard procedure worldwide is that odd-numbered pages are right-hand; even-numbered pages left-hand. ▪ In double-sided publications, the first page (as it is usually an odd number) is never shown as part of a two-page spread. If you want to see it as such, start the numbering with an even number. ▪ Pages can be *numbered* up through 9,999; that is, if you have 20 pages in your publication and you start numbering them with 468, your publication will have pages 468 through 487.
1.31 Renumber the pages, starting with a different number Start page #: 453	▪ From the File menu choose "Page setup." ▪ Change the number in the "Start page #" edit box.	▪ Pages can be *numbered* up through 9,999 (see the note just above).

If you want to do this:	Then follow these steps:	Shortcuts ▾ Notes ▾ Hints

1.32 Format the page numbers

Style: ○ Arabic numeral   1, 2, 3, ...
       ○ Upper Roman   I, II, III, ...
       ● Lower Roman   i, ii, iii, ...
       ○ Upper alphabetic A, B, C, ... AA,
       ○ Lower alphabetic a, b, c, ... aa,

 The page icons that appear in the bottom left portion of the screen, indicating how many pages are in the publication, will always be Arabic no matter what format you choose.

- From the File menu choose "Page setup."
- Click on the button "Numbers...."
- Click in the button to choose your style. *(Be sure to read the notes in the next column)* ☛

- Your choice here will only affect how the *automatic* page numbers (1.147a, b) are displayed. It will have no effect on any page number you type without using the auto feature.
- Roman numeral styles, both upper- and lowercase, can only number as high as 4,999; 5,000 through 9,999 appear as regular Arabic numbers.
- Alphabetic style, both upper- and lowercase, can only number as high as ZZ (52); 53 through 9,999 appear as Arabic numbers.
- No matter what format you choose, the page icons appear as normal (Arabic) numbers.

1.33 Create a prefix for Index and Table of Contents entries

TOC and index prefix: | Section 1: |

- From the File menu choose "Page setup."
- Click on the button "Numbers...."
- Type a prefix of up to 15 characters.

- This prefix will appear in the Table of Contents and in the Index you create (see Section 15). For instance, if you are creating a multi-volume reference with one index, this prefix could define in which volume an item is found, as well as the page number. Or perhaps you want to specify items that are found in the Appendix.
- This prefix is specific only to the *publication* it is created in; that is, since you will typically create each chapter of a book as a separate publication, each one can have its own prefix; e.g., Chapter One: p.14; Appendix B: p. 4.

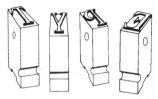

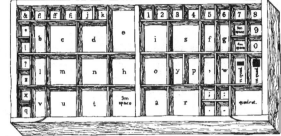

lower case

When type was first being used to print words, each letter was cast on a separate little piece of metal (backwards, of course, so when it printed it would be facing the right direction). These tiny pieces of metal were kept in large, flat, wooden cases, with separate little compartments in each case for each letter. There was one case for the capital letters, and one case for the small letters. To make life easy, all type was stored in the same cabinet, the case for capital letters always above the corresponding case for small letters; thus capitals became known as "uppercase," and small letters became known as "lowercase."

Now, when a printer wanted to create a publication, he would take letters out of their compartments, one by one, and place them in a composing stick until he had enough letters for a whole line, then place that entire line in a chase. When all the lines for the entire page were in, he would lock the chase

composing stick

up tight. If he didn't lock it up tight, the letters might spill all over the floor and it would take a very long time to pick up all those tiny little pieces of type and the boss would probably be angry. Can you imagine each one of the letters, the spaces, and the punctuation marks in this paragraph being each on a separate tiny piece of lead? Can you imagine spilling all those letters on the floor and having to pick them all up and put them back into their special compartments in their case? Can you imagine doing that to backwards letters?

Even if the letters didn't get spilled all over the floor, when that page was completed the movable type had to be broken down anyway and placed back into the little cubbies. Some letters are difficult to distinguish when they're backwards (let alone upside down if you dropped them on the floor), such as b's and d's, or p's and q's. That's where the phrase "Mind your p's and q's" originated—a printer's admonition to his apprentice to make sure things were put back into their proper places. It was probably on a placard placed over the washbasin as a precursor to the ubiquitous "Wash your hands before returning to work."   *—rw*

15

If you want to do this:	Then follow these steps:	Shortcuts ▾ Notes ▾ Hints

1.34 Create a single-sided publication

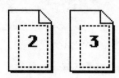

Single-sided with margin guides

- From the File menu choose "Page setup."
- Make sure there is no X in the checkbox next to "Double-sided." If there is, click once in the box to remove it.

- Choosing single-sided will leave your margins exactly the same on every page, as opposed to double-sided (see below). Single-sided assumes the final version of your publication will be copied onto only one side of the paper.

1.35 Create a double-sided publication

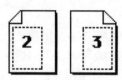

Double-sided with same margin guides

Options: ⊠ **Double-sided**

- From the File menu choose "Page setup."
- Make sure there is an X in the checkbox next to "Double-sided."

- "Double-sided" assumes the final version of your publication will be copied onto two sides, which usually means they will be bound in the inner margin. When you have selected double-sided, notice the margins in the Page Setup do not state Left or Right, but Inside and Outside. When you choose Double-sided, the margins flip-flop, so the inner margin (where you typically leave more space) is always at the bound edge.
- **This does not make your printer print on two sides of the paper**—it only means when you take these originals down to your copy center and have them copied and bound, the layout will have allowed for the binding edge.
- Nor does it automatically create a wider inside margin! That's your responsibility.

> The way to simplicity is hard labor, but it must never seem like hard labor.
> —*Arthur Rubinstein*

If you want to do this:

Then follow these steps:

Shortcuts • Notes • Hints

1.36 Show facing pages

Facing pages

Options: ☒ Double-sided   ☒ Facing pages

- From the File menu choose "Page setup."
- **If** the Double-Sided option is checked (1.35), **then** you can check this box to show the two-page spreads.

- Right-hand pages are always odd-numbered; left-hand pages are always even-numbered.
- Even with Facing Pages checked, the first page (as it is usually an odd number) will stand alone. If you want to see the first two pages of your publication as a two-page spread, put an even number in the "Start page #" box (1.30).

1.37 Set or change the margin

- From the File menu choose "Page setup."
- Select the numbers in the margin boxes and type in your own specifications (press the Tab key to move from edit box to edit box).

- **These margins are only *guidelines* for your text and graphic placements—** anything placed outside of these margins will also print, limited only by the printing area of your printer.
- Margin guides, unlike ruler guides, cannot be changed from the publication page; you must return to "Page setup" (File menu).
- If you later return to Page Setup and change the margins, any *columns* you have customized will be re-centered within the new margins. *And then* if you redo the master page columns, the new columns will not appear on pages that you previously customized (1.61).
- Margins can be set anywhere from 0 to the numbers that add up to just shy of the total width or depth of the page.
- If you want to override the measurement system currently in use, see 1.323.

Rulers and Ruler Guides

1.38   Minimums and maximums:

Item	Minimum	Maximum
Ruler guides	0	40 per page

The maximum of 40 per page includes any master guides. If facing pages are showing, the limit refers to 40 total on the *two* pages.

1.39   Horizontal measurement options:

Standard inches

Decimal inches

Millimeters

Picas (⅙ inch [.167 inch];
   12 points per pica)

Ciceros (4.55 mm [.177 inch];
   12 cicero points per cicero)

1.40   Vertical measurement options:

Standard inches

Decimal inches

Millimeters

Picas (⅙ inch [.167 inch];
   12 points per pica)

Ciceros (4.55 mm [.177 inch];
   12 cicero points per cicero)

Custom (4 to 256 points)

1.41   PageMaker provides a vertical and a horizontal **ruler** for each publication. The measurements in each of these rulers can be customized to your particular preference (e.g., picas instead of inches), and can be re-customized at any time.

1.42   The **ruler guides** are *non-printing*, dotted guidelines that act as a T-square or a non-photo blue pen. They allow you to measure and place objects or text precisely, yet they do not restrict the flow of the text.

1.43
- The horizontal ruler can be set to a different measurement than the vertical ruler.
- Ruler guides can be placed on master pages to show up on every page.
- Ruler guides can be added, moved, or deleted at any time.
- Guides and objects can be made to snap to the ruler measurements.
- You can create an invisible grid and easily align all text and graphics on the grid.
- The zero point can be moved.
- On a color monitor, the guides are opaque and can hide thin lines that are underneath them. See 1.66a to send the guides to the back.

The rulers and ruler guides

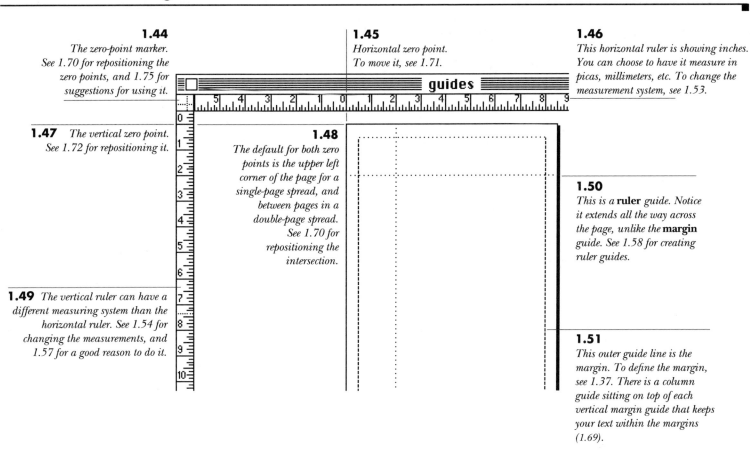

1.44
*The zero-point marker.
See 1.70 for repositioning the
zero points, and 1.75 for
suggestions for using it.*

1.45
*Horizontal zero point.
To move it, see 1.71.*

1.46
*This horizontal ruler is showing inches.
You can choose to have it measure in
picas, millimeters, etc. To change the
measurement system, see 1.53.*

1.47   *The vertical zero point.
See 1.72 for repositioning it.*

1.48
*The default for both zero
points is the upper left
corner of the page for a
single-page spread, and
between pages in a
double-page spread.
See 1.70 for
repositioning the
intersection.*

1.50
*This is a **ruler** guide. Notice
it extends all the way across
the page, unlike the **margin**
guide. See 1.58 for creating
ruler guides.*

1.49   *The vertical ruler can have a
different measuring system than the
horizontal ruler. See 1.54 for
changing the measurements, and
1.57 for a good reason to do it.*

1.51
*This outer guide line is the
margin. To define the margin,
see 1.37. There is a column
guide sitting on top of each
vertical margin guide that keeps
your text within the margins
(1.69).*

If you want to do this:	Then follow these steps:	Shortcuts ▾ Notes ▾ Hints
1.52a Show the rulers	▪ From the Layout menu slide down to "Guides and rulers," then over to the submenu and choose "Rulers"; a checkmark will appear next to the item to indicate they are showing (called "on").	▪ Press Command R.
1.52b Hide the rulers	▪ From the Layout menu slide down to "Guides and rulers," then over to the submenu and choose "Rulers"; the checkmark will disappear, indicating the Rulers are not showing ("off").	▪ Press Command R. ▪ While the rulers are hiding, the "Zero lock" command (1.74) cannot work.
1.53 Change the horizontal ruler measurements 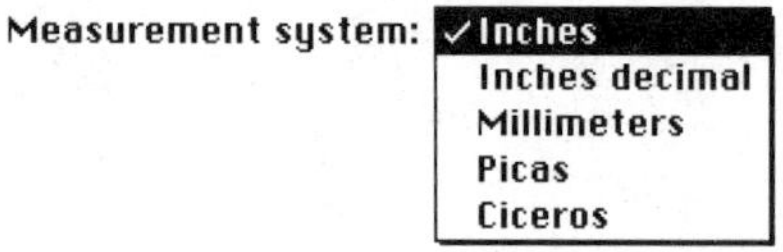 Measurement system: ✓ Inches / Inches decimal / Millimeters / Picas / Ciceros	▪ From the File menu choose "Preferences...." ▪ Press on the box next to "Measurement system" to get the pop-up menu; select the measurement of your choice.	▪ Changing the measuring system here will cause all other measurements in all other dialog boxes to follow the same system; e.g., column guides, paragraph spacing, hyphenation, etc. ▪ Measurements are accurate to $\frac{1}{2880}^{th}$ of an inch, supposedly at any size. ▪ Any measuring system can be temporarily overridden in any dialog box (1.323).
1.54 Change the vertical ruler measurements 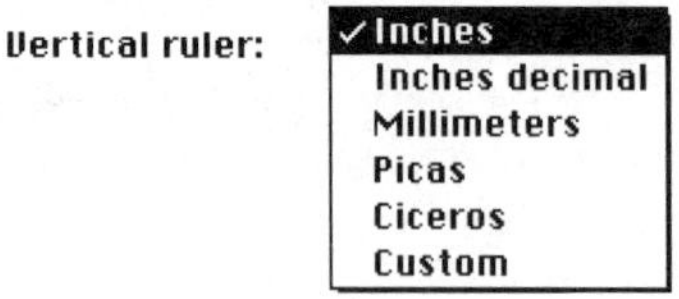 Vertical ruler: ✓ Inches / Inches decimal / Millimeters / Picas / Ciceros / Custom	▪ From the File menu choose "Preferences...." ▪ Press on the box next to "Vertical ruler" to get the pop-up menu; select the measurement of your choice (to work with "Custom," see 1.55).	▪ The vertical ruler measurements choice allows you to have different units of measure in each ruler. ▪ The *vertical measure* applies *only* to the vertical ruler; whereas the *measuring system* applies to every dialog box that uses measures, *as well as* to the horizontal ruler.

If you want to do this:

Then follow these steps:

Shortcuts ▾ Notes ▾ Hints

1.55 Use a custom measurement in the vertical ruler

┌─ Layout ──────────────────────────┐
│ Measurement system: │Inches│   │
│ Vertical ruler: │Custom│ │12│ points │
└───────────────────────────────────┘

- From the File menu choose "Preferences."
- Press on the box next to "Vertical measure" to see the pop-up menu; choose "Custom."
- Now in the box to the right there is a "12"; this is the default. Type in any number of points from 4 to 256.

- If you type in a point value that is the same as your leading, then it will be very easy to align the baselines of your type across the columns (which you really should be doing, you know; see 1.57).
- Use this in conjunction with "Snap to rulers" (1.56) to create an underlying grid that will make it remarkably easy to align all text and graphics at any size view.
- Just remember that when you change measurements, the text and graphics that were already on the page don't move to match the new measurements.

1.56 Use "Snap to rulers"

- From the Layout menu slide down to "Guides and rulers," then over to the submenu; if there is a checkmark next to "Snap to rulers," it is already on.
- If there is no checkmark, choose "Snap to rulers" *or* press Command [.

- With this command, all graphic tools, ruler guides, text blocks, and objects will snap to the tick marks on the rulers, rather than be able to be placed between exact increments. Notice the tick marks get more precise as the view gets larger (at 400% the inch ruler easily shows 32[nds] of an inch).
- Used in conjunction with the vertical ruler set in the point increments of your leading (1.55, this allows you to align the baselines of type across the columns very easily and precisely. In fact, it just does it for you—so take advantage of it (1.57).
- "Snap to rulers" works even if the rulers themselves are not showing.

1.57 SCENARIO #2: ALIGNING BASELINES

A baseline, of course, is the invisible line that type sits on. When there is text in more than one column on a page, it is very important, if the piece is to look unified and professional, that the baselines across the columns be aligned. The bottom of photos and graphics should also align with a baseline. PageMaker makes this very easy for you.

Mrs. Malaprop

The baseline, the imaginary line the type sits on.

- Simply follow the steps in 1.55 to customize the *vertical* ruler—in the "points" box, type the point size of the *leading* of your body text. (If your leading is "Auto," multiply the size of the type by 1.2—that is your leading; 5.59.) Your vertical ruler will now have tick marks in those point increments.
- From the Layout menu, slide down to "Guides and rulers," then over to choose "Snap to rulers" if it isn't already on (the checkmark indicates it is on).
- From the Layout menu, slide down to "Guides and rulers," then over to choose "Snap to guides" if it isn't already on (the checkmark indicates it is on).
- Now as you place ruler guides, text blocks, and graphic objects, they will automatically snap into position, following the ruler increments, and the baselines will be neatly aligned. You'll notice that even the tools (except the pointer and the text tool) will jump across the page, rather than move smoothly—they are jumping from tick mark to tick mark on the rulers.
- If you *do* want to place something *between* tick marks on the rulers, simply turn off the "Snap to rulers" command in the Layout menu and you will have control over the tools again.

If you have added a few extra points of space after paragraphs, or if you have subheads tucked into your body copy, this will throw off the consistency of your baseline alignments. They may align at the top of the page, or at the bottom of the page, but sometimes it is not possible to make them align all the way down, unless you have a thorough working knowledge of grid theory and are using it. If not, you do need to make a conscious decision to align those baselines either at the top or at the bottom, and follow your decision consistently throughout your publication.

There is another option you could use to align the baselines, even if headings and subheads throw them off alignment: the "Grid size" and "Align to grid" features (nested in the Paragraph command from the Type menu, 5.97–5.107, or in the Control palette, 4.306, 4.309). But this method creates uneven gaps, because it forces extra space between paragraphs or after headlines. This "Align to grid" feature does work effectively with inline graphics in many cases, though (5.71; 5.108–5.109).

If you want to do this: ∎	**Then follow these steps:** ∎	**Shortcuts ▾ Notes ▾ Hints** ∎
1.58 Add a ruler guide, either on a master page (1.130–1.135) **or** on any publication page	▪ Make sure the rulers are showing; if they are not, from the Layout menu, slide down to "Guides and rulers," then over to choose "Rulers" (see 1.52a) *or* press Command R. ▪ Using any tool, point in either ruler; the cursor will become an arrow. ▪ *Press* in the ruler; the cursor will become the two-headed arrow. This means you have picked up a ruler guide. Press-and-drag the two-headed arrow onto the screen; the dotted ruler guide will come along with it. Wherever you let go of the mouse button, there you will place the guide.	▪ Guides placed on the master pages will show up on every page. *They can be moved or deleted from any single page, though,* unlike other master page objects, such as text or graphics. ▪ Remember, these ruler guides will not print. You can have 40 per page, including any from the master pages. (This 40 per page actually means 40 per screen—if you have facing pages showing, you can only get 40 for both pages.) ▪ The Control palette displays the position of the pointer tool on the page as you drag ruler guides, helping you place guides precisely.
1.59 Reposition any ruler guide either on a master page (1.130–1.135) **or** on any publication page	▪ You must use the **pointer tool** to reposition a guide. ▪ *Press* on the guide (you should see the two-headed arrow) and drag it to its new position.	▪ *If you don't see the two-headed arrow, you have not picked up the ruler guide!* ▪ If you can't pick up a guide, you may have previously set the guides to stay in the **back** (1.66). If so, find a spot on the guide where nothing is overlapping it (no text block or graphic) and pick it up from there. ▪ Another possibility for not being able to pick up the guides is that you have *locked* them. Check the Layout menu (1.67). ▪ Repositioning or deleting master guides while on a *publication page* will not change them on any other page or on the master page.
1.60 Delete a ruler guide either on a master page (1.130–1.135) **or** on any publication page	▪ You must use the **pointer tool** to remove a guide. ▪ *Press* on the guide (you should see the two-headed arrow) and drag it off any edge of the screen, whether the rulers are showing or not, and let go. If the edge of the page is showing, you can just drop it.	

If you want to do this:	**Then follow these steps:**	**Shortcuts ▾ Notes ▾ Hints**
1.61 Show the master page guide changes on a publication page where they're not showing up	■ On the publication page, from the Layout menu choose "Copy master guides." If the command is gray, it means the current page is already displaying the master guides. If you can't see the guides, maybe they are hidden; see 1.64b.	■ You see, if you go back to the *master page* and change any ruler or column guide, that change *will not appear* on any publication page you have *customized;* that is, on any page where you added or moved or deleted a ruler or a column guide.
1.62 Delete all ruler guides at once, except the master guides	■ From the Layout menu, choose "Copy master guides."	■ If you want to delete **all** the guides from a publication page or facing pages, press the Shift key as you choose "Guides" from the Layout submenu, "Guides and rulers."
1.63 Delete all ruler guides on a page or facing pages	■ Hold down the Shift key; from the Layout menu slide down to "Guides and rulers," then over to choose "Guides."	■ If you do this on a master page instead, you can delete all the master guides on every page by choosing "Copy master guides" from the Layout menu for each page.
1.64a Hide all guides	■ If you can see the guides, then the "Guides and rulers" submenu, under Layout, has "Guides" with a checkmark next to it. Choose "Guides" again to take the checkmark off (or press Command J).	■ This is nice to do regularly to view your work without all the stuff in the way. ■ This gets rid of *all* guides, not just ruler guides. ■ When the guides are not showing, "Snap to guides" from the "Guides and rulers" submenu under the Layout menu will not function, nor can you create new column guides.
1.64b Show all guides	■ If you cannot see the guides, then the "Guides and rulers" submenu, under Layout, has no checkmark next to "Guides." Choose "Guides" again to show them (or press Command J).	

If you want to do this:	Then follow these steps:	Shortcuts • Notes • Hints
1.65a Use "Snap to guides"	▪ From the Layout menu, slide down to "Guides and rulers", then over to choose "Snap to guides" *or* press Command U. (When in effect, there will be a checkmark by the command.)	▪ This command causes any tool (except the pointer and the text tool) and anything you move, be it text or graphics, to snap to any guideline—ruler or column or margin—it gets close to. This doesn't mean you cannot place it *away* from a guide—it just means that if you get close to one, PageMaker will make sure it's placed right on it.
1.65b Turn off "Snap to guides"	▪ From the Layout menu, slide down to "Guides and rulers", then over to choose "Snap to guides" *or* press Command U.	
1.66a Send all guides to the back layer	▪ From the File menu choose "Preferences...." ▪ Under "Guides," click on "Back."	▪ All objects in PageMaker are on separate *layers*, including the guides. The default setting is for the guides to be the top layer. (See 1.189–1.195 for more info on layers.)
1.66b Bring all guides to the front layer	▪ From the File menu choose "Preferences...." ▪ Under "Guides," click on "Front."	▪ Sending the guides to front and back sends *all* guides—rulers, columns, and margins.
1.67a Lock all guides	▪ From the Layout menu, slide down to "Guides and rulers," then over to choose "Lock guides." This will put a checkmark by it.	▪ Locking the guides keeps them in their place so they can't be accidentally moved. This also helps prevent them from getting in the way when trying to pick up something from another layer.
1.67b Unlock all guides	▪ Reselect "Lock guides" as in the above task. This will take the checkmark off.	

1.68   Important note re: locking guides or sending them to the back: at first this seems like a good idea when you find yourself picking up ruler guides instead of drawn lines or objects. The problem is that the guides are so handy and so often used that it becomes more awkward to have them locked or behind. If a guide is in the way of an object, just **hold down the Command key** and you will be able to select the object (1.212). But when the *guides* are *behind,* you cannot grab them without moving the entire overlaying object.

25

If you want to do this:

Then follow these steps:

Shortcuts ▾ Notes ▾ Hints

1.69 Reposition margin guides

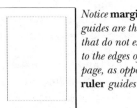

Notice **margin** *guides are the ones that do not extend to the edges of the page, as opposed to* **ruler** *guides (1.44).*

- You can't. Not from the page, anyway.
- But you *can* from the File menu: choose "Page setup."
- Change the values for the margins (1.37).

- Margin guides are the ones that *do not* extend the width/depth of the page.
- They cannot be picked up with any tool.
- When you reposition the margin guides, text that has already been placed *will not* adjust to the new margins—you'll have to do that yourself.
- The left and right *column guide defaults* are directly on top of the left and right *margins.* You *can* press-and-drag to move the *column* edges; you cannot move the margins.

1.70 Reposition the zero point, both horizontally and vertically

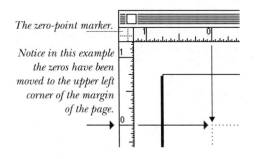

The zero-point marker.

Notice in this example the zeros have been moved to the upper left corner of the margin of the page.

- Check the "Guides and rulers" submenu under the Layout menu, to make sure "Zero lock" has no checkmark by it; if it does, choose "Zero lock" again to unlock.
- There is a white box in the upper left corner where the two rulers intersect, called the *zero-point marker.*
- Press in the zero-point marker, using any tool. Press-and-drag onto your page; intersecting guidelines will follow the mouse movement. The *intersection* is the zero point.
- When the intersection is where you want it, let go of the mouse button; the intersecting guides will disappear and the zeros will align at that point.

- Whenever you want to reposition the zero point, **you must start from the zero point marker again.**
- Changing the zero point is very handy for measuring column widths, measuring sizes of shapes and graphics, comparing items, centering zero on the page, etc.
- See Scenario #3: Using the zero point (1.75).
- The Control palette displays the position of the pointer tool on the screen as you drag the zero point, aiding you in placing it precisely where you want it.
- To put the zero point back in its default location, double-click in the zero point marker (1.73).

If you want to do this:	**Then follow these steps:**	**Shortcuts ▾ Notes ▾ Hints**
1.71 Reposition just the horizontal zero point (1.45)	■ Follow the steps in 1.70, but just drag *straight across* the horizontal ruler.	■ This leaves the vertical zero point intact.
1.72 Reposition just the vertical zero point (1.47)	■ Follow the steps in 1.70, but just drag *straight down* the vertical ruler.	■ This leaves the horizontal zero point intact.
1.73 Reset the zero point to its default position	■ Double-click in the zero-point marker.	■ The default position is the upper left corner of the page on a single page; the top center of a double-page spread.
1.74a Lock the zero point *When the zero point is locked, the zero point marker is blank*	■ From the Layout menu, slide down to "Guides and rulers," then over to choose "Zero lock." Zero lock now has a check-mark next to it on the menu and is "on."	■ Obviously, this locks the zero point in position so you don't accidentally move it.
1.74b Unlock the zero point *When the zero point is unlocked, the zero point marker has little guidelines*	■ From the Layout menu, slide down to "Guides and rulers," then over to choose "Zero lock." This removes the checkmark on the menu and turns it "off."	■ You must unlock the zero point before you can move it.

1.75 **Scenario #3: Using the Zero Point**

The default for the zero point is the upper left corner of the page on a single page, or the center of a double-page spread. Perhaps you are customizing your columns and you want the first column to be exactly two inches wide—you can move the zero point over to the left *margin* edge and measure from there.

The ruler reflects where one edge of the column gutter is—the edge the pointer is pressing on.

I moved the zero point to the upper left corner of the margin. I moved the column in to measure exactly two inches across.

Perhaps you need to draw a keyline or a box the width of the column and 4⁹⁄₁₆" deep. So bring down the *vertical* zero point to the place where the top of the box will start; measure down from there.

I moved the vertical zero point down so I could draw the box to measure.

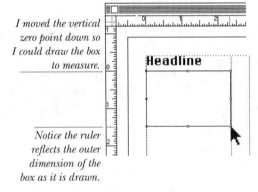

Headline

Notice the ruler reflects the outer dimension of the box as it is drawn.

To center a short rule (line) in the horizontal middle of an 8.5" page, bring the horizontal zero marker over to 4.25 (the center of 8.5). Follow the guidelines in the ruler as you draw the line; you can draw it precisely the same distance on either side of the centered zero.

I moved the zero point to the center of the page. Then I drew the rule equidistant from the zero, starting at -1.25 and ending at +1.25. Notice the ruler reflects the ends of the line.

Columns and Column Guides

1.76 Minimums and maximums:

Item	Minimum	Maximum
Columns	1	20 per page
Column width	.167 (=⅙") (=1 pica) (=12 pts.)	Page width
Space between columns	0	Width between margins

1.77 Column guides vs. margin guides

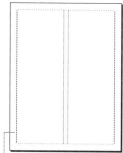

Text will flow between column guides. Margin guides (the outer border) do nothing but provide a visual reference. But remember, what you see here is a **column** *guide directly on top of the outer* **margin** *guide!*

1.78 With column guides you can control the flow of text onto the page—when you *place* text, it pours into the columns. You cannot *place* text (4.28–4.29) into the space between the columns, although you can *manually* insert type into it.

1.79 In PageMaker you can set up to 20 columns per page (typically they are kept within the margins that were determined in the Page Setup (1.37), but they *can* be dragged beyond, out to the edge of the paper).

1.80 After you specify columns, Page-Maker automatically places them on the page in equal widths, centered between the margins. You can customize them at any time to the width and placement of your choice. The column *widths* can all be different, but it is not possible to create columns with differing amounts of space *between* them on one single page.

1.81 It *is* possible, though, to set up a certain number of columns and place text in them, then change the number or width or placement of the columns without disturbing the type already set, and then pour more text into the new columns. The

Aldus manual likens it to wax being poured into a mold—after the mold is removed the wax stays put. This is one way to arrange multiple columns of text on a page.

1.82 If you want the same columns on every page in your publication, set the columns up on your master pages (1.84–1.87; 1.137). Even master columns, though, can always be customized on any single page, so you are not ever stuck with anything.

1.83 When you type directly into PageMaker, the insertion point will always create a text block across the *column* it is placed in, anchoring itself to either edge. Of course, this also can always be overridden if you choose (1.321; 4.62). Isn't it nice how PageMaker always lets *you* have control?

If you want to do this:

Then follow these steps:

Shortcuts ▾ Notes ▾ Hints

1.84   Create equal columns

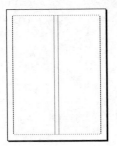

- From the Layout menu, choose "Column guides...."
- If your publication is double-sided and shows facing pages, there is a box that gives you the choice of setting a different number and size of columns for the left and the right pages; check that box if you want to do so.
- Type in a number from 1 to 20 in the box labeled "Number of columns."
- Type in the amount of space you want between the columns in the box labeled "Space between columns."
    If you want no space, type 0;
    If you want to override the current measurement (perhaps you want the space in picas rather than inches), see 1.323.

- If "Column guides..." is gray, it is probably because "Guides" is off. Choose "Guides" again to turn them back on, and "Column guides..." will then be available.
- There is usually a default of at least one column already on the page; it is not possible to have less than one column.
- Notice you can press on either margin edge, get the two-headed arrow, and drag the far outer left and right *column* guide edges anywhere you like (notice the *margin* guides stay put, though; 1.37; 1.77).
- Remember, in the dialog box you can press the Tab key to move from edit box to edit box. Actually, you can do this in any dialog box on the Mac, thus avoiding that reach for the mouse.
- You can create columns on one or both master pages (1.130–1.135) or on each separate publication page. Even if you create columns on a master page, you can still customize, add, or remove them on any publication page.

All you need
is love, love.
Love is all you need.
—John Lennon
Apple Records

If you want to do this:

Then follow these steps:

Shortcuts • Notes • Hints

1.85 Create unequal columns

- Create columns as in 1.84; click "OK," and then:
- On your page, choose the **pointer tool.**
- Press on a column guide (you will see the two-headed arrow) and drag the column to the desired position. Let go when it is where you want it to be placed. If the Control palette is showing, it displays the position of the pointer tool as you drag the column guide.

- The far outer left and right column guide edges sit right on the margin guides (1.77). You can also press-and-drag *those* column guides wherever you like, even outside of the margins. Text will align with the *column edges,* not with the *margin edges* (see 4.19).
- Notice as you move an inner column guide that has space between, both edges of that space come with you.
- When you move a column edge, the dotted line in the horizontal ruler moves *with the column edge the pointer is pressing on.* This allows you to place your column in the exact, measured position you want.
- Use the rulers in conjunction with the larger page views and repositioning with the zero point to measure columns and position them (see 1.70–1.72; 1.75).

1.86 Widen or narrow a column

- With the **pointer tool,** simply press on one edge of the column and drag it.

- Notice the ruler keeps track of the edge that is being dragged. The Control palette, too, displays the position of the pointer tool as it drags the column edge.
- From the page you can change the *width* of the columns, but not the *space between.* To change the space between columns, see 1.87.

If you want to do this:

Then follow these steps:

Shortcuts ▾ Notes ▾ Hints

1.87 Widen or narrow the space between columns

- From the Layout menu choose "Column guides...."
- If there is a *number* in the "Number of columns" box, then just type a new measurement in the "Space between columns" box.
- If it says *Custom* in the "Number of columns" box, you cannot change the space between. You will have to first replace *Custom* with a number, then you can change the space between.

- Remember, you can override the current measurement system if you prefer; for instance, if the dialog box is asking for inches, you could use picas instead (1.323).

- It says *Custom* because you moved a column on that page. Replacing *Custom* with a number will center that number of columns between the margins again.

1.88 Revert the columns to equal widths

- From the Layout menu choose "Column guides...."
- If you have moved any column edge, the "Number of columns" box now says "Custom." Simply type in a number here and PageMaker will reset the columns.

- The columns will be reset to their original formation: centered between the margin guides.

1.89 Change a master page column guide on one publication page

- With the **pointer tool,** simply press-and-drag any column edge to its new position.

- Even though it may be a column that was originally placed on a master page, you can pick it up and move it just like any other guide. *This will not affect the master page columns or columns on any other page.*

1.90 Revert any customized columns back to the master page columns

- On the publication page, from the Layout menu choose "Copy master guides."

- Doing this will replace *all* guides (column and ruler guides) with the master guides.

If you want to do this:	**Then follow these steps:**	**Shortcuts ▾ Notes ▾ Hints**
1.91 Delete all columns	■ From the Layout menu choose "Column Guides...." ■ In the "Number of columns" box type in the number 1 (you cannot have fewer than one column).	■ If you do this on your master pages, it will delete all columns from all the pages *where you did not customize them.* Any customized columns will stay the same. ■ To delete any customized columns after deleting the master columns, from the Layout menu choose "Copy master guides" on each relevant page.
1.92a Hide the column guides	■ From the Layout menu choose "Guides." This will take the checkmark off the command.	■ Doing this will hide or show *all* the guides—rulers, columns, and margins. ■ When the guides are hidden, the "Snap to guides" function doesn't work, nor can you create columns.
1.92b Show the column guides	■ From the Layout menu choose "Guides." This will put a checkmark next to the command.	
1.93a Send the column guides to the back	■ From the File menu choose "Preferences...." ■ Under "Guides," click in the button "Back" to send the guides to the back.	■ Column guides, like all guides, are on the top layer (layers: 1.189–1.195). If you find this irritating because they get in the way when you're trying to grab other objects, send them to the back.
1.93b Bring the column guides to the front	■ From the File menu choose "Preferences...." ■ Under "Guides," click in the button "Front" to bring the guides to the front.	■ *You can select an object under a guide* by pressing the Command key and clicking on the object you want. ■ When guides are at the back, though, there is no way to reach them if they are under any other layer, not even with Command-clicking.

If you want to do this:	**Then follow these steps:**	**Shortcuts ▾ Notes ▾ Hints**
1.94a Lock the column guides in place	▪ From the Layout menu slide down to "Guides and rulers," then over to the submenu to choose "Lock guides." This places a checkmark next to the command.	▪ This command locks *all* guides—rulers, columns, margins. It locks guides that are currently on the page, as well as any new ones that are created. ▪ This is another solution to the problem of the guides being on the top layer. If they are locked, they cannot be moved and thus their layer does not get in the way of selecting objects.
1.94b Unlock the column guides	▪ From the "Guides and rulers" submenu choose "Lock guides." This removes the checkmark from the command.	▪ Actually, though, in general practice it is much easier to Command-click (1.211; 1.212) to get beneath guides than it is to keep locking and unlocking them (or sending them to the back).

Passion without reason is blind; reason without passion is dead.   *—Will Durant, paraphrasing Spinoza*

Pages and Page Views

1.95 A publication in PageMaker can be up to 999 pages long (limited, of course, by your disk storage space). Each page is represented by a page icon. If there are more than 15 or so pages in the publication (depending on the size of your screen), scroll arrows will appear on either end of the line of icons. This subsection details all the ways of moving from one page to another.

1.96 PageMaker provides eight different sizes with which to view your document, plus a custom view magnification. From mini-view (where you can see the entire pasteboard) to 800% (where precision alignment is remarkable), each view has its own advantages.

1.97 Interruptible screen redraw gives you more speed in PageMaker. You can move to a new page and before the page even appears, choose a page view from the menu or with a key command. You can zoom up and down in page magnification without waiting for the screen to redraw in each view—this is especially handy when you want to zoom out to see, and quickly click on an item to zoom in on at a greater magnification.

1.98 In "Page setup" you determined how many pages were to be in your publication. At any time, though, you can add or delete pages. As you do this, the page icons come and go also, and pages are renumbered to adjust for it.

1.99

In a double-sided publication, the page icon indicates whether it is a right-hand page (odd-numbered) or a left-hand page (even-numbered). In a single-sided publication, all pages are right-hand.

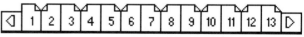

This arrangement indicates that there are more than 13 pages in this publication, and it is set up double-sided with facing pages. Notice the scroll arrows at either end.

If you want to do this:	**Then follow these steps:**	**Shortcuts ▾ Notes ▾ Hints**
1.100 Go to the next page	■ Click on the icon of the next page.	■ Press Command Tab.
1.101 Go to the previous page	■ Click on the icon of the previous page.	■ Press Command Shift Tab.
1.102 Go several pages next	■ Press Command Tab Tab Tab, pressing a quick Tab for each page you want to pass; e.g., three Tabs will take you three pages over.	■ You won't see the pages in-between—you will go directly to the page. ■ If your pages are double-sided, each Tab takes you over one double-page spread.
1.103 Go several pages previous	■ Press Command Shift Tab Tab Tab, pressing a quick Tab for each page you want to go back; e.g., three Shift-Tabs will take you three pages previous.	■ You won't see the pages in-between—you will go directly to the page. ■ If your pages are double-sided, each Tab takes you over one double-page spread.
1.104 Go to any page, if there are fewer than about 15 pages *(meaning all page icons are visible)*	■ Click on the icon of the page.	
1.105 Go to any page, if there are more than about 15 pages *(page icon scroll arrows are visible)*	■ With any tool, press on the scroll arrow at either end of the page icons to find the page number you want; then click on the page icon. • **OR** from the Layout menu choose "Go to page…"; type in the number; click OK.	■ No matter which tool you are using, the cursor will become the arrow when it is on a page icon. ■ Press Command G; type the page number; hit Return.

If you want to do this:	Then follow these steps:	Shortcuts ▾ Notes ▾ Hints

1.106a Show the last page **icon** in the publication
- Hold down the Command key.
- Click on the right arrow at the *end* of the page icons.

Page icon scroll arrows

1.106b Show the first page **icon** in the publication
- Hold down the Command key.
- Click on the left arrow at the *beginning* of the page icons.

- This trick doesn't take you to the *page;* it just makes the page icon visible so you can click on it.

1.107 Jump past half-a-dozen page icons
- Hold down the Shift key.
- Click on one of the page icon arrows.

1.108 Pan through all the pages
- Hold down the Shift key.
- From the Layout menu choose "Go to page..."; let go of the Shift key.
- Click the mouse when you want the cycle to stop.

- Starting at the first page, PageMaker will cycle through all the pages in the publication. When the last page is reached, the cycle will begin again, skipping the master pages.

1.109 From a master page, return to the page you were last working on
- Press Command Tab.

1.110 Change the view of the page you are *going to* into "Fit in Window" size
- Hold down the Shift key while clicking on the page icon.

- When that page appears, it will be in "Fit in Window" size.

1.111 View the entire page in the window *("Fit in window")*
- Press Command W (W for Window); **or** hold the Shift key down and click on the current page icon; **or** while at Actual Size, hold down the Command and Option keys and click anywhere in the window.

- Command W is a good shortcut to keep in mind even if you are already in that view; sometimes at "Fit in window" you move the pages so they are off-center— Command W will place them right back in the middle of the window instantly.

If you want to do this:	Then follow these steps:	Shortcuts ▾ Notes ▾ Hints
1.112 View the entire pasteboard (1.4) (*"Show pasteboard," the mini-view; also known as "Fit in World"*)	■ From the Layout menu slide down to "View"; from the submenu choose "Show pasteboard."	■ In this view you can see the entire pasteboard, which comes in very handy when you're looking for things you placed off to one side earlier. On a large screen you may not notice a big difference between this and the 25% view.
1.113 View the page at 25%	■ From the Layout menu, slide down to "View," then over to the submenu to choose "25%" **or** press Command 0 (zero).	■ 25% depends, of course, on the page size of your document.
1.114 View the page at 50%	■ From the Layout menu, slide down to "View," then over to the submenu to choose "50%," **or** press Command 5 (5 for 50%).	■ 50% is a good view for placing rules and text blocks. If your "Snap to rulers" and "Snap to guides" from the "Guides and rulers" submenu are on, your placements will be extremely precise.
1.115 View the page at 75%	■ From the Layout menu, slide down to "View," then over to the submenu to choose "75%" **or** press Command 7 (7 for 75%).	■ 75% and 50% are great for drawing lines between columns or across the page.
1.116 View the page at Actual Size	■ While in any view and with any tool, **point** to the area you wish to see at Actual Size. ■ Hold down the Command and Option keys. ■ Click.	■ Of course, it is possible to get to Actual Size by choosing that command from the "View" submenu (Layout menu) *or* by pressing Command 1, but those methods don't always take you where you want to go, and you often have to scroll around looking for your work. This method takes you directly to what you want to see.

If you want to do this:	**Then follow these steps:**	**Shortcuts ▾ Notes ▾ Hints**
1.117 View the page at 200% *(twice Actual Size)*	■ While in any view and with any tool, **point** to the area you wish to see at 200%. ■ Hold down the Command, Option, and Shift keys. ■ Click where you are pointing.	■ Of course, it is possible to get to 200% by choosing that command from the "View" submenu (under the Layout menu) *or* by pressing Command 2, but those methods don't always take you where you want to go, and you have to scroll around looking for your work. This method takes you directly to what you want to see. ■ If something is selected, that item will be centered when the view changes to 200% from the menu. ■ 200% view is great for precise alignment!
1.118 View the page at 400%	■ From the Layout menu, slide down to "View," then over to the submenu and choose "400%," **or** press Command 4 (4 for 400%). ■ If something is selected, that item will be centered when the view changes to 400%.	■ 400% *seems* like the place to go for incredibly precise alignment; if your ruler is in picas, each tick mark is 2 points ($\frac{1}{36}$ of an inch). Unfortunately, what you see is not always what you get—you'll notice things look different in Actual Size, in 200%, and in 400%. What you see in 200% seems to be the most accurate.
1.119 Change the view of *all* the pages in the publication	■ Hold down the Option key while choosing a view from the menu.	■ This will change every page to the view of your choice, so the next time you go to any page, it's set the way you want.

If you want to do this:	Then follow these steps:	Shortcuts · Notes · Hints
1.120 Toggle between "Actual size" and "Fit in window" view	■ In the "Actual size" view, with any tool selected, hold down the Command and Option keys and click the mouse button. ■ In the "Fit in window" view, with any tool selected, hold down the Command and Option keys and click the mouse button, while pointing at the area you want to view at "Actual size."	■ In the "Actual size" view, whenever you Command Option click, the view will change to "Fit in window." In any other view, when you Command Option click you will zoom to "Actual size"; see 1.116.
1.121 Toggle between "Actual size" and "200% size"	■ In the "Actual size" view, with any tool selected, hold down the Command, Option, and Shift keys, point to the area you wish to see at 200%, and click the mouse button. ■ In the "200% size," with any tool selected, hold down the Command, Option, and Shift keys, point to the area you wish to see at 100%, and click the mouse button.	■ You can switch to "200% size" in any view with this keyboard shortcut. ■ In the 200% view you can press either Command Option Shift and click, *or* Command Option and click, to view the page at 100%.
1.122 Use the magnifying tool to enlarge the page to the next page view size	■ Press down the Command key, then the Spacebar, ■ Click once on the page.	■ The tool icon turns into a magnifying lens with a plus (+) sign in it. You can also marquee an area with the magnifying tool to custom enlarge it, see 1.124. ■ The magnifying tool will be empty inside when there is no further magnification possible.

If you want to do this:	Then follow these steps:	Shortcuts ▾ Notes ▾ Hints
1.123 Use the reducing tool to reduce the page to the previous page view size	■ Hold down the Command key, then the Option key, then the Spacebar, ■ Click once on the page.	■ Notice the tool icon turns into a magnifying lens with a minus (-) sign in it. Any tool will turn into the reducing tool when you press the Command Option Spacebar combination. ■ The reducing tool will be empty inside when there is no further reduction possible.
1.124 Custom enlarge a section of the page using the magnifying tool	■ Hold down the Command key and the Spacebar, then press-and-drag with the mouse to draw a marquee around the area you want to enlarge.	■ Maximum enlargement is 800%. The amount of magnification depends on the amount of area you marquee. ■ The magnifying tool will be empty when no further magnification is possible.
1.125 View the pages of a publication without the scroll bars showing	■ From the Layout menu slide down to "Guides and rulers," and over to the submenu to choose "Scrollbars."	■ This removes the checkmark next to "Scrollbars." Follow the same directions to reselect the command and see the scrollbars again. ■ To move the page without using the scrollbars, use the grabber hand; see 1.126. ■ The page icons also disappear when the Scrollbars are not showing. You can press Command Tab to move ahead pages, Command Shift Tab to go back pages, or use the "Go to page…" command; see 1.100–1.103, 1.105.

If you want to do this:

Then follow these steps:

Shortcuts ▾ Notes ▾ Hints

1.126 Move the page in any direction without using scroll bars

 The grabber hand cursor

- With any tool selected, hold down the Option key.
- *When you press the mouse,* the tool cursor will become the grabber hand.
- Press-and-drag; the hand will move the page around in any direction for you.
  □ If you hold the Shift key down in addition to the Option key, you will restrain the movement of the hand to just vertical or just horizontal, whichever direction you move first.

- Using the grabber hand allows you to move more freely and with more control
- Using the Shift key makes the grabber hand act just like a scroll bar, but you have more control over the speed.

1.127 Add or insert pages

- Pages are always inserted *before, after,* or *between* the page(s) you are viewing, so go to the appropriate page (1.100–1.105).
- From the Layout menu choose "Insert pages...."
- Choose whether to insert the page *before* the page you are viewing, *after* it, or— if you have facing pages—*between.*
- Click OK.

- You can Undo the insert if you do it *before you click the mouse or switch tools:* from the Edit menu choose "Undo insert pages," or press Command Z.
- If the publication is double-sided, be aware that if you add or delete an *odd* number of pages, all the left-hand pages will become right-hand pages and vice versa; your placed objects will adjust to the switched left and right *margins,* but if there are any differences in column widths or placements, they will all have to be adjusted manually.
- Inserting pages automatically creates new page icons and renumbers any automatically-numbered pages.

If you want to do this:	Then follow these steps:	Shortcuts • Notes • Hints
1.128 Remove or delete pages	■ From the Layout menu choose "Remove pages...." ■ Type in the page number(s) of the page(s) you wish to remove. If you want to remove only one page, type the same page number in both boxes. ■ Click OK; you will get a warning box thoughtfully checking to make sure you really want to do this. If you do, click OK.	■ If you decide you want those pages back, *don't touch a thing!* See 1.129 below. ■ Deleting pages automatically deletes their page icons. ■ If pages have been auto-numbered with Command Option P (1.147a, b), all those numbers will automatically adjust. ■ Be forewarned: in a double-sided publication, if you add or delete an *odd* number of pages, all the left-hand pages will become right-hand pages and vice versa; objects will adjust to the new left and right *margins,* but you will have to make any other adjustments manually.

1.129 Replace pages that were deleted	■ If you haven't made any move since you deleted the pages (screaming is okay), you can use the Edit menu to choose "Undo delete pages."	■ Really, Undo won't work if you do *anything* before you choose to Undo—don't even click the mouse or change tools!
		■ You do have one safety catch: Revert or mini-Revert.
		  □ If you choose "Revert" from the File menu, the publication will revert to the way it was last time you saved, which is why you should save very often, like every three minutes.
		  □ If you hold the Shift key down while you choose "Revert," the publication will revert to the last *mini-save* (the last time you added or deleted a page, etc.; 18.2).

Master Pages

1.130 You can create a PageMaker publication with up to 999 pages. If every page in a publication of this length had an 8-point rule (line) across the top of the page, it would take a long time just to set that up. And then if you changed your mind and wanted a 4-point rule instead, it would take just as long to change it all.

1.131 Well, thank goodness PageMaker has **master pages.** Anything you place on a master page will show up on every page in the publication (which I call *publication pages,* to distinguish them). You can draw that 8-point rule on *one* master page and it will show up on all 999 pages. If you change your mind later, you can change the line to a 4-point rule on that one master page and it is instantly changed on all 999 pages.

1.132 Text, graphics, column guides, ruler guides, text-wrapping attributes, and automatic page numbers can all be placed on a master page. Even though they appear on all pages, you do have the option of ignoring all master elements on any page, hiding any of them, and modifying any master *guides.* You cannot *alter* any master page item (except guides) while you are on a *publication page;* that is, if you want to change or edit objects or text, you must return to the master page.

1.133 Master pages are identified in the bottom left corner of the screen by the pages with the L and R (Left-hand and Right-hand). If your publication is not double-sided, you will see only a right-hand page.

Master page icons for a double-sided document.   *Master page icon for a single-sided document.*

1.134 *Master pages themselves cannot be printed.* It is possible to ask for 0 (zero) pages in Page Setup, and you will still have master pages. But no matter what you put on them, they won't print.

1.135 If you want hard copy of the master page, you must create at least one page (1.127) for a single-sided publication, and two for a double-sided; then you can print those new pages.

If you want to do this:	**Then follow these steps:**	**Shortcuts ▾ Notes ▾ Hints**
1.136 Go to a master page	▪ In the bottom left corner of the window is a page icon marked **R**; if the page setup specifies *double-sided,* then there are two page icons, one **L** and one **R**—these are page icons for the **master pages**. ▪ Click on one of the master page icons to go to that page. ▪ **OR** use the "Go to page…" command from the Layout menu (Command G).	▪ If the publication is *not* double-sided, then anything you place on the one master page will show up on every page. ▪ If the publication *is* double-sided, then you can set up items to appear only on left- or right-hand pages separately. ▪ To return to the publication page you were working on, press Command Tab.
1.137 Set up guides on a master page	▪ Set up margin guides (1.37), ruler guides (1.58), and column guides (1.84–1.85) just as you would on any other page.	▪ These guides will show up on every page, but unlike the graphics or text on a master page, guides can be moved or removed from any publication page with the pointer tool (except, of course, for the margin guides). ▪ If you go back to your master page and change the guides, those changes *will not appear* on any publication page where you have customized (added, removed, or moved) any guides. See 1.138.
1.138 Show newly-created master guides on a previously-created or customized publication page	▪ While viewing the publication page, from the Layout menu choose "Copy master guides."	▪ If you create pages first, then go back and create a master page, you will have to follow this step in order to see the *guides.*
1.139 Place text on a master page	▪ Create text in PageMaker (4.5–4.27) or place text (4.28–4.62) on a master page just as you would on any publication page.	▪ Any text you place on a master page will show up on every page, *but you will not be able to edit or move it on the publication pages.*

If you want to do this:	Then follow these steps:	Shortcuts ▾ Notes ▾ Hints
1.140 Place a graphic on a master page	■ Create graphics in PageMaker (Section 2) or place graphics (10.126) on a master page just as you would on any publication page.	■ Any graphic placed on a master page will show up on every page, *but you will not be able to edit or move it on the publication pages.*
1.141 Set up a graphic to text wrap on a master page	■ Follow the same procedure as you would on any publication page (Section 13).	■ Text on the master page will wrap around the graphic, as will text on every publication page! See 13.38.
1.142 Modify or delete master page items from the master page	■ You must **return** to the master page in order to modify it; click on the **L** or **R** page icon. ■ Modify or delete text (Section 4), graphics (Section 10), or guides (Section 1) just as you would from any other page.	■ You can go back to a master page at any time and modify any element; it will instantly change every publication page— *except* guides (1.138).
1.143 *Remove* master page items from any single page in the publication	■ While viewing any publication page, from the Layout menu choose "Display master items." This will remove the checkmark from the menu command and remove all master page text and graphics from that one page; guidelines will remain.	■ Unfortunately, if you have facing pages showing it is not possible to delete master items from one side and not the other. See 1.144 for a trick to hide some of the objects. See the tip in 21.5 for using the power-paste feature to display specific master page items.

If you want to do this:	**Then follow these steps:**	**Shortcuts · Notes · Hints**
1.144 Hide just *some* of the master page objects so they don't appear on the publication page *(and thus will not print)*	■ With the drawing tools (Section 2), create opaque boxes ("None" line and "Paper" fill) and cover the items you don't want to see or print. Also see 21.5 for another trick along these same lines: hiding all the master page items, but power-pasting the ones you *do* want on the page.	■ Hiding a master page object that has a text wrap attached to it will not prevent text from wrapping around it on the publication page. Only turning off "Display master items" from the Layout menu will stop text wrap on a master object.
1.145 View (display) the master page items on the publication page *(if for some reason they're not visible)*	■ While viewing the publication page, choose "Display master items" from the Layout menu. This will place a checkmark next to the command and will show all text and graphics from the master pages.	■ If there is already a checkmark next to "Display master items," it means they are already visible. If you don't see anything, check your master page to make sure they are there. ■ Also check to make sure there are no opaque boxes covering the master items (with the pointer tool, choose "Select all" from the Edit menu; all handles will show up. Now, are there handles covering the areas where there are supposed to be master items? If so, click once to remove all handles, but remember where the ones are that border the objects you want to get rid of. Then select and remove those opaque boxes; 1.214).

Not only is typeset copy between 20 and 40 percent more readable and legible than typewritten copy, it saves space and is more likely to be read and remembered. *~Allan Haley*

If you want to do this:	**Then follow these steps:**	**Shortcuts ▾ Notes ▾ Hints**

1.146 There are three ways to number your pages in PageMaker:

- Type the number **manually** on any page. This number will never change until you retype it.
- Type an **automatic placeholder** on a *master page*. This number will change as pages are added or deleted. It will appear in the same place on every page (1.147a).
- Type an **automatic placeholder** on the *individual pages*. This number will also change as pages are added or deleted. It can be placed on each page individually (1.147b).

1.147a Automatically number the pages *from the master page* so every page number will be in the same place

- Go to a master page; view at Actual Size (1.116) the spot where you want to place the number.
- Choose the **text tool** (the **A**; 4.10).
- Click to set the insertion point at the approximate placement for the number, **or** create a bounding box to hold it (1.319).
- Press **Command Option P**; this will create an **LM** or an **RM** which is the *placeholder,* standing for Left Master or Right Master. (Don't worry—on every *publication page* LM or RM will turn into the actual number of that page.)
- Select the text with the **text tool** and change the font, style, size, and alignment to suit your fancy (Section 4).
- With the **pointer tool,** reposition the page number text block (press-and-drag it; 4.115) wherever you like.

- You can also type any other text with the page number to create composite numbers, such as *Page 0* or *– 0–* or *4–0* or anything else you like; simply type in the text, then press Command Option P where you want the number to appear.
- If your pages are double-sided, you will have to create one placeholder on *each* of the two master pages, left and right.
- Right-hand pages are *always* even; left-hand pages are *always* odd.
- The page will be numbered with the number that is on its page icon.
- The numbering starts with the number that is entered in the "Page setup" dialog box (1.30), found under the File menu (1.19).
- All pages will automatically renumber when you change the number in the "Start page #" box in the "Page setup" dialog box, or when you add or delete pages.
- See 1.148 for formatting the numbers as Arabic, Roman, or alphabetic.

If you want to do this:	**Then follow these steps:**	**Shortcuts ▾ Notes ▾ Hints**
1.147b Automatically number the pages individually	■ Follow the steps in 1.147a, but do it on any publication page.	■ Well, you might ask, why should you bother using the auto feature on individual pages rather than manually typing each page number? Because auto numbers will automatically change if you insert or delete pages or change the page number you started the publication with. Any page number you type manually will simply stay that very number. ■ Numbering the pages individually allows you to vary the placement and choose which pages are to be numbered. ■ Sometimes you may need to hide the master page items (1.143). You can still set an automatic, individual page number.
1.148 Format the *automatic* page numbers, whether on the master page or on individual pages Style: ◉ Arabic numeral 1, 2, 3, ... ○ Upper Roman I, II, III, ... ○ Lower Roman i, ii, iii, ... ○ Upper alphabetic A, B, C, ... AA, ○ Lower alphabetic a, b, c, ... aa,	■ From the File menu choose "Page setup." ■ Click on the button "Numbers...." ■ Click in the button to choose your style. *Be sure to read the notes in the next column* ☞	■ Roman numeral styles, both upper- and lowercase, can only number as high as 4,999; 5,000 through 9,999 appear as regular Arabic numbers (1, 2, 3...). ■ Alphabetic style, both upper- and lowercase, can only number as high as ZZ (52); 53 through 9,999 appear as Arabic numbers. ■ No matter what format you have, the page icons appear as normal (Arabic) numbers. ■ See 1.149 for the few instances where you can override the format.

If you want to do this:	**Then follow these steps:**	**Shortcuts ▾ Notes ▾ Hints**
1.149 Override the automatic page number **formatting** on pages you have automatically numbered individually	▪ Read the column to the right. ▪ With the **text tool,** on the publication page double-click on the page number to select it. ▪ Press Command Shift K (that's the keyboard shortcut to turn lowercase letters into uppercase letters; you could, of course, go into "Type specs..." from the Type menu and change the "Case"). ▪ To change the numbers back to lower-case again, repeat the process (you can turn lowercase into uppercase and back again, but you can't turn text that has been *typed* as uppercase into lowercase).	▪ The only overriding you can do is to change lowercase Roman or lowercase alphabetic into uppercase (i.e., iii into III, or bb into BB). ▪ You can only override pages that you numbered individually. Well, you *can* override it on the master page, but why bother—if you're going to do that, it makes more sense to just change the formatting style from the "Page setup" dialog box.
1.150 Quick tip for auto-numbering individual pages	Create an automatic page number (type Command Option P) on the pasteboard; it will display **PB** (for pasteboard). ▪ Format it with the font, style, alignment, size, etc., that you want. Size the text block conveniently. ▪ Leave it on the pasteboard, completely off the publication page. Whenever you need it, select it with the **pointer tool,** copy it, and paste it on. Whichever page you paste it onto, the PB will turn into that page number.	▪ Use this as a trick for telling what page you are on when working in a document with more than 999 pages! (The page icons start over with 1 after 999 pages.) Drag any edge of the text block onto the page to see the true page number, 21.33. ▪ Selecting it with the pointer tool rather than the text tool will retain the text block form. If you select it with the text tool and paste it, the text block will conform to the column, as usual.

Multiple Publications

1.151 You can open as many PageMaker publications as your computer can handle. The more RAM (Random Access Memory) you have, the more publications you can have open at one time.

1.152 The advantage is that you can work in more than one publication at a time. You can easily copy text or graphics from one publication to another, or check spelling, or search-and-replace text in all the publications at once. You can even Save or Close them all in one keystroke!

1.153 The Window menu lists the titles of all the open publications. When you choose a title from this list, that publication becomes the active window. A click of the mouse on any part of any publication window also serves to bring it forward and make it the active window.

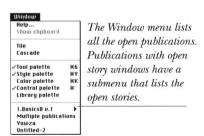

The Window menu lists all the open publications. Publications with open story windows have a submenu that lists the open stories.

1.154 All the usual page "View" options (such as 25%, 50%, Actual size, etc.) are available for displaying the active publication. But you can also choose to display all the open publications on screen in a stacked (cascaded) or tiled fashion.

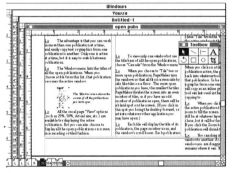

In Cascade view, the open windows are stacked so the title bar of each is visible.

1.155 When you choose **"Cascade"** from the Window menu, all the publications you have open are stacked one in front of the other so that the title bar of each window is visible. The publication that is active when you choose the "Cascade" command, remains active, and is in full window view. The contents of the Style, Color and Control palettes reflect the active publication.

1.156 To make any other publication window active, simply click in its title bar, or select it from the Window menu. When you bring a window forward, it covers the title bars of the windows that were in front of it in cascade view. Choose "Cascade" again, if you wish to see all the title bars.

1.157 To see a cascaded window at full screen view, click in the Zoom box in the upper right-hand corner. The Zoom box acts as a toggle between viewing a window at full size and at the size it is in cascade view. You can also manually change the size of any window by dragging on the size box in the lower right-hand corner.

1.158 Cascading publication windows is useful when you want to make changes in a bunch of publications and want to proceed logically through them all one by one.

1.159 The "Cascade" command is also available in the Story editor for cascading all the open story windows in a publication (see 9.33). When you hold down the Option key before you press on the Window menu, "Cascade" becomes "Cascade all," and *all* the open stories in *all* the open publications are cascaded.

Tiling multiple publications

1.160 When you choose "Tile" from the Window menu, PageMaker will tile the windows side by side, row by row, like tiles on a floor. You can press on an item in one window, drag it to another window, and watch a copy magically appear there.

1.161 PageMaker divides the screen into an even number of tiles, so if you have an odd number of publications open, there will be an empty space on the screen. (If you click in this spot you bring the Finder desktop forward, or activate whatever other application you may have open.) Depending on the number of open publications, and the size of your screen, the tiles may overlap a little, or a lot.

1.162 The publication that is active when you chose "Tile" from the Window menu remains active in the tiled view. You can make any of the publications active by clicking once anywhere in the window or title bar. If you have the Style, Color, or Control palettes displayed on screen, their contents reflect the palette of the active publication.

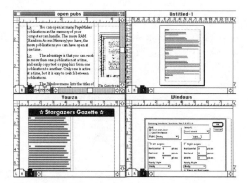

Four open publications in "Tile" view. Each one is at the layout "View" you last chose.

1.163 Each tile displays the title of its publication, the page number icons, and the window's scroll boxes. Each publication appears in its tile on the page and at the size at which you last viewed it. Any choice you make from the menu, such as choosing a "View" from the Layout menu (or using keyboard shortcuts) affects the publication in the active window.

1.164 As you move between tiles, your cursor automatically turns into the pointer tool. When you click on a tile to make it active, the pointer tool reverts to the last tool you used in that publication.

1.165 When you click in the Zoom box of the active publication, that window zooms to fill the screen. The publication stays at whatever layout view you last chose. If you click the Zoom box again, the publication will shrink to its tiled size.

1.166 You can drag objects from one window to another. A copy is placed in the window you are dragging to while the original remains where it was. Remember, though, that in each publication, the last tool you used is still selected. If you drag an object to a publication in which the text tool is selected, it will copy as an inline graphic! (See 1.180.)

1.167 You can drag text blocks from one publication to another. If the insertion point is flashing, the text will paste into the existing text block; if text is selected, the text you are dragging in will replace it.

1.168 In the Story Editor, you can choose to tile all the open story windows. If you hold down the Option key before you press on the Window menu, the tile command becomes "Tile all." All the open stories in all the open publications will tile on screen.

If you want to do this:	**Then follow these steps:**	**Shortcuts ▾ Notes ▾ Hints**
1.169 Open an existing publication	■ If the PageMaker application is not open: □ Double-click on the icon of the file you want to open. ■ If PageMaker is open (you are on the PageMaker desktop): □ From the File menu choose "Open," or press Command O. □ In the "Open publication" dialog box double-click on the file you want, or single click it, then click the "Open" button.	■ When you double-click on a file created in PageMaker it opens the application as well as the file.
1.170 Open more than one publication	■ From the File menu choose "Open," or press Command O. ■ In the "Open publication" dialog box double-click on the file you want, or single click it, then click the Open button. ■ Repeat the procedure for each publication you want to open.	■ Or, from the Finder, you can shift-select several publications and double-click (or choose "Open") to open them all at once. ■ You can open as many publications as the memory (RAM) in your computer can handle. PageMaker will yell at you when there is not enough memory to open another publication.
1.171 Create a "New" publication without closing the active publication	■ From the File menu choose "New." ■ In the "Page setup" dialog box choose the specifications you want the publication to have. ■ Click OK.	■ When you create a new publication, or open an existing one, it becomes the active window. You can easily switch between all the open publications, see 1.172.

If you want to do this:	Then follow these steps:	Shortcuts ▾ Notes ▾ Hints
1.172 Switch between open publications	▪ From the Window menu choose the title of the publication you want to view.	▪ The titles of all the open publications are listed at the bottom of the Window menu. ▪ If you have the Style, Color, or Control palettes displayed on screen, their contents reflect the palette of the active publication.
1.173 Save changes made in all the open publications in one step	▪ Hold down the Option key, then from the File menu choose "Save all."	▪ Of course this could take awhile, especially if you selected "Smaller" in the Save option in the "Preferences" dialog box.
1.174 Close all the open publications in one step	▪ Hold down the Option key, then from the File menu choose "Close all."	▪ PageMaker prompts you with a "Save reminder" for each document that's been changed since the last time you saved.
1.175 Cascade all the open publication windows.	▪ From the Window menu choose "Cascade."	▪ When you choose "Cascade" or "Tile" the active publication remains active.
1.176 View a different window in the cascade layout.	▪ Click once in the title bar of the publication you want to view.	▪ Really you can click on any part of the window that shows. It's just easier to be sure you have the right window if you click the title bar.
1.177 Tile all the open publication windows	▪ From the Window menu choose "Tile."	▪ Notice that "Tile" does not get a checkmark next to it. You cannot go back and deselect "Tile." See the next task for undoing "Tile." You *can* manually resize and/or rearrange the windows.

If you want to do this:	Then follow these steps:	Shortcuts ▾ Notes ▾ Hints
1.178 Bring one window from the tiled layout forward	▪ If the window is not active, click once in the title bar, or anywhere within the publication window, to make it active. ▪ Click in the zoom box in the upper right hand corner of the title bar.	▪ The zoom box acts as a toggle between "Tile" view and full screen view. If you manually resize the window, the Zoom will toggle between the new size and full screen.
1.179 Drag-and-drop an object from one tiled publication to another	▪ If the window is not active, click once in the title bar, or anywhere within the publication window, to make it active. ▪ With the pointer tool press-and-drag the object to the new publication window. ▪ Let go of the mouse when you have the object where you want.	▪ At first it will look as if the original object is moving, but when you let go of the mouse you will see that the original is right where it belongs and a copy of it is in the other publication. ▪ You can drag text blocks from one publication to another. If the insertion point is flashing, or text is selected, the text will paste inline, see 1.180.
1.180 Drag-and-drop an object or text block from one tiled publication and place it inline in another	▪ Set the **insertion point** at the spot in the publication where you want the object or text to go. ▪ Click on the window that contains the object or text you want to copy. (Make sure it becomes the active window before preceding to the next step!) ▪ Select the **pointer tool.** ▪ Press on the object or text block you want to copy and drag it to the other publication window. Let go of the mouse.	▪ If you select the pointer tool while the first window is still active, the insertion point will no longer be flashing in that publication. ▪ If text is *selected* in the publication you are dragging an object or a text block to, it will be replaced with the object or text.

AN ILLEGITIMATE, HOMELESS MAN, DYING IN abject poverty, changes the course of history and his name goes down through the ages as a household word. There's hope for us all. Johannes Gensfleisch zur Laden zum Gutenberg is generally credited with inventing the printing process. Actually, there was already printing of a sort, but Gutenberg perfected the craft with the invention of movable type. (Kind of like there were already computers in the world, then the Mac was invented.) However, back in the 9th century the Chinese were already carving wooden blocks to print prayer scrolls; in the 11th century they developed movable type of clay and metal. In the 13th century the Koreans were casting metal type in sand molds. Movable type is the key thing here—rather than having to carve each page as a separate block, movable type allows one to put together a page of characters, print it, take those characters apart and put them back together in another order for another page. Now, the Chinese and Koreans had an obvious problem—their languages have too many billions of characters to make this process practical. Plus there was no ink invented that could stick to metal. Besides, these Far Easterners just

a 14th century copyist

plain preferred calligraphy anyway. Well, the Europeans in the 15th century didn't know anything about what the Chinese and Koreans had done, so they had to re-invent movable type. Gutenberg was in luck. By the time he came along, the process of papermaking was well-developed; punch-making, which is an important step in creating letters out of metal, was already developed in the gold- and silver-smithing trades (of which Gutenberg was a practitioner); metalcasting was well under way, creating coins and medals; presses were being used for cheese, wine, textile processing, and weaponsmithing. And those industrious Dutch painters, the Van Eycks, had invented an oil-based ink that would adhere to metal. Now isn't it an interesting thought to ponder what might have happened if Johann had been born a hundred years earlier, before the world was ready for him? Or if the boys in the garage had been born fifty years earlier? Eventually someone would have gotten the printing process together, but would we ever have had Macintoshes?

Herr Gutenberg

(continued on page 100)

Selecting, Layering, and Moving

For small erections
may be finished
by their first architects;
grand ones,
true ones,
ever leave the copestone
to posterity.
God keep me
from ever
completing anything.
O, Time,
Strength,
Cash,
and Patience!

Herman Melville,
Moby Dick

1.181 In PageMaker every *object* is on a separate *layer*. Understanding this and using it to your advantage is a key skill in working with this program. Once you know what the layers are and how to select them, move them, group them, and manipulate them, all the rest of PageMaker will make much more sense. In fact, all the other sections in this book assume you understand selecting, layering, and moving objects. So you'd better read this.

Selecting

1.182 *The pointer tool, used for selecting objects.*

```
▤□▤ Toolbox ▤
▶   ╲   ├   A
↺   □   ○   ✄
```

1.183 PageMaker is an "object-oriented" program; that is, each and every item you put on the screen is a separate **object**—each graphic, text block, and line. **Selecting** is the simple process that tells the Mac you are about to do something to an object.

1.184 You *must* select objects before you manipulate them. If you are going to stretch or condense a graphic, make a line longer, delete an object, resize a text block—the basic Macintosh rule is always **select first, then manipulate**.

1.185 Always select objects with the pointer tool. While you use the drawing tools to *create* the objects, you use the **pointer tool** to **select** the objects, such as the entire text block or the separate graphic elements.

1.186 To **de**select anything, just click in any blank space or on any tool in the Toolbox.

1.187 There are three exceptions to the rule that you always select with the pointer tool:

1) **to modify text** (not to remove or stretch the text *block*, but to modify the *characters* themselves, such as when you change font or size or style), you must use the **text tool** to select the particular characters you wish to modify (Section 4);

2) **to rotate an object using the rotating tool,** you can select it with the **rotating tool** (1.219);

3) **to crop a graphic,** you must select it with the **cropping tool** (10.143).

1.188 And remember, no matter how hard you try, you cannot select any master page objects if you are not viewing the master page itself! (You *can* manipulate master page *guides*, though, on any separate publication page.)

Layering

1.189 In object-oriented programs, you can pick up and move each item, modify it, or delete it. You can also *stack* the objects one on top of the other and then change the order of their stacking. It is this stacking, or **layering,** that is often the cause for great consternation.

1.190 It is important to consciously think of every object on the screen as being on a separate layer, as if each were on its own little piece of clear acetate. You can see the outer dimensions of these little pieces of clear acetate when you use the **pointer tool** and click on any item—two to eight *handles* will appear (1.195), depending on whether it is a line or a graphic or a block of text. **An object will show handles when it is ready for moving, modifying, or deleting.**

1.191 When objects overlap, one item may get "lost" behind the other. Don't worry—unless you actually deleted it, *it is still there* and you can easily retrieve it (1.211–1.215) or adjust its layering order (1.216–1.217).

1.192 Unfortunately, it is very simple to inadvertently create an *invisible* layer that gets in your way and causes confusion because you don't know it's there (see 1.214 for finding and deleting it).

1.193 Guides are *always* the top layer, unless you specifically choose to keep them as the back layer (use "Preferences…" from the File menu to send them to the back; see 1.66–1.68, 1.230).

1.194 Once the idea of layering is clear to you, all of PageMaker makes much more sense. You will find it easy to overlay items, send them to the back or bring them to the front to suit your arrangement, temporarily group them together to move them as a unit, dig underneath other layers to find a missing item, remove items from the bottom layer without touching the top, and generally make life easier.

1.195a *This graphic, created in PageMaker, is selected. Notice the eight handles.*

b) *This graphic was also created in PageMaker and is selected, showing its handles. It is on a layer separate from the white box above.*

c) *This text block was created in PageMaker and is selected. Notice its four corner handles and two windowshade loops. It is also on a separate layer.*

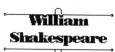

d) *In this image, all three of the layers have been stacked. They are still three separate layers, as shown in e) below.*

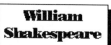

e) *This image shows all three layers with all of their handles.*

Moving Objects

1.196 Once an object is *selected,* you can **move** it by pressing-and-dragging on it. If there are complex graphics or a block of formatted text to move, PageMaker has to gather everything up before it can move it. To accommodate you, there are two ways to move objects: a **fast move** and a **slow move.**

FAST MOVE

1.197 A **fast move** picks up just the *outline* of the information—it looks like a blank box. This is much faster and easier for PageMaker to deal with, and thus faster for you. To do a fast move, press on a selected object or a group of selected objects *and move the mouse instantly;* you will get just the outline. Wherever you let go of the mouse, the outline will stop there and redisplay the objects in their new position. This works well, combined with "Snap to guides," to quickly and precisely align objects in place, even while in the small window view.

In a fast move, you see just an outline of the image.

SLOW MOVE

1.198 A **slow move** picks up the actual visual image of everything selected. This takes longer, but for aligning baselines of text or the border of a graphic, it is indispensable. To do a slow move, with the pointer tool *press* on a selected object or group of selected objects. Hold the mouse button down; at first you will see a watch, which means PageMaker is gathering everything up. After a second or two, depending on how complex the object is, you will see the four-headed arrow. Still holding the mouse button down, drag the objects—you will see every particle of every object as it moves along. This is particularly handy for precise alignments at the larger views.

In a slow move, you see the entire visual image.

BE CAREFUL

1.199 Be careful about moving a group of selected objects, especially in the small views. If there is a text block in the group, your safest bet to move *everything* successfully is to press on that text block to drag the entire group. Avoid pressing on one of the *lines* in a group move; you can easily end up stretching one line instead of moving the whole selected group. **Whenever you are about to move a group, make sure you see the four-headed arrow before you drag, and not a two-headed arrow or a crosshair!**

1.200 If you accidentally stretch or move something out of position, *immediately* press Command Z to Undo, **or** from the Edit menu choose "Undo stretch/move"!! Then try again.

1.201 If the Control palette is displayed, the "Position" option (3.32) shows the on screen position of the object you have selected (according to its reference point). You can type in values to move one or more selected objects, instead of moving the object(s) with the pointer tool (3.87). Section 3 covers the Control palette and the various ways to use it.

If you want to do this:	**Then follow these steps:**	**Shortcuts • Notes • Hints**
1.202 Select a text block 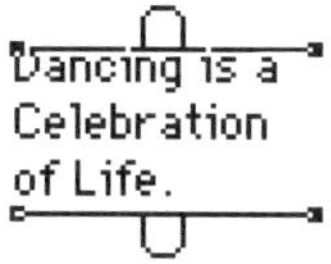 Dancing is a Celebration of Life.	■ With the **pointer tool,** click anywhere in the block of text. You will see handles on all four corners (if all four corners are visible at the view you are in).	■ Also read Section 4 on Text (4.114).
1.203 Select a graphic 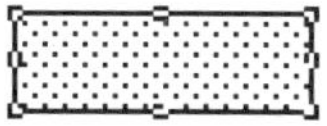	■ With the **pointer tool,** click anywhere on the graphic. You will see eight handles.	■ Also read Section 2 on Drawing Tools (2.24) and Section 10 on Graphics.
1.204 Select a line 	■ With the **pointer tool,** click anywhere on the line. If you can see the *ends* of the lines, you will see a handle on each end.	■ If you pick up a guide when you try to select a line, hold down the Command key while you click on the line.
1.205 Deselect an object *(text blocks, graphics, lines, etc.)*	■ Select a different object; ■ **OR** click in any clear area outside of any object, including outside any text block; ■ **OR** click on any tool in the toolbox.	
1.206 Deselect *all* objects	■ Click in any clear area outside of any object, including outside any space within a text block; ■ **OR** click on any tool in the toolbox.	

What we need is Progress
with an escape hatch.
—John Updike

If you want to do this:

Then follow these steps:

Shortcuts · Notes · Hints

1.207 Select more than one object using the Shift-click method
(See 1.208 to use the marquee method)

- With the **pointer tool,** select the first object by clicking once on it.
- Hold down the Shift key and click on all other objects you want to add to the group.
- To **de**select an object from the group, hold down the Shift key and click on the object again.

- You can use Shift-clicking in combination with Command-clicking (1.211) to pick up objects that are under other layers.
- You can select objects using the rotation tool, and Shift-click to select multiple objects to rotate.

1.208 Select more than one object using the marquee method
(See 1.207 to use the Shift-click method)

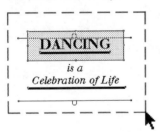

- Position the **pointer tool** in any clear area outside of any object; *make sure you click outside any text block.*
- Press-and-drag to draw the *marquee* (selection rectangle) around all objects to be selected. When they are enclosed within the dotted rectangle, let go.

- The marquee will select only those objects that have *every one of their handles* enclosed in its space (e.g., if your text block has handles that run across the page, you will need to draw the marquee large enough to encompass them). Or just Shift-click if you miss something, as noted in 1.207.
- Because the marquee will select only objects with all handles enclosed in its space, you can use it to select smaller objects that are under a larger layer (1.215).
- To *deselect* an object from the group, hold down the Shift key and click once on the object.
- You can use the rotating tool to marquee objects to select them for rotation.

If you want to do this:	Then follow these steps:	Shortcuts ▾ Notes ▾ Hints
1.209 Add objects to those already selected	■ With the **pointer tool,** hold the Shift key down while you click on other objects.	■ If you change your mind about selecting an object, keep the Shift key down and just click on the object *again* to deselect it.
1.210 Deselect an object or two from a group of selected objects	■ Hold down the Shift key. ■ With the **pointer tool,** click on any object you want to deselect from the group.	■ If you change your mind about deselecting an object, keep the Shift key down and click on the object again to re-select it.
1.211 Select an object that is underneath another object	■ Hold down the Command key. ■ With the **pointer tool,** click on the top object; it will show handles. ■ Click again to select the next layer. ■ Repeat until the desired object is selected.	■ Used in conjunction with the Shift key (1.207), you can dig down through layers and select them into a group along the way. ■ Remember, a graphic with a Fill of "None" must be selected by clicking on its black border, so you may have to hunt around to find it (also see 1.213–1.214).
1.212 Select an object that is under a guide	■ With the **pointer tool,** hold down the Command key and click on the object.	■ Guides are always on the top layer, unless you choose to "Lock guides" from the "Guides and rulers" submenu (in the Layout menu) or send them to the back through "Preferences" in the File menu (1.66–1.68; 1.230).

If you want to do this:	Then follow these steps:	Shortcuts ▾ Notes ▾ Hints
1.213 Select *all* objects on the screen, no matter what layer they are on	■ From the Layout menu, slide down to "View," then over to the submenu to choose "Fit in window" *or* press Command W (you don't *have* to be in this view, but it allows you to see everything on the page). ■ Choose the **pointer tool.** ■ From the Edit menu choose "Select all" *or* press Command A; handles will appear on every object.	■ This picks up everything on the *screen* (whether you can see it or not), not just the *page;* that is, any items on the pasteboard will also be selected. ■ This is a good way to find any invisible graphics or text blocks that may be getting in your way, or to find objects hidden under other opaque objects. ■ When you have selected all objects, you can move, delete, or copy them all at once. ■ If, at this point, you see any objects that do not have handles on them, they must be from the master page (1.130–1.135).
1.214 Select an object that seems to be invisible	■ Select all objects (1.213). ■ Look for any handles that have nothing inside them. ■ Once you find the troublesome item, **de**select all objects by clicking in any blank area, or by clicking on the pointer tool in the Toolbox. ■ With the **pointer tool,** click on the spot where you saw the handles of the invisible object. If you get handles belonging to an object on *top* of the one you want, hold down the Command key and click on them one at a time until the handles on the invisible object you want appear.	■ If the object you want does not show handles, perhaps your screen view is too large to see the handles on either end. Go to "Fit in window" view (press Command W). If you still don't see the handles, the object you want must be on a master page (1.130–1.135). ■ Once the object is selected, you can delete it by pressing the Backspace/Delete key. ■ **OR** you can now copy it, cut it, stretch it, modify it, or do anything else your little heart desires.

If you want to do this:	**Then follow these steps:**	**Shortcuts • Notes • Hints**
1.215 Select an object that is hidden or trapped under another, including a line or border that is under a guide	▪ Hold down the Command key and click with the **pointer tool** to dig down through the layers; with each click you will select the next layer down, then cycle through the layers again; ▪ **OR** with the **pointer tool,** press in a clear area *(make sure you are also outside of any text block)* and drag to produce the *marquee*, or selection rectangle. You'll select anything that is *entirely* enclosed within this marquee. *So,* if you want to select a smaller item under a larger item, draw the marquee too small to capture the entire larger object; you'll select just the smaller object(s) underneath.	▪ This first method will pick up any object under a guide, also. ▪ If you can see little objects under a text block, use this second method: *The joy and pleasure of doing a good job for its own sake has not been discovered by enough people.* *—Ivan Chermayeff*
1.216 Bring an object in front of another	▪ With the **pointer tool,** select the object you want to bring forward to the top layer (click once on it). You may need to Command-click (1.215). ▪ From the Element menu choose "Bring to front" *or* press Command F (F for Front).	▪ When you send an object to the back, you send it *all the way to the back,* not just behind the top layer. So be conscious about what you are sending where. Oftentimes what you need is to bring something else forward, not send the top item back. And conversely, items brought forward are brought all the way forward.
1.217 Send an object behind another	▪ With the **pointer tool,** select the object you want to send behind all the others (click once on it). ▪ From the Element menu choose "Send to back" *or* press Command B (B for Back).	▪ You can select more than one item at a time and send them back or bring them forward. They will stay in their same order.

If you want to do this:	Then follow these steps:	Shortcuts ▾ Notes ▾ Hints
1.218 Select text to modify	■ With the **text tool:** □ Double-click on a word to select the word and the space after it; □ **Or** triple-click to select an entire paragraph; □ **Or** press-and-drag over the characters you want to modify.	■ Be sure to read Section 4 on Text, especially 4.189–4.204. ■ You might also want to check out 1.325–1.326, on how to select text using the numeric keypad.
1.219 Select text or an object to rotate	■ With the **rotating tool,** click once on the text or object. ■ You can Shift click, or marquee objects to select more than one object.	■ You can Command click with the rotating tool to dig through layers of objects. ■ You can select an object with the rotating tool *or* the pointer tool and rotate it through the "Rotating" option in the object-view Control palette; see 3.93.
1.220 Select an imported graphic to crop	■ With the **cropping tool,** click on a graphic (10.143).	■ Graphic information is in Section 10.
1.221 Switch to the pointer tool without deselecting a newly drawn, cropped, or rotated object	■ Hold down the Shift key; click on the pointer tool in the Toolbox, *or* ■ Press Command Spacebar.	■ You can also use the Command Spacebar shortcut to toggle between the pointer tool and the tool you last used. ■ When you press Command Spacebar, you may momentarily see the magnifying tool as it uses the same key combination (1.122). ■ If the Command Spacebar shortcut doesn't work, it may be short-circuited by key commands used by other software.

The "Preferences" dialog box   *(from the File menu, choose "Preferences…")*

1.222 Some very important application and publication default options are found in the "Preferences" dialog box (in the File menu). Choices made here determine how PageMaker is going to handle certain key aspects of your publication including the measuring system, how graphics are handled, typographical standards, etc. If it doesn't all make sense right now, don't worry, it will after you get more familiar with PageMaker.

This measurement system choice affects the horizontal ruler and any dialog box that uses measurements; see 1.224 or 1.53.

You can customize your vertical ruler with points; see 1.226 and 1.55, 1.57.

The vertical ruler measurements can be different than the horizontal ruler; see 1.225 or 1.54.

This refers to the letter and word spacing specifications that PageMaker sometimes has to violate; see 1.227.

This refers to choices you made in the "Paragraph" dialog box; see 1.228.

You can choose on which layer you want the guides; see 1.230, 1.66, or 1.68.

Preferences

Layout
Measurement system: [Picas]
Vertical ruler: [Inches] [ ] **points**

Layout problems
☐ **Show loose/tight lines**
☐ **Show "keeps" violations**

Graphics
○ **Gray out**
◉ **Normal**
○ **High resolution**

Guides
◉ **Front**
○ **Back**

Control palette
Horizontal nudge: [0.01] [Inches]
Vertical nudge: [0.01] [Inches]
☐ **Use "Snap to" constraints**

Save option
◉ **Faster**
○ **Smaller**

[OK]
[Cancel]
[Other…]
[Map fonts…]

Click to see other "Preferences" choices; see 1.223.

See 1.255–1.266.

This determines how graphics are displayed on screen; see 1.229.

Select a unit of measure from these pop-up menus for the nudge buttons in the Control palette; see 3.18.

This allows you to automatically compress the file size, which takes a little longer than a normal Save; see 18.29.

Click to constrain Control palette nudges to guides or rulers depending on which "Snap to" options are checked on the "Guides and rulers" submenu; see 3.16.

Enter a value to specify the nudge amount for Control palette options; see 3.17.

1.223 The "Other preferences" dialog box *(in the "Preferences" dialog box, click the "Other" button)*

Set the maximum amount of memory used to create screen displays for "Normal" graphics; see 1.232.

Click OK or Return

Check to display each page as text is flowed; 1.231.

Press Cancel or Command period to leave the dialog box without making any changes.

Check this option for true typographer's quotation marks and apostrophes; see 1.234.

PageMaker will display an alert message when importing graphics larger than the value entered here; see 1.233.

This determines how text displays in the smaller views; see 1.236.

Select one of these two options when you are working with TrueType; see 1.235.

This is the font that the Story Editor will display text in; you have a choice of any font in your System; see 1.237.

Click to make these options the default settings in the Story editor; see 1.239.

This is the size text the Story Editor will display; see 1.238.

Other preferences

OK

Cancel

Autoflow:
☐ **Display all pages**

Maximum size of internal bitmap: `64` **kBytes**

Alert when storing graphics over: `256` **kBytes**

┌ **Text** ─────────
☐ **Use typographer's quotes**
○ **Preserve line spacing in TrueType**
● **Preserve character shape in TrueType**
Greek text below: `6` **pixels**

┌ **Story editor** ─────────
Font: `Geneva`   ☐ **Display style names**
Size: `12` ▷ **points**   ☐ **Display ¶**

I like work: it fascinates me. I can sit and look at it for hours. —Jerome K. Jerome

If you want to do this: Then follow these steps: Shortcuts • Notes • Hints

Preferences

1.224 Change the unit of measure on the horizontal ruler *and* in the dialog boxes

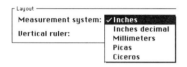

- From the File menu choose "Preferences."
- Under Layout, next to "Measurement system:" press on the shadowed box; this will show the pop-up menu of choices; choose one.

- All measurements in all dialog boxes, such as Page Setup, Column Guides, Paragraph, Indents/tabs, etc., will follow the measurement system you chose here.
- You can temporarily override any measurement system in any dialog box (1.323).
- Measurements are accurate to $\frac{1}{2880}$th of an inch, supposedly at any page view size.

1.225 Change the unit of measure for the vertical ruler

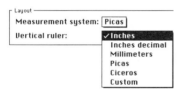

- From the File menu choose "Preferences."
- Under Layout, next to "Vertical ruler:" press on the shadowed box; this will show the pop-up menu of choices; choose one (for "Custom," see 1.226).

- You can, of course, set the vertical and horizontal measures to the same unit. Or perhaps you really like to measure your column widths and line lengths in picas, but want inches vertically. The greatest thing about the vertical ruler measurement is that you can customize it to your leading value, thus making it so easy to align baselines across columns (1.226).

1.226 Customize the measurement of the vertical ruler

- From the File menu choose "Preferences."
- Under Layout, next to "Vertical ruler:" press on the shadowed box; choose "Custom."
- In the points box, type in the number of points you want the vertical ruler divided into, from 4 to 256. Each tick mark will represent that number of points, numbered in groups of fives (not picas!).

- If you set the Custom box to the point size of your leading and use "Snap to rulers" from the "Guides and rulers" submenu, you can make sure the baselines of your text align (see Scenario #2, 1.57).
- You can't override the points to use any other unit of measure (e.g., you can't customize the vertical ruler to half inches).

If you want to do this:	**Then follow these steps:**	**Shortcuts ▾ Notes ▾ Hints**

1.227 Show loosely-spaced and tightly-spaced lines

┌─ Layout problems ──────────
│ ⊠ **Show loose/tight lines**
│ ☐ **Show "keeps" violations**
└──────────────────────────

Generally, only justified text can be forced into tight or loose spacing.

A gray area delineates the text with problems

- From the File menu choose "Preferences."
- Under "Layout problems" click on "Show loose/tight lines."

- This command is directly connected to the spacing limits set in the "Spacing attributes" dialog box (5.10).
- When a line of text or an inline graphic has more spacing (loose lines) or less spacing (tight lines) than the specified limits, a gray or colored bar shades the text (the bar won't print). It is up to you to fix the problem lines yourself by changing spacing, line length, words, etc.
- Generally, only justified text can be forced into tight or loose spacing.

1.228 Show lines that violate the "keeps" commands established in the Paragraph dialog box

┌─ Layout problems ──────────
│ ☐ **Show loose/tight lines**
│ ⊠ **Show "keeps" violations**
└──────────────────────────

- From the File menu choose "Preferences."
- Under "Layout problems" click on "Show 'keeps' violations."

- This command is directly connected to the widow, orphan, or keep-with-next specifications you set in the "Paragraph specifications" dialog box (4.288–4.300).
- Lines of text or inline graphics that violate the commands you set are indicated with a gray or colored bar. It is up to you to fix them yourself by manually bumping lines down, rearranging the lengths of text blocks, changing type specifications, etc.

One ought every day at least, to hear a little song, read a good poem, see a fine picture,

| **If you want to do this:** | **Then follow these steps:** | **Shortcuts ▾ Notes ▾ Hints** |

1.229 Adjust the resolution of detailed, non-PageMaker graphics

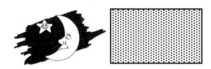

Normal   *Same image grayed out*

- From the File menu choose "Preferences."
- Under "Detailed graphics" choose one of the following:
  Gray out: This provides the fastest screen display; graphics are shown as gray rectangular forms.
  Normal: Graphics, including TIFFs, are shown as low-resolution screen images. PICTs over 64K in size are shown as monochrome TIFF images.
  High-resolution: Graphics, including color images, are shown at full resolution.

- This command affects just the screen display—images will print as usual.
- When placing graphics larger than 256K, or the value you entered in the "Alert when storing graphics over" option, PageMaker gives you the choice of storing a complete copy of the graphic in the publication itself, as opposed to just providing a low-res screen version linked to the original for printing purposes (see 10.101–10.106). Even if you *don't* store the complete copy, choosing high-res will give you a high-res image if you want it.
- With "Gray out" or "Normal" setting, you can choose to view any TIFF at high-res, temporarily, by holding down the Control key as the screen redraws; e.g., when turning pages, changing views, or scrolling.

and, if it were possible, to speak a few reasonable words.   —Goethe

If you want to do this:	**Then follow these steps:**	**Shortcuts ▾ Notes ▾ Hints**

1.230 Send the guides to the *front* or to the *back*

- From the File menu choose "Preferences."
- Under "Guides" choose "Front" or "Back."

- The standard default puts the guides in *front*, which means guides (*all* guides) are always the top layer (see 1.189–1.195 re: layering). This can be irritating when you are trying to pick up a line or other object that is directly under a guide. The easiest solution is to hold down the Command key and click on the object to select it. See 1.66–1.68.
- When guides are at the *back*, though, you cannot dig down through the layers with the Command key to pick them up— whatever is on top of the guides must be physically moved, or you must find someplace to grab the guide where there is nothing on top of it. It's worse than having them in front.

1.231 See each page of a publication as text is placed using the "Autoflow" command

Autoflow:
⊠ Display all pages

- From the File menu choose "Preferences," then click the "Other" button.
- Under "Autoflow," check the box next to "Display all pages."

- Text still flows in automatically on each page when this option is not checked— you just don't see it page by page.
- When unchecked, PageMaker displays only the first and last page(s) of the text.

If you want to do this: ▪

1.232 Set the maximum amount of memory to be used for graphic image screen display

Maximum size of internal bitmap: [64] kBytes

1.233 Set the maximum file size for imported graphics that are being stored in the publication

Alert when storing graphics over: [256] kBytes

Then follow these steps: ▪

- From the File menu choose "Preferences," then click the "Other" button.
- Enter a value up to 1024, in the edit box next to "Maximum size of internal bitmap."

- From the File menu choose "Preferences," then click the "Other" button.
- Enter a value in the edit box next to "Alert when storing graphics over:"

Shortcuts ▾ Notes ▾ Hints ▪

- This setting only applies when the "Preferences" setting for "Graphics" is "Normal."
- This affects the screen display of a graphic, not its print quality (unless PageMaker cannot find a linked graphic and only has this version from which to print; see Section 11; 11.29).
- The smaller the value in the edit box: the lower the screen resolution of the graphic, the smaller the publication, the less memory needed, and the quicker the screen redraws.
- A graphic whose file size is smaller than the current setting will not be affected.
- A graphic whose file size is larger than the current setting will look better on screen if you increase the setting before you import the graphic.

- You will get an alert message when you try to place a graphic that is larger than the value you enter here.
- If you receive the alert box and choose "No," be sure to maintain the link (11.7), otherwise PageMaker will have only the screen version with which to print the graphic. (Section 11 deals with the various ways to store graphics.)

73

If you want to do this:

1.234 Make the inch and foot marks automatically display and print as true quotation marks and apostrophes.

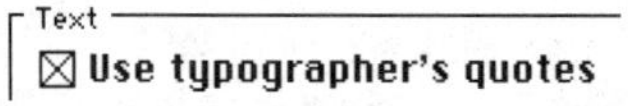

┌─ Text ─────────────────
│ ☒ **Use typographer's quotes**

Then follow these steps:

- From the File menu choose "Preferences," then click the "Other" button.
- Under "Text" check the box next to "Use typographer's quotes."
- PageMaker displays an opening quotation mark if the preceding character is a
  - □ space
  - □ left angle bracket <, left brace {, left bracket [, or left parenthesis (.
- PageMaker displays a closing quotation mark when the preceding character is a
  - □ number
  - □ right angle bracket >, right brace },
  - □ right bracket], or right parenthesis).
  - □ a terminal punctuation mark
  - □ any of the characters displayed above the numbers on the keyboard

Shortcuts ▾ Notes ▾ Hints

- This will not affect marks typed before checking this option.
- You cannot type inch and foot marks while this option is checked! You must deselect the option through the "Preferences" dialog box first.
- You do need to check up on PageMaker. Do not take it for granted that all of your instances of quotation marks fall within PageMaker's range of ability. Also, typos can give PageMaker the wrong clue, like when you forget the punctuation at the end of a quote:
  "Frankly Scarlett, I don't give a damn " said Rhett. PageMaker, of course, can't automatically change the mark when you fix the typos.

Tomorrow,
and tomorrow
and tomorrow,
creeps in this
petty pace
from day
to day.
Shakespeare
MacBeth

If you want to do this: ∎

Then follow these steps: ∎

Shortcuts ▾ Notes ▾ Hints ∎

1.235a Make TrueType stay true to its linespacing

⦿ **Preserve line spacing in TrueType**
○ **Preserve character shape in TrueType**

- From the File menu choose "Preferences," then click the "Other" button.
- Click the radio button next to "Preserve line spacing in TrueType."

- In certain situations, such as setting accent marks, PageMaker must choose between sacrificing the line spacing or sacrificing the character shape of TrueType characters. It is up to you to tell PageMaker which one to give up.

1.235b Make TrueType stay true to its character shape

○ **Preserve line spacing in TrueType**
⦿ **Preserve character shape in TrueType**

- From the File menu choose "Preferences," then click the "Other" button.
- Click the radio button next to "Preserve character shape in TrueType."

- If you select "Preserve line spacing in TrueType," and then set a character with an accent mark over it, PageMaker will adjust the height of the letter (*character shape*) so that the accent does not print above the height of the slug.
- In the same situation, if you select "Preserve character shape in TrueType," PageMaker will adjust the leading (*line spacing*) to prevent the accent from printing above the height of the slug.

1.236 Change the number of pixels for showing "greek" text

Greek text below: **pixels**

"Greek" text

- From the File menu choose "Preferences."
- Type in a value here from 0 to 32,767 (but don't type the comma!); any type smaller than that number of pixels at any view *smaller than Actual Size* will display as "greek."

- A *pixel* is one of the dots (*picture elements*) on the screen—all the images you see are created from these dots. The Mac screen has 72 dots per inch.
- "Greek" text is much easier for PageMaker to draw, thus it can display the screen much more quickly. The default is set at 9 pixels, since type below that size is too difficult to read anyway. If you want your 75% and 50% views to draw more quickly, set the greek text number higher.

If you want to do this:	**Then follow these steps:**	**Shortcuts ▾ Notes ▾ Hints**
1.237 Change the font displayed in the Story Editor Font: New York	▪ From the File menu choose "Preferences." ▪ Under "Story editor," press on the shadowed box next to "Font" to display the pop-up menu of fonts; choose one.	▪ It's a good idea to choose only those fonts with a city name, as they are bit-mapped and designed for the resolution of the screen. They will be clearer and will display faster than non-city-named (which are generally *outline*) fonts.
1.238 Change the font size displayed in the Story Editor Size: 12 ▷ points	▪ From the File menu choose "Preferences." ▪ Under "Story editor," press on the arrow in the box next to "Size" to display the pop-up menu of font sizes; choose a size; **or** type the size of your choice into the edit box.	▪ The clearest size to read will be the font size that is shown in outline format, as that bitmapped size is installed in your System and can be reproduced most efficiently on the screen. (Different fonts have different screen sizes installed.) 9 10 11 12 14 *The 9 and 12 point sizes of this particular font will be the easiest to read on the screen.*
1.239 Automatically display style names and/or nonprinting characters in the Story Editor	▪ From the File menu choose "Preferences." ▪ Under "Story editor," check the box next to "Display style names" and/or "Display ¶."	▪ You can override this option. From the Story menu choose "Display style names" to take the checkmark off, then choose "Display ¶" from the same menu to remove its checkmark.

The "PANOSE font matching" system

1.240 The PANOSE font matching utility lets you use fonts that are available to you as substitutes for fonts that are missing in a publication. You have absolute control over how closely the substituted font matches the one that is missing, and you can approve, cancel, or change any substitution offered.

1.241 This feature can be especially useful when a publication is being shared across platforms like Windows and Macintosh, or, even on two different Macintosh computers that do not have the same fonts installed. PANOSE automatically accounts for fonts that are the same but that are spelled differently on the Mac than in Windows. In all other situations, it offers a font substitute that most closely matches the missing one. From a designer's standpoint, it is usually best not to substitute fonts unless you absolutely have to. However, using a substituted font as a placeholder, just until you have access to the one that is missing, can be helpful. Have you ever opened a document from someone else and found its pages displayed in that dreaded Courier because you don't have the same fonts installed?

1.242 The PANOSE Typeface Matching System classifies fonts according to their visual characteristics. The height of the capital letters, the width of characters, the word and letter spacing, etc, all differ from font to font. These detailed specifications are called the font metrics. When you change or substitute fonts, PageMaker adjusts the type to account for the new font metrics. However, sometimes you will notice afterward that the letterspacing or some other feature is not quite right. To correct this, recompose the stories to ensure that the right font metrics are applied by pressing the Option key and choosing "Hyphenation" from the Type menu.

1.243 It is especially important to recompose a story in which you have installed the original missing font after substituting for it. The degree of recomposition you get will depend upon how closely the substitute font matched the missing one. When you use a substitute font as a placeholder it is okay to go ahead and make editing changes, but don't waste time on typographical fine-tuning such as kerning. You will just need to do it all over again when the missing font shows back up.

1.244 If you have SuperATM installed, you can specify it as the primary or secondary method of substitution (1.257). SuperATM includes a "font emulation" feature that simulates a missing font, whereas PANOSE simply substitutes one font for another. The default font (1.262), which you choose from the fonts always available in your System or currently open in a font managing utility, will be used when neither method can come up with a good match.

1.245 You can also use PANOSE to alert you when fonts are missing. If you check the option "Show mapping results," each time you open a publication with missing fonts, the "PANOSE font matching results" dialog box will list them. If you use a font managing utility, such as Suitcase or MasterJuggler, this will remind you about fonts or sets of fonts that you need to open for a publication. If you don't have the missing fonts, you can either change them (you can use the Find and Change option in the Story Editor), or install them. PANOSE does not alert you of missing fonts within EPS graphics though, including fonts within objects grouped using the "PS Group it" Addition (10.259–10.291).

The "PANOSE font matching" system —*continued*

1.246 Everything about PANOSE is up to you. You can turn it on and turn it off whenever you like. When PANOSE is off, missing fonts are always replaced by the default font (1.262). When PANOSE is on, you control the way missing fonts are substituted when you open publications.

1.247 The slider bar for **"Substitution tolerance"** ranges from 0 to 100. At 0 tolerance, no substitute is offered for a missing font unless it matches it exactly. As you scroll up the slider bar, you loosen the level of tolerance that defines how closely a substitute font must match the missing one. Of course, PageMaker's ability to find a substitute depends on what fonts are available in your System. The default font (1.262) is used whenever PageMaker can't find an appropriate match.

1.248 Missing fonts show in the font menu of a publication with the name of the substituted font in brackets alongside it or, in the case of SuperATM simulations, with a diamond beside the name.

1.249 When you check **"Show mapping results,"** PageMaker alerts you if she opens publications with missing fonts. The beauty behind PANOSE lies in the **"PANOSE font matching results"** dialog box. This dialog box gives you a chance to view, and approve or change, every font substitution Page-Maker offers.

1.250 You can choose to make font substitutions temporary or permanent. With **"Temporary"** substitutions, Page-Maker will still alert you whenever you open a publication and give you the option of changing the substitutes each time. When you make a **"Permanent"** substitu-tion, PageMaker no longer lists a font as missing. The Type menu, though, will still show the missing font name with its substitute in brackets. If a missing font becomes available, both temporary and permanent substitutions are replaced with the original font.

1.251 If you don't check "Show mapping results," PageMaker will not alert you when you open a publication with fonts missing. Instead she goes ahead and makes tempo-rary font substitutions according to the tolerance level you have set.

1.252 To make it easier to share docu-ments across platforms, the **"Spellings"** dialog box keeps a list of Macintosh and Windows fonts that are the same except for how they are spelled. The most commonly shared fonts are already listed, and Page-Maker automatically makes the translation for you. You can add, edit, and remove font names as you need to from the list.

1.253 The **"Exceptions"** dialog box gives you control over all substitutions, and lets you create a list of preferred font substitu-tions for PageMaker to use. Again, you can add, edit, and remove font names, person-alizing the utility for your own needs.

1.254 When you import a document from an application that uses numbers instead of names to specify fonts, any missing font will be listed as "Macintosh font xxx" both in the Type menu and in the PANOSE font matching preview box (see 1.265). This can be very disturbing the first time you see it. It will sometimes happen with Word documents that were saved in a format other than RTF (Rich Text Format, see 17.11).

1.255 The "PANOSE font matching" system *(from the File menu, choose "Preferences…," then click the "Map fonts" button)*

1.257 *The SuperATM option is available only if you have SuperATM installed. SuperATM simulates missing fonts, and can be used as the primary or secondary method of font substitution. The same diamond codes (1.256) apply to SuperATM.*

1.256 *Click the diamond to turn PANOSE on and off. A solid black diamond indicates that PANOSE is on, and is the primary method of substitution. A gray diamond indicates PANOSE is running secondary to SuperATM. A hollow diamond is the off position.*

1.258 *Use the slider bar to designate how closely you want substituted fonts to match the missing font.*

1.259 *Check this box to see the substitution results (1.264) each time PageMaker opens or imports a document with missing fonts. If this box is not checked, font substitutions will be made without alerting you.*

Font matching

◇ SuperATM™ font matching

◆ PANOSE™ font substitution

Substitution tolerance: 50

Exact   Normal   Loose

Default font: Courier

☒ **Show mapping results**

Information
Missing fonts will be substituted using PANOSE™.
If there is no match within the specified tolerance, the Default font will be used.

OK

Cancel

Spellings…

Exceptions…

Help…

1.260 *You can add, edit, and remove fonts from the "Spellings" list, see 1.252.*

1.261 *You can create your own list of font substitutions. See 1.253, 1.270.*

1.262 *Use this pop-up menu to select a Default font. The Default font applies even if PANOSE and SuperATM are both off.*

1.263 *The current status of PANOSE and/or Super ATM is reported here.*

1.264 *In this dialog box you can approve or change the font substitutions, and choose a temporary or permanent status for each substitution.*

PANOSE font matching results

Missing font:	Substituted font:	Status:
P Bodoni Poster	R Walbaum Roman	Temp
Shelley Volante Script	Courier [PANOSE d…	Temp
Macintosh font 523	Courier [PANOSE d…	Temp

OK

Help…

Substituted font: R Walbaum Roman   ● Temporary ○ Permanent

1.265 *When you import a document from an application that specifies fonts by number, you will see it listed as "Macintosh font xxx," both here and in the font menu.*

1.266 *You can choose a different font as a substitute for the highlighted font. The pop-up menu lists all the fonts available in your system. Font substitutions can be made temporary or permanent, see 1.250, 1.269.*

If you want to do this:	Then follow these steps:	Shortcuts ▾ Notes ▾ Hints
1.267 Set PANOSE font matching options	▪ From the File menu, select "Preferences." ▪ In the "Preferences" dialog box click the "Map fonts" button. ▪ If the diamond next to "PANOSE" is not black, click it once to make it black. ▪ Use the slider bar to set the tolerance level for font matching. ▪ Select a Default font. ▪ Check the box next to "Show mapping results" if you want to view the "PANOSE font matching results" dialog box each time fonts are substituted for missing ones. ▪ Uncheck the box next to "Show mapping results" to let PageMaker make substitutions without alerting you; see 1.259.	▪ Choices you make in the PANOSE box become application defaults. ▪ If you want to make sure a font (other than the default font) is always substituted for a missing one, set the tolerance level to "Loose." If you prefer only exact match substitutions, set the tolerance level to "Exact." ▪ In your publication, missing fonts will show in the font menu with the substitute name in brackets alongside it. ▪ To restore the original default PANOSE settings, throw the "PANOSE Preferences" file in the trash (it is in the "Preferences" folder in your System folder). A new preference file, minus all your "Spellings" and "Exceptions" changes, is created the next time you click the "Map fonts" button. ▪ PANOSE and SuperATM can be used together, see 1.244.
1.268 Disable PANOSE font substitution	▪ From the File menu, select "Preferences." ▪ In the "Preferences" dialog box click the "Map fonts" button. ▪ Click the diamond next to "PANOSE," to make it hollow.	▪ A hollow diamond means PANOSE is off. A gray diamond indicates PANOSE is running secondary to SuperATM. The same code applies to the diamond next to SuperATM.

If you want to do this:	Then follow these steps:	Shortcuts ▾ Notes ▾ Hints

1.269 Choose whether to temporarily or permanently accept the font substitutions PageMaker offers for a particular publication 	▪ In the "Font matching" dialog box, "Show mapping results" must be checked (1.267).
	▪ Open your PageMaker publication.
	▪ In the "PANOSE font matching results" dialog box:
	  ☐ Click "Temporary," if you are satisfied with the substitutions for now, *or*
	  ☐ Click "Permanent," if you want to maintain the same substitutions for that publication.
	▪ Click OK.
		▪ Choose "Temporary" if you will be taking the document to a computer that has the missing font, or if you want to reconsider your font options the next time you open the document.
		▪ Choose "Permanent" when you are not sending the publication to another computer, and won't be installing the missing font(s).
		  ☐ If you do install the fonts, PageMaker will replace the substitutions whether they were "Permanent" or "Temporary."

1.270 Create your own font substitutions	▪ From the File menu, select "Preferences." ▪ In the "Preferences" dialog box click the "Map fonts" button. ▪ In the "Font matching" dialog box, click the "Exceptions" button. ▪ Click the "Add" button. ▪ In the "Missing font" edit box, enter the font you want to substitute. ▪ In the "Substituted font" edit box, enter the font you want as a permanent substitute for the font named above. ▪ Click OK. Click "Add" if you want to make other exceptions, or click OK in each dialog box you want to close.	▪ Changes to the "Exceptions" list are not applied to the active publication. You must first close and reopen your publication for the new exceptions to be applied. ▪ PageMaker prompts you to add fonts to the "Exceptions" list when you make substitution changes in the "PANOSE font matching results" dialog box (see 1.271). ▪ Press the Option key as you click the OK button, or press Option Return, to close all the nested dialog boxes and return to your publication.

If you want to do this:

1.271 Select your own substitutions in the "Panose font matching results" dialog box

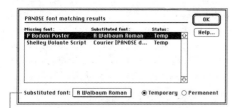

The pop-up menu lists all the fonts presently available in your system.

The "Exceptions" prompt box.

Then follow these steps:

- In the "Font matching" dialog box, "Show mapping results" must be checked (1.267).
- Open your PageMaker publication.
- In the "PANOSE font matching results" dialog box, highlight the font for which you want to change the substitution.
- From the "Substituted font" pop-up menu, select the font you want to use.
  □ Click "Temporary," if you want to reconsider the substitution the next time you open the document.
  □ Click "Permanent," to make that substitution permanent for that publication.
- Click OK.
- In the "Exceptions" prompt box:
  □ Click "No" in the prompt box if you want this substitution to only apply to the current publication.
  □ Click "Yes" if you want PageMaker to add the substitution to the "Exceptions" list, and make the same font substitution for all future publications.
- If necessary, press the Option key and choose "Hyphenation" from the Type menu, to recompose your story.
- From the File menu, choose "Save," to force the recompositition all at once (otherwise PageMaker recomposes as you turn pages).

Shortcuts ▾ Notes ▾ Hints

- Although font substitution goes against the grain of serious typesetting and page design standards, I suppose there could be a reason to keep it selected all the time in your "Preferences…" menu. For one thing, the "PANOSE font matching results" dialog box will prompt you as to which fonts are missing. If you use a font managing utility it will remind you about fonts or sets of fonts that you need to open for a publication. If you don't have the missing fonts, you can either change them or install them. However, used this way, I would always select Courier as the Default font. That way it's easier to remember you are not dealing with the real font. You won't waste your time kerning or tracking, nor will you let it go to final print that way. PANOSE can make it too easy to let a substitute font end up in your final publication. Worse, if you take it to lino, they may have the missing font and replace the substitute with the original one! Since you probably won't get to recompose the text to apply the correct font metrics, the printed publication might not look like you expected.

Miscellaneous

1.272 This miscellaneous subsection covers some last tidbits of useful information. Some of this information is particular to PageMaker, some to basic Macintosh functions that are especially indispensable adjuncts to PageMaker.

a) Cut/Copy/Paste and the Clipboard

These commands work exactly the same in PageMaker as they do in any other Macintosh program, allowing you to remove or copy objects or text and paste them in elsewhere. This section clarifies which tool to use to cut or copy different parts of the publication.

b) Multiple paste

Copy an item to the Clipboard, and then paste multiple copies into your publication. You can paste text or graphics, either independently, inline, or in step-and-repeat patterns.

c) Scrapbook

The Scrapbook works exactly the same as in any other program on the Mac, enabling you to permanently save graphics or text (from PageMaker or from any other program) for use at any time in any publication.

d) Bounding box, or drag-placing

Create a *bounding box* or *drag-place* to control precisely the space that text or a graphic initially occupies—great for placing a lot of things on the pasteboard to have them handy for working on later.

e) Overriding the measurement system

PageMaker, consistent with its philosophy of letting you have control over everything, allows you to override the ruler specifications for any little particular measurement you happen to need at the moment, without changing the rulers; e.g. even though your measurements system may be in inches, you can set your paragraph spacing in points.

f) Numeric keypad

You can use the numeric keypad to type numbers, move the insertion point through the text, or cut and paste. Combined with the Shift key, you can use the keypad to select text for editing.

g) Key Caps

Key Caps is where you find all of the characters the Mac provides to make your type look truly professional.

h) Find File

Don't forget about this great desk accessory for finding 'lost' files on your desktop, or for finding files to Open or folders to Save into while working inside PageMaker.

i) Creating more space in the publication window

This section is simply a tip on how to maximize your viewing area.

Cut/Copy/Paste and the Clipboard 84

Multiple paste 88

Scrapbook 94

Bounding box 98

Overriding ruler measurements 101

Numeric keypad 102

Key Caps 104

Find File 107

Creating more window space 108

Clipboard

1.273 The **Clipboard** is a temporary storage place for text or graphics. Whenever you cut or copy an object or text, it is placed on the Clipboard. It will stay on the Clipboard until you turn off the computer. Whenever you choose to **paste,** PageMaker (and all other Mac programs, actually) pastes a copy of whatever is on the Clipboard. You can paste the item an infinite number of times. *(Deleting or clearing an object or text does* not *place it on the Clipboard.)*

1.274 An important thing to remember about the Clipboard is that *it holds only one selection at a time;* as soon as you cut or copy another item, the new item replaces anything previously on the Clipboard.

1.275 Since the Clipboard is a System tool and not just a PageMaker function, you can put an item into the Clipboard from another program (such as a graphic from SuperPaint), and then paste it into PageMaker.

1.276 The Clipboard is limited by the amount of RAM you have as to how much text you can cut or copy into it. If you try to paste more than that, it will yell at you.

1.277 The Clipboard treats text in two different ways, depending on whether you select the text with the **pointer tool** or with the **text tool.**

1.278 With the **pointer tool:**

a If you select an entire text block *with the pointer tool,* it will paste into the Clipboard with all the formatting intact (size, style, line length, etc.). If you were to view the Clipboard (1.285), you would see the exact text block you copied or cut.

b If you select an entire text block *with the pointer tool* and then paste it into your publication *with no insertion point flashing and no text selected,* it will still be the exact same text block. It will not be threaded to any other text block.

1.279 With the **text tool:**

a If you select text *with the text tool,* it will appear in the Clipboard as 12-point Geneva, no matter what the specifications are. But if you choose to paste that 12-point Geneva text into your publication, all the original formatting and specifications are returned, *except for the line length.*

b When you paste, if there is *no insertion point flashing, or if the insertion point is on the pasteboard or outside of any column,* the text will create its own text block, with the line length being the width of your page margins. All other formatting will stay the same. It will not be threaded to any other text block.

c With **either tool:** If, however, *an insertion point is flashing or text is selected* when you paste, the newly-pasted text will keep its original *character* formatting (font, size, style, etc.), but will adapt to the *paragraph* formatting (line length, tabs and indents, etc.) of the paragraph it is pasted into. (*Selected* text will be *replaced.*)

For more info on cutting, copying, and pasting *text,* see 4.125–4.128.
For more info on cutting, copying, and pasting *graphics,* see 10.132; 10.133.

If you want to do this:	Then follow these steps:	Shortcuts ▾ Notes ▾ Hints
1.280 Cut	▪ To select an *object,* click once on it with the **pointer tool** (1.202–1.221); **or** to select *characters,* press-and-drag over them with the **text tool** (4.203–4.204). ▪ Then from the Edit menu choose "Cut," or press Command X.	▪ **Cut** will **remove** the selected item from the screen and place it on the Clipboard, ready for pasting. If you press the Backspace/Delete key or choose "Clear" from the Edit menu, the item will be removed, but *not* placed on the Clipboard.
1.281 Copy	▪ To select an *object,* click once on it with the **pointer tool** (1.202–1.221); **or** to select *characters,* press-and-drag over them with the **text tool** (4.203–4.204). ▪ From the Edit menu choose "Copy," or press Command C.	▪ **Copy** will **leave** the selected object or text on the screen and place a **copy** of it on the Clipboard, ready for pasting.
1.282 Paste *(see also Paste special 1.286, and Multiple paste, 1.287–1.310.)*	▪ To **paste a graphic or text,** from the Edit menu, simply choose "Paste," or press Command V. ▪ Basically: □ If there is an *insertion point* flashing when you "Paste," text and graphics will be inserted beginning at that insertion point; text will pick up the existing paragraph formatting (1.279c), and graphics will become *inline graphics* (10.125). □ If the *pointer tool* is chosen when you paste, text will create a separate text block (1.279c) and graphics will be independent (10.124).	▪ If "Paste" on the Edit menu is gray, it means the Clipboard is empty. ▪ If you cut or copy a text block or a graphic and paste it back onto the same page, it shows up on the page slightly shifted from the original it was copied from. If you change page views or pages, it pastes into the center of the page. ▪ To paste into the exact position it was cut or copied from, *power-paste with the pointer tool:* **Command Option V** (see 1.283). ▪ When you paste a graphic, if you do not want it to be an *inline graphic* (10.125) connected to a text block, then make sure there is no insertion point flashing!

If you want to do this:	Then follow these steps:	Shortcuts ▾ Notes ▾ Hints
1.283 **Power-paste** a text block or a graphic into the exact position from which it was it was cut or copied	■ With the **pointer tool,** select and cut or copy a text block or graphic as usual (1.280–1.281). ■ Paste the object by pressing Command Option V. ■ Read the column to the right.	■ If you copied an object and it is still visible on the screen, the power-pasted item will land directly on top of the original, which may make you think it didn't happen. It did. ■ Power-pasting like this will work even if you change page views, turn pages, or open another publication before you paste! ■ If the original location is no longer visible, the object will be pasted into the center of the screen. ■ To find out all about Multiple paste, another powerful method of pasting, see 1.287–1.310.
1.284 **Clear,** from the Edit menu, or **Backspace/Delete**	■ Select an object or text (1.202–1.215). ■ From the Edit menu choose "Clear" *or* press the Backspace/Delete key.	■ Both **Clear** and the **Backspace/Delete** key will **remove** the selected object or text from the screen, but *will not* place it on the Clipboard—it's just gone. ■ These commands come in very handy when there is something on the Clipboard you wish to keep, since cutting would replace the Clipboard item. ■ Undo (from the Edit menu, *or* press Command Z) will undo this action, *if* you Undo *before you do anything else.*

If you want to do this:

Then follow these steps:

Shortcuts • Notes • Hints

1.285 View the contents of the Clipboard

- With any tool, choose "Show clipboard" from the Window menu.
- To close it, click in its close box (upper left corner of its window); **or** from the File menu choose "Close"; **or** simply click on the publication page that you see behind the Clipboard.

- Text in the Clipboard is not editable.
- Text sent to the Clipboard with the text tool is displayed in 12-point Geneva; when you paste it back into the publication, though, all its formatting reappears.
- Read 1.277–1.279 for further clarification of what the Clipboard does to text.

1.286 Choose which format PageMaker uses to paste a Clipboard item

The "Paste special" dialog box is explained in detail in Section 10, 10.110–10.119.

- In any program, including PageMaker, copy the item you want to paste.
- From the Edit menu, choose "Paste special...."
- In the "Paste special" dialog box, select the format you want to use for pasting the item.
- Click "Paste."

- The formats that will be available depend upon the type of object and from where it was copied. For example, a PageMaker drawn object becomes available in PageMaker 5.0 format, or PICT format.
- When you choose "Paste" from the Edit menu, PageMaker automatically pastes the Clipboard item in the format at the top of the list in the "Paste special" dialog box, see 10.112.
- If you select a format that makes the "Paste link" button black, the item on the Clipboard is from an OLE server program (11.103). If you click the "Paste link" button, the Clipboard item pastes an OLE-linked object (11.115–11.118). If the "Paste link" button is available, and you click the "Paste" button instead, the item on the Clipboard pastes as an OLE-embedded item (11.111–11.113).

Multiple paste

1.287 The **"Multiple paste..."** command is a powerful editing tool that lets you paste in as many copies of something from the Clipboard as you want. It even lets you specify step-and-repeat patterns for graphics, where each object is pasted a certain distance from the original.

1.288 If the insertion point is flashing when you choose the command, whatever is on the Clipboard pastes inline. With any other tool chosen, each copy that pastes in has its own handles.

1.289 Remember, the Clipboard only holds one selection at a time. If you want to multiple paste an object, or text, it has to be the last thing you copied. "Multiple paste" remembers the position of the copied item too. Unless you are pasting with the insertion point flashing, you have to copy the item in the position you want the copies to paste. For example, if you copy a graphic, then choose to multiple paste 3 copies, .5 inches apart horizontally, the *first* copy will be horizontally offset .5 inches from the *original* graphic you copied.

1.290 The options available to you when you select "Multiple paste..." depend on which tool is selected when you choose the command. When the text tool is selected you can choose the number of copies you want to paste. When any other tool is selected, you can choose the number of copies, plus the distance between each copy you paste. In either dialog box you can enter up to 32,767 as the number of copies you want before you get yelled at!

1.291 With the text tool selected:

Whenever you have the text tool chosen, the "Multiple paste" dialog box will look like this. The results will vary though, depending on whether the insertion point is actually flashing or not.

1.292 Regardless of whether the item on the Clipboard is text or an object, you can only choose how many copies to paste. If the insertion point is flashing within a text block, the copies paste one after the other into the text block. Objects become inline graphics.

1.293 If you choose more than the amount of copies that can fit in the text block, PageMaker will display a message box that tells you it cannot show the insertion point, and only offers a "Continue" button. You may see the message box once for every copy that can't fit. Command period, which can interrupt and cancel most multiple paste sequences, is worthless in this case.

1.294 If you copy text with the text tool, but the insertion point is *not* flashing when you choose "Multiple paste," each copy pastes in as its own text block, one on top of the other. If an object is on the Clipboard (text selected with the pointer tool and copied as a text block, is considered an object), and you have the text tool selected without the insertion point flashing, PageMaker pastes in the number of copies you enter here, but with the offset defaults last entered in the *other* "Multiple paste" dialog box; see 1.300.

The "Multiple paste" dialog box

1.295 Usually the "Multiple paste" dialog box will look like this. With any tool (other than the text tool) selected, you can choose the number of copies you want to paste, and the distance between each copy.

1.296 Press the tab key to move from one Edit box to the next. The values you enter in the edit boxes remain there as publication defaults until you open the dialog box and type in new values.

1.297 You can paste in as many as 32,767 copies at one time. If PageMaker runs out of room when pasting copies, the remaining copies paste one on top of the other. You can press Command Period to cancel the paste sequence in action, but, unfortunately, the "Undo" command is not available after you "Multiple paste."

1.298 You can enter positive or negative values in the "Horizontal offset," and the "Vertical offset" edit boxes to determine the placement of the copies pasted in.

1.299 You can bypass the "Multiple paste" dialog box and copy and multiple paste an object using the settings you last entered in the dialog box; see 1.309.

Click OK or press Return to Multiple paste the item on the Clipboard.

1.300 *Enter the number of copies you want.*

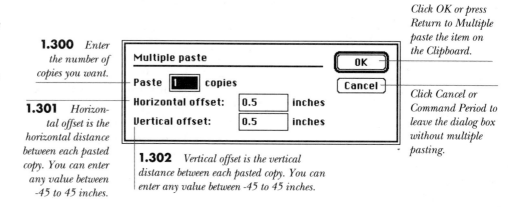

Click Cancel or Command Period to leave the dialog box without multiple pasting.

1.301 *Horizontal offset is the horizontal distance between each pasted copy. You can enter any value between -45 to 45 inches.*

1.302 *Vertical offset is the vertical distance between each pasted copy. You can enter any value between -45 to 45 inches.*

1.303 Positive values in the Horizontal and Vertical offset boxes paste the copies to the right and below the original.

1.304 Negative values in the Horizontal and Vertical offset boxes paste the copies to the left and above the original.

Original

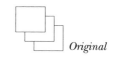

Original

If you want to do this:	**Then follow these steps:**	**Shortcuts ▾ Notes ▾ Hints**

1.305 Multiple paste an object	■ With the **pointer tool** click on the object.
	■ From the Edit menu choose "Copy."
	■ From the Edit menu choose "Multiple paste…."
	■ In the "Multiple paste" dialog box:
	  □ Type a number in the "Paste" box.
	  □ Set a value for the horizontal distance between each copy.
	  □ Set a value for the vertical distance between each copy.
	■ Click OK.
		■ Multiple paste is not undoable! Choose "Save" before multiple pasting—then at least you have "Revert" under the File menu as a way to undo any mistakes.
		■ You cannot go back into the multiple paste dialog box to change the values on copies already pasted in.
		■ If you copy an object, and move it before you select "Multiple paste," the copies still paste in relative to the position the object was in when you copied it.

1.306 Multiple paste objects to the left and above the original
 	
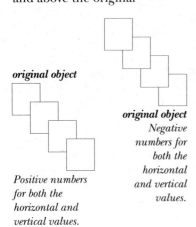
 	
original object
 	
Positive numbers for both the horizontal and vertical values.
 	
original object
Negative numbers for both the horizontal and vertical values.
	■ With the **pointer tool,** click on the object.
	■ From the Edit menu, choose "Copy," or press Command C.
	■ From the Edit menu, choose "Multiple paste…."
	■ In the "Multiple paste" dialog box:
	  □ Type a number in the "Paste" box.
	  □ Type a negative number in the "Horizontal offset" box.
	  □ Type a negative number in the "Vertical offset" box.
		■ Type negative numbers by simply inserting a hyphen before the number.
		■ A positive number in the "Horizontal offset" box sets the copies to the right of the original, a negative number sets the copies to the left.
		■ A positive number in the "Vertical offset" box sets the copies from top to bottom, a negative number sets the copies from bottom to top.

If you want to do this:	**Then follow these steps:**	**Shortcuts ▾ Notes ▾ Hints**
1.307 Multiple paste text	■ With the **text tool,** highlight the text and/or inline graphics you want to copy. ■ From the Edit menu, choose "Copy," or press Command C. ■ Set the **insertion point** where you want the copies to paste. ■ From the Edit menu, choose "Multiple paste…." ■ In the "Multiple paste" dialog box, type the number of copies you want in the Paste box. ■ Click OK.	■ When the text tool is selected, the "Multiple paste" dialog box has only the Paste value box. There are no options for horizontal or vertical offset values when multiple pasting with the text tool. ■ "Undo," from the Edit menu, will only undo the very last copy pasted in—if four copies are pasted in, choosing "Undo" will leave three.
1.308 Multiple paste an object as an inline graphic	■ With the **pointer tool,** select the graphic you want to paste inline. ■ From the Edit menu, choose "Copy," or press Command C. ■ Set the **insertion point** within the text where you want to paste the graphic. ■ From the Edit menu, choose "Multiple paste…." ■ Type a number into the Paste box. ■ Click OK.	■ If you paste an inline graphic into text set with auto leading, the leading will change to accommodate the graphic. Even with fixed leading, the leading value may need to be reset after pasting an inline graphic. (Highlight the text with the text tool, then choose the appropriate leading from the Type menu, the Type specs box, or the Control palette.) See 10.213–10.251 for tips on working with inline graphics. ■ The Control palette has a "Baseline-offset" option that is available when you select the inline graphic with the pointer tool. It's perfect for this. See 10.248.

If you want to do this:

Then follow these steps:

Shortcuts ▾ Notes ▾ Hints

1.309 Multiple paste a graphic or text without reopening the dialog box.

- Select and copy the object or text you want to multiple paste.
- Hold down the Option key as you go to the Edit menu and choose "Multiple paste…."
- PageMaker will use the last values entered in each Edit box.

- PageMaker's default settings for "Multiple paste" (one copy, offset .5 inch both horizontally and vertically), are in effect for every new document (see 1.13 to change application defaults). New values entered in this dialog box when a publication is open, override the application defaults and become the publication's defaults.

1.310 Use "Multiple paste" to create a quick two-tone grid

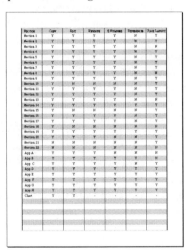

- Create a long, narrow rectangle with a fill that stretches from the left to right margin at the top of the page.
- From the Edit menu choose "Copy," then choose "Multiple paste."
- Enter a number of copies and a vertical offset value equal to the depth of the rectangle, click OK.
- Draw a vertical line at the leftmost edge of your grid, from top to bottom margin.
- From the Edit menu, choose "Copy," then choose "Multiple paste."
- Enter a number of copies and a horizontal offset value, click OK.
- Choose a point size and leading value that places the text within the two-tone rows.

- In the example shown, the page is letter size with a .75 inch margin all the way around.
- The rectangle is .25 inch deep, with a 20% black fill, no line. It was multiple pasted eighteen times, .5 inches apart vertically.
- The vertical line is a 1-point rule, pasted seven times, 1 inch apart.
- The type is 12 point on 18 point leading, with a .125 left indent and center tabs 1 inch apart starting at 1.5 inches.
- When you type on top of the grid, the bars may disappear. Change page views to see the bars again, or select the text block with the pointer tool and from the Element menu choose "Bring to front." You may want to use a bold face type for clarity.

If you want to do this:

1.311 Undo

. . . .

1.312a You *can* Undo:

You can undo these actions:
- Moving ruler guides and column guides
- Adding or deleting ruler guides
- Creating columns
- Moving or resizing graphics or text blocks, including stretching PageMaker-drawn graphics
- Cropping imported graphics
- Changes using the "Object-view" palette
- Editing text

And you can undo these commands:
- "Cut," "Copy," and "Clear" commands from the Edit menu or keyboard
- "Paste" command from the Edit menu or keyboard, *if* it was pasted using the *text tool*
- "Copy master guides" from the Layout menu
- "Insert pages..." and "Remove pages..." from the Layout menu
- "Page setup..." changes

Then follow these steps:

- From the Edit menu choose "Undo ____" **or** press Command Z.

1.312b You *cannot* Undo:

- Pasting while using the pointer tool
- Page view changes or scrolling
- Movement of text tool insertion point, using the mouse or keyboard
- Selecting or canceling selections
- Any changes to line widths, line patterns, and fill patterns
- "Bring to front/back" commands
- Any commands from the Window or Type menus
- Changes using the "Style" or "Color" palettes
- Changes using the "Character-view" or "Paragraph-view" palettes
- Any command from the File menu, except "Page setup..."

Shortcuts ▾ Notes ▾ Hints

- As you do different things in your publication, the Undo command will change, telling you what action will be undone. If the action cannot be undone, "Cannot undo" appears dimmed in the menu.
- You can only Undo *the very last thing you did!* So if you do something you don't like, or if you do something that makes you want to scream, first try Undo. Then scream if necessary.
- Often you can cancel what you just did by doing the opposite; that is, if you pasted a graphic, then while it is still selected just hit the Backspace/Delete key rather than try to Undo it. It really would be nice if we could undo line widths or fill patterns, wouldn't it.
- See Section 18 on Reverting and mini-Reverting for serious undoing.

If you want to do this:

Then follow these steps:

Shortcuts ▾ Notes ▾ Hints

Scrapbook

1.313 Put a graphic into the Scrapbook

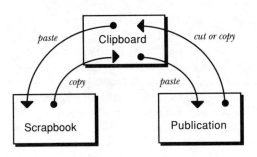

- Select the graphic. If it has more than one layer, be sure to get all the layers. (If you have trouble, read the subsection on Selecting and Layering: 1.181–1.221).
- Copy it (from the Edit menu choose "Copy," *or* press Command C); the graphic is now on the Clipboard (1.273–1.279; 1.281).
- From the Apple menu, choose "Scrapbook."
- While viewing the Scrapbook, from the Edit menu choose "Paste," *or* press Command V.
- Close the Scrapbook window (click in its close box in the upper left corner) to get back to your publication, *or* just click on the PageMaker window under the Scrapbook.

- The Scrapbook is a standard Macintosh desk accessory that permanently stores graphics or text for you. The only way into or out of it is through the Clipboard.
- You could also use the "Cut" command (1.280) to put an object in the Scrapbook.
- You can group together as many objects as you like and paste them all into the Scrapbook at once.

- When you paste any image into the Scrapbook, the current ones move over to make room for it; you're not *replacing* anything.

If you want to do this:	Then follow these steps:	Shortcuts ▾ Notes ▾ Hints
1.314 Put text into the Scrapbook	■ Select text with the **text tool** by pressing-and-dragging over it; **OR** select text with the **pointer tool** by clicking on the text block. ■ From the Edit menu choose "Copy," *or* press Command C. ■ From the Apple menu, choose "Scrapbook." ■ While viewing the Scrapbook, from the Edit menu choose "Paste," *or* press Command V. ■ Close the Scrapbook window (click in its close box) to get back to your publication, *or* just click on the PageMaker window under the Scrapbook.	■ There is an important difference between copying text that has been selected with the *text tool* and copying text that has been selected with the *pointer tool*—the Scrapbook does different things to them, just like the Clipboard (1.277–1.279): 　□ If you select an entire text block with the **pointer tool,** it will paste into the Scrapbook with all the formatting intact (size, style, line length, etc.), and it will come back exactly the same. 　□ If you select text by highlighting it with the **text tool,** it will paste into the Scrapbook as 12-point Geneva, no matter what the specifications were. But if you choose to paste that 12-point Geneva text back into your publication again from the Scrapbook, all the formatting and specifications are returned (except line length)! ■ If there is no insertion point flashing when you paste into the *publication,* the text will create its own text block, which will be the width between the page margins.
1.315 Delete any image from the Scrapbook	■ From the Apple menu choose "Scrapbook." ■ In the open Scrapbook, find the image you want to delete. ■ From the Edit menu choose "Clear."	■ You could, of course, use "Cut" instead, but keep in mind that "Clear" does not put the item on the Clipboard.

If you want to do this: ▪	**Then follow these steps:** ▪	**Shortcuts ▾ Notes ▾ Hints** ▪
1.316 Paste an *object* from the Scrapbook onto a page	▪ From the Apple menu choose "Scrapbook." ▪ Scroll to the image you want to copy onto your page. ▪ While viewing the image, from the Edit menu choose "Copy," *or* press Command C. ▪ Return to your publication (either click in the close box of the Scrapbook window *or* click on the PageMaker window). ▪ From the Edit menu choose "Paste." ▪ *Don't click anywhere!* While the handles are still on the object(s), press on a solid part or directly on text and drag it to its place. ▪ If you change your mind or if you blew it, you can Undo the paste (Command Z) immediately.	▪ You could also choose "Cut," of course, but that would delete it from the Scrapbook. ▪ If the *pointer tool* was chosen before you opened the Scrapbook, the pasted objects will be set right in the middle of the page. ▪ If *any other tool* besides the pointer tool is chosen, and there is no flashing insertion point, when you paste objects they will be set right in the middle of the page and the pointer tool will be chosen for you automatically. ▪ If *an insertion point is flashing,* which means the *text tool* is chosen, the object will be pasted into the text as an *inline graphic* (10.125). Be careful! You'll probably accidentally paste objects as inline graphics at least 23 times before you finally start to remember to watch for that insertion point.
1.317 Paste *text* from the Scrapbook onto a page	▪ Follow the steps in 1.316 above to copy the text and return to the publication. ▪ Using the **text tool,** click to set an insertion point where you want the text to begin (see note to the right ☞). ▪ From the Edit menu choose "Paste," *or* press Command V.	▪ If an insertion point is set *within* an existing text block, the type will flow into that text block. ▪ If an insertion point is set *outside* of any existing text block, the type will create a new text block. ▪ If no insertion point is set, the type will create a new text block. ▪ Also read 1.280–1.282 on cutting and pasting, as well as 4.128.

If you want to do this:

1.318 **Place** Scrapbook items
as graphics

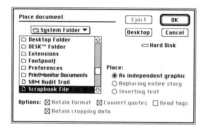

Find the Scrapbook File in the System folder.

  The Scrapbook place icon

Then follow these steps:

- Choose the **pointer tool.**
- From the File menu choose "Place...."
- Find your way to the contents of the System Folder (navigate by clicking on "Desktop" if necessary to access another disk, and double-clicking on folders to open them; see *The Little Mac Book* if you're not clear on finding your way around).
- In the Place dialog box, while viewing the contents of the System Folder, click once on the file called "Scrapbook File."
- Click in the radio button (on the right) to place this as an **independent graphic** (*this is very important—if you don't click that button and there happens to be an insertion point flashing somewhere, the entire contents of your Scrapbook will pour into that text block*).
- Click OK; in your publication, you will see a new cursor with a number on it; the number indicates how many items are loaded into that cursor—the number of items in your Scrapbook.
- Each click of the mouse will place one of the items on the publication page, and the number on the cursor will reduce.
- To evaporate the rest of the items without placing them, click on the pointer tool.

Shortcuts ▪ Notes ▪ Hints

- All PageMaker objects that are placed this way drop in as PICTs (10.23–10.31). You can intentionally turn PageMaker text or graphics into PICTs using the "Paste special" command (10.151).
- Of course, if you have created several different Scrapbook files, you can open the one that you know holds the image you want; it may not necessarily be in the System Folder.
- You don't *really* need to choose the pointer tool first; the crucial thing is that you don't leave a flashing insertion point lying around somewhere. By clicking on the pointer tool, that's just not possible.
- If you are positive there is no insertion point anywhere, then you can shortcut the OK button by simply double-clicking on the file name. Without an insertion point, your only option is an independent graphic anyway.
- If you accidentally placed the entire Scrapbook in a text block, Undo immediately (Command Z). If it's too late to Undo, see 10.242.

If you want to do this: ▪

Then follow these steps: ▪

Shortcuts ▾ Notes ▾ Hints ▪

Bounding Box (or drag-placing)

1.319   Create a bounding box to **type** into

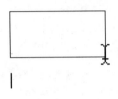

Press-and-drag with the text tool to create a bounding box like this.

When you let go, the box becomes invisible, but it's still there; the insertion point waits.

This text has been typed into an invisible bounding box. The depth will expand as you type, but not the width.

As you type or paste text, it will fill the bounding box.

- Choose the **text tool.**
- Anywhere *outside of any existing text block,* press-and-drag; this will create a *bounding box,* as shown on the left.
- When you let go of the mouse, the box *seems* to disappear, but it is actually just invisible; that perimeter you created is still there!
- The insertion point is flashing in the upper left of this invisible box; type and you will see the text word-wrap as it reaches the outer limits of the bounding box; the depth will expand to accommodate the text.

- This is a particularly useful technique to use when you want to type a headline across two columns—just set up a bounding box across the two and the text will override the column guides. Or when you wish to set page numbers or any other little bit of text, create a tiny little bounding box just big enough to hold your input.

1.320   **Paste** text into a bounding box

- When you are ready to paste text, create a bounding box as above (1.319).
- From the Edit menu choose "Paste," *or* press Command V.
- The text will paste into the bounding box, and the depth will expand to fit.

If you want to do this:

Then follow these steps:

Shortcuts • Notes • Hints

1.321 Drag-place text into a bounding box

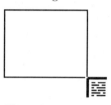

This is the image you will see as you drag a loaded text icon.

- When you are ready to **place** text, get the file as usual (from the file menu choose "Place..."; select the text file to place into PageMaker; see 4.55–4.56; **or** pick up text from a window loop; 4.95; 4.109).
- On your publication page, you should have a loaded text icon (4.88–4.89). With that icon, *don't click!* Instead, press-and-drag to create the bounding box (1.319); when you let up on the mouse, the text will flow into that space.

- Unlike when pasting or typing into a bounding box, *when you place text, the depth does not expand.* The text will flow into *just* that space you created.
- This is a great technique for placing a bunch of stories all over the pasteboard to see what you have to work with— drag-place just a few lines of each story. Even though only a few lines are visible, the text block contains the entire file.

1.322 Drag-place a graphic into a bounding box

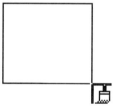

This is the image you will see as you drag a loaded graphic icon. (The icon itself may be different, depending on what type of graphic file you are placing; see 10.126.)

- When you are ready to **place** a graphic, click on the **pointer tool.** Get the file (from the File menu choose "Place..."; and select the graphic file you wish to place into your publication; see 10.126).
- On your publication page, you should see a loaded graphic icon (10.126). With that icon, press-and-drag to create the bounding box (as shown at left); when you let up on the mouse, *the graphic will flow into that space, meaning it will squeeze into whatever shape that space is, which may not be proportional!* Note that it is not cropped or necessarily resized, but has simply filled the space you gave it.

- Using the pointer tool ensures you will not inadvertently place it as an *inline graphic* (10.125).

- If you drag-place a graphic and it is out of proportion, position the tip of the **pointer tool** directly on a handle; hold down the Shift key and *press* the mouse button on that handle. Hold to the count of three; the image will snap back into its original proportions (not necessarily its original *size*, but its original *proportions*).

(continued from page 56)

NYWAY, GUTENBERG (BORN IN 1399 IN MAINZ, Germany) was getting into political trouble with the goldsmithing guilds in the city. So he ran off to Strasbourg, where it seems he began developing his printing equipment in the strictest secrecy. The history books are always wondering why he was so secretive, but is that so unusual? Aren't we still trying to keep PostScript hints and unbreakable codes secrets? **W**ell, the man was obsessive. Driven. An artist. Broke. He went back to Mainz with his perfected system, and in 1450 (at 49 years of age) talked a local financier, Johann Fust, into lending him money – 800 guilders, with the press equipment as security. But Gutenberg was a perfectionist. Besides, he didn't have PageMaker. He couldn't just change his leading with the click of a mouse to make those forty-two lines of type fit on the page. He couldn't press Command-Shift-J and make everything justify. No, he had to have every letter carved and molded backwards out of a separate tiny piece of lead; create other separate letters for the initial caps; take all these backwards letters and arrange them backwards in a wooden flat; insert varying amounts of lead space between each word to justify the text; insert slugs of lead between the lines; ink it up and run it through the press; check for typos, which obviously meant quite a bit of readjusting; then after getting a hundred or so good proofs, take all the letters out of that wooden flat and put them back into their cases (that's movable type) and start all over again with the next page. Whew. And just the thought of keyboarding the Bible is overwhelming. **G**utenberg worked on his project for two years, and Fust got a bit impatient at the lack of progress. Give the guy a break, Fust, he didn't have a Mac IIfx. He didn't even have a typewriter. Fust loaned him 800 more guilders and insisted on becoming a partner. **I**n 1457 Fust had really had it. Seven years. So he took Gutenberg to court and sued for the 1600 guilders he had loaned him, all the type, all the presses and other equipment, all the completed work on the 200 Bibles, plus an extra 426 guilders as interest on his loan. With the judge being another member of the Fust family, Gutenberg didn't stand a chance. **B**ut Fust was a banker – what did he know about printing Bibles? Certainly Gutenberg's most skilled foreman, Peter Schoeffer, wouldn't desert him and traitorously decamp to the buttered side of the press? Alas, Peter was in love with Fust's daughter. Fust and Peter Schoeffer went on to publish what has become known as the first printed piece of work in the world, the 42-line Mazarin Bible. And Peter married the boss's daughter.

(continued on page 191)

If you want to do this:

Then follow these steps:

Shortcuts ▾ Notes ▾ Hints

Overriding ruler measurements

1.323 Override the current ruler measurement in any dialog box that asks for measures

inches
millimeters
picas
points
ciceros
cicero points

After [**0p5**] inches

Example of overriding the inches with points to add extra space between paragraphs.

- No matter what the current measurement system, you can override it with the following abbreviations:

    Inches: type **i** after the value.
    e.g., *2.75 inches = 2.75i*

    Millimeters: type **m** after the value.
    e.g., *3 millimeters = 3m*

    Picas: type **p** after the value.
    e.g., *3 picas = 3p*

    Points: type **0p** before the value (that's a *zero* and a *p*).
    e.g., *6 points = 0p6*

    Picas and points: type a value for picas, type **p**, type the value for points.
    e.g., *2 picas & 6 points = 2p6*

    Ciceros: type **c** after the value.
    e.g., *5 ciceros = 5c*

    Cicero points: type **0c** before the value (that's a *zero* and a *c*).
    e.g., *4 cicero points = 0c4*

    Ciceros and points: type a value for ciceros, type **c**, type the value for points.
    e.g., *5 ciceros & 4 points = 5c4*

- This will leave your rulers intact, but allow you to specify in other measures.
- This is extremely useful, for example, when the measurements are in inches, but you want to specify the space between paragraphs in points, or perhaps the space between columns in picas.
- You can override the measurement, but when you come back to that dialog box you will find that PageMaker has translated the overridden value into the equivalent measure for the system it's currently working in; that is, if you type **1p** to override the inches, the next time you see that dialog box it will no longer say **1p,** but **0.167,** which is the equivalent in inches.
- You can override the measurement system of some options in the Control palette; see 3.114.
- Just for your information:
    □ 1 pica = .167 inch
    □ 1 cicero = .177 inch (4.5 mm)
    □ Picas and ciceros are both divided into 12 points.
    □ In traditional type, 6 picas equals .996 of an inch; in Macintosh type, 6 picas (72 points) is exactly one inch.

101

If you want to do this:

Then follow these steps:

Shortcuts ▾ Notes ▾ Hints

Numeric keypad

1.324   Type numbers with the keypad

- Press Caps Lock down.

- You can also press the Clear key (or Num lock key) instead of Caps Lock to toggle between using the keypad for numbers or for arrow keys (1.325). But there is no visual clue that tells you which mode you are currently in—you just have to type and see what comes up.

1.325   Use the keypad as arrow keys

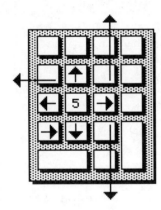

- The insertion point must first be somewhere in the story.
- Make sure Caps Lock is **not** down.

- If you examine the diagram on the left, you'll see that it's pretty logical, really:

  8 takes you up a line
  2 takes you down a line

  7 takes you to the beginning of the line
  1 takes you to the end of a line

  9 takes you up a screen
  3 takes you down a screen

  4 takes you left one character
  6 takes you right one character

  5 always types a 5

- If you get numbers and Caps Lock is not down, press the Clear key.
- When you hold the Command key down in addition, you move in the same direction, but in bigger chunks.

  Command *plus:*
  8 takes you up a paragraph
  2 takes you down a paragraph

  7 takes you to the beginning of the sentence
  1 takes you to the end of a sentence

  9 takes you to the top of a story
  (if it's on the same page or facing page)
  3 takes you to the bottom of a story
  (if it's on the same page or facing page)

  4 takes you left one word
  6 takes you right one word

  5 always types a 5

If you want to do this:	Then follow these steps:	Shortcuts ▾ Notes ▾ Hints
1.326 Select text with the keypad	■ Hold down the Shift key. ■ With the Shift key down, use any of the keypad shortcuts in 1.325 or 1.328; as the cursor moves, the text will be selected.	■ This is particularly great for picking up those little bits that you miss at the end of a selection, or for removing a few characters at the end of a selection: just hold down that Shift key and use the arrow keys (1.328) or keypad keys (1.325) to add to or delete from it.
1.327 Cut and paste with the keypad (*see 1.280–1.282 for more specific info regarding the basic cut-and-paste concept*)	■ Make sure the keypad is giving you arrow keys; if it is giving you numbers, then press the Clear key before you try this. ■ To **Cut:** select the text or graphic as usual; press the decimal point on the keypad. ■ To **Paste:** press the zero on the keypad.	■ Read 1.202–1.215 if you need help selecting text or graphics. Also read 1.326 right above this. ■ See 1.278–1.279 (re: Clipboard) to understand where it will paste.
1.328 Use other keyboard shortcuts to move the insertion point	Left one character: LeftArrow Right one character: RightArrow Left one word: Option LeftArrow Right one word: Option RightArrow Up one line: UpArrow Down one line: DownArrow Up one paragraph: Command UpArrow Down one paragraph: Command DownArrow For the extended keyboards: Up a screen: PageUp Down a screen: PageDown To top of story: Home To bottom of story: End	■ If you press the Shift key in addition to the arrow keys, you will *select* the text as the insertion point moves.

If you want to do this:	Then follow these steps:	Shortcuts ▾ Notes ▾ Hints

Key Caps

1.329 View the Key Caps keyboard layout

- From the Apple menu, choose "Key Caps."

- The Key Caps icon must be in your System Folder (in the Apple Menu Items folder). This desk accessory is just to show you where all those special typographic characters are hiding.

1.330 View all four of the keyboard layouts

- From the Apple menu, choose "Key Caps."
- From the Key Caps menu item that now appears on the far right of the menu, choose the name of the font whose keys you want to see (if you are experimenting right now, choose an outline font; that is, a font without a city name).
- You are looking at all the characters that are accessible in that font without pressing any extra keys (you already know those characters).
- Hold down the Shift key; you are looking at all the Shift characters (you already know those, too).
- Hold down the Option key; you are looking at some of the accent marks and alternate characters available.
- Hold down both the Option and the Shift keys; you see more alternate characters.
- To hide the Key Caps layout, simply click in its close box in the upper left.

- Different fonts sometimes have different characters available. Most of them, though, hide the same characters under the same keys; for instance, ¢ in all fonts is Option 4. City-named (bitmapped/QuickDraw) fonts have fewer characters than non-city-named (which are usually outline/PostScript) fonts. See 19.26–19.38 for more information on fonts.

If you want to do this:

1.331 Use alternate characters in your publication
(for accent marks, see 1.333)

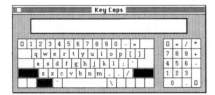

Then follow these steps:

- From the Apple menu, choose Key Caps.
- Choose your font from the menu item that now appears on the far right: Key Caps.
- Find the character you want to use by holding the keys mentioned in 1.330 (Shift, Option, or Shift-Option); then press to find the key your character is hiding beneath (e.g., if you hold Option while you press 7, 8, or 9, you see that the bullet is hiding under the 8).
- Once you know where that character is, close up Key Caps (click in its close box) to return to your publication, or simply click on your publication to return to it and leave Key caps open in the background.
- With the **text tool,** click to set the insertion point where you want the character to appear.
- Press the combination of characters; e.g., hold the Option key down while you press the 8 and you will get a bullet: •.

Shortcuts ▾ Notes ▾ Hints

- Accessing alternate characters is exactly the same as accessing the characters on the keyboards that are above the numbers. For instance, just as you hold the *Shift* key and press 8 to get an asterisk, you can hold the *Option* key and press 8 to get a bullet: •.
- Don't forget about the chart at the end of this book that lists the most common alternate characters.
- There is also a very cool freeware Control panel device (CDEV) called PopChar that lets you pull down a menu with all the characters of a particular font and just pop what you need into your document. The creator of this wonderful little program, Günther Blaschek, just asks that you send him a postcard with a line or two about how it's working for you, maybe with a cool stamp for his son. It's available from various on-line services and user groups.

If you want to do this:	Then follow these steps:	Shortcuts ▾ Notes ▾ Hints
1.332 Insert an alternate character from another font	■ Follow the steps in 1.330 to find the key that holds the character you want; say you need to use this character, ❏, which is only found in the font Zapf Dingbats. ■ On your page, type the appropriate keys in your current font that, if you *were* in Zapf Dingbats, would give you the character you want. Then type the word after it, go back to that character, select it, and change the font to Zapf Dingbats (4.228); ■ **OR** type *up to* that character; change the font; type that character; then change the font back to what you were working with (4.228).	■ Using the first method noted here, the character that initially appears is not what you want; in this case you will type an 'o.' When you change the font, however, it will *become* the character you saw in the Zapf Dingbats keyboard layout. ■ You may find that the character you want is only in another font. Then simply use that font, even in the middle of your current font. (That is sometimes called a "visiting" font.) ■ See 9.77 for a trick to enter a character that you can later find and change automatically throughout the entire publication.
1.333 Use accent marks, as in the word **piñata** *The most common accent marks:* ´ Option e ` Option ~ (tilde) ¨ Option u ~ Option n ^ Option i	■ Follow the steps in 1.330 to find the key that holds the accent mark you need. ■ On your page, type the word that has the accent mark, *but stop right before typing the character that needs the mark over it.* ■ Use the character combination that will create the accent mark—nothing should show up on your page! ■ Now *let go of all keys* and type just the letter to be under the mark—it will appear with the accent mark above it.	**Example** ■ The mark ~ is accessed by holding down the Option key and pressing **n**, as you discovered by looking at Key Caps (or perhaps you used the chart at the end of this book). ■ Type **p i**. ■ Hold down the Option key and press **n**; nothing will appear. ■ Now let go of the Option key and press **n** again. ■ The accent mark will appear *over* the letter: **ñ**. ■ Type the rest of the word: **p i ñ a t a**.

If you want to do this: ▪   Then follow these steps: ▪   Shortcuts ▾ Notes ▾ Hints ▪

Find File

1.334 Use Find File to locate a file while at your Desktop

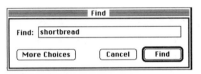

The simple Find window

The "More choices" Find window

- From the File menu, choose "Find…," or press Command F.
- Type in a few letters of the name of the file you want; the more letters, the more specific and the quicker the search.
- Click on the find button, or press Return. A search of all the mounted drives begins.
- When a matching file is found, its window is opened and the file displayed. If a matching file can't be found, you'll hear a beep.
- You can choose to open the file, or if the file isn't exactly the one you want, just leave it there and press Command G (the shortcut for "Find again"). This will put the wrong file away, back where it came from, and another file with the name you want will be displayed. Keep pressing Command G to put the wrong one away and find another one. After the Mac has found every file with that string of characters, you'll hear a beep. At any point you can press Command F to modify or change the file name you are searching for.

- If PageMaker is open, select "Finder" from the Applications menu (in the upper right hand corner of your screen) to go to the Desktop, or simply click on any part of the Desktop that is showing.
- Even if you can't remember the entire name, "Find" will look for any file that has the sequence of characters you specify.
- If you click "More Choices" in the initial "Find" dialog box you can further define the parameters of the search. You can constrain the search to fit other criteria such as by when the file was created, by aliases, or by what word it doesn't contain! If you have more than one drive, you can be specific about which ones to search. You can choose to see all the files found at one time. It can be even more specific than this and is worthy of a read in a good System 7 book.

If you want to do this:

Then follow these steps:

Shortcuts · Notes · Hints

Create more window space

1.335 On a small screen, open up more space in the window

Do any or all of the following:

- If the rulers are showing, hide them by choosing "Rulers" from the "Guides and rulers" submenu under the Layout menu; *or* by pressing Command R.
- If the scroll bars are showing, hide them by choosing "Scroll bars" from the "Guides and rulers" submenu under the Layout menu.
- If the Style palette is showing, hide it by choosing "Style palette" from the Window menu; *or* by pressing Command Y; *or* by clicking in its little close box.
- If the Color palette is showing, hide it by choosing "Color palette" from the Window menu; *or* by pressing Command K; *or* by clicking in its little close box.
- If the Control palette is showing, hide it by choosing "Control palette" from the Window menu; *or* by pressing Command ' (*apostrophe*); *or* by clicking in its close box.
- If the Toolbox is showing, hide it by choosing "Tool palette" from the Window menu; *or* by pressing Command 6; *or* by clicking in its little close box.

- Obviously, hiding all these things can make it awkward to work—it's your choice.
- Without scroll bars, you can still use the grabber hand to move around: while the Option key is down, any tool will turn into the grabber *when the mouse is pressed;* press-and-drag to move the page (1.126).
- When scroll bars are missing, the page icons will be missing too. Use the "Go to page..." command from the Layout menu (or press Command G) to navigate; *or* press Command Tab to go to the next page; Command Shift Tab to go to the previous page (1.100–1.110).
- Press Command Spacebar to toggle between the pointer tool and the last tool you used when the Toolbox was showing (unless that key command is being used by other software).
- The Style list is always available under the Type menu or with Command Y.
- The Color palette can always be brought back with Command K.
- Most of the options on the Control palette are available through the menu.

2 ▾ Drawing Tools

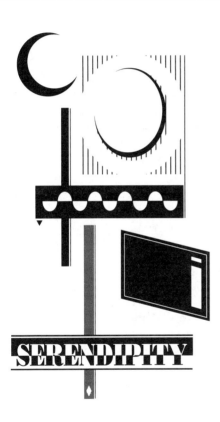

2.1   PageMaker provides several tools for creating simple graphics directly in your publication. They all work in a similar manner; they are all object-oriented and can layer, as explained in Section 1; and you can manipulate their size, shape, and fill pattern at any time.

2.2   You can set the defaults for the lines and fills for all the tools so they automatically draw with whichever line or border width and fill you most regularly use. This way you don't have to select and change them each time. These defaults can be set for the entire PageMaker application or for just the publication you are working on. For instance, you'll find this very handy when you are about to draw several boxes with identical borders and fills; set a publication (temporary) default and you're ready to go. (See 1.6–1.18 for greater detail on defaults.)

2.3   Included here is the Rotating tool. Although it's not really a drawing tool, it can rotate anything you draw and is useful for creating visual effects on the page.

2.4   This section first gives instructions that are common to all the tools, then breaks down into tasks particular to each tool.

The drawing tools 110

Printer examples 112

Lines 119

Rectangles and Squares 120

Ovals and Circles 122

Custom line dialog box 124

Fill and line dialog box 125

Drawing tool defaults 129

The Rotating tool 130

The drawing tools

2.5 To choose any draw tool, simply click on it while the Toolbox is showing (if the Toolbox is not showing, choose "Tool palette" from the Window menu, or press Command 6). Don't press-and-drag to select a tool—just click on it. Your cursor will change (2.12) when you move it away from the Toolbox.

2.6 Diagonal-line tool draws lines at any angle. If you press the Shift key while you draw, you will restrain its movements to only 45° and 90° lines. When you draw vertical and horizontal lines, you can flip the line to draw on either side of the crossbar cursor (see the example in 2.7).

2.7 Perpendicular-line tool draws only 45° and 90° lines; you can flip 90° lines to draw on either side of the crossbar cursor.

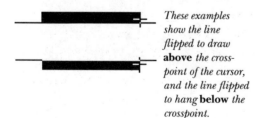

*These examples show the line flipped to draw **above** the cross-point of the cursor, and the line flipped to hang **below** the crosspoint.*

2.8 Rotating tool, not a draw tool per se, rotates anything you can select (including graphics and text blocks) clockwise or counterclockwise. You can use the rotating tool to select one or more items (click, Shift-click, or drag a marquee around the items). Press the starburst cursor on the spot you want the selected object(s) to rotate around, and drag in the direction you want the object(s) to spin. If the Control palette is showing, it displays the degree of rotation. (See 2.88, and 3.35.)

2.9 Rectangle tool draws rectangles with square corners (although you can set a rounded corner style as the default [2.44], or select a rectangle and round the corners in the "Rounded corners" dialog box; see 2.15). The rectangle begins drawing from a corner, with the beginning point anchored to the page. If you press the Shift key while you draw, you will restrain its shape to a square.

I pressed the cursor in the upper left corner and dragged diagonally down to the right.

2.10 Oval/circle tool draws ovals. Pressing the Shift key restrains its shape to a circle. It begins drawing at a "corner" (as opposed to drawing from the center of the circle).

2.11 The Cropping tool is not a draw tool—it is used for cropping imported graphics. Cropping tool information is found in Section 10 on Graphics, 10.143.

2.12 The draw tool cursor is the crossbar icon that appears when you choose a draw tool. The "hot spot," or the point of the tool where the action happens, is right in the center where the two bars meet—that is the point from which lines and boxes will begin drawing. For your convenience, the crossbar will automatically turn back into a pointer when it is in a scroll bar, the Toolbox, the menu, the rulers, the palettes, or on the page icons.

2.13 The basic rule, when using draw tools, is that the tool itself is only used for creating the initial shape; if you want to do anything to that shape (move it, stretch it, delete it, etc.), *you must use the* **pointer tool.**

The drawing tools

2.14
The Toolbox

You can press anywhere in the title bar and drag the Toolbox around on the screen.

Diagonal-line tool (2.6).

Perpendicular-line tool; also known as the Straight-line tool (2.7).

Click in the close box to hide the Toolbox. Press Command 6 to show it again.

Use the pointer tool to manipulate the objects you draw (2.13).

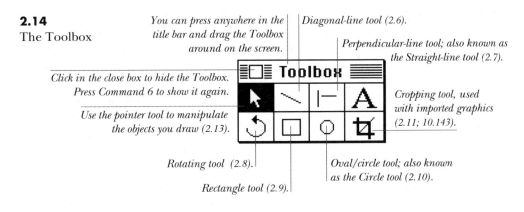

Cropping tool, used with imported graphics (2.11; 10.143).

Rotating tool (2.8).

Oval/circle tool; also known as the Circle tool (2.10).

Rectangle tool (2.9).

2.15 The available corner styles
(from the Element menu, choose "Rounded corners... ")

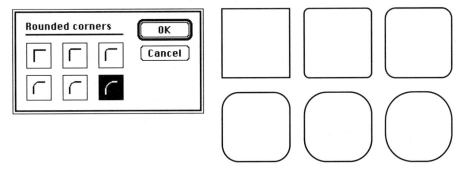

2.16 On a publication page, you can select more than one shape or line together, and then change all their line widths, borders, corners, and fill patterns with the same click.

2.17 You can use the line widths in the "Line" submenu for any kind of line, as well as for the borders of any rectangle, square, oval, or circle. You can also make any one of those lines "Reverse" (the white part of the line turns black and the black part turns white or "paper") or "Transparent" (the white part has no color at all). Take a look at the examples on the following page.

2.18 The line widths shown on the screen are actual size, except "None" and anything ".5 pt." or less. Depending on the resolution of your screen, what you see using those fine lines may not be exactly what prints. Check the examples on the following page for actual printed examples.

2.19 A "fill" is the "color" that fills a shape. The patterns from the Fill submenu are all opaque (except "None") and so will hide anything behind them. As with the line widths, the resolution of your screen does not always show exactly what will print; check the examples on the following page.

2.20
HP DeskWriter: 300 dpi

2.21
LaserWriter Select 360: 600 dpi

2.22
Linotronic 300: 1270 dpi

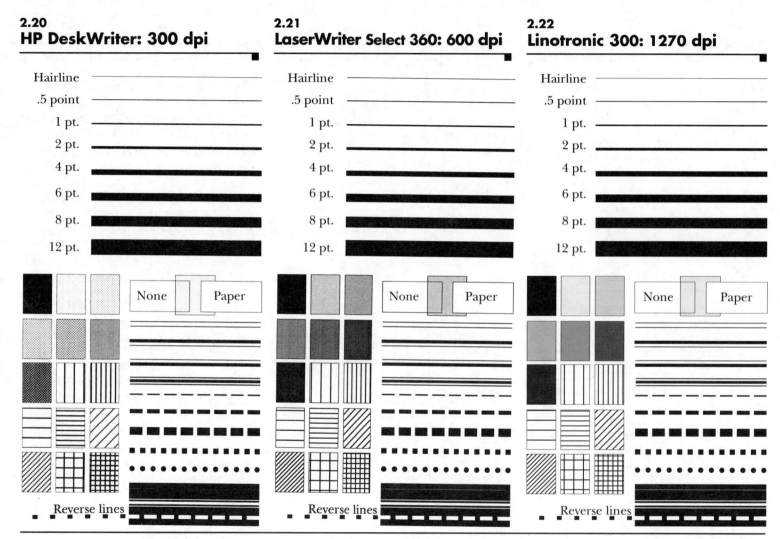

For examples of "Transparent" lines, see 2.62, and 2.76.

If you want to do this:	**Then follow these steps:**	**Shortcuts ▾ Notes ▾ Hints**
2.23 Draw an object 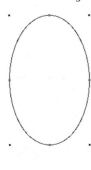 *Notice the eight selection handles on this object— one at each corner and one on each side.* *Lines have only two handles—one at each end.*	■ In the **Toolbox,** click once on the tool of your choice; the cursor will automatically become a crossbar when you leave the Toolbox (2.12). ■ Position the center of the crossbar where you want the object to begin. ■ Press-and-drag until the object is the size you want it; release the mouse button. (If you want to move or resize the object, you must use the *pointer tool*.)	■ As soon as you let go of the mouse button, the object is drawn and will show its selection handles. If you immediately decide you don't want what you've just drawn, **now** is a good time to press the Backspace/Delete key to get rid of it. Or if you want to change its line or border width or inside fill pattern, go up to the Element menu and choose whichever one you want (2.16–2.22). ■ If you click anywhere outside the object, the selection handles disappear. To select it again, see 2.24. The object must be selected before it can be manipulated.
2.24 Select one or more drawn objects (**Important:** *read the section on Selecting: 1.182–1.215. It covers selecting more than one object at a time, as well as selecting hidden or lost objects, invisible objects, objects under other layers, etc.*)	■ With the **pointer tool,** click anywhere on the object (if the object has a fill of "None," you must be sure to click on the border itself, as there is literally nothing inside the border; see the example of "None" in 2.22). ■ To select more than one object, hold the Shift key down while clicking on each one (1.207); **Or** with the **pointer tool,** press in a blank area and drag to draw a marquee around the objects (1.208). The marquee will select only objects with all handles enclosed in its space.	■ If handles don't show up when you click on the object, it may be under another *layer* (1.189–1.194 re: layers). Hold down the Command key and click on the object; with each click you dig down through one layer. You should see handles appear on each layer, including the object you're looking for. ■ If you still can't get handles, the object is probably on a master page. You must go to the master page to change any objects that were placed there (1.130–1.135; 1.142).

If you want to do this:	Then follow these steps:	Shortcuts ▾ Notes ▾ Hints
2.25 Delete a drawn object	▪ With the **pointer tool,** click anywhere on the object to select it (you should see handles). ▪ Hit the Backspace/Delete key, *or* from the Edit menu choose "Clear."	▪ If you have trouble selecting the object, see 2.24, as well as 1.203–1.215. ▪ You can Undo a delete—from the Edit menu choose "Undo delete." Remember, you must Undo *before you do anything else, even before you click again.* If the menu doesn't say "Undo delete," you're too late.
2.26 Delete lots of objects	▪ With the **pointer tool,** hold down the Shift key and click once on each of the objects you want to delete (you should see handles on all of them). ▪ Hit the Backspace/Delete key, *or* from the Edit menu choose "Clear."	▪ The point is, you can select any number of objects and then delete them with the Backspace/Delete key. See 2.24 for a few more hints on selecting. ▪ See 1.203–1.215 for *detailed* information on selecting.
2.27 Move one or more objects ⟷ *When moving objects, you should see this four-headed arrow,* not *a two-headed arrow.*	With the **pointer tool,** click on the object you want to move. For moving more than one, hold down the Shift key and click once on each of the objects (you should see handles on all of them). ▪ Position the very tip of the pointer on a solid part of one of the objects—*not on any handle!* ▪ Press-and-drag to move the object(s); if you have selected more than one, they will all move together. *You should see the four-headed arrow; if you see a two-headed arrow, then let go, Undo (Command Z), and try again.*	▪ You can also use the marquee from the pointer tool to select more than one object; see 1.203–1.215 for info on selecting. ▪ You can Undo a move—if you don't like where you've placed it and want to put it back, from the Edit menu choose "Undo move" (Command Z). ▪ PageMaker has a fast move (press and move quickly—you'll see just the outline) and a slow move (press, wait, then move—you'll see the actual objects). See 1.197, 1.198. ▪ See Section 3, the Control palette, for another way to move objects on the page (3.87).

If you want to do this:	**Then follow these steps:**	**Shortcuts ▾ Notes ▾ Hints**
2.28 Move one or more objects to another page	▪ Follow the steps in 2.24 to select the objects to be moved. Then either: ▫ Cut the objects, go to the page you want to move them to, and paste them onto the new page (see 1.273–1.282 for detailed information about cutting and pasting); ▫ **Or** simply move the objects out to the pasteboard, making sure no handles are connected to the page; then go to the new page and move them on (you will have to re-select the objects after you get to the other page).	▪ You can power-paste objects into exactly the same position as on the page they came from by pressing Command Option V (see 1.283 for more details on power-pasting, and while you're at it, read about "Multiple paste" [1.287–1.310], too). ▪ One of the great features of PageMaker: anything placed on the pasteboard (the area outside the page; see 1.4) will stay there, just as if you were working on your drafting table.
2.29 Move a tiny little object (*when it's so little that the cursor obscures it and you can't see where it's going*)	▪ Create a larger object about an inch away from the one you need to reposition. ▪ Select both objects (Shift-click or use the marquee; 2.24). ▪ With the **pointer tool,** press on the larger object; as you drag the larger one, the smaller one comes along too. ▪ After repositioning the small object, click anywhere outside the objects to deselect them both; then select the larger one (click once on it) and delete it (hit the Backspace/Delete key).	▪ This works great. It'll look like this: *The two objects selected. You can see that if I were to press on the little square, the four-headed cursor would completely cover it.* *The two objects moving. By moving the larger object, I can easily place the smaller one precisely.*

If you want to do this:	**Then follow these steps:**	**Shortcuts ▾ Notes ▾ Hints**
2.30 Move objects in a straight line	■ With the **pointer tool,** select the object(s), as in 2.24. ■ Hold the Shift key while you press-and-drag the objects; the movement will be restrained to just vertical or horizontal, whichever direction you first move.	■ You can keep the mouse button down, but re-press the Shift key to change direction. ■ See Section 3 to learn about the Control palette. You'll find the "Position" option (3.32) offers total precision for positioning objects.
2.31 Draw or move objects in perfect alignment with guide lines	■ From the Layout menu, slide down to "Guides and rulers," then over to the submenu; make sure "Snap to guides" has a checkmark next to it (meaning it's on). If not, choose it to turn it on. ■ As you draw or move, you'll notice that when the cursor gets close to a guideline, it jumps onto it.	■ The "Snap to guides" feature allows you to draw and move objects very precisely, even while in a reduced page view. ■ The Control palette can be used to move objects in conjunction with "Snap to guides." See 3.16.
2.32 Draw or move objects in perfect alignment with the ruler tick marks	■ From the Layout menu, slide down to "Guides and rulers," then over to the submenu; make sure "Snap to guides" has a checkmark next to it (meaning it's on). If not, choose it to turn it on. ■ You'll notice that with "Snap to rulers" on, the cursor kind of jumps around the screen rather than moves smoothly. As you draw with the tools or move objects, they jump from tick mark to tick mark on the ruler—in fact, you cannot position anything *between* the marks.	■ Using "Snap to rulers" makes it so easy, for instance, to place lines every half inch or copy a one-inch box every two inches—objects just stop right on those ruler marks. Check out "Multiple paste" (1.307) to create perfect step-and-repeat patterns. ■ You can customize your vertical ruler in your choice of point increments (1.225; 1.226), thus further enhancing the precision. ■ See Section 3, the Control palette.

If you want to do this:	Then follow these steps:	Shortcuts ▾ Notes ▾ Hints
2.33 Stop the cursor or the objects you are moving from jerking around on the screen	■ From the Layout menu, slide down to "Guides and rulers," then over to the submenu; if there is a checkmark next to either "Snap to rulers" or "Snap to guides," choose them again (one at a time, of course) to turn them off.	■ Read 2.31 and 2.32.
2.34 Change a line width or a border	■ With the **pointer tool,** select the objects that have a line width or border you wish to change. ■ From the Element menu, choose the submenu "Line"; choose any one of those 18 lines, or choose "Custom" to create your own (2.55). You can choose "Transparent" or "Reverse" *in addition* to any line.	■ See 2.24 and 1.203–1.215 if you need info on selecting. ■ Examples of all the line widths and styles on three kinds of printers are found in 2.20–2.22. ■ The white space between double and dotted lines is opaque, unless you also choose "Transparent." See 2.59. ■ Design-jargon for "lines" is "rules."
2.35 Change the line width or the border of a *group* of lines or drawn shapes	■ Just follow the directions above (2.34), first selecting *all* the objects to be changed.	■ Don't neglect this trick—it's a great timesaver.
2.36 Make a patterned line width or border transparent	■ Select one or more drawn objects, as explained in 2.24. ■ From the Element menu slide down to "Line"; then over to the submenu and choose "Transparent."	■ If "Transparent" has a checkmark next to it, it is already chosen. It is one of Page-Maker's original default settings (1.17). ■ Transparent means you can see objects or colors in the layers behind the white areas of double, triple, dotted, or dashed lines. In the "Fill and line" dialog box, it's called "Transparent background" (2.72).

If you want to do this:	**Then follow these steps:**	**Shortcuts ▾ Notes ▾ Hints**
2.37 Reverse a line width or border	■ Select one or more drawn objects, as explained in 2.24. ■ From the Element menu choose the submenu "Line." ■ Choose "Reverse."	■ Reverse (and Transparent) can be used *in combination with* any other line. ■ Any double, triple, dotted, or dashed opaque line will be white where it was black, and black where it was white. See 2.20–2.22. ■ Make sure there is an object selected before you choose "Reverse"; otherwise you will set a default (1.6–1.11) and everything you draw will have a reverse line.
2.38 Find an invisible or "lost" object	■ Reduce the view to Fit in Window size, or at least some size where you can see most of the page where the object is lost. ■ With the **pointer tool,** from the Edit menu choose "Select all." ■ You will see handles on every object, no matter how many layers (1.189–1.195) they may be under. ■ If the object you're looking for is there, you will see its handles; take note of its location. ■ Click once in any blank area or on the pointer tool to release all the handles, then go back and select the lost object. You may need to click around until you hit upon it, or draw a marquee around the area (1.215), or Command-click to find it under another layer (1.211, 1.214) and Bring it to the Front (Element menu; 1.216).	■ Can you find the invisible object and the "lost" object in this melee? 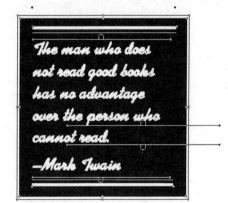

If you want to do this: ■	**Then follow these steps:** ■	**Shortcuts ▾ Notes ▾ Hints** ■

Lines

2.39	Lengthen or shorten a line	■ With the **pointer tool,** click anywhere on the line to select it; handles will appear.	■ If you have trouble selecting the line, read 2.24, as well as 1.203–1.215.

When you press directly on the handle, the pointer will turn into the crossbar cursor again. The part of the crossbar that overlaps the line will turn white.

- Position the very *tip* of the pointer on an end handle.
- Press on the handle; you should see the *crossbar* cursor again. *If you see the four-headed arrow, you are not pressing in the handle; let go and press Command Z to undo any change you may have just made.*
- When you see the crossbar cursor, press-and-drag to the length of your choice.

- **Important:** if the line is perfectly straight (vertically, horizontally, or diagonally 45°) and you want to keep it so, hold the Shift key down while dragging.
- You cannot change the length of more than one line at a time, even if many are selected.
- See Section 3 to learn how to use the Control palette. With the "Line sizing" option you can very precisely lengthen or shorten a line.

2.40 Straighten a crooked line

- With the **pointer tool,** click anywhere on the line to select it; handles will appear.
- Hold down the Shift key; position the very *tip* of the pointer on an end handle.
- Press on that handle and count to three.

- Any line from either line tool can be straightened after it has been drawn. This trick will anchor the end you are *not* pressing, and *your* end will snap out perfectly perpendicular to the anchor.
- If you have trouble selecting the line, read 2.24, as well as 1.203–1.215.

If you want to do this:	Then follow these steps:	Shortcuts ▾ Notes ▾ Hints
2.41 Change the direction of a line	■ With the **pointer tool,** click anywhere on the line to select it; handles will appear. ■ Position the very *tip* of the pointer on an end handle. ■ Press on the handle; you should see the *crossbar* cursor again. *If you see the four-headed arrow, you are not pressing the handle; let go and press Command Z to undo any change you may have just made.* Try again. ■ When you see the crossbar cursor, press-and-drag in any direction.	■ If you have trouble selecting the line, read 2.24, as well as 1.203–1.215. ■ The *other* end of the line will anchor itself to the page and you can move *your* end in whichever direction you choose, even if the line was originally drawn with the perpendicular-line tool. ■ You cannot change the direction of more than one line at a time, even if many are selected.

Rectangles (with and without rounded corners) and Squares

2.42 Draw a perfect square	■ From the Toolbox, click on the **rectangle tool.** ■ Position the center of the crossbar where you want the *corner* of the box to begin. ■ Hold down the Shift key while you press-and-drag to draw the box.	
2.43 Change a drawn rectangle into a perfect square 	■ With the **pointer tool,** select the rectangle to be changed. ■ Hold down the Shift key. ■ With the **pointer tool,** press on any handle and count to three.	■ The opposite side or corner will anchor to the page, and the side or corner you press on will snap into the square. ■ If you have trouble selecting the rectangle, read 2.24, as well as 1.203–1.215.

If you want to do this:	**Then follow these steps:**	**Shortcuts ▾ Notes ▾ Hints**

2.44 Change the corners of one or more rectangles to a different corner

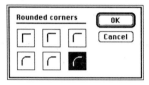

- With the **pointer tool,** select all the rectangles or squares you want to change—either hold down the Shift key and click on each shape, **or** draw the marquee with the pointer tool (1.208).
- From the Element menu choose "Rounded corners...."
- Click on the corner you want; click OK.

- You can do this to any rectangle or square.
- You can set a corner as a default (2.82–2.83) for the rectangle tool by choosing a corner *while no object is selected.*
- If you have trouble selecting the object, read 2.24, as well as 1.203–1.215.

2.45 Resize a rectangle or square
- *Vertically only*
- *Horizontally only*
- *In both directions*

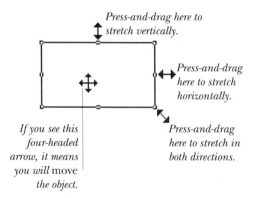

Press-and-drag here to stretch vertically.

Press-and-drag here to stretch horizontally.

If you see this four-headed arrow, it means you will move *the object.*

Press-and-drag here to stretch in both directions.

- With the **pointer tool,** select the rectangle you want to resize by clicking on it.
- To resize **vertically,** use the pointer tool to press-and-drag on a handle in the *middle* of the top or bottom edge; the cursor will become a double-headed, *vertical* arrow.
- To resize **horizontally,** use the pointer tool to press-and-drag on a handle located in the *middle* of the left or right side of the shape; the cursor will become a double-headed, *horizontal* arrow.
- To resize in **both directions,** use the pointer tool to press-and-drag on a *corner* handle; the cursor will become a double-headed, *diagonal* arrow.
- If you see the *four-headed arrow,* you will not resize the object—you will *move* it (2.27).

- If you decide you don't like what you just did, press Command Z to undo the stretch.
- *Do not press the Shift key* when resizing any shape drawn in PageMaker! Although the Shift key will resize *imported* graphics proportionally (10.138), trying it on any rectangle or oval you've drawn in this program will instantly turn it into a square or a circle, respectively. *If that happens accidentally, immediately press Command Z* (or choose "Undo Stretch" from the Edit menu).
- When resizing a *square,* though, keep the Shift key down to retain the shape.
- The Control palette makes it easy to scale objects in a precise fashion. See 3.63–3.74 to learn more about this.

If you want to do this:	Then follow these steps:	Shortcuts ▾ Notes ▾ Hints

2.46 Change the fill pattern

A double-line Reverse border with a 10% fill, placed on top of a black-filled background.

- With the **pointer tool,** select all the rectangles and squares you want to change—either hold down the Shift key and click on each one, **or** enclose them in the marquee using the pointer tool (1.208).
- From the Element menu press on "Fill" to pop out that submenu.
- Choose any one of the 17 patterns as a fill.

- See the examples of available fills in 2.20–2.22. Notice the difference between None and Paper.
- You could choose "Fill and line…" instead and change fills, lines and colors all at once. See 2.63.
- If you have trouble selecting the line, read 2.24, as well as 1.203–1.215.

Ovals and Circles

2.47 Draw a perfect circle

- From the Toolbox, choose the **oval/circle tool.**
- Hold down the Shift key while you press-and-drag to draw.

2.48 Change a drawn oval into a perfect circle

- With the **pointer tool,** select the oval.
- Hold down the Shift key.
- With the **pointer tool,** press on any handle and count to three.

- If you have trouble selecting the oval, read 2.24, as well as 1.203–1.215.
- The opposite side will anchor itself to the page; the corner you press will snap into a circle.

2.49 Change the fill pattern of one or more ovals or circles

This is a double-line Reverse border with a diagonal-line fill, placed on top of a black-filled background.

- With the **pointer tool,** select all the ovals and circles you want to change—either hold down the Shift key and click on each one, **or** enclose them in the marquee using the pointer tool (1.208).
- From the Element menu press on "Fill" to pop out that submenu.
- Choose any one of the 17 patterns as a fill.

- If you have trouble selecting the shape, read 2.24, as well as 1.203–1.215.
- You can choose "Fill and line…" from the Element menu to change both the fill and line at the same time. See 2.63.

If you want to do this:

2.50 Change the shape of an oval or circle
- *Vertically only*
- *Horizontally only*
- *In both directions*

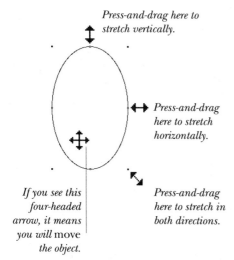

Press-and-drag here to stretch vertically.

Press-and-drag here to stretch horizontally.

If you see this four-headed arrow, it means you will move *the object.*

Press-and-drag here to stretch in both directions.

Then follow these steps:

- To resize the oval, first select it by clicking on it once with the **pointer tool.**
- To resize **vertically,** use the pointer tool to press-and-drag on a handle in the *middle* of the top or bottom curve; the cursor will become a double-headed, *vertical* arrow.
- To resize **horizontally,** use the pointer tool to press-and-drag on a handle located in the *middle* of the left or right curve of the shape; the cursor will become a double-headed, *horizontal* arrow.
- To resize in **both directions,** use the pointer tool to press-and-drag on a *corner* handle; the cursor will become a double-headed, *diagonal* arrow.
- If you see the *four-headed arrow,* you will not resize the object—you will *move* it.

Shortcuts ▾ Notes ▾ Hints

- If you have trouble selecting the oval or circle, read 2.24, as well as 1.203–1.215.
- No matter how many objects you select, you can only resize one at a time.
- *Do not press the Shift key* when resizing any shape drawn in PageMaker! Although the Shift key will resize *imported* graphics proportionally, trying it on any rectangle or oval you've drawn in this program will instantly turn it into a square or a circle, respectively. If that happens accidentally, press Command Z immediately (or from the Edit menu choose "Undo Stretch").
- When resizing a *circle,* though, keep the Shift key down to retain the shape.
- The Control palette makes it easy to scale objects in a precise fashion. Read Section 3 to learn more about this.

The "Custom line" dialog box   *(from the Element menu choose "Line," then slide over to the submenu and choose "Custom…")*

2.51   You can select from a variety of line styles and widths in the "Lines" submenu, or select "Custom" to choose a line style and create a custom width.

2.52   In the "Custom line" dialog box you can create any line weight between 0 and 800 points. A hairline, at 0.2 of a point, is the thinnest line you can accurately print at lower resolutions, while an 800 point line will fill your page with its 11-inch width. Patterned lines (double, triple, dotted, or dashed line styles) will be scaled to match the custom line weight you choose.

2.53   A line can also be made reverse and/or transparent (see 2.59 and 2.60). A **Reverse line** is actually paper-colored—it prevents ink from printing, and allows the paper to show through the line. It works just like choosing a "Paper" fill for an object. A **Transparent line** allows everything behind it to show through, *even another object or the paper itself.* It is the same as selecting "None" as a fill. The white areas in a patterned line are opaque unless you check "Transparent." This is also true for reverse patterned lines.

2.54   The same choice of line styles and weights is available in the "Fill and line" dialog box (2.63).

2.55   **The "Custom line" dialog box.**

2.56   *Choose a line style from this pop-up menu. See the choices in 2.61.*

2.57   *If no object or line is selected when you click OK, the specs set here become the default specifications.*

2.58   *Type in a value from 0 to 800 points. You can specify line weight to the tenth of a point.*

2.59   *This is the same as "Transparent" under the "Line" submenu. When this box is checked all double, triple, dotted, or dashed lines are transparent in the white areas.*

2.60   *When you check this box the black part of a line turns white and the white part turns black.*

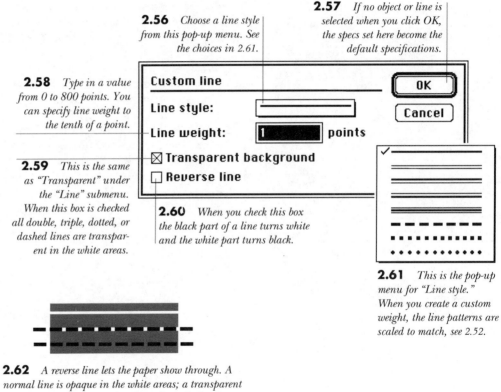

2.61   *This is the pop-up menu for "Line style." When you create a custom weight, the line patterns are scaled to match, see 2.52.*

2.62   *A reverse line lets the paper show through. A normal line is opaque in the white areas; a transparent line allows the background to show through. See the example in 2.76 as well.*

The "Fill and line" dialog box

(from the Element menu choose "Fill and Line…")

2.63 Choose the "Fill and line…" command from the Element menu, or press Command] *(right bracket)*, when you want to set a default for, or change, both fill and line at the same time in PageMaker-drawn objects.

2.64 Most of the options you see here can be found in the Element menu or Color palette. They work here just the same as if you had chosen them from their specific submenu or palette. They are combined here for convenience's sake.

2.65 This is the only place though, where you can choose to "Overprint" selected objects. By default, PageMaker knocks out (doesn't print) the parts of objects that are hidden behind other objects so that the paper shows through and the color prints true. However, when you choose to "Overprint," an object will print right on top of whatever is behind it, mixing the colors or tints and producing a third, new color. (You can choose to always overprint certain **colors** through the "Define colors" dialog box.) See 16.24–16.26 for the overview on overprinting.

2.66 You cannot overprint a reverse line. It is considered the color "Paper," which is not an ink, but the absence of ink; see 2.53.

2.67 *This pop-up menu is the same as the "Fill" submenu under Element.*

2.68 *This pop-up menu is the same as the "Line" submenu under Element.*

2.69 *Click on this pop-up menu to choose a color for the fill. All the colors you have defined in the Color palette will be listed here.*

2.70 *Check this box to make the fill print over objects behind it. See 2.65 for more information.*

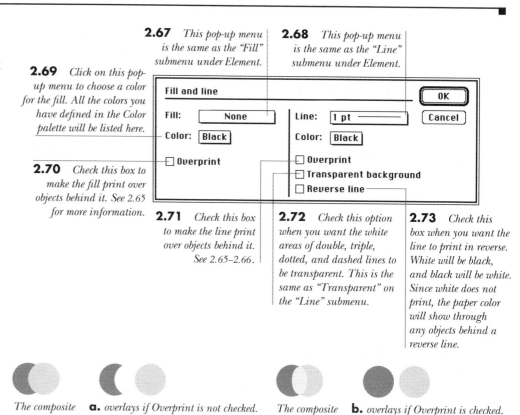

2.71 *Check this box to make the line print over objects behind it. See 2.65–2.66.*

2.72 *Check this option when you want the white areas of double, triple, dotted, and dashed lines to be transparent. This is the same as "Transparent" on the "Line" submenu.*

2.73 *Check this box when you want the line to print in reverse. White will be black, and black will be white. Since white does not print, the paper color will show through any objects behind a reverse line.*

The composite **a.** *overlays if Overprint is not checked.* *The composite* **b.** *overlays if Overprint is checked.*

2.74 *Imagine these two circles are red and blue. PageMaker, by default, will print the bottom (blue) one with a knock out to accommodate the top (red) one. The printed piece will show a red circle on top of a blue one. If you choose "Overprint," the top (red) circle will print over the complete bottom (blue) circle. The result will print as a partial blue circle on the bottom, a partial red circle on top, and a purplish partial circle where the two overlap.*

If you want to do this:

Then follow these steps:

Shortcuts ▾ Notes ▾ Hints

2.75   Create a custom weight line

A 3 point dashed line customized to 8 and 12 points. Notice how the length of the dashes and the space between them is scaled to match the weight of the dash.

- Select the line you want to change.
- From the Element menu slide over to the "Line" submenu and choose "Custom…."
- From the pop-up menu next to "Line style" choose any line style you want.
- In the "Line weight" edit box enter a number between 0 and 800.
- Click in the checkbox next to "Transparent background" and/or "Reverse" if you want the line to have either of these attributes.
- Click OK.

- You can make every line you draw have the same custom specifications—including the lines around shapes. Choose the "Custom" dialog box with no lines or objects selected and set a line style and weight. These specs become the line defaults.
- When you change the weight of a dashed or dotted line, the size of the pattern and the spaces between change to match the weight of the line.

2.76   Let the background show through the lines or patterns of double, triple, dashed, or dotted lines

Neither Reverse or Transparent

Transparent only

Reverse & Transparent

Reverse only

- With the **pointer tool** select all the lines you want to change.
- From the Element menu, slide down to "Line"; then over to the submenu to choose "Transparent."

- You can also make double, triple, dashed, or dotted lines around objects transparent.
- Try the combination of "Reverse" and "Transparent" when placing patterned lines on a background.

If you want to do this:	Then follow these steps:	Shortcuts ▾ Notes ▾ Hints
2.77 Select a line or object that is underneath another line or object	▪ Hold down the Command key ▪ With the **pointer tool** click on the top object; it will show handles. ▪ Click again to select the next layer. ▪ Repeat until the desired object is selected.	▪ If you are having trouble selecting objects see 1.181–1.215. ▪ Press the Shift key too, if you want to select multiple objects as you dig through the layers. ▪ Remember, an object with a fill of "None" can only be selected when you click on its border.
2.78 Change the way two objects are layered	▪ With the **pointer tool** choose the object you want on top. ▪ From the Element menu choose "Bring to front," or press Command F, ▪ **OR** with the **pointer tool** choose the object you want on the bottom. ▪ From the Element menu choose "Send to back," or press Command B.	▪ Of course you can have more than two layers of objects and it is an art to get them in just the order you want. Read more about layered objects in 1.189–1.195.
2.79 Apply a color to the line and/or fill of an object	▪ With the **pointer tool** select the object. ▪ From the Element menu choose "Fill and line…." ▪ Under "Fill," click on the pop-up menu next to "Color" and select a color. ▪ Under "Line," click on the pop-up menu next to "Color" and select a color.	▪ You can select multiple objects and apply one color for all the fills, and the same or a different color for all the lines. ▪ You can give the appearance of more than one color if the objects you select have different tints, or percentage fills. ▪ Please see Section 16 to learn more about using color in PageMaker.

127

If you want to do this:	**Then follow these steps:**	**Shortcuts ▾ Notes ▾ Hints**
2.80 Make an object print over an object underneath it without knocking out any of the bottom object	■ With the **pointer tool** select the object(s) or line(s) that you want to overprint (print on top). ■ From the Element menu choose "Fill and line…" ■ Check the "Overprint" box beneath "Fill" and/or "Line."	■ Overprinting and knockouts are part of the world of color printing. The concepts are touched on here, but you really must read Section 16 to get the full picture. ■ Be careful with objects with a "Paper" fill. "Paper" is not an ink but the absence of ink, so it can't print over other inks. Yet PageMaker lets you set a paper-filled object to overprint. On a composite print, a knockout is created anyway, but if you are printing separations, you may get ink where you expected none.
2.81 Group lines or objects together so they can be copied, moved or resized as one object	■ With the **pointer tool** select all the lines and objects you want to group. ■ From the Utilities menu, slide down to "Aldus Additions," then over to the submenu and choose "PS Group it."	■ PageMaker creates an EPS graphic (or a PICT if you have a non-PostScript printer selected in the Chooser) and replaces the objects with the graphic. A linked file, .PMGx, is created and stored in the folder with your publication. The PMG file is necessary to print a high-resolution version of the EPS graphic, or to run the "PS Ungroup it" Addition. ■ When you run this Addition, PageMaker automatically saves the publication up to that point. ■ "PS Group it," and "PS Ungroup it" can get tricky and are discussed in detail in 10.259–10.291.

If you want to do this:	Then follow these steps:	Shortcuts ▾ Notes ▾ Hints

Set drawing tool defaults

(also see Section 1: Setting Defaults 1.6–1.18)

2.82 Set defaults for any of the lines, fills, or corners *for the current publication*	■ Click on the **pointer tool,** even if it's already chosen. ■ From the Element menu, choose "Fill and line…" (2.63). ■ From the pop-up menus, choose any fill pattern and any line style. Click OK ■ From the Element menu, choose "Rounded corners…"; choose any corner, and click OK.	■ You can actually set the default with any of the other tools, but it is imperative that *no object is selected.* Clicking on the pointer tool ensures nothing is selected. ■ Setting the defaults, as explained in 1.6–1.18, enables you to draw the objects in the style of your choice, rather than having to select and change them afterward.
2.83 Set defaults for any of the lines, fills, or corners *for the entire PageMaker application*	■ Open PageMaker from its icon on the Desktop; **Or** close any publication you currently have open. ■ Follow the steps above, but do it when there is nothing on your screen but the menu bar.	■ Even though you set an *application default,* of course you can change any line or fill or corner or anything else you choose at any time in the open publication.
2.84 Set a text wrap default for drawn objects *(be sure to read Section 13 on Text Wrapping)*	■ With nothing selected *(for a publication default)* or with no publication open *(for an application default),* choose "Text wrap…" from the Element menu. ■ Select the center wrap option, set the standoff, and choose the flow (13.10–13.19). ■ Click OK.	■ Setting a default text wrap means every object you draw in PageMaker, place from the File menu, or paste from the Scrapbook or Clipboard will automatically have a text wrap around it. This might not be what you want. Be sure to read Section 13 on Text Wrapping.

129

The Rotating tool

2.85   The **rotating tool** is not a drawing tool but can rotate anything you create with a draw tool, as well as imported graphics and text blocks. Anything that you can select, you can rotate.

2.86   You can rotate one or more objects 360° in either direction around a fixed point. This **fixed point** can be within or outside the object(s). You can select any place on the screen as the point around which the objects(s) rotate.

2.87   When you select the rotating tool, the cursor turns into a starburst shape. Objects on the page that are selected stay selected when you choose the rotating tool from the Toolbox, but you can also click once on a text block or object with the starburst cursor to select it. You can Shift-click to select more than one object, and you can select any combination of text, objects, and graphics. If absolutely nothing is selected on the page, you can marquee items with the rotating tool to select them.

2.88   To rotate a selected object, press on the spot you want as the fixed point, and drag the cursor *away* from the fixed point in the direction you want to rotate the object.

The fixed point is designated by a stationary hairline cursor. If the Control palette is showing, the degree of rotation will be displayed in the "Rotating" option edit box (see 3.76–3.79 for Control palette info).

2.89   You can rotate objects directly through the Control palette, but the neat thing about the rotating tool is that any point on the object, or on the page or pasteboard, can be the fixed point.

2.90   The farther you drag the starburst cursor away from the fixed point, the longer the rotation lever becomes, and the more control you have when you rotate the object. With a short lever the object tends to jump, while a longer lever helps to rotate the object more smoothly.

2.91   When you rotate multiple objects, all the objects will rotate to the same degree around the same fixed point. If you press the Command key before you begin the rotation, the objects rotate around the center point of the total selected area (2.98).

2.92   When you press the Shift key as you drag the starburst cursor, the objects rotate in 45° increments.

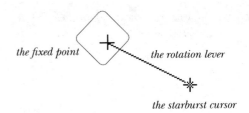

the fixed point   the rotation lever   the starburst cursor

An object can rotate around a fixed point within itself. To rotate the object around its centerpoint, hold down the Command key as you press on the object.

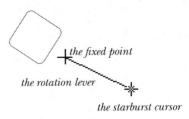

the fixed point   the rotation lever   the starburst cursor

An object can rotate around a fixed point outside itself.

2.93   To keep an object selected after rotating it, press the Shift key as you click on the pointer tool in the Toolbox. You can then modify or move the object without having to select it all over again.

If you want to do this:	Then follow these steps:	Shortcuts ▾ Notes ▾ Hints
2.94 Select and rotate text and/or an object using the rotating tool	▪ Click on the **rotating tool** in the Toolbox. ▪ Click on the text or object you want to rotate. ▪ Press on the spot around which you want the object to rotate. ▪ Drag the starburst cursor away from this fixed point in the direction you want the object to revolve. ▪ Let go of the mouse button when the object is rotated to the position you want.	▪ If the object has a Fill of "None," you must be sure to click on the line of the object to select it, just like with the pointer tool. ▪ The farther away you drag the cursor, the longer the lever, the smoother the rotation. ▪ To rotate the object around its center-point, hold down the Command key as you press on the object. ▪ If the Control palette is showing, the "Rotating" option will display the degree of rotation. See 3.35.
2.95 Select and rotate more than one object using the rotating tool	▪ Click on the **rotating tool** in the Toolbox. ▪ Shift-click on the text and/or objects you want to rotate. ▪ Press on the spot around which you want the objects to rotate. ▪ Drag the starburst cursor away from this fixed point in the direction you want the objects to revolve. ▪ Let go of the mouse button when the group of objects is rotated into position.	▪ You can rotate the objects around any spot on any of the objects, or any spot on the page or pasteboard. ▪ If you hold down the Command key as you rotate the objects, they will rotate around the center point of the selection's bounding box; see 2.98. ▪ The Control palette will display the degree of rotation. See 3.35.
2.96 Keep the rotated object(s) selected while you choose the pointer tool from the Toolbox	▪ Rotate the object(s) as in 2.94 or 2.95. ▪ Hold down the Shift key. ▪ Click on the pointer tool in the Toolbox.	▪ Use this trick to keep objects selected while switching to the pointer tool whenever you use one of PageMaker's draw tools. Objects will stay selected without having to do this when you choose the *rotating* tool, though.

131

If you want to do this:	Then follow these steps:	Shortcuts ▾ Notes ▾ Hints
2.97 Rotate an object in increments of 45°	■ Click on the **rotating tool** in the Toolbox. ■ Click on the text or object you want to rotate. ■ Press on the spot around which you want the object to rotate. ■ Hold down the Shift key. ■ Drag the starburst cursor away from this fixed point in the direction you want the object to revolve. ■ Let go of the mouse button when the object is rotated to the position you want.	■ The rotation lever still moves smoothly around in a circle, but the object jumps only in 45° increments. ■ If you want to change the object with the pointer tool, press the Shift key as you click on the pointer tool in the Toolbox. The object will remain selected (2.96). ■ You can enter values in the "Rotating" option in the Control palette to rotate an object to a predetermined value, see 3.93.
2.98 Rotate a group of objects around the center point of the selected items	■ Click on the **rotating tool** in the Toolbox. ■ Shift-click to select each of the items, **or,** if nothing is selected, use the rotating tool to marquee the items. ■ Hold down the Command key; press-and-drag the starburst cursor in the direction you want the objects to revolve. ■ Let go of the mouse button when the objects are rotated to the position you want.	■ Imagine a bounding box around all of the selected items. The edges of the box are defined by the handle farthest out on each side. The center point is smack in the middle of this imaginary box. ■ If you want to change the objects with the pointer tool, press the Shift key as you click on the pointer tool in the Toolbox. The objects will remain selected (2.96). ■ If a single object is selected, hold down the Command key to rotate the object around its center point.

3 ▾ THE CONTROL PALETTE

3.1 Control palette options:

With a graphic or a text block selected:

Apply — Reflect (flip)

Proxy — Rotate

Position — Skew (tilt)

Size — Nudge

Scale

Imported graphics: Crop

Paint, TIFF graphics: Printer resolution scale

Inline graphic: Baseline offset

With text selected:

Character view

Font — Size

Leading — Type style

Tracking — Kerning

Set width — Baseline shift

Case (CAPS, SMALL CAPS)

Position ($^{superscript,}_{subscript}$)

Paragraph view

Paragraph style — Alignment

Cursor position — Indents

Grid size — Align-to-grid

Paragraph space before and after

3.2 The Control palette is a little window (a windoid, if you like) that gives you instant access to many of PageMaker's standard commands without having to use the menus and dialog boxes. You can change the size and style of type and the leading, resize graphics and text blocks and reposition them, rotate and skew text and graphics, and more. What is displayed in the palette changes depending on whether you have selected an object, text characters, or paragraphs. Since almost every command on the Control palette can also be accomplished through the menus and dialog boxes and with the mouse, the Control palette is simply an easier, faster, and sometimes more precise way to do things. With the Control palette you can measure accurately to within 1/20 (.05) of a point (the rulers, at the most, can measure accurately up to 1/4 (.25) of a point).

3.3 You can click buttons, choose from menus, or type values or text right in the Control palette to make your changes. Or, you can use keyboard shortcuts to select and activate commands. It's a movable window, so you can position it on your screen wherever it's most handy.

3.4 Just like the Style and Color palettes, you can choose to display the Control palette on your screen and then click it away whenever you do not want it. If you want the Control palette to be automatically displayed in every new publication, make it a publication default (3.21).

3.5 Control palette functions are very task-specific. Although this section will introduce you to this wonderful tool, I strongly suggest you study Section 4 and 10 for how to use the Control palette to format text and manipulate imported graphics.

The Control palettes 134

Control palette basics 136

Control palette preferences 137

    Tasks 138

Control palette with object selected .. 142

    The Apply button 144

    The Proxy 144

    Tasks 146

Manipulating objects:

    Control palette options 147

    Tasks 151

Keyboard commands 159

**Scenario #4: Using the keyboard
    to operate the Control Palette** 164

3.6 The Control Palettes

*If a **text block** has been selected with the pointer tool, this is the Control palette you will get. See 3.43.*

Text tool Apply button icon.

Character-view Control palette.

*If **text** has been selected with the text tool, you will see this Control palette. You can change the Control palette from Character-view (type characteristics and formatting) to Paragraph-view (assigning paragraph specifications) by clicking on the "A" or the "¶" (3.44, 4.206–4.224, and 4.300–4.320). Also see Sections 4, 5, 6, 8 and 9.*

Paragraph-view Control palette.

*When a **graphic tool** is chosen (eg., pointer, line, circle, etc.), but no object is selected or drawn, the Apply button icon will change along with the tool. (See 3.9, 3.41.)*

Graphic tool selected; no object selected.

*When a **PageMaker-drawn graphic** is chosen (e.g., line, circle, rectangle), the Apply button will show the graphic selected and the Control palette will display options that can be applied to the object. These can change according to the graphic selected. (See 3.9, 3.42.)*

Line selected Apply button icon.

*If **multiple objects** are selected with the pointer tool, you will see this Control palette. (See 3.9, 3.45.)*

Multiple objects Apply button icon.

The Control Palettes *— continued*

If a **graphic** *is selected with the pointer tool, the kind of Control palette you see will depend upon the kind of graphic that is selected: PageMaker-drawn object, TIFF, EPS, PICT, or Paint. The Apply button icon will change accordingly (3.42). See Sections 2 and 10 for more about graphics.*

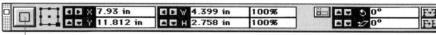

PageMaker-drawn graphic Apply button icon.

The Control palette will offer different options depending upon what tool or object is selected. For instance, the cropping option is available for all graphics **except** *PageMaker-drawn objects (see 3.74 and 10.144) and the printer resolution button is only available when Paint and TIFF images are selected (see 3.75 and 10.142).*

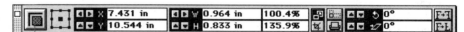

TIFF graphic Apply button icon.   *Printer resolution button.*

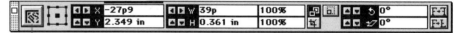

EPS graphic Apply button icon.

Reflecting (flipping) and skewing an object or text block can **only** *be done through the Control palette. See 3.80–3.85 and 10.145.*

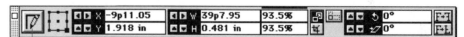

PICT graphic Apply button icon.

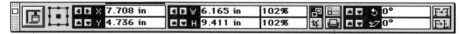

Paint graphic Apply button icon.   *Printer resolution button.*

If, instead of X and Y coordinates, you see the Baseline-offset option, this is your clue that the selected object is an **inline graphic.** *(See 10.221, 10.248.)*

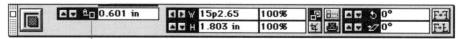

This is your clue that the graphic you have selected is an inline graphic.

Control Palette basics

 3.7 The Control palette is a movable window. Like all windows, you can move it anywhere on the screen you want by pressing on the title bar at the left edge of the palette (the one with the close box) and dragging it. Changes to objects or text can only be implemented through the Control palette when it is active. You can tell if the Control palette is active by the title bar: if it is highlighted it is active (3.20).

3.8 There are several ways to manipulate the options on the Control palette. You can click nudge buttons, press on arrows, or type in edit boxes. Some of the changes take place immediately, while others require that you press the Apply button (or its keyboard shortcuts, the Return or Enter key). You can tell if an option is active by whether or not it has a highlighted bar above or below it.

3.9 The Apply button. The icon for the "Apply" button changes depending on what is selected on the page. For instance, when you select a PageMaker-drawn graphic, the Apply button looks like the object; if you place a paint-type graphic, it looks like a paintbrush. When nothing

in your document is selected, the Apply button shows the tool you have selected.

Click the Apply button to implement the changes you make in the Control palette. (Remember, though, some changes happen immediately and don't need the Apply button.)

3.10 Buttons. When you click a button, such as those that change type style (bold, outline, etc.), or the horizontal and vertical flipping buttons, the change happens immediately.

3.11 Nudge buttons. Most of the options that show a numerical value also have nudge buttons. "Nudging" increases or decreases the value of the option by a predetermined amount. In most cases the nudge amount is a fixed value (see 3.17 for the exceptions). When you nudge a selected item, the change takes place immediately.

A **power-nudge** is 10 times more than a nudge—if the nudge amount is .01 inch, the power-nudge will be .1 inch. To power-nudge, hold down the Command key as you click a nudge button.

3.12 Menus. When you press on a down-pointing arrow (to the right of an option's edit box) a menu pops up with a list of selections for that option. When you select an option from a menu, the change is made immediately.

3.13 Edit boxes. You can type numbers or words to make some changes. Select an edit box, then type the first few characters of that word; PageMaker will display the option that matches it. You must then click the Apply button (or hit the Return key) for the changes to take effect.

3.14 Arithmetic. You can type mathematical expressions in edit boxes to change the value. If you have 10-point type and you want it twice as big, you can type " *2" after the 10 in the type size edit box. Click the Apply button (or press the Return key), and the selected text doubles in size. You can add to, subtract from, multiply, and divide the values in the edit boxes.

The Control Palette and the "Preferences" dialog box *(from the File menu, choose "Preferences...")*

3.15   Any changes you make in the measurement system (3.22) affect the Control palettes just as they affect other measurements in Pagemaker.

3.16   Use 'Snap to' constraints works in conjunction with "Snap to rulers" and "Snap to guides" (both found in the "Guides and rulers" submenu, under the Layout menu). When you check "Use 'Snap to' constraints" along with:

- **Snap to rulers:** PageMaker will constrain to ruler increments all nudges and any new typed-in values.

- **Snap to guides:** PageMaker will snap to the nearest guide any object that you move to within three pixels of a guideline.

- **Both options:** PageMaker will snap objects to ruler increments *or* to any guide positioned in-between ruler increments.

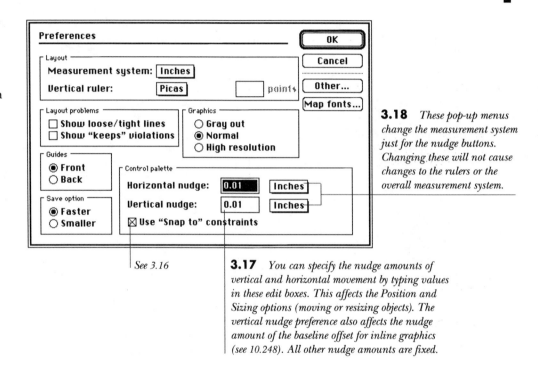

See 3.16

3.18   *These pop-up menus change the measurement system just for the nudge buttons. Changing these will not cause changes to the rulers or the overall measurement system.*

3.17   *You can specify the nudge amounts of vertical and horizontal movement by typing values in these edit boxes. This affects the Position and Sizing options (moving or resizing objects). The vertical nudge preference also affects the nudge amount of the baseline offset for inline graphics (see 10.248). All other nudge amounts are fixed.*

137

If you want to do this:	Then follow these steps:	Shortcuts ▾ Notes ▾ Hints
3.19a Show the Control palette	■ From the Window menu choose "Control palette," *or* press Command ' (*apostrophe; the foot mark*).	■ You cannot change the size of the Control palette. What you see on your screen depends upon how your computer is set up and what monitor you are using.
3.19b Hide the Control palette	■ Press Command ' (*apostrophe*) **or** click in the palette's little close box.	■ The long way to close the palette is to choose it again from the Window menu.
3.20a Make the Control palette active	■ Click on the Control palette, *or* press Command ` (*grave;* the key in the upper left next to the number 1, *or* next to the Spacebar).	■ You can tell the Control palette is active when the little title bar at the left edge is highlighted. Just because you can see the Control palette on your screen doesn't mean it is active. You have to be sure to activate it first before you try to implement any changes. This is especially important if you are making changes with the keyboard (3.101–3.109).
3.20b Make the Control palette inactive	■ Use the mouse to click anywhere on the publication, *or* select a tool from the Toolbox, *or* press Command ` (*grave*).	
3.21 Make the Control palette appear everytime you open a new publication (set it as a publication default)	■ Go to the PageMaker desktop *(when you can see the PageMaker menu but no publication is open, see 1.13).* ■ From the Window menu choose "Control palette." If it already has a checkmark next to it, it's already a publication default.	■ When you open PageMaker by clicking on its application icon, PageMaker opens to its desktop. If you are already in PageMaker, close all open publications to arrive at the PageMaker desktop. ■ Once you've chosen the Control palette as a default, it will be visible in every *new* publication. When you open *existing* documents the Control palette will not be displayed automatically unless it was visible when you last saved the document.

If you want to do this:	**Then follow these steps:**	**Shortcuts ▾ Notes ▾ Hints**
3.22 Change the unit of measure used for the Control palette	▪ From the File menu choose "Preferences…." ▪ In the Preferences dialog box, under "Layout," press on the pop-up menu next to "Measurement system" to choose another unit of measure.	▪ Although in most instances the measurement system is set for the entire publication, the units of measure for certain Control palette options can be changed "on the fly" using keyboard commands; see 3.114.
3.23 Change the unit of measure used for just the nudge buttons 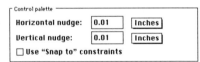	▪ From the File menu choose "Preferences…." ▪ In the Preferences dialog box, under "Control palette," type in the new values in the "Horizontal nudge" and "Vertical nudge" edit boxes.	▪ The measuring system for the rest of the Control palette and the Rulers does not change.
3.24 Change the nudge amount of the Position and Sizing options	▪ From the File menu choose "Preferences…." ▪ In the Preferences dialog box, under "Control palette," press on the pop-up menu next to the "Horizontal nudge:" edit box. Choose a unit of measure. ▪ Do the same for "Vertical nudge:" if desired.	▪ This only affects the nudge buttons for the "Position," "Sizing," and "Baseline-shift" options. ▪ The default nudge amount is 1 point (or .01 inch or 1 millimeter). You can make it anything you want up to 22.75 inches. ▪ The power-nudge value (i.e., 10 times the nudge: 10 points, or .1 inch, or 10 millimeters) will also be changed for these options; see 3.28.

If you want to do this:	**Then follow these steps:**	**Shortcuts ▾ Notes ▾ Hints**
3.25 Constrain objects changed through the Control palette to "Snap to" guides and/or rulers	■ From the File menu choose "Preferences...." ■ In the dialog box, under "Control palette," click the box next to "Use 'Snap to' constraints." Click OK. ■ From the Layout menu slide down to "Guides and rulers" and choose "Snap to rulers" and/or "Snap to guides." See 3.16.	■ Changes you make in the palette will now be constrained to ruler increments and/or objects will snap to the guides. ■ Although you may type a value in the palette, PageMaker may very well override it if you have on "Snap to rulers" or "Snap to Guides." So, if things aren't working like you expected (a nudge button won't move an object or values you type in the palette are changing by themselves) check to see if these options are on. ■ You can temporarily disable the "Snap to" commands without having to go to the Preferences dialog box by choosing them through the Layout menu ("Guides and rulers" submenu) or by using the keyboard commands. (See 1.56 and 1.65).
3.26 Change a selected item by clicking on a button	■ Select the item with the **pointer tool** or **text tool.** ■ Click on the button of the option you want to apply to the selected item.	■ When you make a change with a button, the change takes place immediately.
3.27 Change the value of an option by "nudging" it	■ Select the item with the **pointer, text,** or **rotating tool.** ■ Click the nudge button next to the option you want to change until it displays the value you want.	■ You can also change the rotation and cropping amounts using the nudge buttons. See 3.79, and 10.144–10.145.

If you want to do this:	Then follow these steps:	Shortcuts ▾ Notes ▾ Hints
3.28 Power-nudge a selected item	■ Hold down the Command key as you click the nudge button.	■ Power-nudges are 10 times the amount of a regular nudge.
3.29 Select a Control palette option from a pop-up menu	■ Press on the down-pointing arrow next to the option's edit box, slide down, and select a name or value from the list.	
3.30 Change an option by typing into the edit box	■ Use the mouse to highlight the existing setting in the option's edit box. ■ Type in the number or word that describes the new option in the correct edit box ("H" for Helvetica in the "Font" option, "45" for 45% in the "Rotating" option, etc.).	■ You can make as many changes as you like and then apply them all at once. ■ If you type in a value and then use the mouse to click a nudge button, PageMaker will apply both the nudge *and* the typed-in value all at once.
3.31 Use mathematical formulas to change the value of an option ◄► X 31p1.9*3 ▲▼ Y -2p9.45	■ Set the insertion point immediately after the value in the edit box of the option you want to change. ■ To **increase** the value: □ Type a plus sign (+) and the number you want to add to the value, *or* □ Type an asterisk (*) followed by the number by which you want to multiply the existing number. ■ To **decrease** the value: □ Type a minus sign (-) and the number you want to subtract from the value, *or* □ Type a slash (/) followed by the number by which you want to divide the existing number.	■ You can use either the numeric keypad or the numbers and mathematical signs on the keyboard for this function. If it is more convenient, you can use the Enter key instead of the Return key to apply the values.

The Control Palette options with an object selected

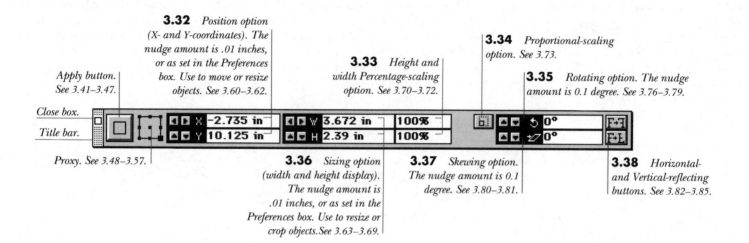

3.32 *Position option (X- and Y-coordinates). The nudge amount is .01 inches, or as set in the Preferences box. Use to move or resize objects. See 3.60–3.62.*

Apply button. See 3.41–3.47.

3.33 *Height and width Percentage-scaling option. See 3.70–3.72.*

3.34 *Proportional-scaling option. See 3.73.*

3.35 *Rotating option. The nudge amount is 0.1 degree. See 3.76–3.79.*

Close box.

Title bar.

Proxy. See 3.48–3.57.

3.36 *Sizing option (width and height display). The nudge amount is .01 inches, or as set in the Preferences box. Use to resize or crop objects. See 3.63–3.69.*

3.37 *Skewing option. The nudge amount is 0.1 degree. See 3.80–3.81.*

3.38 *Horizontal- and Vertical-reflecting buttons. See 3.82–3.85.*

3.39 This is the Control palette in object-view. An object can be a graphic, or a text block, or even a mixed group of both. The Apply button icon changes to represent the kind of object selected (check out the different kinds of palettes you can get in 3.6). The options shown here are always present in the object-view Control palette. Additional options are available for certain types of graphics.

3.40 Although the basic concept and most of the functions of the Control palette are the same throughout all of its views, some of the options are very task specific. Section 3 deals with the general functions of the Control palette, the various ways to manipulate the options in the palette, and, more specifically, the options available in the object-view Control palette.

- See Section 4 for information about the Control palette in character- and paragraph-views (4.206–4.227 and 4.300–4.320).
- See Section 10 for information about the object-view Control palette as it relates to imported graphics.
- All the sections have additional Control palette information included as it relates to the subject at hand.

The Apply button

3.41   The Apply button has two functions. As you can guess from its name, it applies changes you make in the edit boxes. By changing the way it looks, it also lets you know what tool or object you have selected and what is happening on your screen. If nothing in the document is selected, the Apply button just looks like whatever tool is chosen (the same icons as you see in the Toolbox). The position of the tool shows in the Position boxes as X- and Y-coordinates.

When only the pointer tool is selected, all you see is the tool and its position on the page.

3.42   When a **graphic** is selected, the Apply button turns three dimensional with a graphic of the selected object on it. The icons are the same ones you see on the loaded pointer icon when you import graphics, or in the Toolbox when you draw a graphic in PageMaker (See 2.14 and 10.126).

The icon of the selected graphic format is displayed: Paint, PICT, TIFF, EPS, PageMaker-drawn, or OLE.

 3.43   When a **text block** is selected with the pointer tool, the Apply button looks like the text tool in the Toolbox. At this time PageMaker considers a text block an object and you can treat it as such, applying many of the same options to it as you can to any other object.

 3.44   However, when the **text tool** is chosen (with or without text selected), the Apply button shows the text-placing graphic and the Control palette shows the character- or paragraph-view options. See 4.206–4.227 and 4.300–4.320 (and the pages immediately following) for a full discussion on how to use the Control palette for text and paragraph formatting.

3.45   When more than one object is selected in any combination of graphics or text blocks, the Apply button shows **multiple objects**. The only options displayed now are position, rotating and reflecting (flipping).

3.46   The Apply button icon also changes to show the movement of ruler and column guides and the ruler's zero point.

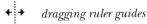 *dragging ruler guides*

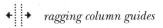 *ragging column guides*

 *dragging the rulers' zero point*

3.47   Clicking the Apply button—or pressing the Return key—implements any changes you type into the Control palette. Remember, many of the changes you make in the Control palette do not take effect immediately. The Return or Enter key is the keyboard shortcut for the Apply button. You can make as many changes as you like in the edit boxes of the Control palette and then apply them all at once.

The Proxy

3.48   The **Proxy**, right next to the Apply button, represents in the Control palette whatever object you have selected in the document. On it are nine reference points that serve as anchor points for the object when you want to make changes to it. No matter what the shape of the object that you have selected (a circle, a rectangle, or a text block), the Proxy will always look like a square.

 **3.49**   The **reference points** (or anchors) on the Proxy look like little black boxes. They let you select from which edge or corner of the object you will be making the change; you can even make changes from the center. They also let you know where the handles of the object are located in relation to the ruler's zero point. That information is displayed as the X- and Y-coordinates.

You can select a corner, the center, or an edge as the active reference point.

3.50   Clicking on any one of the reference points makes it active. The **active reference point** is the point from which all changes will be made. When you select a point on the Proxy, the corresponding handle on the object becomes active. Vice versa, clicking on a handle of the object will change the active reference point on the Proxy. You can use the reference points on the Proxy to move, resize, crop, rotate, skew, or reflect objects (including text blocks).

3.51   The reference point you select will stay active for all subsequent objects until you select a new point on the Proxy or manipulate a handle on another object. You can tell where the active point on any selected object is positioned in the document by looking at the X- and Y-coordinates in the Control palette.

On with the dance!
No sleep til morn . . .
chase the glowing hours
with flying feet.

Lord Byron

Illustration by Michael Hawes
for The Tap Dance Studio

The Proxy —continued

3.52   There are two types of reference points: stationary (a box) and moving (an arrow). When the active reference point is a box, it is the "anchor" on an object from which any changes are made. Changes are measured **from** this reference point as if you dragged the handle **opposite** the reference point.

When the active reference point is a little black box as on the left, it remains stationary when you use the Control palette to make changes. In this example the object is being rotated 30° around its active reference point.

3.53   Therefore, when you enter values in the "Position" edit boxes, the whole object will move to anchor the active reference point to that position on the page. The size of the object is not affected, unless you make other changes in the palette.

3.54   By clicking again on a reference point it turns into a double-headed arrow. Now all changes will occur as if you are directly dragging on the handle to which that reference point corresponds. You are, in effect, transforming the object at the same time as you are assigning the reference point to a new handle from which to make the change (the one directly opposite). The center point turns into a four-way arrow, but the changes will work the same as they do when it is a box. A reference point will remain an arrow (no matter which reference point you make active) until you click again on the active point to change it back to a box.

When the active reference point is an arrow, the corresponding point on the object moves according to the values you enter in the palette. In this example, the object was rotated 30°.

3.55   An arrow reference point, when you enter values in the "Position" edit boxes, causes the handle on the object to move to that position on the page, changing the size of the object.

3.56   The position of the active reference point can affect which "Position," "Sizing," and "Percentage-scaling" options will be available. When a corner reference point is selected, *all* the options are available. However, when a reference point along the vertical side of an object is selected, horizontal measurement options will be dimmed since they have no effect on the active reference point or the movements of the object from that reference point. Similarly, a point along the horizontal side will dim and disable all vertical measurements.

3.57   It is important to know how the reference points work and how they anchor objects on the page or you may find objects behaving differently than you had hoped they would. If it all sounds too complicated, don't worry, just keep your reference points as boxes. It'll all come out the same in the end.

If you want to do this:	Then follow these steps:	Shortcuts ▾ Notes ▾ Hints
3.58 Select an active reference point on the Proxy	■ With an object in the publication selected, use the mouse to click on any point on the Proxy ■ **Or,** with the **pointer tool,** select an object and click on one its handles.	■ The Proxy is only available when an object is selected (a text block, a PageMaker-drawn graphic, or a placed or pasted graphic). When you first draw, place, or paste an object, it is selected. You do not need to select it with the pointer tool to change it through the palette. ■ Anytime you drag the handles of an object on the page, the reference point on the Proxy changes to correspond to the handle you are manipulating. ■ See 3.116 and 3.117 for how to use the keyboard or keypad to select a reference point.
3.59 Change the reference point from a box to an arrow or vice versa	Click once on the reference point that is already active. ■ Click on it again to turn it back to the original symbol.	■ Remember: □ When the active reference point is a box, the point remains stationary through all the changes you make in the palette. □ When the active reference point is an arrow, the point moves with the changes you make in the palette.

Control palette options with an object selected: Position and Sizing options

3.60 Position option: `◄► X 2.004 in` `◄► Y 4.047 in` The "Position" option edit boxes tell you where you are on the screen relative to the document's rulers. The X-coordinate is the horizontal ruler (the Width); the Y-coordinate is the vertical ruler (the Height). When you draw an object, the X and Y values show where you clicked the mouse button to begin drawing. If you have an object selected (either a graphic or a text block) then the X and Y edit boxes show the coordinates of the object's active reference point in relation to the rulers. If you have a tool chosen but no object selected, the coordinates show a continual update of the screen position of the tool.

3.61 You can move or resize a selected object by changing the values in the "Position" option edit boxes (see 3.87–3.89).

3.62 The default nudge amount for the "Position" option is .01 inch (or the chosen unit of measure); the power nudge is .1 inch (press the Command key as you click the nudge button). You can control the amount of nudge by changing the values for "Horizontal" and "Vertical" nudge in the "Preferences" dialog box (see 3.17).

3.63 Sizing option: `◄► W 1.367 in` `◄► H 0.444 in` `◄► L 2.305 in` The width and height of the selected object or the length of a line is displayed in the "Sizing" option edit boxes. You can type new values in these boxes to change the size of the object. How the object changes will depend upon the position and type of active reference point (see 3.56).

3.64 Only those values relative to the active reference point will be available in the Control palette. For instance, if you select a reference point on the Y-axis, then the "Height" option is not available since you are telling PageMaker that you want to modify the vertical nature of the object by moving it horizontally. If you have selected a reference point on the X-axis then the "Width" option is dimmed since you cannot make any modifications to the width of an object by changing its height. It all sounds oh! so complicated, but give it time and you will not know how you ever got along without this wonderful tool.

3.65 The default nudge amount is .01. It can also be changed in the "Preferences" dialog box (3.17).

3.66 PageMaker will not let you enter values which make the width or height equal to 0 (zero) or less. She will also not allow you to make objects so large that they won't fit on the pasteboard.

3.67 If the "Proportional-scaling" option is on (3.92a), it may override whatever you enter in the "Sizing" option box. For example, with "Proportional-scaling" on, if you change the width of an object the height will automatically be changed to maintain the original proportions. To change the width and the height independent of each other you must first turn "Proportional-scaling" off (3.92b). The "Percentage-scaling" option will reflect any changes made in the "Sizing" option.

3.68 The "Sizing" option works differently when a graphic is selected and the "Cropping" or "Printer-resolution" option is on (see 10.142 and 10.144).

3.69 If you enter the wrong value, in most cases you can choose "Undo edit" from the Edit menu (Command Z), to bring back the original value. If you enter a command that is wrong for the option, press the Escape key to return to the last valid entry.

The Control Palette options with an object selected: Scaling and cropping

100% **100%** **3.70 Percentage-scaling option:** This option shows by what percentage objects are reduced or enlarged when they are resized. It is available for all objects including text blocks, objects drawn with PageMaker's tools, or any type of graphic placed or pasted on the page. As you resize objects, you will also notice the values in the "Sizing" option changing to reflect the new dimensions.

3.71 You can also specify the scale you want by typing specific percentages in the edit boxes for an object's width or height. Of course, how something resizes depends on what kind of active reference point you have and where it is on the object. If the active reference point is a box, resizing the selected object doesn't affect the position of the reference point. If the active reference point is an arrow, the reference point will move as the object is resized. See 3.52–3.57.

3.72 Percentage-scaling affects text blocks and PageMaker-drawn objects differently than imported graphics. When you use the Control palette to scale a Page-Maker-drawn object or a text block, the percentage you are changing it will only show while you are editing the object. The next time you select the object the percentage will again read 100%, no matter what. If you press-and-drag *directly* on a drawn object or text block, the percentage in the "Percentage-scaling" option doesn't change at all but stays at 100%. However, with imported graphics, PageMaker will always remember the original size and will show any changes you make to it in the "Percentage-scaling" option. See 10.139.

3.73 Proportional-scaling option: This button is either on or off. When the icon shows a small square within a larger square, the option is on, and any changes made in the "Sizing" or "Percentage-scaling" options will change both the width and height of the object to keep it to its original proportion.

When the button is off you can scale the object's width and height independent of each other, ignoring the object's original proportions. If you scale an object with the button off, then decide you want to return it to its original proportions, *while the object is still selected,* click the button on.

3.74 Scaling and Cropping: These buttons are either on or off, and they are only available for imported graphics—those you either place or paste into your document. They let you access other Control palette options used to resize imported graphics. Selecting an imported graphic with the pointer tool automatically selects the Scaling option. This brings up the Percentage-scaling, Proportional-scaling, and Printer-resolution options (see 10.139–10.142). Selecting the imported graphic with the cropping tool automatically selects the Cropping option. You can now enter the size to which you want to crop the graphic, or, by clicking on the cropping icon in the Toolbox you can change the pointer tool to the cropping tool and manually crop it (see 10.144). See Section 10 for a complete discussion about manipulating imported graphics.

3.75 Printer-resolution-scaling option: This option is only available for graphics imported in a TIFF or Paint format. See 10.142.

Control palette options with an object selected: Rotating and skewing

 3.76 Rotating option: You can use this option to rotate all objects, including text blocks, from -360° to 360° in .01 degree increments. However, the results you get will depend completely on where the active point on the Proxy is located and whether it is a box or an arrow.

- Typing a positive number rotates an object counterclockwise.
- Typing a negative number rotates it clockwise.

3.77 When the active reference point is a box, as in the example below, the selected object will rotate around that reference point. The reference point is the object's "anchor" and it will remain stationary.

The first object was rotated 30°, the second object -30°. The small black square represents the active reference point. Notice it stays in the same position.

3.78 When the active reference point is an arrow, as in this example, the object is rotated by moving the object in an arc. The reference point is no longer a stationary anchor for the object. Instead it moves into a completely new position, swinging the object with it as it does.

With an arrow reference point, the first object was rotated 30°, the second one -30°. (The shadowed images were added to demonstrate the movement of the active reference point.)

3.79 The nudge value is fixed at .1 degree. When you rotate an object, the Proxy rotates with it. The reference points still correspond to the same handles on the object as before. For more information on rotating objects, see 2.85–2.93 and 10.145; for text, 4.271–4.279.

 3.80 Skewing option: You can only skew (slant) objects through the Control palette. Skewing an object tilts it at an angle to the right or the left from 85° to -85° in increments as fine as .01°. When you skew an object, the bottom edge of the object remains still, and the top edge slants. You can slant objects in two ways:

- Typing a positive number slants the object to the right.
- Typing a negative number slants it to the left.

The first object is skewed 30°, the second one -30°.

3.81 When the active reference point is a box, the reference point, and that corner or edge of the object, remains stationary as the object tilts. When the active reference point is an arrow, the reference point, and that corner or edge of the object, moves the specified amount, "sliding" the object along with the reference point. Often, the same effect can be realized even with different reference points chosen.

Control Palette options in object view: Horizontal and vertical reflecting

3.82 Horizontal- and Vertical-reflecting buttons: Any object can be reflected (flipped), but only by using the Control palette. This includes text blocks and all graphics. The top button is the "Horizontal-reflecting" option. Clicking this button turns the selected image around horizontally as if you are viewing it in a mirror. (PageMaker considers this a vertical reflection plus a 180° rotation, so you will notice 180° entered in the rotating edit box after horizontally flipping something.)

3.83 The bottom button is the "Vertical-reflecting" option. Clicking this turns the selected object upside down. (PageMaker doesn't consider this anything special, so no new values will appear in the edit boxes.)

3.84 The type of active reference point you have selected decides how the object will flip. If it is a *box*, the object will flip around the reference point, leaving it and that edge of the object firmly "anchored" in its spot. Don't be confused when the box on the Proxy shifts position. It is just moving with the object as the object flips around it to show the new position of the active reference point on the screen (remember, it's a "mirror" image). If it is an *arrow*, the object *and* the arrow move as the reference point flips and lands in a new position. (An arrow reference point works the same as choosing a box reference point on the opposite edge of the object.)

3.85 After flipping something you will see a black border around the Horizontal and Vertical-reflecting buttons. Unfortunately, this doesn't really tell you much, since if you flip the same object again, even in a new direction, the border disappears. Even if you make an object do multiple flips, the border just keeps toggling on and off.

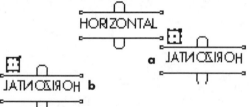

Three text blocks were lined up in a vertical column. The top one is the original, the second and third were flipped with the "Horizontal-reflecting" button. The active reference point was in the top right-hand corner, above the "L." In **a** *(now on the right) the reference point was a box. It anchored the text block to the page at that corner, flipping it over. In* **b** *(now on the left) the same reference point was an arrow, flipping the object and itself over.*

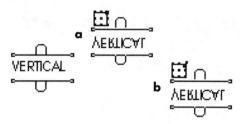

Three text blocks were lined up in a horizontal row. Here, the left one is the original, the second and third were flipped with the "Vertical-reflecting" button. The active reference point was again in the top right-hand corner, above the "L." In **a** *the reference point was a box. It anchored the text block to the page at that corner, flipping it over. In* **b** *the same reference point was an arrow, flipping the object and itself over.*

3.86 Baseline-offset option: This option is only available when you have selected an inline graphic. Numbers you type in the edit box adjust the baseline of the graphic relative to the baseline of the text. See Section 10, especially 10.213–10.233 for complete information about inline graphics.

If you want to do this:	**Then follow these steps:**	**Shortcuts ▾ Notes ▾ Hints**
3.87 Move (change the position of) a selected object	▪ With the **pointer tool,** select the object. ▪ Click the center reference point on the Proxy to make it active. ▪ Use the mouse to highlight the value in the X-coordinate edit box. ▪ Type a new value in the X-coordinate edit box. ▪ Use the mouse to highlight the value in the Y-coordinate edit box. ▪ Type a new value in the Y-coordinate edit box. ▪ Click the Apply button *or* press the Return key.	▪ When the center reference point is active it does not matter if it is a box or an arrow. The object will move just the same either way. ▪ You can choose to activate the Control palette first by either pressing Command ` (*grave*) or sweeping over an edit box. Clicking the Proxy does not activate the palette, but pressing the Tab key will when the palette is in object-view. ▪ See 3.101–3.111 and 3.120 for how to use the keyboard to implement changes in the Control palette without using the mouse.
3.88 Move (change the position of) an object on the page by entering new values for its active reference point	▪ Click the reference point on the Proxy that corresponds to the handle on the object you wish to move, *or* use the pointer tool to click on the handle on the object itself. ▪ Make the active reference point a box (see 3.59). ▪ Activate the Control palette (3.20) and type new values into the X- and/or Y-coordinate edit boxes. ▪ Click the Apply button *or* press the Return key.	▪ If the active reference point is on a corner, both the X- and Y-coordinates can be changed. ▪ If it is on the vertical edge (Y), only the X-coordinate will be available. ▪ If it is on the horizontal edge (X), only the Y-coordinate will be available. ▪ You can also change the value by pressing on a nudge button. ▪ Hold down the Command key as you click on a nudge button to power-nudge. ▪ If you make a mistake you can return to the previous value by selecting Undo edit (Command Z) to return to the original value.

If you want to do this:	Then follow these steps:	Shortcuts ▾ Notes ▾ Hints
3.89 Resize a selected object by entering new values for its active reference point in the Position option edit boxes  *Only the X-coordinate edit box is available because the active reference point is on the Y-axis.*	■ Click the reference point on the Proxy that corresponds to the handle on the object you wish to move, *or* use the pointer tool to click on the handle on the object itself. ■ If the active reference point is a box, click once on it to make it an arrow (3.59). ■ Activate the Control palette (3.20) and type new values into the X- and/or Y-coordinate edit boxes. ■ Click the Apply button *or* press the Return key.	■ As in the last task, which reference point is active will determine whether the X- or Y-coordinate will be available. ■ Another way to turn a box reference point into an arrow is to press the Spacebar when the palette is active and the highlight bar is beneath the Proxy. ■ If "Proportional-scaling" is turned on, it may override your commands for resizing (see 3.67).
3.90 Resize a line ◨◪ L 3.726 in *The "Line" edit box. The "Size" option (width and height) is replaced with the "Line" option when a line is selected.*	■ Select the line. ■ Select the reference point from which you want to extend the line. ■ Make the active reference point an arrow (click once on it if it's a box). ■ Enter a value in the "Line" edit box.	■ If the reference point is a box, it will remain stationary while the other end of the line lengthens or shortens. ■ You can resize a line through the "Position" option box; see 3.89. ■ You can't proportionally scale a line, scale it (using percentages), or skew it.

If you want to do this:	**Then follow these steps:**	**Shortcuts ▾ Notes ▾ Hints**
3.91 Reduce or enlarge an object by a given percent	• Select the object. • Use the mouse to select one of the percentage edit boxes. • Type a new percentage value in the "Width" or "Height Percentage-scaling" option edit box, or in both. • Click the Apply button, *or* press Return.	• If the "Proportional-scaling" button is on, it doesn't matter in which box you enter a new value, both percentages will change. • With text blocks and PageMaker-drawn objects, the "Percentage-scaling" options only display the new percentage while the object is selected. As soon as you de-select it, the edit boxes will again read "100%." • You can also activate the "Percentage-scaling" option using just the keyboard. With the Control palette active (Command `), press the Tab key until the edit box is highlighted. See 3.101–3.120 for more on using keyboard commands.
3.92a Proportionately change an object's width and height *When the proportional button is on it looks like this.*	• Select the object. • Click the "Proportional-scaling" button on. • Change the value in either the "Height" or "Width" edit box—either one will work. • Click the Apply button, *or* press Return.	• With the "Proportional-scaling" button on, both "Height" and "Width" will change commensurately. • You can also use the keyboard to activate the "Proportional-scaling" button. Use the Tab key to move the highlight bar above the icon. Press the Spacebar to turn the button on. See 3.109–3.120 for more about keyboard controls. • Don't forget that the Control palette only affects changes made through the palette. Even if the "Proportional-scaling" button is on, you can press-and-drag directly on an object's handle, re-scaling it at will.
3.92b Change an object's width *or* height independently *When the proportional button is off it looks like this.*	• Select the object. • If the "Proportional-scaling" button is on, click it off. • Change the value in either the "Height" or "Width" edit box, or both. • Click the Apply button, *or* press Return.	

If you want to do this:	Then follow these steps:	Shortcuts ▾ Notes ▾ Hints
3.93a Rotate an object clockwise around a fixed point on the object	■ Select the object. ■ Choose the anchor point around which you want the object to rotate: □ Click directly on a handle on the object; □ **Or** Click the corresponding point on the Proxy in the Control palette. ■ Make the active reference point a box. If it is an arrow click once on it to change it to a box (3.59). ■ Enter a new value in the "Rotating" option edit box: □ Press the Tab key until the highlight bar is above the "Rotating" option and the edit box is highlighted, then type a **negative number;** □ **Or** use the mouse to highlight the edit box, then type in a **negative number.** ■ Click the Apply button *or* press the Return key to apply the rotation.	■ You can rotate anything you can select with the pointer or rotating tool. ■ When you select an object that has already been rotated, the Control palette will display the degree of rotation. ■ If you change the degree of rotation, PageMaker will not add it onto the already existing rotation, but will consider it a new value and rotate the object from 0° again. ■ You can specify rotation for a selected object if the Control palette is active (Command `) by pressing the Tab key until the highlight bar is above the "Rotating" option edit box, *then* typing in the rotation value. ■ You can change a reference point from a box to an arrow if the Control palette is active (Command `). Press the Tab key until the highlight bar is under the Proxy, *then:* Press the Spacebar; **or** press the "S" key.
3.93b Rotate an object counterclockwise around a fixed point on the object	■ Follow the directions in the previous task but type a **positive number** in the "Rotating" option edit box.	■ See 3.101–3.120 for more information about keyboard controls in the Control palette. ■ Use the nudge buttons to rotate the object in .1 of a degree increments.

If you want to do this:

3.94 Rotate an object in an arc by using the arrow reference point (moving the active reference point)

It
was
a
bright
cold
day
in
April,
and
the
clocks
were
stiking
thirteen.

George Orwell
Nineteen Eighty-Four

Then follow these steps:

- Select the object.
- Choose the point around which you want the object to rotate:
  - □ Click directly on a handle of the object;
  - □ **or** click the corresponding point on the Proxy in the Control palette.
- Make the active reference point an arrow. If it is a box, single-click on it to change it to an arrow.
- Enter a value in the "Rotating" option edit box:
  - □ Press the Tab key until the highlight bar is above the "Rotating" option and the edit box is highlighted, then type in either a negative or a positive number;
  - □ **or** use the mouse to highlight the edit box and type in a number.
- Click the Apply button *or* press the Return key to apply the rotation.

Shortcuts ▾ Notes ▾ Hints

- Type in a positive number if you want the object to rotate counterclockwise; a negative number if you want it to rotate clockwise.
- You can use the keyboard to change the active reference point from a box to an arrow: with the Control palette active, press the Tab key until the highlight bar is under the Proxy. Press the Spacebar or the "S" key to change the reference point from a box to an arrow. Also see 3.116.
- Also see 3.93.

If you want to do this:	Then follow these steps:	Shortcuts ▾ Notes ▾ Hints
3.95a Skew (tilt) an object to the right keeping the object anchored in one place (the active reference point stationary)	■ Select the object. ■ Select the active reference point on the Proxy (or on the object) that you want as a stationary anchor. ■ Make the active reference point a box (click on it once if it's an arrow). ■ Type a **positive number** in the "Skewing" option edit box. ■ Click the Apply button *or* press Return.	■ Only the top edge of the object moves. ■ You can make the same thing happen different ways depending on how you choose the active reference point: 　if the upper left corner is a box, it tilts the same as when the lower left corner is an arrow, and vice versa. 　If the upper right corner is a box, it tilts the same as when the lower right corner is an arrow, and vice versa.
3.95b Skew an object to the left keeping it anchored in one place (the active reference point stationary)	■ Follow the directions in the previous task but type a **negative number** in the "Skewing" option edit box.	
3.96 Skew an object to the right or the left, sliding it along the active reference point (moving the active reference point)	■ Select the object. ■ Select the top right or left corner point on the Proxy (or on the object). ■ Make the active reference point an arrow (click on it once if it's a box). ■ Type a value in the "Skewing" option edit box: 　□ Type a positive number if you want the reference point to slide to the right. 　□ Type a negative number if you want the reference point to slide to the left. ■ Click the Apply button or press Return.	■ Selecting the bottom corners as reference points works just the opposite of selecting the top corners: a positive number will move the active reference point to the left. A negative number will move the point to the right.

If you want to do this:	**Then follow these steps:**	**Shortcuts ▾ Notes ▾ Hints**

3.97 Flip an object horizontally around a stationary reference point

 The Horizontal-reflecting button.

HORIZONTAL ⅃AⱠNOƧIᴚOH

- Select the object.
- Select the reference point around which you want the object to flip.
- Make the active reference point a box (click on it once if it's an arrow).
- Click on the "Horizontal-reflecting" button, *or* press the Tab key until the highlight bar is above the "Horizontal-reflecting" option, then press the Spacebar to reflect the object.

- When you select an object that has been flipped, the reflect buttons in the palette will have a black border around them. This border toggles off and on each time you flip an object, so an object that has been flipped both horizontally *and* vertically will show no border. An object flipped *five* times will have a border, but if it's been flipped *six* times, it won't!
- Choosing the center point keeps the object stationary on the page. The object just flips over on itself.
- To flip the object vertically, choose a point on one of the horizontal edges (X); to flip it horizontally, choose a point on one of the vertical edges (Y). The corners are both horizontal *and* vertical anchor points.

3.98 Flip an object horizontally, flipping (moving) the active reference point with it

- Select the object.
- Select the reference point you want to flip.
- Make the active reference point an arrow (click on it once if it's a box).
- Click on the "Horizontal-reflecting" button, *or* use the keyboard controls to flip the object (see 3.111).

- When you change the active reference point to an arrow, it's the same as if you chose an active reference point on the opposite edge. It's much easier to remember, when reflecting objects, to just select a box reference point on the edge you want to anchor.

157

If you want to do this:	**Then follow these steps:**	**Shortcuts ▾ Notes ▾ Hints**

3.99 Flip an object vertically around a stationary reference point

 The Vertical-reflecting tool.

VERTICAL FLIP

ᴧƎᴚꟿICꓴꞀ ꟻꞀIꟼ

- Select the object.
- Select the reference point around which you want the object to flip.
- Make the active reference point a box (click on it once if it's an arrow).
- Click on the "Vertical-reflecting" button, *or* press the Tab key until the highlight bar is below the "Vertical-reflecting" option, then press the Spacebar to reflect the object.

- If, like some people, you find the concept of flipping confusing, it may help to mimic the action you want to achieve with a little flip of the hand. Remember that when you want to apply a vertical action, you must act on the *horizontal* coordinate (X); if you want to apply a horizontal action, you must act on the *vertical* coordinate (Y). When you flip something horizontally, you are actually flipping it around a vertical axis. Watch your reference points for clues as to where you are going.

3.100 Flip an object vertically, flipping (moving) the active reference point with it

- Select the object.
- Select the reference point around which you want the object to flip.
- Make the active reference point an arrow (click on it once if it's a box).
- Click on the "Vertical-reflecting" button, *or* press the Tab key until the highlight bar is below the "Vertical-reflecting" option, then press the Spacebar to reflect the object.

IT'S NEVER TOO EARLY TO HAVE A SECOND CHILDHOOD.
—KENT CALKINS

Control Palette keyboard commands

3.101 Once you get the hang of the Control palette (and see all that it can do) you will want to start using **keyboard commands** to access Control palette options. It is sometimes easier and definitely slicker than using the mouse. The most important thing to remember is to make sure that the Control palette is active first. Fortunately, Command Z (Undo edit) will "undo" a lot of mistakes as you learn.

3.102 Pressing Command ' (*apostrophe*) displays the Control palette. Pressing Command ` (*grave*) makes the palette active; the little title bar at the left of the Control palette will be black (highlighted). The same key command will deactivate it (3.20).

3.103 Pressing the **Tab key** moves you through the Control palette. The highlight bar, a thin black, gray, or colored bar (depending upon your monitor, see 3.110), sits above options that are in the top row of the palette and below those in the bottom row. As you press the Tab key the highlight bar moves from option to option, showing you which one is active.

3.104 This also highlights the edit boxes for the various options as you move to their spot. Only those options available for changes at the moment, however, will be highlighted (this depends upon what kind of object is selected and which reference point is active). Although the highlight bar always shows above or below an option, when an edit box is highlighted it is a sure bet the palette is active (that's the only time an edit box *is* highlighted). See 3.110.

3.105 Pressing the Tab key will take you right through all the options on the palette and back to the beginning. Press Shift-Tab to return to a previous option, or to move backwards through the palette.

3.106 When you want to make more than one change to a selection, you can

- Press the Tab key to apply the change and move to the *next* option in the Control palette.
- Press Shift-Tab to apply the change and move to the *previous* option in the palette.
- Press Shift-Return to apply a change and keep the same palette option active.

3.107 Press Return to apply any changes you made in the object-view Control palette. However, this will also deactivate the palette. So, to make it active again, just press the Tab key to move to the next option. You do not need to keep pressing Command ` (*grave*) after applying changes. You can also tab through the palette, making changes in any or all of the edit boxes as you go, and then press Return to apply them all at once.

3.108 You can make a lot of changes right from the keyboard. You can select options and type into their edit boxes or use the Spacebar to turn certain options on or off (the Proportional- and Printer-resolution scaling, the reflecting buttons, and type style options in the character-view Control palette). When typing in an edit box, you can move the text cursor within the box by using the arrow keys.

3.109 You can also change the measurement system for certain options from the keyboard: "Position," "Sizing," and "Baseline-offset" in the object-view palette; "Baseline-shift" in the character-view palette; "Indent," "Space-before," and "Space-after" in the paragraph-view palette. See 3.114.

If you want to do this:	**Then follow these steps:**	**Shortcuts ▾ Notes ▾ Hints**
3.110 Use the keyboard to move from one option to the next in the Control palette	▪ Press Command ` (*grave*) to activate the palette. ▪ Press the Tab key to move the highlight bar from one option to the next. ▪ Press Shift-Tab to move back to a previous option.	▪ The highlight bar is so narrow that it's pretty hard to see sometimes, even in black and white. If you do have trouble seeing it and have a color or grayscale monitor, try changing its color: □ Select "Color" in the Control Panels folder in the System folder. □ Choose a brighter highlight color if you have a color monitor. (Something like bug-gut green works really well until you get used to seeing the highlight bar. Later you can change it back to a more appealing color.) □ Choose "Black & White" if you have a grayscale monitor.
3.111 Use the keyboard to turn a button in the palette on or off	▪ Press Command ` (*grave*) to activate the palette. ▪ Press the Tab key to move the highlight bar above or beneath the button. ▪ Press the Spacebar.	▪ Pressing the Spacebar toggles options on and off. If an object is selected, the Spacebar can activate some options (like the "Reflecting" buttons). ▪ If the button is one in a series as in the type styles options, use the left and right arrow keys to move between them (4.125). ▪ When you have an object selected on the page, just pressing the Tab key activates the Control palette. But when the insertion point is in text, always, always, *always* press Command ` before you use key commands in the palette.

If you want to do this:	Then follow these steps:	Shortcuts ▾ Notes ▾ Hints
3.112 Apply changes to your document while keeping the palette active and moving to the next option	▪ Select the object or highlight the text you want to change. ▪ Press Command ` (*grave*) to activate the palette. ▪ Press the Tab key to move the highlight bar to the option you want to change. Enter a new value in the edit box. ▪ Press the Tab key again. Enter a new value in this edit box. Do this until you have made all the changes you want. ▪ Press Return to return to the document.	▪ If you are not sure that a change you are making is correct, press Shift-Tab to keep the option highlighted when you apply the palette changes. ▪ When you press the Return key to apply palette changes, the palette becomes deactivated. ▪ You can also press Command `, to deactivate the palette and return to the document.
3.113 Display the last valid entry for a palette option when you enter an invalid value	▪ Click the "Continue" button in the warning box that PageMaker displays. ▪ While the option with the invalid entry is still active press the Escape key (esc).	▪ PageMaker will yell at you when you type in a value that is beyond the parameters of what the edit box can accept.

3.114 Change the measuring system (the unit of measure) "on the fly" for certain options without going into the "Preferences" dialog box	▪ Press Command ` to activate the Control palette, then press the Tab key to highlight the option you want to change.
	▪ **Or** use the mouse to select the option in the palette you want to change.
	▪ Press Command Option M to enter the next available unit of measure.
	▪ Keep pressing Command Option M until you get the correct unit of measure.
		▪ This task works only for
		  ◻ "Position," "Sizing," and "Baseline-offset" in the object-view palette.
		  ◻ "Indent," "Space-before," and "Space-after" in the paragraph-view palette.
		  ◻ "Baseline-shift" in the character-view palette.
		▪ The edit box will keep the new measurement system until you change it again or put the Control palette away.

If you want to do this:	Then follow these steps:	Shortcuts ▾ Notes ▾ Hints
3.115 Use key commands to move an object	■ With the Control palette **inactive,** select the object (or objects) you want to move. ■ Press the arrow keys to nudge the object in the direction you want to go.	■ Do not activate the Control palette. This only works when the palette is inactive! ■ To power-nudge an object, hold down the Command key while pressing the arrow keys.
3.116 Select an active reference point on the Proxy using the arrow keys on the keyboard	■ With an object selected, press Command ` to activate the Control palette. ■ Press the Tab key until the highlight bar is beneath the Proxy. ■ Use the **arrow keys** to switch from one reference point to another.	■ The arrow keys move the active reference point around the Proxy in an orderly fashion according to the direction of the arrow.
3.117 Select an active reference point on the Proxy using the Numeric keypad 7 8 9 4 5 ■ 6 1 2 3	■ With an object selected on the publication page, press Command ` to activate the Control palette. ■ Press the Tab key until the highlight bar is beneath the Proxy. ■ Use the **numbers 1 through 9 on the numeric keypad** to select the reference point.	■ The numbers 1 through 9 each represent a point on the Proxy with "5" as the center point.

If you want to do this:	**Then follow these steps:**	**Shortcuts ▾ Notes ▾ Hints**
3.118 Change the type of active reference point from a box to an arrow (or vice versa) using keyboard commands	▪ With the Control palette active and the highlight bar beneath the Proxy, press the Spacebar once. ▪ **Or** with the Control palette active and the highlight bar beneath the Proxy, press "M" to get the box, press "S" to get the arrow.	▪ The Spacebar toggles the active reference point back and forth between a box and an arrow. ▪ Think of "M" for "Move"—changing the position of an object with a box reference point *moves* the object to the new position. ▪ Think of "S" for "Stretch"—changing the position of an object with an arrow reference point *stretches* the object to the new position.

3.119 Move the cursor through an edit box without using the mouse	▪ With the Control palette active, press the Tab key until the option you want is highlighted.
	▪ Use the arrow keys to move the cursor through the edit box:
	  □ "Up" moves it to the very beginning.
	  □ "Down" moves it to the very end.
	  □ "Left" moves it one character to the left.
	  □ "Right" moves it one character to the right.
	▪ When the cursor is on the right of what you want to change, press the Delete or Backspace key and type in the new number or character.
		▪ This is very much like moving through text with the arrow keys. See 1.325.
		▪ You can use this method to change numbers within values, or even to change the measurement system in an option.

3.120 Scenario #4: Using the keyboard to operate the Control Palette

Using the Control palette can be a pretty slick way to move around a publication. My only caution is that you be sure the Control palette is active before you type commands into it or else you will find some very funny things typed directly into your text! See Appendix I for a complete list of Control palette key commands.

A visionary is the only true realist.
— Federico Fellini

I never took my hands off the keyboard while formatting the quote at the top of the page. How did I do it?

- The first thing I wanted to do after typing in the text and placing the inline graphic, was to assign a font. So I used Command A to select the text block, then pressed Command ` (grave) to make the Control palette active. Now I could use the Tab key to move through the Control palette until the highlight bar showed above the "Font" edit box. I wanted to use Adobe's Myriad Tilt, and so I typed in the letters "m" and "y." That's all PageMaker needed to know. She filled in the edit box with "Myriad Tilt" for me. I hit Shift-Return to apply the font *and* keep the Control palette active; that's all it took. The entire text block was now in Myriad Tilt!

- Next I wanted to make the type size 18 points. I tabbed over to the "Type size" edit box and typed in "18," but this time I just hit Return since I now wanted to go back into the publication and make some changes there.

- I didn't want Federico's name to be as large as the quote. I used Shift-Arrow to select Federico's name, activated the Control palette again, and entered "9" in the "Type size" box, hit Shift-Return (to keep the palette active), then pressed Command Shift ` to change over to the paragraph-view Control palette. Now, using the Tab key and then the RightArrow key, I moved the highlight bar so it was under the "Right-alignment" button, pressed the Spacebar, and *voila!* Fred's name moved over to the right.

- The leading up until this point was still "Auto." That never works well with an inline graphic (see 10.232–10.233), so I deactivated the Control palette, selected the first two lines of the text block using Shift-DownArrow, selected the character-view Control palette (Command Shift `) and activated it (Command `); tabbed over to the "Leading" edit box, typed in the leading I wanted, hit Return. Then I moved to Fred's name and repeated the process all over again. I now had fixed leading. This time, I hit Shift-Tab to apply leading and move *back* to the Type specs buttons, arrowed over to the "Italic" button, hit Shift-Spacebar and italicized his name. Cool, huh?

- Finally, in order to adjust the inline graphic, I selected the text and gave it final tweaks with the "Baseline-shift" option. (I confess that it's a whole lot easier at this point to just select the graphic with the pointer tool and move it into place [10.221, 10.246]. However there are some final adjustments that can be made by selecting the text itself and power nudging the "Baseline-shift" option. See more about adjusting inline graphics in 10.248.)

A wonderful long Chapter concerning the Marvellous; being much the longest of all the explanatory Chapters.

4.1 Minimums and maximums:

Item	Minimum	Maximum
Type size	4 pt.	650 pt.
	(tenth-point increments; .1)	
Leading	.1 pt.	1300 pt.
	(tenth-point increments; .1)	
Replacing text		64K
		(about 25 pages, in one text block)
Small caps size	1% or 1 pt.	200%
	(tenth-percent increments; .1%)	
Super/subscript size	1%	200%
	(tenth-percent increments; .1%)	
Super/subscript position	0%	500%
	(tenth-percent increments; .1%)	

4.2 This section covers all the different ways to work with text directly on the publication page in PageMaker, from creating to formatting. PageMaker gives you incredible control and flexibility in working with type. It's so much fun and so satisfying to perfect it right in front of your very eyes!

4.3 As you can see on the right, this section is broken down into specific aspects of working with the text. You deal with all these aspects at once while you work. But, unlike our brains, books function in a linear fashion, so you may have to do some crossing over between subsections in order to get all your questions answered.

4.4 One of the most important concepts in PageMaker is the **text block.** It is critical that you understand what a text block is and how it operates—if you are new to PageMaker, it would be a good idea to read that part of this section very carefully (4.102–4.129).

Creating text directly on the page 165

Placing text into PageMaker 171

The "Place" dialog box 173

Placing PageMaker files into PageMaker 181

The "Story importer" dialog box 182

Text flow 186

Text blocks 192

Additions for text 206

Selecting and formatting text 216

The "Type specifications" dialog box 222

Character-view Control palette 223

Alignment 234

Rotate text 247

Paragraphs 251

The "Paragraph specifications" dialog box 252

Paragraph-view Control palette 253

Line breaks 261

Special characters 263

Type specification defaults 265

Creating text directly on the page

4.5　PageMaker does not pretend to be a word processor (and word processors should stop pretending to be page layout programs). PageMaker does have the Story Editor, which is discussed at length in Section 9. The Story Editor contains the most important features of a word processor. It's great for writing lengthy text without leaving PageMaker and has a terrific find-and-change feature that has saved me hundreds of hours. Literally.

4.6　If you have more than a small amount of copy, it is best to use the Story Editor or an outside word processing application to write, proof, and edit the text—and then drop it into PageMaker for formatting and layout.

4.7　However, PageMaker is fully capable of creating and editing text right on the screen, so for small amounts of text—such as an advertisement, small package design, flyer, announcement, invitation, etc.—it is usually more efficient to create it directly on the page. It's slower than a word processor because PageMaker uses more complex typographic information to dispay the text on the screen (letter spacing, word spacing, hyphenation, etc.).

4.8　Text is always contained in a **text block**—it cannot be on a page without being in a text block. If you take the pointer tool and click once on any text, you will see the boundaries of the text block and the *handles* at the four corners (this works most visibly at Fit in Window view).

Notice the little square *handles* at each of the four corners of this *text block*.

4.9　It's a good idea to make sure you understand **text blocks** (4.102–4.129) before you start creating text on the page. In some jobs you may want to have the different parts of the text in separate, unconnected text blocks for easier manipulation, as text blocks can be picked up and moved around on the screen. In other jobs, you may want a lengthy story divided into several text blocks that are linked, or *threaded* together.

4.10　The **text tool** (4.11) is used to type or edit text in PageMaker. Click on the **A** in the Toolbox to get the text tool; when you move off of the Toolbox, the cursor becomes the **I-beam** (pronounced eye-beam), as shown in 4.12.

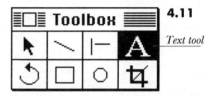

4.11

Text tool

4.12
Text tool cursor: the I-beam
The little crossbar indicates
the baseline (1.57) of the text.

4.13　This I-beam cursor is indicating that you are now in the typing mode—*it is just a pointer,* like any other cursor; it is not the I-beam that tells you where the type will begin.

4.14　When you have the I-beam and click the mouse button once, it sets down a flashing **insertion point.** It is the insertion point that allows you to type. It looks like this: | 　but it flashes.

Watch that insertion point!

4.15   As you type, the text will *begin* at the insertion point, and the insertion point will move along with the characters. If you press the Backspace/Delete key, the insertion point will backspace (and thus delete text) from wherever it is. PageMaker uses the standard Macintosh wordprocessing techniques, so most of this is probably already familiar to you.

4.16   To move the insertion point to another place in the text in order to edit or to start new text, simply use the mouse to position the I-beam where you want to type, and **click once.** The insertion point will move to wherever you click. (You can then move the *I-beam* out of the way, since it has served its purpose.)

4.17   You can also use the arrow keys to move the insertion point. The arrow keys, used in combination with the Shift, Option, and Command keys, can be used to *select* portions of text for editing (4.204; 1.328). The numeric keypad can also function as arrow keys and for selecting text, as well as for typing numbers (1.324–1.327).

4.18   When you click inside a text block, the insertion point lands right where you clicked, unless you clicked in the space at the end of a paragraph or between tabs, in which case it jumps over to the last character in that row.

Note: If you try to click or select text and the insertion point acts funny and won't go where you want it to, there is probably an invisible text block on top of the one you want. See 1.214–1.215 for finding and removing it.

If the insertion point is set, but nothing seems to happen when you type, check to be sure the Control palette is not active. If it is, you are typing commands to it rather than in the document. Click anywhere in the document to deactivate the Control palette (see 3.20).

4.19   When you click *within* the margins on the page, but *not* inside any existing text block, the insertion point will jump to the nearest left column guide (even if *you* think you have no columns on the page— PageMaker always provides at least one column; see 1.79).

If the insertion point does not align on the left when you click, it probably has a *default setting* of either a paragraph indent *or* a centered alignment (4.27). You can reset the default (4.20– 4.23) *or* you can just reset the specs for the moment.

Also see the note in 4.18.

Formatting the insertion point

4.20   When you set the insertion point to begin a *new* text block, it will type with the *defaults* that have been chosen (1.6–1.11). You can check to see what the defaults are:

- Click once on the **pointer tool,** even if it is already selected.
- From the Type menu, press on "Style" (not "Type style"!).
- The "Style" submenu should have a checkmark next to *"No style."* (If there is a checkmark next to anything else, see 4.21).
- Now check out any of the other submenus from the Type menu. Anything that has a checkmark next to it, plus all the specifications in every dialog box, is what PageMaker is using for defaults; that is, that's what the insertion point is automatically formatted with for typing.
- Text you *place* will be formatted with the checked specifications if you choose not to "Retain format" (4.56).
- You can change the defaults whenever you like (see 1.6–1.18 and 4.360–4.366).

4.21   Now if, when you checked the "Style" submenu, there was a checkmark next to any other style than *"No style,"* then *that style* is the default (see Section 8 on Style Sheets). You will type with *those* specifications, and when you place text without retaining the format or reading tags (4.56), it will pour in with those specifications.

To change the Style default to "No style," first click once on the pointer tool. Then choose "No style" from the Style submenu.

4.22   You can also check to see what the defaults are through the Control palette. When the text tool is chosen but there is no insertion point in the text, the Control palette displays the default settings for text. You can change the defaults here too, as long as you make sure the insertion point is not flashing within text (4.366).

4.23   Anytime the insertion point is inserted into existing text, it picks up the formatting *from the character to its left* (unless it is before the first character in a paragraph; then it takes the formatting of the first character). This means it will type in whatever font, style, size, alignment, paragraph specs, style name, etc. of that left character, even if that left character is a blank space! (Blank spaces are formatted just like characters.) Pressing Return pushes the insertion point along, and the insertion point carries all that formatting along with it.

4.24   Now, while that insertion point is *flashing* (whether it is in existing text or beginning a new text block), if you go to any of the menus or the Control palette and change the formatting (specifications), the new formatting *will be poured into the insertion point,* and you will type with those new specifications. You are not setting a default in this case—you are **loading the insertion point.** *If you click anywhere else,* the insertion point again picks up the formatting from the character to its left, or from the existing defaults.

If you want to do this:

Then follow these steps:

Shortcuts ▾ Notes ▾ Hints

4.25 Type onto the page

- Choose the **text tool** (the **A**); the cursor will turn into the **I-beam** when you move away from the Toolbox.
- With the **I-beam,** point to where you want your text to begin; click the mouse to set down a flashing insertion point.
- While it is flashing, simply type.

- If you click on the page outside of any existing text block, the insertion point will jump to the nearest column guide. So, if you click and don't see the insertion point, you may need to move your page over so the column guide is visible.
- If you click outside of any column guides, the insertion point will stay where you click (unless it is not left-aligned; 4.19; 4.27).

4.26 Restrain the size of the text block
*(create a **bounding box** to type in so the handles don't run across the whole page)*

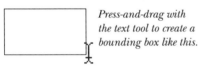

Press-and-drag with the text tool to create a bounding box like this.

When you let go, the box becomes invisible, but it's still there; the insertion point waits.

This text has been typed into an invisible bounding box. The depth will expand as you type, but not the width.

As you type or paste text, it will fill the bounding box.

- Choose the **text tool** from the Toolbox.
- Outside of any existing text block, *point* to where you want the text to begin.
- Press-and-drag in any direction; this will create a rectangle on the screen. Draw the rectangle the length of the line you need. When you let go of the mouse button, this rectangle will disappear, but the invisible form of it is still there! The insertion point will be flashing in the upper left of the invisible box.
- Type your text; it will fit into the line length of the rectangle you created. The depth will increase or decrease as necessary.

- When you click the I-beam outside of any column guides (such as outside the margin boundary or anywhere on the pasteboard), you create a text block that is the width of your margins. This means the handles go shooting across the screen and can be hard to find, sometimes causing problems. Creating a bounding box solves these.
- If the insertion point does not flash in the upper left of the bounding box (and you want it to do so), see 4.27.
- Creating a bounding box is definitely the best way to create text on the page and control the line length (and thus the handles) of the text block!

If you want to do this:	**Then follow these steps:**	**Shortcuts ▾ Notes ▾ Hints**

4.27 Make the insertion point align on the left

Indents:

Left	0	picas
First	1.5	picas
Right	0	picas

The 1.5 entered in the "First" edit box indicates that the first line of each paragraph will be indented 1.5 picas.

Alignment: ✓Left / Center / Right / Justify / Force justify

The alignment also determines where the insertion point flashes.

- With the **insertion point flashing,** from the Type menu choose "Paragraph...."
- In the "Paragraph specifications" dialog box, look under "Indents" at the box next to "First."
- If "First" has any number other than 0 (zero), then change that number to 0 (zero, not the letter O).
- Also check the "Alignment" box; if it says anything besides "Left" in that little box, press on the box to get the pop-up menu. Choose "Left" as the alignment.

- Of course, these directions will also apply if you want to make the insertion point align on the right, or centered, or any other way: instead of choosing "Left," choose the alignment of your choice (4.243–4.248). And instead of typing 0 in the First-line indent box (4.323), type the number of your choice.
- If you follow these directions *while the insertion point is flashing*, you will change the specifications for just this one time. If you want to change the specs more permanently, like every time you start a new text block, then choose the pointer tool before you follow these directions. This ensures there is *no insertion point flashing*. What you are actually doing, then, is setting a new *publication default* (4.360–4.364. 4.366).
- You can also set paragraph indents and alignment through the paragraph-view Control palette, see 4.300.

L*etters are beautiful in themselves.*
 Just like the faces of human beings,
some letters are intricately complex
while others are blank and simple.

—Kiyoshi Awazu

Placing text into PageMaker

4.28 This subsection deals with **placing text** into PageMaker that has been created in an outside word processor (such as Microsoft Word or Works, MacWrite, WriteNow, FullWrite, etc.). For information on placing text that you created in PageMaker's own Story Editor, see Section 9 (9.83). For info on placing stories from another PageMaker publication, see the subsection immediately following this one (4.63–4.86).

4.29 Placing text that has been created elsewhere is one of PageMaker's specialties. Rather than typing a lot of text directly on the page in PageMaker, type it into your word processor where you can edit, spell-check, and proof. Don't bother to format anything; don't space twice between paragraphs; don't spec headlines or captions; don't set up and indent—just type in straight text (of course hitting Return for each new paragraph). Then it is much more efficient to drop your text into PageMaker and use style sheets (Section 8) to format everything. (Style sheets are the most valuable feature in PageMaker. You really must spend the time to learn to use them.)

4.30 Use your word processor (or the Story Editor) for what it does best—word processing. Use PageMaker for what it does best—page layout and text formatting. For this reason, it is not necessary to use a high-powered word-processing application (you don't need a helicopter to cross the street). If you are placing the text into PageMaker, a lot of the high-end word processing power is wasted—the multiple columns, headers and footers, indexing, outlining, tables of contents, etc., from an outside word processor cannot be used by PageMaker. You don't even need to waste your time setting up style sheets in the word processor, since PageMaker can read simple little tags you set (4.38–4.41; 4.60) and automatically style the finished product to your specifications with PageMaker's own style sheets.

4.31 When you place a file, PageMaker calls that file a **story.** The story is the *entire file*, which you may break up into as many separate *text blocks* (4.102–4.113) as necessary. It is important to remember this distinction between a story and a text block.

4.32 Be sure to read the following subsection that goes hand-in-hand with placing text: **Text Flow** (4.87–4.94). Text flow controls how the text is poured onto the page—whether it just keeps pouring until it's finished, whether it stops and waits for you to tell it what to do next, or whether it stops and loads itself back up again. Oh, it's great to be in control.

The Options for placing text

4.33   When you place text that has been created in an outside word processor, you have three options of how that text will format when it pours into PageMaker. You can:

- Retain the format
- Ignore the format
- Read the tags

4.34   When you **retain the format,** PageMaker will hold most of the specifications you set up *in the original file,* but not all:

- Most character formatting will hold, such as font (if that font is in the System that is running PageMaker), type size, type style, paragraph spacing, alignment, etc. Style sheets will be imported too.
- Tabs, indents, and returns are always held, and their ruler placement in PageMaker will match the original's.
- Line lengths will always adjust to the columns in PageMaker.
- Some formatting—such as multiple columns, headers and footers, hidden text, page numbers—are ignored.
- Footnotes from the word processing application will appear at the end of the story in PageMaker.

Basically, any kind of formatting that PageMaker can't do, it will not recognize.

4.35   When you **ignore the format** (which is simply choosing *not* to "Retain format"; 4.56), PageMaker will ignore *any formatting you applied when you created the file in your word processor* (except tabs, indents, and returns—you usually can't get rid of those). The file will be placed into PageMaker following the *default type specifications.* Please read 4.20–4.22 for an explanation of how to find out what the current defaults are.

4.36   Take note of the fact that the specifications are actually taken from the *Style* (as in Style Sheets; Section 8). Typically, the default style is "No style," *but you can set the default to any style you choose.* For instance, if you have set up a style sheet and want the files you place to pour in as your defined "Body text," then set "Body text" as your publication default (simply by using the *pointer tool* to choose "Body text" from the "Style" submenu in the Type menu). Then you won't have to select the text later to apply the style. Again, you really should read 4.20–4.22.

4.37   Tabs and indents from the original file will align themselves to the default tabs and indents in PageMaker, which may not be at all what you want. To prevent insanity, be sure to read Section 6 on Indents and Tabs.

4.38   **Reading tags** works hand-in-hand with Style Sheets (Section 8), so this will probably make more sense if you understand that great feature of PageMaker. Be sure to read Section 8 for a detailed explanation of style sheets, as well as directions on how to create tags (8.75). Briefly, what it will do for you is this:

4.39   In your word processor (or in the Story Editor in a slightly different fashion; see 8.74) you can type *tags.* Tags look like this: **<style name>**. Those are just angle brackets, found above the comma and the period. Between the angle brackets is the name of the style from your style sheet that you want to apply to that paragraph. After you type the tag, type the paragraph. Every time you change the style of a paragraph, you type a new tag in front of it.

4.40   When you place a file with tags into PageMaker and choose "Read tags" (4.52), PageMaker will read the tag, *eliminate it from the text,* and apply the formatting you specified for that style. It's really incredible.

4.41   Be sure to read Scenarios #9 and #10 (8.79–8.81) on using tags and style sheets in your publication!

4.42 The "Place..." dialog box for text *(from the File menu, choose "Place...")*

4.43 *This **label** indicates which folder or which disk you are viewing the contents of.*

4.44 *Click here to go directly to the desktop level to open any other disks or files stored there.*

4.45 *If you are viewing a floppy disk and it doesn't contain what you need, click here to eject it so you can insert another.*

4.46 *The **list box** shows the documents contained in the folder or on the disk named in the label (4.43).*

4.47 *If the icon looks like a little page, you can place it by double-clicking on it.*

4.48 *If the icon looks like a folder, it indicates there may be a file inside that you can place. Double-click on a folder to open it and view the contents.*

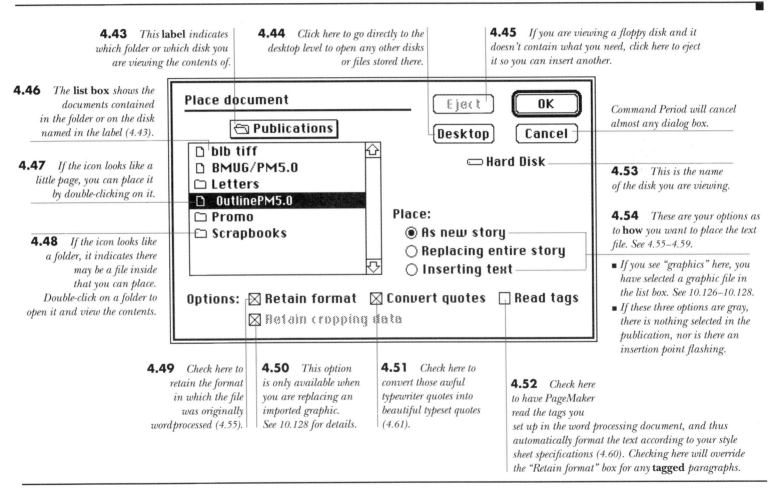

Command Period will cancel almost any dialog box.

4.53 *This is the name of the disk you are viewing.*

4.54 *These are your options as to **how** you want to place the text file. See 4.55–4.59.*

■ *If you see "graphics" here, you have selected a graphic file in the list box. See 10.126–10.128.*

■ *If these three options are gray, there is nothing selected in the publication, nor is there an insertion point flashing.*

4.49 *Check here to retain the format in which the file was originally wordprocessed (4.55).*

4.50 *This option is only available when you are replacing an imported graphic. See 10.128 for details.*

4.51 *Check here to convert those awful typewriter quotes into beautiful typeset quotes (4.61).*

4.52 *Check here to have PageMaker read the tags you set up in the word processing document, and thus automatically format the text according to your style sheet specifications (4.60). Checking here will override the "Retain format" box for any **tagged** paragraphs.*

If you want to do this:

4.55 Place text *as a new story* while *retaining* the format of the original document

Then follow these steps:

- From the File menu choose "Place…," *or* press Command D.
- In the list box (4.46), find the name of the document you wish to place into PageMaker (you may need to switch drives [4.44] or open folders [4.48] to find it).
- Click *once* on the name of the file you want to place.
- There should be an X in the "Retain format" checkbox (4.49); if there isn't, click once on it to put one there.
- If the document was typed using typewriter quotation marks instead of real quote marks (4.61), then by all means make sure "Convert quotes" has a check in it (4.51).
- "Read tags" (4.52) should *not* have a check.
- To place the selected file *as a new story* make sure the button "As new story" is chosen. (If you want to *replace an entire story,* see 4.57; for *inserting text* or to *replace a portion* of a story, see 4.58–4.59.)
- Now, either click the OK button *or* double-click on the name of the file you wish to place.

—continued

Shortcuts ▾ Notes ▾ Hints

- Be sure to read 4.33–4.37 for a discussion on exactly what it means to retain the format. Basically, you are asking PageMaker to retain the same type specifications you used when you originally typed the document.
- If the text has styles (as in style sheets), applied to it, PageMaker will import the styles and add them to your style palette. An imported style has an asterisk next to its name in the style palette. If an imported style has the same name as an existing PageMaker style, the imported style is dropped, and the text takes on the formatting of the PageMaker style.

If you want to do this:	Then follow these steps:	Shortcuts ▾ Notes ▾ Hints
—continued ▣ *The manual flow icon* ▣ *The semi-autoflow icon* ▣ *The autoflow icon*	▪ PageMaker will take you back to your publication and you will have a new pointer—a *loaded text icon* (see left; read 4.87–4.94 for more info about autoflow, semi-autoflow, and manual flow). ▪ Position the loaded text icon where you want the type to begin. ▪ Click once to pour the text onto the page.	▪ Be sure to read 4.90–4.92 about the important differences between manual flow, semi-autoflow, and autoflow before you start to pour text. ▪ If the loaded text icon is positioned inside a column when you click, the text will flow to that column width. ▪ If the loaded text icon is *not* positioned inside a column when you click, the text will create a text block for itself that will be the width of your page margins. ▪ If you want to control the space that the text occupies as you place it, see 4.62.
4.56 Place text *as a new story* **without** retaining the format of the original document	▪ Follow the steps in 4.55 above, but this time make sure the checkbox for "Retain format" (4.49) has **no** check in it (if it does, click once on it to remove it).	▪ *Without* retaining the format, the text will flow in with the specifications of the style that has been chosen from the *style sheet* (Section 8 on Style Sheets). To see which style is chosen: ▫ Click once on the pointer tool. From the Type menu, press "Style" (not "Type style") to get the submenu. ▫ If the style selected is *"No style,"* then the placed text will flow in with the *default* type specs. Please read 4.20–4.21 and 4.35–4.37 for a more detailed explanation of default style sheets.

If you want to do this:	**Then follow these steps:**	**Shortcuts ▾ Notes ▾ Hints**

4.57 Replace an entire story

- With the **pointer tool,** click once on the text block of the story you want to replace; **or** with the **text tool,** click once anywhere in the text to set the insertion point in the story.
- From the File menu choose "Place...," *or* press Command D.
- Locate the file you want to place; click once on the name of it to select it.
- Click in the button "Replacing entire story" (4.54).
- Click OK, **or** double-click on the name of the file to be placed and it shall be done.

- If the "Replacing entire story" button is gray, it's indicating that a story has not been selected. Go back and make sure you did the first step.
- If the story consists of more than one text block, you need to select only *one* block or set the insertion point into *one.* Either method will tell PageMaker to replace the *entire story,* even if it consists of many separate text blocks spanning several pages.
- The text blocks that are being replaced will stay the same size, *except* the last one which will shrink if the new story is shorter, or grow deeper if it's longer.

4.58 *Insert* placed text into a story that is already on the page

- With the **text tool,** click once in the story in the exact spot where you want the text to *begin* inserting. *See the note to the right.* ☛
- From the File menu choose "Place...," *or* press Command D.
- Locate the file you wish to insert and click *once* on it.
- Click on the button "Inserting text" (4.54).
- Click OK, *or* double-click on the name of the file to be inserted and it shall be done.

- If the "Inserting text" button is gray, either (1) there is no insertion point flashing or text selected (4.203–4.204) on the page; go back and do the first step; **or** (2) the file you selected in the list box is not a text file; if you see the word "graphic" in the other buttons, you have selected a graphic file; **or** (3) if *all* the buttons are gray, the file you have selected to place is not place-able in PageMaker, e.g., you cannot place a folder.
- The text will be *inserted* at the spot where the insertion point is flashing. If you are

—*continued*

If you want to do this:

4.59 *Replace a portion* of an existing story

Place:
○ **As new story**
○ **Replacing entire story**
◉ **Replacing selected text**

When you choose to replace a portion of a story, new "Place" options appear in the Place dialog box.

In the fields
of printing
and graphic design
it is generally agreed that
the poet in our midst is the type designer.
—Noel Martin

Then follow these steps:

- With the **text tool,** press-and drag to select the text you wish to *replace* with another file. *See the notes to the right.*
- From the File menu choose "Place...," *or* press Command D.
- Locate the file you wish to replace the selected text with and click *once* on it.
- From the new "Place" options that appear, click on the button "Replacing selected text."
- Click OK, *or* double-click on the name of the file to be inserted and it shall be done.

Shortcuts ▾ Notes ▾ Hints

(—continued)
replacing text (4.59), just the portion that is selected will be *replaced*. All the following text will just thread its way through the text block(s).

- If the insertion point or selected text is *inside* a paragraph, the new text will take on that paragraph's formatting, no matter how the new text was originally set.
- If the insertion point is *in its own* paragraph (meaning you hit a Return and it is flashing on its own line), or if you selected an entire paragraph to *replace,* you can choose to retain the format, read the tags, or let it come in with PageMaker's text defaults, just as when placing any story (page 172). The only difference is that, if you choose *not* to retain the format, the text will always default to "No style," *not* to the style sheet name you set as your style default (4.36).
- Inserting or replacing text this way is *not* Undo-able; that is, you cannot go to the Edit menu and choose "Undo edit." You can, of course, undo it yourself with the standard word processing functions, like cut, copy, delete, etc.

If you want to do this:	Then follow these steps:	Shortcuts ▾ Notes ▾ Hints

4.60 Place text and have PageMaker *read the tags*

- If you are going to *insert* or *replace* text, then either set the insertion point where you want the text inserted, or select the text you want to replace. If you are going to place it as a *new story,* click once on the text tool or the pointer tool to make sure there is no insertion point lying around anywhere.
- From the File menu choose "Place...," *or* press Command D.
- In the list box (4.46), click once on the text file name you wish to place (you may need to switch drives [4.44] or open folders [4.48] to locate the file you want).
- Choose your option (4.55–4.59) to place the text as a new story, as inserted text, replacing a story, or replacing selected text.
- If the checkbox for "Retain format" is checked, "Read tags" will override it, so it doesn't matter if you switch it off or not.
- Of course "Convert quotes" (4.51) should be checked if real quotes or dashes were not used in the original.
- **Put a check in "Read tags"** (4.52).
- Click OK, *or* double-click on the name of the file to be placed; PageMaker will read the tags, eliminate them, and place the text with the formatting you previously specified in your style sheet. Wow.

- Imagine, you just buzz along in your word processor, not formatting anything, just typing in a few tags. Drop it into PageMaker and bingo—all heads are fomatted, body copy is set, charts are tabbed and indented, captions are small and italicized, etc. etc. etc.
- Be sure to read Section 8 on Style Sheets, especially Scenarios #9 and #10 (8.79–8.81) to get a good grip on how to take advantage of this. You will find a very brief explanation in 4.38–4.41.
- You can ask PageMaker to read the tags when you place a file as a new story, as well as when you insert or replace text. But:
  - When you insert or replace text *into an existing paragraph,* the new text will become part of the existing style— it *will not* follow the tag specifications.
  - If you replace *an entire paragraph,* the new text *will* follow the tag specifications.
  - If you insert text *while the insertion point is flashing on its own line* (in its own paragraph), the new text *will* follow the tag specifications.

If you want to do this:

4.61 Convert typewriter quotes (")
to real quotes (" ")

"Scarlett"	"Scarlett"
'Scarlett'	'Scarlett'
Scarlett's	Scarlett's
--Scarlett	—Scarlett
3'4"	3'4"

Then follow these steps:

- You really must get in the habit of typing these in automatically (see 4.355–4.359). But if you didn't do it in the document you want to place, simply click the "Convert quotes" button (4.51) when you "Place...." This will convert all ugly (") marks to beautiful open and closed quotation marks (" and "). It will also convert this mark (') to a real apostrophe (') or to open and closed single quotation marks (' and '). A pair of double hyphens (--) will be converted to an em dash (—).

Shortcuts · Notes · Hints

- This option will only convert the quotation marks from a document that is being *placed* into PageMaker. If you typed the story into the Story Editor, you can "Find and Change" the marks (9.82).
- If you think it is too much trouble to "Find and Change" the marks, you can export the story (17.43) and place it back in, converting quotes along the way!
- The little chart on the left shows what the typewriter marks will transform into. Notice PageMaker is smart enough to leave real foot and inch marks after numbers.
- This is not a foolproof feature, so it is a good idea to double-check your marks. See 4.358 for the key commands for typing these, as well as other special characters.
- You can type real quotes using the keyboard's typewriter marks by setting the "Use Typographer's quotes" option in the "Preferences" dialog box. See 1.234.

179

If you want to do this:

Then follow these steps:

Shortcuts ▾ Notes ▾ Hints

4.62 Place text into a *bounding box* to hold it or to override column guides (**drag-place**)

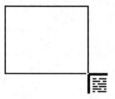

The bounding box created by drag-placing.

When you drag-place, the text stays just inside the bounding box; it doesn't expand. Extra text is

The text that has been drag-placed.

- Follow the steps in 4.55 to get a loaded text icon.
- When the loaded text icon appears, *don't click to place the text*—instead, **press-and-drag.** You will see a bounding box follow the loaded text icon as you drag it across the screen. When you let go, the text will be contained inside that space, even if autoflow is on.

- Great trick—be sure to get this one down! It's very handy for lots of things, such as:
  - ▫ Let's say you have three columns on your page. You want the line length of this new story to be two columns wide—just *drag-place* the text across the two columns. Make the bounding box the size you want the text to fill.
  - ▫ Let's say you are creating a newsletter and you want to have all the stories at hand to puzzle them together. *Drag-place* them all, one at a time, onto the pasteboard, creating a bounding box for each of them that is just big enough to see the first paragraph or so. Then, as you design the pages of the news-letter, you can just pull them in from the pasteboard. Even though you see just a paragraph, the text block holds the entire story.
- Also see 4.26 for using the I-beam to create a bounding box you can type into.

Placing PageMaker files into PageMaker

4.63 You can import stories from other PageMaker 5 publications or from Page-Maker 4 publications using the Story Importer. (If you want to place stories from a PageMaker 3 file, you will first need to convert it into a PageMaker 4 file; see 17.46). The Story Importer, which operates from the "Place..." command in the File menu, is an alternative to opening multiple publications. If you need a PageMaker 4 story but don't want to convert the whole publication, you can use the Story Importer to work around it.

4.64 You can place *all* the stories from another publication, or you can choose just the ones you want. Whichever you choose, they will import as a single story with carriage returns between each original story.

4.65 Often a publication is full of tiny text block stories, such as those containing page numbers, headers, footers, callouts, or captions. The Story Importer allows you the option of filtering out these small ones.

4.66 It is also possible to *view* any story from any other PageMaker publication, copy the text to the Clipboard, and then paste it into PageMaker or any other

application. The on-line documentation does not recommend pasting directly into PageMaker this way because of limitations with the Story Importer, but I haven't had any problem with it yet.

4.67 The Story Importer is limited in its ability to import indices: cross-reference index entries and alternate sort strings cannot be imported, and the range of the index entries is always converted to "Current page" (see Section 15 for info on Indexing).

4.68 You cannot import inline graphics (10.125). You can import rotated text, but it will no longer be rotated when placed.

4.69 If you have the PANOSE typeface matching feature on (1.240–1.266), it will offer substitutions for fonts that are used in the imported stories but that are not currently available in the System. Depending on how you have PANOSE set up, it will either automatically substitute fonts, or offer you the chance to approve or change the suggested substitutions (1.267).

4.70 The Story Importer has a good on-line Help file. See 4.78 for Help.

4.71 Important note: To use this feature, you need to have installed the Story Importer Filter when you originally installed PageMaker 5.0. If not, you will need to go back and install it (see 17.29).

4.72 If you don't know whether the Story Importer Filter is installed or not, you can find out right now:

- Hold down the Command key.
- From the Apple menu, choose "About PageMaker®..." to see the list of installed import and export filters. The Story Importer filters are: Ver. 2.0 PageMaker 5.0 (publication), and Ver. 1.0 PageMaker 4 (publication).

Or you can also check this way:
- From the File menu choose "Place...."
- In the list box (4.46), see if you can locate the name of another PageMaker file.
- If the name of the file shows up, then you have the Filter installed.
- Click Cancel.

4.73 The "Story Importer" dialog box

(from the File menu, choose "Place…"; double-click the name of another PageMaker publication; see 4.71)

4.74 *Click "Select all" to select all the stories in the list box to place (see 4.82).*

4.75 *Press Return or Enter to shortcut OK.*

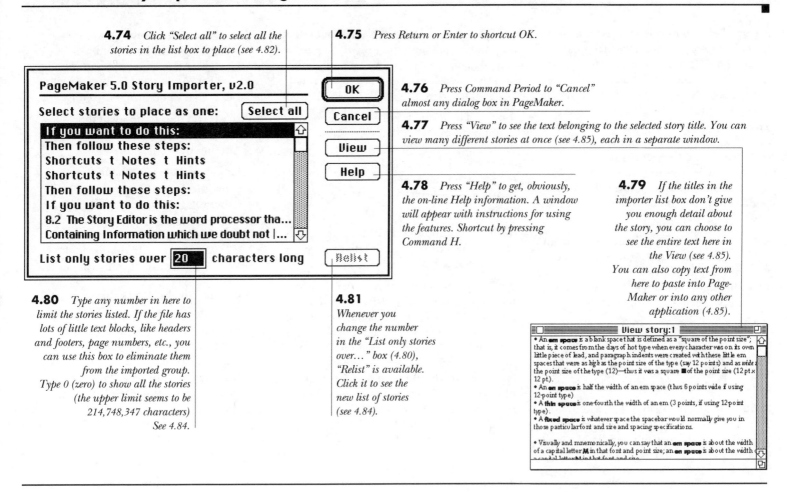

PageMaker 5.0 Story Importer, v2.0

Select stories to place as one: Select all

> If you want to do this:
> Then follow these steps:
> Shortcuts t Notes t Hints
> Shortcuts t Notes t Hints
> Then follow these steps:
> If you want to do this:
> 8.2 The Story Editor is the word processor tha…
> Containing Information which we doubt not |…

List only stories over **20** characters long

OK
Cancel
View
Help
Relist

4.76 *Press Command Period to "Cancel" almost any dialog box in PageMaker.*

4.77 *Press "View" to see the text belonging to the selected story title. You can view many different stories at once (see 4.85), each in a separate window.*

4.78 *Press "Help" to get, obviously, the on-line Help information. A window will appear with instructions for using the features. Shortcut by pressing Command H.*

4.79 *If the titles in the importer list box don't give you enough detail about the story, you can choose to see the entire text here in the View (see 4.85). You can also copy text from here to paste into Page-Maker or into any other application (4.85).*

4.80 *Type any number in here to limit the stories listed. If the file has lots of little text blocks, like headers and footers, page numbers, etc., you can use this box to eliminate them from the imported group. Type 0 (zero) to show all the stories (the upper limit seems to be 214,748,347 characters) See 4.84.*

4.81 *Whenever you change the number in the "List only stories over…" box (4.80), "Relist" is available. Click it to see the new list of stories (see 4.84).*

View story:1

• An em space is a blank space that is defined as a "square of the point size"; that is, it comes from the days of hot type when every character was on its own little piece of lead, and paragraph indents were created with these little em spaces that were as *high* as the point size of the type (say 12 points) and as *wide* the point size of the type (12)—thus it was a square ▪ of the point size (12 pt x 12 pt).
• An **en space** is half the width of an em space (thus 6 points wide if using 12-point type)
• A **thin space** is one-fourth the width of an em (3 points, if using 12-point type).
• A **fixed space** is whatever space the spacebar would normally give you in those particular font and size and spacing specifications.

• Visually and mnemonically, you can say that an **em space** is about the width of a capital letter **M** in that font and point size; an **en space** is about the width

If you want to do this:

4.82 Place (import) an *entire* PageMaker file

Then follow these steps:

- If you are going to *insert* the file into existing text (4.58), *replace a portion* of existing text (4.59), *replace an entire story* (4.57), or place it *as a new story* (4.55–4.56), see the respective task for specifics on where the insertion point should be or how the text should be selected.
- From the File menu choose "Place...."
- Locate the name of the PageMaker file you wish to place (you cannot place any files from the currently open publication).
- In the list box (4.46), click once on the name of the file.
- Choose your options: whether you want to *retain the format* (4.34), *convert quotes* (4.61), or *read tags* (4.38–4.41; 4.60).
- Choose whether you are inserting text, replacing text, or placing a new story, depending on what you did in the first step.
- Click OK, *or* double-click on the file name.
- You should see the Story Importer dialog box, as shown on page 182. Click once in the "Select all" button (see 4.74).
- Click OK, *or* press Return or Enter.
- Depending on whether you are placing a new story or inserting or replacing text, you will either get a loaded text icon to place (4.88–4.92) or the text will automatically insert or replace.

Shortcuts ▾ Notes ▾ Hints

- You can import other PageMaker 5 files and files from any version of PageMaker 4. (the Story Editor dialog box will be titled "PageMaker 4.0–4.2 Story Importer, v.1.02" when you are importing from PageMaker4). To import a PageMaker 3 publication, you must first convert it to a PageMaker 4 file; see 17.42.
- You can treat an imported PageMaker file just as you do any other file you place; i.e., you can insert text, replace text, retain the format, read tags, etc., as detailed in the subsection on "Placing text into PageMaker" (4.28–4.62).
- All the original stories will be imported as one story with carriage returns between each one.
- If the imported story uses fonts not currently in your System, and the PANOSE feature is on, a dialog box may open offering you various choices for font substitution. See 1.264–1.266.
- A shortcut for the "Select all" button is Command A.
- A shortcut to "Cancel" is Command Period. Actually, this great shortcut works on every "Cancel" button in PageMaker (except in the Indents/tabs ruler, and in some Additions).

If you want to do this:	Then follow these steps:	Shortcuts ▾ Notes ▾ Hints
4.83 Place *selected* stories from another PageMaker 5 publication, or a PageMaker 4 publication	■ Follow the steps in 4.82 until you see the Story Importer dialog box. ■ Select the story you want to place by clicking *once* on it. If you want to select more than one story, hold the Shift key down and click once on each story, or press-and-drag down to select sequential stories. ■ If you select a story, then change your mind, you can deselect just that one story by holding the Shift key down and clicking once more on it. ■ When they are all selected, click OK, *or* hit the Return or Enter key. ■ Depending on whether you are placing a new story or inserting or replacing text, you will either get a loaded text icon for placing (4.88–4.92), or the text will insert or replace as you specified in the first step.	■ You can import PageMaker 4 or 5 files. To import a PageMaker 3 publication, you must first convert it to a PageMaker 4 file; see 17.42. ■ The Story Importer dialog box will be titled "PageMaker 4.0–4.2" or "PageMaker 5.0" according to the file you are importing. ■ If you are going to import only one story, you can quickly shortcut by double-clicking on the story name. ■ If you change your mind and want *all* the stories, click on the "Select all" button, *or* press Command A.
4.84 Limit the display of story titles in the list box to just those stories that are greater than a certain number of characters	■ Follow the steps in 4.82 until you see the Story Importer dialog box. ■ In the "List only stories over ___ characters long" box (4.80), type in a number (anything between 0 and 200 million!). Only those stories with more than that number of characters will be displayed ■ The "Relist" button (4.81) will now be active; click on it, *or* press Return or Enter.	■ This feature enables you to eliminate all those tiny little stories that just contain page numbers or captions or call outs, etc. ■ The list shows only the first few words of the story. If you need more, you can View any number of them (4.85). ■ Any story not displayed in the list will not be imported, even if "Select all" is chosen.

If you want to do this:	**Then follow these steps:**	**Shortcuts ▾ Notes ▾ Hints**
4.85 View any story	■ Follow the steps in 4.82 until you see the Story Importer dialog box. ■ Select any number of stories. ■ Click the button "View," *or* press Command V; you will see a view window for each selected story. ■ If you have more than one view window on your screen, they will be in layers. Click on any layer to bring it to the front. ■ Click in the close box (upper left, in the title bar) of each view window to close it, *or* press Command W.	■ The View displays the stories using the original font (if the font is installed in the Macintosh System), type size, type style, and carriage returns. Other attributes such as alignment, indents, etc., are not shown. ■ This View feature is very handy if the title in the list box is not enough for you to identify the story. ■ You can copy text from the View to paste into any other application. Simply press-and-drag to select the text, and press Command C to copy it to the Clipboard.
4.86 Drag-and-drop text between PageMaker 5 publications	■ Open the number of publications you need, and from the Window menu, choose "Tile." ■ Click on the publication to which you are dragging the text. ■ Select the **pointer tool** if you want the text to drag in as its own *text block;* **or** select the **text tool** and set the insertion point where you want the text to copy *inline;* or highlight the text you want to *replace* with the text you are dragging in. ■ Click on the window of the publication that contains the text you want to copy. ■ With the pointer tool, press-and-drag the text block to the other publication. Let go of the mouse when you can see the text block in the new window.	■ At first it will look as if the original text block is moving off the page for good. But when you let go of the mouse you will see that the original is right where it belongs and just a copy of it has moved. ■ Text blocks dragged to a publication bring all their attributes with them including style sheets and color. However, text dragged inline will take on the formatting of the paragraph in which it is placed; text replacing selected text does the same thing. ■ The publication from which you copied the text remains active.

185

Text flow

4.87 In PageMaker you have several options of how you can physically put, or **flow,** the text on the page:

> **manual flow;**
> **semi-autoflow,** and
> **autoflow.**

4.88 When you choose "Place..." from the File menu to place a new story in your publication, the cursor shows a **loaded text icon.** When you click once with this icon anywhere in your publication, the text *flows* onto the page. (Even though your icon is loaded, you can still use the menu, the scroll bars, the rulers, and turn the pages.)

4.89 The three different icons:

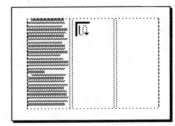 *The manual flow icon*

The semi-autoflow icon

The autoflow icon

4.90 If you use **manual flow,** when you click the mouse the text will flow onto the page until it runs out or hits the bottom margin or a graphic. Then it stops. If there is more text to be placed, a solid, down-pointing arrow will appear in the bottom windowshade loop of the text block (4.109). You must *manually reload the text icon* (by clicking once, lightly, on the arrow) in order to place the rest of the story (4.95).

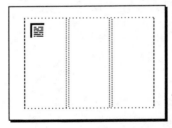

The manual flow icon loaded with text.

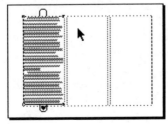

After clicking with manual flow, the arrow symbol in the bottom windowshade loop holds any extra text.

4.91 If you use **semi-autoflow,** when you click the mouse the text will flow onto the page just as in manual flow, but this time, when it bumps into the bottom margin or a graphic, *the pointer automatically loads with the rest of the text.* (Remember, in manual flow you had to manually reload.) In order to flow the rest of the text in semi-autoflow, you still must point-and-click somewhere to continue pouring the text onto the page (4.96).

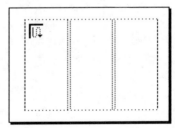

The semi-autoflow icon loaded with text.

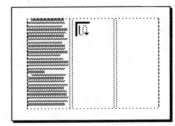

After clicking with semi-autoflow, the icon automatically loads extra text, ready for placing.

Text flow *—continued*

4.92 If you use **autoflow,** when you click the mouse the text will flow onto the page (4.97); when it hits the bottom margin *the text will automatically begin flowing again at the top of the next text column.* If you run out of pages, PageMaker will create more pages for you and continue placing the text. If there are graphics in the way, autoflow will jump over or around them as you have specified in text wrapping (Section 13).

4.93 Autoflow is particularly handy in combination with *reading tags* (4.60; 9.73–9.75): in your word processor, type your document with tags, set up your PageMaker publication with pages and margins and wrapped graphics, and place the document with autoflow—as it pours into the publication, the text formats itself into heads and subheads and body text and pull quotes and wraps itself around graphics just as you previously specified. Tighten up the details and it's done! Magic.

4.94 You'll find yourself using different methods of flow as you work, depending on what you are doing at any particular moment. PageMaker thoughtfully provides keyboard shortcuts so you can switch instantly from one method to another at any time, no matter what the default happens to be (4.98).

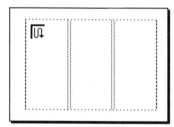

The autoflow icon loaded with text.

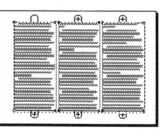

After clicking with autoflow, extra text is poured onto the page in a never-ending stream. Press Command Period to stop the flow.

If you want to do this:

Then follow these steps:

Shortcuts ▾ Notes ▾ Hints

4.95 Place text from a file, **or** place the rest of an existing text block, **using manual flow**

 manual flow icon

*The arrow in the windowshade loop indicates there is more text to that story and that it **is not** threaded into any other text block (4.107–4.110).*

*The + in the windowshade loop indicates there is more text to that story and that it **is** threaded into another text block (4.107–4.110).*

- In the Layout menu, make sure "Autoflow" has no checkmark next to it; if it does, choose it once more to take the checkmark off.
- Follow the steps in 4.55. In your publication, the cursor will become a loaded text icon for placing (see left).
- On the page, click once where you want the text to begin; it will pour itself in.
- If the text bumps into something before it is all placed, such as the bottom margin or a graphic, it will stop and you will see an arrow in a little windowshade loop at the bottom of the text block (see 4.102–4.113 if you need more info on text blocks).
- To pick up the rest of the text manually, position the tip of the pointer on the arrow in the bottom windowshade loop; click *once* quickly and lightly. You will see the loaded text icon again.
- Repeat the previous three steps to place the rest of the text.

- Of course, you can pick up text from any existing text block that shows an arrow or a plus sign in its bottom windowshade loop (with the **pointer tool,** click once on the text itself to see its windowshades—see 4.102–4.113 for more info on text blocks). Picking up extra text this way will give you the same loaded text icon for manual placement.
- An empty loop at the bottom of the windowshade indicates there is no more text to be placed—it's all there.
- Be sure to read the subsection on "Placing text into PageMaker" (4.28–4.62) to understand how the text will be formatted when it pours in.
- Be sure to read 4.98 for info on how to override autoflow or manual flow whenever you feel like it, no matter what it says in the menu or which icon you see.

If you want to do this:	**Then follow these steps:**	**Shortcuts ▪ Notes ▪ Hints**
4.96 Use semi-auto text flow *semi-autoflow icon*	▪ Follow the steps in 4.55 to get the loaded text icon for placing, then: ▪ No matter whether you have a manual text icon or an autoflow text icon, **hold down the Shift key;** the cursor will change to a dotted snake with an arrow head. ▪ Click once to pour the text on the page; if the text hits the bottom margin or a graphic before the entire story is placed, it will stop and *automatically reload* the flow icon for further placement. ▪ Just click at the next point where you want to place more of the text, and keep repeating that sequence until the entire story is placed.	▪ Even if Autoflow is checked in the Layout menu, pressing the Shift key will override it and create semi-autoflow. ▪ You can let go of the Shift key at any time to return it to manual flow or autoflow— whichever it was to begin with.
4.97 Use autoflow *autoflow icon*	▪ From the Layout menu, check to see if "Autoflow" has a checkmark by it; if not, choose "Autoflow" to select it. ▪ Follow the steps in 4.55 to get the loaded text icon for placing, *but don't click yet.* ▪ In your publication, the cursor will show the *autoflow icon;* it looks like a snake with an arrow head (see left). ▪ Click where you want the text to begin. It will pour onto the page, filling column after column, turning pages itself, and even creating more pages if there aren't enough. **To stop, press Command Period.**	▪ **To stop autoflow, press Command Period.** ▪ Autoflow works whether you are placing text from the "Place..." dialog box or picking up extra text at the end of a text block (4.95). ▪ Autoflow will flow between the top and bottom margins and the columns. If you are placing graphic elements, such as rules (lines), be sure to either text wrap them (Section 13) or place them outside the actual margin guidelines; otherwise the text will flow right over them.

If you want to do this:	Then follow these steps:	Shortcuts ▾ Notes ▾ Hints

4.98 Override autoflow or manual flow	■ To temporarily place text **manually** when Autoflow is *on*, hold down the Command key.
	■ To temporarily **autoflow** text when Autoflow is *off*, hold down the Command key.
	■ To temporarily place text **semi-automatically** when *either* manual flow *or* Autoflow is on, hold down the Shift key.
		■ So the gist is this:
		  □ You will get the opposite of either manual flow or autoflow by pressing the Command key.
		  □ You will always get semi-autoflow by pressing the Shift key.
		■ Even while the cursor is showing a loaded text icon, you can go up to the Layout menu and check Autoflow on or off.

4.99 Stop autoflow	■ Press Command Period.	
4.100 Cancel the loaded text icon *without* placing the text	■ With the loaded text icon, click on any tool in the Toolbox.	■ Important trick! ■ This doesn't delete the text; it's still in the loaded windowshade waiting to be picked up again (see 4.95). ■ Warning: Don't roll an unthreaded text block (4.107) up all the way, however, and click on the Toolbox. All your text *will* disappear then and you will have to re-place it.
4.101 Place the text on the pasteboard until you are ready for it	■ With the loaded text icon, draw a small bounding box on the pasteboard. ■ When you're ready to place the text, roll it up completely, click on the loaded windowshade, and place it where you want to.	■ This is handy for when you realize you forgot to turn the page, or set up columns, or whenever you bring in a story before you are quite ready for it.

(continued from page 100)

JOHANNES GUTENBERG ENDED UP HOMELESS IN THE street at the age of 56. Like any obsessive personality, he managed to find some way to carry on his printing in some manner, but he grew increasingly blind. Looking at tiny little pieces of lead all day isn't any better for your eyes than staring at a computer screen, it seems. He never did really get it together again; eventually a local bishop took pity on this destitute inventor and put him on welfare, providing him with a yearly allowance of grain, cloth, and wine. **B**ut what goes around comes around, doesn't it? Even though Fust took over and went on to become rich and to proclaim himself as the publisher of this history-making product, who do we remember? That's right, that impecunious blind old inventor who spent his life struggling for something he believed in. Fust isn't even in the dictionary. **D**evelopers took to the printing press like developers took to the Mac. In less than forty years there were more than a thousand presses operating all over Europe. By 1500 there were 150 presses in Venice alone! More than two million books had been printed. How many people were there in Europe in 1498, anyway? **I**t caught on quickly, but the technology didn't advance very rapidly. Until the early 1970s, everything you saw printed was created using Gutenberg's technique—tiny little movable pieces of lead type. The only significant advancement had been Otto Mergenthaler's Linotype machine in 1882—it could very noisily produce a whole line of type at a time, rather than one character at a time! Wow! **I**n the early '70s a revolution began in the graphic and type world with the advent of electronic type. (The New York Times was printed for the last time by linotype in 1979.) Now things are really moving fast. But, as on a roller coaster, the speed is exhilarating—who cares if you get a little dizzy? *– rw*

" No one can say today how electronics will affect printing. We cannot for the present foresee a complete suppression of book printing with individual movable metal types as discovered by Gutenberg."
Elizabeth Geck, 1968

a 20ᵗʰ century author, designer, typesetter, & publisher

Text blocks

4.102 PageMaker is an "object-oriented" program, which means that every object on the screen is its own little entity and is on its own layer (see 1.189–1.195 about layers). Even text is on a layer.

4.103 Text groups itself into **text blocks.** Every single piece of text, even if it is just one character, or reverse text, or even just blank space in the midst of a story, is in a text block, and each text block is on a separate layer.

4.104 You can see the outer dimensions of the block by clicking once on the text with the **pointer tool.** This shows you the **handles.** There is a handle in each of the four corners; by pressing-and-dragging on one of these handles, you can manipulate the text blocks in various ways—lengthen, shorten, widen, narrow, separate, etc.

4.105

This text is showing all its handles. Notice one in each of the four corners? They show up when you click on the text with the **pointer tool.** This text block is now **selected.**

Corner handle

4.106 At the top and bottom of each text block is a **windowshade loop.** These text boundary markers are called windowshades because they roll up and down just like windowshades. The top and bottom loops give you visual clues as to the text block's connection to other text blocks.

4.107 The **top windowshade loop** will either be empty or will have a plus sign (+) in it.

If the top loop is empty, it indicates that the *story* (4.113) *begins* with that text block.

If the top loop has a plus sign in it, it indicates that this text block is *threaded* (4.110–4.112) to a previous text block that contains more text from the same *story* (4.113).

4.108 If the text block contains the complete *story,* **or** if it contains the last section of a *story* (4.113), the **bottom windowshade loop** will be empty.

4.109 If there is more text than will fit into the current size of the text block, the **bottom windowshade loop** will show either a down-pointing arrow (▼) or a plus sign (+).

The down-pointing arrow indicates that there is more text in the *story* (4.113), but it is not placed into any text block.

The plus sign indicates that there is more text in the *story* (4.113), and it is contained in another text block that is *threaded* (4.110) to this one.

You can click once, lightly, on that ▼ or + symbol to pick up the rest of the text. Then if you click the loaded icon (4.88–4.89), the rest of the text will pour onto the page (4.95).

Text blocks   —*continued*

4.110 When text blocks are **threaded,** as mentioned in 4.107 and 4.109, the text is *connected* through them all, as if a piece of thread runs through every character. As type is edited, deleted, added, or changed in any way in any one text block, the rest of the connected blocks adjust their text accordingly. This will happen whether the threaded text blocks are on the same page or on various pages in the publication.

4.111

The plus sign in the windowshade loop above indicates that this text block is not the beginning of the story, but that it is threaded to a *previous* text block. The plus in the loop below indicates that it is also threaded to a *following* text block. Notice the bottom loop in the textblock in 4.105—it is empty, meaning "that's the end."

4.112 As the text blocks thread, they will not change size, so you needn't worry about your layout being interrupted when you edit —*except:* if changes are made that *decrease* the amount of text, the last text block will decrease in size or disappear, as necessary. If the amount of text *increases,* the last text block will expand to accommodate the extra text, unless you have specifically rolled it up (see 4.117).

4.113 It is important to understand the difference between a **text block** and a **story.** The term *story* is referring to the entire document that was placed or typed into PageMaker. Let's say, for instance, that in your word processor or the Story Editor you type seven separate newsletter articles. You place them into a PageMaker publication one at a time so you can manipulate them easily. Each one of these articles becomes a PageMaker *story.*

You can keep a story in *one text block,* or you may choose to break the story up into *several text blocks.* If there is more than one block, the story is *threaded,* or connected, through them all, even if they are on completely different pages.

A story, then, starts with a text block that has an empty *top* windowshade loop, and ends with the last threaded text block that has an empty *bottom* windowshade loop.

(Excuse me for throwing this drop-shadowed box in here, but I was experimenting. That box is made of two PageMaker boxes pasted inline, 1 point leading, "Keep with next 3 lines" applied. I adjusted the baseline to fit the text inside. Now if I edit text, or roll up or move the text block, that paragraph will always stay inside that box. I learned how to attach one box to text from Steve and Ole in Real World PageMaker, *then spent some time experimenting to get the drop shadow. Zero-point leading does not work.)*

If you want to do this:	**Then follow these steps:**	**Shortcuts ▾ Notes ▾ Hints**
4.114 Select a text block or several text blocks	■ Choose an appropriate page view (from the Layout menu) that will allow you to see the entire text block, or at least the top or bottom portion you need.	■ If you don't see handles, check to make sure the top or bottom edges of the text block are visible in that view.

Letters and characters are communication symbols on one hand, and attractive objects that stimulate sensitivity, on the other.
—*Takenobu Igarashi*

A selected text block shows handles and windowshade loops.

■ With the **pointer tool,** click once on the text whose block you wish to select. You should see handles on all four corners.
■ If you want to select **several** text blocks, hold the Shift key down while you click. To **de**select a block from the group, Shift-click it again.

■ If you still don't see handles on the text of your choice, reduce the page view (Command W); you will see handles *somewhere*—perhaps there is another layer on top of your text that now has handles. If so, move or delete it (4.115; 4.119).
■ If the layering concept is not quite clear to you yet, or if you are unfamiliar with selecting objects, please see 1.181–1.195.

4.115 Move a text block

Letters and characters are communication symbols on one hand, and attractive objects that stimulate sensitivity, on the other.
—*Takenobu Igarashi*

You'll see the four-headed arrow when you move a text block.

■ With the **pointer tool,** click once anywhere on the text to select the block (see 4.114 if you have trouble selecting).
■ With the **pointer tool,** point anywhere in the text; press-and-drag to pick up the text block and move it. When you let go of the mouse button, the text will be in that new position.
■ If you want to restrain the movement of the text block to straight across or straight down, hold the Shift key down while moving; whichever direction you move first will be the one you are limited to. You can let up on the Shift key to switch direction without having to let up on the mouse.

■ To move several text blocks at once, select several (Shift-click; see 4.114).
■ Use a **fast move** (1.197) to move the entire text block quickly across the screen as an outline (press-and-drag with a *quick* start).
■ Use a **slow move** (1.198) when you need to see the actual text in order to align it, as when aligning baselines or images (press, *hold a few seconds* until you see the four-headed arrow, then drag).

If you want to do this:	**Then follow these steps:**	**Shortcuts • Notes • Hints**
4.116 Widen a text block, or make it narrower *(lengthen or shorten the lines of text)*	■ With the **pointer tool,** click once on any part of the text block to select it (see 4.114 if you have trouble selecting). ■ With the **pointer tool,** position the very tip of the pointer on one of the four corner handles. ■ *Press* on the handle—you should see the diagonal, double-headed arrow (see left). ■ Press-and-drag either left or right to lengthen or shorten the line.	■ If you hold the Shift key down while dragging, you won't reposition the text block itself. ■ As you change the line length, the text will word wrap to fit the new length. And the symbol in the bottom windowshade loop may change (4.106–4.109).

Letters and characters are communication symbols on one hand, and attractive objects that stimulate sensitivity, on the other.
—*Takenobu Igarashi*

| **4.117** Shorten a text block | ■ With the **pointer tool,** click once on any part of the text block to select it (see 4.114 if you have trouble selecting). ■ Position the very tip of the **pointer tool** in the middle of one of the windowshade loops—*do not click!* ■ *Press* the mouse button (you should see a double-headed, vertical arrow), and *drag* upward—the windowshade will roll up and stop when you let go. ■ If you accidentally click instead of press, you may get the *loaded text icon* (4.88–4.89). If so, click once on the pointer tool in the Toolbox and try again.   If you get a dialog box that yells at you because there is no more text to place, it means you *clicked* instead of pressed. Just click Continue and try again. | ■ If you drag the *top* loop downward, the bottom shade anchors to the page. Text will thread out of the *bottom* into a connecting text block, or into the arrow in the bottom loop. Dragging from the top *does not* send the first few lines back into a preceding text block! ■ If you drag from the *bottom* loop upward, the *top* shade anchors to the page. Any text that gets rolled up will thread into the connecting text block, if there is one, or else into the arrow in the bottom loop. ■ If the bottom loop was originally empty, it will now have an arrow symbol, indicating there is more to that *story* (4.113). ■ If the bottom loop already had a plus sign in it when you started, it will still have a plus sign when you finish. |

Letters and characters are communication symbols on one hand, and attractive objects that

195

If you want to do this:	Then follow these steps:	Shortcuts ▾ Notes ▾ Hints

4.118 Lengthen a text block

Letters and characters are
communication symbols on one
hand, and attractive objects that

- With the **pointer tool,** click once on any part of the text block to select it (see 4.114 if you have trouble selecting).
- If both top and bottom windowshade loops are empty, *you cannot lengthen the text block*—there is no more to it.
- If there is a symbol in either loop, position the very tip of the **pointer tool** in the middle of one of the loops that has a symbol—*do not click!* (If you accidentally click instead of press, you may get a *loaded text icon* [4.88–4.89]; click once on the pointer tool in the Toolbox and try again.)
- *Press* the mouse button down, and *drag* it outward—the windowshade will roll out and stop when you let go.

- If you pull up on the *top* loop, the bottom shade will anchor to the page and text will be added at the *bottom* of the text block. If you pull down on the *bottom* loop, the top shade will anchor to the page and text will be added at the *bottom* of the text block. If you want to add text at the *top,* you must shorten the *previous,* linked text block.
- No matter how far you pull the last text block handle down, it will snap back up to the last character in the story—you cannot pull it down farther. If you want more open space at the end of the text block, you can hit a few Returns after the last visible character; the Mac sees Returns as solid characters.

4.119 Delete a text block

- With the **pointer tool,** click once on any part of the text block to select it (see 4.114 if you have trouble selecting).
- When you see handles, hit the Backspace/ Delete key (*or,* of course, you could also choose "Clear" from the Edit menu). It's really gone now.

- If you change your mind, you can **Undo** the deletion if you do so *immediately:* from the Edit menu choose "Undo delete," *or* press Command Z.
- See 4.123 for how to remove one or more threaded text blocks.

If you want to do this:	Then follow these steps:	Shortcuts ▾ Notes ▾ Hints
4.120 Delete several text blocks	▪ With the **pointer tool,** click once on any part of the text block to select it (see 4.114 if you have trouble selecting). ▪ Hold the Shift key down and click on other blocks of text; each one you click on will be added to your selection. ▪ When you see all the handles, hit the Backspace/Delete key.	▪ If you want to *deselect* a text block, simply click on it again while holding down the Shift key. ▪ If you change your mind after you delete the text blocks, you can **Undo** the deletion if you do so *immediately:* from the Edit menu choose "Undo delete," *or* press Command Z. See 4.123.
4.121 Delete all the text blocks on the page *(this will also delete everything else on the screen, including any objects on the pasteboard, unless you Shift-click as noted under Shortcuts)*	▪ Click on the **pointer tool** in the Toolbox. ▪ From the Edit menu choose "Select all," *or* press Command A; everything on the screen will have handles (except master page items; 1.130–1.135). ▪ Press the Backspace/Delete key.	▪ If there are some objects you *don't* want to delete, hold down the Shift key and click on them to *deselect* those items before you hit Backspace/Delete. ▪ If you change your mind after you delete, you can **Undo** the deletion if you do so *immediately:* from the Edit menu choose "Undo delete," *or* press Command Z.

Patience is one of those "feminine" qualities which have their origin in our oppression but should be preserved after our liberation.

— S I M O N E   D E   B E A U V O I R

If you want to do this:	**Then follow these steps:**	**Shortcuts ▾ Notes ▾ Hints**

4.122 Divide a text block into two or more parts, keeping the separate text blocks threaded together

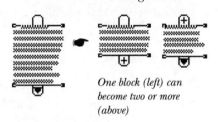

One block (left) can become two or more (above)

- With the **pointer tool,** click once on any part of the text block to select it (see 4.114 if you have trouble selecting).
- If this text block has a plus sign or an arrow in its bottom loop, indicating there is more text to the story, read **part a.**
- If the bottom loop is empty, indicating it is the end of the story, read **part b.**

a) If the text block has a symbol in the bottom windowshade loop

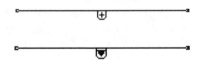

- With the **pointer tool,** click once on the symbol in the bottom windowshade loop; this will give you a loaded text icon (4.88–4.93).
- Wherever you click with that loaded icon, the text will pour itself in, beginning at that point; you will see a + sign in the loop at the *top* of the second text block, indicating the new block is threaded to a preceding one.
- If there is still a symbol in the bottom loop, click once on it to repeat the process. When the bottom windowshade loop is empty, there is no more text to place.

- Remember, the plus sign (+) indicates that the text block is *threaded* to another. If you pick up the text this way and create a new block, the new block will pull text from the *following* connected blocks.
- With a loaded text icon, you can *drag-place* to place the text (press-and-drag to create a bounding box; when you let go, the text will fill that space; 4.62).
- You could, of course, press-and-drag the bottom loop upward to shorten the existing text block before you separate it (4.117).
- As you place text blocks from one story across many (not necessarily sequential) pages, PageMaker threads them all nicely together for you.

If you want to do this:	Then follow these steps:	Shortcuts • Notes • Hints

b) If the text block has an empty bottom windowshade loop

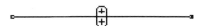

- With the **pointer tool** point to the empty loop, but *don't click yet.*
- *Press* (don't click) on the loop and *drag* upward to the point where you want the text block to end; when you let go, there will be an arrow in the loop.
- Now you can click once with the **pointer tool** directly on the arrow to pick up the extra text and place it somewhere else—just as in **part a** directly preceding this.

- The purpose of this procedure is to shorten the text block so there will be a symbol in the loop, enabling you to pick up the text to start a separate block.

4.123 Remove one or more of several threaded text blocks in a story *without deleting the text in them*

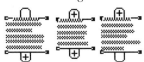

Three text blocks from one story . . .

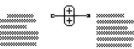

roll one up and click . . .

the block disappears; the text threads on.

- With the **pointer tool,** click once on any part of one text block to select it (see 4.114 if you have trouble selecting).
- Point to the bottom windowshade loop, no matter what symbol it has.
- Press-and-drag upward until the top and bottom windowshade loops meet, like so:

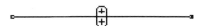

- When they look like this (your loops may have different symbols in them), **click** once anywhere; the handles/loops will disappear and the text that was in that block will thread itself into the other text blocks. **Do not hit the Backspace/ Delete key!**

- Using this technique, the text from the removed block will move into the *following* text blocks, if there are any. They will *not* get any bigger, except the last one, which will expand to accommodate all the extra text. If the last text block already had a down-pointing arrow in its windowshade, you'll need to pull it down or place the extra text that's in it somewhere else.
- Use this technique if you just want to *remove* a text block, but don't want to *delete* the text that was in it.
- If you *delete* a text block that is threaded to another, or between two threaded ones, then that text is gone *permanently.* The other text blocks are still threaded together, but whatever was in that deleted text block will be *missing.* It'll read funny.

199

If you want to do this: ■

Then follow these steps: ■

Shortcuts ▾ Notes ▾ Hints ■

4.124 Put separate, threaded text blocks back into one text block

- If there is room in the column for the entire story, follow **part a;**
  Or if you want to put just one text block back into another, like say the fourth text block back into the third, follow **part a;**
  Or if there is not room in the column or even on the page for the entire story, then read **part b.**

---

a) Reunite separate blocks back into one, *if* there is room in one column

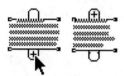

Press in the previous text block's loop and drag downward . . .

to join the text blocks back into one.

- With the **pointer tool,** point to the + sign in the bottom loop of the text block *preceding* the one you want to *add* to it; that is, if you want to add the fourth one into the third, then point to the third. If you want to combine *all the text blocks* into the first one, then point to the first.
- Simply *press* and *drag* the bottom window-shade loop down as far as possible; it will snap up to its end and show the empty loop, indicating there is no more text. Any threaded text blocks following will disappear and their text will thread into this one.
- If you still don't see an empty loop, you need to press-and-drag down further.

- Use this technique anytime you want to combine separate, but threaded, blocks from one story, whether you want to combine them all into one large block, or just join a couple of the multitude together.

If you want to do this:	**Then follow these steps:**	**Shortcuts ▾ Notes ▾ Hints**
b) Reunite several blocks back into one, if there is *not* room in one column for the entire story	■ Follow the steps in 4.123 to remove text blocks, *without deleting any text,* starting at the last text block in the story. ■ Even if the entire story cannot fit into one text block on one page, at least now it is all stored in that arrow symbol at the bottom of the first text block.	■ Remember, the last text block in the story has an *empty* bottom windowshade loop. (See 4.113 for important clarification on the difference between a text block and a story.)
OR Place all the text *except the first block* on the pasteboard	■ Click once in the symbol in the loop at the end of the *first* block to pick up all the following text (it won't disappear yet). ■ If there is room on the pasteboard for the entire story, then click the loaded text icon (not *autoflow*) somewhere on the pasteboard to flow the rest of the story, or *drag-place* to create a bounding box (4.62) large enough to hold the text.	■ Any text blocks that may have held parts of the story will now be gone, no matter how many pages they were spread across, and the entire story will be on the pasteboard.
OR Delete the entire story and re-place it into one block	■ Choose the **text tool;** click once inside any text block belonging to the story. ■ From the Edit menu choose "Select all," *or* press Command A; all the text will be highlighted. ■ Press Command X; every text block of that story will be gone. You have just **cut** the entire story (4.125). ■ With the text tool, set the insertion point where there is room for the entire story; press Command V to paste.	■ You can, of course, just delete the entire story and start from scratch to place the file again, from "Place…" in the File menu (4.55).

If you want to do this:	Then follow these steps:	Shortcuts ▾ Notes ▾ Hints
4.125 Cut a text block	▪ With the **pointer tool,** click once on any part of the text block to select it (see 4.114 if you have trouble selecting). ▪ When you see the handles, from the Edit menu choose "Cut," *or* press Command X.	▪ Remember, anything on the Mac that is **cut** is *removed* from the document and placed on the Clipboard, ready for pasting. Keep in mind that the Clipboard can hold only one object at a time (1.273–1.276).
4.126 Copy a text block	▪ With the **pointer tool,** click once on any part of the text block to select it (see 4.114 if you have trouble selecting). ▪ When you see the handles, from the Edit menu choose "Copy," *or* press Command C.	▪ Remember, anything on the Mac that is **copied** is left in the document and a *copy* of it is placed on the Clipboard, ready for pasting. Keep in mind that the Clipboard can hold only one object at a time (1.273–1.276).
4.127 Delete a text block	▪ See 4.119 through 4.121 for deleting text blocks.	▪ Anything **deleted** is just plain gone—it is *not* placed on the Clipboard (1.273; 1.284).
4.128 Paste a text block	▪ If you want to paste in a text block as a separate block, not threaded to any others, follow **part a;** ▪ **Or** if you want to *insert* the contents of the text block into another text block, follow **part b;** ▪ **Or** if you want to *replace* a portion of the text in another text block, follow **part c.** *—continued*	▪ When you paste text *as a separate block, it is no longer threaded to any other text block.* ▪ When you paste or insert a text block *into another text block,* the new text takes on the formatting and style of the *paragraph* it is inserted into, although the font specifications will remain intact. ▪ If you insert text *into its own paragraph,* though, by pressing Return *before* you insert, all of the original specifications of the text will remain intact (except line length).

If you want to do this:	**Then follow these steps:**	**Shortcuts • Notes • Hints**
a) Paste a text block as its own separate text block	• With the **pointer tool,** cut or copy the text block to the Clipboard (see 4.125–4.126). • To paste it on the page as a separate text block, make sure you have the **pointer tool.** • From the Edit menu choose "Paste," *or* press Command V; the text block will appear slightly offset from the original position, and you will have to move it to where you want it (press-and-drag with the pointer tool; 4.115).	• This block will not be threaded to any other. It will retain all the formatting, including the line length, of the block it was originally copied or cut from. • If the original text block is not visible on the screen, the new text block will paste into the middle of the window. • Press Command Option V to *power paste* (1.283) the text block into exactly the position it was cut or copied from.
b) Paste a text block, inserted into existing text	• With the **pointer tool,** cut or copy the text block to the Clipboard (see 4.125–4.126). • Choose the **text tool** from the Toolbox. • Position the I-beam where you want the text to be inserted; click once to set the flashing insertion point. • From the Edit menu choose "Paste," *or* press Command V.	• *Inserted (pasted) text* will take on the formatting of the paragraph it is inserted into; some font specifications will stay the same, though. • If the text to be pasted has formatting you wish to keep, hit a Return *after* setting the insertion point, but *before* pasting. Since this begins a new paragraph, the inserted text will keep its own formatting, *except* for line length.
c) Replace other text	• With the **pointer tool,** cut or copy the text block to the Clipboard (see 4.125–4.126). • Choose the **text tool** from the Toolbox. • Press-and-drag to select the text you want to replace (4.197). • From the Edit menu choose "Paste," *or* press Command V.	• The text that is selected (highlighted) when you choose to paste will be entirely *replaced* with the new text. No other text in the block will be affected, except to adjust the space.

If you want to do this:

Then follow these steps:

Shortcuts ▾ Notes ▾ Hints

4.129 Separate a text block into two or more parts, making them separate, *unthreaded* stories

- If the text blocks you want to unthread are already in two or more separate but threaded blocks, then follow **part a;**
- **Or** if the text *can* be easily broken into separate text blocks first, do that— separate out what you want to unthread (4.122) and follow **part a;**
- **Or** if the text you want to separate from a block is in the *body* of the text, such as a headline above body copy, follow **part b.**

- **Part a** can help, for instance, when someone gives you one word processing document that contains four different newsletter articles; you really need four separate ones for easier placement and manipulation in PageMaker. Place the entire file, then separate it into smaller stories. (As a precaution, it also would be wise to export each one separately; 17.43.)
- **Part b** is particularly helpful when you find you need to copy a portion of text as a separate story, such as a pull quote, or when you need to cut the headline so it can *span* two columns, while the story is *separated* into two columns.

a) Separate threaded text blocks *(unthread them)*

- With the **pointer tool,** click once on the text block you wish to separate and unthread (see 4.114 if you have trouble).
- When you see the handles of the text block, from the Edit menu choose "Cut," *or* press Command X; the block will disappear.
- From the Edit menu, choose "Paste," *or* press Command V; the new text block will paste in slightly offset from where it originally was and will no longer be threaded to any other block (press-and-drag the new text block to move it; 4.115).

- You could accomplish the same objective with the "Copy" command, realizing that the *original* text block would still be connected and threaded; the new, pasted text block would not be.
- To paste the text block into exactly the same position it was cut or copied from, press Command Option V (that's a *power-paste;* see 1.283).

If you want to do this:

b) Separate a portion of the text from the body of the text block

Then follow these steps:

- With the **text tool,** press-and-drag over the text you wish to cut or copy so you can make a separate text block out of it; you should see light text on a dark background (it's highlighted, or selected; 4.197).
- If you want to *remove* it from the text block, from the Edit menu choose "Cut," *or* press Command X;
  or if you want to leave it in the original text and make a *copy* of it for a new text block, from the Edit menu choose "Copy," *or* press Command C.
- With the **text tool**, click once to set the insertion point where you want the new text to appear (read the column to the right and decide which pasting method is best at the moment).
- From the Edit menu choose "Paste," *or* press Command V.

Shortcuts ▾ Notes ▾ Hints

- If you place the insertion point *in an existing text block*, the new text will become part of that text block and will pick up its formatting.
- If you press-and-drag the I-beam *to create a bounding box* (1.319–1.320), the text will flow into that space and that will be a new text block (great for spanning columns).
- If you place the insertion point *within a column*, the new text block will be the width of the column.
- If you place the insertion point *anywhere outside of any existing text block or outside of a column*, the new text block will be the width of your page margins (unless the insertion point is on the pasteboard to the left of the page, since the text block will stop when it bumps into the page).
- If there is *no insertion point flashing,* **or** *if the pointer tool is chosen,* the text will paste in as a block at the top of the screen and will be the width of the page margins.

Aldus Additions for text

4.130 The Aldus Additions menu is one of the most potentially powerful aspects of PageMaker 5. These little add-ons to the basic PageMaker program were developed to streamline and extend the capabilities of the original program. When you installed PageMaker you had the choice of installing all or some of the Aldus Additions. If you didn't install them and now wish you had, see 20.7.

4.131 The Aldus Additions found in the Utilities menu of the original program fall into three categories: those that help manage text blocks and text, those that help manage page layout, and those that help with printing tasks. While some of the Additions are very straightforward and simple, others may require more study until you get them down. Most of the Additions for text fall in the simple-to-use category.

4.132 The rest of the Additions for text are explained in more appropriate sections. "Expert kerning" and "Edit tracks" are fully discussed in Section 5. "Bullets and numbering" and "Drop cap" each have their own sections in the Additions chapter (Section 20).

"Find overset text"

4.133 "Find overset text" helps you locate text blocks that have hidden text that has not yet been placed. Overset text is simply text that is hiding rolled up in the bottom of a text block somewhere. Instead of having to find, select, and check all the windowshade handles yourself, you can just run this Addition. It finds all those occasions when you forgot to pull on the down-pointing arrow in the bottom windowshade handle of the last text block in a story.

4.134 You don't have to select anything. PageMaker automatically searches all the stories in the publication for you (including text blocks on the pasteboard) and displays the first occurrence of overset text she finds. All you have to do is click and tug on the down-pointing arrow (4.118).

4.135 Although a potentially great idea, this Addition only locates one overset text block at a time. To find them all, you need to keep running it until PageMaker finds all occurrences of overset text in the publication and displays a message box stating "No overset text found." Yes, this means you have to go the menu each and every time until PageMaker finds them all!

"Traverse text blocks..."

4.136 With stories spread out over many different pages in a publication, it can be tricky to keep track of all the threaded text blocks. **"Traverse text blocks..."** lets you follow the thread of a story to find all of its different text blocks in all of their different locations.

4.137 Select any text block in a threaded story (see 4.106–4.113) and run the Addition. You can choose to find the beginning or the end of the story, or either of the adjoining text blocks. PageMaker will locate the requested text block, select it, and display it on-screen in Actual size ready for you work with.

4.138 You may run into trouble running this Addition if the story contains one or more rotated text blocks.

Traverse textblocks	OK
○ First in story	Cancel
○ Previous textblock	
● Next textblock	
○ Last in story	

The "Display story info..." Addition *(from the Utilities menu, slide down to "Aldus Additions," then over to "Display story info...")*

4.139 "Display story info..." gives you specific information about a story including its link, character count, what pages the story is located on, etc. Select any one text block with the **pointer tool** to see information about the whole story.

4.140 The area and depth are shown in the unit of measure that has been selected in the "Preferences" dialog box (1.224). The Total depth of the story is measured in column inches—a standard newspaper measurement that equals an area one column wide by one inch deep.

4.141 When you run this Addition it recomposes the story—for example, if you changed a font, it will apply the new, correct font metrics (1.242).

4.142 *The name of the file the story is linked to, if any. This area will be blank if the story is not linked to an external source.*

4.143 *This dialog box does not cause any changes to happen. Click OK when you have finished viewing the information.*

4.146 *The total number of text blocks in the story.*

4.144 *The page location of the first text block in the story.*

4.147 *The total number of characters in the story. Spaces and punctuation are counted as characters.*

4.148 *Overset characters refers to text that is unplaced—the kind hidden in a text block that shows an arrow in its bottom windowshade. See 4.179 for the overset text remedy.*

4.145 *The page location of the last text block in the story.*

Story info

OK

- **File link:** HERB BK
- **Textblocks:** 4   **First page:** 4
- **Char count:** 4291   **Last page:** 5
- **Overset chars:** 0
- **Total area:** 65.022 sq. inches
- **Total depth:** 30.400 inches

4.149 *The total area of the story is equal to the height of each text block multiplied by its width. A story will measure roughly the same area no matter how you vary the size of its text blocks. Only changing text or paragraph formatting will significantly change this measurement.*

4.150 *The depth of the story in column inches. The width of the text block is not included in this measurement.*

The "Display text block info..." Addition

(from the Utilities menu, slide down to "Aldus Additions," then over to "Display textblock info...")

4.151 "Display text block info..." provides detailed information about a selected *text block*. While the "Story info" dialog box gives you info about all the text blocks in a threaded story, "Display text block info" gives you information about just the selected text block (see 4.113 for the difference between a text block and a story).

4.152 *The name of the file, if any, to which the file is linked. This area will be blank if the story is not linked to an external source.*

4.153 *This dialog box does not cause any changes to happen. Click OK when you have finished viewing the information.*

4.156 *The location of the text block in the story.*

4.157 *The total number of characters in the story, including spaces and punctuation.*

4.158 *The area is equal to the height of the text block multiplied by its width.*

Textblock info   [OK]

File link: HERB BK

Textblock 3 of 4 in story.

Character count: 1296

Area: 20.319 sq. inches

Depth: 9.500 inches

Previous textblock on page: 4

Next textblock on page: 5

4.154 *The page location of the previous text block in a threaded story.*

4.155 *The page location of the next text block in a threaded story.*

4.159 *The depth is measured in column inches (4.140). The width of the column is not included in the measurement.*

The "Add cont'd line..." Addition *(from the Utilities menu, slide down to "Aldus Additions," then over to "Add cont'd line...")*

4.160 "Add cont'd line..." adds jump lines ("Continued on..." and "Continued from...") to the top or bottom of text blocks. Jump lines typically include the page number of the continued text so the reader knows where to find the rest of the story.

4.161 By selecting a threaded text block and running the Addition, a new, unthreaded text block is created called the jump-line story (4.166, 4.167). PageMaker makes room for the jump line by bumping a line from the existing text block and moving it to the next text block in the story. If this is the very last text block of the story, don't forget to pull on the windowshade to display all the text.

4.162 After running "Add cont'd line," you'll find new styles in the style palette—"Cont. from," and "Cont. on." These styles can be edited just like any other style in a style sheet (8.53). You can base one style on the other to make the editing simpler, but if the styles have different paragraph rules (as in the default styles) they will have to be edited independently.

4.163 If you change the page layout, the page numbers in the jump lines are *not* automatically updated. You must manually change them in all the jump-line stories, or delete all the jump-line text blocks and run the Addition again. The most sensible thing, of course, is to wait and run the Addition as one of the very last things you do.

4.166 *Jump-line story.*

Yarrow is a perennial that grows throughout the world. It is found in meadows, along roadsides, and on the edges of woods. It is said to have

Continued on page 2

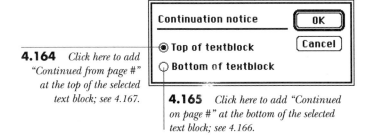

4.164 *Click here to add "Continued from page #" at the top of the selected text block; see 4.167.*

Continuation notice

OK

Cancel

⦿ **Top of textblock**

◯ **Bottom of textblock**

4.165 *Click here to add "Continued on page #" at the bottom of the selected text block; see 4.166.*

4.167 *Jump-line story.*

Continued from page 1

been the favorite herb of Achilles, the famous Greek warrior. Yarrow must be identified with extreme care. It has similarities to wild carrot and hemlock, both of which are poisonous.

The "Balance columns..." Addition *(from the Utilities menu, slide down to "Aldus Additions," then over to "Balance columns...")*

4.168 **"Balance columns..."** tries to even out columns of text in a threaded story by adjusting the number of lines within each column. The text blocks must be threaded (4.110) and selected with the pointer tool before running the Addition. The "Balance columns" dialog box lets you choose how to align the columns and where to put any left over lines.

4.169 When you choose the left icon (4.176) under "Alignment" in the dialog box, the top of each selected text block will line up with the top of the selected text block that sits highest on the page. When you choose the icon on the right (4.175), the bottom of each selected text block will line up with the bottom of the text block that sits lowest on the page.

4.170 When you choose the left icon (4.177) under "Add leftover lines," the *last* column of text will be the shortest if there are not enough lines to make all the columns exactly even. When you choose the icon on the right (4.178), the *first* column will be the shortest if there are not enough lines to fill all the columns evenly. If there are two extra lines, and four columns of text, the last two columns will each have an extra line.

4.171 You don't necessarily want to select every column in a story when you run this Addition. For instance, let's say you have four columns of text and you want three of them to be equal in length with the fourth catching the overflowing text. If you select *all* of them, all four columns will equal out, giving you four short columns.

4.172 Run the "Balance columns..." Addition *before* rotating any text.

4.173 The "Balance columns..." command obeys the choices you made in the "Paragraph" specifications dialog box (4.299). If you selected "Keep lines together" or "Column break before," the columns will balance as best they can within these restrictions.

4.174 Columns that contain inline graphics (10.214), different leading styles, or paragraph space before or after, may not balance perfectly after running this Addition.

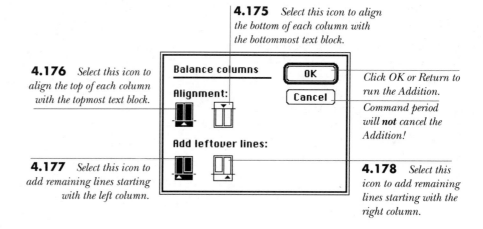

4.175 *Select this icon to align the bottom of each column with the bottommost text block.*

4.176 *Select this icon to align the top of each column with the topmost text block.*

4.177 *Select this icon to add remaining lines starting with the left column.*

Click OK or Return to run the Addition.

*Command period will **not** cancel the Addition!*

4.178 *Select this icon to add remaining lines starting with the right column.*

If you want to do this: Then follow these steps: Shortcuts ▪ Notes ▪ Hints

4.179 Locate all instances of overset text—text blocks that have text hidden in their windowshade

- From the Utilities menu, slide down to "Aldus Additions," then over to the submenu and choose "Find overset text...."
- Click or tug on the down-pointing arrow of the text block, depending on how and where you want to place the extra text.
- Choose the Addition again from the "Aldus Additions" submenu and repeat the procedure until PageMaker tells you that there is no more overset text to be found.

- PageMaker will search the whole publication (including text on the pasteboard), and display the first instance of overset text she finds.
- If you press-and-drag on the down-pointing arrow, the text block will lengthen and fill with the overset text (4.118).
- If you lightly click on the down-pointing arrow, the pointer will become a loaded icon. Place the rest of the text by clicking anywhere on the page (4.95).

4.180 Locate text blocks linked to the one currently selected

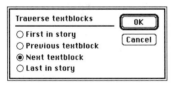

- With the **pointer tool,** select a text block.
- From the Utilities menu, slide down to "Aldus Additions," then over to the submenu and choose "Traverse text blocks...."
- Click the radio button alongside the text block you want to locate, then click OK.

- PageMaker will locate and display that text block on screen.
- You can find the text block that comes before or after the one you have selected, or the first or last text block in the story.

If you want to do this:

Then follow these steps:

Shortcuts ▾ Notes ▾ Hints

4.181 View the **"Story info..."** box for a particular story

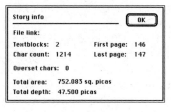

- With the **pointer tool**, select any text block in the story.
- From the Utilities menu, slide down to "Aldus Additions," then over to the sub-menu and choose "Display story info...."
- Click OK or press Return when you are done viewing the information and want to get back to the story.

- It's not easy to keep track of a story, especially in a multiple page document full of text and graphics. This Addition helps you keep track of the linked text blocks that make up a story, and the story's placement, size, and space requirements. It also lets you know when a story contains overset text—text that doesn't get placed properly but stays hidden, rolled up in the bottom of your last text block.
- You can't count on this Addition to show you the proper story info when a rotated text block is selected.

4.182 View the **"Textblock info..."** box about a particular text block

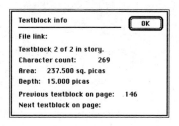

- With the **pointer tool,** click once on the text block.
- From the Utilities menu, slide down to "Aldus Additions," then over to the sub-menu and choose "Display text block info...."
- Click OK or press Return when you are done viewing the information and want to get back to the story.

- This Addition helps you keep track of linked text blocks. It also supplies you with the character count and size (area and depth) of a text block.
- The measurement system used in the "Story info" and the "Textblock info" boxes depends on what is selected in the pop-up menu next to "Measurement system" in the "Preferences" dialog box.

If you want to do this:

Then follow these steps:

Shortcuts • Notes • Hints

4.183 Add the jump-line "Continued on…" to the bottom of a threaded text block

- With the **pointer tool,** click once on the text block.
- From the Utilities menu slide down to "Aldus Additions," then over to the submenu and choose "Add cont'd line…."
- In the "Continuation notice" dialog box click the radio button next to "Bottom of text block."
- Click OK.

- If the text block is not threaded to another text block (4.107–4.109) Page-Maker will tell you she can't find the next text block.
- Some text blocks may need two jump-lines—"Continued from" at the top of the text, and a "Continued on" at the bottom. You can't set both at once, but you can set one right after the other.

4.184 Add the jump-line "Continued from…" to the top of a threaded text block

- With the **pointer tool,** click once on the text block.
- From the Utilities menu slide down to "Aldus Additions," then over to the submenu and choose "Add cont'd line…."
- In the "Continuation notice" dialog box click the radio button next to "Top of text block."
- Click OK.

- Remember the Addition bumps all the text down a line to make room for the jump-line story. Run the "Find overset text…" Addition afterward to locate any instances of text hidden in the last text block of a story; see 4.179.

4.185 Edit the styles of the jump-line stories

- With any tool, from the Type menu choose "Define styles…."
- In the list box, click once on "Cont. on," then click the "Edit" button.
- Click on any of the buttons (Type, Para, Tabs, Color) to make any changes.
- Click OK until you are back at the Define styles box, then Click once on "Cont. from," and repeat the process.

- See Style Sheets, Section 8, for a complete rundown on defining style sheets.
- The existing styles have *paragraph rules* attached to them. If you want to change them be sure to click the Paragraph button, then the Rules button when editing each style. See Section 7 for the whole scoop on working with paragraph rules.

If you want to do this:	**Then follow these steps:**	**Shortcuts ▾ Notes ▾ Hints**
4.186 Balance two or more columns of text in a story, aligning the top of each text block, and adding the extra lines starting in the far left column 	■ Hold down the Shift key as you use the **pointer tool** to select the columns you want to balance. ■ From the Utilities menu slide down to "Aldus Additions" then over to the sub-menu and choose "Balance columns…." ■ Under "Alignment" click on the icon on the left. ■ Under "Add leftover lines" click on the icon on the left.	■ This Addition does not adjust leading or paragraph spacing, it simply tries to even out the number of lines in each paragraph. The columns will all shorten to the average length. ■ You can't run this Addition on rotated text blocks.
4.187 Balance two or more columns of text in a story, aligning the bottom of each text block, and adding extra lines starting in the far right column 	■ Hold down the Shift key as you use the **pointer tool** to select the columns you want to balance. ■ From the Utilities menu slide down to "Aldus Additions" then over to the sub-menu and choose "Balance columns…." ■ Under "Alignment" click on the icon on the right. ■ Under "Add leftover lines" click on the icon on the right.	■ You can mix and match the icons any way that pleases you—align the columns on the top and put the extra lines on the right; align the columns on the bottom and put the extra lines on the left.

Aldus Manutius

Ever wonder why roman type is called roman and italic type is called italic? Well, you can stop losing sleep over it.

Strange as it seems, in 15th century Italy, land of the Romans, very few publications were printed with Roman letters—almost all scholarly or religious works were set in *Greek*. There weren't any other sorts of books anyway, except scholarly or religious works. No romance novels or horror stories yet.

When the man Aldus Manutius entered the publishing business with his company called the Dolphin Press, the printing industry was less than fifty years old. But there were already over a thousand presses operating across Europe, and literally millions of books had been printed. Aldus was proud and protective of his Greek fonts, but a bit sloppy and diffident about his Roman fonts. In fact, most of them were not very well designed, and he used them only for jobs sponsored by wealthy clients or academic friends. In 1496, though, Aldus published an essay for Pietro Bembo, an Italian scholar and friend. The Bembo typeface, with its lighter weight, more pronounced weight stress, and more delicate serifs, was an instant success. Claude Garamond picked it up in France and spread its influence throughout the rest of Europe. This "Aldine roman" affected type design for hundreds of years. *(You are reading the typeface Bembo right now.)*

Aldus himself produced well over 1200 different titles in his 25 years as a publisher. Over 90 percent of the books he produced were Greek classics. Aldus was a well-patronized scholar before he entered the printing and publishing trade, so the classics were close to his heart. His market for the books were the educated, the worldly, the wealthy. Aldus created small books, or *octavos,*

intended for busy people, for nobility traveling across Europe on errands of state, for members of the "educational revolution" that were studying in the growing number of universities. The official writing style of the learned and professional scribes of southern Italy in the late 1400s was a relaxed, oblique, flourishy script called *cancellaresca*. To make his books more appealing to the higher-class market, Aldus took this exclusive writing style and developed a typeface out of it. It was a hit.

Aldus had his new type style copyrighted. He was trying to protect not just the one font—he wanted a monopoly on the cursive sort of style. He got it; he even got a papal decree to protect his rights. But as we all know, that doesn't mean no one will steal it anyway. People did. At least the other Italians called the style "Aldino"; the rest of Europe called it "italic," since it came from Italy. The first italic Aldus ever cut (well, actually, Francesco Griffo cut it) was produced in 1501 in Venice. Does the name Venice ring a bell?

These innovations of Aldus Manutius place him in history as perhaps the most important printer of the Renaissance, next to Gutenberg himself. Popularizing the roman typeface, albeit inadvertently, had a profound influence on typeface development for generations. Prior to Aldus's

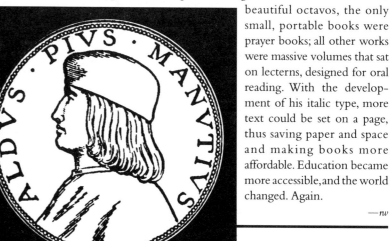

beautiful octavos, the only small, portable books were prayer books; all other works were massive volumes that sat on lecterns, designed for oral reading. With the development of his italic type, more text could be set on a page, thus saving paper and space and making books more affordable. Education became more accessible, and the world changed. Again.

—*nv*

Selecting and formatting text

4.189 PageMaker allows you incredible control over the text on a page. This sub-section covers all the facets of formatting the text characters: type font, type size, type style, case, super- and subscript, set width, as well as rotated text and special characters.

4.190 You can also adjust the space between the lines (leading), the space between the paragraphs, between the letters, between the words. You can kern text and track text. You can define a hyphenation spacing zone. These spacing concepts are a little more complex and need more explanation, so you will find them in their own section, Section 5 on Spacing.

4.191 All of these text manipulations are done with the **text tool** (or the text tool and the Control palette). It is the exception to the rule of using the pointer to change things. But there is no exception to the rule: **select first, then manipulate.** The first part of this section deals with all the different ways to select the text before specifying and formatting.

4.192 When you select the **text tool,** you get the **I-beam** (pronounced eye-beam), as shown below. The I-beam is the visual clue indicating that you are now in the typing, or *text,* mode. It is simply a cursor, just like the pointer.

4.193

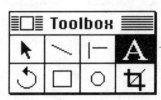

Text tool

Text tool cursor: the I-beam ⎯⎯⎯ ⌶
*(the little crossbar indicates
the baseline [1.57] of the text)*

4.194 And just like the pointer, the I-beam will accomplish nothing until you click the mouse. Click while you have the I-beam and you get the flashing **insertion point:** |

(Be sure to read 4.15–4.24 for a thorough explanation of the insertion point and how it decides what text specifications to type with.)

Selecting text: character formatting *vs.* paragraph formatting

4.195 As noted in 4.191, text must be selected before it can be manipulated. There are two basic ways to select text in PageMaker, depending on whether you are going to change the formatting of the *characters* or of the *paragraph*.

4.196 Character formatting applies *only* to those characters (including blank spaces) that are *selected*.

4.197 You can highlight, or *select* text by pressing-and-dragging the text tool over it, which makes it appear light on a dark background.

> If your text is not light-on-dark like this, try again. You must use the text tool.

4.198 You can add to or delete from a selection, but you cannot select two *unconnected* pieces of text, such as the first paragraph *and* the third paragraph. We all try to do it, thinking that of course there must be some way, but there isn't.

4.199 Text must be highlighted in order to format *characters* for any of the following:

Font	Leading*
Type size	Type style
Case	Position
Set width	Track
Color	No Break, Break
Baseline shift	To cut
To copy	To replace text

*Leading sometimes does and sometimes doesn't affect other characters; be sure to read about leading in Section 5.

4.200 Paragraph formatting applies to entire paragraphs, *whether you select the entire paragraph or not*. For this reason, you don't have to actually highlight the text you want to change—you can just set the insertion point within the paragraph. Of course, if you are changing more than one paragraph, you will need to select at least part of *all* the paragraphs you wish to affect.

4.201 The following are paragraph specific:

Alignment	Style sheets
Indents	Tabs
Hyphenation	Auto pair kerning
Leading method	Auto leading percent
Letter spacing	Word spacing
"Keep with" controls	Grid alignment

Paragraph rules above and below
Paragraph spacing before and after
Dictionary for spell-checking and hyphenation

4.202 Remember, every time you hit a Return key, the Mac sees it as a command to set up a new paragraph. See 4.348–4.354 for more info on this and on the terrific line-break feature.

If you want to do this:	**Then follow these steps:**	**Shortcuts ▾ Notes ▾ Hints**
4.203 Select text using the mouse (*To **deselect text,** click anywhere, even in a highlighted area*)	▪ To select any text at any time, you must use the **text tool.**	▪ See 4.114 for selecting *text blocks,* which is what you would need to do in order to move a block of text or to lengthen lines. ▪ Check out the chart in the back of the book that defines all the keyboard shortcuts. They come in very handy. ▪ See 4.204 and 1.324–1.325 for greater detail on selecting text using the numeric keypad.
a) Select one character	▪ With the **text tool,** position the I-beam to one side of the character to be selected. ▪ Press-and-drag over the character.	▪ **Or** click to set the insertion point, hold the Shift key down, and press the arrow key in that direction.
b) Select one word	▪ With the **text tool,** position the I-beam in the middle of the word. ▪ Double-click. ▪ **Or** if your hands are on the keys anyway and the insertion point is at the end of a word, press Option Shift LeftArrow (use the RightArrow if the insertion point is at the beginning of a word; this will also select the space after the word).	▪ This first technique also selects the blank space *after* a word. If you don't want that blank space selected or affected, use the press-and-drag method in **a)** above. ▪ You see, Option plus the Left or Right-Arrow key moves the insertion point one word; whenever you add the Shift key to an insertion point movement, it *selects* text. This is true in many Mac programs.
c) Select one line	▪ With the **text tool,** position the I-beam at the beginning of the line. ▪ Press-and-drag to the end of the line. ▪ If it is a line without text (the line is a blank), double-click.	▪ **Or** hold down the Shift key and press the number 1 on the numeric keypad, **or** number 7 if the insertion point is at the *end* of the line. (If it types a *number* 1 or 7, press the Clear key and try again.)

If you want to do this:

Then follow these steps:

Shortcuts ▾ Notes ▾ Hints

d) Select one sentence

- With the **text tool,** position the I-beam at the *end* of the sentence; click once to set the insertion point.
- Press Command Shift 7 (on the key*pad*).
- If the insertion point is at the *beginning* of the sentence, press Command Shift 1 (number 1 on the numeric key*pad*).

- This technique selects a sentence. If the insertion point is in the middle of the sentence, the selection will extend to the other end from that point, depending on whether you press 1 or 7. (If you type an actual number, press the Clear key and try again; 4.204, 1.324–1.328.)

e) Select one paragraph

- With the **text tool,** position the I-beam anywhere in the paragraph.
- Triple-click.

- To add other adjoining paragraphs to that selection, press Command Shift and the Up or DownArrow.
- **Or** you can simply hold the Shift key down and click in any other paragraph on the screen in that *story* (4.113), even if it's in another text block—that one and all the paragraphs between will be selected.

f) Select a range of text *(in one story)*

- With the **text tool,** position the I-beam at the beginning point of the range of text to select; click once to set the insertion point.
- If necessary, scroll or change the page view to find the other end of the range of text; position the I-beam there—*don't click yet!*
- Hold down the Shift key and *now* click at this end; everything between the two clicks will be selected, even if they are in separate text blocks (but the text blocks must be part of the same *story;* 4.113).

- See **h)** for adding on to or deleting from this selection.

If you want to do this:	**Then follow these steps:**	**Shortcuts ▾ Notes ▾ Hints**
g) Select an entire story	■ With the **text tool,** click anywhere in any text block belonging to the story. ■ From the Edit menu choose "Select all," *or* press Command A.	■ This technique will select all the text in the *entire story* (4.113), whether you can see it or not, even if it spans several pages and is made up of many text blocks, or even if it is not all placed yet.
h) Extend or shorten the selection	■ After the text has been selected and you decide you need to adjust it, hold down the Shift key. ■ Click once at the point at which you want the selected text shortened or extended, **or** press-and-drag from the *end* of the selection. (A funny thing—you can only adjust the selection from the *end* of where you pressed-and-dragged. That is, if you start pressing at the *beginning* of the paragraph, you can adjust the selection from its *end*. If you pressed at the *end* of the paragraph and selected by dragging upward, you can adjust the text from the selection area at the *beginning* of the paragraph.) ■ You can use this trick in combination with the Command key and the numeric keypad to add characters, sentences, paragraphs, lines, etc., to your selection (1.324–1.328; 4.204).	■ You can also press the Shift key down and *click* beyond or within the end of the selection; everything up to the click will be included in or excluded from the selection. ■ You know those times when you press-and-drag over text to select it, and sometimes you miss the last character or maybe you go a word too far? You don't need to start over again—just use this Shift-key trick!

If you want to do this:	**Then follow these steps:**	**Shortcuts ▾ Notes ▾ Hints**
4.204 Use the keyboard to move the insertion point and to select text	■ With the **text tool,** click to set the insertion point within the text. ■ Hold the Shift key down while using any of these keyboard commands to select the text along the way.	■ *All numbers are numeric keypad numbers—not the numbers along the top of the keyboard!* ■ If you use the numeric keypad and it types a number, press the Clear key to switch it to arrow key mode. ■ Another funny thing—all the numbers on the keypad move the insertion point, except the 5. The 5 key types the number 5. ■ Do you notice the pattern of these key commands? They follow the up-down-left-right placement on the keypad; using the Command key extends their movement. ■ Also see 1.324–1.328 for more info on the numeric keypad.
a) One character to the left	Left arrow, *or* 4 on the keypad.	
c) One character to the right	RightArrow, *or* 6 on the keypad.	
d) One word to the right	Option LeftArrow, *or* Command 4 on the keypad.	
b) One word to the left	Option RightArrow, *or* Command 6 on the keypad.	
e) To the beginning of the line	7 on the keypad.	
f) To the end of the line	1 on the keypad.	
g) To the beginning of the sentence	Command 7 on the keypad.	
h) To the end of the sentence	Command 1 on the keypad.	
i) One line up	UpArrow, *or* 8 on the keypad.	
j) One line down	DownArrow, *or* 2 on the keypad.	
k) One paragraph up	Command UpArrow, *or* Command 8 on the keypad.	
l) One paragraph down	Command DownArrow, *or* Command 2 on the keypad.	
m) Up a screen	9 on the keypad.	
n) Down a screen	3 on the keypad.	
o) To the top of the story	Command 9 on the keypad.	■ If the top or the bottom of the story is not on that page, you will get beeped.
p) To the bottom of the story	Command 3 on the keypad.	

4.205 **The "Type specs..." dialog box** *(from the Type menu, choose "Type specs…," or press Command T)*

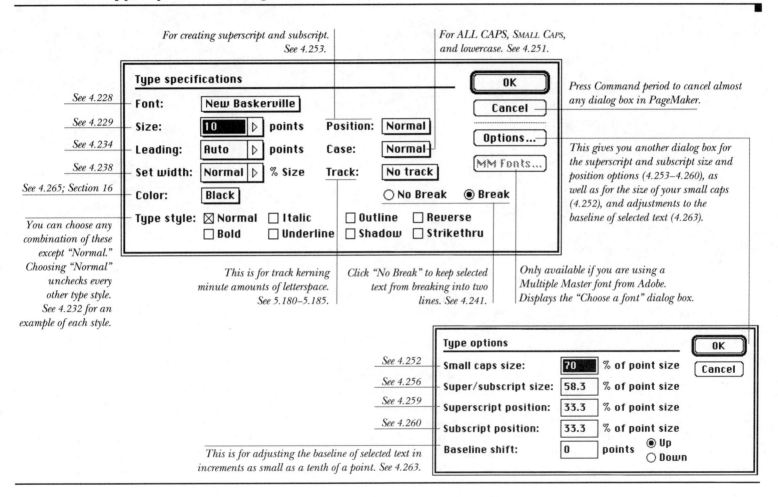

*For creating superscript and subscript.
See 4.253.*

*For ALL CAPS, SMALL CAPS,
and lowercase. See 4.251.*

*Press Command period to cancel almost
any dialog box in PageMaker.*

See 4.228

See 4.229

See 4.234

See 4.238

See 4.265; Section 16

*You can choose any
combination of these
except "Normal."
Choosing "Normal"
unchecks every
other type style.
See 4.232 for an
example of each style.*

*This gives you another dialog box for
the superscript and subscript size and
position options (4.253–4.260), as
well as for the size of your small caps
(4.252), and adjustments to the
baseline of selected text (4.263).*

*This is for track kerning
minute amounts of letterspace.
See 5.180–5.185.*

*Click "No Break" to keep selected
text from breaking into two
lines. See 4.241.*

*Only available if you are using a
Multiple Master font from Adobe.
Displays the "Choose a font" dialog box.*

See 4.252

See 4.256

See 4.259

See 4.260

*This is for adjusting the baseline of selected text in
increments as small as a tenth of a point. See 4.263.*

222

4.206 The character-view Control palette

(from the Window menu, choose "Control palette"; from the Toolbox, choose the text tool; select the character-view button)

4.209 *Character - view button.*

Apply button. See 3.41–3.47

4.210 *Font. Notice the highlight bar indicating that this is the active option.*

4.211 *Type size. The nudge amount is .1 point.*

4.212 *Tracking.*

4.213 *Kerning. The nudge amount is .01 em.*

4.208 *The Close box.*

4.207 *The title bar.*

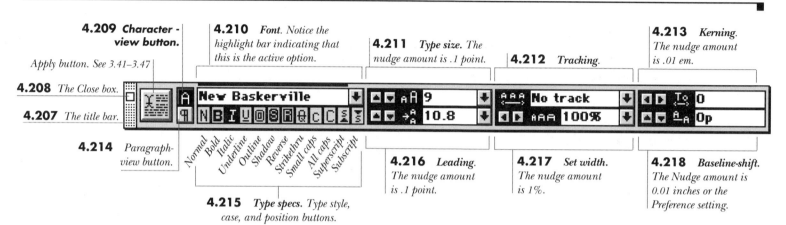

4.214 *Paragraph-view button.*

Normal, Bold, Italic, Underline, Outline, Shadow, Reverse, Strikethru, Small caps, All caps, Superscript, Subscript

4.215 *Type specs. Type style, case, and position buttons.*

4.216 *Leading. The nudge amount is .1 point.*

4.217 *Set width. The nudge amount is 1%.*

4.218 *Baseline-shift. The Nudge amount is 0.01 inches or the Preference setting.*

4.219 The character-view Control palette lets you apply all the same type characteristics that are found in the Type specs dialog box except Color and No Break/Break.

4.220 The character- and paragraph-view Control palettes come into view whenever you choose the text tool. Clicking on the "A" or "¶" buttons, or pressing Command Shift ` *(grave)*, toggles the palette back and forth between character- and paragraph-view. All the characteristics of the currently selected type will be displayed in the character-view palette (font, size, leading, etc.).

4.221 Font, type size, leading, tracking, and set width can be changed either by selecting an option from a pop-up menu or by typing the name or number directly in the edit box. Type style, case, and position are selected by clicking on buttons.

4.222 Kerning and baseline-shift are changed by either typing a value in their edit boxes or by clicking their nudge buttons. Type size, leading, and set width also can be nudged. A power nudge is equal to ten times a regular nudge. See 3.6–3.31 for everything you need to know about Control palette basics.

4.223 If you click a button or select an option from a list, the change will be applied instantly. If you type a change into an edit box, use the Tab key to apply the change and move to the next option all at once (also see 3.106), or just click the Apply button.

4.224 If you are going to change type characteristics by navigating the palette with the keyboard (see 3.101–3.120 and 4.226–4.227), it is important to first know if the Control palette is active or not. If it isn't, you may find yourself typing the name of the new font or inserting a tab into your document instead of into the palette.

If you want to do this:	Then follow these steps:	Shortcuts ▾ Notes ▾ Hints
4.225 Display the character-view Control palette ⬚ (A / ¶ icon)	■ If the Control palette is not on screen, choose it from the Window menu, or press Command ' *(apostrophe)*. ■ From the Toolbox, choose the **text tool.** ■ If the palette is not already in character-view, simply click on the "A" View button or press Command Shift ` *(grave)*.	■ The Control palette automatically becomes active whenever you choose anything from a pop-up list or highlight an option in an edit box.
4.226 Navigate the character-view Control palette using just the keyboard	■ Press Command ` *(grave)* to activate the Control palette. ■ Press the Tab key to move forward through the various options. ■ Press Shift Tab to move backwards through the options.	■ The highlight bar is your clue as to which option is currently active. Be sure you have selected a bright color for your Highlight color (or black for a gray-scale monitor) so you can easily see which option is active (see 3.110). ■ Pressing the Tab key automatically applies changes *and* moves to the next option at the same time. ■ Pressing Shift Tab applies changes and moves to the *previous* option at the same time.
4.227 Turn the type style, case, and position options on and off using just the keyboard	■ Navigate to the Type specs options using the Tab key. ■ Use the left and right arrow keys to move the cursor within the style, case and position options until the one you want is highlighted. ■ Press on the Spacebar to toggle the option buttons on and off.	■ If one of the buttons is dimmed out, it is telling you that the option is not applied to all of the characters in the text you have selected. ■ Clicking Normal removes all the styles you have applied.

If you want to do this:

4.228 Change the font

Then follow these steps:

- With the **text tool,** select the text you want to change (4.203–4.204).
- From the Type menu, slide down to "Font," then slide out to the side and choose the font you want;
  Or from the Type menu, slide down to "Type specs….," press on the Font submenu, and choose the font. Click OK.
  Or from the character-view Control palette, type the font name in the "Font" edit box, or press on the down-pointing arrow to select the font from the pop-up list of fonts.

Shortcuts ▾ Notes ▾ Hints

- If you are going to be making several specification changes at once, such as font and size and style and case, see 4.239.
- If you are printing to a PostScript printer, such as an Apple LaserWriter, don't choose a font with a city name. City-named fonts are usually bitmapped. Their resolution is designed for the lower resolution of the screen and for printers like the ImageWriter; a PostScript printer doesn't know what to do with them. And an imagesetter really freaks out. See 19.5–19.10; 19.26–19.31.
- Be careful you do not have both the TrueType and PostScript versions of the same font installed or you could run into massive printing problems! See 19.36–19.38 for more info on TrueType and PostScript fonts.
- Make sure the Control palette is active before typing any changes into it, and that it is inactive before typing in your document (just click anywhere on the page).
- If you typed in the name for a new font, you must press the Apply button or hit the Return key for it to be applied. Selecting it from the pop-up list automatically applies the change. You only have to type in the first few characters of the font name for PageMaker to know which one you want.

If you want to do this:

4.229 Change the type size

Then follow these steps:

- With the **text tool,** select the text you want to change (4.203–4.204).
- From the Type menu, slide down to "Size," then slide out to the side and choose the size you want.
- If you want a size other than the ones listed, choose "Other..." from that same pop-out menu.
  - ▫ Type in a new point size, from 4 to 650. You can enter .1 increments.
  - ▫ Click OK.
- **Or** from the Type menu, slide down to "Type specs...." Press on the Size submenu and choose a size, or enter a value from 4 to 650, in .1 increments. Click OK.
  Or from the character-view Control palette, type the size you want into the type size box, or press on the down-pointing arrow to select the size from the pop-up list of sizes. You can nudge the type size in .1 point increments by clicking on the up or down nudge buttons.

Shortcuts ▾ Notes ▾ Hints

- There are 72 points per inch. Logically, then, the larger the point size, the larger the type. The Mac screen has a resolution of 72 dots per inch; each dot is one point, so we can see type fairly true to size.
- The type sizes that are in the *outline* style in the menu are the sizes of the PostScript fonts that are *installed* in your system (they can be different for each font). If you don't have ATM, these specific sizes will look best on your screen, although a PostScript printer (such as the Apple LaserWriter) will print clean type no matter what it looks like on your screen (as long as it is not city-named).
- Just about *all* the sizes will show in the outline style if the selected font is a TrueType font.

- See 19.5–19.10 and 19.20–19.38 for info on printers and fonts.

If you want to do this:

4.230 Change the type size from the keyboard

> You
> can do
> a good ad
> without
> good
> typography,
> but you
> can't do
> a great ad
> without
> good
> typography.
>
> —*Herb Lubalin*

Then follow these steps:

- With the **text tool,** select the text you want to change (4.203–4.204).
- **To make the type larger** one point at a time, hold down the Command, Shift, and Option keys all at once; each time you press the > key (above the period), the type will enlarge one point.
- **To make the type smaller** one point at a time, hold down the Command, Shift, and Option keys all at once; each time you press the < key (above the comma), the type will reduce one point.
- **To make the type larger or smaller in standard increments** (PageMaker calls them "graphic art" sizes, the ones you see listed in the size submenu), hold down just the Command and Shift keys while pressing the < or > key. This will change the type to the sizes listed in the Size submenu instead of point by point (e.g., from 14 to 18 to 24 to 30 to 36, etc.).
- **To use the keyboard in combination with the character-view Control palette,** press Command ` *(grave)* to activate the Control palette. Press the Tab key until the Size edit box is highlighted, then type in the new value to the tenth of a point.

Shortcuts ▾ Notes ▾ Hints

- What a great shortcut—watch the size of the type change right in front of your very eyes!
- You can't change tenth-point increments (.1) this way, though. For instance, if the type you have selected is 14.7 point, using the key commands will take it down/up to the next *whole* size and continue from there in whole sizes.
- It's easy to remember which keys enlarge or reduce if you think of the < and > characters as the "less than" and "greater than" symbols, respectively.
- *The "graphic art" sizes*
- If the Control palette is in paragraph-view, press Command Shift ` *(grave)* to move to character-view, (or press the Tab key until the highlight bar is beneath the View buttons, then press any arrow key).
- Pressing the Tab key moves the highlight bar to the next option; pressing Shift Tab moves it to the previous option. The Tab key can also be used in place of the Return key to apply changes (4.226).

227

If you want to do this:	**Then follow these steps:**	**Shortcuts ▾ Notes ▾ Hints**
4.231 Change the type style of selected text *(not to be confused with Style as in Style Sheets!)*	■ With the **text tool,** select the text you want to change (4.203–4.204). ■ From the Type menu, slide down to "Type style," then slide out to the side and choose the style you want (see the examples below); **Or** press Command T to get the "Type specs" dialog box to choose from; **Or** click the desired style button in the character-view Control palette.	■ If you are using *downloadable* (19.39–19.46) fonts, often you cannot change the type style from the Type menu; you need to go into the Font list and choose, for example, the actual italic or bold *font* (4.228). ■ Learn the simple keyboard commands for this process, as shown in the menu and directly below. ■ There are also key commands for most options in the Control palette (3.101–3.120).

4.232 Change the type style of text from the keyboard *before* you type it
(what I call 'loading the insertion point')
	■ Say you are typing and the next word you want to type is to be in Italic, then the rest of the following text will be Normal again. Do this:
	■ Type *up to* the word to be italicized.
	■ Press Command Shift I (which is the keyboard combination for the Italic style).
	■ Type the word—it will be Italic.
	■ Press Command Shift I again; this will take the Italic style *off* and the rest of the text will type Normal again.
	■ Of course this works with changing to any style, including super- and subscript, all caps and small caps, as well as changing point sizes and even alignments.
	
	See the chart in the back of the book for a list of all the keyboard shortcuts.
		■ You don't want to have to pick up the mouse everytime you want to turn a word into italic, right? Follow this simple method to speed your typing.
		■ Normal Command Shift Spacebar
		  Bold Command Shift B
		  Italic Command Shift I
		  <u>Underline</u> Command Shift U
		  ~~Strikethru~~ Command Shift /
		  Outline Command Shift D
		  Shadow Command Shift W
		  Superscript^{hi} Command Shift + (**plus** on the key*board,* not the key*pad!*)
		  Subscript$_{low}$ Command Shift - (**minus** on the key*pad,* or on the key*board; actually* it's the hyphen)
		  ALL CAPS Command Shift K
		  SMALL CAPS Command Shift H

If you want to do this:	**Then follow these steps:**	**Shortcuts ▾ Notes ▾ Hints**
4.233 Change text back to Normal	▪ With the **text tool,** select the text to be changed (4.203–4.204). ▪ From the Type menu, slide down to "Type style" and out to the submenu; choose "Normal"; **Or** after selecting the type, press Command Shift Spacebar; **Or** after selecting the type, click the Normal "Style" button (N) in the character-view Control palette.	▪ Pressing Command Shift Spacebar is the quickest way to return your type back to the original font, even if you had it outlin-shadow-bold-italic (yuck)— just hit these three keys and you're back to Normal. ▪ This does not affect the style changes you don't see in the pop-out menu: super- and subscript (see 4.253 to change), or small caps, all caps, and lowercase (see 4.251).
4.234 Change the leading	▪ With the **text tool,** select the line(s) that have leading you wish to change (see 4.203–4.204 re: selecting). If you want to *decrease* the leading, make sure you select the *entire line* (see 5.27–5.31). ▪ From the Type menu slide down to "Leading" and out to the submenu; choose the leading value, or choose "Other…." ▪ In the "Leading" box, type in the number of points for line space; click OK; ▪ **Or** you can use the "Type specs" dialog box (Command T) to select a standard value or enter your own value. ▪ **Or** enter a value in the "Leading" option box in the character-view Control palette, or select one from the pop-up list, or use the nudge buttons to change the leading in .1-point increments.	▪ Leading can be specified in whole or tenth-point increments (.1), from 0 to 1300 points (don't ever type a comma in the number!). Leading can be larger or smaller than the point size of the type, depending on your objective. ▪ If the "Leading" submenu has no checkmark, or if any of the "Leading" option boxes are empty, it means there is more than one leading value in the selected text. ▪ Leading is a concept that needs to be fully understood in order to take advantage of the capabilities PageMaker gives you for adjusting it. Please read Section 5 on Spacing, especially the Leading section (5.12–5.58). This segment here is just a very brief synopsis.

If you want to do this:	**Then follow these steps:**	**Shortcuts ▾ Notes ▾ Hints**

4.235 Create reverse text

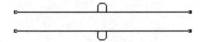

> **Boldness has genius, power, and magic in it.**
> —*Goethe*

- With the **text tool,** select the text you want to reverse (4.203–4.204 re: selecting text).
- From the Type menu slide down to "Type style," then to the pop-out menu on the side and choose "Reverse";
  Or click the Reverse "Style" button (R) in the character-view Control palette.

- Reverse text is white, which means if it is not on a dark background, it is invisible and can easily get lost. See 4.236 for finding it again. See 4.237 to prevent it from getting lost in the first place.
- Unfortunately (or maybe fortunately?) there is no keyboard command to reverse text.

4.236 Finding lost reverse text

An empty text block like this can indicate reverse text. (It can also indicate a text block where the text was removed, but not the extra Returns, so PageMaker still thinks there is something in it. These'll drive you nuts.)

- View the area on the screen where you think the reverse text may have disappeared, **or** from the Layout menu choose "Fit in window."
- Choose the **pointer tool.**
- From the Edit menu choose "Select all," or press Command A.
- You will see handles on every object on every layer (1.189–1.195; 1.214). Look for any handles that are holding an empty text block or that are under another layer— that will be your reverse text.
- Click once on the pointer tool to release all the handles; click in the area where you saw the empty block. Keep clicking until you find it.
- If the reverse text is under another layer, hold down the Command key and click on the layer above it. Click again, and just keep clicking until you get the handles of your object. Then press Command F to bring it to the front (1.216).

- Reverse text may just get lost on a white page, or it may be under another layer. If you don't quite get the layering concept, I strongly suggest you read that subsection in Section 1, 1.182–1.195.

If you want to do this:	Then follow these steps:	Shortcuts ▾ Notes ▾ Hints

4.237 Prevent reverse text from getting lost

> **Reverse Headline•**

Text to be reversed.

> •

Reversed text on the page, with the bullet marking the spot.

> **Reverse Headline**

Reversed text on a black background, with the bullet disappearing.

- At the end of the text to be reversed, type an extra character, like a bullet (Option 8 will give you this bullet: •).
- With the text tool, select the text to reverse it, but don't select the bullet; the bullet will stay black and you will always know where your reverse text is.
- If you are planning to center that text, the bullet will throw off the centered alignment. In that case, simply type the same character at the beginning and the end of the line.

- Of course, this will only work well if you are placing the text on a black background; if the background is only a dark gray or other color, the bullet will show. Of course, you can always shade the bullet or assign it the same color as the background. See 4.265 for info on how to assign color to text.

4.238 Expand or condense the type
(Change the set width)

Expand the limits.

Text expanded 140%

Condense the prose.

Text condensed to 70%

- With the **text tool,** select the text you want to expand or condense (4.203–4.204 re: selecting text).
- From the Type menu, slide down to "Set width" and out to the pop-out menu to choose a percentage.
- Use the "Other..." option to type in any percentage you may want, from 5 to 250 percent, in tenth-point increments (.1).
- To remove the set width from text, select the text and choose "Normal" from the "Set Width" submenu (press Command Shift X).

- You can also set the width in the "Type specs" dialog box (press Command T to get it; 4.205), **or** the Control palette (4.217).
- The set width of your type will affect the chosen letter and word spacing as well.
- This is great for those times when you need special effects for logos or headlines. It also works well when you have an unwanted hyphenated word—you can condense the type 98 or 99 percent, just enough to bring the hyphenated end back up onto the line.

If you want to do this:	**Then follow these steps:**	**Shortcuts ▾ Notes ▾ Hints**
4.239 Make several type specification changes at once	■ Select the text you want to change with the **text tool** (4.203–4.204). ■ From the Type menu, choose "Type specs..." ("specs" is for "specifications"), *or* press Command T. In this dialog box (as shown on page 222) you can specify any or all of those items at once. ■ **Or** make the changes with the Control palette using the style and option buttons, 4.210–4.218. Hit the Apply button (or the Return key) to apply all the changes you made at once.	■ If you are making only one or two changes to the text, such as a font or type style change, it is faster to use the Type menu or the Control palette. But if you want to make several changes without constantly running up to the Type menu or hunting through the Control palette, use "Type specs...." ■ You may find it easier and more efficient to use the Control palette instead of the menu to change type specifications. Most of the Type specs are available in the character-view Control palette. □ It the text tool is chosen but the insertion point is not within text, you will be setting publication defaults. See 4.240.
4.240 Change the type default specifications through the Control palette *(Change the text formatting publication defaults)*	■ Even if it is already the selected tool, click once on the **text tool;** it is important that the insertion point is **not** within text. ■ In the paragraph-view Control palette (4.300), select "No style" from the "Style" option. Enter whatever specs you want in any of the other options. ■ Click the "Character-view" button, or press Command Shift ` *(grave)* to switch to the character-view Control palette. ■ Make any formatting changes you want there. Press Apply or hit Return.	■ Be careful! You are setting new publication defaults. This is the format you will get from now on every time you select the text tool and begin to type. ■ Whenever you set a defined style sheet (other than "No style") as a publication default, the style "No style" picks up all those specifications (this essentially changes your text defaults). To reinstate your text defaults, follow the procedure in this task, or select the pointer tool and set defaults as usual (4.366).

If you want to do this:	**Then follow these steps:**	**Shortcuts ▾ Notes ▾ Hints**

4.241 Keep selected text from breaking at the end of a line

- With the **text tool,** select the words that you want to keep on the same line.
- From the Type menu choose "Type specs…," or press Command T.
- Click the radio button next to "No Break."
- Click OK, or press Return.
- **Or** type non-breaking spaces (a.k.a. hard spaces), between the words that you want to stay together. As you type, press the Option key and the Spacebar together between words.

- The default setting is "Break" which allows lines of text to break normally.
- While this can be very helpful sometimes (such as preventing people's names from being hypenated in weird places) it can also be very frustrating. If lines of text start misbehaving (getting too cozy on a single line, creating skittish line breaks, etc.) select the type and see if "No Break" is selected in the Type specs dialog box (when neither button is selected it means "No Break" is applied to part of the selected type).

4.242 Change the alignment

- With the **text tool,** select the text you want to change (4.203–4.204).
  - ☐ If you are changing just one paragraph, you only need to click once to set the insertion point within the paragraph (remember, PageMaker sees a paragraph every time you press the Return key, so a headline is considered a paragraph).
- From the Type menu, slide down to "Alignment," then over to the submenu and choose your alignment.
- **Or** click on an Alignment button in the paragraph-view Control palette (4.311).

- Notice how easy the keyboard shortcuts are to remember:
  - Align left .... Command Shift **L**
  - Align right ...... Command Shift **R**
  - Align center ... Command Shift **C**
  - Justify .... Command Shift **J**
  - Force justify .... Command Shift **F**
- Just as in 4.232, you can choose an alignment either from the menu or from the keyboard *before* you type. Make sure the insertion point is flashing.
- Be sure to read the following pages for practical information on alignment and its ramifications.

4.243 Alignment

How you choose to align your text plays a vital part in the look and the *readability* of your work (it is not the only factor—font, line length, typeface, style, size, line spacing, and case also contribute).

The term *readability* particularly refers to large amounts of text, as in a newsletter, brochure, magazine, etc. Extensive studies have shown what makes type easy and pleasant to read, and thus what encourages people to read what is written. Type that is not so readable can lose a significant part of its audience.

Sometimes, in short text, as in an advertisement or a package design, you can get away with using a particular design feature that detracts from the readability, but that does add to the attractiveness of the piece (such as extreme letterspacing, or all caps with a justified alignment), if you feel the *look* of the piece is more important than the loss of readability. You just need to be aware of the choice you are making and be able to qualify it.

Alignment in PageMaker is very interconnected with the word spacing, letter spacing, and hyphenation controls, particularly when working with justified text. I know you don't have time, but it would seriously behoove you to read through and understand Section 5.

4.244 Align left

> There is no single voice capable of expressing every idea; romance is still necessary, ornament is necessary, and simplification is not better than complexity.
>
> — Milton Glaser

Text aligned on the left is the most readable, as far as alignment is concerned. It is able to use the "Desired" word spacing and letter spacing (5.112–5.150) that the designer built into the font. With the alignment on the left, as you read, your eye can quickly find the beginning of the next sentence. And in this alignment, you can most easily make corrections and adjust lines when necessary, often without affecting the rest of the text at all.

When you align text left, the ideal is to keep the right, "ragged" side as smooth as possible. Often that means forcing line breaks in order to fill in holes or to prevent long strings from hanging beyond the rest of the lines. For instance, in this paragraph, the word "as" in the second line should be bumped down to the next line so it doesn't hang over like it does. To do that I would put my insertion point directly in front of the "a" and press Shift-Return (4.348–4.353).

4.245 Align right

> There is no single voice capable of expressing every idea; romance is still necessary, ornament is necessary, and simplification is not better than complexity.
>
> — Milton Glaser

Text aligned on the right creates a definite *look*. The letter and word spacing can still retain the "Desired" amount (5.112–5.150), and corrections can still be made fairly easily without affecting the rest of the text. The biggest drop in readability comes from the fact that the left edge, where our eye returns to find the next line to read, is not consistent. In short amounts of text, this isn't a great problem.

If you are using this alignment for the *look* it creates, then you might as well emphasize the look. Don't be a wimp. Rather than try to keep the left, ragged edge as smooth as possible, exaggerate it. There's no excuse to have hyphenated words here; bumping "necessary" down will eliminate a hyphen, as well as make the alignment more interesting. To bump "necessary," press Shift-Return (4.348–4.353) directly in front of it.

4.246 Align center

> There is no single voice capable of
> expressing every idea; romance is
> still necessary, ornament is neces-
> sary, and simplification is not better
> than complexity.
>
> — Milton Glaser

A centered alignment also gives a *look* to text, a more formal, serious sort of look. As with left- and right-aligned, it doesn't affect the letter and word spacing. But, as with right-aligned, if you're going to do it, then do it. Don't let the lines look ambiguous, as if it can't decide if it's justified or centered. A centered alignment gives you a perfect opportunity to group the lines into logical thoughts, rather than letting them fall where they want. Also, varying the line lengths makes it much more visually interesting. And there is never any excuse for hyphenated words. Break the lines with Shift-Returns (4.348–4.353).

> There is no single voice
> capable of expressing every idea;
> romance is still necessary,
> ornament is necessary,
> and simplification
> is not better than complexity.
>
> Milton Glaser

4.247 Justify

> There is no single voice capable of
> expressing every idea; romance is still
> necessary, ornament is necessary, and
> simplification is not better than com-
> plexity.
>
> — Milton Glaser

When you justify text, PageMaker forces the lines to extend to a certain length by adding or deleting space between the words and letters. You can specify the minimum and maximum amount you will allow the spacing to adjust, but if PageMaker can't do it the way you want, she does it the way she wants. (If you check "Loose/tight lines" in the Preferences menu, a colored or gray bar will indicate the lines where PageMaker refused to listen to you; 1.227.)

The biggest problem with justified text is the uneven word spacing; some lines have extra spacing, some less, and this visual irregularity interrupts the maximum readability. The shorter the line length, the worse the problem. It is also more difficult to correct dumb hyphenations and widows, as in the example.

Justify text *only* when the line length is long enough to be able to adjust the spacing equitably.

4.248 Force justify

> There is no single voice capable of
> expressing every idea; romance is still
> necessary, ornament is necessary, and
> simplification is not better than com-
> p   l   e   x   i   t   y   .
>
> — Milton   Glaser

Now this really looks stupid. The worst possible kind of widow (the end of a hyphenated word as the last line of a paragraph) really looks ridiculous when it is force justified. So do those last two words stretched across the line.

In regular justification, the last line of a paragraph retains its regular word and letter spacing. Occasionally the last line may be long enough that you would like it to justify to match the rest, in which case you could safely use force justification. Usually it isn't.

Force justification is a design technique created not so much for paragraphs as for headlines or a short body of letterspaced text. The example below was typed with an Option Spacebar between words, then force justified. See 4.249 for more details.

The Mac is not a typewriter

written   by   Robin   Williams

If you want to do this:

4.249 Force justify display text with wide letterspacing

ZOUNDS!

I   was   never

so   bethump'd

with   words

William   Shakespeare
King   John   ❧   Act   II

I typed this text normally and then force justified it. (The rules, or lines, are part of the paragraph; Section 7.)

ZOUNDS!

I   w a s   n e v e r

s o   b e t h u m p' d

w i t h   w o r d s.

W i l l i a m   S h a k e s p e a r e
K i n g   J o h n   ❧   A c t   I I

I typed this text using the Option Spacebar between words, and then force justified it. (The rules, or lines, are part of the paragraph; Section 7.)

Then follow these steps:

- The trick to stretching text across a line is to make PageMaker think it is one word, which you can do by putting a *hard space*, also called a *non-breaking space*, between the words (5.217–5.238).
- Type each line of text, pressing Option Spacebar (which is a *hard space*) between each word instead of just the Spacebar.
- At the end of each line, where you really want the line to break after it is letterspaced, hit a Return or a Shift-Return (4.348–4.353).
- When you are done, select all the lines with the **text tool.**
- From the Type menu slide down to "Alignment" to get the pop-out menu, and choose "Force justify," **or** press Command Shift F, **or** click the "Force justify" alignment button in the paragraph-view Control palette (4.300).
- **An alternative sequence** is to create a bounding box (4.26) the width you want the text to occupy. With the insertion point flashing, press Command Shift F to force justify what you are about to type. Type, using Option Spacebar between words. This way you can see and decide exactly where lines should break as you type, rather than having to anticipate. *You do need to break the lines yourself,* as the text can't word wrap if it is one huge word.

Shortcuts ▾ Notes ▾ Hints

- Force justify forces *every* line to extend the maximum width of the line length. This differs from regular justification, which doesn't affect any line that has a Return character in it.
- The first thing justifying text affects is the space between words: it adds or removes minute amounts of space. Then, if that isn't enough, it adds or removes space between characters. So, in forcing the justification, if you can make PageMaker think there is just one word on that line, it will letterspace that line nearly perfectly. This is much easier than trying to use the Spacing command.
- If you have already typed the text with Spacebars, or if you can't deal with typing the Option Spacebars, you can use the Story Editor to find and change all the Spacebars to Option Spacebars (9.79). Just make sure you type Returns where you want lines to break, or the entire text will come out as one word and will confuse PageMaker because she can't find that word in her dictionary in order to hyphenate it, in which case it may look something like this:

ZOUNDSIwaseverbethumpdwithwordsWilliamShakespeareKingJohnActII

If you want to do this:

4.250   Set indents or tabs

Then follow these steps:

- With the **text tool,** select the text you want to indent or tab (see 4.203–4.204 re: selecting text). If you just want to adjust a single paragraph, you only need to click the insertion point into the paragraph.
- From the Type menu choose "Indents/ tabs..." *or* press Command I.
- The margin edge of the tab ruler aligns with the margin edge of your text block *if there is space in the window* (otherwise it just plops in the middle of the screen and you have to drag it into position).
- **To set a tab,** click in the ruler at the point where you want the tab to be. Then click on one of the tab alignment icons in the upper left of the ruler. If you want Leaders, choose one while the tab is selected.
- **To set the left or right indent,** press on the bottom half of the large black triangle at either end of the ruler. Press-and-drag on a marker to move it to where you want the text indented.
- **To set a first-line indent,** press on the top half of the left large triangle and move it where you want your first line to indent. The first line after every Return will align with that top marker, and the rest of the text will wrap back to the bottom half of the marker.

Shortcuts ▾ Notes ▾ Hints

- Indents and tabs are so important and so often misunderstood that they rate a separate section of their own. If this brief synopsis isn't enough for you, please read Section 6, where you will find an in-depth explanation of indents and tabs, leaders, the ruler, how and when to use indents and tabs, and much more. Wow.
- You can set indents in the paragraph-view Control palette by typing values in the indent options edit boxes; see 4.321– 4.326.

- You may need to scroll to the right to see the right indent marker.
- The left indent *marker* is made up of two separate triangles; to move the left *indent,* press on the lower one (the top one is the *first-line indent*).

If you want to do this:

4.251 Change the case
(as in uppercase or lowercase)

Case: | ✓**Normal**
All caps
Small caps

a) into UPPERCASE (all caps)

b) into SMALL CAPS
(where typed capitals remain normal-sized capitals, but lowercase letters become small-sized capitals)

c) into lowercase

The "Case" options in the character-view Control palette

Then follow these steps:

- With the **text tool,** select the text you want to change (4.203–4.204).
- From the Type menu choose "Type specs...," *or* press Command T.
- Press on the box next to the label "Case"; you will see a little menu drop down; then:

- To turn *regular lowercase text* or SMALL CAPS into UPPERCASE, choose "All caps."

- To turn *regular lowercase text* into SMALL CAPS, choose "Small caps."
- To turn UPPERCASE into SMALL CAPS, retype it, *using lowercase letters.* Then follow the step directly above.

- To turn SMALL CAPS text into lowercase, choose "Normal."
- To turn UPPERCASE into lowercase, retype it (unless you originally typed it lowercase and transformed it into uppercase; then you can choose "Normal"), *or*
- In the character-view Control palette, click the "Small caps," or "All caps" button.

Shortcuts ▾ Notes ▾ Hints

- Unfortunately, there is no way to turn text that was typed in UPPERCASE into lowercase with just the push of a key—it must simply be retyped. If the text was *originally* typed lowercase and then *transformed* into uppercase with the command, then you can change it back to lowercase with the command.
- To change any text into all caps, select the text and then press Command Shift K; to turn it back into lowercase, press the key sequence again.
- See 4.252 to change the size of the SMALL CAPS. The default is 70% of the point size.
- Keyboard shortcut is Command Shift H.
- You cannot change type typed in all caps into small caps because "Small caps" only affects the lowercase letters.

- The keyboard shortcut to turn SMALL CAPS into lowercase is Command Shift H.
- If you originally typed the text in lowercase and transformed it into uppercase with the command, you can use the keyboard shortcut to turn it back into lowercase: Command Shift K.

If you want to do this:

Then follow these steps:

Shortcuts • Notes • Hints

4.252 Change the size of the SMALL CAPS

Small caps size: **70** % of point size

NOW IS THE TIME *(70%)*

NOW IS THE TIME
(180%)

N. I T. T. *(10%)*

- With the **text tool,** select the text you want to change (4.203–4.204).
- From the Type menu choose "Type specs...," *or* press Command T.
- If the box next to Case does not say "Small caps," then press on it to pop out the menu and choose "Small caps."
- Press on the button "Options...."
- In the box next to "Small caps size," type in a number from 1 to 200; you can use tenth-point increments (.1).

- The keyboard shortcut for creating small caps is Command Shift H. Of course, you must first select the text with the text tool.
- Standard default is 70% of the point size. If you click on the pointer tool before you change that percentage, you can reset the default (4.366).
- Press Option Return to close both dialog boxes with one motion.

4.253 Change the position
(Normal or superscript or subscript)

4ᵗʰ of July   *Superscript (th)*

H₂O   *Superscript (2)*

superscript ▣▣ subscript

The superscript and subscript option buttons in the character-view Control palette

---

- With the **text tool,** select the text you want to change (4.203–4.204).
  - ☐ From the Type menu choose "Type specs...," *or* press Command T.
  - ☐ Press on the box next to the label "Position"; a little menu will pop-up; choose the position you want.
- **Or** use the keyboard shortcuts:
  Superscript: Command Shift +
  (That's the plus sign from the key*board,* above the =)
  Subscript: Command Shift -
  (That's the hyphen, from the key*board;* or the numeric key*pad* minus sign if you're in "arrow key mode"; 4.232.)
- **Or** use the "Position" buttons in the character-view Control palette; see 4.215.

- See 4.254–4.260.
- **Normal** position sets letters on the *baseline,* (4.258) which is the invisible line the type normally sits on.
- **Superscript** sizes text to $\frac{7}{12}$ of the point size (which is 58.3 percent); that is, if the type is 12 points, the superscript size will be 7 points. Then it figures $\frac{1}{3}$ of the point size of the normal text (33%) and puts the superscript baseline just that high *above* the normal baseline. Example: 3rd becomes 3ʳᵈ.
- **Subscript** does the same as superscript, but places the baseline of the subscript character $\frac{1}{3}$ *below* the normal baseline. Example: H2O becomes H_2O.

239

Change the size and placement of superscript and subscript

4.254 To find this dialog box, from the Type menu choose "Type specs…," then click on the "Options…" button.

4.255 As with any character formatting, you must first *select* the text (use the text tool) that is to be super- or subscripted. If you change these settings while no text is selected and while no insertion point is flashing, you will set the defaults for the publication (4.366).

4.256 The **"Super/subscript size"** box defines the actual size of the character. You can enter values from 1% to 200% in tenth-point (.1) increments.

The default percent, 58.3, is $7/12$ of the point size of the type; that is, if the type is 12 points, the super/subscript character will be 7 points. If you change this number to 50%, then in a 12-point font your super/subscript character will be 6 points; in a 30-point font, the scripted character will be 15 points.

4.257 *Do you see a hidden possibility in this sizing option? You can set type up to 1300 points, simply by turning selected text into a superscript at 200%. Set the "position" to 0 (zero). See 21.22.*

See 4.252
See 4.256
See 4.259
See 4.260
See 4.263

Type options

Small caps size:	**70**	% of point size
Super/subscript size:	58.3	% of point size
Superscript position:	33.3	% of point size
Subscript position:	33.3	% of point size
Baseline shift:	0	points ⦿ Up ○ Down

OK
Cancel

4.258 *The line below "Thomas Hardy" defines the invisible baseline from which super- and subscript characters position themselves above (1) and below (2): The normal text itself is positioned with $2/3$ of the character body above the baseline, and $1/3$ below.*

Thomas[1] Hardy[2]

4.259 The **"Superscript position"** box defines where the character will be placed in relation to the baseline of the normal text. The default is 33 percent, which places the baseline of the script character one-third of the way *above* the normal baseline, as shown in 4.258. You can enter any percentage value from 0 to 500 in tenth-point (.1) increments.

4.260 The **"Subscript position"** box defines where the character will be placed in relation to the baseline of the normal text. The default is 33 percent, which places the baseline of the script character one-third of the way *below* the normal baseline, as shown in 4.258. You can enter any percentage value from 0 to 500 in tenth-point (.1) increments.

If you want to do this:

4.261a Set a default for creating beautiful fractions easily

$\frac{7}{8}$ $\quad$ $\frac{15}{16}$ $\qquad$ $9\frac{3}{4}$

Super/subscript size:	70	% of point size
Superscript position:	33.3	% of point size
Subscript position:	0	% of point size

4.261b Type a fraction without having to select characters and open dialog boxes

(See also 4.262)

Superscript

Subscript

The "Position" options in the character-view Control palette.

Then follow these steps:

- Read the column to the right. ➠
- Choose the **pointer tool.**
- Press Command T to get the "Type specs..." dialog box; then click once on the "Options..." button.
- Change the number in the "Super/ subscript size" box to 70.
- Change the number in the last box ("Subscript position") to 0 (zero).
- Press Option Return to close both dialog boxes. You have just set a *publication default* (4.366).

- Set the defaults in the super- and subscript dialog box as shown above. Then use the following keyboard shortcuts:
  - □ Just before typing the top number, press Command Shift +; type the number; press Command Shift + again.
  - □ To type the fraction bar, press Shift Option 1 (that's the number one).
  - □ Press Command Shift - (that's the hyphen); type the bottom number; press Command Shift - again to continue typing in the Normal style.
- **Or** click the appropriate "Position" button in the character-view Control palette.

Shortcuts ▾ Notes ▾ Hints

- **This technique sets a publication default** in the "Type options" dialog box, since creating fractions is probably the most useful way to take advantage of superscripts and subscripts. Setting the default means that whenever you start typing *a new text block,* you will have the new default specifications. As soon as you set your insertion point into a previously-created text block, the specifications from the character to the left of the insertion point take over.
- **If you don't want to set the default,** then just follow the steps to type the fraction. Then select the three characters in the fraction, get the "Type options" dialog box, and type the same numbers (70 and 0) in the same boxes as explained in the directions.
- **If you want to set these defaults for the entire PageMaker application,** simply follow the first five steps *while no publication is open*—you should see just the PageMaker menu, but no open window (4.365).
- You may want to change the size of the super/subscript from the 70 suggested here, depending on the size of your type and how it looks. You may also need to kern (5.151–5.179) to get the spacing correct.

If you want to do this:	Then follow these steps:	Shortcuts ▾ Notes ▾ Hints

4.262 Create a fraction using the "Run script…" Addition
(also see 20.65)

1/2   ¹/₂   ½

A fraction typed as normal text, scripted as a "Fraction," and as a "Horizontal fraction."

ᵃⁿᵈ/ₒᵣ

The "Fraction" script will turn any two words separated by a space into a fraction layout.

- In your publication, type the top number of the fraction, type a slash bar, type the bottom number of the fraction.
- Place the insertion point immediately following the last number (do *not* highlight the numbers).
- From the Utilities menu, slide down to "Aldus Additions," then over to the submenu and choose "Run script…."
- Navigate through your folders to locate and open the "Aldus PageMaker 5.0" folder, then open the "Scripts" folder.
- Select "Fraction" or "Horizontal fraction."
- Click the radio button next to "File."
- Click OK.

- The "Fraction" script can be used for any fraction; the "Horizontal fraction" works only for fractions with single-digit numerators and denominators.
- The "Fraction" script automates the procedure you follow when you manually create beautiful fractions (4.261). In both methods, the fractions may require manual kerning (5.168–5.169).
- Characters you type directly following a fraction may also be subscript. You can avoid this by pressing Command Shift - (hyphen), or clicking the subscript button in the Control palette to turn it off, before you resume typing.
- Although this is kind of a nifty trick, it can be a bit cumbersome to run up to the menu, find all the folders, and then wait for PageMaker to make all the adjustments. It's a lot slicker as you type along to use the keyboard shortcuts outlined in task 4.261b.

It iz better tew know nothing
than tew know what ain't so.

Josh Billings

If you want to do this:

Then follow these steps:

Shortcuts ▾ Notes ▾ Hints

4.263 Shift the baseline of selected text

HOPSCOTCH

Shown within its leading slug, "Hop" has a baseline shift of 5.9 points up.

HOPSCOTCH

Shown within its leading slug, "Hop" has a baseline shift of 5.9 points down.

- With the **text tool,** select the words whose baseline you want to change (4.203–4.204).
- From the Type menu choose "Type specs…," *or* press Command T.
- Click the "Options…" button.
- Enter a value in the "Baseline shift" edit box between 0 and 1600 points in .1 increments.
- Click the radio button next to "Up" or "Down" depending on whether you want to move the baseline up or down.
- Press Option Return to close both boxes.
- **Or,** enter the value you want in the character-view Control palette (4.218).

- Values in the "Baseline shift" edit box are measured in points.
- You may need to switch page views or select the text block and "Bring to front," to see the shifted text. If you delete the text block but the shifted text doesn't seem to go away, simply change page views.
- You can change the measurement system used in the "Baseline-shift" option in the character-view Control palette. With the option active, press Command Option M and then enter the unit of measure you want to use (3.114).

4.264 Create interesting bullets

❖ No ∗ Boring ▾ Bullets ❖

16-point text
7-point Dingbats, with a baseline shift of 1.8 points, as bullets

▲ ▼ ᴬₐ 0 in

The Baseline shift option in the Character-view Control palette.

- Type the character you want to use as a bullet, such as a Zapf Dingbat.
- Select the Dingbat with the **text tool.**
- From the Type menu choose "Type specs…," *or* press Command T.
- In the "Size" box enter the point size you have chosen (one smaller than the text).
- Click once on the "Options…" button.
- In the "Baseline shift" box, type a value.
- Press Option Return to close both dialog boxes.
- **Or** use the options in the character-view Control palette, select and change the size and baseline shift of the character being used as a bullet. See 4.211 and 4.218.

- The standard "bullet" is the round dot you see before *this* paragraph, produced by pressing Option 8 in any font.
- If you simply try to reduce the size of dingbats to use them as bullets, they appear too low in relation to the other characters. However, in some circumstances, it does work just fine (those are 5-point Zapf Dingbats before each paragraph in the tasks sections of this book).
- You can play around with the size and baseline shift value in the "Type specs" boxes to get exactly what you want. The numbers noted here are just suggestions.

If you want to do this:

4.265 Make the text or rules gray

What type shall I use?
The gods refuse to answer.
They refuse because they do not know.

W.A. Dwiggins

The lighter text is 65 percent black.

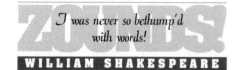

The light background text is 25 percent black;
the 12-point rule is 77 percent black.

Then follow these steps:

- If you haven't done so already, you need to create a Color style. Then you can apply the color to the text, rule, or border:
- From the Element menu, choose "Define colors...."
- Click "New...."
- Click in the radio button next to "Tint."
- Type in a name for this new color, a name that will give you a clue as to what it is, such as "Light Gray," or the percent value of the tint you are creating (e.g., 65%).
- In the "Base Color:" pop-up menu, select "Black."
- In the "Tint" edit box enter a value (like 65).
- Press Option Return to close both boxes.
- From the Window menu, choose "Color palette," or press Command K.
- With the **text tool,** select the text you want to shade gray; **or** with the **pointer tool,** select any number of rules (lines) or borders to shade gray.
- Click once in the color style name that you want to apply to the text or line. Unless you have a color or grayscale monitor, the items won't look any different on the screen, but they will print gray.

Shortcuts ▾ Notes ▾ Hints

- If you have already created the Color style, then you only need to **select** the text or rule, get the Color palette from the Window menu, and choose the color. For text, you can also use the "Type specs" dialog box (press Command T).
- This technique is particularly useful for those of us who deal mostly in one color (black). If you have a color monitor or want to use spot color or any other kind of color, read Section 16 on Color.

- Examples of tints:

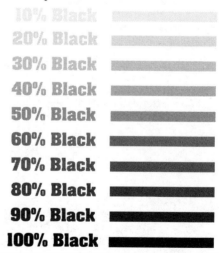

If you want to do this:	**Then follow these steps:**	**Shortcuts ▾ Notes ▾ Hints**
4.266 Delete text	▪ With the **text tool,** select the text you want deleted (see 4.203–4.204 re: selecting). ▪ From the Edit menu, choose "Clear," *or* press the Backspace/Delete key.	▪ **Delete** or **Clear** does *not* put the deleted text on the Clipboard—it is just gone. ▪ If you instantly decide you made a mistake, **UNDO** from the Edit menu. ▪ Shortcut to Undo: Command Z. Note: you can only undo *the very last thing you did* (1.311). If you need more serious undoing, see the info on Reverting, 18.2–18.3 and 18.30–18.31.
4.267 Cut text	▪ With the **text tool,** select the text you want to cut (see 4.203–4.204 re: selecting). ▪ From the Edit menu, choose "Cut," *or* press Command X (easy to remember, since X is like X-ing it out.	▪ **Cutting** removes the text from the publication and places it on the Clipboard (1.273–1.279), ready for pasting (4.269). ▪ If you instantly decide you made a mistake, **UNDO** from the Edit menu. ▪ Shortcut to Undo: Command Z. Note: you can only Undo *the very last thing you did* (1.311).
4.268 Copy text	▪ With the **text tool,** select the text you want to copy (see 4.203–4.204 re: selecting). ▪ From the Edit menu, choose "Copy," *or* press Command C (easy to remember— C for Copy).	▪ **Copying** *leaves* the text in the publication and places a *copy* of it on the Clipboard (1.273–1.279), ready for pasting (4.269).

> **For more info on cutting, copying, and pasting, see 1.273–1.283 and 4.125–4.128.**

If you want to do this:	Then follow these steps:	Shortcuts ▾ Notes ▾ Hints
4.269 Paste text	■ With the **text tool,** cut or copy the text you want to paste (4.267–4.268).	■ For more info on cutting, copying, and pasting, see 1.273–1.284 and 4.125–4.128.
a) Into its own text block	■ If you want to paste the text on the page in its own text block, with the **text tool,** click the insertion point anywhere *outside* of another text block; **Or** press-and-drag with the text tool to create a bounding box for the text to flow into (4.26). ■ From the Edit menu choose "Paste," *or* press Command V. The text will paste in, beginning at the flashing insertion point. The entire story will be contained in the text block.	■ If the insertion point is inside a column, the text block will be the width of the column (1.79–1.85). ■ If you create a bounding box (4.26), the text will be the width of the invisible box, but the depth will expand to fit the text. ■ If the insertion point is neither in a column nor part of a bounding box, the text block will be the width of the page margins (1.79).
b) Into a current story	■ With the **text tool,** click once to set an insertion point in the story at the spot where you want the text to begin. ■ From the Edit menu, choose "Paste," *or* press Command V.	■ Text pasted into a paragraph will take on the formatting of that paragraph—tabs, indents, margins, etc. ■ Text pasted in as its own paragraph (by hitting Return before pasting) will retain its original formatting.
4.270 Replace existing text with the text that you cut or copied onto the Clipboard	■ With the **text tool,** select the text you want to replace by pressing-and-dragging over it (4.203–4.204 re: selecting). *Just the text you select will be replaced.* ■ From the Edit menu, choose "Paste," *or* press Command V; the pasted text will completely *replace* whatever was selected.	■ If you want to replace text with a word processing file, see 4.59. ■ Replacing text works exactly the same if the text you want to use is from the Scrapbook (see 1.314 and 1.317 for info on working with the Scrapbook).

4.271 Rotating text in PageMaker is easy and accurate. At last, she has *full* text rotation capabilities—360° of rotation that can be applied in increments of one one-hundredths (.01) of a degree. Text can be rotated either manually with the rotating tool or, for more control, numerically through the Control palette. Any number and combination of text blocks and objects can by selected and rotated either on their own axis or around another point selected elsewhere on the screen.

4.272 The rotating tool can be used to select text blocks as well as to rotate them. When you click on the rotating tool and move it off the Toolbox, the cursor turns into a starburst. Once a text block is selected, you simply press-and-drag the starburst cursor, causing the text block to rotate.

4.273 For more accurate results, exact degrees of rotation can be specified in the Control palette. After selecting the text block with either the rotating tool or the pointer tool, any degree of rotation between -360° and 360° in .01 increments can be typed into the "Rotating" option edit box in the object-view Control palette (3.35).

4.274 Rotated text can be edited either right on the page or in the Story Editor. Text formatting changes can be made with the text tool selected; the text block and line length can be re-sized when the pointer tool is selected. Any of the options available through any of the Control palettes can be applied to rotated text.

4.275 It is actually the text block itself that is rotated, not the text. Text that is brought into a rotated text block takes on that text block's degree of rotation. If you cut or copy text from a rotated text block, it will not be rotated when you paste it somewhere else (unless you select and cut and paste the *entire* text block with the pointer tool).

4.276 If the rotated text block has any text left to be placed (that is, if there is an arrow or a plus sign in the bottom windowshade handle; 4.109), it, too, will be rotated when you pull down the windowshade. If, however, you click once on the arrow to pick up the rest of the text and place it elsewhere, it will not be rotated.

4.277 If only a single rotated text block is chosen, the degree of rotation shows in the "Rotating" option box in the Control palette. If a new value is typed in, the text block rotates to that degree of rotation. If you select more than one text block or object, the "Rotating" option edit box shows as 0°, regardless of the degree of rotation to which the selected items are rotated (even if they were rotated to the same degree, at the same time; even if one item is rotated and the other isn't). Typing a new value in the "Rotating" option edit box *adds* that value to the existing degree of rotation for each item.

4.278 Text or graphics pasted inline in a rotated text block become rotated; text that contains an inline graphic can be rotated. You can also rotate an inline graphic independent of the text. The same is true for text-wrapped objects: you can rotate both the text and the object, just the text, or just the object.

4.279 Rotated text printed to a non-PostScript printer may look better using ATM or TrueType fonts.

If you want to do this:	Then follow these steps:	Shortcuts ▾ Notes ▾ Hints
4.280 Rotate text using the rotating tool *(See 2.85–2.98 for more info and tasks related to the rotation tool.)*	■ With the **rotating tool,** click once on the text block you want to rotate. ■ Press on the text block and drag the starburst cursor out and then in the direction you want to rotate the text. ■ Let go when the text block is in the position you want it.	■ Hold down the Command key as you press-and-drag the cursor if you want the text block's centerpoint to serve as its fixed point. ■ Hold down the Shift key if you want the text to rotate in 45° increments. ■ The farther you drag the cursor from the text block, the longer the rotation lever becomes. The longer the rotation lever, the smoother the text block rotates. Try it.
4.281 Rotate text using the Control palette *(See 3.76–3.79 and 3.93–3.94 for more info on using the Control palette to rotate objects)*	■ With the **pointer tool,** click once on the text block you want to rotate. ■ Display the Control palette (Command ') if it is not displayed already. Click on a reference point on the proxy to serve as the fixed point. ■ In the "Rotating" option edit box, type the degree of rotation you want. ■ Click the Apply button (or press Return).	■ You can Shift-click to select more than one text block, or text blocks and objects together (See 4.287). ■ Entering a positive number in the edit box rotates the text counter-clockwise; a negative number rotates it clockwise. ■ You can use keyboard shortcuts in the Control Palette to rotate text blocks once they are selected (3.112).
4.282 Unrotate text	■ With the **pointer tool,** or the **rotating tool**, click once on the rotated text block. ■ From the Element menu choose "Remove transformation," ■ **Or**, in the Control palette, type a 0 (zero) in the "Rotating" option edit box; click Return.	■ Pressing Command Z or choosing "Undo rotate" from the Edit menu (or "Undo apply" for text rotated from the Control palette) will immediately undo a rotation. ■ Typing 0 in the "Rotating" edit box when more than one rotated text block is selected will not unrotate the items.

If you want to do this:	**Then follow these steps:**	**Shortcuts ▾ Notes ▾ Hints**
4.283 Edit rotated text	▪ With the **text tool,** highlight the text as usual and make the necessary changes. ▪ **Or,** click the **text tool** within the rotated text. ▪ From the Edit menu choose "Edit story," *or* press Command E. ▪ **Or,** with the **pointer tool,** triple click on the text block. ▪ Edit the text in the story window. ▪ Close the story as usual (9.87–9.88).	▪ Anything you can do to normal text you can do to rotated text. This includes kerning, adding letter or word spacing, changing the width of the characters, applying style sheets, or adding paragraph rules.
4.284 Change the degree of rotation for a single, already-rotated text block	▪ With the **rotating tool** select the text block. ▪ Press-and-drag the starburst cursor in the direction you want the text to rotate. Let go when it is rotated to your liking. ▪ **Or,** with the **pointer tool** select the text block. ▪ In the "Rotating" option edit box in the Control palette, type in the degree of rotation you want to rotate the text. ▪ Click the Apply button or press Return.	▪ Each time you rotate an object through the Control palette, PageMaker starts from 0°. She doesn't just add the new amount to the old one. That means that if you take something that is already at a 45° angle and enter 30° in the "Rotating" option edit box, the object will rotate back to 30°, not up to 75°. It's different, however, when you select more than one rotated object; see 4.287.
4.285 Resize a rotated text block	▪ With the **pointer tool,** click once on the rotated text. ▪ Press-and-drag on one of the text block handles, depending on which direction you want to resize the block.	▪ This is just like resizing any text *block;* the text will word wrap to fill the new size. ▪ If the text block is threaded to other text blocks, the resizing may cause text to flow into or out of the text block. Text that flows into the rotated text block will also be rotated; text that flows out will not. ▪ You can resize a text block through the Control palette; see 3.89.

If you want to do this:

Then follow these steps:

Shortcuts ▾ Notes ▾ Hints

4.286 Wrap rotated text around a graphic

- Text wrap a graphic as usual (Section 13).
- With the **pointer tool,** press-and-drag the rotated text to position it near the text-wrapped object.

- Rotated text will wrap around objects just as any other text will. Lines will break as necessary and the *depth* of the rotated text block will expand as necessary. You can rotate text and graphics together if you want, or rotate just the text, or just the graphic, even after it's been text-wrapped.

4.287 Rotate more than one text block, or text blocks and objects, at the same time

- With the **pointer tool** or the **rotating tool,** shift-click (or marquee) all the text blocks and/or objects you want to rotate.
- With the **rotating tool,** press on the spot you want to serve as the fixed point, and drag the starburst cursor in the direction you want the items to rotate. Let go when you are done.
- **Or,** display the Control palette (Command ') if it is not displayed already.
- Highlight the "Rotating" option edit box, and type in the degree of rotation you want the group of text and/or objects to turn.
- Click the Apply button or press Return.

- To rotate a text block (or any group of items) around its center point, hold down the Command key as you press-and-drag the starburst cursor.
- When you select more than one rotated text block or object at a time, the value in the "Rotating" option edit box will show as 0°, even if everything is rotated to the same degree. If you decide to rotate a group of text blocks some more, the new value you enter in the "Rotating" option box will be added to each object's existing degree of rotation.

Paragraphs

The "Paragraph..." dialog box holds a plethora of possibilities. Most attributes are discussed here; some are discussed more appropriately in Section 5 on Spacing.

4.288 All paragraph attributes apply to an entire paragraph. **Remember, the Mac sees a new paragraph every time you hit the Return or Enter key!** See 4.348–4.354 for intimate details on the paragraph concept and the *line-break* feature that provides the perfect option when you need a new *line,* but not a new *paragraph.*

4.289 Paragraph attributes apply to entire paragraphs. When you want to apply formatting, you only need to set the insertion point anywhere in the paragraph (click once with the text tool) to select it.

4.290 To select more than one paragraph, you must press-and-drag over each one, but you don't need to select *entire* paragraphs—even selecting just one character of each will do. As in any other program on the Mac, it is not possible to select two paragraphs that are not next to each other; e.g., you can't select the first and the third paragraphs, nor can you select the first paragraphs of two separate stories (4.113), even though they may be physically next to each other on the page.

The "Paragraph..." dialog box:

4.291 **"Indents"** is connected to the Indents/Tabs ruler. Use it for indenting left and right margins, as well as for indenting (or "outdenting") the first line of each paragraph. See 4.321–4.326.

4.292 Use **"Paragraph space"** for adding extra space between paragraphs or after heads and subheads, rather than using extra carriage returns. This extremely important and useful concept is covered in 5.72–5.96.

4.293 Use **"Alignment"** to determine whether text aligns on the left, the right, or both sides; is centered, or force justified. See 4.243–4.249 for examples and information on the uses of the different alignments, and 4.327 for using this dialog box to control it.

4.294 Use **"Dictionary"** to choose one of the many foreign language or specialized dictionaries for hyphenation and spell-checking. You can use more than one dictionary (up to seventeen) per publication, but additional dictionaries do slow down the composition and the spell-checker. (Spell-checking info is in 9.90–9.100; 9.105–9.126. Dictionary info is in 9.97–9.103. Hyphenation info is in 5.229–5.255.)

4.295 Use **"Options"** to control where columns and paragraphs break. Use it also to avoid widows and orphans (lines of a paragraph that straggle alone at the top or bottom of columns). See 4.329–4.347.

4.296 Use **"Rules..."** to place rules (or "lines," as they are called in the Element menu) at the top or bottom of a paragraph. This is a terrific feature. It takes a bit of time to learn to use properly, but I guarantee it's worth every minute of the effort. Section 7 is entirely devoted to Paragraph Rules.

4.297 Use **"Spacing..."** to fine tune the space between letters, between words, and between lines (leading). This entire dialog box and its concepts are discussed in Section 5 on Spacing. You really should read it.

4.298 Some of the options in the "Paragraph" dialog box are also available in the paragraph-view Control palette. See 4.300 for a diagram of this palette and Section 3 for an in-depth look at the full potential of the Control palette.

4.299 The "Paragraph specifications..." dialog box *(from the Type menu, choose "Paragraph...," or press Command M)*

"Paragraph space" Before and After is discussed in Section 5 on Spacing. See 4.292; 5.72–5.96.

Paragraph specifications

See 4.291 — **Indents:**

See 4.321 — **Left** `0` **inches**

See 4.323–4.325 — **First** `0` **inches**

See 4.322 — **Right** `0` **inches**

Paragraph space:

Before `0` **inches**

After `0` **inches**

See 4.327 — **Alignment:** `Right`

Dictionary: `US English`

See 4.329–4.347 — **Options:**

See 4.334 — ☐ **Keep lines together**

See 4.335 — ☐ **Column break before**

See 4.336 — ☐ **Page break before**

☐ **Keep with next** `0` **lines**

☐ **Widow control** `0` **lines**

☐ **Orphan control** `0` **lines**

☐ **Include in table of contents**

OK

Cancel

Rules...

Spacing...

Press Command Period to shortcut.

One of PageMaker's greatest features! See Section 7.

See 4.297. This dialog box is discussed in detail in Section 5 on Spacing.

See 4.294; 4.328

See 4.337

See 4.340–4.347

See 4.340–4.347

This automatically adds the paragraph to the Table of Contents list. See 4.338, as well as Section 15 on Book Publications; 15.32–15.36.

4.300 The paragraph-view Control palette

(from the Window menu, choose "Control palette"; from the Toolbox, choose the text tool; select the paragraph-view button)

4.302 *Character-view button.*

4.301 *Apply button. See 3.41–3.47*

4.303 *Style edit box and menu.*

4.304 *Cursor-position indicator.*

4.305 *First-line indent.*

4.306 *Paragraph space-before. See 5.72–5.85*

4.307 *Grid-size.*

4.308 *Close box.*

4.309 *Title bar.*

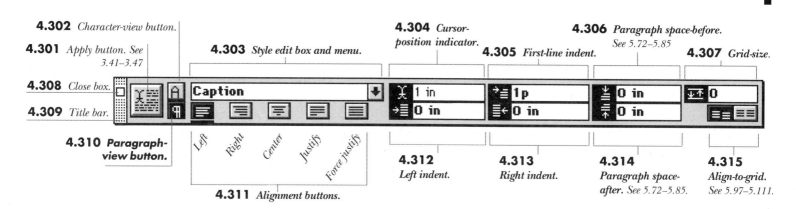

4.310 *Paragraph-view button.*

Left   Right   Center   Justify   Force justify

4.311 *Alignment buttons.*

4.312 *Left indent.*

4.313 *Right indent.*

4.314 *Paragraph space-after. See 5.72–5.85.*

4.315 *Align-to-grid. See 5.97–5.111.*

4.316 The paragraph-view Control palette lets you control many paragraph specific options without having to continually open the Paragraph specifications dialog box. The text tool must be chosen to display the text Control palettes; simply click the "¶" View button in the Control palette to view this palette. It displays many of the characteristics of the currently selected paragraph as well as the position of the cursor on the page. Toggle back and forth between character- and paragraph-view by pressing Command Shift ` (grave). You can navigate this Control palette with the keyboard just as you can all the others. See 3.101–3.119 for a guide to keyboard commands.

4.317 Apply text alignment by selecting the paragraph and then clicking on one of the Alignment buttons. The Indents and Space-before or -after options accept numerical values. Check out 5.72–5.96 for more information on paragraph spacing.

4.318 The Cursor-position indicator doesn't do anything *to* your document, it just tracks your cursor on the page. It can come in real handy, though, for placing indents. Just position the cursor wherever you want the indent to be, read the value from the indicator option box, and enter it into the Indent edit box. Pretty nifty. See Section 6 for all the scoop on Indents and Tabs.

4.319 You can apply and edit paragraph styles without ever having to leave the Control palette. Choose paragraph styles either from the pop-up list or by typing the style name directly into the edit box. To create a new style, select the text and then type a new, never-before-used name into the edit box. To edit an existing style, hold down the Command key while clicking on the style name. See Section 8 for more information on paragraph styles.

4.320 For information on using Align-to-grid and Grid-size see 5.97–5.111. For information on using the Control palette while in the Story Editor see 9.44.

If you want to do this:	**Then follow these steps:**	**Shortcuts ▪ Notes ▪ Hints**

4.321 Indent a paragraph on the left
(To use the Indents/tabs ruler, also see 6.58; 6.80)

This paragraph has no indents. The text word wraps from one edge of the text block to the other.
　　　Now this paragraph has a **left indent** of .25—it is indented .25 inch from the left edge of the text block.

`→≣ 0.25 in`

The "Left indent" option in the paragraph-view Control palette.

4.322 Indent a paragraph on the right
To use the Indents/tabs ruler, also see 6.57; 6.81)

This paragraph has no indents. The text word wraps from one edge of the text block to the other.
Now this paragraph has a **right indent** of .5—it is indented .5 inch from the right edge of the text block.

`≣← 0.5 in`

The "Right indent" option in the paragraph-view Control palette.

- With the **text tool,** select the paragraph(s) you want to indent (see 4.289–4.290 re: selecting paragraphs).
- From the Type menu, choose "Paragraph...," *or* press Command M.
- In the "Left" indent box, type a measurement for the indent. If "First" and "Right" are at 0, it will look similar to the example shown on the left, often called a "nested indent."
- **Or** in the paragraph-view Control palette, type a value in the "Left indent" edit box; click the Apply button (or press Return).

- With the **text tool,** select the paragraph(s) you want to indent (see 4.289–4.290 re: selecting paragraphs).
- From the Type menu, choose "Paragraph...," *or* press Command M.
- In the "Right" indent box, type a measurement for the indent. If "Left" and "First" are at 0, it will look similar to the example shown on the left.
- **Or** in the paragraph-view Control palette, type a value in the "Right indent" edit box; click the Apply button (or press Return).

- **Indents** refer to how far the text is indented *from the edges of the text block.* They have nothing to do with column guides or margins or anything else—only text block edges as defined by the handles. See 6.57–6.60 for examples.
- These indents are all explained at great length in Section 6 on Indents and Tabs. There you will see examples of each indent, a Scenario using indents, and explanations on how to use them in combination with tabs to format your work most easily.
- The indent spacings you set here will be reflected in the Indents/Tabs ruler, and, conversely, any indents you set in the Indents/Tabs ruler will show up here.
- An advantage to setting your indents in the Paragraph specs box (or the Control palette), rather than in the Indents/Tabs ruler, is that you can enter a specific measurement, and even override the current measurement system being used (1.323). For instance, it is only here that you can get a *one-em indent* for paragraphs (4.325); which is what you really should be using if you're indenting first lines.
- Often, though, it is easier to use the Indents/Tabs ruler because you can actually see the physical width of indents.

If you want to do this:	Then follow these steps:	Shortcuts ▾ Notes ▾ Hints
4.323 Indent the first line of every paragraph *(To use the Indents/tabs ruler, also see 6.23–6.32, 6.54–6.56)* I put a .25-inch **first-line indent** in these paragraphs. The text word wraps between the left and right indents, which are at zero. 　Every time I hit a Return, the first line of the next paragraph automatically indents a quarter-inch. 　This is a terrific function. Use it. **⁚≣⁚0.25 in** *The "First-line indent" option in the paragraph-view Control palette.*	▪ With the **text tool,** select the paragraph(s) you want to indent (see 4.289–4.290 re: selecting paragraphs). ▪ From the Type menu, choose "Paragraph...," *or* press Command M. ▪ In the "First" indent box, type in a measurement. *This measurement will be added onto the "Left" indent,* since the first-line indent will indent itself *from the left indent, not from the edge of the text block* (e.g., if "Left" is .25 and "First" is .25, the indent will be actually .5 inch from the edge of the text block). ▪ **Or** in the paragraph-view Control palette, type a value in the "First-line indent" edit box; click the Apply button (or press Return).	▪ The "Left" and "Right" indents reference themselves from the left and right edges of the text block (6.54–6.61). "First," though, references itself from the "Left" indent. So then, the first-line indent can be to the left (a negative number) or to the right (a positive number) *of the left indent.* A negative number creates a hanging indent (as in 4.324), while a number larger than the left indent value creates a typical indent, as shown here in the first column.
4.324 Create a hanging indent *(To use the Indents/tabs ruler, also see 6.60)* I put a .25-inch "Left" indent in these paragraphs so the text will word wrap at the right margin, then indent .25 inch on the left. I put a –.25-inch (that's a minus, or hyphen) indent in "First" so the first line will begin .25 inch to the *left* of the left indent. Remember that the first-line indent references itself from the *left indent, not* from the left edge of the text block.	▪ With the **text tool,** select the paragraph(s) you want to indent (see 4.289–4.290 re: selecting paragraphs). ▪ From the Type menu, choose "Paragraph...," *or* press Command M. ▪ Set a left indent by typing a number in "Left." That is where the text will align as it word wraps. ▪ In the "First" box, type in a *negative* number. That negative number can be no larger than the positive number in "Left" (that is, if the left indent is .25-inch, the first-line indent can be no more [less?] than –.25-inch).	▪ As noted in 4.323 above, a first-line indent to the *left* of the "Left" indent must be a *negative* number, since the first-line indent relates directly to the Left *indent,* not the left *margin* ("margin" as indicated by the edge of the text block). ▪ You can also enter these values in the "Left indent" edit box and the "First-line indent" edit box in the paragraph-view Control palette. 　To use a different unit of measure for the indents, highlight the edit box and press Command Option M (see 3.114).

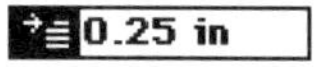

If you want to do this:	Then follow these steps:	Shortcuts ▾ Notes ▾ Hints
4.325 Set a one-em indent for first lines	■ *Before* you select the paragraph(s), know the point size of your text ■ With the **text tool,** select the paragraph(s) you want to indent (see 4.289–4.290 re: selecting paragraphs). ■ From the Type menu, choose "Paragraph…," *or* press Command M. ■ In the "First" box, type a **0** (zero), then a **p**, then the point size of your type (e.g., **0p10**). There are variations of this, but this technique will work no matter what measurement system you are using and no matter what size your type is. If you change the size of your type, though, you will have to adjust this indent. ■ **Or,** type the value in the "First-line indent" edit box in the paragraph-view Control palette.	■ Traditional typographic aesthetics long ago determined that a *one-em indent* is the most visually pleasing. An *em* is a typographic measure. When type was set with little pieces of metal, a typesetter would insert a little blank square of metal at the beginning of each paragraph. That little square was an *em* (also called a *mutton*). It is *approximately* the size of a capital letter M; it is *precisely* the size of the point size of the type. That is, if your type is 12 points, an em is 12 points wide. If your type is 36 points, an em is 36 points wide. Paragraphs that are indented more than an em space generally look awkward and clunky. Yes, an em space is much less than the five spaces or the half-inch we were taught to indent on a typewriter.
4.326 Set up paragraph indents *before* typing the paragraphs	■ With the **text tool,** click to set the insertion point flashing anywhere except in another paragraph. ■ From the Type menu, choose "Paragraph…," *or* press Command M. ■ Type in the values for the First, Left, and Right indents; click OK. As long as you do not click the mouse anywhere else before typing, the insertion point is loaded with these specs, and they will be applied.	■ If an insertion point is *not* flashing and if there is no text selected, then any specifications you set in the "Paragraph" dialog box will become the publication defaults (4.360–4.366). ■ You can also enter these values in the "Indent" edit boxes in the paragraph-view Control palette.

If you want to do this:

Then follow these steps:

Shortcuts ▾ Notes ▾ Hints

4.327 Change the alignment of a paragraph

The "Alignment" icons in the paragraph-view Control palette.

- With the **text tool,** select the paragraph(s) you want to align.
- From the Type menu, choose "Paragraph...," *or* press Command M.
- Press in the box next to "Alignment" to see the pop-up menu; choose the alignment.
- **Or** click on the "Alignment" button you want in the paragraph-view Control palette.

- I strongly suggest you read 4.243–4.248 for examples of each alignment and how each one affects readability.
- As in 4.326, you can also load this function into the insertion point before you begin typing.
- You can also select a palette alignment button with the space bar; see 3.111.

4.328 Change the dictionary, or add another one

Dictionary:
✓US English
Deutsch
Français
Español
Italiano
UK English
Svenska
Dansk
Norsk
Nederlands
Portuguès
Brazileiro

- With the **text tool,** select the paragraph(s) whose dictionary you want to change (see 4.289–4.290 re: selecting paragraphs).
- At any time, from the Type menu choose "Paragraph...," *or* press Command M.
- Press in the box next to "Dictionary" to see the pop-up menu; choose the language.

- Dictionaries are paragraph-specific; that is, the dictionary you choose applies only to the paragraphs you selected before you went to the dialog box.
- The dictionary you choose here will be the one used in spell-checking that paragraph in the Story Editor (9.90–9.126). It is also used for guiding PageMaker in hyphenation (5.229–5.255).
- You can use up to seventeen dictionaries per publication, although the more you use, the slower everything will become.
- If the names of the dictionaries are gray, you do not have them installed. Only the US English dictionary comes with PageMaker; you can buy others separately. Specialized dictionaries, such as medical or legal, are available as well as foreign language ones.
- See 9.97–9.103 for more info.

The Paragraph dialog box "Options"

Options:
☐ Keep lines together ☐ Keep with next ⬚ lines
☐ Column break before ☐ Widow control ⬚ lines
☐ Page break before ☐ Orphan control ⬚ lines
☐ Include in table of contents

4.329 The "Options" section of the Paragraph dialog box is something many people ignore because what it will achieve is not instantly clear, and if it is not instantly clear most of us don't have time to figure it out so we ignore it. So here are three pages of instant clarification. It's really quite simple.

4.330 These controls are often nicknamed "keeps," even though they are not all "keep" commands. All "keeps" are *paragraph specific;* that is, they will apply to the entire paragraph that is selected.

4.331 You set these paragraph controls and PageMaker tries to do what you say. But sometimes she can't. In the "Preferences" dialog box (1.222; 1.228) from the File menu, under "Layout problems" you can check "Show 'keeps' violations." Any line(s) where PageMaker has had to ignore your specs, you will see a gray bar (a yellow bar on a color monitor). That's just an indication to you that she had to think for herself, and it is your choice to leave it the way it is or to fix it manually. (The colored bar will not print.)

4.332 If your text starts to act funny, like jumps around on the page, or rolls itself up and refuses to budge, or appears and disappears as you type, there may be some paragraph option applied. To discover any applied options, don't select *all* of the paragraphs involved—select the suspects one at a time, then press Command M to get the dialog box. If you select more than one paragraph and they have different settings applied, PageMaker gets confused and will tell you that no options are applied at all.

What? You can't check the paragraph because the text block won't unroll? See 22.11.

4.333 If, however, you want to remove *all* paragraph keeps controls from selected paragraphs or the entire story, do this:

- Press-and-drag to select the paragraphs you want to affect;
  or select the entire story: click once anywhere in the story with the **text tool,** then press Command A.
- Press Command M to get the Paragraph dialog box.
- Click in any "Options" checkbox to turn it on, then click in it again to turn it off (there should be no "X").
- Click OK.

4.334 Keep lines together: When this option is checked, PageMaker will not break the lines of the selected paragraph into different columns, from page to page, or over text-wrapped graphics. This is an appropriate control for paragraphs of body text, but isn't really applicable to one-line paragraphs, such as headings (4.337).

"Options" —continued

4.335 Column break before: When you autoflow text, any paragraph with this option checked will jump to the next column, even if the next column is on the next page (and it will keep turning pages until it finds a blank column). If you are using manual or semi-autoflow, it will stop as usual and wait for you to place the rest of the text. If you apply this option to text you have already placed, paragraphs may disappear suddenly as they instantly go to find the top of a column.

It would not be a good idea to apply "Column break before" to the body text under a head, as it will leave the head stranded at the end of the previous column. It would make much more sense to apply it to the head itself. And it would be silly to bother applying this control to the first paragraph in a story.

4.336 Page break before: When you autoflow text, any paragraph you have applied this option to will jump to the next page, even if there is no next page (autoflow will create one). If you are using manual or semi-autoflow, the text will stop as usual and wait for you to place the rest. Even if you want to, PageMaker will not *allow* you to place a paragraph with this attribute on the same page as the paragraph before. If you try, it will just roll itself up and obstinately refuse to unroll until you move it to another page or to the pasteboard.

4.337 Keep with next __lines: This option enables you to keep the selected paragraph connected to the next 1, 2, or 3 lines of the following paragraph, which is great for making sure you don't have a headline stuck all by itself at the bottom of a column—at least it will have 1, 2, or 3 lines with it. If the 1, 2, or 3 lines won't fit at the end of the column with the head, the head will pop over to the next column to stay with its lines. If you want the head attached to the entire next paragraph, not just to a few lines, then also apply the "Keep lines together" (4.334) option to the paragraph *following* the head.

4.338 Include in table of contents: When you apply this to a selected paragraph, that entire paragraph will automatically be included when you create the publication's table of contents (see Section 15 on Book Publications; 15.33–15.35). If you have chapter heads, or perhaps subheads that you will be using to annotate the Contents page with, just add this to your head and subhead style sheets (Section 8).

4.339 Some of these controls are quite handy to add to your style sheets (Section 8). Look them over carefully; they can save quite a bit of time and trouble, like "Include in table of contents" for a style denoting chapter heads, or "Keep with next __ lines" for a subhead style.

"Options" and widows and orphans

4.340 There seems to be great puzzlement over the precise definition of a **widow** and of an **orphan**. Here is the low-down:

4.341 A **widow** is a very short last line of a paragraph, one that contains fewer than seven characters. The worst kind of widow is the last part of a hyphenated word, even if it is longer than seven characters. It's obnoxious.

Unfortunately, you see it all the time.

4.342 An **orphan** is the last line of a paragraph that is all by itself at the top of the next column, separated from the preceeding lines of its paragraph.

Unfortunately, you see that all the time, too.

4.343 The widow and orphan controls in the "Paragraph specifications" dialog box are designed to control these bereft creatures.

4.344 Orphan control ___ lines: This works great. Type in a 1, a 2, or a 3. If you enter a 1, you are telling PageMaker never to let this paragraph leave one line alone at the top of a column (of a text block, actually)— you'll have at least two lines at the top. If you enter a 2, you'll have at least three lines; and if you enter a 3, you'll have at least four lines.

4.345 Widow control ___ lines: This does *not* mean that PageMaker will prevent leaving fewer than seven characters or a hyphenated word as the last line of a paragraph. Unfortunately, PageMaker has a bit of a mistaken notion of widows. She defines it as a small number of lines left at the bottom of a column, while the rest of the paragraph continues in the next text block.

4.346 You can type 1, 2, or 3 in the widow control box. If you type 1, PageMaker will not leave one lonely line from that paragraph at the bottom of the text block; the line will jump over to its mates in the following text block. If you type 2, PageMaker will not leave two lines; the two lines will jump over to the following text block. And I bet you can guess what will happen if you type 3.

There is no way in PageMaker to get rid of a real widow.

4.347 Now, it may or may not be obvious that if you "Keep lines together," exercising "Widow and/or Orphan control" in addition becomes redundant. If you do check them both, the entire paragraph will generally put itself at the top of the next text block.

Line breaks

4.348 The **line break** feature is a very small, yet very significant, addition to PageMaker. When you press Shift-Return, you cause the line of text to end, or *break*, but it does not start a new paragraph. Until you need it, this may not seem like much.

4.349 In almost every Macintosh program, every time you hit the Return key you are creating a new paragraph. A Return key makes what is called a "hard Return," meaning that when you edit the text, the line will always break at that point. This is opposed to a "soft Return," which is when the text automatically word-wraps at the margin edge. You can see the visual representation of each sort of Return character in the Story Editor (Section 9):

```
Soft·returns·show·no·visible·characters;·
they·just·bump·into·the·edge·and·move·on.◦

A·hard·return·is·represented·by·the·
paragraph·symbol,·as·it·shows·the·end·of·
one·paragraph.¶

A·line·break,·which·creates·a·new·line·
but·does·not·end·the·paragraph,·is·
represented·by·a·right-pointing·arrow.↵
```

4.350 That hard Return character (¶) holds all the paragraph formatting. Whenever you hit a Return, that little Return character goes marching forward, bringing with it all the paragraph formatting to apply to the next paragraph. Paragraph formatting includes:

- Styles from the style sheet (Section 8), including whether to apply a "Next style" (8.28–8.32);
- Extra paragraph space before and/or after (5.72–5.96);
- First-line indent (6.55; 4.323–4.325);
- Paragraph rules (Section 7);
- Tabs and indents (Section 6);
- Hyphenation controls (5.229–5.247);
- Letter and word spacing specs (5.10);
- Alignment (4.243–4.248);
- Paragraph "Keeps" options (4.329–4.347).

4.351 This is where the **line break** comes in. By pressing Shift-Return, you can get a new line, *but you don't create a new paragraph* and all those things that come along with a new paragraph. In essence, if you press a Shift-Return you will get a new line that will **not:**

- Apply a "Next style";
- Add any extra paragraph space before or after;
- Create a new first-line indent;
- Create any paragraph rules.

4.352 But the new line **will** keep the tabs and indents, the hyphenation controls, the letter and word spacing, the alignment, and the "Keeps" options—thus making it *appear* to be the same paragraph. And actually, PageMaker also sees it as the same paragraph (see 4.354).

4.353 A line break will not word-wrap, though, so if you edit text that has line breaks, the sentences will retain the line endings.

- See the Scenario on the next page for instances of when to use the line break.

4.354 Scenario #5: Using the line break feature

Let's say you are typing a nice letter. You are very efficient: you choose your font and type specifications before you even begin to type. You put an extra 5 points of space between paragraphs. Now when you type the return address, every time you hit the Return key your lines are separated by those extra 5 points. Like this:

Ms. Scarlett Florence Williams

Toad Hall Annex

Santa Rosa, California 95404

But that's not what you want. So you retype it, this time using a Shift-Return at the end of each line instead of a Return. Now it looks like this:

Ms. Scarlett Florence Williams
Toad Hall Annex
Santa Rosa, California 95404

This also retains these three lines as one single paragraph! If you triple click with the text tool, all three lines will be selected.

Of course, you could just *replace* the Returns in your first address with Shift-Returns. Either backspace over the Returns and replace them with Shift-Returns, or use "Change" in the Story Editor (9.82).

Sometimes you may find a word that is hyphenated in a stupid place, as in the following paragraph:

> For my part, I travel not to go an-
> ywhere, but to go. I travel for travel's
> sake. The great affair is to move.
> *Robert Louis Stevenson*

So put your insertion point directly before the **a** in **an-** and press Shift-Return. The Shift-Return will just break the line without giving you the first-line indent. It also keeps the sentences as one entire paragraph.

> For my part, I travel not to go
> anywhere, but to go. I travel for
> travel's sake. The great affair is
> to move.
> *Robert Louis Stevenson*

*Just to let you know, you could also type a discretionary hyphen (Command Hyphen) in front of the **a** to prevent the word from hyphenating (5.234; 5.251).*

The Shift-Return line breaks can make it much easier to reformat columns of tabular material. At the end of each line, press Shift-Return instead of Return. This will retain all those separate lines as one paragraph. You can reformat all the rows of columns as easily as you reformat a single paragraph.

One➡	Two➡	Three⏎
Einz➡	Zwie➡	Drei⏎
Un➡	Deux➡	Trois⏎
Uno➡	Dos➡	Tres¶

In the Story Editor notice the right-pointing arrows (➡), indicating tabs. Notice the left-pointing arrows (⏎), indicating Shift-Returns. Notice the paragraph symbol (¶), indicating the *end* of the one paragraph.

4.355 Take advantage of the special characters the Macintosh keyboard provides to make your work look more professional.

4.356 In all of these keyboard sequences, **hold down** the Command key and/or Shift key and/or Option key while you press the other character.

4.357 The ellipsis (…) is a handy character, as it combines the three dots into one character and thus won't break at the end of a sentence (leaving you with one period at the end of one line and the other two on the line below). Professionally, though, typesetters still prefer a nicely-spaced ellipsis. You can create a nicely-spaced ellipsis that won't break by putting a non-breaking thin space (Command Shift T; see 5.225) between each period . . .

- Don't forget about the handy chart in Appendix E, located at the back of the book. It lists every special character currently available and how to type it.
- Also see Key Caps, 1.329–1.333. And be sure to read *The Mac is not a typewriter.*

4.358 To type a special character: Press these keys:

opening double quotation mark	"	Option [
closing double quotation mark	"	Option Shift [
opening single quotation mark	'	Option]
closing single quote mark; apostrophe	'	Option Shift]
en dash	–	Option hyphen
em dash	—	Option Shift hyphen
ellipsis	…	Option ;
bullet	•	Option 8
tiny bullet (a raised period)	·	Option Shift 9
copyright symbol	©	Option g
trademark symbol	™	Option 2
registered trademark symbol	®	Option r
degree symbol	°	Option Shift 8
cents symbol	¢	Option 4 *(the $, logically)*
fraction bar	/	Option Shift 1
ligature of f and i	fi	Option Shift 5
ligature of f and l	fl	Option Shift 6
inverted exclamation point	¡	Option 1 *(one, or !)*
inverted question mark	¿	Option Shift ?
monetary pound sign	£	Option 3 *(the #, or pound, sign)*
cedilla, lowercase	ç	Option c
cedilla, uppercase	Ç	Option Shift C

If you want to do this:	**Then follow these steps:**	**Shortcuts ▾ Notes ▾ Hints**

4.359 Accent marks

- Find the key combination that will create the accent mark—either check the list below, the chart in Appendix F, or look in Key Caps (1.329–1.333).
- Type the word *up to* the letter that goes under the accent mark.
- Type the key combination that will produce the accent mark—*you did it right if nothing shows up on the page!* If you see the accent mark at this point, delete the word and start over.
- Now type the letter that is to be under the accent mark—*they will show up together;* type the rest of the word as usual.
  □ Example: to type **résumé:**
  · Type **r** .
  · Press **Option e.**
  · Type **e** .
  · Type the rest of the word (**sum**), and repeat the accent mark over the last letter **e**; you should see **résumé.**

   ´   Option e
   `   Option ~ (upper left or next to the spacebar)
   ¨   Option u
   ~   Option n
   ^   Option i

- Now you have no excuse, as you did on a typewriter, not to take advantage of accent marks. If a word is supposed to have one, then use it.

Type specification defaults

4.360 When you type directly into PageMaker (but not into some text already on the page), the font specifications that show up are the ones that have been set as the **defaults;** that is, *there has to be* some sort of specifications, and if *you* don't *choose* what they are to be, you get the defaults.

4.361 In addition to the font itself, you can set the text to default to a different alignment, reverse type (be careful!), specific tabs and indents, autoflow or not, extra paragraph spacing, dictionary choices, "keeps" options, etc.—anything to do with the text can be set as a default, so every time you type you get those particular specifications.

4.362 See 1.6–1.10 and 1.118 for a list of the specifications that can be set as defaults, and for more detailed info. Basically, anything you see that is not gray when the pointer tool is selected can be set as a default.

4.363 Don't forget—text wrapping can also be set as a default (13.43); everything you draw, place, or paste in PageMaker as a graphic will then come in with a boundary around it. This can be very frustrating.

4.364 Control palette options will use whatever measuring system defaults you have set for the publication. However, some units of measure can be changed "on the fly" by pressing Command Option M after highlighting the edit box with the measurement system you want to change (3.114). By repeatedly pressing the key command, you can cycle through all the units of measure that are available for that particular option. In the paragraph-view Control palette the only options that do this are the Indent edit boxes.

Life
is
uncertain.
Eat
dessert
first.
Christian
Nelson

If you want to do this:	**Then follow these steps:**	**Shortcuts ▾ Notes ▾ Hints**
4.365 Set the default type specifications for the entire PageMaker application	■ Open PageMaker from the icon on the Desktop; **Or** if PageMaker is already open, close any publication that may be on the screen. You should be looking at a *blank* screen with the PageMaker menu bar. ■ With the **pointer tool**, from the Type menu choose the font, size, leading, and style of your choice (or choose "Type specs..." and make your choices there). (See the subsection from 4.189–4.260 for info on setting specifications.)	■ Any text specifications you choose while in PageMaker, *but with no publication open* (just the blank PageMaker screen), will be the new *application* defaults. Every publication you open from then on will *default to,* or automatically set you up with those specifications. ■ New application defaults do not affect any previously-created documents.
4.366 Set the default type specifications for the publication you are in	■ At any point while the publication is open, choose the **pointer tool.** ■ From the Type menu choose the font, size, leading, and style of your choice (or choose "Type specs..." and make your choices there). (See the subsection from 4.1189–4.260 for info on setting specifications.) ■ **Or** click once on the **text tool,** even if it is already selected (to ensure that the insertion point is not within text), and make your type specification choices from the character- and paragraph-view Control palettes.	■ Any text specifications you choose with the **pointer tool** (with nothing whatsoever selected) *while a publication is open* will be the *publication* defaults. Just while you are in that publication, those are the specifications to which it will automatically revert. ■ Publication defaults do not affect any other document, whether previously created or yet to be created.

5 ▾ Text Spacing

5.1   Minimums and maximums:

Item	Minimum	Maximum
Leading	.1 pt.	1300 pt.
(tenth-point increments; .1)		
Autoleading	0%	200%
Para. space	0 pt.	1300 pt.
(tenth-point increments; .1)		
Word space	0%	500%
(1% increments)		
Letter space	-200%	+200%
(1% increments)		

Kerning	¹⁄₁₀ᵗʰ units	¹⁄₂₅ᵗʰ units	¹⁄₁₀₀ᵗʰ units
	(.1 of an em)	(.04 of an em)	(.01 of an em)

Item	Minimum	Maximum
Set width	5%	250%
(.1% increments)		
Hyphenation zone	0	12 picas (2 inches)
(.1 increments)		
Number of consec. hyphens	1	255 or "No limit"
Word added to user dictionary	1	31 characters

5.2   PageMaker allows you to control practically *everything*. Now, you don't *have* to be in control—the default (automatic) settings for spacing are quite good for the average advertisement, flyer, or invitation. In fact, you could live a long time, never read this chapter, and never notice the lack of it in your life. If learning PageMaker itself is overwhelming you, *don't* read this yet. You'll get along fine for a long while. But when you're ready to really tap into the fine tuning, come back and study this section.

5.3   You'll know it's time to take control of spacing when you find yourself thinking, "Hmm . . . that's really too much space between those paragraphs," or "I wish I could tighten up that headline," or "I sure would like to set this copy with lots of white space between the letters and the lines." Understanding and using the spacing controls not only will make you a happier, more powerful person, but also will give your work a more professional appearance.

5.4   Even though I present each aspect of spacing in its own little subsection here, all aspects interweave. The leading affects the paragraph spacing, the letter spacing affects the word spacing, the kerning affects the tracking, the tracking affects the letter spacing, and on and on. It's a lot to grasp. Take it one space at a time.

Leading 270
Paragraph spacing 285
Align to grid 291
Word spacing 295
Letter spacing 299
Kerning 304
Expert kerning Addition 310
Tracking 313
Edit tracks Addition 317
Set width 321
Hard spaces (non-breaking) 323
Hyphenation 325

5.5 What's the difference?

Leading is the space between every line of type, measured in points.

Paragraph spacing is the extra space you can add between paragraphs instead of using a double return.

Word spacing is the amount of space between words; **letter spacing** is the amount of space between letters. Both are measured relative to the ideal spacing built into the characters by the font designer. Both apply to entire paragraphs and are typically used over a range of text, either for special effects or to correct spacing problems.

Auto kerning is an automatic adjustment to the letterspacing over a range of text based on built-in font specifications.

Manual kerning is the fine-tuning adjustment you apply between two characters to obtain visually-consistent letterspacing.

Range kerning is the same as manual kerning except it applies to the entire range of characters you select.

Tracking is an adjustment that automatically increases *or* decreases the letter and word space based on the built-in kerning pairs and depending on the point size of the type. Tracking applies only to the selected characters.

Points and picas

5.6   Type size, leading, and paragraph space are measured in points. In case you are not clear on what **points** and **picas** are, here is the low-down:

A **pica** is the unit of measure used in typesetting instead of inches. There are **6 picas per inch.**

Each pica is divided into **12 points.** Thus 72 points equal 1 inch.*

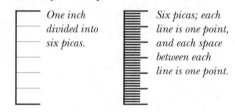

One inch divided into six picas.

Six picas; each line is one point, and each space between each line is one point.

5.7   Once you get beyond the basics in PageMaker, you will usually find it easier to set your measurement system to picas (5.9). If you still want to cling to inches, it's possible to leave your measurement system in inches but set your vertical ruler in points and picas (or go all the way and customize the vertical ruler; 1.226).

---

* *For those of you versed in traditional typography, 72 points do equal **exactly** one inch, not .996/inch, because the original Mac screen was 72 dots per inch.*

Measurement system

5.8   In all the dialog boxes that deal with spacing attributes, it is easier to work with points and picas since that is what most of the spacing functions are based on.

5.9   To change your measurement system to picas, from the File menu choose "Preferences...."

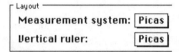

Next to "Measurement system," press on the submenu and choose "Picas." (This will affect all dialog boxes that have measurements in them, as well as the page rulers and the indents and tabs ruler.)

Next to "Vertical ruler," press on the submenu and choose "Picas." (This will affect just the vertical page ruler; see 1.225.)

Click OK.

5.10 "Spacing attributes" dialog box *(from the Type menu, choose "Paragraph..."; click on the "Spacing..." button)*

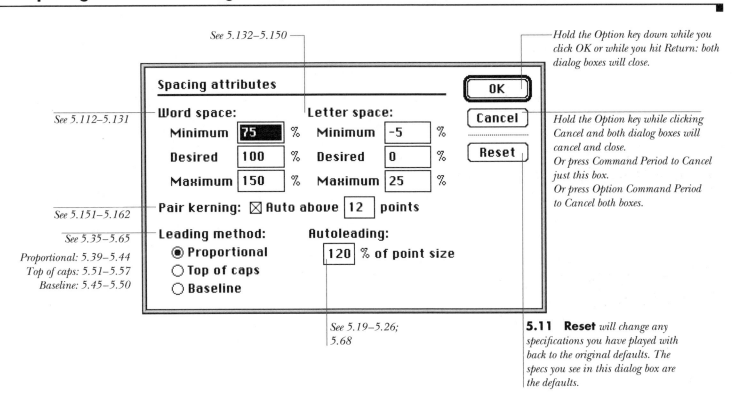

See 5.132–5.150

Hold the Option key down while you click OK or while you hit Return: both dialog boxes will close.

See 5.112–5.131

Spacing attributes

Word space:

Minimum `75` %

Desired `100` %

Maximum `150` %

Letter space:

Minimum `-5` %

Desired `0` %

Maximum `25` %

OK

Cancel

Reset

Hold the Option key while clicking Cancel and both dialog boxes will cancel and close.
Or press Command Period to Cancel just this box.
Or press Option Command Period to Cancel both boxes.

See 5.151–5.162

Pair kerning: ☒ **Auto above** `12` **points**

See 5.35–5.65
Proportional: 5.39–5.44
Top of caps: 5.51–5.57
Baseline: 5.45–5.50

Leading method:

⦿ **Proportional**

○ **Top of caps**

○ **Baseline**

Autoleading:

`120` **% of point size**

See 5.19–5.26;
5.68

5.11 Reset *will change any specifications you have played with back to the original defaults. The specs you see in this dialog box are the defaults.*

Leading

(pronounced 'ledding')

5.12   It's very important to understand the concept of **leading**—what it is, what it is doing for the type, and how it is figured—before you can understand how to manipulate it aesthetically and sensibly and without going insane. It is easier to understand the *concept* if you understand its *physical origin*.

5.13   The term **leading** is a holdover from the days when all type was cast in metal. Literally, every single letter, space, and punctuation mark was on a separate piece of metal (guess what kind of metal they used). And type foundries had to make a complete set of metal characters for each point size of type. The typesetter lined up all these tiny lead letters and spaces in little rows. Then, between each row, or line, of type, he inserted a thin strip of **lead** to separate the lines. Leading, therefore, is a term referring to the space between the lines of type.

5.14   Type has been measured in points (5.6) for a long time. Leading (the strip of lead), is also measured in points. If the typesetter wanted an extra 4 points of space between the lines of type, he inserted a thin strip of lead that was 4 points thick. That's easy enough, right? Now here's where you have to start paying attention because it directly relates to what you have to work with in PageMaker's menu.

5.15   The typesetter would get out the case of 12-point letters to set a small booklet. He set the lines of 12-point type, and between the lines he put thin strips of lead that were 2 points thick. Now, you would think that he would call that a 2-point leading, right? Wrong.

5.16   The size of the leading is added onto the point size of the type, and we call the leading (in this example) 14 point. That's why you don't see 2 or 3 or 4 points of leading listed in the leading submenu in PageMaker. *What you see are the leading values that have been added together with the point size of the type you are working with.*

5.17   If you have 18-point type with an extra 4 points of space between the lines, you have a leading of 22 (written 18/22; spoken 18 on 22). If you have 30-point type with no extra space between the lines (30/30), you have a leading of 0, which we call *set solid*.

5.18   Today we can go even further with leading than the metal typesetters were able to—we can have *negative* leading. We can have 30-point type with a leading of 26 (30/26), which is –4, right? (Which is why, at this point in time, *leading* should really be called *linespace*.)

Auto leading

5.19 As with most things in life, leading has a standard from which we can deviate. **The standard value for leading is 20 percent of the point size of the type.** For instance, if you are using 10-point type, the standard leading value to use is 12 point (20 percent of 10, added to the 10, equals 12).

5.20 PageMaker's standard value for automatic leading is 120 percent (which gives the same results as *adding* 20 percent, or multiplying by 1.2). So when you see a leading value of **Auto** in any dialog box or menu, that Auto means 120 percent of the point size of your type rounded off to the nearest tenth (.1).

5.21 An easy way to find out what the Auto leading value is that PageMaker is applying to selected text, is to press Command ' *(apostrophe)* to get the Control palette (3.19). Even if Auto leading is applied, the Control palette will display the exact numerical value. *Just because the value shown is a number, does not mean the leading value is "fixed"! (see 5.25)*

5.22 *The 120 percent default autoleading value can be changed to suit your need for more or less auto-linespace (5.68). It is paragraph specific, meaning the autoleading value will only apply to the paragraphs you select.*

Auto leading applied

5.23 Whenever the leading applied in a paragraph is Auto, *the space between the lines will adapt to any larger point sizes introduced into a line.* The characters with the largest amount of Auto leading take over the whole line. For instance, if the paragraph is 9-point type with Auto leading and you insert an 18-point capital at the beginning of the paragraph, the leading on that entire first line will increase to the Auto specifications for 18 point. It will look like this:

In the time of your life, live . . . so that in that wondrous time you shall not add to the misery and sorrow of the world, but smile to the infinite delight and mystery of it.
—William Saroyan

5.24 Does that awkward line space look familiar? With Auto leading applied, Page-Maker will take the Auto leading of the largest character on the line and apply it to the entire line.

Fixed leading

5.25 The solution to what you see in 5.23 is to use **proportional** (see 5.39–5.44) and **fixed leading.** Fixed leading is any leading amount that you *choose*, either from the Leading submenu or by typing in a value in a dialog box, *as long as it is not the word "Auto."* Even if you type in the exact amount that PageMaker is already using for Auto, the fixed amount you enter does not adapt. It stays fixed. (You can't use the Control palette, though, to fix the leading with the same value as Auto; use the menu.)

5.26 In 5.23, I selected the entire paragraph (shown below) and changed the leading to 10.8, which is the exact amount PageMaker was automatically applying through "Auto" for the 9-point type (9 x 1.2). But by typing in the value, I *fixed* the leading amount. Then, when I changed the first letter to 18 point, it stayed fixed (see below). It doesn't matter whether you fix the leading *before* or *after* you change the type size.

In the time of your life, live . . . so that in that wondrous time you shall not add to the misery and sorrow of the world, but smile to the infinite delight and mystery of it.
—William Saroyan

p.s. Not even fixed leading will help text that uses the "Top of caps" leading method (5.51–5.57).

Selecting text to change the leading

5.27 There is one important trick to remember when selecting the text whose leading you want to change: *you must select the entire line,* not just the characters that are visible. It is entirely possible (and it happens all the time) that any leftover blank spaces will have a different leading value or a larger point size. It is not so much a problem when you are *increasing* the leading, as PageMaker will apply the larger value. But if you try to *decrease* the leading you will run into problems.

5.28 Here is an example. I wanted to decrease the linespace in this two-line headline, set at 12 point with Auto leading.

Never take anything too seriously.

At first, not knowing better, I selected the *characters* in the first line, ignoring the spaces at the end. ────────

Never take anything too seriously.

When I changed the leading to 6 point (yes, that is radical leading), nothing happened! That's because those blank spaces after the word *"anything"* are also 12 point with Auto leading, just like the visible characters. Since PageMaker applies the largest leading value *to the entire line,* that larger Auto leading holds the linespace intact.

5.29 So I got more intelligent. This time I selected the entire line of text, all the way to the right margin. (The easiest way to select the entire line is to position the insertion point just before the first character in the line, and then drag *straight down* just a bit. Really. Try it. ────────

Never take anything too seriously.

This time when I changed the leading of the first line to 6 point it closed up the line space.

Never take anything too seriously.

5.30 When you want to change the leading of an entire *paragraph,* it's safest to triple-click on it (with the text tool), rather than press-and-drag. That way you are guaranteed that everything will be selected.

5.31 A quick way to select more paragraphs in addition to the first one is to hold down the Command and the Shift keys and press the Up or DownArrow.

Slugs

5.32 Leading values determine the size of the **slug** of type. When you press-and-drag over a line of type, what you see highlighted is the slug.

This slug shows 10-point type with Auto leading:

Dancing is a celebration of Life.

This slug shows 10-point type with a leading value of 20:

Dancing is a celebration of Life.

(Both of these slug examples are using the proportional leading method.)

If you find this fascinating and really want to read more about slugs, check out 7.15–7.19.

The leading submenu

5.33 This is just a tiny little tip regarding the "Leading" submenu in the Type menu. Since the leading depends on the size of the type, you first need to know what size the type is in order to adjust the leading. Well, Aldus added this thoughtful little touch:

When you choose the "Leading" submenu, you are usually* offered a list of possible leading values depending on the point size of the text that is selected. One of those numbers is in bold type—that number indicates the point size of the selected text. Isn't that nice?

Leading ▶	Other...
	✓Auto ⇧⌘A
	9
	9.5
	10
	10.5
	11
	11.5
	12
	15
	20
	30

* If you only get the options for Other and Auto in this submenu, it is because the selected text has more than one leading value applied to it.

5.34 Of course, you can always check the Control palette to view the size of your type and leading, or the Type specs dialog box. If the palette is not on your screen, press Command ' *(apostrophe)*.

Leading methods

5.35 PageMaker offers three ways to work with leading; one is inept and the others are a little better. The following pages explain the three methods in great detail. You can switch from one method to the other per paragraph, and you can define the method in your style sheets (Chapter 8).

5.36 The inept method is called **Top of caps.** Earlier versions of PageMaker (before 3.0) used this method, and it is included in 5.0 in case you used it in 4.0. Generally, you won't use "Top of caps" (see 5.56 for an instant clue why not). It does have *one* great function, however (see 5.57).

5.37 The **Baseline** method is PageMaker's attempt to recreate the baseline-to-baseline method we became accustomed to in photo-typesetting. Except they got it backwards. Some people actually like this method.

5.38 The third method is **Proportional.** This is much easier to deal with than the other two methods, and when you understand what proportional leading is doing and how to manipulate it, you can actually predict the results accurately.

"Proportional" leading and examples

5.39   When you use the **proportional** leading method, PageMaker divides the leading value into thirds. Two-thirds of that value is placed *above* the baseline, and one-third *below* the baseline. Like so:

Isn't this the most beautiful Q you've ever seen?

baseline

5.40   The example above is 36-point type on 36-point leading. The slug (5.32) is exactly 36 points deep; 24 points of the leading value (⅔) are *above* the baseline, and 12 points of it (⅓) are *below* the baseline.

If the leading for the same example were 30, then 20 points of it would be placed above the baseline and 10 points below.   The characters, of course, sit directly on the baseline at all times.

5.41   This is very consistent and predictable. In proportional leading, the leading slug arranges itself around the baseline. The slug of the largest leading value will take over, and any smaller type will just sit on the larger type's baseline.

5.42   This does present one problem. When you change the leading of a line, it does not just change the space *below* the line; it changes the space *above*, as well. This means if you adjust the leading between two lines of a headline, both

5.43   The examples below show how proportional leading can affect the same two lines so differently depending on where you apply it.

5.44   *This control headline is set with 10 point type and Auto leading (10/Auto). In the following examples, notice how the different leading values affect the text depending on whether you change the first line, the second line, or both lines (the lower guideline through the examples is where the original text block ended). The discrepancy is because proportional leading applies the leading to **both** the space **above** the baseline, as well as **below** the baseline.*

lines may move out of position up or down. It can be very frustrating.

Every home should have a stage and a dance floor

Every home should have a stage and a dance floor

a) *First line:*   10/18
   Second line: 10/Auto

Every home should have a stage and a dance floor

b) *First line:*   10/Auto
   Second line: 10/18

Every home should have a stage and a dance floor

c) *First line:*   10/18
   Second line: 10/18

Every home should have a stage and a dance floor

d) *First line:*   10/8
   Second line: 10/Auto

Every home should have a stage and a dance floor

e) *First line:*   10/Auto
   Second line: 10/8

Every home should have a stage and a dance floor

f) *First line:*   10/8
   Second line: 10/8

"Baseline" leading and examples

5.45   When you use the **baseline** leading method, PageMaker applies the leading value from the baseline *upwards*. Like so:

baseline

5.46   The example above is 36-point type on 36-point leading. The slug (5.32) is exactly 36 points deep; the entire value is placed *above* the baseline.

If the leading for the same example were 30 points, all 30 points of it would be placed above the baseline. The characters, as usual, sit directly on the baseline at all times.

5.47   This is consistent and predictable. The leading slug arranges itself around the baseline. The slug of the largest leading value will take over, and any smaller type will just sit on the larger type's baseline.

5.48   Now, this baseline leading method was included in PageMaker because so many of us who were accustomed to working with baseline-to-baseline leading in phototypesetting clamoured for it. But in phototypeset baseline-to-baseline leading,

the leading value measured from the baseline of that line of type down to the *next* baseline. If you set 36/40, the line of text would be 36 point type and the machine would drop 40 points down to the next baseline for the next line of text. As you can see, PageMaker does the opposite; it applies 40 points *up* to the baseline above.

5.49   This creates two problems: text of different sizes will not align across the top of a page, even though their text blocks are aligned; and you will often get totally unacceptable spacing between lines of differently sized text unless you really know how to control line and paragraph spacing. Baseline leading is not for the beginner.

Every home should have
a stage and a dance floor

5.50   *This control headline is set with 10 point type and Auto leading (10/Auto). In the examples, notice how the different leading values affect the text, depending on whether you change the first line, the second line, or both lines (the lower guideline through the examples is where the original text block ended).* **Notice also how the descenders are always chopped off, which drives me NUTS.** *To show the descenders again, redraw the screen (5.70).*

Every home should have
a stage and a dance floor

a) *First line: 10/18*
Second line: 10/Auto

Every home should have
a stage and a dance floor

b) *First line: 10/Auto*
Second line: 10/18

Every home should have
a stage and a dance floor

c) *First line: 10/18*
Second line: 10/18

Every home should have
a stage and a dance floor

d) *First line: 10/8*
Second line: 10/Auto

Every home should have
a stage and a dance floor

e) *First line: 10/Auto*
Second line: 10/8

Every home should have
a stage and a dance floor

f) *First line: 10/8*
Second line: 10/8

"Top of caps" leading and examples

5.51 **Top of caps** leading is a holdover from earlier versions of PageMaker. In this method, the slug (5.32) extends down from the top of the tallest *ascender* on the line. Now, that needs some explanation.

5.52 An *ascender* is the part of a letter that extends above the height of the letter **x.** The letters h, f, and b each have an ascender. *Ascenders are sometimes taller than the capital letters of the same font,* as in the example in 5.55. (So I don't know why they call it "Top of *caps,*" when really the slug begins at the top of the *ascender.*)

5.53 Even if there is no letter with an ascender on that line, the slug begins where the ascender would be if it *were* there. If you have more than one point size of type on a line, the slug will begin at the top of the tallest ascender that *would* be there from the largest point size of type. (Now, remember, blank spaces also have sizes; 5.27–5.28.)

5.54 Because the leading slug begins at the ascender height and drops down from there, it is difficult to make the space between lines consistent if there are varying point sizes in a line. In fact, it is so inept that you will very rarely want to use it (5.56).

5.55 Here are a few examples of slugs indicating the leading values using the "Top of caps" method. Notice how the slug stays in place along the top of the ascenders and only the space *below* the line adjusts. (When you see a number like 10/12, it's pronounced "ten on twelve." The first number is the point size of the type; the second number is the leading.)

10/Auto When in doubt, don't.

10/20 When in doubt, don't.

10/6 When in doubt, don't.

5.56 Here is an example of a paragraph using "Top of caps" leading method. The text is 10/12 (fixed leading; 5.25). In the fourth line is a bullet •. This bullet is 14 point. Even with fixed leading, that line has a slug reaching from the top of the ascender that *would* be there in that 14-point type. So it takes the 12 points of fixed leading and puts most of it above the type with very little left for the linespace below. Then the line below moves its slug up to meet the one above. This is very difficult—and sometimes impossible—to correct.

5.57 Although you are able to control *proportional* leading (5.39–5.44) more accurately than "Top of caps," there is one particular instance where "Top of caps" will help you retain your sanity.

You may have run across the problem of trying to change the amount of space between two or three lines in a headline. Using the default *proportional* leading, when you change the leading with the intent to bring the second line up closer to the first, you find that the first line also moves up, away from the second. That can be very annoying (below, and 5.44).

But if you apply the "Top of caps" method to the paragraph, the first line stays right in place when you change the leading, and the second line will move up to meet it.

10/Auto **PERFECT** IS GOOD ENOUGH

10/6 **PERFECT** IS GOOD ENOUGH
*Proportional leading; first **and** second line moved up.*

10/6 **PERFECT** IS GOOD ENOUGH
Top of caps leading; second line moved up.

5.58 **Comparison of leading examples**

⌐All the text blocks are hanging from this "clothesline."

I wish my brain was a computer

by Robin Williams

I awoke one morning out of an interesting dream. In my half-sleep, I found myself wondering if I should store that dream on my hard disk or on a floppy. When I awoke completely, of course, I realized how silly that was—why, that dream was in full color and couldn't possibly fit on a floppy.

Adapter boards

When my sister-in-law got a new job, it seemed the logical thing to do would be to remove the board with the job chips from her predecessor's brain and insert it into the slot in my sister-in-law's brain. That way she would instantly know all the key contacts, their histories, where everything is filed, where the bathrooms are, and who's sleeping with whom.

Proportional leading. *Because the leading is spread out above and below the text, beginners can use default leading values and not have problems.*

I wish my brain was a computer

by Robin Williams

I awoke one morning out of an interesting dream. In my half-sleep, I found myself wondering if I should store that dream on my hard disk or on a floppy. When I awoke completely, of course, I realized how silly that was—why, that dream was in full color and couldn't possibly fit on a floppy.

Adapter boards

When my sister-in-law got a new job, it seemed the logical thing to do would be to remove the board with the job chips from her predecessor's brain and insert it into the slot in my sister-in-law's brain. That way she would instantly know all the key contacts, their histories, where everything is filed, where the bathrooms are, and who's sleeping with whom.

Baseline leading. *As you can see in the headline, baseline leading creates a problem when there is large type above small type. You have to know how to fix it. This example is a screen shot so you can see baseline leading's annoying habit of chopping off the descenders.*

I wish my brain was a computer

by Robin Williams

I awoke one morning out of an interesting dream. In my half-sleep, I found myself wondering if I should store that dream on my hard disk or on a floppy. When I awoke completely, of course, I realized how silly that was—why, that dream was in full color and couldn't possibly fit on a floppy.

Adapter boards

When my sister-in-law got a new job, it seemed the logical thing to do would be to remove the board with the job chips from her predecessor's brain and insert it into the slot in my sister-in-law's brain. That way she would instantly know all the key contacts, their histories, where everything is filed, where the bathrooms are, and who's sleeping with whom.

Top of caps leading. *The most unacceptable feature of tops of caps leading is that you cannot have more than one size of type per paragraph, even if you fix the leading value—notice the larger W in the first paragraph (text: 9/11)*

If you want to do this:	**Then follow these steps:**	**Shortcuts ▾ Notes ▾ Hints**
5.59 Figure out the actual value of "Auto" leading in a line of text *(the old-fashioned method)*	▪ With the **text tool,** click in a word. ▪ You need to know the point size of the type. From the Type menu, choose "Size" and see where the checkmark is. If the checkmark is next to "Other...," then slide over and see what it is; click Cancel. ▪ From the Apple menu, choose "Calculator." Multiply the point size of the type by 1.2. The answer, rounded off to the tenth of a point (.1), is the actual leading value. ▪ Put the calculator away by pressing Command W.	▪ If there is no checkmark next to any number, and the "Other..." box is blank, there is more than one point size in the text you have selected.
5.60 Figure out the actual value of "Auto" leading (or any leading) in a line of text *using the Control palette*	▪ With the **text tool,** click in a word. ▪ If the Control palette is not already on your screen, press Command ' *(apostrophe);* press Command Shift ` *(grave)* to get it in character-view if necessary. ▪ The leading value is displayed in the leading edit box, as shown below. The Control palette *does not display the word Auto*—it just gives you the value, even if the leading is set at Auto. ▪ If you want to remove the Control palette, press Command ' again.	▪ You cannot "fix" the leading (5.25) to the same point value as the Auto leading *through the Control palette*. That is, if the Auto leading value is 12, you can type "12" in the menu leading box or in the Type specs dialog box, and the leading value will be fixed at 12. But if you type "12" in the Control palette leading box, the leading remains "Auto"—it's not really a fixed 12. (Of course, you have to understand the importance of fixed leading before this statement will make sense.)

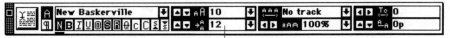

This box displays the leading value.

If you want to do this:	Then follow these steps:	Shortcuts ▾ Notes ▾ Hints

5.61 Figure out the current leading value of the selected text	■ With the **text tool,** select the text you want to check.
	■ From the Type menu, choose "Leading."
	  ☐ If there is a number checked, that is the current leading value.
	  ☐ If "Other..." is checked, choose it to see the value; click Cancel.
	  ☐ If "Auto" is checked, follow the steps in 5.59 or 5.60 to find the value.
	  ☐ If the menu only shows "Other..." and "Auto," with no check next to either one of them, *or* if it shows the complete list but with nothing checked, there is more than one leading value in the selected text. You need to select a smaller portion of text to check.
		■ You can just click the insertion point in any text or blank space to check the leading at that spot. If you think there may be varying amounts of leading in the text, press-and-drag to select and confirm it.
		■ If the menu indicates that you have more than one leading value selected, select a smaller portion of text. If necessary, check separately to see what the other values are.
		■ If you type a value into the "Leading" edit box in "Type specs" or into "Other..." in the submenu at this point, you will change the leading of the *selected* text.
		■ **Or** use the character-view Control palette to check the leading value, as in 5.60.

5.62 Increase or decrease the leading	■ With the **text tool,** select the entire line(s) you want to affect.
	■ Get the *current* leading value. See 5.61, or check the Control palette (5.60).
	■ From the Type menu, choose "Leading," then choose the number you want;
	  ☐ **Or** choose "Other..." and type in a leading value; or type it into the Control palette.
	  ☐ **Or** choose "Type specs...," then press Tab (just a shortcut to the Leading edit box) and enter a leading value; click OK.
		■ The higher the leading number, the greater the line space. You can apply leading from 0 to 1300 points, in tenth of a point increments (.1). Don't type a comma in the number.

If you want to do this:	**Then follow these steps:**	**Shortcuts ▾ Notes ▾ Hints**
5.63 Use the *proportional* leading method (5.39–5.44) Leading method: ◉ Proportional ○ Top of caps ○ Baseline	■ With the **text tool,** select the paragraph(s) you want to affect. ■ From the Type menu, choose "Paragraph...." ■ Click in the "Spacing..." button. ■ Click the "Proportional" button. ■ Click OK twice, *or* press Option Return.	■ "Proportional" leading is *paragraph-specific,* meaning that it will apply *to the entire paragraph* that has the insertion point in it, *or* to all paragraphs that have been highlighted (selected) with the text tool. ■ This is PageMaker's default method of leading.
5.64 Use the *top of caps* leading method (5.51–5.57) Leading method: ○ Proportional ◉ Top of caps ○ Baseline	■ With the **text tool,** select the paragraph(s) you want to affect. ■ From the Type menu, choose "Paragraph...." ■ Click in the "Spacing..." button. ■ Click the "Top of caps" button. ■ Click OK twice, *or* press Option Return.	■ "Top of caps" leading is *paragraph-specific,* just like "Proportional," as mentioned in the paragraph above. ■ The default method is *proportional.* Of course, if you like to create obstacles in your path just for the thrill of overcoming them, or if there is someone in your office you really don't like, set the application default to "Top of caps."
5.65 Use the *baseline* leading method (5.45–5.50) Leading method: ○ Proportional ○ Top of caps ◉ Baseline	■ With the **text tool,** select the paragraph(s) you want to affect. ■ From the Type menu, choose "Paragraph ...." ■ Click in the "Spacing..." button. ■ Click the "Baseline" button. ■ Click OK twice, *or* press Option Return.	■ "Baseline" leading is *paragraph-specific,* just like "Proportional," as mentioned in the paragraph at the top. ■ Before you use baseline leading, be sure you read the information about it (5.45–5.50) and understand the kinds of problems you may encounter. The "problems" are only problems if you don't quite understand how to adjust your line spacing and paragraph spacing. Otherwise you might like baseline leading.

If you want to do this:

Then follow these steps:

Shortcuts ▾ Notes ▾ Hints

5.66 Adjust the leading of a paragraph so it is consistent

- If you already know the leading value you want the entire paragraph to have, skip the next step.
- If you want to match the inconsistent lines with the rest of the lines, then with the **text tool** double-click on a word that seems to hold the leading value you want. Follow the steps in 5.61 to discover its actual value.
- With the **text tool,** triple-click to select the entire paragraph.
- From the Type menu, choose "Leading," then choose a value;
  Or choose "Other..." and type in a value; click OK;
  Or from the Type menu, choose "Type specs...," then press Tab and type in the leading value for the entire paragraph; click OK;
  Or show the Control palette (press Command ') and either choose a leading value from the submenu or type a value into the leading edit box (as shown in 5.60).

- This is a common procedure that you will need to follow whenever you increase the size of a character within a paragraph (see 5.23–5.26).

- Pressing the Tab key in this step is only to select the Leading edit box. You could, of course, just double-click in the box.

If you want to do this:	Then follow these steps:	Shortcuts ▾ Notes ▾ Hints
5.67 Adjust the leading above the last line of a paragraph of body text	■ Occasionally you will have a paragraph that seems to have more linespace above the last line than there is above the rest of the lines, yet the entire paragraph has the same leading value. ■ With the **text tool,** set your insertion point directly after the last character in the paragraph. ■ Hit a Return. This will bump the last line up to match the rest of the linespacing. ■ If you have too much space between paragraphs now, hit the DownArrow key once, then press the Backspace/Delete key to remove the extra line you just inserted. **Or,** with the **text tool,** double-click on the *blank* line and delete it.	■ Make sure the paragraph is using the proportional leading method (5.63). ■ Hitting the DownArrow key is meant to place the insertion point directly *in front of the first character* on the next line. Check to make sure that's where it is before you Backspace/Delete.
5.68 Change the Auto leading value **Autoleading:** [120] % of point size	■ Read the notes to the right. ☛ ■ From the Type menu, choose "Paragraph…," *or* press Command M. ■ Click the "Spacing…" button. ■ Double-click in the edit box below "Autoleading." ■ Enter a value between 0% and 200%, in 1% increments. ■ Click OK.	■ If the *insertion point* is flashing, you will set the auto leading for *that* paragraph. ■ If there is any amount of *text selected,* you will set the auto leading for the *paragraphs* that contain the selected text. ■ If you follow these steps when the *pointer tool* is selected, you will set a publication default (1.6–1.11). ■ Include this spec in your style sheet (Section 8) for paragraphs that you always want with loose (extra) or tight (less) leading.

If you want to do this:

5.69 You want to change the leading, but it won't change

Then follow these steps:

- If you are changing the leading of one line, make sure you select the *entire line,* including any white space at the end, before you change the leading value. You must highlight the line *clear to the end of the text block,* even if you have indents set (6.24–6.25).
- If you are changing the leading of a *paragraph,* make sure you select the *entire paragraph,* including any white space at the end, before you change the leading value. The most efficient method is to triple-click on the paragraph with the **text tool.**
- If you selected the text properly and it still doesn't change, check these: With the text selected, press Command M to get the Paragraph dialog box.
  - ☐ Any numbers in the "Before" or "After" edit box can affect your leading. Change them to zeros, if necessary.
  - ☐ Any "Options" applied don't really affect your leading, but they can make your type act very strange (4.332).
  - ☐ Click on the button "Rules...." Any rules applied to a paragraph affect the visible linespace.
  - ☐ While in the "Rules" dialog box, click on the button "Options...." A checkmark next to "Align to grid" will affect your leading. Deselect it, if necessary.

Shortcuts ▾ Notes ▾ Hints

- To select the entire line, not just the words you can see, drag the mouse *downward,* not across. Really.
- Make sure your leading method is "Proportional" (5.63). Using "Top of caps" can really mess you up (5.51–5.57).
- Sometimes the leading is really doing just what you told it, but you are *expecting* something else. Be sure to read 5.39–5.44 for examples of how proportional leading will affect the lines.

- If either the "Before" or "After" edit boxes in the Paragraph dialog box are *blank* (that is, they don't even have *zeros* in them), the selected paragraphs have *some* amount of space applied before or after, but the amounts differ in the different paragraphs. If you type a zero (or any other value) into either box, you will change the amount for all selected paragraphs.

If you want to do this:	Then follow these steps:	Shortcuts ▾ Notes ▾ Hints

5.70 Make the letters reappear after you decrease the leading or when using the Baseline leading method

HELP — *The letters couldn't fit on the leading slug anymore.*

HELP — *Just redraw the screen*

- With the **pointer tool,** click once on the text block. From the Element menu, choose "Bring to front," *or* press Command F. This will redraw just the text block.
  Or with any tool, select a new page view from the Page menu, or even select the same view.
  Or click in the zoom box with any tool you happen to have (the zoom box is the tiny little box way up in the upper right corner of the window: ⊟). These last two methods will redraw the entire screen.

- Parts of the characters disappear because they are either out of the text block or hidden under the white space of the leading. No matter why, it is easy to make the character parts reappear.
- Actually, the letters will reappear whenever the screen is redrawn, as when the view is resized or scrolled across. These are just a couple of methods for redrawing the screen.
- Even if parts of the characters are missing on the screen, they will print.

5.71 Adjust the leading on an inline graphic so it doesn't make the linespace inconsistent

- With the **text tool,** click to set the insertion point on either side of the inline graphic.
- From the Type menu, choose "Paragraph...."
- Click on the button "Rules..."; then click on the button "Options...."
- Click on the checkbox "Align to grid."
- Next to "Grid size," type in the leading value of the text you are working with.
- Press Option Return to close all the boxes.
- **Or** in the paragraph-view control palette enter the leading value in the "Grid-size" option (4.307). The "Align-to-grid" button (4.315) will automatically be selected.

- Inline graphics are discussed in great detail in Section 10 on Graphics; the task on this page is just meant for quick reference.
- Note: this process works in conjunction with paragraph returns. Text will realign on the grid *after* you hit a Return. For a full explanation of the purpose of "Align to grid" and what it is doing here, please see 5.97–5.109.
- Shortcut: typing in a value or selecting one from the submenu will automatically put a checkmark next to "Align to grid."

Paragraph spacing

(from the Type menu, choose "Paragraph…," or press Command M)

5.72 The **paragraph spacing** feature is terrific. On a typewriter, when we wanted extra space between paragraphs, we hit the carriage return twice—our only option. You may have noticed that now, with the professional-level type you are creating, those double spaces look a bit large and clunky. PageMaker provides you with the option of putting as much or as little space as you want between your paragraphs *automatically,* with just *one* press of the Return key.

5.73 The amount of space between paragraphs is determined in the "Paragraph specifications" dialog box ("Paragraph…" from the Type menu, or Command M). The only part of that confusing dialog box you need to be concerned with here is the "Paragraph space" section.

5.74 Let's start with the paragraph space **After,** as it's easier to understand. For the text you are working on, decide how much extra space you want between the paragraphs. A general rule is to add about half a line's worth of extra space. For instance, if you are working with 12 point type, the Auto leading is 14.5 points (5.20). If you pressed a Return key twice, you would have a blank line of 14.4 points between the paragraphs. You want only half of that; you want a line space of about 6 or 7 points.

5.75 So *instead* of pressing the Return key twice, go to the "Paragraph space" dialog box and enter **0p6** (that's a zero, the letter p for picas, and the number of points you want; see 5.87) into the "After" edit box.

5.76 Every time you hit a Return, Page-Maker thinks you just finished one paragraph and are about to start a new one. Once you have entered a number into the "After" box, you get those extra points of space *after* each paragraph.

5.77 The paragraph space **Before** is very similiar to "After," but *Before* inserts the extra points of space *above* the next line of type.

5.78 A classic case for applying extra space before is in a subhead. Typically a subhead follows several paragraphs of body copy, right? The body copy usually has extra space between its paragraphs. But after the last paragraph, you want even a little *more* space. You don't want to have to put extra space after that last paragraph every time you come to a subhead, do you? No. So you put extra space *before* the subhead. (See 5.85, as well as 5.92, Scenario 6).

5.79 Paragraph space before and after should be a natural part of your style sheets (Section 8). The example in 5.78 above would be a perfect situation in which to set up a style for body text with its extra space "After," and another style for the subhead with its extra space "Before."

5.80 A paragraph can certainly have space "After" in addition to any space "Before" which would be particularly appropriate for the subhead we were just talking about. It would *not* be appropriate for paragraphs of body text, though; see 5.81–5.85 for an important message.

An Important Note

5.81 *Paragraph space before, paragraph space after, and leading are cumulative.* That is, any values you enter into the "Before" and/or "After" edit boxes are added onto the literal leading value.

5.82 Let me explain. If your text is 12 point and you have 15-point leading, you actually (literally) have 3 extra points of space between the lines, right? (See 5.12–5.18). If you add an extra 5 points of space "After," the 5 points *are added onto the 3 points* that naturally come with the lines of text; you really have 8 points of space between the paragraphs (3 + 5).

5.83 So your paragraph has 3 literal points of leading and an extra 5 points of space "After." Then a subhead comes along that has an extra 4 points of space "Before." That space "Before" gets added onto all the other space—the 3 literal points of leading and the 5 extra points of paragraph space. So the subhead will actually have an extra *12 points* of visual space above it (3 + 5 + 4).

5.84 *Space before and after is literal.* That is, it does not get spread out through the slug as the leading does (5.32–5.33). It literally sits under or over the leading slug. You can count on it.

5.85 Paragraph space examples

This Headline is 18 point

The headline above is 18-point type with a leading of 18 points. It has no extra space "After."

These paragraphs of body copy are 11 point with 15-point leading (11/15). They have no extra space "After."

Subhead Number One

Subhead Number One is also 11/15, with no extra points of space "After."

This is just to show you a comparison.

This Headline is 18 point

The headline above is 18-point type with a leading of 18 points. It has a space "After" of 8 point. The dotted lines indicate the *extra* 8-point slug (5.32).

These paragraphs are 11 point with 15-point leading (11/15). They have a space "After" of 5 points. The dotted lines directly above indicate the *extra* 5-point slug.

Subhead Number One

Subhead Number One is also 11/15, with 5 points of space "After." But to separate it from the paragraphs above, it has an extra 4 points of space "Before." The dotted lines above the Subhead indicate the *combination* of the extra 5 points from the second paragraph, plus the extra 4 points "Before" from the Subhead.

Use points to override the measurement system

5.86 Since the basic unit of leading is points (5.6–5.7), the relationship between paragraph spacing and leading (linespace) seems clearer if you also use points for paragraph space. If you don't want to change your entire measurement system to picas (1.224; 5.91), you can override the existing measurement system by entering values in picas and points in the edit boxes.

5.87 If the value is less than one pica (less than 12 points), enter a **0** (zero), then the letter **p** (for picas), then the number of **points** (**0p5**). The **p** tells PageMaker not to use the current measuring system but to use picas instead.

If the value is one pica or more, enter the **number,** then the letter **p** (**2p**). If there are points also, enter those after the **p** (**2p7** means 2 picas and 7 points).

5.88 The only problem with overriding is that when you return to the dialog box you'll find that PageMaker has automatically translated those points and picas into the current measuring system (see 5.89–5.91). Then, if you want to change the space by a tenth point or several points, it is difficult to figure.

5.89 Overriding the measurement system looks like this. Notice it says "inches," but the value entered in the edit box is in picas and points.

Paragraph space:		
Before	0	inches
After	0p5	inches

5.90 When you return to the dialog box, you'll find that PageMaker has turned the picas and points into the value of the current measurement system. That can make it difficult to work with.

Paragraph space:		
Before	0	inches
After	0.069	inches

5.91 To see the actual value that you originally entered, go to the "Preferences" dialog box (from the File menu) and change the "Measurement system" to "Picas." When you go back to the "Paragraph space" dialog box, the value will have reverted to picas and points. *(This will change the entire measurement system to picas, including the horizontal ruler, the Indents/tabs ruler, and all dialog boxes. See 1.224.)*

Paragraph space:		
Before	0	picas
After	0p5	picas

Or change the measurement system in the space-before and -after edit boxes on the Control palette "on the fly"; 3.109 and 3.114.

Mai: It would all be folly.
Mrs. Brown: Tell me, Mai, what's wrong with folly?

National Velvet

5.92 Scenario #6: Paragraph space "before" and "after"

Take note, in the example, of the spaces *before* and *after* the subheads, as compared to the spaces *between* the paragraphs.

I set the **body copy paragraphs** with an extra 2 points of space **after** each (5.93). This means that every time I pressed the Return key, an extra 2 points of space was inserted *after* that last line. This 2-point space was *added onto* the current leading: the type size is 10-point with 12-point leading, so the space between the paragraphs is now 14 point.

I set the **subheads** with an extra 4 points of space **after,** because it usually looks best to have a slight bit more separation after a subhead than there is between paragraphs. Again, these points were *added onto* the leading of the subhead.

Now, to emphasize the connection of the subhead with the following text, I inserted a little bit of extra space **before** the subhead. The examples here have an extra 6 points. These 6 points are *added onto the leading of the line above it*—thus (read this carefully), the *leading* of the paragraph above, the *after* of the paragraph above, and the *before* of the subhead, are *all added together* to create that space above the subhead.

JOHN BASKERVILLE

A type design

In 1780 the 'transitional' typeface *Baskerville* was introduced to the world. Nobody liked it.

Baskerville is called a transitional typeface because its characteristics were crossing the threshold from the 'oldstyle' typefaces that were currently in use, to the 'modern' typefaces with their extreme contrasts of thick-and-thin strokes. But the public wasn't ready for this cold, dry look—they wanted the warmth of the oldstyles.

An inventor

John loved those thin strokes of his new font, made possible with the new technology of copperplate engraving. But the paper technology was not ready yet to accept those thin lines—when printed, paper was so absorbent that the lines mushed up and lost their fine quality.

So John had to invent a new paper process—*calendaring*—that is still used today to create a smoother finish for printing.

An entrepreneur

John was a wealthy man, making his money in the japanning trade of the 1700s—*japan* is a hard, durable, black varnish originating, of course, in Japan. At the age of forty, when he became a typefounder, John lost his fortune because nobody liked his typeface. They preferred Caslon.

A coincidence

Baskerville (the font) was lost to the world for the next 150 years. In 1923 The Monotype Corporation revived this lovely typeface, and it went on to become the most popular type in the world. The coincidence is that the country where Baskerville has been used most extensively is Japan, to whom John originally owed his fortune.

An aside

This book is set in ITC Baskerville, 10/12, from Adobe Systems Incorporated.

If you want to do this:

5.93 Add space *after* a paragraph

Paragraph space:

Before `0` picas

After `0p5` picas

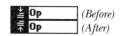
(Before)
(After)

The "Paragraph space" options in the paragraph-view Control palette

5.94 Add space *before* a paragraph

Paragraph space:

Before `0p3` picas

After `0` picas

Then follow these steps:

- With the **text tool,** select the paragraph(s) to which you want to apply extra space (you can select just one paragraph simply by clicking the insertion point in it).
- From the Type menu, choose "Paragraph...," *or* press Command M.
- Enter the value for the amount of *extra* space you want in the "After" edit box. If your measurement system is in inches, you may find it easier to override the inches (5.8–5.88) or to change your measurement system to picas (5.9).
- **Or** in the paragraph-view Control palette, enter a value in the "Paragraph space after" option box, see 4.314.

- Follow the steps in 5.93 above. Enter the value for the amount of *extra* space you want in the "Before" edit box. Be sure to read 5.77–5.85 to understand what you are doing and what to expect.

Shortcuts ▾ Notes ▾ Hints

- Remember, a *paragraph* on the Mac is any line or group of lines that has a Return at the end of it (4.348–4.354). See 4.289–4.290 re: selecting paragraphs.
- If the Control palette is not already on your screen, press Command ' (*apostrophe*). To toggle between character-view and paragraph-view, press Command Shift ` (*grave*).
- You can override the measurement system in the Control palette the same as you can in the "Paragraph" dialog box (5.86–5.88, 5.9). However, you can also change the measuring system for certain options "on the fly," and the option will keep the measurement system you choose, see 3.109; 3.114.

- See 4.289–4.290 re: selecting paragraphs.

If you want to do this:	Then follow these steps:	Shortcuts ▾ Notes ▾ Hints
5.95 Break a line *without* adding a paragraph space	■ Every time you press the Return key, Page-Maker thinks you want a new paragraph and so adds on any extra space before and/or after that you have specified. Sometimes you don't want that extra space. Instead of pressing a Return, press **Shift Return.** You will get a hard line break that will not add any extra space.	■ See 4.348–4.354 for more info on the Shift Return line break.
5.96 Remove paragraph space	■ With the **text tool,** select any and all paragraphs from which you want to remove any extra space. ■ From the Type menu, choose "Paragraph...," *or* press Command M. ■ The "Before" and "After" edit boxes may be blank or they may have values in them. Either way, to remove space from either one, type a 0 (zero) into it. You don't need to change both the "Before" and "After" edit boxes. If one of the edit boxes is blank, you can leave it blank if you choose. **But:** *you **cannot** remove a value from an edit box and **then** leave it blank.* PageMaker will yell at you. ■ **Or** in the paragraph-view Control palette, delete the values in the "Paragraph space" option edit boxes.	■ See 4.289–4.290 re: selecting paragraphs. ■ If you remove the paragaraph space and there is still more space than you want, there may be something else going on. See 4.332. ■ Press Command ' *(apostrophe)* to display the Control palette on screen if it is not already showing. Press Command Shift ` *(grave)* to change from character-view to paragraph-view, and vice versa.

Align to grid

(from the Type menu, choose "Paragraph…"; click on the "Rules" button; click on the "Options" button)

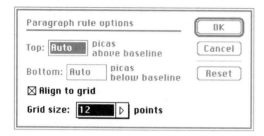

5.97   Some to-do has been made over what some people think is PageMaker's *vertical justification* feature. Well, this is it, but it isn't. Ideally, a vertical justification feature would take a column of text and align it vertically to fill a certain depth, just as horizontal justification aligns text to fill a certain width. PageMaker has always been capable of vertically aligning text by feathering in tiny increments of leading (well, always since 3.0). This "Align to grid" feature, though, does something quite different.

5.98   **Align to grid's** principal claim to fame is that *you can force lines of text across columns to align on the same baseline.* Some people feel very strongly that every baseline (1.57) of every column should align on one common grid, as the baselines of this paragraph align with the baselines of the paragraph to the right. I believe there are other visual factors that are oftentimes more important. You can read this unbiased (ha!) report and make up your own mind.

5.99   With "Align to grid" on, PageMaker does not feather lines of text to fill a certain depth. No—instead, extra points of space are added after headlines, subheads, and between paragraphs. So then your body copy baselines are aligned, but you have another problem: the space between your paragraphs and headlines is inconsistent. Personally, I feel *that* is often a more flagrant visual inconsistency than baselines not aligning.

5.100   This is basically how "Align to grid" works: In your text, including any style sheets you may have created, you have set up a certain point size and leading for your body copy, and a different sort of size and leading for your headlines and subheads. You have probably incorporated a bit of extra space between your paragraphs, after your heads, and before your subheads (5.72–5.85). Well, with this extra space here and there, you find that your baselines across the columns do not match after a while, just like the columns on this page. The first part of this paragraph, as shown by the dotted lines above, aligns with the column to the left because the type is the same size with the same leading. But there are a few extra points of space after each paragraph, so now, at this point, the baselines of the two columns are no longer aligned.

Align to grid   *—continued*

5.101 With "Align to grid" turned on and your leading grid established, PageMaker will automatically insert extra space wherever it's needed to keep those baselines on the grid. The grid, according to this feature, is a set of invisible lines that you define using the leading value of your body copy. If your text is 12-point with 14-point leading, you would set your grid to 14 point.

5.102 On the previous page, I *could* select the text in the second column and align it to the grid so it would match the third column. PageMaker would insert extra points of space *between the paragraphs* until the baselines of the second paragraph matched the baselines directly across from it. But, personally, I don't want to do that because I don't want that much space between my paragraphs. If I did, I would have set them up that way myself. In this case, it is more important to me that I have half a linespace between paragraphs, rather than have a large, clunky space.

5.103 "Align to grid" assumes you know how to work with a *grid*. A grid is an underlying structure, a framework, upon which to base your layout. Once a grid is established, all the elements of the job are aligned with it. The more complex the layout, the more essential a grid becomes. Grid theory is a very exciting and important part of graphic design. If you have studied grid theory, you will be able to take advantage of what the "Align to grid" feature has to offer without running into the problems it causes, or without having to use it at all.

5.104 You can set up your text to align with the grid at any point in the creation of your publication. You can apply it as a default, either for the publication or for the application (1.13, 1.16). Or you can apply it to the appropriate styles in your style sheet. Or you can apply it as you go along. Or you can layout all the pages of your publication *without* using "Align to grid" and just apply it where it seems necessary (which is my preference).

Outside of a dog,
a book is a man's best friend.
Inside of a dog,
it's too dark to read.

—Groucho Marx

Notes ▪

5.105 The "Align to grid" feature will "work" most appropriately if:

- The body copy (the main text) all has the same leading.
- The text blocks all begin at a common point (they all hang from a "clothesline"), or at least they all "Snap to rulers" with the rulers having been customized to your leading increment (1.55; 5.107).
- You don't mind if PageMaker inserts extra linespace above the misaligned paragraph in order to stay on the grid.

5.106 "Align to grid" is paragraph-specific; that is, it is applied to the entire paragraph no matter how few characters in that paragraph have been selected. In fact, it will apply to any paragraph that merely has the insertion point flashing in it. Since it is paragraph-specific, you can also include it in a style sheet.

With "Snap to rulers" ▪

5.107 Using **Snap to rulers** is indispensable in conjunction with "Align to grid." Turn "Snap to rulers" on from the "Guides and rulers" submenu, under the Layout menu, then:

- In the "Preferences" dialog box (from the File menu), choose a "Custom" vertical ruler.
- Type in a point value that equals the point value of the leading of your body copy (5.61); click OK.

Now you will find as you move text blocks or graphics around on the page, they sort of hop from tick mark to tick mark on the rulers. In fact, you *cannot* place anything *between* tick marks. Since the markings on the vertical ruler are in the increments of your body text leading, it is not possible to place a text block anywhere but on one of the "grid" lines (also see 1.56).

With inline graphics ▪

5.108 "Align to grid" is most practical when you are using *inline graphics.* An inline graphic is a graphic that you have placed as part of the text block. It can have leading and paragraph space applied to it, will conform to tabs and indents, and will move along with the text as you edit and format. The biggest problem with inline graphics is that they can throw off the leading. For instance, in this book, all the graphics you see in the first columns are inline (as in 5.93). The baseline of the first column is designed to align with the baseline of the second column. But when there is an inline graphic, it throws off that alignment.

5.109 So I select each inline graphic and align it to the grid (I check "Align to grid" and enter the leading value of the text). PageMaker then adds enough points to the space after the graphic (because now the graphic is a paragraph) to make the *next* line of text stay on the 12-point grid that aligns it with the adjacent column. The extra space is not a problem in this case, because the space below the inline graphic is so variable anyway.

See Section 10, 10.213–10.233 for more info on inline graphics.

If you want to do this:	**Then follow these steps:**	**Shortcuts ▾ Notes ▾ Hints**
5.110 Align text to a leading grid	■ First, make sure you know the point size of your leading (5.61). Then . . .	■ The paragraph-view Control palette offers the most direct method for setting align-to-grid values. If the palette is in character-view, click the "Paragraph-view" button *or* press Command Shift ` *(grave)* to change it to paragraph-view. Simply type the leading value in the "Grid-size" option edit box (4.307). The "Align-to-grid" button (4.315) will automatically be selected.

"Grid-size" option

┌─────────┐
│ ↓↑ 12 │
│ ≣ ≣≣ │
└─────────┘

"Align-to-grid" button

Faster than a nested dialog box, you can simply type your leading value in the paragraph-view Control palette.

■ With the **text tool,** select the paragraphs you want to align to a grid.
■ From the Type menu, choose "Paragraph...."
■ Click on the "Rules..." button.
■ Click on the "Options..." button.
■ Click in the checkbox next to "Align to grid."
■ Type in the leading value of your body text in the "Grid size" edit box.
■ Press Option Return to *OK* all three dialog boxes (press Command Option Period to *Cancel* all three dialog boxes).
■ Customize your vertical ruler to the same leading value you set in "Align to grid" (5.107).

■ From the Layout menu, make sure "Snap to rulers" is on (5.107).
■ With the **pointer tool,** press near the *top* of the text block and drag it into position. The text block will snap to the nearest ruler tick mark.

■ "Snap to rulers" is located in the "Guides and rulers" submenu, under the Layout menu.

5.111 Align graphics to a leading grid *(or to any other kind of grid)*

■ Customize your vertical ruler to the leading of your body text (5.107; 1.55).
■ From the Layout menu, make sure "Snap to rulers" is on (5.107).
■ Now as you move and resize graphics, they will snap to the grid.

■ You don't have to set your grid with a *leading* value; you can customize the vertical ruler with any measurement, such as half-inches (36 points) or quarter-inches (18 points).

Word spacing

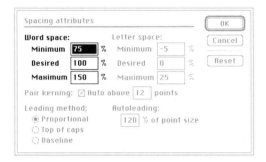

5.112 To get the "Spacing attributes" dialog box, choose "Paragraph..." from the Type menu, then click on the "Spacing..." button. In that overwhelming dialog box, only those three little boxes on the left deal with word spacing (see above). Ignore all the rest for now.

5.113 Word spacing applies to entire paragraphs, not just to selected text. Even if you have just a few of the characters selected, any changes entered here will affect the entire paragraph.

5.114 The **Word spacing** segment of the "Spacing attributes" dialog box is concerned with the space *between the words.* When you hit the Spacebar, you create a space, right? That is a **word space.** A technical term for it is the *space band.*

5.115 When designers create fonts, they not only design the characters, but they also determine the ideal amount of space that should separate the letters and the words in that font and at each particular size.

5.116 The default value in the **Desired** edit box is 100%. That 100% indicates the ideal that the designer built into the font. If you leave that value at 100%, the text consistently retains that amount of space between words, *as long as the text is not justified.*

5.117 If you change the Desired default to another value, such as 80%, PageMaker will set the text using 80% of the ideal space between the words, *as long as the text is not justified.*

5.118 If your text *is not justified,* then it doesn't matter what values are in the Minimum and Maximum boxes; PageMaker will use the Desired value (unless you use an excessively large amount of space and the words can't fit on the line easily).

5.119 Any applied *word* spacing will *not* affect the *letter* space. Be careful, because too much or too little word space without appropriate letterspace can really make your text look dumb.

—continued

5.120 *This is an example of a font that needs to have its word spacing adjusted to make it more readable.*

"I believe that everyone should have a chance at an extravagant piece of folly."
14-point type with default word spacing
~Mrs. Brown, National Velvet

"I believe that everyone should have a chance at an extravagant piece of folly."
14-point type with 150% word spacing
~Mrs. Brown, National Velvet

Word spacing —*continued*

5.121 When text is **justified** (aligned at both margins; 4.247), PageMaker increases or decreases space between the *words* in order to align the margins. In this process, often it can't use the 100% word space you desire.

5.122 The default value in the **Minimum** edit box is 50%. That 50% means that you won't mind if PageMaker has to squeeze the desired word space down to *half* of what the designer originally built into the space band.

5.123 The default value in the **Maximum** edit box is 200%. That 200% means that you won't mind if PageMaker has to increase the desired word space up to *twice the amount* of what the designer originally built into the space band.

5.124 You can change the values in either the Desired, the Minimum, or the Maximum edit boxes, with these rules:

- You can set a Minimum of anywhere from 0 to 500 percent (1% increments).
- You can set a Maximum of anywhere from 0 to 500 percent (1% increments).
- The Desired spacing must be *equal to or between* the Minimum and the Maximum.

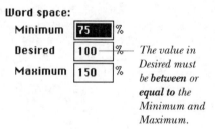

Word space:
Minimum [75] %
Desired [100] % — *The value in Desired must be **between** or **equal to** the Minimum and Maximum.*
Maximum [150] %

5.125 PageMaker tries very hard to follow your word spacing specifications. But sometimes it just can't. PageMaker will let you know which lines disobey your rules *if* you have checked "Show loose/tight lines" in the Preferences dialog box (from the File menu). Problem lines will have a gray or colored bar behind them (see 5.128). The bar does not print; it is just a clue suggesting that perhaps you should take a closer look at that line. You may need to rewrite it, change the spacing, change the alignment, etc. But then again, the spacing might not bother you and you can just leave it as is.

5.126 Most of the time you can safely ignore the word spacing as the Desired amount is generally adequate. Occasionally you may come across a font that looks a little too tight, or maybe it sets too loose. Then, of course, adjust it.

5.127 Rarely do you find that you can adjust the word spacing without adjusting the letter spacing as well. Extra word space with normal letter space usually looks like you don't know what you're doing. If you add extra letter space (5.139; 5.143), don't forget that letter spacing also affects the word spacing.

5.128 Examples of word spacing   *All of the following examples use the font Futura Book (sans serif) or Goudy (serif), 12/Auto leading.*

This column is **left aligned.**

This column is **justified, sans serif font.**

This column is **justified, serif font.**

Min: 50   Des: **100**   Max: 200

Thou art thy mother's glass, and she in thee calls back the lovely April of her prime.

Min: 50   Des: **100**   Max: 200

Thou art thy mother's glass, and she in thee calls back the lovely April of her prime.

Min: 50   Des: **100**   Max: 200

Thou art thy mother's glass, and she in thee calls back the lovely April of her prime.

Min: 50   Des: **200**   Max: 200

Thou art thy mother's glass, and she in thee calls back the lovely April of her prime.

Min: 50   Des: **200**   Max: 200

Thou art thy mother's glass, and she in thee calls back the lovely April of her prime.

Min: 50   Des: **200**   Max: 200

Thou art thy mother's glass, and she in thee calls back the lovely April of her prime.

Min: 50   Des: **500**   Max: **500**

Thou   art   thy   mother's glass,   and   she   in   thee calls   back   the   lovely April   of   her   prime.   *(see 5.125)*

Min: 50   Des: **500**   Max: **500**

Thou   art   thy   mother's   glass, and   she   in   thee   calls   back the   lovely   April   of   her   prime.

Min: 50   Des: **500**   Max: **500**

Thou   art   thy   mother's   glass,   and she   in   thee   calls   back   the   lovely April   of   her   prime.

Min: **0**   Des: **50**   Max: 200

Thou art thy mother's glass, and she in thee calls back the lovely April of her prime.

Min: **0**   Des: **50**   Max: 200

Thou art thy mother's glass, and she in thee calls back the lovely April of her prime.

Min: **0**   Des: **50**   Max: 200

Thouartthymother'sglass,andsheinthee callsbackthelovelyAprilofherprime.

297

If you want to do this:	Then follow these steps:	Shortcuts ▾ Notes ▾ Hints
5.129 Increase the word space	■ With the **text tool,** select the paragraph(s). ■ From the Type menu, choose "Paragraph...," *or* press Command M. ■ Click on the "Spacing..." button. ■ Increase the value in the "Desired" edit box (e.g., 300% will increase the word space three times the normal amount). ■ Increase the value in "Maximum" to at least as large as the value in "Desired." ■ Click OK; click OK (or press Option Return to close both boxes).	■ You can set Minimum or Maximum values anywhere from 0 to 500 percent, in increments of 1%. The Desired value must be *between,* or equal to, the Minimum and the Maximum. ■ Be sure to read 5.112–5.127 to understand what you are doing.
5.130 Decrease the word space	■ With the **text tool,** select the paragraph(s). ■ From the Type menu, choose "Paragraph...," *or* press Command M. ■ Click on the "Spacing..." button. ■ Decrease the value in the "Desired" edit box (e.g., 25% will decrease the word space to one-fourth the normal spacing). ■ Decrease the value in "Minimum" to at least as small as the value in "Desired." ■ Click OK; click OK (or press Option Return).	■ You can set Minimum or Maximum values anywhere from 0 to 500 percent, in increments of 1%. The Desired value must be *between,* or equal to, the Minimum and the Maximum. ■ Be sure to read 5.112–5.127 to understand what you are doing.
5.131 Reset all the word space back to the original default **Word space:** Minimum `75` % Desired `100` % Maximum `150` %	■ With the **text tool,** select the paragraph(s). ■ From the Type menu, choose "Paragraph...," *or* press Command M. ■ Click on the "Spacing..." button. ■ Enter the values shown on the left. ■ Click OK twice, or press Option Return.	■ If the word spacing edit boxes are empty, it indicates that there is more than one value set for the selected paragraphs. What you enter will change *all* the selected paragraphs. ■ See 5.11.

Letter spacing

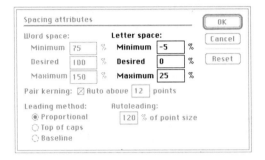

5.132 To get the "Spacing attributes" dialog box, choose "Paragraph..." from the Type menu, then click on the "Spacing..." button. In that overwhelming dialog box, only those three little boxes on the right deal with letter spacing (see above). Ignore all the rest for now.

5.133 Letter spacing applies to entire paragraphs; you cannot apply it to just a few words that are part of a larger paragraph. Using the letter spacing attributes is an easy way to get nicely "letterspaced" text, often so pretty. You can also include letter spacing attributes in your style sheets (Section 8), which is a great boon.

5.134 The **Letter spacing** segment of the "Spacing attributes" dialog box is concerned with the space *between the letters*. A technical term for it is the *pen advance,* a term for the amount of space you must move your pen before you begin the next letter.

5.135 When designers create fonts, they not only design the characters, but they also determine the ideal amount of space that the "pen" should advance before the *computer* creates the next letter; in other words, the designer decides how much space should surround each letter in a particular font and at a particular size.

5.136 The default value in the **Desired** edit box is 0%. That 0% indicates that *you do not want to deviate* from the ideal that the designer has built into the font. If you leave that value at 0%, then as text composes on the screen it keeps that consistent space between letters, *as long as the text is not justified.*

5.137 If you change the Desired default to another value, such as 20%, then Page-Maker will set the text using 20% *more* than the ideal space between the letters, *as long as the text is not justified.*

5.138 If your text *is not justified,* then it doesn't matter what values are in the Minimum and Maximum boxes; PageMaker will use the Desired value. Just remember: Desired must be *between* or equal to the Minimum and Maximum.

5.139 Letter space *does* affect the word space as well. It affects it because the space between words is just a Spacebar character. To us, it appears to be invisible. But to the Mac, it is a character; PageMaker doesn't know we can't see it. So as the letter space expands or condenses, the word space will expand or condense proportionally.

Letter spacing   *—continued*

5.140   To make the *justified* lines of text align at both margins, PageMaker first increases or decreases space between the *words,* according to the values set for word space (5.112–5.127). If PageMaker cannot justify the lines within the minimum and maximum word space settings, then it starts to work with the letter spacing settings.

5.141   The default value in the **Minimum** edit box is –5%. That –5% means that, when you choose to justify text, you won't mind if PageMaker has to squeeze up to 5% of the desired letter space *out* of what the designer originally built into the pen advance (5.134).

5.142   The default value in the **Maximum** edit box is 25%. That 25% means that when you choose to justify text, you won't mind if PageMaker has to increase the desired letter space up to 25% *more* than what the designer originally built into the pen advance (5.134).

5.143   You can change the values in either the Desired, the Minimum, or the Maximum edit boxes according to these rules:

- You can set a Minimum from –200 to 200 percent (1% increments).
- You can set a Maximum from –200 to 200 percent (1% increments).
- The Desired spacing must be *between,* or equal to, the Minimum and the Maximum.

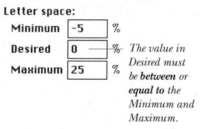

*The value in Desired must be **between** or **equal to** the Minimum and Maximum.*

5.144   PageMaker tries very hard to follow your word and letter spacing specifications. But sometimes she just can't. PageMaker will let you know which lines disobey your rules *if* you have checked "Loose/tight lines" in the Preferences dialog box (from the File menu). Problem lines will have a gray or colored bar behind them (5.128). The bar does not print; it is just a clue suggesting that perhaps you should take a closer look at that line and adjust it, if necessary (rewrite it, change the spacing, change the alignment, etc.). But then again, it may looks just fine to you the way it is.

5.145   Most of the time you can safely ignore the letter spacing as the Desired amount is generally adequate. Occasionally you may come across a font that looks a little too tight, or maybe it sets too loose. Then, of course, adjust it.

5.146 Examples of letter spacing *All of the following examples use the font Futura Book (sans serif) or Goudy (serif), 12/Auto leading.*

This column is **left aligned.**

Min: –5 Des: **0** Max: 25

Thou art thy mother's glass, and she in thee calls back the lovely April of her prime.

Min: –5 Des: **25** Max: 25

Thou art thy mother's glass, and she in thee calls back the lovely April of her prime.

Min: –5 Des: **75** Max: **100**

Thou art thy mother's glass, and she in thee calls back the lovely April of her prime.

Min: **–25** Des: **–25** Max: 25

Thou art thy mother's glass, and she in thee calls back the lovely April of her prime.

This column is **justified, sans serif font.**

Min: –5 Des: **0** Max: 25

Thou art thy mother's glass, and she in thee calls back the lovely April of her prime.

Min: –5 Des: **25** Max: 25

Thou art thy mother's glass, and she in thee calls back the lovely April of her prime.

Min: –5 Des: **75** Max: **100**

Thou art thy mother's glass, and she in thee calls back the lovely April of her prime.

Min: **–25** Des: **–25** Max: 25

Thou art thy mother's glass, and she in thee calls back the lovely April of her prime.

This column is **justified, serif font.**

Min: –5 Des: **0** Max: 25

Thou art thy mother's glass, and she in thee calls back the lovely April of her prime.

Min: –5 Des: **25** Max: 25

Thou art thy mother's glass, and she in thee calls back the lovely April of her prime.

Min: –5 Des: **75** Max: **100**

Thou art thy mother's glass, and she in thee calls back the lovely April of her prime.

Min: **–25** Des: **–25** Max: 25

Thou art thy mother's glass, and she in thee calls back the lovely April of her prime.

If you want to do this:	Then follow these steps:	Shortcuts ▪ Notes ▪ Hints
5.147 Increase the letter space	■ With the **text tool,** select the paragraph(s). ■ From the Type menu, choose "Paragraph...," *or* press Command M. ■ Click on the "Spacing..." button. ■ Increase the value in the "Desired" edit box (e.g., 50% will increase the letter space half again as much as normal). ■ Increase the value in "Maximum" to a value at least as large as the one in "Desired." ■ Click OK; click OK (*or* press Option Return to close both boxes).	■ You can set Minimum or Maximum values anywhere from –200 to 200 percent, in increments of 1%. The Desired value must be *between,* or equal to, the Minimum and the Maximum. ■ Be sure to read 5.132–5.145 to understand what you are doing.
5.148 Decrease the letter space	■ With the **text tool,** select the paragraph(s). ■ From the Type menu, choose "Paragraph...," *or* press Command M. ■ Click on the "Spacing..." button. ■ Decrease the value in the "Desired" edit box (e.g., –25% will decrease the letter space by one-fourth the normal amount). ■ Decrease the value in "Minimum" to one at least as small as the value in "Desired." ■ Click OK; click OK (*or* press Option Return).	■ You can set Minimum or Maximum values anywhere from –200 to 200 percent, in increments of 1%. The Desired value must be *between,* or equal to, the Minimum and the Maximum. ■ Be sure to read 5.132–5.145 to understand what you are doing.
5.149 Reset all the letter space values back to the original defaults Letter space: Minimum [-5] % Desired [0] % Maximum [25] %	■ With the **text tool,** select the paragraph(s). ■ From the Type menu, choose "Paragraph...," *or* press Command M. ■ Click on the "Spacing..." button. ■ Enter the values shown on the left. ■ Click OK twice, *or* press Option Return.	■ If the letter spacing edit boxes are empty, there is more than one value set for the selected paragraphs. What you enter will change all the selected paragraphs. ■ See 5.11.

If you want to do this:

5.150 Letterspace a headline

YOU CAN'T LET THE SEEDS
STOP YOU FROM ENJOYING
THE WATERMELON

Then follow these steps:

This really has nothing to do with the letter space segment of the "Spacing attributes" dialog box, but since you might look in this section for this information, here it is.

- Type the headline. **But** instead of just hitting the Spacebar between words, press the Option key while you hit the Spacebar. This creates a hard, or *non-breaking* space (5.217–5.222). If the headline is more than one line, *do* type a Return or a Shift Return (5.95) between lines.
- When you are done typing, select all the lines of the text (if you used Shift-Returns, you only need to have the insertion point somewhere in the text).
- From the Type menu, slide down to "Alignment," then out to the submenu and choose "Force justify"; **or** press Command Shift F; **or** click the "Force justify" alignment button in the paragraph-view Control palette (4.311).

Shortcuts ▾ Notes ▾ Hints

- Also see 4.248 and 4.249 for other examples of letterspaced heads, using this same technique.
- You can use the letter space controls in the "Spacing attributes" dialog box to create this same effect, but it's a matter of trial and error to make it justify at both margins. Using the technique detailed here, the letters will spread or tighten to whatever length you widen or narrow the text block.

Kerning

5.151 Kerning is the process of adjusting the space between characters. It is slightly different from the *letter spacing* you may have just read about (5.132–5.139), in that kerning is *character* formatting directly applied *between individual letters* rather than entire paragraphs. Kerning is a fine tuning control rather than a general attribute.

5.152 You may have read, here and there throughout this book, about the hot metal process used for centuries (until the 1970s), where every character was created on a separate little piece of metal (lead). These letters were lined up in rows to ready them for printing. Obviously, if each character was on its own little piece of lead, it could only get just so close to the one next to it. If a metal typesetter wanted letters closer to each other, he had to take a knife and trim the tiny blocks of lead. He didn't do it very often. You can pick up an old newspaper or magazine and instantly tell that it's old, right? A large part of the look that dates it is the loose letter spacing. The trend for the past twenty years has been to set tighter and tighter letter spacing (fortunately, this trend is changing toward more readable spacing).

Watermelon
Watermelon

Watermelon

Watermelon

Watermelon

Watermelon

5.153 The example to the left shows how the letters would be spaced if they were each on a separate block of lead. Notice particularly the gaps between the **Wa** and around the **o.** Curved letters and letters with extra white space, such as **T, W, A** (as opposed to letters like **H, I,** and **E**), always need kerning.

5.154 This example shows 18-point type set with no kerning.

5.155 This shows the same type set with *auto pair kerning;* the computer kerned the characters automatically (5.160–5.162; 5.166).

5.156 This example shows the same type set with *auto pair kerning,* then refined with *manual kerning* (5.160–5.165).

5.157 This example shows the same type set with the "Expert kerning" addition applied with a kern strength of 1.5 (5.173–5.178). Notice it still needs some adjustment.

The point: visually consistent

5.158 The term *kerning* originally meant *reducing* the space between characters, but it has now come to mean *increasing* the space beween characters as well, or simply *adjusting* the space.

5.159 The end result should be *visually consistent letter spacing* because consistent spacing strengthens the readability of the text. Whether that means you increase space between tight letters or decrease space between loose letters, the spacing must be consistent. The eye should not stumble over spacing inconsistencies.

Auto kerning pairs

5.160 Most fonts have *kerning pairs* built into them. That is, as designers create fonts, they build in tighter spacing around certain *pairs* of letters that are known to cause inconsistent gaps—such as Ta, To, Yo, we, and many others.

5.161 You can have PageMaker automatically kern those pairs *(auto pair kerning)* as you type. Auto kerning slows down the text composition on the screen, plus it is usually only applicable to larger sizes of type (above 12 or 14 point). You can choose to have PageMaker kern only type above a certain point size, or you can choose to turn it off altogether (5.166; 5.167). You can add "auto pair kerning" to a style sheet (great for headlines) or you can set it as a default for your entire publication (1.16). **Auto pair kerning applies to the entire paragraph.**

5.162 Not all fonts have kerning pairs built in, and some have poorly adjusted pairs. Some fonts have 200–300 kerning pairs, others have over a thousand. Just because a font has an excessive amount of kerning pairs does not mean it's better. In fact, where there are thousands of pairs it takes an interminable length of time to compose the text.

Manual kerning

5.163 Kerning is a totally visual skill. The computer does the best it can with what it has to work with, but the end result, especially for display type (type over 14 point), depends entirely on your judgment. So PageMaker also gives you the option to **manually kern** type (5.168–5.172). You can manually kern between two characters or over a selection (range) of text.

5.164 The space is increased or decreased between letters in units of an *em*. An em is a space the width of the point size of the type. That is, if you are using 12-point type, an em space is 12 points wide. If you are using 36-point type, an em is 36 points wide.

PageMaker divides the em into 10, 25, or 100 *units; thus* you can kern in $\frac{1}{10}$th, $\frac{1}{25}$th, or $\frac{1}{100}$th units of an em, depending on the key combination or Control palette button you use (5.168–5.169). Because the amount of space is so tiny, often you won't see the result on the screen, but you will when you print.

5.165 Yes, that means you must print the page to check your kerning. If it's not right, you kern again and check again. (One of the greatest reasons to invest in Adobe Type Manager is that it allows you to see the effects of your kerning on the screen.)

If you want to do this:	Then follow these steps:	Shortcuts ▾ Notes ▾ Hints
5.166 Turn auto kerning on or off Pair kerning: ☒ Auto above `12` points	▪ If you want to turn auto kerning on or off for the entire publication, then follow these steps after you click once on the **pointer tool** (click once on the pointer tool, even if it is already selected). **Or,** if you want to turn auto kerning on or off for just one or more paragraphs, then select the paragraph(s) with the **text tool.** ▪ From the Type menu, choose "Paragraph...," *or* press Command M. ▪ Click once on the "Spacing..." button. ▪ Find "Pair kerning." If you *do* want PageMaker to automatically pair kern, make sure there is a checkmark in the box for "Auto above." If you *don't* want auto pair kerning, make sure there is *no* checkmark in the "Auto above" box. ▪ Hold the Option key down as you click OK to close both dialog boxes (*or* press Option Return).	▪ The auto kerning function is *paragraph specific;* that is, it applies to an entire paragraph, not to individual characters. Turning it on or off while certain characters are selected will turn it on or off for the entire paragraph that the selected characters are part of.
5.167 Determine the point size of type that will be auto kerned Pair kerning: ☒ Auto above `12` points	▪ Follow the steps in 5.166 above. After you turn pair kerning *on,* enter the minimum point size of the type *above which* you want to auto kern. ▪ Hold the Option key down as you click OK to close both dialog boxes (*or* press Option Return).	

If you want to do this:

5.168 Decrease the space between two characters

Then follow these steps:

- With the **text tool,** click once to set the insertion point *between* the two characters you want to kern together.

- To decrease the space in **fine** amounts (¹⁄₁₀₀th units of an em; .01): press Option Backspace/Delete; **or** press Command Shift LeftArrow **or** show the character-view Control Palette (press Command '), then click the left "Kerning" nudge button (see below).

- To decrease the space in **coarse** amounts (¹⁄₂₅th units of an em; .04): press Command Backspace/Delete; **or** press Command LeftArrow.

- To decrease the space in **big chunks** (¹⁄₁₀th units of an em; .1): show the Control Palette (press Command '), then hold down the Command key and click the left nudge button (see below).

Or you can show the Control Palette and type in any negative number you like from −.01 to −1 into the "Kerning" option edit box.

Shortcuts ▾ Notes ▾ Hints

- You can kern in the Story Editor using the nudge buttons or typing a value in the edit box of the "Kern" option in the Control palette. You can't see the results of your work though you can see the kern amount in the Control palette.
- You can't include manual kerning as part of a style sheet.
- Kerning is cumulative with auto pair kerning, with letter spacing applied using the "Spacing attributes" dialog box, and with tracking (see 5.180–5.186).
- Press Command ` *(grave)* to shift between the character-view and paragraph-view Control palette.

Kerning nudge buttons   *Kerning edit box*

New Baskerville	24	No track	0
N B I U O S R e c C	28.8	100%	0p

307

If you want to do this:

5.169 Increase the space between
two characters

Then follow these steps:

- With the **text tool,** click once to set the
insertion point *between* the two characters
you want to kern apart.

- To increase the space in **fine** amounts
($\frac{1}{100}^{\text{th}}$ units of an em; .01):
press Option Shift Backspace/Delete;
or press Command Shift RightArrow
or show the character-view Control
Palette (press Command '), then click
the right "Kerning" nudge button (see
below).

- To increase the space in **coarse** amounts
($\frac{1}{25}^{\text{th}}$ units of an em; .04):
press Command Shift Backspace/Delete;
or press Command RightArrow.

- To increase the space in **big chunks**
($\frac{1}{10}^{\text{th}}$ units of an em; .1): show the
Control Palette (press Command '), then
hold down the Command key and click
the right nudge button (see below).

Or you can show the Control Palette and
type in any positive number you like
from .01 to 1 into the "Kerning" option
edit box.

Shortcuts ▾ Notes ▾ Hints

- You can kern in the Story Editor which
works great if you already know the kern
amount you want (5.168).
- You cannot include manual kerning as
part of a style sheet.
- Kerning is cumulative with auto pair
kerning, with letter spacing applied using
the "Spacing attributes" dialog box, and
with tracking (see 5.180–5.186).
- Press Command ` *(grave)* to shift between
the character-view and paragraph-view
Control palette.

Kerning nudge buttons ———— | *Kerning edit box*

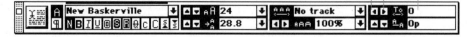

If you want to do this:	Then follow these steps:	Shortcuts ▾ Notes ▾ Hints
5.170 Decrease or increase the spacing over a range of text	▪ With the **text tool,** press-and-drag over the range of text to be kerned. ▪ Follow the steps as in kerning between two characters (5.168; 5.169).	▪ Retyping the text will also remove any kerning that had been applied.
5.171 Remove all kerning from selected text	▪ With the **text tool,** press-and-drag to select the text from which you want to remove kerning. ▪ Press Command Option K, **or** press Command Option Shift Delete, **or** enter 0 in the "Kerning" option edit box in the character-view Control palette.	▪ When you have a range of text selected, the "Kerning" option in the Control palette shows the kerning value between the first two selected characters (if indeed the text has had any kerning yet applied).
	▪ You can enter or remove values in the "Kerning" option in the Control palette, or click the nudge buttons.	▪ You won't see the effects of kerning except in the Control palette.

Phone Call

To _____

Date _____ Time _____

While you were out

_____ called

Of _____

Phone No. _____

Message

☐ Please call
☐ Will call again
☐ Returned your call

	Initials

01-142 (0594)

...black box. I raised the baseline of
...reated a paragraph rule behind

Expert kerning Addition

5.173 The "Expert kerning" Addition is specifically for larger point sizes of text. I suppose the point of this Addition is to give beginners a feeling of security, knowing their type has been "expertly" kerned, but no machine can do a perfect kerning job. Even after running this Addition on your text, you are going to need to use your eyes and fine-tune the spacing. If you want to use it anyway, you should read the following.

5.174 Know these things:

- This is meant for large sizes, particularly larger than about 18 point.
- This only works on PostScript Type 1 fonts—not on TrueType. Plus, you must have the printer font *installed* on your computer, which means you cannot run it on the standard "Laser-Writer 35" (Palatino, Avant Garde, Bookman, etc.) unless you have bought and installed their printer fonts. If you use ATM, you probably have the Times and Helvetica printer fonts installed, but let's hope you are not using the

bitmaps designed for the TrueType versions that were automatically installed with System 7 (confused? Read *How to Boss Your Fonts Around*).

- You must have a *range* of text selected— this doesn't work with the insertion point flashing between two characters.
- Remove any tracking values that may have been applied to the text (select the text and press Command Shift Q).
- Turn off the auto-kern feature (select the text, press Command M to get the Paragraph specs dialog box, click the "Spacing" button, uncheck the "Pair kerning" box). The Addition will automatically remove any manual kerning that was applied.
- Don't do this on body text. Besides the fact that smaller point sizes of type (below 12 point) usually don't need much kerning, running the Expert Kerning Addition on text is very slow— it took 3.5 minutes to expert-kern three lines in the paragraph above!

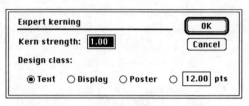

5.175 Enter a "Kern strength" value from 0.00 through 2.00; the higher the number, the tighter the kerning. The larger your text, the tighter it needs to be spaced.

5.176 The "Design class" option needs some explanation. PageMaker wants to know the *original design source* and expectations of the font. Most of the fonts you buy are in the text category, meant to be used in sizes less than 24 or even 14 point. When a font is *meant* to be used in *larger* sizes, it *should* be redesigned (see examples on the next page). The redesign includes different kerning pairs (5.160–5.162) and different spacing values (larger type needs less space between letters) which affects the expert kerning.

If you did not consciously buy a specifically designed display or a poster face, choose the "Text" button.

Expert kerning Addition — *continued*

Scarlett
Scarlett

thinner joins

more delicate
thin strokes

smaller serifs
and terminals

slightly thinner
vertical strokes

more open
counters

thinner
crossbars

Minion Regular, 72 point. *Notice how heavy the face looks. That's because the weight has been designed for small text sizes, and the strokes have been enlarged in proportion.*

Minion Display Regular, 72 point. *At larger sizes, the thin strokes can be thinner. If you reduced these thin strokes to 10 point text, they would disappear, or at least they would be difficult to print. Notice also the letter spacing is naturally tighter (this has not been kerned, except for auto-pair kerning).*

5.177 While the kerning is going on, you can move this little windoid out of the way, and you can cancel at any time. If you cancel, some kerning may have already been applied. To remove it, select the text and press Command Option K.

Press and drag in this title bar to move this box.

Expert Kerning

Kerning in progress

Cancel

Click here, or press Command Period.

5.178 Use the Expert kerning Addition

- With the **text tool,** select the text you want to kern.
- From the Utilities menu, choose "Aldus Additions" and slide out and down to "Expert kerning...."
- Enter a kerning value (5.175) and choose a design class (5.176). Click OK.

- Be sure and read the preceding information so you know what you are doing.
- When the Addition has finished running, go back in and fine-tune the spacing manually.

5.179 Remove the expert kerning

- With the **text tool,** select the text from which you want to remove the kerning.
- Press Command Option K.

- This does not remove any auto pair-kerning; you must go into the Paragraph specs dialog box to remove that (5.166).

311

etaoin shrdlu

By Herb Caen
OF THE SAN FRANCISCO CHRONICLE

It just occurred to me, with the usual thull dud, that "etaoin shrdlu" is dead. If you are under a certain age, this will mean nothing to you, more's the pity. If you are over that age, and are a printfreak besides, the mere mention of "etaoin shrdlu" may bring a tear to your peepers—the same tear that is drawn by the mere mention of such words as "running board," "25-cent martini" and, well, OK, "peepers." In the pioneer days of print journalism, the intriguing "etaoin shrdlu," pronounced roughly "Etwan Sherdlu," was the most famous and most frequent of all typographical errors. And needless to say, The Old Chronicle had more than its share.

Once upon a time, children, reporters wrote their stories on typewriters. The result, called "copy" or "jeez that's awful," depending, was edited by copy editors (drunk, grizzled) using pencils. The copy, ruined or vastly improved by editing, depending, went to the composing room, where it was set into type by Linotype machines. These machines made wonderful, delicate tinkling noises as the operators' skilled fingers flew over the keys. The machines' hot lead, in great pots, was transformed into columns of type. The type, beautiful to see and touch, was transferred in trays to a metal frame, where compositors arranged it into a page, the layout of which had been sketched by a makeup editor, grizzled, drunk.

Every now and then, a Linotype operator would make a mistake. He would then run his finger down the two left-hand columns of the lower-case keyboard, producing the matrices "etaoin shrdlu," which filled out one line. Or, these words would be used as a guide on a galley of type, under the slug, say of "Caen." The compositor, a fellow who could read type upside down and backwards but no other way, was supposed to remove the slug and the "etaoin shrdlu." But in many cases, after too many trips to Hanno's, the M&M, or Breen's, the compositor would forget. And a front-page story would read: "The Mayor, shocked at reports that he would be indicted for mopery, called in reporters and said etaoin shrdlu." Or "Bryant Townsend II, socialite sportsman, announced his engagement to Miss etaoin shrdlu." The Chronicle became so famous for these it was sometimes called The Daily Shrdlu.

(continued on page 766)

Linotype keyboard

San Francisco Chronicle

cument

of War ongress Told

tained in a 27-page document prepared for the Senate Foreign Relations and Armed Services Committees, now considering the troops-to-Europe issue.

The document was drafted by legal experts of the White House and the State, Defense and Justice Departments. It spelled out arguments to support the view that President Truman has constitutional power to send troops to Korea in United Nations action and to assign troops to the North Atlantic Treaty defense force.

Clay Pleads For Europe

Senate Urged To Understand 'Little Man'

By VANCE JOHNSON
Washington Correspondent, The Chronicle

WASHINGTON, Feb. 28— Public hearings on the troops-for-Europe issue ended today with a three-star general begging Senators to look to the "little man" of Europe for the answer to their misgivings.

The witness was Lieutenant General Lucius D. Clay, retired, former commander of American occupation forces in Germany, now a deputy director of the Office of Defense Mobilization.

Pleading with the Senate Foreign Relations and Armed Services Committees not "to value freedom and Allies on the basis of two divisions to one division, or 10 dollars against 1 dollar," the general expressed the opinion that if the Europeans are given a chance they will prove themselves.

Limits, ratios or strings to American aid, said Clay, not only will fail to produce vigorous European rearmament but well might defeat the whole program.

Marines Attack

Stiff Fight in Center Sector; Han Crossed

By the Associated Press

TOKYO, March 1 — U. Marines led a powerful att today (Thursday) by All troops and planes along a mile front in Central Ko against the heart of Chin Red defenses.

Simultaneously, U. S. 3d Divis infantrymen on the Western fr crossed the Han river in assaboats and attacked a two-mile-l sand island southeast of Red-h Seoul.

Both actions met fierce en resistance.

Primary purpose of the big c tral front assault: make the Chi either attack and fight or withd from the one sector best suited any enemy counteroffensive.

Purpose of the 3d Division ac was: get troops across the south loop of the Han; establish a bri head; then move tanks across shallow northern loop of the r into flatland southeast of Seoul

ISLAND BATTLE

Third Division soldiers ran hard-fighting Reds near Sinc on the north side of the island Chamsil near the southern shor

The central front assault ga ground despite bitter opositio U. S. 1st Marine Division tro spearheading the assault, qui captured 800-foot "Clover Leaf h a strategic height in the Hoeng area. A Marine spokesman said attack was progressing on schedu

The drive by American, Br Commonwealth and South Ko troops was timed at heavily ma Communist mountain positions n of the road hub of Hoengsong, Correspondent Stan Swinton ported from U. S. Eighth A headquarters.

WEST OF HOENGSONG

The 25-mile attack front exte: generally westward from Hoeng The new attack amounted

1950s' hot lead

Tracking
(from the Type menu)

Track ▶	✓No track ⇧⌘Q
	Very loose
	Loose
	Normal
	Tight
	Very tight

5.180 Tracking (also known as track kerning) at first seems very similar to PageMaker's *letter spacing* in that you are adjusting the space between the letters. There are several differences, though.

5.181 Letter spacing applies to entire paragraphs; tracking applies only to the selected characters. Letter spacing is an arbitrary, overall measurement; tracking is dependent on the point size of the type and on the kern pairs built into each font. Letter spacing can be adjusted in .1 percent increments from –200 to +200 percent; tracking offers you five options (although you can edit the tracking values). And perhaps the most significant difference: it takes time to figure out how to use letter spacing; tracking provides instant gratification.

5.182 Tracking can be included in your style sheet (Section 8). Tracking can also be applied in the Story Editor, although you won't see any changes until you return to the page layout.

5.183 More history: Remember those little pieces of lead from which type used to be printed? Every single font and every single point size of type had its own set of characters. When a typecutter made a 9-point font set, he built into it the appropriate letter spacing for 9-point. When he made a 36-point set, he built into it the appropriate letter spacing for 36-point *which was not the same, relatively, as that for 9-point.* The larger the type size, the *less* space we need between the characters, proportionally. If you take 9-point text and enlarge it on a camera to 36-point, you can clearly see the loose letter space that results (see below, 5.186).

Computerized typesetting, though, does not create a separate font for each size with its attendant adjustments in letter spacing as well as in stroke width and proportions. Computers use one size as a standard, and all other sizes are created from that size.

5.184 Macintosh programs that work with proportional text and spacing use a *linear calculation* to determine the amount of space between words. That is, they take a size, such as 12-point, and proclaim that as the standard. With 6-point, they use half the amount of letterspacing that 12-point used. With 36-point type, they use three times as much letterspacing than 12-point used. This creates too much space in large type, and too little space in small type.

5.185 For the best readability, large type needs less space, small type needs more space. Tracking addresses this problem. A "Normal" track *reduces* the amount of letter space in large sizes and *adds* letter space to small sizes. It does slow the text composition, so it's best to use it for what it is intended rather than applying it to all your text indiscriminately. If you want a slightly tighter or looser letterspacing over a *broad* range of text, use the "Letter space" function (5.132–5.149).

5.186 *The small text is 9-point. I turned it into a graphic and enlarged it to 36-point. Notice how loose the same letter spacing appears at the larger size.* The world, dear Agnes, is a strange affair. *Molière*

The world, dear Agnes,

Examples of tracking

5.187   *36-point type with "No track"*
("Molière" is 24-point)

The world, dear Agnes, is a strange affair. *Molière*

36-point type with "Very loose" tracking

The world, dear Agnes, is a strange affair. *Molière*

36-point type with "Loose" tracking

The world, dear Agnes, is a strange affair. *Molière*

36-point type with "Normal" tracking

The world, dear Agnes, is a strange affair. *Molière*

Examples of tracking   —*continued*

36-point type with "Tight" tracking

The world, dear Agnes, is a strange affair. *Molière*

36-point type with "Very tight" tracking

The world, dear Agnes, is a strange affair. *Molière*

5.188

5 point; "No track" — The world, dear Agnes, is a strange affair. *Molière*

5 point; "Very loose" track — The world, dear Agnes, is a strange affair. *Molière*

5 point; "Loose" track — The world, dear Agnes, is a strange affair. *Molière*

5 point; "Normal" track — The world, dear Agnes, is a strange affair. *Molière*

5 point; "Tight" track — The world, dear Agnes, is a strange affair. *Molière*

5 point; "Very tight" track — The world, dear Agnes, is a strange affair. *Molière*

5.189

10 point; "No track" The world, dear Agnes, is a strange affair. *Molière*

10 point; "Very loose" track The world, dear Agnes, is a strange affair. *Molière*

10 point; "Loose" track The world, dear Agnes, is a strange affair. *Molière*

10 point; "Normal" track The world, dear Agnes, is a strange affair. *Molière*

10 point; "Tight" track The world, dear Agnes, is a strange affair. *Molière*

10 point; "Very tight" track The world, dear Agnes, is a strange affair. *Molière*

Notice how a "Normal" track on the 10-point type and especially on the 5-point size **increased** *the letter spacing. "Normal" on the 36-point* **decreased** *the letter spacing.*

315

If you want to do this:	**Then follow these steps:**	**Shortcuts ▾ Notes ▾ Hints**
5.190 Apply tracking to selected text	■ With the **text tool,** select the text. Tracking will only apply to the high-lighted (selected) text. ■ If the insertion point is flashing when you choose a track, then you are loading the insertion point and everything you type from that point on will track *until you click the insertion point somewhere else.* ■ From the Type menu, slide down to "Track," then out to the side to select the track value. See 5.187–5.189 for examples of the effects on different sizes of type.	■ Don't forget the character-view Control palette has a Tracking option. You can select a track value from the pop-up menu, or type the desired track value in the edit box, see 4.212.
5.191 Change the tracking	■ Just repeat 5.190 to change the tracking.	
5.192 Remove any tracking	■ With the **text tool,** select the text from which you want to remove tracking. If you are not sure exactly which characters have a track applied, it's okay to select extra text. ■ If the insertion point is flashing when you remove tracking, there will be no tracking in any text you type from that point on *until you click somewhere else.* ■ You can go up to the Type menu, down to "Track," and choose "No track," *or* it is much easier to just press Command Shift Q. *(Q? How'd they come up with Q?)*	■ Of course, you can scoot over to the character-view Control palette if you have it on screen, and select "No track" from the pop-up menu in the "Track" option.

Edit tracks Addition

5.193 Tracking, as mentioned before, adjusts the spacing between letters. Range kerning, where you select a range of text and add or decrease space, adds or removes the same amount between each character. Tracking, however, adds or deletes space depending on the point size of the type and on the built-in kerning pairs.

5.194 PageMaker has five built-in levels of tracking to choose from. For most people, these are sufficient. But for those who want tighter controls, you can edit the five existing tracks. Perhaps you're using a 72-point face in a major headline and you apply the Very tight tracking to it (because, as you know, the larger the point size, the tighter the letterspacing needs to be), but it's not quite tight enough. So you edit the track. Or perhaps you are working on a form with lots of small print and the Normal track is too tight but the Loose track is too loose. So edit it.

I suggest you read through all the info on the next couple of pages before you march in and start whacking away at the tracks.

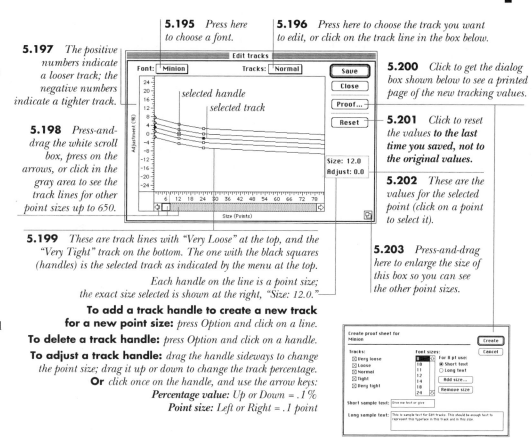

5.195 *Press here to choose a font.*

5.196 *Press here to choose the track you want to edit, or click on the track line in the box below.*

5.197 *The positive numbers indicate a looser track; the negative numbers indicate a tighter track.*

5.198 *Press-and-drag the white scroll box, press on the arrows, or click in the gray area to see the track lines for other point sizes up to 650.*

5.200 *Click to get the dialog box shown below to see a printed page of the new tracking values.*

5.201 *Click to reset the values **to the last time you saved, not to the original values.***

5.202 *These are the values for the selected point (click on a point to select it).*

5.203 *Press-and-drag here to enlarge the size of this box so you can see the other point sizes.*

5.199 *These are track lines with "Very Loose" at the top, and the "Very Tight" track on the bottom. The one with the black squares (handles) is the selected track as indicated by the menu at the top.*

Each handle on the line is a point size; the exact size selected is shown at the right, "Size: 12.0."

To add a track handle to create a new track for a new point size: *press Option and click on a line.*

To delete a track handle: *press Option and click on a handle.*

To adjust a track handle: *drag the handle sideways to change the point size; drag it up or down to change the track percentage.*
Or *click once on the handle, and use the arrow keys:*
***Percentage value:** Up or Down = .1%*
***Point size:** Left or Right = .1 point*

If you want to do this:

Then follow these steps:

Shortcuts ▾ Notes ▾ Hints

5.204 Important!
Copy the "Tracking Values" file before changing the tracking of a font

Tracking Values

- When you edit tracks, you permanently change PageMaker's original tracking values for that font. If this is what you want, skip this task. But if you want to edit the values for this font only when it is used in a particular publication, read on.
- If you haven't already, create a folder and put your **closed** publication in it.
- Open the System Folder, then open the Aldus folder. Find the file called "Tracking Values."
- Hold the Option key down and drag the Tracking Values icon over to your folder that contains the publication. This will make a *copy* of Tracking Values.
- Close the windows and **now open** your publication to edit the tracks.

- When you open a publication, Page-Maker looks for the Tracking Values file. It first looks in the same folder as the publication. If there isn't one there, it looks in the Aldus folder inside the System Folder. This means you can have several Tracking Values files, each stored with its pertinent publication without affecting the original file.
- ***Never rename the Tracking Values file or PageMaker won't be able to find it!*** Well, you can temporarily rename it, but be sure to name it "Tracking Values" again before you want to use it.
- If this publication will be printed on another computer, you must take the Tracking Values file with it!

5.205 Edit the tracking values

- From the Utilities menu, choose "Aldus Additions," then over to "Edit tracks...."
- From the font menu choose the font whose tracks you want to edit.
- Read the diagram on the previous page to choose a track, create new handles (which indicate point sizes), and make the track looser or tighter.
- Click "Save," or choose a new font to edit which will give you the option to save before you edit the next one.

- **Read the task above to know whether you want to make a copy of the Tracking Values file before you edit tracks!**
- You can do this whether or not there is a publication open on the screen; you don't have to be in the pub in which you are using the font *unless you are editing the tracks of the Tracking Values file for this publication only.*

If you want to do this:	Then follow these steps:	Shortcuts ▾ Notes ▾ Hints
5.206 Copy the tracking values from one font to another	■ While you are editing the tracks (see the previous task), select the name of the font in the dialog box (5.195) that has the values you want to copy. ■ Press Command C to copy. ■ Choose the name of the font to which you want to apply these tracking values. Press Command V.	■ When you copy the values, you copy all five tracks. There is no way to copy or paste single tracks.
5.207 Proof (take a look at in print) your new tracking values 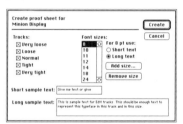	■ Edit the values (5.205), or choose a font whose values you have already edited. ■ Click the "Proof..." button. You'll see the dialog box shown on the left. ■ Choose the font sizes you want to see. PageMaker will print *all* the sizes listed in that box, so be sure to remove or add the sizes you do or don't want to print. ■ Click on a font size then choose whether you want to print a short amount of text or a long amount. Choose the tracks you want to see. Do this for each point size. ■ You can select the sample text and type in your own. ■ Click the "Create" button. PageMaker will make a new, untitled document and put the text on the page in all the point sizes and all the tracks you requested. You can print it and save it.	■ You don't have to actually *edit* any tracks before you proof—you can proof any existing tracks at any time. ■ If your open publication is very large, don't do this when you're in a hurry. Don't even click the button just to see what's there unless you have some time to spare. Even if you cancel you will have to save your publication so it doesn't keep recomposing every time you turn a page. ■ In the proof publication, PageMaker creates style sheets for each point size and track you requested. If the style palette was open on your screen when you chose to proof it will automatically be open in the new publication.

If you want to do this:	**Then follow these steps:**	**Shortcuts ▾ Notes ▾ Hints**
5.208 Print with the font for which you have changed the tracking values	■ If you have edited the tracks, or if you are taking your publication to a computer where you suspect someone has edited *their* tracks, it is critical that you bring the "Tracking Values" file with you. ■ If you followed the directions in 5.204, your Tracking Values file is already in the folder with the publication. If you go to another computer, bring that file with you. ■ If the Tracking Values file is *not* in the folder already, open your publication, go to the File menu and choose "Save As...." Click the button that says, "Files for remote printing." This will copy the Tracking Values file into the same folder as it is copying (or replacing) the current publication. Take this tracking file with you in the folder when you go somewhere else to print.	■ If someone else is printing this for you, be sure and tell them you have edited the tracking files. They must open the publication from the same folder in which the tracking file is stored. Of course, you only need to worry about the altered tracks if you actually *applied* a new track to text in the publication. ■ If your publication is accidentally opened without the correct Tracking Values file in the folder, you may need to recompose the text when you reopen it with the correct tracking file (select the pointer tool, hold down the Option key and from the Type menu choose "Hyphenation"; then save your publication).
5.209 Reset the tracking values to the original values	■ When you are editing fonts, you can click the "Reset" button to reset the values *to the last ones you saved*. This does *not* reset the values to the original settings! The only way you can get the original, PageMaker default tracking values back is to reinstall it, or borrow a copy of someone else's unaltered Tracking Values file and replace the one in your Aldus Folder.	■ You can reinstall the original Tracking Values file from Disk 3 of your PageMaker 5 application disks. Double-click on the file to run the Installer, and save the file to the Aldus folder in your System folder. Although it gives you a chance to rename the file, it installs with the filename "Tracking Values" anyway, and will copy over any existing file with the same name.

Set width

5.214 Examples of set width

5.210 Set width is not really a spacing function, but it is included here because it interconnects with and affects the other spacing values.

5.211 The "Set width" command actually expands and condenses the type: you can expand characters up to 250 percent, and you can condense them down to 5 percent, in .1 percent increments. Set width can be included in your style sheet. It can also be applied while in the Story Editor (Section 9), although of course you won't see the results until you return to the page layout.

5.212 When a designer creates an expanded or condensed font, she redraws the original characters that are in the Roman (straight) version, creating subtle differences in the strokes, the stress, the line weights, the thick/thin contrasts, the connections, etc. When the *computer* creates an expanded or condensed font, it just squishes or stretches the existing font—thus it is not a good typographic procedure.

5.213 Set width is *character specific;* that is, the width changes apply to just the characters that are selected with the text tool, not to the entire paragraph.

"Open Sesame—I want to get out!" ~Stanislaw J. Lee	20%
"Open Sesame—I want to get out!" ~Stanislaw J. Lee	50%
"Open Sesame—I want to get out!" ~Stanislaw J. Lee	70%
"Open Sesame—I want to get out!" ~Stanislaw J. Lee	80%
"Open Sesame—I want to get out!" ~Stanislaw J. Lee	90%
"Open Sesame—I want to get out!" ~Stanislaw J. Lee	Normal
"Open Sesame—I want to get out!" ~Stanislaw J. Lee	110%
"Open Sesame—I want to get out!" ~Stanislaw J. Lee	120%
"Open Sesame—I want to get out!" ~Stanislaw J. Lee	130%
"Open Sesame—I want to get out!"	175%
"Open Sesame—I want to get out!" ~Stanislaw J. Lee	250%

If you want to do this:	**Then follow these steps:**	**Shortcuts ▾ Notes ▾ Hints**
5.215 Apply a set width to selected text, or change the set width of selected text	■ With the **text tool,** select the text. A set width will only apply to the highlighted (selected) text. ■ If the insertion point is flashing when you choose a width, then you are loading the insertion point and everything you type from that point on will condense or expand *until you click the insertion point somewhere else.* ■ From the Type menu, slide down to "Set width," then out to the side to select the value. If you want a value other than those shown, choose "Other..." and type in a value of your choice from 5% to 250%, in .1 increments. See 5.214 for examples of the different effects.	■ Of course, if the character-view Control palette is on screen you can enter a value in the "Set width" option edit box (4.217), or choose a width from the pop-up menu. ■ You can also apply a set width to selected text through the "Type specifications" dialog box: choose "Type specs..." from the Type menu, or press Command T.
5.216 Remove any set width	■ With the **text tool,** select the text from which you want to remove a set width. If you are not sure exactly which characters have a width applied, select lots of text. ■ If the insertion point is flashing, you will just be applying the normal width to any text typed from that point on *until you click somewhere else.* ■ You can go up to the Type menu, down to "Set width," and choose "Normal," *or* it is much easier to just press Command Shift X.	■ You can also apply a set width to selected text through the character-view Control palette (4.217), or the "Type specifications" dialog box (Command T). ■ If you accidentally pressed Command X and your text disappeared, Undo immediately (from the File menu). If you are too late to Undo, do a mini-Revert: hold the Shift key down while you choose "Revert" from the File menu. Click OK. Your publication will revert to the way it was just before you removed the text.

Hard spaces (non-breaking)

5.217 PageMaker provides more than one way to get a blank space. Again, we go back to our historical roots. When printers were creating a page of type with those tiny little pieces of lead, they would use tiny little *blank* pieces to separate words and sentences, as well as to indent and to hang punctuation (21.10). These blank pieces came in several standard sizes, among them, **ems, ens,** and **thins.**

5.218 When the printer was setting a page, he would insert one **em** quad as a paragraph indent. An em quad was a little square of lead; it was as *tall* and as *wide* as the point size of the type (thus it was a *square* of the point size). On that 12-point page, then, the indent would be 12 points, the width of a 12-point em. If the type was 8 point, the em space would be 8 point. He could put several ems together to create a larger space.

5.219 An **en space** was the same as an em, but half the *width*. Thus a 12-point en was 12 points tall (as tall as the type) but only 6 points wide. And a **thin space** was one-quarter the width of an em. Thus a 12-point thin was 3 points wide.

5.220 Phototype and electronic type carried over the ems and ens and thins. We also have a *fixed space,* or *hard space;* that is, a non-breaking space the width of a normal space between the words, just like the Spacebar. "Set width" (5.210–5.216) affects the size of these special spaces; they will expand or contract at the same proportion at which you set the text.

5.221 Ems, ens, thins, and fixed spaces are all **non-breaking.** That is, even though they appear to be blank, the computer thinks of them as characters. If they are used between words, the words will not *break;* for instance, if you put a fixed space between *Ms.* and *Wollstonecraft,* the two words will never split at the end of a line.

5.222 When would you use ems and ens and thins? One very important use is for hanging punctuation (21.10). Or use them whenever you want a quick, dependable amount of space and don't necessarily want to set a tab. A thin can be used before leaders in tabs to customize the leaders (6.72; 6.73). A fixed space can be used between words to letterspace a headline (4.248–4.249; 5.150) or to prevent an awkward line break (5.221). These spaces can be formatted with any text formatting you would use for regular characters, so you can select a hard space and make it smaller, for instance, if you need a tiny space less than the thin in your current point size.

An **em** was also called a "mutton," to distinguish it from an **en,** which was also called a "nut."

323

If you want to do this:	Then follow these steps:	Shortcuts ▾ Notes ▾ Hints
5.223 Create an em space	■ With the **text tool,** select the space you want to replace, **or** set the insertion point at the spot you want it to appear. ■ Press Command Shift M.	■ Hey! Is that an **M** for **em** space?
5.224 Create an en space	■ See the first step, above. ■ Press Command Shift N.	■ An **N** for **en** space!
5.225 Create a thin space	■ See the first step in 5.223. ■ Press Command Shift T.	■ A **T** for **thin** space!
5.226 Create a fixed space	■ See the first step in 5.223. ■ Press Option Spacebar.	■ See 5.221.
5.227 Create a non-breaking hyphen	■ See the first step in 5.223. ■ Press Command Option Hyphen.	■ This hyphen will not allow the word to break at the hyphen at the end of a line.
5.228 Create a non-breaking slash	■ See the first step in 5.223. ■ Press Command Option /.	■ This slash will not allow the word to break at the slash at the end of a line.

Hyphenation *(from the Type menu, choose "Hyphenation...")*

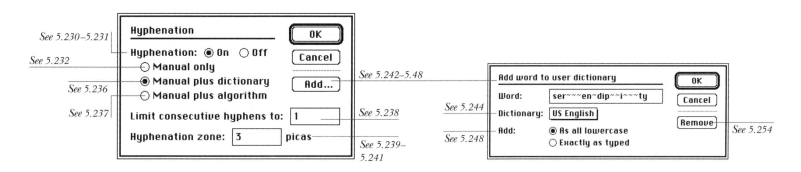

See 5.230–5.231

See 5.232

See 5.236

See 5.237

Hyphenation

Hyphenation: ● On ○ Off
○ Manual only
● Manual plus dictionary
○ Manual plus algorithm

Limit consecutive hyphens to: [1]

Hyphenation zone: [3] picas

OK

Cancel

Add...

See 5.242–5.48

See 5.238

*See 5.239–
5.241*

See 5.244

See 5.248

Add word to user dictionary

Word: [ser~~~en~dip~~i~~~ty]

Dictionary: [US English]

Add: ● As all lowercase
○ Exactly as typed

OK

Cancel

Remove

See 5.254

5.229 PageMaker has options to control whether there is any hyphenation allowed in the selected paragraph(s), where words will be hyphenated, how many line endings can hyphenate in a row, and how close to the right margin a word has to get in order to be allowed to hyphenate. You can also add words to the user dictionary so it will know where to hyphenate them. These hyphenation controls are *paragraph specific* (they affect just the *selected* paragraph). The controls can be built into your style sheet. You can set the controls as application or publication defaults, or you can just change the settings per paragraph in your text before or after you create it.

5.230 Hyphenation off tells PageMaker not to hyphenate anything at all. In fact, you can't even *manually* hyphenate words (unless you insert a real hyphen; 5.232). Although, words that are just born with a hyphen in them will still break at the end of a line at the hyphen (such as tongue-tied).

5.231 If you turn hyphenation **on,** you have these three choices, as you can see in the dialog box: *Manual only, Manual plus dictionary,* and *Manual plus algorithm.* These options determine how PageMaker makes decision about where to hyphenate words. They are explained on the following pages.

Manual only

5.232 Manual only means that Page-Maker will not automatically hyphenate words for you. You have to do it yourself. *That does not mean that you insert hyphens in words you want to hyphenate!* Oh no. If you type a regular hyphen to break a word at the end of the line, that hyphen will stay there when the text is edited. I'm sure you've seen this before:

> I declare! Sometimes it seems to me that every time a new piece of machin- ery comes in at the door, some of our wits fly out at the window.
>
> *(Aunt Abigail in* Understood Betsy*) Dorothy Canfield Fisher*

5.233 Somebody entered a hyphen to break the word at the end of the line. Then when the text was edited, or the line length changed, or the point size increased, or any number of things that made the text reflow, the hyphen stayed there. See 5.234 for a solution.

Discretionary hyphens

5.234 To prevent the problem illustrated in 5.232, use a **discretionary hyphen** instead of a regular hyphen: press Command Hyphen. A discretionary hyphen is invisible until you need it. If the word has room to break at the end of a line, it will break and PageMaker will insert a visible hyphen. If the text reflows so that the word is no longer at the end of a line, the hyphen becomes invisible. It will wait there in the word until you need it again.

5.235 So with **Manual only** turned on, any words you want hyphenated you must hyphenate yourself with *discretionary hyphens* (see 5.249–5.251).

If you insert a discretionary hyphen and it doesn't hyphenate the word, it is because your hyphenation zone is too wide. See 5.239–5.241; 5.252.

PageMaker has a dictionary choice of "None." If you apply the dictionary choice "None" through the "Paragraph specifica-tions" dialog box (9.124), then the only option available to you in "Hyphenation" is "Manual." If you want either of the other methods of hyphenation, apply a different dictionary to the paragraph (9.124).

Manual plus dictionary

5.236 The second option, **Manual plus dictionary,** in addition to allowing Page-Maker to hyphenate at discretionary hyphens, also permits it to look words up in the dictionary and check the ranking of hyphenation breaks (5.246–5.247). If a word has a first, a second, and a third preference for hyphenating, PageMaker will try to hyhenate according to that order. If you have more than one dictionary installed, it will look in the dictionary that you have specified for that paragraph in the "Paragraph specifications" dialog box, plus its accompanying user dictionary (5.242).

Manual plus algorithm*

5.237 The **Manual plus algorithm** option allows PageMaker to hyphenate any word containing a discretionary hyphen (5.234), *plus* any word it finds in the dictionary *plus* any word that is not in the dictionary, but which it can figure out how to hyphenate by using a dictionary algorithm.* This option gives PageMaker full range, which you may need to watch out for (such as two-character hyphen-ations, like words broken at "-ed" or "-ly" endings, or hyphenating "jus-tif-i-ca-to-ry" as if it were the same as "jus-ti-fi-cate"). At this point, the text layout itself and the hyphenation zone (5.239) will influence the hyphenation most seriously.

*Algorithm: a set of rules for solving a problem. Remember those rules we learned in the third grade about where to hyphenate words? PageMaker uses similar rules.

Limit consecutive hyphens

5.238 The option **Limit consecutive hyphens to** is a very important control. It allows you to control the number of con-secutive hyphens per paragraph, anywhere from 1 hyphen to 255, or, for some strange reason, you can type in "No limit." Really, you never want to have more than one hyphen in a row. It looks very tacky to have stacks of hyphens (called "ladders"), and it is not difficult to avoid them. Sometimes it takes a little copy editing, sometimes a little tracking (5.180–5.192), sometimes a little adjusting of the line length, but it must be done. You don't want to look tacky. Limit your consecutive hyphens to 1.

Hyphenation zone

5.239 In the **Hyphenation zone** you determine how far away from the end of the line a word has to be in order to hyphenate. For instance, if you enter 3 picas (.5 inch) as your hyphenation zone, nothing will be hyphenated *within that last half inch of the line.* You automatically weed out those two- and three-letter word breaks. If you enter .25 inch (or any equivalent, such as 1p6, which is 1 pica and 6 points), the beginning of a word can get to within a quarter-inch from the end of the line and still hyphenate. Obviously, that means shorter portions of the word can be left on the line above. You can enter any value from 0 to 12 picas (2 inches) in .1 increments.

5.240 *The smaller the hyphenation zone, the more PageMaker will hyphenate.* With greater ability to hyphenate, justified text can have more consistent word spacing and unjusti-fied text can have a smoother right margin. But there will be too many hyphenated words.

5.241 *The larger the hyphenation zone, the less PageMaker will hyphenate.* With less hyphenation, justified text will have more inconsistent word spacing. Unjustified text will have a more ragged margin.

Adding words to the user dictionary *(from the Type menu, choose "Hyphenation...," click on the "Add..." button)*

```
┌─────────────────────────────────────────────┐
│  Add word to user dictionary        ┌──────┐ │
│                                     │  OK  │ │
│  Word:     [ser~~~en~dip~~i~~~ty  ] └──────┘ │
│                                    ┌────────┐│
│  Dictionary: [US English]          │ Cancel ││
│                                    └────────┘│
│  Add:      ● As all lowercase      ┌────────┐│
│            ○ Exactly as typed      │ Remove ││
│                                    └────────┘│
└─────────────────────────────────────────────┘
```

5.242 PageMaker allows you to add words to the *user dictionary* (also see 9.97–9.103), not to the main dictionary. The *main* dictionary has 100,000 words; the *user* dictionary is where you can add words that are not in the main dictionary but that you use regularly, such as jargon, technical terms, proper names, etc. PageMaker looks through both the main and the user dictionaries for hyphenating and spell-checking, so by adding your words to the user dictionary, PageMaker will be able to hyphenate them. Also, if a word is in neither dictionary, it is considered misspelled, so having the words in the user dictionary will prevent their being flagged as wrong.

5.243 This dialog box is the same one you see in the spell checker in the Story Editor; they operate the same way and they accomplish the same thing (9.120–9.122). You can add words to the user dictionary using the Dictionary Editor too, see 9.127–9.136.

5.244 If you have more than one *language* dictionary, each language has its own, separate user dictionary. You can choose the user dictionary in which to add the word by pressing on the submenu next to "Dictionary" (page 325). If you have the Legal or the Medical dictionary, they both share the same user dictionary as the US English one.

5.245 The main purpose of this little dialog box is to define where you want a word to be hyphenated as you add it to the user dictionary. You can also change the hyphenation points in words that are in the main dictionary (actually, you are really *adding* them to the user dictionary, but since PageMaker checks the user dictionary first, what it finds there will take precedence over what is in the main dictionary).

5.246 Type in the word you want to add. The tilde is the symbol used for **ranking** the hyphenation points: ~ . It is on the upper left of some keyboards, or next to the Spacebar on the MacPlus keyboards; use it with the Shift key. (See the example in the dialog box, upper left.)

5.247 To rank the hyphenation points:
- Enter **one tilde** at the point in the word where it is most desirable to hyphenate.
- Enter **two tildes** at permissible hyphenation points.
- Enter **three tildes** where you want PageMaker to hyphenate the word only if it's absolutely necessary.
- **Remove all tildes** if you never want the word to hyphenate.

5.248 If you click **As all lowercase,** then no matter where you use capital letters as you type the word into the edit box, the word will be entered into the user dictionary as lowercase. PageMaker will spell check and hyphenate any occurrence of that word whether it contains capital letters or not.

If you choose **Exactly as typed,** then the word in the edit box will be entered into the user dictionary, *case-specific.* That is, Page-Maker will spell check and hyphenate only the occurrences of that word that include the same capitalized and lowercase letters.

If you want to do this:	Then follow these steps:	Shortcuts ▾ Notes ▾ Hints
5.249 Enter a discretionary hyphen	▪ First make sure the hyphenation feature is turned on: with the **text tool,** select the paragraph(s) containing the word(s) you want to hyphenate; press Command H; click in the "On" checkbox button if it isn't already checked; click OK. ▪ With the **text tool,** click in the word at the exact spot you want to enter the discretionary hyphen. ▪ Press Command Hyphen.	▪ The hyphenation feature defaults to "On" with "Manual plus dictionary" selected. If you haven't changed it, it is probably still set. ▪ If entering a discretionary hyphen still doesn't hyphenate the word, you need to widen the hyphenation zone; see 5.235; 5.252.
5.250 Remove a discretionary hyphen	▪ With the **text tool,** click in the word, directly to the *right* of the discretionary hyphen. Even if you can't *see* the discretionary hyphen, you can do this—just click to the right of where it would be if you *could* see it. ▪ Press the Backspace/Delete key.	
5.251 Prevent a word from hyphenating	▪ Follow the steps in 5.249 to enter a discretionary hyphen, but place it *in front of the word.* That particular occurrence of that word will never hyphenate.	▪ Also see 5.253 to add a word to the user dictionary so it *never* hyphenates.

If you want to do this:	Then follow these steps:	Shortcuts ▾ Notes ▾ Hints
5.252 Change the hyphenation zone	■ Select the paragraph(s) you want to affect. ■ From the Type menu choose "Hyphenation…," *or* press Command H. ■ In the "Hyphenation zone" edit box, change the value. The larger the value, the less PageMaker will hyphenate; the lower the value, the more hyphenation will occur. Please see 5.239–5.241. • Click OK.	■ For instance, if the hyphenation zone is .5 inch and you want more words to hyphenate, change .5 inch to .25 inch. ■ Remember, anything you change in the "Hyphenation" dialog box is paragraph-specific; it applies only to the paragraphs that are selected when you choose the dialog box.
5.253 Add a word to the user dictionary, setting and ranking the hyphenation points	■ From the Type menu choose "Hyphenation…," *or* press Command H. ■ Click the "Add…" button. ■ In the "Word" edit box, type the word you want to add to the dictionary. ■ Insert tildes (~; 5.246) where you want the word to hyphenate: 　□ **One tilde:** preferred hyphenation. 　□ **Two tildes:** less preferable, but acceptable. 　□ **Three tildes:** least acceptable; hyphenate at this point only if necessary. 　□ **No tildes:** never hyphenate this word. ■ Make sure you've selected the proper dictionary if you have more than one (5.244). ■ Select "As all lowercase" or "Exactly as typed"; see 5.248. ■ Click OK twice, *or* press Option Return.	■ Personally, I don't even bother entering tildes at the least acceptable point. Except for very lengthy words, I generally put one tilde at the only point where I would accept a hyphenation and don't even let PageMaker have any other options. ■ You can enter a maximum of 31 characters as a word.

If you want to do this:

5.254 Remove a word from the user dictionary

If the word is not in the user dictionary, you will get this dialog box when you try to remove it:

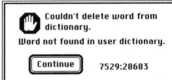

| Couldn't delete word from dictionary. |
| Word not found in user dictionary. |
| Continue   7529:28683 |

Then follow these steps:

- From the Type menu, choose "Hyphenation...," **or** press Command H.
- Click the "Add..." button (yes, the Add button).
- In the "Word" edit box, type the word you want to remove from the dictionary.
- Choose the dictionary from which you want to remove it.
- Click the "Remove" button. Click the OK button of the next dialog box.
- You can only remove words from the *user dictionary*. This means that if you or someone else did not input the word into the user dictionary, it cannot be removed from there. It is not possible to remove words from the main dictionary.

Shortcuts ▾ Notes ▾ Hints

- If you are told "Word not found in user dictionary" and you know you entered it earlier, you may have misspelled it either when you entered it or just now when you tried to remove it (this can be a problem—ha!). Remember, even blank spaces are characters, so if you hit the Spacebar after the word when you entered it, you have to type it with a Spacebar if you want to remove it.

  Also, each separate dictionary has its own user dictionary (except for Legal, Medical, and US English which all share one). If you are switching dictionaries around on different paragraphs, you may have entered the word originally into another user dictionary.
- The Dictionary Editor, the cool little utility tucked away in the Utility folder (in the Aldus folder, in your System folder) is the easiest way to remove misspelled words from the user dictionary. You can simply scroll through the user dictionary, removing words as need be, or use the "Find" command. See 9.127–9.141.

If you want to do this:

5.255 Change the hyphenation points of a word that is already in the dictionary

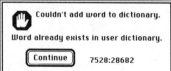

Then follow these steps:

■ If the word you want to add is typed on the screen, select it with the **text tool.** Don't select any extra spaces at the end of the word, or any punctuation—just the word itself. It will be in the "Add word to user dictionary" dialog box when you get there (press Command H, then click "Add..."). Change the tildes as in 5.253. Click OK, and the new hyphenation points will take precedence over the original ones.

■ If the word you want to change is not on the screen, you can add the word with the new hyphenation points to the user dictionary as usual (5.253). Since Page-Maker checks the user dictionary first, the new version will take precedence over the original points.

■ If you get a message telling you the word is already in the user dictionary, then first *remove* the word (5.254). You don't have to click the last OK button; just click the "Add..." button again and add the word with its new hyphenation.

Shortcuts ▾ Notes ▾ Hints

■ A great exercise would be to change the hyphenation of the word "dictionary." The main dictionary within PageMaker hyphenates it wrong (see 9.101). You should also change "dictionaries."

■ Check out the "Dictionary Editor" information in Section 9. It's a utility that comes with PageMaker for accessing the user dictionaries.

6 ▼ Indents & Tabs

6.1   Minimums and maximums:

Item	Minimum	Maximum
Tabs	0	40 per parag.*
	Can be as close as $\frac{1}{32}$"	
Indents	The left and right indents cannot get closer than $\frac{11}{32}$" to each other	

* The tab limitation of 40 per paragraph is literally 40 per paragraph, not 40 per story or text block.

Note: *Indents and tabs can be very frustrating if you don't understand their logic. Once you understand it, you will find they are extremely consistent and dependable. You must keep in mind that tabs do exactly what you tell them. The problem is, we often don't know what we're telling them. If you find yourself screaming and yelling at tabs and indents, remember they are doing what you told them. It is your responsibility to* understand *what you are telling them.*

6.2   Indents and tabs are extremely important when working with *proportional type,* such as the type created on a Macintosh. On a typewriter, the text is *monospaced;* that is, each character takes up the same amount of space—the letter **i** takes up as much space as the letter **m.** When type is *proportional,* the letter **i** takes up about *one-fifth* the space of the letter **m.**

With monospaced typewriter type, you know that pressing the spacebar five times at one place will create exactly the same amount of space as pressing the spacebar five times somewhere else on the page. When working with proportional type, though (which means any font on the Mac except Courier and Monaco), using the spacebar is not accurate.

1. I inserted two spaces here after the period, and then spaced in this line.
2. Often it may look aligned on the screen.
3. But when it is printed, the misalignments are sadly obvious.

However, using tabs:

1. This is the first paragraph.
2. It will look aligned on the screen.
3. And when it is tabbed, you can rest assured it will really align when printed.

6.3   ***Never* use the spacebar to align text. *Always* tab.**

Having trouble? 334
Tabs and the line-break command ... 335
Examples of tab alignments 335
How the tabs work 336
Defaults and Miscellaneous info 337
Using the ruler 338
The Indents/tabs ruler 339
More on tabs 340
Indents and examples 342
Scenario #7: Indents & tabs together 343
Scenario #8: Nested indents 344
Tabs: Tasks 345
Indents: Tasks 354
Indents using the Control palette: Tasks 358
Miscellaneous: Tasks 359

If you find you have trouble with indents and tabs, review the following principles:

6.4 ▪ You must have the **text tool** chosen in order to set indents or tabs, and you must select the text *before* you try to create indents or tabs.

6.5 ▪ Indents and tabs affect **only:**
  - the flashing insertion point; **or**
  - the paragraph in which the insertion point is flashing; **or**
  - all *paragraphs* in which at least one character has been selected with the text tool.

  A new paragraph is created every time you press the Return key—a return address of three lines is actually three paragraphs (see 6.10).

6.6 ▪ If any *portion* of any number of paragraphs is selected with the text tool, then the indent/tab formatting will affect *all* those paragraphs.

6.7 ▪ Remember, no matter how many tabs you set in the ruler, in your text you must press the Tab *key* to move the insertion point over to the set tab before you begin to type!

6.8 ▪ If the insertion point is flashing and it is not imbedded in any paragraph *but is sitting alone on its own line (and thus is its own paragraph),* then all the tab/indent formatting *will be put into that insertion point*—anything typed after that point will follow those specifications.

☛ ▪ *But,* let's say you format the insertion point, then move the mouse and *click* the insertion point down somewhere else, whether in another text block, the same paragraph, or even just a few characters over—*the second insertion point will not hold the formatting you just put into the first one* (6.9).

6.9 ▪ Don't forget—standard Macintosh convention is that the insertion point *picks up the formatting of the character to its left.** That is, whatever font, style, size, leading, tabs, indents, paragraph spacing, etc., is in the character to the left of the flashing insertion point, even if that character is a blank space, that formatting will follow the insertion point as you create new characters.

So once you have your tabs and indents set up, as long as you press Returns you will carry on that formatting. Again, if you set your insertion point down somewhere else, you will lose it all—it will pick up its left neighbor's formatting.

* *If the insertion point is the first thing in a text block, it will pick up the formatting from the first character. If the insertion point begins a new text block, it will pick up the formatting from the defaults (1.6–1.9).*

Also read 6.14–6.17 and 6.49–6.52

Tabs and the line-break command

6.10 Tab formatting is *paragraph-specific;* that is, it applies to the *entire paragraph,* no matter what portion of it is selected. At the same time, it applies *only* to the paragraph that is selected. Of course, on a Mac every time you press a Return you create a new paragraph. Thus, changing a tab for a column of text means you must select every line of the entire column.

6.11 However, PageMaker offers a way to create separate lines of text, but keep them contained as a single paragraph. If you *do* need a new line of text, but you don't want to start a new *paragraph,* then use the **line-break** command: press **Shift-Return** instead of a regular Return. Doing this will create a hard line-break, but it will retain the line as part of the paragraph. See 4.348–4.354 for more info on this great little feature.

6.12

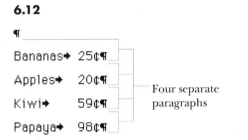

Four separate paragraphs

In the list of fruit (with tabs indicated by right arrows), I ended each line with a Return key, indicated by the ¶ marker. From the bottom of one marker to the bottom of the next is one paragraph.

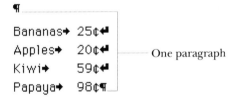

One paragraph

In the same list, I used a Shift-Return at the end of each line, indicated by the left-pointing arrows. This creates a line break, as you can see, but retains the text as one paragraph, between the two ¶ markers. Now I can format the entire unit as one paragraph.

6.13
Examples of tab alignments

↧
This text
is set
to a
**left-aligned
tab**

↧
This text
is set
to a
**right-aligned
tab**

↓
This text
is set
to a
**centered
tab**

↧
These numbers
are set to a **decimal tab**.
12.56
123.76
.0067
789.
56478.45903
*(if there is no period or
decimal point,
this tab functions
as a right-aligned tab)*

335

How the tabs work:

Be sure to read the following pages for a thorough explanation of the ruler. See 6.13 for examples of the tab alignments.

6.14   When setting tabs in the Indents/tabs ruler, you must, in this order:
- **First** select the text you want to affect (6.5).
- **Then** get the Indents/tabs ruler (from the Type menu).
- **Click** in the ruler to set the tab.
- **Choose** a tab alignment (6.38).
- **Always** check to make sure the tail of the tab indicates the tab setting you want (6.13).
- Click the **Apply** button to see the changes without leaving the dialog box.
- Click OK.

6.15   PageMaker's **internal pre-set tabs** are set every half inch, indicated by tiny triangles (6.18a), so even if you haven't set any tabs yourself, hitting the Tab key will move the insertion point a half inch each time. As soon as you set one of your own tabs, all the internal pre-set tabs to the *left* of that one are eliminated; there are still internal pre-set tabs to the *right* of any you set yourself (6.18b/c).

6.16   Now, the following concept can be confusing, but it is a key to understanding tabs. Read it slowly and carefully:

Tabs are seen by the Mac as characters, the same as any other characters; they just have a different visual representation on the screen—to us they are invisible. When you press the Tab key one or more times before typing a word, that word hangs on to those Tabs, as shown in the word Hello below. Tab keys are indicated by the right arrows.

a) *In the Story Editor, you can see the visual representation of the Tab keys as little arrows (6.51). These three tabs will stay with* Hello *until you physically delete them.*

If no new tabs have been set in the Indents/tabs ruler, then Hello will align with the third pre-set tab.

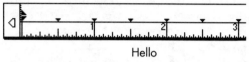

b) *The third pre-set tab is at 1.5 inches*

6.17   The tabs in a line are *cumulative;* for example, in the figure below: Mary will go to the first tab, Denny will go to the second tab, and Janyce will go to the third tab, wherever those tabs may be found.

Also read 6.29–6.32

The Indents/tabs ruler from the Type menu: Defaults and other important miscellaneous info

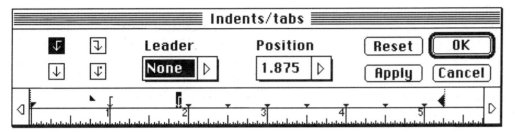

6.18 There are three kinds of **default tabs** that can be set in this ruler:

a) PageMaker's **internal pre-set default tabs,** set every half inch, indicated by the tiny triangles, as seen above. Clicking "Reset" eliminates all other tabs and restores these.

b) **Application default tabs,** indicated by regular tab markers (6.43). Set these defaults when there is no publication open (6.86). These will override the pre-set tabs and will apply to every new publication you create.

c) **Publication default tabs,** also indicated by regular tab markers. Set these defaults when a publication is open and the pointer tool is selected (6.85). These will override the application defaults, but will only apply to *new* text created in the current publication.

d) **Paragraph-specific tabs** are set while text is selected with the text tool (6.63). They are **not defaults,** and apply only to the selected paragraphs, overriding all other defaults.

Miscellaneous info:

6.19   The ruler always appears directly above the spot where the insertion point is flashing, with the zero point (6.40) aligned at the left edge of the text block. If the left edge is not visible or if there isn't enough space, the ruler places itself in the center of the screen.

It's not a bad idea to position the text you want to tab and indent so it is visible in the lower left part of the screen; this will enable you to see the entire ruler when it appears.

6.20   The ruler is actually a window; you can press-and-drag in its title bar (the top portion with the lines in it; 6.37) to move it around. If it isn't already, place the ruler so the zero point is sitting directly on top of the left margin of your text block, as shown in the examples 6.57 through 6.60. Use the ruler scroll bars also (6.39a/b), to help position the zero point.

6.21   The spacing and breakdown of the ruler markings changes with your page view, as the ruler adjusts itself according to the view at the moment; e.g., if you are viewing your page at 200%, the ruler will also show a 200% view. Thus, if you want to precisely place tabs and indents, get the ruler while in a larger view.

6.22   The measurement system of the ruler is determined by the measurement system used in the rest of the publication; i.e., if your page ruler is in inches, your tabs ruler will be in inches; if your page ruler is in picas, your tabs ruler will be in picas, etc. You can change this with the Preferences command (1.222; 1.224–1.226).

Using the ruler

6.23   The Indents/tabs ruler has absolutely nothing to do with the horizontal ruler on the screen. In the Indents/tabs ruler you will see *dotted lines* (6.48). These dotted lines indicate *the outer edges of your text block*—the edges where the handles appear. If you don't see them on either end, press the little *scroll arrows* (6.39) to move the ruler back and forth.

6.24   The large right triangle, which is the *right indent* (6.47), is where all the text will align, within the handles.

6.25   The left triangle is made of two separate triangles: the top half is the *first-line indent* (6.42); the bottom half is the *left indent* (6.41). You can drag the top half back and forth by itself, but the bottom half always drags along the top half with it.

6.26   To move the bottom half of the left indent independently, hold the Shift key down, then drag.

6.27   Changes in your text will not be made until the OK button is clicked. The "Apply" button lets you see what the text will look like with the changes. You can keep making changes until you hit the OK button.

6.28   With the OK button, changes are not Undo-able (meaning you cannot use the *menu* to Undo changes)—you just have to go back and fix them.

6.29   The **"Apply"** button lets you change the indents and tabs of selected text and view the effects of the changes without leaving the dialog box. You can change the settings a zillion times and click the "Apply" button (or press Command A) each time to view the effect. If you don't like the changes you can Cancel out of the dialog box to restore the original settings. If you do create a format you like, simply click OK to store the settings and close the ruler.

6.30   Be careful not to click the "Reset" button unless you want PageMaker's internal pre-set tabs. It's easy to think that "Reset" will put the tabs back the way they were before you started changing them. No way. "Reset" has only one setting and that's half-inch tabs all the way across the ruler.

6.31   You must have text selected, or the insertion point within a paragraph, for the "Apply" button to cause changes. And if you are working with tabs, the text must have tab characters inserted within it, in order for the text to jump to the settings you are creating or changing. If you click the "Apply" button and nothing seems to happen it's probably because you never pressed the Tab key in the selected text.

6.32   You can only set tabs through the Indents/tabs ruler, but indent options are available in the Paragraph dialog box and the Control palette (6.83). If you change the left, right, or first-line indent on the ruler, the changes will be reflected in both the Paragraph dialog box and the paragraph-view Control palette. Likewise, if you change the indents through the Paragraph dialog box or the Control palette, the changes will show up in the Indents/tabs ruler. The indents for selected text can be changed through any of these methods, and each method will override any previous settings.

6.33 The Indents/tabs ruler

6.34 *Choice of leaders (see 6.71 for examples); press the arrow to see the menu. For custom leaders, type in any two characters (6.72).*

6.35 *Click Apply, or press Command A, to see how the indent and tab changes affect the text. See 6.29.*

6.36 *Click Reset to restore PageMaker's internal pre-set tabs every half inch (6.30).*

6.37 *Title bar. Notice this ruler is a window—press-and-drag in its title bar to move it around (6.20).*

6.38 *Choice of four tab alignments (see 6.13).*

6.39a *Left scroll arrow.*

6.40 *Zero point.*

Press Command Period to Cancel.

6.39b *Right scroll arrow.*

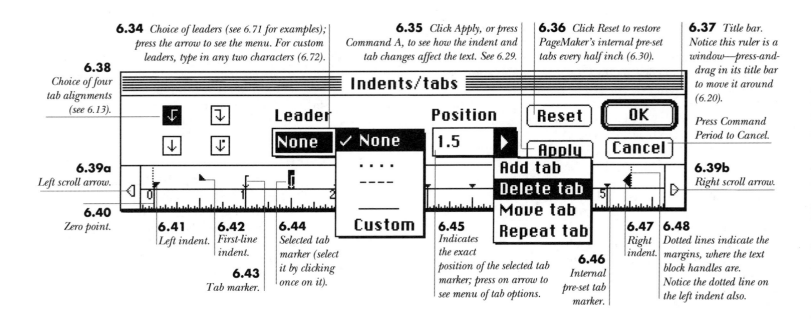

6.41 *Left indent.*

6.42 *First-line indent.*

6.43 *Tab marker.*

6.44 *Selected tab marker (select it by clicking once on it).*

6.45 *Indicates the exact position of the selected tab marker; press on arrow to see menu of tab options.*

6.46 *Internal pre-set tab marker.*

6.47 *Right indent.*

6.48 *Dotted lines indicate the margins, where the text block handles are. Notice the dotted line on the left indent also.*

More on tabs

6.49   Has something like this ever happened to your text?

- In your text, you hit the Tab key three times and arrived at the 1.5" default tab; you typed the word "Hello" (as in 6.16a).
- Then you went to the indents/tabs ruler, set a tab at 1.5", and clicked OK.
- Your tabbed info jumped over to 2.5", not 1.5"!
- That's because you had put *three* tabs into the word "Hello"; Hello said to itself, "I'm going to the third tab—no matter where I find it, even if it's on the next line, I'm going to the third tab."
- Setting a tab at 1.5" deleted all the default tabs to its left, causing the tab at 1.5" to become the *first* tab.
- But remember, the default at 2" is still there, which is now the *second* tab. The default at 2.5" is also still there, which is now the *third* tab. Since the word "Hello" was told to go to the *third* tab, it goes to 2.5".

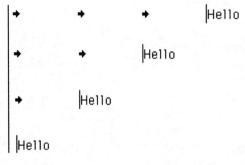

The defaults to the left of 1.5" disappear, making the 1.5" tab the first one.

6.50   To delete those extra tab characters, in the text simply backspace from the H in Hello—*tabbed spaces are deleted just as if they were characters,* whether you can see the arrows or not, and whether you are in the Story Editor or on the publication page.

Set the insertion point to the left of the H; backspace once for each tab you want to delete.

6.51   In the Story Editor (Section 9) you can choose to see the tabs as visible characters, as in 6.50 (while in the Story Editor, from the Story menu choose "Display ¶"). This can help impress upon you that every time you hit the Tab key, you are creating a character that will stay there until you remove it. And as long as a Tab character is there, it will always try to find its spot on the ruler. You can also use the Story Editor to find and remove unwanted tabs (9.82).

6.52   The moral of the story: don't press the Tab key more than once per word/column until you get your tabs set up and know where you are going. You can always go back and adjust either the Tab characters or the tab settings if you decide later that they need to be moved.

YOU THINK YOU HAVE TROUBLE WITH POINTS AND PICAS?

The points-and-picas measuring system often confuses people who are just beginning to work with type. But take a look at what typographers had to work with until just before the 20th century—they used *names* to denote the sizes of type and the spaces between. ↦

Can you imagine pulling down a menu and setting your headline text as Double English with a Double Pica line spacing, an extra Minion after, and a Nonpariel-plus-a-German for the space before?

My goodness. Thanks, Nelson!
(Nelson Hawks, that is, who conceived of the points-and-picas system; see page 496.)

point size (approximately)	name
1	American
1.5	German
2	Saxon
2.5	Norse
3	Brilliant
3.5	Ruby
4	Excelsior
4.5	Diamond
5	Pearl
5.5	Agate
6	Nonpareil
7	Minion
8	Brevier
9	Bourgeois
10	Long Primer
11	Small Pica
12	Pica
14	English
16	Columbian
18	Great Primer
20	Paragon
22	Double Small Pica
24	Double Pica
28	Double English
32	Double Columbian
etc.	etc.

Indents

6.54 You can **Indent** from the left or right *margin*. The margin, in this function, is not referring to any *page* or *column* margin, but to the margins of the *text block* as defined by its handles (for resizing the text block, see 4.104; 4.116–4.118). The margins show up in the indents/tabs ruler as dotted lines at either end, the left always being at zero. Neither indents nor tabs can be placed beyond either margin.

6.55 The **first-line indent** is only activated *on the first line after the Return key is pressed*. This is great for automatically indenting all paragraphs in body copy: you can either set up the indent before you begin typing so every paragraph will automatically indent, or select all the text afterward and set the indent. All first lines will be affected. (You can always re-adjust it at any time.)

6.56 Typical typewriter procedure was to use a tab for paragraph indents. The advantage of using the first-line indent instead of a tab is that you don't need to press the Tab key to activate it; it just happens on a Return. Also, you can more easily eliminate it from, or add it to, blocks of text, as it isn't dependent on your having pressed the Tab key.

Examples of indents

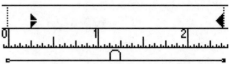

On the far right is a **solid dark triangle**—that is the **right indent.** If you move that triangle to the left, all the selected text will move in that far from the right margin edge.

6.57 *Right indent*

On the far left is a **split dark triangle**—that is the **left indent.** If you press on the bottom half and move *both* the top and the bottom parts of the left triangle, the entire paragraph will *indent* to that point. Remember, the *margin* is still at the boundary defined by the text block handles, indicated on the ruler by the dotted line at either end.

6.58 *Left indent*

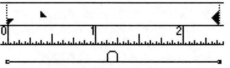

The **top half** of the split triangle is the **first-line indent.** If you move this top half to the right, the *first line* of each paragraph of the selected text will move in that far from the left margin edge.

6.59 *First-line indent*

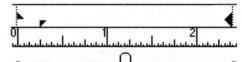

The **bottom half** of the triangle is the **left indent.** If you press the Shift key and move just the bottom half to the right, all lines of the selected text *except* the first line of each paragraph will move in that far from the left edge, or margin, where the text block handles are located.

6.60 *Hanging indent*

6.61   Scenario #7: Indents & tabs together—creating numbered paragraphs

a)

b)

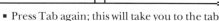

1. A numbered paragraph needs the *first-line indent* set at the margin, and the *left indent* set far enough to the right to allow for the numbering, as shown above, **a).**

2. Notice in this arrangement there is also a *tab* set directly on top of the left indent. This is to get the first word of the text over to the indent.

3. When typing the text, type the number and then the period.

4. Next press Tab to get to the left indent (the bottom triangle), which is where all the type is going to align.

5. As you type, the text will *word wrap at the right indent, and align at the left indent,* just as you see here.

8. If the numbers are going to go beyond one digit, as in the number 10, then you must use *another* tab in order to keep the numbers aligned and to prevent this look:
   8. Aligned.
   9. Aligned.
   10. Not aligned. Oops.

9. So, even before typing the first number, set the ruler in this manner, shown in **b):**
   - Set the first-line indent (top triangle) all the way to the left margin.
   - Set the left indent (bottom triangle) to where text will align (allow room for increasing numbers).
   - Set a decimal tab *between* the two indents (allow more room on the left side of the tab for numbers to grow larger). If you're not using a decimal or a period, you can set a right-aligned tab to produce the same effect.
   - Set a left-aligned tab directly on top of the left indent (bottom triangle).

10. When typing the text, follow these steps:
    - Between numbered paragraphs, hit Return.
    - Press Tab; this will take you to the decimal tab; type the number and the period.

- Press Tab again; this will take you to the tab on the left indent; begin typing.
- As your text word wraps, it will come back to the left indent (the bottom half of the triangle) and align there, making your text look like these last three numbered paragraphs (without the bullets).

11. Remember, **never** use the space bar to align text or numbers—**always** use a tab, even if you're aligning only one or two spaces.

6.62   Scenario #8: Example of nested indents

Nested indents is a term used for indents within indents, such as in this column. Oftentimes this necessitates changing the ruler formatting several times in one document.

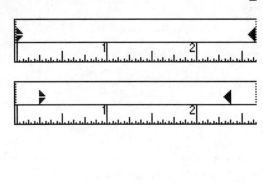

To nest *this* paragraph, I pressed the Return key after the word *document,* then set a new ruler. In the new ruler, I moved *both* the left and right indents inward from the margins. Since the Return key had created a new paragraph, the indents/tabs ruler only affected the text *following* the insertion point.

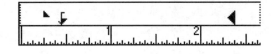

- Now, on *these* bulleted paragraphs I used a combination of the tabs and indents.
- I placed the first-line indent marker where you see the bullet.
- I placed the left indent marker where I wanted the text to align.
- I put a tab directly on top of the left indent marker, so I could tab the first line to the spot where I wanted the rest of the text to align.
- I left the right indent marker right where it was.

Now, in this paragraph I set the indents back out to the margins, returning to the format of the first paragraph. You may have also noticed I deleted the extra space between those paragraphs (5.96) in the bulleted section to further emphasize their grouping.

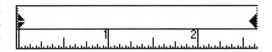

IS IT APPROPRIATE?

BUT

edward gottschall

If you want to do this:

Then follow these steps:

Shortcuts ▾ Notes ▾ Hints

Tabs

6.63 Set a new tab,
or add a tab

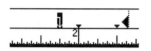

Tab marker, selected, in the ruler

*Choice of tab alignments (see 6.13
for examples of each alignment)*

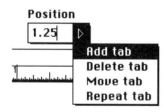

- With the **text tool,** click to set an
insertion point;
or select *all* the paragraphs in which
a tab is to be set.
- From the Type menu, choose "Indents/
tabs…" *or* press Command I.

Either Manually:
- In the Indents/tabs ruler, click at the
point on the ruler markings where you
want to set the tab; a tab marker as shown
at left should appear.
- In the upper left of the ruler, click on
the tab icon (as shown at left) symbolizing
the alignment you want (6.13); click OK.

Or using the Position box:
- Type in the exact measurement for where
you want the tab to appear;
- Press on the arrow in the box;
- Slide down and choose "Add tab."
- In the upper left, click on the tab icon
symbolizing the alignment you want
(6.13); click OK.

- Remember, the Indents/tabs function
only applies to the **paragraph** that has
the insertion point in it, or the paragraphs you have selected. Mac sees a
new paragraph *every* time you press the
Return key, so if you have a column
of information, each *line* is a separate
paragraph—unless you have used the
Shift-Return line break (6.11).
- Check to make sure the tail of the tab
is indicative of the type of tab you want
(see 6.13). If it isn't, **change** that tab
by selecting a new icon (6.67). You can
always click the "Apply" button (or press
Command A) to view the changes
without leaving the dialog box. Then
if you don't like what you see you can
change the tabs or indents and click
"Apply" again. When you are satisfied
with the results, click OK.

If you want to do this:

Then follow these steps:

Shortcuts ▾ Notes ▾ Hints

6.64 Set a tab directly on top of an indent marker

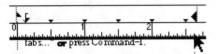

Click here in the tick marks, and the tab will pop up to the top of the ruler.

- Follow the same procedure as 6.63, but this time click in the ruler markings on the *bottom* half of the ruler, directly under the indent marker—the tab will slide right up the tick mark and land directly on top of the indent marker. Sometimes if the right indent marker is directly on the right margin, you must set the tab in just a fraction of an inch.

- If the two halves of the left indent are separated, you cannot place a tab on the left-most one; and it doesn't make sense to place anything except a right-aligned tab on the right indent.
- If you still have trouble setting a tab directly on top of an indent marker, set a tab anywhere else and just drag it over on top of the indent.

6.65 Delete a tab

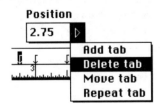

- With the **text tool,** click to set an insertion point in the paragraph; **or** select *all* the paragraphs from which you want to delete the tab(s).
- From the Type menu, choose "Indents/tabs…" **or** press Command I.

Either Manually:
- *Press* on the tab you wish to delete and drag it *down* off the ruler; when you let go of it, the tab will disappear.

Or use the Position box:
- Click once on the tab;
- Press on the Position box arrow; choose "Delete tab."
- **Or** in the Position box, type in the ruler measurement of the tab you want to delete;
  - □ Press on the arrow; choose "Delete tab."

- **Note:** You cannot delete the internal pre-set tabs—those tiny triangles (6.18a).
- Deleting a right-most tab that *you* have set causes all pre-set tabs to reappear that were originally between the deleted tab and the next tab to the left.
- Now, you must understand that this only deletes *the tab marker in the ruler*—it does *not* delete the tab character you typed into your text! Even though you delete a marker, the text is still going to look for another tab marker to jump to. To delete the tab character itself from your text, backspace it, just as if it were a visible character (6.50).

If you want to do this:

Then follow these steps:

Shortcuts ▾ Notes ▾ Hints

6.66   Move a tab

■ With the **text tool,** click to set an insertion point in the paragraph; **or** select *all* the paragraphs in which you want to move the tab.

■ From the Type menu, choose "Indents/tabs...," *or* press Command I.

Either Manually:

■ Simply *press* on the tab you wish to reposition and drag it to its new location; you can drag any tab marker right across any others without bothering them.

Or use the Position box:

■ Click once on the tab to select it;

■ Type the new ruler measurement into the Position box;

■ Press on the Position box arrow; choose "Move tab."

■ You can't move the internal pre-set tabs (the tiny little triangles).

■ You *can* set new *application* defaults (6.18b) or override the pre-set tabs with *publication* defaults (6.18c).

■ Remember, pre-set tabs will appear and disappear as the right-most tab is moved.

■ Specifying a measurement in the Position box is great for getting precise placement, even in a small view.

6.67   Change a tab from one alignment to another

■ With the **text tool,** click to set an insertion point in the paragraph; **or** select *all* the paragraphs in which you want to change the tab.

■ From the Type menu, choose "Indents/tabs...," *or* press Command I.

■ Click once on the tab *marker* you wish to change.

■ In the upper left of the ruler, click on the new tab alignment (6.13) you wish to change to; click OK.

■ This particular step cannot be done from the Position box—*you must select the tab itself* by clicking once on it; that is, typing a tab's ruler measurement in the Position box and then clicking on a new tab alignment will *not* change the tab specified in the Position box.

If you want to do this:	**Then follow these steps:**	**Shortcuts ▾ Notes ▾ Hints**

6.68 Repeat a tab

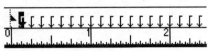

a) Notice the tabs are repeating the space between the selected tab and the zero point.

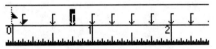

b) Notice the tabs repeat the space between the selected tab and the tab to its left.

- With the **text tool,** select *all* the paragraphs in which you want tabs; **or** just set an insertion point at the point where you want new text to begin.
- From the Type menu, choose "Indents/tabs…," *or* press Command I.
- Either set a tab (6.63) or select an existing tab by clicking once on it.
- Press on the arrow in the Position box.
- Choose "Repeat tab."
- Read the next column ☞

- Ever try to set a tab every ³⁄₁₆"? Well, this procedure sets up a series of tabs that will repeat an equidistant measure across the ruler. That distance is determined by either the space between the zero point and the first tab *(figure a)*, or between the tab selected and the tab to its left *(figure b)*.
- If there are currently tabs to the right of the tab selected to repeat, they will be *replaced* by the repeated tabs.
- If you change your mind and you want the ruler you had originally set, you must *Cancel;* choosing *Reset* will *not* reset your original ruler! (6.69)

6.69 Reset the tabs

[**Reset**]

- With the **text tool,** select *all* the paragraphs in which you want tabs reset; **or** just set the insertion point in the one paragraph you want to affect.
- From the Type menu, choose "Indents/tabs…," *or* press Command I.
- Click the "Reset" button; click OK.

- Resetting the tabs deletes all *publication and application* tabs (6.18b/c) and restores all the *internal pre-set* tabs (the tiny triangles; 6.18a); it does not affect the indents.
- Resetting *when no text is selected* will reset the default tabs back to the *internal pre-set* tabs (6.18a).

6.70 Clear all tabs

- With the **text tool**, select *all* the paragraphs in which you want to clear all tabs.
- From the Type menu, choose "Indents/tabs…," *or* press Command I.
- Click the Reset button.

- Clearing all the tabs *does not mean you have no tabs;* you can't get rid of the internal pre-set tabs. You can't even set a default of zero tabs—there must be at least one.

If you want to do this:

Then follow these steps:

Shortcuts ▾ Notes ▾ Hints

6.71 Set a tab with leaders

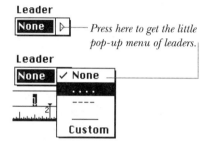

Press here to get the little
pop-up menu of leaders.

Example of dot leaders 1

Example of dash leaders ——————— 2

Example of line leaders_____ 3

Example of custom leaders•••••• 4
This custom example is a bullet and
an en-space combination

*The line leaders are great for quick forms;
just hit a Return at the end of each line,
instead of a number. Move the tab to
make the lines longer or shorter. Change
the leading or paragraph space to change
the space between the lines.*

- With the **text tool,** select *all* the paragraphs in which you want tabs with leaders;
  or just set an insertion point at the point where you want new text to begin.
- From the Type menu, choose "Indents/tabs..." **or** press Command I.
- If you don't want the current tabs, click Reset;
  or at least delete any tabs to the left that you don't need.
- As usual, click in the ruler to set a new tab; **or** type a ruler measurement in the Position box; press on the arrow and choose "Add tab."
- Click on a tab alignment icon (6.38) to choose the alignment; typically, with leaders you want a **right-aligned** tab ⬇.
- Press on the arrow next to the Leaders box; choose the leader of your choice (for custom leaders, see 6.72); click OK.
- On your publication page, type the text that precedes the leaders; press Tab—if you don't see the leaders yet, that's okay!
- Type the text that is to be on the other end of the leaders—the leaders will then appear if they haven't already.

- The font, size, and style of the text at the *end* of the leaders can be different than that at the *beginning* of them; the leaders themselves will always be in the same font, etc., as the last character they *follow* (see 6.73 for tips on circumventing this situation).
- The "Custom" choice allows you to create leaders from any single character on the keyboard, or any combination of two characters, including a space (6.72; 6.73).
- If you want leaders with nothing at the end and the leaders won't show up until you type something, then insert whichever of these invisible characters works for your project:

Spacebar ....
(just the Spacebar)
Fixed space ....
(Option–Spacebar)
Thin space ....
(Command Shift t)
En space ....
(Command Shift n)
Em space ....
(Command Shift m)
Return ....
(Return)
Line break ....
(Shift-Return)

If you want to do this:

Then follow these steps:

Shortcuts ▾ Notes ▾ Hints

6.72 Create your own custom leaders

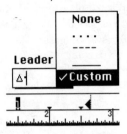

- With the **text tool,** select *all* the paragraphs in which you want to have custom leaders;
  or set the insertion point at the point where you want to begin using leaders.
- From the Type menu, choose "Indents/ tabs…" **or** press Command I.
- If you don't want the current tabs, click Reset; **or** at least delete any tabs to the left that you don't need.
- Either set a new tab or click once on the one you want to add custom leaders to (usually a right-aligned tab).
- While the tab marker is selected, in the Leaders box press on the arrow; choose "Custom."
- Type any two characters of your choice, including any of the non-breaking spaces or alternate characters (4.358, or see Appendix E); click OK.
- On the publication page, type the text; press Tab—*you will probably not see the leaders!* Type the text at the end of the leaders—the leaders will then appear (if they haven't already). Also see 6.73.

- The font, size, and style of the text at the *end* of the leaders can be different than that at the *beginning* of them; the leaders themselves will always be in the same font, etc., *as the last character they follow.* If this is a problem, see 6.73 for solutions.

- Even though the alternate character may appear as just an empty square or some other strange symbol in the entry box in the ruler, it will turn into the corresponding character in the font of your text.

If you want to do this:

6.73 Create fancy custom leaders, where the font of the leaders is different than the font before or after the leaders

Examples:

Isn't this fancy? ✒✒✒✒ Oh my yes!

Get practical .... OK

Leader

This is the character I entered to get the diamond leaders in the second example. Then in the line of text, I typed the thin space, selected it, and turned it into 6-point Zapf Dingbats. (Extra trick: to get the diamond so small, I subscripted it and changed the size to 50 percent. Unfortunately, you can't change the baseline of the leader this way. See 4.253–4.260 for super- and subscripts.)

Then follow these steps:

- Create custom leaders as in 6.72. In the Leader box, type in the character you want to be your leader. Don't worry if it's an alternate character that appears as a blank box or some other strange symbol. (For instance, in the first example to the left, the text font is Futura, but to get the little hand in the Zapf Dingbats font, I typed Shift 8, which looks amazingly like an asterisk.) Click OK.
- Type your info, press Tab, type the text at the end of the leader. Of course the leader at this point is still in the text font.
- Just after the last character *before* the Tab (in the first example, just after the question mark), insert a thin space (Command Shift T).
- Select that blank thin space and change its font (in these examples, to Zapf Dingbats). The leaders will pick up that font. You do have that little extra space, though. If you don't like it you can always select it and reduce the point size, thus reducing the point size of the leaders also. You can also kern between the last character and the thin space (5.168).

Shortcuts ▾ Notes ▾ Hints

- Use this trick also for those times when you need consistent leaders, but the preceding text is not always consistent; e.g., sometimes bold, sometimes light:

Tostadas **$1.95**
Enchiladas
   with green sauce **$2.50**
   with red sauce **$2.25**

Insert a consistent thin space (say, an 8-point light italic) after each item, before the leaders:

Tostadas **$1.95**
Enchiladas
   with green sauce **$2.50**
   with red sauce **$2.25**

- The easiest way to select that thin space you inserted, if your insertion point is still there just after it, is to hold down the Shift key and press the left arrow key.
- You may want to kern (5.168) between the last character and the inserted thin space.

If you want to do this:	**Then follow these steps:**	**Shortcuts ▾ Notes ▾ Hints**
6.74 Remove the leaders, not the tab	■ Select the paragraph(s) as noted in 6.72. ■ Click once on the tab that holds the leaders. ■ In the Leader box, press on the arrow; choose "None"; click OK.	
6.75 Set a tab with leaders that go right over the top of a text-wrapped object	■ Follow the steps for creating a tab with leaders (6.71; 6.72). ■ Just make sure that *both ends* of the tabbed line are *beyond the borders* of the text wrapping boundary.	■ The leaders can go in front of or in back of the text-wrapped object (select the text block with the *pointer tool,* and from the Element menu choose "Bring to front" or "Send to back"). ■ If the leaders don't all appear, you may need to redraw your screen—simply change page view sizes, click in the zoom box in the upper right corner of the window (⊡), **or** select the text block with the *pointer tool* and from the Element menu choose "Bring to Front."

Ted's Moonshine Madness

Green leaf .... 79¢
Red leaf .... 89¢
Butter lettuce .... 79¢
Arugula .... 99¢
Endive .... 89¢

If you want to do this:	Then follow these steps:	Shortcuts ▾ Notes ▾ Hints
6.76 Use a tab to create text that is both left and right justified	■ Type the text you want left justified, press the tab key, then type the text you want right justified. Hit Shift Returns or regular Returns between the lines as needed.	■ This is a handy for setting up documents such as price lists and menus (see the graphic in 6.75). You don't even need to set a tab in the Indents/tabs ruler, unless you want a leader tab. The trick: the last tab in a paragraph assumes the paragraph's alignment.

a. *Breakfast*   *8 am*

Lunch   *12 pm*

Dinner   *6 pm*

b. *Breakfast*   *8 am*

Lunch   *12 pm*

Dinner   *6 pm*

c. *Party:* **T o a d H a l l**

When: **J u n e 2 1**

Why: **S o l s t i c e**

Examples **a** *and* **b** *are the same, but the text block handles are extended further out in* **b**. *Example* **c** *is left justified and force justified type in one line. Remember to press Option Spacebar between words that are force justified.*

■ With the **text tool**, click to set the insertion point within the text, *or* if there is more than one paragraph select them all.
■ Change the alignment to flush right:
  □ From the Type menu, slide down to "Alignment," then over to the submenu and choose "Align right," *or* press Command Shift R, *or*
  □ In the paragraph-view Control palette, click on the right alignment icon.
■ With the **pointer tool**, narrow or widen the tabbed space:
    drag the text block handles in or out.
■ With the **text tool**, narrow or widen the tabbed space:
  □ move the tab marker in the Indents/ tabs ruler.
■ If you want leaders in the text, select the text, go to the Indents/tabs ruler, and set a tab. While the tab marker is highlighted, select a leader; see 6.71; 6.72; 6.73.

■ Select the text again and try other type alignments.

If you want to do this:	**Then follow these steps:**	**Shortcuts ▾ Notes ▾ Hints**

Indents

6.77 Set a first-line indent
(example and ruler: 6.59)

This paragraph has a first-line indent; that is, the first line indents to the right of the main body of text.

- With the **text tool**, click to set an insertion point in the paragraph;
or select *all* the paragraphs in which you want to have a first-line indent;
or set the insertion point at the point where you want text to begin.
- From the Type menu, choose "Indents/tabs…," *or* press Command I.
- Press on the **top** half of the large triangle on the far left of the Indents/tabs ruler; press-and-drag it to the spot on that ruler where you want the first lines to indent; click "Apply," *or* press Command A, if you want to view the effect without closing the dialog box.
- Click OK.

- Remember, a *first line* is any line you type after pressing the Return key (6.55).
- As you hit Return, the next paragraph will pick up the same ruler formatting.
- You can also set your first-line indents from the Paragraph dialog box (4.323), **or** within your Style Sheets (Section 8).
- Typographic standards traditionally dictate a *one-em indent;* that is, an indent equivalent in width to the point size of your type—in 12-point type, the indent should be 12 points wide.
- You can set an indent in points in the Paragraph dialog box (from the Type menu; 4.323); override the current ruler measurement if necessary (1.323).

6.78 Set a hanging indent
(example and ruler: 6.60)

This paragraph has a hanging indent; that is, the first line is to the left of the main body of text.

- Select the text as in 6.77.
- From the Type menu, choose "Indents/tabs…," *or* press Command I.
- Hold the Shift key down and press on the **bottom** half of the large split triangle on the far left of the Indents/tabs ruler; press-and-drag it to the spot on that ruler where you want the **body** of the paragraph to align; click "Apply" (Command A) if you want to see the effect, then click OK.

- Remember, a *first line* is any line after pressing the Return key (6.55). The first line will align at the **top half** of the triangle; the rest of the text will word-wrap to align at the **bottom half** of the triangle.
- If the top half is at zero, the bottom half will not move to the left unless you hold down the Shift key while dragging.

If you want to do this:

6.79 Delete any first-line indent or hanging indent

If both halves are at the zero marker, there will be no indents of any kind.

Then follow these steps:

- With the **text tool**, click to set an insertion point in the paragraph;
  or select *all* the paragraphs in which you want to have a first-line indent;
  or set the insertion point at the point where you want text to begin.
- From the Type menu, choose "Indents/tabs…," *or* press Command I.
- Press on the **top** half of the large split triangle; press-and-drag it to place it *directly on top of* the bottom half of the triangle.
- If necessary, press-and-drag on the **bottom** half of the black triangle to drag them *both* to wherever you want the text to align.

Shortcuts ▾ Notes ▾ Hints

- The "Apply" button gives you the opportunity to test-drive indents or tabs which you are setting, changing or deleting. If you aren't sure you want to delete an indent or tab, try it first in the ruler, then press the "Apply" button (or press Command A), to see how it looks. If you don't like it you can always Cancel out of the dialog box and the text will remain unchanged.

- Take them both back to the zero point if you don't want to have any indent at all.

Experience is what you get—when you don't get what you want. Richard Thomas Cella

355

If you want to do this:

Then follow these steps:

Shortcuts ▾ Notes ▾ Hints

6.80 Indent from the left margin
(example and ruler: 6.58)

This first paragraph has no indent; that is, everything aligns with the left edge, or margin, *of the text block handles.*

This second paragraph, however, is indented from the left margin of the same text block.

And this paragraph is reverted back to the specifications of the first one.

- With the **text tool**, set the insertion point in the paragraph;
  or select *all* the paragraphs you want to have indented;
  or set the insertion point at the point where you want text to begin.
- From the Type menu, choose "Indents/tabs...," *or* press Command I.
- If the top half of the left large triangle is not on top of the bottom half, then press-and-drag to place it on top.
- Press on the *bottom* half of the triangle (both halves will now move together); press-and-drag to the spot on the ruler where you want the text indented.

- Remember, the term "left *margin*" is *not* referring to the page margins or the column margins you set up, nor is it necessarily where the text is aligned in the text block—the left *margin* is where the left-side *handles* of the text block are. See the example in 6.58.

- Or hold the Shift key down and just drag the bottom half to meet under the top half.
- Take them both back to the zero marker if you don't want to have any indent at all.
- Use the "Apply" button (Command A) to check it out.

6.81 Indent from the right margin
(example and ruler: 6.57)

This paragraph has no indent; that is, the text is justified with both edges, or margins, *of the text block handles.*

This second paragraph, however, is indented from the *right* margin of the same text block.

And this paragraph is reverted back to the specifications of the first one.

- Select the text as in 6.80 above.
- From the Type menu, choose "Indents/tabs...," *or* press Command I.
- If you don't see the large solid right triangle in the ruler, press on the right scroll arrow.
- When you find the large solid triangle, press-and-drag it to the spot on the ruler where you want the text indented.

- Remember, the term "right *margin*" is *not* referring to the page margins or the column margins you set up, nor is it necessarily where the text is aligned in the text block—the right *margin* is where the right-side *handles* of the text block are. See the example in 6.57.
- Use the "Apply" button (Command A) to see how the indent will look without leaving the dialog box.

If you want to do this:

6.82   Remove any indents

There
is
no
duty
we
so
much
underrate
as
the
duty
of
being
happy.

Robert Louis Stevenson

Then follow these steps:

- With the **text tool**, set the insertion point in the paragraph;
  or select *all* the paragraphs you want to remove indents from;
  or set the insertion point at the point where you want text to begin with no indents.
- From the Type menu, choose "Indents/tabs…," *or* press Command I.
- To remove the **right indent,** press-and-drag the large solid right triangle (if you don't see it, press on the right scroll arrow); drag the triangle all the way back to the dotted line on the right, which indicates the edge of your text block.
- To remove the **left indent,** press-and-drag both halves of the large left triangle back to the zero point. Hold down the Shift key to drag the bottom half, if necessary.

Shortcuts ▾ Notes ▾ Hints

- Remember, the term "*margin*" is *not* referring to the page margins or the column margins you set up, nor is it necessarily where the text is aligned in the text block—the *margins* of your text are defined by the *handles* of the text block. See the examples in 6.57 to 6.60.
- You can press the "Apply" button, *or* press Command A, to see the effect of your changes without closing the dialog box.

If you want to do this:

Then follow these steps:

Shortcuts ▾ Notes ▾ Hints

Indents using the Control palette

6.83   Set an indent using the paragraph-view Control palette

(please see Section 3 for more complete information on the Control palette.)

first-line indent

left indent   *right indent*

- With the **text tool**, set the insertion point in the paragraph;
  or select *all* the paragraphs you want to have an indent;
  or set the insertion point at the point where you want text to begin with indents.
- Click the Paragraph button on the Control palette if it is not already in paragraph-view.
- Type a value into any or all of the indent option boxes.
- Press the Return key to implement the changes and return to the document.

- If the Control palette is not already on screen, choose it from the Window menu, *or* press Command ' (*apostrophe*).
- There are different ways to manipulate the Control palette. Read the section about the Control palette if *you* want to be in total control of *it*.
- You don't have the luxury of test-driving your indents like you do with the Indents/tabs ruler. Remember the original settings so you can return the text to its previous format if you don't like the changes you make.
- The Indent options on the palette will always reflect changes you make to the indents through the Indents/tabs ruler or through the Paragraph dialog box.

If you want to do this:	Then follow these steps:	Shortcuts ▾ Notes ▾ Hints

Miscellaneous tab and indent info

6.84 Copy the entire tab/indent formatting to other *adjacent* paragraphs

- Select the text with the **text tool.** The trick here is to select the paragraph that has the formatting you want to apply to the others, *and* the paragraphs that you want to apply it to. You can drag up or down to select the separate, adjacent paragraphs, *but it is the ruler formatting in the paragraph **at the top of the selection** that will apply to all the other selected paragraphs.*
- From the Type menu choose "Indents/ tabs…," *or* press Command I.
- The ruler shows the format for the *topmost* paragraph you selected; just click OK and that formatting will be applied to the other selected paragraphs.

- Unfortunately, there is no way simply to copy the ruler formatting from one paragraph and apply it to other paragraphs that are not sequential. If you copy *text* from one format and paste it (using the text tool) into another, the pasted text takes on the formatting of the paragraph it is pasted *into.*
- You can, though, select some text that has the formatting you wish to copy, *create a style name,* and apply that *style* to other paragraphs (see Section 8 on Style Sheets).

6.85 Set the default tabs and indents for the current open publication

- While the publication is open, choose the **pointer tool,** even if it's already chosen.
- From the Type menu choose "Indents/ tabs…," *or* press Command I.
- Set any tabs and indents you like. PageMaker's *internal pre-set* tabs will still be the tiny triangles, and your publication defaults will look like regular tab markers. These defaults will apply only to this particular publication.

- Clicking "Reset" in the ruler will restore the tiny triangles—the *internal PageMaker pre-set tabs*—every half inch, *not the application defaults you may have set!*
- Set publication default tabs when you find you regularly need a particular set-up; for instance, rather than every half inch, you really need tabs every 1.25 inches.

If you want to do this:	Then follow these steps:	Shortcuts ▾ Notes ▾ Hints
6.86 Set the default tabs and indents for the entire application	■ *While no publication is open,* from the Type menu choose "Indents/tabs…." ■ Set any tabs and indents you like. You'll notice your application and default tabs look like regular tab markers, as opposed to the triangular, pre-set internal PageMaker tabs every half inch.	■ If a publication is open, close it. You need to be looking at PageMaker's empty desktop, with no publication open—and the PageMaker menu along the top. ■ If you click the "Reset" button in the ruler, you will reset all the tabs back to the *pre-set internal PageMaker tabs,* indicated by the tiny triangles every half inch. ■ See 1.6–1.18 for more info on setting defaults in general.
6.87 Reset the tiny triangular pre-set tabs	■ You can't.	
6.88 Replace spaces with tabs throughout an entire story, where someone spaced more than twice, or remove tabs that someone entered in the wrong places	■ Use the Story Editor (Section 9). Task 9.82 specifically walks you through finding and changing invisible characters, like tabs.	
6.89 Deselect a tab in the Indents/tabs ruler	■ Click once in the white space above the measuring part of the ruler, like next to the word "Leader" or next to "Apply."	

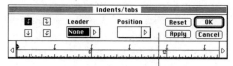

Click anywhere in the space above the measurements.

Containing matter of such Import
as will Astound and Delight
the User.

7 ▼ PARAGRAPH RULES

7.1 Minimums and maximums:

Item	Minimum	Maximum
Length	-22.75 inches	+22.75 inches
	(indented or extended beyond the text or the text block)	
Above or below the baseline	0 inches	22.75 inches

Marry, sir,

she's the kitchen wench

and all grease.

I know not what use to put her to,

but to make a lamp of her

and run from her

by her own light!

Dromio
The Comedy of Errors
William Shakespeare

7.2 This section deals with the incredible paragraph rules. No, these are not rules like "Every paragraph must contain a beginning thought, a developed idea, and a conclusion." "Rules," in design jargon, means "Lines." In PageMaker, in the Element menu they are called Lines, and in the Paragraph dialog box they are called Rules. Hmmm . . .

7.3 Anyway, this Rules feature is one of the greatest little inventions. Absolutely terrific. Now you can put rules under and over text, and as you edit the text, enlarge or reduce the type size, change the font, or move the text block, the rules come right along with it. Getting the rules placed in exactly the right position can take a little figuring and trial-and-error, but it is definitely very well worth the time spent.

7.4 In this book, every line you see embedded within text is actually a rule applied to the paragraph. Take a look at the little chart on page 179 or the quote on page 236. Or, hey, take a look at the far left column on this page. One amazing thing about these rules is that *they can extend beyond the borders of the text block!* I had a hard time believing they could be that wonderful. In this book, created entirely in PageMaker (really—I never touched Word), each column is a separate text block, threaded through all the pages of one section. But there are those hairline rules between each task that span all three columns. At first I was drawing them in. Then, of course, when I edited text I had to move them all. Now I have a style in my style sheet (see Style Sheets, Section 8) called "Hairline" that consists of a paragraph rule that starts in the left column and extends across the page; I just click the style name and it appears. I rearrange the text and it follows along. I'm so happy now.

The "Paragraph rules" dialog box 362

Notes about paragraph rules 364

Points and picas 364

How paragraph rules work 365

The "Paragraph rule options" dialog box 366

Baseline leading 367

Line styles and point sizes 367

Tasks 368

7.5 The "Paragraph rules..." dialog box *(from the Type menu, choose "Paragraph..."; click on the "Rules..." button)*

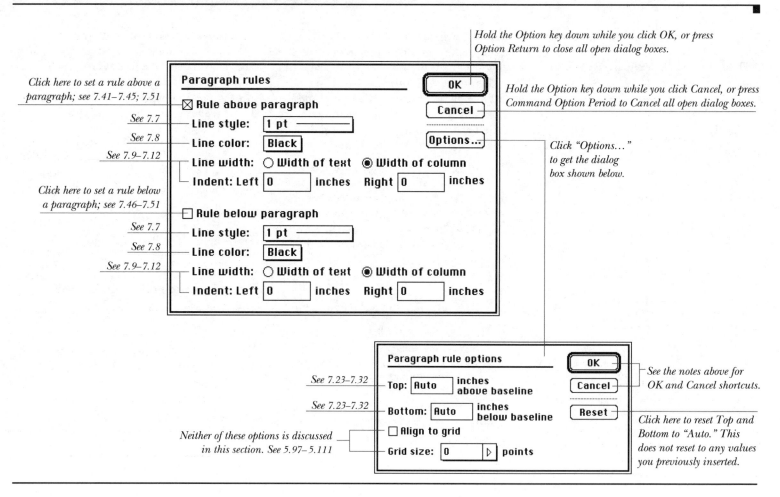

Hold the Option key down while you click OK, or press Option Return to close all open dialog boxes.

Click here to set a rule above a paragraph; see 7.41–7.45; 7.51

Paragraph rules

☒ **Rule above paragraph**

See 7.7 — **Line style:** | 1 pt ———— |

See 7.8 — **Line color:** | Black |

See 7.9–7.12 — **Line width:** ○ **Width of text** ⊙ **Width of column**

└ **Indent: Left** | 0 | **inches** **Right** | 0 | **inches**

Click here to set a rule below a paragraph; see 7.46–7.51

☐ **Rule below paragraph**

See 7.7 — **Line style:** | 1 pt ———— |

See 7.8 — **Line color:** | Black |

See 7.9–7.12 — **Line width:** ○ **Width of text** ⊙ **Width of column**

└ **Indent: Left** | 0 | **inches** **Right** | 0 | **inches**

[OK]

[Cancel]

[Options...]

Hold the Option key down while you click Cancel, or press Command Option Period to Cancel all open dialog boxes.

Click "Options..." to get the dialog box shown below.

Paragraph rule options

See 7.23–7.32 — **Top:** | Auto | **inches above baseline**

See 7.23–7.32 — **Bottom:** | Auto | **inches below baseline**

☐ **Align to grid**

Grid size: | 0 | ▷ | **points**

[OK]

[Cancel]

[Reset]

See the notes above for OK and Cancel shortcuts.

Click here to reset Top and Bottom to "Auto." This does not reset to any values you previously inserted.

Neither of these options is discussed in this section. See 5.97–5.111

The "Paragraph rules" dialog box —*continued*

7.6 The "Paragraph rules" dialog box is where you define the look and length of the line (rule). The choices "Rule above paragraph" and "Rule below paragraph" look exactly the same, but can have different specs in them.

7.7 Line style is simply the same pop-up menu you are accustomed to using from the Element menu. See 7.36–7.40 for examples and point sizes of the patterned lines.

7.8 Line color is the same menu that appears in the "Color palette" (from the Window menu), which holds all the default colors plus the ones you defined (16.105). See 7.57 for specifics on how to make your rules in colors or in shades of gray.

7.9 Line width offers you two choices. If you choose to extend the line the width of the *text,* then the rule will lengthen or shorten as you edit the words. If you choose to extend the line the width of the *column,* the line will lengthen or shorten as you change the width of the *text block* (which really has nothing to do with the *column*).

7.10 Indent allows you to indent the width of the line a certain distance from the beginning and end of the words (if you have "Width of text" chosen), or from the edges of the text block (if you have "Width of column" chosen). You can enter positive or negative values in the Left and Right boxes. **You can specify any value up to ±22.75 inches** (but you might not see the whole rule on the screen).

7.11 If you have chosen **"Width of column,"** the value **0 (zero)** in the "Indents" boxes will extend the line exactly the width of the **text block.**

YOUR ATTITUDE IS YOUR LIFE.

If you type in a **positive** value, such as .5, the rules will *indent* that amount from the left and right edges of the text block.

YOUR ATTITUDE IS YOUR LIFE.

If you type a **negative** value, such as -.5, the rules will *extend* that far beyond the text block! *You may not see it on the screen,* but it will print.

YOUR ATTITUDE IS YOUR LIFE.

7.12 If you have chosen **"Width of text,"** the value **0 (zero)** in the "Indents" boxes will extend the line exactly the width of the words it is directly above or below. "Text," or words, includes any tabs or spaces!

YOUR ATTITUDE IS YOUR LIFE.

If you type in a **positive** value, such as .5, the rules will *indent* that amount from the beginning and end of the words.

YOUR ATTITUDE IS YOUR LIFE.

If you type a **negative** value, such as -.5, the rules will *extend* that amount from the from the beginning and end of the words. Notice this can also extend beyond the boundaries of the text block!

YOUR ATTITUDE IS YOUR LIFE.

7.13 Notes about paragraph rules

❖ Rules can be applied to style sheet definitions (Section 8).

❖ Rules can have a color applied to them (7.57).

❖ You cannot select paragraph rules with the pointer tool.

❖ You cannot edit rules (change anything about them) except through the Paragraph dialog box from the Type menu, or, if the rule is part of a style you created, the Paragraph dialog box found in "Define styles...."

❖ Paragraph rules will text wrap just like text (Section 13).

❖ The extra space for positioning the rule is added onto any space "before" or any space "after" (5.72– 5.84).

❖ The rules are actually *behind* the text, so you can put reverse text over black or colored rules and create other fancy effects.

The text to the left has the following specs:

Column width:	*15.75 picas (2.625 inches)*
Body text:	*Baskerville 10/auto (12)*
Bullet:	*Zapf Dingbats, Shift E; 10/auto (12); reverse; 2.5 point baseline-shift*
Indents:	*Left: 3p5*
	First: -3p5
	Right: 0p7
Space after:	*0*
Rule above:	*12 point*
	Color: black
	Width of column
	Indent left: 1p11
	Indent right: 13p
Rule below:	*Hairline*
	Color: black
	Width of column
	Indent left: 2p
	Indent right: 0
Top of rule:	*1p above*
Bottom of rule:	*0p6 below*

p.s. Tabs are set at 2 picas and 3p5 picas. There is a tab before and after each Zapf Dingbat. (Sometimes tabs and rules don't get along. If tabs cause the text to disappear try using hard spaces instead.)

7.14 Points and picas

To work efficiently with paragraph rules, it helps to understand points and picas.

In typesetting, inches are not used at all. Instead, the measuring system is **picas.**

There are **six picas in one inch;** one pica equals .167 of an inch (have you seen that number before?). Picas are generally used to measure width (as of columns or line lengths), or depth (as in columns, text blocks, or ad space). Anytime you would typically use inches, you can use picas.

Each pica is divided into twelve points. Type size is measured in points; linespace (leading) is measured in points. There are, of course, seventy-two points in one inch.

Typing a value like **3p6** means you want 3 picas and 6 points. If you want less than one pica's worth, you must type the 0 (zero) before the p: **0p7** means 7 points.

One inch divided into 6 picas.

One inch divided into 72 points. Each line and each space between the lines is 1 point.

How paragraph rules work

7.15 Paragraph rules are actually attached to the paragraph. (Remember, one paragraph ends and another one begins when you press Return, and not before.) The rules are paragraph-specific, meaning they apply to the entire paragraph, even if only a portion of it is selected. To understand exactly where they attach, you need to understand *slugs*.

7.16 When you press-and-drag with the text tool over a line of type to select it, the black area you see is the line *slug*, a term held over from metal type.

This is not a banana slug.

7.17 The example directly above is 10-point type with auto leading (auto leading would be 12 points; 5.20–5.21). If you add more leading, the line slug will enlarge, because the slug in PageMaker is actually the size of the line of *leading*, not the size of the type. The slug below shows 10-point type with 20-point leading.

Visit the Guerneville Slug Fest.

7.18 Now, a *paragraph* slug (triple click with the text tool) also shows any "space after" you have set, as well as any "space before" from the following paragraph (5.72–5.84), as shown below.

Every year in Sonoma County we celebrate slugs at the Slug Fest: slug races, beauty contests, and prizes for the best slug recipes. You've just got to try Banana Slug Bread with walnuts, or Black Slugs Sautéed with garlic and our world-class wines. Yum.

7.19 Paragraph rules are automatically placed at the top and bottom of the *line* slugs, though, not the *paragraph* slugs. Here are the three previous examples with the default "Auto" rule specifications above and below.

This is not a banana slug.

Visit the Guerneville Slug Fest.

Every year in Sonoma County we celebrate slugs at the Slug Fest: slug races, beauty contests, and prizes for the best slug recipes. You've just got to try Banana Slug Bread with walnuts, or Black Slugs Sautéed with garlic and our world-class wines. Yum.

7.20 Obviously, the default specs are not usually what you will want. So we need to discuss the *baseline* of text lines, because you position the rules up or down from the baseline. The baseline is simply the invisible line that the letters sit on:

Slugs for Supper! *baseline*

7.21 **No matter what the leading or the type size, the baseline stays the same.** With proportional leading (5.39–5.41), PageMaker takes the point size of the leading and divides it into thirds. Approximately two-thirds of it is positioned above the baseline, and one-third is positioned below the baseline. *That defines the slugs you see in 7.16–7.17, which in turn determines where the rules are automatically placed.* The **type size** is also divided the same way—two-thirds above and one-third below. For instance, with 24-point type, PageMaker puts 16 points above the baseline and 8 points below.

7.22 So, if you want the rules placed somewhere other than where those "Auto" defaults place them, you need to insert a measurement in the "Paragraph rule options" dialog box (7.24–7.32).

The "Paragraph rule options" dialog box *(from the Type menu, choose "Paragraph…"; click "Rules…"; click "Options…")*

```
┌─────────────────────────────────────────┐
│  Paragraph rule options          ┌──────┐│
│                                  │  OK  ││
│  Top: [Auto▾]  picas             └──────┘│
│                above baseline    ┌──────┐│
│                                  │Cancel││
│  Bottom: [Auto]  picas           └──────┘│
│                  below baseline  ┌──────┐│
│  ☐ Align to grid                 │Reset ││
│                                  └──────┘│
│  Grid size: [0    ▷] points              │
└─────────────────────────────────────────┘
```

7.23   Read page 365.

7.24   "Top" affects the rules above, and "Bottom" affects the rules below (the ones you specified in the "Paragraph rules" dialog box). If you chose no rules, these values do nothing.

7.25   It is generally easier to work with the "Paragraph rule options" if you have your measuring system set to picas. To do that, from the Edit menu choose "Preferences…." Press on the box next to "Measuring systems" to get the pop-up menu, then choose "Picas." Click OK. (For more info on the "Preferences" dialog box, see 1.222, and 1.224–1.226.) No matter what your measuring system is, though, if you use the **0p__** sorts of values that I'll be mentioning here (**zero, p** for picas, then a **point** value), they will override whatever system is currently in effect (1.323).

7.26   The values you enter in the "Top" or "Bottom" boxes determine how far above and below the baseline the rule will be placed. You have seen where "Auto" places the rules (7.19). **"Auto" places the rules on the slug boundaries, but any** *values you type in* **are literal. Note:** If you enter any value in "Top" or "Bottom" besides "Auto," then the placement of your rules will not be affected if you later decide to change the leading (see 7.32).

7.27   The values are literal; that is, if you specify 2p in the "Top" box, the rule will begin literally two picas above the baseline. That is, the *top* of the rule will begin two picas above the baseline, and the thickness of it will *hang down* from there (7.31).

7.28   If you specify 1p in the "Bottom" box, the rule will begin literally one pica below the last baseline: the *bottom* of the rule will begin one pica below the baseline, and the thickness of it will *build up* from there (7.31).

7.29   So you must take into consideration the size of the type. Since two-thirds of the point size of the type is above the baseline, and one-third is below the baseline (7.21), add up those figures plus the point size of the rule (7.40) to determine the exact distance above or below. You'll probably still have to experiment.

Maximize Your Options
2 picas
1 pica

7.30   *These hairline rules are set at 2 picas above and 1 pica below the baselines (type is 24/23). You can see that these measurements are literal.*

Maximize Your Options
2 picas
1 pica

7.31   *The paragraph now has 4-point rules. Notice the top rule hangs **down** from the top of the 2 picas, and the bottom rule **builds up** from the bottom of the 1 pica specification.*

Maximize Your Options
2 picas
extra leading
1 pica

7.32   *Notice that changing the leading does not affect the relative positions of the rules. Neither will changing the font size. That's usually good.*

Baseline leading

7.33 Basically, paragraph rules work the same with baseline leading as with proportional leading. What you have to be aware of though, is that the line slug is different for the two types of leading. And the line slug is what determines where the rules are automatically placed.

7.34 In baseline leading the line slug sits directly on the baseline. The descenders hang below the slug! When you increase the leading the slug increases too, but only above the baseline, since that is where all the leading is placed.

7.35 So you can see that if you set rules with the "Bottom" option edit box set to "Auto," the bottom rule will sit directly on the baseline and cut through any descenders in the text; see 7.58.

Line styles and point sizes

7.36 Line styles are shown at their actual size on-screen, except Hairline, .5 point, and anything smaller because of the resolution of most screens. See 2.20–2.22 for examples of actual printed lines, which may look slightly different than what you see on your screen.

7.37 You can create a rule from 0 to 800 points wide by choosing "Custom" from the "Line style" pop-up menu. You can change the weight of the single solid rule or any of the patterned rules by typing a value in the "Line weight" edit box.

7.38 Reversing type out of a wide solid paragraph rule looks wonderful and can save you time—the type and rule will always remain together as you move or edit the text. Although you wouldn't want to set large amounts of text this way, it's great for headlines, subheads, and the like.

7.39 When you change the weight of a patterned rule, the value you type in the "Line weight" edit box is the total width of the rule. The lines, dashes, and dots of the rule enlarge proportionally according the weight you specify. Patterned lines can now be transparent between the black areas,

allowing any layers beneath the rule to show through.

7.40 Below are the literal point sizes of the patterned rules, so you can figure out how far to place them above and below the baseline. Custom lines have a point size total of the value you enter in the "Line weight" edit box.

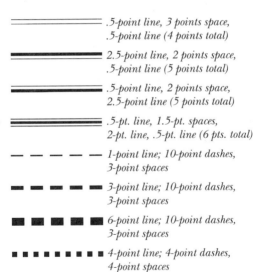

.5-point line, 3 points space, .5-point line (4 points total)

2.5-point line, 2 points space, .5-point line (5 points total)

.5-point line, 2 points space, 2.5-point line (5 points total)

.5-pt. line, 1.5-pt. spaces, 2-pt. line, .5-pt. line (6 pts. total)

1-point line; 10-point dashes, 3-point spaces

3-point line; 10-point dashes, 3-point spaces

6-point line; 10-point dashes, 3-point spaces

4-point line; 4-point dashes, 4-point spaces

4-point line; 4-point dots, 4-point spaces

If you want to do this:

Then follow these steps:

Shortcuts ▾ Notes ▾ Hints

7.41 Set a paragraph rule **above** that is the width of the column or of the text

• • • • • • • • • •

This paragraph rule
is the width of the text.

• •
We
• • • • • • • • • •
haven't the money,
• • • • • • • • • •
so we've got to think.

Lord Rutherford

Paragraph rule: column width

Font size: 10 point/Auto

Extra paragraph space after: 0p2.5

Rule position: 1p1.5 above

Text indent: left 2p

- With the **text tool,** select the paragraph(s).
- From the Type menu, choose "Paragraph...," **or** press Command M.
- Click on the "Rules..." button.
- Under "Rule above paragraph," press on the "Line style" pop-up menu and choose a line width or pattern (this will automatically put a check in the "Rule above paragraph" box).
- ★ Click in either the "Width of text" or "Width of column" box.
- Click on the "Options..." button.
- Next to "Top," type in the number of picas and points that measure how far above the baseline you want to position the rule. Allow for two-thirds of the point size of the type, plus the point size of the rule (7.40), plus a few points for space. You can use the **0p__** format, no matter what measuring system is currently in use (7.25; 1.323).
- Click all the OK buttons; *or* hold the Option key down while you click one OK button; *or* press Option Return once.
- Check it out. You may need to return to the paragraph rules dialog boxes to adjust the precise placement of the rules.
- Paragraphs with rules *above* often need to have a few points of paragraph space added *after* (5.72–5.84).

- You have to be careful about pressing on the "Line style" submenu in the dialog box. You may *think* you are just checking things out, but pressing on this submenu automatically puts a rule above the selected paragraph for you, whether you notice or not. That's another reason to always *Cancel* out of boxes you were just nosing around in, rather than click OK. (If you are in nested dialog boxes, press Option Cancel to close them all at once.)
- A problem with overriding the current measuring system rather than changing it to picas (7.25), is that PageMaker converts your overriding measure into the current measure. For instance, say you are using inches for the measurement system and you type in 0p4 because you want a rule 4 points below the baseline. You click OK to go check it out. The next day you decide you want more space, so you go back to the dialog box. Now the dialog box says 0.056 inches and you haven't the foggiest idea how many points you inserted originally. Just change the whole measurement system to picas.

If you want to do this:	**Then follow these steps:**	**Shortcuts ▾ Notes ▾ Hints**

7.42 Set a paragraph rule **above,** *indenting* from the width of the column

This paragraph rule is the width of the column, indented 3p from the left and 3p from the right. The text is 9 point, with 3p of paragraph space after. The rule is 1p5 above the baseline.

With a paragraph rule above, every time you hit the Return key, the paragraph will start with that rule.

This group of paragraphs may look like they have a rule above and also a rule below, but they are fooling you.

- Follow the steps in 7.41 until you get to the star (★).
- Click in the "Width of column" button.
- In the Left and/or Right indent boxes, type a **positive** number. If you type a number in both boxes, make sure they don't add up to more than the width of the text block.
- Go back to 7.41 and continue on with the steps to position the rule above.

- Though PageMaker calls this the "Width of column," it is actually the width of the *text block*. The rule doesn't give a darn what your *column* measurements are.
- As you widen or narrow your text block, this rule will adapt to the new width.
- The "Width of column" ignores any tabs or indents set for the text.
- The example to the left looks like it has a rule *below* the last paragraph. Actually, it is just the rule *above* from the next paragraph (but the next paragraph has no text, obviously).

7.43 Set a paragraph rule **above,** *extending* beyond the width of the column

This paragraph rule is the width of the column. It is extended −1p5 from the left and −1p5 from the right. The text is 9 point and the rule is placed 1p5 above the baseline. The dotted lines on either side indicate the text block edges.

- Follow the steps in 7.41 until you get to the star (★).
- Click in the "Width of column" button.
- In the Left and/or Right indent boxes, type a **negative** number. You can enter up to −22.75 inches on either side.
- Go back to 7.41 and continue on with the steps to position the rule above.

- If your rules extend beyond the text block, you may not see them on the screen. In fact, you probably won't. If you redraw the screen, they usually show up (change the page view; click in the zoom box (⊡); click on the text block with the pointer tool and press Command F).
  The rules seem to be very trustworthy, though, and will show up on your page when you print.

If you want to do this:	**Then follow these steps:**	**Shortcuts ▾ Notes ▾ Hints**

7.44 Set a paragraph rule **above,** *indenting* from the width of the text

• • • • • • • • •
You can't let the seeds
• • • • • •
stop you from enjoying
• • •
the watermelon.
• •

- Follow the steps in 7.41 until you get to the star (★).
- Click in the "Width of text" button.
- In the Left and/or Right indent boxes, type a **positive** number. If you type a number in both boxes, make sure they don't add up to more than the width of the first line of text in each paragraph.
- Go back to 7.41 and continue on with the steps to position the rule above.

- When it is the width of text, the rule reads *every* character, including spaces, hard spaces, and tabs. This can be to your advantage or not. In the example, the indent was 2p on both sides. There are dots after the last line because I hit a Return, then typed em spaces (Command Shift M). I also inserted an em space on either side of the first line to make PageMaker think there was more text, thus making more dots.

7.45 Set a paragraph rule **above,** *extending beyond* the width of the text

▬ ▬ ▬ ▬ ▬ ▬ ▬
Tahiti people say:
▬ ▬ ▬ ▬ ▬ ▬ ▬
You eat Life,
▬ ▬ ▬ ▬
or
▬ ▬ ▬ ▬ ▬ ▬ ▬
Life eats You.
▬ ▬ ▬ ▬ ▬ ▬ ▬

Mutiny on the Bounty

- Follow the steps in 7.41 until you get to the star (★).
- Click in the "Width of text" button.
- In the Left and/or Right indent boxes, type a **negative** number. You can extend the line -22.75 inches on either side.
- Go back to 7.41 and continue on with the steps to position the rule above.

- If extending the rule beyond the text also extends it beyond the text block, the full length of the rule may not show up on your screen. It will print, though. You can usually see most of the rule if you redraw the screen: click in the zoom box, located in the upper right corner of your screen (回); *or* change the page view (or select the same view you are looking at already); *or* just redraw the text block by clicking on it with the pointer tool and pressing Command F.

If you want to do this:

7.46 Set a paragraph rule **below** that is the width of the column or of the text

When a rule below is the **width of the text,** it will be as long as the last line in the paragraph.

_____

When a rule below is the **width of the column,** it stretches the width of the text block, no matter what the text does.

So you can have the same paragraph rule specs, but adjust the tabs and indents to suit your fancy.

This gives you a great deal of flexibility. You'll start trying to dream up work to do just so you can play with paragraph rules.

On all paragraph rules above and below, you may want to add a few points of paragraph space before or after (see 5.72–5.84).

This is 9-point type, with an extra 6.5 points of paragraph space added before (see 5.94). The rules are .5 point, positioned 0p7.5 below.

Then follow these steps:

- With the **text tool,** select the paragraph(s).
- From the Type menu, choose "Paragraph...," *or* press Command M.
- Click on the "Rules..." button.
- Under "Rule below paragraph," press on the "Line style" pop-up menu and choose a line width or pattern (this will automatically put a check in the "Rule below paragraph" box).
- ★ Click in either the "Width of text" or "Width of column" box.
- Click on the "Options..." button.
- Next to "Bottom," type in the number of picas and points that measure how far below the baseline you want to position the rule. Allow for one-third of the point size of the type, plus the point size of the rule (7.40), plus a few points for space. You can use the **Op__** format, no matter what measuring system you're currently using (7.25; 1.323).
- Click all the OK buttons; *or* hold the Option key down while you click one OK button; *or* press Option Return once.
- Check it out. You may need to return to the paragraph rules dialog boxes to adjust the precise placement of the rules.
- Paragraphs with rules positioned *below* often need to have a few points of paragraph space added before (5.72–5.84).

Shortcuts ▾ Notes ▾ Hints

- In the second example, do you wonder how there can be a rule *above* the first paragraph in the example, if it is supposed to contain only a rule *below?* Actually, that line is just a paragraph with no text. Hitting the Return key makes PageMaker think there is a paragraph, so she throws in a rule.

If you want to do this:	**Then follow these steps:**	**Shortcuts ▾ Notes ▾ Hints**
7.47 Set a paragraph rule **below,** *indenting* from the width of the column	▪ Follow the steps in 7.46 until you get to the star (★). ▪ Click in the "Width of column" button. ▪ In the Left and/or Right indent boxes, type a **positive** number. If you type a number in both boxes, make sure they don't add up to more than the width of the text block. ▪ Go back to 7.46 and continue on with the steps to position the rule below.	▪ The example is 9-point Futura Book on 20-point leading. The rule is a hairline indented 4 picas from the left, positioned 1.5 points below the baseline.
Question 1 _____ Question 2 _____ Question 3 _____ _____		
7.48 Set a paragraph rule **below,** *extending beyond* the width of the column	▪ Follow the steps in 7.46 until you get to the star (★). ▪ Click in the "Width of column" button. ▪ In the Left and/or Right indent boxes, type a **negative** number. You can extend the line up to –22.75 inches. ▪ Go back to 7.46 and continue on with the steps to position the rule below.	▪ Rules extending beyond the width of the text block may not show up on the screen. Don't worry, though, they print. ▪ The specs for this example are the same as for the one above (7.47), except that it now has a –17p-right indent which takes the rules 17 picas past the right margin, out of their 16-pica text block, so they span the second column.
Question 1 _____ Question 2 _____ Question 3 _____ _____		

If you want to do this:	**Then follow these steps:**	**Shortcuts ▾ Notes ▾ Hints**
7.49 Set a paragraph rule **below,** *indenting* from the width of the text	■ Follow the steps in 7.46 until you get to the star (★). ■ Click in the "Width of text" button. ■ In the Left and/or Right indent boxes, type a **positive** number. If you type a number in both boxes, make sure they don't add up to more than the width of the last line of text in each paragraph. ■ Go back to 7.46 and continue on with the steps to position the rule below the baseline.	■ The specs for the example: 9-point Futura Book, auto leading; an extra 9 points of space between paragraphs (5.93); a 2-point rule, indented 3 picas from the left; positioned 5.5 points below the baseline. Notice that this position (5.5 points below the baseline) works here because the text has no *descenders* (those parts of the letters that hang below the baseline, as in p, q, y, g, etc.). If there were descenders, I would have had to allow more space for them.
A Points:		
B Picas:		
C Ems:		
D Ens:		
E Thins:		

7.50 Set a paragraph rule **below,** *extending beyond* the width of the text	■ Follow the steps in 7.46 until you get to the star (★). ■ Click in the "Width of text" button. ■ In the Left and/or Right indent boxes, type a **negative** number. You can input a value as low as –22.75 inches. ■ Go back to 7.46 and continue on with the steps to position the rule below the baseline.	■ The specs for the example are the same as those above (7.49), *except* that the left indent is extended –1p6 beyond the text, which takes it beyond the text block itself. The right rule indent is still set at zero, but the text is now aligned at a right tab (Section 6 on Indents and Tabs, 6.63).
A Points:		
B Picas:		
C Ems:		
D Ens:		
E Thins:		

This dotted line indicates the edge of the text block.

373

| **If you want to do this:** | **Then follow these steps:** | **Shortcuts ▾ Notes ▾ Hints** |

7.51 Set paragraph rules **above and below**

The Three Rules of Life

Rule 1: Your attitude is your life.

Rule 2: Maximize your options.

Rule 3: Never take anything too seriously.

■ **Rousseau** Myself alone . . . I am not made like anyone of those who exist. If I am not better, at least I am different.

■ **Voltaire** Everything must end; meanwhile, we must amuse ourselves.

■ **Kazantzakis** I'm laughing at the thought of you laughing, and that's how laughing never stops in this world.

Those little black boxes are actually 8-point paragraph rules. They are indented from the right, so they appear to be little boxes. They automatically show up when I hit the Return key.

- With the **text tool,** select the paragraph(s).
- From the Type menu, choose "Paragraph...," *or* press Command M.
- Click on the "Rules..." button.
- Choose line widths or patterns from both "Line style" pop-up menus (this will automatically put checks in the "Rule above/ below paragraph" boxes).
- Click in either the "Width of text" or "Width of column" buttons.
- Enter values for indenting or extending the rules (7.42–7.45; 7.47–7.50).
- Click on the "Options..." button.
- Next to "Top," type in the number of picas and points you want the rule to be positioned *above* the text. Allow for two-thirds of the point size of the type, plus the point size of the rule (7.40), plus a few points for space.
- Next to "Bottom," type in the number of picas and points you want the rule to be positioned *below* the text. Allow for one-third of the point size of the type, plus the point size of the rule (7.40), plus a few points for space.
- Click all the OK buttons; *or* hold the Option key down while you click one OK button; or press Option Return once.

- You may need to fuss around with extra paragraph space (5.72–5.84) and/or leading values (5.12–5.71) to get the precise amount of white space above and below the rules.

- The specs for the first example: Futura Book and Bold, 8-point type; 20-point leading; 15.75 pica column. Extra paragraph space of 0p4. Rule above is 4 point; width of column; indented from the right 13p3; positioned 1p2 above the baseline. The rule below is a hairline; width of column; no indents; positioned 0p8 below the baseline. I removed the rule above from the first paragraph.

- The specs for the second example: Futura Book and Bold, 8-point type; auto leading; 15.75 pica column. Extra paragraph space of 0p6.5. There is an 8-point rule above; width of column; indented 15p3 from the right; positioned 0p7 above the baseline. The rule below is .5 point; width of column; indented from the left 7p; positioned 0p8 below the baseline. There is also a left paragraph indent of 7 picas, and a first-line indent of -5p9.

If you want to do this:

7.52   Create reverse text in a rule

Herb Lubalin said:

It stinks.

Christophero Sly: Come, madame wife, sit by my side and let the world slip; we shall never be younger.

Taming of the Shrew

Child	Birthdate
Ryan	12/2/77
Jimmy	4/19/82
Scarlett	5/01/86

Then follow these steps:

- Follow the steps in 7.41, 7.46, or 7.51 to position rules above and/or below.
- From either "Line style" pop-up menu, choose "Custom." Select the single solid line and enter a value in the "Line weight" edit box. You will need to experiment with the point size and placement of the rule (in the "Paragraph rule options" box), to be sure the text fits neatly within it.
- You can put the rule above or below the paragraph. Keep in mind: the rule above *hangs down* from the value you type into "Top," and the rule below *grows up* from the value you type in "Bottom" (7.27–7.28).

    You can type a value as low as 0 (zero) into "Top," which means the rule will start at the baseline and hang down from there; essentially it is hanging down over the next line of type, even though it is a rule "above."

    In "Bottom" you can type a value that is less than the point size of the rule (down to zero, in fact), thereby making the rule grow up and over the baseline into the text above.
- So then, if a black rule is positioned over text, obviously you must select the text and reverse it (from the Type menu, choose the submenu "Type style," then choose "Reverse"). (See 4.231–4.232.)

Shortcuts ▾ Notes ▾ Hints

- See page 380 for specs of the examples.
- You don't have to create a custom line. If one of the standard lines is wide enough for your type to fit, go for it.
- Make sure the rule is wide (tall) enough so the ascenders and descenders don't stick out of it. Experiment with the weight of the rule, and the value in the "Top" or "Bottom" edit boxes to change the amount of rule that is above and below the type.
- The rules are actually on a separate layer, *behind* the text (see 1.189–1.195 re: layers). Sometimes they pop forward and cover the text. If the text disappears redraw the screen: click in the zoom box, located in the upper right corner of your screen (⊡); *or* change the page view (or select the same view you are looking at already); *or* just redraw the text block by clicking on it with the pointer tool and pressing Command F.
- Tabs can create a problem with reverse text, typically with the text just *in front* of the tab. Not always, but sometimes. If your text won't come forward, take out any tabs and replace them with hard spaces (5.217–5.226). If your text isn't visible because of a tab, *it won't print!*

If you want to do this:

7.53   Remove rules

Then follow these steps:

- To **remove** rules, select the text with the **text tool,** go back to the paragraph dialog box, click the "Rules" button, then:
- ☛ If you selected *one paragraph,* you can uncheck the Rule checkboxes.
- ☛ If you selected more than one paragraph *but they all have the exact same specs,* you can uncheck the Rule checkboxes.
- ☛ If you selected more than one paragraph *and the paragraphs have different rule specifications,* the options in the "Paragraph rules" dialog box may come up blank. If the checkboxes are blank, click twice (the first click turns it on, the second click turns it off) in the "Rule above paragraph" box and twice in the "Rule below paragraph" box to remove all the rules in the selected text.

Shortcuts ▾ Notes ▾ Hints

- If you select text that has different paragraph rules in it, PageMaker will only provide information on the options that are the same for each paragraph. The options that are different in each paragraph will be empty (*like the Font menu that won't show a font checked if the selected text contains more than one font*). The indent boxes though, may show the value of the rule indents of the first selected paragraph (*like the Indents/tabs ruler that will display the specs of the first paragraph even though the selected text has many different indents or tabs*). Confusing, huh?
- If by chance there is a checkmark in one of the "Rule above," or "Rule below" boxes (which means a rule is exactly the same in all the paragraphs), then simply uncheck it with a single click. At any rate, the idea is to end up with the Rules boxes unchecked for every paragraph selected.

The difference between the almost right word and the right word is really a large matter — 'tis the difference between the lightening-bug and the lightening.
— Mark Twain

If you want to do this:

7.54   Change the rule and/or its
position

Then follow these steps:

- Now, you already know that to **change** something, you select it and go back to the paragraph dialog boxes, input new information, and click all the OK buttons.
- ☛If you select *one paragraph,* you can go into the dialog boxes and change the specs.
- ☛If you select more than one paragraph *that all have the exact same specs,* you can go into the dialog boxes and change the specs.
- ☛If you select more than one paragraph *and the paragraphs have different rule specifications,* some of the options in the "Paragraph rules" dialog box may be empty. But you can still make changes:
- You can make one or more options the same in all the rules by changing only the specifications for the option you want to be the consistent in each rule. Each paragraph will keep the original specifications for all the other options.
- You can make the same rules appear in all the paragraphs. You must select a style, click a radio button, or type a value into each and every option box, even if it is merely a repeat of what is already selected or entered. In this way you override any specifications a paragraph is holding onto.

Shortcuts ▾ Notes ▾ Hints

- You can select text with different paragraph rules and make changes, but you have to be smart about it. *Each paragraph will hang on to its original rule specifications, unless you instruct it otherwise.* Only the options for which you set new specs will change in each rule; each rule will keep all its other specifications.
- If you attend to every option in the "Paragraph rule" dialog box (Line style, Line color, Line width, and the Indent boxes), and to the Top and Bottom measurements in the "Paragraph rule options" dialog box, you will get the same rules in all the paragraphs of the selected text.
- This is worth checking out. Create a few short paragraphs (one line per paragraph will do), and give them each different paragraph rules, including different "Line styles." Select them all and go into the "Paragraph rules" dialog box again. Choose a line style again (even though the box is empty the pop-up menu is still there). Click Option OK (or Option Return). All the rules should now be the same line style, but with the original line width, color, indents, and distance from the baseline.

If you want to do this:	**Then follow these steps:**	**Shortcuts ▾ Notes ▾ Hints**

7.55 Create a Custom rule

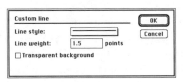

- With the **text tool,** select the paragraph(s).
- From the Type menu, choose "Paragraph...," *or* press Command M.
- Click on the "Rules..." button.
- From either "Line style" pop-up menu, choose "Custom." (This will automatically put a check in the Rule checkbox and open the "Custom line" dialog box.)
- From the "Line style" pop-up menu, choose a line style.
- In the "Line weight" edit box type a value between 0 and 800, to one-tenth of a point.
- If desired, check "Transparent background."
- Click OK and set the other rule specs.

- If you choose a double, triple, dashed, or dotted line style, the white areas will be opaque and will print white over anything behind the rule. If you check "Transparent background," the white areas will be transparent and allow any layers behind the rule to show through.
- When you change the line weight of a patterned rule, the value you enter becomes the total amount of point space the rule will take up. The lines, dashes, or dots within the line will enlarge in proportion to the total line weight. See 2.52–2.62 and 2.75 for all the details on custom lines.

7.56 Create a reverse rule

Robert Louis Stevenson

- Ah—so you noticed that the line style submenu is missing the "Reverse" option! But that's easy to take care of.
- Select the paragraphs and position the rules as in 7.41, 7.46, or 7.51. Before you click the final OK, press on the submenu next to "Color" and choose "Paper."
- Of course, the paper-colored rule must be over a dark background in order to be visible. The dark background can be an object you draw with the PageMaker tools or any graphic you import. Or you can overlap the white rule on a dark rule, as in the example to the left.

- Specs for the example: Futura Bold 7 pt.; 11.5 leading; paragraph indent of 3 picas. Rule above: 12 pt.; width of column; right indent of 5.3p; positioned 0p8 above baseline. Rule below: .5 pt.; width of text; no indents; positioned 0p4 below baseline. I extended the first and last paragraph rules by inserting em spaces (Command Shift M), since the rules follow the width of the text. I removed the rule below the last paragraph.
- Remember, paragraph rules require hard returns. Word wrap or Shift Returns will not create rules above and below each line, but above and below the entire paragraph!

If you want to do this:	**Then follow these steps:**	**Shortcuts ▾ Notes ▾ Hints**

7.57 Change the rule to a color or to a shade of gray

they: used with an indefinite singular antecedent in place of the definite masculine "he" or the definite feminine "she."

The Random House College Dictionary

- Select the paragraphs and position the rules as in 7.41, 7.46, or 7.51.
- In the "Paragraph rules" dialog box, press on the submenu next to "Color." This menu holds all the default colors, as well as any colors you defined in the "Define colors..." dialog box (16.69). Choosing one will change the color of the rule for that paragraph.
- On a monochrome screen, even a gray rule may appear as solid black, but it will print in the tint percentage. (Avoid using tabs after the word(s) that overprint a gray rule; 7.52).

- It's very easy to make a gray rule. Details are in Section 16, but here is a brief synopsis:
  - ❑ From the Element menu, choose "Define colors...."
  - ❑ Click "New." Click the "Tint" button. Select "Black" as the "Base Color." Type a value in the "Tint" box (like 15 for a 15% tint of black). In the "Name:" box type a name for your color (it is wise to include the percentage of tint and the base color). Click OK, OK. Now this color will show up in the "Paragraph rules" dialog box.
- You can create tints of any spot or process color in your palette; see 16.106.

7.58 Create a rule for text with baseline leading.

Typography

Notice the slug around a line of type (10 point type, auto leading) that uses the baseline leading method. Compare it to the slug around the same type with proportional leading:

Typography

- Select the paragraphs and position the rules as in 7.41, 7.46, or 7.51.
- If you are creating a bottom rule, press the "Options" button.
- In the "Paragraph rule options" dialog box, enter a value in the "Bottom" edit box. The larger the value, the further below the baseline the rule will sit.
- A setting of "Auto" in the "Bottom" edit box is equivalent to 0 (no distance from the baseline).

- Paragraph rules work the same with baseline leading except the line slug is different. PageMaker positions the whole slug on and above the baseline. The slug will enlarge if you add more leading, but it will still remain completely above the baseline. The paragraph rules are automatically placed at the top and bottom of the line slugs. This means a setting of "Auto" in the "Bottom" edit box is equal to 0, placing the rule directly on the baseline. Ugh.

7.59 Specs for the examples on page 375

Herb Lubalin said:

It stinks.

Christophero Sly: Come, madame wife, sit by my side and let the world slip; we shall never be younger.

Taming of the Shrew

Child	Birthdate
Ryan	12/2/77
Jimmy	4/19/82
Scarlett	5/01/86

- In these two lines (each a paragraph), there is no extra paragraph space before or after, and no extra leading. It's the hairline rule 1p6 above the second paragraph that extends the line slug (7.19) to create that nice white space, since the line uses auto leading.
"Herb Lubalin said:"
- Futura Bold, 14-point type, auto leading. **Rule above:** Custom, 24-point; width of text; left and right indents –0p2; positioned 1p6 above the baseline.
"It stinks."
- Futura Book, 9-point type, auto leading. **Rule above:** Hairline; width of column; positioned 1p6 above the baseline.

- *You could place both of these rules above and below the first paragraph to achieve the same effect. The rule below would need to be 6 points (0p6) below the baseline to tuck under the thick rule from above, and you'd have to add paragraph space or leading, too.*

- Futura Book; 9-point type with 13-point leading; "Christophero Sly:" is 8-point Bold. **Rule above:** 12-point; width of column; indented from the right 9 picas; positioned 0p8.5 above the baseline. Notice it is a 12-point rule positioned only 8.5 points above the baseline, which means a few points will hang down below the baseline, covering the descenders.
- There is a paragraph left indent of 0p6.

- Except for the first line, the specs are Futura Book, 9-point type on 13-point leading. There is no extra paragraph space before or after. There is a left paragraph indent of 0p7.
Rule above: 12-point; width of column; left indent of 10p; positioned 0p9 above the baseline.
Rule below: .5-point; width of column; no indents; positioned 1p1.5 below the baseline.
- **First line:** (Child...Birthdate) The first line has the same specs, except that the font is 8-point Futura Bold, and the rule above has no left indent.

A Chapter very full of learning,
nicely adapted to the present taste and times,
and calculated for the
Instruction and Improvement of the User.

8.1   Style sheets have got to be the most
wonderful invention since the Mac and
the LaserWriter—it's hard to imagine how
we ever lived without them. Even on a one-
page document, style sheets can save hours
of time and frustration. It doesn't take long
to learn how to use them, and the time
spent is one of the best investments you
could make for yourself. If you are not
using style sheets, you are not tapping
into the true power of PageMaker.

8.2   What style sheets allow you to do
is label, or *tag*, paragraphs with a *style name*,
or *definition*. That name, or definition, tells
a paragraph exactly what form to take. You
can apply any text formatting (8.33). Once a
style definition has been set up, you simply
click in a paragraph and choose the style
name (from the Style palette, the paragraph-
view Control palette, or the "Style" submenu
in the Type menu), and all the formatting
will be applied to that paragraph. At any
time later you can change the specifications
in that style *definition,* and all paragraphs
that have had that particular tag, or name,
applied also change instantly. (See the
Scenarios, 8.79–8.82.)

8.3   Even though a paragraph has a style
definition attached to it, you can certainly
customize any paragraph; you can italicize
words, add tabs, create indents, specify paragraph rules, change the track, etc. These are
overrides (8.35; 8.38–8.43).

8.4   You can even *tag* the text in your
word processor (8.75) as you create it,
labeling text with the style definitions.
When you place the document into Page-
Maker, all the appropriate formatting will
automatically be applied!

8.5   Style sheets are saved along with
each publication or template. So if you set
up a style sheet in a template (Section 14),
each new publication you create from that
template will be perfectly consistent with the
original. Or you can copy the style sheets
(8.56–8.58) from one publication into
another rather than recreate them all from
scratch. Or copy and then edit them to suit.
Oh, it is just amazing what you can do with
style sheets.

8.6   **Be careful:** Don't get *style sheets*
confused with *type styles* (they should have
named them something else). *Type styles* are
things like bold, italic, underline, etc.

The "Define styles" dialog box 382

New, Edit, and Copy buttons 383

Based on 384

Next style 385

Formatting options 386

Overrides and imported styles 386

The "List Styles Used" Addition 387

Tasks 388

Scenario #9: Using style sheets
(the "create as you go" method) 410

Scenario #10: Using style sheets
(the "I know what I want" method) 411

Wow 412

Please note:

*The procedures in this section assume you
understand how to use the tabs and indents
ruler, the type specification dialog box, the
paragraph dialog box, the Control palette,
and the color specifications. When a direction
assumes something, I've added references to
the specific paragraphs where you'll find the
other information.*

8.7 The "Define styles..." dialog box *(from the Type menu, choose "Define styles...," or press Command 3)*

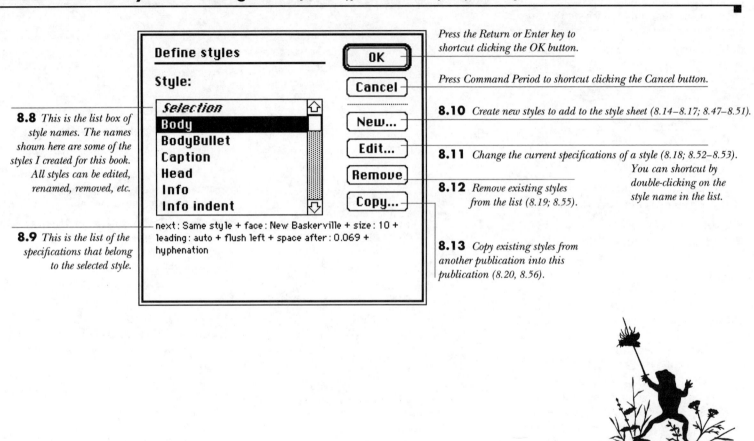

Define styles

OK

Press the Return or Enter key to shortcut clicking the OK button.

Cancel

Press Command Period to shortcut clicking the Cancel button.

Style:

Selection
Body
BodyBullet
Caption
Head
Info
Info indent

8.8 *This is the list box of style names. The names shown here are some of the styles I created for this book. All styles can be edited, renamed, removed, etc.*

New...

8.10 *Create new styles to add to the style sheet (8.14–8.17; 8.47–8.51).*

Edit...

8.11 *Change the current specifications of a style (8.18; 8.52–8.53). You can shortcut by double-clicking on the style name in the list.*

Remove

8.12 *Remove existing styles from the list (8.19; 8.55).*

Copy...

next : Same style + face : New Baskerville + size : 10 + leading : auto + flush left + space after : 0.069 + hyphenation

8.9 *This is the list of the specifications that belong to the selected style.*

8.13 *Copy existing styles from another publication into this publication (8.20, 8.56).*

Make definite assertions. William Strunk, Jr.

New...

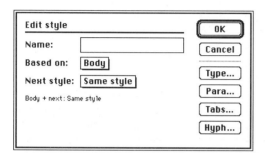

Edit...

Copy...

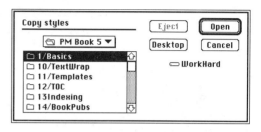

8.14 If you click the **New...** button, you will get this dialog box. You need to type in a name (it's a good idea to give it a descriptive name so you will have a clue as to what it will do).

8.15 The name that appears automatically in **Based on:** is the name that was highlighted in the list when you clicked "New...." See 8.21–8.27 on the importance of the name in that box.

8.16 The name selected for **Next style:** is the style *that PageMaker will switch to automatically* when you hit the Return key (8.28–8.32).

8.17 The buttons along the side (*Type...*, *Para...*, *Tabs...*, and *Hyph...*) will give you the standard dialog boxes that you already know and love (8.47–8.48).

8.18 If you click the **Edit...** button, you will get this dialog box. It's exactly the same as the "New..." box, except that the name of the style-to-be-edited is already entered. Notice at the bottom you see the specifications that have been already defined for this style. Use this box to make any changes to an existing style (8.53).

8.19 If you click the **Remove** button, you will not get a dialog box (8.55). You will not even get an alert box asking if you really want to remove the selected style. It's just gone. Instantly. If you decide that was *not* a smart thing to do, **click the Cancel button.**

8.20 If you click the **Copy...** button, you will get this dialog box. It's just like any other "Open" dialog box you see on the Mac, and you navigate the same way. Double-click on any PageMaker file and you will copy all style sheets from that publication into the current one. If any styles you are copying have exactly the same name as *existing* styles in your current publication, PageMaker will ask if you want to copy over existing styles; if you click OK, the specifications of the publication you are copying *from* will *replace* your current specifications. All other copied styles will be *added* to your list; nothing will be removed.

You can also drag or copy text from one publication to another to add only specific, selected styles to a publication, see 8.57–8.58.

Based on:

8.21   A style can be **based on** another style. This is a very important concept to grasp and to take advantage of, as it can either help you tremendously or foul you up royally.

8.22   The basic idea is that you can *base* a new style on an existing one. That means you don't need to go through and re-specify all the formatting for the new style—it will pick up all the formatting from the one it is *based on.* Then you can adapt the *new* one to make it different than the original. For instance, let's say you have a style for Headlines. You want your subheads to have all the same formatting as the headlines, except a smaller size. So you base your new style Subhead on the existing style Headline, and change only the *size* of the style Subheads.

8.23   This has another advantage besides making it faster to create the style. Let's say your font for Headlines is Times Bold. Your client now wants you to change it to Palatino Bold. So you go to your style sheet and change the Headline font. *All styles that are based on Headline will also change to Palatino Bold.* Your Subheads will change to Palatino Bold, *but they will stay the smaller size.*

8.24   Take a look at the specifications at the bottom of this "Edit style" dialog box.

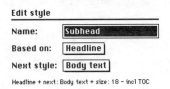

You see that it is based on "Headline," then the specs show a plus sign and more formatting. Anything I change in "Headline" will also change in "Subhead," *but "Subhead" will retain all the formatting listed after the plus sign.*

You can also *remove* parts of the "Based on" style that you don't want to apply to the new style. For instance, anything tagged with the style Headline is to be included in the Table of Contents (a specification in the paragraph dialog box). In the new style Subhead, I *removed* "Include in Table of contents," as indicated in the example above by the notation "– incl TOC."

8.25   The power of this is that you can make global changes to a publication with only a few seconds of work. *It also means you can inadvertently change styles you didn't mean*

to if you based one style on another without understanding the purpose of "Based on."

8.26   If you *remove* a style from your style sheet, all paragraphs that had been previously tagged with that style *will revert to whatever the removed style had been based on.* Now, this does not mean they will turn into that style, though. *They will retain the formatting of the style that was removed,* but they will be *tagged* with the "based on" style name. If you click in one of those paragraphs and take a look at the style sheet palette (Command Y), you will see a plus sign after the style name, indicating that the paragraph has an override (8.34–8.35) in it. These paragraphs *will* respond to any changes you make in the style they are now tagged with, but they will keep their overrides.

8.27   If you remove a style, and you *do* want to revert all those paragraphs with the overrides back to the original formatting that is in the "based-on" style, see 8.55 and 8.68–8.70.

Next style:

8.28 The **Next style** feature is hot. You gotta get this one down. You can set up your style sheet and include in the specifications which style you want to appear *next,* when you hit the Return key. Let's say that in your work you see that every time you tag a paragraph with your Subhead style, the next style you work with is Body Text. If you set your style Subhead to include a "Next style" of Body Text (as you can see noted in the example in 8.24), then this will happen: You choose Subhead from your style sheet and type the subhead text; when you hit the Return key to go to the next line, *the text automatically turns into the style Body Text.* Body Text would most likely have a "Next style" of "Same style," since you will probably have several paragraphs of Body Text before you need to switch back (manually) to your Subhead style.

8.29 You can get very tricky with this. You can set your Subhead style to follow next with First Paragraph style, a paragraph formatting you have set up that does not include an indent (which is a standard typographic format). Then First Paragraph has a "Next style" of Body Text, which *does*

have a one-em indent, as is typical of body copy. So: you type the Subhead, hit Return; then type the next text, which is now *automatically* First Paragraph, hit Return; and then type the rest of the text, which is now *automatically* Body Text.

8.30 In a parts list, a catalog, a program, a résumé, or any publication where certain styles often follow other styles, you can set up your "Next styles" and just buzz along, watching the formatting appear before your very eyes. Take a look at 8.82 for one example of this feature, and see Scenario #9 (8.79). Oh, it's truly wonderful.

8.31 *"Next style" only goes into effect as you are typing.* That is, let's say you have several paragraphs already on the page. You create a style that has a "Next style" in its formatting. If you apply that style to the first of the paragraphs that have already been typed, the second existing paragraph *will not* become whatever is the "Next style." If you go back and edit a style and change its "Next style," that change *will not be reflected anywhere*—it will only appear as you type new text with that style.

8.32 If you don't want the "Next style" to be applied to the next line of text, then use a **line break** instead of a Return; that is, press Shift-Return (hold the Shift key down while you press Return; 4.348–4.354). This will break the line, but will *keep* the current paragraph formatting and style. For instance, you may want to force a line break in your subhead so it doesn't hyphenate. If you hit a Return, you will get the "Next style." But if you hit Shift-Return, you will get a line break, and retain the Subhead style.

Formatting options

8.33   This is a list of the format options you can apply to each style name:

> Font
> Size
> Leading
> Set Width
> Position
> Case
> Track
> Type style
> Baseline-shift
> Left indent
> Right indent
> First-line indent
> Alignment
> Paragraph space before
> Paragraph space after
> Word spacing
> Letter spacing
> Auto pair kerning
> Leading method
> Auto leading percent
> Paragraph keeps options
> Paragraph rules
> Tabs
> Hyphenation
> Color
> Next style
> Include in table of contents

The + and the * (overrides and imported styles)

8.34   A style applies to an entire *paragraph* (remember, you create a new paragraph every time you press the Return key). Whenever the insertion point is in a paragraph, the style belonging to that paragraph will be highlighted in the Style palette (if the palette is showing; Command Y) or in the menu ("Style" in the Type menu). Style names are also displayed in the Style edit box in the paragraph-view Control palette (8.64, 4.303, 4.319). You may see a plus sign (**+**, indicating an *override*), or an asterisk (*, indicating an *imported* style) after a style name.

Style name in the paragraph-view Control palette.

8.35   Because styles apply to entire paragraphs, if you change the formatting of even one character (italicize a word, or make it bold, or change the font, or add a tab, etc.), that paragraph no longer carries the pure style formatting—it has an **override** in it. It is that *override* that makes the plus sign (**+**) appear in the Style palette. (If the override is from local *character* formatting, such as bold or italic, the plus sign will only appear

if the insertion point *is in the word itself* that is creating the override.) Overrides are fully discussed in 8.38–8.43.

8.36   If you place text into PageMaker that has been prepared in a word processing program, and that program also uses style sheets, the styles imbedded in the text will be added to your list as **imported** styles (8.59). They are indicated with the asterisk (*). *If an imported style name matches the name of one of your PageMaker styles, the formatting from PageMaker will take over.*

Microsoft Word automatically applies the style "Normal" to text, even if you think you have never used style sheets. This can create a problem; see 8.60. Also see 8.59 for more info on importing styles.

8.37   You can selectively add styles from other PageMaker publications (8.57–8.58). When you copy or drag-and-drop text from one publication to another, the style sheets imbedded in the text will be added to the existing style palette. However, if one of the new style names matches an existing style name, PageMaker ignores the new style and applies the existing style to the imported paragraphs tagged with the same name.

Overrides: temporary and permanent

8.38 Styles apply to entire paragraphs, although it is possible to **override** them. In other words, even though the paragraph is set up as ITC Baskerville 10 point, for example, you can throw in an italicized word or perhaps another font altogether. These changes *(local formatting)*, are called *overrides.* It is important to understand how the overrides work so they won't frustrate you. There are two kinds: **temporary** and **permanent**.

8.39 If a paragraph contains a **temporary** override, when you *apply a new style* or when you *reapply the same style,* the temporary override (local formatting), *disappears* and the characters revert back to the standard for that style.

8.40 *Temporary* overrides are created using any type specifications *except type style* (that is, bold, italic, outline, etc.) either from the menu or any of the dialog boxes, or from the character- or paragraph-view Control palettes. Specifications such as paragraph spacing, leading, size, tabs and indents, alignments, font changes, etc., *and the type style Reverse,* will all disappear when the style belonging to the paragraph changes.

8.41 A **permanent** override not only stays through the change, but adapts itself to its purpose—e.g., if you *underline* a word for emphasis and then change the style definition to underline, the underline override you made earlier becomes *not underlined* so it is still emphasized! Amazing. How does it know?

8.42 *Permanent* overrides are created when you use any of the *type styles* (except Reverse) from the Type menu, **or** from the Type specs dialog box, **or** from the character-view Control palette. *Case* options (caps, small caps, or lowercase) and *position* options (superscript and subscript) are also permanent in that they will stay in place when the style definition is changed, although they don't adapt themselves by reversing as the *type styles* do.

8.43 When you change the style of a paragraph, you can choose to hang onto any override (8.66). You can also get rid of permanent overrides (8.69–8.70).

"List styles used"

8.44 The Aldus Addition **"List styles used..."** is an easy way to get an instant overview of all the styles used in a story. The Addition creates a list of the styles along with the total number of paragraphs tagged with that style. The list shows each style name formatted in its own style. You may want to keep the list on the pasteboard as a handy visual reference.

8.45 You can select any text block with the pointer tool and the Addition will check all the paragraphs in all the text blocks in that particular story (4.113). PageMaker places the style list as its own text block, right next to the one you selected. If there is no room on the page, she places the list on the pasteboard. If you are working in column format she puts it in the next available column on the page, even if that means putting it down on top of another text block.

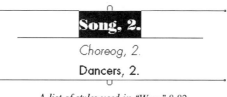

A list of styles used in "Wow," 8.82.

If you want to do this: ■	Then follow these steps: ■	Shortcuts ▾ Notes ▾ Hints ■
8.46a Show the Style palette	■ From the Window menu choose "Style palette," *or* press Command Y.	■ It is very handy to have this on your screen. The paragraph-view Control palette also affords easy access to style names (4.319).
8.46b Hide the Style palette	■ From the Window menu choose "Style palette," *or* press Command Y.	■ Since the palette is a window, you can also click in its little close box (upper left).
8.47 Create a new style from scratch **One method** *(also see 8.48, 8.49)* *Be sure to read Scenario #9 and Scenario #10 (8.79–8.81)* Based on: No style / ✓Body / BodyBullet / Caption / Hairline / Info Next style: Same style / No style / ✓Body / BodyBullet / Caption / Hairline / Info	■ From the Type menu choose "Define styles...," *or* press Command 3. ■ From the "Define styles" dialog box that appears, click "New" (8.10) to get to the "Edit style" dialog box for a new style (8.18). ■ Type in the name of your new style where it says "Name"; any name that describes the purpose of this new style will do. ■ To use "Based on," press on the box to get the submenu of other styles in your style sheet; choose the style you want to base this new style on. If you don't want it based on any style, then choose "No style." Read 8.21–8.27 to clarify this option. ■ For "Next style," press on the box to get the submenu of other styles in your style sheet; choose the style you want to automatically appear next. If you don't want a different style to follow next, then choose "Same style." Read 8.28–8.32 to clarify this option. *—continued*	■ Use this method when you have a defnite idea of what the specifications should be. You can always change things later. ■ The name should be something that will identify the style's purpose when you see it in a list. Don't make it too vague, such as "#1."

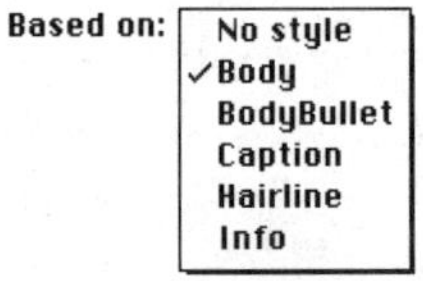

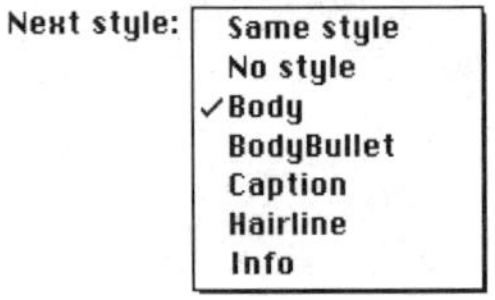

If you want to do this:	Then follow these steps:	Shortcuts ▾ Notes ▾ Hints
—continued	▪ Click the button "Type..." to get the type specifications dialog box; choose any of the specifications you see (4.205), including color or varying shades of gray for your text (4.265); click OK. You are still creating/editing.	
	▪ Click the button "Para..."; set any specifications you see (4.299; 5.72–5.96). Don't forget about those amazing paragraph rules (Section 7)—take advantage of using them in a style sheet! Click OK; you are still creating the style.	▪ If you set indents in the "Para..." box, they will show up in the tabs ruler.
	▪ If you want any tabs or indents, click the button "Tabs..." (6.63); you can set your indents here rather than in the "Para..." box. Click OK; you are still creating the new style.	▪ If you choose to set the indent in the tabs ruler, the specs will also appear in the "Para..." box.
	▪ If you want control over the hyphenation that is different than the default controls, click the button "Hyph..." (5.229–5.241); click OK.	▪ You can use this opportunity to add a new word to the user dictionary.
	▪ Click all the OKs to close the "Define styles..." dialog boxes and you've got it!	▪ If you are nested deep in these dialog boxes, you can hold the Option key and either press OK *or* hit Return (or Enter) and all the dialog boxes will close. **Or** you can press Command Option Return.
	▪ This process just *defined* the style. Now you must go to your text and *apply* the styles, also called *tagging* the paragraphs (8.62).	▪ To Cancel out of *all* the boxes, hold the Option key down while you click Cancel, **or** press Command Option Period. Command Period will cancel just one box at a time.

If you want to do this:

8.48 Create a new style from scratch
A second method *(also see 8.47, 8.49)*

See Scenario #10 (8.80–8.81)

Then follow these steps:

- With the text on the page, format a paragraph the way you want it—set the font, size, leading, tabs, spacing, rules, etc.
- With the **text tool,** click the I-beam within the formatted text.
- From the Type menu choose "Define styles...," *or* press Command 3.
- "Selection" should be highlighted in the list box; click on "New..." to get the "Edit style" dialog box (*or* just double-click on "Selection").
- Type in a name that will give you a clue as to the purpose of this new style.
- "Based on": read 8.21–8.27 to clarify this option. Since you are creating the style this way and not as in 8.47, you probably want it based on "No style."
- "Next style": read 8.28–8.32 to clarify this option. Press on the box to get the submenu of other styles in your style sheet; choose the style you want to appear next automatically. If you don't want a different style to follow next, then choose "Same style."
- Click all the OK buttons.

Shortcuts ▾ Notes ▾ Hints

- With this method you are setting up all your specifications in the text itself, watching what you are doing. It is often easier to do it this way, where you can make instant changes to the appearance, than to do it from inside a dialog box. Then when it meets your standards, create the new style and it will hold all the formatting you set. Of course, you can always go back and edit changes later. That's the whole idea.
- When formatting the paragraph to create a style, *make sure you are using only **one** specification from each category.* That is, the paragraph cannot have some words bold and some italic; it cannot have two variations of leading or spacing, etc. You can override things later with local formatting (8.38–8.43; 8.65) if you choose.
- If you are nested deep in these dialog boxes, you can hold the Option key and press OK *or* hit Return (or Enter) and all the dialog boxes will close. *Or* you can press Command Option Return.
- To Cancel out of *all* the boxes, hold the Option key down while you click Cancel. *Or* press Command Option Period. Command Period will cancel just one box at a time.

If you want to do this:	**Then follow these steps:**	**Shortcuts ▾ Notes ▾ Hints**
8.49 Create a new style from scratch using the paragraph-view Control palette **A third method** *(also see 8.47, 8.48)*	■ With the text on the page, format a paragraph the way you want it—set the font, size, leading, tabs, spacing, rules, etc. ■ With the **text tool,** click the I-beam within the formatted text. ■ Press Command ' *(apostrophe)* to display the Control palette if it is not on-screen already, then click the paragraph-view button to display the paragraph options. ■ Type a new style name in the Paragraph style option box. ■ Click the Apply button, *or* press the Return key. Click OK (or press Return) to close the dialog box that comes up to announce the creation of a new style.	■ Remember, you can make all of your formatting changes through the Control palette. Highlight the text, make changes in the character-view Control palette, then press Command Shift ` *(grave)* to switch to the paragraph-view option to complete the formatting. Finish up by naming the style. See Section 3 for the ins and outs of the Control palette. ■ With this method you don't have access to the "Based on," or "Next style" options. ■ When the text tool is selected but the insertion point is not within text, the Control palette displays the default settings for text in that publication.
8.50 Create a new style based on an existing style, using the paragraph-view Control palette **One method** *(also see 8.51)*	■ With the **text tool,** highlight a paragraph that has the style on which you want to base your new one. ■ Make the formatting changes you want in the new style. ■ In the paragraph-view Control palette, type a new style name in the Paragraph style option box. ■ Click the Apply button, *or* press the Return or Tab key. Click OK (or press Return) to close the dialog box that comes up to announce the creation of a new style.	■ The original style is automatically entered for the "Based on" and "Next style" options. ■ One drawback with this method is that the paragraph on which you base your formatting changes will reflect the new style (if necessary, you can re-tag the style with its original style name when you are done). ■ With the methods outlined in 8.51, the selected paragraph will retain its style unless you tag it with the new style.

If you want to do this:	**Then follow these steps:**	**Shortcuts ▾ Notes ▾ Hints**
8.51 Create a new style **based on** an existing style **Other methods** (also see 8.50)	**Either:** ■ With any tool, from the Type menu choose "Define styles…," or press Command 3. ■ In the list box, click once on the style name you want the new style to be *based on.* ■ Click "New" in the "Edit style" dialog box; make your format changes the same as with a new style (8.47–8.48). *See Notes* ☛	■ Each of these methods automatically puts the style name of the *selected* text in the "Based on" submenu for your new style. All the formatting from the "Based on" style automatically applies to this new style you are creating—you only need to *revise* it. ■ If one style is "Based on" another, when *the original style it is based on* is changed, this one changes too. Be sure to read 8.21–8.27 to understand this important concept.
	Or: ■ With the **text tool,** click in a paragraph that has the style on which you want to base your new one. ■ From the Type menu choose "Define styles…," or press Command 3. ■ Click "New" in the "Edit style" dialog box; make your format changes the same as with a new style (8.47–8.48). *See Notes above* ☛	
	Or: ■ With the **text tool,** click in a paragraph that has the style on which you want to base your new one. ■ If the Style palette is not showing, press Command Y. Hold the Command key down and click once on the style "No style." ■ This shortcuts to the "Edit style" dialog box; make your format changes the same as with a new style (8.47–8.48). *See Notes above* ☛	■ This is the quickest and easiest method. You will not replace the style "No style," as it is part of the PageMaker program. (Actually, "No style" holds the type spec defaults for the publication; 1.6–1.9.).

If you want to do this:	**Then follow these steps:**	**Shortcuts ▾ Notes ▾ Hints**
8.52 Rename a style	▪ If the Style palette is showing (press Command Y), hold down the Command key and click once on the name you wish to change; you will get the "Edit style" dialog box. Type the new name; click OK. ▪ **Or** if the insertion point is within the style, hold down the Command key and click once on the style name in the paragraph-view Control palette; you will get the "Edit style" dialog box. Type the new name; click OK.	▪ If you prefer the long way: from the Type menu choose "Define styles...." Double-click on the name you wish to change (which is a shortcut to the "Edit style" dialog box). Type in the new name; click the OK buttons, *or* press Option Return.
8.53 Edit an existing style (*Change its definition*)	▪ With any tool, from the Type menu choose "Define styles...," *or* press Command 3. ▪ In the list box, click once on the style name you want to edit; then click the "Edit..." button (*or* just double-click on the style name); you will see the "Edit style" dialog box. □ **Or** with the **text tool,** click in a paragraph that has the style you want to edit. □ In the paragraph-view Control palette, Command click on the style name. ▪ Click on any of the buttons (Type, Para, Tabs, Color) to make any changes. ▪ Click the OK buttons, *or* press Return to close one box at a time, *or* press Option Return to close all boxes.	▪ A great shortcut to the "Edit style" dialog box: in the Style palette (Command Y) or with the paragraph-view Control palette active (Command Shift `), hold down the Command key and click once on the style name. ▪ A point to remember: changing the specs for a style *will not automatically change any local formatting* (overrides; 8.34–8.43) that you previously made in a paragraph, whether the overrides were permanent or temporary. The changes will, of course, take effect in any new text created with this style, and in any existing paragraph that you *re-apply* this style to (click in the paragraph, click again on the style name).

If you want to do this:	Then follow these steps:	Shortcuts ▾ Notes ▾ Hints
8.54 Replace an existing style	■ Follow the steps in 8.47, 8.48, or 8.49 to create a new style. ■ Name it exactly the same as the one you want to replace; click OK. ■ You will get an alert box asking if you want to replace this one; click OK; then click OK again.	■ Sometimes it's easier to start from scratch and just *replace* an existing style, than to try to Edit the entire thing. Any paragraphs that were tagged with the original style name will turn into the new style with the same name. ■ Also see 8.61 about having one existing style transform, or merge, into another.
8.55 Remove any style	■ From the Type menu, choose "Define styles...," *or* press Command 3. ■ Click once on the name of the style you want to remove. ■ Click the button "Remove." **Be careful**— this is inconsistent with our Macintosh expectations. Typically, if you are going to do something potentially disastrous you get an alert box asking if you really want to do this. Not here—it just gets instantly removed and is never seen again. *If you accidentally Remove something you really do want, click* **Cancel.** ■ If you want the style removed, click OK.	■ When you Remove a style, every paragraph that had that style attached to it *changes its tag* to the style the Removed one was *based on.* But *the text formatting will not change;* that is, existing text will not look any different, as PageMaker will consider the old formatting as overrides (8.34–8.43) to the new style. If the removed style was *not* based on anything, all paragraphs that were tagged with the Removed style will change to "No style," which means it really has no tag of any style at all. Be sure to read 8.21–8.27 about the "Based on" concept.

If you want to do this:

Then follow these steps:

Shortcuts ▾ Notes ▾ Hints

8.56 Copy all the styles from another PageMaker publication

- From the Type menu choose "Define styles....," or press Command 3.
- In the dialog box, click the button "Copy." You see the same kind of dialog box you get with "Open" or "Save as..." and you navigate around in it the same way (opening folders, changing disks, etc.; see page 718).
- Find the publication that has the style sheet you want to copy; double-click on its name. If there are styles with the same name, PageMaker will ask if you want the new ones to copy over existing styles, giving you a chance to Cancel; click OK.

- Be sure to read 8.20 to understand exactly what copying styles does for you. Any changes will be implemented throughout the entire publication as soon as you click the OK button, or hit Return.
- If you change your mind before you click OK, click Cancel!
- It's a good idea to **Save** your publication right before you Copy styles, just in case you change your mind *after* you click OK. Copying styles *is not Undo-able,* but you *can* Revert to the last time you saved (18.30), or mini-Revert to the last update on the mini-Save (18.31).

8.57 Import just certain selected styles from another PageMaker publication

- With the **text tool,** select the paragraphs that contain the style(s) you want to copy, and from the Edit menu, choose "Copy" (Command C).
- In the publication into which you want to copy the style(s), from the Edit menu, choose "Paste" (Command V).
- **Or** with the **pointer tool,** click on the text block that contains the styles you want to copy.
- Drag the text block to the publication to which you want to copy the styles.

- Text pasted or placed inline will take on the formatting of the paragraph into which it is pasted, but in both methods, the styles will be added to the Style palette regardless of whether the text is inline or in its own text block.
- **If a style has the exact same name as a style in the publication to which you are copying it, PageMaker ignores the one you copy and applies the already existing style to the text you bring in. To get the new style, you need to first rename it (8.52).**

If you want to do this:	**Then follow these steps:**	**Shortcuts ▾ Notes ▾ Hints**

8.58 Copy styles from one publication to another using the Library palette

(See also Section 12, Library palette)

- From the Window menu, choose the Library palette if it is not already on screen.
- With the **pointer tool,** select the text block that contains the style(s) you want to copy.
- Click the plus sign in the Library palette.
- To add the style(s) to a publication, press-and-drag the text that contains the style(s) from the Library palette to the publication page; let go of the mouse.
- You can delete the text, the styles will remain in the style palette.

- Again, if a style has exactly the same name as a style in the publication to which you are copying it, PageMaker ignores the style you copied, and applies the already existing style to the text you brought in.
- You may want to name the item in your Library palette with the name of the style the text contains, or any name that helps you identify the style sheets that are included.
- You can create a Library palette in which to save favorite styles. To learn more about the Library palette, read Section 12.

8.59 Import styles from a word processing program

An asterisk next to a style name indicates that style was imported from another document. See the note in 8.61!

- When you *place* a word processed document in PageMaker (4.33), any styles you applied to the original incoming document are *added* to PageMaker's style sheet. These **imported styles** are indicated in the Style palette with an asterisk (*).
- If you choose to "Retain format" when you place, the document places with the text formatted and tagged with the word processing style names. If you do *not* choose to "Retain format," the document places with PageMaker's default style (8.78); you will usually see a plus sign (**+**; 8.34–8.36) in the Style palette, in addition to the asterisk.

- If there are style names in that word processing style sheet that are not *used* in the document, they will not be imported.
- **If an imported style has exactly the same name as a PageMaker style, the formatting of the PageMaker style takes over.**
- Not all features of the imported style can be applied; basically the features for which PageMaker does not have an equivalent will be lost, such as hidden text, bar tabs, headers and footers, etc.
- All other tabs, Returns, and first-line indents will carry over, whether "Retain format" is checked or not.

If you want to do this:	Then follow these steps:	Shortcuts ▾ Notes ▾ Hints

8.60 Fix a "Bad record index"
*(Thanks to Ole and Steve,
in* Real World PageMaker,
for this great tip!)

- Read the column to the right.
- If you don't have the Style palette on your screen, press Command Y.
- Check each style to see if it is confused. Start with the imported styles (the ones with an asterisk [*] next to their names): Hold down the Command key and click once on the style name; you will see the "Edit style" dialog box.
- Click OK; if you *do not* get a "Bad record index" message, this style feels fine.
- If you *do* get the message, hold down the Command key and click on the style *"No style."* Type the *exact* name (but not the * or the ✦) of the confused style you just found. Click OK and PageMaker will ask if you want to replace the original one; click OK.
- After changing all the offending styles, use "Save as…" to compress and protect your publication (18.29).
- Now go to the "Define styles…" dialog box (Command 3) and *remove* those styles you just renamed (click on the style name, then click the Remove button).
- Use "Save as…" again to compress and protect your publication (18.29).

- **Note:** A good preventive measure to protect yourself from a bad record index is to make sure you turn imported styles (8.59) into PageMaker styles as soon as they appear. Imported styles are indicated with an asterisk (*) next to the style name. To turn them into PageMaker styles, simply hold the Command key down and click once on the style name in the Style palette; when you see the Edit dialog box, click OK.

  Remove any imported styles that you don't use, need, or want (8.55).

- A bad record index is indicated by an alert box, often after you've been in your "Define styles…" dialog box and made changes to styles; after you click OK, PageMaker tells you the changes couldn't be made. Or she may tell you that you "Cannot turn the page" when you try to define styles. If you start getting funny (yeah, very funny) messages, go through the procedure noted to the left.
- A bad record index is most often the result of imported word processing styles getting confused. Whenever you place a file into PageMaker that was created in Microsoft Word, you bring in the style "Normal," whether you used style sheets or not. If you *did* use style sheets in Word or another program, those styles are *also* imported when you place the file. If any of these styles have the same name, like "Normal," but not the exact same specifications, they try to come into PageMaker, but the existing imported styles do not really belong to PageMaker, so they are not replaced and PageMaker gets confused and freaks out. These alien styles sneak into your PageMaker document whether you have clicked "Retain format" in the Place dialog box or not. *They will not come in if you choose to "Read tags," whether there are actually tags to be read or not* (4.38–4.41).

397

| **If you want to do this:** | **Then follow these steps:** | **Shortcuts ▾ Notes ▾ Hints** |

8.61 Transform one existing style (Style A) into another existing style (Style B)
(Another valuable technique from Steve and Ole, of Real World PageMaker*)*

Note: *You may find it easier to use the Story Editor to find all paragraphs tagged with a certain style, and change them all into another style (8.72). There may be a time when find-and-change will not work effectively, in which case you can always use this technique.*

To transform Style A into Style B:

- Click once on the **pointer tool,** *even if it is already selected.*
- If the Style palette is not showing, press Command Y. Click once on **Style B.**
- Press Command 3 to get the "Define styles…" dialog box.
- Double-click on the style name "Selection." You will see the "Edit style" dialog box, but with a blank name, *based on* **Style B.**
- Type in the *exact* name of **Style A.** Click OK; when PageMaker asks if you want to replace the existing style, click OK again. *Don't close the "Define styles…" box yet!*
- Double-click on **Style A;** you will see the "Edit style" dialog box. Type in the *exact* name of **Style B** (replacing Style A's name).
- Change "Based on" to "No style."
- Click OK; click OK again when Page-Maker asks if you want to replace the existing style of that name.
- Now you can click OK to close the "Define styles…" dialog box. Everything that was previously tagged **Style A** is now tagged **Style B.** Not only are they tagged, but they have changed their formatting to **Style B.**
- Permanent overrides will be kept through this transformation, and temporary overrides will disappear (8.39–8.40).

- Use this technique when you want to take two separate, existing styles and eliminate one of them, *transforming* it into the other style. Perhaps you have two separate styles, like Subhead1 and Subhead2, and you want to turn them all into Subhead2. Or perhaps you want to turn all the stupid Normal text into Body Copy. If you follow the procedure outlined here, you will not only change the two style *names* into one, but you will transform all the *text* of the two separate styles into the one style.
- You may think: If I just *base* (8.21–8.27) Subhead1 on Subhead2, then I can *remove* Subhead1. All the paragraphs that were Subhead1 will then *become* Subhead2, since that's what they were *based on*. Well, that's true to a certain extent—all the paragraphs that were Subhead1 will be *tagged* with the style Subhead2, *but their actual formatting won't change*. They will still *look like* Subhead1 and the old formatting will be thought of as *overrides* (8.38–8.43).
- What you are actually doing here is making the two styles identical, except for their names. Then you are making their names identical as well, so they actually become one.

If you want to do this:

Then follow these steps:

Shortcuts ▾ Notes ▾ Hints

8.62   Apply a style to a paragraph

- With the **text tool,** select the text:
  - □ if you want to **select just one paragraph,** simply click the I-beam anywhere in it;
  - □ if you want to **select more than one consecutive paragraph,** press-and-drag to select all of them;
  - □ if you want to **select an entire story,** click with the I-beam anywhere in the text block, then press Command A to "Select all."
- From the Type menu, slide down to "Style" (near the very bottom—*not* "Type style!"); move out to the right and choose the Style of your fancy. **Or** press Command Y to show the Style palette; click on the style name to apply it to the selected paragraph (s). **Or** select the style name from the Paragraph style option list in the paragraph-view Control palette.

- Applying a style removes any other fonts and formatting that were in the text. Permanent overrides are preserved (8.41–8.43).
- After you apply a style to a paragraph, that paragraph is now considered *tagged*.
- To apply or change styles completely from the keyboard, see 8.64.

- You can also type the style name in the Paragraph style edit box in the Control palette. See 4.300 and 8.64 for how to use the Control palette to apply paragraph styles.

8.63   Change a paragraph's style

- Changing a paragraph's style is exactly the same as applying a new style (8.62).
- If you want to change the *definition,* or specifications of the style, see 8.53.

- Changing the style, though, may have an effect on any overrides (8.38–8.43) that may be in the paragraphs. To preserve the temporary overrides, see 8.66.

If you want to do this:

8.64 Apply or change a style from the keyboard

The Control palette is active in paragraph-view. The Style option edit box is high-lighted, ready to accept an entry.

Then follow these steps:

- With the **text tool,** select the text as in 8.62.
- Press Command ' (*apostrophe*) to display the Control palette if it is not on screen.
- Press Command ` (*grave*) to activate the Control palette.
- If the palette is not in paragraph-view, hold down the Command and Shift keys and then press the grave key, *or* press the Tab key until the highlight bar is below the paragraph icon (¶), then press any arrow key.
- Press the Tab key to move to the Style option edit box.
- Enter the first few characters of the style name you want.
- Press the Return key to apply the style and deactivate the Control palette.

Shortcuts ▾ Notes ▾ Hints

- If you find this too confusing, read the Control palette section first (Section 3), then come back and try it.
- The highlight bar is just a little tiny black or colored bar (depending on what kind of monitor you have) that indicates the active option. It's easy to notice it when it causes an edit box to highlight, but easy to miss when it is below a small button option like the paragraph icon. See 3.110 to change the color of the highlight bar if you have a hard time seeing it.
- Press the Tab key to move forward in the Control palette (from left to right). Press Shift Tab to move backward (from right to left, 3.110).
- When you type names (or fonts) in Control palette option boxes, PageMaker displays the first alphabetical possibility for the word you are spelling as soon as she is able to recognize it (3.30). This means you can get away without knowing the exact spelling: "Su" will display "Subhead." If you spell the style name wrong, however, Pagemaker will not be able to match it at all.

"What type shall I use? The gods refuse to answer.

If you want to do this:	Then follow these steps:	Shortcuts • Notes • Hints
8.65 Override the style sheet *(change the formatting in any paragraph)*	■ If you want to change any specifications in the paragraph itself, just go ahead and do it—size, font, tabs, indents, etc. ■ Be sure to read about temporary and permanent overrides (8.38–8.43) to see how they will affect future changes in style names or in paragraph formatting.	■ A plus sign (**+**) next to the style name on the Style palette indicates the presence of an override (8.38–8.43). *That plus sign will only appear, though,* when the insertion point is in the actual word or section of text that is creating the override.
8.66 Preserve temporary overrides (8.39–8.40) when changing a paragraph's style	■ If you want to retain the temporary overrides in a paragraph, press the Shift key when changing the style.	■ Changing the *definition*, or specifications of a style ("Edit…" from the "Define styles…" dialog box) *will not change any overrides, even if they are temporary (see 8.67).*
8.67 Include overrides as part of a style	■ With the **text tool**, highlight the text that has the overrides you want to become part of the style. ■ Hold down the Command and Shift keys; click on the style name in the paragraph-view Control palette. ■ Click OK (or press Return) in the dialog box that confirms you are updating the style.	■ This will only work if the overrides are consistent—there cannot be any conflicting specifications in the text. The plus sign must remain next to the style name when all of the text is highlighted before updating it. If the text specs are not consistent, PageMaker will act as if she is going to update the style, but then will display a message box stating that the text has conflicting specs.

They refuse because they do not know. ”
— *W.A. Dwiggins*

If you want to do this:	Then follow these steps:	Shortcuts ▾ Notes ▾ Hints
8.68 Eliminate all temporary overrides from tagged paragraphs	■ With the **text tool,** click once in the paragraph, *or* press-and-drag to select more than one paragraph, *or* click once in any paragraph and press Command A to select the entire story. ■ From the Type menu, pop out the sub-menu "Style" and choose the style for the selected text, *even if it is already checked.* **Or** show the Style palette (Command Y) and click once on the style name, *even if it is already highlighted.* The plus sign should disappear (unless there are also *permanent* overrides in that paragraph; 8.69). **Or** in the paragraph-view Control palette, press on the down-pointing arrow to select the style name from the pop-up list *even if it is already checked.*	■ The plus sign (**+**) in the Style palette indicates an override (8.34–8.43), whether temporary or permanent. ■ A temporary override is any formatting except type style (bold, italic, outline, etc., as well as case [caps vs. lowercase] and position [super- and subscript; 4.253–4.260]). Temporary overrides include reverse, size, leading, font, paragraph specs, tracking, set width, and tabs and indents, etc.
8.69 Eliminate permanent overrides from tagged paragraphs *(bold, italic, underline, strikethru, outline, and shadow)* *(See **8.70** to get rid of case and position overrides)*	■ Some permanent overrides are trickier to get rid of than others. To get rid of the easy ones—the type styles you see listed in the menu (bold, italic, underline, strike-thru, outline, and shadow)—do this: ■ Select the text with the **text tool.** ■ From the Type menu, pop out the "Type style" submenu and choose "Normal," **or** just press Command Shift Spacebar, **or** just click the "Normal" button in the character-view Control palette.	■ These type style overrides are easy to get rid of. It is not Undo-able though; that is, after you eliminate the type styles this way you cannot go to the Edit menu and choose Undo (Command Z) to bring them back.

If you want to do this:	**Then follow these steps:**	**Shortcuts ▾ Notes ▾ Hints**
8.70 Eliminate really permanent overrides from tagged paragraphs (*case,* as in uppercase or lowercase; and *position,* as in superscript or subscript) (See **8.69** to get rid of type style overrides)	■ These permanent overrides are trickier to get rid of than the simple type style formatting. You will have to change all the selected text into the same case or position, then change it back again. ■ Save your publication before you do anything, just in case you blow it. Then if you do blow it, from the File menu you can choose "Revert" (18.30). ■ Select the text by pressing-and-dragging over it, *or* click once in any paragraph and press Command A to select the entire story. ■ Now, *you have to change the entire selection of text into the offending override.* For example, if you have some text *that you typed in lowercase and used the menu to transform into all caps,* you can turn everything back into lowercase: select it and turn it *all* into uppercase (Command Shift K), then back into lowercase (same keys). You can do the same for text in small caps (Command Shift H).	■ All caps, small caps, superscript, and subscript really hang in there; you need to go to extra lengths to get rid of them. ■ Remember, you can only turn all caps into lowercase *if the text was originally typed in lowercase and then turned into all caps through the menu, the keyboard shortcut, or the character-view Control palette.* If you *typed* the text all caps, then the only way to transform it back into lowercase is to retype it. Really. ■ If you have just a few of these overrides, of course you can select just the specific pieces of text and change them one at a time. Use the technique explained here when you want to eliminate several instances of the override throughout the story. *The paragraphs you select do not have to be tagged with all the same style.* ■ You can use keyboard shortcuts or click the "Case" and "Option" buttons in the character-view Control palette on and off to turn the selected text into the offending override and back again.
8.71 View a list of all the styles applied in a story	■ With the **pointer tool,** select a text block in the story. ■ From the Utilities menu slide down to "Aldus Additions," then over to the submenu and choose "List styles used...."	■ This places a new text block with a list of all the styles used in your story on the page or the pasteboard (8.44–8.45). Don't leave it sitting somewhere awkward when you print!

403

If you want to do this:	**Then follow these steps:**	**Shortcuts • Notes • Hints**
8.72 Use the Story Editor to find and change local formatting (overrides; 8.34–8.43)	■ If you are not familiar with using the Story Editor, first read Section 9; 9.80. ■ For instance, if you want to get rid of all the italic overrides throughout the publication, leave the "Change" box empty, and just select the "Attributes" for the text you want to change. You can set it to change any italic it finds, in any font or a specific font, in any size or a specific size, etc. You can find and change bold text to normal, or all occurences of 12-point text to 10-point text. ■ You can also change specific text to local formatting. Let's say you are writing about a book titled *The Mac is not a typewriter*. You can just speed type the initials "tm." Then go to the Story Editor, find any occurence of "tm," and change it into the full title in the italic font of your choice, thus overriding the style sheet with ease and elegance (9.79).	■ In this book, style sheets were used for all text. In the first column, though, you can see that style has an override in every paragraph; the main text is 10-point Baskerville, but the number is 9-point Futura Bold. Also scattered throughout the text are various references, also in 9-point Futura Bold. Changing text into 9-point Futura Bold is a multi-step process: First I have to select the text, then go to the menu and change the font, reduce the point size, and make the style bold. But by using the Story Editor in combination with style sheets, I was able to save hours of time: 　　As I typed the text, I used the keyboard command to underline all the characters I knew would eventually be Futura Bold; that is, I typed along, then pressed Command Shift U *before* I typed the characters that were to change, then pressed Command Shift U again *after* I typed the characters, to turn the following text back to Normal. When I finished the chapter, I opened the Story Editor and changed all the underlined text into 9-point Futura Bold in all stories. Wow. I'm impressed. Thank you Aldus.
8.73 Use local formatting (overrides; 8.34–8.43) intentionally, then use the Story Editor to find and change it	■ Taking advantage of the Story Editor, you can *intentionally* insert overrides in your text, especially the ones using keyboard commands, as you can do those so quickly. Then you can use the Story Editor to change all those easy keyboard overrides into more complex formatting (see the column to the right).	

If you want to do this:

8.74 Apply styles to text in the Story Editor

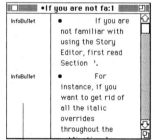

The sidebar in the Story Editor, displaying the style names.

Then follow these steps:

- Apply the style name to paragraphs while you are in the Story Editor just as you would while on the publication page:
- Click in the paragraph, or select a series of paragraphs.
- You can still use the Type menu, although using the Style palette is so much easier and quicker (Command Y to show the Style palette). Just click on the name in the style sheet list. You can use the Paragraph style option in the paragraph-view Control palette, see the note on the right.
- While in the Story Editor, *you will not see any type changes.* They will not appear until you place or close the story. Yes, that can be frustrating. You will see the *type styles,* though, if your style specifications include any of those (bold, italic, underline, strike-thru, outline, and shadow; not Reverse).
- While in the Story Editor, if you choose "Display style names" from the Story menu, you will see the style names tagged to each paragraph; they will be in a list in the sidebar on the left. If there is no style attached to a paragraph, you will see a bullet (•) in the sidebar.

Shortcuts ▾ Notes ▾ Hints

- Be sure to read Section 9 on the Story Editor for all the details on this great adjunct to PageMaker.
- You can apply styles while in the Story Editor, and you can create them there as well. Of course, you can't see the results of what you're doing until you get back to the page layout.
- You can apply styles to text while in the Story Editor using the paragraph-view Control palette. Simply select a style name from the "Paragraph style" option list, or type the style name directly in the edit box (you only need to type the first few characters, enough for PageMaker to distinguish which style you want). You can even do it without your hands ever leaving the keyboard (8.64). See Section 3 for the complete details on using the Control palette.

If you want to do this:

8.75 **Create** a word processing document so PageMaker can read the tags
Also read Scenario #10; 8.81

(See 8.74 for word processing with style sheets in PageMaker's Story Editor)

Then follow these steps:

- In your word processing document, don't format anything—don't bother to change fonts or sizes or set paragraph spacing or indents. Just type the text with your favorite city-named font. Use Returns only when you want a paragraph break (4.348–4.354). Read Section 6 to understand tabs and indents; don't *format* with tabs, just *insert* them where you know you will need them later to work with them. Let the word processor do what it does best—process words.
- At the beginning of each paragraph that will have a new style attached, type in the style name that you want PageMaker to read, and enclose it between angle brackets, like so:

    ```
    <Headline>William Strunk, Jr.
    <Body text>If you don't know
    how to pronounce a word, say
    it loud.
    ```

- Not *every* paragraph needs a tag—just the first one in that style. Any paragraph following will pick up the same specifications as the one above it until a new tag is applied.
- It doesn't matter which letters are capitals.
- Leave no space or tab between the tag and the first word of the paragraph, unless you want it to appear in the final version.

Shortcuts ▾ Notes ▾ Hints

- Actually, this is the best way (from my point of view, which you are stuck with in this book) to prepare text for placement in PageMaker.
- **Either use style names you have already created in the PageMaker publication, or make up style names in the word processor; then when you get to PageMaker, create styles using those same names (of course, *before* you place this document).**
- With the tags in position, when you place this document PageMaker will *read the tags* (if you checked that Option in "Place..."; 8.76), *eliminate the tags* from the text, and *apply that style* to the paragraphs. Do you realize what this means? You can type, for instance, 66 pages in MacWrite II, tag the heads and subheads and indented tables and body text and captions and pull quotes without ever having to select text and use the menus, then drop it into PageMaker (where you have set up your style sheet), and all 66 pages will instantly have its final formatting. Amazing! Used with Autoflow (4.92–4.93) and text wrapping (Section 13), PageMaker will just pour text in and make new pages for you as she needs them.
- If your word processor can do it, set up a macro or a glossary entry to input the tags.

If you want to do this:

8.76 Place a word processed document that has been tagged with style names

Then follow these steps:

- In the PageMaker publication, set up your style sheet (8.47–8.49), **or** copy it in from another publication (8.50–8.51); **or** open a template that already has style sheets prepared.
- From the File menu choose "Place...."
- Navigate, if necessary, to find the tagged document you want to place (page 718).
- Click once on the name of the file you want to place.
- Uncheck "Retain format" by clicking once on it.
- Click on "Read tags" to check it.
- Double-click on the name of the file you want to place, or click OK.
- With the loaded text icon that is now on the screen, click to start pouring the text. (Read 4.28–4.62 for detailed info about placing text.)

Shortcuts ▾ Notes ▾ Hints

- Make sure the names on the PageMaker style sheet *exactly* match the tags you used in the word processor!
- You can always go in and edit the styles after the document has been placed.

- If "Retain format" and "Read tags" are both checked, "Read tags" will take precedence on paragraphs that are tagged. Untagged paragraphs will retain the format in which they were originally word processed.
- See 8.75 for info on putting the tags in the word processing document.
- If any tags come in as text, check the formatting of the characters (including the brackets) of the style name tag. If the formatting is mixed, say one of the brackets is bold, PageMaker will import it as text instead of interpreting it as a tag.

The good type designer knows that, for a new font to be successful, it has to be so good that only a few recognize its novelty.   —*Stanley Morison*

If you want to do this:	Then follow these steps:	Shortcuts ▾ Notes ▾ Hints

8.77 Export a story, tagging it with the style sheet names

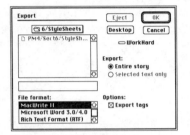

The "Export" dialog box; also see 17.43.

- With the **text tool,** click once in any paragraph in the story. If you want to export just a selected portion of the story, then press-and-drag over that portion.
- From the File menu, choose "Export…"; you'll see the dialog box shown at the left.
- Click the appropriate "Export" button, depending on whether you want to export the entire story or just the portion you selected. If you didn't select a portion, the "Selected text only" button will not be available.
- Click the "Export tags" box under "Options."
- Choose the "File format," which is the word processing format or application you want the story to be converted into.
- Type a name for the file. Make sure you are putting it in the right folder; navigate if necessary (see page 718).
- Click OK. There will be an icon or file name on your disk representing this file, and the document will contain all the tags in angle brackets; i.e., <Headline>.

- The exported story will have tags, that is, angle brackets with the name of the paragraph style: <Body Copy>. You'll see them typed in front of each paragraph. This file can then be placed into any other PageMaker publication that carries the same style sheets with the exact same names. (The tags themselves are simply *text;* they do not indicate formatting that is applied. These tags *will not be added to the style sheet* of any PageMaker publication.)
- When you place one of these files, remember to click the "Read tags" button, or the text will come in with a tag still visible in front of each paragraph.
- The "File format" list displays the export filters you installed when you first loaded PageMaker onto your Mac. If you need another filter, you can copy just the filter icon onto your disk at any time. Put the filter in the "Aldus Filters" folder, which is in the "Aldus Folder," which is in the System Folder on your hard disk. I know, you don't remember making that folder. You didn't—PageMaker did when you installed her.

If you want to do this:

8.78 Set a particular style as the publication default when typing in PageMaker, *or* when placing text from a word processor

SANITY IS A COZY LIE.
SUSAN SONTAG

Then follow these steps:

- With the **pointer tool,** choose a style from the Style sheet submenu, either at the bottom of the Type menu, or from the Style palette, if it is showing (Command Y).
- **Or**, if the **text tool** is selected but the insertion point is not within text, you can choose a style name from the paragraph-view Control palette.
- Take advantage of this. For instance, if you are going to type several captions, default to your Caption style. When you are about to go through your publication and write pull quotes, default to the style you previously set up for pull quotes.

Shortcuts ▾ Notes ▾ Hints

- Every time you click the insertion point *outside* of a text block and begin to type, PageMaker uses the text specifications from the style that has been set as the default. Typically the default is *"No style."*
- You can check to see what the current default is: click once on the pointer tool, then check the Style submenu to see which style name is checked, *or* see which style is highlighted in the Style palette. The paragraph-view Control palette will also display the default style, if the insertion point is not within text.
- When you *place* text into PageMaker, if there is **no** check in the "Retain format" checkbox, the text will transform itself into the specifications of whichever style from the style sheet is the default.
- The specs for *"No style"* are whatever you choose while the pointer tool is selected; see 4.20–4.21. You can change them at any time.
- Whenever you set a style as the default, the style *"No style"* picks up all those specifications (which essentially changes your "standard" text defaults).

Scenario #9: Using Style Sheets—the "create as you go" method

8.79 Scene One: OK. You're about to create a résumé. You have a blank, one-page publication open on the screen. Since there is not a significant amount of text involved in a résumé, you decide to just create it on screen. So you type in a head, hit a Return, and type some supporting information.

Before you go too much further, you start playing around with fonts, styles, spacing, leading, set widths, paragraph rules, etc. You format the head and finally are fairly happy with something. So you select the head text, press Command 3, double-click on *Selection,* name it **Head**, and click OK. While you're there, you can remove all the default styles PageMaker provided you with. You click OK again, and apply that new style to the selected head.

Well, you like that **Head** all right. So now you format the supporting text with a lighter weight font, less space after, no set width, etc. You go back to the "Define styles…" dialog box and name this new one **Support.** While you are there, you also set the "Next style" for **Head** to be **Support,** so as you type a Return after each head, the formatting automatically transforms into the **Support** style.

As you create this résumé, you start to notice a pattern. You notice that after each **Support** line, the next two or three lines are always indented. So you name a new style, **Indent,** *based on* **Support,** and actually you set the *next style* as **Support,** also. And you edit the **Support** style so the *next style* is **Indent.**

Now you can type a **Head.** When you hit the Return key, the style automatically switches to **Support** and you type a supporting line of text. When you hit Return, the style automatically switches to **Indent.** You want to type two or three lines indented, but Indent's *next style* is specified as **Support.** Well, you don't want a **Support** paragraph yet, so instead of pressing Return, you press Shift-Return to get a line break but not a new paragraph. So with the Shift-Returns you type a few lines of **Indent.** Then you hit Return and it switches to **Support.**

Now the résumé is all keyed in. You want to make some refinements in the look of it, like you want the Heads to be a little larger and bolder. You want the paragraph rule to be a little closer to the text. So you edit the **Head** style and all the changes are made to the page. You decide you want a completely

different font for the **Support** and **Indent** text. So you edit **Support**—change the font. Because **Indent** was *based on* **Support,** the font in **Indent** *automatically* changes. Oh, life has never been so easy.

This beautiful résumé is so wildly successful that people are begging you to create a similar one for them. So you save the original document as a *template,* as well as a publication (14.14). Now, when you open the *template,* the style sheet you so laboriously created is still there and you can whip out those résumés like cookies.

Scenario #10: Using Style Sheets—the "I know what I want" method

8.80 Scene Two: All right, so you know what you want. You're doing a six-page brochure and you've already decided in your loose comps what all the text formatting will be. You create six blank pages. You create a style sheet for Headlines, Subheads, Body Copy, Pull Quotes, and Captions.

Unfortunately, whoever input the text in the word processor didn't know how to add tags (8.75). So after you place each file you are going to have to select the paragraphs and apply the styles.

To make life a little easier, you set a new default style. Since most of your text is going to be Body Copy, you set Body Copy as the default (simply by clicking once on the pointer tool, then selecting Body Copy from the Style palette). Now when you *place* each story for the brochure, you make sure the "Retain format" box is *not* checked. When the text drops into PageMaker, the entire story will turn into Body Copy. (To *tag* it with the style though, insert the text tool anywhere in the story, and press Command A. Click on Body Copy in the Style palette or choose it in the Control palette.) Now you only need to select the heads, subheads, pull quotes, etc., and apply their styles.

8.81 Scene Three: Your office is working on an annual report, about thirty pages long. A typist is inputting the text and you will be doing the layout in Page-Maker. Since you are so smart, you have taught the typist how to input the tags.

You don't know exactly what the text formatting will eventually be, but you do know there will be Heads, Subheads, Body Copy, Tables, and ByLines. So in the rough copy from which the typist will be keyboarding, you mark the spots where he is to insert tags.

As the typist types, when he sees one of your callouts, he types the tag so: <Heads>. He types the text following the tag, with no space between the tag and the text. You've trained him not to put any *extra* carriage returns between paragraphs—you will specify extra paragraph space in the style sheet. You've trained him not to indent—you will specify indents in the style sheet. You've trained him not to input any extra tabs; he is to hit the Tab key *once* before each item in each column, *even if on the screen in the word processor it doesn't line up*—you will specify the tabs in the style sheet.

By the way, you've also given him the book *The Mac is not a typewriter* so he doesn't put two spaces after periods, or use two hyphens instead of a dash, and so he knows where to use an en dash, and whether a comma goes inside the quotation marks or not, etc. etc. etc. He's so grateful.

You see (and thank goodness you know this), if someone inputs extra carriage returns, tabs, indents, spaces, etc., you will have to go through the text when it gets to PageMaker and delete them all. It is possible to use the Story Editor to find and change those extra characters, even those invisible ones (9.78). But it's wise, as well as more efficient, to keyboard it in the most efficient manner to take advantage of the style sheets.

While your typist is keyboarding, you are busy preparing the thirty-page PageMaker publication in which to place the finished document. You're setting up your master pages with columns, guidelines, and auto-numbering; you're creating text wraps to control the text flow, and definitions for the style sheets. And you're thinking about what you are going to do with all the time you will save by using style sheets.

8.82 Wow

Opus One

choreographed by Vicki Suemnicht

Betsy Waliszewski, Harrah Argentine, Ronni Madrid, Anne Marie Ginella, Jimmy Thomas, Mary Grady, John B. Rose

Anything Goes

choreographed by Nina Raggio

Marjori Cerletti, Barbara Sikora, Robin Williams, David Peters, Gary B. Jones, Janyce Bodeson, Shannon Mills, Ryan Williams, Vicki Calkins, Beverly Scherf

To the left is an example of how using style sheets with paragraph rules (Section 7), saved countless hours. I created a twelve-page program for the Tap Dance Studio, listing thirty-two dances. I created three styles in my style sheet: one for the song title with the reverse text on the black rules; one for the choreography by-line, which placed the hairline rule above; and one for the list of dancers. *Combined with the feature "Next style"* (8.28–8.32), I was able to type the song title, hit a Return, type the choreography line, hit a Return, type the list of dancers, hit Shift-Returns (4.348–4.354) until the last name, then hit a Return and start over with the next song title. As I typed, *all* the formatting, including the rules and the reverse text, just appeared. As I edited, all the rules adjusted automatically. I could roll up the text block and pour it somewhere else, and all the rules came right along. Awesome.

9 ▾ STORY EDITOR

9.1 Minimums and maximums:

Item	Minimum	Maximum
Open story windows	1	approximately 15 *(depends on computer memory)*
Number of char. to change	0	32,767

Type
is one of the most eloquent means of expression in every epoch of style. Next to architecture, it gives the most characteristic portrait of a period and the most severe testimony of a nation's intellectual status.

—Peter Behrens

9.2 The **Story Editor** is the word processor that is built into PageMaker. Yes, people have complained that it is clunky and inelegant. But personally, I think it's terrific. This entire book was done entirely within PageMaker—I never even looked at Word. (Actually, if I was going to use a separate word processor, I would have used MacWrite II anyway.)

9.3 The Story Editor allows you to create text much more quickly than it can appear on the layout page. What upsets some people is that the text formatting you see in the Story Editor is *not* what you see on the Layout page. But I say, "So what." Use the word processor to process words, not to format your text. Use it to find and change words. Use it to check your spelling.

9.4 Use it to find and change text attributes; for instance, use it to find all instances of Baskerville Italic and change them all to Franklin Gothic Bold. Or find all text that is tagged with a Subhead1 style and change them to the Subhead2 style. Oh, it is the most marvelous invention. Please see Scenarios #11 and #12 for other ways to take advantage of this great feature.

About the Story Editor 414
The Story Editor menu 416
Opening windows, editing: Tasks 417
"Find" 427
Scenario #11: Using "Find" 428
    Tasks 429
"Change" 434
Scenario #12: Finding and changing text 435
    Tasks 436
Closing windows, placing the text: Tasks 441
The spell checker 444
The user dictionary and other dictionaries 445
    The Spelling window 446
    Tasks 448
The Dictionary Editor 456

About the Story Editor

9.5 Move *a window by dragging in its title bar.* **Resize** *a window by dragging in its size box. This shows several windows open in the Story Editor. Notice in the background you can see the page layout window as well.*

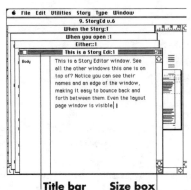

Title bar   Size box

9.6   When you open the Story Editor (9.29–9.30), you are looking at the **story view.** The actual PageMaker publication page is referred to as the **layout view.** I will also refer to it as the *page layout view* or the *publication page* to make it as clear as possible here.

9.7   What you see when you open the Story Editor is a **window** that operates just like any other window on the Mac. It has a title bar, a scroll bar, a zoom box, a size box, and a close box (if you are not familiar with these parts and how to operate them, you really should read *The Little Mac Book*). The Toolbox disappears, because you don't need it.

9.8   Each window holds only one story (if you are not clear on the difference between a *text block* and a *story,* please pop over to 3.113). You can get a window for each and every story in the entire publication, including every little pull-quote and caption, no matter how small. In addition, each is named with the first few characters in the first paragraph of the story. If there is more than one story that begins with the same characters, the title bar will number them (Hello:1; Hello:2; etc.).

9.9   You can open stories in any of the publications you have open. You can have up to twenty story windows open at a time, each holding a different story, from the same or different publications. As is typical with windows, they will layer over the top of each other. You can easily get to the different windows by clicking on the visible part of the one you want (it will come forward), **or** by choosing it from the Window menu. All open publications will be listed in the Window menu, each with a submenu listing all its open story windows (9.27–9.28).

Window tricks: To move a window all the way to the back, hold the Option key down and click in its title bar. To move a window without making it active (in front), hold the Command key down as you drag its title bar. You can cascade and tile story windows; see 9.33–9.34.

9.10   You can open story windows only when a publication is open. You can open new blank story windows, or story windows for text that already exists in the publication. In the layout view you can run the Aldus Addition "Open stories…" to open all the stories (*fifteen or so at one time*) of the currently active publication (9.46). You cannot **print** the document directly from a story window; the story must be placed on a page (9.83).

9.11   When you close the publication, all *unplaced* (9.85) story windows close also. Only *unplaced* stories will automatically open again when you re-open the publication. PageMaker considers any story as *unplaced* that has not been put on a publication page—it exists only in the Story Editor.

9.12   PageMaker automatically saves all *unplaced* stories (9.85) and re-opens them along with the publication.

The Story Editor   *—continued*

9.13   The **font** (typeface) displayed in the Story Editor defaults to 12-point Geneva. This means that *everything* you type is in 12-point Geneva. Even if you select text and change its font to 36-point Garamond Ultra, it will appear as 12-point Geneva in the window. Neither will you see line breaks, columns, letter or word spacing, hyphenation, text color, rotation, or kerning. Just 12-point Geneva text. You *will* see any type *style* changes (bold, italic, etc., except reverse), and you will see some kind of blank space where a tab or indent has been set.

9.14   As you type, though, PageMaker keeps track of any changes, and when you close the story window, the text with all its attributes will flow onto the page. When you are in the Story Editor, you may notice, if it is visible, that the story on the layout page is gray when its window is open.

9.15   You can change the font in which the Story Editor displays to any other font in your System (9.48). But you will find it easier to read a bitmapped font, as they are designed for the resolution of the screen. Almost all bitmapped fonts have city names (Geneva, Boston, New York, Chicago, etc.). Also, to make it easiest to read, choose a font size that is installed in your System. You can tell which sizes are installed by looking in the Size submenu: the numbers in outline form indicate installed sizes.

9.16   The Style palette, the Color palette, and the Control palette are available while you are in the Story Editor. You can use them to apply styles to paragraphs, and color and other character and paragraph formatting to text, but you won't see the effect. You *can* choose to see the *name* of the applied style in the sidebar next to the paragraph, though (from the Story menu, choose "Display style names").

9.17   This is a great little feature: if you choose "Display ¶" from the Story Editor Story menu, you can hide or show all those invisible characters, like Returns, Tabs, Line breaks, and Spaces. This is great for those times when you are trying to discover why your tabs are acting bizarrely, or where someone has used spaces instead of first-line indents. You can also find-and-change any misformatting (Scenario 12).

9.18   An inline graphic (10.125) in the Story Editor will appear as a little box (▨), just a placeholder. Index entries (Section 15) will appear as ◊. Automatic page-number markers (1.147a) will appear as #. The end of the story is indicated by a small, vertical bar ( ).

9.19   **Important note:** When you place a story into PageMaker that you created in an outside word processor, you know you can always throw away the version you have in PageMaker because the word processed version is still on the disk and you can place it again. **But,** if you create a story directly in the Story Editor and then place it on a page, **there is no other copy of it.** The Story Editor just gives you another view of what is on the page. If you eliminate the story on the layout page, you eliminate the story view of it also. If you want to keep an outside copy of the story, export it (9.39).

9.20   You can close all the open story windows of the active publication at one time by pressing the Option key as you click the close box of the active story window. All the stories that have been placed will close. If you have any unplaced stories PageMaker will notify you and keep them open until you to decide what to do with each one (9.83).

The Story Editor menu   *(from the Edit menu, choose "Edit Story," or press Command E)*

9.21   When the Story Editor is open, you will see a slightly different menu bar:

9.22   The File *menu commands work the same as in layout view. "Place…," though, imports stories directly to the Story Editor. You can place a new story within a current story (9.35) or in a new story window. If it is a new story window, the text will eventually need to be placed in the layout view.*

9.23   *When you're in the story view, the last command is "Edit layout," to return to the page layout. When you're in the layout view, this command is "Edit story."*

9.24   *In the Story Editor, the "Find," "Change," and "Spelling" commands are black and available (in the layout view, they are always gray). Indexing and creating tables of contents can be done from the story view (Section 15).*

9.25   *From the Story menu you can open a new, blank story window (9.29), and close an existing one (9.83). You can also choose to see the style sheet names, as well as invisible characters (9.42).*

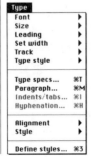

9.26   *You can use almost any of the type specifications, just as in the layout view, except indents and tabs and the hyphenation controls. Remember, though, you won't see any of your specs in the story window (9.13). You can use the Control palette to format text, too (9.44).*

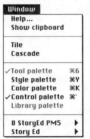

9.27   *From the Window menu you can choose to "Cascade" (9.33) or "Tile" (9.34) all the open story windows, and show and hide the palettes. All the open publications are listed at the bottom of the menu.*

9.28   *Publications with open stories have a submenu that lists all their open story windows, including the page layout view window. If you leave the Story Editor by choosing the layout page, all those story windows just go behind the publication page; they are actually still open back there.*

If you want to do this:	**Then follow these steps:**	**Shortcuts ▾ Notes ▾ Hints**

Opening windows; editing

9.29 From the publication page, open the Story Editor to a new, blank story window *(If you are already in the Story Editor, just choose "New story" from the Story menu)*	■ **Either:** With the **text tool,** click once *outside of any existing text block;* **Or:** Click once on the **pointer tool,** even if you already have the pointer tool selected. ■ **Then:** From the Edit menu, choose "Edit story," *or* press Command E. ■ In the story view you will get a blank window that is named "Untitled:1."	■ Every existing text block already has its own story window that will open if there is an insertion point anywhere in it, or if any of its text is selected, so the trick to begin a new, *blank* text block is to click the insertion point somewhere else, or make sure no text block has been selected with the pointer tool.
9.30 Open the Story Editor to view a particular story you want to edit:	There are several ways to do this, depending on exactly what you want to view in the story:	
a) So that the insertion point is flashing before the first character of that text block, even if it is not the first text block in the story	**a)** With the **pointer tool,** triple-click on the text block. ■ **Or,** with the **pointer tool,** click once on a text block to select it, then from the Edit menu choose "Edit story," *or* press Command E.	
b) So that the insertion point is flashing in the story window at the same spot it was flashing in the layout	**b)** With the **text tool,** click once at the particular spot you want to start editing. ■ From the Edit menu, choose "Edit story," *or* press Command E.	■ You can also select text (press-and-drag over it) and then press Command E. The selected text will still be highlighted when it appears in the Story Editor.
c) If you previously opened this window and it is now tucked behind the layout view	**c)** With any tool, from the Window menu choose the name of the story (the "name" is the first few letters of the story); *or,* if you can see the story window edge behind the layout, click once on it.	■ Whichever window is *active,* or on the top layer, determines whether you are in story view or layout view (9.6). You can resize your publication window so you can see the story windows behind it (9.5).

417

If you want to do this:	Then follow these steps:	Shortcuts ▾ Notes ▾ Hints
9.31 While the Story Editor is active, bring to the front a story window that is already open, but is buried under other windows	■ From the Window menu choose the name of the story from the submenu next to the publication name; ■ **Or,** if it is already open you should be able to see its title bar (with the name in it); just click in the title bar.	■ To send a window behind all the others, hold the Option key and click its title bar. To move a window without making it come to the front, hold the Command key and press-and-drag in its title bar (actually, this trick works on any window on the Mac).
9.32 While the Story Editor is active, open a story that is still on the layout page	■ To open a story window for an existing text block, you must return to the page layout view. *This does not mean you must close the story view.* Just click once on the exposed portion of the publication page; **or** choose the publication name from the Window menu. ■ Find the story you want to open, and then open it as usual (triple-click on it with the pointer tool, or click the insertion point in it and press Command E). You will return to the Story Editor, and all the other windows that were open will still be open.	■ It does seem a little awkward to have to go back to the layout view to get another story. If you know you will be working in all the stories, in the layout view you can run the Addition "Open stories," to open all the story windows at one time (up to approximately fifteen; 9.46). Then you can easily pop from one story window to another (9.31).
9.33a While the Story Editor is active, stack all the open story windows of the current publication so you can see the title of each window	■ From the Window menu choose "Cascade."	■ You can click in the Zoom box of the active story window to zoom the window to full screen. Click in it again to toggle back to the cascaded view.
9.33b While the Story Editor is active, stack all the open story windows of all the open publications	■ Hold down the Option key and then choose "Cascade all" from the Window menu.	■ "Cascade" turns to "Cascade all" when you hold down the Option key *before* you press on the Window menu.

If you want to do this:	**Then follow these steps:**	**Shortcuts · Notes · Hints**
9.34a While the Story Editor is active, tile all the open stories of the current open publication	■ From the Window menu choose "Tile."	■ The "Tile" command places all the open windows side by side in rows. The more windows you want to tile, the smaller each window will be. ■ You can click in the Zoom box of the active story window to zoom the window to full screen. Click in it again to toggle back to the tiled view.
9.34b While the Story Editor is active, tile all the open stories of all the open publications	■ Hold down the Option key and then choose "Tile all" from the Window menu.	■ "Tile" turns to "Tile all" when you hold down the Option key *before* you press on the Window menu. ■ Tiled and cascaded windows can be moved and resized manually just like any other windows.
9.35 While the Story Editor is active, place a file from a word processing program outside of PageMaker into its own separate window *(see the dialog box in 9.36)*	■ From the File menu choose "Place...." ■ Other than the title "Import to Story Editor," it is the same dialog box as "Place..." in the layout view (4.42–4.52). You use it the same way here. Find the name of the document you wish to import, check your options at the bottom (9.36; 4.49, 4.51–5.52), and double-click on the file name. You will get a new window with your imported story in it.	■ Placing into the Story Editor is just like placing into the publication (4.28–4.83), except that you don't get a loaded text icon—you get a story window.

If you want to do this:	Then follow these steps:	Shortcuts ▾ Notes ▾ Hints

9.36 Import a story, *inserting* the text into the current story, *replacing the entire story,* or *replacing a portion* of the current story

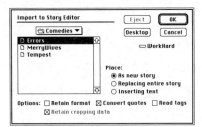

- Open the story that you want to edit (9.30).
- If you want to **insert new text** into the existing text, click once to set the insertion point where you want the new text to begin;
  - □ **or** if you want to **replace an entire story,** click once anywhere in the story;
  - □ **or** if you want to **replace a portion of text,** select the portion you want to replace (press-and-drag, or see 9.40).
- From the File menu, choose "Place...."
- In the dialog box, find the file to import and click once on its name.
- Under "Place:" click in the button of your choice. If you left an insertion point flashing in your story window instead of selected text, there will be a button "Inserting text."
- Choose whether you want to "Retain format" (4.55–4.56), "Convert quotes" (4.61; always, really), or "Read tags" (4.60; 8.75–8.76).
- Click OK, or double-click on the file name.

- If you have trouble "navigating" to find other files, you may want to spend some time studying page 718. Or use Find File (1.334).

9.37 Import stories from another PageMaker publication

- This works exactly the same as it does in the layout view, so please see 4.63–4.85. The only difference is that the file you're importing drops into the story window as text, rather than as a loaded icon on the layout page.

- You can import stories from any Page-Maker 4 or 5 publication.
- You can open the other publication and drag the story from one window to the other, but the import method can save you time, and RAM.

If you want to do this:

9.38 Import a graphic into a story, either as a *new* inline graphic or to *replace an existing* inline graphic

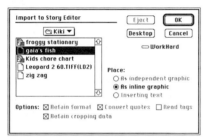

Then follow these steps:

- Open the story window where you want to insert or replace a graphic (9.30).
- If you want to **insert an inline graphic,** then just click the insertion point at the spot you want it inserted; **Or** if you want to **replace an inline graphic,** then select the little icon (▓) representing the graphic you want to replace (double-click it, or press-and-drag over it).
- From the File menu choose "Place...."
- Find the graphic file you want to import. You will know the file is a graphic when you click once on it: the buttons "As inline graphic" or "Replacing entire graphic" will show up and be black. The story window cannot accept an independent graphic (10.124).
- Click once on the file name, then click OK; *or* double-click on the file name.
- In the Story Editor window the graphic will appear as that little icon (▓). I know, you can't tell one from the other. But it works.
- If you are replacing one graphic with another, remember that *the new one will assume the size and proportions of the one it is replacing,* which may or may not be what you want.

Shortcuts ▾ Notes ▾ Hints

- The only kind of graphics you can have in the story window are *inline graphics.* Inline graphics are those that are imbedded within the text. They move along with the text as you edit, and are actually part of the text block. Inline graphics are too cool. Learn to take advantage of them (10.213–10.251).

- If the replaced graphic in the page layout view is not proportioned properly, you can do this: Get the **pointer tool.** Click once on the graphic. Hold the Shift key down. *Press* on any handle and count to three. It will snap back to the original proportions (not the original size) it was created in.

If you want to do this:	Then follow these steps:	Shortcuts ▾ Notes ▾ Hints

9.39 Export and link a story, either the *entire* story, or a *selected portion* of the story

(for complete info on linking, see Section 11 on Linking Text and Graphics)

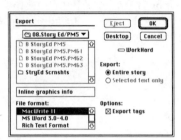

- Open the story window you want to export.
- If you want to export the **entire story,** just click the insertion point anywhere;
- **Or** if you want to export just a **portion of the story,** select just a portion (press-and-drag, or see 9.40).
- From the File menu choose "Export...."
- If there is already a name in the edit box (directly above "File format:"), then this file is already linked to something. If you can see the same name in the list box, you will be asked if you want to replace the existing file.
  - □ If you change the name, you create a second version of this same file, *but the story will still be linked to the first version.*
  - □ If there is no name in the edit box, then type one in.
- Click the button to export the entire story or selected text only. Even if text is selected in the story, you can choose to export the entire story anyway.
- Choose the file format you want the exported document to be in (17.18–17.19).
- Click "Export tags" if you used them and want to keep them.
- Click OK. The link (11.2–11.12) is established automatically.

- When you export a story you are putting it into a format that can be read by a word processor.
- The link is established automatically. See Section 11 for detailed information on linking text and graphics. The basic idea is that if you make any changes in the linked word processing or graphic document after you close PageMaker, the changes can be automatically updated.
- **But** if you make changes in the *PageMaker version* after establishing the link, and then choose to update the changes that were made in the *word processing version,* you will lose all those changes you made in the *PageMaker version.*
- Each story must be exported as a separate document. You can't expect to name two or three files with the same name and have them funnel into one—they won't.
- Exporting from the Story Editor is exactly the same as exporting from the page layout view, actually. If you need more information, please see Section 11 on Linking and Section 17 on Exporting.

If you want to do this:	**Then follow these steps:**	**Shortcuts ▾ Notes ▾ Hints**
9.40 Select text in a story	Selecting text in a story window is similar to selecting text in the layout text blocks (4.195–4.204).	■ If you miss a few characters at the end when you press-and-drag to select, or if you go a few characters too far, hold the Shift key down and pick up the drag at the end to add to or delete from the selection. You can only do this from the *end* of the selection; that is, if you press-and-drag upward, the *end* is on the up side. Try it!

■ You can, of course, press-and-drag to select text.

■ You can use the arrow keys or the keypad keys in combination with the Shift key to select text in increments of characters, words, lines, sentences, paragraphs, screens, or the entire story (1.326; 1.328).

■ Command A selects the entire story, whether it is all visible or not.

■ If the style names are showing in the sidebar (from the Story menu, choose "Display style names"; 9.43), you can use them to select paragraphs: Click once on the style sheet name (even if it is just the bullet indicating "No style") that appears in the sidebar. You can't press-and-drag down through those style names, not even with the Shift key, but you *can* Shift-click to add to the selection. That is, click once on a style name. If you want to add the next three paragraphs to the selection, hold down the Shift key and click on the style name three paragraphs below. You can also select upward.

■ On the keypad, the 3 and the 9 work a little differently in the story view than they do on the publication page:

☐ If you press 3 or 9, the screen moves, *but not the insertion point.*

☐ Hold Shift and press 3 to select all the text *visible* in the window *above* the insertion point (the window may scroll up so you don't see the selected text; if so, press on the down scroll arrow). Hold Command Shift and press 3 to select all the text *below* the insertion point, whether it is visible or not. Hold Shift and press 9 to select everything visible in the window, *plus* one window up. Hold Command Shift and press 9 to select from the insertion point *all* the way up to the beginning of the story.

Who? Me?

Alisandra Brewer

If you want to do this:	**Then follow these steps:**	**Shortcuts ▾ Notes ▾ Hints**
9.41 Edit in a story window	■ Edit in a story window just like you edit in a text block. The only difference is that you won't see any formatting changes except type style. ■ You can't use keyboard shortcuts to change text size, but you can make good use of the Control palette for most text changes. ■ You can press Option Backspace/Delete to delete the character to the *right* of the insertion point (see note on right).	■ Just remember the basic Mac rule (Rule #2): Select first, *then* operate. Select the text you want to edit, then use the menu, the Control palette, or keyboard commands to change it. Also, remember to set the insertion point down first before you begin to type or delete. ■ Option Backspace/Delete in the page layout view, though, will *kern* in small increments (5.168–5.170).

9.42 Display or hide invisible text characters *Spaces* · (a raised period) *Return* ¶ *Line break* ↵ (*Shift-Return*) *Tab* ➡	■ To display the invisible characters while in a story window, from the Story menu choose "Display ¶"; a checkmark will appear next to it. ■ To hide the invisible characters, from the Story menu choose "Display ¶"; the checkmark will disappear.	■ Any kind of space is symbolized with the little raised period: normal spaces with the Spacebar, hard (fixed) spaces, and em, en, and thin spaces (5.217–5.226). ■ See 9.60 for a chart of the symbols to input into the Find box in order to find these characters. ■ This view makes it much easier to remove troubling tabs or Returns.

9.43 Use style sheets in the Story Editor *This is the sidebar where the style names will appear.*	■ **Create** style sheets just as you would in the layout view (Section 8). ■ **Use** style sheets in the Story Editor just as you would in the layout view: Select the paragraph(s), then choose the style name from the Style palette, *or* the "Style option" in the paragraph-view Control palette, *or* the "Style" submenu under Type.	■ You won't see any effect of the style sheet while you are in the Story Editor. ■ You can choose to see the style names in the sidebar: From the Story menu, choose "Display style names." ■ You can choose to show or to hide the Style palette or the Control palette from the Window menu.

If you want to do this:	**Then follow these steps:**	**Shortcuts ▾ Notes ▾ Hints**
9.44 Use the Control palette to format text in the Story Editor	▪ In the story view press Command ' (*apostrophe*) to display the Control palette, if it is not already showing. ▪ Select text (9.40) and use any of the options on the palette. Press Command Shift ` (*grave*) to switch between the character-view palette and the paragraph-view palette.	▪ The Story Editor shows type style changes, position changes (super- and subscript), and paragraph indents (though not true to size). However, many of the other formatting changes do not show until you place the story or return to it on the layout page. ▪ You can make changes in the Control palette with the mouse or from the keyboard. Please see Section 3 for specific directions on using the palette.
9.45 Move a story window without making it active (that is, without bringing it to the top layer)	▪ Hold down the Command key. ▪ Press-and-drag in the title bar of the window you want to move. You will be able to move it, but it won't come forward.	▪ This comes in handy quite often, actually. It's a good trick to know as it works on any window on the Mac.
9.46 In the layout view, open all the stories in the current publication using the "Open stories" Addition	▪ From the Utilities menu slide down to "Aldus Additions," then over to the submenu and choose "Open stories." ▪ Work within the story windows as usual. ▪ To close all the story windows at once, press the Option key as you click in the close box of the active story window.	▪ The "Open stories" Addition opens a separate story window for each story in the active publication (up to approximately fifteen stories) and displays the windows in cascaded view (9.33). ▪ PageMaker will open a story window for every text block, no matter how few or how many characters it has. ▪ PageMaker displays an alert box when she has reached the maximum amount of stories she can open. She also tells you how many stories are left to open.

If you want to do this:	Then follow these steps:	Shortcuts ▾ Notes ▾ Hints
9.47 In the story view, close all the open stories in the current publication	■ Press the Option key and click in the close box of the active story.	■ PageMaker will not close any stories that have not been placed. See 9.83–9.85, and 9.89 for ways to deal with unplaced stories.
9.48 Change the font and/or size text that the Story Editor displays 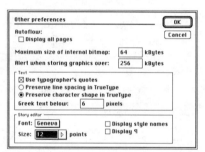	■ In either the story view or the layout view (9.6), from the File menu, choose "Preferences...." ■ In the "Preferences" dialog box click the "Other" button. ■ Under "Story editor," next to "Font," press on the box to get the font submenu and choose a font. ■ Next to "Size," either type a size into the size box, **or** press on the little arrow to get the size submenu and choose a size. ■ Click OK, *or* press Return or Enter. (To Cancel, press Command Period.)	■ As noted in 9.15, city-named fonts are bit-mapped and easier to read on the screen (fonts such as Geneva, Boston, New York, Chicago, etc.). Personally, I prefer to use New York or Boston. ■ Also be sure to choose a size that you have installed in your System. You can tell which sizes are installed: they are in outline style. Sizes 10 and 12 are good and legible.
9.49 Set Story Editor display defaults	■ In either the story view or the layout view (9.6), from the File menu, choose "Preferences...." ■ In the "Preferences" dialog box click the "Other" button. ■ Under "Story editor," click the checkboxes next to "Display style names" and/or "Display ¶."	■ This sets a publication default. Every story you open in Story Editor will automatically show style names and hidden characters. From the Story menu you can deselect these options to turn them off in any particular story. ■ You can set these options as application defaults if you open the "Preferences" dialog box and select them when no PageMaker publication is open.

"Find..."

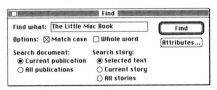

9.50 The **Find** window enables you to instantly find any occurrence of a word or any part of a word, or even of alternate or invisible characters, such as Returns, tabs, and em spaces (9.61–9.66). Notice it is just a *window,* and so can be moved around on the screen. It can also get lost behind other windows, but if it does, just choose it again from the menu, or press Command 8.

9.51 Now, "Find" goes one step beyond just finding characters: You can find text **attributes.** For instance, you can search for occurrences of any 18-point type, or any italics, or any paragraphs that are tagged with a certain style from your style sheet, or any font, or any combination (9.63). You can find text set in all caps, small caps, subscript and superscript (9.62).

9.52 You can combine finding words with finding attributes (9.62). For instance, you can find just the word *rat* that is in 24-point Bodoni Bold, and the Story Editor will ignore any other *rat*.

9.53 If **Match case** is checked the Story Editor will only find those words with capital letters that exactly match the capital letters you have typed here. Otherwise it is *case insensitive,* meaning it will ignore whether letters are capital or not, both in how you typed it in the "Find" box and in the words it finds.

9.54 If **Whole word** is *not* checked, the Story Editor will find any word that has that string of characters in it. For instance, looking for *rat* will also find you *brat* and *rather.* Now, the string includes any spaces you type, also. That means you have to be careful—if you ask to find *"rat "* with a space after it, you will find *brat* but not *rats.*

9.55 If **Whole word** *is* checked, the Story Editor will only find words that *exactly* match the words you have typed.

9.56 **Whole word** and **Match case** are checkboxes: You can select either one or *both* of them.

9.57 You can choose to **search** for the characters or attributes in the current active publication only, or in all the open publications. When you choose to search the **Current publication,** you can search in

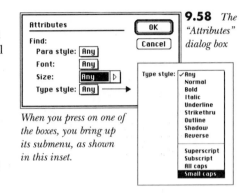

9.58 *The "Attributes" dialog box*

When you press on one of the boxes, you bring up its submenu, as shown in this inset.

three ways: In **Selected text** (provided you had some text selected *before* you chose "Find"); in the **Current story;** or in **All stories** in the entire publication. When you choose to search **All publications**, the **All stories** button is automatically selected. The more text it has to search, though, the longer it will take.

9.59 As the Story Editor finds the characters, it displays their story window on the screen. The characters are highlighted, ready for you to deal with. When you click on the highlighted text to do something to it, the "Find" window will disappear behind the other windows. Just press Command 8 to bring it forward again.

9.60 Scenario #11: Using "Find..."

Let's say you have a 130-page publication. You need to edit the story about the walruses that have been beaching themselves in Bodega Bay. So when you open PageMaker, rather than try to find the page with that story on it, you simply press Command E. This brings up the Story Editor, with a blank window. You then press Command 8 to get the "Find" window. You type *walrus*, choose the button "All stories," and hit the Return key (which, you know, is a shortcut for the "Find" button, since the "Find" button has a dark border around it). Oops, PageMaker shows you a poem about *The Walrus and the Pussycat*. The "Find" button has now turned into the "Find next" button, so you just click again. *Now* the story about the walrus and Bodega Bay is on the screen and you can edit away.

The sexophones wailed
    like melodious cats under the moon.
        Aldous Huxley · *Brave New World*

So you have edited that story, but now you need to find the photo of Ms. Hassenpfeffer because you have a new TIFF file you want to replace it with. You can't "find" specific graphics, but you know the caption had her name in it. So in the "Find" window you type *hassen*. You only type part of the name because you're not sure if it's spelled right in the caption or if you even know how to spell it right anyway. The search finds and shows you the story window for the caption on the screen. You press Command E and PageMaker takes you right to the page that has that caption story on it. Neato.

Turns out Ms. Hassenpfeffer made it into a few other publications, and you're still not sure how her name was spelled. But you're not worried because you can find them all at one time. Open each of the publications, press Command E to open the Story Editor, and then Command 8 to bring up the "Find" window. Just like before you type *hassen* in the edit box, but this time under "Search document" you click the radio button for "All publications." It might take a while, but you will find each instance of Ms. Hassenpfeffer, and can correct any misspellings.

You created a four-page newsletter and took it to your service bureau for output. They say you have the font New York somewhere in your file and you need to get rid of it, but you can't see it anywhere. Since you did place some MacWrite II files in the newsletter that someone else wrote, you think perhaps there may be some blank spaces or blank lines that are still formatted as New York.

So, in the "Find" window, you don't type anything. You leave it completely blank, with not even a spacebar. You click on the "Attributes..." button and choose the font New York from the submenu. You click OK, click "All stories," and then click "Find." Et voilà! All those darn little New York buggers will show up and you can choose to do whatever you want with them, like delete them or turn them into Times.

Also use the Story Editor to find all those paragraphs that are still tagged with that irritating style "Normal*" that got imported from Word (we're talking *style sheet Normal*, not *type style Normal*).

If you want to do this:

Then follow these steps:

Shortcuts ▾ Notes ▾ Hints

Find

9.61 Find a word or words with no particular text attributes

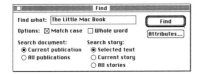

- You must be in the Story Editor to **Find.**
  - □ If you want to search only **Selected text,** then select that portion (9.40);
  - □ If you want to search the **Current story,** then make sure the story is in the *active* window; click the "Current story" button;
  - □ If you want to search **All stories** in the publication, click the "All stories" button.
  - □ If you want to search all stories in **All publications** that are open, just click the "All publications" button.
- From the Utilities menu, choose "Find...," *or* press Command 8.
- Type the characters you want to find. Be careful not to type any superfluous spaces.
- If there is an underline under "Find what:," hold the Option key down and click once on the "Attributes..." button.
- Click "Match case" and/or "Whole word" as needed (9.53–9.56).
- Click the "Find" button, *or* press Return.
- If you get the "Continue from beginning of story?" alert box, make your choice. ☛
- To put "Find" away, click in its close box *or* press Command W. Clicking on another window will simply *hide* "Find" behind a larger window.

- If "Find..." is not available in the menu, it means the "Change" window is open somewhere. If you don't see the "Change" window, then choose it from the Utilities menu or press Command 9. Then close it with the close box, or press Command W —don't just click on another window to make it disappear.
- An underline under "Find what" indicates that there are some attributes applied to the characters to be found. This will limit your search. Using the Option-click, as mentioned, changes all the attributes back to "Any."
- Once you have found characters, in order to do anything to them you need to click in their window. This makes that window *active,* and may hide the "Find" window. To bring the "Find" window back, choose it again from the menu, or press Command 8.
- If you are searching just the current story, the search starts at the insertion point and goes to the end. There you will be asked if you want to "Continue from beginning of story?" in order to search back to where "Find" started from.

If you want to do this:

9.62 Find characters with special text attributes

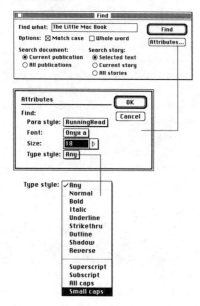

Then follow these steps:

- Follow the steps and read the info in 9.61.
- Before you click the "Find" button, click the "Attributes..." button. You will see the dialog box shown on the left.
- Each of the little boxes is a submenu that you can choose from.
  - ☐ **Para style** has all the style sheets that are in the current publication.
  - ☐ **Font** has all the fonts installed in your System.
  - ☐ **Size** has all the standard font sizes. Or you can type in any size you like, from 4-point to 650-point, in tenth-point (.1) increments (as usual).
  - ☐ **Type style** has the standard styles, plus position and case options. This is the only submenu where you can choose more than one attribute. Choose the first one, then go back and choose others. A plus sign (✦) will appear next to the style name, indicating there is more than one style selected. To take away one of them, choose it again. To take away all of them, choose "Any." Choose "Normal" to remove the standard styles, but leave the case and position options selected.
- Click OK.
- Choose the other "Search" and "Options" choices as in 9.61, and then click "Find."

Shortcuts ▾ Notes ▾ Hints

- As soon as you choose any other attribute besides "Any," you'll see an underline beneath "Find what." It's a great little visual clue that tells you an attribute is selected, without having to check the dialog box.
- To return all the attributes back to "Any," hold down the Option key and click once on the "Attributes..." button. The underline beneath "Find what" will disappear.
- If you haven't done so yet, you may want to read Scenario #11 for some ideas about when this feature comes in handy.
- The "Find what" edit box (where you type in the characters) will not reflect any of the attributes—it will always stay 12-point Chicago.

- When you choose "Any," all of the selected attributes for Type style are removed. When you choose "Normal," the standard type style attributes go away, but the position and case options remain checked. A plus sign will appear next to Normal if a case or position option is selected.

If you want to do this:

9.63 Find just attributes

9.64 Change all the attributes
back to "Any"

Find what: [   ]

Change to: [   ]

*The underline indicates that some
attributes are applied.*

Find what: [   ]

Change to: [   ]

*No underline indicates that no
attributes are applied.*

Then follow these steps:

■ If you want to search for just text attributes, no matter what words they belong to, then **leave the edit box blank** and choose the attributes. *Make sure the edit box is really blank;* the flashing insertion point must be all the way to the left. Otherwise, if you have even a blank space in the edit box, the Story Editor will search for blank spaces with the necessary attributes.

■ Notice that if there are attributes selected, "Find what:" is underlined.

■ Hold down the Option key and click once on the "Attributes..." button. The underline beneath "Find what:" will disappear.

Shortcuts ▾ Notes ▾ Hints

■ To return all the attributes back to "Any," hold down the Option key and click once on the "Attributes..." button.

■ You can select more than one attribute for the "Type style" option (see 9.62).

■ You will not be able to use the "All caps" attribute to find words that have been typed with the Caps lock key down. This attribute will only find text that was set as all caps using the "Case" option in the Type specs box, using the key command Command Shift K, or by clicking the "Caps" button in the character-view Control palette.

■ As the example on the left shows, you can also use this method in the "Change" window to remove the attributes for "Find" as well as "Change."

If you want to do this:

9.65 Find invisible or special characters

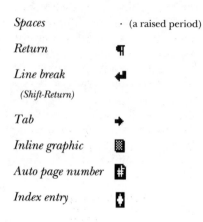

Spaces   · (a raised period)

Return   ¶

Line break   ⏎
  (Shift-Return)

Tab   ➔

Inline graphic   ▨

Auto page number   #

Index entry   ◊

Then follow these steps:

- See 9.61 and 9.62 for the general steps.
- To find some of the invisible and special characters, you need to type in a code (the ^ symbol, a caret, is Shift 6).
- To find a **Spacebar space,** type a space.
- To find a **non-breaking space,** type a non-breaking space (Option Spacebar)
  or type: ^S *or* ^s

Non-breaking slash   ^/
Non-breaking hyphen   ^~
Em space   ^M *or* ^m
En space   ^>
Thin space   ^<
Any kind of blank,
  white space   ^W *or* ^w
En dash   ^=
Em dash   ^_ *(Shift Hyphen)*
Return   ^P *or* ^p
Line break   ^N *or* ^n
Tab   ^T *or* ^t
Discretionary hyphen   ^-
Caret   ^^
Automatic page number   ^# *or* ^3
Index entry   ^;
Inline graphic   Control Q
    (in the edit box, it will look like the Command key symbol: ⌘)

Shortcuts ▾ Notes ▾ Hints

- Any special characters that are not in this list can be found by simply typing the standard keys for that character (see Appendices D and E for a complete list).
- Some special characters may appear as empty boxes (□) in the edit box because Chicago (which is the only font you will see in the edit box) doesn't have all those special characters. Don't worry—as long as you type in the correct key combination, PageMaker knows what you actually want and can find it.

If you want to do this:

9.66   To find a wildcard character

Then follow these steps:

- See 9.61 and 9.62 for steps on the general process of finding characters.
- In the edit box, type ^? (that's Shift 6 and a question mark) in place of the wildcard character. You can use attributes with it.

Shortcuts ▾ Notes ▾ Hints

- A wildcard character allows you to find words that may be misspelled, or ones that you just don't know quite how to spell. For instance, if you want to find *Allen,* but you are not sure if it is spelled *Allen* or *Allan,* you could search for *All^?n* and PageMaker would find either one.
- You can use any number of wildcard characters in a string of characters. Wildcard characters will indicate any character, including spaces, except Returns and Tabs.

I remember that T.M. Cleland, the famous American typographer, once showed me a very beautiful layout for a Cadillac booklet involving decorations in colour. He did not have the actual text to work with in drawing up his specimen pages, so he had set the lines in Latin. This was not only for the reason that you will all think of, if you have seen the old type foundries' famous Quousque tandem copy (i.e., that Latin has few descenders and thus gives a remarkably even line). No, he had told me that originally he had set up the dullest "wording" that he could find, and yet he discovered that the man to whom he submitted it would start reading and making comments on the text. I made some remark on the mentality of Boards of Directors, but Mr. Cleland said, "No, you're wrong; if the reader had not been practically forced to read—if he had not seen those words suddenly imbued with glamour and significance—then the layout would have been a failure. Setting it in Italian or Latin is only an easy way of saying, 'This is not the text as it will appear.'"

Beatrice Warde, *Printing Should Be Invisible,* 1927

"Change..."

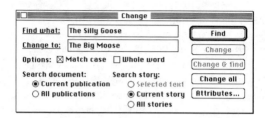

9.67   The **Change** window enables you to instantly find any occurrence of a word or any part of a word, or even of invisible or alternate characters, such as Returns, tabs, and em spaces (9.78–9.80), and *change* them into any other characters.

9.68   "Change," like "Find," goes one step beyond just finding characters: it can find and change certain text **attributes** (formatting). For instance, you can search for occurrences of any 18-point bold type and change it into 12-point italic in another font (9.82).

9.69   You can combine finding words with finding attributes (9.79). For instance, you can find just the word *dog* that is in 24-point Bodoni Bold, set in small caps, and the Story Editor will ignore any other *dog*s.

9.70   If **Match case** is checked, the Story Editor will only find those words with capital letters that exactly match the capital letters you have typed here. Otherwise it is *case insensitive*, meaning it will ignore whether letters are capital or not, both in how you typed it and in the words it finds. But words will always **change** into the case you type in.

9.71   If **Whole word** is *not* checked, the Story Editor will find any word that has that string of characters in it. For instance, looking for *dog* will also find you *hotdog* and *dogfood*. If you change *dog* to *cat*, you will get *hotcat* and *catfood*. Now, that includes any spaces you type, also. That means you have to be careful—if you ask to find *"dog "* with a space, you will find *hotdog* but not *dogfood*, because *hotdog* will have a space after it. If you find *dog* and change it to *"cat "* (with a space), *dogfood* will become *cat food*.

9.72   If **Whole word** *is* checked, the Story Editor will only find words that *exactly* match the words you have typed and will *replace* them with exactly the words you have typed.

9.73   **Whole word** and **Match case** are checkboxes, which indicates that you can select either one or *both* of them.

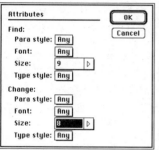

9.74   *The "Attributes" dialog box; the top half identifies attributes you want to find, and the bottom half identifies attributes to which you want to change the found words. Each little box is a submenu.*

9.75   You can choose to **search** for the characters or attributes in the current active publication only, or in all the open publications. When you choose to search the **Current publication,** you can search in three ways: In **Selected text** (provided you had some text selected *before* you chose "Change"); in the **Current story;** or in **All stories** in the entire publication. When you choose to search **All publications**, the **All stories** button is automatically selected. Of course, the more text the Story Editor has to search, the longer it will take.

9.76   Notice the "Change" box is just a *window;* you can move it around on the screen. It can also get lost behind other windows, but if it does, just choose it again from the menu (Command 9).

9.77 Scenario #12: Finding and changing text

This is the greatest thing. You have probably noticed that the text in this book is Baskerville, 10 point. But every paragraph has a number and many important words in 9-point Futura Bold. Well, when I originally started drafting this book in PageMaker 3.02, I had to press-and-drag over those words, go to the Type specs dialog box, and change the selected text to 9 point, Futura, and bold. What a pain in the you-know-what.

Well, this is what I do now: I just type away in my 10-point Baskerville paragraphs (which are all tagged with a style definition, of course; Section 8). When I come to a word that is to be 9-point Futura Bold, I press the keyboard shortcut to underline it *before* I type the word(s). Then I type the word(s). Then I press the keyboard shortcut again to take the underline off.

When I am finished with the entire section, I open the Story Editor. I tell it to go find all the underlined words and turn them into 9-point Futura Bold with no underline. Then I tell it to go find every occurrence of **fi** and **fl**, no matter what the attributes ("Any") and change them into the ligatures **fi** (Option Shift 5) and **fl** (Option Shift 6). Oh my gosh. It's too wonderful.

Let's say you are working on a form. There are lots of little checkboxes: . You know the checkbox is just a Zapf Dingbat letter **n,** outlined. You can type an **n** wherever you are going to want the box to appear. Then, when you are done with the form, you go into the Story Editor and change all the **n**'s into Zapf Dingbats, outline, and maybe a point size or two larger or smaller. But first make sure to check the box "Whole word." That way the words that contain the letter "**n**" won't be affected. You could also check the box "Match case," to limit the changes to lowercase **n**'s.

If you have several files in which you are designing similar forms, you could wait until they are all done, open each publication on screen, and change all the **n**'s to boxes at the same time. Just choose "All publications" under "Search document" in the "Change" dialog box. "All stories" is automatically selected for you.

Or, let's imagine someone else has input the copy for the entire 16-page tabloid you are responsible for editing. They haven't read *The Mac is not a typewriter* yet, so the copy is full of typewriter mentality. The first thing you do is give them that book to read so you won't have to repeat this chore next month. Then you set to work with the Story Editor and find-and-change.

You find every *Period Space Space* with "Any" attributes, and change them all into *Period Space* (just type a period and hit the space bar twice for two, once for one) with "Any" attributes. You then find all the double hyphens and change them into em dashes (9.82). You find any text than has an underline and turn it into italic. You find all the **fi** and **fl** combinations and turn them into the fi and fl ligatures (9.82). You find every instance of where the typist typed five spaces for a paragraph indent, and you remove them (change them into nothingness by typing nothing in the "Change to:" box). Later you will set a paragraph indent in your style sheet. You find all the foot marks (') that some people use as an apostrophe, and turn them all into true apostrophes ('), watching out, of course, for any numbers that really need the foot mark. You find . . .

If you want to do this:	Then follow these steps:	Shortcuts ▾ Notes ▾ Hints

Change

9.78 Change characters, regardless of their particular attributes

- You must be in the Story Editor (9.29–9.30) to **Change.**
  - ☐ If you want to search only **Selected text,** then select that portion of text (9.40); click the "Selected text" button.
  - ☐ If you want to search the **Current story,** then make sure the story is in the *active* window (you should be able to see the horizontal lines in its title bar; 9.7; 9.9); click the "Current story" button.
  - ☐ If you want to search **All stories** in the publication, then it doesn't matter which story window is active or if any text is selected; click the "All stories" button.
  - ☐ If you want to search all stories in **All publications** that are open, click the "All publications" button.
- From the Edit menu, choose "Change...," *or* press Command 9.
- Type the characters you want to find. Be careful not to type any superfluous spaces.
- If there is an underline under "Find what:" hold the Option key down and click once on the "Attributes..." button.
- Click "Match case" and/or "Whole word" if necessary (9.70–9.73).

—continued

- If "Change..." is not available in the menu, it means the "Find" window is open somewhere *or* that you are in layout view. If you don't see the "Find" window, then choose it from the Edit menu or press Command 8. Then close it with the close box or press Command W—don't just click on another window to make it disappear.
- An underline under "Find what:" indicates that there are some attributes applied to the characters to be found. This will limit your search. Use the Option-click, as mentioned, to change all the attributes back to "Any" (9.80).
- Once you change all the occurrences, you cannot undo those changes simply by choosing Undo from the menu. If you seriously need to undo, you can Revert; see 18.30–18.31.

If you want to do this:

—continued

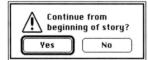

Then follow these steps:

- If you want to change every occurrence of the characters, then click "Change all."
- If you want to be selective about the characters you are changing, then click the **Find** button, *or* press Return.
- If you are being selective and have found the first occurrence of the characters, you then have a choice:
  □ The "Find" button turns into a **Find**
  □ **next** button. This allows you to skip
  □ the change and go find the next one.
  □ Click the **Change** button to change it and stay right there on that selected word. This allows you to pop into the story window if you like and work with the selected text. The "Find" button turns into a "Find next" button.
  □ Click the **Change & find** button to change it and move on to the next one.
- If you are searching just the current story, the search starts at the insertion point and goes to the end. You may be asked if you want to "Continue from beginning of story?" in order to search back to where it started from.
- To put "Change" away, click in its close box, *or* press Command W.

Shortcuts ▾ Notes ▾ Hints

- Remember, when you put away the Story Editor by choosing "Edit layout" from the Edit menu, or by pressing Command E, you are simply *hiding* the story windows, including the Change window, behind the page layout view. If you want to close the Change window, or any story window, press Command W once for each window. If you want to close all the story windows of the active publication at one time, press the Option key as you click in the close box of one of the story windows. (You cannot do this with the close box of the Change window.)

- Clicking on another window, including the publication window, will simply hide "Change" behind a larger window; it will not put it away.

If you want to do this:	Then follow these steps:	Shortcuts ▾ Notes ▾ Hints

9.79 Find and change characters with text attributes

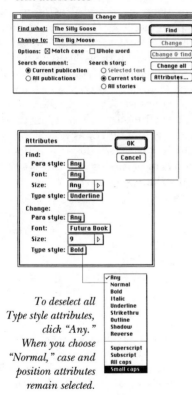

To deselect all Type style attributes, click "Any." When you choose "Normal," case and position attributes remain selected.

- Follow the steps in 9.78 to get the "Change" window.
- Input the characters you want to find, then input what you want to change them to.
- Select your choices for "Options," "Search document," and "Search story" (9.70–9.75).
- Click the button "Attributes...." In the "Attributes" dialog box press on the little boxes to pop up the submenus.
  - □ **Para style** has all the style sheets that are in the current publication.
  - □ **Font** has all the fonts in your System.
  - □ **Size** has all the standard font sizes, *or* you can type in any size you like, from 4-point to 650-point, in tenth-point (.1) increments (as usual).
  - □ **Type style** has the standard styles, plus position and case options. This is the only submenu where you can choose more than one attribute. Choose the first one, then go back and choose others. A plus sign (✦) will appear next to the type style name, indicating there is more than one style selected. To deselect one of them, choose it again. To deselect all of them, choose "Any."
- Now go through your finding and changing as described in 9.78.

- The text in the edit box will always be 12-point Chicago, no matter what attributes you apply to it, so don't worry if it doesn't look like what you want.
- Unfortunately, you can't apply such attributes as set width or tracking. But you can search for, and apply, the attributes of super- and subscript, all caps and small caps.
- If you have applied attributes to the characters you want to *find*, you will see an underline below "Find what."

  If you have applied attributes to the characters you want to *change into*, you will see an underline below "Change to."

  It's important to be aware of whether there are attributes applied or not because they can seriously affect the search. To remove all applied attributes (turn all the little boxes back to "Any"), hold the Option key down as you click once on the "Attributes..." button. You will see the underlines disappear.
- When you choose "Normal" all the standard style attributes will be removed, but the case and position options will remain selected. A plus sign will appear next to Normal, indicating that another option is selected.

If you want to do this:	**Then follow these steps:**	**Shortcuts ▾ Notes ▾ Hints**
9.80 Find and change just text attributes	▪ Follow the steps in 9.78 to get the "Change" window. ▪ If you want to search for just text attributes, no matter what words they belong to, then just **leave the edit boxes blank** and choose the attributes, *both* for finding and changing. *Make sure the edit boxes are really blank;* the flashing insertion point must be all the way to the left. If you have even a blank space in the edit boxes, the Story Editor will search for and/or change blank spaces with the necessary attributes. ▪ **If you don't select any "Change" attributes (if they all remain as "Any"), then all characters with the "Find" attributes will be *eliminated!*** ▪ If there are attributes selected, "Find what:" and "Change to:" *are underlined.*	▪ To return all the attributes back to "Any," hold down the Option key and click once on the "Attributes..." button. ▪ You can select more than one attribute for the "Type style" option (see 9.79). For example, you can change all instances of words set in bold, italic, all caps to outline small caps, with an underline if you want to be that outrageous. ▪ You will not be able to use the "All caps" attribute to change words that have been typed with the Caps lock key down. This attribute will only find text that was set as all caps using the "Case" option in the Type specs box, using the key command Command Shift K, or by selecting the "Caps" button in the character-view Control palette.
9.81 Find and **eliminate** characters and/or text attributes	▪ Follow the steps in 9.78 to get the "Change" window. ▪ The deal is this: if there is no text in the "Change to" edit box, and if there are no "Change" attributes selected (no underline below "Change to"), then any text or any attributes from the "Find what" edit box will just be *eliminated.*	▪ If you are asking to find just attributes, *then any text with those attributes will be eliminated.* Although this can be scary, you can certainly use it to your advantage. ▪ Watch those visual clues: if there is no underline below "Change to," then there are no attributes selected.

If you want to do this:

9.82 Find and change special characters

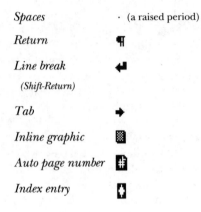

Spaces	· (a raised period)
Return	¶
Line break	↵
(Shift-Return)	
Tab	➡
Inline graphic	▓
Auto page number	▦
Index entry	◘

Then follow these steps:

- See 9.78 and 9.79 for the general steps.
- To find some of the invisible and special characters, you need to type in a code (the ^ symbol, a caret, is Shift 6).
- To find a **Spacebar space,** type a space.
- To find a **non-breaking space,** type a non-breaking space (Option Spacebar)
  or type: ^S *or* ^s

Non-breaking slash	^/
Non-breaking hyphen	^~
Em space	^M *or* ^m
En space	^>
Thin space	^<
Any kind of blank, white space	^W *or* ^w
En dash	^=
Em dash	^_ *(Shift Hyphen)*
Return	^P *or* ^p
Line break	^N *or* ^n
Tab	^T *or* ^t
Discretionary hyphen	^-
Caret	^^
Automatic page number	^# *or* ^3
Index entry	^;
Inline graphic	Control Q

(in the edit box, it will look like the Command key symbol: ⌘)

Shortcuts ▾ Notes ▾ Hints

- Any special characters that are not in this list can be found by simply typing the standard keys for that character (see Appendices D and E for a complete list of codes and special characters).
- The text in the edit box is always 12-point Chicago, no matter what attributes are applied. Many special characters will appear as empty boxes (□) in the edit box because Chicago doesn't have all those special characters. Don't worry—PageMaker knows what you actually want and can find it.

If you want to do this:	**Then follow these steps:**	**Shortcuts ▾ Notes ▾ Hints**

Closing windows; placing text

9.83 Place a *new* story
(*Untitled or imported; 9.29; 9.35; 9.37*)

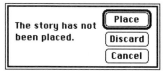

This alert box appears if the story has never been on the publication page before.

- To place a new story, the new story must be the *active* window (in the front, with horizontal lines its title bar). There are three ways to place it; choose one:
  □ From the Edit menu, choose "Edit layout" (or press Command E). You will get the standard loaded text icon (4.88– 4.89). Click to flow the text onto the page.
  □ **Or** you can just click in the close box (tiny box in the upper left of the window);
  □ **Or** from the Story menu, choose "Close story" (or press Command W). Either way, you will get an alert box warning you that the story has not yet been placed. Click the "Place" button and you will get the standard loaded text icon. Flow the text onto the page as usual (4.87–4.100).

- You can always tell if a story is *new* because the name in the title bar is "Untitled:1." If there is more than one new story, they will be called "Untitled:1," "Untitled:2," etc.
- If you do not place a story before you quit PageMaker, it will still be saved along with the publication (as long as you didn't "Discard" it!). Next time you open PageMaker, that story will be the active window, right in front of your face, reminding you that it is still unplaced.
- If this new story is the only story window open, then placing it will close the Story Editor. Otherwise, if there are more windows open, the Story Editor will stay open and all the story windows will just hide behind the page layout window.
- Remember, you can turn or create pages with a loaded text icon if you need to place the story on another page.

9.84 Discard a *new* story
(*Untitled or imported*)

- To discard a new story, click in its close box (the tiny box in the upper left of the window). You will get an alert box warning you that the story has not yet been placed. Click the "Discard" button. *This is not Undo-able—it is really gone.*

- **Note:** If you created the story in the Story Editor, then you have no other copy of it! If you discard this story, this story is destroyed. See 9.19.

441

If you want to do this:	**Then follow these steps:**	**Shortcuts ▾ Notes ▾ Hints**
9.85 Leave a new story (Untitled or imported) *without* placing or discarding it	■ Don't *close* the Untitled window; just click on the layout page of your publication, *or* from the Window menu, choose the name of your publication. Either way, the Story Editor will actually stay open, and it and all the other windows will hide behind the publication page window.	■ If you do not place a new story before you *quit* PageMaker, it will still be saved along with the publication. Next time you open PageMaker, that story will be the active window, right in front of your face, reminding you that it is still unplaced.
9.86 Return to the layout view	■ If you open a story window for a story that already exists on the layout page, there are three ways to return to the layout page with the edited version: □ Click in the story window close box; □ **or** choose "Edit layout" from the Edit menu, *or* press Command E; □ **or** click on the publication layout page. ■ You will *not* get a loaded text icon; the text will just flow into the text block it came from, whether you can see it on the current page or not. See 9.88 for returning to the layout view and, at the same time, turning to the page the story is on.	■ The story window closes only if you click in its close box. When you choose "Edit layout" or you click on the publication page, you return to the layout view, but the story window remains open. When you are in layout view, all open story windows hide behind the publication window.
9.87 Return to where you left off in the layout view	■ No matter which story you are editing, you can return to the exact page you left before you entered the Story Editor simply by clicking on the publication page window, or by choosing "Layout" from the Window submenu.	

If you want to do this:

Then follow these steps:

Shortcuts ▾ Notes ▾ Hints

9.88 Return to the layout view in the exact spot in the story you are currently editing

(You can't do this with an untitled or imported story.)

- When you are finished editing in a story window, *don't* click on the publication page, and *don't* choose the publication name from the Window menu. *Instead,* from the Edit menu, choose "Edit layout," *or* press Command E.
- The entire Story Editor will hide, the pages will turn, if necessary, and you will arrive at the page where your insertion point was flashing in the story window, and with any new changes applied.

- The insertion point will be flashing in the story in the new position, but if you are returning to the same page in the layout view that you were on before you worked in the Story Editor, you may need to scroll the window to see it.

9.89 Save a new (Untitled or imported) story *without* placing or discarding it

- To save the story without actually placing it on the page, *don't* hide the Story Editor (that means, *don't* choose "Edit layout" from the Edit menu, and do not press Command E). *Instead,* click on the publication layout page, or choose the name of the publication from the Window menu.
- Now you can go ahead and close the publication or quit PageMaker. When you open PageMaker next time, any untitled or imported-but-not-yet-placed windows will appear in front of you.

- If you press the Option key and click in the close box of the active story window, PageMaker will close all the stories that are already placed on the publication page. An alert box will inform you if there are unplaced stories, but they will be left alone unless you specifically place or discard each one. You can close the publication and/or quit PageMaker, and the unplaced stories will still be there when you reopen the publication.

The spell checker

9.90 I do like PageMaker's spelling checker. It is simple, complete enough, and fairly clever. It takes about five minutes to figure out. You probably don't even need to read this.

9.91 Remember, a spell checker is always limited. It will check for obviously misspelled words, but it cannot tell you if you should be using *pair* where you typed *pear,* or if you mean *effect* where you typed *affect.* You still need someone with a spelling brain to proof the text.

9.92 Besides spelling, the spell checker will check for other errors, such as duplicate words (the the), or for words that should be capitalized.

9.93 If the potentially misspelled word is capitalized, all the suggestions for correct spelling replacements are also capitalized. (Deplorably, though, whenever the dictionary has an apostrophe in its word, it uses the typewriter symbol ['] instead of a true apostrophe ['] unless the word you are replacing has a true apostrophe in it—in that case, the true apostrophe will carry over into the new word as necessary.)

9.94 The spell checker is in a **window,** not a dialog box (pages 446–447). If you like, you can move the window around on the screen so it is out of the way. While it is open you can still use the menus and desk accessories. If you click on another window to make it *active,* the spell checker may hide behind the active window. Just choose it again from the menu (or press Command L) to bring it forward.

9.95 When you installed PageMaker, you automatically installed the 100,000 word US English dictionary. What? You don't see it? Didn't you look in the US English folder, which is in the Proximity folder, which is in the Aldus folder, which is in the System folder, which is on your hard disk? If you don't have a dictionary installed when you ask to check spelling, PageMaker will yell at you (9.119). See 9.100 for installing any dictionary.

9.96 You can buy other dictionaries from Aldus, such as Legal and Medical, as well as foreign languages. Be sure to read the following page regarding the installation of these dictionaries and how they operate. One **important note:** although you can have up to seventeen dictionaries installed, *you can only use one at a time.* The dictionaries are **paragraph-specific;** that is, you must choose one dictionary per paragraph, and you must choose it from the "Paragraph" dialog box (9.123–9.125). It is that particular, chosen dictionary that the spell checker will use for that paragraph, both for spell-checking and for hyphenation. Because dictionaries are paragraph-specific, you can include them in a style sheet (Section 8). If you want PageMaker to search more than one dictionary in a paragraph, see 9.123.

PageMaker includes an option of not using any dictionary at all, called "None." PageMaker will not spell check or hyphenate paragraphs with "None" applied.

The user dictionary and other dictionaries (foreign, legal, and medical)

9.97 PageMaker uses a 100,000-word Merriam-Webster dictionary. That's a lot of words, but in most of our work, there are always words that are not in a standard dictionary, such as jargon, nicknames, proper names, etc. ("PageMaker" isn't even in the dictionary, and thus it can't be hyphenated). To prevent PageMaker from constantly reporting those words as misspelled, you can add them to a **user dictionary.** Whenever you use the hyphenation dialog box or the spell checker to add words, those words are added to the *user dictionary,* not to the main dictionary. When you remove words, they are removed from the *user dictionary.*

9.98 PageMaker checks both the English dictionary and the user dictionary whenever you spell check in the Story Editor or whenever a word needs to be hyphenated.

9.99 It is possible to create more than one user dictionary, but you can only access one at a time (see 9.141 for installing other user dictionaries). However, a specialized user dictionary may come in handy sometime for a particular project. You can copy any customized user dictionary into someone else's dictionary folder so they can use it also (9.126; 9.139).

9.100 If you order **foreign dictionaries** from Aldus, you must *install* them, not just copy them into the Proximity folder, as the dictionaries are compressed files. Just click on the "Install" icon on your dictionary disk and it will walk you through the process. Each foreign dictionary is in its own folder. *Each foreign dictionary will have its own user dictionary.* As you spell check or add words for hyphenation while using a foreign dictionary, the words will automatically be added to the user dictionary for that particular language.

9.101 Aldus recommends that you don't have more than one dictionary in the same language installed. If you install the US English Legal or Medical dictionary when the PageMaker application is not open, the US English dictionary will disappear (actually, the dictionary disappears, but its folder and user dictionary remain). This is okay because both the Legal and Medical dictionaries contain the English dictionary. In fact, the Medical dictionary contains the Legal dictionary, too. So, by installing the Medical dictionary you have them all.

Dictionary:
None
✓US English
UK English
Deutsch
Deutsch CH
Français
français canadien
Español
Italiano
Dansk
Svenska
Norsk
Nynorsk
Suomi
Nederlands
Português
Português brasileiro
Catalans

9.102 *This shows the list of dictionaries Aldus has available. If you have installed the US English Legal or Medical dictionary, it will be listed only as "US English" in the "Paragraph" dialog box.*

9.103 Although you essentially have three dictionaries rolled into one, you will only have one user dictionary for the set. If you created user dictionaries when using either the standard English or the Legal dictionary, you can access them through the Dictionary Editor (9.134, 9.141).

Look where the dictionary hyphenates the word "dictionary"! This would be good practice—go into the "Hyphenation" dialog box and change the hyphenation of that word so it doesn't look stupid (5.254).

9.104 **The "Spelling" window** *(from the Utilities menu, while the Story Editor is open, choose "Spelling…")*

9.105a *Watch this* **message;** *it changes frequently to tell you what's going on.*

9.106 *The selected wrong spelling (9.105b) will change into whatever is in this* **edit box.**

9.107 *By default both of these are selected, but you can speed up the spell check by turning one or both off.* **Alternate spellings** *provides suggested spellings for words PageMaker does not recognize.* **Show duplicates** *looks for two of the same words in a row.*

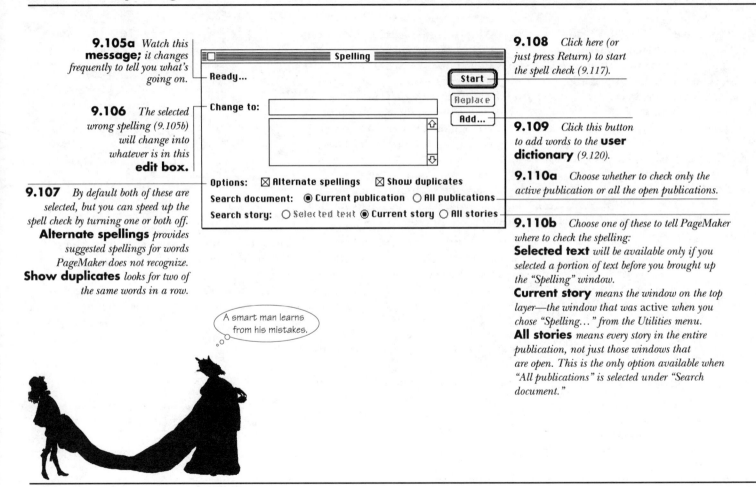

A smart man learns from his mistakes.

9.108 *Click here (or just press Return) to start the spell check (9.117).*

9.109 *Click this button to add words to the* **user dictionary** *(9.120).*

9.110a *Choose whether to check only the active publication or all the open publications.*

9.110b *Choose one of these to tell PageMaker where to check the spelling:*
Selected text *will be available only if you selected a portion of text before you brought up the "Spelling" window.*
Current story *means the window on the top layer—the window that was* active *when you chose "Spelling…" from the Utilities menu.*
All stories *means every story in the entire publication, not just those windows that are open. This is the only option available when "All publications" is selected under "Search document."*

The "Spelling" window —continued

9.105b *Now the* **message** *tells you there is a misspelled (unknown) word.*

9.111 *The* **title bar;** *press-and-drag here to move the window around.*

9.114 *Click here to skip the word and move on. Ignored words will be remembered and ignored again until you close the publication.*

9.112 *The* **edit box** *shows a possible correct spelling. You can type into this box.*

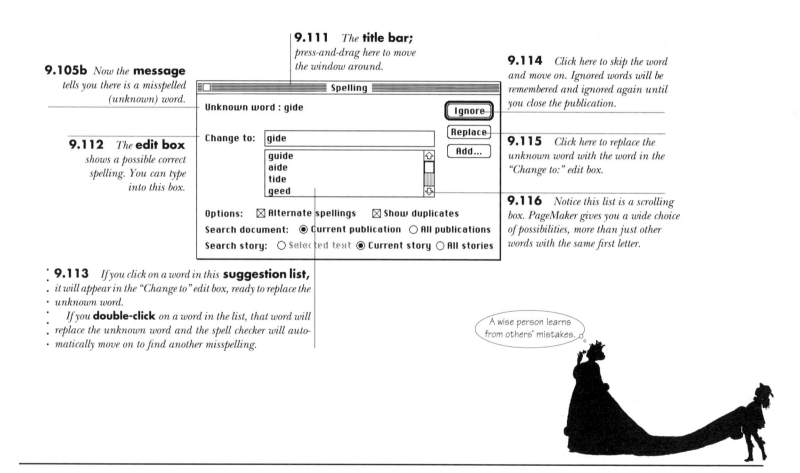

9.115 *Click here to replace the unknown word with the word in the "Change to:" edit box.*

9.116 *Notice this list is a scrolling box. PageMaker gives you a wide choice of possibilities, more than just other words with the same first letter.*

9.113 *If you click on a word in this* **suggestion list,** *it will appear in the "Change to" edit box, ready to replace the unknown word.*

If you **double-click** *on a word in the list, that word will replace the unknown word and the spell checker will automatically move on to find another misspelling.*

A wise person learns from others' mistakes.

If you want to do this:

Then follow these steps:

Shortcuts ▾ Notes ▾ Hints

9.117 Check spelling
Notice the messages in the upper left corner of each of these examples

a) *The spell checker, ready to start.*

b) *A misspelled word has been found. Notice that the "unknown" word is in the edit box.*

c) *An* improper *word has been found. Notice the most likely proper word is in the edit box.*

- If you want to check the *entire active publication* or *all the open publications* press Command E; **or** with the **pointer tool,** triple-click on any text block.
- **Or,** if you just want to check *one story,* either triple-click on that story with the **pointer tool; or,** with the **text tool** click once in the story and then press Command E.
- **Or,** if you want to check just *a selected portion of text,* either select the text on the page (press-and-drag over it with the text tool) and then press Command E; **or** open the story window first (click once in the story with the text tool, and press Command E) and then select the text.
- While a Story Editor window is on the screen, from the Utilities menu choose "Spelling...," *or* press Command L. You will see the Spelling window (**a**).
- Click the "Options" (9.107) and "Search" buttons of your choice (9.110); then click the "Start" button, or press Return.
- If the spell checker finds a misspelled word, the window contents will change to look something like **b** or **c.** Always check the little message in the top left corner (**9.105a/b**).
- If you want to skip this word, click the **Ignore** button (9.114). *—continued*

- My father would have been so happy with a spell checker. He always complained: "How can anyone look up the correct spelling in the dictionary if he doesn't know how to spell it?" Now he would be able to type "sikology" and the spell checker would suggest politely that perhaps he meant "psychology."

- Notice in **b** and **c** that the Return key default (the button with the dark border) is different. When you select a word from the list to replace the unknown word, the "Replace" button gets the dark border.
- Pressing Command Period automatically selects "Replace."

If you want to do this:

d)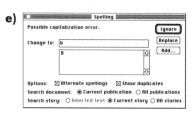

e)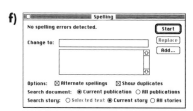

f)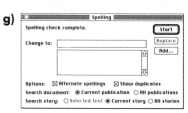

g)

Then follow these steps:

- If you want to replace the unknown word with the word in the "Change to:" edit box, then click "Replace." You can, of course, edit the word in the edit box first.
- If you want to replace the unknown word with a word from the list, click once on the list word, then click "Replace," *or* just double-click on the list word (9.113).
- If the spell checker finds two of the same words in a row, the second is selected as an unknown and the "Change to:" box will be empty (**d**). Click "Replace," which will *remove* the duplicate word (you are actually replacing the duplicate word with the nothingness in the "Change to:" edit box).
- Other messages may appear in the window, depending on what the checker finds (**e**).
- If there are no spelling errors, you will get a message in the spell checking window informing you so (**f**).
- No matter where the insertion point is flashing, the spell checker will check the entire area you asked it to search (9.110). When it is finished, the message will tell you so (**g**).
- You can leave the spell-checking window open off to the side somewhere (press-and-drag in its title bar), **or** click in its close box to put it away.

Shortcuts ▾ Notes ▾ Hints

- If you double-click on a word in the list, the unknown or misspelled word will be replaced and the spell checker will move on to find another word.

- You can send the Story Editor and the Spelling window behind the layout view: just select "Layout" from the submenu next to the story name under the Window menu (9.28). When you want the Spelling window back, you can either select the Story Editor from the same submenu then press Command L; or just press Command E, Command L.

If you want to do this:	**Then follow these steps:**	**Shortcuts ▾ Notes ▾ Hints**
9.118 Check the spelling of just one word	■ To check just one word, you need to select the word and have the spell checker go through its motions for the "Selected text." It may seem, at first, like a lot to go through, but if you use the keyboard commands, you can check a word in less than four seconds.	■ If you previously clicked the "Selected text" button, the spell checker will stay in that mode. Then you can really speed along— just press Command E and then L and hit Return, without even waiting for anything to appear. It will catch up to you.

■ **If you are in the layout view,** do this:
- Double-click on the word;
- Press Command E then L (one after the other). Click in the "Selected text" button, if it isn't already on; then hit Return.
- Find the correct spelling in the suggestion list and double-click on it;
- Press Command E again, **or** just click once on the layout page.

■ **If you are in the story view,** do this:
- Double-click on the word.
- Press Command L (even if the window is visible; these keys will make it *active*). Click in the "Selected text" button, if it isn't already on; then hit Return.
- Find the correct spelling in the suggestion list and double-click on it.
- Click once on your story window to make it active again.

■ You don't need to worry about that extra space after the word that PageMaker selects when you double-click on a word. The spell checker knows to ignore it.
■ Of course, if the correct word is not in the suggestion list, you may have to spend a few seconds typing the correction.

If you want to do this:

9.119 Find out why you get the "Error accessing dictionary" or "Cannot open dictionary for this paragraph" message

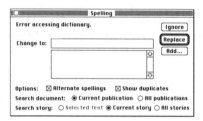

Then follow these steps:

- This message will appear if PageMaker cannot find a dictionary with which to spell check or hyphenate.
  □ You may have accidentally selected "None" in the "Dictionary" pop-up menu in the "Paragraph" dialog box. You may have tagged selected paragraphs "None" or, if nothing was selected, set "None" as the default dictionary.
  □ The paragraph may be tagged with a dictionary that is not installed on your computer. Of course, this is a possibility only if you received the file from someone who had other dictionaries installed.

Shortcuts ▾ Notes ▾ Hints

- The dictionary icons looks like this when they are on the floppy disk:

ALDUSN00.VPX ALDUSN.BPX

They look like this after they have been installed:

AldUsn00.vpx   AldUsn.bpx

- When you originally installed PageMaker, the dictionary was automatically installed into the Proximity folder in the Aldus folder in the System folder. If you have the Medical/Legal dictionary set, installing the Medical dictionary will provide you with the US English, the Legal, *and* the Medical dictionaries.
- To install a new dictionary, just click on the "Install" icon that is on the same disk. It will walk you through the process.

If you want to do this:

9.120 Add words to the user dictionary from within PageMaker
(See also Dictionary Editor, 9.137)

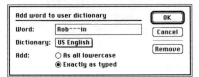

Then follow these steps:

- You need to be in the Story Editor, with the spell checker up (9.117).
- If the word you want to add is already in the spell checker's "Change to:" box, then click the "Add" button.

    Even if the "Change to:" box is empty or contains a word you don't want to add to the user dictionary, click the "Add" button.
- You will see the dialog box shown on the left. Any word in the "Change to:" box appears here with tildes (~) indicating hyphenation points. You can change the tildes: zero tildes prevents hyphenation; one tilde indicates the best hyphenation; two is okay; three is the least desirable.

    If the "Change to:" edit box was empty, the "Word:" box here will be empty. Type the word and insert tildes as you prefer.
- Click "As all lowercase" if you want to enter the word as lowercase, no matter how you typed it. This allows the spell checker to find the same word with caps or lowercase.
- Click "Exactly as typed" if you want to enter the word with the capital letters as you specify.
- You can choose to which language dictionary you want to add these words, although the words are not added to the dictionary itself, but to the supplemental user dictionary (9.97–9.99).

Shortcuts ▾ Notes ▾ Hints

- Depending on the keyboard, the tilde is found either in the upper left corner or next to the spacebar. Hold the Shift key down and press the tilde key.
- See 5.229–5.255 for more info on the hyphenation system in PageMaker.
- You cannot add words to the main Merriam-Webster 100,000 word dictionary. You *can* add words to the *user dictionary*. PageMaker automatically checks the user dictionary first *in addition* to any language dictionary whenever she checks spelling and hyphenation.
- In the user dictionary you can permanently set up all your technical terms, proper names, swear words, etc., so you don't have to keep clicking the "Ignore" button.
- Choosing a dictionary here does not tell PageMaker which dictionary to use to check spelling—that choice is made from the "Paragraph" dialog box (Command M; 9.125).
- You can also create or modify PageMaker user dictionaries with the stand-alone utility the Dictionary Editor, see 9.127–9.141.

If you want to do this:	**Then follow these steps:**	**Shortcuts ▾ Notes ▾ Hints**

9.121 Hyphenate a word you are adding to the user dictionary

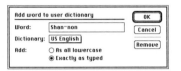

- When the word is in the "Add" edit box (9.120), you may see tildes (~) indicating the points where PageMaker will hyphenate the word. One tilde indicates the ideal point to hyphenate; three the least. You can add or delete them as you see fit.
- In this dialog box, if you never want the word to hyphenate, take out all the tildes.

- Depending on the keyboard, the tilde is found either in the upper left corner or next to the spacebar. Hold the Shift key down and press the tilde key.
- See 5.229–5.255 for more info on the hyphenation system in PageMaker.
- See 9.138 to hyphenate words using the Dictionary Editor.

9.122 Remove a word from the user dictionary

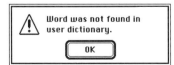

- You need to be in the Story Editor, with the spell checker up (9.117).
- If the word you want to remove is already in the spell checker's "Change to:" box, then click the "Add" button.

    Even if the "Change to:" box is empty or contains a word you don't want to remove, click the "Add" button.

    The point is, you want to see the "Add word to user dictionary" dialog box.
- If the word is not already in the edit box, then type it in.
- Click the "Remove" button. If it worked, you'll get a message "Word removed." If PageMaker could not find that exact word, you'll get a message "Word was not found in user dictionary." Maybe you mistyped it, or it may not be in the *user* dictionary.

- You are removing this word from the *user dictionary,* not from the main dictionary (9.92–9.99).
- To remove misspelled words from the user dictionary, it may be easier to use the Dictionary Editor (9.137) so that you don't have to try to recreate the misspelling!
- If you want to get rid of your user dictionary, and start over, you can throw out the "ALDUSN.UDC" file in the Proximity folder in the Aldus folder in your System folder. The next time you add a word to the user dictionary, a new file "ALDUSN.UDC" will be created, tucked away deep in that same folder.

If you want to do this:	**Then follow these steps:**	**Shortcuts ▾ Notes ▾ Hints**
9.123 Check spelling, using more than one dictionary	• This segment will only apply if you have any foreign dictionaries installed. • While you are in the Story Editor, check the spelling as usual (9.117). • Then *select* the paragraphs (9.40) that you want to check with another dictionary. • While the paragraphs are selected, from the Type menu, choose "Paragraph...," *or* press Command M. • Press on the "Dictionary" submenu and choose another dictionary. Click OK. • Press Command L to bring back the spell checker. • Check the selected text again. • If you will be editing that text again, you may want to select the paragraphs again and reapply the original dictionary to them.	• The spelling is checked using the dictionary that was applied to the paragraph through the "Paragraph" dialog box (from the Type menu). I know, you probably think you didn't apply one. But just like everything else, if you didn't change it yourself, a default was applied. If you only have one dictionary installed (typically US English), then that is your only choice. • If you do have a foreign dictionary and are checking occasional foreign words, it works best to select just the foreign words in question and spell check just the selected text. Otherwise, the foreign dictionary will think every English word is a misspelling.
9.124 Change dictionaries in a paragraph	• With the **text tool,** select the paragraph(s) in which you want to change the dictionary. • From the Type menu, choose "Paragraph...," *or* press Command M. • Press on the submenu next to "Dictionary" and choose another dictionary. • Click OK. PageMaker will now look through *this* dictionary when you choose to spell check in the Story Editor.	

If you want to do this:	Then follow these steps:	Shortcuts ▾ Notes ▾ Hints
9.125 Change the default dictionary	■ To change the **application default,** follow this procedure when there is no publication open; all you should see on the screen is the PageMaker menu. ■ To change the **publication default,** follow this procedure when a publication is open. Click once on the pointer tool (even if it is already chosen) before you follow this procedure. 　□ From the Type menu, choose "Paragraph...," *or* press Command M. 　□ Press on the "Dictionary" submenu and choose another dictionary. Click OK.	■ Changing the default dictionary does not change anything in any text that is already on the page. ■ PageMaker will check both spelling and hyphenation from the dictionary that is chosen in the "Paragraph specifications" dialog box. ■ To change the *user dictionary* that the default dictionary works with, see 9.139, and 9.141.
9.126 Copy the user dictionary to give to someone else	■ At the Desktop, open your System folder, open the Aldus Folder, open the Proximity folder, then open the US English folder. *(If you are working with the US Legal or US Medical dictionary, open its specific folder instead.)* ■ Click once on the file "ALDUSN.UDC," and drag the file to a floppy disk. ■ To install the user dictionary on another computer, go through the same procedure of opening files to reach the US English folder *(or Legal, or Medical folder).* Copy the file to the new computer.	■ You can create, install and edit user dictionaries through the Dictionary Editor. To share user dictionaries you still need to follow this procedure to copy it, but there is another method for installation. See 9.127–9.141. ■ If you are working with a language other than English, follow the directions using that language folder instead. ■ If you wanted to get rid of your user dictionary, and start over, you can simply throw the "ALDUSN.UDC" file out. The next time you add a word to the user dictionary, a new file will be created, tucked away deep in that same folder.

455

The "Dictionary Editor" utility

(in the System folder, open the Aldus folder, then open the Utilities folder and double-click on the Dictionary Editor icon)

9.127 Nested deep within your System folder is the Aldus Dictionary Editor. This stand-alone utility lets you make new user dictionaries as well as edit existing ones. You can either type the words into its dialog box, or import word lists from text-only (ASCII) files (9.140). You can also export dictionaries as an ASCII file to use in other applications. If you want, you can print out a copy of your dictionary to keep as a reference or give out as a style manual with a job. And you don't even need to be working within PageMaker to do any of this. You can also add, remove, edit, and custom-hyphenate words that you already access through the spell checker or "Hyphenation" box by using the Dictionary Editor. You *must* have a user dictionary installed to use Page-Maker's spelling and hyphenation features.

9.128 A user dictionary is automatically created when you first select a dictionary in the "Paragraph" dialog box (9.124), or "Add" a word in the "Spelling" or "Hyphenation" dialog boxes (9.120–9.121). Within the Dictionary Editor you can open and modify this user dictionary or create new ones.

9.129 Adding a list of words to an existing user dictionary is easy. Just type them into the "Word" edit box. Now you either let PageMaker decide how they will be hyphenated by choosing "Hyphenation" (to use the built-in algorithm) or you can choose the hyphenation points yourself (9.138).

9.130 To further edit hyphenation in a word that is already in a dictionary list, double-click on it to bring it up into the edit box. Click "Replace" to put it back in the list.

9.131 The "Find" command easily locates words in the dictionary. It works just like the one in the Story Editor. If you have more than one dictionary open, the "Find" command will search the dictionary in the last window that was active.

9.132 The "Import" command lets you bring into a user dictionary a list of words from any file saved as text-only. The dictionary will recognize as individual words those entries separated by a space, tab, or return. The "DictEd" document (9.137) in the Utilities folder gives details on how to correctly prepare text-only word lists.

9.133 You can export words in a user dictionary to other programs as text-only files through the "Export" command. Also use "Export…" in conjunction with the "Import" command to move words from one user dictionary to another.

9.134 Since PageMaker can only access one user dictionary at a time *per language,* use the Dictionary Editor to switch user dictionaries. "Install…" puts the dictionary you want to use into the correct folder and moves the current one into another folder of your choice. If you think you will be switching user dictionaries regularly, create a folder for storing those that are disabled.

9.135 You can open user dictionaries from previous versions of PageMaker through the "Open" command. However, doing so converts it for PageMaker 5 use and renders it unusable for versions earlier than 4.2. It is therefore wise to make a back-up copy first in case you need to use it in older files.

9.136 Although the Dictionary Editor cannot open dictionaries that exceed 15,000 words, you can continue to access one larger than this and add words to it through "Spelling" in the Story Editor and "Hyphenation" in the Type menu (9.120; 5.253).

If you want to do this:

9.137 Add, remove, or edit words in the user dictionary with the Dictionary Editor utility

Dictionary Editor

The "Find" dialog box is similar to the one in the Story Editor.

Then follow these steps:

- Open your System folder, open the Aldus folder, open the Utilities folder. Double-click on the Dictionary Editor icon.
- To open the existing user dictionary, from the File menu, choose "Open."
- Open the Proximity folder (in the Aldus folder, in the System folder), then open the US English folder. Double-click on the file ALDUSN.UDC.
- If you have not added words through the "Hyphenation" or "Spelling" commands, the dialog box will be empty.
- To add a word, enter it in the "Word:" edit box, then click the "Add" button.
- To remove a word, simply select it in the list and click "Remove."
- To find a word in the list, from the Edit menu choose "Find." Enter the word, check the appropriate boxes and click the "Find" button.
- To edit a word, double-click it in the list to enter it in the edit box. Make your changes and click the "Replace" button.
- From the File menu choose "Save."
- When you are done, from the File menu choose "Close," or click in the close box of the dictionary window.
- From the File menu choose "Quit" to quit the utility.

Shortcuts ▾ Notes ▾ Hints

- Also within the Utilities folder is "DictED," a six-page PageMaker 5 document that provides information on how to use the Dictionary Editor.
- If you become a regular Dictionary Editor user, you may want to make an alias of the application and keep it in a handy place (on your desktop or in the Apple Menu Items folder, etc.).
- Instead of adding words one by one to a dictionary, you can create a list of words in a word processing program and then import them into your user dictionary (9.140).
- You can customize the hyphenation of any words you add to the dictionary; see 9.138.
- In the "Find" dialog box, check "Whole word" to find only those words that match the one you entered character for character. Check "Match upper/lowercase" to find only those words that are capitalized exactly as you typed them.

- PageMaker prompts you to save changes to a dictionary if you "Close" or "Quit" without saving.

If you want to do this:	Then follow these steps:	Shortcuts ▾ Notes ▾ Hints
9.138 Specify how a word you are adding to a user dictionary will be hyphenated	■ Enter the word in the "Word:" edit box, *or* if it is already in the list, double-click on it. ■ Insert tilde characters (or press the Option key as you click the insertion point) to indicate where you want the word to hyphenate; ■ **Or** from the Edit menu, choose "Hyphenation," to use the built-in algorithm.	■ One tilde indicates the ideal hyphenation point, two indicates the next acceptable point, and three tildes indicates the least preferable point. ■ If you don't want the word to ever hyphenate, don't add any tildes to it. This is useful for proper names. ■ The built-in algorithm does not always hyphenate a word at a syllable break.
9.139 Create another user dictionary 	■ First create a folder in which to store user dictionaries: □ From the desktop, open your System folder, open the Aldus folder, and open the Proximity folder. Create a new folder within the Proximity folder, and title it for user dictionaries. ■ In the Aldus folder, open the Utilities folder, then double-click on the application "Dictionary Editor." ■ From the File menu choose "New." ■ In the dialog box, make sure the folder you just created is open at the top. Title your new dictionary, choose a language if necessary, and click OK. ■ You can enter and add words directly in this window (9.137) or import words from a text-only file (9.140).	■ PageMaker will add the extension ".udc" to a dictionary, even if you don't include it in the title. ■ You can create, copy, and trash user dictionaries. You may want to create specific dictionaries to go with specific projects. You may want to share a user dictionary with co-workers to keep the spelling, capitalization, and hyphenation of words used in a particular publication consistent, or, as part of a style manual (9.126). If you trash the "ALDUSN.UDC" user dictionary without installing a new dictionary in the US English folder, a new "ALDUSN.UDC" dictionary will be created the next time you add a word through the "Spelling" or "Hyphenation" commands.

If you want to do this:

Then follow these steps:

Shortcuts ▾ Notes ▾ Hints

9.140 Import a text-only file to your user dictionary

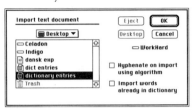

- From the File menu, choose "Save."
- Open the Dictionary Editor application. From the File menu, choose "Open."
- Open the user dictionary to which you want to import text, and from the File menu, choose "Import."
- Locate the file you want to import (only text-only files will show); click OK.

- Check "Hyphenate on import using algorithm," to use the built-in algorithm for hyphenation. This will not apply to words that you hyphenated with tildes.
- Check "Import words already in dictionary" if you want to replace words that are spelled the same in both lists with those you are importing.

9.141 Install a user dictionary
(Switch user dictionaries)

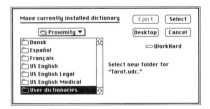

- Open the Dictionary Editor application.
- From the File menu, choose "Open." Open the folder that contains your user dictionaries and double-click on the one you want to install.
- From the File menu choose "Install."
- Click the "Install" button in the Alert box that shows the current dictionary set-up.
- PageMaker asks where to move the currently installed dictionary. Click *once* on the folder you created to store user dictionaries (don't open the folder!), and click the "Select" button.
- "Close" or "Quit" the Dictionary Editor as necessary.

- You can bypass the Dictionary Editor if you want, and switch from one user dictionary to the another by putting the one you want to use into the US English folder which is inside the Proximity folder, inside the Aldus folder, inside the System folder. Take the user dictionary (remember, user dictionaries always have the filename extension .udc) that is in the US English folder and stash it somewhere else (preferably in the folder you created for user dictionaries; see 9.139).
- These directions assume you are working with the US English dictionary. If you are working with any foreign dictionaries (9.100–9.103), you need to go into its dictionary folder, of course, which will also be found in the Proximity folder.

A discourse between the Poet and the Player: of no other use in this manual but to divert the reader.

A special blessing expressing praise of the new printing technology.

LESSED BE HE WHO FORMS MAN WITH KNOWLEDGE

AND TEACHES HUMANS UNDERSTANDING,

WHO AMPLIFIED HIS GRACE WITH A GREAT INVENTION,

ONE THAT IS USEFUL FOR ALL INHABITANTS OF THE WORLD,

THERE IS NONE BESIDE IT AND NOTHING CAN EQUAL IT

IN ALL THE WISDOM AND CLEVERNESS

FROM THE DAY WHEN GOD CREATED MAN ON EARTH.

R. David Gans ❧ 1592 ❧ Prague
(the first Hebrew histographer)

10 ▾ GRAPHICS

10.1 Minimums and maximums:

Item	Minimum	Maximum
Graphic file size automatically stored in publication	0	32,767K
Lines/inch	5	300
Screen angle	0°	360°

10.2 Compatible graphic file formats

Macintosh

MacPaint (PNT, PNTNG)

TIFF (.SEP, CMYK)

PICT and PICT 2

EPS (EPSF)

Photo CD

TWAIN

Other

OGM

DXF

BMP

WMF

10.3 There are two general categories of graphics in PageMaker: 1) those you create within PageMaker with the drawing tools; and 2) those you create in other software programs and then bring into PageMaker. Section 2 covers the first category of graphics; this section covers the second.

10.4 There are three ways you can bring in graphics that were created outside PageMaker. You can *paste* them in from the Clipboard. You can *place* them from a graphic file. Or you can subscribe to a graphic file published in another program (11.79–11.102). Files that are pasted include those that come from the Scrapbook or that are OLE-embedded or -linked (see 11.103–11.132). Files that are placed fall into one of two categories: scanned images; and images created in paint, draw, or illustration programs.

10.5 PageMaker can read files saved in MacPaint (PNT), TIFF, PICT, or EPS (all of which are explained in the following pages) as well as Photo CD, video images, and various CAD, 3D, and Windows formats. For PostScript printers, TIFF or EPS graphics are the preferred format.

The basics 462
Paint-type graphics 463
PICT graphics 464
TIFF graphics 465
EPS graphics 466
Photo CD images 467
Other graphic formats 467
Scanned images 468
Line art scans 469
Halftones, grayscales,
   and scanning 470
Halftone examples 472
Rules of thumb for grayscale scans ... 473
The best way to save a graphic
   for placement into PageMaker 474
"Include complete copy?" 475
Update original copy 475
Paste and Paste special 476
Insert Object and
   Publish and Subscribe 477
Independent vs. inline graphics 477
Independent graphics: Tasks 478
Image control 497
   Tasks 503
Inline graphics 506
   Tasks 509
Additions for graphics 520
   Tasks 524

Graphics: the basics

10.6   Choosing up front which graphic format to use for files you will be bringing into PageMaker is important to the final outcome of the printed publication. Also important is the "Target printer resolution" you select in "Page setup" (10.141). Not only does this determine which graphics will print best, but it sets a number of the default settings that are used in conjunction with editing and manipulating imported graphics.

10.7   For those who are printing to non-PostScript printers, MacPaint or PICT formats will give the best printed resolution.

10.8   There are various ways for getting a graphic into your PageMaker document. Pasting and placing graphics are the most common methods of importing graphics. *Placing* a graphic automatically establishes a link with the original object **whether you store a copy of the graphic in the publication or not.** This is valuable if you want to later edit or revise the original graphic.

10.9   PageMaker can place graphics **inline;** that is, you can embed a graphic into a text block and it will move along as you edit text (10.213–10.251).

10.10   One of PageMaker's particularly exciting features is her ability to automatically update linked graphics that are edited outside PageMaker in another program (10.146– 10.147). There are options for automatically updating the placed graphic either in the "Links…" dialog box under "File" *or* in "Link options" in the "Element" menu (see 11.55– 11.57). When you *paste* a graphic, any editing to the original file must be done in the source program and then it must be re-pasted into your document.

10.11   PageMaker now supports Microsoft's OLE (pronounced Olé) technology. This lets you import files that are not PageMaker compatible by using the OLE-linking ("Paste link") or OLE-embedding ("Paste special…") commands. (You can also just plain "Paste" a file from an OLE server program. Confused? See Section 11 for all you need to know about linking). Although this may be useful for bringing in certain graphics, tables, or charts from Windows or Microsoft programs, almost everything *you* create can be converted in another program into a graphic format that PageMaker can read and import (10.2, 10.5).

10.12   PageMaker also supports Apple's System 7 Publish and Subscribe which lets you "subscribe to," or access, commonly held files (including graphics). Although useful to people on a network, the rest of us can do the same kind of thing by relying on PageMaker's linking capabilities. See Section 11 for the whole scoop on Publish and Subscribe and other ways of linking.

10.13   You will find a list of graphic files supported by PageMaker in the "Help" file under the Window submenu (Importing Files). You can see what import filters you have installed by holding down the Command key and selecting "About PageMaker…" under the Apple menu. See Section 17 for more about importing files.

10.14   The Control palette is a slick and easy way to work with graphics and it gives you visual clues as to the kind of graphic with which you are working (3.42). The Control palette is also the only means by which you can skew or reflect (flip) graphics (3.37–3.38 and 10.145).

Paint-type graphics

10.15 A paint-type graphic is always **bitmapped.** Bitmapped means it is made out of the bits of dots (pixels) on the screen; 72 dots per inch (dpi), to be precise. The screen is made up of all those tiny dots, and a bitmapped image tells the screen which dots to turn on (black) and which dots to turn off (white). Here is an image that was created as a paint-type graphic:

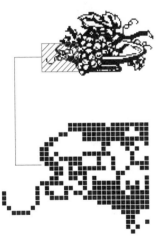

This is an enlarged view of the bottom left part of this image. It shows clearly how the image is made of a collection of pixels, either on or off.

10.16 Paint-type graphics are always black-and-white (meaning pixels are either on or off). You can *assign* color to the pixels). Paint-type are always 72 dots per inch. Their white background is usually transparent. You can create a paint graphic in most any *paint* program (such as MacPaint, SuperPaint, DeskPaint, or Photoshop; 10.95). The biggest problem with paint-type graphics is that when you enlarge them, the dots get bigger; when you reduce them, the dots smoosh together.

10.17   When you save a file in a paint program, save it in the file format "MacPaint" or "PNT."

10.18 PageMaker can *read* any bitmapped MacPaint graphic file, but once it is *placed* or *pasted* into PageMaker, it is no longer literally bitmapped. The image still holds onto its pixel-by-pixel *look*, but the graphic itself actually becomes a TIFF, even though PageMaker displays a paintbrush icon in the Control palette. If a paint image is *placed* from the Scrapbook, it becomes a PICT (10.24).

10.19 When you place a paint graphic, the cursor changes to a paintbrush, giving you a visual clue as to what type of graphic you are about to lay on your page:

10.20 When you resize a 72-dot-per-inch paint-type graphic, any patterns that may be in the graphic get scrunched or expanded, often creating a moiré pattern or a series of odd lines through the image. PageMaker provides a way to resize the graphic so the dots will match the resolution of the printer on which you will create the final output. It will still be a 72-dot-per-inch image, but it will be resized so the printer resolution can best accommodate it. PageMaker calls this "magic-resizing." See 10.141 and 10.142.

10.22 *A paint-type graphic resized normally.*

10.22 *A paint-type graphic resized using the "magic-resize" technique.*

PICT graphics 🖋

10.23 PICT graphics are not bitmapped, they are **object-oriented.** PICTs are created in draw-type programs, such as Canvas, MacDraw Pro, DeskDraw, or the draw portion of ClarisWorks. *Paint* graphics are created by turning dots on and off; *PICT* graphics are created as entire *objects,* defined by a mathematical formula. When a PICT is resized, it is not the dots that get larger or smaller. Using the formula, the computer actually redraws the image in a different size, so the resolution stays exactly the same. It is the *object* that gets resized, not the dots.

10.24 Almost any paint-type graphic can also be saved as a PICT; *this does not mean that it turns the existing paint dots into a math formula for a clearer image!* It just means that now, instead of being read dot-by-dot, the entire bunch of dots has been grouped into one inseparable image. If the image was created with paint dots to begin with, the dots will get bigger as the image is resized. Paint-type graphics placed from the Scrapbook are turned into PICTs (as shown directly below).

10.25 You cannot use image control (10.162–10.211) on a PICT, nor can you magic-resize it (10.33; 10.141–10.142).

10.26 There are two basic PICT formats: PICT and PICT 2 (color PICTs). Nowadays, you'll usually find both lumped together simply as PICTs. The PICT 2 format (if that's an option in the software you're using) has more enhanced capabilities, including high-resolution color. PageMaker can read both.

10.27 PICTs are not as dependable nor as precise as the other file types. The graphic on the right was created in the draw portion of SuperPaint and saved as a PICT and also as a MacPaint file. The MacPaint file has faithfully reproduced the original, the only problem being the bitmapped type (which *can* be a major drawback). The PICT, on the other hand, has unpredictably changed a number of elements, including the font. Whenever possible, save objects created in draw programs as EPS (10.39–10.46).

10.28 **As a general rule,** avoid saving files as PICTs unless that is your only choice. If you must save as a PICT, limit the image to *objects;* that is, don't try to include paint-type graphics in them, such as from the paint

10.29 *A paint-type file, created in the draw portion of SuperPaint and saved in the MacPaint format (the cat and rug are bitmapped).*

10.30 *This is the exact image as above, but saved as a PICT file.*

portion of SuperPaint. If you set type within the graphic, avoid *downloadable* fonts (19.33–19.35)—stick to the fonts that are installed in the printer's ROM (such as Helvetica, Times, Bookman, Avant Garde, etc.).

10.31 When printing to a PostScript printer, it is best, if you can, to convert PICTs to EPS or TIFF graphics through another program like Photoshop or Canvas. You *can* use the "PS Group it" Addition to group PICT images into an EPS file (see 10.259–10.291), but it probably *still* won't print the way you expect.

TIFF graphics

10.32 TIFF (tagged image file format) images are all bitmapped images, although they can be any size and resolution, and even grayscale or color. TIFFs come in three varieties:

- Black-and-white bitmaps (bi-level), usually created in a paint program and saved as a TIFF, or scanned in as line art (10.59).
- Palette-color TIFFs created in paint programs (16- or 256-color images).
- Grayscale or full-color TIFFs, created by scanning photographs or artwork (10.72).

10.33 Once a black-and-white or grayscale TIFF is placed in PageMaker, you can use image control on it (10.162–10.211). You can magic-resize (magic-stretch) bi-level TIFFs (10.20–10.22; 10.141–10.142). TIFF is the best format in which to save scanned images (10.54–10.65).

10.34 TIFFs can be quite large, so Page-Maker allows you to **compress** them (10.152). The printing quality is the same, and the compression can be sizable, so I recommend you get in the habit of regularly compressing the files as you place them. PageMaker also

gives you a choice when the file is large, of whether or not to include the entire file within the publication (10.101–10.106).

10.35 A color TIFF image will display as a grayscale image on a grayscale monitor, and will print as a grayscale on a black-and-white printer.

10.36 In the "Preferences" dialog box (from the File menu) you have a choice of viewing your detailed graphics on screen as gray boxes ("Gray out"), as "Normal" low-res versions, or as "High resolution" (10.155–10.157). The "High-resolution" *vs.* "Normal" choices visibly affect TIFFs more than any other format. If you've selected "High resolution," you'll find that it takes a great deal of time to redraw high-res TIFFs as you are working on the page. However, you can set your preference to "Normal," enjoy a quick-drawing screen, but at any time still *temporarily* view the images in high resolution just until you redraw the screen again: simply hold down the Control key (yes, that's Control, not Command) as the screen redraws (as when you resize an image, text wrap, change views, etc.; 10.158).

10.37 *Black-and-white bitmapped TIFFs, scanned as line art.*

10.38 *Scanned photograph, saved as a grayscale TIFF.*

EPS graphics

10.39 EPS graphics (Encapsulated Post-Script; aka EPSF) are created with high-end drawing programs, such as Adobe Illustrator or Aldus Freehand. *PostScript* is a page description language that can be read by PostScript printers, such as Apple and HP LaserWriters or linotronic imagesetters, and the output is smooth and clean and beautiful. Other printers use other languages, such as *QuickDraw* or *QuickScript,* and oftentimes can't interpret EPS files. Your printouts of EPS graphics from these printers will usually show just the low-resolution screen version, or they may ignore the image altogether.

10.40 It's possible to save a scanned image as an EPS, but the files are huge and you can't image control them. And it's not recommended that you save any bitmapped images as EPS, especially color bitmaps. On the plus side, some draw programs allow you to save images as EPS, which is often more preferable than those undependable PICTs. In PageMaker, you can also save a group of objects (10.284) or an entire publication page as an EPS file (10.160), and then place it into any other PageMaker publication as a graphic image (10.126).

10.41 An EPS file is actually made up of two parts—the high-resolution PostScript code and the low-resolution screen version. The PostScript code is a text document that tells a Postscript printer how to print the high-res image on paper. The low-res version is what you see on the screen. A non-PostScript printer can generally output only the low-res screen version.

10.42 If you're a programmer, you can write your own code to create or to edit EPS files. If you're mortal like the rest of us, you can create an EPS image in a software package like Aldus Freehand or Adobe Illustrator (see 10.97 and 10.98 for tips on how to best save those images so PageMaker can read them).

10.43 It is possible to place into PageMaker just the EPS code, rather than the screen version. This would happen if you inadvertently saved the graphic without following the advice in 10.97 or 10.98, or if you imported an EPS graphic created in another platform (probably Windows). Even though you may see only the code, the graphic itself will print—if you're

printing to a PostScript printer. It is a little disconcerting, though. If you are printing to a non-PostScript printer, all you will get is whatever you see on the screen.

10.44 *This is what an EPS file will look like on your screen if the screen version is not available.*

TITLE ToadHallLogo.ps
CREATOR: Freehand
CR DATE: 7/11/90 12

10.45 *Even if your screen shows just the code, as above, the graphic will print to a PostScript printer.*

Toad Hall
on Montecito

10.46 PANOSE does not recognize those fonts used in EPS graphics which are also missing from your System. When confronted with this situation it prints Courier. It is a good idea to get into the habit of converting fonts embedded within EPS graphics into objects (outlines) while still in the PostScript drawing program.

An EPS file, created in Illustrator by Tuan Pham. Based on the logo for The Tap Dance Studio.

Photo CD images ▨

10.47 Photo CD images are probably one of the most exciting things currently on the graphics horizon. Now you can access a file of color stock photography stored on CD-ROM. Or, have your own photographs transferred to CD-ROM disk by specialty service bureaus and photo developing labs. PageMaker lets you place photo images directly from your CD-ROM drive into your PageMaker document. Well, actually, she establishes a link between your publication and the Photo CD image.

10.48 Photo CD image files are huge, taking up between three to five or more megabytes of precious disk space. PageMaker *never* stores a Photo CD file within the publication. That means that if you are going to output your publication at a service bureau (which only makes sense anyway if you're printing a photograph), you need to take along the CD-ROM disk that has on it the image you used. If your service bureau doesn't have CD-ROM capabilities, you will have to transfer the image from the CD-ROM disk through an image enhancement program like Photoshop or PhotoStyler onto another type of storage disk (like a Syquest cartridge) and take *that* with you.

10.49 Photo CD images come into PageMaker through the "Place" dialog box just like any other graphic. Really, they are just an RGB color TIFF (16.141). Choosing "OVERVIEW.PCD" in the list box in the dialog box gives you a choice of images to select from a series of thumbnail previews. "PCD" is the tag for Photo CD files.

10.50 Always let PageMaker choose the resolution and color for you; she will automatically decide which resolution best matches the target printer you have selected and will bring in the graphic in its native color format. If you want to use the Photo CD image for a four-color printing job, you need to take it first into an image enhancement program that can convert it to a CMYK TIFF. (PageMaker cannot separate RGB color images, the default color format for Photo CD.) Better yet, have your service bureau do it for you.

Other graphic formats

10.51 The Library palette: Graphics can be collected in the Library palette and then simply dragged-and-dropped into a publication. Anything within a PageMaker document that you can copy to the Clipboard is fair game. All linking information is also copied. It doesn't get much simpler than this. See Section 12 for more information about how it works.

10.52 Other file formats: Although PageMaker is able to import file formats from a number of non-PageMaker compatible programs (including PC programs), most of us normal people will do just fine with the ones outlined here. But, if you get stuck, PageMaker has a good on-line guide to graphic file formats. See "Importing Files" in "Help Topics," the first Help dialog box (under the Window menu).

10.53 Video "grabs": For the truly adventurous with all the right equipment, PageMaker will import images captured from a video or television. Of course, you are stuck with the inherent low-resolution and PICT format that accompanies them, but, if you have all the equipment, you probably already know more about this than I do anyway.

Scanned images

10.54 Scanned images are images that have been created outside the computer and brought onto the screen through scanning hardware and software, rather than having been created in a graphics program and just placed or pasted onto the screen. The following recommendations are only for using with PageMaker; other programs may have different needs.

10.55 Scans come in three basic varieties: **line art, halftone,** and **grayscale**. Each variety can usually be saved as a TIFF (10.32–10.38), as an EPS (10.39–10.46), or as a PICT (10.23–10.31). **The preferred format is TIFF,** developed especially for scanning. Bit-mapped EPS files are huge and ungainly, plus you cannot image control them in PageMaker. PICTs are unreliable, and cannot be image controlled.

10.56 When you're scanning, it's generally best to scan as close to the finished size as possible, perhaps just a little bigger. You can always resize it in PageMaker, but you'll get the best results and save disk space if you don't have to make a radical correction.

10.57 Also, crop the image as much as possible when you create the scan. You can,

of course, crop it in PageMaker (10.143), but PageMaker holds onto the entire image, even the part that has been cropped off.

Thus, the file size remains just as hefty for a small portion of the graphic as it does for the entire image.

10.58

Scan as Line Art:	Advantages	Disadvantages
· Anything black-and-white, any image from a book or newspaper, pen-and-ink drawings, engravings, most clip art, almost any logo.	· It's easy to create good quality images. · Files are small. · They print quickly. · They resize well.	· Image has no gray values. · It's sometimes difficult to hold both the fine lines *and* the detail in the dark areas.
Scan as Halftone:	**Advantages**	**Disadvantages**
· Any image that has shades of gray or color, such as pencil or charcoal drawings, photographs. · If you are printing to a non-PostScript printer, it is usually best to use a halftone scan.	· You can usually control the pattern. · Files are small. · They print quickly. · Some scanning software corrects for laser printers, in which case it can be better than grayscale when printed on a laser printer.	· Must be scaled integrally (magic-resized; 10.20–22). · Difficult to edit. · Prints the same at high-res or low-res. · Cannot adjust contrast or brightness in PageMaker.
Scan as Grayscale:	**Advantages**	**Disadvantages**
· Any image that has shades of gray or color, such as pencil or charcoal drawings, photographs. · If you are printing to a high-res PostScript printer, use grayscale scan.	· Can edit and scale well. · Can adjust contrast and brightness in Page-Maker. · Can scan at lower res. · Extremely high quality available on high-res printer.	· Large files. · Slower printing. · White areas are opaque in PageMaker. · Usually requires large amounts of memory.

Line art scans

10.59 Scan black-and-white images as **line art TIFFs,** at the highest resolution possible. A black-and-white image is one that has no shades of gray. Sometimes an area may appear gray, but it is really an illusion, with small black or white dots—when little black dots are in a white space, or vice versa, it *appears* gray. Anything that has previously been printed is black-and-white, actually. Any clip art you find in books, any photo in a newspaper, any logo that has been printed on a page—these are all black-and-white line art. (Keep in mind that if it has been printed before, it may be copyrighted! Check.)

10.60 When scanning a black-and-white image, it doesn't do any good to adjust the "Contrast," because there is only one form of contrast and it's already there: black vs. white.

You *can* adjust the "Brightness," though. It's always a trade-off. You can brighten the image as you scan it to get more detail in the dark areas or to drop out dirt on the original. But fine lines in the light areas will fall apart. You can decrease the brightness to pick up fine details, but the dark areas will fill in. Below are examples.

10.61 Occasionally you may want to save a scanned black-and-white image as a grayscale in order to pick up the fine details (10.72). Again, it's a trade-off, this time between sharp, visual clarity and the detail in the darker areas. When making your choice, you'll also want to remember that white areas in line art are transparent; white areas in grayscale images are opaque (as shown by the black line below).

10.62 *Scanned with -12% brightness. Lines are heavier and blacks more solid. Notice the tiny spots where it's picking up dust on the page.*

10.63 *Normal line art scan with no adjustments made. White areas are transparent.*

10.64 *Scanned with +12% brightness. Notice the added detail in the dark areas, but the fine lines are falling apart.*

10.65 *Scanned as a grayscale TIFF. There's more detail, but it is also halftoned. White areas are opaque.*

Halftones, grayscales . . .

10.66 With digital halftoning, things can get complex, what with the different resolutions and halftone/dithering options and gray levels and screen frequencies all affecting each other. **This segment is meant only as a guide.** There are entire books written on scanning, halftones, and the variables and variations. You will always need to experiment to get your image just right, but my hope is that this section will cut down on the time and frustration it takes.

10.67 Any image that is not strictly black-and-white, such as a pencil or charcoal drawing, a color image, or an actual photograph, must be turned into black-and-white so it can be printed. Neither the laser printer nor the printing press can print shades of gray with black ink (or black toner)—each only prints a black-and-white *illusion* of gray. This has been true since printing began, and it will be true for a while to come.

10.68 So, in order to get a charcoal drawing or a photograph printed, you must turn those shades of gray into black dots. Tiny black dots on a white background look light gray; big black dots with less white area in the background look much darker—it's in this way that a printer is able to replicate various shades of gray, using only black ink or toner on white paper. An image that has had its shades turned into dots is **halftoned** (giving it half the tone it started with), or **screened.**

10.69 A halftone can have a very fine *screen* or a very coarse *screen* (or anything in-between). The fineness of the screen is measured in **lines per inch.** A halftone with a 53-line screen would have 53 rows of dots per inch; a 133-line screen would have 133 rows of dots per inch. You can see from the examples below that the 53-line screen is much coarser.

10.70 No matter which of the following methods you choose to halftone your image (10.74), you need to know what line screen

105-line screen   *53-line screen*

your commercial press will need in order to produce your job. Newspapers generally use a 75- or 85-line screen (look carefully at a newspaper photo and you can easily see the dots that create the image). Any printing press with the word *speedy, quick,* or *instant* in its name generally uses an 85- to 100-line screen (copy machines deal best with that frequency, also). Glossy magazines generally use 120- or 133-line screens. High-quality art books use 150- or 175-line screens. Line screens over 110 should be printed onto film.

10.71 When you choose to scan an image as a **halftone** (10.54–10.65), the scanner turns the gray tones into printer-readable black-and-white dots: each dot on the screen is either black or white. The scanned halftone is then called a "flat" or "bi-level" bitmap.

10.72 When you choose to scan an image as a **grayscale,** each dot on the screen holds more information than just whether it is black or white; it goes four to eight levels deep, and each dot can register a different depth, or gray value. Sort of like looking into a pond—where the water is deep, it looks darker; where it is shallow, it looks lighter. The many levels of gray it contains are

...and scanning

trying to approximate the *continuous gray tone,* the gradual blend of black to white, of which photographs are comprised. *In order to print a grayscale image, either on your laser printer or on a commercial press, you must still halftone the grayscale image (10.74–10.78)*

10.73 There is a complex connection between the printer resolution, the line screen, and the number of gray levels an image can have. Generally you will hear about 16-level and 256-level grayscale values. Some scanners let you choose the grayscale depth level, and some just give you the deepest possible and let you monkey with the levels that will eventually be visible as you change the line screen and the printer.

10.74 There are three ways to halftone an image you want to work with in PageMaker:

- You can halftone it when you scan it.
- You can scan the image as a *grayscale* and halftone it on the PageMaker publication page through "Image control" (10.162–10.211).
- You can scan the image as a *grayscale* and let the PostScript printer halftone it as it gets printed (10.77).

10.75 As a rule of thumb, **it's best to scan the image as a grayscale** and then halftone it in PageMaker or on the printer. If you scan it as a halftone, the file will be nice and small, as it turns into just a black-and-white image. But you will always be stuck with the line screen you scanned it in with, and you won't be able to adjust the brightness or the contrast. You have more options using a grayscale.

10.76 You should still halftone a grayscale image before you print it. One way to do this is through the "Image control" dialog box (10.162–10.167), which allows you to give your image the line screen and the angle you want, as well as to adjust the brightness and the contrast (10.18–10.203).

10.77 Or you can let a PostScript printer halftone it for you. A 300-dpi LaserWriter will apply a 53-line screen (see 10.86) to any grayscale image it finds that doesn't have a screen already applied. It doesn't have high enough resolution to distinguish between 16 and 256 levels of gray. If your final output will be to a laser printer, save the image as a 16-level TIFF (if your scanning software lets you) to keep the file size to a minimum. It will look as good as a 256-level image.

10.78 High-resolution imagesetters can take advantage of the information provided in a 256-level grayscale. They have a much higher default line screen; for instance, a Linotronic will automatically apply a default of a 150-line halftone screen. Most service bureaus reset the default to around 105 (see 10.70), as 150-line is too fine for most work. If you want a different line screen than the imagesetter's default, you can apply it through the "Image control" dialog box (10.162–10.195) to each grayscale image, one at a time. Or you can ask the service bureau to change the PPD (19.11) so all the images will use the same line screen automatically.

10.79 By the way, the printer's default line screen (in laser printers, as well as in high-resolution imagesetters) applies to any and all screens in a publication—drawn boxes with fills, gray tints applied to text or lines, etc.

Halftone examples

*(**Always** magic-resize images that have been scanned as halftones! See 10.20–10.22; 10.141–10.142)*

Scanned as a halftone *(10.66–10.71)*

10.80 *Halftoned with a 53-line screen; Apple LaserWriter IINT. If you don't like the way a scanned halftone looks after you print it, you have to rescan it; you can't adjust it within PageMaker.*

10.81 *Halftoned with a 71-line screen; Apple LaserWriter IINT.*

10.82 *Halftoned with a 71-line screen; Linotronic (1270 dpi).*

Scanned as a grayscale, halftoned through Image control *(10.162–10.167)*

10.83 *Grayscale; Apple LaserWriter IINT; 53-line screen applied. Notice it looks the same as when the LaserWriter applies the screen itself (10.86).*

10.84 *Grayscale; HP Deskwriter; 53-line screen applied. Any screen you apply in "Image control" will override the printer's default screen.*

10.85 *Grayscale; Linotronic (1270 dpi); 85-line screen applied. Any screen you apply in "Image control" will override the printer's default screen.*

Scanned as a grayscale, halftoned through the printer *(10.77–10.79)*

10.86 *Grayscale; Apple LaserWriter IINT; 53-line screen default.*

10.87 *Grayscale; HP DeskWriter; 53-line screen default.*

10.88 *Grayscale; Linotronic (1270 dpi); 105-line screen default.*

yes, that's me in 1953.

Rules of thumb for grayscale scans

10.89 In general, don't halftone at the scanner; apply the halftone in the "Image control" dialog box (10.162–10.167) **or** let the printer halftone it (10.77–10.78).

10.90 When you scan an image as a grayscale, set the dpi (dots per inch) at no more than twice the line screen at which it will be printed. For instance, even though a LaserWriter has a resolution of 300 dpi, the default line screen for halftoning is **53 lines per inch.** So, scan the image at around 106 dpi. Extra image data that is more than twice the line screen is ignored, and just makes your file larger. To find out the default line screen of your printer, you can read your PPD file (19.11) or ask your printer's Tech Support.

Scanned at 210 dpi; printed with 105-line screen.   *Scanned at 300 dpi; printed with 105-line screen.*

10.91 What a grayscale image looks like on the screen doesn't have much to do with what it will look like when printed. That's not very comforting, I know.

This is what the photo in 10.88 looked like on my screen at Actual Size.

10.92 If you will be printing to a high-resolution imagesetter, the output on the laser printer will not give you a very good representation of what to expect from the imagesetter. That's not very comforting, either. Below, the first photo was printed on an Apple LaserWriter IINT; the second photo, with the same image-control settings, was printed on a Linotronic 300.

 LaserWriter

 Linotronic

10.93 When a halftone is printed on a commercial press or on a copy machine, the tiny little black dots you see in the white

areas will drop out (disappear). The tiny little white dots you see in the black areas will clog up. So inevitably, every image that comes out of any imagesetter is going to develop more contrast when it's finally reproduced—the lights will be lighter and the darks will be darker. **It's important to adjust for this** by image-controlling the TIFF so it comes out of *your* printer rather gray and flat-looking. When you first start working with halftones, it's hard to make yourself create a flat-looking image; we want to see it sharp and crispy. Control yourself. The photo below, on the left, was gray and dull on the screen, as well as from the LaserWriter. The photo on the right was adjusted so it looked crispy on the screen, with dark blacks and light whites. But after going through the imagesetter and then the printing press, the crispy one has lost too much detail in both the dark and light areas; the grayer one on the left picked up contrast in the process. See 10.199 for a standard setting for producing a decent halftone.

The best way to save a graphic image for placement into PageMaker

10.94 When you create a graphic in a graphic program, you generally have a choice of file formats in which to save the image. You make the choice as you "Save as…" and name the file. If you have already created and saved the graphic with a name, you can open it in its program and choose "Save as…" again, give it another name, and thus save a copy in another format. It's a good idea to include the type of file format in the name, so when you see the name in a list box you will know what you are looking at (e.g., Cats/macpaint, or Cats/tiff).

10.95 Paint programs: Save as a **Mac-Paint** file. Even in SuperPaint you must save it as a MacPaint file if you want PageMaker to read it. Paint programs are the ones where you can use brushes to wipe a pattern across the screen, and an eraser to remove things. Fractal Painter, Canvas, and SuperPaint are paint programs. Believe it or not, so is Photoshop. They are bitmapped. Some can save files in a variety of formats including TIFF or EPS. Don't save paint images as PICTs (10.28).

10.96 Draw programs: Save as a **PICT** file, or, if your software lets you, as an **EPS**. Draw programs are *object-oriented*. If the images you create have handles on them, like PageMaker-drawn boxes, and you select items by clicking on them with a pointer tool, then it is a draw program. MacDraw and DeskDraw are draw programs. Save as a PICT if the image contains only object-oriented graphics or type (preferably ROM fonts; 10.28)—if you add any paint stuff to it, the PICT will be very undependable (10.27–10.31), and you may be better off saving it as a MacPaint or EPS file.

10.97 Adobe Illustrator: Illustrator files automatically save as **EPS** files. You have a choice of whether to include the screen version along with the PostScript code in the file (10.41–10.46). If you want to make sure you will be able to see the graphic itself on the screen, rather than just the structuring comments in a gray box, then make a selection in the "Include preview for"—select either "Black and White Macintosh" or "Color Macintosh," depending on the screen on which you will be viewing it. If you placed other EPS files within this graphic, then also click the checkbox to "Include copy of placed EPS files for other applications."

10.98 Aldus Freehand: PageMaker cannot read a Freehand file. You must use the "Export…" command under the File menu. This gives you the "Export as Encapsulated PostScript" dialog box. With PageMaker's "hotlinks" feature, if you update the original illustration, the EPS version is automatically updated along with it (10.109)!

10.99 DeskPaint: With most other graphic programs, it is always safe to save as a TIFF (preferably) or as an EPS or MacPaint file. A TIFF is usually preferable because you can get a higher resolution than a PAINT file in the image and see image enhancement right on the screen (see 10.33).

10.100 Photoshop: There are photo enhancement and graphic conversion programs available like Photoshop and Graphic Converter that can save files in a PageMaker compatible format (including converting PICTs to EPS or TIFF files). Some of the PAINT programs (like Canvas and SuperPaint) can even open and save files in a variety of formats. If you don't have these programs, ask your service bureau if they can do this for you.

"Include complete copy?"

10.101 Even though PageMaker links *all* placed graphics to the original by default, she also stores a copy in the publication unless you go in and specifically change the linking options. When placing a large graphic file, you may see this alert box:

10.102 The links let PageMaker update the files you placed in the publication with any changes you make in the original files. Pretty amazing.

10.103 The default link option is to "Store copy in publication." This means that PageMaker will keep a copy of the graphic as part of the publication itself, as opposed to keeping only a low-resolution screen version in the publication. If only the low-res version is stored, PageMaker follows the link to the external, original file when she needs complete information in order to display or print the publication. See Section 11 for an in-depth look at Linking.

10.104 However, if a graphic file is larger than 256K (or whatever size you specified in the "Preferences" dialog box; see 1.232–1.233), PageMaker will ask if you really do want to store the whole thing in the publication, even if "Store copy in publication" is checked. If you choose "Yes," your publication size will increase by that amount. This can be significant if you have more than a couple of graphic images. The larger and more ungainly the publication size, the slower PageMaker operates.

10.105 You will also see this alert box when you update an existing publication file that is over the file size you specified in Preferences, or when the update will enlarge the file to more than you specified.

10.106 If you are not using large files, or if you don't care about updating changes in them, then you can ignore or break the links (11.3; 11.64). All your graphics can be stored in the publication, and everything will act just the same as it did before linking was invented.

p.s. All OLE-embedded files are always stored in the publication anyway, whether you like it or not (11.111–11.114).

Update original copy

10.107 If you *place* a graphic (this includes OLE linking and embedding and Publish and Subscribe), you can update the copy within PageMaker every time you change the original. That means whenever you open a PageMaker document, you will immediately see any little changes or additions to a logo, a scan, or a chart that you made in the original graphics program. Automatic updating of a file can be disabled through the "Link options…" dialog box in the Element menu. See 11.55–11.57.

10.108 You can also edit the originals of linked graphics while in PageMaker through "Edit original" in the Edit menu. Just by selecting the graphic and double-clicking on it (or using the "Editions" submenu under "Edit" for "Subscribed to" graphics) you can launch the original program in which the graphic was created. If you don't have access to the original program, you may be able to launch another, compatible program, all right from within PageMaker (10.147).

10.109 Graphics created in Freehand 3.1, Persuasion 2.1, PhotoStyler 1.1, PrePrint 1.5, or ColorStudio 1.5 *or later* are "hotlinked" and are updated everytime you make a "Save" in the original graphic.

Paste and Paste special...

10.110 Pasting a graphic from the Clipboard into PageMaker is usually a pretty straightforward process: select and copy the graphic and then paste it into the publication by choosing "Paste" from the Edit menu. But if you want to guarantee the integrity of the graphic format you bring into your publication, you have to pay attention to how the Clipboard works.

10.111 Programs copy items to the Clipboard in a variety of formats so they will be accessible to a variety of different applications. When you paste a copied graphic into a program, it automatically selects the format it reads best. If you are copying and pasting within PageMaker this works just fine.

10.112 When pasting from the Clipboard in PageMaker, she automatically selects the richest file format that holds the most information. When you are pasting text, PageMaker selects a format that gives you editing power but also preserves the formatting. When you are pasting graphics, she picks the one that will best preserve the integrity of the original graphic. But what PageMaker also lets you do is override her decision, if you want to, through "Paste

special" (from the Edit menu) and choose the file format in which *you* want to place the Clipboard object. Of course, your choices are limited to formats PageMaker supports.

10.113 These choices depend on what is on the Clipboard. If more than one format is available, they are listed in descending order with the richest at the top of the list and the less desirable ones at the bottom. If it's an image you copied from a paint program, for example, the only choice is

probably "PICT" because that's the common ground between the paint program and PageMaker. If it's a paint image you copied from another PageMaker publication, however, you also have the choice of "Page-Maker 5.0 format" which pastes the graphic in with its paint format intact. If it's an EPS graphic from another PageMaker publication, PageMaker picks its own PageMaker format, but it also offers you a choice of selecting, in descending order, either EPS or PICT. If you copy it from another program, your only choice will be PICT.

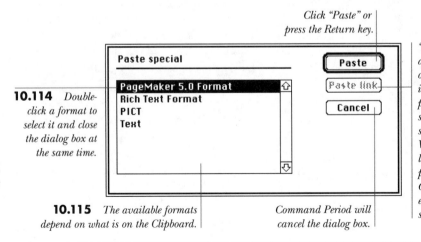

Click "Paste" or press the Return key.

"Paste link" is available when the object on the Clipboard is from an OLE server program, and you select the format that supports the link. When you "Paste link," the object is pasted in with an OLE-link to its external file; see 11.124.

10.114 *Double-click a format to select it and close the dialog box at the same time.*

10.115 *The available formats depend on what is on the Clipboard.*

Command Period will cancel the dialog box.

...Insert object and Publish and Subscribe

10.116 Select a format by simply clicking on it and then clicking the "Paste" button. The object pastes into the publication without any link to any external file.

10.117 When a graphic is not in a compatible format, PageMaker can't simply paste or place it. That's when you turn to OLE-linking or -embedding and Publish and Subscribe ("Editions"), also found in the Edit menu.

10.118 If the object on the Clipboard is from an OLE server program, the "Paste link" command in the "Paste special" dialog box becomes available. This is the same command as the one directly under the Edit menu (see 11.124).

10.119 Choosing "Paste" from the "Paste special…" dialog box breaks all links to the original file. "Paste link" establishes an OLE-link. Of course, this only works if the source file was an OLE file to begin with.

10.120 OLE-linking and -embedding require graphic programs that support Microsoft's OLE technology (such as Word and Excel or various Windows software). An OLE-*embedded* graphic lets you update the object without having to establish and maintain a link with the original graphic. OLE-*linked* graphics require regular linking updates just like all other graphics. See Section 11 for more on linking.

10.121 By choosing "Insert object…" and a graphic type, the OLE program that can create that graphic starts up, gives you a new, untitled document with which you can create the graphic, and embeds it right in the publication (11.126–11.132).

10.122 "Publish and Subscribe" works outside the OLE-savvy environment with graphics programs that do *not* produce PageMaker compatible graphic formats but that *do* publish editions. This includes Freehand, Canvas, Photoshop, Illustrator, and MacDraw Pro. It can be particularly useful for network users who want to subscribe to a commonly held graphic like a company logo, or to commonly used graphics that are periodically updated such as those that might be used in a promotional campaign. See Section 11 for info on "P and S."

Independent *vs.* inline graphics

10.123 Any kind of graphic in PageMaker can be placed or pasted on the page in one of two ways: either as an **independent** graphic or as an **inline** graphic.

10.124 An **independent** graphic is one that is not embedded in any text block, but is just sitting on the page all by itself, just like you would expect it to. If you move the graphic, nothing else moves with it. If you do anything to any other element on the page (such as cut, delete, copy, rotate, or resize), the action doesn't affect the independent graphic.

10.125 An **inline** graphic is one that you place or paste directly into a text block, just as you would a text character. You can apply some text attributes to it, but you can still treat it as a graphic in other respects, such as rotating or cropping it independently from the text. As part of the text, it will move along just like a character as you edit. You can roll it up in a windowshade, or cut it along with the text block. See 10.213–10.251 for full details.

If you want to do this:

Then follow these steps:

Shortcuts ▾ Notes ▾ Hints

Independent graphics

10.126 Place a graphic

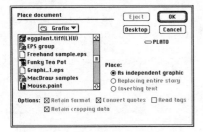

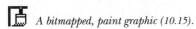

A bitmapped, paint graphic (10.15).

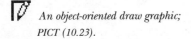

An object-oriented draw graphic; PICT (10.23).

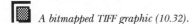

A bitmapped TIFF graphic (10.32).

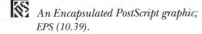

An Encapsulated PostScript graphic; EPS (10.39).

A Scrapbook PICT graphic (10.130).

- Click once on the **pointer tool** even if the pointer tool is already selected. This is to prevent accidentally placing the graphic inline.
- From the File menu choose "Place...."
- Find the name of the graphic file in the list box; you may need to switch drives and folders to find it. You will know it is a graphic when you click once on it, because the top button under "Place" will become "As independent graphic."
- Click once on the name of the file, then click OK; **or** double-click on the name of the file.
- Depending on the file format of the graphic, you will get one of the cursors shown on the left (a loaded graphic icon). Simply click the loaded cursor on the page and the graphic will pour on; the top left corner of the graphic will be positioned wherever you click.
- If you immediately decide you don't want it at all, just hit the Backspace/Delete key.

- See 10.123–10.125 to understand the difference between independent graphics and inline graphics. Basically, an independent graphic is its own little entity on the page, separate from anything else. An inline graphic is actually part of the text block, and will reflow with any text editing.
- When an object is selected, you will see the same graphic icons on the Control palette "Apply" button. This is a good visual clue as to the kind of graphic with which you are working.
- Use the Control palette to guide you in precisely placing an object: drag-place the loaded icon (10.127) and use the X- and Y-coordinates to tell you where your icon is on the publication page, and the H and W sizing options to tell you the exact size of the object as you drag it into place (3.32–3.33 and 3.36).

If you want to do this:	**Then follow these steps:**	**Shortcuts ▾ Notes ▾ Hints**
10.127 Drag-place a graphic	■ Select a file to place, just as in 10.126. ■ Instead of clicking to put the graphic on the page, press-and-drag with the loaded graphic icon. You will see a bounding box. When you let go of the mouse button, the graphic will flow into the space you created.	■ Unfortunately, you can't use the Shift key to restrain the bounding box to the proper proportions of the graphic. If you don't like the proportions, see 10.140.
10.128 Replace a graphic 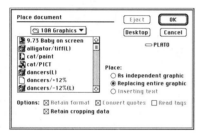	■ On the publication page, select the graphic you want to replace (click once on it with the **pointer tool**). ■ From the File menu choose "Place...." ■ Find the name of the file you want to place; click once on it. ■ On the right, under "Place," you will have an option of "Replacing entire graphic." Click in that button. ■ Next to "Options" you can check "Retain cropping data." Check this box if you want the new graphic to retain the same cropping and proportions of the original one. ■ Click OK, *or* double-click on the file name. ■ You won't get a loaded graphic icon this time; PageMaker will just go ahead and get rid of the graphic on the page that you selected earlier, and replace it with this one. *This new one will take on the size and shape of the one it is replacing.* If the new one has the wrong proportions, see 10.140.	■ The new graphic will replace the selected graphic, taking on the size and shape of the selected one. If you are replacing a file with the *same one* in a new, updated version, the new one will drop in with the same cropping as the old one it is replacing. ■ All cropping information from the original graphic is automatically retained for all linked, hotlinked, OLE-linked, or embedded graphics, or for editions (see 10.109, 11.03–11.08, 11.69, and 11.79–11.87).

If you want to do this:	Then follow these steps:	Shortcuts ▾ Notes ▾ Hints

10.129 Paste a graphic from the Scrapbook

- Choose the **pointer tool.**
- From the Apple menu choose "Scrapbook."
- Find the image you want to paste. From the Edit menu choose "Copy," *or* press Command C. Click in the close box.
- While on the publication page, from the Edit menu choose "Paste," *or* press Command V.

- Graphics from the Scrapbook will retain their format when they paste into PageMaker.

10.130 Place a graphic from the Scrapbook

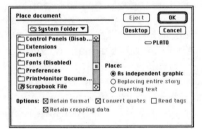

The Scrapbook File is in the System Folder, as you can see in the list box above.

 This is the loaded graphic icon you will see when you place the Scrapbook. The number indicates the number of items loaded into the icon. Each time you click, this number will decrease.

- Click once on the **pointer tool.**
- Make sure the Scrapbook is *closed,* not just hiding behind the PageMaker window (click in the Scrapbook close box).
- From the File menu, choose "Place...."
- Navigate to the System folder (see 18.7– 18.10 if you need help).
- Click once on "Scrapbook File."
- Under "Place," make sure the button "As independent graphic" is clicked on.
- Double-click on the "Scrapbook File."
- You will get a loaded graphic icon, as shown on the left. The number indicates the number of items in the Scrapbook.
- Each time you click the mouse, the next item in the Scrapbook will place on the page, starting with the first.
- When you don't want any more items, click the pointer tool in the Toolbox to absorb the extras.

- It's extremely important to make sure you click on that pointer tool to ensure that there is no insertion point lying around somewhere. You can inadvertently place an entire Scrapbook into an insertion point that may even be on another page altogether. You probably won't even know it because the text block can't figure out what to do with all those things that were in your Scrapbook, so it rolls itself up and you can't figure out where the heck the stuff went. So maybe you even try it again and then you're really in trouble 'cause you can't even unroll the text block to remove the stuff once you figure out where it landed. Do you wonder how I know about this dilemma? See 10.242 for a tip on how to deal with it.
- Any lines finer than 1 point will be converted into 1-point lines when placed.

If you want to do this:	Then follow these steps:	Shortcuts · Notes · Hints
10.131 Place a graphic from the Library palette	■ If it is not already open, choose the Library palette from the Window menu. ■ Scroll through the Library palette until you find the graphic you want. ■ With any tool, select the graphic and drag it to the spot you want on your publication page. The icon will stay loaded until you release the graphic.	■ See Section 12 about the Library palette. ■ Colors in EPS and PageMaker-drawn graphics drop into the new publication's Color palette.
10.132 Paste a graphic from the Clipboard	■ In any program, you can put any graphic on the Clipboard: select it and cut or copy it as usual. See 10.133 and 1.280–1.281. ■ Quit that program and open PageMaker. ■ Just press Command V to paste the graphic right on the page. You have to remember not to cut or copy anything else before you paste into PageMaker.	■ The Clipboard is part of the Macintosh System; it is not part of any particular program. So whatever you put into it in one application (say, SuperPaint) will stay right there while you go to another program (say, PageMaker). When you turn off the Mac, anything that was on the Clipboard will disappear. ■ You can **power paste** a graphic into the exact position it was cut or copied from by pressing Command Option V. It will land directly on top of the original unless the original location is no longer visible, then it will paste into the center of the screen.
10.133 Cut or copy a graphic	■ First select the graphic with the **pointer tool.** Cut or copy it just as you cut or copy anything on the Mac. ■ From the Edit menu choose "Cut" (Command X) or "Copy" (Command C).	■ See Section 1, Basics, for info on cutting, copying, pasting, and the Clipboard: 1.273–1.276 and 1.280–1.286.

If you want to do this:

Then follow these steps:

Shortcuts ▾ Notes ▾ Hints

10.134 Copy a graphic by dragging-and-dropping it between PageMaker 5 publications

- Open the publications you want to copy a graphic from and to in "Tile" view (under the Window menu).
- Make sure the **pointer tool** is selected in the publication to which you are dragging the graphic.
- With the **pointer tool** select the graphic in the original publication and with the mouse button pressed down, drag it into the new publication.
- When you see the graphic appear in the new publication, let go of the mouse.

- You can drag-and-drop any object between open publications: graphics, PageMaker-drawn objects, text blocks, even groups of objects (1.179–1.180).

10.135 Choose a paste format for a Clipboard item

- The item you want to paste must be on the Clipboard 1.273–1.279).
- From the Edit menu choose "Paste special…."
- In the "Paste special" dialog box select the format you want, then click the "Paste" button, *or* press Return;
- **Or** double-click on the format to select it and close the dialog box at the same time (10.114).

- To see what is on the Clipboard, choose "Show Clipboard" from the Window menu. Click the close box to put the window away, or select "Close" from the File menu (Command W).
- Anything copied from a PageMaker publication is automatically given "PageMaker 5.0 Format."
- If you choose "Paste," or Command V, instead of "Paste special," PageMaker will select the format at the top of the list.

10.136 Delete a graphic

- Delete a graphic as you delete anything on the Mac: click once on it with the **pointer tool,** then hit the Backspace/Delete key (*or* choose "Clear" from the Edit menu).

- When you cut or copy a graphic, it goes onto the Clipboard. When you "Clear" or Backspace/Delete it, it is really gone. You can immediately Command Z to Undo.

If you want to do this:

Then follow these steps:

Shortcuts ▾ Notes ▾ Hints

10.137 Move a graphic

✛ *The four-headed arrow, indicating the graphic is in moving mode.*

- With the **pointer tool,** press-and-drag on the graphic. *Make sure you don't press on any handle.* You should see a four-headed arrow; if you see a two-headed arrow, you have grabbed a handle and will end up *stretching,* not *moving,* the graphic (10.138).
- If you press-and-drag *quickly,* you will see just a rectangular outline as you move the graphic. This is a **fast move** (1.197).
- If you press and *hold it,* waiting until you see the watch cursor, *then* the four-headed arrow, you will see the entire graphic as you move it. This is a **slow move** (1.198).

- If you see this symbol when you press: ⊞ it means the graphic is an *inline* graphic. You cannot move it the same way as an independent graphic; see 10.232–10.233.
- If you accidentally stretch the graphic, instantly press Command Z to Undo the stretch.
- You can also move objects with the Control palette; see 3.87 and 3.88. By entering values in the edit boxes of the Control palette, you can move objects with precision for those publications that demand that kind of attention.

10.138 Resize a graphic

Original graphic.

Stretched horizontally.

Stretched vertically.

Stretched proportionally with the Shift key.

- With the **pointer tool,** click once on the graphic.
- With the very tip of the **pointer tool,** press-and-drag on a handle.
  - Pressing on a side handle will resize the graphic horizontally.
  - Pressing on a top or bottom handle will resize the graphic vertically.
  - Pressing on a corner handle will resize the graphic in both directions.
- To resize the graphic **proportionally,** hold down the Shift key while stretching on any handle.

- Again, you can use the Control palette for precise resizing by entering new values for the graphic's reference point in the "Position" option (3.89).
- Click on "Proportional-scaling" in the Control palette to resize a graphic proportionally. All amounts or percentages entered in one dimension will automatically determine the amounts for the other dimension in order to keep the graphic proportional. See 3.73 and 3.92 for more about the "Proportional-scaling" option.

If you want to do this:	Then follow these steps:	Shortcuts ▾ Notes ▾ Hints

10.139 Resize a graphic using the Scaling option on the Control palette

 The Scaling option sits above the Cropping option. You can toggle back and forth between the two when one of them is selected by pressing the arrow keys. See 3.74.

- With the **pointer tool,** click once on the graphic. Notice that the "Scaling" option button in the Control palette is automatically highlighted.
- Select a reference point on the "Proxy" from which to resize the graphic.
- Enter either the percentage by which you want to resize the graphic in the "Percentage-scaling" option edit box;
- **Or,** enter the amount by which you want to resize the graphic in the "Sizing" option edit box;
- **Or,** click the Nudge buttons next to either edit box.
- Click on the "Apply" button *or* hit Return.

- You can resize a graphic by entering a percentage amount in the "Percentage-scaling" edit box, or by entering actual measurements in the "Sizing" option edit boxes.
- Notice that the Sizing options (H and W) and their corresponding "Percentage-scaling" options are active according to which reference point is active on the Proxy: a point along the top of the Proxy makes the height active; a point along the side makes the width active; a point on the corners or in the center makes both options active.
- The point selected on the Proxy can affect the graphic in very strange ways if you don't fully understand how the active reference point works. Review the section on the Proxy in the Control palette section, 3.48–3.59.

10.140 Resize a graphic back into its original proportions

- With the **pointer tool,** click once on the graphic.
- Position the very tip of the pointer on one of the handles.
- Hold the Shift key down and *press* on that corner handle to the count of three. The graphic will pop back into its original *proportions,* although not its original *size.*

- If you prefer to use the Control palette, you can resize the graphic back to its original proportions by clicking on the "Proportional-scaling" button. See 3.34, 3.73 and 3.92.

If you want to do this:	Then follow these steps:	Shortcuts ▾ Notes ▾ Hints

10.141 "Magic-resize" a bi-level graphic

A graphic resized normally.

A graphic resized magically.

- From the File menu choose "Page setup...."
- Select your final output resolution from the pop-up menu next to "Target printer resolution." If the proper resolution is not listed, just type it into the edit box.
- Follow the steps in 10.138 to resize a graphic, either vertically, horizontally, or both. *Before you press-and-drag, though, hold down the* **Command** *key.* The graphic will resize in jumps.
- To magic-resize *proportionally,* hold down both the Command *and* the Shift keys.
- **Or**, use the "Printer-resolution-scaling" button *along with* the "Proportional-scaling" button on the Control palette. See 10.142, below.

- Magic-resizing only works on black-and-white bitmapped images (paint-type or black-and-white TIFF images); it does not work on PICTs, even if they hold a bitmapped image, and it doesn't need to work on EPS files.
- Magic-resizing is a technique to enhance the look of bitmapped graphics by matching the screen pattern of the graphic with the resolution of the printer. This means, though, that PageMaker must know the resolution of the printer on which you are going to print *the final output.* For instance, if you are doing proofs on a laser printer, but you are going to an imagesetter for the final output, you need to resize the graphics for the imagesetter.
- Magic-resizing works on files that have been *placed* or *pasted.* You will know if it's working or not because when you magic-resize, the image jumps from size to size in big leaps. Thus your image size is more limited than when you are resizing normally. The higher the printer resolution, the more sizes you can adjust to.
- If you change the "Target printer resolution" after resizing images, you need to go back and resize them again for the new printer resolution you have selected.

10.142 "Magic-resize" a bi-level graphic using the "Printer-resolution" option on the Control palette

Printer-resolution option on

Printer-resolution option off

- With the graphic selected, turn on the "Printer-resolution-scaling" option by clicking on it before resizing the graphic.
- If "Proportional-scaling" is also on, PageMaker will sacrifice proportion and adjust the object first to the correct printer resolution.
- When the "Printer-resolution" option is active, you can toggle it on and off by pressing the Spacebar.

If you want to do this:	**Then follow these steps:**	**Shortcuts ▾ Notes ▾ Hints**

10.143 Crop a graphic, uncrop a graphic, and pan a graphic

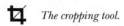

The cropping tool.

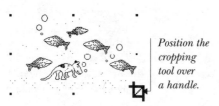

Position the cropping tool over a handle.

*When you press on a **handle** with the cropping tool, you will get an arrow to crop with.*

*When you press on the **image** with the cropping tool, you will get the grabber hand. Press-and-drag to pan (move) the image within the frame.*

- With the **cropping tool,** click once on the graphic. The handles you see will look like standard handles.
- Center the *inside* of the cropping tool directly over one of the handles (see left).
- Press-and-drag the handle in toward the center. This does not *resize* the image; it actually chops off, or *crops*, the part you drag over. Dragging the side handles will crop just horizontally or just vertically, the same as when you resize. Dragging a corner handle will crop in both directions at once.
- Cropping is not like using scissors; if you want to **uncrop the image,** simply drag back out. You can uncrop it even after you have resized it, or cut and pasted the image. Even though you can't see the entire image, it will always hang onto its whole self and you can pull it back out any time.
- After you have cropped it down to the necessary size, you can **pan the image.** This is too cool, you really must try it. After it's cropped, with the **cropping tool,** *press* on the center of the image. The tool will turn into the grabber hand and you can move the image around *within the frame.* Even after you cut and paste a cropped image, you can always go in and pan the pasted version again.

- The cropping tool icon is derived from the L-shaped pieces of cardboard that designers and photographers have traditionally used for making decisions as to where an image should be *cropped,* or chopped off. We put the two Ls together, as shown in the cropping tool icon, and moved them in and out from each other to frame just the part of the image to keep. An image is rarely used full-frame, unless the photographer has a great design sense, or unless the photos have been very tightly directed by an art director. Even so, often it is necessary to crop out an awkward corner, or a bit off the top, or some fingers along the bottom that happened to get stuck in the photo. Or the original has three people in it and you want only one person's face. Or often you may find a little piece of something useless attached to some clip art you copy in from somewhere else. These are all typical uses of the cropping tool.
- In general, though, avoid major cropping. Whenever possible, take the image into a graphic program and remove what you don't need. Even though you may see only a fraction of the original graphic, the entire image is still there, taking up lots of space and potentially causing printing problems.

If you want to do this:

Then follow these steps:

Shortcuts ▾ Notes ▾ Hints

10.144 Crop a graphic using the "Cropping" option in the Control palette

- With the **cropping tool,** click once on the graphic;
- **Or,** with the **pointer tool,** click once on the graphic and then on the **"Cropping" option** in the Control palette.
- Select a reference point on the Proxy and enter new size values for the graphic in the "Sizing" option.
- Selecting the center point on the Proxy will crop the graphic in equally from all edges by the specified amount.
- Click the Nudge buttons to crop in miniscule increments.
- Click on the "Apply" button, *or* hit Return.
- **Pan the image** if necessary in the normal manner (10.143).

- You cannot specify a size that will make the graphic exceed its original boundary.
- If the "Scaling" option is already highlighted, toggle between it and the "Cropping" option with the arrow keys (any of them will work).
- This requires a little experimentation to get it down. If the reference point is a box, the corresponding handle on the graphic stays put. If it is an arrow, the corresponding handle moves to create the crop. You really have to understand how the reference points on the Proxy work to be able to use the "Cropping" option effectively. Re-read Section 3.

10.145 Transform a graphic (*skew, rotate, or reflect*) using the Control palette

Skewed   *Rotated*   *Reflected*

This teapot was transformed by 30° in all three instances on the center reference point.

- Select the graphic with the **pointer tool.**
- Click on the "Reflecting" buttons to flip, or invert, the graphic.
- Enter a value (or click a Nudge button) in the "Skewing" option box to distort the graphic.
- Enter a value (or click a Nudge button) in the "Rotating" option box to rotate the graphic by a specific percentage.
- Click on the Apply button or hit Return.

- Transforming objects with the Control palette is throughly discussed in the Control palette Section, 3.76–3.86 and 3.93–3.100. Anything you can do with the Control palette to PageMaker-drawn objects or text blocks you can do with an imported graphic as well.
- To remove any and all transformations of a selected object, simply choose "Remove transformations," under the Element menu.

If you want to do this:	Then follow these steps:	Shortcuts ▾ Notes ▾ Hints
10.146 Edit the original copy of a graphic from within PageMaker	■ With the **pointer tool,** select the graphic you want to edit. ■ From the Edit menu choose "Edit original"; ■ **Or** double-click on the object while holding down the Option key. ■ Make the editing changes to the graphic and save the graphic in the original graphic program before quitting.	■ If the graphic is not linked, the option "Edit original" will not be available. ■ If the graphic is an edition (see Publish and Subscribe, Section 11) and you want to make sure the changes take effect immediately when you return to the layout view, be sure "Update automatically" is checked in the "Link options" dialog box. Now, when PageMaker returns, the new version of the graphic will be in place, with the same position, cropping, and transformations as the old graphic.
10.147 Edit the original copy of a graphic from within PageMaker when you do not have the originating graphic program	■ With the **pointer tool,** select the graphic you want to edit. ■ Option double-click on the object; click OK in the alert box that asks if you want to choose another application. ■ Choose a graphic program from the list offered in the "Choose editor" dialog box (navigate to find the application you want, if necessary). ■ Click on Launch or double-click on the application name.	■ With an OLE graphic displayed, the command "Edit original" changes into the name of the object itself. See 11.123. ■ To save time and the frustration of navigating through all your folders when the original application is not available, make aliases of those programs you will want to use ahead of time and store them in the Editor Alias folder (in the Aldus folder in the System folder).
10.148 Edit the original copy of a graphic from within the Story Editor	■ With the Story Editor open, select just the inline graphic icon. ■ Choose "Edit original" from the Edit menu. ■ Make the editing changes to the graphic and save the graphic in the original graphic program before quitting.	■ See 10.222 and 10.238 for more about inline graphics in the Story Editor. See Section 9 for complete Story Editor info.

If you want to do this:

Then follow these steps:

Shortcuts ▾ Notes ▾ Hints

10.149 Text wrap a graphic

The "Text wrap" dialog box. The standoff has been defined as .2 picas.

a)

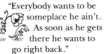

"Everybody wants to be someplace he ain't. As soon as he gets there he wants to go right back."
Henry Ford

A rectangular text wrap with a standoff of .2 picas.

b)

"Everybody wants to be someplace he ain't. As soon as he gets there he wants to go right back."
Henry Ford

A custom text wrap.

- With the **pointer tool,** click on the graphic.
- From the Element menu choose "Text wrap...."
- Under "Wrap option" click on the middle icon, as shown at left.
- Under "Text flow" the third icon will automatically select itself, as shown at left.
- Enter values in the "Standoff" boxes for the amount of space you want between the graphic boundary and the text wrap boundary (as seen in **a**). Click OK.
- If you want a custom wrap (**b**), then use the **pointer tool** to click on the dotted line around the graphic (the wrap boundary). Each click will create a new point. Press-and-drag to move the point. (See 13.30.)
- With each move, the text will reflow. To pause the reflow until you finish moving the points, hold down the Spacebar while you press-and-drag. When you let go of the Spacebar, the text will re-wrap.

- Text wrapping is explained in great detail in Section 13. This segment is just a brief synopsis of the process.
- You cannot text wrap inline graphics. You can text wrap any other graphic, whether you have placed it, pasted it from the Clipboard or Scrapbook, subscribed to it, or drawn it in PageMaker (including lines).

10.150 Remove text wrapping from a graphic

Wrap option:

Text flow:

- With the **pointer tool,** click once on the graphic.
- From the Element menu choose "Text wrap...."
- Under "Wrap option" click on the first icon, as shown at left.
- Click OK.

- If everything you place or paste drops into PageMaker with a text wrap, there is a default set. To remove a text wrap default, click once on the pointer tool *instead* of on the graphic (click on the pointer even if it's already selected). Then follow the rest of the steps. See 13.44.

If you want to do this:

Then follow these steps:

Shortcuts ▾ Notes ▾ Hints

10.151 Turn text into a graphic

a) *Type the text into its own text block.*

b) *This shows the list of format possibilities available.*

c) *Notice the text now has graphic handles.*

d) *Stretch it just like a graphic. 'Cuz it is one.*

- With the **text tool,** draw a bounding box and type in the letter(s) you want to use as a graphic **(a)**. It's easiest, although not imperative, if you make the text as close to the finished size as you can. Make any style changes (font, bold, italic, etc.).
- With the **pointer tool,** click once on the text block.
- From the Edit menu choose "Copy" (*or* press Command C).
- From the Edit menu choose "Paste special….".
- Choose "PICT" from the list of available formats **(b)**.
- Click on "Paste."
- Now your text is a graphic, complete with graphic handles, as shown at left **(c)**. You can stretch and maneuver it just like any

- This is the perfect trick to use when you want to text wrap an initial cap: first turn the letter into a graphic, then apply the text wrap (10.149; Section 13).
- When you turn a PostScript letter into a graphic this way, it becomes a PICT. When printed, it will retain the same smooth edges it would have had as a plain ol' letter, no matter how you may resize it.
- PageMaker will still ask for the font you transformed even though it is now a graphic! Remember, PICTs are not very dependable, especially if they have downloadable fonts in them (10.28). Be sure you include the font you are transforming with any files you take to your service bureau, and to include it for downloading if printing the graphic to your laser printer. Some fonts behave better than others (some just won't print this way at all).

If you want to do this:

10.152 Compress a TIFF file to save space on the disk

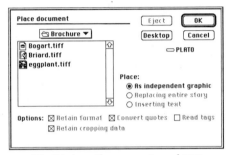

The list shows three uncompressed TIFFs.

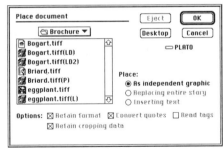

The list now shows compressed copies of the original TIFFs.

Then follow these steps:

- Click once on the **pointer tool,** even if the pointer tool is already chosen.
- From the File menu choose "Place...."
- Locate the TIFF file you want to compress and click once on it.
  - □ To create a **moderately-compressed** copy, hold down the Command and Option keys. Click on the OK button (or hit Return), *and keep holding those two keys down to the count of two.*
  - □ For **maximum** compression, hold down the Command, Option, and Shift keys. Click on the OK button (or hit Return), *and keep holding those three keys down to the count of two.*
- You will get the typical TIFF loaded icon with which to place the graphic. Click as usual to put it on the page.
- Now there is a new file on your disk. If you go back to the File menu and choose "Place...," you will see it listed. PageMaker has added an initial after the file name to indicate what you did to it (see the chart on the right).

Shortcuts ▾ Notes ▾ Hints

- This procedure does not compress the *original* TIFF; it creates a compressed *copy.* In order to take advantage of the extra disk space the compression creates, you need to remove the original TIFF from the disk (to a back-up disk, right?). PageMaker will automatically link (Section 11) the publication version to the compressed copy.
- The amount a file can be compressed depends on the complexity and size of the original. I've seen a TIFF reduce from as much as 1267K down to 206K.
- You can always decompress any compressed TIFF (10.154). Most other programs cannot read a TIFF that was reduced in PageMaker.
- You can also compress paint files. When you next place that compressed paint file, you'll notice it has turned into a TIFF.

P	=	Moderate compression of black-and-white or palette-color TIFFs
LD	=	Moderate compression of grayscale or color TIFFs
L	=	Maximum compression of black-and-white or palette-color TIFFs
LD2	=	Maximum compression of grayscale or color TIFFs
U	=	Decompressed TIFF of any sort

If you want to do this:	Then follow these steps:	Shortcuts ▾ Notes ▾ Hints

10.153 Replace a TIFF file on the page with a compressed TIFF file	■ Follow the steps in 10.152 to compress a TIFF, but with these exceptions:
	  ☐ Before you go to the File menu, with the **pointer tool,** click on the graphic you want to replace.
	  ☐ In the "Place…" dialog box, after you click on the file name, click in the button "Replacing entire graphic."
	  ☐ Make sure "Retain cropping data" is checked if you want the new file to be cropped the same as the old one.
		■ This trick will eliminate the current graphic image from the page (whether it is a TIFF or not) and replace it with the compressed version as you create it from the "Place…" dialog box. If you are replacing the current graphic with the same file compressed, it will drop in with the exact size, cropping, and image control settings.
		■ If you don't check "Retain cropping data," the new file may distort to fit within the frame of the old file.

10.154 Decompress a TIFF file	■ Click once on the **pointer tool,** even if the pointer tool is already chosen. ■ From the File menu choose "Place…." ■ Locate the compressed TIFF file you want to decompress and click once on it. You will know the file is compressed by the letter in parentheses after its name; see 10.152. ■ Hold down the Command key and click OK. *Keep holding the Command key down to the count of two.* ■ You will get the typical TIFF loaded icon to place the image. Click on the page. **If you don't want to place it, click on the pointer tool.** The decompressed copy will stay on your disk, even if you don't actually place the file on the page.	■ This decompressing technique does not decompress the compressed file—it creates an *additional* copy that is decompressed. If you return to the "Place…" dialog box you will see the previously-compressed file listed, this time with a (U) after its name, in addition to the original compression code (P, LD, L, or LD2; see 10.152).

If you want to do this:	Then follow these steps:	Shortcuts ・ Notes ・ Hints
10.155 Display all graphics as gray boxes for fastest screen display 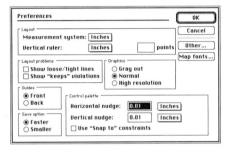	■ From the File menu choose "Preferences...." ■ Under "Graphics" select the radio button next to "Gray out." ■ Click OK.	■ If your graphics are merely placeholders, or if you are in a major rush, turn this option on. It will change the graphic: becomes: ■ When you print the publication with this option turned on, PageMaker will still print the real graphics; this preference is just for quick screen display.
10.156 Display all graphics as low-resolution screen images 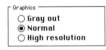	■ This option is actually the default, so you won't need to reset it, unless someone has gone in and changed it. If so: ■ From the File menu choose "Preferences...." ■ Under "Graphics," select the radio button next to "Normal." ■ Click OK.	■ This option places TIFF images as low-resolution screen versions. You can temporarily view the graphic at high-res at any time; see 10.158.
10.157 Display all graphics at high-resolution 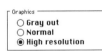	■ From the File menu choose "Preferences...." ■ Under "Graphics," select the radio button next to "High resolution." ■ Click OK.	■ This will make all graphics display at their highest resolution, which can significantly slow down your work on the screen. It's best to leave this option at "Normal" and display the high-res version only when it's necessary. See 10.158 for displaying high-res images one at a time temporarily.

If you want to do this:	Then follow these steps:	Shortcuts ▾ Notes ▾ Hints
10.158 Display a single graphic at high-resolution	■ This technique won't work if the "Graphics" option in the "Preferences" dialog box is set to "Gray out." ■ To display a high-res version of a graphic, hold down the **Control** key as you place the graphic or as the screen redraws. (The screen redraws anytime you change views, use the scroll bars, resize an image, click in the zoom box, etc. You can hold down the Command and Shift keys as if you were going to resize an image, hold down the Control key also, and press on a corner handle to re-display in high-res.)	■ Actually, this will display any and all of the high-res graphics that happen to be on the screen, not just the one image. ■ Notice this technique uses the **Control** key, not the Command key. That means if you have a keyboard that does not have a Control key you can't do this.
10.159 Apply color to a graphic	■ With the **pointer tool** click once on the graphic(s). ■ If the Color palette is not showing, press Command K (or choose it from the Windows menu). ■ Select the color to apply to the graphic(s).	■ See Section 16 for details on using color in your publication. This segment is just a brief synopsis. ■ Black-and-white and grayscale TIFFs and paint-type graphics will display the colors you apply. PICT and EPS graphics can have color applied to them, but they will not show their assigned colors on screen. ■ You cannot apply color to objects through the "Define colors..." dialog box. That box is just for *creating* colors.

A PERFECT BEAUTY OF A SUNFLOWER!
A PERFECT EXCELLENT LOVELY SUNFLOWER EXISTENCE!
A SWEET NATURAL EYE TO THE NEW HIP MOON,
WOKE UP ALIVE AND EXCITED GRASPING IN THE
SUNSET SHADOW SUNRISE GOLDEN MONTHLY BREEZE!

ALLEN GINSBERG · SUNFLOWER SUTRA

If you want to do this:

10.160 Create an EPS file of a PageMaker page

These are the options for writing a PostScript file to disk.

This is an EPS graphic of a 4" x 6" page from another PageMaker publication.

Then follow these steps:

- You need to be in the publication that has the page you want to make into a file. You don't have to be viewing that page, though; just know its page number.
- From the File menu choose "Print...," *or* press Command P.
- Select the type of printer on which you will eventually print the EPS file.
- Select printing options just as if you were going to print the file regularly, including the page numbers or range for which you want EPS files.
- Click the "Options" button in the "Print document" dialog box.
- Click "Write PostScript to file"; check "EPS."
- If you have used non-resident fonts in the publication, check the option "Include downloadable fonts" (see 19.103).
- If you want, select "Save as..." to navigate and save the file to a new location.
- Click the "Save" button.
- You will see messages flash across the screen similar to those you see during a regular printing session. When the process is done, you can go to the "Place" dialog box (from the File menu) and see the new file listed. It will place just like any other graphic.

Shortcuts ▾ Notes ▾ Hints

- This procedure allows you to create a graphic image of any PageMaker pages. You can then place the image in any PageMaker publication. As an EPS file, you can resize it, stretch it, crop it, etc., just like any other graphic.
- *The graphic will be as large as the page it was created on.* If you want a smaller-sized graphic, change the page size in the "Page setup" dialog box (from the File menu) to as small as you can get away with.
- You can only rename a file if you are printing a single page. If you are printing more than one page to disk, you must accept PageMaker's default name. Each page will print as a separate file and will be numbered by its page number in the original document. Cool, huh?

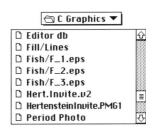

Each page of the 3-page document "Fish" was automatically printed as an EPS file and numbered with the correct page number.

- See Section 19 for a complete discussion about printing to disk.

Nelson Hawks

"In the 1600s, type foundries grew out of the printing trade. There was no order to the new foundries' product offerings and nothing matched from one foundry to another. If printers limited themselves to one foundry's products, the situation was usually under control; but as soon as another foundry's type was introduced, havoc resulted. No type from any two foundries aligned the same, was the same size, or was even consistent in height; nothing matched. The same faces from different foundries simply could not be used together, and careful attention had to be paid not to mix various foundries' faces when storing type. Even spacing material did not match, which meant that printers had to purchase multiple sets of everything." *

Does that scenario sound familiar? Read it again, substituting "1990s" for "1600s," "vendor" for "foundry," and "Mac user" for "printer."

In the 1400s when a print shop had a job to do, they made their own type for that job. Every print shop made their own type. It wasn't until the early 1600s that Claude Garamond had the idea to create type and sell it to others—the very first type foundry. But as other type foundries developed, type was made in all sorts of ways, as there were no established standards. By the 1800s there were thousands and thousands of print shops all over the world, each with thousands of pounds of metal type that couldn't be consolidated in any way. Oftentimes even the same typeface from the same foundry ordered on two different days didn't match each other. One printer complained in the late 1880s that "there are no two foundries . . . whose body types, either in depth, or in width, are cast by the same standard."

In 1877, Nelson Hawks was a junior partner in Marder, Luse and Company, a large type foundry in Chicago. Nelson was sent to San Francisco to establish a branch office. He was directly confronted with the inventory problems of metal type. So, being a very simple and practical man, he created a solution. Nelson came up with a workable standard, the one we now know and love: points and picas. All he had to do was convince all the printers in the country to adopt the new system.

Mr. Hawks presented the idea to his boss, Mr. Marder. Mr. Marder saw that the time was ripe for this sort of change, and since all their type had been melted in the Great Chicago Fire anyway, he wanted to go into production immediately, patent the system, and establish a monopoly. Marder told Nelson to keep this a great secret.

But Nelson was enthusiastic and altruistic and he thought everyone should know about this new system because it would make everyone's life easier. So when Mr. Marder went back to Chicago, Nelson stayed in California (Alameda, actually) and vigorously promoted this new idea all over the west coast. Of course this irritated his cantankerous partners in Chicago, so Nelson just up and quit. Sold out his interest in 1882 for $12,000. Then he got to do what he really wanted to do: evangelize the point system. He traveled all over America, meeting with the owners of the largest foundries, taking out ads in trade journals, writing letters to every type foundry in the United States. He didn't do it for money—he did it because it was the right thing to do.

Nelson's system did become the standard in America and in Britain, and he was fortunate enough to live to see the day (in fact, he lived to be 89). At the age of 80, Nelson remarked, "The only benefit I have derived from it lies in the satisfaction of having been successful in giving the printing craft something useful and lasting."
Thank you, Nelson.

This passage is from Allan Haley's article in U&lc, May, 1985. Many thanks to Mr. Haley and his historical research for the basis of this article.

EXPLANATION
OF THE
POINT SYSTEM
OF PRINTING

TYPE

WITH
SPECIMENS
IN THE OFFICE OF THE ISLAND CITY PRESS
ALAMEDA, CALIFORNIA

Image control   *(with the pointer tool, click on a TIFF or paint-type image; from the Element menu, choose "Image control...")*

10.162   Image control is a dialog box that allows you to control several aspects of bitmapped graphics (which in PageMaker are the TIFF or paint-type images). You can use it to change the screen pattern (dots vs. lines), adjust the contrast of the darks and lights, alter the lightness or darkness of the entire image, and change the dot-screen angle and lines-per-inch frequency.

10.163   Image control only works on one image at a time. It doesn't work at all on PICTs, color TIFFs, EPS graphics, or graphics placed from the Scrapbook (PageMaker turns them into PICTs). If you really need to apply image control to a PICT, you can copy the item into another program, save it as a TIFF or as a MacPaint file, and then bring it back into PageMaker (10.31).

10.164   The Control palette can tell you the format of the *selected* graphic. Just select the graphic and check out the icon on the "Apply" button. A TIFF will look like this: Or you can just pull down the Element menu and see if the "Image control..." command is black; if it is, the *selected* image is a TIFF (*or*, a paint-type graphic).

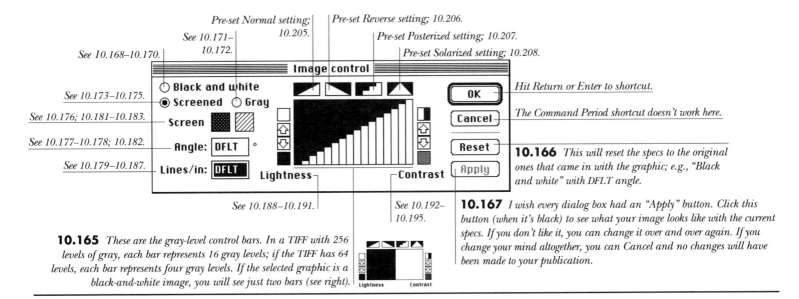

Pre-set Normal setting; 10.205.

Pre-set Reverse setting; 10.206.

Pre-set Posterized setting; 10.207.

See 10.171– 10.172.

Pre-set Solarized setting; 10.208.

See 10.168–10.170.

See 10.173–10.175.

See 10.176; 10.181–10.183.

See 10.177–10.178; 10.182.

See 10.179–10.187.

Hit Return or Enter to shortcut.

The Command Period shortcut doesn't work here.

10.166   *This will reset the specs to the original ones that came in with the graphic; e.g., "Black and white" with DFLT angle.*

See 10.188–10.191.

See 10.192– 10.195.

10.167   *I wish every dialog box had an "Apply" button. Click this button (when it's black) to see what your image looks like with the current specs. If you don't like it, you can change it over and over again. If you change your mind altogether, you can Cancel and no changes will have been made to your publication.*

10.165   *These are the gray-level control bars. In a TIFF with 256 levels of gray, each bar represents 16 gray levels; if the TIFF has 64 levels, each bar represents four gray levels. If the selected graphic is a black-and-white image, you will see just two bars (see right).*

Image control:
Black and white ∎

10.168 The **Black and white** button is automatically chosen if the selected graphic is a bi-level bitmap (10.15), meaning it is strictly black-and-white with no gray levels.

10.169 If the image is already "Screened" or "Gray," clicking on the "Black and white" button will convert it to a bi-level image.

"Gray"   *"Black and white"*

10.170 If an image is black-and-white, your only option in "Image control" is to reverse it; that is, what is black will be white and what is white will be black (10.206).

Image control:
Gray ∎

10.171 The **Gray** button will only be available if the selected graphic is a gray-scale TIFF *and* you have a grayscale or color monitor that has the gray levels or color turned on (from the Control Panel). Without a color or grayscale monitor, or with a monitor set to "Black & White," the "Gray" button will be dim, and the "Screened" button will be selected. You can still adjust the gray levels (10.173–10.175; 10.195), you just won't see the effect so clearly on the screen. (Grayscale TIFFs sure do look pretty on a grayscale monitor.)

10.172 With the gray-level control bars (10.165; 10.188–10.195) you can control the lightness and the darkness of the pixels. See 10.196–10.203 for examples.

Image control:
Screened ∎

10.173 The **Screened** button is automatically chosen if you have selected a grayscale TIFF image but you don't have a grayscale monitor. If you leave the "Screen," "Angle," and "Lines/in" options as they are, the grayscale image will reproduce the same as if you had the option of the "Gray" button.

10.174 If the selected object is a black-and-white TIFF, you can click the "Screened" button to apply a halftone to it. This can occasionally bring out some extra detail in the image (10.209), but it comes in most handy when you want to lighten the image. You can lighten it just a touch so the image is not so harsh, or you can lighten it quite a bit so the image becomes just a shadow on the page (10.210).

10.175 If the selected object is a grayscale TIFF, you can use the "Screened" button to apply a halftone to *override* the default settings of the designated printer. For instance, if your LaserWriter defaults to a dot pattern, 45° angle, and 53 lines/inch, you might want to apply a line pattern (10.182–10.183) with 30 lines/inch for a special effect; it will replace the LaserWriter's defaults for that particular image.

Image control:
Screen (or pattern)

Screen
Standard dot pattern | Line pattern

10.176 If you applied a halftone screen as you scanned your image, you probably had options as to what sort of pattern to use. If you scanned the image as a grayscale TIFF (which is preferable), PageMaker also gives you options: the standard dot pattern or a line pattern. (They are usually called "dot screens" and "line screens," but many other things are also called screens; to keep the confusion down at the moment, I will refer to them as patterns.) As you click on either of the patterns, it is instantly applied to the image.

Image control:
Angle

Angle: 90 °

10.177 **Angle** refers to the direction in which the dots or lines are lined up. The standard default for black-and-white half-tones is 45°. You will rarely need to change it, unless you are doing special effects, or you are fine-tuning patterns on different colors that will be overlaying each other.

10.178 You can specify any angle from 0° through 360°. When the value in this box is **DFLT,** the angle will adjust to whatever the default is for the printer that is printing the publication. Your service bureau can change its imagesetter's default, if necessary.

Image control:
Lines/in

Lines/in: 53

10.179 **Lines/in** refers to the *line frequency,* or how many rows of dots or lines there are in one **inch.** The higher the number, the finer the dot. The finer the dot, the more difficult to print.

10.180 A PostScript printer will automatically apply a default line/inch value as it goes through the printer. Generally, a 300 dpi LaserWriter uses 53 lines per inch; a 600 dpi LaserWriter uses 71 lines per inch; a Linotronic uses 150 lines per inch (10.186). **Any number you enter in this box will override the printer's default.**

10.181 *The image below is 105 lines per inch, using the standard dot pattern at the standard 45° angle.*

10.182 *The image below is 45 lines per inch, using a line pattern at a 90° angle.**

10.183 *The image below is 53 lines per inch, using a line pattern at a 0° angle.**

*No, that's not a typo. If you define an angle on your screen and then print the page Wide, the angle doesn't change to match the screen's orientation! That is, a 90° angle on your screen will print at 0° in the Wide orientation, and vice versa. Very interesting.

Image control:
Lines/in —continued
∎

10.184 You can enter a line frequency from 5 through 300 lines per inch. You must keep in mind, however, the printing method you'll be using for final reproduction.

10.185 If you will be using a copy machine to reproduce the work, use a line frequency of not more than 60 to 80. You can go towards the higher end (70 to 80) if the paper from the laser printer and the copy machine are both smooth (not plain ol' copy paper), or if you are printing to a high-resolution imagesetter.

10.186 If you are printing to a high-res imagesetter and a commercial press will be making reproductions, *ask the presspeople* what line screen (frequency) they will prefer for the press. You can either enter that number here in the "Lines/in" edit box (see page 497), **or** tell your service bureau to print all the screens in your publication at that frequency (10.78, 19.109).

10.187 When the value in the edit box is **DFLT,** the frequency will adjust to whatever the default is for the printer that will eventually print the publication.

Image control:
Lightness
∎

10.188 The **Lightness** control bar adjusts the brightness of the **dark pixels** (dots).

10.189 If your image is **Black-and-white,** you can only adjust this to all or nothing— either your image is black-and-white or it is white-and-black. Click towards the top of the large black bar to switch settings, or click in the pre-set Reverse button (10.206).

10.190 Even though your image is black-and-white, you can click in the "Screened" button and adjust the *lightness.* You still cannot adjust the *contrast,* even though you can move the bar up or down.

10.191 If the **Screened** or **Gray** buttons are selected, you can adjust the varying levels of gray. You can use the little scroll arrow to move the bars, but you will have more control over the individual bars if you just press-and-drag on them. You can start from one bar and just sweep across—the bars will follow the pointer. See the following pages for examples of lightness and contrast settings and how they affect an image.

Image control:
Contrast
∎

10.192 The **Contrast** control bar adjusts the brightness of the **light pixels** (dots).

10.193 If your image is **Black-and-white,** you can only adjust this to all or nothing— either your image is black-and-white or it is white-and-black. Click towards the top of the black chunk to switch settings, or click in the pre-set Reverse button (10.206).

10.194 Even if you halftone your black-and-white image by clicking in the "Screened" button, you can't adjust the contrast because there is no contrast to adjust. Either a pixel is black or it is white; you cannot adjust the levels in-between to make black less of a contrast to white.

10.195 If the **Screened** or **Gray** buttons are selected, you can adjust the varying levels of gray. You can use the little scroll arrow to move the bars (10.165), but you will have more control over the individual bars if you just press-and-drag on them. You can start from one bar and just sweep across—the bars will follow the pointer. See the following pages for examples of lightness and contrast settings and how they affect an image (10.198–10.203).

Image control lightness and contrast settings

10.196 The following are some examples of what to expect with different lightness and contrast settings. These are all printed on a Linotronic (1270 dpi) at a default angle and line frequency (105) unless otherwise noted. Remember, avoid the tendency to make the image appear sharp and crisp on the screen (10.93). In your laser printer proof, you want to be able to see a few white dots in the black areas and a few black dots in the white areas, realizing that those few tiny dots will probably disappear when it gets reproduced and the general contrast will be sharpened even more when it goes through the printing press or the copy machine.

10.197 It takes a good deal of experimentation and experience to get these controls adjusted so you know what to expect. And even then, often it's a surprise. And you're never quite satisfied. Well, that's what we get for being on the cutting edge. I'm sure Gutenberg felt the same way trying to get the ink just right for the impressions on varying types of paper.

10.198 *Normal default. For this photo, normal is much too dark.*

10.199 *Not bad.*

10.200 *The light pixels are getting too dark.*

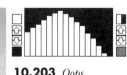

10.201 *Too flat. Needs more contrast.*

10.202 *Too dark.*

10.203 *Oops.*

Pre-set settings

10.204 For any of these pre-set settings, simply click in the little icon in the "Image control" diaog box. Then you can adjust individual bars if necessary. These were all printed on a Linotronic, 1270 dpi, with a 105-line screen (frequency) with the default angle.

Normal

10.205 *This is a Normal setting for comparison. This is Serena Pickering Catt, my great-great-great-grandmother. My alter ego. They say I'm her spittin' image.*

Reverse

10.206 *This is a pre-set Reverse setting. All the white pixels are now black and all the black pixels are now white. This is probably a fair representation of what Serena looks like at the moment.*

Posterized

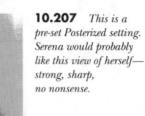

10.207 *This is a pre-set Posterized setting. Serena would probably like this view of herself— strong, sharp, no nonsense.*

Solarized

10.208 *This is a pre-set Solarized setting. A little too psychedelic for Serena.*

If you want to do this:	**Then follow these steps:**	**Shortcuts · Notes · Hints**

Image control

10.209 Adjust the appearance of a TIFF image

- With the **pointer tool,** click once on *one* graphic.
- From the Element menu choose "Image control...." If the command is gray, either you have selected more than one graphic or the image you selected is not a bitmapped (TIFF) image. If it's not a TIFF, you can't image control it.
- In the "Image control" dialog box adjust everything to your liking. Segments 10.162–10.208 explain, and give examples for, all those mysterious controls.
- Regularly click the "Apply" button to see how you are affecting the image. When you like it, or at least when you are through controlling it, click OK.

- See 10.100 for guidelines on turning EPS and PICT graphics into TIFFs in order to image control them.

Moby Dick
—Herman Melville

you perhaps think for.

than that man in more is there sure be him, about able-laugh bountifully anything has that man the and way, that in spent be to and spend to himself allow cheerfully him let but backward, be not him let anybody, to joke good a for stuff afford person, proper own his in man, one any if So, pity, the more's the thing; good a scarce too rather and thing, good mighty a is laugh good ▼

If you want to do this:	Then follow these steps:	Shortcuts ▾ Notes ▾ Hints
10.210 Lighten a TIFF or paint-type image to a shadow so you can print text right over the top of it	▪ Select the graphic and open the "Image control" dialog box as noted in 10.209.	▪ Image control cannot be applied to PICTs or EPS graphics.

10.210　Lighten a TIFF or paint-type image to a shadow so you can print text right over the top of it

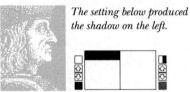

The setting below produced the shadow on the left.

Black-and-white TIFF

The setting below produced the shadow on the left.

Grayscale TIFF

▪ Select the graphic and open the "Image control" dialog box as noted in 10.209.
▪ If the image is **black-and-white,** click the button "Screened."
  ▫ Choose whether you want the dot screen or the line screen (10.176–10.183).
  ▫ Drag the first control bar, the "Lightness" bar, upward. You can use the little scroll arrows but you'll have more control if you just press-and-drag the bar itself (10.165).
  ▫ Press the "Apply" button to see the effect. When it's appropriate, click OK.
▪ If the image is a **grayscale,** the button "Gray" should already be selected.
  ▫ Position the pointer tool in the first of the bars on the far left. Press the mouse button and sweep across the bars to get the same general pattern you see on the left. You can also adjust each bar individually.
  ▫ Experiment with the bars, clicking "Apply" regularly to check it out. When you like it, click OK.
▪ You can return to "Image control" at any time (when the image is selected, of course) and re-adjust the settings.

▪ Image control cannot be applied to PICTs or EPS graphics.
▪ Color tint screens from the Color palette can be applied to TIFFs (black-and-white and grayscale but *not* color), PICTs, paint, *and* EPS graphics. See 10.212, 16.7–16.8, and 16.106.

If you want to do this:

Then follow these steps:

Shortcuts ▾ Notes ▾ Hints

10.211 Return a TIFF image to its original specifications

- With the **pointer tool,** click on the graphic.
- From the Element menu choose "Image control...."
- Click the "Reset" button. Click OK.

- This Reset button will return the graphic to the specs with which it came into PageMaker.

10.212 Lighten a PICT or EPS graphic to a shadow

PICT graphic.

EPS graphic.

Although these looked just plain black on the screen, they printed as a gray tint.

- You can't use image control on a PICT or EPS graphic, but you *can* apply a black tint screen. If you have black tint screens already in your Color palette, just select the image and then select the tint. If you need to make a tint to apply, follow these steps:
- Under Element, choose "Define colors...."
- Click "Black." Click "New."
- Click the "Tint" button.
- Type in a name (it's best to type the name of the base color, then the tint percentage so you always know what it is).
- Change the percentage value in the "Tint" edit box from "100" to the tint value you want. To see the new color, click in the *top half* of the Color box on the right.
- Press Option Return (to close both boxes).
- From the Window menu choose "Color palette," *or* press Command K.
- With the **pointer tool,** click once on the graphic you want to lighten.
- In the Color palette click on the name of the tint you just made.

- This doesn't really come under the topic of "Image control," but I thought you might get frustrated trying to screen back (lighten) an image other than a TIFF, so I included it here. You'll find more detailed info on tints in Section 16 on Color.
- Although color can be applied to PICTs and EPS graphics they won't show on the screen as tints. However, on a PostScript printer they will print as tints. Trust me!

Inline graphics

10.213   Inline graphics are one of the very greatest features of PageMaker. Any graphic that can be placed, pasted, or otherwise imported independently, or that can be drawn in PageMaker, can also be placed, pasted, or otherwise imported *inline* (including subscribing or OLE-linking or -embedding); that is, imbedded as part of the text. When it is inline, a graphic will move along with the text as it is edited. And then it can also be cut, copied, and pasted along with the text it rides with, all the while retaining its original links. However, the graphic will disappear if the *story's* link is changed or updated (see 11.15, 11.63, 11.66).

10.214   An inline graphic can take on some text attributes, but can also be manipulated as a graphic. To apply text attributes, select the inline graphic with the text tool; to apply graphic attributes, select the inline graphic with the pointer tool. (Selecting an inline graphic with the pointer tool selects *just* the graphic, not the text block; to select the text block, click in the text area or Command-click on the graphic until you see handles on the text block.)

10.215   Since an inline graphic is part of the text, you can include it in tracking, kerning, leading, leading method, word and letter spacing, and color. It will align with tabs, will move over with the spacebar or any hard spaces (5.217–5.228), and will respond to Returns and indents. It will listen to paragraph-level formatting, such as space before and after, keeps controls, and alignment.

10.216   You cannot apply a point size to inline graphics, nor a font, nor a style such as bold or italic. You cannot use super- or subscript options to reposition the graphic nor apply the Drop Cap Addition (20.42) to it.

10.217   As a graphic, you can crop it; resize it; cut, copy, and paste i;, adjust the resolution; apply color; transform it (independently or as part of the text block); and modify it with image control (if it's a TIFF). If the graphic is a PageMaker-drawn object, you can change its line widths and corners.

10.218   You *cannot* apply a text wrap. The "Bring to front" and "Send to back" commands don't work on inline graphics, either, except as part of the entire text block.

10.219   Anything you can do with the Control palette to an independent graphic you can do to an inline graphic: scale, crop, rotate, skew, reflect, and magic-resize. (However, there is no Proxy available.) Any text attributes that can be assigned to an inline graphic can also be assigned through the Control palette.

10.220   An inline graphic has a *boundary* around it, just like any other graphic, indicated by its handles. This boundary is sometimes wrapped directly around the image itself, but oftentimes is much larger than the graphic. This can create problems, because the boundary is what determines the space between the graphic and the text, the tab, the indent, etc. The simple solution is to crop the excess away from the graphic (10.143, 10.144).

The text cannot get closer to the actual image than the boundary (indicated by the eight handles).

After cropping the boundary away, you have more options for spacing the graphic.

Inline graphics —*continued*

10.221 An inline graphic also has its own *baseline,* which is two-thirds of the distance from the top of the graphic boundary, no matter what leading method you use. You can actually adjust the baseline of the graphic by moving the graphic up or down (10.232–10.233; 10.246) or with the "Baseline-offset" option in the Control palette (10.248).

10.222 In the **Story Editor** (Section 9), an inline graphic will appear as a little box (■), as shown below. You can place (or paste or link or what-have-you) a graphic inline just as you do in the layout view; see 10.238. The Story Editor is a good place to find all those inline graphics that were supposed to be independent graphics.

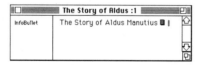

A Story Editor window, showing what an inline graphic looks like in a window view.

10.223 Inline graphics, like paragraph rules or oversized initial caps, can hang outside of the text block. Whenever anything hangs outside the text block, it usually disappears until you redraw the screen. So if part of your graphic melts on you, either click in the zoom box (upper right of the window), change page views, re-choose the same page view (it's quick and easy to use the Command-key equivalent), or select the text block with the pointer tool and press Command F ("Bring to front").

10.224 Because the graphic is actually part of the text block, when you place or paste it, the graphic drops in at the insertion point, just as with text. This means that you have to be conscious of whether and where the insertion point is flashing, even (and especially) if you are not *intending* to set an inline graphic.

10.225 Count how many times you accidentally place an inline graphic when you want an independent one, before you finally get in the habit of clicking the pointer tool before you paste or place. It's important to be conscious of where you are placing your graphics; if you accidentally place a large graphic inline that is too big for the text block, the text block rolls up and you don't see what happened. Or, what's really killer is leaving a flashing insertion point *on another page,* and pasting a graphic. You don't see the graphic anywhere, so you think maybe you did something wrong and you paste it again. Eventually you figure it out, but by then the text block on the other page has rolled up and you can't find the images. Or if the graphic was really big, you can't even unroll the text block big enough to find the graphic and delete it. One of my favorite learning experiences was when I inadvertently placed my entire Scrapbook of forty-three items into a text block. See 10.242 for some tips on how to get out of predicaments like that (use the Story Editor). Yes, as Mr. Cella said, "Experience is what you get—when you don't get what you want."

10.226 A most important tip: If the graphic is large and you need to significantly resize it, do the resizing *before* you paste it inline. If you don't, the graphic sometimes can't find room to squeeze in and so it keeps going deeper and deeper into the text block. I've lost 'em over seventeen inches deep.

What to expect with inline graphics

10.227 Most of the images you see in this book are inline, especially the ones in the "If you want to do this" column, or the ones right in the text line itself, like this: . As the text gets edited, reformatted, cut and pasted, moved, etc., the graphic just goes right along with the flow. Amazing.

10.228 Even a little graphic, as the one in the paragraph above, usually carries with it a larger leading than in the text. As you know, the line will adjust to the larger

leading, creating this sort of look between the lines, which probably isn't quite what you want. The solution is exactly the same as with text that has a larger character in it: use fixed instead of auto leading. Adjust the leading and tracking of inline graphics either through the Type menu or the "Inline specifications" box (10.243).

10.229 If the graphic is significantly larger than the text, though, even the fixed-leading technique won't work because the graphic will overlap the text. On the screen at first it may look like the graphic is getting chopped off, but as soon as the screen redraws the graphic pops out in full. It may be transparent or it may be opaque.

10.230 Because the graphic is basically a large text character, it's not so easy to put a couple of lines directly next to it, like a caption. This is what generally happens, even with the second line tabbed over:

 Alien creatures found

frolicking in the park.

10.231 You can, though, with intelligent use of the Indents/tabs ruler, create a "hanging" graphic off the side of a paragraph (10.251), like so *(this greatest of tricks was invented by Olav Martin Kvern)*:

 The crow doth sing as sweetly as the lark, when neither is attended, and I think the nightingale, if she should sing by day, when every goose is cackling, would be thought no better a musician than the wren. How many things by season season'd are to their right praise and true perfection!

 A man may fish with the worm that hath eat of a king, and eat of the fish that hath fed of that worm.

William Shakespeare

10.232 When an inline graphic is in a text block, it is possible to adjust its baseline in connection with the other text on the line; that is, you can move it up and down to a certain extent. The following paragraph has an inline graphic with *Auto leading:*

 I am a woman of the world, Hector;

and I can assure you that if you will only take the trouble always to do the perfectly correct thing, and to say the perfectly correct thing, you can do just what you like.

George Bernard Shaw
Heartbreak House

10.233 If you use *fixed leading*, you can use the pointer tool to press-and-drag on the graphic up or down, above or below its natural baseline (or use the "Baseline-offset" option on the Control palette, see 10.248). Notice the difference in this version:

 I am a woman of the world, Hector; and I can assure you that if you will only take the trouble always to do the perfectly correct thing, and to say the perfectly correct thing, you can do just what you like.

George Bernard Shaw
Heartbreak House

If you want to do this:	**Then follow these steps:**	**Shortcuts ▾ Notes ▾ Hints**

Inline graphics

10.234 Paste a graphic inline

- This task assumes you already have something on the Clipboard to paste (1.273–1.281).
- With the **text tool,** click in the text at the point where you want to insert the graphic. You can create a *new* text block for the graphic (click outside of any existing text) or create a bounding box (4.62).
- With the insertion point flashing, press Command V, *or* from the Edit menu, choose "Paste."
- You may need to adjust the graphic; see the following tasks for resizing, replacing, moving, etc.

- If the graphic is fairly large, paste it on the page as an independent graphic first (simply by clicking on the **pointer tool** before you paste). Resize and crop the graphic to approximately the size you will need (10.138–10.144), cut it, *then* follow these steps to paste it in.

10.235 Place a graphic inline

- With the **text tool,** click in the text at the point where you want to insert the graphic. You can create a *new* text block for the graphic (click outside of any existing text) or create a bounding box (4.62).
- From the File menu choose "Place...."
- Find the graphic file you want to place and click once on it.
- Select the button "As inline graphic."
- Click OK, *or* double-click on the file name. It will appear at the insertion point.

- Placing a graphic inline involves exactly the same process as placing a graphic independently (except you start with the **text tool**), or as placing text. If the graphic is fairly large, you might want to take note of the tip directly above (10.234).

If you want to do this:	Then follow these steps:	Shortcuts ▾ Notes ▾ Hints
10.236 Replace an existing inline graphic with another graphic file	■ With the **pointer tool,** click once on the inline graphic; **or** with the **text tool,** double-click on the inline graphic. If you have more than one graphic *in a row* to select, you must press-and-drag with the text tool, as you cannot use the Shift-click technique to select more than one inline graphic at a time. ■ From the File menu choose "Place...." ■ Find the file you want to place and click once on it. ■ Click in the button "Replacing entire graphic." ■ Click OK, *or* double-click on the file name. ■ The new graphic will replace the old one, and will take on all its formatting—size, image control, cropping, etc.	■ Please note an important distinction between replacing an existing inline graphic by *placing* a graphic file or by *pasting* an item from the Clipboard or Scrapbook (10.129). When you *place,* the new graphic takes on the size and formatting of the old one. When you *paste,* the new graphic just drops in, ignoring any specifications of the old one, including its size, cropping, and any transformations.
10.237 Replace an existing inline graphic with another graphic from the Clipboard	■ In order to replace the inline graphic with a graphic from the Clipboard, you must select the existing one with the **text tool,** not the pointer tool. Either double-click on it or press-and-drag over it. ■ From the Edit menu, choose "Paste," *or* press Command V. ■ When you *paste* the new graphic, it does *not* take on the formatting of the one it replaces.	■ See the note above (10.236).

If you want to do this:	**Then follow these steps:**	**Shortcuts ▾ Notes ▾ Hints**

10.238 Import (place) an inline graphic into the Story Editor

```
┌─────────────────────────────┐
│▤▢▭▭ To the right you se:1 ▭▭▭┤▢▭│
├──────┬──────────────────────┼──┤
│Body  │To the right you see  │⇧│
│      │the charming face of  │ │
│      │Charles Lindberg:  ▨  │ │
│Body  │What a cutie-patootie.§│⇩│
│      │                      │▢│
└──────┴──────────────────────┴──┘
```

■ While in the Story Editor (Section 9), click in the text at the point where you want the graphic to be placed.
■ From the File menu choose "Place...," *or* press Command D.
■ Find the graphic file you want to place and click once on it.
■ The button "As inline graphic" will be selected. That's your only choice.
■ Click OK, *or* double-click on the file name. You won't get the loaded graphic icon— you will just see the little box appear at the insertion point. When you go back to layout view you'll see the graphic in all its splendor. Which may surprise you.

■ See Section 9 for full details on the Story Editor.

10.239 Resize an inline graphic

■ In the Layout view, with the **pointer tool,** click on the graphic.
■ Resize an inline graphic just as you resize any graphic (10.138–10.142). It will respond to Shift-resizing to keep its proportions. If the graphic is a TIFF or paint-type, you can Command Shift-resize to adjust the resolution to match the "Target printer resolution" (10.141).

■ Inline graphics can be resized and manipulated with the Control palette just like independent graphics can. See 10.138–10.139 regarding resizing graphics with the Control palette.
■ Inline graphics can also be magic-resized by using the "Printer-resolution" button on the Control palette (10.142).

If you want to do this:	**Then follow these steps:**	**Shortcuts ▾ Notes ▾ Hints**
10.240 Cut or copy an inline graphic	■ With the **text tool,** double-click on the graphic, or press-and-drag over it; **or** with the **pointer tool,** click once on the graphic. ■ From the Edit menu, cut or copy as usual.	■ No matter which tool you use, the graphic will paste back in at the size it was when you cut or copied. It will even keep any cropping changes.
10.241 Delete an inline graphic	■ With the **text tool,** double-click on the graphic, or press-and-drag over it; **or** with the **pointer tool,** click once on the graphic. ■ Hit the Backspace/Delete key.	■ You cannot Shift-click with the pointer tool to select a group of inline graphics. It *is* possible to press-and-drag over several of them in a row with the text tool.
10.242 Delete an inline graphic you can't see because it is too big or it disappeared somewhere or there are so many of them you can't select them all at once	■ You can try widening the text block to find the graphic, and then delete it as above. **Or,** if that's not possible, do this: ■ With the **pointer tool,** triple-click on the text block, just above where you think the graphic disappeared; **or** with the **text tool,** click the insertion point in the text and press Command E. Either method will bring up the Story Editor. ■ In the Story Editor you will see little boxes (▨). Each one represents an inline graphic. ■ Select the graphic by double-clicking on it, or pressing-and-dragging over a group. Unfortunately, you can't tell one graphic from another in the Story Editor. But by the time you resort to this trick, you often don't care. Get rid of 'em all and start over. ■ Press Command E to get back to the publication page.	■ I must be sadistic. I love to see a roomful of people going nuts because they keep accidentally pasting graphics inline. It just cracks me up to see those bewildered and sometimes panic-stricken faces. I guess I enjoy seeing it because I have done it myself so many times that I find it satisfying to know it's not really stupidity that causes that to happen.

If you want to do this:	Then follow these steps:	Shortcuts ▾ Notes ▾ Hints
10.243 Adjust the leading and tracking of an inline graphic using the "Inline specifications" dialog box 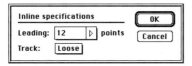	■ With the **text tool,** brush over and select *just* the inline graphic. ■ From the Type menu select "Type specs…," *or* press Command T. ■ Enter the leading in the edit box; choose the tracking you want from the pop-up list. ■ Click OK *or* hit Return.	■ The same thing can be down by selecting the options individually from the Type menu. ■ Leading of an inline graphic can also be changed using the Control palette.

10.244 Move an inline graphic horizontally	■ You can't *drag* the graphic horizontally with the pointer tool, but you can *push* it over with hard spaces (5.217–5.228).
	  □ If the graphic is left-aligned and you want to move it to the right, insert hard spaces *before* the graphic.
	  □ If the graphic is right-aligned and you want to move it to the left, insert hard spaces *after* the graphic.
	■ You can also use tabs; in fact, you can get incredibly precise placement with tabs, since the Indents/tabs ruler allows you to type in exact measurements (6.63).
	■ If you place the graphic in its own paragraph (hit a Return before and after you place it), you can then align it left, right, or centered (10.249) between the text block handles.
		■ Each graphic has a boundary around it. Some graphics have quite a bit of excess boundary area, while others have handles directly on the edges of the image itself (10.220). It is the *boundary* that is aligned on the left or right or top or bottom, *not* the actual image that you can see (10.247). If there is too much space around your graphic, use the cropping tool and crop that excess away (10.143; 10.247).
		■ Some horizontal adjustment can be made in the "Inline specifications" dialog box (10.243).

If you want to do this:

10.245 Step-and-repeat inline graphics horizontally, like so:

There's no end to what you can do with inline graphics and Multiple paste. Watch out! These little guys can slow you down and load up your file in no time.

Then follow these steps:

- Actually, the rows of ducks were created simply by pasting the images in with PageMaker's Multiple paste feature. First resize your image small enough (10.138), and crop the excess boundary, if necessary (10.143; 10.220). Copy the graphic to the Clipboard (click on it with the **pointer tool** and press Command C).
- With the **text tool,** click to set an insertion point where you are going to paste.
- From the Edit menu, choose "Multiple paste…."
- Since you are pasting *within text,* you are not offered any choices except the number of copies you want to paste in.
- Hit OK, and watch the graphics paste inline, one right after another.
- Hit the Return key to start another line, choose "Multiple paste…" again, and another line will paste in. Keep doing this until you have as many rows of inline graphics as you want. Or, you can just copy the first line and continue to paste it in.
- Now you can go back in and adjust the spacing either by tabbing, or spacing, or kerning.

Shortcuts ▾ Notes ▾ Hints

- Once you have your ducks all in a row, you can space them, apply color to them, and transform them any way you want to get the effect you want.
- Hold down the Option key while choosing "Multiple paste…" to bypass the dialog box. The graphic will paste in according to the last set of specifications entered.
- Command Period will cancel the multiple paste operation in mid-stream.
- Check out 1.287–1.310 for the whole scoop on Multiple paste.

If you want to do this:

10.246 Adjust the baseline of an inline graphic
(See also 10.248)

WORK HARD. THERE IS NO SHORTCUT.
Alfred P. Sloan, Jr.

WORK HARD. THERE IS NO SHORTCUT.
Alfred P. Sloan, Jr.

WORK HARD. THERE IS NO SHORTCUT.

Alfred P. Sloan, Jr.

Then follow these steps:

- With the **pointer tool,** press on an inline graphic. You will see the pointer turn into this cursor:
- This cursor symbolizes the graphic, with the baseline positioned two-thirds of the way from the top no matter what type of leading method you are using (5.58). As you press, you can drag the graphic up and down on its baseline.
- Play with this for a while to see how adjoining text reacts to the graphic as it moves—sometimes it goes up, sometimes it goes down, sometimes it seems like it bounces right back where it came from. The examples on the left all have exactly the same text formatting—same leading (Auto), size, paragraph space, etc.; the only difference is that the frog has been moved up or down.
- The frog graphic is seen as one large character on the line, and its Auto leading takes over. When you use an inline graphic in a body of text, you will usually want to use fixed leading, rather than Auto leading (5.19–5.26). The examples in 10.233 and 10.251 both use fixed leading.

Shortcuts ▾ Notes ▾ Hints

- Remember, the baseline is determined by the size of the graphic *boundary* (10.220). If there is excess white space inside the boundary of the graphic, you may want to crop it away (10.143–10.144).
- If you change an inline graphic into an independent one and then back again, it will remember the baseline information you originally gave it. See also 10.248.
- Read about "Align to grid" (5.108–5.109) and inline graphics when you want paragraphs *following* an inline graphic to stay on your leading grid.

If you want to do this:

10.247 Precisely adjust the space above and below an inline graphic *that is in its own paragraph*

a) *An inline graphic showing its boundary handles, and the leading slug that adds the Auto leading value (in this example, 120%) onto the graphic.*

b) *The same inline graphic with its excess boundary cropped, and with the Auto leading changed to 100%.*

Then follow these steps:

■ An inline graphic has its own baseline. Its baseline, as with text, is determined by the leading slug (5.32). In a graphic, the leading (autoleading of 120%; 5.20) is added onto the outer boundary (10.220). The outer boundary may be larger than the image itself, as shown on the left. Thus it is difficult to determine the precise baseline, and to add or delete specific amounts of linespace above or below the image.

■ So, there are two things you can do for yourself. I'd advise you to do both.
  □ One, crop the boundary down to as close to the actual image as possible (10.143; 10.220).
  □ Two, change the Auto leading value from the default 120% to 100%:
    ▾ With the **text tool,** select the graphic.
    ▾ From the Type menu choose "Paragraph...," *or* press Command M.
    ▾ Click on the "Spacing..." button.
    ▾ In the "Auto leading" edit box type in the number 100. Press Option Return to close both dialog boxes.

■ Now the leading slug will be the exact size of the graphic. You can then add paragraph space before and after (5.72–5.96) to create exactly as much space above and below your graphic as you like.

Shortcuts ▾ Notes ▾ Hints

■ If you find you need to use this technique on a regular basis, create a style (Section 8) with an Auto leading of 100% that you can apply to the paragraph containing the graphic. You will still have to crop any excess boundary space yourself.

■ When you create the graphic in whatever program, push the image into the upper left corner before you save. This simple move will often save you the trouble of having to crop off the excess boundary space later.

This "feature" was first discovered by Olav Martin Kvern. Thanks, Ole!

If you want to do this:

10.248 Adjust the baseline of an inline graphic using the Control palette

— WILLIAM WORDSWORTH

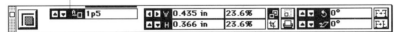

"Baseline-offset" option.

Then follow these steps:

- With the **pointer tool** select the inline graphic.
- Enter a value in the "Baseline-offset" option box that will move the graphic into the position you want. Zero (0) lines the base of the graphic up with the baseline of the text.
  - □ You cannot enter a number greater than the height of the graphic.
- You can further adjust the baseline of the graphic using the nudge buttons (3.17). The default amount is .01 inches, or as set in "Preferences."

Shortcuts ▾ Notes ▾ Hints

- **Note:** There are two baseline adjustment options on the Control palette: "Baseline-offset" on the object-view Control palette which adjusts the baseline alignment of inline graphics and "Baseline-shift" on the character-view Control palette which adjusts the baseline alignment of text (see 4.218, 4.263). An inline graphic can be further adjusted with the "Baseline-shift" option only if it is selected along with one or more *text* characters in the paragraph. In effect, you are moving the baseline of the text in relation to the graphic.
- You cannot move a baseline graphic in an amount less than zero or more than its height. (However, changes you make through the character-view Control palette regarding baseline-shift in general will further affect the shift of any inline graphics.)
- If you change an inline graphic to an independent graphic and then back again, PageMaker will remember the baseline information you originally gave it.
- All in all, you may find it easier (though much less precise) to just select and move the inline graphic visually as in 10.246!

If you want to do this:	**Then follow these steps:**	**Shortcuts ▾ Notes ▾ Hints**

10.249 Perfectly center an inline graphic in a text block

Remember, this is centered between the text block handles. If you want to center it on a column *you must stretch the text block handles to align with the column guides.*

- Simply paste the graphic into its own text block (or its own paragraph in an existing text block, if that will work). Make sure both the left and right handles of the text block are on the guidelines between which you want to center the image.
- Crop (10.143–10.144) any excess boundary space (10.220), as it will affect the way the graphic centers.
- With the insertion point flashing in the graphic's paragraph, press Command M to get the "Paragraph specifications" dialog box.
- Make sure the "Indents" edit boxes all have zeros in them. If not, enter zeros.
- Next to "Alignment," press to get the submenu; choose "Center." Click OK.
- If the graphic still doesn't look quite centered, check to make sure you haven't added any spaces in front of or following the graphic, as PageMaker will center those along with the image itself.

- It's frustrating to try to center a graphic horizontally on the page, isn't it? Those nice little centered handles that show up when you select a graphic always disappear when you try to move the image. Whenever it's possible to use this technique, it sure works great.
- As with any centered alignment, PageMaker centers the item *between the text handles,* not between any guidelines or column guides.

10.250 Use image control on or apply color to an inline graphic

- Use image control on or apply color to an inline graphic just exactly as you would on an independent graphic (10.162–10.212). The same limitations and restrictions apply.

If you want to do this:

10.251 Set an inline graphic to the side of a paragraph

Aldus Manutius
The dictionary defines this man as "an Italian printer and classical scholar." See page 215 for an in-depth account of this interesting human being.

Claude Garamond
You probably thought Claude designed the typeface *Garamond,* which is the official typeface of Apple Computer, Inc. Wrong again, dear. Beatrice Ward successfully proved, in 1926, that Jean Jannon was the artful designer, 80 years after Claude himself died in 1561.

Scarlett Williams
Isn't she the cutest little thing you ever did see? And she is just as sweet as she is cute.

Then follow these steps:

- Each of the examples to the left have the same tab and indent setup. The inline graphic has been moved up or down (10.246, 10.248). The first example uses auto leading; the other two use fixed leading (5.19–5.26).
- This paragraph is set up with a hanging indent (6.60). If you want a similar effect, this is how to arrange the ruler:

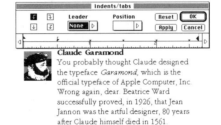

- Set the first-line indent (top triangle) at the far left margin.
- Set the left indent (bottom triangle) where you want the text to align.
- Position a tab directly on the left indent (½").
- Paste in the graphic at the first-line indent (at zero). Hit a tab to move the insertion point to the left indent. Then type the text, and as it word wraps, it will align at the left indent. Fix the leading and adjust the baseline, if necessary. Piece of cake.

Shortcuts ▾ Notes ▾ Hints

- **Re: Auto and fixed leading:**
  When a line uses Auto leading, the space between the lines will adjust to accommodate the largest character; in the case of mixing inline graphics with text, the graphic is generally the largest character. When you paste or place a graphic inline, the larger Auto leading of the graphic will override any existing fixed leading *(any leading value other than "Auto")* that may be attributed to the rest of the text. *So,* the thing to do is fix the leading *after* you place or paste the graphic, get the graphic into the paragraph, then triple-click on the paragraph with the text tool and apply the leading value (5.25).
  □ You cannot "fix" the leading to the same point value as the Auto leading through the Control palette (5.60). Also, be aware that the Control palette displays a numerical value for leading even when "Auto" leading is applied (5.21).

Additions for graphics

10.252   There are four Additions under the Utilities menu that can be used effectively with graphics: Acquire Image, PS Group it/PS Ungroup it, and Create keyline.

10.253   "Acquire Image" is a special Addition useful with *some* types of scanning software. Basically, it lets you scan images "on the fly" without ever having to leave PageMaker to scan and place the image. Called TWAIN, this technology is not PageMaker specific, although she does provide the vehicle for using it if it is available to you (10.303–10.305).

10.254   The two Additions "PS Group it" and "PS Ungroup it" work together to group and later ungroup objects into a graphic unit. The resulting object is an EPS file (or a PICT if you are printing to a non-PostScript printer). It can be useful for grouping objects together on a page to be simultaneously manipulated. Or you might want to group separate graphic elements, such as lines and dingbats, into a single graphic. See 10.259–10.291.

10.255   Although "Create keyline…" can be used in the more traditional sense to create traps and keylines for printing (see 16.23–16.30), it is also useful for creating interesting design effects like borders, boxes, and screens. See 10.292–10.302; 10.306–10.307.

10.256   All the Additions are accessed through "Aldus Additions" under the Utilities menu.

10.257   If you didn't install these Page-Maker Additions when you originally installed the program, you can install them now; see 20.7. See Section 20 for general information about PageMaker's Additions.

10.258   Other Additions that could be useful with graphics are the "Drop cap…" and the "Bullets and numbering…" Additions, Section 20, and "Create color library…," Section 16.

*You see things; and you say, "Why?"
But I dream things that never were; and I say, "Why not?"*

George Bernard Shaw • Back to Methuselah

The "PS Group it" Addition

10.259 The "PS Group it" Addition is PageMaker's way of combining an assortment of text and/or objects (drawn or imported) into one graphic element. Click once on the group to select it and you'll find only one set of handles framing all the objects. If you later need to ungroup them, run the "PS Ungroup it" Addition. While they are very simple Additions to run, the process itself is somewhat cumbersome and it produces large files and demanding links. However, it is a handy Addition that is worth learning.

10.260 "PS Group it" creates a single EPS graphic (or a PICT graphic in the case of non-PostScript printers) out of a group of objects which then replaces the objects themselves. The graphic is linked to a PMG (PageMaker Group) file that is automatically stored with your publication in its folder (10.268–10.270).

10.261 To run the Addition, you must be working in a publication that's been saved at least once. Check to make sure all the links in your group are up to date (11.67). If you are grouping color objects, make sure you have selected a color PostScript PPD in the "Print" dialog box or the group will print in black-and-white.

10.262 Once the objects are grouped, you can manipulate them as a unit the same as you can any other EPS object. You can apply all the options in the object-view Control palette to it including rotate, skew, reflect, and scale. You can even add groups to one another. You can copy and paste groups, but first you need to make sure you understand how the PMG link works and what its limitations are (10.268–10.283).

10.263 While you can group text and objects together, text nested in an EPS file is not always reliable. If you used any downloadable fonts (19.33–19.34), you need to remember to include them in your System. PageMaker's font substitution feature, PANOSE (1.240–1.266), will not warn you of fonts in nested EPS files (10.46). (This is, after all, just another EPS file with embedded fonts.)

10.264 At actual size, the screen preview of grouped items displays accurately. At all other page views, the screen appearance may be off but the group will still print clearly. (This is the trade-off PageMaker uses to help minimize the size of the PMG file to which the group is linked.)

10.265 *This shirt was drawn line by line in PageMaker and then grouped. It was grouped again with the text and then rotated. It's one item now, easily selected and moved or modified. Its PMG file is 102k.*

10.266 It's important that you read the next page to understand what happens when you group objects, and how to handle the PMG file to guarantee high-quality printing.

10.267 PS stands for PostScript. Both the "PS Group it" and "PS Ungroup it" Additions have been optimized for use with PostScript printers. If you are printing to a non-PostScript printer (or you have a non-PostScript printer selected in the Chooser), you will end up with a PICT. PageMaker warns you when you run the Addition that she is creating a PICT and that it may not print correctly.

The PMG file

10.268 When you group items, PageMaker creates a whole new EPS file to replace the original objects. This file, like all EPS files, is composed of two parts—the screen version and the high-resolution printing information file. To print or ungroup the EPS group, PageMaker must be able to access the information in the high-resolution file.

10.269 The screen version is linked to the high-resolution file stored with your publication. This is crucial to understand as this link affects the future of your original objects. It's labeled with the publication name and the extension ".PMGx" (PageMaker Group with x representing a different number for each existing PMG file in the publication). The PMG file retains all the *original* information about each object in the group such as the line and fill attributes, and the position and stacking order. Changes you make to the screen version of the EPS group (like transformations or resizing) do not affect the PMG file (10.271).

10.270 The "Links" dialog box lists the PMG file and its status just like it lists any other graphic that is linked to an external file. PageMaker needs this file to print a high-resolution version of the EPS group.

The PMG file is stored externally by default, but you can choose to store it in the publication using the "Link options" dialog box. Generally speaking, EPS files are rather large, and you are best off just maintaining the link to the external file. (If you don't understand linking, read Section 11. Linking is one of Pagemaker's finer points, and if you work much with graphics it's a concept well worth mastering.) You can print an EPS group whose file is stored internally without having the PMG file, but you will not be able to ungroup it.

10.271 The "PS Ungroup it" Addition uses the PMG file to restore the objects exactly as they were before you grouped them—any modifications or transformations you made to the EPS group are gone. Because the PMG file was created from the original objects *before* you made any transformations, the only thing the objects retain from their grouped status is their position on the publication page.

10.272 "PS Ungroup it" is where the process gets a little confusing. Now, you can choose to delete the PMG file when you ungroup the EPS group (10.279). This is absolutely what you want to do if this is the

only copy of the group. PMG files can be a source of serious clutter! You want to learn to trash the ones you don't need. Yet, if you placed or pasted in other copies of the same EPS group, you need the PMG file to print or ungroup them! In *that* case you *don't* want to delete the PMG file (10.280).

10.273 PMG clutter can be a problem if you delete groups from your publication page. Since the PMG file is not deleted along with it, you may have to ungroup the objects first, delete the PMG file as you ungroup, and then delete all the individual objects from the page. If your publication has more than one grouped object, you can check the "Link info" dialog box to note the number of the PMG file linked to the group you want to delete. Now you can delete the group and go back later and trash the corresponding PMG file.

10.274 PMG files can be imported into other PageMaker 5 publications, and into any application that supports EPS graphics. EPS files created in PageMaker are larger than files created in other programs (like Freehand), and they can only be ungrouped in PageMaker.

10.275 The "PS Ungroup it" Addition dialog box

10.276 To edit text or change the way objects are layered, you must first ungroup them. PageMaker uses the PMG file to recreate the original objects. In the "PS Ungroup it" dialog box you can choose whether or not to delete the PMG file as the objects ungroup. If you delete a file, any other existing copies of the group can never be printed at high-resolution nor be ungrouped.

10.277 You can disable the "PS Ungroup it" dialog box if you want and set a default that either always or never deletes the PMG file. If you disable the dialog box, you can revert to the original defaults by dragging the "PS Group it preferences" file to the trash; see 10.289.

10.281 *You can choose to disable this dialog box and set a default that always or never deletes the PMG file; see 10.288. To see the message box again, throw out the "PS Group it preferences" file in the Additions folder; see 10.289.*

10.278 *This refers to the PMG group file PageMaker creates for every group. It is stored on disk in the same location as the publication file and is called by the same name as the publication with the extension ".PMGx" (the "x" changes for each grouped object). The PMG group file retains the original attributes of all the objects in the group, thus supplying the information necessary to ungroup or print a grouped object.*

10.279 *If you choose "Yes" the grouped objects will ungroup and appear on the page in the same location as the group, but with their original attributes restored. The PMG group file will be deleted as well, so any other copies of the grouped objects cannot be ungrouped or printed at high-resolution.*

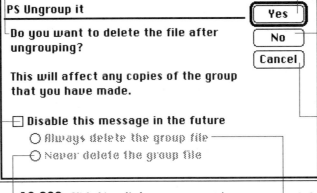

10.280 *If you click "No" the objects will ungroup and the PMG group file will remain intact so that you can ungroup or print other copies of the group.*

Click Cancel or Command Period to leave the dialog box without ungrouping the selected group.

10.282 *Click this radio button to ungroup items without deleting the PMG group file. This means that if copies of the group exist, they can be ungrouped or printed at high-resolution. It also means you may have non-essential PMG files hanging around in the folder with your publication cluttering things up.*

10.283 *Click this radio button to delete the PMG group file every time you ungroup items. This means that if copies of the group exist, they can never be ungrouped or printed at high-resolution.*

If you want to do this:	**Then follow these steps:**	**Shortcuts ▾ Notes ▾ Hints**
10.284 Group two or more objects	■ With the **pointer tool** select the objects you want to group. ■ From the Utilities menu slide down to "Aldus Additions" then over to the submenu and choose "PS Group it...."	■ The "Apply" button, in the Control palette, will change from the multiple objects icon to the PS (Postscript) icon. ■ PageMaker puts a PMG file in the folder along with the publication in which you are working; see 10.260. Watch out! This file can be big. ■ If you do not have a PostScript printer selected in the Chooser, PageMaker creates a PICT instead of an EPS graphic. ■ To group color objects you must have a color PostScript PPD selected in the "Print" dialog box.

10.285 Ungroup a group	■ Click once on the group to select it.
	■ From the Utilities menu slide down to "Aldus Additions" then over to the submenu and choose "PS Ungroup it...."
	■ In the dialog box:
	   □ Click "Yes" if this is the only copy of the grouped file.
	   □ Click "No" if there are other copies of the group that you may want to modify at some other time.
		■ Whether you click "Yes" or "No," the objects will ungroup and appear on the page in the exact same place as where the group was, but **without** any of the changes you made to the group. Each object will be its original shape, size, and proportion.
		■ If you click "Yes" the PMG file is deleted, and no other copy of the group can be ungrouped or printed at high-resolution.
		■ If you click "No" you preserve the PMG file to use with other existing copies of the group.
		■ Beware of the "Disable" option. See 10.288–10.289.

If you want to do this:	**Then follow these steps:**	**Shortcuts ▾ Notes ▾ Hints**
10.286 Make changes to an object within a group, and then group it again	■ With the **pointer tool** select the group. ■ From the Utilities menu slide down to "Aldus Additions" then over to the submenu and choose "PS Ungroup it…." ■ Click "Yes" in the dialog box. ■ Deselect the objects by clicking elsewhere on the page and then click on the object you want to change (or Shift-click to deselect all the objects except the one you want to change). ■ Make the changes to the selected object. ■ Shift-click or marquee all the objects you want to group. ■ From the Utilities menu slide down to "Aldus Additions" then over to the submenu and choose "PS Group it…."	■ Definitely get rid of each PMG file while you are still modifying the grouped objects. You only need the very last one—the one that goes with the grouped objects that you decide to keep. ■ If you change the name or location of a PMG file, in order to print or ungroup the objects you must relink it (in the "Link info" dialog box; see 11.51–11.54).
10.287 Add an object, objects, or group of objects to a group	■ With the **pointer tool** select the object, objects, or groups you want to make into one group. ■ From the Utilities menu slide down to "Aldus Additions" then over to the submenu and choose "PS Group it…."	■ Now you have two layers of grouped objects. If you choose to ungroup, only the last group will separate. You have to select the original group and run the "PS Ungroup it" Addition again to ungroup that one as well. ■ You can only ungroup one group at a time.

If you want to do this:	Then follow these steps:	Shortcuts ▾ Notes ▾ Hints

10.288 Disable the "PS Ungroup it" dialog box and set a PMG file default	■ With the **pointer tool** select a group to ungroup.
	■ From the Utilities menu slide down to "Aldus Additions" then over to the submenu and choose "PS Ungroup it...."
	■ In the dialog box:
	  ▫ If you want to *always* delete the PMG file when you ungroup an object, click in the radio button next to "Always delete the group file."
	  ▫ If you *never* want to delete the PMG file when you ungroup an object, click in the radio button next to "Never delete the group file."
	■ For just this last time you have a choice of whether to delete the PMG file or not. Click "Yes" to delete it, or "No" to save it.
		■ This is the last you will see of the "PS Ungroup it" dialog box. From now on, anytime you ungroup, whether you are in an existing or a new publication, the Addition will run according to the default you just set.
		■ You can get this dialog box back, though. See the next task (10.289).

10.289 Display the "PS Ungroup it" dialog box again	■ At the Finder/Desktop, open your System folder. ■ Navigate to the Aldus folder. Open it, then locate and open the Additions folder. ■ Drag the file "PS Group it preferences" to the trash. ■ Return to PageMaker.	■ Be careful! Don't throw out the Addition (PS Group it.add); throw out only the *preferences* file. ■ The "PS Group it..." preferences document will reappear in your System folder *after* the next time you run the "PS Ungroup it" Addition.

If you want to do this:	Then follow these steps:	Shortcuts ▾ Notes ▾ Hints
10.290 Manipulate a group	■ With the **pointer tool** select the group you want to change. ■ You can press-and-drag directly on the group to move it or click directly on the handles to resize or stretch the group. You can use the rotating tool to rotate it. ■ Press Command ' (*apostrophe*) to display the Control palette if it is not already showing. ■ Through the palette you can move, resize, stretch, scale, crop, rotate, tilt, and reflect the group. ■ From the Element menu you can choose the "Remove transformation" command to undo rotation, skewing, and reflecting.	■ PageMaker remembers the original size of a grouped object, just like it does of an imported graphic. The "Percentage-scaling" option on the palette will always display the amount the group has been modified relative to its original size (see 3.72). You can enter 100% to bring the group back to its original size. ■ The reference point on the Proxy will work the same as it does for any other type of object. See 3.50–3.57 to read about the active reference point.

10.291 Take a publication that contains grouped objects to a service bureau for printing	■ From the File menu choose "Save as...."
	  □ To copy all files that are linked to the publication click the radio button "All linked files."
	  □ To copy only the files that are linked to the publication and not stored in the publication, click the button "Files for remote printing."
	■ Name the publication, choose where to save it, and click "Save" *or* press Return.
		■ You can change the default in the "Link options" dialog box (11.55) to "Store copy in publication" if you don't mind dealing with larger file sizes (PMG files are considerably large) and don't want to than deal with external links.
		■ The "Save as..." options are discussed in Section 18.
		■ Be careful if you have text or fonts included in your group. EPS groups handle nested fonts just like any other EPS graphic does. Bring along copies of any fonts you used. (Even then it may not print exactly as you expected.) See 10.46.

Old age ain't no place for sissies.   Bette Davis

527

The "Create keyline..." Addition

10.292 A keyline is used in traditional printing to create traps between adjacent colors, or to mark a spot on the mechanical (the camera-ready artwork) so the printer knows exactly where to drop in halftones or artwork. An accurate keyline, as the name implies, can be an important "key" for accurate positioning and for precise traps and spreads. Should you want to do your own pre-press work, PageMaker offers the "Create keyline..." Addition. (See my warning about traps first, though, in the Color Section, 16.127.) I'd personally suggest leaving trapping and other intricate pre-press work to the printing professionals and use this Addition for purely decorative purposes. However, if you want to use it to prepare your work for film separations, be sure to thoroughly check out the *Commercial Printing Guide* that came with your PageMaker program.

10.293 *Enter the distance you want the keyline to be from the handles of an object. You can enter a positive or negative number, to the tenth of a point. See 10.300.*

Click OK or press Return to create the keyline.

10.294 *Click a radio button to put the keyline in front of or behind the object.*

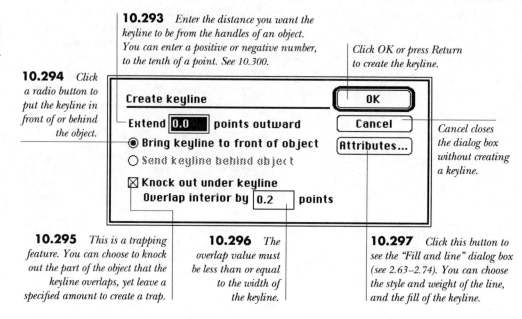

Cancel closes the dialog box without creating a keyline.

10.295 *This is a trapping feature. You can choose to knock out the part of the object that the keyline overlaps, yet leave a specified amount to create a trap.*

10.296 *The overlap value must be less than or equal to the width of the keyline.*

10.297 *Click this button to see the "Fill and line" dialog box (see 2.63–2.74). You can choose the style and weight of the line, and the fill of the keyline.*

10.298   The "Create keyline..." Addition basically just draws a border around a selected object, either a graphic or a text *block*. You can place the keyline in front of or behind the object. It remains a separate object with its own handles, unless you choose to group it with the object (10.284).

10.299   You choose the fill and the line style and weight for the box under "Attributes..." (10.297). It is just like drawing a box around the object with the rectangle tool but there is no worrying about precise centering of the object. All you have to do is tell PageMaker how far to place the keyline from the object's *handles* and the measurement will be the same all the way around the object. This means that you have to pay careful attention to the cropping of imported graphics.

10.300   The distance the keyline is placed from the object determines its size. If you enter 0 (zero) in the "Extend" edit box, the keyline will be the exact size as the object and its handles will be directly on top of the object's handles. A positive number makes the keyline larger than the object; a negative number makes the keyline smaller.

10.301   Beware when you put a keyline around an inline graphic. The graphic will move if you edit the text, but the keyline will hold fast to its original position. You can pick it up and move it manually, but what's the point? You can group the two items and then paste the object inline; see 10.284 and 10.234.

10.302   You can add screened boxes behind call outs or frames to simple graphics. You can choose to overlap the keyline and the object with a trap and/or a knockout to allow separate color overlays to print correctly on the press. A trap is a thin line where the keyline and object overlap to prevent a gap between the two colors. See 16.24–16.29 for more information. A knockout removes a portion of the object underneath the keyline by creating and placing a *mask* beneath the keyline but in front of the object. If you choose to delete a keyline with a knockout, be sure to also select and delete the mask.

10.303   The "Acquire Image..." Addition supports TWAIN technology, a new development in scanning software that lets you scan and place a TIFF image into PageMaker (and other programs that support TWAIN) without ever having to leave the program *or* the publication you are working in. This works, of course, only if you have scanning equipment (or a digital camera) that supports TWAIN and if the data source file of your equipment is in your System.

10.304   When you choose the Addition, it will display a dialog box asking you to choose a device (if you have more than one), the name of the image you want to acquire, and where you want the image stored. This in turn brings up a dialog box specific to your scanning device. If you have installed the Aldus TWAIN filter you can accomplish the same thing by using the "Place..." command. However, "Acquire Image..." is quicker and slicker to use.

10.305   Using "Acquire Image..." presupposes you will not be making any enhancements to the TIFF except for those that are available right in PageMaker.

If you want to do this:	Then follow these steps:	Shortcuts ▾ Notes ▾ Hints
10.306 Create a keyline to mark the position for a halftone or artwork to be dropped in by your printer	▪ With the **pointer tool,** select the object you want to surround with a keyline. ▪ From the Utilities menu slide down to "Aldus Additions" then over to the submenu and choose "Create keyline…." ▪ Enter a value for how far you want the keyline to extend away from the object. ▪ Click the "Attributes…" button; select fill and line attributes for the keyline box. ▪ Check the box next to "Knock out under keyline" if you want to trap the keyline to the object. ☐ Enter a value for the amount you want the outside edge of the keyline to knock out the object. (The rest of the keyline overprints the object below it.)	▪ If you output your job as camera-ready artwork from which a printer will make negatives for you, the keyline will serve as a guide for him or her to know where to strip in the halftones or stats from photos or artwork you supply. Typically, a keyline is either an open or solid box with information printed within it that identifies the image to be used in that spot. If you will be outputting your job to *film*, then it is *your* responsibility to be sure all your images are scanned, placed, *and trapped* accurately. This can get a little hairy in multicolored jobs. See my warning regarding trapping: 16.127.
10.307 Create a keyline to use as a frame or decorative box  *The outer border of this PS group of objects is a keyline. Notice how it was created in reference to the perimeter of the grouped objects (it was inset -14 points). The keyline can be moved independently of the group.*	▪ With the **pointer tool,** select the object you want to frame. ▪ From the Utilities menu choose the Addition "Create keyline…." ▪ Enter a value for how far you want the keyline to extend away from or in towards the object. ▪ Click the "Attributes…" button; select fill and line attributes for the keyline box. ▪ Select and delete the box and re-run the Addition if it isn't what you want (there is no "Undo").	▪ PageMaker uses the handles of the object as reference points. The larger the number you enter in the "Extend" box, the farther the keyline is from the object's handles. Negative numbers in the "Extend" box place the keyline inside of the object's handles. ▪ The line weight you choose for the keyline is measured *in* from the perimeter of the keyline box (the same as assigning a line weight to PageMaker-drawn objects).

Where the good-natured User
will see something
that will give him no little Pleasure.

11 ▾ LINKING TEXT & GRAPHICS

11.1   Methods of Linking:

Place (Sections 3, 4, 8, 9, 10)

Placed text and graphics are automatically linked to their original, external files. By default, PageMaker stores a complete copy of the object in your publication which can then be updated manually or automatically. If you choose not to store the object within the publication, you can easily maintain the link to the external file. The object will update automatically when the original is revised.

Publish and Subscribe (11.79–11.102)

PageMaker can "subscribe" to "editions" published in other Macintosh applications. Files are linked and can be updated automatically, or as you choose. You can update the edition in more than one publication at the same time.

OLE, Object-linking and -embedding (11.103–11.132)

OLE, object linking and embedding, is a method of linking text or graphics *copied* from an OLE server program, usually a Windows or Microsoft program such as Microsoft Word, or Excel. Embedded files are stored within your publication; linked files are stored externally, and can be updated automatically, or as you choose.

Paste special (10.110–10.119)

Paste linking comes available when the object on the Clipboard is from an OLE server program.

11.2   PageMaker 5 automatically **links** all text and graphics that you place in your publication to their original, external files. Through the link, PageMaker keeps track of any changes that you make in the original text or graphic file and generally gives you a *choice* (11.66) of whether to update the publication version with the original, changed version.

11.3   The benefits of linking are twofold: you can easily update the information in a PageMaker publication, and you can manage the size of your publication by storing memory-intensive graphics externally. If you choose, however, you can completely ignore the linking function and everything will operate as if linking didn't exist. If you don't change the link defaults (11.77), you'll never know it's working and it will never bother you.

11.4   If you are working in a group, where several writers are revising text, several artists are working on graphics, and others are laying out the publication, the linking feature can be invaluable. With sensible use of it, you can keep track of which versions of the text or graphics have been updated, which have been modified but are not updated, which

are missing their original versions, and other link management tasks.

11.5   PageMaker supports three systems of linking: her own "Place" command (the most reliable), Apple's System 7 "Publish and Subscribe," and Microsoft's "OLE" (pronounced olé) or Object Linking and Embedding. The general information in this section about linking pertains to *all* methods with a few noted exceptions about OLE. Specific information about Publish and Subscribe is in 11.79–11.102; OLE is dealt with in detail in 11.103–11.132.

About linking 532
Managing links 533
Updating links, ... 534
Missing links 535
Printing linked files 535
The "Links" dialog box 536
Status chart and indicators 537
Avoiding trouble in workgroups 538
The "Link info" and "Link options"
    dialog boxes 539
Tasks 540
Publish and Subscribe 553
OLE 557
"Insert object" 561

About linking

11.6   There are several ways to import graphics or text into PageMaker that will establish linked files. You can link files when you **Place** them in either the layout view or in the Story Editor. You can utilize the "Import" and "Update" commands under the Edit menu if you **Subscribe to** an edition with Publish and Subscribe (11.79–11.102). Or you can **Paste link** OLE objects through the Clipboard (11.103–11.132).

11.7   In each of these import methods, text and graphics are *automatically* linked as you drop them into PageMaker. As soon as the imported document is in PageMaker, she sees it as having two parts, an internal file on the publication page and an external file tucked away on a disk somewhere. PageMaker keeps track of the *name* and the *location* of each external file (that is, in which folder and on which disk, whether hard or floppy). It's important to remember that, while PageMaker keeps track of the name and the location, if you change the name of the external file or if you move it then the link will be broken. You can, however, always re-establish a broken link (11.65).

11.8   Graphics or text that you *copy* from any other program or from the Scrapbook and then *paste* into PageMaker will *not* have any links established. You can manually link copied items if the original is a separate file stored on a disk.

11.9   However, if you cut or copy graphics or an entire story from your PageMaker publication—*graphics or stories that already have links established*—the link information will also transfer when you paste them; that is, the pasted text or graphics will also be linked to the *original*, external files. The same holds true for graphics or text you drag-and-drop from one PageMaker publication to another.

11.10   You can also *change* the links (11.52; 11.63). PageMaker doesn't really care what you link to what; if you say, "Link this to that," she'll do it (as long as you connect a graphic to a graphic and text to text). The link is only connected to a file with that particular name in that particular folder on that particular disk. If you put another file in the same location with the same name, then *that* new file is the one that will be linked to the publication. When you open the publication, PageMaker will notice that something has been changed and will ask if you want to update to the new version.

11.11   Text typed directly in PageMaker has no link to an external file, nor do graphics created in PageMaker. However, if necessary, you can create an external link for text; see 11.70.

11.12   If you happen to remove or lose or throw away an external file that is linked to a PageMaker publication, in most cases it is not a big deal (as long as you don't need the external changes). All text files have their complete copies stored within the publication anyway (11.16–11.23), so what you see in the publication will print. Any graphic that is stored in the publication will also print as you see it. So the only problem you may run into is if you lose the external version of a high-resolution graphic file that you placed or subscribed to and didn't store in the publication. In this case, all you will be able to print is the low-res screen version.

Managing links

11.13 When you open a publication in 5.0, PageMaker looks for any links that have been established and then follows your instructions on how to deal with them. If you have never gone into any of the Links dialog boxes and fiddled around, then you won't notice any difference between opening a publication with links and opening one without links. See also 11.16–11.23.

11.14 If you do want to be in control of the links and take advantage of their power, you need to establish a *management system* (which is only a fancy term for deciding whether to update the files or not). You can choose to update the internal file in one of several ways:

a) You can set an **application default** (11.77) that will check every link whenever a publication is opened and, if there are changes to an external file, will update the internal file. You can choose to have this done automatically upon opening a publication, or you can choose to have PageMaker ask if you really do want each update. As an application default, it will apply to every publication you create *from that point on.*

b) You can set a **publication default** (11.78) for the link update options that will do the same as an application default, but it will only apply to the current publication. That is, the next time you open that particular publication, all links will either be automatically updated or you will be asked for permission to update. A publication default will override any application default.

c) You can set **separate** link update options for each text or graphic file (11.60) within the publication. When the publication is next opened, these options instruct PageMaker whether to update the link automatically or to let you know before it gets updated. Individualized options will override any defaults.

d) While you are working within a publication, you can choose to instantly update any or all files that you know (or you discover) have been changed externally (11.66).

e) Also, while you are working within a publication, you can choose to link an internal file to a *different* file altogether. This not only changes the link, it changes the internal file itself, right in front of your very eyes (11.63). Keep in mind, though, that as soon as you change the link, the new text or graphic file drops into the place of the first one. If it is a story, the new file takes on all the existing text attributes of the one it is replacing in the publication (unless you "Retained the format" when you originally placed it; 4.55). If it is a graphic image, the new file takes on the size and proportions of the one it is replacing.

11.15 Important note: If you made changes to the *internal version* of a Page-Maker story while in the publication, and then updated it with the changes that came from the *external version*, any alterations you made to the *internal version* will be lost. There is no automatic way to combine the revisions made within PageMaker with the revisions in the external file—the *external file* will always override the *internal file.* (See 11.68 to update the external version with the internal version.)

Updating links

11.16 PageMaker always stores complete copies of any text files directly in the publication; that is, they just become part of the publication itself. If you copy the publication to another disk, all the text files that are part of it will be included in that copy. PageMaker maintains a link to their external files, though, in case you want to make any updates.

11.17 You can choose, through the "Link options" dialog box, whether or not to store a complete copy of graphic files in the publication (11.55). If you do choose to store them, the publication size will grow that much larger, which can cause PageMaker to slow down, as well as cause the pub to become so large you would have trouble backing it up conveniently. (Remember to compress TIFF files before you place them; 10.152–10.153.)

11.18 If you choose *not* to store graphic files, you will see the low-resolution version on the screen (to view a temporary high-res version of grayscale TIFFs, see 10.158). When you print, PageMaker will find the external, linked, complete version and use that data for printing, regardless of the screen version. So make sure you keep all your links

connected by not renaming them or removing them from their folder. If you do have to rename or move them, be sure to re-establish the links (11.65).

11.19 Now, there seems to be a Catch-22 here. As PageMaker opens the publication, any file that is stored *within* is left as is. If there is a file that has its only copy stored *outside* the publication, that external file is the only one PageMaker can use to open the publication. Thus, any revisions to the original, external file *are automatically transferred to the publication version, without even asking your permission!* If you do not store a copy in the publication, you cannot *choose* to update and be alerted. As the pub opens, you will see a tiny, brief message flash by, then lo and behold, your image is changed. The response to this can range anywhere from surprise to irritation to homocidal threats.

11.20 There are three ways to prevent surprise revisions. One is to store the copy in the publication, then choose to update and be alerted before the update. But storing all of the graphics in the pub can create gargantuan files (in this book, Section 10, without storing the files and with every TIFF compressed, is almost five megabytes—aack!).

11.21 A second way to prevent surprise revisions is to store the copy outside the publication, then make sure that any revisions that are not final do not *replace* the original, external version. You can do this by naming them something different, like "Graphic 2.1" and "Graphic 2.2." When you decide you *do* want to update, change the link to the new version (11.63).

11.22 A third way is to temporarily break the link to the external file using the "Unlink" button in the "Links" dialog box (11.35). However, when you are ready to print the publication, you must diligently relink the file (11.65). Of course, if the file is stored within the publication you only need to relink if you want to update it.

11.23 OLE-linked objects are always stored externally, but there is enough information in the internal file that PageMaker does not need the external copy to open the publication. Therefore, revisions to the original file are not automatically transferred unless you want them to be. If you decide that you do, then choose "Update automatically" in the "Links option" dialog box (11.55) and, if you want, instruct PageMaker to alert you first (11.56).

Missing links

11.24 As PageMaker opens the publication, she looks for the links for all imported files. If she **cannot find a link** to a file that is **stored** in the publication, she quietly puts a question mark next to the file name in the "Links" dialog box (11.31). If you previously selected an automatic update on that file (11.60), PageMaker will ask you to find the missing link. When you establish a new link by selecting a file in the list, the internal file gets updated.

11.25 If PageMaker **can't find a link** to a file that is **not stored** in the pub, she gives you an alert box informing you that the link can't be found and asking you whether she ought to ignore or re-establish the link. If you previously selected the update option, the file will be updated automatically as the link is re-established. If you don't re-establish the link, PageMaker puts a question mark next to the file name in the "Links" dialog box (11.31).

11.26 PageMaker will not alert you about missing links for OLE objects. She will simply place a question mark next to the file name in the "Links" dialog box (11.31).

Printing linked files

11.27 When you choose to print, PageMaker first looks for all the linked files in the places where they are supposed to be. If they are not there, she then checks the folder that holds the publication itself. If they are not there, she gives you a warning:

> ⚠ One or more of the linked items in this publication may not print as expected. See the 'Links...' dialog for more information.
>
> [Print pub]
> [Cancel print]

11.28 You can Cancel the printing and go back to re-establish the missing links (11.65) or update the file (11.66), and try printing again. Or you can ignore the warning and print anyway. You will see this warning even if you are printing only one page out of a multi-page publication. *It doesn't necessarily mean that the page you are printing is missing a link;* it just means that somewhere in the entire publication some link is amiss.

11.29 If you are taking your publication to another printer for output, either to a service bureau or to a do-it-yourself place, you must make sure to bring all the linked files. If PageMaker cannot find the external version of a high-resolution graphic, the printer will only print the low-resolution screen version. (Actually, the only linked files that are critical are the graphic files that have been placed or subscribed to, and that do not have copies stored in the publication.)

11.30 See 11.73 for an easy way to make sure you get all the linked files into one place so you can take them to the remote printer. You can choose to copy all the linked files or just those linked files that are not stored in the publication. If you are going to a service bureau (19.134–19.136 and 19.150–19.161), ask them what they need from you.

11.31 The "Links" dialog box   *(from the File menu, choose "Links…"; or press Command =)*

11.32   *This dialog box gives a list of the text and graphic documents in the publication. The symbol in the margin indicates their link status; see 11.40–11.48.*

An edition is "Subscribed to" through the Publish and Subscribe command; see 11.79–11.102.

See 11.103–11.132 for info on embedded and linked Word documents (OLE objects).

"PS Group it" creates an external EPS file (10.254). In all other cases, text or graphics that have been created within PageMaker are not linked (text can be linked if you export it; 11.70).

11.33   *This button will show the "Link info" box for the selected file; 11.51–11.54.*

Links

Document	Kind	Page
◆ **About linking**	🗋 **Text**	**410**
alligator/tiff(L)	🗋 **TIFF**	**PB**
JMS Edition	▢ **Encapsulated PostScript**	**PB**
◇ **PM4/Sect3/TextA**	🗋 **Text**	**409**
NA	⇄ **Embedded Word Docum…**	**409**
PerfAppraisal	⇄ **Linked Word Document**	**411**
Violets.PMG1	🗋 **Encapsulated PostScript**	**416**

OK

Status : The linked document has been modified since the last time it was placed. However, automatic updates have not been requested.

[**Info…**]   [**Options…**]   [**Unlink**]   [**Update**]   [**Update all**]

11.39   *OK does not make anything happen in this dialog box! It will just close the box for you— nothing will be updated or changed unless you have clicked any of the buttons (or buttons within buttons) below. Notice you cannot Cancel any updates you make. If you make a mistake, you can Revert (18.30– 18.31).*

11.38   *The status of the linked object is spelled out for you here in addition to the symbol denoting the status under "Document" (11.32).*

11.34   *This button will show the "Link options" box for the selected file; 11.55–11.57.*

11.35   *This button will break the link between the selected file and its external version; 11.64.*

11.36   *This button will immediately update the selected internal file with its current external version; see 11.66.*

11.37   *This button will immediately update all files that have modified links **and** that have the option "Update automatically" checked in their "Link options" dialog box; see 11.67. (When you open the publication, you know the files will be updated. But these Update buttons allow you to update the files without having to close the publication.)*

11.40 Status chart

Status indicators

blank   This item is not linked, or the link is up-to-date *(check the status;* 11.38; 11.42).

◊   The external file has been modified, but you haven't requested an automatic update (11.43).

♦   The external file has been modified; the internal version will be updated automatically the next time you open the publication (11.44).

△   Both the external file and the internal file have been modified (if it is updated, the internal changes will be lost; 11.45).

?   PageMaker cannot find the external, linked file (11.46).

>   A link in a file converted from Windows PageMaker is not fully supported in Macintosh PageMaker (11.47).

¿   A file may not print at high-resolution for various reasons (11.48).

These indicators are intended to provide at-a-glance info. For more specific info, click on the name of the file; below the list box you will see the precise, current status (11.38).

11.41   The narrow space, or column, to the left of the list of file names, displays the symbols that indicate the current status of all files in the publication. It's a guide to the publication at a glance. You can always click once on a file to get more detailed information in the "Status" info bar (11.38).

11.42   If the status column is **blank,** you have no problems—all the external, linked files are the same as the ones in the publication.

11.43   If the status column shows a **hollow diamond** (◊), it means that the external file (the source file) has been changed, but the link options for that file have *not* been set to update it automatically. You may want to check with whoever made the changes and see if they are really meant to be included in your publication. If they are, you can click the "Update" button to make the changes.

11.44   If the status column shows a **black diamond** (♦), it means that the external file (the source file) has been changed and the link option has been set to automatically update it. Again, you may want to check to make sure the changes are really meant to be included in the pub. If they are, you can click the "Update" button or you can just wait until the next time you open the

publication, as the changes will be made automatically at that time.

11.45   If the status column shows a **hollow triangle** (△), you may have a problem. This means that *both* the internal file and the external file have been changed. (If you have rewritten copy, reformatted, or even kerned characters in the publication itself, the internal file is considered changed.) If you ask for an update, the external changes will override any internal changes. It's a good idea to remove any "Update automatically" links from that file, then find out which set of changes (internal or external) takes precedence. If both, you have some manual work to do combining the changes.

11.46   If the status column displays a **question mark** (?), it means the linked, external file can't be found. It may have been moved from its folder, or the name may have been changed. If it is a text file and you never find it, it only means you won't be able to update any changes that may have been made in the external file; PageMaker will print what you see in the pub. If it is a high-res graphic and the link is missing, you will only be able to print the low-res screen version.
—continued

Status indicators *—continued*

11.47 A **greater than symbol** (>) means that a link in a file converted from *Windows* PageMaker is not fully supported in *Macintosh* PageMaker. This could have to do with the options you selected when you translated the file or with the filter required to print that graphic format. Click once on the file to get more info in the "Status" info bar. (See 17.47 for information on opening a Windows PageMaker file in Macintosh PageMaker.)

11.48 An **upside down question mark** (¿) means that an object may print at high resolution but without the expected results, or it may not print at high-res at all. There are a variety of reasons that could cause this status including a modified linked file for which your publication has not been updated, a missing link, an improper image translation (PC to Mac), or missing import filters.

Kind indicators

◻ Indicates a Placed item, whether it is text or a graphic. The file type that follows is more specific (11.31).

▧ Indicates an Edition: a file to which you have subscribed. See Publish & Subscribe; 11.79–11.102.

⮂ Indicates the object is OLE-embedded, or OLE-linked. See OLE; 11.103–11.132.

Page location

LM	The left master page.
RM	The right master page.
PB	The pasteboard.
OV	The object is within overset text—text that is hidden in a rolled up windowshade.
UN	The object has not yet been placed on a publication page from the Story Editor.

11.49 *PageMaker's visual indicators help you keep track of the kind of links in your publication and the location of each, even when an item is not on a page.*

Avoiding trouble in workgroups

11.50 One of the biggest problems that seems to arise in workgroup publishing is keeping track of all the versions of the stories and graphics and knowing which one is, or should be, in the current publication. If one person takes a copy of the linked word-processing file and tweaks it, then another person takes a different copy of the same file and tweaks it, pretty soon you have an incredible mess. There is undeniably a lot of cooperation and organization that must evolve in any group, and groups must work it out among themselves. But one tip regarding links management can help any group, and that is based on the Conch System. Remember *Lord of the Flies*? "He who has the Conch, speaks." In this case, "S/He who holds the File Folder containing the hard copy of the document, can tweak." If you don't have that file folder in your hand, you can't touch the document. If you do, then you and you alone are authorized to make changes. Put the hard copy for the current changes in the Conch folder, preferably with name, date, time, and notes. The person working on the PageMaker publication cannot update changes unless the appropriate Conch folder is in their hands.

11.51 The "Link info" and "Link options" dialog boxes

(With the pointer tool, click on a text block or graphic, then from the Element menu choose "Link info..." or "Link options...."; or in the "Links" dialog box [File menu], click the "Info..." or "Options..." buttons)

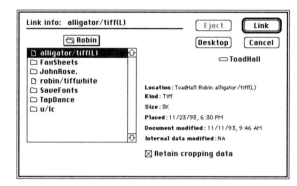

11.52 *Use the "Link info" dialog box to:*
a) *Find information about an item.*
  (NA stands for "Not applicable.")
b) *Change the link (11.63).*

11.53 *If you are just checking the information, click Cancel (or press Command Period) instead of hitting the Return key, as Return will activate the "Link" button, linking the item to whatever file is selected in the list box (if you do accidentally hit Return, you will have a chance to cancel, though).*

11.54 *If the "Link info..." command from the Element menu is gray, it means either nothing has been selected with the pointer tool or the text tool, or the item selected is not linked to anything because it was created within PageMaker.*

11.55 *Use the "Link options" dialog box to customize the options for the selected item. Each option is dependent on the one above it being selected; that is, you cannot "Update automatically" unless you first choose to "Store copy in publication" (11.16– 11.17). This does not mean you can't update the file—it just means the process won't take place automatically; you will have to request it (11.60).*

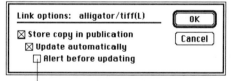

11.56 *If you choose to "Alert before updating," the next time the publication is opened and PageMaker notices that the original version has been altered, PageMaker will first ask you if you really do want to update the file.*

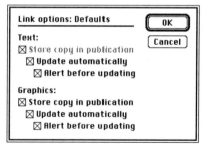

11.57 *If there is nothing selected and no insertion point flashing, the "Link options" dialog box (above) allows you to set the defaults (11.77–11.78). "Store copy in publication" for text is gray because text is **always** stored in the publication (11.16).*

If you want to do this:	Then follow these steps:	Shortcuts ▾ Notes ▾ Hints
11.58 Establish a link to a file that has been placed	■ You already did. Really. To prove it, choose "Links…" from the File menu. Every text and graphic file you placed or imported into the publication is listed (11.32).	■ Actually, the *link* itself is automatically established as soon as you place the file into PageMaker. What is *not* automatically established is how you want to deal with that link; see 11.55. ■ With certain programs (such as newer versions of FreeHand and PhotoStyler) PageMaker establishes a "hotlink"—all PageMaker updates are automatic when you save the original document (11.69).
11.59 Edit a linked item in its original application	■ With the **pointer tool** select the object. ■ From the Edit menu select "Edit original." ■ In the original application, make your changes. Save and quit the application. ■ From the Applications menu choose PageMaker, *or* click on your PageMaker window to make it active. ■ Objects that were set to "Update automatically" in the "Link options" dialog box, as well as Editions, will be updated when you return to the publication. Update the link in the "Links" dialog box for all other files (11.66–11.67).	■ The command is greyed out if you select an object that is not linked. If you select an OLE object, the command name changes to reflect the object you have selected (11.123). ■ In the Story Editor, set the insertion point within the text you want to revise, or select the marker of an inline graphic, then choose "Edit original" from the Edit menu. ■ Another way to launch the original program is to hold down the Option key and double-click on a linked object. A simple double-click on a selected OLE object will launch its server program. ■ See 11.75 to edit a linked object in an application other than the one in which it was created. ■ Also see Graphics, 10.146 and 10.148.

If you want to do this:	Then follow these steps:	Shortcuts ▾ Notes ▾ Hints

11.60 Set the link options for a file
(for "Editions" see also 11.93, 11.101)

- With the **text tool** click anywhere in the story **or,** with the **pointer tool** click on any text block in the story or on any graphic.
- From the Element menu choose "Link options...."
- If the selected file is text, the first option "Store copy in publication" is gray because text files are always stored in the publication. If the selected file is a graphic, you can choose to have its copy stored in the publication (11.16–11.23).
- If the copy is stored in the publication, the next option becomes available to you: "Update automatically." If you check this box, any changes that are made in the original, external file will be automatically transferred to the internal file when the publication is next opened. If you do not check it, you will still be able to update the internal file (11.66)—it just won't happen automatically.
- If you choose to update automatically, the next option becomes available to you: "Alert before updating." If you select it, the next time you open this publication you will get a warning before the file is updated automatically, with an option to ignore the update.

- If "Link options..." is gray, the object (text block or graphic) you selected has no external link. Objects pasted from the Clipboard (and OLE-embedded objects) contain all the information they need and don't need an external link (see 11.111). Text or graphics created within Page-Maker don't have an external link unless you create one. You can create an external link for text (11.70). Grouping items using the "PS Group it" Addition (10.254) creates an external link for PageMaker graphics.
- The "Link options" dialog box looks slightly different for text than it does for graphics: the option "Store copy in publication" is gray and already chosen because text files are *always* stored in the publication (11.16).
- "Store copy in publication" is gray *and* checked for OLE-linked objects. Although these files are never stored in the publication, you have the option to update as if they were.
- Objects imported with the Publish and Subscribe command set link options in yet another way; see 11.93.

If you want to do this:	Then follow these steps:	Shortcuts ▾ Notes ▾ Hints

11.61 Determine the status of a file

- With the **text tool** click anywhere in the story **or,** with the **pointer tool** click on any text block in the story or on any graphic.
- From the Element menu choose "Link info...."
- The "Link info" dialog box will tell you all about your file (11.51–11.54).
- You can also get this dialog box for any individual file by following the steps in 11.62.

- Be careful about hitting the Return key to get out of this dialog box—the default button here is "Link," which will link the file that is selected on the publication page with the file that is highlighted in the list box. If you accidentally hit Return (and therefore "Link"), and the selected file is not the one you want to link to, an alert box will appear and offer you a chance to Cancel the link change.

11.62 Determine the status of any and all files

- From the File menu choose "Links...," *or* press Command = .
- Check the status code for any file (11.40–11.49).
- Click once on any file name to see the exact status of the file spelled out for you at the bottom (11.38).
- Click once on a file, then click the "Info…" button to get the "Link info" dialog box for further details about the file (11.51–11.54); *or* just double-click on the file name to get that dialog box.
- Click once on a file, then click the "Options..." button to get the dialog box to change your storing and updating options (11.55–11.56).
- Click OK, *or* press Return.

- You can't Cancel out of the "Links" box; although the keyboard shortcut for canceling (Command Period) will close it, any changes you made in the "Links" dialog box will be retained. Clicking OK is a little disturbing in this dialog box, because we are used to OK buttons making things happen. In this case, nothing happens—the box just goes away.
- If you accidentally update or change something you really didn't mean to, you can choose "Revert" from the File menu (18.30–18.31).

If you want to do this:

Then follow these steps:

Shortcuts ▾ Notes ▾ Hints

11.63 Change a link

- From the File menu choose "Links...,"
  or press Command = .
- Double-click on the file name, *or* click once on it then click the "Info..." button to get the "Link info" dialog box.
- Double-click on the file name you want linked to your internal file.
- You must connect a graphic file to a graphic file, and a text file to a text file. Other than those parameters, you can switch any internal file to link up with any external file.
- If the newly-linked file is different than the file in the original link, PageMaker will ask you if you want to change the linkage. If you click "Yes," the new link is estab-lished and the file in the publication is instantly updated to the new, external file.

- This is really kind of fun. Just by changing the links you can drop new graphics or text into your publication! A new graphic takes on all the proportions and transfor-mations of the one it's replacing; text will fill the same width text block as the previous text.
- If the option "Retain cropping data" is checked in the "Link info" dialog box, a new graphic will keep the same cropping info as the one it is replacing.

11.64 Unlink a file

- From the File menu choose "Links...,"
  or press Command = .
- Click once on the file name you want to unlink.
- Click the "Unlink" button.

- PageMaker will not check or update the status of a file that has been unlinked.
- If you unlink an OLE-linked object it becomes an OLE-embedded object (11.111).
- If you unlink an Edition, it will take on all the attributes of having been pasted in from the Clipboard. If it was not stored within the publication, PageMaker will offer you a chance to do so before she unlinks the file.

If you want to do this:	Then follow these steps:	Shortcuts ▾ Notes ▾ Hints
11.65 Re-establish a broken link	■ From the File menu choose "Links...," *or* press Command = . ■ Any file that has a question mark to the left of its name is missing its link (11.46). Double-click on the file name, *or* click once on it then click the "Info..." button; you will get the "Link info" dialog box. ■ You can navigate through this dialog box just as you navigate through any other "Place" or "Save as" dialog box—open folders, switch disks, etc.—to find the external file with which to link up. When you find the external file name, double-click on it, *or* click once, then click the "Link" button or hit Return. ■ Click OK, *or* press Return.	■ If the link is missing because the external file has been renamed, you can simply name that external file with the original, linked name again. If the link is missing because the external file has been moved, put the file back into the folder in which PageMaker keeps looking for it. Or you could put it in the same folder as the publication, as PageMaker always looks there for linked files if she can't find them where they belong. ■ You can also relink any internal file to the external file with the new name or the new location. You can also change the link altogether and link the internal file to any other external file you want. See 11.63 to change a link.

Another method:
■ If you know which file is missing its link, click once on it with the **pointer tool.**
■ From the Element menu choose "Link info...."
■ Navigate through the folders and disks to find the missing link (the external file). When you find it, double-click on the file name, *or* click once, then click the "Link" button or hit Return.

If you want to do this:	**Then follow these steps:**	**Shortcuts ▾ Notes ▾ Hints**
11.66 Update one file immediately	■ With the **text tool,** click anywhere in the story **or,** with the **pointer tool,** click on any text block in the story or on any graphic. ■ From the Element menu choose "Link info...." ■ Find the name of the external file in the list box. Double-click on it, *or* click once on it and click the "Link" button or hit Return. The internal file will immediately be revised to the external version. **Another method:** ■ From the File menu choose "Links," *or* press Command = . ■ If the file has an external version that has been changed, you will see a black or a hollow diamond to the left of its name (11.40–11.44). Click once on the file name, then click the "Update" button. ■ Click OK.	■ Read 11.13–11.15 on all the ways to automatically update files each time the publication is opened. ■ If you update a file and then realize you really didn't want to do that, you can Revert (18.30; 18.31).
11.67 Update all files immediately	■ From the File menu, choose "Links," *or* press Command = . ■ If any file has an external version that has been changed, you will see a black or a hollow diamond to the left of its name (11.40–11.44). Click the "Update all" button. ■ Click OK.	■ Read 11.13–11.15 on all the ways to automatically update files each time the publication is opened.

If you want to do this:	**Then follow these steps:**	**Shortcuts ▾ Notes ▾ Hints**

11.68 Update the external version of a text file with the internal version

- With the **pointer tool,** click once anywhere in the story.
- From the File menu choose "Export...."
- Under "File format" choose the word processor that you typically work with.
- Under "Export" click "Entire story."
- In the list box, find the name of the external version you want to update.
- Where the insertion point is flashing, type in the *exact* name of the external version you want to update.
- Hit Return, or click OK.
- In response to the alert "Replace existing '_____'?," click "Yes." The external version is now the same as the internal version.
- If you didn't get the "Replace . . ." alert, either you did not type the exact name, or the file you want to update was not in the list box. Either way, you did not *update* the external version, but created a *new* external version. The internal file is still linked to the *first* external version.

- This procedure is actually *exporting* the internal text with the same name as the external file you want to update/replace.
- See Section 17 for more details on importing and exporting.

- The file name may already be in the edit box if you originally placed the story using the options "A new story" or "Replacing entire story." Selecting either of these retains the original file name.

Life
is either
a daring
adventure
or nothing.

—Helen Keller

If you want to do this:	Then follow these steps:	Shortcuts ▾ Notes ▾ Hints
11.69 Establish a "hotlink"	■ Create a graphic in FreeHand (3.1 or later), Persuasion (2.1 or later), PhotoStyler (1.1 or later), PrePrint, or ColorStudio (1.5 or later). ■ In PageMaker, from the File menu, choose "Place." ■ Select and place the graphic created in one of the programs named above.	■ A hotlink updates your publication whenever you save the original document. ■ From within PageMaker, you can launch the original program and edit the object (11.59). The update in your PageMaker publication will occur as you are saving the original document.
11.70 Establish an external link to text that was typed directly in PageMaker	■ In order to establish an external link, you need to **export** the PageMaker file: ■ With the **text tool,** click once anywhere in the story. ■ From the File menu choose "Export...." ■ Choose a file format from the list of word processors (17.10–17.11 and 17.13–17.16). ■ Make sure the Export button "Entire story" is selected. ■ Click "Export tags" if you like (8.77). ■ Make sure you are saving it into the folder you want to keep it in (18.6–18.10). Name it with a title that identifies the file. ■ Click OK, *or* press Return. You now have an external version and it is linked.	■ In effect, you are turning PageMaker text into a word processed file, thereby creating a source file that can serve as a common link for other publications. ■ The internal version will be linked to the external version from now on. Any changes you make in the *internal* version will not be recognized by the *external* version, though. If you choose to update, the *external file* will replace the *internal file*. ■ You can place the external version into other publications. Many different publications can all have files linked to the same external file. ■ See Section 17 for detailed info on exporting; see 17.43 in particular.

If you want to do this:

Then follow these steps:

Shortcuts ▾ Notes ▾ Hints

11.71 Establish a link to a graphic that came in through the Clipboard

If the graphic that came in through the Clipboard has an external version of its own (a MacPaint file, a PhotoShop file, etc.), then you just need to establish a link:

- With the **pointer tool** click once on the graphic.
- From the Element menu choose "Link info...."
- Find the external file to which you want to link the graphic; double-click on it. It will be updated to the new link instantly!

- Be careful! When you copy and paste through the Clipboard you usually choose just part of the file to import. If you later go and link to the complete file, you'll end up importing the whole thing! It will come in scaled to fit within the boundaries of the original object.
- If the graphic has no original, external version, copy and paste the image into a graphic program and save it in a file format PageMaker can read (10.94–10.100). Go back to the PageMaker publication and place the new file you just created.

11.72 Copy linked documents when saving a PageMaker file

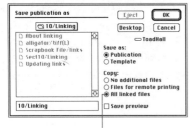

Click this radio button.

- From the File menu choose "Save as...."
- If there are stories or graphics in the publication that are linked to the original stories or graphics outside of PageMaker, then the option "All linked files" will be available. Click on the radio button next to it.
- Name the file, if necessary. Click OK.

- PageMaker will find the originals to all the internally and externally linked text and graphics in your publication and put copies of them on the disk or into the folder that is storing this PageMaker publication.
- See also 11.73.

If you want to do this:

11.73 Copy the files linked to your publication for remote printing (taking it to a service bureau or laserprint shop)

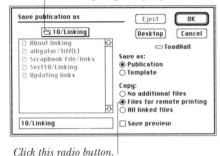

This is the label where you should see the name of the folder you just created.

Click this radio button.

Then follow these steps:

- At the Finder/Desktop, create an empty folder (Command N) and name it something appropriate to your project.
- Open your publication if it is not already open. Make sure there are no missing links (11.61; 11.62).
- I hope you've been using "Save as…" to compress the publication size all this time (18.29). Choose "Save as…" one more time. This time click the radio button next to "Files for remote printing."
- In the list box, find the name of the new *folder* you just created. Double-click on it; you will see the folder's name in the label, as shown in the example to the left.
- Click OK, *or* hit Return. This will copy the publication *and all the externally linked files into that folder.* Quit PageMaker.
- If you are sending the publication through a modem, send the entire folder. If you are taking a disk to a service bureau and that folder will fit onto one disk, do it. If you need more than one disk, go ahead and split up the files. The service bureau will copy all the files into one folder on their hard disk and print from there.

Shortcuts ▾ Notes ▾ Hints

- This procedure copies all files needed to print the publication properly, including a file called "Tracking Values" which some service bureaus may need. See 19.134–19.136 and 19.150–19.161 for details on using a service bureau.
- If all the files are in the same folder as the publication, it doesn't matter where you initially set up the links. PageMaker will look for them where you said they would be; but if they are not there, she will look for them in the same folder as the publication.
- Only the external, linked files that are *not* stored in the publication are copied, (with the exception of OLE-linked files which are not stored in the publication, but are not needed for printing either, 11.116). If you want to copy all the linked files *including* the ones stored internally and the OLE-linked files, click the radio button "All linked files"; see 11.72.

If you want to do this:

11.74 Create a template with linked files that will automatically update

Then follow these steps:

- Let's say you created a membership directory of names and phone numbers. Someone typed all the names and numbers in a word processor and you placed that file in the publication. When you are finished with the first publication, make a template out of it (which is just the same as creating a publication but when you choose to "Save as...," click the "Template" button; 14.14).
- Now it's time to do the quarterly update on the membership list. You can do either of two things:
  □ Open the original word processing list of names and numbers and revise it.
  □ Then open the PageMaker template. As it opens, PageMaker will ask if you want to update the internal stories. Yes you do. All the new names and numbers appear and you just have to fine-tune the publication.
- **Or:** You can create a *new* word processing file with updated names and numbers.
  □ Open the PageMaker template. Change the link of the existing text; link it to the new list of names and numbers (11.63). The new names will pour right onto the page.

Shortcuts ▾ Notes ▾ Hints

- This comes in handy in repetitive projects like directories or parts lists where everything but specific data stays the same.

—Swiss Proverb

If you want to do this:

11.75 Edit an imported item in an application other than the original one

11.76 Set a default to store large graphic files externally

Then follow these steps:

- With the **pointer tool** select the object.
- To open the "Choose editor" dialog box, hold down the Shift key and select "Edit original" from the Edit menu, *or* hold down the Option and Shift keys as you double-click on the object.
- In the Editor Aliases folder choose the application you want to use (if the folder is empty, navigate through your folders to locate the program you want to use). The status information tells you if the selected program can open the document.
- Click the "Launch" button.

- With the **pointer tool,** from the File menu, choose "Preferences"; click the "Other" button.
- Enter a value in the edit box next to "Alert when storing graphics over___" specifying the largest size graphic file you want stored internally.
- In your PageMaker publication, when you "Place" a graphic larger than this value, PageMaker will give you the option of storing the particular graphic externally no matter what defaults are set.

Shortcuts ▾ Notes ▾ Hints

- The Editor Aliases folder is in the Aldus folder in the System folder. The folder is empty until you store aliases of your programs there.
- This method bypasses the "application is missing" alert box you get when you choose "Edit original" from the Edit menu.

- You can increase or decrease the file size noted in the "Alert" preferences box. If you increase the file size, PageMaker will store larger graphics internally without checking with you. If you decrease the file size, PageMaker will ask for confirmation before storing any graphics larger than the value you enter.
- If you deselect "Store copy in publication" as a publication or application default (11.77–11.78), it does not matter what value is in the "Alert" preferences box.

If you want to do this:

Then follow these steps:

Shortcuts ▾ Notes ▾ Hints

11.77 Set link options as **application** defaults

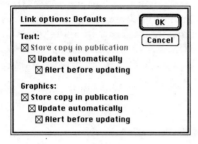

- Have PageMaker open, but no publication on the screen. All you should see is the PageMaker menu across the top.
- From the Element menu choose "Link options...."
- Click checkmarks in the commands you want to set as defaults.
- Click OK.

- As application defaults, the commands you set here will affect every *new* publication you create. Application defaults will be overridden by any publication defaults you set later (11.78), or by individual link options (11.60).
- New application defaults will not affect editions subscribed to using Publish & Subscribe; 11.85.

11.78 Set link options as **publication** defaults

- Open the publication for which you want to set defaults.
- From the Element menu choose "Link options...."
- Click checkmarks in the commands you want to set as defaults.
- Click OK.

- As *publication* defaults, the commands you choose here will affect only the publication in which you set the defaults. These new defaults will only affect files that are placed on the page *after* the defaults have been set; they will not affect any files already on the page.
- Publication defaults will not affect objects brought in through Publish & Subscribe. You must change these options individually for each edition; see 11.85.
- Individual link options (11.60) will override any publication defaults.

Publish and Subscribe

11.79 Publish and Subscribe is Apple's System 7-based "live" copy and paste feature; "live" because you can continually update the copied object. From within a program that supports this technology, you can "publish" (copy) a document or part of a document as a separate file, called an edition, to which you can "Subscribe to" (paste) in another program. The beauty is that now there is a link between the original and the "published" copy (the edition) to which any number of people on a network can subscribe. These editions can automatically be updated by a single user, *and,* if you update the original, all the editions in all the subscribing documents will be updated automatically when the pub is opened. Amazing! What's more, you can even subscribe to yourself!

11.80 PageMaker is one of many programs that support Publish and Suscribe as a "Subscriber." Using the commmand under the "Editions" submenu, you can subscribe to editions published in a myriad of applications that includes Aldus FreeHand, Microsoft Word and Excel, Claris Works, Canvas, PhotoShop, Illustrator, MacDraw Pro, etc.

11.81 Although subscribing is really just another method of placing and linking, it has a number of very cool features. For example, there is a preview window that gives you an advance look at exactly what you are subscribing to. And, editions subscribed to by multiple users can all be updated simultaneously. (The latter can also be a drag, though, as it *increases the time required to save in the publishing file.*)

11.82 In the "Subscribe to" dialog box (11.88), the preview window displays a thumbnail of the selected edition. Editions are generally text, PICT, or EPS formats. Careful, though, because PICTs have a reputation for being unreliable, especially when printing to an Imagesetter.

11.83 When you bring an edition into your PageMaker publication, your publication is the "Subscribing file," and the edition within your publication is called the "Subscriber"; see (11.100).

11.84 The link options available through the "Subscriber options" dialog box (11.93) are a combination of the options in the "Link options" dialog box (Element menu), and the "Links" dialog box (File menu). Link options you set in any of these dialog boxes will be reflected in the other two boxes. It can get rather confusing. Basically, if you are already familiar with PageMaker's link dialog boxes, stick with them; if you want to know more about the "Subscriber options" dialog box, see 11.93–11.99.

11.85 When you subscribe to an edition, the default is to store it in the publication and update it automatically. You can select a subscriber and change the link options; however, you can't change the application or publication defaults.

11.86 "Stop all editions" temporarily stops updates to subscribers that have selected "Automatically" in the "Subscriber options." This prevents updates without having to select and change the link options for each and every subscriber. It is in effect for existing subscribers in all the publications you open and close until you deselect the option or restart your computer (new subscribers are still updated by default). See 11.102.

11.87 To edit an edition, select it and choose "Edit original" from the Edit menu or, in the "Subscriber options" dialog box (11.93), click the "Open publisher" button (11.98; see also 11.101).

The "Subscribe to" and "Subscriber options" dialog boxes

(from the Edit menu, slide down to Editions then over to "Subscribe to" or "Subscriber options")

11.88 **The "Subscribe to" dialog box.**

11.89 *Navigate through folders to find the object to which you want to subscribe.*

11.90 *The Preview window displays a thumbnail of the selected edition.*

11.92 *Click "Subscribe" to import the selected edition into your PageMaker publication.*

11.91 *Select an edition to view it in the Preview window. You can double-click on an edition to subscribe to it and close the dialog box.*

11.94 *Shows the file name of the edition. Press on the pop-up menu to see where the edition is located.*

11.99 *Click "Cancel Subscriber" to unlink the file. This has the same effect as clicking the "Unlink" button in the "Links" dialog box; see 11.35 and 11.64.*

11.93 **The "Subscriber options" dialog box.**

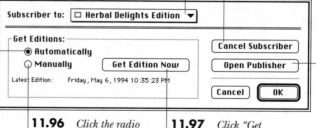

11.95 *Click the radio button next to "Automatically" if you want the subscriber in your publication to update whenever the original file is modified. This is the default setting.*

11.98 *Click "Open Publisher" to launch or switch to the publishing program and open the publishing file.*

11.96 *Click the radio button next to "Manually" to control all the updates. The edition will now be stored in the publication.*

11.97 *Click "Get Edition Now" to update the subscriber with the most recent version of the edition.*

If you want to do this:	Then follow these steps:	Shortcuts ▼ Notes ▼ Hints
11.100 Subscribe to an edition	■ With the **text tool** click where you want the edition to be inserted; ■ **Or,** select the **pointer tool** if you don't want to place the subscriber inline (just to make sure the insertion point is not flashing). ■ From the Edit menu slide down to "Editions," then over to the submenu and choose "Subscribe to...." ■ In the "Subscribe to..." dialog box, select the edition file you want, then click the "Subscribe" button; **Or** double-click on the edition name to select it and close the dialog box at the same time. ■ If the edition is an inline graphic it will automatically appear in the text. ■ If the edition is not an inline graphic, click the loaded icon down on the page where you want the upper-left corner of the subsciber to be; **Or** press-and-drag to define the size of the subscriber. Let go of the mouse button when the bounding box is the size you want the edition to be.	■ Only graphic editions can be pasted inline; when you subscribe to a text edition, you always get a loaded pointer icon. ■ PageMaker uses the default settings in the "Link options" dialog box. Text editions are stored in the publication; graphic files are stored internally but can be stored externally if you choose. PageMaker adds a default of "Update automatically" (11.55–11.56). ■ The "Edition" is the file that results when you publish text or graphics. The *file* the edition came from is called the **Publishing file** while the original text or graphic that you published from that file is called the **Publisher.** Your PageMaker publication is called the **Subscribing file,** and the edition within your publication is called the **Subscriber.** ■ To import a text edition as a PICT graphic, hold down the Shift key as you click "Subscribe." ■ You can use the "Subscribe to" command while working in the Story Editor. ■ The "Subscribe to..." dialog box automatically opens to a list including the most readily available editions.

If you want to do this:	Then follow these steps:	Shortcuts ▾ Notes ▾ Hints
11.101 Choose "Subscriber options" for a selected subscriber	■ With the **pointer tool** select the subscriber. ■ From the Edit menu slide down to "Editions," then over to the submenu and choose "Subscriber options...." ■ In the "Subscriber options..." dialog box: □ When you choose to "Manually" update a subscriber, the option in the "Link options" dialog box defaults to "Store in publication." ■ Click "Get Edition Now" if you want the subscriber to be updated now (11.97). ■ Choose "Open Publisher" to activate the program the edition came from and open the original publishing file (11.98). ■ Choose "Cancel Subscriber" if you want to unlink the file (11.99).	■ Choose "Automatically" if you want the subscriber to update each time you modify the original file. Choose "Manually" if you want to store the subscriber in the publication and initiate all updates yourself. ■ You can update a subscriber through the "Links" dialog box, too (11.31). If you choose to "Update all," then editions set to update "Manually" in the "Subscriber options..." dialog box will *not* be updated. ■ You can also open the edition's original file and program by selecting the subscriber and Option-double-clicking on it. ■ An unlinked subscriber is the equivalent of a graphic pasted in from the Clipboard. ■ You can relink subscribers the same as you can other linked files (11.65). The rule of linking only text files to text files and graphic files to graphic files still applies.
11.102 Stop all editions from updating	■ From the Edit menu slide down to "Editions," then over to the submenu and choose "Stop all editions." ■ Reselect "Stop all editions" to turn on automatic updating again. All updates will apply immediately. □ To prevent *pending* updates from happening, press the Shift key as you choose "Stop all editions."	■ This applies to all publications, both opened and closed, until you restart. It does not apply to new subscribers which are automatically updated by default. ■ You can override the "Stop all editions" command for one or all of the subscribers in a publication. In the "Links" dialog box, click "Update" or "Update all" (11.36–11.37).

OLE, Object-linking and -embedding

11.103 OLE, object-linking and -embedding, is Windows' and Microsoft's copy and paste version of importing (placing) by which you can bring text or graphics into a PageMaker publication through the Clipboard and yet still create a link. You can object-link or -embed anything that can be copied from an OLE server program to the Clipboard. Both Microsoft Word 5.0 and Excel 3.0 (and newer) are OLE server programs, but they also support System 7's Publish and Suscribe technology. At this time, OLE is used almost exclusively on the Windows platform.

11.104 Because you *are* copying and pasting, you can choose just what part of a file you want to have in your PageMaker publication. Unfortunately, in Word you are limited to what fits on a page; in Excel you are limited to what will fit on a pair of facing pages in PageMaker.

11.105 All OLE objects are pasted in as graphic elements (the screen representation of an OLE object is a PICT). Therefore, tables, charts, etc., hold all their formatting. Even OLE text that you paste into an existing text block in your publication is pasted in as a graphic element.

11.106 Since PageMaker can't edit OLE-linked and -embedded objects directly, a simple double-click on an embedded or linked file opens a window in the original source program. (If your file is converted from Windows 3.1, OLE-linked or -embedded objects in the file can be edited in the Macintosh version of the source program.)

11.107 Check the link information of an OLE object by selecting the object and choosing "Link info…" from the Element menu or by choosing "Links…" from the File menu.

11.108 Importing through the Clipboard may require more RAM than "Placing." If "Insufficient memory" dialog boxes haunt you, try placing the file or object with which you are working.

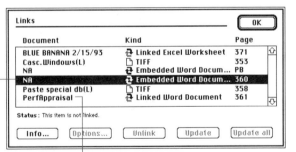

11.109 *An OLE-embedded object shows an embedded symbol and the name of the program it comes from. The file itself is labeled "NA" for not available, even if the file is from a saved original. The "Options…" and "Unlink" buttons are dimmed when an embedded object is highlighted in the dialog box. Embedded objects are never linked.*

11.110 *The symbol is slightly different for a linked object—the dimmed arrow lets you know that some of the information is elsewhere. The name of the source program is listed and the file is labeled with the name of the original document. OLE-linked objects can be managed in the same way as other linked objects; see 11.14.*

Object-embedding

11.111 OLE-embedded objects contain all their overhead information, relieving you of the need to keep track of an original file. In fact, the object may have been created in an unsaved file, or you might have thrown out the original version. It doesn't matter. All you need to do is create the object in an OLE server program, copy it, and then paste it into a PageMaker publication.

11.112 Because they contain all the information necessary to edit or print, embedded objects can add considerable size to your publication. Without a link, when you edit the object only that one copy will update; any other copies of the object are not affected.

11.113 You can choose "Paste" directly under the Edit menu to embed an OLE object, but you run the risk of PageMaker choosing Rich Text Format (RTF) from the Clipboard formats. A surer bet is to use the "Paste special…" dialog box; see 11.122.

11.114 An alternative method is to create an OLE object "on the fly" from within PageMaker. It's a great way to create and add a Word table or an Excel spreadsheet to a publication. See the "Insert object" command, 11.126–11.132.

"Paste link"

11.115 Rather then embed an OLE object in its entirety, you can "Paste link" it. The "Paste link" command is only available when the object on the Clipboard is from a saved file in an OLE server program. OLE-linked objects can be managed in the same way as other linked objects (see 11.14).

11.116 OLE-linked objects are never stored in your PageMaker publication. They are linked to the original file no matter how little or much of that file you pasted into PageMaker. It's up to you to maintain the link (11.7) if you want to be able to edit the object. However, the linked file is not necessary for printing, which does leave one to wonder about the reliability of printing these puppies.

11.117 When you unlink an OLE object, it becomes embedded. Unfortunately, an unlinked OLE object from Word cannot be edited, although it can be printed.

11.118 In general, use OLE for text or a graphic that fits on a page or pair of facing pages. The current source programs do not support multiple-page OLE text objects (11.104).

OLE reliability

11.119 Although there are situations in which OLE-linking and -embedding may be invaluable, PageMaker's "Place" command is a far more dependable method of importing. OLE was designed for the Windows platform to let you import objects from programs not supported by PageMaker or the Apple operating system. Well, currently on the Mac platform there are only two programs that support OLE, Word and Excel. And Page-Maker has import filters for both of them.

11.120 Still, it can be frustrating to import a Word table or an Excel spreadsheet using the "Place" command because the original formatting doesn't always hold. Since OLE imports text or graphics as a graphic object, you usually get all the formatting as it was in the original file in a format *similar to a PICT*—it is not entirely reliable, especially when printing to an imagesetter.

11.121 In the overall picture OLE works fine for importing objects from Windows programs or to publications whose final output is the laser printer. Although your table or chart may appear the same as it did in the original file, do check it carefully to make sure the text and/or graphics are complete.

If you want to do this:	Then follow these steps:	Shortcuts ▾ Notes ▾ Hints
11.122 Embed an OLE object	▪ In the OLE server program, copy the item to the Clipboard. ▪ Launch PageMaker or, if it is already open, select it from the Applications menu in the upper right hand corner of your Mac. ▪ In your PageMaker publication: ☐ Insert the **text tool** within text if you want the OLE object to paste as an inline graphic; ☐ **Or,** choose the **pointer tool** if you want the object to paste in independently. ▪ In your PageMaker publication choose "Paste special…" from the Edit menu. ▪ Select a format that makes the "Paste link" button available, but click "Paste."	▪ Simply selecting "Paste" from the Edit menu, or pressing Command V, will also embed the object, unless the object is text. If it's text, it's possible that it was also copied to the Clipboard in Rich Text Format (RTF). PageMaker will paste that format by default since it can be edited in PageMaker (and is therefore considered more advantageous to the user). ▪ When you paste art, animation, or sound created in a *Windows* program that supports OLE, PageMaker embeds an OLE object. ▪ You can "Multiple paste…" OLE objects (1.287–1.304).
11.123 Edit an OLE-embedded object *The Apply button on the object-view Control palette when an OLE object is selected.*	▪ Select the object with the **pointer tool,** then select the last menu item under the Edit menu, **or** simply double-click on the object. ▪ After you edit the object, select "Update" from the server program's menu (usually under the File menu) to update the object in your PageMaker publication. ▪ You can either quit the program or leave it open and choose PageMaker from the Applications menu.	▪ When the object is an OLE object, the last menu item of the Edit menu, "Edit original," is replaced by the object format, such as "Word Document object" or "Excel Worksheet object." ▪ A temporary file in the server program opens. The file does not exist anywhere else, and does not need to be saved. ▪ In Word, click the close box of the temporary file to close the file, update the embedded object in PageMaker, but leave the server program open.

If you want to do this:

Then follow these steps:

Shortcuts ▾ Notes ▾ Hints

11.124 Paste link an OLE object

The Apply button on the object-view Control palette when an OLE object is selected.

- In the OLE server program, copy the item to the Clipboard.
- From the Applications menu in the upper right hand corner of your Mac select PageMaker.
- In your PageMaker publication:
  □ Insert the **text tool** within text if you want the OLE object to paste as an inline graphic;
  □ **Or,** choose the **pointer tool** if you want the object to paste in independently.
- From the Edit menu choose "Paste link...."

- The "Paste link..." command is also available in the "Paste special" dialog box.
- If the "Paste link..." command is dimmed, it can mean one of two things:
  □ the program from which you copied does not support OLE (see 11.115);
  □ the file from which you copied was not saved.
- You cannot paste link a Word document that has an apostrophe in its filename. Change the filename, then copy the object you want to paste link.

11.125 Edit an OLE-linked object

You can choose to be alerted before updates occur and then to allow or ignore the updates.

- Select the object with the **pointer tool**, then from the Edit menu select the last menu item, **or** simply double-click on the object.
- Edit the object and save the document.
- Quit the OLE server program or choose PageMaker from the Applications menu.
- The object will update according to the options you set in the "Link options" dialog box (11.55).

- This can eat up RAM. If you get stuck, you may be better off avoiding it altogether.
- If you have trouble getting the original program to launch, try copying and pasting something small to clear RAM.
- Please read the general information about linking. An OLE-linked object is the *same* as other linked objects since the original document and source program are still necessary to edit the object and you must maintain the link in order to update the object. An OLE-linked object *differs* from other linked objects in that it cannot be stored in the publication, it won't update unless you request it, and the original file is not needed for printing.

11.126 The "Insert object" command is a way to embed an OLE object without it even existing yet. It is created "on the fly" from within PageMaker.

11.127 Located under the Edit menu, the "Insert object" command lets you open another program from within PageMaker. You don't need to go to the desktop, or the Apple menu, or the Applications menu. However, only OLE-compatible programs are available through the "Insert object" dialog box (at this time that is either Word or Excel or certain Windows programs).

11.128 When you select the type of object you want to create and click OK, the program that can create the object is opened. If the program is already open, it is brought to the foreground. In either case, a new, untitled document is opened for you.

11.129 Once you have created the object you can choose "Update" from the OLE program's File menu and then close or quit the program. PageMaker automatically inserts the object into your publication as an OLE-embedded object.

11.130 Since the "Insert object" command embeds OLE objects, it has the same limitations:

- Text is imported as a graphic and cannot be edited in PageMaker.

- The object is not linked, so you cannot update multiple copies of an object at the same time.

- Since the object is automatically stored in the publication, the size of the publication is increased.

- The source program must support OLE-embedding.

- Importing through the Clipboard may require more RAM than importing through the "Place" command.

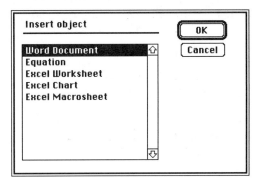

11.131 *Select "Word Document" to create an object in Microsoft Word, select any of the Excel options to create an object in Microsoft Excel. If you do not have the program, the format option will not be displayed here.*

If you want to do this:

Then follow these steps:

Shortcuts ▾ Notes ▾ Hints

11.132 Use the "Insert object" command to create and embed an object

The Apply button on the object-view Control palette when an OLE object is selected.

- With the **text tool** click where you want the object to be inserted;
- **Or,** if you do not want the object inserted as an inline graphic, select the **pointer tool.**
- From the Edit menu choose "Insert object."
- In the dialog box, highlight one of the format options to open a temporary file. Click OK;
- **Or,** double-click on any of the options to select it and close the dialog box.
- Create the object in the OLE program.
- In the OLE server program, from the File menu choose "Update" or "Quit and update," depending on what is available.
- Choose PageMaker from the Applications menu, *or* click on any visible part of the PageMaker window to make it active.

- At the moment, the only two Macintosh OLE server programs are Microsoft Word 5.0 and Excel 3.0 or later.
- In Word, you can simply click the window away. This inserts the object in PageMaker, but leaves the OLE server program open. Click on any part of the PageMaker window to make it active.
- You can double-click on an OLE-embedded object to launch the server program and edit the object in a temporary file.
- The "Insert object" command is not available in the Story Editor.

Our life is frittered away by detail... Simplify, simplify.

Henry David Thoreau

Containing a discourse on this most
Beneficial of Utilities, which may afford
a useful lesson to all Users.

12 ▾ LIBRARY PALETTE

12.1 Minimums and maximums:

Item	Minimum	Maximum
Palettes	0	Limited by disk space only
Items	0	Limited by disk space only

12.2 PageMaker's Library palette is simple to create, and simple to use. With it you can catalog and keep handy on the screen all the collections of text and graphics that you repeatedly use for various projects. When you want something, you just drag-and-drop whatever it is into your publication. You may even want to use it to group graphics by kinds (all your TIFFs in one palette, all your Paints in another, etc.), or to keep a handy reference of bits of information you can never seeem to find (a name and address, a by-line or credit, or a copyright notice).

12.3 You custom design each library to suit your needs. You decide what goes in it and you decide how to organize it. Items are added to it and dragged from it with a simple point and click. Keywords and other information can be added to the items in a library so you can search for specific categories of items. You can create as many Libraries as you need: one with the logo and business graphics of a regular client, another with frequently used text and graphics for a monthly newsletter.

12.4 The Library palette is a movable window and it will layer over any of the other palettes on screen. You can resize the palette window to view as many of its objects at once as you wish. Or you can choose to view just a list of items by name only (12.60).

12.5 Library palettes are not stored within publications. When you create a new library you choose where you want to store it, and you can access it from within any publication you want. However, you can only display one palette at a time.

12.6 Anything that can be copied to the Clipboard, can be added to the Library palette. PageMaker copies all the linked information about the object, so that you can count on all your updates to happen as you planned (11.14). Best of all, graphics retain their file format—no more "PICTs" when you least expect them.

12.7 To open the Library palette for the very first time, see 12.51.

Library palette basics 564
The Library palette window 566
Preferences & Item information 567
The "Search library" command 572

THE CHALLENGE OF TYPOGRAPHY, LIKE THE CHALLENGE OF ARCHITECTURE, IS THE INTEGRATION OF THE MATERIALS INTO A STRUCTURE WHICH WILL PERFORM A DESIRED FUNCTION. CARL DAIR · DESIGN WITH TYPE

Library palette basics

12.8 The command that lets you create a new library or open an existing one is found in the Library palette itself. You first must select "Library palette" from the Window menu. To open the Library palette for the first time, see 12.51.

12.9 To create a new library, select the "New library" command from the "Options" menu in the Library palette. After you name your new library and choose where to save it, you can add items to it from within your publication. You never have to intentionally save it again, although you should compress a library after you remove items from it (see 12.56). You may want to create a library folder in which you store all your libraries, or you may want to store a library in the folder with its publication.

12.10 Although you can create as many libraries as you want, only one library can be open at a time. Whenever you open an existing library, or create a new one, the library previously open closes.

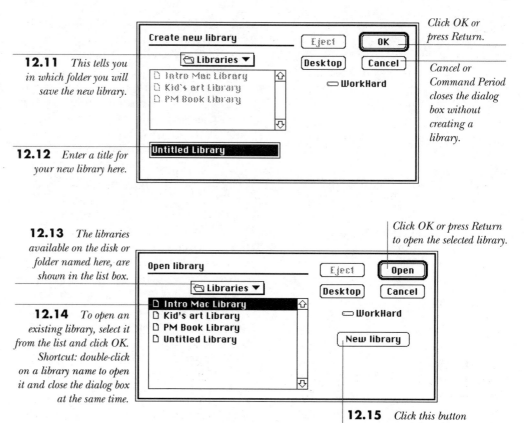

12.11 *This tells you in which folder you will save the new library.*

12.12 *Enter a title for your new library here.*

Click OK or press Return.

Cancel or Command Period closes the dialog box without creating a library.

12.13 *The libraries available on the disk or folder named here, are shown in the list box.*

12.14 *To open an existing library, select it from the list and click OK. Shortcut: double-click on a library name to open it and close the dialog box at the same time.*

Click OK or press Return to open the selected library.

12.15 *Click this button to create a new library.*

Library palette basics —*continued*

12.16 To add an item to a Library palette, use the pointer tool to select the object(s) on the page; then click the plus sign in the upper left-hand corner of the palette. The new item is added to the end of all the items; you may have to scroll the window to see it.

12.17 You can scroll through the library just as you would any window. You can press-and-drag on the resize button to enlarge the window and see more library objects. Click on an object in the palette to select it. It doesn't matter what tool you use, every tool turns into the pointer tool in the Library palette.

12.18 Use the **"Item information"** dialog box (12.46–12.50) to catalog information about objects in the library. You can name objects, and note the author, title, and any keywords that will make it easier to locate an object or a group of objects during a search (12.63). The "Preferences…" menu lets you choose whether or not this dialog box is automatically displayed each time you add an item to the library; see 12.57.

12.19 To place a Library palette item in your publication, you just press-and-drag it from the palette to where you want it in the publication. The cursor will show as a loaded graphic icon with an "X" on it (see 10.126). Position the icon on the page where you want the item and let go of the mouse button. You can unload the icon *without* placing the item by clicking on any tool in the Toolbox.

12.20 You can shift-click to select and add more than one object to the library at a time. Although they will copy into the library as a group, later, when you drag the group from the palette to a publication, each item will still have its own handles and you can select and manipulate each one individually.

12.21 When PageMaker copies a graphic to the library, she copies all the information that goes with it. If the graphic's link option is "Store copy in publication," then the library will also store the complete graphic.

12.22 If you are working with a graphic that is stored outside the publication, then PageMaker will copy the link info to the library (see Section 11 for info on linking).

As long as the original file to which the graphic is linked remains available, your library copy remains viable. If the link is broken, you can still place the graphic into your publication. However, it may not print as expected since it won't have all the information it needs. Network items in a library may not be placed at all if their link has been broken.

12.23 You can select multiple text blocks that are threaded together (4.107–4.109) and copy them to the library as one unit. They will remain threaded when you copy them from the palette to your publication. Selecting and adding just one text block of a story to the library isolates it. Likewise, a text block with overset text (text hidden in the rolled up part of the window; 4.109) no longer contains its hidden text when you drag it from the library into a publication.

12.24 Style sheets can be transferred from one publication to another through the library. When you drag text tagged with a style from the library into a publication, the style sheet is added to the existing Style palette. If the style name already exists in the current publication, the new style is ignored, and the text takes on the formatting of the current publication's style.

The Library palette window

12.25 *The close box.*

12.26 *Give your library a title that will identify its contents.*

12.27 *Press-and-drag on the "Resize box" to change the window size of the palette.*

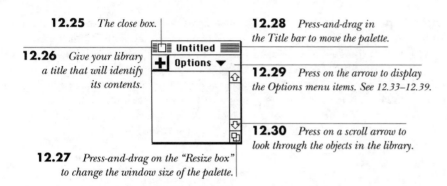

12.28 *Press-and-drag in the Title bar to move the palette.*

12.29 *Press on the arrow to display the Options menu items. See 12.33–12.39.*

12.30 *Press on a scroll arrow to look through the objects in the library.*

12.31 Although it looks like a typical palette window, the Library palette is in a league of its own. Other palettes list choices and have simple pop-up menus; the Library palette serves as a visual database and has a menu chock-full of commands.

12.32 *Click the "Add" button (the plus sign) to add selected items to the library. See 12.16.*

12.33 *Click "Remove item…" to delete an object from the library. See 12.55.*

12.34 *Choose "Show all items" to display all the library items after you have completed a "Search …."*

12.35 *Choose a display option to specify whether objects will appear on the palette as thumbnail images, as a list of names, or as both image and name.*

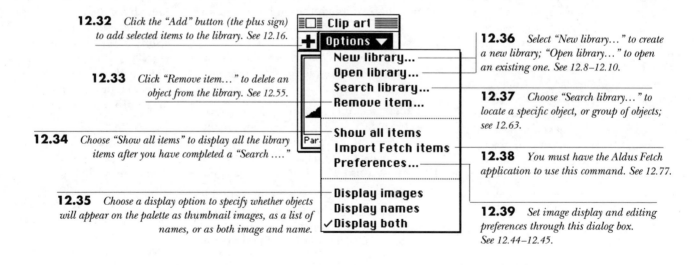

12.36 *Select "New library…" to create a new library; "Open library…" to open an existing one. See 12.8–12.10.*

12.37 *Choose "Search library…" to locate a specific object, or group of objects; see 12.63.*

12.38 *You must have the Aldus Fetch application to use this command. See 12.77.*

12.39 *Set image display and editing preferences through this dialog box. See 12.44–12.45.*

Cataloging information: the "Preferences" and "Item information" dialog boxes

12.40 Whatever "Library Preferences" you select when you first open the Library palette become the preferences for all libraries you subsequently open or create.

12.41 Checking the box next to "Edit items after adding," displays the "Item information" dialog box every time you add another item to the palette. You can enter any information you need to catalog your libraries, or to help you later locate the object (see 12.63).

12.42 You can leave this box unchecked and still add information to items in the library. Double-clicking on an item in the palette displays the "Item information" dialog box. You can now enter any additional information about an item, or edit information you have previously entered.

12.43 The more information you type in the "Item information" box, the more power you will have when searching for items (12.64). Try creating a keyword strategy to make your searches more effective.

12.44 *Items in the library retain their original colors but can be stored as color or black and white thumbnails. To see color thumbnails, the "Make color thumbnails" option must be checked **before** you add the item to the library.*

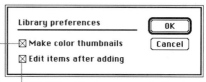

12.45 *Check to automatically view the "Item information" dialog box each time you add an item to a library, 12.46–12.50.*

12.46 *The title is the name of the image that will be displayed in the palette. Both the "Title" and "Author" can be used as search criteria.*

12.47 *If you click Cancel in this dialog box when you are **adding** an item to the library, the item will not be added. If you are entering information about an item already in the library, only the new information you entered will be canceled.*

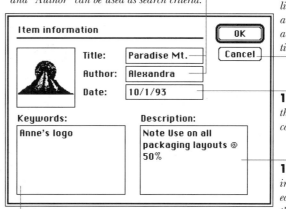

12.48 *The date the object is copied to the palette is entered automatically. You can change it if you want.*

12.49 *You can enter about 12 lines in the "Description" and "Keywords" edit boxes. You can type more than that, but it probably won't all be there the next time you look!*

12.50 *Type one or more keywords that describe the object. You can use keywords to locate an object, or categories of objects, with the "Search library" command.*

If you want to do this:	Then follow these steps:	Shortcuts ▾ Notes ▾ Hints
12.51 Open the Library palette for the first time	▪ From the Window menu, choose "Library palette." ▪ PageMaker will display the "Open library" dialog box. Click the "New library" button on the right of the box. ▪ In the "New library" dialog box, type a name in the highlighted edit box. ▪ Choose where to save the library. ▪ Click OK or press Return.	▪ Whenever you select the "Library palette" command from the Window menu, it will display the library that was last opened. ▪ Occasionally you will open a publication and find the "Open library" dialog box in your face, for no apparent reason. Just click Cancel.
12.52 Create a new Library palette once the Library palette has been established	▪ From the Window menu, choose "Library palette." ▪ In the Library palette, press on the Options menu and slide down to choose "New library...." ▪ In the "Create new library" dialog box, type a library name in the highlighted edit box. ▪ Choose where to save the library. ▪ Click OK or press Return.	▪ You can create a new library or open another library anytime you want. The library currently open will close and be replaced by the new one you are opening.
12.53 Add text or an object to the library palette	▪ With the **pointer tool,** select the object in your publication that you want to add to the palette ▪ Click the plus sign in the upper left hand corner of the Library palette.	▪ You can select and add more than one object at a time. In fact, you can add a whole page of items to the palette at once. But, when you drag them out of the palette to a publication, each object will have its own handles and can be manipulated separately.

If you want to do this:	Then follow these steps:	Shortcuts ▾ Notes ▾ Hints
12.54 Place a library object in your current publication	■ Open the library that contains the object you want to place in your publication (12.61). ■ Open your publication to the page on which you want to place the object. ■ Press-and-drag the object from the palette, onto the publication page. Let go when the object is where you want it.	■ The object appears exactly as it was when you selected it and added it to the palette: same proportions, crop, etc. ■ You can manipulate the object in your publication in any way you wish. It will in no way affect the corresponding object on the palette. ■ If the object is a graphic, you can check the "Link info…" dialog box to see the path to the original object, its file format, etc.
12.55 Delete an object from a Library palette	■ Click once on the object in the palette that you want to remove. ■ In the Library palette, press on the Options menu and slide down to choose "Remove item…." ■ Click Yes, or press Return, in the message box that's asking you whether you are sure you want to permanently remove this object.	■ When you select an item in the palette it is surrounded by a dark border. ■ An object remains selected until you select another one. When you remove an object, PageMaker automatically selects the next object in line. ■ The library doesn't automatically get smaller when you delete objects, but you can compact the palette, see 12.56.
12.56 Compress the library after removing items	■ Hold down the Option key. ■ In the Library palette, press on the Options menu and slide down to choose "Preferences…." ■ PageMaker displays a message box as its compacts the library.	■ This doesn't compress the individual items in the palette, but rather compacts the palette itself after one or more items have been removed.

If you want to do this:	Then follow these steps:	Shortcuts ▾ Notes ▾ Hints
12.57 Add information in the "Item information" dialog box each time you add an item to the Library palette	■ In the Library palette, press on the Options menu and slide down to choose "Preferences…." ■ In the "Preferences" dialog box, check the box next to the "Edit items after adding."	■ If you Cancel out of the "Item information" box when adding an item to the library, the item will not be added. If you double-click on an item in the library to open this dialog box, then Cancel out, information added at that time will not be added.
12.58 Add a title, author, date, keywords, or description to an object already in the library	■ Double-click on the item in the library that you want to attach information to. ■ In the "Item information" dialog box enter the information in the appropriate edit boxes.	■ You can use this method to provide information about an object for the first time, or to edit information that has already been entered.
12.59 Add color or grayscale images to the library, and view them as color or grayscale thumbnails	■ In the Library palette, press on the Options menu and slide down to choose "Preferences…." ■ In the "Preferences" dialog box, check the box next "Make color thumbnails."	■ This option must be selected *before* you add the images you want as color thumbnails. Images added to the palette when this option is checked remain in color even if you deselect this option. ■ If this option is not checked, all color images added to the Library palette will be displayed as black and white thumbnails, but will be placed in your publication in their original colors. ■ Of course your monitor must be set to "Color" to show color, and must be at least a grayscale monitor to see shades of gray. ■ The options you select in the "Preferences" dialog box will remain selected in all your libraries until you choose to change them.

If you want to do this:	Then follow these steps:	Shortcuts ▾ Notes ▾ Hints
12.60 See a list of all the objects in the Library palette	■ In the Library palette, press on the Options menu and slide down to choose "Display names."	■ When you view the objects by name only, you can see a longer list of the library contents in a smaller window. All the information remains the same, just the display is changed.
12.61 Open an existing library	■ Choose the Library palette from the Window menu. ■ In the Library palette, press on the Options menu and slide down to choose "Open library...." ■ In the "Open library" dialog box, find the name of the library you want to open. ■ Click on the name and click "Open" (or press Return), *or* double-click on the name to open it and close the dialog box.	■ This is just like opening a file. Find the library by opening folders or switching disks as necessary. ■ Sometimes the "Open library" dialog box will appear unbidden when you are simply opening a publication (most often if a linked item had been transferred through the library to that publication). Just click the Cancel button.
12.62 Add text to the library	■ Choose the Library palette from the Window menu. ■ With the **pointer tool,** click on the text you want to add to the library. ■ Click the plus sign in the upper left corner of the Library palette.	■ Text blocks that you wish to maintain as a story must be selected together and added to the library at the same time. ■ When you drag text from the library into a publication, it always copies in as its own text block, even if you left the insertion point flashing within text. ■ Style sheets are transferred through the library. It is a great way to intentionally copy a single style to another publication Fortunately, PageMaker won't let you unintentionally copy over existing styles.

The "Search library..." dialog box

12.63 Perhaps your library has grown so large you hate the thought of scrolling through it. Perhaps you want to find all the objects that share certain keywords, or were added to the palette by the same author. No problem—the Library palette comes with its own search feature.

12.64 You can search for an object by name (title), author, keyword(s), or any combination of these. This is a very powerful feature, but it's up to you to enter information about your library objects in the first place that will make a search productive.

12.65 If you choose to search by keyword, you can further define the search by selecting a search operator and entering another keyword. When you choose "And" as an operator, the search finds all the items that contain *both* keywords. When you choose "Or" the search finds all the objects that contain *either one* of the keywords, resulting in a larger group of items. When you choose "But not" the search can focus in on items related to the keyword in a more specific way (12.76).

12.66 After a search, the library will display only those objects that fulfill all the search options. To display the full palette again, choose "Show all items" from the Options menu.

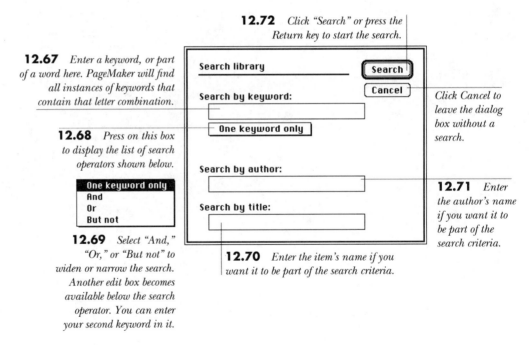

12.72 *Click "Search" or press the Return key to start the search.*

12.67 *Enter a keyword, or part of a word here. PageMaker will find all instances of keywords that contain that letter combination.*

12.68 *Press on this box to display the list of search operators shown below.*

12.69 *Select "And," "Or," or "But not" to widen or narrow the search. Another edit box becomes available below the search operator. You can enter your second keyword in it.*

12.70 *Enter the item's name if you want it to be part of the search criteria.*

12.71 *Enter the author's name if you want it to be part of the search criteria.*

Click Cancel to leave the dialog box without a search.

If you want to do this:	Then follow these steps:	Shortcuts ▾ Notes ▾ Hints
12.73 Search for a specific object in the library	■ In the Library palette, press on the Options menu and slide down to choose "Search library…." ■ In the "Search library" dialog box, enter the title, author, and/or keyword that identifies the object you want to find. ■ Click "Search."	■ The more information you enter in the "Search library" dialog box, the more defined the search will be, and the more likely PageMaker will find exactly the object you want. ■ You don't have to type a whole word in the keyword edit boxes. PageMaker will match up combinations of letters. For example, if you enter "man" as the keyword search criteria, objects with the keyword "woman" will also be displayed.
12.74 Search the library for a group of related objects	■ In the Library palette, press on the Options menu and slide down to choose "Search library…." ■ In the "Search library" dialog box, enter all the information that the objects have in common. ■ Click "Search."	■ PageMaker displays the objects that match *all* of the search criteria.
12.75 Have all the items in the library show again after a search	■ In the Library palette, press on the Options menu and slide down to choose "Show all items."	

If you want to do this:	Then follow these steps:	Shortcuts ▾ Notes ▾ Hints
12.76 Search for an object or group of objects using a search operator to further define the search	■ In the Library palette, press on the Options menu and slide down to choose "Search library...." ■ In the "Search library" dialog box, enter a keyword in the first edit box. ■ Press on "One keyword only" to display the search operator menu; slide down to select one. ■ Enter a second keyword in the new edit box. ■ Enter other information as appropriate. ■ Click "Search."	■ "And" finds all the objects that contain both the keywords you entered. ■ "Or" finds all the objects that contain either keyword, and thus locates a larger group of items than "And." ■ "But not" narrows a search by defining what items to eliminate from the search. In the search for items with the keyword "man," you can select the operator "But not" and enter "woman" to prevent finding items with that keyword.
12.77 Add an Aldus Fetch item to your library	■ From within Aldus Fetch, open a catalog and select the item(s) you want to import to your library in PageMaker. ■ From the Fetch Edit menu, slide down to "Copy References," then over to the submenu to select "Include thumbnails." ■ Open PageMaker, or if it is already open, make it active by clicking on a PageMaker window. ■ From the Window menu, choose "Library palette." ■ From the Options menu on the Library palette, choose "Import Fetch items." ■ Scroll to the bottom of the palette window to see the imported item(s).	■ Aldus Fetch is an image database on a grand scale. It can handle all types of file formats, including multi-media. ■ In PageMaker, you can import these file formats from Fetch: PICT, EPS, TIFF, Photo CD, MacPaint, or an Edition. ■ You can copy up to 125 items at one time. ■ You can't import sounds or QuickTime movies into the library.

> A short and sweet Chapter,
> but very full of Matter.

13.1 Minimums and maximums:

Item	Minimum	Maximum
Handles	3	As many as you can squeeze in
Standoff	-22.75 inches (.01 increments)	22.75 inches

Through
typographic
means, the designer now
presents, in one image, both
the message and the pictorial
idea. Sometimes, this 'playing'
with type   has resulted
in the loss of   a certain
amount of   legibility.
Researchers   consider this
a deplorable   state of affairs;
but, on the other hand, the
excitement created by a novel
image sometimes more than
compensates for the slight
difficulty in readability.

—Herb Lubalin

An example of wrapped text.

13.2   Text wrapping is the process of forcing text to wrap around certain boundaries of a *graphic* element. Without text wrap applied to a graphic, text will flow right over the top of the image.

13.3   You can apply a text wrap to any graphic you draw with the PageMaker drawing tools, to any image you paste in from the Scrapbook or the Clipboard, and to any graphic file you place from any other program. You can even create a *space*, or a place-holder, with a text wrap by making an *invisible* box (using a line of "None") with the Page-Maker drawing tools. One thing you *cannot* do is apply a text wrap to *text*, like an initial cap (but see 13.40).

13.4   When you apply a text wrap to a graphic, it sets up *boundaries*. You can control how far from the edge of the graphic these boundaries appear (13.9), and the text will wrap around the outside of them. The boundary initially appears as a rectangle, but you can customize its shape endlessly (13.30). In addition, you can put a text wrap on a master page, and all text on the publication pages will wrap around it (13.38). And it is even possible to turn the wrap inside out and have the text wrap *inside* the boundaries (13.41).

13.5   Text wrapping does slow down the process of redrawing the screen every time you change views or scroll. Small price to pay.

The "Text wrap" dialog box 576
Wrap options and text flow 577
Standoff 578
Examples of text wrapping 579
Tasks 580
**Scenario #13: Using text wrap
    on master pages** 585

13.6 **The "Text wrap" dialog box** *(from the Element menu, choose "Text wrap...")*

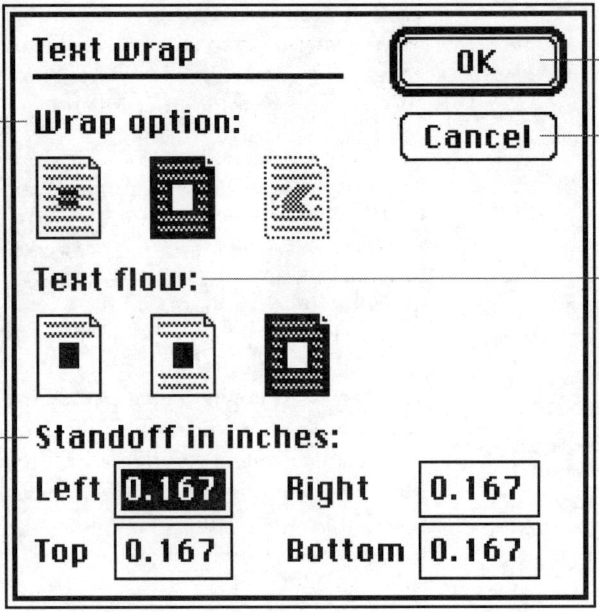

13.7 *The "Wrap option" provides a choice of whether the text will flow right over the top of (13.10) **or** around (13.11) the selected graphic. You cannot choose the third icon; it will be automatically selected when you customize a boundary (13.12).*

Text wrap

OK

You can press Return or Enter instead of clicking OK.

Wrap option:

Cancel

Press Command Period to shortcut

Text flow:

13.8 *The "Text flow" option provides choices as to how the text will flow around the graphic (13.13–13.15). If the "No wrap" icon (the first of the three icons above; 13.10) is selected, these icons will be gray and inaccessible.*

Standoff in inches:

13.9 *If the "Standard wrap" icon (the middle wrap option icon; 13.11) is selected, as shown above (13.7), you will be able to input values here to determine how far from the edge of the graphic the text wrap boundary will appear (13.16–13.20). The measurement system (here it is inches) is determined by your choice in "Preferences..."; see 1.224). The value .167 is one pica (5.6–5.7).*

Left 0.167   **Right** 0.167
Top 0.167   **Bottom** 0.167

Wrap option

Wrap option:

13.10   The first icon, which is the default selection, indicates there is **no text wrap** applied. If you ever want to remove a wrap from an object, this is the icon to select (13.42). Since this icon means no text wrap, when it is selected the "Text flow" icons are blank.

Wrap option:

13.11   The second icon indicates the **standard rectangular text wrap.** If you select this icon, you can then choose a "Text flow" option and can insert values for the standoff (13.8–13.9).

Wrap option:

13.12   The third icon indicates a **custom-ized wrap.** You cannot *select* this icon. After you have customized a standard wrap (13.30), this icon will be automatically selected.

Text flow

Text flow:

13.13   The first text flow icon indicates a **column break.** When the text reaches an object that has this column break applied, the text will stop flowing and will jump over to continue at the top of the next empty column (13.38).

Text flow:

13.14   The second text flow icon is the **jump-over** icon (example: 13.23). When text reaches a graphic that has the jump-over wrap applied, the text will jump over it and con-tinue on below the graphic, leaving white space on both sides. The values you enter as the top and bottom standoff (13.16–13.20) determine how far above and below the graphic the text will stop and then continue.

Text flow:

13.15   The third text flow icon is the **wrap-all-sides** icon. Text will flow around all sides of an object with this wrap, whether rectangular or customized. The values you enter as the standoffs (13.16–13.20) deter-mine how close the text will get to the graphic. See the example of the fish on page 575, and other examples in 13.19, 13.25, and 13.30.

Standoff

Standoff in inches:

Left `0.167` Right `0.167`
Top `0.167` Bottom `0.167`

13.16 The **standoff** boxes are where you determine how close you want the text to get to the object. You can enter a value from -22.75 inches up to 22.75 inches, in .01 increments. You can input a different value in each box. Specify 0 (zero) if you want the text to bump up right against the edge of the graphic boundary, or specify a negative value if you want the text to overlap the graphic. If you resize the graphic, the standoff remains the same.

13.17 The standoff is measured *from the edge of the rectangular **graphic** boundary*. Most often a graphic has a boundary that is larger than the actual graphic itself, especially if the graphic itself is not rectangular.

13.18 *The eight inner, unconnected handles belong to the graphic object. The dotted line is the text wrap boundary (its handles are diamond-shaped); the distance between the two sets of handles is the* **standoff** *(13.9).*

13.19 *I added more of the diamond-shaped handles to this text wrap boundary, and customized its shape (13.30). Notice the graphic still has its eight square handles in their original places.*

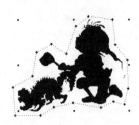

13.20 Since the standoff can be anywhere from -22.75 to 22.75 inches, you can actually create a text wrap that is on a completely separate part of the page than the actual graphic, or even across the other side of a two-page spread. I can't imagine why you would ever need to do that, but it's possible.

 Listed below are the standoff values for this graphic, values that place the text wrap over there:

Left: -3	*Right: 4*
Top: 1.5	*Bottom: -1*
(using inches)	

Examples of text wrapping

13.21 Standard rectangular text wrap on all sides (13.11)

In graphic design, as in all creative expression, art evolves from craft. In typographic design, craft deals with points, lines, planes, picas, ciceros, leads, quads, serifs, letters, words, folios, pages, signatures, paper, ink, color, printing, and there is no art without without rules, so too without fantasy, with-child's art is much craft. It is the fusion of the two that makes the difference.

—*Paul Rand*

13.22 Inside-out text wrap (13.41)

In graphic design, as in all creative expression, art evolves from craft. In typo-graphic design, craft deals with points, lines, planes, picas, ciceros, leads, quads, serifs, letters, words, folios, pages, signa-tures, paper, ink, color, printing, and binding. Just as there is no art without craft and no craft without rules, so too there is no art without fantasy, without ideas. A child's art is much fantasy but little craft. It is the fusion of the two that makes the difference.

P A U L ❧ R A N D

13.23 Standard rectangular text wrap jumping over the graphic (13.14)

In graphic design, as in all creative expression, art evolves from craft. In typographic design, craft deals with points, lines, planes, picas, ciceros, leads, quads, serifs, letters, words, folios, pages, signatures, paper, ink, color, printing,

and binding. Just as there is no art without craft and no craft without rules, so too there is no art without fantasy, without ideas. A child's art is much fantasy but little craft. It is the fusion of the two that makes the difference. —*Paul Rand*

13.24 Text wrap around an initial cap (13.40)

*I*n graphic design, as in all creative expression, art evolves from craft. In typographic design, craft deals with points, lines, planes, picas, ciceros, leads, quads, serifs, letters, words, folios, pages, signatures, paper, ink, color, printing, and binding. Just as there is no art without craft and no craft without rules, so too there is no art without fantasy, without ideas. A child's art is much fantasy but little craft. It is the fusion of the two that makes the difference. —*Paul Rand*

13.25 Custom text wrap (13.30)

In graphic design, as in all creative expression, art evolves from craft. In typographic design, craft deals with points, lines, planes, picas, ciceros, leads, quads, serifs, letters, words, folios, pages, signatures, paper, ink, color, printing, and bind-ing. Just as there is no art without craft and no craft without rules, so too there is no art without fantasy, without ideas. A child's art is much fantasy but little craft. It is the fusion of the two that makes the difference.

—*Paul Rand*

13.26 Text wrap around a placeholder with room for a caption (13.36)

In graphic design, as in all creative expression, art evolves from craft. In typographic design, craft deals with points, lines, planes, picas, ciceros, leads, quads, serifs, letters, words, folios, pages, signa-tures, paper, ink, color, printing, and binding. Just as there is no art without craft and no craft without rules, so too there is no art without fantasy, without ideas. A child's art is much fantasy but little craft. It is the fusion of the two that makes the difference. —*Paul Rand*

photo caption

If you want to do this:	**Then follow these steps:**	**Shortcuts ▾ Notes ▾ Hints**
13.27 Create a standard rectangular text wrap around an object or around a group of objects 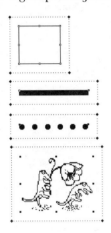	■ With the **pointer tool,** select the object(s). ■ From the Element menu, choose "Text wrap…." ■ Under "Wrap option," click on the middle icon (standard rectangular wrap; 13.11). ■ Under "Text flow," click on the flow of your choice (see 13.13–13.15). ■ If you want space between the boundary of the object and the boundary of the text, type a values into the "Standoff in (measurement)" boxes (13.17). Remember, you can override the current measurement system (1.323), you can insert values from –22.75 inches to 22.75 inches, and you can always adjust the standoff manually on the screen or return here to change it. ■ Click OK.	■ You can select more than one object and apply a text wrap to them all simultaneously. They will all have the same text wrap specifications. ■ You can pick up and move any object with a text wrap applied. The text the object leaves behind will word wrap back into place. The text the object drops into will wrap around the standoff you set. ■ If you copy and paste a graphic with text wrap, the text may not always wrap correctly. You can move the image slightly to force the text to wrap, or recompose the text: hold down the Option key and select "Hyphenation" from the Type menu. Save afterward.
13.28 Change the text wrap standoff *from the dialog box (also see 13.29)* **Standoff in inches:** Left `0.167` Right `0.167` Top `0.167` Bottom `0.167`	■ With the **pointer tool,** select the object(s). ■ From the Element menu, choose "Text wrap…." ■ Under "Wrap option," click on the middle icon (13.11). If either the "no wrap" or "custom wrap" icon is chosen, you cannot change the standoff from the dialog box. ■ Type in new values in the "Standoff" boxes. ■ Click OK.	■ You can enter values from –22.75 inches to 22.75 inches. You can override the current measurement system (1.323). ■ If the "Custom wrap" icon is selected, the "Standoff" boxes delude you into thinking you can change them—they are blank and the insertion point is flashing. If you enter values in them and click OK, PageMaker will completely ignore you. If you go back to the dialog box you will see the boxes are empty again.

If you want to do this:

13.29 Change the text wrap standoff
on the object itself (also see 13.30)

a)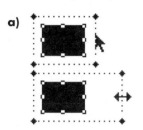

b)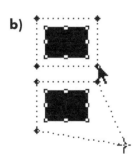

c)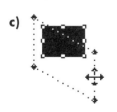

Then follow these steps:

- With the **pointer tool,** select the object.

To move one boundary edge (a):
- Point the tip of the pointer directly on the dotted boundary line; don't click!
- *Press*-and-drag; you should see the double-headed arrow (↔), pointing in the direction you are dragging (vertical or horizontal).

To move a corner (b):
- Point the tip of the pointer directly on any corner handle.
- *Press*-and-drag; you should see the crossbar cursor (+).

To move two sides and keep them parallel (c):
- First you must press-and-drag any corner handle at least a pixel (which is just a teeny bit). Let go.
- Now point to any edge with the **pointer tool;** *press* (don't click!) and it will become the four-headed arrow (⊕).
- Press-and-drag that four-headed arrow; you can even move it beyond the opposite side.

Shortcuts ▾ Notes ▾ Hints

- Every time you move a boundary, the text on the screen will reflow. This can get boring. Hold down the Spacebar while moving the boundaries; when you want to see the text reflow, let go of the Spacebar.
- As soon as you move a boundary, even if you put it back right where it came from, PageMaker labels it "customized." If you go back into the text wrap dialog box while that graphic is selected, you will see the "custom" icon selected.
- If you don't like how you moved the boundaries and you want to return it back to a rectangular wrap, select the graphic, get the text wrap dialog box, and click the middle wrap option again (13.11).
- To create more handles so you can tug the boundary in a greater variety of ways, see 13.31.

If you want to do this:

Then follow these steps:

Shortcuts ▾ Notes ▾ Hints

13.30 Customize the text wrap to an odd shape

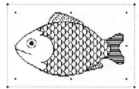

Graphic with a standard text wrap, standoff of .1 inch.

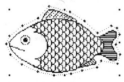

The same graphic with a customized text wrap. This is how the fish on page 575 were wrapped.

- Follow the steps in 13.27 to select a graphic object and apply a standard rectangular wrap with any width of standoff you choose. Then:
- See 13.29 for changing the boundaries, using the sides and the four handles that already exist.
- Now you need to **create more handles** on the text wrap boundary so you can push and pull at other points besides the corners: with the **pointer tool,** click once on the dotted line at the spot where you want a new handle. *Do not press-and-drag,* as that will move the entire segment, not create a new handle. **Click, and then let go.**
- When you let go, you will see a new diamond-shaped handle. *Now* you can press-and-drag on that handle (vertex) to move that segment. You can press-and-drag the handle to move it *along* the segment, or you can move it out and about to *pull* the segment along with it.
- **To get rid of a handle,** press-and-drag it onto the top of another handle.
- **To get rid of all extra handles** and take the wrap back to a plain ol' ordinary rectangle: select the object, get the text wrap dialog box from the Element menu, and choose the middle wrap option (13.11).

- As soon as you make any adjustments to the text wrap boundary, it becomes "customized." If you take a peek at the dialog box, you will see the "Custom wrap" option selected.
- At the risk of being repetitious, I want to remind you that you can hold the Spacebar down while you add handles and move them. This will prevent the text from reflowing every time you make a change. Let up on the Spacebar to reflow the text when you are done or when you just want to check out the wrap and see how it's doing.

If you want to do this:	Then follow these steps:	Shortcuts ▾ Notes ▾ Hints
13.31 Add handles (vertices) to a text wrap boundary	■ Follow the steps in 13.27 to get a standard rectangular text wrap. ■ With the **pointer tool,** *click* once at any point along the dotted line. *Do not drag—* just click. Click as many handles as you want.	■ There seems to be no limit to the number of handles you can have, except for the limit of space along the dotted boundary. Of course, the more handles, the more memory the graphic takes up.
13.32 Move the handles (vertices) on a text wrap boundary	■ With the **pointer tool,** press-and-drag on any *wrap boundary* handles and you will be able to move it right along the line segment. A corner handle won't slide along the line until you add a new handle to either side of it.	■ The movement depends on the direction you drag the pointer. If you move it *in* or *out,* you'll drag the boundary with it. If you move the handle *along* the line segment, it just runs right up and down the dotted line.
13.33 Delete the handles (vertices) on a text wrap boundary	■ With the **pointer tool,** press-and-drag on a handle and place it right on top of another handle. That will make it disappear.	■ **If you want to delete *all* the handles,** except for the original four corners: select the object; go back to the dialog box; choose the standard rectangular wrap (the middle option).
13.34 Delay the text reflowing until you finish changing the boundary	■ Hold down the Spacebar while you add, delete, or move the handles. The text will not recompose until you let go of the Spacebar.	■ Indispensable trick.
13.35 Resize the graphic object without affecting the text wrap boundary	■ With the **pointer tool,** press-and-drag on any of the *graphic* handles (any of the eight *square* handles) as you would normally (10.138). The standoff and custom wrap will resize in proportion.	■ Use the Shift key to keep the graphic proportional (10.138) and the Command key to magic-resize a bi-level graphic (10.141). Text-wrapped graphics can be treated like any other graphic.

If you want to do this:	**Then follow these steps:**	**Shortcuts ▾ Notes ▾ Hints**

13.36 Put text, such as a caption, inside a text-wrapped object

- As long as the handles *on both ends of the text block* are tucked *inside* the text wrap boundary, the text will just sit there patiently. Either enter a standoff value (13.28) that gives you enough space for the text, or drag the boundary to the size you need (13.29).
- Then, either create a little bounding box (1.319; 4.26) in the space provided and type in the text, **or** create the text outside the text wrap, size it small, and move it in.

- This is great for putting the captions running up the side of the photo—just specify a standoff wide enough, rotate the caption (4.280, 4.281), and slide it in.

13.37 Set a tabbed leader that goes right over the top of a wrapped object

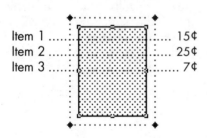

Item 1 .... 15¢
Item 2 .... 25¢
Item 3 .... 7¢

- See Section 6 (6.71–6.75) on Indents and Tabs to create the tabbed leaders.
- As long as the beginning and end of the leaders *are outside the wrap boundary,* the leaders will ignore the wrap and just march right over the top of the graphic.
- If the leaders disappear, the graphic is probably just sitting on top of them. To make the leaders visible again, click once on the wrapped graphic with the **pointer tool** and send it to the back (press Command B; 1.217).

- "Leaders" are the little dots or bullets or dashes that lead from one item to the next, as in a table of contents. They're explained fully in Section 6.

13.38 Scenario #13: Using text wrap on master pages

Besides the obvious technique of wrapping a graphic that will appear on every page, you can take advantage of text wrapping on a master page in several other ways, some of which are yet to be discovered. Remember: anything you are able to do on a publication page, you can apply to all pages by doing it on your master page(s) (1.130–1.150).

Column breaks

Maybe you have a thin outer column on each page that you don't want text to flow into. Draw an invisible line or box at the top of the thin column. Apply the "Column break" text wrap to it. As you autoflow text (4.92–4.93), the text will bump into that line or box and immediately jump over to the top of the next column.

Perhaps the right-hand page on your two-page spreads is strictly for illustrations. Use the column-break text wrap to force text to ignore the entire page as it flows.

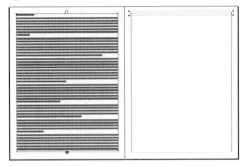

Invisible text wraps to manipulate white space on pages

Let's say you have several columns that you will be flowing text into, but you want to leave a four-inch spot at the bottom of the left column on every left page. So create an invisible box, or even a visible one if you prefer, and apply a rectangular text wrap to it. The text will flow around that box on every page, leaving you with four inches to do with what you will, including manually place text.

Carrying the previous example a little further, you can create several text-wrapped boxes to control the text in interesting ways.

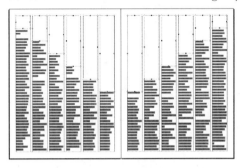

Create inside-out text wraps (13.41), or set up a master page text wrap for angled margins (13.39). Oh, there are so many possiblities. It's too much fun.

If you want to do this:

Then follow these steps:

Shortcuts ▾ Notes ▾ Hints

13.39 Use text wrap to create angled margins

Notice the text block handles are all the way out to the sides. Select the boxes and give them a line of "None" so they are invisible.

The best
remedy for
a bruised heart
is not, as so many
people seem to think,
repose upon a manly bosom.
Much more efficacious
are honest work, physical activity,
and the sudden acquisition of wealth.
Dorothy L. Sayers wrote that.

- Use PageMaker's drawing tools (Section 2) to draw a thick line or a small box.
- Follow the steps in 13.27 to apply a text wrap to the line or box.
- Follow the steps in 13.30 to customize the text wrap boundary. Shape it into the angle you need. If necessary, create another shape on the other side at the same angle.
- Place the text next to the angled object. Make sure the top left of the text block is over far enough to allow all the text to flow along the angle (see note at left). when the text is all placed, select the line or box and choose "None" from the Line submenu (under Element).

- Once you know this trick, you may wonder why you hadn't used it many times before. It comes in handy regularly, and it's so easy.

13.40 Text wrap an initial cap

*O*nce upon
a time there was a mother
and her three children. They
lived in a little house and were very,
very happy.

- You cannot create a text wrap around text, so you must turn the text into a graphic:
- Type the letter into a single text block. Size it close to what the final size will be.
- Select the letter with the **pointer tool;** from the Edit menu, choose Copy (Command C).
- From the Edit menu, choose "Paste special."
- In the "Paste special" dialog box, select the "PICT" format, then click OK.
- The text is now a graphic and can be text wrapped as usual (13.27–13.30).

- When you copy an object to the Clipboard it is placed there in a variety of formats. When you choose to "Paste" the object, PageMaker, by default, chooses the format at the top of the list. "Paste special" allows you to choose the format on the Clipboard that you would prefer to work with. See Section 10 (10.110–10.115).

If you want to do this:

13.41 *Wrap* text *inside* a graphic object (also known as an *inside-out text wrap*)

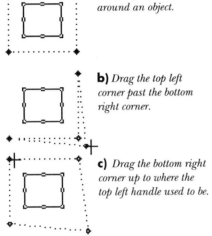

a) *Set up a text wrap around an object.*

b) *Drag the top left corner past the bottom right corner.*

c) *Drag the bottom right corner up to where the top left handle used to be.*

d) *If you have made some wild and crazy shape, make sure there is a little trap for the top left text block handle. Notice the trap here, and the little pathway that is too small for the actual text.*

Then follow these steps:

- Follow the steps in 13.27 to create a rectangular text wrap that flows on all sides of an object. You don't really need any standoff (13.16) for this, but that's up to your particular project.
- Press on the **top left corner handle** and drag it a bit beyond the diagonally opposite corner handle (bottom right).
- Press on the **bottom right corner handle** and drag it back to where the top left handle used to be. (Actually, it doesn't matter which corner you drag, as long as you reverse two opposite corners.)
- Now the wrap is inside out and the text will flow *within* the borders. If you drew a box and don't need to see it anymore, just change the Line weight to "None" (2.34).
- The only limitation is that the top left text block handle *must be inside the wrap somewhere.* This sometimes necessitates creating a little trap for it, a trap large enough to hold the corner handle, but too small for the text to flow into; see **d.**

Shortcuts ▾ Notes ▾ Hints

- This is a great trick. Typically a text wrap *repels* the text *away* from its borders. If you turn it inside out, the wrap will *contain* the text *inside* its borders.
- The Herb Lubalin quote on page 575 is an inside-out text wrap, with an inner, oval, regular text wrap. The example in 13.22 is an inside-out wrap also.
- This kind of wrap is also a good alternate method for creating those angled margins, as in 13.39.
- If you ever find that you have "lost" the invisible text wrap, there are a few tricks mentioned in 1.214–1.215 or 2.38 that can help you find it.

If you want to do this:	Then follow these steps:	Shortcuts ▾ Notes ▾ Hints
13.42 Remove all text wrapping from an object or group of objects *This is the "No text wrap" icon*	▪ With the **pointer tool,** select the object(s) you wish to remove the wrap from. ▪ From the Element menu, choose "Text wrap…." ▪ Click on the first "Wrap option" icon, which is the "No text wrap" icon (13.10). ▪ Click OK.	▪ As soon as you click OK, any text that was surrounding or inside the object(s) will reflow. If the graphic is now under a layer of text and you need to grab it, hold down the Command key and click to select the layer underneath (1.211; 2.38).
13.43 Set text wrapping as a default (defaults: 1.6–1.18)	▪ Click once on the **pointer tool,** even if the pointer is already selected. ▪ From the Element menu, choose "Text wrap…." ▪ Click on the middle "Wrap option" icon, which is the "Standard rectangular text wrap" icon (13.11). ▪ Fill in values for the standoff (13.16–13.20). ▪ Click OK.	▪ Once you have set a text wrap as a default, every time you *paste* a graphic from the Scrapbook or Clipboard, every time you *place* a graphic file, and every time you *draw* any line or shape, the image will appear with a text wrap around it. ▪ This procedure sets a **publication** default. To set the **application** default, follow the same steps *when there is no publication open* (1.13).
13.44 Delete the text wrapping default	▪ Click once on the **pointer tool,** even if the pointer is already selected. ▪ From the Element menu, choose "Text wrap…." ▪ Click on the first "Wrap option" icon, which is the "No text wrap" icon (13.10). ▪ Click OK.	▪ To delete an *application* default, follow the same steps *when there is no publication open* (1.11, 1.13).

14 ▾ TEMPLATES

14.1   This is a list of the templates PageMaker provides for you.

Avery labels

Brochure 1

Brochure 2

Calendar *(see 14.29)*

Cassette labels

Cassette liner

CD liner

CD notes

Diskette labels

Envelope *(see 14.35)*

Fax cover sheet *(see 14.36)*

Invoice

Manual

Newsletter 1 *(see 14.37)*

Newsletter 2

Purchase order

Videocassette labels

14.2   A **template** is a fake (or dummy) publication that is already set up with the specifications necessary for production. PageMaker provides over fifteen pre-made templates, and you can turn any of your own publications into a template at any time.

14.3   A template may include formatted text, guidelines, columns, style sheets, graphics, etc. The text and graphics act as **placeholders.** When you use one of the pre-made Page-Maker templates, it is up to you to replace the existing text with new stories, adjust the style sheets and guides to suit your own style, replace the existing graphics with your own graphics, or eliminate items altogether. When you use a template you created for yourself, you'll be basically replacing your old text with your new text (14.17–14.18), and leaving the format the way you previously arranged it.

14.4   When you open a template, the original template document *stays intact on the disk;* PageMaker opens a **copy** of the original, and you save and work on the *copy.* This protects that original template from being changed inadvertently. Next time you need the template, it is still there, intact.

14.5   There are two advantages to using a template. One is that all the work that goes into the initial setup of a project—the design decisions, typographic decisions, guidelines, columns, style sheet specs, layout, masthead, logo placement, etc.,—are already done for you. You just need to come in and modify details, change text and graphics, et voilà—on to the next project. Or lunch.

14.6   The second advantage is that a template provides a way to keep all similar documents consistent. For instance, if you create a four-page newsletter every month, you may think, "Why create a template? I'll just take last month's, since we don't need it anymore, and replace the text." The problem here is that soon you lose the consistent look of the publication. Some months the four pages turns into five pages, or perhaps two pages. Some months there is too much text or too little text and so point sizes and leading are adjusted. If you keep changing one publication over and over again, even with those minor changes, you soon forget what the original specifications were. With a template, no matter what adjustments you need to make monthly, you can consistently start with an intact original.

Scenario #14: When, why, and how to create your own template

14.7   Create your own template for any project that you will be repeating more than once. For instance, this book was created in twenty-five separate publications. I set up the first section; I created the layout and the page design, put the guidelines in place, made a style sheet, and built the master pages. Then I saved it as a template. Every time I started a new section of the book, I opened a copy of the *template* and built from there. Thus each chapter is consistent, and I didn't have to repeat the same work twenty-four times.

14.8   If you write memos regularly, you'll want to set up a template with the standard memo information on the master page. The easiest way to do it is to just *do* the first one; that is, just put the memo together as you normally would, print it up, and send it off. But before you quit PageMaker, go back to "Save as…" and save it again, this time as a **template** (14.14; I'm assuming you previously saved it as a publication earlier in the process).

14.9   Another appropriate time to make a template is when you need to create multiple documents all based on the same design and layout. Let's say you work for a travel agency that sends people to various fly-fishing spots all over the world, and you are in charge of promoting those spots. You need to make a four-page brochure for each of them. Just like with the memo, go ahead and create the first one. When it's complete, save it again, this time as a template (14.14). For the next fly-fishing hot spot, open the *template* and just change the necessary items. Often in a case like this, much of the information is the same and does not even need re-keyboarding.

14.10   Several reports that are going to more than one office may perhaps contain generally the same information (with just a different cover sheet, letter, and some data, for instance) would best be done as a template. Calendars, forms that are constantly changing, letterhead, invoices, literally anything you are creating more than one of, can easily be done as a template, saving you many hours of work.

14.11   I have suggested several times in this series of Scenarios to go ahead and build the first publication and *then* save it as a template. Another method is to create a template specifically as a template; that is, know what you want, put it together, and then use the template to build even the first publication.

14.12   The reason I have come to prefer the first method is that even though you may think you know exactly what you want, many finely-tuned design and typographic decisions are made during the process of creating an actual publication. Many of these decisions are not necessary when you are just setting up a style sheet, putting in guidelines, and placing phony text. When it comes to creating the actual publication, you will probably find (as I do every time) that some slight adjustments should be made in the template itself. And adjusting them in the *template* is much preferable to (and more efficient than) having to slightly adjust things every time you create a new publication based on this template. Working through the process of bringing a project to completion allows you to tighten up all the details *before* making the template. You can always, of course, go back to the original template and adjust it.

If you want to do this:

14.13 Open a copy of a template

Template Icon   Publication Icon

Then follow these steps:

- **If you are at the Finder/desktop** find the template icon. (If you are not viewing the window by icon, then you may have a difficult time distinguishing between templates and regular documents. It is a good idea, whenever naming a template, to include the word "template" in its name to prevent this problem.)
- Double-click on the icon; this will put an *Untitled* copy on the screen. Be sure to save it as a *publication*, with a different name than that of the template.

- **If PageMaker is already open,** from the File menu, choose "Open...."
- Find the name of the template. If you can't remember whether a document is a publication or a template, click once on the file name; if it is a template, the little button in the lower right will switch from "Original" to "Copy."
- Either click once on the template name, then click OK, **or** double-click on the template name. This will put an *Untitled* copy on the screen. Be sure to save it as a *publication*, with a different name than that of the template.

Shortcuts ▾ Notes ▾ Hints

- This is the method to open templates you create. PageMaker comes with seventeen pre-designed templates. If you installed the "Open template" Addition when you installed PageMaker, you can access those particular templates through the "Aldus Additions" submenu, see 14.21.
- If you view the window by "Name" or "Kind," etc., the little template icon shows up as having two pages; the publication icon shows up as one page. You just have to look closer.
- These same icons will be visible in the "Open publication" dialog box.

    ▯ **Letterhead**
    ▯ **Brookwood Mort.LH**

- **Note:** If the publication is not labeled "Untitled" after it opens, then you have opened the original template, not a *copy* of the template.
- To save the file as a publication, just make sure the "Publication" button is checked when you "Save as...."

If you want to do this:	Then follow these steps:	Shortcuts ▾ Notes ▾ Hints
14.14 Save your PageMaker document as a template 	■ From the File menu, choose "Save as...." ■ In the mid right portion of the dialog box, click on the "Template" button. ■ Give the template a name that will tell you it's a template, even if you can't see its icon (e.g., LooseGoose.tmp). *Remember, as when saving any publication, if there is already a publication with the same name, you will be* replacing *the first one (Section 18).* ■ Click OK.	■ You can choose to save a document as a template at any point, even if it has previously been saved as a publication. ■ If you are working on a previously-saved publication and now save it as a template *with a different name,* PageMaker will put the *publication* away, safe on the disk, and the *template,* with its new name, will be on your screen. If you save it as a template *and give it the same name as the publication,* then PageMaker will *replace* the publication with the template (if they're in the same folder). You will get an alert box to verify the save.
14.15 Open the original template	■ You cannot open the *original* of the template from the Desktop; you can only open a *copy.* So, first you must open PageMaker. Then ... ■ From the File menu, choose "Open...." ■ Find the name of the template in the list box. (If you're not sure whether a document is a publication or a template, click once on it; if it is a template, the little button in the lower right will switch from "Original" to "Copy.") ■ Click *once* on the name. On the right, the button will automatically jump to "Copy"; click on "Original." ■ Click OK.	■ *It's not possible to shortcut this procedure!* That is, you can't use the double-click-on-the-file-name trick: you can't click on the file name, click the "Original" button, and then double-click on the file name, because as soon as you click on the file name again, the button switches back to "Copy." So you must use the OK button. ■ You can always tell if you opened the original or a copy— if it's a copy, the title bar at the top of the window will show "Untitled."

If you want to do this:	Then follow these steps:	Shortcuts ▾ Notes ▾ Hints
14.16 Replace a template headline with your headline	■ Just as you replace text anywhere, select the text with the **text tool** by pressing-and-dragging over it. ■ While the type is highlighted, type in your own headline. You do not need to delete the existing text first; it will disappear as soon as you type the first letter.	■ If the headline uses text in two different styles, such as bold and light, select just the bold text and type the replacement; then select just the light text and type the replacement.
14.17 Replace an entire template story with your story 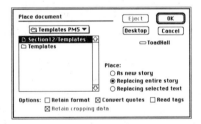	■ With the **text tool,** click anywhere in any text block of the story you want to replace. ■ From the File menu, choose "Place...." ■ Find the name of the story in the list box; click *once* on it. ■ On the right, click in the button for "Replacing entire story." ■ Make sure there are no checkmarks in "Retain format" (4.49) or "Read tags" (4.52). Click OK.	■ Make sure you understand the difference between a *text block* and a *story* (4.113). ■ This procedure is exactly the same as replacing any story in any publication. See 4.57 for full details. ■ Replacing the entire story without retaining the format ensures that the story you are bringing in will pick up all the text formatting of the story it is replacing.
14.18 Replace a selected portion of template text with new text 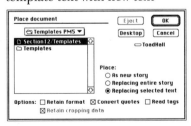	■ With the **text tool,** select the text you want to replace (use any of the selection methods detailed in 4.203–4.204). ■ Then either simply retype text, as in 14.16; **or** use the "Place..." dialog box, as in 14.17, to replace it with an outside file, making sure you click the "Replacing selected text" button (4.59).	■ The new text will retain the format of the text it is replacing.

If you want to do this:	Then follow these steps:	Shortcuts ▪ Notes ▪ Hints
14.19a Replace an **independent** graphic with another graphic from the Clipboard or the Scrapbook *(see 10.123–10.125 re: independent vs. inline graphics)*	▪ First you need to *eliminate* the existing graphic: click once on it with the **pointer tool,** then hit the Backspace/Delete key. ▪ After it is gone, copy and paste the new one in as usual (Command V) and move it into position, cropping and resizing as necessary (see notes at right).	▪ If there was a text wrap applied to the existing graphic, when you delete it you will also delete the text wrap, which will make the text reflow. You may want to first paste the new graphic, resize it, apply a new text flow, put it in position, and *then* delete the existing graphic underneath. To get rid of the one underneath, hold the Command key down. With the pointer tool, click in the graphic area until you see the handles that belong to the graphic underneath. Then hit the Backspace/Delete key.
14.19b Replace an **inline** graphic with another graphic from the Clipboard or the Scrapbook	▪ To replace an *inline* graphic, select it with the text tool. When you paste, the new graphic will replace the existing one and will also be inline (see 10.213–10.251 for detailed info about inline graphics).	
14.20 Replace a template graphic with a graphic file 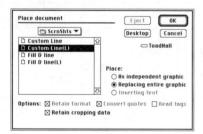	▪ If the graphic has its own file on disk, such as a MacPaint file or a TIFF file, then it is possible to *replace* the existing graphic, dropping the new one into its place. The new graphic will take on the same size, placement, proportions, text wrap, and transformations as the graphic currently on the page. ▪ With the **pointer tool,** click once on the graphic to be replaced. ▪ From the File menu, choose "Place...." ▪ Find the graphic file in the list box. Click once on the file name. ▪ On the right, click in the button "Replacing entire graphic," click OK.	▪ You won't get a loaded graphic icon with this procedure (10.126); the graphic on the page will just instantly be replaced with the new graphic file. ▪ You may not want the exact same size and proportions as the graphic already on the page. But once it is there in position, you can easily adjust it (see Section 10). ▪ If you also select "Retain cropping data," your new graphic will come in cropped to exactly the same proportions as the original. If not, it will come in in its entirety, sacrificing proportion, if necessary, to match the original size. See 10.128.

"Open template..." Addition *(from the Utilities menu, slide down to Aldus Additions, then over to the submenu to choose "Open template...")*

14.21 The "Open template" Addition gives you access to PageMaker's pre-designed templates. Rather than take up disk space with actual publication templates, the Addition runs a *script* that generates the template you select. (In simple terms, a script is a set of directions written in the PageMaker scripting language, that tells PageMaker what to do and how to do it.) The templates cover a range of common publishing tasks such as newsletter formats, brochures, invoices, and fax cover sheets. Most of the templates require that the fonts Helvetica and Times be available in your System.

14.22 When you choose a template from the list, a thumbnail image is displayed in the "Preview" window. The "Language" pop-up menu displays the default dictionary. If you have installed other dictionaries (9.100) you will see them here.

14.23 The "Page size" pop-up menu displays a choice of common page sizes for the selected template. When "Avery labels" is selected, the pop-up menu displays nine choices of templates, each a grid for a different size label.

14.24 Like all templates, PageMaker opens a copy of the file and presents you with a new "Untitled" document. It is up to you to "Save as…" and name your document. You can save it as a publication, or work the quirks out of a template and then save it as a new template.

14.28 *Click OK to open the template you have highlighted. You can also double-click on the file name to open the template and close the dialog box.*

14.25 *Choose from the list of 17 templates.*

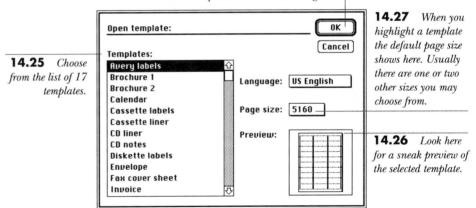

14.27 *When you highlight a template the default page size shows here. Usually there are one or two other sizes you may choose from.*

14.26 *Look here for a sneak preview of the selected template.*

If you want to do this:	Then follow these steps:	Shortcuts ▾ Notes ▾ Hints
14.29 Open a PageMaker template	■ From the Utilities menu, slide down to "Aldus Additions," then over to the submenu and choose "Open template…." ■ Single-click on a file name of the type of publication you want. ■ Select a dictionary, if necessary. ■ Select a page size if you want one different than the template default. ■ Click OK. ■ Save your new document as a publication or a template. If you save your *new* file as a template, you won't need to run that particular script again to access that template.	■ Each template is a script that tells Page-Maker how to set it up. At first you may think things have gone awry—PageMaker seems to be piling all the text and graphics on top of one another! PageMaker doesn't assemble the layout until *after* she accounts for every text block and place-holder the template requires. ■ You must have Helvetica and Times installed in your System to open a template that contains text (all except the Avery label templates). It doesn't matter that you intend, rightly enough, to replace those fonts the minute you work in the template. Even with the PANOSE font matching system turned on, PageMaker will freak out if she can't find those two fonts. ■ The Calendar template comes with 24 months of Calendar updates (through 1994). The updates are scripts that you run as per the instructions on the pasteboard in the Calendar template publication. Run the scripts you want before you make changes to the template! The "Days" folder deep within the "Calendar update scripts" folder (within "Templates," within "Additions," within your System folder) offers another method of updating, see "Days Read me," within the "Days" folder.

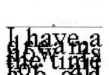

What's this? This is a paragraph full of drop caps. It's what you'll get if you sweep over text that starts with a drop cap and type over it or replace it with another story! See 14.37.

How to use the templates that PageMaker provides

14.30 You can open one of PageMaker's pre-designed templates from the PageMaker desktop; you don't need to be within a publication, nor do you use the "Open" command under the File menu. Simply open PageMaker and select "Open template…" from the Aldus Additions submenu, under the Utilities menu.

14.31 The basic process for using the templates is this: Replace the existing "greek" text with your own stories; replace the "Title" with your own title (14.16); replace the masthead or logo with your masthead or logo (14.19); replace the boxes representing graphics with graphics and photographs of your own (14.19); delete pages or add pages as necessary (1.127–1.128); change the style sheets (Section 8) to take advantage of your own great collection of fonts (rather than use Times and Helvetica and thus scream to the world that your publication was created on a Mac).

14.32 The idea behind these PageMaker-provided templates is that since they have been professionally designed, people with little or no design background can easily put together nice-looking publications. Supposedly, you don't need to know Page-Maker intimately, either, in order to use the templates. That's true *to some extent*. But I found instances in these particular templates where a beginner could get into trouble if she didn't know all the ins and outs of text blocks and story continuity, or of adapting style sheets. A couple of potential problems are noted in the following examples.

14.33 When you open a template, view the Master pages to aquaint yourself with the master items. Then view each page in the publication and with the pointer tool selected, choose "Select all" from the Edit menu. It's very important to see all the handles on each template, because they tell you a lot about how the publication is built and what you can expect when you start replacing things. You can see how many separate stories are in a publication or how long the story is that you may be replacing. You can see which graphics have a text wrap applied, and where the template has ignored the guidelines.

14.34 In longer publications, such as the Newsletters, you may want to select a text block and run some of the Additions for text to get an overview of the story layout. "Display story info" (4.139–4.150) shows you the total amount of text blocks in the story, and on what page the story begins and ends. Use "Traverse textblocks" (4.136–4.138) to follow the thread in a story from text block to text block.

14.35 Envelope template

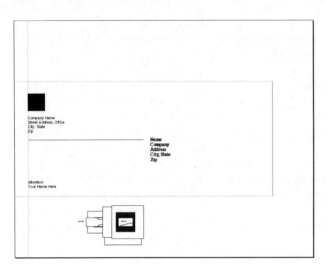

The template doesn't provide for very creative typography—Helvetica for one address, Times for the other—but you can use the style sheet to change the type to whatever you want. Use Shift-Returns in Address 2, unless you *want* a rule before every line in the address. (The "Run script" Addition opens a similar document.)

The cute little printer (drawn entirely in PageMaker), tells you to insert the envelopes face up with the flap facing down on the right. Of course, you may need to adjust this to accomodate your printer.

Style Sheet:
- Address 1
- Address 2
- Caption

Specs:
- 8.5 x 11 page size, *or* 8.27 x 11.69 (A-4) Wide
- Single-sided
- 1 page in template

Master pages:
- Guideline

14.36 Fax cover sheet template

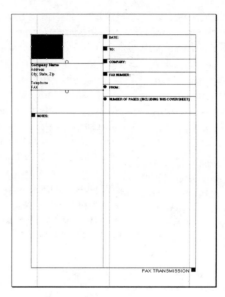

Style Sheet:
- Address 1
- Address 2
- Field heading
- Heading 1
- Note

Specs:
- 8.5 x 11 page size, *or* 8.27 x 11.69 (A-4) Tall
- Single-sided
- 1 page in template

Master pages:
- Field headings
- Head 1
- Rules and small boxes
- Guidelines
- 2 custom columns

If you will be using the keyboard to enter the fax info on this cover sheet, (if your fax machine is a fax/modem within your computer) you might want to develop a style with paragraph space that lets you type inside just one text block to fill in all the data.

Drop in your logo and company name and save this as a new template. If you send faxes frequently, you may want to make an alias of the template and put it in your Apple Menu Items folder, so you can access it any time you want from within any program.

14.37 Newsletter 1 template

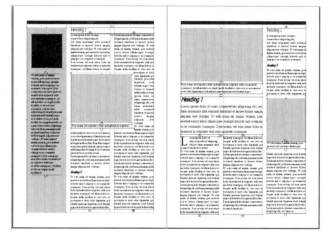

Style Sheet:

- Caption
- Header
- Heading 1
- Heading 2
- Heading 3
- Paragraph 1
- Paragraph 2
- Title
- TOC Heading 1
- TOC Heading 2
- TOC Heading 3
- TOC Title

Specs:

- 8.5 x 11 page size, *or* 8.27 x 11.69 (A-4) Tall
- 3 columns
- Double-sided
- 4 pages in template

Master pages:

- Column guides
- Header

Each page is one long, connected *story* (4.113), excluding the captions which are separate, unlinked text blocks. There is a text wrap applied to four of the graphic placeholders, each of which include room for a caption.

If you were to sweep over the text starting with one of the drop caps, and place or type in new text, all the text would take on the formatting of the drop cap! Create new drop caps (see 20.59) as one of the last steps in the production of the publication.

It wouldn't hurt to run the "Display publication info…" Addition (19.188) to check out the "Based on," and "Next styles" incorporated into these style sheets. Styles were created for the Table of contents, but none of the Headings have "include in the TOC" in their style sheets. To be able to generate the Table of Contents automatically, add "Include in TOC" to the Heading 1 style sheet, the other headings are based on it. The style "Title" is based on Heading 1 too, so deselect the TOC option in that style sheet.

14.38 What is a grid?

A **grid** is a framework of guidelines that provides a structure upon which to build a publication. Grids can be simple or quite involved and technical. A well-thought out grid is really the only solution when designing a lengthy, complex project, such as an encyclopedia or informational atlas, that involves a number of different elements. But you will also find it invaluable for any publication of more than one page that needs a unified, professional appearance.

A well-designed grid is based on an interplay between all the possible demands of the text and the graphics. That is, a grid is based on the point size of the text type and its leading. The point size and leading of the headlines, subheads, captions, and pullquotes should all be based on multiples of the body text. For instance, if the body text is 10/12, the grid will be based on 12-point units of space. So headlines, in order to fit the grid, will work at sizes such as 24/24, or perhaps 34/36. Captions could be italic, 9/12, etc. Text blocks should always align with the grid. Graphics should be cropped or scaled to fit within the grid.

In the Newsletter template in 14.37, the grid is a simple three column format. Some of the graphics, though, override the grid. Really, the secret to creating a successful, dynamic publication with a grid is knowing how and when to override the grid, while still keeping the continuity, the unity, the clarity, and the organization that the framework of the grid provides.

You can create grids from scratch, or from publications you have already created. Margin guides (1.37) help define a grid, as do column guides (1.78) and ruler guides (1.42) placed on the master page(s)(1.137) of the publication or template. You can lock the guides (1.67), and the zero point (1.74), and turn on "Snap to guides" (1.65) and "Snap to rulers" (1.56). Customize the vertical ruler (1.55) to 12 points, or to the leading measurement you use most often. Enter a "Grid size," and check the option "Align to grid" (5.97–5.111) if you want PageMaker to force alignment of text and graphics to the leading grid.

Save a grid as a template and use it the same way you use a template. Take advantage of the framework that is provided. Align text along the top of the rectangles, scale and crop graphics to fit within the rectangles, align captions and pull quotes to match body text baselines, etc. Keep in mind that white areas help organize the material, and don't aim to fill every square of the grid!

Grid theory is one of the most fascinating studies in graphic design. If you have any interest in pursing this topic, I strongly recommend you read these classics:

Grid Systems in Graphic Design, Josef Müller-Brockmann. Second revised edition. New York: Hastings House Publishers, Inc. 1985.

The Grid, Allen Hurlburt. New York: Van Nostrand Reinhold Company, 1978.

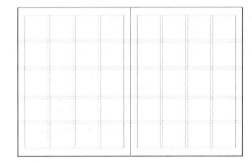

14.39 *An example of a grid. The page size is 8.5 x 11; the grid is 4 columns x 5 rows.*

15 ▾ BOOK PUBLICATIONS

15.1   Minimums and maximums:

Item	Minimum	Maximum
Number of books in a book list	1	Unlimited
Index entry	1 char.	50 char.
Table of Contents entry	1	over 4,000
Table of Contents or Index titles	0 char.	30 char.

15.2   PageMaker 5 has several features specifically geared toward the publication of long documents: the Book List, Table of Contents, and Indexing features.

15.3   In order to create either a Table of Contents or an Index for a book that is comprised of more than one PageMaker publication, you need to know how to create and use a Book List. This feature lets you handle multiple documents as if they were one publication. It'll take you about five minutes to learn.

15.4   The Table of Contents feature is very straightforward and easy to use. If you take advantage of your style sheets as you create the table of contents, you can whip up a great Table in no time, with all your headings and subheads referenced to their appropriate page numbers. As you edit, add, or delete pages, PageMaker keeps track of the changes and allows you to instantly update to the new page numbers.

15.5   The Indexing feature is not so straightforward, but it is really remarkable, once you figure out how to use it. You can just buzz through your publications (thoughtfully, of course), entering index

entries, many with just a keystroke. After you've created indices for all the publications that make up your entire book, you can then create one major index for the whole thing, complete with cross-references and subentries. The index drops in fully formatted, complete with style sheets you can edit, one- and two-em indents for subentries, en dashes between page ranges, etc. It's too cool. As you edit, add, or delete pages, PageMaker keeps track of the entries and allows you to instantly update to the new page numbers.

Note: When either the Table of Contents or the Index becomes large, PageMaker can take an incredibly long time to create and show it. I mean seriously long, like half an hour for an index consisting of a couple thousand entries. Even editing in the "Show index" dialog box becomes tedious.

The Book List 602
    Tasks 604
Tables of Contents 612
    Tasks 617
Indexing 623
    Tasks 634

The Book List

15.6 You can create a single PageMaker publication up to 999 pages. Big deal—you would never want to create one file that large. It would get awkward and ungainly, and would be difficult to back up, maneuver, keep track of, etc., etc., etc. This book in your hands has fewer than 999 pages, but weighs in at 45 megabytes, not including the fonts necessary to print it.

15.7 You will probably want to divide any book or document longer than about fifty pages into sections or chapters. For these lengthy works it's better to create a separate PageMaker file for each of its sections, plus a separate file for the table of contents and the index sections (some people like to combine those two into one file; I like to keep a separate file for each). You can then create a **Book List** to connect all the separate files and work with them as one publication for printing and generating an index and a table of contents.

15.8 The Book List contains a list of all the publications that belong to the entire book, listed in the order you want them to print. (Any publication may be listed in more than one Book List.) Typically you will set up your Book List in only one of the separate publications, most likely in the table of contents pub. If you would like to have it in any of the other separate publications, PageMaker has a keyboard command to copy the existing Book List into every publication in the list (15.25).

15.9 The Book List allows you to print every publication, one after another, without having to open each one separately. You can generate a table of contents (15.32–15.67) and an index (15.68–15.207) that encompass every section. The table of contents and the index will automatically include the page number of each item. As you add or delete pages in the publication, the page numbers recorded in the internal table of contents and the index will change accordingly.

15.10 The separate sections can be automatically and consecutively numbered as you print the entire Book List. The buttons in the "Book publication list" dialog box (15.19) allow you a variety of ways to automatically number the pages in each of your publications as they print (15.29).

15.11 The Book List is actually just a list that tells PageMaker where to *find* the publication. If you move or rename the publication after you have added it to a Book List, PageMaker will ask you to find it when you try to print or generate a table of contents or an index.

15.12 Be sure to take advantage of creating templates (Section 14) and copying style sheets (8.20; 8.56) to keep each publication in the book consistent. That is really one of the secrets of a professional-looking piece—consistency—because it creates a unified work that looks like the creators knew what they were doing.

15.13 "Book publication list" dialog box *(from the File menu, choose "Book...")*

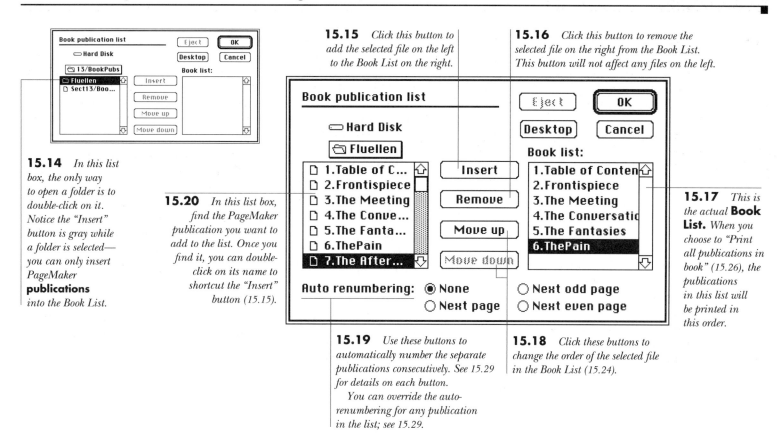

15.15 *Click this button to add the selected file on the left to the Book List on the right.*

15.16 *Click this button to remove the selected file on the right from the Book List. This button will not affect any files on the left.*

15.14 *In this list box, the only way to open a folder is to double-click on it. Notice the "Insert" button is gray while a folder is selected—you can only insert PageMaker* **publications** *into the Book List.*

15.20 *In this list box, find the PageMaker publication you want to add to the list. Once you find it, you can double-click on its name to shortcut the "Insert" button (15.15).*

15.17 *This is the actual* **Book List.** *When you choose to "Print all publications in book" (15.26), the publications in this list will be printed in this order.*

15.19 *Use these buttons to automatically number the separate publications consecutively. See 15.29 for details on each button.*
You can override the auto-renumbering for any publication in the list; see 15.29.

15.18 *Click these buttons to change the order of the selected file in the Book List (15.24).*

If you want to do this:

15.21   Create a Book List

Then follow these steps:

- Open any one of the publications that comprise the whole book (preferably the first publication in the group, just so you always know where the Book List is).
- From the File menu, choose "Book...."
- In the "Book publication list" dialog box, there are two list boxes. On the left, navigate through your disks and folders to find the publication you want to add to the Book List (the publication you are currently in will already be visible in this list). *The only way to open a folder in the left-hand list box is to double-click on it.*
- Once you find the publication that you want to include in the list, click once on its name, then click the "Insert" button (or double-click on its name). The publication will be added to the Book List on the right side.
- Once it is on the Book List, you can move the publication up higher on the list: select it (click once on its name); click the "Move up" button as many times as necessary. Click the "Move down" button to move the publication below any other file in the list.
- Before you click OK, you can navigate through your folders to find any other publications to add to the list.
- Click OK.

Shortcuts ▾ Notes ▾ Hints

- Actually, the publication is not always added to the *end* of the Book List; it is added directly after whichever publication in the Book List is *selected* (highlighted). So if you want to control the order of the publications without the extra steps of moving them up or down, simply select the name in the Book List that you want the new publication to *follow* (click once on it; see the illustrations in 15.22). When you insert the next publication, it will appear directly after the selected name.
- A publication can only contain one Book List at a time. Yes, a publication can be listed in more than one Book List, but you can only have one Book List per publication.
- Book lists are lost in files converted from PageMaker 4.x. You will have to recreate the Book List in the 5.0 publication. However, only PageMaker 5 publications can be added to the Book List.

If you want to do this:

Then follow these steps:

Shortcuts ▾ Notes ▾ Hints

15.22 Add a publication to the Book List

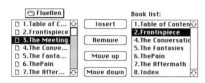

If you want to add a new publication directly below one that is already in the list, click once on the pub in the Book List.

When you insert the new pub, it will appear directly below the one that was previously selected.

- Open the publication that contains the Book List.
- From the File menu, choose "Book...."
- Just as in 15.21, navigate through the disks and folders in the left-hand list box to find the publication you want to add to the list.
- The existing Book List is in a particular order—you will probably want it in the order in which the book is to be read. If you want to add a publication to that list in a certain spot in the order rather than at the bottom, do this:
  - In the Book List on the right, click once on the name of the publication that you want the new one to *follow*.
  - In the publication list on the left, double-click on the pub you want to add (or select it and click the "Insert" button). The new publication will be added to the Book List directly *after* the one that was selected.
- If the publication is added to the *bottom* of the Book List and you want it in a different order, you can move the selected publication up or down in the list order by clicking the "Move up" or "Move down" buttons.
- Click OK.

If you want to do this:	Then follow these steps:	Shortcuts ▾ Notes ▾ Hints
15.23 Remove a publication from the Book List	▪ Open the publication that contains the Book List. ▪ From the File menu, choose "Book...." ▪ In the Book List shown on the right of the dialog box, click once on the publication you want to remove. ▪ Click the "Remove" button. You will not get an alert box asking if you really want to do this. If you didn't want to remove it, but you did, you can either Cancel this dialog box (which will cancel any other changes you made here), or you can simply find the publication and insert it again. ▪ Click OK.	▪ Removing a publication from the Book List does not affect the original publication in the left-hand box (15.16).
15.24 Change the order of the publications in the Book List	▪ Open the publication that contains the Book List. ▪ From the File menu, choose "Book...." ▪ In the Book List shown on the right, click once on the publication whose order you want to change. ▪ Click either the "Move up" or "Move down" buttons. Click OK.	
15.25 Copy the Book List into every other publication in the list  `[======      ] Cancel` Copying book publication list. Publication: 5.The Fantasies	▪ Press the Command key as you choose "Book..." from the File menu. You won't get the actual dialog box; you will just see a progress report of the copying process.	▪ The current publication must have a Book List, of course, and the pub must be titled (not "Untitled"). This process will replace any existing book lists that may already be in the other publications.

If you want to do this:

15.26 Print all the publications
on the Book List

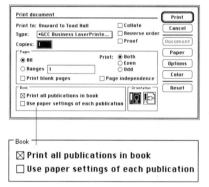

*The "Book" options are found in the
"Print document" dialog box.*

Then follow these steps:

- From the "File" menu open the publication that contains the Book List.
- If you want to automatically renumber the pages in each publication in the Book List, see 15.29.
- From the File menu choose "Print...," *or* press Command P.
- Check the box next to "Print all publications in book" (this is only available in publications that contain a Book List).
- Set up the "Print" dialog boxes any way you like. All the specs you choose here will apply to every publication in the list, regardless of their individual print specifications except:
  - ▫ Each publication will maintain its paper orientation.
  - ▫ Each publication will keep its own "Source" and "Size" settings in the "Paper" printing dialog box if you check "Use paper settings of each publication" (15.27).
  - ▫ All the pages in each publication will print if "All" is selected. If "Ranges" is selected only the page ranges specified in each publication will print.
  - ▫ You cannot select individual inks to print if you choose to print "Separations."
- Click "Print," *or* hit Return.

Shortcuts ▾ Notes ▾ Hints

- The publications will print in the order they are listed, even if the one on the screen is not the first in the list (even if the one on the screen is not *in* the list).
- **Important note:** All the pubs will print with the print specifications that are in the publication from which you are printing, even if the current publication is not in the list. (If you want to print multiple publications and maintain individual print specifications, see the "Printer styles..." Addition; 19.191–19.216.)
- If you select "Reverse," the Book List will print in reverse order **and** each publication will print in reverse order.
- You can print more than one copy of each publication and still have it collated. PageMaker will print one collated copy of each publication in the list, and then start all over from the beginning.
- If your publication is oversized, you can check the "Tile" box in the "Paper" printing dialog box and the "Auto" radio button to automatically tile each publication.
- See Section 19 for more information on printing publications.

If you want to do this:	**Then follow these steps:**	**Shortcuts ▾ Notes ▾ Hints**

15.27 Print all the publications on the Book List but keep each publication's "Size" and "Source" settings

┌ Book ─────────────────────────┐
☒ **Print all publications in book**
☒ **Use paper settings of each publication**
└───────────────────────────────┘

■ Follow the steps in 15.26, but check the box next to "Use paper settings of each publication."

■ This option is not available on non-PostScript printers.
■ The "Size" and "Source" settings are found in the "Paper" printing dialog box. They define the size of the paper used for that publication and the printer tray from which the paper is fed. These settings will be stored with the publication if you previously printed and then saved the publication (if you cancelled the printing the settings were not stored). The settings will be stored without printing if you pressed the Shift key as you clicked the "Print" button; then saved the publication.

15.28 Print just some of the publications on the Book List

┌ Book ─────────────────────────┐
☒ **Print all publications in book**
☐ **Use paper settings of each publication**
└───────────────────────────────┘

■ If you don't want to print every pub on the list, change the list. You can always change it back later.
■ **Or** move the publications that you do want to print into the first positions (15.24). After those pages come out of the printer, Cancel the printing (click on the "Cancel" button, or press Command Period).
■ **Or** open another publication and create another Book List that contains just the pubs you want to print. Any publication can be in any number of Book lists, because the Book List is just a list that tells PageMaker where to *find* the actual pub.

■ Remember, no matter which publication contains the Book List, when you print the entire Book, the printing proceeds only in the order on the list and includes only those publications listed there. So you can actually have a publication open that contains a Book List that doesn't even list the pub that is open! But from within this publication, you can print any other PageMaker file on your disk. That's a good trick. Just remember to remove the file when you're through printing if you don't want it as a permanent member of the Book List.

If you want to do this:

15.29 Automatically and consecutively renumber all the pages in the publications printed from the Book List

Auto renumbering:

⦿ None ○ Next odd page
○ Next page ○ Next even page

Then follow these steps:

■ Before you print, from the File menu, choose "Book...."
■ Click one of the buttons for "Auto renumbering":
  □ **None:** This is the default setting. Page-Maker will not renumber the pages.
  □ **Next page:** The following publication will begin with a page number that is in exact sequence with the previous publication in the list.
  □ **Next odd page:** This is just like "Next page" except that it forces each new publication to begin printing on an odd page (which is a right-hand page). The publication will end on an even-numbered page (left-hand). PageMaker will insert pages, if necessary, at the beginning and end to accomplish this. Since she is inserting blank pages, they will not print unless you check the "Print blank pages" box in the "Options" dialog box before you print (19.60). They won't print with any page numbers on them.
  □ **Next even page:** This works exactly like "Next odd page" above, except that the first page will always be even (left-hand).

Shortcuts ▾ Notes ▾ Hints

■ This automatic renumbering feature actually changes the page numbers on the publication pages. That is, if you had five publications of six pages each, each numbered from 1 to 6, after you print with this automatic renumbering in effect, those pages will be numbered 1 to 6, 7 to 12, 13 to 18, etc.
■ **If you want to override the auto page numbering for any publication in the Book List,** you need to click the "Restart page numbering" checkbox in that particular publication's "Page setup" dialog box (from the File menu). This will cause the pub to retain its own numbering.
■ If you are going nuts trying to figure out why publications on a Book List won't renumber, check the "Page setup" dialog box (1.23) in each publication to see if the "Restart page numbering" option is checked.

If you want to do this:

15.30 Print a selected range of pages in each of the publications in the Book List

◉ **Ranges** | 4-7, 11 |

Then follow these steps:

- Open the publication that contains the Book List.
- From the File menu, choose "Print...," *or* press Command P.
- Check the box "Print all publications in book."
- Click the radio button next to "Ranges," under "Pages" in the "Print document" dialog box. Enter the pages you want to print from this publication.
  - ☐ Each publication in the Book List will print according to the last setting used for "Pages" in its own "Print document" dialog box.
- Set up the "Print " dialog boxes any way you like.
- Click "Print" *or* hit Return.

Shortcuts ▾ Notes ▾ Hints

- PageMaker will not renumber pages when the "Ranges" button is selected.
- Each publication will print the same page ranges as the last time you printed and saved in that publication. (If the "All" radio button was last selected, all the pages in that particular publication will print this time too.) You can only change the page range settings for the publication you are printing from.
- However, you *can* change the page range setting in each publication if you open it and Shift-Print to save print specs. In the "Print" dialog box of each publication, enter the page range needed, then press the Shift key as you click the "Print" button. Save and close the publication, and print as usual from the publication with the Book List. Do be aware that the print specs remain saved until you change them again.

> If you ain't the lead dog, the scenery never changes.
> — E. Wilson

If you want to do this:

15.31 Print an entire book to disk as a PostScript file

The "Postscript" options are in the "Options" Print dialog box.

Then follow these steps:

- From the File menu open the publication that contains the Book List.
- From the File menu, choose "Print...," *or* press Command P.
- Check the box next to "Print all publications in book."
- Click the "Options" button on the right-hand side of the dialog box.
- Under "PostScript" click the box next to "Write PostScript to file."
  - ▢ Click the radio button next to "Normal" to save the book as a single PostScript file.
  - ▢ Click the radio button next to "For separations," to save each publication in the book as a file with a .SEP extension.
- Set all the other printing options as desired and click "Print."

Shortcuts ▾ Notes ▾ Hints

- The "EPS" option is not available when you choose to print all publications in a Book List.

Tables of Contents (TOC)

15.32 PageMaker makes it incredibly easy to generate a table of contents. It does involve foresight and planning, however, and you really should have a working knowledge of style sheets (Section 8) in order to use this feature without frustration.

15.33 The **Table of Contents (TOC)** feature works in this way: In any publication, whether it is complete in itself or part of an entire book, you choose which *paragraphs* you want to include in a table of contents. Remember, on the Mac any text that ends with a Return key is one *paragraph;* each separate one of your chapter titles, headings, subheads, etc., is considered a separate *paragraph.* PageMaker can compile all the paragraphs you choose and create a table of contents for the current publication, or for the entire Book List, all accurately paginated and set up with leader tabs (see the examples on page 616).

15.34 You can choose whether a paragraph should be included in the table of contents in either of two ways:

- You can select the individual paragraph (just click in it with the text tool), then bring up the "Paragraph specifications" dialog box (from the Type menu, choose "Paragraph..."). Click in the checkbox next to "Include in table of contents."

- Or you can include the option "Include in table of contents" right into your style sheet so it will automatically build every instance of that style (be it headline, subhead, etc.) into your table of contents.

Click this checkbox, whether individually or through your style sheet definitions (Section 8).

15.35 It is best, really, to plan on using your style sheets to help define the table. Then you know nothing will be forgotten; plus, it keeps everything consistent. It does mean you have to be aware that every time you apply that particular style the tagged paragraph will be added to the table of contents *(which can be edited, though).* And if you base any other styles (8.21–8.27) on that particular style, those paragraphs will also be included in the table of contents.

15.36 That's not the only reason you need to understand your style sheets. When the table of contents is generated, PageMaker creates and applies a style to each level (see 15.42–15.43). It will rarely look exactly like you want, so you need to know how to edit the style sheet to your satisfaction.

The process of creating a Table of Contents

15.37 First, you must tag all the paragraphs that you want included in the table of contents (15.34; 15.59). You can create a table for just one individual publication, or you can create a table that spans every publication in the Book List (15.62–15.63). Or you can do both, as I did in this book.

15.38 You can apply a prefix to the page numbers; the prefix will appear only in the table of contents and the index (not on the pages themselves). For instance, you may have your publication divided into sections A, B, and C. You can set up a prefix, using the "Page numbering" dialog box (15.61), that will precede each number with the section letter; e.g., A1, A2, A3, etc. Or perhaps you want to label your appendix pages or your front matter pages (table of contents, intro, etc.) differently than the regular pages. These prefixes are specific to each publication.

15.39 If you are working with one individual publication, after you are finished and everything has been tagged, you can choose "Create TOC..." from the Utilities menu and create the table (15.62).

15.40 If you are working with several publications as part of a book, there are several other factors to deal with:

a) You can choose to include all the publications that appear in the Book List contained within the open publication.

b) If you decide to include the entire Book List, the items in the table of contents *will be in the order of the Book List*, not in their page number order. That is, if your Book List shows Sections 1, 2, 4, 3, your table of contents will reflect that same order.

c) If you want PageMaker to automatically number your pages in consecutive order, make sure "None" is not selected next to "Auto numbering" in the Book List.

15.41 When you choose "Create TOC..." PageMaker gathers up all the paragraphs that have been tagged, either in the individual publication or in all the pubs in the Book List (15.63). She arranges them in the order they appear in the publication and in the order the publications appear in the list.

15.42 Each item in the table is tagged with a style that PageMaker creates; these styles are automatically added to your style sheet. Each style is named with the prefix "TOC," followed by the name of the style with which the item is already tagged. That is, if Subhead 1 is checked to include table of contents items, then when those tagged items are generated into a Table of Contents, each will then be tagged with the style "TOC Subhead 1."

15.43 All TOC styles default to a tab with a dot leader (which you can change; 15.65) leading over to the page number. The size, type style, other tab stops, and the alignment are the same as they are in the style from which they were generated.

That is, if the style "Subhead 1" is 18-point Garamond Bold, then in the generated table of contents the corresponding "TOC Subhead 1" will use 18-point Garamond Bold. That's why it is important for you to know how to work with and edit your style sheets. Change the style sheets to your heart's content, *but don't change the style names!!* (15.45)

—continued

The process —*continued*

15.44 When you click OK in the "Create table of contents" dialog box (15.62–15.63), PageMaker generates the table.

- If you are on a publication page, you will get a loaded text icon. Click on the page to place the table of contents story.
- If you are in the Story Editor (Section 8), you will get a new story window displaying the table of contents. Select "Edit layout" from the Edit menu, or press Command E to get the loaded icon; click to place the story on the publication page.

15.45 You will undoubtedly need to edit the TOC style sheets to arrange the text aesthetically and legibly. Edit the styles all you want, *but don't change the style names!!* When you update the Table of Contents, you can choose to have PageMaker replace the current version with the new version; the new version will reuse the customized style sheet *if the styles have the same names as PageMaker originally gave them.*

15.46 If a paragraph that is included in the table of contents is not tagged with a style, PageMaker will format it, but will not assign it a style (it will be "No style").

15.47 In the "Create table of contents" dialog box (15.51), you have an option of creating a title for the table of contents page. The standard title is "Contents," and that is the default PageMaker supplies. You can change that edit box (15.52), though, to any title you choose, up to 30 characters in length. Or you can just leave it blank.

15.48 If you decide to have a title, Page-Maker will assign it a style, "TOC title." Because of this, it is best not to name any of your own styles *(ones that will be included in the table of contents)* with the name "Title," or you may end up confused.

15.49 If you will be adding the Table of Contents to the beginning of an existing publication, be sure you allow enough pages for it. Take into consideration the fact that, if you have to add pages to make room for your TOC, your page numbers will all change, including the first page of your first chapter. That may or may not be a problem for you.

15.50 If you really want the TOC to be included in the same publication as the rest of the pages, consider adding the Table of Contents at the end of the publication, without page numbers. That way the first chapter can start on page one, yet your Table of Contents can expand as necessary.

15.51   The "Create table of contents" dialog box   *(from the Utilities menu, choose "Create TOC...")*

15.52   *You can enter up to 30 characters in the "Title" edit box. This will be the title at the top of the table. You do not have to have a title at all, if you so choose; you can just leave it blank; see 15.47.*

15.53   *This is only available if there is an existing Table of Contents; see 15.66.*

15.54   *This is available only if the current publication contains a Book List (15.6–15.31); see 15.63.*

15.55   *You can choose the basic format of the number placement, or even whether to have numbers at all; see 15.64.*

Create table of contents

OK

Cancel

Title: **Contents**

☐ Replace existing table of contents

☒ Include book publications

Format: ○ No page number
○ Page number before entry
● Page number after entry

Between entry and page number: ^t

15.56   *You can specify how you want the space formatted between the entry and its page number. You can enter up to seven characters here. What is shown is the default, a code for creating a tab; the style sheet contains a right-aligned leader tab to match. See 15.65 for more information on this option. See 15.200 and Appendix D for entering other formatting codes.*

Examples of Tables of Contents

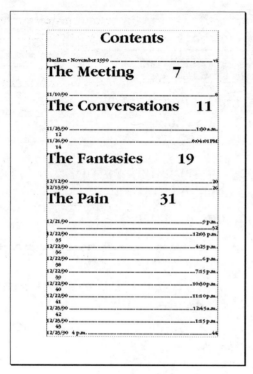

15.57   *This is an example of a typical table of contents for a Book List, using PageMaker's defaults (15.63), including "Page number after entry." Notice that the Table needs some adjusting.*

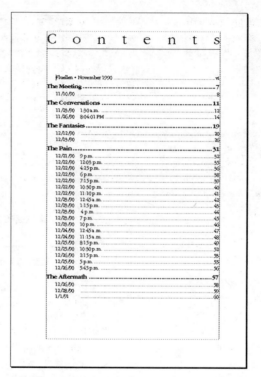

15.58   *This is the same Table as in 15.57 (left), but the style sheets have been customized to my specifications. When I update (replace) this Table of Contents, PageMaker will re-use my customized style sheets.*

If you want to do this:	Then follow these steps:	Shortcuts ▾ Notes ▾ Hints
15.59 Tag individual paragraphs to be included in the Table of Contents	■ With the **text tool** click in the paragraph you want to include. ■ From the Type menu choose "Paragraph…," *or* press Command M. ■ At the bottom of the "Paragraph specifications" dialog box, click in the checkbox "Include in table of contents" (15.34). ■ Click OK.	■ Remember, a **paragraph** on the Mac is anything that has a Return after it. Paragraphs can be single words on one line, or they can even be blank lines. The kinds of items that typically go into tables of contents, such as Headlines, Subheads, etc., are one line.

15.60 Use a style sheet to tag paragraphs to be included in a table of contents	■ Go to the "Edit style" dialog box for the style you want to include by one of these methods. Either:
	  □ From the Type menu, choose "Define styles…," *or* press Command 3. Double-click on the style name you want to edit.
	  □ **Or:** Show the Style palette (choose it from the Window menu, *or* press Command Y). Hold down the Command key; click once on the style you want to edit.
	  □ **Or:** If the text tool is within the style you want to edit, Command-click on the style name in the paragraph-view Control palette (4.303).
	■ Click on the "Para…" button.
	■ In the "Paragraph specifications" dialog box, click in the checkbox "Include in table of contents" (see left).
	■ Press Option Return to close both boxes.
		■ **Be careful:** if you "base" any other styles on this one (8.21–8.27), the other styles will also be included in the Table of contents. It doesn't matter how many characters are in the paragraph—I created a table of contents entry that had over 4,000 characters in it. Use "Based on" wisely.
		■ See Section 8 for complete details on Style Sheets.

Edit style

Name: `Info`

Based on: `Body`

Next style: `Same style`

OK · Cancel · Type… · Para… · Tabs… · Hyph…

Body + next: Same style + left indent: 0.5 + first indent: -0.5 + space after: 0 + incl TOC

Click these buttons.

Paragraph specifications

Indents:
Left `5` picas
First `-3` picas
Right `0` picas

Paragraph space:
Before `0` picas
After `0` picas

OK · Cancel · Rules… · Spacing…

Alignment: `Left`   Dictionary: `US English …`

Options:
☐ Keep lines together   ☐ Keep with next `0` lines
☐ Column break before   ☐ Widow control `0` lines
☐ Page break before   ☐ Orphan control `0` lines
☒ Include in table of contents

If you want to do this:	Then follow these steps:	Shortcuts ▾ Notes ▾ Hints

15.61 Define a prefix for the page numbers in the Table of Contents *(optional)*

- From the File menu open the publication with the Table of Contents to which you want to add a page number prefix (such as the appendices, index, or perhaps volumes).
- From the File menu choose "Page setup."
- Click on the button "Numbers...."
- In the "TOC and index prefix" edit box, enter the characters that you want to precede the page number (you can enter up to fifteen characters). Be sure to also type any spaces you need, such as the space directly before the number.
- Hit the Return key twice, *or* press Option Return to close both dialog boxes.

- This optional format is *publication-specific;* that is, it will apply only to the page numbers from this one publication. If you are creating a table of contents for an entire Book List, then you must follow this procedure for every separate publication for which you want prefixes.
- You can always press Command Option Period to Cancel out of nested dialog boxes.

15.62 Create a Table of Contents for just the current publication, using PageMaker's defaults

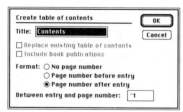

If the publication does not contain a Book List, the option to "Include book publications" is not even available.

- Go to the page where you want to set up the Table of Contents.
- If you have tagged paragraphs (15.37; 15.59–15.60), then from the Utilities menu choose "Create TOC...."
- If you are updating (replacing) a table, see 15.66. If you want to change any of the defaults shown, see 15.64 and 15.65. Then simply click the OK button. You will get a loaded text icon; click on the page to place the story, just as you would place any story.
- Edit the style sheets as necessary (15.67).

- If you have not tagged any paragraphs to be included in the table of contents (15.59; 15.60), then your Table of Contents will be empty except for the title "Contents."
- You can also do this while in the **Story Editor** (Section 9). Instead of a loaded text icon, you will get a new story window displaying the table of contents. Press Command E to place this story on the page. You will get the loaded text icon; click with the icon to pour the story onto the layout page, just as you would place any story.

If you want to do this:

15.63 Create the Table of Contents for an entire Book List, using PageMaker's defaults

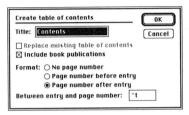

Then follow these steps:

- Open the publication in which you want to set up the Table of Contents. The publication must contain a Book List. If there isn't one there already, create one now (15.6–15.12; 15.21), or copy it in (15.25).
- If you have tagged paragraphs (15.59–15.60) in each publication in the Book List, then from the Utilities menu choose "Create TOC...."
- The checkbox "Include book publications" should be checked on.
  - □ If you are updating or replacing a table, see 15.66. If you want to change any of the defaults shown, see 15.64 and 15.65. Then simply click the OK button.
- PageMaker will collect all the entries and you will eventually get a loaded text icon. Click on the page to place the story, just as you would place any story.
- Edit the style sheets as necessary (15.67). If you edited them in another publication and want to use the same format, just "Copy" the style sheet (8.56–8.58).

Shortcuts ▾ Notes ▾ Hints

- If you have not tagged any paragraphs to be included in the table of contents (15.40; 15.59–15.60), then your Table of Contents will be empty except for the title "Contents."
- You can also do this while in the **Story Editor** (Section 9). Instead of a loaded text icon, you will get a new story window displaying the Table of Contents. Press Command E to place this story on the page. You will get the loaded text icon; click with the icon to pour the story onto the layout page, just as you would place any story.

If you want to do this:

Then follow these steps:

Shortcuts ▾ Notes ▾ Hints

15.64 Change the presentation of the page numbers in the TOC

Format: ◉ No page number
○ Page number before entry
○ Page number after entry

Between entry and page number: [^t]

If you choose "No page number," you will get a nice list of the contents.

Fluellen • November 1990
The Meeting
11/10/90
The Conversations
11/28/90   1:30 a.m.
11/26/90   8:04:01 PM
The Fantasies
12/12/90
12/13/90
The Pain
12/21/90   9 p.m.
12/22/90   12:03 p.m.

vi   Fluellen • November 1990
7 ....**The Meeting**
8   11/10/90
11 ....**The Conversations**
12   11/28/90 ....1:30 a.m.
14   11/26/90 ....8:04:01 PM
19 ....**The Fantasies**
20   12/12/90
26   12/13/90

If you choose "Page number before entry," the page numbers will be on the left, with the default tab leader leading to the item. You will need to do some style sheet editing.

■ Follow the steps in 15.62 or 15.63 to create a table of contents. Before you click OK, decide what format you want the numbers to have.

☐ If you choose "No page number," then of course you will see no page number. This is handy when you just want to generate a list of items. When you choose this option, the "Between entry and page number" option is gone.

☐ If you choose "Page number before entry," then the page number will be on the left side of the page, left-aligned (numbers really should be right-aligned). You will need to edit your style sheet and will probably need to insert tabs (Section 6) to align the numbers.

☐ The default option is "Page number after entry," which gives you the standard look, as shown in 15.57.

■ I created the list of tasks in Appendix B by using this TOC feature with no page numbers.

If you want to do this:

15.65 Format the space between the entry and the page number

Between entry and page number: | ^t |

The Conversations page 11
  11/23/90 page 12
  11/26/90 page 14

In this example, "page " was entered in the edit box.

The Fantasies   ······19
  12/12/90 ······20
  12/13/90 ······26

In this example, the raised period was entered (Option Shift 9).

The Pain   ·•·•·•31
  12/21/90 ·•·•·•32
  12/22/90 ·•·•·•35
  12/22/90 ·•·•·•36

In this example, periods and bullets (Option 8) were entered.

Then follow these steps:

- Prepare to create a table of contents as in 15.62 or 15.63.
- In the "Create table of contents" dialog box, enter up to seven characters in the "Between entry and page number" edit box. You can enter more, but they will be ignored.
  - ☐ The default character (^t) is a tab; the style sheet sets it as a right-aligned leader tab. Even if you change this existing tab character, the tab ruler in the corresponding style sheet still retains a right-aligned tab marker. (That tab marker is difficult to see in the ruler because it is directly on top of the right margin marker.)
  - ☐ See 15.200 and Appendix D for a list of the codes to enter to create the special characters, such as Returns, tabs, non-breaking spaces, line breaks, etc.
- When you click OK, the table of contents will be created using those characters before the page number. To the left are several examples. Be sure to enter any spaces you also need; e.g., in the first example, five characters were entered: "page " (the four letters in *page,* plus a space).

Shortcuts ▾ Notes ▾ Hints

- Anything you enter in this entry box will apply to every page number in the table of contents. Notice the text formatting of the characters is the same as that of the text itself. You can even use the "Change" feature in the Story Editor to change the formatting (9.67–9.77). I'd advise you to wait until you are sure the current table of contents is the final version before you do this, because if you update the table later all the changes will be replaced.
- If you want to add characters to the page numbers of just certain publications, such as "Volume A," define a prefix in the "Page numbering" dialog box (15.61).
- Remember, you can also customize those leaders; see 6.71–6.73.

621

If you want to do this:	Then follow these steps:	Shortcuts ▼ Notes ▼ Hints
15.66 Update (replace) an existing Table of Contents	• Open the publication that contains the existing Table of Contents. You don't have to actually be viewing the page that the table is on, although it is nice to see what you're doing. If you are not on the TOC page, PageMaker will take you to it when she replaces the text, anyway. • From the Utilities menu choose "Create TOC...." • Click in the checkbox "Replace existing table of contents." • Change the other specs in this dialog box as you wish. • Click OK. You won't get a loaded text icon. PageMaker will recreate the table, removing the one that is currently on the page and automatically replacing it with the new one. The new one will pick up all the style sheet changes that you have made. *But the new one will not pick up any editing changes or revisions that were made in the previous table!* That's why it's a good idea to leave the editing until you create the final version.	• There can only be *one* Table of Contents story in the publication. You can create what looks like more than one; I mean, you can place two or three or four on the page, but PageMaker will consider only the very latest one the *actual* Table of Contents. It is the latest one that will be updated; the rest are just plain ol' text blocks.
15.67 Edit the TOC styles to format the table of contents	• Press Command Y to get the Style palette. Hold the Command key down and click on the style name to get the "Edit style" dialog box. See 8.53 for details.	• Section 8 explains style sheets in detail. Style sheets are probably the most important thing you could learn to master in PageMaker. And paragraph rules.

The dialog box shown reads:

```
Create table of contents                    [ OK ]
Title: [Contents                ]           [Cancel]
☒ Replace existing table of contents
☒ Include book publications
Format:  ○ No page number
         ○ Page number before entry
         ◉ Page number after entry
Between entry and page number: [^t]
```

Indexing

15.68 This is a pretty amazing feature. You can quickly and easily compile a great index, either as you write or at the very end of the publication. PageMaker will alphabetize it for you, indent for secondary and tertiary entries, create bold headings, and even set up cross-referencing cues. PageMaker keeps track of the pages on which each entry is found; as you edit text and as page numbers change, you can instantly update the index to include the changes automatically. You can create an index for just the current publication, or you can combine the indices from each publication in the Book List (15.6–15.12) into one large index.

15.69 This is not just a search-and-add process, where every occurrence of a word or phrase is added to the index (although you can do that, too, see 15.157). *You* control which occurrences of each item are entered into the index by selecting an item and then entering it (15.143). PageMaker relies on your intelligence and simply provides you with a tool, replacing a type-writer and thousands of index cards.

15.70 You can use the index feature on several different levels, from simple to complex. That is, if you have just a small, simple indexing job to complete, don't be scared away by the complexity and potential power of this feature. I completed the index on the right in less than fifteen minutes, using only one keyboard command and never looking at a dialog box. I just repeatedly selected text and hit a keystroke; when I finished entering items, I chose "Create index..." and hit Return; the index you see on the right appeared on the page. I did some minor editing. For this quick, easy method, see the ultra-zippy shortcut in 15.143.

15.71 Just as when you generate a table of contents (15.37–15.50), PageMaker adds styles to your style sheet to format the index. The styles are preceded with the identifying label "Index"; e.g., "Index level 1" or "Index section." You do need to know how to work with style sheets (Section 8) in order to take advantage of this most important convenience.

Index

A
abdominal pain 21
acute pediatric illness 12
acute surgical abdomen 20
Artificial Intelligence 12
B
bronchiospasm 20
C
collapse 20
conclusion 22
D
data collection 18
de novo 19, 22
DeDombal 21
double-blind 19
E
ear infection 20
educational tool 12
EKG 21
emergencies 19
encyclopedia 14
expert systems 21
F
fever 15
First Opinion 12
FORTH 13, 15
G
glitches 20
H
HyperCard 17
I
IBM PC 17
"if/then" rules 16
K
knowledge base 20, 13

L
lab tests 19
M
Macintosh 17
medical expert systems 12
N
nasal stuffiness 20
non-emergency 20
O
otitis media 15
P
physical exam 19
post-history 20
pulmonary function 21
R
references 23
respiratory distress 20
results 20
S
SA-4 inference engine 13, 15
self-resolving situations 19
sore throat 20
Sphinx 21
study methods 19
surgical findings 21
symptom-based indices 14
symptomatology 20
T
Torasso 21
triage 12, 20, 21
Triage Assessment option 19
W
well-child care 19
Y
yes/no questions 18

The basic process

15.72 The index commands are found in the Utilities menu. They can be rather intimidating, and they are definitely not intuitive: the "Index entry..." command has three dialog boxes; the "Show index..." command has five dialog boxes, some of which look the same as those in "Index entry"; the "Create index..." command has two dialog boxes. Each dialog box has a very specific and different function, even though several of them look exactly alike.

15.73 Use the "Index entry..." command to create the list of entries, to add to the list of entries, to create topic references, and to set up cross-references.

15.74 Use the "Show index..." command after the list is created, to review the existing list, or to edit, cross-reference, or remove entries. You cannot add new entries to the index with this command *(well, you can add them, but they won't have a page number locator).*

15.75 If you are creating a book that is comprised of several separate publications, build an index for each publication (you don't even need to place it on a page). Make a new publication just for the index pages (or perhaps for the index and the table of contents pages). In that new pub make a Book List of all the publications whose indices you want to include (15.21). Now when you create the index you can choose to include the book publications and you will have one cohesive index covering the entire book (15.185). Wow.

15.76 Use the "Create index..." command to generate the actual index in story form to place on the page. This is also where you will format the look of the index, defining how many spaces between the entry and the number, whether the secondary entries nest or run-on into each other, etc. As you add or edit entries, use the "Create index..." command to automatically update the index on the page.

15.77 Once an entry is made into the index, it is keyed to the text on that page. If the text on that page is moved to another page, the index will change to reflect the new page number. If the text is deleted, the index entry will disappear. If you have already placed the index on the page as a story, you will not see the changes in that story; the changes are made to the *internal* index. When you *update* the index story, you will see the revisions; 15.182; 15.202.

15.78 Once you place the index as a story on a page, you will undoubtedly find things you want to change. *Don't spend any time editing the index on the page, since all changes will be lost as soon as you update it!*

Instead, **edit the internal index.** Edit the index entries through "Show index..." (15.164). Edit the format of the index through "Create index..." (15.188–15.200). Edit the text specifications through the style sheets (Section 8).

When you are completely finished with the book and the index entries, and you have the final version on the page, *then* it is worthwhile to spend time revising the index story directly on the publication page.

15.79 "Add index entry" dialog box (with text selected or the insertion point flashing)

(from the Utilities menu, choose "Index entry…," or press Command ;)

15.80 *This is an example of the formatting for first-, second-, and third-level entries.*

> **F** *(index section marker)*
> Primary entry (first-level)
>   secondary entry (second-level)
>   tertiary entry (third-level)
> Primary again (first-level)

15.81 *To make a primary entry into a secondary entry, or a secondary into a tertiary, or a tertiary into a primary, click this button. It just moves the entered text into the next box in line; 15.128.*

15.82 *Click the "Cross-reference" button to cross-reference an entry. See the dialog box on page 627.*

15.83 *Use "Sort" to alphabetize an entry under separate characters, such as "St." under "Saint." See 15.129–15.134; 15.170–15.171.*

15.84 *The OK button is only available if there is text selected on the page, or if the insertion point is flashing in an **existing** text block and you type an entry into the "Topic" primary-level edit box (15.89). If no text is selected and no insertion point is flashing within text, you will see the dialog box on page 627.*

15.89 *If text was selected before you pulled up this dialog box, it will be entered here. This first box is for primary entries (also known as first-level); 15.143.*

Secondary entries (second-level); 15.147–15.149.

Tertiary entries (third-level); 15.150–15.152.

Add index entry

Type: ⦿ Page reference ◯ Cross-reference

Topic: Sort:

Book Publications

Page range: ⦿ Current page
     ◯ To next style change
     ◯ To next use of style: `Body`
     ◯ For next `1` paragraphs
     ◯ Suppress page range

Page # override: ☐ Bold ☐ Italic ☐ Underline

[OK] [Cancel] [Add] [Topic…]

Press Command Period to shortcut.

15.85 *The "Add" button (which is black when there is text in a "Topic" edit box) allows you to index multiple entries, without having to leave and enter the dialog box each time. This is great for sorting with several different entries and for cross-referencing. Anything you add will all be referenced to the same page number. "Cancel" does not cancel anything you have added. See 15.141.*

15.88 *The page range refers to the expanse of text where the new entry is the topic. If the range spans several pages and you indicate that expanse here, PageMaker will list all the appropriate pages in the index (e.g., 37–43). You can also choose to not show the page range. See 15.90–15.97.*

15.87 *You can override the format for page numbers, setting them apart from the index entries. The same choices are available for "X-ref override" (15.104). When you select them here they also stay selected for cross-references; see 15.175.*

15.86 *This will bring up the "Select topic" dialog box; see 15.114–15.118.*

Page range

15.90   The **Page range** option tells Page-Maker which pages to reference in the index. The range *applies to the newest entry in that dialog box.*

Say you entered "Dogs" at one point, and you gave it a range of "To next style change," which covers several pages. Later, you add a secondary entry of "Labradors" under the same topic of "Dogs" (15.147). When you are in the dialog box for the *second* time, creating that *secondary* entry of "Labradors," the range you now select will apply to that *new* entry "Labradors." "Dogs" will retain its original page range, and "Labradors" will pick up the *new* page range.

15.91   If you chose "Index entry…" but do not see any "Page range" or "Page override" choices, you have not selected text or placed an insertion point within an existing text block. Instead, you have automatically been moved to the Cross-referencing options and your only option now is to cross-reference an existing topic (15.97).

15.92   Current page: This is the default choice. If this button is on, the entry in the completed index will reference just the one page that contains the **paragraph** in which the entry is mentioned.

15.93   To next style change: Click this button if you want the entry referenced to all the pages of information that continue until the *style* (as in Style Sheet; Section 8) changes. For instance, perhaps "Labradors" is mentioned several times under a subhead of "Working Dogs." The text that talks about Labs is tagged with the style Body Text. You know that when the next subhead appears, the text of which is tagged Subhead 1, the topic moves on to "Froofroo Dogs," thus ending the discussion on Labradors. By clicking the "To next style change" button PageMaker will list all the pages with the relevant information, starting from the page number on which you initially created the entry, and ending on the page number where the style sheet changes.

15.94   To next use of style ___: Click this button if you want the reference to continue on past other style changes (see above, 15.93) until it meets text that has been tagged with the *particular* style that you chose here from the mini-menu of your style sheet, such as "Headline."

15.95   For next ___ paragraphs: Click this button if you want the reference to cover a certain length of text, regardless of style changes. You can enter a number from 1 through 255.

15.96   Suppress page range: If you click this button the index will not display the page number. You will see the number in the dialog box with parentheses around it, but it will not print in the index.

15.97   Cross-reference: Click on this button at the top of the dialog box if you want to cross-reference the entry. The "Page range" option will be replaced with the "Denoted by" option, see 15.105. Similar to applying a page range, you are applying the cross-reference to the entry for which you set up this dialog box. That is, if you are creating a *secondary* entry (15.147), that secondary entry is what the cross-reference will apply to, not to the primary (first-level) topic. See 15.98–15.113, and 15.172–15.175 for complete details on cross-referencing.

15.98 **"Add index entry" dialog box** (without text selected or the insertion point flashing) *(from the Utilities menu, choose "Index entry…"; or press Command ;)*

15.99 You can access this dialog box in two ways. It will be displayed automatically if no text has been selected and there is no insertion point flashing when you choose the "Index entry…" command. Or you can click the "Cross-reference" radio button (15.82) in the dialog box on the previous page to get this dialog box.

15.100 *In this dialog box the only thing you can do is cross-reference. You can enter text as a topic, but PageMaker will not be able to give it a page number location.*

Add index entry

Type: ○ Page reference ● Cross-reference

Topic: **Sort:**

[   ] [↕] [   ]

[   ]   [   ]

[   ]   [   ]

Denoted by: ● See [also]
○ See
○ See also
○ See herein
○ See also herein

X-ref override: □ **Bold**   □ **Italic**   □ **Underline**

[OK]
[Cancel]
[Add]
[Topic...]
[X-ref...]

15.101 *This is the same as the "Add" button in 15.85. Also see 15.141.*

15.102 *This will bring up the "Select topic" dialog box; see 15.114–15.118.*

15.103 *This will bring up the "Select cross-reference topic" dialog box; see 15.117–15.118. It is only available when the "Cross-reference" button is selected.*

15.105 *You can choose how your cross-references will read; see 15.174.*

15.104 *The same overrides are available for the cross references as for the page numbers. The "X-ref override" option allows you to format the cross-referenced topics to set them apart from the index entry; see 15.175.*

Cross-reference options and methods

15.106 When you choose to cross-reference a topic you can also choose what type of cross-reference you prefer. By default, "See [also]" is selected. With this option, PageMaker inserts "See also" when you cross-reference a topic with a page number. If you cross-reference a topic without a page number, PageMaker inserts just plain "See."

> **E**
> earthling 5. *See also humans*
> experiment. *See Garden of Eden*

15.107 You can control whether the cross-reference reads "See" or "See also" by selecting either of those radio buttons. "See" refers the reader directly to the cross-reference topic, while "See also" directs the reader to the page number of the entry and to the topic mentioned in the cross-reference.

15.108 The last two choices direct the reader to subentries within the entry. Again, "See herein" refers the reader directly to a subentry, while "See herein also" refers the reader to the page number of the entry itself and to the subentry listed in the cross-reference.

15.109 In the "Add index entry" dialog box, there are two buttons, "Topic..." and "X-ref...." They bring up dialog boxes that appear to be exactly the same (15.114); they both have a list of all the topics that have been entered into the index or that have been *imported* (15.116; 15.124–15.126; 15.154). You can use the "Select topic" list to select primary-level topics that you want to enter as secondary or tertiary entries (15.147; 15.150). Use the "Select cross-reference topic" list to establish a cross-reference to an existing topic (15.172–15.173).

15.110 Topic section: This is a little menu that lists the alphabet. Slide up or down to choose the letter representing the particular *section* of the index you want to view. Topics starting with the letter you choose will appear in the list.

From the "Show index..." (15.120) command, this same mini-menu is called **Index section.** They are exactly the same.

15.111 Next section: This button presents the next alphabetical *section* of the index that has any entries, skipping all those alphabetical sections that are empty. It's a shortcut to the "Topic section" or "Index section" mini-menus.

15.112 After you have gone through a publication creating the index entries, you can use the "Select topic" dialog box and the "Select cross-reference topic" dialog box to add cross-references to your index. Choose the pointer tool to be sure no text is selected and the insertion point is not flashing within text. You can then choose the "Index entry..." command to go directly to the cross-reference version of the "Add index entry" dialog box. Click the "Topic" button and select a topic from the topic list; click OK. Click the "X-ref..." button and select a cross-reference from the list in that dialog box; click OK. Click "Add" back in the "Select topic" dialog box, then, repeat the process for every topic to which you wish to add a cross-reference.

15.113 Unfortunately, the method is not foolproof. You see, topics can exist that have no page references anywhere in the index. Uh-oh. It may be handy to create and print a version of the index (and click "Remove unreferenced topics" to at least get those out of the way in your topics list), to which you can refer as you create cross-references.

15.114 "Select topic" and "Select cross-reference topic" dialog boxes

(from the Utilities menu, choose "Index entry…";
click the "Topic…" or the "X-ref…" button)

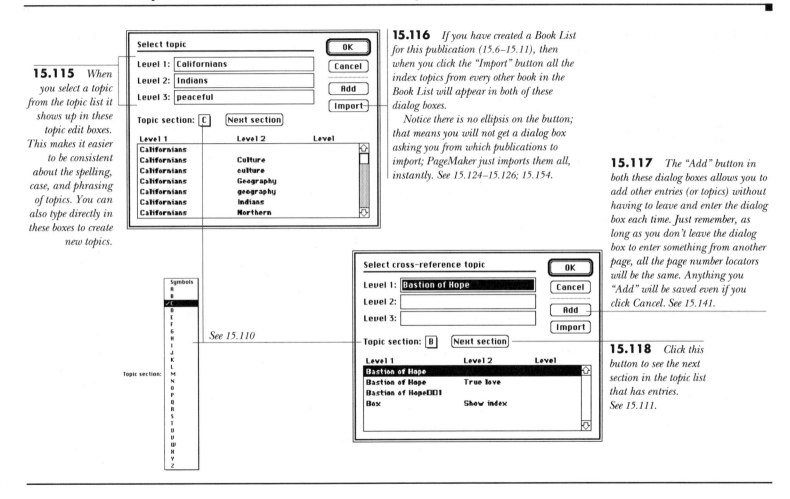

15.115 *When you select a topic from the topic list it shows up in these topic edit boxes. This makes it easier to be consistent about the spelling, case, and phrasing of topics. You can also type directly in these boxes to create new topics.*

See 15.110

15.116 *If you have created a Book List for this publication (15.6–15.11), then when you click the "Import" button all the index topics from every other book in the Book List will appear in both of these dialog boxes.*

Notice there is no ellipsis on the button; that means you will not get a dialog box asking you from which publications to import; PageMaker just imports them all, instantly. See 15.124–15.126; 15.154.

15.117 *The "Add" button in both these dialog boxes allows you to add other entries (or topics) without having to leave and enter the dialog box each time. Just remember, as long as you don't leave the dialog box to enter something from another page, all the page number locators will be the same. Anything you "Add" will be saved even if you click Cancel. See 15.141.*

15.118 *Click this button to see the next section in the topic list that has entries. See 15.111.*

15.119 **"Show index" dialog boxes** *(from the Utilities menu, choose "Show index…")*

15.120   Do you find this confusing? It is. Just follow the directions for the task you want to complete—they'll take you through step-by-step.

By the way, the "Index section" list starts with "Symbols." However, the pop-up menu will display the first section that has entries.

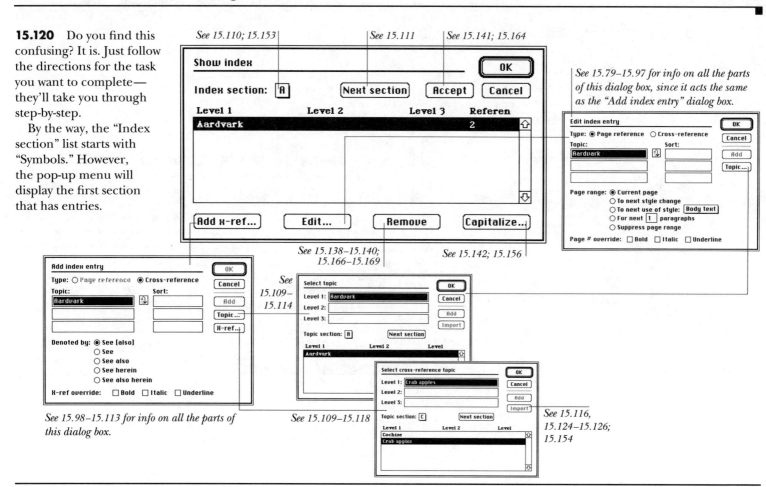

See 15.110; 15.153

See 15.111

See 15.141; 15.164

See 15.79–15.97 for info on all the parts of this dialog box, since it acts the same as the "Add index entry" dialog box.

See 15.138–15.140; 15.166–15.169

See 15.142; 15.156

See 15.109– 15.114

See 15.98–15.113 for info on all the parts of this dialog box.

See 15.109–15.118

See 15.116, 15.124–15.126; 15.154

Topic vs. entry

15.121 There is a subtle distinction between the terms *topic* and *entry*. **Topic** always refers to a primary-level entry. It is often a general category that has subentries below it. The Topic and Cross-reference lists are organized by these topics.

15.122 An **entry** is anything you have entered into the index. All primary-level, secondary, and tertiary information that you input is considered an entry. Primary-level text, then, can be referred to as an entry *or* as a topic.

15.123 In the dialog boxes, you will see the topic entered a separate time for each subentry connected with it. As long as the topic is spelled exactly the same (including capitals), they will all combine into one group. The page number you see in the "Show index" dialog box is the page number for the lowest-level entry.

Import

15.124 Import: If you look at the Topic or Cross-reference lists from the "Index entry..." command (15.114), you will see the "Import" button. This button imports all the indexed topics from every other publication that is *listed in the current publication's Book list (15.116)*. You only need to import once—unless you have added another publication to the Book List, or if you have added other entries to the other publications. Be aware that you will be stuck with these topics forever. When you create the index, you can remove the unreferenced topics. The rest you are stuck with.

15.125 If you look at the Topic or Cross-reference lists from the "Show index..." command (15.120), you will also see the "Import" button, but it is always gray. This is because the "Show index" dialog box and topics lists *automatically* display all topics from every publication in the Book List.

15.126 It's possible to limit the "Show index" dialog box to just the entries that you created in the current publication; hold down the Command key while you select "Show index..." from the Utilities menu. If you do this, the "Import" button will be available.

Index prefix

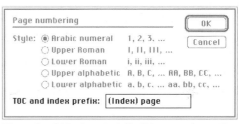

To get this dialog box, from the File menu choose "Page setup...." Click on the "Numbers..." button.

15.127 From this dialog box, you can apply a prefix to the page numbers in the index or in the table of contents (not the numbers on the layout pages themselves).

For instance, you may have divided your book into three segments: A, B, and C; each segment is set up as a separate publication. Using the dialog box shown above, you can create a prefix in each publication. Then each page number in the index or table of contents in that publication will be preceded by the segment letter; e.g., A1, A2, A3, etc. (15.61).

Or you can use this feature to label your appendix pages or your front matter pages (in the index or table of contents) differently than on the layout pages. These prefixes are specific to each publication.

⬇ Move-down button

15.128 You will sometimes use this button when creating secondary and tertiary entries (15.148; 15.151). It moves entries up or down in the three-level edit boxes. Actually, it won't move anything *up;* it just keeps moving the text down until it cycles back up into the top edit box again.

Topic:

| Move down | | ⬇ |

| | |

| | |

With one click, the first-level entry becomes a second-level (secondary) entry.

Topic:

| | ⬇ |

| Move down | |

| | |

Now you can type a first-level entry into the edit box, and the secondary entry will still be referenced to its page number (15.148).

p.s. If you call Aldus Tech Support, don't refer to this button as the "Move-down" button. I had to make that name up because its actual title is not in any documentation, and no one in Tech Support knew what it is called.

Sort *(alphabetize)*

15.129 In an index, sometimes words need to be alphabetized (sorted) by characters other than the first several characters in the entry itself. For instance, "St." is usually sorted as if it was spelled out "Saint"; "Mt." is usually sorted as "Mount." PageMaker gives you the option of assigning different sorting characters to each entry (also see 15.170).

15.130 Use the edit boxes under "Sort" to change the characters used to alphabetize an entry. Each Sort edit box refers only to the entry in the Topic edit box to its left.

- If there is nothing in the Sort edit box across from the entry, then the entry will be sorted as usual, by its own characters as entered in the Topic box.

- If there *is* an entry in the Sort edit box, then the entry will be alphabetized by what is in the Sort box, not by its own characters. **In the index, it will still be *spelled* as it is in the Topic box, though.**

15.131 For instance, in the example above right, the number 11 would be sorted in ASCII order (15.134), before letters. By typing "eleven" into the Sort box, it will be entered in the index under "E."

Topic:

| 11/22/90 | ⬇ |
| McNab's Day |
| St. Martha |

Sort:

| eleven |
| M |
| Saint |

15.132 You can have one entry sorted in several different ways, to make sure a reader will find it, but you have to create each entry separately; see 15.171.

15.133 Characters sort in this order:
- Blank spaces always come first;
- Symbols next ($#*), in random order;
- Numbers, in ASCII order (15.134);
- Letters in alphabetical order.

15.134 When dealing with numbers, take note that *ASCII sort order is not numerical!* It's more like alphabetical: it will list all the numbers that start with 1, then all the numbers that start with 2, etc. For example, these numbers are sorted in ASCII order: 1, 100, 11, 110, 111, 2, 20, 207, 22, 3, 30, etc. If you need numbers in numerical order, use the Sort edit boxes to alphabetize them this way: 001, 002, 003, 011, 020, 022, 030, 100, 110, 111, 207, etc. Use as many place holders as the largest number (e.g., if there are numbers in the thousands, use 0001).

"Show index"

15.135 Use the "Index entry..." command (15.143–15.152) to enter topics and subentries; use the **Show index...** command to edit and cross-reference those entries.

15.136 The "Show index" list box will show you the entries that will actually print in the index; it includes all the entries from every publication in the Book List. You can choose to edit, cross-reference, or remove any entry. You cannot *add* new entries here, even though you get a dialog box similar to the one in which you created entries. You *can* add *cross-references* to existing topics (15.172). You can add *words* to the index here, but the words will not be referenced to page numbers (15.164).

15.137 You may notice that the "Topic" list and the "X-ref" list appear to be the same. And you may notice that they *appear* to be the same ones you had from the "Index entry..." command. And the "Edit index entry" dialog box looks just like the "Add index entry" dialog box. Yes. It can be terribly confusing. The safest thing to do is to find the task you want to complete (enter an entry, delete an entry, add a secondary entry, cross-reference, etc.) and then just follow the directions for that task *(tasks begin on the next page).*

Remove

15.138 You can remove any topic from the index by selecting it in the "Show index" list and clicking the **Remove** button. This will also remove it from both the Topic and the Cross–reference lists after you click OK.

15.139 You can remove, or undo, the most recent index entry additions. You can also undo the index entries you recently removed (see 15.165).

15.140 Please note: "Remove" does not remove any entries from the "Topic" or "X-ref" lists *in the "Index entry..." command!* You can only remove **unreferenced** topics from these lists when you create the index. In the "Create index" dialog box (15.184) select "Remove unreferenced topics" (you can create the index even if you are not finished indexing. Either delete it and create it again, or update it when you are finished). This will remove all the topics in the "Index entry" lists that are not referenced in the active publication or in any of the publications in the Book List. But unless you do this each time you remove a topic (and that would be absurdly time-consuming), it is possible for you to cross-reference an entry to a topic *that has actually been removed from the index.*

Add, Accept, and Capitalize

15.141 The **Add** and **Accept** buttons both function in the same way. As you enter or edit entries, you can click whichever of these buttons you see in the dialog box to add your entry to the index. This allows you to add multiple entries or cross-references without having to close the dialog box each time. If you Cancel out of the dialog box, anything that has been "Added" or "Accepted" will not be cancelled. The "Add" button in the "Select topic" dialog box, though, does not add entries to the index, but adds topics to the Topic list. These new topics do not show up in the index until you use them to create an index entry.

15.142 The **Capitalize** button is only in the "Show index" dialog box, and it is only available when you generate an index from a single publication. You can choose to capitalize the selected entry, all Level 1 entries, or all entries (see 15.156).

If you want to do this:

Then follow these steps:

Shortcuts ▾ Notes ▾ Hints

15.143 Add an index entry using an existing, selected word or words

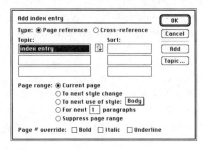

- With the **text tool** select the text you want to enter into the index. If it is just one word, simply double-click on the word.
- From the Utilities menu choose "Index entry...," *or* press Command **;** *(semicolon).*
- In the "Add index entry" dialog box you will see the selected word in the *primary level* edit box. If you need to capitalize it or change the spelling (e.g., *Fox hunting* to *Fox hunt*), do so now.
- Choose the "Page range" for which you want PageMaker to reference a page number (see 15.90–15.97).
- Click OK.

- **Ultra-zippy shortcut:** If you want the "Current page" range and you don't need to edit the text at this moment, then you can do this: Select the text (double-click if it's one word). Press Command Shift **;** *(semicolon).* You won't even see a dialog box—the text simply gets entered straight into the index.
- Use this method to enter into the index words that you have directly located.
- See 15.156 for a way to automatically capitalize entries.

15.144 Add an index entry, entering your own word(s) that you want referenced to this paragraph

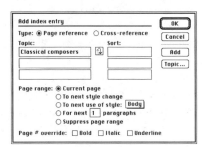

- With the **text tool** click once in the paragraph that contains the information you want to reference.
- From the Utilities menu, choose "Index entry...," *or* press Command **;** .
- In the "Add index entry" dialog box type the text you want to reference to the information in this paragraph into the *primary-level* edit box (the top one, first-level; 15.89).
- Choose the "Page range" for which you want PageMaker to reference a page number (see 15.90–15.97).
- Click OK.

- Use this method to enter words that *refer* to a topic in a paragraph, but where the word itself isn't directly mentioned in the paragraph. For instance, the paragraph may discuss Chopin's music, and you want to enter a general index reference locating "Classical composers."
- You can click the "Add" button to add the current entry, then retype and add another without having to close the dialog box. Remember, though, any other entries you add will still be referenced to the same paragraph you originally started from.

If you want to do this:	**Then follow these steps:**	**Shortcuts ▾ Notes ▾ Hints**
15.145 Enter a list of topics with no page numbers *(useful as an outline, or to be used later for topics and cross-referencing)*	■ With the **text tool** type a list of the topics you want to enter. ■ With the **text tool** select one topic (if the topic is only one word, double-click on it). ■ Press Command Shift **;** *(semicolon).* This enters the entry in the index. ■ Repeat those two steps with the next word on the list. ■ When the list is completely entered, choose the **pointer tool.** Click on the text block that contains the list, and delete it (hit the Backspace/Delete key). ■ The topics are now in the Topic list and the Cross-reference list that you find in the "Index entry..." command (from the Utilities menu). The topics will not appear in the "Show index" lists. Only the topics that you choose to place in the primary Topic edit box (15.89) or that you cross-reference with another entry (15.97) will actually appear in the final index.	■ You can enter topics of up to fifty characters. ■ If you delete the text block, the entries will be deleted from the Topic and Edit lists in the "Show index" dialog box. They will still be in the Topic and Edit Lists in the "Add index entry" dialog box. They will be removed from these lists if you check "Remove unreferenced topics" when you "Create index." ■ See 15.146 for adding an index entry with no page number reference.
15.146 Add an index entry with no page number reference Level 1 Level 2 Level 3 Reference no page number (505)	■ Follow the steps in 15.143 or 15.144 to add an index entry. ■ Click the "Suppress page range" button. ■ Click OK. The entry will appear in the index when you place it on the page, but it will have no number locating it.	■ The page number will appear in parentheses in the "Show index" dialog box list, but the number will not appear in the actual index when you place it on the page.

If you want to do this:

15.147 Create a secondary (second-level) entry (*one method*)

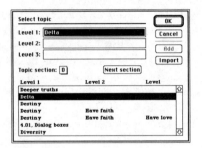

a) *The "D" section of the Topic List.*

b) *Type in the secondary entry.*

Then follow these steps:

- With the **text tool** click once in the paragraph you want to reference.
- From the Utilities menu, choose "Index entry...," *or* press Command **;** *(semicolon)*.
- Click the "Topic..." button to get the list of topics that you have already entered.
- Press on the "Topic section" mini-menu (15.110) to choose the alphabetical section you wish to view, *or* click the "Next section" button to view the next section that contains topic entries.
- In the list, find the topic (**a**) for which you want to create the secondary entry. Double-click on the topic, *or* click on it once, then click OK or hit Return.
- Now *that* chosen topic is in the primary Topic edit box (**b**) in the "Add index entry" dialog box. Type the second-level entry into the next edit box. Don't try to type a third-level entry; see 15.150–15.152.
- Click OK.

Shortcuts ▾ Notes ▾ Hints

- This method involves manually typing the second-level entry. The second method (15.148) involves manually typing the primary topic. *Either way, the primary topic must already have been entered into the index.*
- The advantage to this first method is that you never have to worry about misspelling the primary topic. If you do misspell it, you will have separate topics, each with its own subentry, rather than one primary entry with a combined list of subentries.
- You can also single-click the topic, add the secondary entry in the topic edit boxes right in the "Select topic" dialog box, and click Option Return (*or* Option OK, *or* OK, OK). It's the OK in the "Add index entry" dialog box that adds the entry to the index.
- If you have removed topics from the list through the "Show index" command, they are not removed from this topic list! Thus it is possible to create subentries and cross-references to topics that are non-existent. This is a bug. A cockroach. See 15.140 and 15.179 for a way to avoid this.

If you want to do this: Then follow these steps: Shortcuts ▾ Notes ▾ Hints

15.148 Create a secondary (second-level) entry *(another method)*

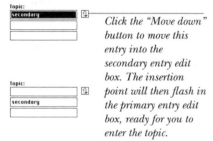

Click the "Move down" button to move this entry into the secondary entry edit box. The insertion point will then flash in the primary entry edit box, ready for you to enter the topic.

S
Show   503
    secondary   504

This is what a secondary entry looks like when the index is placed on the page.

- You must know the exact spelling of the primary topic under which you want to create this secondary entry, including caps.
- With the **text tool** select the text you want to enter into the index, *or* click once in the paragraph you want to reference.
- From the Utilities menu choose "Index entry...," *or* press Command **;** *(semicolon).*
- If the insertion point is flashing, hit the Tab key to send it to the second-level edit box; if the selected word appears in the first-level edit box, click on the "Move down" button (see left; also see 15.81).
- Now this is the trick: you have to manually *type* the primary-level topic into that edit box. If it's not exactly correct, that's okay, because you can always edit it later (15.164). Don't try to enter a third-level entry at this point; see 15.150–15.152.
- Click OK.

- PageMaker can only locate one page number per entry in the dialog box. Thus you can only simultaneously reference a primary-level entry *plus* a secondary entry, or a secondary *plus* a tertiary if they are all in the same paragraph (or on the same page and you are finished editing). In this case you can click the "Add" button for each entry. Otherwise, you just have to accept the fact that you need to OK this dialog box and come back again to create the next entry.
- If you want to add entries into more than one level, you must click the "Add" button after each entry for which you want to have a page number; only the lowest-level entry will have a page number attached. The other entries will be in the index, but they won't have page references unless they, too, were added as the lowest level.

15.149 Add another secondary entry under the same primary topic

- Repeat the steps in 15.147 or 15.148. If the primary topic is the same each time, all the secondary entries will be listed under the one primary topic. *That's why you need to spell all the primary topics the same way!* (See 15.164 for editing existing entries.)

- You can click the "Add" button to add the current entry, then retype and add another without having to close the dialog box. Remember, though, any other entries you add will still be referenced to the same paragraph from which you originally started.

If you want to do this:

15.150 Create a tertiary (third-level) entry *(one method)*

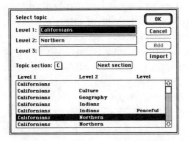

a) *The "C" section of the topic list.*

b) *Type in the tertiary entry.*

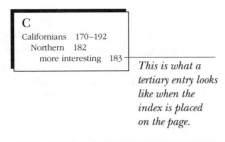

This is what a tertiary entry looks like when the index is placed on the page.

Then follow these steps:

■ With the **text tool** click once in the paragraph you want to reference.
■ From the Utilities menu choose "Index entry...," *or* press Command **;** *(semicolon)*.
■ Click the "Topic..." button to get the list of topics that have already been entered.
■ Press on the "Topic section" mini-menu (15.110) to choose the alphabetical section you wish to view, *or* click the "Next section" button to view the next section that contains topic entries.
■ In the list, find the topic (**a**) for which you want to create the tertiary entry. *The topic you choose must already have a secondary entry.* Double-click on the topic, *or* click on it once, then click OK or hit Return.
■ Now *that* chosen topic is in the primary topic edit box (**b**), with the secondary entry in its own edit box. Type the third-level entry into the last edit box.
■ Click OK.
■ **Or** you can single-click the topic, add the tertiary entry in the topic edit boxes right in the "Select topic" dialog box, and press Option Return (or Option OK; *or* OK, OK). It's the OK in the "Add index entry" dialog box that adds the entry to the index. Obviously, you can't add more than one entry this way.

Shortcuts ▾ Notes ▾ Hints

■ You can type any other words into the primary and secondary edit boxes, rather than choose a topic from the topic list, but anything you type in will not be located to a page number.
■ If you choose a topic that does not have a secondary entry, you will have to type a secondary entry before PageMaker will accept it; it is not possible to have only a primary plus a tertiary entry. If you *type* a secondary entry, though, that entry will not be referenced to any page number. *PageMaker will only reference the lowest-level entry* (primary level being the highest).
■ You can click the "Add" button in the "Add index entry" box to add the current entry, then retype and add another without having to close the dialog box. Remember, though, any other entries you add will still be referenced to the same paragraph from which you originally started.
■ The "Add" button in the "Select topic" dialog box is for adding topics to the topic list (see 15.141). You cannot add index entries with this "Add" button.

If you want to do this:

Then follow these steps:

Shortcuts ▾ Notes ▾ Hints

15.151 Create a tertiary (third-level) entry *(another method)*

Click the "Move down" button to move this entry into the tertiary entry edit box. The insertion point will then flash in the primary entry edit box, ready for you to enter the topic.

S

Show 503
  secondary 504
    tertiary 506

This is what a tertiary entry looks like when the index is placed on the page.

- With the **text tool** select the text you want to enter into the index, *or* click once in the paragraph you want to reference.
- From the Utilities menu choose "Index entry...," *or* press Command **;** *(semicolon).*
- If the insertion point is flashing, hit the Tab key to send it to the third-level edit box; if the selected word appears in the first-level edit box, click twice on the "Move down" button (see left; also 15.81).
- You have to actually *type* the primary-level topic *and* the existing secondary entry into that edit box. You *must* enter a secondary entry. (If the spelling is not exactly correct, you *can* edit it later; 15.164.)
- Click OK.

- You must know the exact spelling of the primary topic *and* the secondary entry under which you want to create this third-level entry. You can click the "Topic" button to look it up (15.86). This is handy for those times when you need to enter a complex word and you are sure you will misspell it if you have to retype it, like diethymethoxylate-19-psq.
- You can click the "Add" button to add the current entry, then retype and add another without having to close the dialog box. Remember, though, any other entries you add will still be referenced to the same paragraph from which you originally started.

15.152 Add another tertiary entry under the same secondary topic

- Start all over again and repeat the steps in 15.150 or 15.151. If you enter the same primary and secondary entries each time, all the tertiary entries will be listed under the one primary topic. *That's why you need to spell all the primary and secondary entries the same way!*

- See the note directly above, regarding adding multiple entries.
- See 15.164 for editing existing entries.

If you want to do this:	Then follow these steps:	Shortcuts ▾ Notes ▾ Hints
15.153 Check the Topic list to see what's available  *Anything you select in the Topic list will be placed in the edit box:* **Topic:** 	▪ In the "Add index entry" dialog box, just click on the "Topic…" button to get the list of topics. ▪ Press on the "Topic section" mini-menu to choose the letter under which you want to view the entries, *or* you can click the "Next section" button to jump to the next section that contains entries. ▪ The entry that is selected when you click OK will be entered in the primary topic edit box. Any accompanying secondary and tertiary entries will also be entered. *Anything already existing in those edit boxes will be replaced.* So, if you don't want to actually put the selected topic into the dialog box, click Cancel.	▪ The topics are alphabetized by the primary-level entry. ▪ This Topic list is especially handy when you are entering secondary or tertiary entries, when you need to go get a topic, or when you need to check to see how the primary topic was actually spelled; e.g., to see whether you spelled the entry *Pharaoh* or *Pharoah*, or whether the topic is *Create entropy* or *Creating entropy*.
15.154 Import topics *(also see 15.116; 15.124–15.126)* 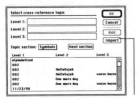 *The "Import" button is in both the "Select topic" dialog box (Topic list, see 15.153) and the "Select cross-reference topic" dialog box (Cross-reference list).*	▪ You can only import topics from the indices belonging to the other publications that are in the current publication's Book List (15.6–15.12). Create a Book List, if necessary (15.21). ▪ To import topics into either the Topic list or the Cross-reference list, click the "Import" button. Only the topics for which you actually create subentries or that you cross-reference will appear in the final, placed index.	▪ The purpose of importing is to give you access to the other topics in the other publications that are part of the Book, topics you may need for cross-referencing or for creating subentries. ▪ Once you click the "Import" button, those topics are in the lists forever. Even if you Cancel both dialog boxes, *even if you eliminate the topics from the original publication,* they are in the lists. Which means there is potential for cross-referencing to topics that aren't really there. Uh oh.

If you want to do this:

Then follow these steps:

Shortcuts ▾ Notes ▾ Hints

15.155 Automatically index proper names

- *All words in the selected text are names.*
- *All names are in either of these formats: "FirstName LastName" or "LastName, FirstName."*
- *If there is no comma between FirstName LastName, the second name is considered the last name.*
- *If a first or last name is a multiple word, the two parts of the name must be connected with a non-breaking space (Option Spacebar) or a non-breaking hyphen (Command Option Hyphen).*
- *A unique character (such as a comma, a semicolon, or a return) must separate the names in a list.*

- You can select any single name or a lengthy list of names and instantly enter the entire list. Each name will be a separate entry, and will be formatted as LastName, FirstName. The single name or the list of names must abide by the rules as noted in the left column.
- Select the name, or the entire list of names.
- Press Command Shift Z. You won't *see* anything happen (the dialog box will not appear) but if you check out the Topic list, you will see all the names. Wow.

- Each name is indexed separately as a primary-level entry.
- Each entry will have a page range of "Current page" (15.92).
- PageMaker handles some name extensions properly, like Jr. or Sr., but you should check.
- PageMaker will consider titles after names as separate names, so you need to index (or at least edit) those manually.

15.156 Automatically capitalize index entries

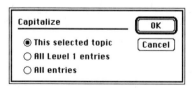

- From the Utilities menu, choose "Show index...."
- Click on the "Capitalize..." button.
- Choose a radio button.
  - □ "This selected topic" is only available if a topic is selected in the topics list.
  - □ Click "All Level 1 entries" to capitalize all primary entries.
  - □ Click "All entries" to capitalize all levels of all entries.
- Click OK.

- The "Capitalize..." button is not available if the current publication has a Book List.
- This will only capitalize the existing entries; it will not affect any entries you add in the future.
- If you have already placed your index on the page, you will have to update it in order to see the capitalization changes (15.202).

If you want to do this:

15.157 Index all occurrences of key words

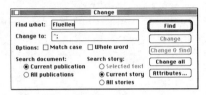

The "Change" feature can index all instances of a key word.

F

Fluellen 2, 3, 4

An example of the index entry of a key word indexed through the "Change" window.

Then follow these steps:

- In the Story Editor click the insertion point within any story in the publication that you want to index.
- From the Utilities menu choose "Change," *or* press Command 9.
- In the "Find what" edit box, type the key word you want to index.
- In the "Change to" edit box, type ^; (that's a *carat* [shift 6] plus a *semicolon*).
- Select your choices for "Options," "Search document," and "Search story (9.70–9.75).
- Set any of the "Attributes" options that you wish (9.79).
- Click "Change all" if you wish to index all instances of the key word.
- **Or** if you prefer to decide whether each instance of the key word should be entered in the index, press "Find."
  - □ If you want to index the selected instance of the key word, press "Change," then press "Find next" to continue the process (*or* choose "Change & find" to do both at once).
  - □ If you don't want to index that instance of the word, just press "Find next."
- Without leaving the "Change" window, you can repeat this procedure for other key words. Just type over the word in the "Find what" edit box.

Shortcuts ▾ Notes ▾ Hints

- If the story is in layout view, simply click the insertion point within the text and press Command E (Edit story).
- An index marker ⬦ is inserted in front of all words that are included in the index. If you include a word more than once (for example, as a primary entry and then again at the secondary level), there will be a marker for every entry. The marker is part of the text. It moves as the text is edited, but it is not part of the indexed word. If you delete the word but not the marker, the index entry still remains. Index markers are only visible in the Story Editor, not in the document. You can Cut, Copy, and Paste index markers, and you can view their contents; see 15.161, and 15.162.

- With this method you can customize an entry at any time during the search; see 15.158.

If you want to do this:	Then follow these steps:	Shortcuts ▾ Notes ▾ Hints
15.158 Customize entries made for key words	■ Follow the directions in the previous task, finding and changing each instance of the key word separately. ■ When you get to a key word you want to customize, choose "Index entry…" from the Utilities menu (or press Command ;). ■ Select the options you want in the "Index entry" dialog box, click OK to add the entry. ■ Press the "Find next" button to continue the key word indexing.	■ If you change the "Page range" option, it will affect only that instance of the key word. ■ If you change the "Page # overrides" it will affect all the following key word entries. It will not affect entries already completed. ■ You can add a cross-reference but be aware that it may not follow the page number of that particular entry. It will be listed at the end of all the page number references for that keyword.
15.159 Index a key word in more than one publication at the same time Search document: ○ Current publication ◉ All publications Search story: ○ Selected text ○ Current story ◉ All stories	■ Open all the publications that contain the key word you want to index. ■ With the **text tool,** set the insertion point within the text of a story, and press Command E (Edit story). ■ From the Utilities menu, choose "Change" *or* press Command 9. ■ Type the key word into the "Find what" edit box. ■ Type ^; *(carat semicolon)* in the "Change to" edit box. ■ Under "Search document," select "All publications." ■ Click "Change all," or "Find" if you prefer to enter the key word one by one.	■ When you select "All publications" the option "All stories" is automatically selected. You have no choice. ■ Each publication will have its own index. Only the publications with a Book List will show index entries from any other publications (in the "Show index" dialog box).

If you want to do this:

15.160 Create secondary entries for a key word indexed through the "Change" dialog box

Then follow these steps:

- Follow the directions in the previous task, finding and changing each instance of the key word separately.
- When you get to a word you want to have a secondary level entry, choose "Index entry…" from the Utilities menu (*or* press Command ;).
- Type an entry in the secondary edit box, then click OK. This creates an entry with the page reference attached to the secondary entry.
- If you want to also enter that key word at a primary level entry, press "Change & find" to enter it and proceed with the indexing.
- If you do not want it entered at the primary level, press "Find next."
- **Or** when you find an instance of the key word, hit "Change" to enter it at the primary level, then choose "Index entry"; type in the secondary-level entry, click OK. Then, click "Find next" to keep going.
- **Or** "Find" an instance of the key word, choose "Index entry," click "Add" (which enters it at the primary level), type in the secondary level entry, click OK, then carry on, pressing "Find next."

Shortcuts ▾ Notes ▾ Hints

- This is not foolproof. You may need to coax the finding along after adding the entry with the secondary level. Page-Maker may declare that the "Search is complete," when you know it is not. In this case, click OK and click the "Find" button again. PageMaker may also ask to "Continue search from the beginning?" even if it has already searched there— and it will add another index marker to text already marked, until returning to the key word with the secondary entry!
- You can cross-reference the secondary entry. Click "Add" instead of OK after you enter the text, then cross-reference as usual (15.172–15.173).
- You can also switch it around and make the key word the secondary instance and enter a different topic at the primary level. In the "Index entry" dialog box, click the "Move down" button to bump the key word to the secondary level. Type an entry in the first-level edit box; click OK.
- The Return key of course, can be pressed as a keyboard shortcut for any button with a dark border around it.

If you want to do this:	**Then follow these steps:**	**Shortcuts ▾ Notes ▾ Hints**
15.161 See the contents of an index marker	■ In the Story Editor select the index marker (you can select it as you would any ordinary character). ■ From the Utilities menu choose "Index entry…" *or* press Command ; *(semicolon)*. ■ View the contents of the index marker in the "Edit index entry" dialog box. ■ You can edit the contents if you wish.	■ If you select any other characters along with the index marker, the "Add index entry" dialog box will be displayed instead of the "Edit index entry." If you click OK, a new index entry is created (and you will see another marker alongside the first in the text). Click Cancel to avoid this, and select the index marker again.
15.162 Move an index entry	■ In the Story Editor select the index marker (you can select as you would any ordinary character). ■ From the Edit menu choose "Cut," *or* press Command X. ■ Click the insertion point in the story where you want the index marker to be. ■ From the Edit menu choose "Paste," *or* press Command V.	■ The index marker will retain all its information, but its page reference will now reflect its new location.

Beautiful colors fill my mind with dreams of things that don't exist.

Gaia Sikora

If you want to do this:

15.163 Show all the entries before generating the actual index

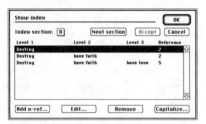

The section shown above will produce the index entries shown below:

Then follow these steps:

- From the Utilities menu choose "Show index...." This command shows what is in the index for all the publications *that are in the Book List,* so if the current publication is not in the list, you will not see its index!
  - □ You can *add* the current publication to the Book List (15.22), or you can choose to *view just the index for the current publication:* hold down the Command key before you choose "Show index..." from the Utilities menu.
- What you see in the "Show index" dialog box is what you will get in the final index. In the example to the left, you see *Destiny* three separate times: once with a page number, once with a secondary entry and its page number, once with a tertiary entry and its page number. *Destiny* will appear as one entry with its corresponding secondary and tertiary entries, as shown, **if** *all primary and secondary entries are spelled exactly the same, including capital letters.*
- If you need to edit entries so they are the same, see 15.164.

Shortcuts ▾ Notes ▾ Hints

- Use the "Show index..." command when you want to review and edit the index.
- What you see in that first dialog box is what will print. What you see in the Topic list and in the Cross-reference list is not what will be in the final index; they are just the possible topics to which you can cross-reference or add secondary and tertiary entries. If you choose to remove entries (15.166), they will be removed from the "Show index" dialog box, not from the Topic or Cross-reference lists.

If you want to do this:

15.164 Edit index entries

(especially necessary to amalgamate all primary topics with their respective secondary and tertiary entries; 15.80)

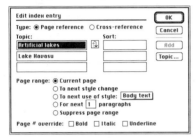

Then follow these steps:

- From the Utilities menu choose "Show index...."
- In the dialog box, press on the "Index section" mini-menu; choose the letter of the alphabetical section that contains the entry you wish to edit.
- Click once on the entry you want to edit, then click the "Edit..." button, *or* just double-click on the entry itself.
- This is the "*Edit* index entry" dialog box; you cannot enter *new* entries here! (Well, you can type them in, but they won't have page numbers.) Check spelling, etc.
- Click OK. If you want to edit others, find and edit them in the same way. When you are finished, close all the dialog boxes and PageMaker will update the entries.
- If you want to edit more than one entry, click the "Accept" button (15.141) after each edit. This adds it to the index immediately, without having to click OK and close the dialog box. If you later Cancel, you will only Cancel the editing that occurred after the last time you clicked "Accept."

Shortcuts ▾ Notes ▾ Hints

- You do need to go through the entire index and combine all those like items that may be phrased slightly differently, or perhaps capitalized differently. Otherwise each entry will be completely separate; e.g., *horses* will be separate from *Horses*.
- You can also edit entries through the "Index entry..." command from the Utilities menu, but I suggest you do your editing through "Show index...." The "Show index" dialog box (15.163) is the only place where you see a true account of the actual *entries*. Keep in mind that the Topic and Cross-references lists can contain *topics* that will not appear in the index itself when it is placed on the page (see "topics vs. entries," 15.121–15.123).
- If your publication has a Book List and you want to see and edit the entries of *the active publication only,* hold down the Command key as you select "Show index..." from the Utilities menu.

If you want to do this:	Then follow these steps:	Shortcuts ▾ Notes ▾ Hints
15.165 Undo the latest index additions or deletions	• This trick will only undo the editing changes you have made in the "Show index" dialog box. It will not affect any changes that you have added to the index by clicking the "Accept" button or that were already in the index when you opened the dialog box. ▢ **To undo additions:** hold down the Option key and click "Add x-ref...." ▢ **To undo deletions:** hold down the Option key and click "Remove."	
15.166 Remove entries from the index	• From the Utilities menu choose "Show index...." • In the dialog box press on the "Index section" mini-menu; choose the letter of the alphabetical section from which you wish to remove an entry. • Click once on the entry you want to remove. • Click the "Remove" button. You will not get an alert button asking if you really want to do this. ▢ If you change your mind, press the Option key and click "Remove." All index entries you have deleted since the last time you clicked "Accept" or OK will be reinstated.	• "Remove" automatically removes the entry from the Topic and Cross-reference lists that are accessed through the "Show index..." command (after you click "Accept" or OK). It will *not* remove entries from the similar-looking lists of the same names that are accessed through the "Index entry..." command. You can remove unreferenced topics from those lists when you create the index (15.179). • Also see 15.138–15.140 and 15.167–15.169.

If you want to do this:

Phone Call

To _____

Date _____ Time _____

While you were out

_____ called

Of _____

Phone No. _____

Message

☐ Please call
☐ Will call again
☐ Returned your call

| Initials |

01-142 (0594)

enced
e index
right!)

enced
e index
right!)

enced
entries from
ch means
index)
right!)

Then follow these steps:

- From the Utilities menu choose "Show index…."
- Hold down the Command and the Option keys while you click the "Remove" button.
- If you change your mind, immediately click the "Cancel" button.

- From the Utilities menu choose "Show index…."
- Hold down the Command and the Shift keys while you click "Remove."
- If you change your mind, immediately click the "Cancel" button.

- From the Utilities menu choose "Show index…."
- Hold down the Command, Shift, and Option keys while you click "Remove."
- If you change your mind, immediately click the "Cancel" button.

Shortcuts ▾ Notes ▾ Hints

- **Warning!!** Each of these tasks (15.167–15.169) eliminates the entries *from every publication in the Book List!* Really. If you do one of these removals and then open up another of the publications that is on the Book List, you will find that it is missing its entries. **Task 15.169, then, eliminates the entire index from the entire book.** Be careful!

*L*ife
is
too
short
to
figure
it
out.

Tom
Serianni

If you want to do this:	**Then follow these steps:**	**Shortcuts ▾ Notes ▾ Hints**
15.170 Sort an entry by characters different than the entry's original characters Topic: [11/22/90] ⭷ [eleven] [McNab's Day] [M] [St. Martha] [Saint] Sort: *In these examples, 11/22/90 will be alphabetized as "eleven"; "McNab" will be alphabetized as the letter "M," meaning it will be placed before "Mac," since empty spaces come before letters; "St." will be alphabetized as "Saint," rather than being placed towards the end of the list as "St."*	■ Read 15.129–15.134 to understand what "Sort" accomplishes. ■ Simply type the characters you want the entry to be alphabetized by in the edit box directly across from it. That is, the primary topic will be sorted by what is in the first edit box under "Sort"; the secondary entry will be sorted by what is in the *second* "Sort" edit box; and the tertiary entry will be sorted by what is in the *third* "Sort" edit box. You are not allowed to have a sort character in the "Sort" edit boxes unless there is a corresponding entry on the left.	■ Whenever there is an entry in any edit box, in either the "Add index entry" or the "Edit index entry" dialog boxes, you can apply a new sort character. You can do this at any time, either right when you enter it or later.
15.171 Sort an entry by several different sets of characters Topic: Sort: [11/22/90] ⭷ [ ] [ ] [ ] [ ] [ ] Topic: Sort: [11/22/90] ⭷ [November] [ ] [ ] [ ] [ ] *Each separate sort must be entered into the index separately.*	■ To sort an entry by its own first character, leave the "Sort" edit box blank; click "Add." ■ Then, to sort the same entry by another character, *as well as* by its own first character, type the other characters you want the entry alphabetized by in its corresponding "Sort" edit box; click "Add." ■ To sort the entry by a third category, type the next set of characters you want the entry alphabetized by in its corresponding "Sort" box; click "Add." ■ Get it? Just keep adding them separately, and when you are done click OK.	■ If there is no character in the "Sort" edit box, then the entry will be sorted as usual, in ASCII sort order (15.134). If you want to sort the entry by other characters, *as well as* by its own first character, you must create and "Add" a sort entry for each one.

If you want to do this:

15.172 Cross-reference an entry

a)

b)

c)

d)

Then follow these steps:

- From the Utilities menu choose "Show index...."
- Using the "Index section" mini-menu (15.110), find the topic to which you want to attach a cross-reference. Click once to select it (**a**).

  Note: Notice in this section that *Fluellen* is listed four times. It will actually print in the index only once, with its corresponding page number (**a**). The second *Fluellen* listed indicates a secondary entry and its page number. The third *Fluellen* listed indicates a tertiary entry, under *friend*. The fourth *Fluellen* listed indicates another secondary entry.

  The cross-reference will apply to the lowest entry in the topic you select. That is, if you select the first *Fluellen*, the cross-reference will apply to the primary topic. In the example, the topic selected has a *secondary* (lower) entry, so the cross-reference will apply to the *secondary* entry.

- Click the "Add x-ref..." button to get the "Add index entry" dialog box. The entry you just selected will be in the edit box(es) and the "Cross-reference" radio button will be selected already (**b**).

—continued

Shortcuts ▾ Notes ▾ Hints

- It is best to have all or at least most of the entries entered into the index before you start to cross-reference.
- "Show index" will show you all index entries that are included in every publication that is listed in the current publication's Book List (15.6–15.11). It is possible to remove entries from the "Show index" list. But keep in mind that removing them from the "Show index" list *does not remove them from the Cross-reference List!* Thus it is possible to cross-reference entries to topics that are no longer in the index. For instance, maybe yesterday you eliminated all mentions of Fluellen's poetry from the book and also from the index. *Poet* is still in the Cross-reference List. In the example to the left, *Fluellen* is cross-referenced to *Poet*. But if someone were to look up *Poet* in the index she would find no such entry.
- See 15.175 regarding the text format for the cross-reference.

If you want to do this:	Then follow these steps:	Shortcuts ▾ Notes ▾ Hints

—*continued*

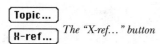

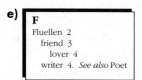

The "X-ref..." button

e)

- Select an option for "Denoted by."
- Click the "X-ref..." button (on the right).
- In the "Select cross-reference topic" list (**c**), find the topic you want cross-referenced to the entry. Select it and click OK (*or* double-click on the entry); you will return to the "Add index entry" dialog box. Click OK again to get back to the "Show index" dialog box.
- Now in "Show index" you can see the cross-reference listed (**d**). Click "Accept" if you want to continue adding cross-references to this or to another entry. When you are done cross-referencing and editing, click OK.
- When you generate the index and place it on the page, the cross-referencing will appear as shown on the left (**e**).

- See 15.174 for information about the different ways of cross-referencing that are available under "Denoted by." When the default option, "See [also]" is selected, the cross-reference for an entry with a page number reads "See also." A cross-reference for an entry without a page number reads "See."

- Clicking the "Accept" button will enter the new information yet leave you in the dialog box if you want to continue working there.

If you want to do this:	Then follow these steps:	Shortcuts ▾ Notes ▾ Hints
15.173 Cross-reference a secondary or tertiary entry *as you create the entry (another method, similar to 15.172)*	▪ Create a secondary **or** a tertiary entry (see 15.147–15.152) using the "Add" button to enter it. Then select the "Cross-reference" radio button (above the "Sort" boxes). ▪ Select an option for "Denoted by" (15.174). ▪ Click the "X-ref..." button. ▪ From the list, find the topic to which you want to cross-reference. Double-click on it. ▪ If you like, override the current cross-reference format (15.175). ▪ Click OK in the "Add index entry" dialog box.	▪ You cannot cross-reference both a secondary *and* a tertiary entry in the same listing. PageMaker will only make reference to the lowest-level entry. ▪ You can cross-reference a secondary entry, create a tertiary level for that entry and cross-reference *that*, all in one visit to the "Index entry" dialog boxes. Just make sure the insertion point is in the same paragraph as the tertiary entry. ▪ Be careful about cross-referencing to topics that no longer exist in the index (see notes in 15.140; 15.147; 15.172).
15.174 Choose the type of cross-reference option you want Denoted by: ⦿ See [also] 　　　　　○ See 　　　　　○ See also 　　　　　○ See herein 　　　　　○ See also herein	▪ Follow the steps in 15.172 to create a cross-reference, but instead of the default option of "See [also]," select another option for "Denoted by." 　▫ "See" refers the reader to other topics in the book. 　▫ "See also" refers the reader to the current topic and to the cross-reference topic. 　▫ "See herein" refers the reader to subentries (level 2 or 3) within the topic. 　▫ "See also herein" refers the reader to the entry itself and to subentries within the topic.	▪ When you select the default option of "See [also]," PageMaker decides whether to use "See" or "See also." If the topic you are cross-referencing has a page reference, the cross-reference will read "See also such-and-such." If the topic has no page number, the cross-reference will read "See such-and-such."

If you want to do this:	Then follow these steps:	Shortcuts ▾ Notes ▾ Hints

15.175 Format the type style in which the cross-reference text or the page numbers appear

X-ref override: ☐ **Bold** ☐ **Italic** ☐ **Underline**

> **E**
> Entropy 1. *See also* Xanadu

No override.

> **E**
> Entropy 1. *See also* **Xanadu**

Bold override.

> **E**
> Entropy 1. *See also* Xanadu

Italic override.

Page # override: ☐ **Bold** ☐ **Italic** ☐ **Underline**

You can override the page numbers in the same way.

- In either the "Add index entry" (15.98) or the "Edit index entry" (15.119) dialog boxes, you can format the cross-reference text. These buttons only apply to cross-references. After you have created the cross-reference, simply click in the override of your choice. It will override whatever type style you've defined in the style sheet for this paragraph. Notice in the examples on the left that the override affects just the text following *See* or *See also.*
- The choices are cumulative; you can choose one, two, or all three of the options (but see the note to the right).
- If you change your style sheet so the entries are already formatted in bold, then clicking the "Bold" checkbox will have just the opposite effect: the cross-reference will be Normal. The same holds true for the italic and underline overrides.

- You can also choose to override the type specifications for the page numbers, as well as for cross-references.
- Although one choice for the override is underline, I do hope you realize that text never looks good when it has an underline style applied. I don't know why that is even an option. The underline bumps into the descenders and it is too heavy for the small text in an index. Besides, underlining is a primitive holdover from typewriters, where it was one of the few options available for emphasizing words. An underline's actual purpose is to indicate that the underlined words should really be italicized, since the typewriter couldn't create italics. Knowing that, you can see how redundant it would be to check underline *and* italic.
- The override options will remain checked until you deselect them. This means you can set a default for the cross-reference and page number override. However, the default will apply to both; you cannot set separate defaults for references and page numbers.

If you want to do this:

15.176 Show all the index entries

15.177 Show the index for the active publication only

15.178 Locate an index entry according to its reference in the "Show index" dialog box

Then follow these steps:

- From the Utilities menu choose "Show index...." The entries you see in *this* dialog box are the entries that will actually place on the page. It includes all entries from each publication listed in the Book List (15.6–15.11) in the current publication.
- Click the "Next section" button to view each section.

- Hold the Command key down.
- From the Utilities menu choose "Show index..." while still holding the Command key.

- From the Utilities menu, choose "Show index...."
- The "Reference" column will list the page number of the indexed entry, *or*
  - ☐ PB for entries on the Pasteboard.
  - ☐ LM for entries on the Left Master page.
  - ☐ RM for entries on the Right Master page.
  - ☐ UN for entries in an unplaced story.
  - ☐ OV for entries within overset text.
  - ☐ "?" for entries included in a page range that may have changed.

Shortcuts ▾ Notes ▾ Hints

- Remember, it is possible to have topics in both the Topic List and the Cross-reference List that are not actually entries in the index. The actual entries are only what you see in the "Show index" dialog box list.
- If the active publication is not listed in the Book List, its index will not be included in the "Show index" dialog box.

- If you have established cross-references to topics in other publications in your Book List, those topic entries are considered to be part of this publication now.

- Page numbers in parentheses denote entries with a suppressed page range, see 15.146.
- PageMaker will not include entries on the pasteboard, the master pages, in an unplaced story, or within overset text when she generates the final index. Be sure to check the "Show index" dialog box for any listings with these references.

If you want to do this:

15.179 Get rid of all those useless topics that you don't need anymore in the "Index entry..." Topic and Cross-references Lists

Then follow these steps:

- From the Utilities menu choose "Create index...."
  - □ You can create the index even if you are not finished indexing. You can either delete it and create it again when you are finished, or just replace it with an updated index later.
- Check the box next to "Remove unreferenced topics."
- Check the other options as desired, then click OK.
- Place the index (see 15.201–15.203).

Shortcuts ▾ Notes ▾ Hints

- This will get rid of all the topics that have no page numbers or cross-references in the current publication (but not entries with the option "Suppress page references"). They may be topics you entered manually or imported from the other publications in the Book List; topics for which all index entries were removed, or topics that had their index marker removed in the publication.
- Topics that are page- or cross-referenced in the other publications in the Book List will still show up in the Topic list in the "Show index" dialog boxes.
- **Note:** Don't check this option if you are creating an unfinished version of the index, and need to keep the topics to complete the index.
- See the notes in 15.140 and 15.166.

Formatting and placing the actual index

15.180 As you place the index for the first time, PageMaker creates style sheets for each level, as well as for the section headings (the letters defining each alphabetical section) and for the index title. You can edit the style sheets; when you update the index, PageMaker will re-use your customized style sheets *as long as you haven't renamed them.*

15.181 PageMaker offers you a lot of control over the appearance of your index through the "Index format" dialog box (see next page). You also have control over which parts of the index you want to show up, as indicated below.

15.182 Replace existing index: If there is no existing index in the publication, this option is not available (it's gray). If this box is checked and there is an index somewhere in the publication, even if only one character of it is visible, PageMaker will replace that existing index with this newer version.

15.183 You can *place* more than one index in the publication, but PageMaker will only recognize the latest version as the true index. It is the latest version that will be updated.

15.184 "Create index" dialog box *(from the Utilities menu, choose "Create index…").*

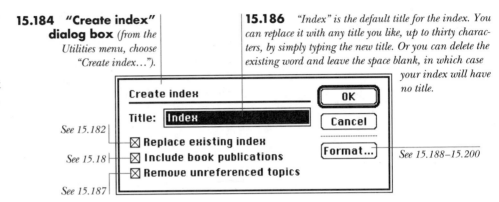

See 15.182
See 15.18
See 15.187

15.186 *"Index" is the default title for the index. You can replace it with any title you like, up to thirty characters, by simply typing the new title. Or you can delete the existing word and leave the space blank, in which case your index will have no title.*

See 15.188–15.200

15.185 Include book publications: If the current publication does not contain a Book List (15.6–15.11), this option is not available (it's gray). If there is an existing Book List, you can check this box to include the index entries from all the other publications in the List. If this box is not checked, only the entries from the current publication will be included in the printed index.

15.187 Remove unreferenced topics: If you check this box, PageMaker will not place any primary topics that have no page locators, subentries, or cross-references. (It will still place entries created with "Suppress page range" selected.) It also removes these unreferenced entries from the *internal* index of the active publication and the internal index of any publications in the Book List. This includes all unreferenced topics whether they have been imported into the active publication or not!

657

"Index format" dialog box *(from the Utilities menu, choose "Create index…"; click the "Format…" button)*

15.188 With a few simple clicks in this "Index format" dialog box, you can format the entire index consistently. You only need to set these specs once. If you decide you don't like something, you can always change it and simply update the index (15.202) to show the changes.

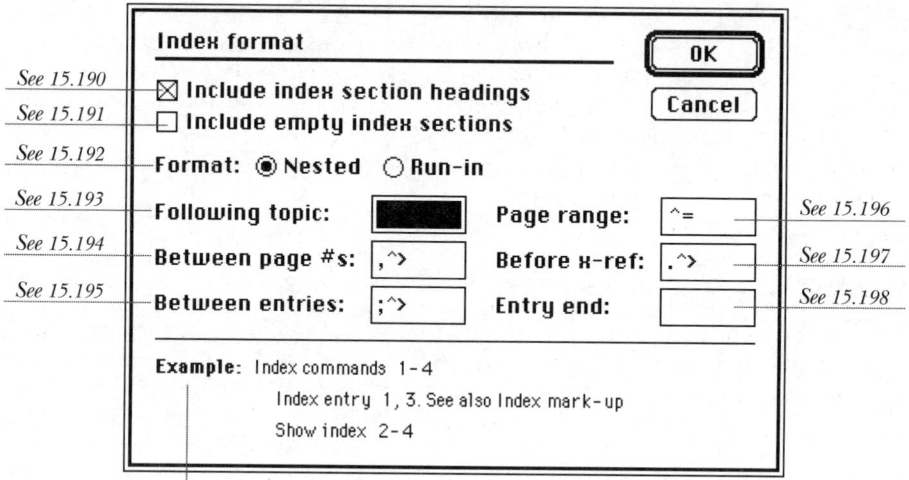

See 15.190
See 15.191
See 15.192
See 15.193
See 15.194
See 15.195

Index format

OK

Cancel

☒ Include index section headings
☐ Include empty index sections

Format: ● Nested   ○ Run-in

Following topic: ▮   Page range: `^=`   *See 15.196*

Between page #s: `,^>`   Before x-ref: `.^>`   *See 15.197*

Between entries: `;^>`   Entry end: *See 15.198*

Example: Index commands 1–4
Index entry 1, 3. See also Index mark-up
Show index 2–4

See 15.199. The format displayed here changes as you make changes in the edit boxes above. It displays how the index will appear with your chosen specifications.

The whole world admits unhesitatingly,
and there can be no doubt about this,
that Gutenberg's invention
is the incomparably greatest event
in the history of the world.

Mark Twain

Index format specifications

15.189 As you change any of the specifications in the "Index format" dialog box, you will see the changes reflected in the bottom portion of the box, under "Example." Those cryptic symbols in the edit boxes are codes for entering special characters; you will find a complete list of the codes in Appendix D. In 15.200 I've detailed several of those you're most likely to use.

15.190 Include index section headings:
The "index section headings" are the large capital letters that break the index into alphabetical sections. If you uncheck this box you won't see any letters, but there will still be extra space to separate the sections.

15.191 Include empty index sections:
If this box is not checked, PageMaker will only place section headings over the sections that actually contain entries. If this box is checked, all 27 section headings (the alphabet, plus "Symbol") will appear in the index, whether or not they contain entries. If the section is empty, PageMaker will insert *"no entries."*

An empty index section.

15.192 Format (Nested or Run-in):
As you click in either button in the dialog box, you can see an example of the format reflected in the bottom portion of the dialog box.

- A **Nested** index lists all the subentries on their own indented lines, one per line. It is much easier to find items this way. (The index in this book is nested.)

- A **Run-in** index lists all the subentries in paragraphs, one entry after another.

15.193 Following topic:
Whatever is entered in this edit box will separate any index entry from its first page number. The box appears empty, but it contains two regular spaces. This default will allow line breaks to occur between the topic and its first page number. You may want to change this to a non-breaking space (such as an en or em space) so the entry will never be separated from its page number. To set a new default for all future publications, change this specification when no PageMaker publications are open.

15.194 Between page #s:
When an entry is referenced to more than one page number, the page numbers will be separated by whatever is entered in this edit box. The default is a comma and an en space. Remember, the en space won't break (PageMaker will think all the numbers are one word), so if you have a lot of numbers for an entry, I would suggest using a comma and a regular space. Just type "**,** " (Comma Spacebar).

15.195 Between entries:
Whatever is entered in this edit box is what will separate the multiple secondary entries in the "Run-in" format, as well as any multiple cross-references in either format. The default is a semicolon and an en space. Again, I would suggest using a regular space to make it easier on PageMaker to break the lines at reasonable places, especially considering that index columns are generally rather narrow. (To separate the secondary entries in a "Nested" format, use "Entry end"; see 15.198.)

Index format specs —continued

15.196 Page range: Sometimes index entries have a *range* of pages where the information can be found, such as "35–39" (15.90–15.96). Whatever is in the "Page range" edit box is what will separate those numbers. The default is an en dash, which is the appropriate mark to show a range of information.

15.197 Before x-ref: Whatever is in this edit box is what will separate an index entry from its corresponding cross-reference. The default is a period and an en space. Again, you might want to consider a normal space rather than an en space, which will make it easier for PageMaker to break the lines.

15.198 Entry end: Whatever is in this edit box is what will appear at the end of every entry in a "Nested" format. In a "Run-in" format, this character will appear at the end of the last reference in each topic. The default is no character at all, because we typically see the end of the line as denoting the end of the information. But you may want to have a stronger visual marker for the end of the entry, such as a bullet of some sort. See the examples in 15.199.

15.199 Remember, you can enter characters in these edit boxes and instantly see how they will affect the index. You'll see an example of the proposed format in the bottom portion of the dialog box:

Example: Index commands 1-4 ●
　　　　　Index entry 1, 3. See also Index mark-up ●
　　　　　Show index 2-4 ●

This is an example of a "Nested" format with a thin space and a bullet used in "Entry end."

Example: Index commands 1-4; Index entry 1, 3.
　　　　　See also Index mark-up; Show index 2-4;
　　　　　Create index 1, 3-4 ●

This is an example of a "Run-in" format with a thin space and a bullet used in "Entry end."

Character codes

15.200 Here is a brief list of some of the codes you can enter into the edit boxes in order to create special characters within the index. Notice that these are different than what you type to put that same character on the page. You'll find a complete chart in Appendix D. *(Type the caret [^] by pressing Shift 6.)*

To get a:	Type:
Normal space	Spacebar
Non-breaking space	Option Spacebar *or* ^s *or* ^S
Em space	^m *or* ^M
En space	^> (> is above the period)
Thin space	^< (< is above the comma)
Em dash	^_ (_ is next to zero)
En dash	^=
Tab	^t *or* ^T
Return	^p *or* ^P
Line break	^n *or* ^N
Non-wordbreaking slash	^/
Non-wordbreaking hyphen	^~
Bullet	Option 8
Raised period	Option Shift 9
Apple	Option Shift K

If you want to do this:

Then follow these steps:

Shortcuts ▾ Notes ▾ Hints

15.201 Create/place the index
for the first time
(actually put it on the page)

- Open the publication that you want to place the index in. It would be easiest if you are on the correct page, also.
- If there is no Book List in this publication, create one (see note to the right). Include all the publications that have entries you want to include in this index.
- From the Utilities menu choose "Create index...."
- Read 15.185–15.187 and decide if you want to include the entries from all publications in the Book List or if you want to remove all unreferenced topics.
- If you want to change the title, type the change.
- Click the "Format..." button and format the index entries (see 15.189–15.200). Click OK. If you just want to accept the defaults, you can skip this step.
- Click OK in the "Create index" dialog box.
- If you are on a layout page, you will get a loaded text icon, just as if you were placing an outside text file. Click on the page to place the text.
- If you are in the Story Editor, PageMaker will create a new story window with the index in it. To get the loaded text icon to place the index on the layout page, press Command E.

- Of course, you only need to have a Book List (15.6–15.11) if you are compiling one comprehensive index that includes entries from more than one PageMaker publication.

If you want to do this:	Then follow these steps:	Shortcuts ▾ Notes ▾ Hints
15.202 Update an existing index, *replacing* the existing one	■ You must be in the publication with the existing index that you want to update. You don't have to be on the same page as the existing index; PageMaker will automatically take you there as soon as you update it. ■ From the Utilities menu, choose "Create index...." ■ Put a check in the checkbox, "Replace existing index." ■ Set up the rest of this dialog box and the "Format" dialog box as you like. Any changes you make here will override whatever is in the existing index. ■ Click all the OK buttons you find. You won't get the loaded text icon this time; PageMaker will wipe out the existing index and replace it with the updated version using the same style sheet.	■ It is entirely possible to place the updated index on the page without *replacing* the existing index. Just don't check the "Replace existing index" button (15.165). ■ If you have placed more than one index on the page without *replacing* (updating) any, then PageMaker will update the last one you placed. If by chance you have eliminated the last one, then PageMaker thinks you don't have an index at all and the "Replace existing index" option will be gray (unavailable).
15.203 Update an existing index *without* replacing the existing one	■ Follow the steps in 15.202, above. This time do *not* put a check in the "Replace existing index" checkbox. Click all the OK buttons you find. ■ You will get a loaded text icon if you are on a layout page, or a new story window if you are in the Story Editor, just as you did the first time (15.201).	■ It is not possible to have more than one index that PageMaker recognizes; that is, as you place more than one index on the page, only the latest version will be considered the actual index. The others simply become plain ol' stories that can never again be updated even if you delete the latest version.

If you want to do this:

15.204 Search the index for an entry

Then follow these steps:

- First you must place the index in the publication (15.201).
- If you are not already in the Story Editor, viewing the index story, then get there:
  - ☐ With the **pointer tool** triple-click on the index story;
  - ☐ **or** with the **text tool** click once in the story, then press Command E.
- From the Utilities menu, choose "Find...," *or* press Command 8.
- In the "Find" dialog box, type the word, or at least several characters of the word you want to find. If you know the style with which it is tagged with, you can narrow the search by applying that attribute to the word (click the "Attributes..." button and choose the style from the mini-menu).
- Click the "Find" button. If PageMaker finds a word that is not the precise word you were looking for, click the "Find next" button. Keep clicking until you find it.
- If you want to go straight to that word on the layout page, press Command E while the word is selected in the Story Editor.
- See Section 9 on the Story Editor for full details on using "Find."

Shortcuts ▾ Notes ▾ Hints

- The basic idea here is to go into the Story Editor, view the index story window, and then use "Find." The directions here are very abbreviated; for detailed info on the Story Editor, see Section 9. For specifics on the Find command, see 9.50–9.66. For details on using Find-and-Change, see 9.67–9.82.

If you want to do this:	Then follow these steps:	Shortcuts ▾ Notes ▾ Hints
15.205 Define a prefix for the page numbers in the index *(optional)*	▪ Open the publication in which you want to add a prefix to the index page numbers (such as the appendices, charts, or perhaps volumes; see 15.118). ▪ From the File menu, choose "Page setup." ▪ Click on the button "Numbers...." ▪ In the edit box, enter the characters (up to 15) that you want to precede the page numbers. Be sure to type any spaces you need, such as the space directly before the number. ▪ Hit the Return key twice, *or* press Option Return to close both dialog boxes.	▪ Remember, if you want appendices, charts, volumes, etc. to have separate prefixes, they each need to be a separate publication. ▪ This optional format is *publication-specific;* that is, it will apply only to the page numbers from this one publication. If you are creating an index for an entire Book List, then you must follow this procedure for every separate publication that you want prefixes for. ▪ You can press Command Option Period to cancel out of both boxes.
15.206 Eliminate the entire index *(the internal index, not the index that has been placed on the page)* **Caution! Read the notes** ☞	▪ From the Utilities menu choose "Show index...." ▪ Hold down the Command, Option, and Shift keys while you click the "Remove" Button. Click OK.	▪ This will remove all entries *from every index in the current Book List.* I mean, seriously— when you return to another publication (in that Book List) for which you laboriously created entries, those entries will be **gone.** ▪ See also 15.138–15.140 and 15.167–15.169.
15.207 Eliminate the index in the current publication *(the internal index, not the index that has been placed on the page)*	▪ Hold down the Command key. From the Utilities menu, choose "Show index...." ▪ Hold down the Command, Option, and Shift keys while you click the "Remove" Button. Click OK.	▪ When you hold the Command key down, PageMaker assembles only the entries from the current publication into the "Show index" dialog boxes. If you remove these entries, no other publication will be affected.

Of which you are desired to Read
no more than you like.

16.1 Minimums and maximums:

Item	Minimum	Maximum
Colors in Color palette	3	65,280
Hue (measured in)	0°	359°
Values in Color Wheel edit boxes	0	65535
	low intensity	high intensity

I strongly suggest you read the Aldus publication that came with PageMaker 5, called "Commercial Printing Guide." It's an excellent booklet that explains color and the printing process in much greater depth and with more illustrations than I can do here.

16.2 There are several ways of working with color in PageMaker. Even on a black-and-white monitor, you can apply certain types of color and print spot color overlays, or even drop in full-color images.

16.3 PageMaker offers you the option of working with one of three different color *models* (16.42–16.49). The one you choose to work with depends on the reproduction process you will use to produce the publication (16.37–16.41). Color is a very complex creature, in both color theory and how to design *with* it, as well as in color technology and how to design *for* it. It is beyond the scope of this book to provide theory or technology. In the next few pages I cover the very basics of how to work with color presses to reproduce your job, and how to prepare your PageMaker publication appropriately.

16.4 If you have no idea what the terms *four-color process* or *color separations* mean, you probably will not be using them and can ignore all references to that information, if you so choose. Sometimes our brains just get full.

The basics of color reproduction:	
One color, tints	666
Spot color, multicolor	667
Four-color, process colors	670
Separations	668
Knockouts and traps	669
Color models: which one to use	671
RGB	672
HLS	672
CMYK	672
Color Libraries	673
Apple Color Wheel	674
The color Registration, the color Paper, and the fill Paper	675
The "Define colors" dialog box	676
The "Edit color" dialog boxes	677
The Color palette	678
Color defaults	679
Tasks	680
Create a custom color library	693
The dialog box for printing color	694

The basics of color reproduction: one color, tints

16.5   To work with color in PageMaker, you will find it helps to have an understanding of how the color will be put on the paper when it is reproduced. This is a ten-minute rendition of a complex topic, geared to people with no previous background in any type of printing technology.

16.6   Let's start with **one color.** When a job is termed a "one-color" job, that means it will go through the printing press one time. One color of ink will be loaded onto the press; the paper will go through the press one time to print one side (it may, of course, go back through on the other side later). It doesn't matter what color of ink is on the press—it may be black, it may be purple, it may be a PMS color. The point is, *there is only one color of ink.* You might use a different color of paper, so when the job is finished, it *looks* like it is two color (e.g., brown ink on pink paper). *But the color of the paper is entirely irrelevant; **a one-color job uses one color of ink.*** If you are using a copy machine, the concept is equivalent: there is only one color of toner being laid onto the page; the paper goes through the machine only once.

16.7   One way to get variations out of a single color is to apply a **tint** (often called a **percentage value** or a **screen**) to objects or to text. A tint creates the *appearance* of a lighter shade (16.106). A "percentage value" means you are only getting a percentage of the full color. For instance, if you create and apply a 50% tint to a black shape, PageMaker breaks up the black area into dots in such a way that only 50% of the black is still there. The other 50% is the white space around the dots. This is an enlarged example:

Below, the box on the left is black. The box on the right has been assigned a 20% tint. It *appears* to be gray, because the tiny black dots it was printed with (look closely) blend with the white paper, making your eye *think* it is gray.

If these two boxes had been printed with red ink, the left box would be red and the right box would appear to be pink. Your job can have an endless number of these tints, an endless array of variations of red and pink, *yet still the job is considered one color.*

16.8   The color of the paper you print on will affect any tints, of course, because in your eye the paper color blends with the ink color. A 40% red on white paper will appear to be a different color than a 40% red on purple paper.

16.9   If you are creating a one-color job and you know it will be printed in, say, blue ink, *it is entirely unnecessary* to assign a blue color to everything in the publication! The laser printer or the imagesetter (19.5–19.10) can only output your publication in black, anyway. You take your black-and-white pages to the press, and the press person uses the black-and-white pages to make the *printing plates* that get put on the press. The press person then puts the color of ink you choose on the press and applies that ink to the paper. So, no matter what color you want the finished product to be, if you're planning a one-color job you can just leave everything on your screen black-and-white.

The basics of color reproduction: spot color, multicolor

16.10 This brief intro discusses **two- or three-color jobs.** The information also applies to publications with four, five, or six colors, as long as they are *spot colors* rather than *four-color process.* **Spot color** is when you select text or an object and apply a pre-mixed color to it, using the Color palette found in the Window menu, or when you place or paste a one-color image. *Four-color process* is the technology the press will use when you reproduce color photographs or illustrations (explained on the next page).

16.11 There is one abiding rule about printing multicolor jobs: **talk to the printer first.** I don't mean talk to your laser printer; I mean talk to the commercial press printer who will reproduce the publication for you. Ask how they would like you to prepare the pages of your publication so the press can print the job most efficiently. Depending on where the colors are, whether or not they bump into other colors, and a few other factors, the printer may want you to prepare *separations, knockouts,* or *traps,* or they may just want you to point out where the other colors go. Whatever they want, prepare it that way!

Different presses may require slightly different preparations, so make sure you prepare it for the press that will actually be reproducing the job.

16.12 When a multicolor job is printed on a one-color press, the paper goes through the press once for each color. The press operator has to wash the ink off the roller and prepare it for printing the next color. A multicolor press has more than one roller; each roller can have a different color ink.

No matter what kind of press is used in a multicolor job, the press person must make a separate printing *plate* with which to print each color. To make those plates, the printer may ask you to provide a *separation* for each color. In PageMaker, you can print separations automatically; each color prints on a separate page (16.16–16.22; 16.130). For instance, the red objects will come out of the laser printer on one page, the green objects will be on another page, etc.

16.13 If the separate colors DO NOT touch each other, it is entirely possible your commercial printer would not need or want separations. For instance, if all the

headlines are to be pale blue and all the body copy is to be dark gray, the two colors (headline and body copy) won't touch each other. Most presses won't need you to provide separations in this case. This is especially true if you are not going to a "quick" printer (a "quick" printer is any printshop with the word speedy, quick, fast, instant, etc., in its name). *Talk to your printer first.*

16.14 If the separate colors DO touch each other (a red box overlaps a green circle, for instance), then you must create separations. Also, the printer may ask if you can provide a *knockout* and perhaps even a *trap* (16.23–16.30).

16.15 With multicolor, you can use varying tints (16.7–16.9) to give the appearance of even more colors by overlapping tints on top of each other, or you can overlap a percentage of one color on an area of a solid, different color. You must be careful when you overlap two different tints, though; you may end up with *moiré* patterns (10.20–10.22) and so will need to adjust the angle (16.139).

Separations   *(please read the next page, also, for information very related to separations)*

16.16   When you take your pages to a commercial print shop, they print multiple copies on a press: they take the pages of your publication, make a *plate* of each page, and put that plate on a roller on the press. Each roller on a printing press can print only one color at a time.

16.17   If you have a multicolor job, each of the colors in the job must be on its own separate roller. If it is a one-color press (with only one roller), that means the printer has to clean off one color of ink, put the next plate on, and put the next color of ink on. That's one of the reasons why printing more than one color is costly.

16.18   Each printing plate that goes on each roller must have just the elements on it that will be printed in the same color. Since the printing plates are made from the pages you give the press, each of the elements of like colors must be on its own page. For instance, let's say all the text is going to print black, and all the headlines and rules are going to print light blue. Then all the black text must be on one page *without* the headlines and rules. All the headlines and rules must be on another page *without* the text (but see 16.13).

16.19   PageMaker makes this easy for you through the "Separations" option when you print (16.130–16.140). PageMaker will separate the colors for you (say the black and the light blue I just mentioned), and put each color on a separate page; the pages are considered **separations** (what PageMaker 4 called "overlays," harkening back to our graphic roots).

16.20   Now, when your laser printer or the imagesetter prints the separation pages, they always come out of the printer black and white, right? It doesn't even matter what color they were on your screen. It doesn't matter what color you specified. The output is always black and white, and that makes the commercial printer happy because she can only make a plate from a black-and-white original. After the plate is on the roller, she can put whatever color of ink you like on that roller. Or, when you copy your page in the copy machine, you can set the machine to print any color of toner you like.

16.21   Remember, we are talking about *spot colors:* text or objects to which you have applied a solid or tinted color, such as Red, Green, Blue, or perhaps a Pantone or Toyo color. When working with spot color you typically don't want to use more than two or three different colors because of the expense (see 16.7–16.8 for some tips on how to make it *appear* that you are using more colors). If you want more than three or four colors, you should probably use *process colors* (16.31–16.36).

16.22   You know what? If you are going to reproduce the job at a higher-quality commercial press (as opposed to a "quick" printer), *you do not need to make separations if the two (or more) colors do not touch each other.* For instance, headlines and rules generally do not touch the body text. Just tape a piece of translucent tissue paper over the top of the finished laser proof of the page and neatly indicate the items you want inked in a second or third color. ***Talk to your printer about it first!***

Knockouts and traps   *(if you don't know the purpose of separations, please read the previous page first)*

16.23 If your publication contains more than one spot color, and those colors touch each other, you need to create *separations*.

16.24 If the colors overlap each other at any point, you have two choices regarding those separations:

a You can let one color print on top of the other color, called **overprinting.** This usually results in a mismatched effect, where the color underneath discolors the one above (16.26). (You won't see the discoloration on the screen because the PageMaker objects, unlike the inks, are really opaque.)

b Or you can remove the portion of whatever is beneath the first color, which is called a **knockout.** The color underneath is being knocked out of the color above (16.27). (PageMaker, by default, knocks out all colors under the top color.)

16.25 For instance, let's say you are printing a yellow square that is partially on top of a red rectangle, sort of like this:

16.26 If you were to *overprint*, the final product would look like this:

16.27 A commercial printer would *knock out* the portion of the red rectangle that is overlapped by the yellow square, so the yellow square will print onto the white paper and the red "rectangle" will print right up next to it. PageMaker automatically creates knockouts for you. These two shapes, printed on two separate pages with a knockout, will show up on their respective pages like this:

first separation   *second separation*

16.28 The problem inherent in Page-Maker's knockouts is that this image is now dependent on the press registering these two colors to each other *perfectly;* that is, these two colors must now be *exactly* lined up with each other on the press or a white line will show where the colors didn't quite connect.

16.29 A commercial printer rarely creates a knockout without a **trap.** A trap is the thin line where the two colors overlap, giving the press a tiny bit of leeway where the two colors abut. A camera person at the printshop puts the images through photographic contortions like "chokes" and "spreads" to create the trap. They like to do that because it makes printing the job much easier. Commercial printers will most likely not be very happy with you if you try to give them separations with PageMaker's knockouts. *Talk to your printer first!* Ask if they want the knockouts, being sure to explain that there are absolutely no traps provided.

16.30 You can put *yourself* through contortions to create your own trap, making this a touch bigger and that a touch smaller and aligning everything just perfectly. Often, you and everyone else will be happier if you let the commercial press prepare them for you, or have your service bureau trap objects using Aldus TrapWise.

The basics of color reproduction: four-color process, process colors

I must remind you once again that this is an extremely brief introduction to a very complex subject. I highly recommend you read the "Commercial Printing Guide" included in your PageMaker package.

16.31 *Spot color* refers to single, pre-mixed colors, such as green, blue, daffodil, plum. A color photograph or multicolor illustration is not spot color; it is *full color*. Full-color images cannot be separated into spot-color separations; that is, you cannot tell Page-Maker to print the daffodil on one page, the plum on another, the peach on another, etc. There are too many millions of possible colors. Full-color images have always gone through a **four-color separation process.**

16.32 In the traditional process, powerful, high-tech machines scan the full-color image and separate all those millions of colors into the three process primary colors, plus black, that together make up the full-color image. The process colors are Cyan (blue), Magenta (the closest thing to red in process colors), Yellow, and Black (which provide the initials for CMYK). The machine finds all the cyan, for instance, in the image, whether it is embedded in the color purple or green or violet or whatever, and represents that layer on a piece of film in varying degrees of dark to light. It then finds all the magenta, all the yellow, and all the black, and separates each layer of color onto a separate piece of film. The colors are transparent, so when these four layers of film are laid over one another, the full-color image appears. Where dark cyan overlaps dark magenta, the image is dark purple; where light yellow overlaps a mid-blue with a touch of magenta, the image is a rich green.

16.33 The full-color image is reproduced by printing these four colors onto paper, one color at a time (one color per roller, anyway). By combining these four colors in millions of varieties, virtually any color can be reproduced. If you use a magnifying glass (printers use a special *loupe*) to take a look at any color photo in any magazine, you will see combinations of the four-colors overlapping each other to produce the colors your naked eye sees. You will see little *dots* of color, because the principle is the same as printing various tints (16.7) in one color—the press can lay down only a solid layer of ink, so by using dots we can make the colors *appear* to be lighter.

16.34 Four-color process printing is a very exacting procedure. Each of the four colors is printed on the paper as miniscule dots. The dots are lined up in rows. Each color must have its rows of dots lined up at very precise angles to avoid a *moiré* pattern. A moiré pattern is the strange pattern that appears when the lines of dots overlap each other at random angles. Although the patterns may be very interesting, generally they are undesirable (10.20–10.22).

16.35 The four-color process recreates most colors. It does not make a very good red, though, so oftentimes a true red is added as a fifth color, a spot color. Metallics (silver, gold, etc.) or other spot colors are also often added as fifth or sixth colors.

16.36 PageMaker can separate CMYK TIFFs, DCS images, and EPS files. PageMaker cannot separate RGB TIFFs, but you can use Aldus PrePrint to separate them. PICT files, especially color PICT files, are extremely unreliable and should not be used if you are going to press.

Color models: which one to use *(the color models are explained on the following pages)*

16.37 PageMaker offers several different **color models** (16.42–16.49) to work with. A color model is a method of describing the type of color you want to apply. The model you choose to work with depends on how you are going to reproduce the publication. You have a choice of RGB, HLS, CMYK, or a color matching system, all of which are explained on the next few pages.

16.38 If you know you will be reproducing the publication either on a **slide recorder** or on a **color printer,** use the RGB or HLS color model (including the Apple Color Wheel, if you like; 16.54–16.61). For instance, perhaps you will be printing directly to a color printer to get a full-color comp to show a client, or because you only need six printed copies of this job. Or perhaps you are designing a presentation that will be output onto color slides.

16.39 If you are going to take your PostScript-printed pages to a **copy machine** or a **commercial press** to have one, two, or three different colors of ink or toner applied, you can use any color model you like, *except* CMYK. Just make sure you make a spot color separation for each separate color (16.16–16.22; 16.140). This method will also work for four, five, or six colors, as long as you are not trying to separate a full-color photograph or illustration.

16.40 If you will be taking your publication to a **commercial press** and you want to use a specific color matching system (16.51), then specify your colors using a color from the library. When you print, create a separation for each color.

16.41 If you have a publication with **full-color photographs** or **illustrations** in it, which of course will be going to a commercial press, use the CMYK color model (these are called *process colors*) and/or choose a process color matching system from a color library (16.53).

EXPERIENCE
*teaches you
to recognize a mistake
when you've made it again.*

See 16.76–16.84 for editing colors using any of these models.

RGB

Edit color | **OK**
Name: purple | **Cancel**
Type: ● Spot ○ Process ○ Tint
Model: ● RGB ○ HLS ○ CMYK
☐ Overprint | Libraries: ▷
Red: [22] %
Green: [0] %
Blue: [75] %

16.42 RGB stands for **Red, Green,** and **Blue.** The RGB model is actually not a color standard for printing to paper, but is based on the balance of colors used to create color photographic prints from color negatives and for creating video and television displays. Color Mac monitors use the RGB model to display what you see on the screen.

16.43 If you are going to print straight to a color printer to see what your publication looks like, or if you are going to print slides, use the RGB model. If you are going to need to separate those colors for printing on a press, use the CMYK color model instead.

HLS

Edit color | **OK**
Name: purple | **Cancel**
Type: ● Spot ○ Process ○ Tint
Model: ○ RGB ● HLS ○ CMYK
☐ Overprint | Libraries: ▷
Hue: [257] °
Lightness: [37] %
Saturation: [100] %

16.44 HLS stands for **Hue, Lightness,** and **Saturation** (also known as HSB for Hue, Saturation, and Brightness; same thing).

16.45 Hue refers to the color itself, such as whether the color is blue or green or orange, etc. **Lightness** refers to how much white is added to the color; the more white, the lighter the color. **Saturation** refers to the intensity, or purity, of the color. Typically, the more saturated the color is, the richer and deeper it appears.

16.46 Notice that the color purple as defined in RGB (top left) automatically translates into certain values here in HLS. You will rarely use the HLS model.

CMYK

Edit color | **OK**
Name: purple | **Cancel**
Type: ○ Spot ● Process ○ Tint
Model: ○ RGB ○ HLS ● CMYK
☐ Overprint | Libraries: ▷
Cyan: [78] %
Magenta: [100] %
Yellow: [25] %
Black: [0] %

16.47 CMYK stands for **Cyan, Magenta, Yellow,** and **Black** (see 16.32). This model uses *process colors* and is the standard for printing full-color jobs (16.31–16.36).

16.48 Notice that no matter which model you use to define a color, all the other models enter their appropriate values for that color. The example above shows the CMYK values for the color purple that I originally defined in RGB. Fortunately, PageMaker keeps track of those colors in its process palette, so if you initially defined colors using RGB and/or HLS for color proofs, and then you change your mind and want to print it using four-color process, just change the color model to CMYK.

Color Libraries

16.49 The **Color Libraries** are internationally-recognized color identification systems used by ink manufacturers, designers, and commercial printers. Color names such as teal, forest green, or sky blue are always open to misinterpretation. But with these libraries of matching systems, you can identify the exact color you want by checking a color swatch book or catalog available from art supply houses or directly from your commercial press. Each color is identified with a number. You can then specify that number to almost any printer in the world and be guaranteed the color will match what you had in mind.

16.50 Even if you have a black-and-white monitor, you can choose a color from the swatch book or catalog, then find the corresponding color in PageMaker and add it to your Color palette (16.105). When you print with separations (16.140), each color will print on a separate page.

16.51 How do you know which library to choose from? *Talk to the commercial press that will be printing your job!!!* Ask them which color matching system they use, then choose colors from that library.

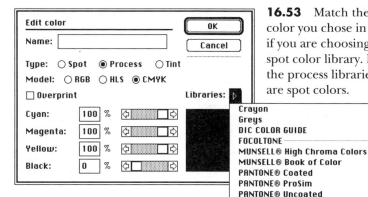

16.52 *Because computer monitors use RGB for display, the color you see on your screen is not an exact match to the color that will output from a color printer, which is also not an exact match to the true color of that same name or number that the press will use to reproduce your job.* It is critical that you accept this fact. If you are accustomed to working with spot color and process colors, you are probably accustomed to having color proofs and chromes made before going to press. Don't skip that process now! In fact, it's even more critical now, since the RGB color computer screen can delude you.

16.53 Match the library with the *type* of color you chose in the dialog box. That is, if you are choosing a spot color, choose a spot color library. In the menu list below, the process libraries are marked. All others are spot colors.

Process color libraries.

The terms "Coated" or "Uncoated" refer to the kind of paper you plan to print your final piece on.

16.54 Apple Color Wheel   *(also known as the Apple Color Picker; press the Shift key as you click "Edit" in the "Edit color" dialog box, or hold both the Command and the Shift keys down as you click on a color [not Black, Paper, or Registration] in the Color palette)*

16.55 If you have a grayscale or color monitor, you can tap into the Apple Color Wheel. With the color wheel, you can just buzz around and pick up the color you want. The specs for it will automatically drop into each of the color models. (Notice the Apple Color Wheel uses an HSB model while PageMaker uses the comparable HLS; see 16.44).

16.56 The color wheel can display 16.8 million colors (who counted them, I want to know), although a press can only reproduce a fraction of those. You can view the color wheel on a black-and-white monitor; you see little initial letter clues telling you where each color would be if you could see it. That's not a whole lot of help.

16.61 To define the color values:

Hue *(the color)***:** Press the mouse button and move the pointer around on the color wheel. The selected color will appear in the top half of the Color Box (16.58).

Saturation *(the purity or intensity of the color)***:** Click toward or away from the center of the wheel. There is actually a very thin line running from the outer edge of the circle towards the center, along which the hue stays the same. For example, you can click on the outside edge and pick up hue 35944, and then click towards the center and pick up the same hue with less saturation. It's easier, though, to pick a hue in the color wheel, and then use the arrows (16.60) to control the saturation and brightness.

Lightness (brightness) *(how much white is in the color)***:** Use the scroll bar on the right. The up arrow lightens/brightens the color; the down arrow darkens/shades the color, all the way down to black.

Also see 16.60.

16.57   *This is the name of the color that was selected when you clicked the Edit button.*

16.58   *The bottom half of this Color Box shows the original color. The top half shows how the color changes as you edit it. Click on the bottom half of the Color Box to return to the original color.*

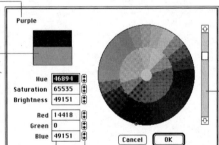

16.59   *To adjust the brightness (lightness), press on the scroll arrows, drag the scroll box, or click in the gray scroll bar.*

16.60   *You can press the arrows to change any of the specs; the color wheel will change right before your eyes.*

You can also **type** *a value from 0 (low intensity) to 65535 (high intensity). You will not see the color change until you click somewhere in the dialog box; click anywhere except in the bottom half of the color box (16.58).*

The color Registration, the color Paper, and the fill Paper

16.62 "Registration" isn't even a color, actually it is a *tag*. When you are printing separations, any text or object that has had **Registration** applied to it *(tagged)* will appear on *every* separation page. For instance, if you created one page with six different multicolor business cards on it, you probably made tick marks to define the boundaries of the cards. If you apply the color "Registration" to the tick marks, the marks will show up on every page when you print the separate colors.

16.63 The **color Paper** (from the Color palette) actually is the color of the paper you are working on. Usually it is white because PageMaker gives you a white page whenever you create a new publication. You can change the color of Paper, though, to anything you like! If you have a color monitor and will be printing the job on a pale peach stock, you can change Paper to pale peach. The pages on your screen will be pale peach, giving you a clearer indication of how all the various colors will react together. On a black-and-white laser printer or imagesetter, Paper will always print as white, though.

16.64 *Paper is no ink at all.* However, you can use the color or fill Paper to mask out areas from solids (see 16.67) or to knock out other objects. It keeps other colors from printing. How it prints when you make separations for the printer depends upon how you use it. Although you can edit the **color** Paper (16.63) you must be careful not to assign a color to the **fill** Paper (16.122). It may look just fine on your screen, but it will print differently than it looks. (Fill makes a tint or pattern inside of PageMaker-drawn objects. A fill of "None" makes a transparent shape; a fill of "Paper" makes a mask of the shape *so the paper shows through*. Also see 2.63–2.74). Since Paper is no ink, you cannot overprint Paper ("Knockout" is the default; see 16.24).

16.65 When you change the *color* Paper, the **fill Paper** (from the "Fill" or "Fill and Line" submenu in the Element menu) also changes. The two Papers function the same, a major departure from PageMaker 4.

16.66 When you print separations, an object with a fill **or** color of Paper will appear on all the separations. It will knock out and obscure *all* other objects on any layer beneath it. The border, however, will only appear on the separation with the border color.

If the border of a Paper-filled or -colored object is Registration colored, the object *and* the border will print on every separation.

16.67 All this can come in very handy. Say you want a crescent shape, so you overlay one dark circle with a Paper-filled or -colored circle. If you print separations, the dark circle will print with a white "chunk" out of it, even on the separation page.

Black circle with white circle on top to create a crescent.

Separation result if white circle is Paper-filled or -colored.

16.68 If you change the Paper *color* in the Color palette, the new color *does* affect every object already in the publication that has a *fill* of Paper, as well as objects with the *color* Paper already applied.

The "Define colors" dialog box *(from the Element menu, choose "Define colors...")*

16.69 The style sheet for colors works the same as the style sheet for text. To apply a color to a graphic object or to text, simply select the object or the text with the appropriate tool, then click on the color shown in the Color palette (graphic: 16.123; text: 16.120–16.121). This is also called *tagging* an object with a color, or *applying* a color.

If you edit (change) that color in the color style sheet, then everything that has had that color applied to it will automatically and instantly change throughout the publication. Any tints that were based on that color (16.106) will also change to be tints based on the new, edited color.

16.70 *On a color monitor, this bar will display the selected color.*

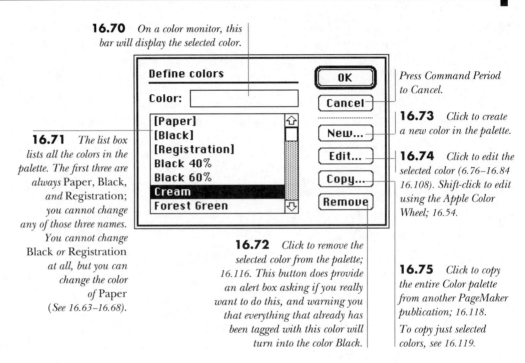

16.71 *The list box lists all the colors in the palette. The first three are always* Paper, Black, *and* Registration; *you cannot change any of those three names. You cannot change* Black *or* Registration *at all, but you can change the color of* Paper *(See 16.63–16.68).*

16.72 *Click to remove the selected color from the palette; 16.116. This button does provide an alert box asking if you really want to do this, and warning you that everything that already has been tagged with this color will turn into the color Black.*

Press Command Period to Cancel.

16.73 *Click to create a new color in the palette.*

16.74 *Click to edit the selected color (6.76–16.84 16.108). Shift-click to edit using the Apple Color Wheel; 16.54.*

16.75 *Click to copy the entire Color palette from another PageMaker publication; 16.118.*

To copy just selected colors, see 16.119.

You look rather rash my dear, your colors don't quite match your face. **—Ms. Daisy Ashford**

The "Edit color" dialog boxes

16.76 This example shows the CMYK edit box, but the edit box for each color model works exactly the same.

16.77 If the Color palette is showing on your screen (press Command K if not), you can shortcut to the edit box for any color: hold down the Command key and click once on the color name. The only limitation in the "Edit color" dialog box is that it doesn't allow you to change the name of the color; to do that you must go through the "Define colors..." command (16.105).

16.78 Remember, these colors are like style sheets. If you apply a color to an object or to text, that object or text is considered *tagged*. If you edit any color, all objects or text with that color applied (tagged) will be changed to the new version of that color.

See 16.10, 16.31, and 16.7

16.80 *By default, all colors will "knockout" of any other colors that are on top of them (see 16.23–16.30). If you want this color to **always** overprint (print right over the top of the other colors) instead of knocking out, check this box.*

If you want this color to overprint just occasionally, use the "Fill and line..." dialog box (2.70–2.71). Also see 16.107.

16.79 *Type the name of the color here. If you select a color from one of the color matching systems (from the Libraries), its name will appear here. It's a good idea to keep that official name rather than change it, as that name will appear on the separation pages.*

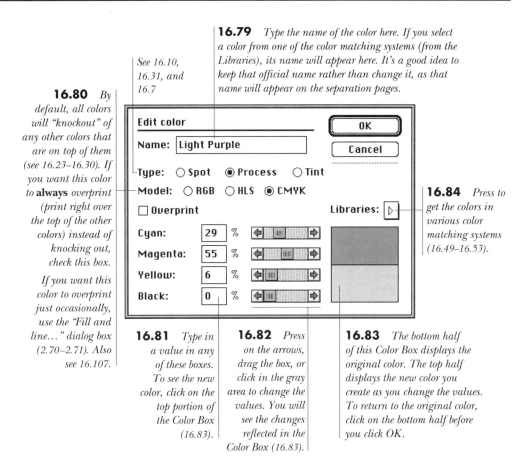

16.84 *Press to get the colors in various color matching systems (16.49–16.53).*

16.81 *Type in a value in any of these boxes. To see the new color, click on the top portion of the Color Box (16.83).*

16.82 *Press on the arrows, drag the box, or click in the gray area to change the values. You will see the changes reflected in the Color Box (16.83).*

16.83 *The bottom half of this Color Box displays the original color. The top half displays the new color you create as you change the values. To return to the original color, click on the bottom half before you click OK.*

The Color palette

16.85 PageMaker's Color palette gives you a lot of information. You can instantly tell which colors are spot colors, which are process colors, which colors have been imported from a placed EPS graphic, which colors are tints, and you get to see a little swatch of the actual color.

16.86 When you place an EPS file, any *spot* colors it contains are automatically added to the Color palette so you can use them elsewhere in your publication. You can even edit those spot colors and change the colors in the imported EPS file (see 16.124).

If the EPS graphic is from FreeHand, PageMaker will also add any *process* colors in the graphic to your Color palette (as shown by the Cream color in the example). Because there is no standard for creating process colors in various applications, PageMaker cannot add process colors from programs other than FreeHand. You cannot edit these EPS process colors nor can you delete them.

16.87 All new colors you define will appear in the Color palette, in the "Type specifications" dialog box, and in the "Paragraph rules" dialog box.

16.89 *Click here to put the Color palette away, or press Command K.*

16.90 *These color swatches indicate the color.*

16.91 *A color name in italic indicates it is a process color.*

16.92 *Color names in regular type (not italic) are spot colors, not process colors.*

16.93 *The percent symbol indicates this color is a tint based on another color.*

16.88 *This menu offers you the choice to apply the color to the inside fill, to the outside line, or to both.*

Press-and-drag here to move the palette around your screen.

Colors

Line ▼

[Paper]
[Black]
[Registration]
% *Black 40%*
% *Black 60%*
Cream
Forest Green
Peach
Purple
% Purple 25%
Rooster Red

16.94 *Instead of using the little menu, you can click on the left button to choose to apply the color to the fill, or the right button to apply the color to the border (line).*

Hold the Shift key down and press on either button to select both.

16.95 *When I placed this EPS graphic (created in FreeHand) into PageMaker, its colors were added to the Color palette, as you can see to the left.*

16.96 *This symbol indicates the* **spot** *color has been brought in with an EPS graphic and added to the palette. If you remove the EPS graphic, these colors remain, but the PS symbol disappears.*

PageMaker only imports **process** *colors from FreeHand or other PageMaker-created graphics.*

The Red Hen

Color defaults

16.97 You can add any color in the Color palette to any paragraph style in your style sheet (16.121; see Section 8 on Style Sheets). For instance, you may want all your Headlines to be Purple. Just remember that before you can add a color to a style, you first need to define it so it appears in your Color palette (16.105).

16.98 You can set a default color that will automatically apply to text.

You can set a *separate* default color that will automatically apply to objects.

16.99 Step-by-step directions for setting a text default color are found in 16.126. The basic concept is that you are just adding a further specification to the text defaults that already exist (4.36). The current text color default is probably Black; you can change it to *any* color in the Color palette. Then whenever you type using the default style "No style," your text will be in that particular chosen color.

16.100 You can always temporarily override a paragraph style sheet by simply selecting text and choosing a color, or by choosing a color while the insertion point is flashing (see 8.38–8.43 regarding overrides). This temporary override is in effect only until you click the insertion point somewhere else. Removing these colorful temporary style sheet overrides is easy: with the insertion point flashing in the paragraph, click on the style name again (8.68).

16.101 You can set a default color that will apply to any graphics you draw in Page-Maker (that is, any line, box, or oval; 16.125). This default will also automatically apply to any graphic you paste in from the Clipboard (as long as it did not come from the Scrapbook), and also to any external graphic file you *place,* **if** the graphic has not had a color assigned to it previously.

16.102 It's important to know about color defaults because it is so easy to change them inadvertently, and if your screen is black-and-white you won't even know the color has changed. On my grayscale monitor (which is set to black-and-white so it will redraw faster), I unknowingly pasted in every screen shot in the entire publication with a 20% tint. I didn't catch it until I printed the pages.

It's a very good idea, when you are working with colors on a monochrome monitor, to leave your Color palette visible on the screen (press Command K). That way you can see the color selection jump from one to another as you place, paste, and create.

If you want to do this:	Then follow these steps:	Shortcuts ▾ Notes ▾ Hints
16.103 Show the Color palette	■ From the Window menu, choose "Color palette," *or* press Command K.	■ If there is a checkmark in the Window menu next to the command "Color palette," it means the palette is on the screen. ***If you don't see it, check behind the Style palette.***
16.104 Hide the Color palette	■ From the Window menu, choose "Color palette," *or* press Command K.	
16.105 Create/define a new color	■ From the Element menu, choose "Define colors...." ■ Click the "New..." button. The specifications you see in the edit boxes are those from whichever color in the palette was highlighted when you clicked "New...." Changing the specs will not affect any existing color. ■ Name the color. It's a good idea to set up a system of naming colors that gives you an indication of which model the color was created in (16.79). ■ In the "Edit color" dialog box, click on the radio button to choose the color model you want to use (see 16.37–16.53 to decide on the appropriate model). ■ Adjust the specifications: type in values, (16.81), use the scroll bars (16.82), or choose a color from one of the libraries (16.84). See 16.76–16.84 for detailed info on using the "Edit color" dialog box. ■ Click OK, click OK, *or* press Option Return to close both boxes.	■ **Extra-zippy shortcut:** ▫ If the Color palette is not already on the screen, press Command K (16.103). ▫ Hold the Command key down and click on "Black" or "Registration." This brings up the "Edit color" dialog box. ▫ Define the color. Click OK. ▫ This extra-zippy shortcut does not *apply* the color to anything on the page. You can just keep Command-clicking "Black" to create new colors. ■ If the OK button in the "Edit color" dialog box is not black, it means you have not named the color. ■ If you click on the bottom half of the Color Box (16.83), you cancel your new specs and remove the name. The dialog box stays, though. ■ Read 16.80 to know if you want to check the "Overprint" button.

If you want to do this:	**Then follow these steps:**	**Shortcuts ▾ Notes ▾ Hints**

16.106 Create a tint of any color

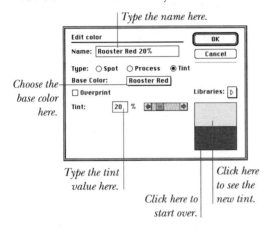

Type the name here.

Choose the base color here.

Type the tint value here.

Click here to start over.

Click here to see the new tint.

Before you can create a *tint* of a color, you must first create the *base* color (16.105).

- Once the base color is created, go into the "Define colors" dialog box. Click "Black." Click "New." Click "Tint."
- There is a little menu next to "Base Color." Press on it and choose the color for which you want to make a tint.
- Type a name (it's best to type the name of the base color, then the tint percentage so you always know what it is).
- Change the percentage value in the Tint edit box from "100" to the tint value you want. To see the new color, click in the *top half* of the Color Box on the right. Click OK.

- You cannot *edit* a color into a tint— you must *create a new one.*
- If the OK button in the "Edit color" dialog box is not black, it means you have not named the color.
- If you click on the bottom half of the Color Box (16.83), you cancel your new specs and remove the name. The dialog box stays, though.
- All tints will print on the same separation page as the base color. You can choose their line screen (lpi ruling; 16.135).
- If you change the base color, all tints will change to become tints of the new base color. Too cool.

16.107 Create a color that sometimes overprints and sometimes doesn't

- First create the color that *isn't* going to overprint (16.105 to make a new color).
- Now create the color again, but check the "Overprint" box.
- Name it something that distinguishes it from the first color (such as "OP Blue," etc.). Click OK.

- When a color "overprints" it prints directly *on top* of any other colors that may be underneath. This can change the appearance of the color, which might be what you want. When a color does *not* overprint, all colors underneath knock-out (become white where that color will eventually print); see 16.23–16.30.
- By giving the same color two different names, you fool PageMaker into thinking that it is two different colors. In a way it is: one overprints, one knocks out.

If you want to do this:	**Then follow these steps:**	**Shortcuts ▾ Notes ▾ Hints**

16.108 Edit (change) a color in the Color palette	• From the Element menu, choose "Define colors...."
	• Click once on the name of the color you want to edit, then click the "Edit..." button, *or* just double-click on the color name.
	• Editing a color is basically the same as creating a new color. You can change its name, any of the values, or even the color model. See 16.76–16.84 if you need further help on using the "Edit color" dialog box.
	• Click OK, click OK, *or* press Option Return.
		• **Extra-zippy shortcut:**
		  ☐ If the Color palette is not already on the screen, press Command K.
		  ☐ Hold the Command key down and click once on the color name to bring up its "Edit color" dialog box.
		  ☐ Edit the color. Click OK. *(You can't change the name of the color; see 16.109.)*
		• Any changes you make to this color will then instantly be applied to all text or objects that have been tagged with this color (16.69; 16.78).
		• All tints based on this color will change to tints of the new color.

16.109 Change the name of a color	• From the Element menu, choose "Define colors...." • Click once on the name of the color you want to edit, then click the "Edit..." button, *or* just double-click on the color name. • In the "Edit color" dialog box, type in the new name. • Click OK, click OK, *or* press Option Return.	• You cannot use the extra-zippy shortcut (mentioned above) to change the name of a color. If you Command-click a color in the Color palette, you will be able to edit any of the specifications *except* the name.

T i m e   i s   w h a t   k e e p s   e v e r y t h i n g   f r o m   h a p p e n i n g   a t   o n c e .

If you want to do this:	Then follow these steps:	Shortcuts ▾ Notes ▾ Hints
16.110 Use the Apple Color Wheel to edit an existing color (grayscale or color monitors only)	■ From the Element menu choose "Define colors...." ■ Click once on the name of the color you want to edit; hold down the Shift key and click on the "Edit..." button; **or** hold the Shift key down and double-click on the color name. ■ See 16.54–16.61 for specifics on how to choose and change the values. ■ Click OK to get back to the "Edit color" dialog box. Continue editing, if necessary, *or* press Option Return to close both dialog boxes.	■ **Extra-zippy shortcut** to the color wheel: If the Color palette is not showing, press Command K (if you still don't see it, look behind the Style palette). Then hold the Command and Shift keys and click once on the name in the Color palette. □ You can only use the Color Wheel to *edit* an existing color—you can't get to the wheel through the "New..." button. You *can* create a new color and click OK in the "Edit color" dialog box. Then hold the Shift key down and double-click on the name of that new color to get the Color Wheel.
16.111 Use a color from one of the color matching systems (one of the Libraries)	■ From the Element menu, choose "Define colors...." ■ Click the "New..." button to define a new color, or double-click on an existing color to change it to a color in the library. ■ Click the Spot button for spot color, the Process button for process color. If you're going to print to paper (not to a color printer, slides, etc.), click CMYK. ■ Press on the "Libraries..." arrow, and slide down to select the matching system your press has recommended (16.49–16.53). ■ Scroll to find the color you want, or type in the number, if you know it. Click OK.	■ It is entirely possible to define a color as any color in the matching system and then change its values. This means the color you see on the screen is *really* not going to match the printer's ink of that same name/number (16.49). *Make sure you rename the color if you change its values!* ■ If you go and open a different library, it will open to the color in its color matching system that most closely resembles the one you originally selected.

683

If you want to do this:	Then follow these steps:	Shortcuts ▾ Notes ▾ Hints
16.112 Change the color "Registration"	▪ You can't.	▪ "Registration" isn't even a color, really. It is just a tag to apply to those items that you want to show up on every page of the separations (16.62).
16.113 Change the color "Black"	▪ You can't.	▪ You may have noticed that if you Command-click on either "Registration" or "Black" in the Color palette, as if to edit the color, the name is missing. If you make any changes in this "Edit color" dialog box, you will not be changing "Black" or "Registration," but you will be defining a new color.
16.114 Change the color "Paper"	▪ You can get the "Define colors…" dialog box and edit "Paper," just as you would any other color (16.108). **Or:** □ If the Color palette is not showing, press Command K to show it. □ Hold the Command key down and click once on the color "Paper." □ In the resulting "Edit box," change the color using any of the color models you like (16.37–16.53). □ Click OK.	▪ Changing the color "Paper" *actually changes the color of your paper on the screen!* "Paper" is a color you can apply to text or objects, but it also refers to the color of the paper you are creating your publication on (your page itself doesn't show up as a separation, though). See 16.63–16.68. ▪ Whatever color you change "Paper" to will also apply to the *fill* "Paper" in the Element menu.

If you want to do this:

Then follow these steps:

Shortcuts ▾ Notes ▾ Hints

16.115 Change the color "Paper" back to its original color (white)

- From the Element menu, choose "Define colors...."
- Click once on "Paper," then click the "Edit..." button, *or* double-click on "Paper."
- Change the values in all the edit boxes to 0 (zero), either by typing the number or by dragging the scroll boxes to the left.
- Click OK.

- If the Color palette is visible on your screen (press Command K to show it), Command-click on "Paper" to get the "Edit color" dialog box.
- If you type 0 (zero) and you don't see the change reflected in the Color Box on the right, click in the top half of it (16.83).

16.116 Remove a color from the Color palette

- From the Element menu, choose "Define colors...."
- Click once on the name of the color you want to remove, then click the "Remove" button.
- Thoughtfully, PageMaker asks if you really want to do this, even warning you that any objects that have had this color applied will turn black. Click OK, if you really do want to remove it.
- Click OK to close the "Edit color" dialog box (Cancel, of course, if you have changed your mind).

- Instead of removing a color, which makes everything that had that color applied to it turn black, you can *replace* one color with another; for instance, you can replace green with another color in your palette, like blue. In this case, everything that was green turns blue, including any tints based on green; see 16.117.
- Since you probably read *The Little Mac Book,* you know that Rule Number One on the Mac is Save Often. You really should be especially conscious of saving just before you do something potentially drastic, like removing colors. If you have saved, you can always Revert (18.30).

If you want to do this:

16.117 Change one color into another existing color
(rather than remove a color)

Then follow these steps:

- From the Element menu, choose "Define colors...."
- Double-click on the name of the color you want to get rid of.
- In the dialog box, change the name of this color to the name of the color that you want to take its place. Click OK.
- You will get a little message box verifying that this is what you want to do. Make sure you are changing the right color into the right color. If so, click OK.

Shortcuts ▾ Notes ▾ Hints

- Any tints based on the original color will turn into tints based on the new color.
- Of course, before you ever do anything drastic like this you should **save** your publication. Then if you really blow it with a task, you can always Revert (from the File menu; 18.30).

The primeval essence of color is a phantasmagorical resonance, light becomes music.

At the moment when thought, concept, formulation, touch upon color,

its spell is broken, and we hold in our hands a corpse.

≫≪

Johannes Itten

If you want to do this:

16.118 Copy a Color palette from another publication

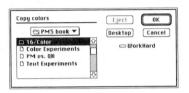

The dialog box allows you to choose the publication that contains the color styles you want to copy into the current publication.

PageMaker will warn you before replacing any existing colors.

Then follow these steps:

- From the Element menu, choose "Define colors...."
- Click the button "Copy...." This takes you to a dialog box where you can look for the PageMaker publication that contains the Color palette you want to copy into the current publication. Switch disks and/or open folders to find it.
- When you find the PageMaker publication, double-click on it. All the colors in that file's Color palette will be added to the current Color palette. (You could, of course, single-click on the file name and then click the OK button.)
- If the palette you are copying from has a color with the same name as a color in the current palette, PageMaker will ask if you want to replace the current color. If you click the Cancel button here, you will just cancel that one replacement; you will not be canceling the entire copy process. You will get a separate little alert box for every color with the same name (regardless of caps and lower case).
- Click OK if you are done. You can Copy a palette from another file; you can Cancel if you decide this was not a smart thing to do; you can Remove any colors that you now see need to be removed (16.116).

Shortcuts ▾ Notes ▾ Hints

- When you copy a Color palette from another PageMaker publication, the other colors are *added* to the current Color palette. If any colors have the same name (regardless of capital letters), PageMaker will ask if you want to replace the current color with the copied one. If you *replace* a color, remember, all objects that have had that color applied will change into the new, copied version of that color, as well as all tints based on that color.
- Copying colors comes in very handy when you are working on several publications in which you want similar colors.
- Since the color you see on the screen is not what prints on the color printer, nor is it what will print on the press, you may want to create a custom library that contains a set of colors you have adjusted to specifications that you know will print (see 16.128). For instance, maybe your company uses a particular color for its logo. After much trial and experimentation and frustration, you finally found exactly the right combination of CMYK that creates exactly that color on the press. If you store it in a library, you can always use that color in any other publication.

If you want to do this:	Then follow these steps:	Shortcuts ▾ Notes ▾ Hints
16.119 Copy just one or two colors from another Color palette	■ While your current publication is open, also open the publication that contains the color you want. ■ Draw a small object with one of Page-Maker's drawing tools, then apply to this object the color(s) you want to take to the other publication. ■ From the Window menu, choose "Tile" so both publications will be side-by-side. ■ With the **pointer tool,** press on the colored object and drag it across your screen; drop it into the current publication. Et voilà, the colors in that object will appear in your Color palette. You can delete the small object and the colors will remain.	■ If you want to copy *all* the colors from another publication, see the previous task, 16.118. Also check out 16.128 for instuctions on how to create your own custom library of colors. ■ When you bring color TIFF or EPS graphics into a publication from the Library palette, their colors will be copied into the new publication.
16.120 Apply colors to text	You can only *apply* colors that you have previously *created* (16.105). ■ Get the Colors palette, if it isn't already visible: from the Window menu, choose "Color palette," *or* press Command K. ■ With the **text tool,** select the text you want to color. ■ Click on the color in the Color palette. **Or,** select the text, then get "Type specs…" from the Type menu. Choose the color from the "Color" submenu. Click OK.	■ If the insertion point is flashing, any color you choose will be poured into that insertion point; text you type from that point on will be in color. ■ All colors you define will also appear in the "Type specifications" and the "Define styles" dialog boxes, and from either of these boxes you can apply color to text. All colors you define will also be available in the "Paragraph rules" dialog box for coloring rules (lines).

If you want to do this:	Then follow these steps:	Shortcuts ▾ Notes ▾ Hints
16.121 Apply colors to text through style sheets	■ If your Style palette is showing, just Command-click on the style you want to add color to. If the Style palette is not showing, from the Type menu, choose "Define styles..." and double-click on the style name. ■ Click the "Type..." button. ■ From the Color submenu, choose the one you want. All colors from the Color palette will show up here. ■ Click as many OK buttons as necessary; or press Option Return.	■ To show the Style palette, you can choose it from the Window menu, *or* press Command Y. ■ Of course, if you are starting a new style from scratch (8.47–8.49), you can just build color into it from the beginning. See Section 8 on Style Sheets. ■ If you sometimes see a white box behind the colored text, don't worry about it—simply redraw the screen (resize the view, click in the zoom box, etc.) and the white box will go away.
16.122 Create a shape with a colored border and a fill of a different color	■ Create a shape with one of PageMaker's drawing tools (2.9–2.10). ■ If the shape is not selected, click once on it with the **pointer tool.** ■ From the Element menu, choose "Fill and line..." *or* press Command]. ■ Choose the fill you want— *but don't choose Paper.* Choose the color. ■ Choose the line width and the color (see 2.70–2.73 for details on what the "transparent," "reverse," and "overprint" checkboxes mean). ■ Click OK or press Return. You can only *apply* colors that you have previously *created* (16.105).	■ Even if you chose "None" as a fill, when you apply a color to the inside, the color will apply. ■ Of course, if the object is already created on your page, you can always use the "Fill and line" menu command or the Color palette (press Command K to show it) to apply the colors. ■ If you're having trouble assigning color to a shape, check and be sure you haven't chosen "Paper" as the fill. ***You can't assign color to Paper fill. If you try to do so, you will create havoc if you then print separations.***

If you want to do this:	**Then follow these steps:**	**Shortcuts ▾ Notes ▾ Hints**
16.123 Apply colors to an imported graphic	■ Get the Colors palette, if it isn't already visible: from the Window menu, choose "Color palette," *or* press Command K. ■ With the **pointer tool,** select the graphic you want to color. ■ In the Color palette, click on the name of the color you want to apply. You did that, but the color didn't show up on the screen? Yeah, the color will only show up on a grayscale or monochrome TIFF or paint-type image; all other graphics won't look any different, although the color *will* print on the proper separation.	■ Don't bother to apply color to RGB TIFF or CMYK TIFF graphics, or to DCS files— these graphics will always print with their own colors. ■ You *can* apply colors to black-and-white or grayscale EPS, TIFF, or paint-type graphics (PAINT, MacPaint), and to PICT or PICT2 files. *You won't actually always* **see** *the colors on the screen, but they will appear on their proper spot or process color separation.* ■ If you want to edit *spot* colors in an imported EPS graphic, see 16.124, below. ■ Choose "Restore original color" (from the Element menu) to remove any color you applied *in PageMaker* to an imported color graphic. Just choose "Black" from the Color palette to remove color you applied to monochrome bitmaps or grayscale TIFFs.
16.124 Edit an imported EPS spot color	■ Edit a spot color in an EPS graphic just as you would edit any color (16.108). ■ Read the notes to the right.	■ Notice this task mentions specifically "spot" color. If the graphic is a color file from FreeHand, the process colors will be imported into PageMaker, but you cannot edit nor delete them. ■ *You won't see a change on the screen,* but the color will print on the proper separation. ■ If you want the EPS graphic to print using its original colors, click the "Preserve EPS colors" checkbox before you print (16.136).

If you want to do this:	**Then follow these steps:**	**Shortcuts ▾ Notes ▾ Hints**
16.125 Set a default color for graphics	■ If the Color palette is not showing, press Command K (or choose it from the Window menu). ■ Click once on the **pointer tool.** ■ Click once on the color you want as a graphic default. The color you choose is the color in which all PageMaker-drawn objects will be automatically drawn, all graphics from the Clipboard or the Scrapbook will be pasted, and all graphic files will be placed (as long as the graphic was not assigned a color previously, either in PageMaker or in another program).	■ If you read the section on defaults (1.6–1.18), you know there are two levels of defaults for most items in PageMaker: *application* defaults that apply to the entire program, and *publication* defaults that apply just to the current publication. The color choice default can be applied only to the current publication; you cannot set it as the application default. That's probably a good, safe thing.
16.126 Set a default color for text	■ If the Color palette is not showing, press Command K. ■ If the Style palette is not showing, press Command Y. ■ Click once on the **text tool.** ■ In the Style palette, click once on the style "No style." (If any other style is selected, you will set a temporary override in that particular paragraph style.) ■ Click once on the color you want as a text default. When you type with the style "No style" selected, the text will be that color.	■ If you find you have inadvertently set a color *override* (8.38–8.43) in a paragraph style, rather than a new text default color, simply click on the text tool and then click in the style name. ■ If text is on the page that has a paragraph style applied, but you accidentally changed its color, simply click inside the paragraph with the text tool, then click on the style name in the Style palette. The original color will be returned. ■ See 4.360–4.366 re: text defaults in general.

If you want to do this:	**Then follow these steps:**	**Shortcuts ▾ Notes ▾ Hints**

16.127 Trap a color

- There are explicit step-by-step directions in the online Help section that go into more detail than I can do here for various trapping scenarios.
  - □ From the Window menu, choose "Help...."
  - □ Click the button "Keyword."
  - □ Type "trap" quickly to instantly select the topic "Trapping."
  - □ On the right side, click on the topic you want to know about.

- If you seriously want to trap, you should read the "Commercial Printing Guide" that came in your PageMaker box. It is a great little booklet that explains the entire process in much greater and better detail than I can possibly do here. In fact, it is just not possible to explain in a couple of paragraphs "How to trap a color."
- You might also want to consider letting your pre-press provider use Aldus Trap-Wise on your project, in which case you would make an EPS file of your publication (19.142; 19.148). Talk to your service bureau or pre-press consultant first.

You know,
color trapping is an incredibly complex topic.
Questions enter in like: what is trapping; when do you need to
trap and when is it not necessary; at which stage of the pre-press process
should you trap; should you do it yourself or let the commercial press do it; should
you trap the lighter color or the darker color and is green or purple darker anyway; should
you trap with shared colors or should you trap with a third color; what trapping values should you use
(values like .0077, .0025, or .0152), which depends on the printing press and the printer's expertise and the
paper it's to be printed on; and other questions. Within PageMaker you can create simple traps around simple objects
by making one object a tiny bit larger than the knockout area, by creating keylines around ovals and rectangles and overprinting
the keylines, or by using other common techniques. There are so many variables, and I do think the topic is serious and important enough
that I don't want to lead you astray with superficial information. —rw

If you want to do this:

Then follow these steps:

Shortcuts ▾ Notes ▾ Hints

Create color library Addition

16.128 Use the "Create color library" Addition to create and use a custom color library

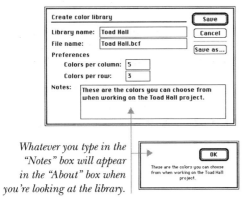

Whatever you type in the "Notes" box will appear in the "About" box when you're looking at the library.

ToadHall.BCF

When you click "Save, PageMaker stores this file in the Color folder, which is in the Aldus Folder, which is in the System Folder. You can save it somewhere else, if you choose, by clicking on the "Save as..." button, but PageMaker can't use the library unless this file is in the Color folder.

- To make a custom library, you first must build a Color palette with all the colors you want in it (16.105). This Color palette can be in a publication you're working on, in a template, or in a blank document. You can use spot colors, process colors, or colors from any of the other libraries.
- If it isn't open already, open the publication that contains the Color palette with all the colors you want in your own library.
- From the Utilities menu press on "Aldus Additions" and slide down to "Create color library...." You will get the dialog box you see to the left.
- Enter a library name.
- Enter a file name that is similar to or the same as the library name so you will recognize it if you ever need to find it.
- Choose the number of rows and columns, up to 10 by 10. Type a note, if you like.
- Click Save.
- When you want to use this library in another publication, create a new color, as usual (16.105), and choose your new library. Hold the Shift key down and drag over all the colors. Click OK.

- Rather than having to create the same colors over and over again, or having to copy unneeded colors into a new Color palette, you can create your own library, then choose just the colors you want from that customized library. This is handy if you have special colors for special jobs or corporate identities, or perhaps you've finally figured out the exact CMYK combination for your logo.

- The name of your new library will appear in the "Libraries" section of the "Edit Color" dialog box (16.84).
- If you don't add the ".bcf" after the file name when you type it in, PageMaker will add it for you. You can, if you like, leave the file name as "Custom.bcf," but then if you create *another* custom library and save it as "Custom.bcf," your new library will replace the existing one.
- Rather than dragging over *all* the colors, as suggested in this last step, you can of course just select the individual colors you want—you certainly don't have to add all of them.

The dialog box for printing color

16.129   *Click Composite and Grayscale to see a gray proof of your color page.*

16.130   *Click Separations to print each ink on a separate page, ready for making plates. (Do this on your laser printer to proof your job to make sure everything is printing on the correct separation.)*

16.131   *If an ink has a checkmark, PageMaker will print (in black) all pages with that color on it.*

16.132   *Double-click an ink color to select it for printing or to de-select it, **or** click once on the color, then click the "Print this ink" checkbox.*

16.133   *PageMaker will only print as many pages as necessary to create the colors on the separations. But if you click the checkbox "Print blank pages" (under Document), then PageMaker will print a separation for every color for every page. For instance, if you are printing the color "Forest Green," but page 3 doesn't contain Forest Green, PageMaker will print a blank page for that separation anyway. If you also check "Print page information" (under Options), then this identifiable blank page becomes a handy item to give the press so they understand it's not just a mistake that the "Forest Green" separation for page 3 is missing.*

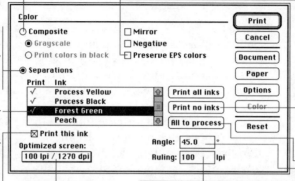

16.134   *If you have chosen a high-resolution printer or imagesetter in the Document section, then you have a great number of choices in this mini-menu. PageMaker has chosen the best screen frequency ("lines per inch," or "ruling") and resolution, according to the installed PPD, but you can choose another. Talk to the service bureau first before you change this!*

16.135   *"Ruling," or "lines per inch" (lpi) refers to how fine the dots in a color or gray image appear. See 10.69 and 10.179– 10.188 for details and examples.*

In this box, PageMaker has determined for you the best ruling for the printer you have chosen and for the "Optimized screen" you have selected (to the left, 16.134). If you choose another printer (under Document), this ruling may change.

You can change the ruling, but talk to the commercial press who will be printing the job! Ask them what "lines per inch" they prefer.

16.136   *If you have edited any of the spot colors in an imported EPS graphic (16.124), you can click this button to print the original colors instead of the edited colors.*

16.137   *Of course you wouldn't print pages with no inks, because you'd print blank pages (actually, **nothing** prints if there are no inks selected). Use this button to remove all the checkmarks from the list of inks, then double-click each ink you really do want to print.*

16.138   *If you click this button, **all** spot colors will temporarily print as the equivalent colors using CMYK values, which may not look quite like the colors you expect! If you really want some spot colors turned into process, it is better to use the "Edit Color" dialog box (16.76). Clicking this button will also remove any "Overprint" overrides you may have applied to borders or boxes.*

16.139   *When printing process colors, the angle of the dots is very important. PageMaker applies the standard angles (click the different colors to see the different angles). You can, if you choose, change this angle, but don't do it without first consulting the commercial press that will be printing the job!*

If you have applied any angles to TIFF images through "Image control" (10.176–10.183), probably for special effects, those angles will override any angles set in this box.

If you want to do this:

16.140 Print color separations directly from PageMaker

Options

Graphics
- ○ Normal
- ● Optimized
- ○ Low TIFF resolution
- ○ Omit TIFF files

Markings
- ☐ Printer's marks
- ☒ Page information

Then follow these steps:

- From the File menu, choose "Print...," *or* press Command P.
- Set up the "Print document" dialog box the way you need it (19.47).
- Click the "Options" button (19.50–19.64).
  - □ Click "Normal."
  - □ Click "Printer's marks" and "Page information" if you like (see notes to right).
- Click the "Color" button.
  - □ Click "Separations" (16.130).
  - □ Make sure there is a checkmark next to each color ink you want to print on a separate page (see 16.131–16.133). Double-click to add a checkmark; double-click to remove a checkmark. All tints will print on the same page as the base color.
- Read the information on the previous page to decide if you need to click any other buttons or choose any other options here.
- Click the OK buttons to start printing. Each color will print on a separate page.

Shortcuts ▾ Notes ▾ Hints

- See Section 19 for in-depth info on all sorts of printing.
- The color "Paper" will not print as a separate page.
- Check "Printer's marks" to print registration marks, crop marks, color-control bars, and density control bars. Check "Page information" to print the color of the separation, the filename information, the date, and the page number on each printed page. *To print these marks, though, the paper must be bigger than the page size,* which might or might not be possible on your printer.
- Most commercial printers ignore the registration marks that are provided on any job, so don't worry too much about them. *Talk to your printer* (16.11–16.13).

If you want to do this:

Then follow these steps:

Shortcuts ▾ Notes ▾ Hints

16.141 Print separations of a file that contains an RGB TIFF

- Well, PageMaker can't create separations for RGB TIFFs. You will have to use Aldus PrePrint or some other post-processor.
- You can, though, take the RGB TIFF back into an imaging application, such as PhotoShop, and turn it into a CMYK TIFF, then update the graphic in PageMaker (10.000, 10.107–10.108, 11.66). PageMaker can separate it as a CMYK TIFF.

- Another file format that every application has trouble with in regard to printing on PostScript devices is PICT, especially color PICTs. Avoid PICTs if you are going to be printing pages. If your publication is designed to stay on the screen, feel free to use PICTs.

 foolish consistency is the hobgoblin of little minds, adored by little statesmen and philosophers and divines. With consistency a great soul has simply nothing to do.

Ralph Waldo Emerson

Being almost the shortest,
but not the least significant,
Chapter in this Book.

17 ▾ IMPORTING & EXPORTING

17.1   Methods of importing:

Paste (1.273–1.282)

Copy and paste text or graphics through the Clipboard. Use when a link to the original file is not necessary.

Place (Sections 3, 4, 8, 9, 10, 15)

Imports text and graphics from all applications and in all file formats for which PageMaker has a filter. This is the most reliable method of importing.

Paste special (10.110–10.119)

Copy and paste through the Clipboard, but choose the file format you prefer according to what is available.

Publish and Subscribe (11.79–11.102)

A System 7 feature for sharing text or graphics between applications. Limited to Text, EPS, and PICT file formats. Useful when you need just part of a file, or when a file is being shared across multiple applications.

OLE, Object-linking and -embedding (11.103–11.132)

Paste or Paste link objects copied from an OLE server program. Use when PageMaker does not have an import filter that suits your purpose, or when you want to import just part of a file.

17.2   PageMaker gives you access to a wide range of text and graphic file formats for both importing and exporting without ever having to leave your publication. The ease and efficiency with which she handles both lets you incorporate bits and pieces of different programs into one, nice, PageMaker package.

17.3   If linking is not an issue, then using **Paste** is the most direct method of importing. PageMaker automatically selects the best format for pasting objects that have been copied to the Clipboard or Scrapbook, or you can choose a format with "Paste special."

17.4   If linking *is* an issue, you can, in most cases, simply **Place** an object. A variety of word processsing and graphic filters were automatically installed when you installed PageMaker (17.8–17.19). PageMaker selects the correct filter for you and establishes a link between the original document and the copy in your publication (see Section 11 for all the info on linking.)

17.5   Placing is covered in various places throughout the book. You can place both text (4.28–4.83) and graphics (10.126–10.130) directly on a publication page or in the Story Editor (9.35–9.38).

17.6   For files that are not PageMaker compatible, you can either **Subscribe** to them (see Publish and Subscribe, 11.79–11.102) or OLE-link or -embed them using **Paste link** or **Insert object** (see 11.103–11.132). Both methods maintain links that in most cases let you edit the object from right within your PageMaker publication.

17.7   Of course, it's a cinch to take text and graphics from one PageMaker publication to another. You can copy and paste text and graphics through the Clipboard, drag-and-drop them between open windows, or drag them in from the Library palette. And you can import other PageMaker stories (including those from PageMaker 4 and Windows PageMaker 5).

Import and export filters 698
"Smart ASCII import filter" dialog box .. 700
Tasks 701
**Converting 4.x publications into
    5.0 publications** 713
**Converting PC 5.0 PageMaker
    publications into Mac 5.0
    PageMaker publications** 714

Import and export filters

17.8   Import and **export filters** let PageMaker import and export files to and from the most popular word processing software packages. You can choose to install filters when you install PageMaker or at any time afterward. When a new or upgraded word processing software program is released, Aldus will just create a new filter for it rather than update the PageMaker program itself.

17.9   When you install PageMaker, you are offered a list of import and export filters. The list, to the uninitiated, looks a bit intimidating. You are asked to choose which ones you want to install. If you have disk space and you don't want to waste brain time trying to decipher the list, go ahead and install all of them (1.1 megs worth of space) and you will be ready for almost anything anybody wants you to place into PageMaker. If you need to conserve disk space, then take a close look at the list. You will notice it is nothing more than the names of word processing programs and their version numbers. Just select the filters for the word processing programs you use.

If you have already installed PageMaker, you can go back and check which filters you have installed; see 17.28.

17.10   You can choose to **import** from these Mac programs* *(see 17.40 for info on PC import filters)*:

- Acta Advantage 1.0
- MacWrite II
- Microsoft Word 1.05, 3.0, and 4.0–5.0
- Microsoft Works 1.0 and 2.0
- Microsoft Excel 3.0 and 4.0
- PageMaker 4.x and 5.0
- WordPerfect 1.0 and 2.x
- WriteNow 2.0 and 3.0

Also: RTF (Rich Text Format; 17.11) and Smart ASCII (17.11) text-only format. MacWrite Pro filter available.*

17.11   In addition to the filters for the word processing programs you use, also install these:

- **ASCII export** and **Smart ASCII import** filters. ASCII (pronounced *askee*) is the simplest and most universal file format for text. Smart ASCII is an import format used specifically by PageMaker that allows you to retain more of the formatting of imported text than does a regular ASCII filter. These filters allow PageMaker to read almost any text file and to export PageMaker stories in a format that can be read by almost any other program.
  Text only = ASCII.
- **RTF** filters. RTF is similar to ASCII, but it holds onto more of the typeset formatting.
- **Story Importers 4 and 5.** Don't forget to install these. They allow you to import any PageMaker story from any PageMaker 4.x or 5 publication.

17.12   PageMaker automatically installs some graphic import filters (TIFF, PICT, Paint, and Editions), but gives you the option of installing these *(see 17.40 for info on PC graphic import filters)*:

- EPS Import
- EPS Import Nested DCS
- Photo CD Import
- TWAIN Image Importer

See 10.1–10.13 and 10.126–10.130 for the scoop on importing graphics.

The update patch, PageMaker 5.0a, offers additional import filters. Check your on-line service, or call Aldus for more information. New filters are available all the time.

Filters —*continued*

17.13 When you choose to import or place a file, you don't need to know which filter to use—PageMaker automatically gets the one it needs. If the necessary filter is not installed, you will get this alert box:

17.14 If you get this alert, you will have to install the filter for that document before you can place or import it into PageMaker (17.29). If that is not possible for some reason, you can try opening the file in the program it was created in and save it in a different format, one for which you have a filter.

17.15 There may be some formatting in the imported file that PageMaker cannot deal with, such as hidden text or vertical tab rules. These will be lost in the version you see in PageMaker. However, if you export it

back to its word processing program, the formatting will usually be returned to it, *depending* on the program it came from and what the formatting is.

17.16 To find out what format attributes PageMaker does support, look in her extensive on-line "Help" file. In the "Help" window, click on "Importing files"; then click on "Text filters." Here you'll find a list of the most common word processing programs and their attributes listed under the subheads "Character," "Paragraph," "Style, tab and hyphenation," and "Other."

MICROSOFT WORD CHARACTER SPECS

Character attributes	Import
Font	√
Size:	
Range	4-127
Increment	1
Leading	Note
Width	√
Color	√
Position:	
Superscript	√
Subscript	√

17.17 *Simply click on a program's attribute subhead to see a list of specific formatting attributes. PageMaker supports the ones that are checked. In the Help window, you can click on any underlined word, such as* Note, *to get more info.*

17.18 You can choose to **export** any story in PageMaker. You can export it in any of several different file formats, depending on which program you want to be able to read it. PageMaker provides these export filters:

- MacWrite II
- Microsoft Word 2.0, 3.0/4.0
- WriteNow 2.0, 3.0
- Rich Text Format (RTF) (PC or Mac)
- ASCII (text-only) format (PC or Mac)
- DCA/RFT (Document Content Architecture; for PCs)
- XyWrite III (PC)

17.19 If you are exporting a story to be read by a word processing program other than one listed here, then try exporting it first as an RTF file (Rich Text Format) since most programs can now read this format. If it can't, then export it as "Text only." That turns the story into an ASCII file that almost *anything* can read (17.11). ASCII files do not export with any text attributes.

17.20 When you export text, you are actually creating a new file that will have its own icon on your disk. It does not affect or remove the text in your publication, nor does it change any established link (11.2–11.12); it simply makes a copy of the story.

"Text-only import filter" dialog box   *(this dialog box automatically appears when you import or place a text-only file)*

17.21   When you choose to import a text-only file, either onto your publication page or into the Story Editor, PageMaker automatically displays this dialog box, allowing you some control over the formatting. This is especially useful when you're importing a file that has been converted from a PC.

17.22   *A typical ASCII file puts a carriage return at the end of every line, not just at the end of paragraphs. This option gives you a choice of retaining or deleting those returns (usually you do **not** want a return at the end of every line).*

17.23   *If you check "Between paragraphs," this filter will remove all but one carriage return between paragraphs.*

17.24   *If you have checked either of the first two options, this option becomes available. If there are lines of text that begin with spaces or tabs, or if a line contains embedded tabs, PageMaker will not remove the carriage returns from them.*

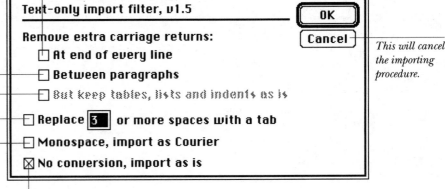

17.25   *If the person who input the text used spaces instead of tabs, you can turn those spaces into tabs with this option. You can input a value from 3 through 80.*

Some programs, in converting text from one format to another, automatically replace tabs with spaces. This option will turn them back into tabs.

17.26   *This option turns all your text into Courier, a mono-spaced PostScript font that looks like typewriter text. The only reason you would ever want to do this is if you are receiving formatted files (tables, charts, etc.) from either an on-line service or certain IBM computers and you want to see what the existing format looks like. See 17.33.*

This will cancel the importing procedure.

17.27   *This is the default option. You cannot manually click it off. As soon as any other box is checked, this option automatically becomes unavailable.*

If you want to do this:	**Then follow these steps:**	**Shortcuts ▾ Notes ▾ Hints**
17.28 Check to see which import and export filters are installed 	■ Hold down the Command key. ■ From the Apple menu choose "About PageMaker®...." ■ You will see a list of all the installed Additions, import filters, export filters, dictionaries, and a few other odds and ends.	■ If you hold down the Command and Shift keys when you choose "About PageMaker®..." you will see the names of the people who developed PageMaker. ■ Hold down the Shift key and choose "About PageMaker®..." to see a special memorial dedication to a PageMaker engineer.
17.29 Install a filter that was not originally installed *Filter icon.* MacWrite II Import.flt  *The Aldus Filters folder is located in the Aldus folder in your System folder.*	■ Insert Disk 1 of the original PageMaker disks (or your back-up disks). ■ If the "Utilities" window is open, close it. ■ Double-click on the AldusFilters folder. ■ The filters in this folder are all com-pressed. Find the one you want to install and double-click on it. You will get a dialog box (shown left). ■ Single-click the "Desktop" button. Double-click on your hard drive's name. ■ Double-click on the System Folder (scroll, if necessary, to find it in the list). ■ Double-click on the Aldus folder. ■ Double-click on the Aldus Filters folder. ■ Click the "Save" button. ■ When you're done, close the windows and eject the disk (drag it to the trash *or* press Command E).	■ There are more filters in yet another Aldus filters folder on Disk 3. ■ You cannot install a filter by dragging it into the folder. All that will happen is that you will copy the *compressed* file onto your hard disk. You must go through this mini-install process. ■ Actually, you can install more than one filter at a time. Shift-click or use the marquee (1.207–1.208) to select all the filters you want to install. (You still double-click on just one to open the Installer.) When you click the "Save" button, PageMaker will install the first one, then bring you back to that dialog box so you can click "Save" again. This will be repeated until all the filters you chose are installed.

701

If you want to do this:	**Then follow these steps:**	**Shortcuts ▾ Notes ▾ Hints**
17.30 Import a word processed file	▪ From the File menu choose "Place...." ▪ In the list box, find the file you want to import into PageMaker. You may need to scroll to find it. Double-click on the file name, *or* single-click and click OK. ▪ You will get a loaded text icon. Click on the publication page to pour the text onto the page.	▪ If the insertion point is flashing or text is selected when you choose the "Place" command, you have choices as to how the imported text places (4.49. 4.51–4.52, and 4.54–4.56). ▪ This is an extraordinarily brief synopsis of the process. It is covered in great depth in Section 4 on Text, 4.28–4.62. You really should read that section. There is really so much more involved than just clicking.
17.31 Import a word processed file into the Story Editor 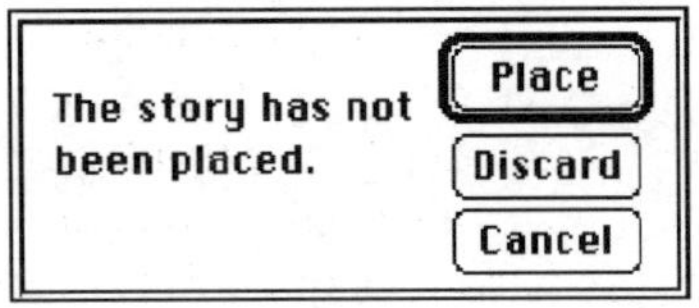	▪ From the File menu choose "Place...." ▪ Click the radio button "As new story." ▪ In the list box, find the file you want to import into PageMaker. You may need to scroll to find it. Double-click on the file name, *or* single-click and click OK. ▪ PageMaker will create a new story window for the file where you can edit it. When you are ready to put it on the layout page, either choose "Close story..." from the Story menu, *or* click the Close box, *or* press Command W. You will get the alert box shown on the left. Click "Place" or hit Return. You will get a loaded text icon and you can then place the text in the usual manner (4.28–4.62).	▪ You can import text to a new story window (9.35), into an existing story as new text, or to replace text (9.36). ▪ Again, this is an extraordinarily brief synopsis of the process. You really must read Section 9 on the Story Editor, 9.6–9.20.

The story has not been placed.
Place
Discard
Cancel

If you want to do this:	**Then follow these steps:**	**Shortcuts ▾ Notes ▾ Hints**
17.32 Import a graphic ▨ *This is what an imported graphic looks like in the story view.*	■ Importing a graphic **in the layout view** is just another term for "placing" the graphic. See Section 10, 10.126–10.130. ■ Importing a graphic **in the story view** is the same as importing text (17.31) **in the layout view**. The difference is that in the story view you can only import a graphic as an *inline* graphic (10.213–10.226), never as an *independent* graphic. The inline graphic will appear in the story window as a little box (see left). When you place the story itself on the publication page (17.31; 9.83) you will see the actual graphic.	
17.33 Import a text-only file	■ From the File menu choose "Place...." ■ Double-click on the file name you want to import/place. ■ You will get the "Text-only import filter" dialog box. See 17.21–17.27 for details on the available options. Check the boxes of your choice. Click OK. ■ Place the file as usual (see 17.30–17.31).	■ You don't have to know beforehand whether the file is text-only or not; PageMaker knows. You will know it, too, when you see the "Text-only import filter" dialog box appear. ■ The procedure is the same for importing a text-only file to the Story Editor. ■ If you are bringing in monospaced text (either downloaded from an on-line service or received from an IBM computer that uses monospaced type) that has been formatted as a chart or table, you may want to preview it first to see how it is to be set up; "Monospace, import as Courier" is the only way to get the original formatting.

If you want to do this:

17.34 Import a Microsoft Word file, with control over the Table of Contents entries, index entries, character spacing, and "Page break before" setting

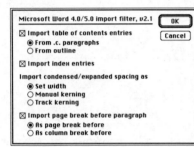

Then follow these steps:

- From the File menu choose "Place...";
- Locate the file you want to import. Click once on it. Hold the Shift key down while you click OK (or while you double-click the file name). You will get the dialog box shown on the left.
- To "Import table of contents entries," click the box and specify how you entered them ("From .c. paragraphs" or "From outline").
- Check "Import index entries" if you want.
- If you condensed or expanded any letter spacing in Word, you need to translate it into something PageMaker can format:
  - □ "Set width" retains Word's line length, and expands or condenses the *characters* to fit (5.210–5.216).
  - □ "Manual kerning" tries to match Word's letter spacing with PageMaker's pair-kerning values (5.163–5.165).
  - □ "Track kerning" tries to match Word's letter spacing with one of PageMaker's six tracking values (5.180–5.185).
- PageMaker does not retain Word's automatic or forced page breaks inserted in the text; she will only read "Page break before" specified from Word's "Paragraph" dialog box. You can choose to import these page breaks either "As page break

—continued

Shortcuts ▾ Notes ▾ Hints

- How come only Word gets this special, secret little filter?
- The reason you have to convert the letter spacing when you import is because Word measures spacing between letters in *points,* and PageMaker measures it in percentages of the font size.
- PageMaker may crash when importing a Word file that had "Fast Save" checked in Word's "Preferences" dialog box.

If you want to do this:	Then follow these steps:	Shortcuts ▾ Notes ▾ Hints
—continued	before," in which case text will jump to the top of the next available page (4.336), or "As column break before," in which case the text will jump to the top of the next available column (4.335). ■ Click OK, and you can continue to place as usual (17.30; 17.31).	■ Really, paragraphs specified with "As page break before" absolutely *cannot* physically be placed on the same page as the previous text. The text block will "exhibit puzzling behavior," such as roll itself up and refuse to unroll.

17.35 Import a Microsoft Word (4 or 5) table as a graphic (PICT)

On Government	On Politicians	On Diplomacy
It is dangerous to be right when the government is wrong.	Ninety percent of the politicians give the other ten percent a bad reputation.	Diplomacy is the art of saying "nice doggy" until you can find a rock.
Voltaire	*Henry Kissinger*	*Will Rogers*

A Word table imported as a graphic.

Then follow these steps:

■ In Microsoft Word, after you have created and saved the table, go to the Tools menu and choose "Preferences."

■ In the "View" option, turn off "Show Hidden Text" and "Show Table Gridlines." Click the close box, *or* press Command W.

■ Select the entire table (press-and-drag from one corner to the diagonally-opposite corner). Don't select any lines above or below the table, even if they are blank.

■ Press Command Option D. This puts the table into the Clipboard.

■ Close or quit Word and select your PageMaker publication.

■ Click once on the **pointer tool.** From the Edit menu choose "Paste Special," choose "PICT," then click on the "Paste" button. If the insertion point is flashing, you can paste the table as an inline graphic (10.213–10.226). The table is now a PICT graphic (10.23–10.31).

Shortcuts ▾ Notes ▾ Hints

■ Once the table is in PageMaker it is a graphic, so you can resize or stretch it just like any other graphic.

■ To **OLE-embed** the table (11.103), press Command V (or choose "Paste" from the Edit menu) instead of selecting "Paste Special." This way you can double-click on it in PageMaker to open a temporary file in Word. You edit it in Word and the table in PageMaker updates immediately.

■ If you have trouble editing an OLE object, try copying and pasting a small item or a few characters in PageMaker. This clears the OLE object off the Clipboard and frees up RAM.

■ See Publish and Subscribe (11.79–11.102) to *subscribe* to a table you published in Word. To create a Word table "on the fly" from within PageMaker, see "Insert object" (11.126–11.132).

If you want to do this:

17.36 Import a Microsoft Word table as text (tab-delimited)

Actor	Role	Year
David Garrick	Richard III	1783
Charlotte Cushman	Romeo	1852
Sarah Bernhardt	Hamlet	1899

◀ *The original table in Word.*

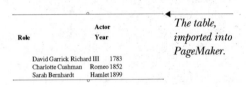

◀ *The table, imported into PageMaker.*

◀ *The same table, showing the Tabs and Returns.*

Actor	Role	Year
David Garrick	Richard III	1783
Charlotte Cushman	Romeo	1852
Sarah Bernhardt	Hamlet	1899

▲ *The same table, with the Tabs customized in PageMaker.*

Then follow these steps:

- In Microsoft Word, open the document that contains the table.
- Insert a new line right before the table, and type a capital letter **T** in the line.
- Select the **T**.
- From the Format menu, choose "Character...."
- In the "Style" section of the dialog box, check "Hidden." Click OK.
- Save and close the Word document.
- Select your PageMaker publication.
- Place or import the file as usual (17.30; 17.31).
- The placed file will not look like the original table (see left).
  - □ Borders are eliminated.
  - □ The type style in the first cell in each row is applied to the entire row.
  - □ The left edge of each column comes in as a left-aligned tab (including the first column), and other text in the cell is aligned to that tab.
  - □ The rows are separated by paragraph Returns.

Shortcuts ▾ Notes ▾ Hints

- Obviously, the text from this kind of importing needs some editing.
- If you want to edit the table in PageMaker, import it using this method. If you would rather the table look exactly like it does in Word, and you don't mind making the editing changes from within Word, publish it as an edition and subscribe to it in PageMaker (11.100), or import the table as an OLE object (17.35, and 11.103–11.132). Either of these latter methods will allow you to access the original Word file from within PageMaker.

I think that I shall never see

If you want to do this:

17.37 "Place" a Microsoft Excel spreadsheet

```
┌─────────────────────────────────────────┐
│ Place Excel range:              ┌──────┐ │
│ File: excel Fri                 │  OK  │ │
│                                 └──────┘ │
│ Cell range:    [A1:K24]  [▶]    ┌──────┐ │
│ Tab alignment: [Decimal ▼] Places: [2]  │
│                                 │Cancel│ │
│ ⊠ Apply XLS style  ☐ Truncate to cell boundary │
└─────────────────────────────────────────┘
```

A properly executed apostrophe.

—*Anonymous copy editor; John Grimes*

Then follow these steps:

- From the File menu choose "Place…."
- Select the spreadsheet you want to import.
- Click OK.
- In the "Place Excel range" dialog box, enter the range name, select one from the list, or enter coordinates.
  - Coordinates must be entered in the Excel convention. For example, A1:K24.
- If desired, choose a "Tab alignment" to override the tab alignments set in the spreadsheet.
  - If you chose a decimal tab, you can enter a value from 0 to 20 to designate how many places the number should extend to the right of the decimal point (only cells with number values will be affected).
- Check the option "Truncate to cell boundary" if you want to limit the number of characters in a spreadsheet cell to the width of the cell.
- Check the option "Apply XLS style" if you want PageMaker to create and apply a style sheet based on the font you used in Excel.
- Click OK.
- Position the loaded text icon where you want the type to begin; click once to pour the text onto the page.

Shortcuts ▾ Notes ▾ Hints

- Each row in the spreadsheet will be converted to a paragraph, and the columns will be separated by tabs. You cannot import more than 40 columns. PageMaker places tabs based on the column width (hence the 40 column limit; PageMaker has a maximum of 40 tabs per paragraph).
- The option "Truncate to cell boundary" can improve the appearance of a spreadsheet, but it does so at the risk of losing data. Data that extends beyond the cell boundary will not be imported when this option is checked.
- You can create an "XLS" style sheet before you import the spreadsheet and except for tabs, PageMaker will apply the attributes you set. The tabs PageMaker creates when she imports the spreadsheet will override the style sheet. Simply select all the text and click once on the style name to eliminate this override.
- You can import spreadsheets from other applications as well. If you used hyphens to underline data in your spreadsheet, and you want to retain the underline, uncheck the option "Convert quotes" in the "Place document" dialog box.

If you want to do this:	Then follow these steps:	Shortcuts ▾ Notes ▾ Hints
17.38 Import an Excel spreadsheet as a PICT	▪ In Microsoft Excel 3.0 or above, open the spreadsheet document. ▪ Select the spreadsheet. ▪ Hold down the Shift key and choose "Copy picture" from the Edit menu. ▪ Select "As Shown when Printed" (unless you want to import it in color and/or with all the cells, grids, etc. included). ▪ Open PageMaker, or, if it is already open, activate your publication (choose PageMaker from the Applications menu, *or* click on the PageMaker window). ▪ In PageMaker, choose "Paste" from the Edit menu, *or* press Command V.	▪ This method imports an unlinked PICT into your PageMaker publication. ▪ If you need to make changes to the spreadsheet (or chart, or worksheet) you will have to return to Excel, make the changes, then copy the revised version into PageMaker once again, replacing the existing one. ▪ "As Shown on Screen" imports the entire screen representation of the spreadsheet as a color PICT; "As Shown when Printed" imports it as a grayscale PICT. ▪ If you would rather have a linked version of the spreadsheet that you can update automatically, see the next task.
17.39 Import an Excel spreadsheet as an OLE object *This is the Apply button icon you will see on the Control palette when you select an OLE graphic.*	▪ In Microsoft Excel, open the document that contains the spreadsheet. ▪ Select the spreadsheet. From the Edit menu choose "Copy" (Command C). ▪ Open PageMaker, or if it is already open, activate your publication. ▪ In PageMaker, from the Edit menu choose "Paste special" to OLE embed the object, *or* "Paste link" to link the object to its original file.	▪ An OLE-embedded object is self-contained and has all the information it needs to edit and print the object. It is not linked to the original file. ▪ An OLE-linked object is linked to the original file. To edit the file you must maintain the link. However, you can print the object without the original file. ▪ Read 11.103–11.132 to learn more about OLE. ▪ Publish and Subscribe is another method for importing linked files from Excel. See 11.79–11.102.

If you want to do this:

17.40   Import a text file from a PC
   (*except from Microsoft Word; see 17.41*)

Available filters:
- **DCA** (for programs that create Document Content Architecture, such as Samna Word, IBM DisplayWrite 4, WordStar 3000, Volkswriter 3)
  extension: .DCA

- **WordPerfect** 4.2
  extension: .WP

- **WordPerfect** 5.x
  extension: .WP5

- **XyWrite III (Plus)**
  extension: .XY3

- **RTF** (for programs that save files in Microsoft Rich Text Format)
  extension: .RTF

- **Smart ASCII** (for programs that save files in ASCII format from PC AT-compatible computers)
  extension: .TXT

Graphic formats PageMaker supports:
- **Windows Metafile (WMF)**
- **Windows Bitmap (BMP)**
- **Computer Graphics Metafiles (CGM)**
- **Dynamic Exchange format (DXF)**

Then follow these steps:

- Make sure you have installed the correct filter for the file you want to import (see list at left).
- The file you want to import must have the correct filename extension (see list).
- Use a communications bridge to transfer the document as a binary file, or use a utility such as Apple File Exchange to transfer the file.
- Import the file as you would any other (17.30; 17.31).

Shortcuts ▾ Notes ▾ Hints

- When you pop a PC disk in your Macintosh, PageMaker will let you know that she can't read it. By opening Apple File Exchange first (on any Mac with a SuperDrive), *then* popping in the disk, you can access the contents of the PC disk. If you are DOS-savvy you may already have a utility such as AccessPC or DOS Mounter which can create icons for the PC disk (and its folders and files) for even easier access to the files. There's also MacLink-Plus which translates files between platforms.
- The PC character sets are different than the Mac characters sets, so some of the special characters you inserted in the PC file may not duplicate properly. If you don't change them, they will be retained when you transfer the file back to the PC.
- You can find Apple File Exchange on your System 7 "Tidbits" disk.

If you want to do this:	Then follow these steps:	Shortcuts ▾ Notes ▾ Hints
17.41 Import a Microsoft Word text file from a PC *Import from:* MS-DOS: Microsoft Word 3.0, 4.0, 5.0 OS/2: Microsoft Word 5.0	▪ **If** you have saved the Word file as ASCII (text-only) or as ASCII with line breaks (both with the extension .TXT), or as RTF (.RTF): ☐ Transfer the file to your Macintosh. ☐ Import as usual (17.30; 17.31). ▪ **If** you have saved the DOS or OS/2 Word file in Normal format: ☐ Transfer the file to your Macintosh. ☐ Open the file in Word 4.0 or 5.0 for the Mac. Save it. Quit. ☐ Import as usual (17.30; 17.31).	▪ When you save DOS or OS/2 Word files as RTF or Normal, they retain almost all their formatting when you import them into PageMaker.
17.42 Import stories from a PageMaker 4 or 5 publication	▪ You must have the Story Importer filters installed to do this (see 17.28 to check). ▪ From the File menu choose "Place...." ▪ Find the name of the PageMaker publication and double-click on it. ▪ From this list select the stories you want to place/import. You can Shift-click to select more than one, or Shift-and-drag. ▪ Click OK. You will get a loaded text icon if you are in the layout view, **or** the stories will put themselves into a new story window if you are in the Story Editor. All the stories you select will be combined into one story with paragraph returns between them.	▪ It's called the Story Importer when you install it, and it's listed as the Story Importer in the Aldus Filters folder in your System folder. If you check out the filters through the Apple menu (17.28; 4.72), though, the filters are called: ☐ Ver. 2.0 PageMaker 5.0 (publication) ☐ Ver. 1.0 PageMaker 4.0 (publication) ▪ This is a brief synopsis of the procedure. You will find great detail in 4.63–4.85. ▪ The Story Importer dialog box appears twice when you are importing a story from 4.x. Just select what you want and click OK twice. If you want to import a 3.0 story and you don't have the 3.0 to 5.0 filter, convert it first to a 4.0 publication (17.46).

If you want to do this:

17.43 Export a PageMaker story as a text document

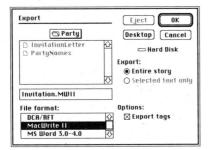

The "Export" dialog box. Notice the name of the file has an extension so I can remember under which file format I saved it.

Then follow these steps:

- You can export a story in any file format for which you have a filter (17.8–17.20).
- Click once on the **text tool.**
  - □ To export the entire story, click once anywhere in any text block of the story.
  - □ To export a selected portion of the story, select the portion.
- From the File menu choose "Export...."
- Name the file. You may want to add an extension to the name to indicate the file format under which it is saved.
- In the "File format" list, select the format in which you want to export this file.
- Under "Export," choose the appropriate option ("Selected text only" is available only if you selected a portion of text before you brought up this dialog box).
- If you have applied paragraph style tags from your style sheet, you may want to click the checkbox "Export tags." If the program you are exporting to supports style sheets, it will be able to read *most* of the formatting. Also, if you export the tags, PageMaker will be able to read them and re-apply the style formatting if the file is imported back into PageMaker.
- Make sure you are about to save into the proper folder so you will be able to find this file again (18.6–18.15); click OK.

Shortcuts ▾ Notes ▾ Hints

- When a file is exported to MacWrite II (my favorite word processor), all the em and en dashes (4.358) are turned into hyphens.
- If you export tags and the word processor cannot translate them, they will appear as text: `<Body text>`. If you place this file back into PageMaker, PageMaker will read those tags, eliminate them, and apply the style to the paragraph (see 8.75–8.76).
- You can use this method to export graphics, but, you are limited to PICT graphics placed inline. You must save the file in a Word or RTF file format and you can only export it to a program that can deal with inline graphics.

- Basically, PageMaker and the other program can read each other's common formatting. That is, PageMaker cannot import formatting she cannot do, such as vertical-line tabs or hidden text. The word processing program probably can't read the set widths or tracking values.

If you want to do this:	**Then follow these steps:**	**Shortcuts ▾ Notes ▾ Hints**
17.44 Drag-and-drop objects from one PageMaker publication to another	▪ From the File menu open the publications you want. ▪ From the Window menu choose "Tile" to view the open pubs on screen at the same time. ▪ Click on the window that contains the object you want to copy to make it active. With the **pointer tool,** select the text or graphic you want and simply drag it into the window of the other publication. Let go of the mouse when it is in the correct position. ▪ The window from which you dragged the object remains the active window.	▪ At first it will look as if the original object is moving, but when you let go of the mouse you will see that the original is right where it belongs and a copy of it is in the other publication. ▪ To copy text or graphics inline, you still use the pointer tool to select the object. But before you do, leave the insertion point flashing in the publication to which you are dragging the object (1.180). ▪ Objects dragged from one publication to another can bring colors, style sheets, and links with them.
17.45 Import text or graphics through the Library palette *(to open a Library palette for the first time, see 12.51)* 	▪ From the Window menu choose "Library palette." ▪ If the Library you want is different than the one that opens up, from the "Option" menu choose "Open" to locate the Library you want. ▪ Find the object in the Library. ▪ Press-and-drag it from the palette onto the publication page. The cursor will turn into a box with an "X" on it: ⊠. Let go of the mouse when the object is where you want it.	▪ Please see Section 12 for all the whole scoop on the Library palette. Basically, if the object copied to the palette was stored in the publication, you are now copying the complete copy into your current publication. If the original object was stored externally only, the copy you are importing now will be stored externally and will include all its link info. ▪ Objects dragged from the Library palette can bring colors, style sheets, and links with them.

If you want to do this:	**Then follow these steps:**	**Shortcuts ▾ Notes ▾ Hints**

Converting 4.0 Mac or PC to 5.0 Mac

17.46 Convert a Macintosh PageMaker 4.01, or 4.2 publication (both hereinafter referred to as 4.x) into a PageMaker 5.0 publication

- Open PageMaker 5 (the application itself).
- From the File menu choose "Open...."
- Find the name of the 4.x publication. Double-click on it. It will open as an "Untitled" publication.
- From the File menu choose "Save as...." Give the file a name.
  - □ If you name this file with exactly the same name as the 4.x publication and click OK, you will get an alert box asking if you want to replace the other file of the same name. If you click "Yes," the 4.x version of the publication will be eliminated.
  - □ If you name this file with a different name than the 4.x version (or save into a different folder), then you will have two copies, one in 5.0 and one still in 4.x.
- Click OK.
- It is advisable to recompose the text: Hold down the Option key and choose "Hyphenation..." from the Type menu. This process adjusts any odd letter or word spacing that occurred during conversion. (PageMaker will do this automatically if you don't. See note on the right.)
- Save again.

- The bigger your 4.x publication, the more room on your hard drive Page-Maker needs to convert it. It is best to have plenty of free RAM as well.
- Tracking is looser in PageMaker 5.0; this may cause a problem if you used "Tracking" in your original layout. Simple solution: copy the "Kern Tracks" from PageMaker 4.x, rather than fiddle with all the line breaks; see 17.48.
- Publication defaults (1.9–1.11) are retained in the conversion, but Book Lists (15.21) are not.
- Check your publication through carefully, especially regarding graphics and color. Watch for knockouts (PageMaker 5's default) where you wanted overprinting (PageMaker 4's default).
- You cannot open PageMaker 3.0 documents in PageMaker 5.0 unless you obtain a special converter from Aldus. Otherwise open a 3.0 document in 4.x, save it, and then open it in 5.0.
- PageMaker 5.0 checks for defects during the conversion process and recomposes the text in your converted publication every time you turn the page.

If you want to do this:	Then follow these steps:	Shortcuts ▾ Notes ▾ Hints
17.47 Transfer a PC PageMaker 5.0 publication to a Mac PageMaker 5.0 publication	• If the publication is PC PageMaker **4.0,** in either Windows or OS/2, you must first convert it to a PC PageMaker **5.0** publication (follow the Mac steps; 17.46). • You will get the best type specification results if you set a PostScript printer as the target printer for both the PC and the Mac. • You will get the best graphic results if you work with TIFF or EPS file formats. • Translate the file into a Macintosh-readable format using Apple File Exchange or the utility AccessPC if you have it, or use a communications bridge (such as TOPS, Daynafile II, PC MacBridge, or MacLinkPlus) to transfer the publication as a binary file. • Open PageMaker on your Mac. From the File menu select "Open," then locate and open the PC file. • If you are moving the publication to the Mac permanently, in the "Translation options" dialog box: ▫ Check "Translate filenames in links." PageMaker will look for the linked files on the Mac (in effect, this breaks the link on the PC side). ▫ Check the option "Translate Metafiles to PICTs" and "For printing and viewing." This affects the screen and print	• Once it has been transferred, you can open a PC PageMaker publication with the same version of Macintosh PageMaker. (you can't transfer a 4.2 PC publication and then open it in PageMaker 5.0 for the Mac). • The PC character sets (ANSI) are different than the Mac characters sets, so some of the special characters you inserted in the PC file may not duplicate properly. If you don't change those special characters, they will be retained if you transfer the file back to the PC. • Here's where the "Font matching results" dialog box comes in real handy. The "Spellings" list (1.252) will translate the fonts into their Mac counterparts whenever possible. If you accept PageMaker's substitutions for fonts that aren't available in the current system, the original specs are saved and will be returned to the publication if it is transferred back to the PC.

—continued

If you want to do this:

—continued

Then follow these steps:

representation of all Metafiles stored in the publication.
- If you are moving the publication to the Mac temporarily, in the "Translation options" dialog box:
  - ☐ Don't check "Translate filenames in links." PageMaker will not update the links nor produce high-resolution output, but the links will be automatically reestablished when the pub is opened on the Windows platform.
  - ☐ If you need to view the graphics, check the "Translate Metafiles to PICTs" and "For viewing" options. If you don't need to view them, leave the options unchecked.

Little ones who light our eyes, have you come to make us wise?
Showing us the child, asleep within us all, help us find our way back home...
—John Sikora

Shortcuts ▾ Notes ▾ Hints

- Low-res screen versions of scanned graphics and graphics that have their complete copy stored in the publication will be automatically transferred. All bitmapped graphic formats can be transferred and printed across platforms, and both platforms support TIFF and EPS files.
- Linked graphics and text files are not automatically converted; you must transfer them separately and relink them (11.65). If you check the option "Translate filenames in links," graphics that were placed should be easy to relink.
- Photo CD images do not transfer and will need to be placed separately and relinked.
- OLE-embedded objects are automatically transferred, but OLE-linked files must be transferred manually. However, you only need to relink the file if you want to edit the object. In that case the Mac equivalent source program must be available.
- Tables created in the Table Editor on the Windows platform are Metafiles that will convert as PICTs.
- Items grouped using the "PS Group it" Addition should be ungrouped before transferring the file. Regroup them on the Mac platform.

If you want to do this:

17.48 Use the tracking information from a previous version of PageMaker

Kern Tracks

The PageMaker 4.2 version of tracking values. Simply rename the file to use it as the tracking file in PageMaker 5.0.

Tracking Values

The PageMaker 5.0 version of tracking values.

Then follow these steps:

- Find the "Kern Tracks" file from PageMaker 4.0 or 4.2. If you have a back-up file of the Aldus folder from *before* you installed PageMaker 5.0, you will find it there; if not, look on your original 4.0 or 4.2 program disks.
- Rename the file "Tracking Values."
- To change the tracking values on an application level, place the file in the Aldus folder in your System folder, replacing the 5.0 file;
- **Or,** to change the values for a publication, place the "Tracking Values" file in the folder with your publication. If the publication is open, close and reopen it to give PageMaker a chance to see the new tracking file (or do a "Save as" to that folder).

Shortcuts ▾ Notes ▾ Hints

- Use this trick if you are attempting to maintain the original line breaks in imported stories or publications converted from 4.x. (Without this procedure, revising this book would have been an even harder job. Whew.)
- In version 5.0 tracking is looser so you have more control. Before you change the tracking values on an application level, take the 5.0 "Tracking Values" file and stash it somewhere accessible in case you want to upgrade to it. Of course, you can always retrieve it from the original program disk, too. It is compressed on Disk 3. Double-click on it to run the Aldus Installer and save it to your Aldus folder.

The brain is a wonderful organ; it starts working the moment you get up in the morning and does not stop until you get to the office.
Robert Frost

18 ▾ SAVE and REVERT

Read this, even if you think you know everything about Saving on the Macintosh!

18.1   Saving, of course, is the process of taking the pages of your publication out of their temporary holding place in RAM and storing them more permanently on the disk (hard or floppy). It is good practice to "Save as..." your publication to a disk immediately upon beginning, then Save the changes every few minutes—*literally, every few minutes*—to avoid losing any data in the event of a catastrophe of any considerable dimension.

Unlike most software applications, Page-Maker has this wonderful system built into itself that is very forgiving and advantageous in the event of a catastrophe. You see, Page-Maker actually saves *two* versions of each publication. One version is the regular one you create when you "Save as...," the version that is stored on your disk and updated each time you press Command S or choose "Save" from the File menu. It is this version that PageMaker will return to when you choose "Revert" from the File menu (18.30).

18.2   But PageMaker also creates a "mini-save" file. Every time you turn a page, insert a page, delete a page, change the page setup, click the icon of the page you are currently on, switch between layout view and story view, paste, or print, PageMaker updates the mini-save. It is this version that PageMaker will return to *when recovering from a power loss or malfunction!* Even if you never saved your document in the first place, even if it is still Untitled when the power goes out, you can usually retrieve it (18.33). You can also choose to Revert to this mini-version at any time (18.31).

18.3   Each version is a complete publica-tion, which is one reason PageMaker files are so large. Even if you delete text, graphics, or pages, the files grow larger! But, thought-fully, along with this problem of large files, there is a solution. Every time you use "Save as...," the current *mini-version* is deleted (18.29). **This significantly reduces the size of the publication—anywhere from 20 to 60 percent!** It's too wonderful.

18.4   The mini-version instantly creates itself again, as soon as you touch the page. **To keep the file small, to prevent Mac from crashing, and to prevent the file from getting so large that PageMaker can't even open it (which I have seen happen to two-page files), "Save as..." every half hour or so (18.29). Really.**

18.5   In the "Preferences" dialog box you can choose to make every "Save" a "Save as":

```
┌─ Save option ────┐
│  ○ Faster        │
│  ◉ Smaller       │
└──────────────────┘
```

If you click the **Faster** button, everything will function just as it always has. You will grow mini-versions and you can mini-revert back to them. When you press Command S, PageMaker will save the latest changes.

If you click the **Smaller** button, Page-Maker will automatically compress the file (by deleting the mini-version) every time you do a regular Save (from the File menu, *or* by pressing Command S). This takes longer than the regular, faster save.

18.6 **The "Save as..." dialog box** *(from the File menu)*

18.7 *Always look here! This* **label** *tells you exactly which folder you will be saving into. Notice the open folder icon? If you were not in a folder, this icon would be a disk.*

18.8 *If there is a folder icon showing in this* **label**, *pressing on the name will drop down a* **menu** *with a* **list** *of all the folders and the name of the disk they are on (the "hierarchy," as shown to the right). Slide down the menu to go into another folder or back to the face of the disk itself (18.18).*

The menu, as mentioned in 18.7, and 18.8.

18.9 *This is the* **list box,** *showing you the folders and documents that are in the folder or on the disk that is named in the* **label** *(18.7; 18.8).*

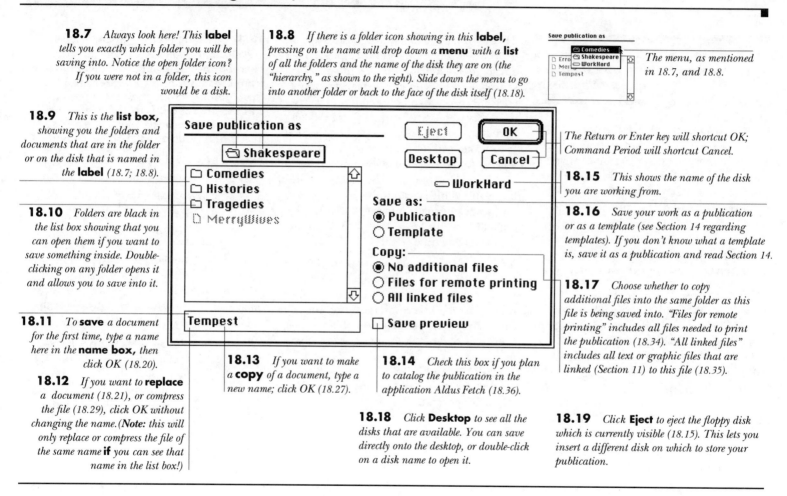

The Return or Enter key will shortcut OK; Command Period will shortcut Cancel.

18.15 *This shows the name of the disk you are working from.*

18.10 *Folders are black in the list box showing that you can open them if you want to save something inside. Double-clicking on any folder opens it and allows you to save into it.*

18.16 *Save your work as a publication or as a template (see Section 14 regarding templates). If you don't know what a template is, save it as a publication and read Section 14.*

18.17 *Choose whether to copy additional files into the same folder as this file is being saved into. "Files for remote printing" includes all files needed to print the publication (18.34). "All linked files" includes all text or graphic files that are linked (Section 11) to this file (18.35).*

18.11 *To* **save** *a document for the first time, type a name here in the* **name box,** *then click OK (18.20).*

18.12 *If you want to* **replace** *a document (18.21), or compress the file (18.29), click OK without changing the name.(**Note:** this will only replace or compress the file of the same name* **if** *you can see that name in the list box!)*

18.13 *If you want to make a* **copy** *of a document, type a new name; click OK (18.27).*

18.14 *Check this box if you plan to catalog the publication in the application Aldus Fetch (18.36).*

18.18 *Click* **Desktop** *to see all the disks that are available. You can save directly onto the desktop, or double-click on a disk name to open it.*

18.19 *Click* **Eject** *to eject the floppy disk which is currently visible (18.15). This lets you insert a different disk on which to store your publication.*

If you want to do this:	**Then follow these steps:**	**Shortcuts ▾ Notes ▾ Hints**
18.20 Save a **publication** Publication Icon	■ From the File menu choose "Save as...." ■ You *must* name the publication; just type a descriptive name (no colons allowed). ■ Check to make sure the button next to "Publication" is checked. ■ Click OK, or press Return; your publication will now show its name in the title bar, and an icon will be on your disk when you quit. ■ Be sure to update changes every few minutes (press Command S) and compress the file regularly (18.29).	■ Be sure you are saving your document onto the right disk and into the right folder! If you don't get into that habit, documents end up all over the place and some may never be found again. If it's not clear to you how to save something into the folder you want, studying the previous page may help. ■ If you haven't named the file, choosing "Save" *or* pressing Command S will give you the same dialog box as "Save as...."
18.21 Save changes to the **publication** *(see also 18.5)*	■ From the File menu choose "Save," *or* press Command S. ■ Once you've named your publication, you do not need to go back to "Save as..." again, unless you want to make other versions based on this publication (18.26–18.27) or unless you want to compress the file (18.29).	■ You won't see much happen: the File menu will flash, and you may see the watch cursor. But any changes you created since the last save have been saved onto the original version. *Yes, this does replace the original.* If you want to make copies *without* affecting an original, see 18.26–18.27.
18.22 Save changes to **all the open publications**	■ Hold down the Option key; ■ From the File menu choose "Save all."	■ "Save" will only change to "Save all" if more than one publication is open. ■ Sorry, no keyboard shortcut for this, though the menu gives you hope.

If you want to do this:	Then follow these steps:	Shortcuts ▾ Notes ▾ Hints
18.23 Save a **template** Template Icon	■ From the File menu choose "Save as...." ■ You *must* name the template; just type a descriptive name (no colons allowed). ■ Click the button next to "Template." ■ Click OK; your template will now have its name showing in the title bar, and a white icon will be on your disk when you quit.	■ Read all about templates in Section 14. ■ If you ever want to open the original template again, you must go through the "Open..." dialog box inside PageMaker (18.25).
18.24 Save changes to the **template** *before* it has ever been closed	■ Once the template has been given a name, you do not need to go back to "Save as..." again, unless you want to make other versions based on this template (18.13) or unless you want to compress the file (18.29). ■ From the File menu choose "Save" *or* press Command S.	■ You won't see much happen: the File menu will flash, and you may see the watch cursor. But any changes you've created since the last save have been saved onto the original template. *Yes, this does replace the original.* If you want to make copies *without* affecting an original, see 18.26–18.27.
18.25 Open the original **template** again in order to create and save changes	You must open the *original* template in order to make changes in it. Once the template has been closed there is only one way to open the original again: ■ Open PageMaker. ■ From the File menu choose "Open...." ■ Find the name of the template to open; click **once** on its name. ■ "Copy" is already selected—click on "Original"; click OK.	■ The trick here is not to shortcut by double-clicking. Double-clicking on the template icon at the Desktop (Finder) will open a *copy*. Double-clicking in the "Open..." dialog box will open a *copy*. You must use this OK method from inside PageMaker. ■ Be sure to read Section 14 on Templates.

If you want to do this:	Then follow these steps:	Shortcuts • Notes • Hints
18.26 Save a copy of the **publication** or **template,** *with the same name,* into a different folder or onto a different disk	▪ From the File menu choose "Save as...." ▪ The current name of the publication is highlighted in the name box. Navigate to the other disk and/or folder. Click Drive to find the other disks, and double-click on folders, if necessary, to open them. ▪ When you see the name of the disk you want (18.15) and the name of your folder in the label (18.7; 18.8), click OK.	▪ This process leaves the original publication intact, with its icon right where you left it last time you saved. ▪ After you click OK you will see the same name in the title bar—but this is now a *different* publication with its own icon! ▪ Any changes you make in this publication will have absolutely no effect on the one you started with.
18.27 Save a copy (a separate version) of the **publication** or **template,** *with a different name,* into any folder or onto any disk	▪ From the File menu choose "Save as...." ▪ The current name of the publication is highlighted. To prevent your new copy from replacing that original file, you must rename it. Typing any character after the current name, such as a period or a number *or even a blank space,* will effectively change the name.	▪ This process leaves the original publication intact, with its icon right where you left it last time you saved. ▪ After you click OK you will see the new name in the title bar—this is now a *different* publication with its own icon! ▪ Any changes you make in this publication will have absolutely no effect on the version you started with.
18.28 Reduce the size of a publication each time you save it ┌─ Save option ─────┐ ○ **Faster** ◉ **Smaller** └───────────────────┘	▪ From the File menu choose "Preferences...." ▪ Under "Save option," click the radio button next to "Smaller." ▪ In your publication choose "Save" from the File menu, or press Command S.	▪ Each time you "Save," PageMaker will automatically compress the file by deleting all the mini-saves and saving only the current information. This takes longer than a regular save, and is actually the equivalent of "Save as..." but you skip the "Save publication as" dialog box.

If you want to do this:	Then follow these steps:	Shortcuts ▾ Notes ▾ Hints

18.29 Reduce the size of a PageMaker publication (*see also 18.5; 18.28*)

- While the publication is open on the screen, from the File menu choose "Save as...."
- Make sure you see the name of the current document in the list box! (It will be gray. If you don't see the name, change disks or folders until you see it listed.)
- The name of the current document should be in the name box. If for some reason it isn't (like you accidentally hit the spacebar), type the *exact* name again.
- Click OK; you will get an alert box asking if you want to *replace* the item with the same name; **click Replace.**
- If you did not get the alert box, then you created a separate (and reduced) version because there was no file of that same name in the list box. When you get back to your Desktop, you can replace the larger publication with the smaller one.

- If you don't remember where the original is stored, use Find File (1.334).
- If the disk is already very full, PageMaker cannot "Save as...," even though doing so would reduce the file size (she has to have room to create another one, then replace the first one). Switch drives and save to another disk; later back at your Desktop, replace the large one with the smaller version. It's a good idea to label the reduced version (by renaming the second, saved-as one) so you don't get the two files mixed up.
- If the two files have the same name and you don't remember which is the larger, Get Info will give you the file size: at the Desktop, click once on the file icon; from the File menu, choose "Get Info." Or change the window views to "By size."

18.30 Revert to the last saved version

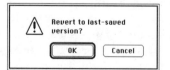

- From the File menu choose "Revert." You will get an alert box to verify your decision ("Revert" will be gray if you have just saved).
- Click OK.

- This reverts to the last time you saved the publication, either with "Save" or with "Save as...." Any changes made since that point will not be recorded: another good reason to save often.
- It is not possible to revert just a portion of the publication—it's all or nothing.
- This cannot be undone!

If you want to do this:

Then follow these steps:

Shortcuts ▾ Notes ▾ Hints

18.31 Revert to the last mini-save version

- Hold down the Shift key (you *must* press the Shift key *before* you go up to the File menu).
- From the File menu choose "Revert" while the Shift key is still held down. You will get an alert box to verify your decision.
  □ If the message doesn't say "mini-save" then you probably weren't holding down the Shift key before you went to the menu. Cancel and try again.
  □ If the message still doesn't say "mini-save" then perhaps you have not done anything to update the mini-version, such as turn a page, delete a page, paste, etc.; see the note on the right.
- In the alert box, click OK.

- This will revert to the last time you clicked on a page icon, turned a page, inserted or deleted a page, switched between layout view and Story Editor, changed the page setup, pasted, or printed.
- This is great, for several reasons. One is that if there was a power failure or system crash and you haven't saved for a while, you could bring back your document to the mini-save point (18.33). Another is that sometimes you want to revert, but not all the way back to the last time you saved. You could take advantage of the mini-save consciously, to develop various layout ideas along the way until you're ready for the Big One.

18.32 Close the publication or quit PageMaker *without* saving changes

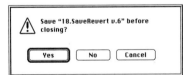

- To **Close,** simply click in the close box in the upper left of the publication window, *or* choose "Close" from the File menu.
- To **Quit,** from the File menu choose "Quit," *or* press Command Q.
- Either way, if you did not save your latest changes (even if you just clicked on another page icon or changed views) PageMaker will display a save reminder box and offer you a chance to do so.
- Just click your choice. "Cancel" will take you back to your publication.

- Remember, Close just closes the current open publication. If you press the Option key before you press on the File menu you can choose "Close all," to close all the open publications at once. PageMaker will display the save reminder box for each file. If you click Cancel in a reminder box, PageMaker will stop closing files and take you to the file you canceled closing.
- Quit will close all the open files, plus take you back to your Desktop. You will see a save reminder box for each unsaved file.

If you want to do this:

18.33 Open a publication that was closed due to a power failure or system malfunction
(this will not work on a damaged disk)

Then follow these steps:

If you did not have a chance to save the publication before the failure:
- Restart the computer.
- In the Trash you will see a "Rescued items from (your disk name here)" folder. It should contain two files: one named ALDTMP00; one named ALDTMP01.
- Drag ALDTMP01 out of the Trash. Put it on the Desktop, or on your drive.
- Double-click on ALDTMP01; this will start PageMaker and place the publication on the screen in the last *mini-saved* version.

If you did save the publication before the failure:
- In the folder you were working from you will find your document. Double-click; it will open to the last *mini-saved* version.
- Save it immediately. In fact, do a "Save as..." just to be safe.

Shortcuts ▾ Notes ▾ Hints

- Can you believe this? Even if the document was Untitled because you never even got to "Save as...," you can salvage up until you last clicked a page icon, deleted or added pages, changed the page setup, printed, or pasted. What a thoughtful feature.
- Of course, you can also start PageMaker and then open the ALDTMP01 file from the File menu (you do have to drag it out of the Trash before you can open it, though).
- After you've re-opened it, you can also choose to "Revert" to the last real save.

The greatest discovery of my generation is that a human being can alter his life by altering his attitude.
—William James

If you want to do this:

Then follow these steps:

Shortcuts ▾ Notes ▾ Hints

18.34 Copy files for remote printing when saving a PageMaker file

- From the File menu, choose "Save as...."
- Click the radio button next to "Files for remote printing."
- Name the PageMaker file, if necessary.
- Click OK.

- PageMaker must have access to any file (such as a graphic file) that is not stored in the publication; otherwise PageMaker cannot print it properly. When you click this radio button, PageMaker will copy into the same folder *only* those linked files that are *not* stored in the publication (11.16–11.26), including a file called "Tracking Values" which some service bureaus may need. See 19.150–19.161 for details on using a service bureau.

18.35 Copy linked documents when saving a PageMaker file

- From the File menu, choose "Save as...."
- If there are stories or graphics in the publication that are linked to the original stories or graphics outside of PageMaker (see Section 11 on Linking Text and Graphics), then the option "All linked files" will be available. Click on the radio button next to it.
- Name the file, if necessary. Click OK.

- If you choose to copy linked files, then PageMaker will find the originals to all the internally and externally linked text and graphics in your publication and put copies of them into the folder that is storing this PageMaker publication.
- The links will still be connected to the original linked file, not to the one you copied into this folder. PageMaker will look for the original files to print, but will settle for the ones stored in the same folder as the publication.
- This is a handy technique for gathering up all the files in one place, as you may need to do to take the publication to a service bureau (19.150–19.161) or to give to a client.

If you want to do this:

18.36 Save a screen version of the first page of your publication to catalog it in the application Aldus Fetch

Check this box.

Then follow these steps:

- From the File menu, choose "Save as...."
- Check the box next to "Save preview."
- Save your publication in the usual manner: name it, and select the appropriate button under "Copy as."
- Click OK.

Shortcuts ▾ Notes ▾ Hints

- Aldus Fetch is an application for storing and retrieving items. It doesn't store the original item, but a thumbnail image of it, and a pointer to the source file. Fetch provides a visual database of the catalogued items and can search files to find the item you want.

L E T T E R S

are symbols

which turn matter

into spirit.

Alphonse de Lamartine

Which treats of Matters
of a very different Kind
from those in the preceding Chapters.

19 ▾ PRINTING

19.1 Minimums and maximums:

Item	Minimum	Maximum
Page size	Depends on printer	
Print area	Depends on printer	
Number of publication pages to print	Limited only by the amount of memory in the printer	
Number of copies	1	32,000
Manual tile overlap	0 pts. 0 inches (.1 increments)	360 pts. 30 inches
Thumbnails per page	1 (increments of 1 or 2)	1,000
Scaling	5% (.1 increments)	1600%

19.2 When you get right down to it, printing is the proof of the pudding. No matter how stunning your publication, you have to print it to be able to use it. Some of the decisions you make about your publication depend on the printer you will be using for your final output, so it is a good idea to be familiar with the printing aspects of PageMaker before you begin creating.

19.3 Even though many of us will always "go to lino" with many of our publications, many more of us will rely upon the laser printer to print much of what we do. And no matter what, we still rely on desktop printers to proof our publications.

19.4 Laser printers use an immense amount of power, kind of like refrigerators. It's recommended that you let a laser printer have its own power source rather than plug it into an outlet strip. If energy conservation or electric bills concern you, don't keep a laser printer on unnecessarily and utilize any energy saving features available for your model. If you don't want to waste paper and toner on the startup page that most laser printers automatically spit out when you start them up, use a LaserWriter utility program to turn it off.

Printers 728
PPDs 729
LaserWriter 8 729
Print spoolers 729
Setting up a PostScript printer 730
Fonts
    Bitmapped and outline 731
    Screen and printer 731
    Resident and downloadable 732
    TrueType 732
Downloading the downloadables 733
"Print" dialog box
    "Document" 734
    "Paper" 738
    "Options" 742
    "Color" 746
Printing to a non-PostScript printer 749
Tasks 750
Making a PostScript file (printing to disk) 758
    Tasks 760
Using a service bureau 762
Troubleshooting 765
Additions for Printing 767
    "Update PPD" 768
    "Display pub info" 770
    "Printer styles" 772
    "Build booklet" 779

Printers: Laser printers, QuickDraw printers, and PostScript imagesetters

19.5 Printers can be divided into three categories, each providing a different level of quality: PostScript laser printers, QuickDraw printers, and PostScript imagesetters.

19.6 PostScript laser printers, such as the Apple LaserWriter, Apple LaserWriter Pro, or HP LaserJet 4 series, read **PostScript,** a page-description language. The visual images you see on the screen are sent to the printer in the PostScript language. The printer interprets the information and creates the images on "plain paper" in resolutions of 300 to 600 dots per inch. This resolution is perfectly adequate for many publications, especially if you use smooth (not glossy) paper that has been specially formulated for laser printers. To prevent text from looking heavy and to keep the small areas (called "counters," such as inside the letter *e*) from filling in, keep the toner level down to the minimum necessary for good blacks.

19.7 QuickDraw printers, such as the Apple StyleWriter, some of the Apple LaserWriter Select series (not the 360), or the HP DeskWriter, use the Mac's own **QuickDraw** drawing language to create the printed pages. Their resolution is generally between 72 and 360 dots per inch. The different printers can vary widely in what they require from a font in order to print text; you need to check your printer documentation.

19.8 Because QuickDraw printers cannot read PostScript, they cannot print EPS graphics very well, if at all (Encapsulated PostScript graphics; 10.39–10.46). They can usually print the PICT screen representation of an EPS image, though (10.39–10.41). It is up to you to decide whether the image quality of this version is satisfactory for your publication.

19.9 PostScript imagesetters, such as the Linotronic 330, AGFA ProSet 9600, or Varityper 4300P, read PostScript and print at resolutions of between 1000 and 2540 dots per inch. They use resin-coated paper, as traditional typesetters do, as opposed to the "plain paper" that is used by personal laser printers. Besides providing the best possible quality for text and graphics, output on resin-coated paper is much more durable if you are going to paste-up with rubber cement or wax.

19.10 Imagesetters are found in **service bureaus.** You can take your disk to a service bureau, leave it there for a few hours or overnight, and then return later and pick up your finished publication pages. Or you can send your file over a modem. Please see 19.150–19.161 for tips on how to prepare your publication for a service bureau.

EPS graphic printed on an Apple LaserWriter, 300 dpi.

EPS graphic printed on an HP DeskWriter, 300 dpi.

EPS graphic printed on a Linotronic, 1270 dpi.

Illustrations by Tuan Pham

PPDs LaserWriter Pro 630

19.11 A PPD is a **PostScript Printer Description** file. Each printer must have its own PPD, which looks (to mortals) like a text document. It is. It contains information about the printer that PageMaker reads before it sends the publication over to be printed. This information tells PageMaker such things as the name of the printer model, the paper sizes that particular printer can handle, the image area for each paper size, the paper trays that are available, the fonts that are resident (19.34) in the printer, and any other special features or options.

19.12 You can only print to printers whose PPDs are in the Printer Descriptions folder* (in the Extensions folder, in the System folder). The PPD folder was created when you installed PageMaker. If you need to add a PPD to the folder, see 19.137. Be sure to add the PPD for the printer your service bureau uses. Without the PPD, you cannot choose the printer for "Type" in the "Print" dialog box and thus you will not be able print to disk using its specifications (19.138–19.148).

If there is no PPD for your printer, try using the "General" PPD. See the Addition "Update PPD" to enhance the performance of your printer (19.171).

LaserWriter 8

19.13 LaserWriter 8 is the new PostScript printer driver developed by Apple and Adobe. (*If you received the driver from Adobe it's called PS Printer 8.*) PageMaker is one of the first software developers to take full advantage of this new, faster driver. LaserWriter 8 replaces the need for the Aldus driver and its companion file, AldusPrep, that were used with previous versions of PageMaker.

19.14 The LaserWriter 8 printer driver was automatically installed during the PageMaker installation. All you need to do is set it up to match your printer. See 19.20–19.25. Be sure you are running version 8.01 or later to avoid the buggy 8.0 version that originally shipped. If you bought an early release of PageMaker 5, you can get a LaserWriter upgrade through Apple, an authorized Apple dealer, Aldus, or on-line services. Apple System disks ship with the most recent version of LaserWriter 8.

19.15 Although most other applications will print just fine using the LaserWriter 8 driver, you may want to keep a previous version of LaserWriter in your Extensions folder to use with older applications and fonts.

Print spoolers

19.16 A **print spooler** is a software program that allows you to work on the screen while the job is printing.

19.17 Normally, when you tell PageMaker to print, the Mac sends the information to the printer at a fairly rapid rate, but the printer processes the information at a much slower rate than it is received thus tying up your screen while it figures out how to produce the page. If you use a spooler, the information goes to the spooler which takes care of funneling the information to the printer at the printer's slower speed, and you get your screen back much faster.

19.18 LaserWriter 8 also spools information to the printer, but it does so in the *foreground,* tying up your computer as it does its thing. If you turn on "Background Printing" (Apple's computer-resident spooler found in the Chooser, 19.127, and, really, a better choice than a third-party spooler), LaserWriter 8 sends the information to the "Print Monitor" which sends the info to the printer in the *background* and you get your screen back sooner.

19.19 PageMaker also works well with network spoolers. Select the spooler name in the Chooser, instead of your printer's name.

Setting up a PostScript printer

19.20 To print to a PostScript printer, you must establish a link between your printer and PageMaker via the LaserWriter 8 PostScript printer driver.

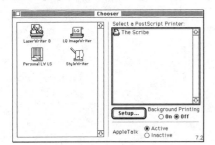

19.21 In the "Chooser" dialog box, click on the LaserWriter 8 icon. Only those printer drivers whose icons are in the Extensions folder in your System folder (19.12) will appear here. Then, in the right hand box, click on your printer's name (turn on your printer first). Next click the "Setup…" button.

19.22 Click "Auto Setup" to open the link between your printer and LaserWriter 8. The PPD for your printer is automatically selected. In most cases this is all you need to do. Simply click OK when the process is done and close the "Chooser."

19.23 If you want to control which PPD file is selected, click "More Choices," then click "Select PPD…" instead of "Auto Setup." In the Printer Descriptions folder (19.12), choose the PPD file* with the features that most closely match those of your printer and click "Select." Click OK and close the "Chooser," or continue the setup.

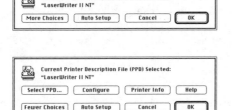

The "Setup" dialog box available through the "Chooser." Click "More Choices" to view the box on the bottom, click "Fewer Choices" to view the top box.

19.24 Click the "Printer Info" button to get the all the lowdown about your printer or any other PPDs you installed. If there is more than one PPD file available for your printer, you can use the PostScript version number of your printer as a guide to help decide which PPD file to choose.

19.25 The setup process, whether it is done automatically with "Auto Setup" or manually with "Select PPD…" tells Page-Maker the printer is a PostScript printer. You can still print from PageMaker without going through one of these processes, but there will be no PPD (PostScript information) available and the "Print" dialog box will only offer non-PostScript printer options (19.122–19.126). Be sure the LaserWriter icon is displayed in front of your printer's name in the "Chooser."

If a PPD file is not available for your printer, do whatever it takes to get one: write to the manufacturer or hunt on-line for one. When printing to a PPD other than the one for your printer, especially the "General" PPD, PageMaker may be unable to take full advantage of all your printer's features.

Fonts: Bitmapped and outline; screen and printer; resident and downloadable

19.26 The subject of fonts (or typefaces) on the Mac can be as confusing to people with a background in typography as it is to people with no type background. On these few pages is a *brief* synopsis of the font technology that you really need to know to work effectively in PageMaker. If you want to go beyond the basics, read *How to Boss Your Fonts Around.* Another excellent source of in-depth information is *The Macintosh Font Book* by Erfert Fenton.

19.27 There are three kinds of type most commonly used: **bitmapped**, **outline,** and **TrueType.**

19.28 Bitmapped fonts are created using the QuickDraw display language. They are built out of the little dots on the screen, and are designed to take advantage of the 72-dot-per-inch screen resolution. Bitmapped fonts are always *(well, there are a couple of rare exceptions)* named for a city: Geneva, New York, Monaco, Athens, Cairo, etc., are all bitmapped fonts. **Never use a font with a city name** unless you are printing to a QuickDraw printer. Laser printers and image-setters cannot read bitmapped fonts. Service bureaus will not be happy if you provide them with files that include bitmapped fonts.

19.29 Outline fonts, often called Post-Script fonts, have been designed with mathematical formulas written in the PostScript language, rather than with little square dots. Reading the formula, any PostScript printer can create the fonts and scale them to any size and any resolution within reason. PostScript fonts print beautifully, and if you use Adobe Type Manager (ATM) they will look good on your screen too. Outline fonts are never *(well, there are a couple of rare exceptions)* named for a city. Avant Garde, Bookman, Helvetica, Times, etc., are all outline fonts.

19.30 Outline fonts are actually made up of two parts. One part is a **screen font** that is actually *(now, don't get confused!)* a *bitmapped* version of the outline font. The *computer* uses the screen font to display the type on the screen (see 19.31). The other part of an outline font is the **printer font,** which is the technical data that the *PostScript printer* uses to print the typeface on the page (see 19.32).

Futura Book 10   FuturBoo

B Futura Bold 10   FuturBol

Every PostScript screen font has a corresponding printer font.

19.31 The **screen font** is what you see on the screen; it's the bitmapped portion of the outline font that the *computer* reads. Screen fonts are bitmapped because they must be represented with the dots on the screen. Even though they are just a visual representation of the outline font that will actually print on your page, you must have the bitmapped screen font installed to use the outline font for printing.

Screen fonts are often stored in little suitcases with the letter A on them (see below). You can double click on the suitcase to open it, then double-click on a screen font to view a sample of the font.

Futura family

*A **bitmapped** font (19.28) is stored in a "suitcase." Every **outline** font (19.30) has a corresponding bitmapped, or screen font, also stored in a suitcase. Some people interchange the terms bitmapped and screen fonts. It's a tricky distinction.*

Double-clicking on the screen font icon displays a sample of the font.

—continued

Fonts —*continued*

19.32 The **printer font** is the portion of the outline font that the *PostScript printer* reads in order to print the type on the page. Printer fonts have their own icons, and each font vendor's icon looks different:

Goudy

TypoUpr

ModulSer

| Printer font: | | | |
| Vendor: | *Adobe* | *Bitstream* | *Emigre* |

19.33 Fonts must be stored directly in the System folder (or the Extensions folder within the System folder) in System 7.0x, and in the Fonts folder in the System folder in System 7.1. When you choose to print, PageMaker gets the outline information and **downloads** it into the printer so the printer knows how to create the font.

19.34 You might notice, though, that some fonts don't ever get downloaded. Most laser printers have *read-only memory* (ROM) that has certain fonts **resident** in it. The outline information for those fonts is stored permanently in a chip in the printer so the printer can use them whenever it likes. These fonts are often **resident:** Avant Garde, Bookman, Helvetica, New Century Schoolbook, Palatino, Times, Symbol, Courier, Zapf Chancery, and Zapf Dingbats. Most other outline fonts are termed **downloadable,** and you must buy them from a font vendor.

19.35 If you have a lot of downloadable fonts, your font menu becomes long and unwieldly. Plus there is a limit to the number of fonts the System will allow. If you get to that point, you really must invest in a font handler utility, such as Suitcase II™ (Fifth Generation Software) or Master Juggler™ (AlSoft, Inc.). These utilities allow you to organize and consolidate your font menu by families. They also resolve font conflicts—if you have a lot of fonts, you run the considerable risk of the fonts having mistaken identity crises: Korinna thinks it is Lubalin Graph, etc.

Futura family

FuturBoo

FuturLig

FuturBol

FuturBooObl

FuturLigObl

FuturBolObl

With a font utility, you can create a folder for every font family in which to store the suitcase of screen fonts and all their respective printer fonts.

TrueType

19.36 On the other hand, **TrueType fonts,** Apple's font technology, look smooth on the screen at all sizes and print without needing any printer font icons at all. All you need is a single icon stored wherever you store all your other fonts. TrueType icons have three letter A's on them.

Times

Palatino

Each TrueType font has only one part.

19.37 TrueType fonts print clearly and legibly on any printer, and if you print to a non-PostScript printer you may really love them. However, imagesetters, remember, are PostScript, and most service bureaus will only want to see PostScript fonts.

19.38 You can use both TrueType and PostScript fonts, but if you do, read one of the recommended font books (19.26)! Especially, never, *ever*, mix PostScript and TrueType fonts of the same name together. For instance, do not have both TrueType Helvetica *and* PostScript Helvetica installed in your System.

Downloading the downloadables

19.39 If you never use any other fonts except the standard residents (19.34), you needn't bother reading this page, except for this note: if you use only the resident fonts, your work will scream THIS WAS DONE ON A MACINTOSH! That's perfectly okay; many, many people need never go beyond Times and Helvetica. However, if you want to give your work a professional, creative appearance, you really should invest in downloadable fonts. You also should read *The Mac is not a typewriter* or your work will still scream "Mac!"

19.40 You know what downloadable fonts are (19.33–19.39). Now you need to know how PageMaker and the printer deal with them so you can work most efficiently. Downloadable fonts have to be downloaded into the printer's *random-access memory* (RAM). Resident fonts, remember, are stored in the printer's ROM, which is *permanent* (19.34). RAM is a *temporary* storage place that is emptied whenever you turn off the power.

19.41 Font downloading is only necessary when you print to a PostScript printer (19.6; 19.9). Other printers just print the bitmapped screen fonts or their own specially-developed printer fonts. For those printers, the Adobe Type Manager program (ATM, from Adobe, Inc.) can significantly improve the look of the printed pages as well as how the type looks on the screen.

19.42 Font downloading can be handled **automatically,** which is probably what has been happening all this time. If your fonts are properly installed in your System folder, when you choose to print to a PostScript printer, PageMaker goes into the System folder, gets the printer font, and downloads it into the printer's memory. If the memory gets full because you used a lot of fonts in your publication, PageMaker has to remove a font (flush it from memory) to make room for the new one.

19.43 Automatic downloading works quite well, particularly if your printer has two or three megabytes of RAM available and your publication doesn't use more than three or four fonts. *Remember,* Goudy is one font, Goudy Italic is another font, Goudy Bold is another font, etc. etc. etc. However, there are times when you want to speed up the process, and not wait around for fonts to be downloaded.

19.44 When you buy downloadable fonts, the font vendor always sends you a *font downloader utility.* This is what the Adobe downloader looks like:

Font Downloader

19.45 You can use this utility to **manually download** the fonts in your publication. Although it appears complicated, it is really an easy process. Just double-click on the downloader and it will walk you through the process. It's a bit tricky to get PageMaker to acknowledge that the fonts are there in RAM—but it is possible; see 19.132 and 21.34.

19.46 There is one **permanent** way of downloading fonts to your printer, and that is buying a PostScript printer that allows you to connect a hard disk that holds all your downloadable fonts (printers such as the Apple LaserWriter Pro, the NewGen Systems, or any imagesetter). Once on that special hard disk, all your fonts will act just like resident fonts (19.34). Remember to run the "Update PPD" Addition (19.171–19.178) to create a PPD "Include" file that tells PageMaker the fonts are there.

19.47 "Document" in the "Print..." dialog box *(from the File menu, choose "Print...," or press Command P)*

19.48 If a Post-Script printer has been selected in "Chooser" (19.21), this is the dialog box you will see when you choose "Print..." from the File menu.

19.49 If a Quick-Draw printer (19.7) has been selected in "Chooser" or if you hold down the Option key when you choose "Print...," you will get a different series of dialog boxes; see page 749.

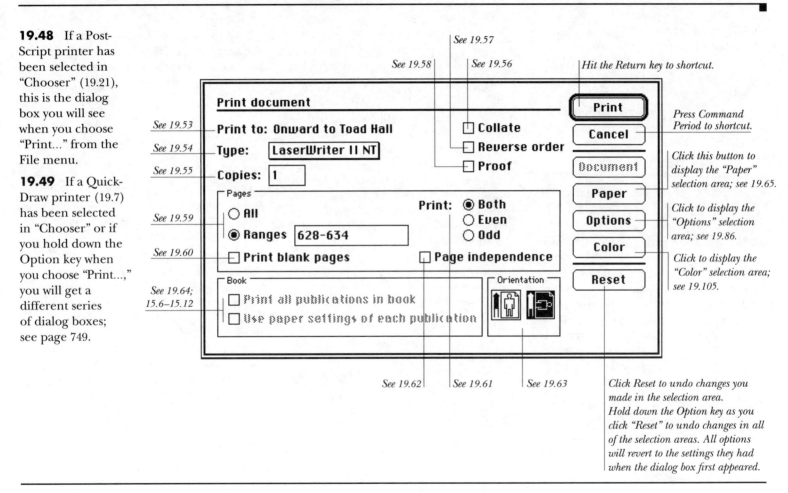

See 19.57

See 19.58   *See 19.56*

Hit the Return key to shortcut.

See 19.53

See 19.54

See 19.55

See 19.59

See 19.60

See 19.64;
15.6–15.12

Print document

Print to: Onward to Toad Hall

Type: LaserWriter II NT

Copies: 1

Pages
○ All
◉ Ranges 628-634
☐ Print blank pages

Print: ◉ Both
○ Even
○ Odd

☐ Collate
☐ Reverse order
☐ Proof

☐ Page independence

Book
☐ Print all publications in book
☐ Use paper settings of each publication

Orientation

Print
Cancel
Document
Paper
Options
Color
Reset

Press Command Period to shortcut.

Click this button to display the "Paper" selection area; see 19.65.

Click to display the "Options" selection area; see 19.86.

Click to display the "Color" selection area; see 19.105.

See 19.62   *See 19.61*   *See 19.63*

Click Reset to undo changes you made in the selection area. Hold down the Option key as you click "Reset" to undo changes in all of the selection areas. All options will revert to the settings they had when the dialog box first appeared.

"Document" options specifications

19.50 Once you decide to print something, PageMaker offers you a whole range of options from which to choose. Within the "Print" dialog box are other, more detailed dialog boxes. Well, they are not *really* dialog boxes, but they act just like them. Along the right side of the dialog box are buttons that *control* the options available in the *selection area* on the left.

19.51 Everything you select stays selected throughout the publication until you change it unless, of course, you hit "Cancel." You can even save your print settings without actually printing anything: hold down the Shift key as you click the "Print" button (19.130).

19.52 After your first printing, you can buzz into your next printing in the same publication by hitting Command P, then instantly hitting the Return key. You won't even see the dialog box. If you need to specify a range of pages, do this: Press Command P; hit Tab; type the number of the first page to print; type a *hyphen*; type the number of the last page to print; hit Return. It's very satisfying when you can do it so fast the dialog box doesn't even appear.

19.53 Print to: The name of the printer you chose in the Chooser shows at the top of the dialog box, after "Print to" (in the example on the previous page, the name of my printer is "Onward to Toad Hall"). You can't change this from within PageMaker, although you can override it by choosing another PPD next to "Type"; see 19.54.

19.54 Type: The "Type" pop-up menu displays the printers whose PPDs you installed (19.11–19.12). The printer you choose from this menu affects some of the other options, such as the print area or the paper sizes available. Typically, you choose the same printer here that you have selected in the "Chooser." Exceptions would include the selection of custom PPDs for specific printing tasks (as in downloaded fonts; 19.132; 21.34), and setting up the "Print to" dialog box for remote printing at a service bureau (19.133–19.134; 19.147).

19.55 Copies: Type the number of copies that you want to print (up to 32,000).

Notice how the relative print area and the possible paper sizes change with the different printers. These options are from the "Document" and "Paper" selection areas.

19.56 Collate: Check this box if you are making more than one copy of multiple pages and you want the printer to collate the pages for you. To collate a publication, though, the printer has to build a page, print it, build the next page, print it, etc., for the entire publication, then repeat the process for the next collated collection. Checking the collate button will slow down printing significantly. If you do collate, make sure you know which order your designated printer will print: last page first or first page last, and check the "Reverse order" button (19.57) as needed.

—continued

"Document" options specifications —continued

19.57 Reverse order: The printer's PPD (19.11–19.12) determines in which order the pages are printed—back to front or front to back. Whichever order your printer normally prints, checking this button will reverse it.

19.58 Proof: With this option checked only text prints. Graphics print as boxes with Xs through them. If your publication contains a lot of graphics but you just want to proofread the text or check the layout, check "Proof" to dramatically speed up the printing process.

19.59 Pages: You can print all or any of the pages in your publication including single non-sequential pages and various page ranges, all at the same time. This is one of the niftiest things about PageMaker 5. Click the "All" button to print every page in the publication or book. Click the "Ranges" button when you want to print just certain pages and/or page ranges (19.129). You can even combine them, printing one page here and another page there and then a range of pages immediately after, all with the same Print command. Individual page numbers, separated by commas, can be typed in the order you want them printed.

Hyphens designate a range of pages. If you type -5, all the pages up to and including 5, will print. If you type 5-, page 5 and all the following pages will print. Type a hyphen between two numbers (always in ascending order, 4-9, not 9-4) to print all the pages in that range, and always type the full number. You can't get away with typing 122-24. Use commas to separate page ranges.

You can type up to sixty-four characters in the "Ranges" edit box. You can't always see all the page numbers you have entered, however, as the edit box can't show sixty-four characters all at once. Sometimes you can get the cursor to highlight in reverse, but sometimes you just have to trust that the page numbers you entered are there.

19.60 Print blank pages: Unless you put a check in this box, PageMaker will not print any blank pages in the publication. "Blank" means *really* blank: master page items count as "something" on the page, as do white, "invisible" boxes or reverse lines.

19.61 Print: Choosing to print **Odd** or **Even** pages also prints those blank pages whether there is a check in the "Print blank pages" option or not. You cannot print odd or even pages if either "Thumbnail" or "Tile" is selected. Use this feature to print both sides of a paper if your printer doesn't feature the "Duplex" printing (see 19.85).

19.62 Page independence: If you check this box, PageMaker will download font information separately for each page. Normally you can ignore this option and let PageMaker handle the font downloading as necessary. If your publication is headed for a post-processing program, ask your service bureau if you need to check this option.

"Document" options specifications —*continued*

19.63 Orientation: The icons refer to the way the information is printed on the page. The right-side up person represents the "tall" (portrait) mode and the sideways person represents the "wide" (landscape) mode.

Your choice of printing orientation in this dialog box should usually match the orientation you chose in the "Page setup" dialog box. If the choices do not match, the orientation checked in the "Print document" dialog box will take precedence over that in the "Page setup" dialog box.

19.64 Book: These options are only available if there is a Book List (15.6–15.12) in *this* publication. If you check "Print all publications in book," every publication that is in the Book List will print in the order you have specified. You will only be allowed to make one copy, and certain options will not be available to you.

For the most part, each publication will print according to the specifications you set in the active publication's "Print" dialog box. However, each publication will print in its correct orientation, and you can check "Use paper settings of each publication" so that each publication will use the "Size" and "Source" settings saved in its own "Print" dialog box.

When you choose to print "All" pages in the active publication, PageMaker prints all the pages in *each* publication. She can even consecutively renumber the pages if you want (15.29). If you specify a range of pages, PageMaker does *not* renumber the pages and prints only the ranges specified within each publication.

"Write PostScript to file" in the "Options" area prints the Book to disk as a PostScript file. "Normal" saves the entire Book List as a single PostScript file; "For separations" saves each publication as a separate file. You will not be able to select which inks will print even if "Separations" in the "Color" options dialog box is selected. All the ink colors in the book will be printed.

See Section 15 on Book Publications for more in-depth information on this feature (15.26–15.28 for printing a whole book).

The origins of printing are almost as obscure as the origins of writing, and for much the same reason—its inventors never used their new medium to record the process.

—Sean Morrison

19.65 "Paper" in the "Print..." dialog box *(from the File menu, choose "Print..."; click the "Paper" button in the control area)*

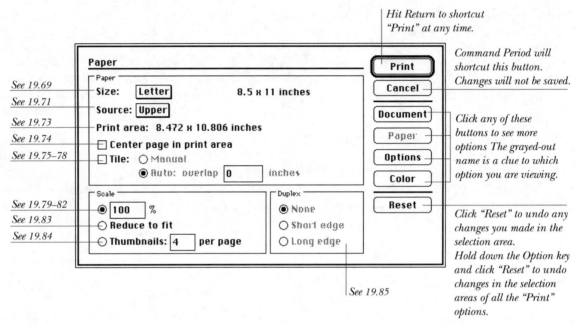

Hit Return to shortcut "Print" at any time.

Command Period will shortcut this button. Changes will not be saved.

See 19.69
See 19.71
See 19.73
See 19.74
See 19.75–78

Paper
┌ Paper
Size: **Letter**   8.5 × 11 inches
Source: **Upper**
Print area: 8.472 × 10.806 inches
☐ Center page in print area
☐ Tile: ○ Manual
       ◉ Auto: overlap **0**   inches

Print
Cancel
Document
Paper
Options
Color
Reset

Click any of these buttons to see more options The grayed-out name is a clue to which option you are viewing.

See 19.79–82
See 19.83
See 19.84

┌ Scale
◉ **100** %
○ Reduce to fit
○ Thumbnails: **4** per page

┌ Duplex
◉ None
○ Short edge
○ Long edge

Click "Reset" to undo any changes you made in the selection area.
Hold down the Option key and click "Reset" to undo changes in the selection areas of all the "Print" options.

See 19.85

19.66 If you click "Print" while in an options dialog box, any changes you made will stay with the publication for all subsequent printing (unless you Cancel before it's completely finished printing).

If you click "Cancel," the dialog box will disappear along with any changes you may have made.

19.67 To save print specifications as publication defaults *without* printing the publication, hold down the Shift key as you click the "Print" button. The publication will not print, but all the selections you made in the dialog boxes will stay until you go back and change them (19.130).

"Paper" options specifications

19.68 Much of what you can choose in the "Paper" option depends upon the printer you are using (the PPD you selected in the "Document" options, 19.54). There is a big difference between printing at your station to a PostScript printer and taking something to "lino."

19.69 Size: Choose the paper size you want to print on from this pop-up menu. Notice that when you choose a paper, its actual size is displayed to the right. This *paper size* may be different than the *page size* you specified in the "Page setup" dialog box. Whatever *page size* you set up will be centered on the *paper size* you select here. The unit of measure that is used is determined by the measurement system you chose in the "Preferences" dialog box (1.224–1.225).

For some printers, such as imagesetters, the "Size" option may include "Custom…."

19.70 Imagesetters don't use single sheets of paper—they print onto *rolls* of resin-coated paper. If you are printing to an imagesetter using the "tall" orientation (19.63) for letter-sized pages or smaller, you can get more pages in less space on the roll if you choose the paper size option "Letter transverse." This makes the pages print perpendicular to the roll, wasting much less paper. *Check with your service bureau, though, before you change any of the print options for an imagesetter!* (*See service bureau tips: 19.150–19.161.*)

19.71 Source: Paper tray sources depend upon the PPD you have selected. In many cases you don't even need special trays to print other paper sizes. Simply feed in odd-sized paper, legal paper, or envelopes through the manual feed slot. You must still choose the correct size from the "Size" pop-up menu, though (19.69).

19.72 Card stock is paper that is heavier than normal; it often has problems wrapping around the drum as it goes through the printer. Most printers have a tray that opens out the back end especially made to solve that problem. With that tray open, the paper rolls right on through, flat, out into the flat tray (envelopes and transparencies work well with the back end open, also). Note that this will reverse the order, though! Pages that would otherwise wrap around the drum and come out face down on the bottom of the pile, will now come out face up on the bottom of the pile.

19.73 Print area: This is the *area that can actually be printed* for that paper in that printer and varies from printer to printer. Most laser printers cannot print all the way out to the edge of the paper, while imagesetters, because they print on a roll, can use the entire space, even beyond the actual image area specified. Generally, anything you want to print must fit within the print area. This includes printer's marks. See 19.131 for a nice trick for getting things printed on the sheet but outside the actual page size.

—continued

"Paper" options specifications: Tiling and image size

19.74 Center page in print area:
Check this box when you want to center the publication page within the *printable* area of the designated printer. Usually the print area is centered within the paper size anyway, so this option is unnecessary except with those printers that have an asymmetrically offset print area. With the option unchecked, the publication page will center within the paper size.

19.75 Tile: You have to use this option when the *page size* of your publication is greater than the *paper size* that comes out of your printer, or if you *scale* the page to print larger (19.79–19.82). For instance, if you are creating a tabloid-sized newsletter (11 inches x 17 inches) and printing to an Apple LaserWriter, you must Tile in order to print each 11- x 17-inch page. The 11- x 17-inch page will be divided into equal sections, and PageMaker will print each section on a separate 8.5- x 11-inch piece of paper. After the pages come out of the printer, you need to manually *(aack—manually?)* piece the sections together to create one 11 x 17 page. Different printers can accommodate different paper sizes.

19.76 When you print with the "Tile" option and the **Auto overlap ___ inches** button checked, PageMaker computes the amount of tiles needed to print the entire page and starts printing at the upper left corner of the publication page. Each page is overlapped by the amount you enter in the "Auto overlap" edit box. The overlap makes it possible for you to paste the pieces together precisely (on a light table, paste one page over the other, exactly aligning what is visible on the overlap; trim the excess). When PageMaker displays the printing status she indicates how many tiles will print.

19.77 The **Manual** button in the "Tile" option causes the page to print differently than does "Auto overlap." With "Manual," the printer will print *one* sheet of paper no matter what the page size. The upper left corner of the page will begin wherever the *zero point* (1.44; 1.70–1.73) is located on the screen. It will *literally* begin at that corner, which means a certain portion of the image may not print as most laser printers cannot print all the way to the edge of the paper. When you set the zero point for Manual tiling, be sure to allow space for that non-

printing area. Manual tiling ignores any amount that may be entered in the "Auto overlap" edit box.

19.78 Manual tiling is a great way to reprint just certain sections of that larger page size since with Auto tiling you get every section, even if some are blank, whether you want them or not. It's also great for those times when you want to enlarge just a portion of a page, like perhaps a graphic image (19.77–19.80).

19.79 Scale: You can enter a value from 5% to 1600% (in 0.1% increments) to reduce or enlarge the printed pages. If a page is **reduced** it will be centered on the paper, in which case you should choose to show the "Printer's marks" (19.95). If you don't show the "Crop marks," you won't know where the boundaries of the reduced page are (19.96).

19.80 If you **enlarge the page** and it exceeds the width or depth of the paper size, you may need to "Tile" in order to print all of the image. The page will be printed onto several sheets of paper that you will need to paste together (19.75–19.78). If you only need to **enlarge a portion** of the page and don't care about printing the rest

Tiling and image size —*continued*

of it, you still might want to read the tiling information to make sure that the image you want enlarged will show up on the paper when you print.

19.81 If you only want to **enlarge a portion** and don't want to bother tiling, place the image in the center of the page (19.74).

19.82 Some people like to print their pages slightly enlarged, say 125%, and then have the commercial press reduce the pages when they make the printing plates for reproduction. This gives the effect of a higher resolution.

19.83 Reduce to Fit: Click this option whenever you want to force a publication to fit on a smaller paper size. For instance, if you want to fit a single, tabloid-sized page onto a letter-sized piece of paper, just click "Reduce to fit." If you have "Printer's marks" or "Page information" also selected (from the "Options" dialog box, 19.86), the publication will be scaled even smaller so these, too, will fit on the page. To make sure your publication page fits within the "Print area," also check "Center page in print area" (19.74).

19.84 Thumbnails: Thumbnails are small, "thumbnail"-sized reproductions of the pages and are useful for viewing the layout of the overall project to check for consistency, concept, missing elements, etc. You can ask for anywhere from 1 to 1000 per page, bearing in mind that the size of the thumbnail will depend on how many you request per page (the fewer the number, the larger the images). If you request sixteen per page, but you only print four pages, the four thumbnails will be as small as if there were sixteen. Each thumbnail representation of a page is numbered for you and has a nice border with a drop-shadow to define it. Thumbnails are really a neat way to view your project.

PageMaker will print all the pages in the publication or just the ranges you specify. Each range of pages starts a new page of thumbnails. Blank pages will be included, even if you don't check that box (19.60). It takes just as long to print thumbnails as it does to print full-sized pages!

19.85 Duplex: This option is available for those printers that can print on both sides of a piece of paper with only one pass through the printer. The "Short edge" option prints the pages so that they read correctly when bound on the shorter side of the paper. The "Long edge" option prints the pages so they read correctly when bound on the longer edge of the paper. When this option is dimmed it means your selected printer can't do it.

The rest of us make do with the "Even/ Odd" option (19.61). First print the **even**-numbered pages. Then take those pages, turn them around, put them back in the printer tray, and print the **odd**-numbered pages. The exact way you place them back into the paper tray depends entirely on your printer. You will probably need to experiment on the first few pages; when you figure it out, write it down so you don't have to figure it out all over again next time. I wish I had done that.

My plan was to kiss her with every lip on my face.
Steve Martin, in Dead Men Don't Wear Plaid

19.86 "Options" in the "Print..." dialog box   *(from the File menu, choose "Print..."; click the "Options" button in the control area)*

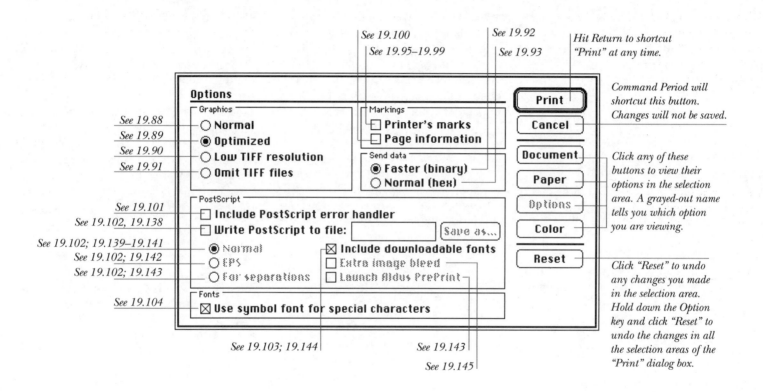

See 19.100
See 19.95–19.99

See 19.92
See 19.93

Hit Return to shortcut
"Print" at any time.

Options

*Command Period will
shortcut this button.
Changes will not be saved.*

Graphics

See 19.88 ○ **Normal**
See 19.89 ◉ **Optimized**
See 19.90 ○ **Low TIFF resolution**
See 19.91 ○ **Omit TIFF files**

Markings

☐ **Printer's marks**
☐ **Page information**

Send data
◉ **Faster (binary)**
○ **Normal (hex)**

PostScript

See 19.101 ☐ **Include PostScript error handler**
See 19.102, 19.138 ☐ **Write PostScript to file:** ⎣ Save as... ⎦

See 19.102; 19.139–19.141 ◉ Normal
See 19.102; 19.142 ○ EPS
See 19.102; 19.143 ○ For separations

☒ **Include downloadable fonts**
☐ Extra image bleed
☐ Launch Aldus PrePrint

Fonts

See 19.104 ☒ **Use symbol font for special characters**

Print
Cancel
Document
Paper
Options
Color
Reset

*Click any of these
buttons to view their
options in the selection
area. A grayed-out name
tells you which option
you are viewing.*

*Click "Reset" to undo
any changes you made
in the selection area.
Hold down the Option
key and click "Reset" to
undo the changes in all
the selection areas of the
"Print" dialog box.*

See 19.103; 19.144
See 19.143
See 19.145

"Options" specifications: Graphics

19.87 Clicking the "Options" button takes you to one of the selection areas where many pre-press specifications are made ("Color" is the other one). Choices made in the "Graphics" box decide the quality of printed images as well as the time it takes to print them. The choices you make in the "Markings" box tell PageMaker whether or not to include file data and other pre-press information on the printed piece.

19.88 Normal: When this button is clicked all the imported, bitmapped graphics (TIFF and paint-type images) in your publication will be sent to the printer with all their image data.

19.89 Optimized: Sometimes your bitmapped images have more information then you need at the moment. Perhaps you scanned an image at a resolution higher than the printer on which you are proofing it. Select the "Optimized" button to tell PageMaker to remove any image data that is not needed by the selected printer.

Although this speeds up printing time, it can occasionally yield results different from what is expected. It is useful, though, for proofing high-resolution graphics (like scans) on a low resolution printer (300–600 dpi).

19.90 Low TIFF resolution: TIFFs are usually represented in low-resolution on the screen. When the page prints, PageMaker finds the linked file and prints the high-resolution version. Perhaps you want to place the image manually or speed up the printing for proofing and don't need the high-res version at this point. Checking this option instructs the printer to just print the low-resolution screen version "for position only" (FPO) to indicate where on the page the final version should be placed. If it's checked on, you don't need to include the publication's linked TIFF files.

If you are printing to disk for color separations, leave this box **un**checked.

19.91 Omit TIFF files: Click this option to prevent any and all TIFF files from printing. It is especially useful when you are printing to disk and want to link high-resolution versions of the images to the publication at print time.

19.92 Send data Faster: Faster means image data (TIFF and paint-type graphics) is sent in binary format (0s and 1s) to the printer. The sending is faster but it requires the same processing time. If printing errors occur in this format switch to "Normal."

19.93 Send data Normal: Image data is sent to the printer in hexadecimal format. (Hexadecimal format uses the numbers 0 through 9, and the letters A to F.) It gets to the printer slower than binary data, but the printer processing time is the same.

—continued

"Options" specifications: Page markings

19.94 These options let you choose to include any file data you want along with the proofs or finals you crank out of your laser printer or through lino. They can be good for tracking jobs of repeat clients or projects, establishing visual clues and references for printing, or for controlling imaging specifications of graphic elements.

19.95 Printer's marks: Check this box to print crop marks, registration marks, density-control bars, and color-control strips on every page of your work. These marks need room to print, though, and will only show if the paper size you are printing on is at least three-quarters inch larger on all sides than the size of your publication page. (For example, for marks to show on 8.5- x 11-inch paper, your publication *page* size must be 7 x 9.5 inches or smaller.)

To proof work, you can force printer's marks to print on any page; click the radio button next to "Reduce to fit" under "Scale" in the "Paper" options area (19.83).

19.96 Crop marks: If the *page size* you defined in the "Page setup" dialog box (from the File menu) is smaller than the *paper size* it will be printed on, your page will be centered on the paper when it is printed. Since the page boundaries that you see on the screen don't show up on the paper when you print, you have no way of knowing where your actual page begins and ends. When you choose "Printer's marks," crop marks define the original page boundaries and can be used as guides for trimming the paper to its proper page size.

19.97 Registration marks: With color separated documents, a separate page is printed for each color. Registration marks help the commercial printer align the separate pages correctly when printing.

19.98 Density-control bars: Also called calibration bars, the density-control bars are used to verify that the output device (printer or press) is printing at the correct degree of darkness. Each process or spot color in the document in displayed in 10% value increments.

19.99 Color-control strip: This strip shows 100% and 50% tints of the process-color inks and combinations of cyan and magenta, cyan and yellow, and magenta and yellow. Use the color-control strip to check color accuracy when you print a composite on a color printer or to check a composite color proof.

19.100 Page information: This feature can help you keep your hard copy (or negs) organized. With this option checked, each publication page prints with its filename, page number, current date, and spot- or process-color separation name (when printing a composite it will say "Composite" instead). All the information is printed starting in the lower-left corner of the page, in 8-point Helvetica. Your *paper* size must be one-half inch bigger on the bottom edge than your *page* size for the info to show.

"Options" specification: PostScript information; the Symbol font

19.101 Include PostScript error handler:
If you run into printing problems, you may want to use this option to help you research and "debug" the file. What it does is copy PageMaker's PostScript error handler to your printer (or to your file when you "Write PostScript to file"). Error messages describing the error type, the PostScript command that caused the error, *and* suggestions on how to fix the problem, will now be printed on those pages on which the error occurred. Be sure to check with your service bureau before sending them files with this option checked.

19.102 Write PostScript to file: When you choose "Write PostScript to file," PageMaker creates a printer file on a disk with the PostScript code needed to print the publication at a later date. This is one way to take a file to a service bureau (19.147) or other remote printer. You can name the file whatever you like, but by default PageMaker wisely gives it the publication name followed by an extension that notes what kind of file it is.

The term "Write PostScript to file" is the same as "print to disk."

Normal saves the *entire file* with all the same specifications it would normally send to the printer. The extension ".ps" is added to the file name. **EPS** saves *each page* as a separate EPS file. Both the page number and the extension ".eps" are added to the file name. **For separations** saves a PostScript file that can be opened in a post-processing program or that can be printed as separations by your service bureau. The extension ".sep" is added to the file name.

See 19.138–19.149 for more information on how to write PostScript to disk, including information on the options **Extra image bleed** and **Launch Aldus PrePrint.**

19.103 Include downloadable fonts:
If your publication includes fonts that are not resident in your printer (19.33–19.35), PageMaker needs to download the fonts at print time. By default, this option is checked **on.** The only time you need to uncheck it is if you have manually downloaded all the fonts in your publication, and you want to prevent PageMaker from downloading the fonts again (19.132).

If you are printing to disk, be sure to see 19.144.

19.104 Use symbol font for special characters: The more common alternate symbols, like ®,©, ™, and ±, will print in most any font, but there are a few alternate characters that may show up on your screen in any font but will not print. Sometimes what you see is *not* what you get! If you check this option, the font "Symbol" will substitute for any symbol character in a font that will not print.

®	©	™	°	μ	¬	÷	±
π	∏	∂	Δ	Ω	◊	∫	≈
√	≠	∞	≤	≥	Σ	🍎	

The top row of symbols would print in any font; the bottom two rows required Symbol font substitution.

Of course, this option can get you unexpected results as well *since it is on by default.* Proof your work closely, especially if you customize fonts.

19.105 "Color" in the "Print..." dialog box

(from the File menu, choose "Print..."; click on the "Color" button in the control area)

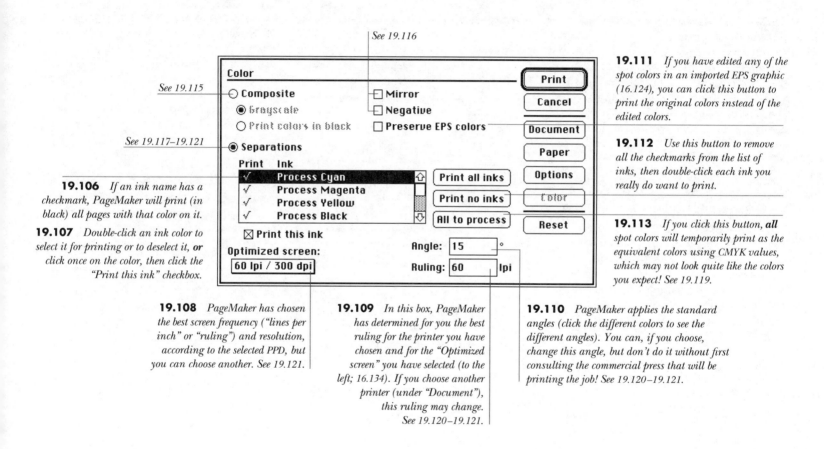

See 19.116

See 19.115

See 19.117–19.121

19.111 *If you have edited any of the spot colors in an imported EPS graphic (16.124), you can click this button to print the original colors instead of the edited colors.*

19.112 *Use this button to remove all the checkmarks from the list of inks, then double-click each ink you really do want to print.*

19.106 *If an ink name has a checkmark, PageMaker will print (in black) all pages with that color on it.*

19.107 *Double-click an ink color to select it for printing or to deselect it, **or** click once on the color, then click the "Print this ink" checkbox.*

19.113 *If you click this button, **all** spot colors will temporarily print as the equivalent colors using CMYK values, which may not look quite like the colors you expect! See 19.119.*

19.108 *PageMaker has chosen the best screen frequency ("lines per inch" or "ruling") and resolution, according to the selected PPD, but you can choose another. See 19.121.*

19.109 *In this box, PageMaker has determined for you the best ruling for the printer you have chosen and for the "Optimized screen" you have selected (to the left; 16.134). If you choose another printer (under "Document"), this ruling may change. See 19.120–19.121.*

19.110 *PageMaker applies the standard angles (click the different colors to see the different angles). You can, if you choose, change this angle, but don't do it without first consulting the commercial press that will be printing the job! See 19.120–19.121.*

"Color" options specifications

19.114 PageMaker can separate your publication at print time into color plates whether you use spot color or process colors. Most of us can learn to separate simple jobs with "loose" registration, but more complex jobs requiring "traps" and "spreads" and "chokes" benefit from the expertise of trained, pre-press professionals (16.127).

The basics are easy enough to learn and essential for proofing separations before you go to lino. An understanding of how color is printed on paper and how to work with color in PageMaker provides a foundation for understanding the "Color" print dialog box. You might want to depend on your service bureau to handle the final "Color" dialog box settings for you, however. *Talk to them!* **Note:** Read Section 16 thoroughly first if you haven't already done so.

19.115 No matter how many colors are used in a publication, you can always choose to print it as a **Composite.** A composite prints all the colors on a page at once to give you an overall perspective of the design. Of course, if you are printing to a black-and-white printer, your colors will be just shades of gray.

Select **Grayscale** when printing color on a color printer (yes! grayscale!) or to print in shades of gray that simulate the real colors on a black-and-white-printer: a 20% tint of red will correctly print with a different intensity than a 20% tint of black.

Select **Print colors in black** when you are printing spot-color separations with only one or two colors and you want PageMaker to print each color as the tint of black that is necessary to print the color correctly on film. PageMaker ignores the base color, so a 20% tint of red prints with the same intensity as a 20% tint of black. Always check with your commercial printer before sending them a file specced this way.

19.116 Mirror, and **Negative** may or may not be necessary options. Discuss them with your commercial printer and your service bureau first. "Mirror" flips the page so it is printed backwards as if you were looking in a mirror. "Negative" will print the reverse of what is on the screen: what is white will be black and what is black will be white.

Aldus offers this chart to help you determine when to check the "Mirror" option:

	Right reading		Wrong reading	
Emulsion:	Up	Down	Up	Down
Set "Mirror":	Off	On	On	Off

If you understand the printing terms "right reading," "wrong reading," "emulsion up," and "emulsion down," you have an idea what these options are for. Check with the press you are working with to determine the correct settings for your publication. If you have never heard these terms, do not mess with these options. Instead call the commercial press with whom you are working and ask them what they prefer. Then, when you send your job to lino, give the service bureau the information from the commercial press and let them determine the correct settings for your publication.

—continued

"Color" options specifications: printing Separations

19.117 Choose **Separations** to print each spot or process color in your publication on a separate piece of paper or film. Again, you may prefer to use the services of trained, pre-press professionals. As final output, you will probably produce these separations on an imagesetter and so can count on your service bureau to set the options correctly. However, you need to at least know the basics so you can proof your work *before* you go to lino! Color separations can be produced on a laser printer (or a non-PostScript printer) to make sure that objects are printing on the correct separation, and colors are layering as you expected (knockouts and overprints especially, see 16.24–16.27). The dialog box looks more complicated than it really is, and, in fact, PageMaker will automatically make some of your choices for you.

19.118 You can choose to print all or some of the colors in the ink list. A separate piece of paper or film (a "neg") is output for every color you select. When an ink color has a check next to its name, it will be printed. Double-click ink colors to select or deselect them, or highlight an ink color and check or uncheck the "Print this ink" box. You can click "Print all inks" to select all the ink colors, and "Print no inks" to deselect them all. (Publications printed from a Book List have "Print all inks" automatically selected; see 15.26.)

Please read 16.133 for valuable information on "Print blank pages" and "Print page information."

19.119 Clicking the button **All to process** temporarily converts spot colors to their equivalent process colors and prints your publication entirely as process-color separations (16.31–16.36). The process color, though, may not match the spot color exactly and overprinting and trapping effects may be lost. The "All to process" button will become "Revert to spot" so that you can restore your spot colors to the ink list. Permanently convert a spot color to a process color in the "Edit color" dialog box; 16.77.

19.120 Each process color must be printed at a certain angle and ruling to avoid creating moiré patterns when layered with the other colors (16.34). Fortunately, PageMaker can take care of this for you. Read on.

19.121 The seemingly intimidating choices at the bottom of the "Color" dialog box (19.109) are actually selected for you according to which PPD you have chosen in the "Document" selection area of the "Print" dialog box. You see, each PPD has its own information already written into its code that tells PageMaker which screen frequency and angle will give the best results for the printer you are using. It is therefore critical that you choose the PPD that will be used for your final output! When printing composites (or separations from a laser printer) screen rulings may not look like they will when they finally print.

The pop-up menu under "Optimized screen" may have many choices available. When you change the screen, the default selections for "Angle" and "Ruling" automatically change also. You can change the angle or ruling without changing the "Optimized screen," but the default values will usually give the best results. See 16.134–16.135 and 16.139 for more information.

The bottom line: talk to both your commercial printer and your service bureau before making changes in these options.

19.122 Printing to a non-PostScript (QuickDraw) printer

19.123 Selecting a non-PostScript printer in the Chooser gives you a whole different series of print dialog boxes. The "Document," "Options," and "Color" selection areas are available but with only limited choices. Anything that deals with PostScript language (EPS graphics, downloading fonts, substituting fonts, etc.) is not available.

However, you can "trick" PageMaker into thinking you have a PostScript printer so you can prepare files for remote printing by choosing a PostScript printer in the Chooser (see 19.127).

19.124 Click the "Setup…" button to display the standard Apple page setup and dialog boxes for your printer.

19.125 If you want to bypass PageMaker's PostScript options (see 22.47) and print your publication using just the LaserWriter 8 driver, you can. Hold down the Option key while selecting "Print" from the File menu. You will see the same dialog boxes as below, but the "Setup…" button will display the LaserWriter 8 dialog boxes with *their* PostScript options.

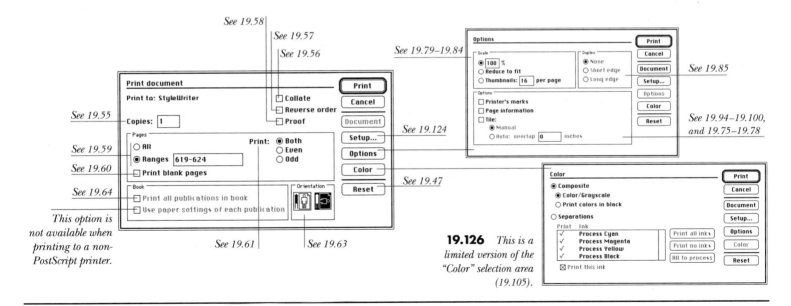

See 19.58
See 19.57
See 19.56
See 19.79–19.84
See 19.85
See 19.55
See 19.124
See 19.94–19.100, and 19.75–19.78
See 19.59
See 19.60
See 19.47
See 19.64

This option is not available when printing to a non-PostScript printer.

See 19.61
See 19.63

19.126 *This is a limited version of the "Color" selection area (19.105).*

If you want to do this:	Then follow these steps:	Shortcuts ▾ Notes ▾ Hints

19.127 Use Chooser to select a PostScript printer 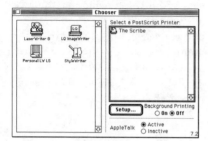 *The Chooser window found under the Apple menu.*	• Before you print, select "Chooser" from the Apple menu (see the note ☞).
	
	• On the left, click on the LaserWriter 8 icon. After you click on a printer icon, the name(s) of the printers of that type will appear on the right.
	
	• On the right, click on the name of the particular printer you want to send your publication through (it may already be selected).
	
	• If this is your first visit to the Chooser since you installed PageMaker 5, click the "Setup" button (see 19.22–19.25).
	  □ Click "Auto Setup" to have a PPD file for your printer chosen automatically.
	  □ Click "Select PPD..." to manually choose a PPD (see 19.23).
	  □ Click OK.
	
	• When you are using a PostScript laser printer, or if you are connected to more than one printer, AppleTalk must be Active.
	
	• Turn on "Background Printing" if you want to continue working as you print files.
	
	• It feels like there should be an OK button in this window, but there isn't. When you click in the close box (upper left), the Chooser sends the information to the driver which lets PageMaker know what printer to use.
		• You do not need to go to Chooser every time you print. You only need to go there when you print to a certain printer for the first time. After that, the information is stored, even if you turn off the computer and/or the printer. You need never go back to Chooser again until you want to print to a different printer or unless you want to change the default PPD file selected in the "Setup" dialog box (for example, if you run the "Update PPD" Addition you may want the updated PPD as the default setting; 19.175).
		
		• The Chooser will display the printer icons of any printer drivers you have in the Extensions folder in your System folder. If a printer driver is not in the Extensions folder, you cannot print to it.
		
		• With "Background Printing" turned on, the LaserWriter 8 spools *all* the print information before printing begins. In effect, this increases the time it takes to begin printing, however, once pages start to spit out of your printer your computer is free for you to work again.

If you want to do this:

19.128 Print a publication

Where the bee sucks,
There suck I
In a cowslip's bell I lie;
There I couch when owls do cry
On the bat's back I do fly
After summer merrily.
Merrily, merrily shall I live now
Under the blossom
That hangs on the bough.

— *Shakespeare*

Then follow these steps:

- Always Save just before you print—the ever-necessary precaution.
- From the File menu choose "Print...," *or* press Command P.
- Make your choices in the selection area of the "Print document" dialog box; see 19.47–19.64.
  - □ To print the entire publication click the radio button next to "All."
  - □ To print a range of pages, click the radio button next to "Ranges." In the edit box, enter the page number of the first page you want to print, type a hyphen, then enter the page number of the last page you want to print.
  - □ To print non-consecutive pages, enter the page numbers of all the pages you want to print in the "Ranges" edit box, separating them with commas.
- Click the "Paper" button to choose paper and scaling options; see 19.65–19.85.
- Click the "Options" button to choose from a variety of print options; see 19.86–19.104.
- Click the "Color" button to choose various color specifications; see 19.105–19.121.
- Click the "Print" button *or* press Return.

Shortcuts ▾ Notes ▾ Hints

- If you chose a PostScript printer (19.6; 19.9) in the Chooser (19.21; 19.127), you will get the "Print document" dialog box shown in 19.47.
- If you chose a QuickDraw or other non-PostScript printer (19.7–19.8) in Chooser, you will get the "Print document" dialog box shown in 19.122.
- Once you have set up the "Print" dialog boxes and printed, the information will stay intact—you do not have to redo the specifications each time you print. Just press Command P and hit the Return key (shortcut for OK) to start the process.
- You can set print publication defaults without printing the document by holding down the Shift key as you select "Print" from the menu; see 19.130.
- PageMaker has two Additions to enhance printing. If you have upgraded your printer, be sure to see the "Update PPD" Addition, 19.171–19.178. If you want to print multiple publications see the "Printer styles" Addition, 19.191–19.225.

If you want to do this:	**Then follow these steps:**	**Shortcuts ▾ Notes ▾ Hints**
19.129 Print a variety of page ranges and non-consecutive pages	• From the File menu choose "Print...," *or* press Command P. • Set all of the options in the "Print" dialog boxes the way you want them. • In the "Ranges" edit box: □ To print all the pages *up to* a certain number starting with the first page, type a hyphen followed by the last page you want to print. □ To print all the pages *after* a certain number, enter the page number with which you want to start, followed by a hyphen. □ To print more than one range of pages, enter commas between the ranges. □ To print random pages, enter page numbers separated by commas. • Although you can enter up to 64 characters in the edit box, you can't see them all; the numbers in the edit box scroll to the left as you keep entering numbers.	• Page ranges must be separated by a hyphen and must be listed in ascending order (4-9, not 9-4). • Although non-consecutive pages must be separated by a comma, they can be listed in any order. • You can enter up to 64 characters in the "Ranges" edit box in any combination of page ranges and separate pages. You do not need to enter spaces between page entries (spaces count as characters). Even though you can no longer see the page numbers in the edit box, they are still there! • If you choose to print "Even" or "Odd" pages, PageMaker prints only the even or odd pages within the specified page ranges.
19.130 Save print specifications without printing the publication	• From the File menu, choose "Print...," *or* press Command P. • Set all of the options in the "Print" dialog boxes the way you want them. • Hold down the Shift key and click the "Print" button. The "Print" dialog box will close, saving the specs you just set.	• Whenever you actually print a publication, the print specifications are saved as publication defaults. With this method you can save print publication defaults without printing. This is good for going back in and adjusting specs you forgot to save.

If you want to do this:

19.131 Print items outside the boundary of the page

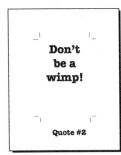

This is the 4 x 6 page in PageMaker. Notice the text block handle of "Quote #2" is within the page boundary, but the text itself is on the pasteboard (1.4).

Quote #2

When printed on 8.5 x 11 paper, the text appears outside the 4 x 6 boundary, but within the 8.5 x 11 page.

Don't be a wimp!

Quote #2

Registration mark with a white box behind it. The white box needs a line of "None."

"Paste special" the reg mark as a PICT to combine all the separate pieces into one graphic.

Then follow these steps:

- As long as at least one handle of the object is placed within the page boundary, the object will print.
- To print **text:** In front of the first character in the text block, hit a couple of Returns to make the text block larger on the top. Place the text block on the page so the top handles touch the page itself, but the rest of the text block hangs into the pasteboard area (1.4). The text block could also hang off either side, in the same manner; use indents (Section 6) to give you space on the sides.
- To print **graphics:** If the graphic has any white space within its boundary, then it is very easy to place an edge of the graphic on the page and hang the image itself on the pasteboard.
- If the graphic is a composite one you created in PageMaker, such as a registration mark (⊕), you can do this:
  □ Create the reg mark. Put a white (paper-filled) box behind it. Give the box a line of "None." Select it all, and copy it. Choose "Paste special" from the Edit menu, and double-click the format "PICT," to paste the graphic as one element. Hang the edge of the reg mark on the page.

Shortcuts ▼ Notes ▼ Hints

- If the page size you established in the "Page setup" dialog box (from the File menu) *is at least a half-inch less than the paper size you are printing on,* it is possible to print items that are outside the boundary of the smaller page size. This is great for placing automatic page numbers or other notes that you need in order to identify the pages but that you don't want to appear on the actual, cropped page itself.
- PageMaker does offer two options— "Printer's marks," (19.95–19.99) and "Page information" (19.100)—as a way to add identifying information to a printout.

- A registration mark tagged with the color "Registration" will show up on all separations of a color file (16.62).
- You could select the mark and the box and put them in the Scrapbook as item number one, then *Place* the first item in the Scrapbook (10.130) when you want a reg mark. The reg mark can be stored permanently in the Scrapbook. With "Paste special" it's only available until you copy or cut something else.

If you want to do this:

Then follow these steps:

Shortcuts ▾ Notes ▾ Hints

19.132 Manually download all the fonts in your publication

- Open your font downloading utility (19.44).
- Follow the steps to download the fonts you want, making sure to download all the downloadable fonts in your pub.
- If you are using the LaserWriter Font Utility that comes on your System 7 tidbits disk,
  - □ Double-click on the LaserWriter Font Utility to launch it.
  - □ From the File menu choose "Download fonts...."
  - □ Click "Add"; navigate to your fonts.
  - □ Select the fonts you want to download; click "Add"; click "Done" when you've added all the ones you want to.
  - □ Click "Download." You will see a progress report as the fonts are downloaded to your printer; click OK when done.
  - □ "Display available fonts" from the File menu shows all the fonts available at your printer.
  - □ To erase the fonts from the printer's memory, select "Restart Printer" from the Utilities menu, or turn off your printer.
- In PageMaker, when you are ready to print, deselect the option "Include downloadable fonts" (19.103) in the "Print options" (19.86) dialog box.

- **You** are responsible for all the fonts in the pub. PageMaker will not download **any** fonts when the "Include downloadable fonts" option is not selected.
- In order to speed up printing time, Page-Maker no longer queries the printer to find out what is in RAM each time you print. So PageMaker never *knows* you downloaded those fonts, she simply doesn't send them because you told her not to.
- If your printer memory is limited, make sure you turn off the printer, then turn it back on again just before you download. This empties the RAM so you will have the maximum space available.
- If your publication won't print, the printer may not have enough memory to handle the fonts and the publication. Try printing less pages at a time.
- If your font downloading utility is not a current version, it might not recognize LaserWriter 8. To work around this, temporarily select an earlier version of the LaserWriter in the Chooser.
- If you are working in a publication that uses a certain set of fonts consistently, you can create a custom PPD file that tells PageMaker those fonts are at the printer; see 21.34.

If you want to do this:

19.133 Prepare a publication for do-it-yourself remote printing (printing on a Mac at a copy center, for instance)

Then follow these steps:

- If you have a Mac at home for creating the publication, but you don't have a laser printer, sometimes you must take the pub to someone else's place for printing (*remote* printing).
- Proof your pub on your own machine as carefully as possible. At a copy or service center you will be charged for every page that is printed whether it has typos or not. Plus, you will usually be charged for the time it takes you to fix them.
- Call the copy center to make sure the Mac you will be using has the same version of PageMaker you used to create your publication. Also ask which fonts they have installed. If they don't have the fonts you used, you are usually out of luck because copy centers don't like you to install your own fonts on their machines (see the note, though, in the right column).
- Put a blank disk in your drive, then open the publication.
  - □ From the File menu choose "Save as...."
  - □ Click the radio button "Files for remote printing" (see note at right).
  - □ Click the "Desktop" button to get to the floppy disk.
  - □ Name the publication; click OK.

Shortcuts ▾ Notes ▾ Hints

- Of course, if you have to take your file somewhere else to print, you need to make sure it fits onto a floppy disk or other portable storage medium (such as a SyQuest cartridge) if the copy or service center handles that medium.
- **Important tip:** Copy or service centers that have Macs you can rent by the hour sometimes don't keep up on the latest versions of everything, and their stock of fonts is often limited. If you want to bypass their limitations altogether and ensure that your file prints exactly as you set it up, create a PostScript file by printing to disk ("Normal"); see 19.147. Then you can download it into their printer (if you have a downloader utility with you, 19.149) and it will print exactly as you prepared it no matter what they have on their Mac (even if they don't even have PageMaker!).
- "Files for remote printing" copies all the files that are linked to the publication but *that are not stored within* the publication. This may just be the Tracking Values file, or it may be a large graphic you chose not to store in your pub. See 19.135 for more info.

If you want to do this:

Then follow these steps:

Shortcuts ▾ Notes ▾ Hints

19.134 Prepare a publication as a **PageMaker file** for remote printing at a service bureau *(as opposed to preparing it as a PostScript file; 19.147)*

- Before you open the publication, make a new folder on your hard disk (Command N) and give it a very identifiable name.
- Open the publication. Proof it carefully. At a service bureau you will be charged for every page that is printed, whether it has typos, comes out blank, etc.
- From the File menu choose "Save as...."
- Locate the new folder you created earlier on your hard disk; double-click on its name so it appears at the top of the list box (18.10).
- Click in the checkbox "All linked files" (11.72). This will copy all the files that are linked to the publication (see the note in the next column**).
- Name the publication and click OK. Quit PageMaker.
- Create a fonts folder. Copy both the screen (19.31) and printer fonts (19.32) you used in the publication into the folder.
- Copy both the font folder and the publication folder onto a disk. You may need more than one disk to hold all the files; that's okay—you can now take them out of the folders and use as many disks as you need. Just make sure that you include everything.

- If you relied on PANOSE (1.269) for font substitution be sure you have changed the fonts as necessary and recomposed the text (1.242). If not, any font substitutions you specified may be replaced with the actual font (should the service bureau have it), possibly playing havoc with your layout.
- Don't worry about links being broken when you copy the linked documents out of their original location. If PageMaker can't find the link in its original spot, she checks the folder that the publication itself is in. When you take your folder to the service bureau, they put the publication and all the companion files into one folder so PageMaker can always connect the links.
- You will probably find service bureaus listed in the phone book under "Typesetting," "Printing," "Graphic Design," or perhaps, if your phone book is forward-thinking, under "Desktop Publishing and Service Bureaus."
** If the service bureau tells you all they want are the files *that are not stored in the publication,* then click the radio button for "Files for remote printing." PageMaker will copy into the folder *only* those linked files that do not have a copy stored in the publication (11.15–11.28; 11.73; 19.136).

Never underestimate the number of choices you have.
Donald K. Lee

If you want to do this:	Then follow these steps:	Shortcuts ▾ Notes ▾ Hints
19.135 Copy the publication's Tracking Values for remote printing **Or** **19.136** Copy only the linked files that are not stored in the publication	▪ Follow the steps in 19.134 to prepare your file for remote printing. ▪ From the File menu choose "Save as…." ▪ Click the radio button next to "Files for remote printing." ▪ When you click OK, PageMaker will copy only the files that are linked to the publication but that are not stored in the publication (this includes the Tracking Values file).	▪ If you created your own tracking values with the "Edit tracking" Addition, or have replaced PageMaker 5's Tracking Values with those of PageMaker 4 (17.48), make sure to follow this procedure when saving a file for remote printing. ▪ If you want to copy both the Tracking Values *and* all the linked files for remote printing, you will need to follow 19.134 to "Save as…" and copy the linked files. Then "Save as…" *again* following the technique outlined here to put the Tracking Values in the same folder. (Alternatively, you can simply drag a copy of the Tracking Values file into the folder with your publication and its linked files.)
19.137 Install another PPD	▪ At the Desktop, insert and open Disk 6 of the back-up copies of your original PageMaker application disks. ▪ Open the Extensions folder; open the Printer Descriptions folder. ▪ Double-click on the PPD you want to install. This launches the Aldus Installer. ▪ In the resulting dialog box, save the file to the "Printer Descriptions" folder in your Extensions folder within your System folder.	▪ Make sure you are saving the new PPD to the Printer Descriptions folder within the Extensions folder within your System folder. ▪ On-line services, such as CompuServe, America Online, and eWorld are another source of the most current PPDs. ▪ If you upgrade to a newer version of LaserWriter 8, some PPD files may automatically update, too. Any PPD file that is locked needs to be unlocked before the update can take place.

Making a PostScript file (printing to disk)

19.138 Printing your PageMaker publication straight to a printer or imagesetter is not the only way to get output. You can also **print to disk,** called **Write PostScript to file.** The publication is changed into a PostScript text file; you or the service bureau can send that file to a PostScript printer which reads and translates the text into the graphic publication. Many service bureaus *prefer* that you bring your publication as a PostScript file; some even offer discounts when you do. Printing to disk is easy to do.

You can write a PostScript file in three separate and distinct ways, each used for a particular purpose: "Normal," "EPS" (one page per file), or "For separations."

19.139 When you make a **Normal** PostScript file (19.147), PageMaker creates a straight-text copy of your publication. The text is in the PostScript language that a PostScript imagesetter can read and translate back into your actual publication. For any one of a number of reasons, your service bureau may want you to provide them with a PostScript file instead of, *or in addition to,* the actual PageMaker publication.

19.140 If you provide the service bureau with a "Normal" PostScript file, you don't need to worry about whether the links are still connected or what System or software version it was created in. All the information to print the entire publication is contained in the PostScript. Make sure to check "Include downloadable fonts" (19.144).

19.141 It is critical, though, to set up your print specifications correctly in the dialog boxes before making a "Normal" Postscript file. Set up the file as if you were printing normally, but in the "Type" option (19.54) choose the printer your service bureau uses (see PPDs, 19.11–19.12). Click "All" to save the whole publication to disk or enter page range numbers in the "Ranges" edit box. The service bureau can't make any changes, corrections, or additions to the file once it is PostScript—it's like one huge graphic. *The final word on which options you really need should come from your service bureau.*

By default the file is saved with its publication name followed by the extension ".ps." Click the "Save as…" button (19.146) to specify where to save the file and to rename it, if necessary.

19.142 You can print your publication to disk as a series of **EPS** files (19.148). PageMaker creates a straight-text PostScript copy, *plus* a screen version of the image (just like any other EPS graphic; 10.39–10.46): it basically just turns a page into a graphic image. PageMaker will make a separate EPS file for each page you print. Click "All" to print the whole publication, or enter page numbers or ranges as usual in the "Ranges" option. Each file will have the publication name (up to six characters), followed by an underscore, the page number being printed to disk, and the extension ".eps."

You cannot print to disk as an EPS when you are printing a book (19.64). The "Tile" option is unavailable when the "EPS" option is selected, and EPS files ignore options under "Scale" (see 10.160).

Use this option to prepare files for postprocessing programs such as TrapWise, or to place the file as a graphic within another program that reads the EPS format. PageMaker-created EPS files, though, are much larger than EPS files created in other programs such as Freehand or Illustrator.

—continued

Making a PostScript file —*continued*

19.143 When you choose to print the file to disk **For separations,** PageMaker creates a PostScript file that is readable by Aldus PrePrint or other separation software. The file is set up specifically to provide four-color separations (see 16.31–16.36). If you don't know what four-color separations are, you probably don't need to click this button.

Launch Aldus PrePrint is only available when printing separations to disk. When you click the "Save…" button in the "Print…" dialog box, PageMaker will launch Aldus PrePrint with the file open.

Print.sep

The default file name when creating a PostScript file "For separations."

19.144 Check **Extra image bleed** when you are sending pages to Aldus TrapWise or another post-processing program, and you want to extend the image bleed of TIFF images to one inch. This option is not available when making a Normal PostScript file.

19.145 Check **Include downloadable fonts** for any PostScript file that contains downloadable fonts (any fonts that are not resident in the printer to which you are sending the file; see 19.34). Checking this option makes the file larger, but it means you can print to any printer regardless of the fonts it has. *If you are taking the file to a service bureau and disk space is a concern, tell them which fonts you used (include the vendor and version number if possible) and ask whether it is necessary to check this option or not.*

19.146 Click the **Save as…** button to choose where you want to save the file you are writing to disk. The dialog box also offers a "New folder" button.

While you can change the name of any publication you write to disk, it is a good idea to keep the extension the same as it is in the default name. It will help you to identify your file later.

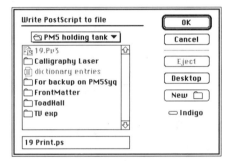

When you "Write PostScript to file" and click the "Save as…" button, you will see this dialog box. Name the file, choose where to save it and click OK. Then click the "Save" button in the "Print" dialog box to actually create the PostScript file.

If you want to do this:

19.147 Prepare a publication as a
PostScript file ("Normal" or
"For separations") for remote
printing at a service bureau
*(as opposed to preparing it
as a PageMaker file; 19.134)*

Print dialog box, "Options" selection area:

*The "Print" button in this dialog box turns
into a "Save" button when you choose the
"Write PostScript to file" checkbox.*

*When printing to disk "For separations,"
other options become available.*

Then follow these steps:

- Open the publication.
- Make sure you have chosen a PostScript
  printer in Chooser (19.127; also see right).
- From the File menu, choose "Print...."
  Set up the specifications in all the selec-
  tion areas *exactly* as if you were going to
  print as usual.
- In the "Options..." selection area check
  the "Write PostScript to file" box. Set the
  PostScript specifications appropriately
  (19.139–19.141).
  - □ If you select "For separations," the
    "Extra image bleed" and "Launch
    Aldus PrePrint" options become
    available (19.143; 19.145).
- Check the box for "Include downloadable
  fonts" if you used downloadable fonts in
  your publication (19.144).
- Click the "Save as..." button, name the file
  (or accept the default name), and decide
  where to save it. Click OK.
- Click "Save."

Shortcuts ▾ Notes ▾ Hints

- You don't have to be *hooked up* to a Post-
  Script printer or even have one in your
  office or home; you just need to have
  a PostScript printer icon sitting in your
  Extensions folder. As long as the icon is in
  your Extensions folder, you can select it in
  Chooser and then print to disk.
- PostScript files are very large. This chapter,
  at fifty-seven pages, is normally 1,370K. As
  a PostScript file it weighs in at a hefty six
  megabytes! Of course, this can present a
  problem when trying to transport files on
  disks. A popular way to transport large files
  is on a removable-cartridge disk. Check
  with your service bureau to see if they can
  accommodate a cartridge, and make sure
  you get one for yourself that is compatible
  with theirs.
- Your service bureau may ask you to provide a regular PageMaker version of the
  publication *in addition to the PostScript file*
  just in case there is a simple problem they
  can fix for you.

If you want to do this:	Then follow these steps:	Shortcuts ▾ Notes ▾ Hints
19.148 Create an EPS file of one page or individual EPS files of specific pages in a publication **Print_619.eps** *The default filename includes the publication name and the page number.*	■ Follow the steps in 19.147 to create a PostScript file. In the "Document" selection area enter the page numbers and/or range of pages in the edit box next to "Ranges." Also make sure you have not checked any of the following options: □ Thumbnails, Tile, Proof, or Scaling other than 100%. ■ In the "Options" selection area (19.86) click "Write PostScript to file" and then click the "EPS" button. ■ Click the "Save as..." button to choose where to save the file. Rename the file if necessary; click OK. ■ Click the "Save" button.	■ PageMaker makes a separate EPS file for each page. The default file name will include the page number. ■ The "Tile" and "Proof" options will gray out after you select "EPS." ■ Once you have made an EPS file of a PageMaker page, you can then place it on the page just like any other EPS graphic (10.39–10.46; 10.126). The image on page 495 is an EPS file of a PageMaker page. ■ Use this method for preparing color files for post-processing in a program such as Aldus TrapWise.
19.149 Print a "Normal" PostScript file yourself Font Downloader LaserWriter Font Utility *Utilities such as these will download your PostScript file to the printer.*	■ To print a "Normal" PostScript file yourself you need a **downloader.** You can use the same downloader you use to download fonts into your printer (19.44). If you have bought PostScript fonts from any vendor, you will find a downloader on the disk. ■ Double-click on the downloader, then follow the directions. There will be either a button to click or a menu command to choose to download a PostScript file to the printer.	■ You may never need (or want) to print a PostScript file yourself. Then again, you may want to print it to verify your specifications before sending it to the service bureau. Or you may want to take this file and your downloader to a copy center or service center where you can print it to their laser printer yourself. ■ You'll find the LaserWriter Font Utility on the System 7 Tidbits disk.

Using a service bureau

19.150 A **desktop publishing service bureau** is a new type of service, just invented in the last few years. Isn't it interesting—such dire predictions were made that the computer would put so many people out of work, and instead an entire new industry was spawned, with jobs for everyone. Why, thousands of people make a living just building booths for all the computer trade shows.

19.151 A service bureau is where you take your publication on a disk (or send it by modem) when you want a higher quality output than your laser printer or QuickDraw printer can provide. Service bureaus use **imagesetters** (19.9–19.10) that output your pages onto resin-coated paper at extremely high resolutions. There are some things you should know about taking your job to a service bureau.

19.152 Be nice. Be nice, be friendly. It goes a long way. If you are rude and demanding, or even just plain cold, you can only expect that human nature will respond in kind. If you are pleasant and accommodating, your rush jobs will always be done on time and you will be notified of potential problems before they happen. Besides, it's just more fun to be nice.

19.153 Find a service bureau you like and stick with them. Work with them, ask questions, find out how they operate so you can provide jobs on disk just the way *they* like them so you can get your jobs back just the way *you* like them. A good service bureau is happy to teach you the most efficient, economical, and foolproof way to prepare your documents for remote printing. If you establish a good relationship, you can usually count on the bureau as a technical resource.

19.154 Fill out the job ticket thoroughly. A service bureau usually has you fill out a job ticket for each job you bring in. This ticket asks for extremely important information, but to be of any use, it must be complete and precise. Make sure you have the necessary information before you go in:

a) When the ticket asks for the fonts you used, *list each and every font, including the vendor's name.* For instance, if you used Goudy from Bitstream as the basis for your publication, list Goudy Regular, as well as Goudy Bold, Goudy Italic, and Goudy Bold Italic if you used them at all anywhere in the entire publication, and tell them it is the version made by Bitstream. Ask the service bureau if they would like to know the *package number* of the fonts you have used; this may help.

b) Write the exact file name of the publication you want printed. Be precise; don't say, "Oh, print the brochure."

c) Write the number (amount) of pages you want printed, and their page numbers.

d) Write the kind of machine on which you created the publication, the System version, and the software version.

e) State *clearly* when you need the job returned. Don't write "Tomorrow" or "ASAP." Be specific. And clear it with the service bureau to be sure they can even turn it around for you in the time you need.

f) Remember to leave your name and phone number. Always.

19.155 Label the disk. Disks all look the same. It's *critical* that you label the disk with your name, your phone number, the name of the job, the date, etc.

19.156 Give them a clean disk. Make sure you have *only* the publication (and its companion files; 19.157) that you want to print. Don't leave a bunch of unrelated junk on the disk.

Service bureaus —*continued*

19.157 Include any companion files. Companion files are those external files that are linked (Section 11) to items in the publication. You don't need to include all the text files, as they are stored in the publication (11.16), but bring all TIFF, PICT, MacPaint, and EPS files that you have placed into the pub. You won't really need them all, but they should be there just in case. Put all the files into one folder along with the publication (19.134–19.136) and label the folder appropriately. Don't worry about PageMaker not being able to find the links—the service bureau will put all the files into one folder on their hard disk. PageMaker can always find the linked files if they are in the same folder as the publication itself.

If your file is really huge (this book, for instance, is over 40 megs, not including the fonts), you may want to take it to the service bureau on a removable cartridge hard disk, rather than on fifty floppies. Check with the service bureau first, of course, to make sure your cartridge is compatible with their machine.

If you are sending the bureau a *PostScript file* (19.138; 19.147), you will not need to provide the external, linked files.

19.158 Ask if you need to provide the fonts. If the service bureau does not own the fonts you use in the publication, you will need to bring to them the screen fonts (in a suitcase*), as well as the corresponding printer fonts (separate icons; 19.30–19.33). In my Utilities folder I keep a suitcase called "ScreenFontsToGo" in which I load up any necessary fonts. *(Be sure you understand your license agreement with the font vendor.)*

If you are sending the bureau a *PostScript file* (19.138–19.147), you will not need to provide any fonts.

*If you don't know how to copy screen fonts into a suitcase, you will find step-by-step directions in both The Little Mac Book *and* How to Boss Your Fonts Around, *or in the Macintosh manual. Basically, you just copy the fonts you need into an empty suitcase.*

19.159 Let them know you're coming. If the job involves just one or two pages, this step isn't always necessary. But if it is a major job—a manual, a book, a large or complex graphic file, an annual report, etc.—it is thoughtful and often critical to call the service bureau to let them know it will be arriving in a day or two. This helps them schedule their workload and helps ensure you can get your job back when you need it.

19.160 Confirm the price. Get it straight exactly what the costs will be so you won't be surprised and upset when you pick up the job. Many service bureaus charge for downloading fonts or switching files or having to clean up your mistakes, etc. Know what to expect.

Ask what the normal turnaround time is (the time between when you bring the job in and when it is ready for you to pick up). If you need it faster, clarify any rush charges. There may be varying rush charges, depending on how big a rush you're in.

19.161 You can also use a modem. Most service bureaus love it when you send the file over the modem. There are fewer disks floating around, there is less foot traffic, and less disruption. Plus it saves you a few trips. To do this, you need to set up an account with the bureau and let a consultant there tell you exactly how to send the file. Generally, they prefer that you put all the files into one folder and compress it with a file compression utility. *Give the folder a clearly identifiable name.* The service bureau can even fax you a finished copy for approval and overnight-mail the final job directly to you (or to the commercial press or other destination of your choice).

TEN WAYS TO DRIVE YOUR SERVICE BUREAU NUTS

1. Always, **always** wait until the last possible moment to bring your work to the imagesetter. Be sure you have an ironclad printer deadline you can tell the service bureau about so if they have trouble outputting your job or something else goes wrong, they can know in their hearts they are ruining your whole production schedule.

2. Complain loudly if they charge you a rush charge and threaten to take your work elsewhere, even though they have bailed you out countless times in the past. This helps to build mutual trust and ensures that they will try **really** hard to please you in the future.

3. Don't bother to call them to let them know you are coming with the rush job—they love surprises like that. Keeps them from becoming bored. Or do call and tell them it's a bona-fide life-and-death situation so they'll pull your job and run it ahead of everyone else. Then don't go to pick it up for a week or so.

4. Bring the job in on an unlabeled diskette. The service bureau deals with hundreds of diskettes daily and they love having unidentified ones floating around.

5. Don't bother to fill out the order form completely. Whatever you do, don't put your phone number on it . . . that way if they need to talk to you they can add some adventure to their lives by roaming through the phone book, calling mutual acquaintances, etc., trying to find you. They don't have anything else to do anyway. Don't tell them what fonts you used in your document, either. They love to guess.

6. Put a lot of different files on the diskette you bring in and forget exactly which one it is that you want printed. Write on the order form "I'm not sure what the name of the file I need is, but it's the one that says 'Little Bo Peep' in the lower right-hand corner of page three." Even better, ask if you can just look at the files on the service bureau's computer, just for *one minute*. The operator won't mind interrupting whatever s/he happens to be working on right then so you can figure out the name of the file you need.

7. Don't bother to bring all those companion files and other junk like Tracking Values or linked files with you. That way, when the job tries to print and asks for this additional data, the operator can call you on the phone and enjoy a leisurely chat. They don't take enough breaks anyway.

8. Use lots of obscure fonts manufactured by companies that don't understand the rules about fonts. Then "forget" to bring the font with you to the service bureau. Better yet, bring only one part, i.e., the screen (bitmap) part or the printer (outline) part.

9. Don't bother to upgrade your software. So what if you do all your work in ReadySetGo 1.0 with Cricket Draw graphics. The service bureau loves to load up old versions of software so they can print your job.

10. When you send a file by modem, don't bother to compress it. The service bureau's other clients won't mind getting a busy signal for two hours because the modem is busy receiving your file. Also, give the file a name like MXRVB.sit so the operator can identify your job right away. This will get you preferential service for sure.

But seriously, folks . . . most service bureaus will bend over backwards to help you get your job out, whatever it takes. Just remember, as in all your business dealings, a little thoughtfulness and consideration go a long way!

BY JANET BUTCHER
Petaluma Imagesetting, Inc.

Troubleshooting

19.162 If a job won't print all the way through on your laser printer, it's probably because your printer doesn't have enough memory to deal with your page. Some things that make pages extra complicated are:

- Too many text wraps on a page, or the text wraps are too complex (too many points).
- Too much text has been expanded or condensed with "Set width."
- Too many rotated objects or text blocks.
- Too many TIFF, EPS, or PICT files.
- One or more TIFF, EPS, or PICT files are too complex.
- Too many downloadable fonts.
- The publication itself is too complex, possibly due to a failure on your part to "Save as..." in order to compress the file size (see 18.4–18.5; 18.29).

19.163 Service bureaus generally don't have as much trouble printing PageMaker publications on their imagesetters because imagesetters have more memory. Even if *you* can't get it to print, it may print just fine at your service bureau. *Don't always count on it though*, especially if you are under a heavy deadline. If a file is complex, it may take more time to run (and remember that service bureaus do charge extra for long-running files).

19.164 You can try these troubleshooting measures with your laser printer:

- Use "Save as..." to compress the file (18.29). Compressing it makes it less complicated and so sometimes makes the printer happier.
- If you did not compress your TIFFs as you placed them, replace them with compressed versions (10.153).
- Turn the printer off, wait a minute or two, then turn it back on again. This clears out the RAM, which gives you the maximum amount of memory. If you have downloaded fonts into the RAM, try manually downloading fewer fonts next time.
- Check the option "Include PostScript error handler" (19.101) to identify the problem.
- In the "Print document" dialog box, check the "Proof" box. Then if the job prints okay, you will at least know that the problem is in the graphics.

- Print only a couple of pages at a time. If the problem is with one particular page, the printer will usually print up to that page, then freak out. Try printing just that one particular page alone, then continue printing the rest.
- If the printer gets stuck on one page, then obviously that page has a problem. Try removing one of the graphics, then printing. If the graphics are causing problems, see if there is any way for you to simplify them. If a graphic has heavy cropping (10.143–10.144; 10.220), take the image back into the appropriate graphic program and trim off the excess there, rather than cropping it in PageMaker. If a graphic is a TIFF, make sure you compress it as you place it (10.152). (I have had to remove a graphic, print the page, remove everything else on the page, put the graphic back and reprint.)
- If one page is really stuck, try printing that one page to disk (19.147) and then downloading it to print (19.149).
- Hold down the Option key as you choose "Print" to bypass the PPD (19.125).
- Try printing the job through someone else's Mac and printer.

etaoin shrdlu (continued from page 312)

Like everything else, the newspaper business has changed. It became a business. It used to be "the newspaper game," a term that made us feel better about our ridiculous wages. Who gets paid for having fun except ball-players and maybe some hookers? (Hookers are "turned out" and newspaper people are "broken in" but otherwise there isn't much difference, hence the term presstitute.) In the old days we pounded out the copy with two fingers and hollered "Boy!" to rush this hot stuff to the composing room. Today you yell "Boy!" and a girl arrives along with a member of the union grievance committee. It's silly to holler "Person!" so nobody yells any more.

Gone are the magnificent men on their Linotype machines, gone the galley proofs smelling of fresh ink, gone the paperweights with your name in 90-point type, the gift of a friendly printer. Gone the "Boy!"s of yesterday, gone with the wind, gone with the Winchell, gone with the demon rewrite man with phone cradled to ear and cigaret burning his lips as he pounds out a perfect, tight, non-editable "new lede" (never "lead") on a fast-breaking story. Gone—yes, the very TYPEWRITERS.

When cold type replaced hot lead, the manual typewriter was doomed. The scanner—ours, at least—would "accept" only the IBM Selectric, which doesn't have keys that jam, like a proper typewriter, but a golfball device that runs back and forth like a mouse in a maze. Now, the Selectric is being phased out for VDTs, which is not police shorthand for someone with a social disease plus the shakes. The initials stand for Video Display Terminal.

Although I am generally spineless, I rose off my knees in protest at both the Selectric and the VDT. Old dog, new tricks and all that. Since I do use only two fingers while typing, the Selectric is too much machine for me, and the VDT is either above or below contempt, I forget which. I have thus been allowed to go on using my ancient and beloved Royal manual—metal, not plastic—and living in the past. I edit my copy with an Eagle 314, just as in the old days. I go on writing, and yelling "Boy!" as though it were still 1941. You may have noticed. Where have you gone, etaoin shrdlu? Operator, gimme rewrite! Stop the press—uh, scanner—I gotta story here that'll shake this old town right off its foundations. Boy! Boy? Uh . . .

Typewriter of the '50s

Additions for printing

19.165 Of the twenty-five Additions that shipped with PageMaker 5, three of them can help you get your publication printed easier and more efficiently. A fourth printing Addition is a utility that is crucial to run if you have upgraded your printer in any way.

19.166 The **Update PPD** Addition (19.171–19.178) is important if you have installed additional memory or added a hard drive with permanently installed fonts to your laser printer. Running this Addition creates a custom PPD telling PageMaker what new information is now available at the printer.

19.167 The **Display pub info** Addition (19.179–19.190) lets you view on screen (or print out) a list of all the fonts, links, and style sheets in a publication. (If you need a visual reference of your style sheet *formatting*, try the "List styles used" Addition discussed in Section 8.)

19.168 With the **Printer styles** Addition (19.191–19.225) you can set up multiple "Print" dialog boxes and save the specifications as a printing style. Just like you can tag a paragraph with a style sheet, you can tag a publication with a printer style. You can send multiple publications to the printer all at once and, since they are tagged with their own printer specifications, they will print accurately without you ever having to fuss over them.

19.169 If the terms mock-up, imposition, and signature are familiar to you, then the **Build booklet** Addition (19.226–19.248) may be a welcome ally. If not, some time spent learning the principles on which this Addition runs may help you master the ins and outs of bindery techniques. "Build booklet" automates the process of correctly ordering the pages of a publication for printing and binding. It is a rather complicated Addition, though, so read about it carefully and try it first on some simple experiments. Even though PageMaker automates the process, it is still valuable to create a dummy (mock-up) so *you* know what the outcome should be.

19.170 If you are not sure which Additions you installed, simply check out the "Aldus Additions" submenu under the Utilities menu. Any Additions you didn't install can be added at any time (20.7). A complete listing of PageMaker's Additions is shown on page 785. Don't forget there's a whole market of third-party Additions available (see Appendix J).

The "Update PPD..." Addition

19.171 PageMaker no longer sets up a running conversation with your printer during printing jobs, querying your printer each time you print for needed information. Instead, she now reads the information provided *about* your printer in the selected PPD (PostScript printer description). What if this PPD text file doesn't accurately reflect the current status of your printer? If you have upgraded your printer with RAM or added a hard disk of fonts, you need to run the "Update PPD" Addition to bring your PPD current with the new printer information. *(If you are using a network spooler, "Update PPD..." does not work.)*

19.172 "Update PPD..." gets the new information from your printer and creates an up-to-date PPD "Include" file. PageMaker reads this new "Include" file together with the original PPD file to determine how to best send information to your printer.

19.173 The "Update PPD" dialog box has a pop-up menu of all the PPDs installed on your hard disk (19.12). In the event you can't find a PPD for your printer, choose "General" or a PPD for a printer model whose features most closely resemble the features on yours. You may receive an alert message if the PPD file name and your printer model name do not match exactly. That's okay, the process will still work.

19.174 When you click the "Update" button, PageMaker creates the "Include" file and prompts you to save the new PPD in the Printer Descriptions folder in the Extensions folder in your System folder.

19.175 The custom PPD will now show in the pop-up menu next to "Type" in the "Print" dialog box. If you prefer that the PPD be set as an application default in the "Print" dialog box, run through the LaserWriter setup explained on page 730 using the "Select PPD..." option in 19.23.

19.176 Since PageMaker no longer has a direct line of communication with your printer, one wonders how she recognizes manually downloaded fonts (19.45). She doesn't. And unfortunately the "Update PPD" Addition doesn't recognize fonts in the printer's RAM either. Supposedly, LaserWriter 8 is fast enough that we won't miss our font downloading capabilities, but, if you should, there are a couple of work-arounds.

19.177 One is to simply download all the fonts in your publication and deselect the option "Include downloadable fonts" in the "Print" dialog box; see 19.132. Or you can go in and edit a PPD file to include fonts that you plan to manually download; see 21.34. Although it sounds intimidating, it's really not that hard, especially if you edit an updated PPD (these are simple "Include" files as opposed to the original long and complex PPD files). Another option, if you are brave, is to use the resource editing program "ResEdit" to customize the "Update PPD" Addition so it queries for RAM-resident fonts.

If you want to do this:	**Then follow these steps:**	**Shortcuts ▾ Notes ▾ Hints**

19.178 Run the "Update PPD" Addition

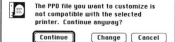

- Turn on your printer if it is not on already.
- Make sure the LaserWriter 8 icon and your printer is selected in the Chooser.
- From the Utilities menu, slide down to "Aldus Additions," then slide over to the submenu and choose "Update PPD...."
- In the pop-up menu next to "Select PPD," choose the PPD file that best fits your printer.
- Click "Update."
- If you receive an alert box click the "Continue" button.
- In the "Save as" dialog box, accept or change the default name PageMaker offers for the "Include" file. The Printer Descriptions folder should already be open for you. Click "Save."
- Click OK.
- Open a new or existing publication. To rebuild the Printer list hold down the Shift key while selecting "Print" from the File menu.
- Select the new PPD from the list and print as usual.

- If you don't have a specific PPD file for your printer, you can substitute another PPD file as long as it is for a printer that is similar to yours.
- The bullet placed before the default PPD name places it at the top of the PPD list in the "Print document" dialog box.
- You can go to the Chooser and change the PPD file through the "Setup" dialog box (19.23) if you want the new PPD to be selected by default in all your new PageMaker publications. Otherwise you can simply select the PPD of your choice directly in the "Print document" dialog box.

If you can keep your head when all about you are losing theirs, it's just possible you haven't grasped the situation. —Jean Kerr

The "Display pub info..." Addition

(from the Utilities menu, slide down to "Aldus Additions," then over to the submenu and choose "Display pub info...")

19.179 When it comes time to print your publication, it helps to know as much about it as you can. "Display pub info" lets you review, on screen, all the fonts, links, and styles that are in your active publication. You can, if you want to, save this info as a TeachText file and print it for future reference or to take with you to the service bureau. You may even want to use it as a reference manual in workgroup situations or for a series of publications that require consistency.

19.180 PageMaker displays the fonts used in the publication followed by all those available in the system. "Y" stands for yes, it's there; "N" stands for no, it's not.

Font:	In Pub	In System
Futura Book	Y	Y
Zapf Dingbats	Y	Y
New Baskerville	Y	Y
BernhMod	Y	N
B Futura Bold	Y	Y
L Futura Light	Y	Y
Times	Y	Y
Present	N	Y

Notice that Bernhard is in the publication but not in the system; Present is in the system but not in the publication. If "BernhMod" is available, it can be accessed through a font management utility. If it is not available, PANOSE can substitute a similar, available typeface (1.240), or you can change the font yourself.

19.181 *Click "Save..." to save the information as a TeachText document. You can then print it as a reference; see 19.190.*

19.182 *Path to the document.*

19.183 *The list for each linked item includes the path to the original item, the kind of file it is, and the page on which it is placed.*

19.184 *The "Styles" info lists all the styles in the publication.*

19.185 *When you run the Addition, all the options are automatically displayed. You can deselect any of the options to shorten the list for viewing and/or saving.*

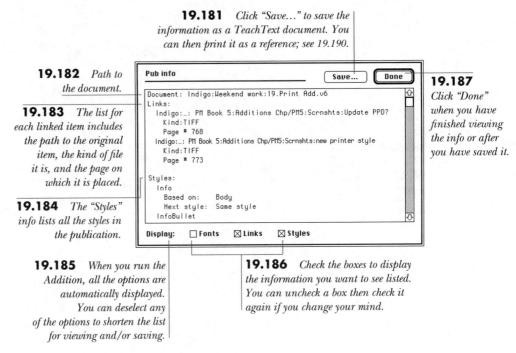

19.187 *Click "Done" when you have finished viewing the info or after you have saved it.*

19.186 *Check the boxes to display the information you want to see listed. You can uncheck a box then check it again if you change your mind.*

If you want to do this:	Then follow these steps:	Shortcuts ▾ Notes ▾ Hints
19.188 Display the publication info for your active publication	▪ With **any tool** selected, go to the Utilities menu, slide down to "Aldus Additions," then over to the submenu to choose "Display pub info…." ▪ Use the scroll bars to read the whole list. ▪ Click "Done" when you have finished viewing the information.	▪ By default, all the "Display" options (Fonts, Links, Styles) are checked each time you run the Addition. Unchecking these options doesn't affect the choices the next time you run the Addition.
19.189 Save the information in the "Pub info" dialog box	▪ With **any tool** selected, go to the Utilities menu, slide down to "Aldus Additions," then over to the submenu to choose "Display pub info…." ▪ Uncheck any options you don't want to save. ▪ Click the "Save…" button and name the file.	▪ The default publication name is the file name with the extension ".info." ▪ The "New folder" button lets you create a new folder in which to save the publication info.
19.190 Print the publication information	▪ Double-click on the file you saved. ▪ While in TeachText, choose "Print…" from the File menu.	▪ If you want a more aesthethic printout of the info, you can place the file in PageMaker instead. Then you can change the font, add tabs, etc. See 4.28–4.56 if you need to review how to place a story. ▫ In the "Text-only import filter" dialog box, check the box "Replace 3 or more spaces with a tab." You can then line up all those "Y's" and "N's" using the Indents/tabs ruler (6.63).

The "Printer styles..." Addition

(from the Utilities menu, slide down to "Aldus Additions," then over to the submenu and choose "Printer styles...")

19.191 The "Printer styles..." Addition is too cool. With it you can line up multiple publications to print one right after the other automatically. You can create "Print styles" and then print publications without ever looking at the "Print" dialog boxes.

19.192 Use the "Define..." button to save print dialog box settings as print styles. The styles can then be applied to a publication (just like a paragraph style) instead of selecting the options individually in the "Print" dialog boxes. You can create as many styles as you want, easily edit them, and temporarily override them when necessary.

19.193 Creating a print queue is very similar to creating a Book List. Navigate through your disks and folders to locate a publication you want in the list and assign it a "Print style" from the "Style" pop-up menu. You can change or override print styles assigned to publications and you can rearrange the list using the "Item up" and "Item down" buttons.

19.194 The Addition also has a feature for keeping a record of each job you print and for tracking the print time of each job in the queue (19.214–19.216).

19.195 *Select a publication to add to the print queue.*

19.196 *Click "Add" to add a selected file from the list on the left to the print queue on the right.*

19.197 *Click "Print" to send the files in the queue to the printer.*

19.198 *Click to close the dialog box. Print styles you create are available each time you run the Addition.*

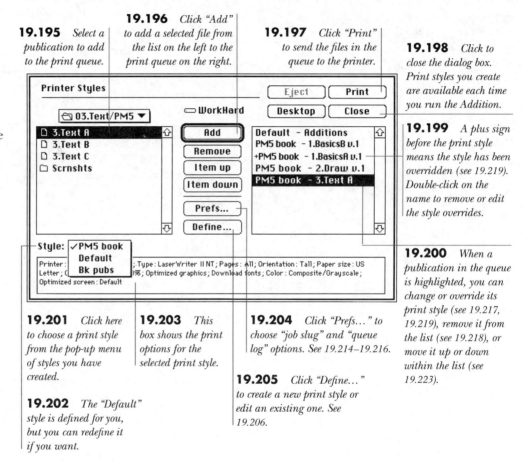

19.199 *A plus sign before the print style means the style has been overridden (see 19.219). Double-click on the name to remove or edit the style overrides.*

19.200 *When a publication in the queue is highlighted, you can change or override its print style (see 19.217, 19.219), remove it from the list (see 19.218), or move it up or down within the list (see 19.223).*

19.201 *Click here to choose a print style from the pop-up menu of styles you have created.*

19.202 *The "Default" style is defined for you, but you can redefine it if you want.*

19.203 *This box shows the print options for the selected print style.*

19.204 *Click "Prefs..." to choose "job slug" and "queue log" options. See 19.214–19.216.*

19.205 *Click "Define..." to create a new print style or edit an existing one. See 19.206.*

Defining print styles   *(in the "Printer Styles" dialog box, click the "Define" button)*

19.206 Creating a print style is easy. Click the "New" button and name the style; PageMaker will display the "Print" dialog boxes for you. It's just like creating a style sheet.

19.210 Type in a name and click OK. PageMaker automatically displays the "Print" dialog boxes for you to choose the style settings.

Click OK to return to the "Printer styles" dialog box.

19.207 The "Define printer styles" dialog box lists all the print styles available. Each style you create is given a .PQ extension and placed in the PSTYLES folder, in the Additions folder, in the Aldus folder, in your System folder.

19.211 Click "Edit" to view the "Print" dialog boxes and make changes to the selected print style.

19.208 You can copy the print styles from the PSTYLES folder to place in the PSTYLES folder on another computer.

19.212 Click "Remove" to remove the selected print style from the list.

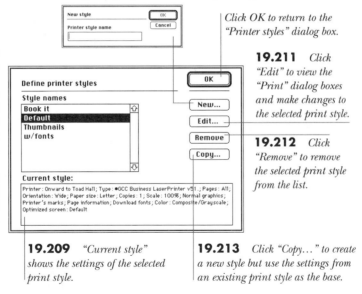

19.209 "Current style" shows the settings of the selected print style.

19.213 Click "Copy…" to create a new style but use the settings from an existing print style as the base.

"Job slugs" and "Queue logs"

19.214 "Slugs" and "logs" help you keep records of all the work you output. You can print or save a file about each job in a queue. When you select "Include job slugs," the options you check are printed at the end of each publication on a separate page.

19.215 Check the box next to "Create queue log" to save a text file that contains information about each file printed and the printing time of the entire queue. The text file is stored in the PSTYLES folder (see 19.207) and is named POLOG000.TXT (the zeros become numbers as you create queue logs). You can open the file in TeachText or place it in a PageMaker document.

19.216 Choices you make in the "Preferences" dialog box are in effect each time you print using "Printer styles."

If you want to do this:

19.217 Create and print a queue of publications

Then follow these steps:

- Make sure that all the publications' fonts and links are available. Alert boxes for either will interrupt the print queue.
- From the Utilities menu slide down to "Aldus Additions" then over to the submenu and choose "Printer styles...."
- Click once on a publication in the left hand box that you want to add to the print queue.
- From the "Style" pop-up menu select a print style.
- Click "Add."
- Navigate through folders as necessary to select other publications you wish to print and repeat the above process.
- If necessary, rearrange the print queue by selecting a publication in the queue and clicking the "Move up" or "Move down" button.
- Click the "Prefs..." button. Check the "Include job slugs" and "Create queue log" options as desired (19.214–19.216). Click OK.
- Click "Print."
- When the printing is complete, click "No" or "Yes" in PageMaker's very considerate dialog box (see left).

Shortcuts ▾ Notes ▾ Hints

- You can run the Addition from either the PageMaker desktop (no pubs open) or from within any PageMaker publication.
- If you haven't created any print styles yet, the only choice in the "Style" pop-up menu will be "Default" containing basic PageMaker print settings.
- If the print style you want is showing in the "Styles" menu, you can double-click on a publication name to add it to the queue with that style.
- You can also change the print style assigned to a publication *after* it has been added to the print queue. Click on the pub name then choose another style.
- You can add a publication to the queue list more than once. If you assign it the same print style, PageMaker will ask if that is what you really want to do. You can also assign it different print styles. This comes in handy when you want to print a publication in different formats. For this book I created a four-to-a-page thumbnail style. When printing sections, I often printed them twice: once at full size for editing purposes, and once as thumbnails to view the layout and flow of material. "Printer styles" made this effortless.

If you want to do this:	Then follow these steps:	Shortcuts ▾ Notes ▾ Hints
19.218 Remove a publication from the print queue	▪ Select the publication in the print queue. ▪ Click "Remove."	▪ Of course this only removes the publication from the print queue; it still exists wherever it came from.
19.219 Temporarily override the print style assigned to a publication in the queue	▪ Double-click on the publication in the print queue. ▪ In the "Print" dialog boxes, change the print settings how you want and click OK.	▪ This is good for modifications to a print style such as a change of page range or the number of copies to be printed.
19.220 Create a print style	▪ From the Utilities menu slide down to "Aldus Additions" then over to the submenu to choose "Printer styles...." ▪ Click the "Define..." button. ▪ In the "Define printer styles" dialog box, click "New." ▪ Enter a name for the print style; click OK. ▪ Cruise through the "Print" dialog boxes selecting the options you want as part of the print style. Click OK when you are done. ▪ Click OK in the "Define printer styles" dialog box. ▪ You can create other print styles, create and print a queue list, or just "Close" the "Printer Styles" dialog box.	▪ In the "Print" dialog boxes, the "Print" button modifies to an OK button. The "Book" option is not available when defining a style except as an override (see 19.219). ▪ Once you create a print style, it is stored deep within your System folder (see 19.207), and is available each time you run the "Printer styles" Addition. ▪ You can create a style for all sorts of handy printing features: thumbnails, separations, print to disk, etc. You can even get a PPD file from your service bureau and create a style for printing to their imagesetter. ▪ You can modify a print style with temporary overrides; see 19.219. ▪ You can create a style based on an exisiting style by clicking on the original style then clicking "Copy"; give it a new name in the "New style" dialog box.

If you want to do this:	Then follow these steps:	Shortcuts ▾ Notes ▾ Hints
19.221 Edit a print style	▪ From the Utilities menu slide down to "Aldus Additions" then over to the submenu and choose "Printer styles…." ▪ Click the "Define…" button. ▪ In the "Define printer styles" dialog box, click on the style you want to edit, then click the "Edit…" button. ▪ In the "Print" dialog boxes, change any of the print settings; click OK. ▪ Click OK in the "Define printer styles" dialog box.	▪ When you edit a style, publications in the queue with that assigned style assume the edit changes. (Unless the style has an override. A style with a plus sign before it doesn't assume editing changes made to the original style.)
19.222 Remove a print style	▪ From the Utilities menu slide down to "Aldus Additions" then over to the submenu and choose "Printer styles…." ▪ Click the "Define…" button. ▪ In the "Define printer styles" dialog box, click on the style you want to remove then click the "Remove" button. ▪ Click OK in the alert box.	▪ If you have created a print queue, you can't remove a style that is assigned to a publication in the queue. ▪ PageMaker displays an alert box before removing the style just in case you didn't *really* mean to remove it.
19.223 Rearrange the order of publications in the print queue	▪ Select a publication in the queue list. ▪ Click "Item up" or "Item down." ▪ Repeat the process as necessary to create the order in which you want the publications to print.	▪ If PageMaker opens a publication with missing links or PANOSE font substitutions when printing a queue, she displays an alert box. Printing will not continue until you deal with the alert message.

If you want to do this:	**Then follow these steps:**	**Shortcuts ▾ Notes ▾ Hints**
19.224 Print an informational page at the end of every publication	▪ From the Utilities menu slide down to "Aldus Additions" then over to the submenu and choose "Printer styles...." ▪ Set up the print queue as desired. ▪ Click the "Prefs..." button (see 19.204). ▪ In the "Preferences" dialog box make sure the box next to "Include job slugs" is checked. ▪ Check all the information options you want to include; click OK. ▪ Back in the "Printer Styles" dialog box, click "Print."	▪ You can select as many of the "job slug" options as you wish. A page prints after each publication listing all the options you chose. ▪ You can choose to save a queue log at the same time as you choose it print it.

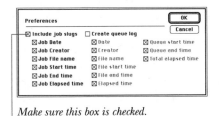

Make sure this box is checked.

19.225 Save a queue log—a text file that contains information about the publications printed.	▪ From the Utilities menu slide down to "Aldus Additions" then over to the submenu and choose "Printer styles...." ▪ Set up the print queue as desired. ▪ Click the "Prefs..." button. ▪ In the "Preferences" dialog box make sure the box next to "Create queue log" is checked. ▪ Check all the information options you want to include; click OK. ▪ Back in the "Printer Styles" dialog box, click "Print."	▪ This information does not print with the publications but is stored as a TeachText file, in the PSTYLES folder, in the Additions folder, in the Aldus folder, in the System folder. Whew. You can double-click on the file name to open it in TeachText, or you can "Place" it in a PageMaker document. ▪ The "queue log" information can contain the same info as the "job slugs" plus the start, finish, and total printing time of the entire queue. Unfortunately, neither "job slugs" nor "queue log" provide an option for the number of pages printed.

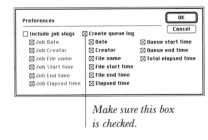

Make sure this box is checked.

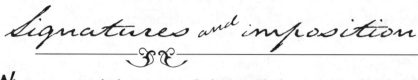

Signatures and imposition

When printers print a book, or a magazine, they use large, parent-sized (larger 'n' life) sheets of paper on which they print a number of pages, on both the back and the front, which they then fold up into **signatures**, cut into pages, and stitch into a book. All we as authors have to do is write the book; it's up to the printer to figure out how to take all the pages we write and arrange them so that when he folds the **signatures** they all come out right. It never fails to amaze me that printers know how to make page 237 follow page 236, or even how to make sure a book begins with page 1 and ends with page 256 (or 936! or whatever page your book ends on) ✎

A signature can be made up of any number of pages depending upon the thickness of the paper being used. The most common signatures are a **folio**, or 2-up (folded once); a **quatro**, or 4-up (folded twice); and an **octavo**, or 8-up (folded three times) ✎

To the inexperienced eye the **imposition**, how the pages are arranged on each parent-sized sheet of paper, looks like a hodgepodge of pages randomly grouped together on a single piece of paper (the parent sheet). But to the experienced printer it all makes sense. He knows that once the **imposition** is printed, he will have one signature that can be folded and inserted inside another folded signature, ad infinitum (nauseam!), until he has your book ready to bind ✎

Perfect bound books are **signatures** bound together along the spine. Traditionally the signatures were sewn together and then elegantly hand-finished. Nowadays, they more often use glue. Paperback books or the thicker magazines are quite commonly put together in this manner ✎

When a book is **saddle-stitched**, on the other hand, the imposed pages (printed "2-up," or 2 book-size pages to a sheet of paper) are sewn (in the good old days) or stapled through the middle of the center fold. It's simple, inexpensive, and lets the pages lie flat. Many magazines are bound this way ✎

When doing either kind of binding, especially 2-up with a lot of pages, the printer needs to take a number of things into account. One of these is **creep**. The thicker the book gets, the more of a "fan" of pages there will be that need to be trimmed. That's all fine and good, except when you **trim** the pages, more of the paper on the inside pages is lost than on the outside pages. This is the creep amount and it must be anticipated and figured into the layout of the **signatures** ✎

And this is just scratching the surface. The art of bookbinding—and it **is** an art—is not to be taken lightly. Imagine the horror of opening a book to the first page and beginning a tale at the middle of a story. Or of discovering the solution to the perfect crime right there in the middle of the book ✎

—*ve*

The "Build booklet..." Addition

19.226 The "Build booklet..." Addition was developed to take the confusion out of designing and producing double-sided, multi-paged, bound publications. Although the Addition holds much potential for designers, there is much to be said for the art of printing and bookbinding that makes me advise most of you to utilize the services of a professional when designing and producing such publications. *Talk to your printer and service bureau first!* However, "Build booklet..." may be the perfect solution for simple binding scenarios such as smaller booklets or programs and multi-paneled brochures.

Now, instead of dividing a page layout into columns and painstakingly measuring for cut and fold lines and panel widths, you can create a document page by page (read panel by panel) that can then be automatically assembled in the correct order. The very first step, however, no matter how little or big the publication is, is to create a hard copy "mock-up" or "dummy" to help you visualize the proper arrangement of the pages. This will help assure that all the pages will be printed in the right order, and facing in the right direction.

19.227 PageMaker creates a whole new publication when you run the "Build booklet" Addition. No changes are made to your original publication (other than a last chance to save changes). A copy of the original publication is made, the pages are **imposed**, and any changes specified in the "Build booklet" dialog box are made. A new, untitled publication opens on screen, hopefully ready to print.

19.228 In the new publication all master page items, including page numbers, are transferred to each page of the publication. The master pages are blank.

19.229 There are limits to "Build booklet...." It can only handle publications with less than 500 pages (which really is rather admirable) and you cannot create impositions for more than one publication at a time. Be sure you have plenty of RAM and enough memory allocated to PageMaker (21.45) as otherwise the Addition can cause PageMaker to crash.

19.230 PageMaker offers five different page impositions. They can all widen the spread size (signature) but never make it taller. No imposition can be wider than PageMaker's maximum page size of 42 inches. Really, though, what's even more important is your printer or service bureau's maximum page size. If you are printing to film, or do not want to tile the publication for any other reason, make sure both the output device and printing press can accommodate the signature you have chosen. *Talk to your printer and service bureau first!*

19.231 The "Build booklet..." dialog box

(from the Utilities menu, slide down to "Aldus Additions," then over to the submenu and choose "Build booklet...")

19.232 *The spread size adjusts automatically according to the page size and the page layout you choose. You can also manually change the page size or the spread size by entering new values.*

19.233 *Path to the publication.*

Click OK or press Return to run the Addition.

Command Period cancels the dialog box.

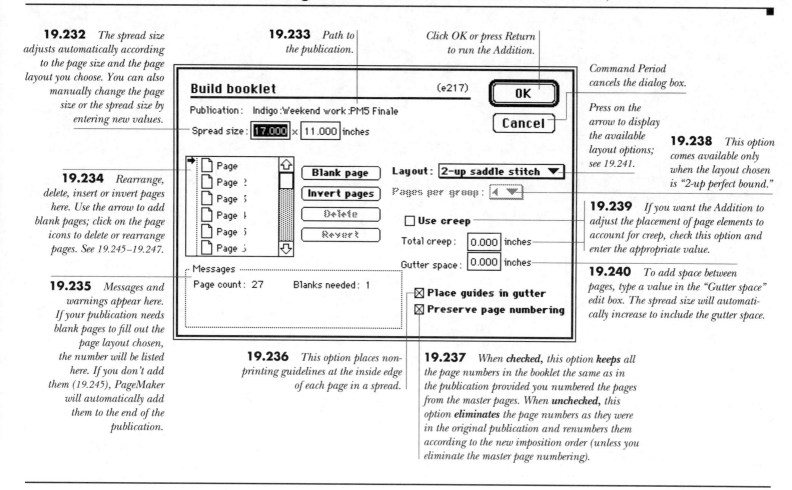

19.234 *Rearrange, delete, insert or invert pages here. Use the arrow to add blank pages; click on the page icons to delete or rearrange pages. See 19.245–19.247.*

19.235 *Messages and warnings appear here. If your publication needs blank pages to fill out the page layout chosen, the number will be listed here. If you don't add them (19.245), PageMaker will automatically add them to the end of the publication.*

Press on the arrow to display the available layout options; see 19.241.

19.238 *This option comes available only when the layout chosen is "2-up perfect bound."*

19.239 *If you want the Addition to adjust the placement of page elements to account for creep, check this option and enter the appropriate value.*

19.240 *To add space between pages, type a value in the "Gutter space" edit box. The spread size will automatically increase to include the gutter space.*

19.236 *This option places non-printing guidelines at the inside edge of each page in a spread.*

19.237 *When **checked**, this option **keeps** all the page numbers in the booklet the same as in the publication provided you numbered the pages from the master pages. When **unchecked**, this option **eliminates** the page numbers as they were in the original publication and renumbers them according to the new imposition order (unless you eliminate the master page numbering).*

"Build booklet" guidelines

19.241 Running "Build booklet…" closes the original publication and creates a new untitled copy of it (the original version of the publication is left unchanged). There is no way to undo a booklet, you can only start over again. Here are a few guidelines to check through before running it.

- Make sure your text and layout is complete. Although you can make all the changes you want, anything more than minor editing may disrupt the new page layout.

- Generate and place any tables of contents and index stories *first* so that they reflect the original page numbers. Even when you preserve the page numbering, PageMaker will still recognize the pages according to the page on which they land in the new layout. *(For example, in a four-page booklet imposed for 2-up saddle stitching, pages 4 and 1 will land on page 1. Even though they are labeled 4 and 1, from now on PageMaker will see both pages as page 1.)*

- If you will be using the 2-up **saddle stitch** or 2-up **perfect** layout, make sure the page numbering starts on an odd-numbered page. If it doesn't, insert a blank page before the first page either directly in the publication or in the "Build booklet" dialog box (see 19.245).

- In the page setup dialog box, the page size should be equal to the page size of each individual page in the booklet. The **spread size** is created when you choose a layout imposition. PageMaker's maximum page width is 42 inches. You should also be aware of the maximum printable area of your output device and of the press that will run the job. Some impositions may need to be tiled (see 19.75) in order to be printed. *Always talk to your service bureau and your printer first.*

- Since the Addition creates a new publication, you need to have enough room on your floppy disk or hard drive to accommodate it. To be on the safe side you should have an amount two-and-one-half times the size of the original publication.

- Always save your publication before running the Addition. (PageMaker will alert you and ask you to save it when you run the Addition.) If you don't, any changes you made since the last Save will not show up in the new publication.

"Layout" options

19.242 The **2-up saddle stitch** and **2-up perfect bound** options combine two pages onto a single sheet; see 19.244. The **2-, 3-, or 4-up consecutive** options combine two, three, or four pages onto a single page. See 19.248 to create a three-panel brochure.

Layout:	
✓None	
2-up saddle stitch	
2-up perfect bound	
2-up consecutive	
3-up consecutive	
4-up consecutive	

19.243 None is also an option. If you choose "None" a new untitled publication opens, but the spread size and the page layout doesn't automatically change. You can still add blank pages (see 19.245), delete pages (see 19.246), and rearrange the pages manually (see 19.247). You can also change the individual page size for the new publication by entering new values in the "Spread size" edit boxes (see 19.232).

If you want to do this:	**Then follow these steps:**	**Shortcuts ▾ Notes ▾ Hints**
19.244 Turn a publication into a booklet ready for printing and binding	■ Complete the publication and do a final "Save as…" to reduce the memory size of the publication. ■ From the Utilities menu slide down to "Aldus Additions," then over to the submenu and choose "Build booklet…." ■ In the "Build booklet" dialog box press on the pop-up menu next to "Layout." Select the page imposition you want. ■ Check the "Messages" box to see if blanks are needed to fill out the imposition. Add them if necessary (see 19.245). ■ Folded booklets may require a creep adjustment. Estimating creep requires that you create a "dummy" and measure the offset distance of the inner page to the outer page. Enter the value in the "Total creep" edit box. ■ Type a value in the "Gutter space" edit box if you want to add space between pages that print on the same sheet (19.240). ■ Check the box next to "Place guides in gutter" if you want a guideline to designate the inside edge of each page (19.236). ■ Check the box next to "Preserve page numbering" if you want the new layout to include the same page numbering as the original layout (19.237). ■ Click OK, *or* press Return.	■ The "2-up saddle stitch," "2-up perfect bound," and "4-up consecutive" options all require the total number of pages to be a multiple of four (4, 8, 12, 16, 20…). The "2-up consecutive" imposition requires the page total to be a multiple of two, while the "3-up consecutive" imposition requires the page total to be a multiple of three. PageMaker will add any necessary blank pages to the end of a publication if you do not designate where to put them. ■ The "2-up saddle stitch" and the "2-up perfect bound" create a *signature* in which the first and last page are on the same sheet of paper, and the second and the second-to-last page are on the same sheet, etc. When these sheets are printed (or photocopied) front-to-back and folded once, the pages are in proper sequence. With the "2-up perfect bound" signature however, instead of creating one booklet for the whole publication, you can specify the amount of pages per signature. The Addition will create the number of signatures necessary to produce the publication. The folded signatures can then be stacked and bound.

If you want to do this:	**Then follow these steps:**	**Shortcuts ▪ Notes ▪ Hints**
19.245 Add blank pages to a publication	▪ From the Utilities menu slide down to "Aldus Additions," then over to the submenu and choose "Build booklet...." ▪ In the dialog box use the scroll bar on the page icon window to see where you want to insert a blank page. ▪ In the narrow column left of the page icon window, click to set the arrow where you want to insert a blank page. ▪ Click the "Blank page" button. ▪ Click OK to run the Addition after you have made all the necessary selections.	▪ The arrow can only be positioned between pages. ▪ You can click the "Revert" button to return the pages to the order they were in when the dialog box first opened. ▪ If you Cancel out of the dialog box, no pages will be added to the publication. But if you click OK with "None" selected as the layout option you will get a new untitled copy of your publication with the blank pages added.
19.246 Delete pages in a publication	▪ In the "Build booklet...." dialog box (19.231), click on the page icon to highlight it. Shift-click to select multiple consecutive pages; Command-click to select multiple non-consecutive pages. ▪ Click the "Delete" button.	▪ The "Delete" button is gray until a page icon is selected. ▪ The "Revert" button will return the pages to the order they were in when the dialog box first opened.
19.247 Move pages in a publication	▪ In the "Build booklet...." dialog box (19.231), select the page icon(s) you want to move. ▪ Press the Option key as you drag the icons to the new position. ▪ Click OK to run the Addition after you have made all other necessary selections.	▪ Shift-click to select more than one page if they are in consecutive order; Command-click if the pages you want are in non-consecutive order. ▪ Non-consecutive pages will be placed consecutively in the new position. ▪ You can rearrange the pages without changing the publication's imposition by choosing "None" as the layout option.

If you want to do this:

19.248 Use "Build booklet" to create a three-panel brochure

Page 1	Page 2	Page 3
right leaf	*back panel*	*front cover*

Outside

Page 4	Page 5	Page 6
left panel	*middle panel*	*right panel*

Inside

By default, "Build booklet" imposes pages based upon this model.

Then follow these steps:

- Create a dummy of the brochure showing all the folds, the page numbers, and the content of each page (including any blank pages).
- In PageMaker, set up a six-page publication with the page size equal to that of one panel of the brochure.
- Completely design and finish your piece including placing all the graphics and editing all the text.
- Do a final "Save as…" to reduce the size of the publication.
- From the Utilities menu slide down to "Aldus Additions," then over to the submenu and choose "Build booklet…."
- In the "Build booklet" dialog box:
  □ select "3-up consecutive" next to "Layout";
  □ check "Place guides in gutter";
  □ uncheck "Preserve page numbering";
- Look in the "Messages" box for information relevant to the pub (it should show a page count of six; also check for any warnings regarding the spread size).
- Adjust the spread size as necessary.
- Rearrange pages if necessary (19.247).
- Click OK.
- Save your new publication.

Shortcuts ▾ Notes ▾ Hints

- An accurate dummy is the key to successful imposition. See the model on the left.
- Build booklet can also run impositions for two- and four-panel brochures. It cannot, however, run impositions for off-center folds although you can manipulate the margins on the original design and then manipulate the gutters on the booklet to create an off-center effect. Your imagination is your only limit.
- If your dummy and design are accurate, the final imposed publication should have all the panels in their proper places and printed at the correct size with the correct margins and gutters. Bleeds will print over the edges of the new booklet if you designed them to do that. (In this case PageMaker may warn you that items are crossing over gutters as the Addition runs.)
- The publication size (displayed next to "Spread size") should equal the desired size of the finished piece. If it does not, go back to the original pub and recalculate the individual page dimensions.
- If your *original* publication setup does not follow the default model, you will have to move pages before running the Addition (19.247).

20 ▾ ALDUS ADDITIONS

20.1 Aldus Additions:

Acquire image (*10.253*)

Add cont'd line (*4.160*)

Balance columns (*4.168*)

Build Booklet (*19.169*)

Bullets and numbering (*20.8*)

Create color library (*16.128*)

Create keyline (*10.255*)

Display pub info (*19.167*)

Display story info (*4.139*)

Display textblock info (*4.151*)

Drop cap (*20.42*)

Edit tracks (*5.193*)

Expert kerning (*5.173*)

Find overset text (*4.133*)

List styles used (*8.44*)

Open stories (*9.46*)

Open template (*14.21*)

PS Group it (*10.254*)

PS Ungroup it (*10.254*)

Printer styles (*19.168*)

Run script (*20.65*)

Running headers\footers (*20.101*)

Sort pages (*20.125*)

Traverse textblocks (*4.136*)

Update PPD (*19.166*)

20.2 Additions are one of the most potentially powerful aspects of PageMaker 5. They are extra PageMaker features that automate or customize tasks, often with a single menu command. There are additions you access through PageMaker's menus, scripts you write yourself, and stand-alone modules developed independent of Aldus. Most of them you'll find lumped together in the "Aldus Additions" submenu (under "Utilities"). New Additions can be added to PageMaker at any time.

20.3 PageMaker comes standard with more than twenty menu Additions. **Aldus Additions** add a hefty chunk to the program, however (1.5 megs—in the System folder!). There are Additions for text, for page layout, and for printing. Instructions for using many of them are spread throughout the book according to their specific use; refer to the column on the left to locate them. The remainder of the Additions are explained here. There are some you'll love and some you'll hate—don't be afraid to use the ones you love and trash the ones you don't.

20.4 Once you see how well the good ones work, you may want to write a few of your own using the "Run Script" Addition, a powerhouse Addition that shows just how friendly PageMaker's scripting language really is.

20.5 There are also **Independent Additions** (developed and marketed by small, independent software companies) which address the specialized design needs of some users. Additions that can instantly create UPC bar codes or packaging templates or that let you customize grids are a few examples. See Appendix J.

20.6 Check the "Aldus Additions" submenu under the Utilities menu to see which Additions were installed when you installed PageMaker 5 ("Easy install" installs them all). You can add Additions to PageMaker at any time; see 20.07.

Bullets and numbering 787

Drop cap 792

Run Script 797

Running headers\footers 801

Sort pages 809

If you want to do this:

20.7 Install Aldus Additions after you have already installed PageMaker

DropCap.add

The Additions are compressed files. When you double-click on the icon, it runs the Installer which copies a decompressed version of the Addition to your disk.

Make sure to save the Addition in the "Additions" folder in the "Aldus" folder in your System folder.

Then follow these steps:

- Open Disk 5 of the original PageMaker 5 application disks.
- Double-click on the "Additions" folder.
- Double-click on the Addition you want to install.
- In the "Save as…" dialog box, click the "Desktop" button to view your hard drive. Locate your System folder, and double-click on it to open it.
- Double-click on the "Aldus" folder.
- Double-click on the "Additions" folder.
- Click the "Save" button.

Shortcuts ▾ Notes ▾ Hints

- Of course, it is always best to use back-up copies of the PageMaker application disks, rather than the originals.
- By default, all the Additions are installed when you installed PageMaker.
- Even if you did a custom install and chose not to install any Additions, PageMaker still created the "Additions" folder for the Additions she uses behind the scenes. "Run script" was automatically installed too.

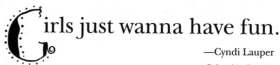

Girls just wanna have fun.

—Cyndi Lauper
Columbia Records

The "Bullets and numbering..." Addition

(from the Utilities menu, slide down to "Aldus Additions";
from the submenu, choose "Bullets and Numbering...")

20.8 The **"Bullets and numbering..."** Addition is a real time-saver. With it, you can come along after you've finished a document and enter all those pesky bullets and paragraph numbers that can be so time consuming when you're typing. PageMaker lets you use any character in any font as a bullet, and all the same numbering characters that she offers for page numbering (1.148). You have a range of choices regarding how to place the bullets or numbers—from every paragraph to just a select few. Tentative designers take heart. This dialog box sports a Remove button!

20.9 To run the Addition, the insertion point must be flashing within the story you are bulleting or numbering. Page-Maker will always place the bullet or number on the margin or indent of the first line, bumping the rest of the text to the first available tab marker. Tabs can be adjusted with the Indents/tabs ruler to control the distance between the bullet and the text either before or after you run the Addition.

20.10 Clicking on the "Edit" button opens the "Edit bullet" dialog box. Here you will find all the characters on the keyboard from which you can choose a bullet style (20.25). However, you are limited to just those sizes listed in the pop-up menu (unless you go back in later and change them through the "Change" command, see 20.37).

20.11 Characters that sit on the baseline as normal text will still sit on the baseline as a bullet. You can go back in and adjust them later just like any other character.

20.12 This Addition may change line breaks; be sure to check for overset text afterwards (4.179).

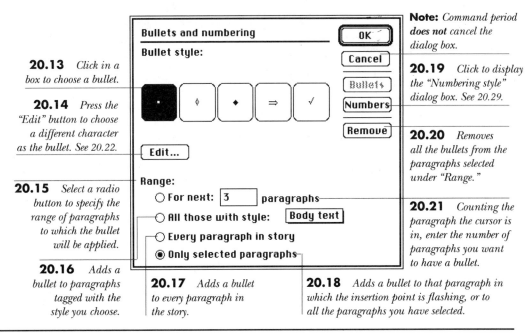

20.13 *Click in a box to choose a bullet.*

20.14 *Press the "Edit" button to choose a different character as the bullet. See 20.22.*

20.15 *Select a radio button to specify the range of paragraphs to which the bullet will be applied.*

20.16 *Adds a bullet to paragraphs tagged with the style you choose.*

20.17 *Adds a bullet to every paragraph in the story.*

20.18 *Adds a bullet to that paragraph in which the insertion point is flashing, or to all the paragraphs you have selected.*

Note: *Command period* **does not** *cancel the dialog box.*

20.19 *Click to display the "Numbering style" dialog box. See 20.29.*

20.20 *Removes all the bullets from the paragraphs selected under "Range."*

20.21 *Counting the paragraph the cursor is in, enter the number of paragraphs you want to have a bullet.*

"Bullets and numbering..." dialog boxes

(from the "Bullets and numbering" dialog box, click on the "Edit..." or "Numbers" button)

20.22 The "Edit bullet" dialog box.

20.23 *Press on the pop-up menu to choose a font from those available in your system.*

20.26 *Click OK to enter the selected bullet in the "Bullets" dialog box.*

20.27 *Click Cancel to return to the "Bullet style" dialog box without implementing any changes.*

20.24 *Press on the pop-up menu to choose a point size from 6 to 72. You are limited strictly to the sizes shown here.*

20.28 *Displays the bullet in the font and size chosen.*

20.25 *Displays all the available characters in a font. Click on a character to select it as a bullet.*

20.29 The "Numbering style" dialog box.

20.30 *Click a radio button to choose a style.*

20.31 *Choose a symbol from the pop-up menu to separate the number from the text.*

Click OK or Return to run the Addition.

Note:
*Command Period **does not** cancel the dialog box.*

20.34
Displays the "Bullet style" dialog box.

20.32 *Start the "Numbering style" with any number or character in the sequence, but enter it as an Arabic number here (20.38–20.39).*

20.33 *Same choices as in the "Bullet style" dialog box; see 20.15–20.21.*

20.35
Removes numbers from the paragraphs selected under "Range."

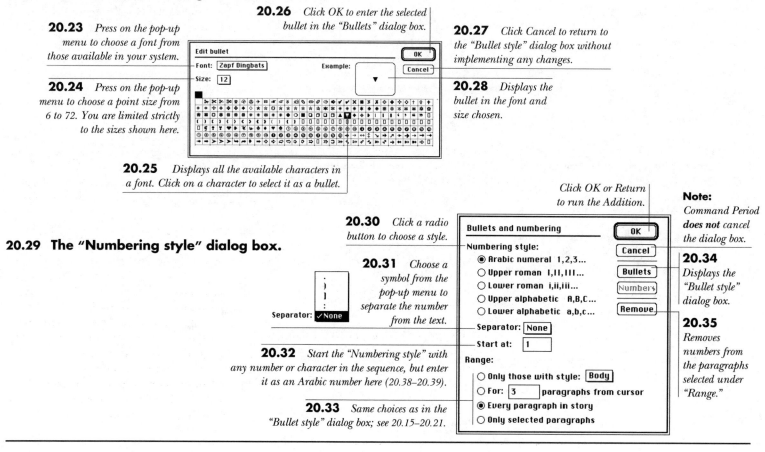

If you want to do this:	Then follow these steps:	Shortcuts ▾ Notes ▾ Hints
20.36 Add bullets to paragraphs in a story	■ Set the **insertion point** in the first paragraph that you want to have bullets. ■ From the Utilities menu, slide down to "Aldus Additions," then slide over to select "Bullets and numbering…" from the submenu. ■ If you get the "Numbering style" box, click on the "Bullets" button. ■ Click on one of the bullets displayed to select a bullet style. ★ Under "Range," click a radio button to select which paragraphs will have bullets. ■ Click OK.	■ **Note:** It doesn't matter where the insertion point is in the story if you are adding bullets to all the paragraphs or to those with a certain style. However, it *does* matter if you select "Only selected paragraphs" or "For next __paragraphs." ■ You can adjust the baseline of a bullet using the "Type specs…" dialog box (4.205) or the "Baseline-shift" option in the character-view Control palette (4.218). Unfortunately, you will have to change each bullet individually. You can adjust one bullet, copy it, then paste it over each of the other bullets, but it is still a pain.

20.37 Edit a bullet style	■ Follow the directions in 20.36 until you get to the star (★).
	■ Click the "Edit" button.
	  □ Click on a character, and/or
	  □ Choose another font, and/or
	  □ Choose another point size.
	  □ Click OK.
	■ Under "Range," click a radio button to select which paragraphs will have bullets.
	■ Click OK.
		■ New bullets you create stay in the "Bullet style" edit boxes until you select new ones.
		■ You can use "Change" in the Story Editor along with the Addition to create special bullets like the outline boxes in the column to the left. You will need to know the keyboard position of the character you used as a bullet. You can even change all the bullets to superscript if you want to raise them off the baseline. See 9.67–9.76 for more info on using the "Change" dialog box, and specifically 9.79 for finding and changing characters with text attributes.

If you want to do this:	Then follow these steps:	Shortcuts ▾ Notes ▾ Hints
20.38 Consecutively number paragraphs in a story, starting with 1 (or I, i, A, or a)	▪ Set the **insertion point** within the first paragraph you want to number. ▪ From the Utilities menu, slide down to "Aldus Additions," then over to the submenu and choose "Bullets and numbering…." ▪ Click on the "Numbers" button if "Numbering style" is not already showing. ▪ Click the radio button next to the style of numbering you want to use. ▪ Next to "Separator," press the pop-up menu and select the symbol you want to use to separate the number from the rest of the text. ★ Next to "Start at:" type in 1. ▪ Under "Range," click a radio button to select which paragraphs will have numbers. ▪ Click OK.	▪ You can use the Tab key to move the cursor from the "Start at" edit box to the "For next__paragraphs" edit box. ▪ The "Bullets and numbering" dialog box will open directly either to "Bullet style" or "Numbering style," depending on which one you used last.
20.39 Consecutively number paragraphs in a story starting with a number other than 1 (or I, i, A, or a)	▪ Follow the directions in 20.38 until you get to the star (★). ▪ Next to "Start at:" type in the number with which you want to start. Use Arabic numerals (regular numbers) no matter which numbering style you choose. ▪ Under "Range" click a radio button to select which paragraphs you want numbered. ▪ Click OK.	▪ If you type "3" as the "Start at:" number, Roman numerals will begin at "III" or "iii"; alphabetic numbering will begin at "C" or "c," because C is the third letter of the alphabet. If you make a mistake, you can go back and remove the numbers and renumber the paragraphs (20.41).

If you want to do this:	**Then follow these steps:**	**Shortcuts · Notes · Hints**
20.40 Change the tab of the text after you've inserted bullets or numbers	■ Add bullets (20.36) or numbers (20.39) as desired. ■ With the **text tool,** highlight all the paragraphs involved. ■ From the Type menu choose "Indents/tabs." ■ Set a left tab as close or as far from the first line marker as you wish. ■ Click "Apply," or press Command A, if you want to view the changes before you leave the dialog box. ■ Click OK.	■ PageMaker sends the text to the first available tab, whether it's a default tab or a tab you intentionally set. ■ Leave enough room between the first line marker and the tab for the bullet or number to fit! ■ If you are working with style sheets, use the style sheet to access the Indents/tabs ruler to make the tab consistent in all paragraphs tagged the same. ■ See Section 6 for everything you need to know about indents and tabs.

20.41 Remove bullets or numbers from a story	■ Set the **insertion point** within the story.
	■ From the Utilities menu slide down to "Aldus Additions," then over to the submenu and choose "Bullets and numbering…."
	   □ If you are in the "Bullet style" dialog box and you want to remove numbers, click the "Numbers" button.
	   □ If you are in the "Numbering style" dialog box and want to remove bullets, click the "Bullets" button.
	■ Under "Range" click the radio button to choose from which paragraphs you want the bullets or numbers removed.
	■ Click the "Remove" button.
	■ Click OK in the alert box.
		■ After you click "Remove," PageMaker will ask you if you want to remove a bullet or number from each paragraph you selected. If you aren't sure you checked the right radio button (or if you forgot all together), press "Cancel," check the range of paragraphs you want, then click "Remove" again.
		■ During the process of removing the bullets or numbers, PageMaker displays a message box that will let you stop the process at any point.

The "Drop cap..." Addition

As invisible as good typography should be, it should also invite the reader in. Drop caps are one method of doing this. They create visual interest on the page while breaking the text into readable sections.

20.42 Drop caps are letters larger than the rest of the type. The "Drop cap..." Addition sets the initial cap neatly into the paragraph—the top of the letter aligns with the top of the text, and the baseline aligns with a baseline of text.

20.43 To insert a drop cap is simple enough. All *you* have to do is decide how many lines of text deep you want the cap to be. PageMaker does the rest.

20.44 What she does is change the size of the first character in the selected paragraph and wrap the remaining text around it. The more lines you choose to wrap, the bigger the character becomes. When the drop cap character is highlighted, you can see both its size and leading in the character-view Control palette or in the "Type specs..." dialog box. Do be aware that the bigger the drop cap, the more space it needs on the line and therefore

the more words it will bump down a line. (Here's another Addition that profits from running "Find overset text" afterwards.)

20.45 PageMaker also gives the character a subscript position. It then sets it at the correct distance from its original baseline so that it lines up with the baseline of the text you specified in the "Size" box.

20.46 Tabs are inserted into the rest of the text to make room for the drop cap. Line breaks, equivalent to Shift-Returns, are placed at the end of each line of wrapping text. You need to know this—you may have to manually fuss with them if you later make changes in paragraphs that have been formatted with the "Drop cap..." Addition.

20.47 The "Drop cap..." Addition does a pretty good job, but you may want to kern between the drop cap character and the next letter or word. You may also want to change the line breaks or tweak the tabs a bit, too. If you want the tabs different around the cap so that it imitates a text wrap, you must first change the Shift-Returns to regular Returns.

20.48 To run the Addition, the insertion point must be flashing within a paragraph that is aligned either left, justified, or force justified. You can go back in later and change the alignment of a paragraph to whatever you wish after the drop cap is set.

20.49 PageMaker is very particular about some things when running this Addition. It will seem as if it is running okay, but when you click OK or "Apply" you get the "Addition error" dialog box. Note that you can't set a drop cap when:

- The text is right or center aligned.
- "Top of caps" leading is checked in the Paragraph spacing dialog box.
- The first character in the paragraph is an inline graphic (10.213), or a space of any kind (a regular space, an en or em space, a tab, etc.).

All other characters can be used including quotation marks, bullets, and numbers.

20.50 PageMaker always turns the *first* character of a paragraph into a drop cap no matter where you put the insertion point, nor if you highlight another character.

20.51 **The "Drop cap" dialog box** *(from the Utilities menu, slide down to "Aldus Additions"; from the submenu, choose "Drop cap…")*

20.53 *You can click here to see what the drop cap looks like without leaving the dialog box.*

20.54 *These buttons allow you to change drop caps in more than one paragraph at a time. See 20.62.*

20.55 *OK changes to "Close" after using the "Apply" button.*

20.52 *Press-and-drag on the title bar to move the window.*

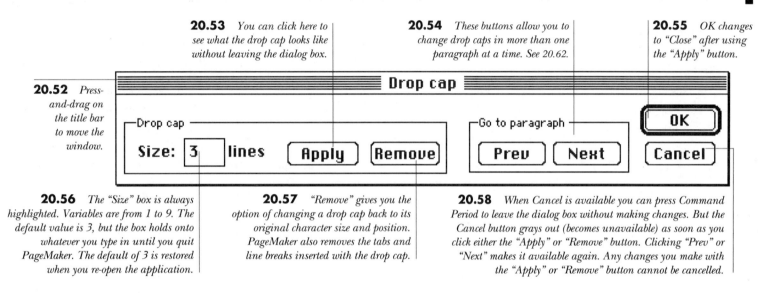

20.56 *The "Size" box is always highlighted. Variables are from 1 to 9. The default value is 3, but the box holds onto whatever you type in until you quit PageMaker. The default of 3 is restored when you re-open the application.*

20.57 *"Remove" gives you the option of changing a drop cap back to its original character size and position. PageMaker also removes the tabs and line breaks inserted with the drop cap.*

20.58 *When Cancel is available you can press Command Period to leave the dialog box without making changes. But the Cancel button grays out (becomes unavailable) as soon as you click either the "Apply" or "Remove" button. Clicking "Prev" or "Next" makes it available again. Any changes you make with the "Apply" or "Remove" button cannot be cancelled.*

> *A*ll the problems of the world could be settled easily if men were only willing to think. The trouble is that men very often resort to all sorts of devices in order not to think, because thinking is such hard work. —Thomas Watson

(Note the gender spoken of in this quote!)

If you want to do this:

Then follow these steps:

Shortcuts ▾ Notes ▾ Hints

20.59 Create a drop cap

T he unfortunate thing about this world is that good habits are so much easier to give up than bad ones.

–W. Somerset Maugham

Two-line drop cap.

- With the **text tool,** click in a paragraph.
- From the Utilities menu, slide down to "Aldus Additions" then over to choose "Drop cap…" from the submenu.
- Enter a number, from 1 to 9, in the "Size" box. The cap will be as tall as the number of lines you enter.
  - ☐ Click the "Apply" button.
  - ☐ If you like how it looks, click "Close."
  - ☐ Otherwise choose "Remove," and then enter a different number in the "Size" box. Use the "Apply" button to see the layout change without making a commitment to it.
- Click "Close."

- The "Apply" and "Remove" buttons are the guardian angels of this dialog box. You can experiment freely without ever leaving the dialog box. But even so, the wise designer waits until the text is stable (all rewrites and editing completed) before creating drop caps.
- If the drop cap creates awkward line breaks, you can drag the text window handles inward or outward, and fuss with the tabs. You may prefer to remove the cap, change the line length, and simply run the Addition again.
- PageMaker inserts line breaks (Shift-Returns) even if the text doesn't need them. This may create blank lines that you will have to manually delete.

20.60 Select only the drop cap

L ife is what we make it, always has been always will be.

–Grandma Moses

- With the **text tool,** click to set the insertion point before the *second* letter in the paragraph.
- Hold down the **Shift key** and click on the **left arrow,** *or*
- With the **text tool** click anywhere in the paragraph. Hold down the **Command key** and press the 8 on the numeric keypad (caps lock must be off). Hold down the **Shift key** and click on the **right arrow.**

- Notice that only the top portion of the drop cap is highlighted when it is selected. That's okay.
- The simple method of sweeping over a letter with the text tool works, too. Don't try to select the whole letter, just press-and-drag the cursor where the letter would be if it were a normal character.
- You can dress up your drop cap by applying a color or shading it gray (see 4.265).

If you want to do this:	**Then follow these steps:**	**Shortcuts ▾ Notes ▾ Hints**
20.61 Remove a drop cap from a paragraph	■ With the **text tool,** click in the paragraph containing the drop cap. ■ From the Utilities menu, slide down to "Aldus Additions" then over to choose "Drop cap…" from the submenu. ■ Click "Remove." • Click "Close."	■ The number in the size box does not necessarily reflect the line wrap value of the paragraph the cursor is in. It doesn't matter what number is in the size box when you are *removing* drop caps. ■ The line breaks and tabs that were inserted with the drop cap are also removed.

20.62 Create or remove drop caps in more than one paragraph at the same time	■ With the **text tool,** click in a paragraph.
	■ From the Utilities menu, slide down to "Aldus Additions" then over to choose "Drop cap…" from the submenu
	■ To create drop caps:
	  □ Enter a number in the "Size" box (see 20.56).
	  □ Click "Apply" and approve the changes.
	  □ Click "Prev" or "Next" to jump to the other paragraphs you want to format.
	  □ Click "Apply" for each drop cap you are formatting.
	■ To remove drop caps:
	  □ Click the "Remove" button.
	  □ Click "Prev" or "Next" to jump to other paragraphs.
	  □ Click "Remove" for each drop cap you want to remove.
	■ Click "Close" when you are done.
		■ You can press and drag on the title bar to move the "Drop cap" window around on screen.
		■ PageMaker will automatically turn pages in the document to find "Prev" and "Next" paragraphs. This is a very cool feature. Of course, if the paragraphs you want to format are pages and pages apart, it may be quicker to leave the dialog box each time and manually insert the cursor tool in the next paragraph.
		■ Check out the method of creating a drop or initial cap in 21.15, and 10.151 (using "Paste special…" to turn text into a graphic), for more personal control over the size and positioning of the letter. You can also change text to a graphic and text wrap it (13.40) for a neat variation on the drop cap theme.

If you want to do this:

Then follow these steps:

Shortcuts ▾ Notes ▾ Hints

20.63 Change the leading, point size, or font of a paragraph with a drop cap

- Highlight all the text **except** the drop cap.
- Change the leading value, or point size, or font of the selected text.
- From the Utilities menu, slide down to "Aldus Additions" then over to choose "Drop cap…" from the submenu.
- Click "Remove."
- Check the "Size" box to be sure it has the line wrap you want, then choose "Apply."
- Click "Close."

- This method removes and reapplies the drop cap giving PageMaker a chance to evaluate the paragraph's new formatting.
- Really it's best to create the drop caps after all the formatting and editing is done, but it's always good to know the work-arounds just in case!
- You can change the font or type style of the drop cap too. Just select it separately from the rest of the paragraph, as in 20.60. Follow the procedure here to remove and reapply the drop cap so that PageMaker can adjust the text to fit the dimensions of the new character.

20.64 Edit the word that has the drop cap

Always put off for tomorrow what you can do today.

Nlways put off for tomorrow what you can do today.

- With the **text tool**, select only the drop cap character (see 20.60).
- Type in the new character.
- With the **text tool** select the rest of the word to be edited.
- Type in the new characters.

Nlways put off for tomorrow what you can do today.

- If you select the entire word and attempt to edit it, you will get all drop cap characters; the insertion point always takes on the formatting of the character to its left!

Never put off for tomorrow what you can do today.

The "Run script..." Addition

(from the Utilities menu, slide down to "Aldus Additions"; from the submenu choose "Run script...")

20.65 The "Run script..." Addition uses scripts (yours or others) to put PageMaker on automatic pilot to handle time-consuming tasks. Although they sound mysterious, scripts are just a list of commands written in a text format called "Script language" that automatically performs mundane tasks that you would otherwise have to do manually. PageMaker offers nine ready-made scripts for you to use. You can either use them just as they are, modify them to suit your own needs, or use them as models to create your own.

20.66 It's easy to run one of PageMaker's ready-made scripts: just find it in the Scripts folder in the PageMaker folder and click OK. PageMaker does the rest. Most of the sample scripts won't affect your current publication; instead they open a new, untitled publication. Only "Crayon Me" (which adds a selection of ready-made colors to the Color palette) and the fraction scripts (which turn ugly fractions into proper ones, see 4.262) affect the active publication.

20.67 You can write your own scripts either right in PageMaker or in any program that can save files as text-only. Checking "Trace" lets you perform the script step-by-step to test and debug it.

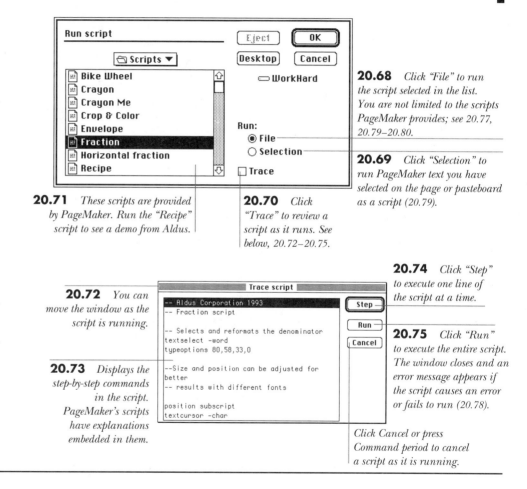

20.71 *These scripts are provided by PageMaker. Run the "Recipe" script to see a demo from Aldus.*

20.70 *Click "Trace" to review a script as it runs. See below, 20.72–20.75.*

20.68 *Click "File" to run the script selected in the list. You are not limited to the scripts PageMaker provides; see 20.77, 20.79–20.80.*

20.69 *Click "Selection" to run PageMaker text you have selected on the page or pasteboard as a script (20.79).*

20.72 *You can move the window as the script is running.*

20.73 *Displays the step-by-step commands in the script. PageMaker's scripts have explanations embedded in them.*

20.74 *Click "Step" to execute one line of the script at a time.*

20.75 *Click "Run" to execute the entire script. The window closes and an error message appears if the script causes an error or fails to run (20.78).*

Click Cancel or press Command period to cancel a script as it is running.

797

If you want to do this:	**Then follow these steps:**	**Shortcuts ▾ Notes ▾ Hints**
20.76 Run the "Star Wrap" script to get a star-shaped object with a custom wrap *AQUARIUS–The visionary reformer who brings a love for the future. Indulge impulses to change for the better. PISCES– She feels the unconscious links be-tween us all. Pay attention to your dreams & your imagination. ARIES– She has the ability to evoke the true essential core of any situation. Let looseyour creativity, show your talents. TAURUS– She loves being grounded and in touch with the growing earth. Honor keepers of the earth.*	■ From the Utilities menu, slide down to "Aldus Additions," then over to the submenu and choose "Run script…." ■ Navigate through your folders to locate and open the "Aldus PageMaker 5.0" folder, then open the "Scripts" folder. ■ Select "Star Wrap." ■ Click the radio button next to "File." ■ Click OK. A new, untitled publication opens. ■ Create or import text into your new publication, or drag-and-drop the star shape into another publication window. ■ Drag a text block on top of or next to the star shape to create the text wrap.	■ It's easy to loose this text wrap shape on the page, and hard to move it even when it is selected. To see and move it better, marquee it right away and change "Line" in the Element menu from "None" to "Hairline." Now you can see the box around it to select the star and move it. Don't forget to change the box back to "None" before printing! ■ Press the Shift key and drag in or out on one of the corner handles to resize it. ■ You can *place* any of PageMaker's sample scripts into a PageMaker publication to read it or modify the tasks. For example, with "Star Wrap" you could change the values of the numbers following "textwrappoly" to change the shape of the star in this script. Just experiment, it's fun.
20.77 Run a script created in another program	■ From the Utilities menu, slide down to "Aldus Additions," then over to the sub-menu and choose "Run script…." ■ Navigate through your disks and folders to locate the script. Click once on it. ■ Click the radio button next to "File." ■ Click OK.	■ To run a script that was written in another program, the script must have been saved as a text-only file. ■ An alternative method is to place the script as a new story in your PageMaker publication (17.33), and follow the directions in 20.79 to run the script.

If you want to do this:

20.78 Trace a script

Then follow these steps:

- From the Utilities menu, slide down to "Aldus Additions," then over to the submenu and choose "Run script...."
- Click once on a script to select it.
- Click the radio button next to "File."
- Check the box next to "Trace."
- Click OK.
- In the "Trace script" dialog box:
  - ☐ Click "Step" to execute the selected line of the script. Continue to click "Step" to run the script line by line.
  - ☐ Click "Run" to execute the entire script.

Shortcuts ▼ Notes ▼ Hints

- This process is valuable for test-running a new script. The window lets you review each step of a script, one step at a time. The "Trace script" window will close if it comes to a line that causes an error, and it may display an error message.
- You can cancel a script while it is running if the "Trace script" window is on screen.
- This process is also valuable to those intimidated by the idea of writing a script. If you run the sample scripts with the "Trace" option selected, you will see how simple and straightforward the process is. There are comments embedded in the scripts that explain what each section of commands tells PageMaker to do. If the process intrigues you and you want to know more about writing scripts yourself, send for the *PageMaker 5.0 Script Language Guide*. It's free from Aldus.

If you want to do this:	Then follow these steps:	Shortcuts ▾ Notes ▾ Hints
20.79 Write and run your own script created in PageMaker	■ Write the script either on the pasteboard of the document you are working in, or in another or new PageMaker document. ■ With the **pointer tool,** click on the script, or with the **text tool,** highlight the text of the script (either the whole thing or just the part you want to run). ■ From the Utilities menu, slide down to "Aldus Additions" then over to the submenu and choose "Run script…." ■ Click on the radio button next to "Selection" and click OK.	■ Writing a script sounds harder than it really is. Accuracy is essential, however. You must be sure to spell and write out all the commands and queries just exactly the way they are listed in Aldus's *Script Language Guide.* ■ Scripts written in the Story Editor must be placed before they can be run. ■ You can create a number of helpful scripts that could cover such mundane tasks as opening, printing, and closing frequently-opened files or changing preferences "on the fly." In the guide there are examples already listed out for you to copy and try out.
20.80 Write and run your own script created in another program and saved as text	■ Write the script in a word processing program that will save files as text-only; ■ **Or** write the script in PageMaker and export it as a text-only file. ■ From the Utilities menu, slide down to "Aldus Additions" then over to the submenu and choose "Run script…." ■ Find and highlight the file of the script you want. ■ Click on the radio button next to "File" and click OK.	■ If a script has been written or saved as a text-only file, you can alternatively place it into PageMaker and follow the directions in 20.79. ■ Click "Trace" to run your script one step at a time and test it for bugs.

The "Running headers\footers..." Addition

20.81 The "Running headers\footers..." Addition automatically creates headers and footers that reflect the contents of a page. It's important to remember that this Addition only works with **threaded text blocks** and by using paragraph styles. (If you want a header or footer that is the same on each page, create a master page item; 1.139.) Even if you don't write dictionaries, this Addition is handy for glossaries, employee and phone directories, etc.

20.82 To run this Addition your publication has to have a title (saved at least once) and contain style sheets. PageMaker selects text for the header/footer content by searching for a specific paragraph style.

20.83 Beginning with the text block you select, the Addition creates a header/footer for every page that follows that has a text block threaded to the one you selected. It cannot follow the story backward to any threaded text blocks that come before the one you select.

20.84 When you run the Addition, Page-Maker creates and saves a special file in the folder with your publication labeled with the file name and the extension ".HDR."

You cannot modify or redo the existing headers/footers without this file; however, it is not linked to the document, or necessary for printing.

20.85 Whether it's a header or a footer is determined by the value you enter in the "Vertical" edit box (20.94). If the vertical measurement places the text at the top of the page, it's a header; if it places it at the bottom, it's a footer. You can run the Addition twice on the same story and change the "Vertical" value (along with any other selection changes you want) to add both headers and footers (see 20.121, 20.122).

20.86 The content of the headers/footers will not change if you edit the text in the publication. You can manually edit them if need be, but, as with many of the Additions, it is best to run it in the final stages of designing the publication to avoid unnecessary work.

20.87 To successfully place headers and footers, you may need to increase the amount of memory given to PageMaker (22.45). And be sure to save your publication *before* you run the Addition just in case (see 20.106).

20.88 *A story with a header from the first instance of a style and a footer from the last instance of the same style. The "Insert" option was "First word."*

Benefit

Benefit Plan - Refers to the specific services available to an enrollee under the HMO agreement with the employer.

Capitated Services - Those services listed in the Covered Services of the I.P.A./Medical Group and hospital contracts which the I.P.A./Medical Group and hospital are each responsible for providing for a fixed amount of reimbursement per member per month.

Capitation - A prepaid monthly fee made to the I.P.A./Medical Group and hospital for each enrollee in exchange for the provision of comprehensive health care services to enrolled members.

Concurrent Review - Review of a patient's hospital chart including verification of necessity of treatment and need for continued treatment in the hospital.

Conversion Factor - The dollar amount to be applied to each relative value unit in the CRVS to determine the payment value of physician services.

Co-Payment - A supplemental charge to a patient receiving medical care to be collected by the provider of care.

Coordination of Benefits - When a patient is covered by two or more group health plans, coordination of benefits divides the responsibility of payment.

Coordination

20.89 **The "Running headers\footers..." dialog box**   *(from the Utilities menu, slide down to "Aldus Additions"; from the submenu, choose "Running headers\footers...")*

20.90 *In the "Find" box, choose the type of search and the paragraph style for PageMaker to find. You can find the first or last instance of a particular style.*

20.91 *From this pop-up menu choose what part of the text to insert as the header/footer content. See 20.111–20.114.*

20.92 *Click the Edit button to customize the header or footer content. See 20.115–20.120.*

20.97 *Choose the style you want the Addition to find. The pop-up menu lists all the style sheets in your publication except "No style."*

20.98 *If your publication has only right-hand pages (single-sided), all the left-hand page options will be dimmed. When available, the options work the same as the right page options. See 20.93–20.95.*

20.99 *Choose the style you want to apply to the header/footer. All the style sheets in your publication are listed here except "No style." You can set different styles for left and right pages.*

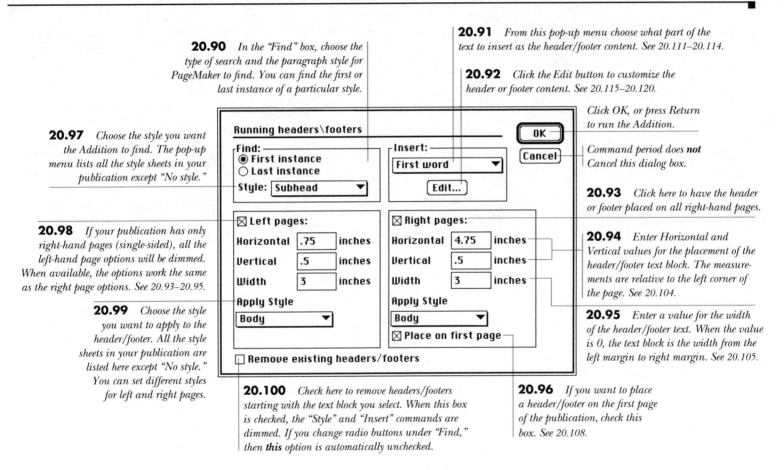

Click OK, or press Return to run the Addition.

*Command period does **not** Cancel this dialog box.*

20.93 *Click here to have the header or footer placed on all right-hand pages.*

20.94 *Enter Horizontal and Vertical values for the placement of the header/footer text block. The measurements are relative to the left corner of the page. See 20.104.*

20.95 *Enter a value for the width of the header/footer text. When the value is 0, the text block is the width from the left margin to right margin. See 20.105.*

20.100 *Check here to remove headers/footers starting with the text block you select. When this box is checked, the "Style" and "Insert" commands are dimmed. If you change radio buttons under "Find," then **this** option is automatically unchecked.*

20.96 *If you want to place a header/footer on the first page of the publication, check this box. See 20.108.*

The "Running headers\footers..." dialog box options

20.101 Find tells the Addition what to search for. You choose what paragraph style to find and whether it should be the first instance of that style on the page, or the last instance. This is where the content of the header/footer will come from.

20.102 Under **Insert** you choose what part of the paragraph you want as the content of the header/footer. The pop-up menu offers a pre-defined group of options that should cover most straightforward headers and footers. Choices range from inserting just the first two characters to inserting the whole paragraph (see 20.111). The **Edit** button opens a dialog box that lets you edit the Text patterns that define the "Insert" options (see 20.115). You can edit the existing patterns to create new "Insert" options, or use the existing patterns as a template for creating new ones (see 20.123). You can never delete or overwrite a style from the pre-defined group of options, so it is safe to experiment.

20.103 You can place the headers/footers on the left-hand pages of your publication, the right-hand pages, or both. Check the box next to **Left pages** and/or **Right pages.**

20.104 The Addition creates a new text block for the header/footer. You specify where you want that text block relative to the upper left corner of the page. The **Horizontal** measurement determines the position of the leftmost handles of the text block. The **Vertical** measurement determines where the top of the header/footer text block aligns.

20.105 Enter a value in the **Width** edit box to specify the total width of the header/footer text block. If the header/footer contains more text than fits in the width you specify, when the text block is selected, it will show a down-pointing arrow. By default, the header/footer text block is the width of the page from margin to margin, even if the text block is not placed on the margin.

20.106 When the Addition is running, it will alert you if the header/footer overlaps existing text. You can choose to continue anyway, or to skip that header/footer. Headers/footers that overlap text may cause that text to be deleted. (There is no alert for headers/footers that start away from text, and then overlap it.) You can't cancel the Addition as it is running, and you can't undo

it. Save before you run the Addition, so you can "Revert" if text is inadvertently deleted.

20.107 Select a paragraph style for the header/footer under **Apply style.** You can create a style sheet to use specifically for the headers/footers before you run the Addition, or choose one from your existing styles. If you modify the style at all, the headers/footers will pick up the modifications. You can override the style sheets as usual (see Section 8).

20.108 If you want the first page of your publication to have a header/footer, you must select the text block on the first page when you run the Addition, *and* check the box next to **Place on first page.**

20.109 You can **remove existing headers/footers** by checking the box and running the Addition. The "Running headers\footers…" dialog box will retain the values you entered the last time you ran the Addition, including different measurements for "First instance" and "Last instance." If you have moved the headers/footers, enter the new location measurements before you click OK. See 20.124.

20.110   Creating the content of headers and footers

20.111   *From the "Insert:" pop-up menu, choose which characters or words you want as the content of the header or footer.*

Insert:
- ✓First word
- First two words
- Entire paragraph
- First word, no articles
- First character, no articles
- First two characters
- First three characters
- Swap first two words
- Swap first two words plus sp.
- Second word of paragraph
- Your text plus paragraph

20.112   *"No articles" means PageMaker will skip over words like "A" and "The" and select the next word or character.*

20.113   *If you choose this option, you can add repeating text to the header or footer. See 20.123.*

20.114   *This option switches around the first two words in the paragraph. The next option does the same, plus it inserts a space between the two words.*

20.116   *You can view the Text pattern of any of the core group options. Whenever you edit a text pattern you must give it a unique name. That prevents you from overwriting an existing pattern.*

20.115   The "Create custom content" dialog box.
(in the "Running headers\footers" dialog box, click the "Edit..." button)

20.117   *When you edit or create a Text pattern you can add it to the list of options under "Insert."*

20.120   *You can create new patterns by editing the characters in this box. In this pattern you could add another question mark and create a Text pattern for inserting the first four characters. You can copy and paste characters from the other Text patterns. When you name and save a custom Text pattern (20.117), a new file is stored in the Additions folder. See 20.123.*

Create custom content: Ver 1.0 B1 E4

OK

Cancel

Add

Delete

Name:
First three characters ▶

Find:
{???}

Insert:
\1

20.118   *You can delete patterns that you edit or create, but you can't delete any of the pre-defined options.*

20.119   *This box tells PageMaker what to insert. The backslash says to override the Text pattern and treat it as normal character. If you delete the backslash your header/footer would be the actual characters in the "Find:" edit box! The "1" tells PageMaker to insert the information in the "Find:" edit box.*

If you want to do this:	Then follow these steps:	Shortcuts ▾ Notes ▾ Hints
20.121 Set a header on every right-hand page of a publication, using the first instance of a style	▪ With the **pointer tool** select the first text block in the story, *or* insert the **text tool** within the first text block of the story. ▪ From the Utilities menu slide down to "Aldus Additions," then over to the submenu and choose "Running headers\footers…." ▪ In the "Find" box click the radio button next to "First instance." ▪ From the pop-up menu next to "Style" choose the style from which you want the headers text to come. ★ In the "Insert" box choose which words or characters you want as the headers content. ▪ Click the box next to "Right pages" (20.93). ▪ Measuring from the left corner of the page, enter a horizontal measurement for the header text block. Enter a value for the Vertical measurement. ▪ Enter a maximum width for the header text block if necessary. ▪ Under "Apply style" choose a style for the header. ▪ Click the box next to "Placc on first page" if you want a header on the first page of the publication. ▪ Click OK, or press Return. Whew!	▪ Remember to select the first text block in the story if you want headers from the beginning to the end of the story. If your story is in columns, select the first column on the page. ▪ The left handles of the header text block are placed on the ruler measurement you enter in the "Horizontal" edit box. The top of the text block hangs from the ruler measurement you enter in the "Vertical" edit box. Know the printable area of your page (19.73). You don't want your headers to be cut off in printing. ▪ If you want headers *and* footers in a publication, you must run the Addition twice—remember to change the "Find" and "Insert" information as necessary, and definitely change the "Vertical" placement value. ▪ The Addition may not find the correct style consistently if the style is imported from another program. To turn an imported style into a PageMaker style, hold down the Command key and click once on the style name in the Style palette; when you see the Edit dialog box, click OK.

If you want to do this:

20.122 Set a footer on every page of a publication using the last instance of a style

Then follow these steps:

- With the **pointer tool** select the first text block in the story, *or* insert the **text tool** within the first text block of the story.
- From the Utilities menu slide down to "Aldus Additions," then over to the submenu and choose "Running headers\footers…."
- In the "Find" box click the radio button next to "Last instance."
- From the pop-up menu next to "Style" choose the style from which you want the footers text to come.
- ★ In the "Insert" box choose which option you want as the content of the footers.
- Click the box next to "Left pages." Enter horizontal and vertical measurements for the footers text block, and a maximum width. Under "Apply style" choose a style for the left page footers.
- Click the box next to "Right pages." Enter a horizontal and vertical measurement for the footer text block, and a maximum width. Under "Apply style" choose a style for the right page footers.
- Click the box next to "Place on first page" if you want a footer on the first page of the publication.
- Click OK, or press Return.

Shortcuts ▾ Notes ▾ Hints

- It's a footer if you place it at the bottom of the page! Remember to measure from the top left corner of the page to the spot where you want the top of the text block to be. (The Aldus manual says the *baseline* is placed on the vertical measurement, but I haven't found that to be true.)
- The vertical measurement of footers (or headers) should be the same on both the right and left pages, but the horizontal measurement may be different. Perhaps you want the headers or footers to be on the outside edge of each page. In that case the left pages might have a horizontal measurement of 1 inch (1 inch in from the edge of the page), while the right pages might have a horizontal measurement of 5 or 6 inches in from the left edge of the page.
- Another way to place headers or footers on the outside edges of left and right pages is to design two headers/footers styles in which everything is the same except the alignment. Make the style you use for the left pages flush left, and the style for the right page headers/footers flush right.

If you want to do this:

20.123 Add repeating text to the
headers/footers

```
Create custom content: Uer 1.0 B1 E4      [ OK ]
                                          [Cancel]
Name:
[ Your text plus paragraph        ] ▶     [ Add ]
                                          [Delete]
Find:
[ <(?+)>                               ]
Insert:
[ Your text here \1                    ]
```

*Add the text you want to repeat in each
header/footer here.*

Then follow these steps:

- Follow the directions in 20.121 or 20.122
  until the ★.
- In the "Insert" box choose "Your text
  plus paragraph."
- Click the "Edit" button.
- In the "Create custom content" dialog
  box, under "Insert," replace the words
  "Your text here" with the text you want to
  repeat in each header/footer.
- Make sure the "\1" characters follow your
  text. Click OK, or press Return.
- In the "Running headers\footers…"
  dialog box, check the box next to "Left
  pages," "Right pages," or both.
- Enter values in the "Horizontal," "Vertical," and "Width" boxes.
- Under "Apply style" choose and apply a
  style to the headers/footers.
- Check the box next to "Place on first
  page" if you have selected a text block on
  the first right page of the publication and
  you want a header/footer on that page.
- Click OK, or press Return.

Shortcuts ▾ Notes ▾ Hints

- Perhaps you don't want the whole
  paragraph to follow your text. You can
  edit this option to be "Your text plus first
  word." If you are adventurous try this:
  - In the "Create custom content" dialog
    box, under "Name," choose "First word."
    Highlight and copy the Text pattern
    characters in the "Find" edit box.
  - Under "Name" choose "Your text plus
    paragraph."
  - Now under "Find," highlight the Text
    pattern and press Command V, or
    choose "Paste" from the Edit menu.
  - Under "Insert," replace the words
    "Your text here" with the text you want
    to repeat in each header/footer.
  - Make sure the "\1" characters follow
    your text. Name your custom pattern;
    click "Add" to store it. Click OK.
  - Complete the options in the "Running
    headers\footers…" dialog box.
  - Click OK, or press Return.
- When you name and save a customized
  Text pattern (20.117), information about
  it is stored in the "Header.ini" file in your
  "Additions" folder. To use your custom
  header on another computer, you need
  to move the "Header.ini" file to the
  "Additions" folder on that computer.

If you want to do this:	Then follow these steps:	Shortcuts ▾ Notes ▾ Hints

20.124 Remove headers\footers

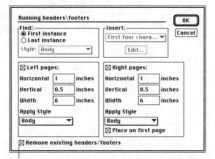

Make sure this box is checked. It deselects itself if you change radio buttons under "Find."

- With the **pointer tool** select the text block from which you ran the Addition, *or* insert the **text tool** within it.
- From the Utilities menu slide down to "Aldus Additions," then over to the submenu and choose "Running headers\footers…."
- At the very bottom of the dialog box, check the box next to "Remove existing headers\footers."
- If you manually moved the headers or footers on the publication page, enter the new location measurements in the "Horizontal" and "Vertical" edit boxes.
- Click OK, or press Return.

- The Addition will only remove headers/footers to the end of the story starting with whatever text block you select. If you don't want to remove all of the headers/footers, don't select the initial text block from which you ran the Addition.

I would live all my life in nonchalance and insouciance
Were it not for making a living, which is rather a nouciance.
—Ogden Nash

The "Sort pages..." Addition

20.125 The "Sort pages..." Addition lets you move pages from one place in a document to another without having to copy, remove, insert, and re-paste entire pages of information. "Sort pages" lets you view your whole publication as numbered thumbnails that you can rearrange just by selecting and dragging.

20.126 You can simply click on a page and drag it to a new position between other pages, or at the beginning or end of a row. A flashing black bar at the new location indicates where the page will go when you return to layout view.

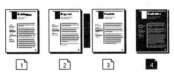

The black bar indicates where the page will be inserted.

20.127 You can Shift-click to select more than one page at a time. Facing pages will move as a unit unless you press the Command key to select and move just one of them. Similarly, if you press the Command key before you move page icons, you can insert pages between a pair of facing ones.

20.128 Once a page is moved, the original number icon dims, and one with the new page number appears. The dimmed icon with the original number always remains, though, as a visual reminder of the original page order no matter how many times you shuffle the pages around. The folded corner on the number icons tells you whether it is a right- or a left-hand page and how your rearrangement of pages affects the left- or right-hand page status of the publication. This is one of the tricky things to watch for when using the "Sort pages..." Addition.

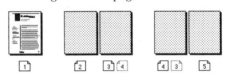

In this example, page 4, a left-hand page, was moved into the position of page 3, a right-hand page. This causes the original page 3 to become page 4. Note how the page-status of both pages is changed.

20.129 How the page elements are placed is an important consideration if your publication is double-sided *and* the inside and outside margins are different. If a page changes from a left-hand page to a right-hand page (or vice versa), the text and graphics may fit incorrectly on the new page.

You can compensate for this, though, by *unchecking* "Don't move elements" in the "Options" dialog box to make PageMaker automatically adjust the page elements to fit correctly on the new page. *Check* the box if you want the page elements to stay in the same position no matter how the page and its margins and guides change.

20.130 Sorting pages can change the order of text blocks in a story that spans several pages. It is up to you to be aware of the order and placement of threaded text blocks. Although the text in a story is never altered when you sort pages, there is nothing PageMaker can do to prevent you from mixing up the order of the text blocks themselves.

20.131 Although PageMaker makes it easy to rearrange pages, think it through before you actually do it. Take into account the effect resorting the pages may have on the rest of the publication. Pages designed to be left-facing can look just plain awful facing right. And who knows what havoc you may wreak on a threaded story without even realizing it? Always check your publication carefully afterward.

The "Sort pages..." dialog box

(from the Utilities menu, slide down to "Aldus Additions"; from the submenu, choose "Sort pages...")

20.132 The "Sort pages..." dialog box is a window that you can resize, zoom, and move around on-screen. The "Magnifying" icon and the "Detail" buttons control how you view the page icons. Clicking the magnifying and reduction icons switches between four levels of viewing magnification. You can view the thumbnails in detail individually or as a group through the "Options" dialog box.

20.133 In the "Options" dialog box, you can change the setup of your publication from single-sided to double-sided (either as individual pages or as two-page spreads). These options affect the setup of the actual publication as well as the "Sort pages" view.

20.134 This Addition is a real memory hog—be sure to give PageMaker as much memory as possible (22.46) if you will be using "Sort pages," and always, always, always save your publication before running it (or any other Addition, for that matter) so you can bail out with a "Revert" (18.30) if the results are not what you expected!

20.135 *Page icons (thumbnails) in detailed view.*

20.136 *Hold down the Command key to select a single page in a pair of facing pages.*

20.137 *Hold down the Command key to insert pages between facing pages.*

20.138 *Magnifying and reduction icons.*

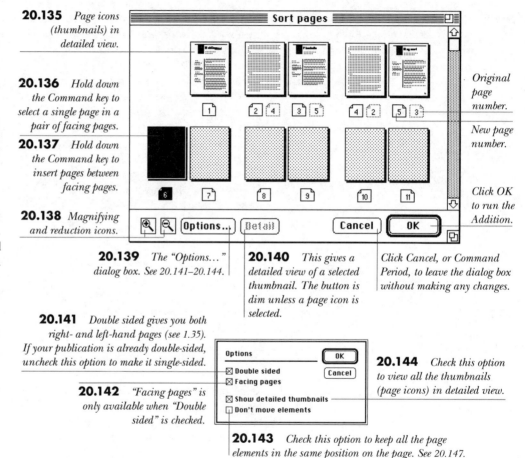

Original page number.

New page number.

Click OK to run the Addition.

20.139 *The "Options..." dialog box. See 20.141–20.144.*

20.140 *This gives a detailed view of a selected thumbnail. The button is dim unless a page icon is selected.*

Click Cancel, or Command Period, to leave the dialog box without making any changes.

20.141 *Double sided gives you both right- and left-hand pages (see 1.35). If your publication is already double-sided, uncheck this option to make it single-sided.*

20.142 *"Facing pages" is only available when "Double sided" is checked.*

20.144 *Check this option to view all the thumbnails (page icons) in detailed view.*

20.143 *Check this option to keep all the page elements in the same position on the page. See 20.147.*

If you want to do this:	Then follow these steps:	Shortcuts ▾ Notes ▾ Hints
20.145 Rearrange the pages in a publication	■ With **any tool** selected, go to the Utilities menu, slide down to "Aldus Additions," then over to the submenu and choose "Sort pages…." ■ In the dialog box, click on the page icon or icons you want to move. Drag it (or them) to their new position. A black bar indicates where the first one will be inserted. Let go. ■ Click OK. The Addition will run a bar graph indicating that it is sorting pages and cleaning up.	■ Shift-click to select more than one icon at a time, *or* press-and-drag with the pointer tool to select a range of pages within the marqueed area. ■ Press the Command key to select one page from a pair of facing pages. ■ To insert a selection between facing pages, press the Command key and drag the selection in between the pages. ■ In short publications PageMaker may not run the bar graph. ■ If you have any trouble running this Addition, try giving PageMaker more memory. Click once on the application icon when PageMaker is not open. From the File menu, choose "Get info" and increase the amount of memory next to "Preferred size" (System 7.1) or "Current size" (System 7.0).
20.146 Enlarge or reduce the size of the page icons	■ Open the "Sort pages" dialog box. ■ To enlarge the size of the page icons: □ Click on the magnifying icon (20.138), *or* press Command Shift > (above the period). ■ To reduce the size of the page icons: □ Click on the reduction icon (20.138), *or* press Command Shift < (above the comma).	■ There are four levels of magnification. At each view, PageMaker will fit as many page icons as she can in a row. You can click the zoom box, or press-and-drag the resize box to change the size of the window. Use the vertical scroll bar to view page icons not visible in the window. ■ Use larger point sizes for display text (about 18 points and up) to read the page icons at lower magnifications.

If you want to do this:	Then follow these steps:	Shortcuts ▾ Notes ▾ Hints
20.147 Rearrange the pages without moving any of the elements on the page	▪ With **any tool** selected, go to the Utilities menu, slide down to "Aldus Additions," then over to the submenu and choose "Sort pages...." ▪ Click the "Options" button. ▪ Check the box next to "Don't move elements" (20.143). Click OK. ▪ In the dialog box, click on the page icon(s) you want to move. Drag the icons to their new positions. ▪ Click OK.	▪ This option has no effect if the publication's inside and outside (or right and left) margins are the same. ▪ You can select this option either before or after you rearrange the page icons as long as it's before you hit the final OK.
20.148 Rearrange the pages so the elements fit within the new margins and guides	▪ With **any tool** selected, go to the Utilities menu, slide down to "Aldus Additions," then over to the submenu and choose "Sort pages...." ▪ Click the "Options" button. ▪ Make sure the box next to "Don't move elements" (20.143) is *not checked*. Click OK. ▪ In the dialog box, click on the page icon(s) you want to move. Drag the icon(s) to their new positions. ▪ Click OK.	▪ When you first rearrange the icons, it will look just like it does when "Don't move elements" is checked. The adjustments for the margins do not show up until after you click OK, and you are back in layout view.
20.149 View one or more of the page icons in detail	▪ In the "Sort pages..." dialog box, click on the icon(s) you want to see in detail. ▪ Click the "Detail" button.	▪ The "Detail" button is gray until an icon is selected. ▪ You can see all the icons in detail by checking "Show detailed thumbnails" in the "Options" dialog box (20.144).

Containing several clear Matters,
but which flow from the same Fount
as those in the preceding Chapters.

21 ▾ Special Techniques

21.1   I have tried, throughout this book, to include any special techniques directly in the section to which they pertain. So the first part of this section is just a list of possible special techniques in which you may be interested, along with references for where to find their detailed directions in other parts of the book. The second part is a list of techniques that didn't seem to have a proper pigeonhole. If you have any neat tricks, let me know and I'll add them to this section (with due credit, of course).

SOMETIMES THE SEAS ARE CALM

AND THAT'S WONDERFUL.

SOMETIMES THE SEAS ARE NOT CALM

AND THAT'S THE WAY IT IS.

RABBI NATHAN SEAGULL

21.2 Techniques in the book

General publication tips

- Begin page numbering with a number other than one: 1.30

- Show the first two pages of a publication as a double-page spread: 1.36

- Change the horizontal ruler measurements: 1.53

- Tricks with page turning and viewing: 1.100–1.124

- View a page at actual size at the exact spot you want: 1.116

- View a page at 200% size at the exact spot you want: 1.117

- View a section of the page at up to 800% magnification: 1.124

- Auto number individual pages: 1.150

- Drag-and-drop items between PageMaker publications: 1.179, 1.180, 4.86, 10.134

- Override ruler measurements: 1.323

- Activate the Control palette: 3.20

- Change the Control palette measurement system "on the fly": 3.114

- Print a publication other than the one that is on the screen: 15.26; 19.217

- Shortcut to the "Edit color" dialog box: 16.77

- Open a Mac PageMaker 4.x publication in PageMaker 5: 17.46

- Open a PC PageMaker publication in Mac PageMaker: 17.47

- Reduce the size of a publication: 18.28–18.29

- Prevent a laser printer from printing a test page every time you turn it on: 19.4

- Define printing styles: 19.220–19.222

- Scale large-sized pages onto letter-sized paper when printing: 19.79, 19.83

- Print items that fall outside the boundary of a page: 19.131

Text tips

- Letterspace text across a text block: 4.248; 4.249; 5.150

- Step-and-repeat graphics or text blocks: 1.305; 10.245

- Turn text into a graphic: 10.151, 13.40

- Create a confined space in which to place text: 1.319; 4.26

- Type numbers with the keypad: 1.324

- Use the keypad as arrow keys: 1.325

- Select text with keyboard: 1.326; 4.204

- Cut and paste with the keypad: 1.327

- Create a confined space to type text into, or create a text block to override any existing columns: 4.26

- Place stories from another PageMaker publication: 4.63–4.86

- Override auto or manual flow: 4.98

- Cancel a loaded text icon: 4.100

- Drag-and-drop text from one PageMaker publication window to another: 4.86

- Combine several separate text blocks into one text block: 4.124

- Separate one text block into several, unconnected text blocks: 4.129

- Add to or delete from the text selection: 4.203

- Create beautiful fractions: 4.261–4.262

- Create interesting bullets: 4.264

- Apply a color to text: 4.265; 16.120; 16.121

- Set a one-em indent for first lines: 4.325

- Break a line of text without getting a new paragraph: 4.348–4.353

Techniques in the book *—continued*

- Create a nicely spaced non-breaking ellipsis: 4.358
- Create non-breaking spaces: 5.217–5.228
- Make the linespacing consistent when there are different points sizes of type in the same paragraph: 5.23–5.26
- Prevent a word from hyphenating: 5.251
- Move the left margin marker independently in the Indents/tabs ruler: 6.26
- Use tab leaders to create forms or fill-in blanks: 6.71
- Create custom leaders: 6.72–6.73
- Copy tab and indent formatting into other contiguous paragraphs: 6.84
- Create a new style through the Control palette: 8.49
- Transform one style sheet definition into another: 8.51
- Find-and-change keyboard formatting: 9.62; 9.65
- Find invisible characters through the Story Editor: 9.65
- Place the table of contents and/or index from a Word file: 17.34

- Place a table or chart from a Word or Excel file into PageMaker as a graphic: 17.35, 17.38
- Create a Drop capital: 20.59

Graphic tips

- Select an object that is underneath another object: 1.211
- Select a line that is under a guide line: 1.212
- Step-and-repeat graphics or text blocks: 1.305; 10.245
- Turn text into a graphic: 10.151, 13.40, 17.35, 17.38
- Restore a distorted graphic to its original proportions: 1.322; 10.140
- Move a tiny little object: 2.29
- Move or draw objects in perfect alignment with the ruler tick marks: 2.32
- Change the line widths or the fills of more than one line or border at a time: 2.35
- Cancel a loaded text or graphic icon: 4.100
- Make an EPS graphic out of a PageMaker page: 10.160

- Re-size bitmapped graphics and halftoned scans to the printer resolution (to prevent unwanted patterns): 10.141–10.142
- Compress TIFFs: 10.152–10.153
- View a grayscale TIFF temporarily at high resolution: 10.158
- Make graphics gray (which, when printed in colored ink or toner, will appear to be a tint): 10.159; 16.123
- Lighten a PICT or an EPS to a shadow: 10.212
- Adjust the space above and below an inline graphic: 5.108–5.109; 10.246–10.248
- Center an inline graphic in a text block: 10.249
- Create an inline graphic as the first character in a hanging indent: 10.251
- Turn a text wrap inside out (so text will wrap inside the shape): 13.41
- Access the Apple color wheel: 16.54
- Edit a graphic without leaving PageMaker: 10.146–10.148
- Make a decorative border: 10.307

If you want to do this:	**Then follow these steps:**	**Shortcuts ▾ Notes ▾ Hints**
21.3 Custom enlarge the page view	■ Choose any tool; hold down the Command key and Spacebar. Use the magnifying tool that appears to drag a marquee around the area you wish to enlarge.	■ The amount of the page that is enlarged depends upon the size of the area you select. Maximum magnification is 800%. See 1.112–1.124 for other page view info.
21.4 Make Zapf Dingbat arrows point to the left, up, or down 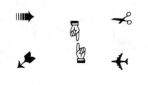	All arrows in the font Zapf Dingbats point to the right. To make them point in other directions, simply put them in their own little text blocks, then rotate the text: ■ Type the dingbat in a separate text block. ■ Click once on the **pointer tool;** click once on the text block. ■ In the Control palette enter a value in the "Rotating" option box. ■ Click the Apply button or press Return.	■ Enter a positive value to rotate the dingbat counter-clockwise; a negative value to rotate it clockwise. ■ You can also use the rotating tool to select and rotate the dingbat: click on the rotating tool, click on the dingbat to select it, then press and drag in the direction you want it to revolve. ■ Read 4.271–4.287 for more details regarding rotated text.
21.5 Eliminate *some* master page items from a publication page, but leave others	■ View the page you want to customize. Turn off the master page items (Layout menu). ■ Go to the master pages. ■ With the **pointer tool,** Shift-click to select the items you *do* want to display on the publication page. ■ Press Command C (to copy). Press Command Tab to return to the page. ■ Press Command Option V. The master page items will paste onto the page in exactly the same position as they were on the master page.	■ Use this is in lieu of making opaque boxes to cover up master page items you don't want to show. ■ Command Option V is the power-paste command (1.283). It pastes any cut or copied items into exactly the same position they were in when they were first cut or copied (provided the same space is visible on the screen).

If you want to do this:

Then follow these steps:

Shortcuts ▾ Notes ▾ Hints

21.6 Remove a headline from a story and make it span several columns

| The Alphabet More powerful than all poetry, more pervasive than all science, more profound | than all philosophy are the letters of the alphabet, twenty-six pillars of strength upon which our culture rests. Olof Lagercrants |

◄— *Original story. Select the headline and cut it. This may leave an extra line at the top of the body copy that you will have to delete (double-click on the blank line; press the Backspace/Delete key).*

| More powerful than all poetry, more pervasive than all science, more profound than all philosophy are the letters of the | alphabet, twenty-six pillars of strength upon which our culture rests. Olof Lagercrants |

| More powerful than all poetry, more pervasive than all science, more profound than all philosophy are the letters of the | alphabet, twenty-six pillars of strength upon which our culture rests. Olof Lagercrants |

The bounding box will look like this box, with the I-beam at the end of it, until you let go of the mouse. Then the insertion point jumps to the left and the bounding box seems to disappear. But, really, it's still there. Just paste, and the headline will paste into the bounding box which overrides the columns.

| The Alphabet More powerful than all poetry, more pervasive than all science, more profound than all philosophy are | the letters of the alphabet, twenty-six pillars of strength upon which our culture rests. Olof Lagercrants |

With this first method, the headline is not threaded to the body text.

- With the **text tool** select the headline.
- Press Command X to cut it (this removes it permanently from the story; if you want it back in, press Command Z immediately to Undo, or paste it back in again at anytime as long as you don't copy anything else to the Clipboard).
- With the **text tool** press-and-drag to create a bounding box across the columns.
- Press Command V to paste the headline into that bounding box.

If you want the headline to remain threaded:

- With the **pointer tool** roll up the entire text block.
- Click once, lightly, on the plus sign in the bottom windowshade loop.
- With the resulting loaded text icon, press-and-drag across the columns, dragging just deep enough to accommodate the headline. Let go at the right edge.
- Click once, lightly, on the arrow sign in the bottom windowshade loop of the headline text block.
- With the loaded text icon, click in the column to pour in the text as usual. You can also press-and-drag bounding boxes for the columns of text.

- *Threaded* means the text in one text block is connected to the text in another text block. As you edit, the changes can affect all connected, or *threaded*, text blocks (4.106–4.113).
- Read 1.319–1.322 and 4.26 for more details on the text bounding box.

If you want to do this:	**Then follow these steps:**	**Shortcuts ▾ Notes ▾ Hints**

21.7   Adjust line breaks

With money in your pocket,
you are wise and you are
handsome, and you sing well
too.
                     Yiddish proverb

With money in your pocket, you
are wise and you are handsome,
and you sing well too.
                     Yiddish proverb

In the first text block, the line breaks are awkward, plus there is a widow ("too"). I extended the text block, which wrapped the words into a better arrangement.

With money in your pocket,
you are wise and you are
handsome, and you sing well
too.
                     Yiddish proverb

With money in your pocket, you
are wise and you are handsome,
and you sing well too.
                     Yiddish proverb

Perhaps it's not possible to extend the text block. In this example, I selected the first couple of lines and tracked it to "Normal." This tightened up the letter spacing just enough to pull the words into a better arrangement.

To uphold the standards of typographic excellence, you really must be conscious of how lines are breaking—not only in headlines, but in body text as well. I touched on this topic in 4.348–4.353. There are several ways to adjust line breaks:

- Rewrite the copy. Sometimes it just takes a word added or deleted several lines back.
- Lengthen or shorten the line length just a hair (by dragging the text block handle in or out a touch).
- If you need to squeeze a few more letters on the line, select the line and set the track to "Normal" (from the Type menu). Or if it's already "Normal" and you need to bump a couple more letters to the next line, select the line and give it "No track."
- If you need to bump a word down to the next line, you can:
  □ Hit the Tab key before the word to bump it down to the next line. This will not work on justified or right-aligned text.
  □ Press the Spacebar a few times in front of the word to bump it down (okay with justified text).
  □ Position the insertion point just before the word and press Shift-Return (4.348; great with justified text). —*continued*

- Be conscious of rag right (left-aligned) body copy lines getting *too* ragged as when a very short word hangs out above the next line. Usually you can bump the word down to fill in the space and thus smooth out the right edge a little. Notice the second line in this paragraph: you can bump the word *as* down to the next line to fill in the space.

- "Normal" tracking is looser in PageMaker 5 than in 4.x. If you have converted documents from 4 to 5 and the line breaks are driving you crazy, see 17.48.

If you want to do this:

Never learn to do anything. If you don't learn, you will always find someone else to do it for you.

Mark Twain

Never learn to do anything. If you don't learn, you will always find someone else to do it for you.

Mark Twain

The word "If" needs to bump down to the next line, as well as the word "to." I bumped "If" down with a Shift Return (line break); I bumped "to" down by attaching it to the word "do" with a hard space. (Then I noticed that the name "Mark Twain" was hanging out too far, so I put a couple of em spaces after his name [after his name because he is right-aligned] to scoot him over. It's so much fun to be fussy.)

Then follow these steps:

(Each of the above methods will show a visible space when you edit the text, or change the margins, indents, font, size, etc.; see the example to the right.)

☐ You can also try this to adjust those unseemly breaks: select the blank space directly *after* the word you want to bump down (press-and-drag over the space, *or* position the insertion point directly after the word and press the Shift and RightArrow key), press Option Spacebar to create a hard space (5.226). As you edit the text, this won't leave a visible, open space behind (but those two words, now connected with a hard space, will always be seen by the computer as one word).

■ Sometimes you need to adjust the lines *preceding* the awkward line break, and then the awkward line break will fix itself.

Shortcuts ▾ Notes ▾ Hints

■ Below is an example of what happens when you adjust the line breaks and then edit the text, change the margin, etc. I forced a line break with a tab in the following text and then changed the point size; the tab space is visible.

All things are ready if our minds be so.
King Henry the Fifth

All things are ready   if our minds be so.
King Henry the Fifth

If you want to do this:

Then follow these steps:

Shortcuts ▾ Notes ▾ Hints

21.8 Maintain consistent linespace between two separate text blocks

Very few things
happen at the right
time, and the rest do
not happen at all. The

▲ *Position a ruler guide along the bottom windowshade handles.*

Position the top windowshade handles of the next text block along that guide line.

Very few things
happen at the right
time, and the rest do
not happen at all. The
conscientious historian will correct these defects.
Herodotus 483–425 B.C.

▼

Sometimes you have to separate a text block into more than one part, with one part aligned directly under the other and with the exact same amount of linespace between the two text blocks as there is between the lines of text.

- Separate the two blocks. With the **pointer tool** click once on the top block.
- Press in the horizontal ruler and bring down a ruler guide. Position it directly along the bottom windowshade handles of the text block.
- With the **pointer tool** move the lower text block into position under the one above. Position the top windowshade handles of the *lower* text block directly on the guide line. The space between the two text blocks is now exactly one linespace.

Who

knows

where

we're

going,

but

we'll

get

there.

Keasley Jones

If you want to do this:

Then follow these steps:

Shortcuts ▾ Notes ▾ Hints

21.9 Keep linespacing consistent when an inline graphic has been added

Alice was beginning to get very tired of sitting by her sister on the bank, and of having nothing to do:

9-point text with "Auto" leading once or twice she had peeped into the book her sister was reading, but it had no pictures or conversation in it, "and what is the use of a book," thought Alice, "without pictures or conversations?

Alice was beginning to get very tired of sitting by her sister on the bank,

9-point text with 14-point leading and of having nothing to do: once or twice she had peeped into the book her sister was reading, but it had no pictures or conversation in it, "and what is the use of a book," thought Alice, "without pictures or conversations?"

You can do several things.

- One is to remove any excess boundary that may be surrounding the graphic. Just click on it with the cropping tool and crop it away (10.143; 10.216, 10.220).
- Another thing to do is to *fix* the leading, rather than use Auto leading. Triple-click on the paragraph the graphic is in, then change the leading to anything you like *except Auto* (see 5.12–5.26).
- You can also fix just the leading of the inline graphic: select it (*just the graphic*) with the text tool and press Command T. Enter the leading you want in the edit box (see 10.243).
- Use "Align to grid" (5.97–5.111) as another way to adjust errant inline graphics. See 5.108–5.109 for "Align to grid" information specific to inline graphics.

- Inline graphics drop in with a boundary around them, and this boundary uses a slug, just like text (5.32–5.34). The slug has its own Auto leading, and when you drop the graphic into text it can throw the linespacing off: baselines will not align across columns anymore.
- You may have to adjust the graphic vertically once you have fixed the leading (10.246).
- If your graphic looks fragmented, just redraw the screen (change views, etc.).
- See 10.247 for a tip on how to precisely align the space above and below an inline graphic that is in its own paragraph.
- See 10.248 for information on how to use the object-view Control palette to precisely adjust the baseline-offset of an inline graphic. You can further trick PageMaker into letting you exceed the range of adjustment by using the Baseline-shift option on the character-view Control palette to apply precise baseline shift amounts to a range of lines (see 4.263). Just select a line that is correctly linespaced and note its measurement in the Baseline-shift edit box. Now select the lines with the inline graphic and enter that same amount into their edit boxes.

| **If you want to do this:** | **Then follow these steps:** | **Shortcuts ▾ Notes ▾ Hints** |

21.10 Hang the punctuation

"**Time is Money,
and the way to buy Time
is Money.**"
Chip Swanson

"**Time is Money,
and the way to buy Time
is Money.**"
Chip Swanson

In the first example the punctuation is not hung, making the sentence appear to be indented. The second example shows how quotation marks can actually hang outside the text block using the first technique in the next column.

(I also reduced the size of the quotation marks and the period, kerned the space open a touch between the first quotation mark and the T, and closed up the spacing around the punctuation. Yes, I am fussy with my letters. But my house is a mess.)

There are several ways to hang punctuation depending on the situation. Use one of the following methods after first typing the text.

- Even if the punctuation mark is in the middle of a paragraph you can use this method:
  □ **If the text is left-aligned or justified,** type a hard space (Option Spacebar) in front (to the left) of the punctuation mark.
  □ Kern (see 5.163–5.171 for all the ways to kern) until the punctuation mark is hung properly. The mark will temporarily disappear—that's okay!! Redraw the screen (click in the zoom box in the upper right) to make the mark re-appear.
  □ **If the text is right-aligned,** type a hard space (Option Spacebar) *after* the punctuation. Hit the LeftArrow key once to move the insertion point next to the punctuation. Kern.

—*continued*

- In large-size text (14-point or above) or in quoted material, always hang the punctuation (*hang* it outside the aligned edge of text, whether on the left or the right). If you don't hang the punctuation, it makes the aligned edge look unaligned.
- Hanging the punctuation is always the very last thing to do because if you have to edit the text *after* you've taken care of the punctuation, ya gotta start all over again (unless you use the indent method).
- Notice in the example I aligned the second and third lines with the *stem* of the T, not the *bar*. That's because in this case the stem was visually stronger.

If you want to do this:	**Then follow these steps:**	**Shortcuts ▾ Notes ▾ Hints**
—continued	■ **Or** you can indent the other lines that *don't* have punctuation by either of these methods: □ Insert hard spaces (ems, ens, or thins; 5.217–5.228) to bump the line over. You can select those hard spaces and reduce or enlarge them increments of a point, if necessary, for perfect alignment. □ **Or** if the hanging needs to be done on the left and only on the first line, you can set a first-line indent flush left, and set the left indent in just to where the rest of the text should align. (See 6.54–6.60 re: indents.) You could create a style sheet for this (Section 8).	
21.11 Start a publication on a left-hand page or on a double-page spread	■ From the File menu, choose "Page setup…." ■ In the "Start page #" edit box enter an even number. ■ This will, of course, change your automatic page numbers. If you are not going to automatically number the pages then you have nothing to worry about. If you are going to have PageMaker number the pages, then before you print you will have to go back to the "Page setup" dialog box and change "Start page #" back to the actual number of the first page.	■ This works great for those times when you have only two pages in your publication and you want to view them together. Unless you use this little trick, they will never display side-by-side on the screen. (Remember, to view pages side-by-side, you must choose "Double-sided" and "Facing pages" in the "Page setup" dialog box; 1.35, 1.36).

If you want to do this:	**Then follow these steps:**	**Shortcuts ▾ Notes ▾ Hints**
21.12 Let go of the text or graphics that are in the loaded text icon without placing them on the page	▪ With any loaded icon (text or graphics), simply click on any tool in the Toolbox, *or* press Command Spacebar.	▪ Or hold down the Command and Spacebar keys until the loaded icon turns into the magnifying tool, and then let go.
21.13 Prevent a word from hyphenating	▪ With the **text tool,** click the insertion point directly in front of the first character of the word you don't want to hyphenate. ▪ Press Command Hyphen; this creates a *discretionary hyphen* (5.234) that prevents the word from hyphenating in this paragraph. You will not *see* the discretionary hyphen. ▪ To remove that discretionary hyphen, backspace over it, even though you can't even see it.	▪ Instead you could select the word, go to the "Type specs" dialog box and click the radio button next to "No Break." ▪ If you *never* want that word to hyphenate, add it to the user dictionary specifying no hyphenation (5.253).
21.14 Proportionally re-size a PageMaker-drawn rectangle 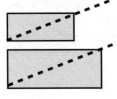 *This is what the "Proportional-scaling" button looks like when it is on.*	▪ Select the rectangle. ▪ In the Control palette turn on the "Proportional-scaling" button (3.92). ▪ Type the percentage by which you want to enlarge the rectangle in the "Width" or "Height" edit boxes. ▪ Click the Apply button, or press Return.	▪ To display the Control palette if it is not already on screen, choose it from the Window menu, or press Command ' *(apostrophe).*

If you want to do this:

21.15 Use Baseline-shift for special effects

The smaller letters are shifted up (each with different specs) but unkerned.

After kerning.

This is just to show that the type effect is really one text block.

Then follow these steps:

- The example on the left shows two different ways of using baseline-shift and kerning to create interesting type effects.
  - □ The first word, *Limousine,* has a Typo Upright (Bitstream font) letter *L* at 48 points. The rest of the word is 9-point Walbaum Roman (Adobe font). I selected *imousine* and entered the value .12 in the "Baseline-shift" option edit box in the Control palette (4.218). Then I set the insertion point between the *L* and the *i* and kerned using Command Delete (repeatedly pressing Delete while holding down the Command key) until the word appeared as you see it.
  - □ The second word, *Service,* has a 48-point Typo Upright letter *S* and 9-point Walbaum Roman *ervice.* I selected *ervice* and entered the value .27 in the "Baseline-shift" option edit box in the Control palette. Then I kerned it.

Shortcuts ▾ Notes ▾ Hints

- You can also shift the baseline of selected text in the "Type options" dialog box found in "Type specs" under the Type menu (4.205), or set a baseline-shift value as a default. See 5.151–5.179 for more info on kerning.

書 book

is like a garden

carried in the pocket.

—*C h i n e s e   p r o v e r b*

If you want to do this:

21.16 Adjust the height of parentheses, hyphens, quotations marks, etc.

(parentheses) hy-phen

Parentheses and hyphens are designed for use with lowercase letters.

(RAM) (RAM)

Notice in the first RAM how the parentheses hit the top of the caps, but seem to drop too low below the baseline. In the second example, I raised the parentheses a bit.

(707) 570-1564
(707) 570-1564

In the first example, the hyphen seems too low. The parentheses have the same problem around numbers as they do around caps. In the second example, both the hyphen and the parentheses have been raised (and I kerned the hyphen away from the zero).

Then follow these steps:

- After the text has been typed, select a parenthesis or a hyphen (press-and-drag over it or press Shift Arrow key).
- Press Command T to get the "Type specifications" dialog box.
- Click the "Options" button.
- In the "Baseline-shift" edit box enter 1.5; click the radio button next to "Up."
  - □ This raised the one parenthesis or hyphen. If there are others you want to adjust, you can follow the same procedure for each one.
  - □ **Or,** you can copy the adjusted character, select another character and paste in the adjusted one. (If you paste a left parenthesis where a right parenthesis should go, just select the new one and type the right parenthesis back in; that space, even after you delete the adjusted character, retains the formatting.)

Shortcuts ▾ Notes ▾ Hints

- Parentheses and hyphens are designed, by default, to be used with lowercase letters since that is what they do most often. But when parentheses and hyphens are used with capital letters or with numbers they appear too low.
- Another method is to use Find-and-Change to globally search for and replace parentheses and hyphens with a superscript version. This only works *if* you change the default size and position of superscript type first:
  - □ With the text tool chosen, press Command T.
  - □ In the "Position" pop-up menu, choose "Superscript."
  - □ Click the "Options" button.
  - □ Hit the Tab key once to select the "Super/subscript size" edit box. Enter **100.**
  - □ Hit the Tab key once more to select the "Superscript position" edit box. Enter **9.**
  - □ Click OK, click OK; *or* press Option Return to close both dialog boxes.
  - □ See 9.79 for changing characters with special attributes.

If you want to do this:

21.17 Use leaders for creating lines that end evenly (when you don't want to, or can't, use paragraph rules)

Hello

My name is_____

My favorite book is_____

I hate _____

When I grow up I want to be_____

The title of my autobiography will be____

_____

The example above uses the line leader; the example below uses the dots.

Hello

My name is ....

My favorite book is....................................

I hate ....

When I grow up I want to be.......................

The title of my autobiography will be.............

....

Then follow these steps:

Section 6 on Indents and Tabs details all the explicit steps for creating tabs with leaders. See 6.34 and 6.71.

- The basic idea is that you set a right-aligned tab at the end of the line and assign a leader to it.
- Type the text, hit Tab. You probably won't see the leader until you hit a Return.
- Continue typing text and hitting Tabs and Returns. The lines will always end at the same place.
- If you shorten the text block with the text handles, you may need to move the tab over to the left, as well. If you have a 3-inch text block and you set a tab at 2.5 inches, the tab is defined at 2.5 inches; it is not defined as being .5 inches from the end of the text block, as paragraph rules are. If you shorten the text block to 2 inches, the tab at 2.5 inches is gone. If you stretch the text block back out to 3 inches, the tab will return.

Shortcuts ▾ Notes ▾ Hints

- The great thing about using leaders is that they are so incredibly easy: you can lengthen or shorten them instantly, you can customize them, you're always assured they'll end neatly, and when you change the point size or the leading, you know the leaders will move right along with the type—just like paragraph rules. In the example on the left, leaders have an advantage over paragraph rules because they can start wherever the text ends without having to spec each line. The disadvantage is that you cannot control the point size of the line. You can customize the leader character, though; see 6.71–6.73.

If you want to do this:	Then follow these steps:	Shortcuts ▾ Notes ▾ Hints

21.18 Print one PageMaker publication while inside another	■ From the File menu, choose "Book…."
	■ If there are any publications listed on the right-hand side, under "Book list," then select and remove them (click on the name, then click "Remove").
	■ Using the left-hand list box, locate the publication you want to print. Double-click on its name, and it will appear in the right-hand list.
	■ Click OK.
	■ From the File menu, choose "Print…."
	■ Under "Book," check the box "Print all publications in book."
	■ If you click "Print" right now, PageMaker will not print the current publication, but will print *only* the publication that is in the Book List. That particular publication will print with the specifications you set in this dialog box.
	  □ To keep the "Size" and "Source" settings of the original publication, check "Use paper settings of each publication."
	  □ To print only certain page ranges, see 15.30.
		■ If you want to print more than one publication, than transfer the name of more than one publication into the Book List (see 15.6–15.31 for more info on the Book List). PageMaker will print the publications in the order they appear in the List. If you want to renumber the pages in the publication you are about to print, see 15.29.
		■ You can also print one or more publications from within another one by using the "Printer styles" Addition; you do not need to have a publication open, and you can print as many publications as you want. You can use a pre-defined set of print specifications (a "print style"), or define the print specs on the spot; see 19.191–19.225.

If you want to do this:	**Then follow these steps:**	**Shortcuts ▾ Notes ▾ Hints**

21.19 Automatically number the pages but prevent the front matter (title page, introduction, etc.) from being included in the numbering

■ Often in a publication you have a title page and perhaps some other front matter that you don't want numbered. But then when you automatically number the pages, the *real* first page does not get labeled as page one. To solve that problem simply put the front matter at the *end* of the publication. That is, create the page that you want numbered as page one *on* page one. Create the rest of the pages in their order.

At the end of the publication, say pages 14, 15, and 16, create the front matter (the title page, the introduction, etc.). On those end pages, **either:**

□ Remove the master page numbers on the current page by deselecting "Display master items" from the Layout menu. This will remove *all* the master page items on the screen, not just the page numbers (1.143).

□ **Or** cover the master page numbers with opaque boxes drawn with PageMaker's drawing tools (1.144).

Without knowing the force of words, it is impossible to know men.

Confucious

If you want to do this:	**Then follow these steps:**	**Shortcuts ▾ Notes ▾ Hints**
21.20 Keep track of certain information about a publication such as time spent, client comments, etc.	▪ Simply create a little text block on the pasteboard. Make it a chart, if you like, detailing the time you opened the publication, the time you closed it, the changes you made, etc. Then each time you open and close the publication, fill in the chart to keep a running total of time and current information on the project. To print the chart, just make an extra page at the end of the publication and move the text block onto it. Also see 19.131 for a tip on how to print something off the page.	
21.21 Arrange text in several sets of columns on one page, e.g., in a three-column format across the top two-thirds of the page and a five-column format on the bottom third	▪ Set up your column guides and place the text for one of the column formats, say three columns. Then change the columns. The text in the first columns will not move. ▪ **Or** you could set up a multiple column format, like six columns, and then drag-place the text into the special column sizes you want. See 1.321 and 4.62 for details on drag-placing.	▪ No, this is not a very elegant trick, but it is the only way to accomplish a multiple column format.

If you want to do this:

Then follow these steps:

Shortcuts ▾ Notes ▾ Hints

21.22 Create text up to 1300 points

- Size the type to one-half of the final size you want. For instance, if you want 900-point type, size it to 450. Select the text.
- Press Command T to get the type specs.
- Change the "Position" to "Superscript."
- Click on the "Options…" button. Change the "Superscript size" to 200%. Change the "Superscript position" to 0 (zero).
- Click the OK buttons.

- Of course, you could change the super-script size to anything from 100% to 200%, instead of always 200%.
- See 4.253–4.261 for full details on super- and subscript.

21.23 Create a line of text that is longer than 22.75 inches

- Make the text as large as it can possibly be while staying completely within the maximum text block width of 22.75 inches.
- With the **pointer tool,** select the text block and copy it.
- From the Edit menu choose "Paste special…."
- In the "Paste special" dialog box, double-click on the format name "PICT."
- Back in your publication, stretch the PICT to create the desired line length. Keep pressing the Shift key to retain the correct proportion.

- For example, to fit "Happy Birthday" within the maximum text block size in Goudy Bold, type the message at 220 points. Be sure if you are taking the text up this large, that you specify a page in "Page setup" large enough to handle it (42 x 42 inches is Page-Maker's maximum page size) and that you choose "Tile" when you want to print it (19.75–19.78).
- See 10.151, for more info on turning text into graphics to manipulate it.
- You could also use the "PS Group it " Addition (10.259–10.267) if you are working with more than one object. (If not, you can fake a group by creating a reverse rule, or a box filled with paper or None to select along with your type.) However, this increases the size of your publication *and* creates an external link needed for printing.

If you want to do this:	Then follow these steps:	Shortcuts ▾ Notes ▾ Hints
21.24 Prevent the last text block from expanding as text is edited	▪ The last text block will expand if it has not been intentionally rolled up. To prevent the block from expanding, hit an extra return after the last line of text, then roll up the text block one line.	▪ Sometimes you want the last text block in the story to expand as you edit, sometimes you don't. You have a choice.
21.25 Delete multiple items as you select them	▪ With the **pointer tool,** hold down the Delete/Backspace key and click on each item you want to delete. ▪ **Or,** hold down the Delete key as you drag a marquee around all the items. They will all disappear when you let go of the mouse.	▪ You have to be careful with this method—it's quite easy to get trigger-happy and delete something you didn't want to. Command Z will undo the last deletion, of course.
21.26 Apply the same Image Control settings to several TIFFs	▪ Set up a TIFF on the page and apply the Image Control settings you want to recreate. Make a couple copies of it and move them into position. ▪ With the **pointer tool,** click once on one of the copies of the TIFF graphic. ▪ *Place* the new TIFF as usual (10.126), but be sure to first click the button "Replacing entire graphic" (10.128). The new graphic will replace the selected one *and* it will drop in with the same Image Control settings and cropped size as the selected graphic. ▪ Repeat the process for the other TIFFs.	▪ This technique will work with TIFFs that you *place* from the File menu; it will not work with TIFFs that you try to *paste* from the Clipboard. ▪ It will not work if you replace a grayscale TIFF with a black-and-white TIFF, or vice versa. ▪ If you want the new TIFF to also retain the same cropping data (meaning not only will it be the same size as the graphic it is replacing, but it will also be cropped in the same manner), make sure the button is selected for "Retain cropping data."

If you want to do this:	**Then follow these steps:**	**Shortcuts ▾ Notes ▾ Hints**
21.27 Recompose all the text in the publication	■ Hold down the Option key and choose "Hyphenation…" from the Type menu. It will take a few minutes. ■ If you get the "Hyphenation" dialog box, just click Cancel. ■ Press Command S to save the publication again or the text will recompose every time you turn a page (a very time-consuming process).	■ If you find that your text has weird spacing problems because you changed fonts or converted the file from another program, or because you opened the publication on someone else's computer, try this global recompose.
21.28 Run a diagnostic on the publication in addition to recomposing all the text	■ Choose the **pointer tool.** ■ Hold both the Shift and the Option keys down. From the Type menu, choose "Hyphenation…." 　□ If you hear **one beep,** PageMaker did not find any problems. 　□ If you hear **two beeps,** PageMaker found a problem and fixed it. 　□ If you hear **three beeps,** PageMaker found a problem but could not fix it. ■ Save your publication again.	■ This diagnostic sometimes fixes things like bad links or bad styles. If your publication is giving you grief about something or other, start with this diagnostic to see if PageMaker can take care of the problem. ■ See 22.48 for more information about damaged publications.

A man is known by the books he reads. Emerson

833

If you want to do this:

Then follow these steps:

Shortcuts ▾ Notes ▾ Hints

21.29 Create paragraph rules that *begin* outside the text block

a

They are ill discoverers Francis Bacon
that think there is no land,
when they can see nothing
but sea.

b

They are ill discoverers Francis Bacon
that think there is no land,
when they can see nothing
but sea.

c

They are ill discoverers Francis Bacon
that think there is no land,
when they can see nothing
but sea.

Really, this is too cool. You can set up paragraph rules that actually begin and end *outside* of the text block.

- Create the rule as usual (see Section 7).
- In the "Paragraph rules" dialog box, set the "Indent" for one side that extends *beyond* the column width or the text (the value for the indent should be a negative number).
- Set the "Indent" for the opposite side as a positive number. It is the positive indent that bumps the negative indent out of the text block. Here's an example:
  - □ In **a,** I put a rule in the paragraph *Francis Bacon.* I clicked "Width of text" (I could have used "Width of column" if I chose). The left indent is –8p6; the right indent is 0. So the rule starts at the end of the text (the right indent) and continues 8p6 out to the left of the text (left indent).
  - □ In **b,** I set the right indent at 4p5. So the rule *starts* 4p5 from the right, which bumps the right end of the rule over, outside the text block.
  - □ In **c,** I set the right indent at 7 picas. So the indent bumps the beginning of the rule over even farther.

- See Section 7 for all the details on creating paragraph rules.
- You may not *see* the whole rule at first. When you redraw the screen though (when you change page views for instance), it will appear. Also, a rule attached to a text block you deleted may not disappear until you change page views.
- I used this in a newsletter of PageMaker tips. The far left column had the heads. In the style sheet for the heads, I built a paragraph rule that started a pica-and-a-half outside the headline text block and extended over the next two columns to the right, above the story that belonged to the head. Then, whenever I applied that style, the rule went shooting over the columns right where it belonged.

If you want to do this:	**Then follow these steps:**	**Shortcuts ▾ Notes ▾ Hints**

21.30 "Crop" a graphic into an oval or circular shape

On the left is the oval with the thick line enclosing the photograph. On the right, the thick line has been reversed.

- All you need to do is choose the **oval/circle tool** and draw an oval with a thick line, like 12 point.
- With the **pointer tool,** click once on the oval. From the Element menu go to the "Fill and line" dialog box. Choose "Reverse line" for the Line and "None" for the Fill. Then position the shape so that it frames (crops) your graphic.
- If you need more coverage, create a custom line width in the "Custom line" dialog box (select "Custom…" in the Line submenu or in the "Line" pop-up menu in the "Fill and line" dialog box).

21.31 Set text flush left and right so it will adjust if the text block changes width

Party at Toad Hall   June I

Party at Toad Hall   June I

- On the left side of the text block, type the text you want flush left.
- Hit Tab. It doesn't matter where the text goes as long as there is a tab set somewhere on the line.
- Type the text you want to be flush right.
- With the insertion point still flashing in that line press Command Shift R (that's the keyboard shortcut for right-aligned text). Now if you resize the text block, the text will adjust to the left and right sides.

Dance is a perpendicular expression of a horizontal desire. —George Bernard Shaw

If you want to do this:

Then follow these steps:

Shortcuts ▾ Notes ▾ Hints

21.32 Create two separate paragraphs on the same line so you can create columns, as shown below, but still retain each one as a paragraph with style sheets

Petruchio	Good morrow, Kate; for that's your name, I hear.
Katherina	Well have you heard, but something hard of hearing: they call me Katherina that do talk of me.
Petruchio	Hearing thy mildness praised in every town, they virtues spoke of, and thy beauty sounded, myself am moved to woo thee for my wife.
▆▆▆▆▆▆ **Katherina**	Moved! In good time: let him that moved you hither remove you hence.

The text for the left "column" is actually in the space above what you see on the screen, as shown by this slug. If you want to change the text, you must select and change the blank space. Or, click in the text block, press Command E to get into the Story Editor, and edit your text there.

- The trick here is that the text in the left "column" has a negative baseline shift (4.263). The text is actually typed on the line *above* the paragraph of body text but it has been told to drop down to the next baseline.
- The body text has an indent (4.321) so it *appears* to be in a separate column. The leading is "fixed" (5.25–5.26), meaning I applied a specific number, not "Auto."
- The text in the left column also has fixed leading. It doesn't really matter at *what* you fix the leading values, but the leading will affect how much you drop the baseline.
- If you want to decrease the amount of space between the sections, decrease the leading value of the left "column." Of course, you're using style sheets for this, right? (See Section 8 on Style Sheets.)

- The "Baseline-shift" option is available in the "Type specs" dialog box (4.205) and the character-view Control palette (4.218).
- Because the text is not where it is really supposed to be (that is, it is below the baseline) it may freak out and disappear now and then. That's okay—just redraw the screen and it will reappear, or just redraw the text block (click on it with the pointer tool then press Command F).

If you want to do this:

21.33 Find out what page you're on when there are more than 999 pages in your publication

998 999 0 1 2 3

More pleasant far to me the broom
  That blows sae fair on Cowden Knowes
For sure sae sweet, sae soft a bloom;
  Elsewhere there never grows.
                              Scottish Song

Then follow these steps:

- From the Layout menu choose "Remove pages..."; it will tell you what page(s) you are viewing, then you can just Cancel it.
- **Or,** this is a good trick:
  □ With the *text tool,* create a small text block (1.319) that has all four handles on the pasteboard.
  □ Type **Page**, spacebar, and press Command Option P. It should look like this: **Page PB** (PB for pasteboard).
  □ Size this text large enough that you can read it at "Fit in window" size.
  □ With the **pointer tool,** drag any edge of the text block onto any page; the **PB** will turn into the number of that page. Then move the text block back onto the pasteboard to use on another page.

Shortcuts ▾ Notes ▾ Hints

- After page 999, the page icons start over again at 0. So when you're on page 1783, the page icon says 83—you don't know if it's page 1783 or 4583 or 9883. *(Yes, you're right; this is a trick you probably won't need very often. One never knows, though.)*
- The automatic page numbers will *print* correctly—it's just the icons that have trouble.

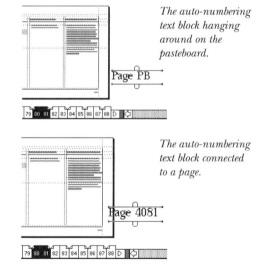

The auto-numbering text block hanging around on the pasteboard.

The auto-numbering text block connected to a page.

If you want to do this:

21.34 Create a custom PPD file that prevents PageMaker from re-downloading fonts you have already downloaded

```
¶
*Font·Futura-Bold:·Standard·RAM¶
*Font·NewBaskerville-Roman:·Standard·RAM¶
*Font·NewBaskerville-Italic:·Standard·RAM¶
¶
¶
*Include:·"LaserWriter·IINT"¶
¶
*%·End·of·Aldus·PPD·local·customization·file.¶
```

Then follow these steps:

- Manually download the fonts to your printer as in 19.132 but, as you do, write down the PostScript names of the fonts as they appear in the utility dialog box.
- In PageMaker, update a PPD as in 19.178.
- Double-click on the PPD you just updated (in the System folder, in the Extensions folder, in the "Printer Descriptions" folder) to edit the file in Teachtext.
  - □ **Or,** open any word-processing file and choose "Open" from its menu.
  - □ Open the PPD file you just updated.
  - □ In the "Select a Converter" dialog box, click "Text."
- At the end of the file, before the line that starts "Include," type:
  *Font xxx: Standard RAM
- Hit returns between lines and type in the names of the fonts you downloaded.
- Save the file in text-only format, give it a distinguishable name, and save it in the "Printer Descriptions" folder.
- In PageMaker, in the "Print document" dialog box, next to "Type," select the PPD you just customized and named.
- If you have other downloadable fonts in your publication you want included, check "Include downloadable fonts" in the "Print options" dialog box.

Shortcuts ▾ Notes ▾ Hints

- It's important to get the name of the printer font, not the name of the screen font that appears in your font folder. You choose "Display available fonts" from the font utility's menu after the fonts are downloaded. Copy the PostScript names of the downloaded fonts from this list.
- I know this seems intimidating but it's also empowering. If you goof, PageMaker will yell at you when you try to print, telling you exactly what you did wrong and how to fix it. Just throw out the file and try again. Never work on an original PPD, but it might help to open one to see how the fonts are listed. You can copy and paste between PPD files—copy fonts from one, paste in the one you are modifying, then highlight and change just the font names to the ones you are manually download-ing. In this way you know that all the asterisks, colons, and spaces are correct.
- PageMaker reads the customized PPD and acknowledges the fonts in RAM. When you check "Include downloadable fonts," you cover your bases for any fonts in the pub that you *didn't* manually download.
- **Remember** to manually download the fonts *first* each time you plan to use this custom PPD.

22 ▾ Help!

22.1   This section is a compilation of the most common problems I have seen hundreds upon hundreds of people struggle with in PageMaker as I taught them to use the program. I built many of the answers to these problems into the appropriate sections in this book, but I have also included some of them here so you don't have to go digging through the pages (there are always reference numbers, of course). If you don't find your specific problem here, check the index for information on the most closely-related topic.

22.2   PageMaker provides an online Help file for getting information about every command and various topics. See 22.3 for specific details on accessing the Help file.

The ability to simplify means to eliminate the unnecessary so that the necessary may speak.   *—Hans Hoffman*

If:	Then follow these steps:	Shortcuts ▾ Notes ▾ Hints

22.3 You want to use PageMaker's online Help file

PageMaker's online Help screen.

? *The Help cursor.*

■ From the Window menu choose "Help...."
■ In the Help window select "Using Pagemaker Help" for details on exactly how to get the information you need.

■ An alternate way to use the Help screen and to go straight to the information about a command is to use the **menu-sensitive Help:**
  □ Press Command **?** *or* press the Help key on an extended keyboard. This turns your cursor into a question mark.
  □ With the **question mark cursor,** choose any item from any menu to get basic information on that command (for commands with submenus, go into the submenu before you let go of the mouse button).
  □ If you have the question mark cursor and you don't want any help, just click once on the pointer tool to get your pointer back.

■ If you have the Help cursor and you want to get rid of it, either click on any tool *or* press Command Period (this turns it into the pointer tool).

When I am in a good space, I see obstructions as instructions. When I am in a bad space, even instructions look like obstructions. Norm Howe

If:	Then follow these steps:	Shortcuts ▾ Notes ▾ Hints
22.4 You want to reduce the file size of the publication	■ Use "Save as..." to reduce the file size. See 18.1–18.4 for information on why your files get so large and why "Save as..." reduces them. See 18.29 for the specific steps to actually compress the file. Basically, all you need to do is choose "Save as..." from the File menu, don't change the name of the publication, click OK, and click "Replace" when you are asked if you want to replace the existing file.	■ Through the "Preferences" dialog box, you have the option of automatically compressing the file size every time you save, just as if you went through the "Save as..." procedure. It takes a bit longer, though. See 18.5 for information on this option.
22.5 There is not enough room on the disk to "Save as..." 	Even though "Save as..." makes the file smaller, PageMaker initially must have extra room on the disk to work the changes. If there is no room on the disk, you will have to save onto another disk: ■ Click Desktop to view the disks available; you may need to eject a floppy disk and insert another. ■ After you "Save as..." onto another disk, you can always replace the larger file with the newer, smaller version later (just copy the smaller one back onto the disk). Even though PageMaker wouldn't let you actually compress the file on the original disk, the smaller file will usually fit on the original disk *after* it has been saved.	

If:	Then follow these steps:	Shortcuts ▾ Notes ▾ Hints
22.6 The OK button is gray when you try to "Save as…"	The OK button will be gray if you try to save changes to a file on a locked disk. **To unlock a disk** so you can save changes: ▪ In the "Save as…" dialog box, click "Eject" to spit out the disk. ▪ On the back of the disk is a little hole with a tab that covers or uncovers it. If you can see through the hole, the disk is locked. Slide the tab over the hole to close it. ▪ Insert the disk back into the drive. Continue saving as usual.	▪ When you open a file on a locked disk, PageMaker opens a template of the file called "Untitled–1." ▪ On high-density disks you will see two holes, one with a tab and one without. The tabbed hole locks the disk; the other hole tells the computer that this disk is high-density.
22.7 A file won't complete the "Save as…" process  *Click here to unlock a file.*	If PageMaker acts as if she will replace the file, but then displays a message stating "the file already exists, the file may be locked." **To unlock a file** so you can save changes: ▪ Go to the Desktop (Finder). ▪ Click once on the file that is locked; Select "Get Info" from the File menu (Command I) to get the Get Info dialog box. ▪ In the lower left corner, the "Locked" checkbox has a check in it; click in the checkbox to remove the check. ▪ Close the Get Info box; go back to your publication. Now you can "Save as…."	▪ When you open a file that is locked, PageMaker will warn you that you won't be able to save changes, and then opens a template of the file called "Untitled–1." ▪ Remember to lock the file again if it is important that changes are not inadvertently made to it.

If:	**Then follow these steps:**	**Shortcuts ▾ Notes ▾ Hints**
22.8 You click the I-beam, but you don't see the insertion point	The insertion point will always jump over to the column edge. Usually the type default is left-aligned, so it jumps to the left edge. If you don't see the insertion point, check these things: ▪ Make sure the **text tool** has been chosen. Then click the I-beam once more on the page before you check the rest of these possibilities. ▪ Type a couple of words. The screen will usually jump to the text. ▪ From the Type menu, check the "Alignment" submenu. If the text is right- or center-aligned, then the insertion point is jumping to the center of the text block or to the right edge. Can you see the right edge or the center? If you can't, change your page view to something smaller. ▪ In a small view, such as Fit in Window, you may need to look carefully to see the insertion point flashing. If you are inside the page margins, it will generally flash right on top of the guide lines. If you are outside the page margins, the insertion point may be far over on the right, depending on your alignment and page margins (see note at right).	▪ If you have changed the color Paper (on a color monitor) to something other than white, you may find that you cannot see the insertion point. Type a few words and you will find its hiding place. ▪ When you click the I-beam within the page margins, PageMaker creates a text block the width of the column (there is always at least one column on the page). The insertion point will place itself in reference to the text block edges, according to the specified alignment. If you click the I-beam outside the page margins, PageMaker automatically sets up a text block that is the width of the space within the margins. That is, if the page is 8.5 inches x 11 inches, but you specified a one-inch margin left and right, then the width of the space within the margins is 6.5 inches. So any text block outside these page margins will automatically be 6.5 inches. ▪ If you click on the pasteboard (1.4) to the left of the page, the text block will bump into the page and stop, in which case the text block *won't* be as wide as the margins. ▪ Be sure to read about text blocks and how to control them (4.102–4.129). Especially get the trick about creating bounding boxes: 4.26; 4.62.

If:	**Then follow these steps:**	**Shortcuts ▾ Notes ▾ Hints**
22.9 You can see the insertion point, but it is not at the left edge where you really want it	■ The alignment is not left-aligned. From the Type menu choose "Alignment," then slide out and choose "Align left." **Or** in the paragraph-view Control palette, click the left alignment button. ■ If you choose that command while the insertion point is flashing, the alignment will be changed for just that one paragraph of text. ■ If you choose that command while no insertion point is flashing (click once on the text tool, just to make sure), then you will be setting a new alignment *default* (see 4.360–4.366).	■ You could also use the keyboard command, Command Shift L, to change the alignment to "Align left."
22.10 You can't see the guides that you are bringing in	One of two things is probably happening: ■ The guides have been turned off. Check the "Guides and rulers" submenu, under the Layout menu; if there is no checkmark next to "Guides," they are turned off. Choose "Guides" again to turn them back on. ■ The guides have all been sent to the back, and thus they can hide behind solid objects. If you want to bring them to the front so you can always see them: □ From the File menu choose "Preferences...." Under "Guides" click the "Front" button. Click OK.	■ If you turned off the guides, or if you sent all the guides to the back because they were irritating you, then you may want to read 1.189–1.195 about layering and getting beneath the layers. If a guide is on top and you want to select something beneath it, hold the Command key down. You can then select the object under the guide (1.212; 1.230). ■ If you can't pull *any* ruler guides from the rulers, you may have reached the maximum number of guides per page (40). Drag some guides off the page, or simply re-use the ones already on the page.

If:

22.11 You can't unroll a text block, or the text block "exhibits puzzling behavior"

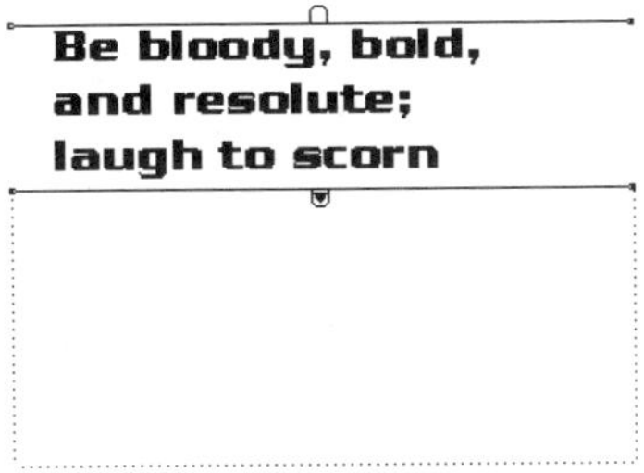
Be bloody, bold,
and resolute;
laugh to scorn

One example of "puzzling behavior" is when you cannot unroll a text block.

Then follow these steps:

- Did you add any **paragraph rules** to the text? What measurement did you enter in the edit boxes for placing the rules above or below the baseline? Did you add any **"paragraph space before or after"**? What measurement did you enter? Go back and check. It is very easy to insert 15 *picas* or *inches,* when you really wanted 15 *points.* If you think you may have added too much space before or after paragraphs or rules, but now you can't unroll the text block to check the paragraph, use the Story Editor (with the text tool, click in the last paragraph you can find, then press Command E).
- **Or** click the insertion point in the last paragraph. Press Command E to get the Story Editor so you can see everything in the story. Do you see any of these **symbols** in the troublesome area: ▩ ? These represent inline graphics (10.125). If you see one of these symbols in the paragraph following the last part of the text you are able to get on the screen, that graphic is probably the thing that is causing you trouble. Select it (press-and-drag over it) and hit the Backspace/Delete key to remove it. Press Command E again to get back to your page. Now can you unroll the text block?

—continued

Shortcuts ▾ Notes ▾ Hints

- See 1.323 for details on how to override the measurement systems in any dialog box or Control palette(that is, if the measurement spec says "inches," you can temporarily override it by entering values in points, picas, ciceros, millimeters, etc.).
- If you need to select a rolled-up text block you can't see anymore, see 22.12.
- If the inline graphic is causing you trouble, it may be because it is too large. Place or paste the object as an independent graphic first (by choosing the pointer tool before you place or paste). Reduce the size of the graphic, and then cut-and-paste it into the text.

If:	**Then follow these steps:**	**Shortcuts ▾ Notes ▾ Hints**

— "Puzzling behavior" continued

■ In the Story Editor, click in the paragraph *following* the last one you can see on the screen. Press Command M. Are any of the "Options" checked? Before you uncheck any of the options, make sure you understand what the option is accomplishing; perhaps you want to leave it applied and work with its purpose (see 4.329–4.347 for info on the options, often called "keeps").

■ **If any of these specifications keep recurring** (like every time you start to type text, the space between the paragraphs gives you trouble), then it means someone *(not you, of course)* has accidentally set an inappropriate default **or** has set the problematic specification in a style sheet.

　□ **To fix a style sheet:** Check the style sheet in the problem paragraph. Delete the problem specs.

　□ **To change a default:** Click on the **pointer tool.** From the Type menu, slide down to "Style" and choose "No style." Then go into the dialog box that holds the problem specification and delete the specs.

■ If the text acts funny when it gets near a graphic image or a line or box, the graphic may have a *text wrap* applied. See 22.22 for a solution.

■ These paragraph options can really make your text act weird: text blocks won't unroll, they'll hop right off the page, etc.

■ See Section 8 on Style Sheets; see 8.53 for editing a style definition.

■ See 1.6–1.18 for general information on defaults. See 4.360–4.366 for information on text defaults.

■ For detailed information on text wrapping, see Section 13.

If:	Then follow these steps:	Shortcuts ▾ Notes ▾ Hints
22.12 You lost a text block—you rolled it up (or maybe it rolled itself up) and now it has disappeared	■ As long as you didn't hit the Backspace/Delete key to actually *delete* the text block, it is still there. Press Command W to view the page at window size (assuming the lost text block was within that space). ■ Click on the **pointer tool.** ■ Press Command A to select all. Do you see the rolled up windowshade of the lost text block? It will look like this: ■ After you find it, click in any blank area to deselect all the objects. ■ With the **pointer tool,** press-and-drag to create a marquee around the area where you saw this lost block. You may have to do this several times in order to capture it. Remember, you must enclose both ends of the rolled-up text block within the marquee. ■ Once you have the rolled-up text block selected, see if you can unroll it. □ If you can't, press Command E while it is selected. This will open the text block in the Story Editor. Now read 22.11 and see if you have any formatting or inline graphics that are causing problems. ■ If all else fails, Revert to the last time you saved or mini-Revert to the last mini-save (18.30–18.31).	■ If you think the lost text block may be on the pasteboard somewhere, then select "Show pasteboard" from the View submenu (under the Layout menu) instead of pressing Command W. Now follow the rest of the steps. ■ If the text block is *really* lost, try running the "Find overset text" Addition (4.133–4.135). If the text block has unplaced text, this just may work. ■ If you don't quite understand how to use the marquee to select objects, see 1.208. ■ If there are only a few items on your page, you can "Select all," then hold down the Shift key and click on each item one by one until you have deselected everything except the text block you want. ■ Of course, reverting will only help if you saved or mini-saved before this trouble occurred.

If:	Then follow these steps:	Shortcuts ▾ Notes ▾ Hints
22.13 You can't tell what page you are on	■ This will only occur if your pages happen to be numbered beyond 1000; you can't tell if the page is 1234, 4234, etc., because the icons can only fit three numbers in them. See 21.33 for the solution.	
22.14 You can't align objects exactly where you want because they jump around	■ Check the "Guides and rulers" submenu under the Layout menu. □ If "Snap to guides" is on (has a check-mark next to it), then the handles of the objects will jump to any guideline they get close to. Choose "Snap to guides" again to turn it off. □ If "Snap to rulers" is on, then the handles of the objects *will jump to the tick marks of the rulers.* Choose "Snap to rulers" again to turn the command off.	■ In fact, the draw-tool cursor itself will jump to the guidelines. ■ Again, the draw-tool cursor itself will jump to the ruler tick marks. You can take advantage of this by customizing your rulers, essentially creating a "snap-on" grid (1.56; 5.97–5.104; 5.107).
22.15 You want to unload the text or graphic that is in the loaded icon, but you don't want to put it on the page	■ Click on any tool in the Toolbox *or* press Command Spacebar. The loaded icon is now gone and you have the tool cursor. ■ **Or** press-and-drag the text or graphic into a small bounding box on the pasteboard (1.321–1.322).	■ If you press Command Spacebar, you will briefly see the magnifying tool first; wait until the loaded icon turns into the magnifying tool before letting go. ■ Placing the graphic or a small chunk of the text on the pasteboard makes it handy to use later.

If:	**Then follow these steps:**	**Shortcuts ▾ Notes ▾ Hints**
22.16 You type, but no text appears on the screen	▪ The most likely cause is that the type is Reverse. With the insertion point still flashing, go up to the Type menu, down to "Type style," and see if "Reverse" has a checkmark next to it. If so, choose "Reverse" again to turn it off; now all text you type in that text block will be visible. If there is text on the page you still can't see, select it and choose "Reverse" again. *You do need to check to make sure "Reverse" is not a default:* □ Click once on the **text tool,** even if it is already selected. Check again to see if "Reverse" has a checkmark next to it. If so, choose it again to turn it off.	▪ If the Control palette is on screen, you can check the "Reverse" button in the character-view palette instead of going to the Type menu. If it *is* selected, click it once to deselect it. ▪ See 1.6–1.18 for info on defaults in general; see 4.360–4.366 for info on text defaults. Basically, if there is no text selected and no insertion point flashing, then whatever you choose from the menus or the Control palette (4.240) will become the new defaults. ▪ It is also possible that a "Baseline-shift" value has been entered in either the "Type options" dialog box (4.205) or the character-view Control palette (4.218).
22.17 Some reverse text you created is now lost and you want to find it	▪ You'll find detailed directions for solving this problem in 4.236.	
22.18 Every time you type, the text shows up in a font you don't want	▪ Click once on the pointer tool. ▪ From the Type menu, go to the "Font" submenu and choose the font that you do want to show up (as the default). **Or** click once on the text tool (even if it is already selected, it is important the insertion point is not set somewhere), then choose a font in the character-view Control palette.	▪ You need to learn how to control Page-Maker's defaults. See 1.6–1.18 and 4.360–4.366. Check the application defaults as well as the publication defaults.

If:	Then follow these steps:	Shortcuts ▾ Notes ▾ Hints
22.19 You draw a line, but it doesn't show up	■ The Line default is "Reverse." To make the current line show up (if you can still see its handles), go to the Lines submenu and uncheck "Reverse" (select it again). ■ To change the default, click once on the **pointer tool** or either **line tool.** ■ From the Element menu, get the Lines submenu. If there is a checkmark next to "Reverse," choose "Reverse" again to remove the check.	■ See 1.6–1.18 for general info on defaults; see 2.82–2.84 for info on the defaults for the drawing tools.
22.20 You think you created a bunch of reverse lines and you want to get rid of them	■ Click once on the **pointer tool.** ■ Press Command A to select all. Do you see handles with nothing between? Note where the invisible lines are. Click once in a blank area to deselect everything. ■ Go back to where you saw the invisible objects and try to select them (click around, or use the marquee to grab objects within an area; see 1.208). ■ Once you have their handles, hit the Backspace/Delete key to remove them.	■ If there are no other lines or boxes on the page, you can un-reverse the lines without having to deselect everything. "Reverse" from the Lines submenu will not affect text or non-PageMaker-drawn objects. ■ If there are only a few objects on the page, deselect everything but the lines using the shortcut method described in 22.12.
22.21 Every time you draw a line or a box, it shows up in a line width or a fill you don't want	■ Learn to control the defaults. See 1.6–1.18 for general info on defaults; see 2.82–2.84 for info on the defaults for the drawing tools.	

If:	Then follow these steps:	Shortcuts ▾ Notes ▾ Hints

22.22 Everything you draw or paste or place shows up with a text wrap around it *(that is, the text jumps away from every graphic you put on the page)*

- Someone inadvertently set a text wrap default. To remove the text wrap from the objects on the page:
  - □ With the **pointer tool,** click once on the graphic, *or* Shift-click to select more than one at a time.
  - □ From the Element menu choose "Text wrap...."
  - □ Click on the first icon under "Wrap option":   Click OK.
- To change the default so this doesn't happen again, follow the same steps, just make sure *there is no object selected* before you go to the Element menu (click once on the pointer tool to make sure).

- If your text is "exhibiting puzzling behavior," also check 22.11.

22.23 The last line of a paragraph has too much linespace above it

- Choose the **text tool.**
- Position the I-beam directly after the last character in the paragraph; click to set the insertion point.
- Hit a Return. This will bump the last line up to match the linespace of the rest of the paragraph.
- This may give you an extra blank line after the paragraph that you don't want. If so, move the insertion point down to the beginning of the next line of text and hit the Backspace/Delete key.

If:	Then follow these steps:	Shortcuts ▾ Notes ▾ Hints
22.24 You enlarged a character in a paragraph (like an initial cap) **or** you inserted an inline graphic, and it changed the linespace in a way you don't like	■ The linespace changed because the leading is Auto leading (5.20–5.24). You need to *fix* the leading (5.25–5.26). Fix it *after* the larger character or the graphic has been added to the paragraph, not *before*. ■ With the **text tool,** triple-click in the paragraph. ■ From the Type menu go down to "Leading," then out to the submenu. Either choose one of the leading values listed or choose "Other..." and enter your own value. As long as you choose any value other than "Auto," the linespace in the paragraph will be consistent.	■ See 5.12–5.58 for detailed information on leading, both fixed and auto. ■ If you create an initial cap using the "Drop cap" Addition (20.42), the linespace will not change even if it is Auto leading. ■ If the Control palette is on screen, you can choose a leading value from the pop-up menu, or enter a leading value (other than one equal to that of Auto leading) in the "Leading" option edit box (4.216).
22.25 You changed the master page guides, but they didn't change on your publication page	■ On the publication page, go up to the Layout menu and choose "Copy master guides." (If that command is gray, it indicates that the page already has the master page guides on it.)	■ If you have added, deleted, or moved any guides on a publication page, PageMaker leaves your custom ones there and does not switch them to the new master page guides.
22.26 You changed the leading and now the tops of the letters have disappeared	■ This is not really a problem because the letters will print anyway. But it is disturbing. Anytime the screen redraws (as when you change views or pages, etc.), the letter tops will reappear. I find the simplest thing to do is to click once on the text block with the **pointer tool,** then press Command F (to Bring to Front).	

If:	Then follow these steps:	Shortcuts ▾ Notes ▾ Hints
22.27 You specified paragraph rules that extend beyond the text block, but they don't show up on the screen	■ Don't worry—they will show up when you print. Things have trouble when they leave the text block; it's like they go into the Twilight Zone. Large inline graphics, long paragraph rules, and text with little leading all freak out, but they do print all right. Reversed text on top of a paragraph rule also disappears, but prints. You can try changing the view; it sometimes makes the rule appear temporarily.	■ Not being able to see the outer boundaries of a paragraph rule presents only one problem: you cannot tell if the rule reaches to exactly the point you need it to. You will have to print a few proofs to get the length exactly right.
22.28 Paragraph rules show up where you don't want them	■ If this problem recurs regularly, the paragraph rule is embedded in a style sheet, **or** there is a default somewhere. ■ With the insertion point in the text that is giving you trouble, look at "Style" in the Type menu; the checked style is the one with the problem. Change the paragraph rules in that style sheet (8.53). ■ If the style is "No style," the problem is a publication default: with the **pointer tool** selected, go into the "Paragraph rules" dialog box and uncheck the rule (7.53).	■ See Section 7 for detailed information about rules.
22.29 You converted a publication from PageMaker 4.x and the line breaks are not the same as in the original	■ Tracking is looser in 5.0. If you used tracking values in the original publication, the lines will adjust to the new track value. Not as many words will fit on a line, causing different line breaks.	■ If you prefer to maintain the original line breaks, you can copy the tracking values from PageMaker 4 into the folder with your publication, see 17.48.

If:

22.30   When you type, the text squishes up

Then follow these steps:

- First of all, check the text block to see where its handles are:
  - ☐ With the **pointer tool,** click once on the text block. Is the text block excessively short? Does the text unsquish when you widen the block? (Press on any corner handle and drag outward.)
- If you lengthen the text block and the text still does not unsquish, check the indents:
  - ☐ With the **text tool,** click once in the line of text. Press Command I to get the Indents/tabs ruler. If you don't see the large right-indent triangle, scroll the ruler until you do. Is the triangle directly on the dotted line (6.54, 6.57)? If not, press-and-drag the triangle as far to the right as it will go. Click OK.
- If this problem recurs regularly, the problem is a default somewhere, *or* it is embedded in a style sheet. Check the style sheet of the paragraph in which this is occurring: with the insertion point in the text that is giving you trouble, check out "Style" in the Type menu; the checked style is the one with the problem. Change the indent in that style sheet. If the style is "No style," the problem is a publication default; with the **pointer tool** selected, change the indent.

rite with your spade,
and garden with your pen
—Roy Campbell—

Shortcuts ▾ Notes ▾ Hints

- There's a difference between *squished* and *condensed. Condensing* type is a conscious act; you can choose to condense type from the "Set width" submenu (4.205, or 4.217; 4.238). *Squishing* is an accident; it indicates something is not right.

Normal:	Scarlett Williams
Condensed:	Scarlett Williams
Squished	ScarlettWilliams

- See 6.77–6.83 for information about indents. See 8.18 and 8.53 for information about editing a style sheet.

- If the Style palette is showing, the offending style name will be highlighted when the insertion point is within the paragraph; if the Control palette is on screen, the "Style" option box will also display the style name.

If:	Then follow these steps:	Shortcuts ▾ Notes ▾ Hints
22.31 You lengthened the text block to lengthen the line, but the line length didn't change	■ There is probably a right indent set. With the **text tool,** click once in the text. ■ Press Command I to get the Indents/ Tabs ruler. If the right-indent triangle is anywhere but on the dotted line, press-and-drag the triangle as far to the right as it will go. Click OK.	■ See Section 6 for everything you ever wanted to know about indents.
22.32 You want to type numbers with the numeric keypad	■ Press down the Caps Lock key or, on the extended keyboard, the Num Lock key. ■ If the Caps Lock or Num Lock key is not down and the numeric keypad types numbers anyway, see 22.33, below.	■ The number 5 always types a number 5; it never moves the insertion point.
22.33 Sometimes the numeric keypad types numbers and sometimes it moves the insertion point	■ With Caps Lock or Num Lock down, the keypad will always type numbers. With them up, the Clear key is in control: ■ Pressing the Clear key on the keypad switches the function back and forth between typing numbers and moving the insertion point. If it is performing the function you don't want, press the Clear key again. Unfortunately, there is no visible sign to indicate which function is currently on on standard keyboards; the only way to tell is to press a number on the keypad and see what you get.	■ The number 5 always types a number 5; it never moves the insertion point. ■ The Num Lock key doesn't lock into position like the Caps Lock key does so you may have to toggle it to see if it is on or off. ■ See 1.324–1.328 for details on using the keypad to move the insertion point and to select text.

If:	Then follow these steps:	Shortcuts ▾ Notes ▾ Hints
22.34 You pasted or placed a graphic and it is inverted (reversed; black instead of white) *Click on this icon.* 	▪ With the **pointer tool,** click on the graphic. ▪ From the Element menu choose "Image control...." ▪ Click on the left-most icon above the image control bars (see left). ▪ Click OK.	▪ If one graphic is selected and the "Image control..." command is gray, then the graphic cannot be reversed. You will have to take it back into a graphics program that can switch it. ▪ See 10.162–10.212 for details on Image Control.
22.35 Everything you place, paste, or draw is automatically tagged with a color	▪ A color has been set as a default for graphics. See 16.97–16.102 for details on how to change the default back to black.	
22.36 A dialog box yells at you because it thinks you have inserted incorrect values, but you don't know which values it's talking about	▪ Check Appendices A1–A8 for views of all the defaults in all the dialog boxes. Then select the edit box in the dialog box that is giving you grief, and input the values you see in the appendix. ▪ **Or** you can always just Cancel the dialog box. If you had made some changes you want to keep, you will just have to go back and enter them again.	

If:	Then follow these steps:	Shortcuts ▾ Notes ▾ Hints
22.37 You entered an invalid value in the Control palette and you want to reinstate the previous value	▪ In the dialog box telling you about the invalid value press "Continue," *or* hit Return. ▪ Press the Esc key to reinstate the previous value in the offending option box.	
22.38 You placed or pasted a graphic, but you don't see it anywhere	▪ Is the text tool selected? If it is, then you probably pasted the graphic inline somewhere, possibly even on another page. If there is an insertion point flashing, PageMaker will paste or place the graphic *inline* (10.125; 10.213–10.233); the graphic will be pasted right into the text block where that insertion point was. The frightening thing is: *the insertion point can be flashing on another page altogether!* It may be flashing seventeen pages away. See 10.242 for a solution to this dilemma. ▪ To prevent this problem from ever happening, always click once on the **pointer tool** before you paste or place a graphic (unless you *want* an inline graphic).	Boring graphic design is the moral equivalent of ergonomic lovemaking. —John Grimes

If:	**Then follow these steps:**	**Shortcuts ▾ Notes ▾ Hints**
22.39 You accidentally placed a giant-sized graphic in your text (or perhaps you placed the entire Scrapbook) and now your text block won't unroll	▪ With the **text too,** click in the last paragraph you see in the text block, then press Command E. If the text block is completely rolled up and all you can see are its handles, press Command E. If you lost the text block altogether and can't even find its handles, see 22.12. ▪ The Command E will bring you to the Story Editor. You will see the graphic represented by this symbol: ▓. Select that symbol (press-and-drag over it) and hit the Backspace/Delete key. Press Command W to get back to the layout page.	
22.40 When you try to import or place a graphic or text, PageMaker tells you "Unknown file format" 	▪ PageMaker can only import files for which you have installed the proper filter. See 17.8–17.20 for information on the filters you need. See 17.29 for instructions on how to install the proper filter.	▪ To see a list of all the filters you have installed, hold down the Command key and choose "About PageMaker…" from the Apple menu. Scroll past the Aldus Additions to see the import filters. ▪ Aldus makes new filters available through on-line sources.

Let the hands of life push you gently along on the currents of your beliefs.

—John Sikora

If:	Then follow these steps:	Shortcuts ▾ Notes ▾ Hints
22.41 You can't change the style sheet specifications; PageMaker tells you there is a bad record index	■ This problem and its solution is explained in detail in Section 8 on Style Sheets: 8.60.	
22.42 In the Story Editor, the "Find" command or the "Change" command is gray	■ If the command is gray, the dialog box is already open. If you don't see it, the box is hiding behind another window. Use the keyboard commands to bring them forward: Command 8 to bring up the "Find" dialog box; Command 9 to bring up the "Change" dialog box.	
22.43 The Story Editor cannot find something that you know is there **Find what:** ▯ **Change to:** ▯ *If there is an underline beneath "Find what," it indicates there are attributes applied to the search.*	■ The problem may lie in the "Attributes" that are applied. Maybe you didn't even know there were any applied. An underline under "Find what" indicates that PageMaker is looking for text with attributes. To eliminate any attributes in the search, hold down the Option key and click once on the "Attributes" button.	
22.44 The cursor is jumpy on screen even when you are making choices in dialog boxes	■ Are you printing in the background? If you have Background printing turned on, PageMaker's tools may not function as smoothly as usual when something is being printed.	■ The command for Background printing is in the Chooser (19.18). If you don't mind a little skittish behavior on the part of the tools, you can work while publications print.

If:

22.45 You can't find a graphic or text block that you dragged onto the pasteboard

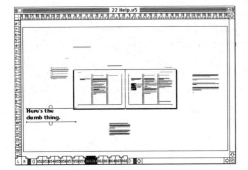

Then follow these steps:

The handles of the text block or graphic are probably touching a page. Even though most of the object is on the pasteboard, you will only be able to see it when you are on the page it is touching. There are a couple things you can try, though.

- If it is an overset text block (4.109), then you can run the "Find overset text" Addition to locate it (4.133–4.135).
- If it is a linked graphic, you can go into the "Links…" dialog box where you will find it listed along with the number of the page it is touching.
- **Or** you can always go through your publication page by page until you find it, or print your publication and look for a wayward object in the margin of one of the pages.

Shortcuts ▾ Notes ▾ Hints

*O*ur moments of inspiration are not lost though we have no particular poem to show for them; for those experiences have left an indelible impression, and we are ever and anon reminded of them.

—Henry David Thoreau

If:

22.46 You receive "Low memory" or "Out of memory" alerts, or PageMaker crashes when running certain Additions

2750k is the default memory allocation. PageMaker prefers a memory partition of 3000 to 6000k.

Then follow these steps:

- Save and close all open publications.
- Quit PageMaker. If you can give PageMaker more memory, do so:
  □ From the desktop, click once on the PageMaker application icon.
  □ From the File menu, choose "Get info" (Command I).
  □ Enter a higher value in "Preferred size" in the "Memory Requirements" box. Click the close box to put away the info window.
  □ Restart PageMaker.
- If you don't have memory to spare, quit and restart PageMaker and open fewer publications at one time. The heftier Additions such as "Build booklet," "Open templates," "Printer styles," and "Sort pages" may not run with lower memory.

Shortcuts ▾ Notes ▾ Hints

- In System 7.0 or 7.01, memory allocation is changed through "Current size" in the "Memory" box.
- The amount of memory you can give PageMaker depends on what else you are running at the same time.
- Although it may seem like a good idea to give PageMaker all your free RAM all the time, she will take everything you give her. This leaves no memory left for moving around on the Desktop, opening other applications or the Chooser, etc.

If:	**Then follow these steps:**	**Shortcuts ▾ Notes ▾ Hints**

22.47 Your computer randomly crashes, freezes, displays error messages, or otherwise acts weird and drives you crazy

Although there are a lot of different things that can make a computer behave in this unconscionable manner, some things are found to cause trouble more than others.

- Trying to run PageMaker without giving her enough memory may cause her to quit unexpectedly or exhibit other strange behavior while running certain features. See 22.46.
- Running a computer with an 68040 chip (or a PowerPC) with out-of-date filters from previous versions of PageMaker is a no-no.
  - □ Open the System folder, then open the Aldus folder.
  - □ Open the "Aldus Filters" folder and trash any filters dated earlier than 1993.
- A System or init conflict (rather than something to do with PageMaker) can cause big problems.
  - □ Try running PageMaker with no extensions on and then re-introducing them one by one to try to isolate the problem.
- If all else fails, you can always try throwing out your Preferences and Default files (in your System folder). There's no reason this should work, but sometimes it does!

continued—

- Filters particularly known to cause a problem are ASCII Text Export; MS Word 4.0 Import; RTF Import; Smart ASCII Import; Story Importer 1.0.
- You can try running PageMaker with all Extensions turned off (hold down the Shift key as you restart your computer) to see if the problem resolves itself. If it does, then you know it is probably one of your extensions that is the culprit.

If:

—"Computer crashes" continued

Fontificate: (V. fon tiff i kate) n. 1. To desktop publish in a pompous or dogmatic manner. 2. to discharge the duties of a fontiff. e.g., "Bob, your report is in 72-point type, all caps, bold, underlined, centered, italic!! Would you please stop fontificating."

—John Grimes

Then follow these steps:

If you incur crashes or error messages while printing, then the problem *probably* lies with your fonts or your printer driver.

- A corrupted font will not print. Try dragging the font to the trash, emptying the trash, and then reinstalling the font from its original disk.
- In PageMaker, LaserWriter 8 cannot download some Type 3 fonts. However, the PageMaker 5.0a patch corrects for this problem; see Appendix C.
- Font ID conflicts or using both TrueType and PostScript versions of the same font can create real havoc. Have only one kind of one font installed at any one time.
- Trying to print a publication with too many downloadable fonts, graphics, screens, and/or filled boxes can overload your printer. Try Option-printing.
  - Hold down the Option key as you select "Print" from the File menu.
  - Click the "Setup" button. Set the LaserWriter 8 print options as you want.
  - Click the "Print" button in the LaserWriter dialog box.
  - Check the options as usual. There are limited choices with this method of printing (19.125–19.126).
  - Click the "Print" button.

Shortcuts ▾ Notes ▾ Hints

- Normally, PageMaker generates the PostScript code and the LaserWriter 8 driver simply spools it to the printer.
- Option Print has been recommended as a diagnostic tool when printing troubles prevail. A file that won't "Print," but will Option Print, tells you there is trouble in the way PageMaker is generating the code, or in its interface with the LaserWriter driver.
- The LaserWriter bypasses the PPD and instead queries the printer. A side effect of this is that manually downloaded fonts are recognized without the work-arounds suggested in 19.177.
- If the file prints, proof it carefully. The LaserWriter driver cannot handle everything that PageMaker specifies, like some color features.
- If you continue to have problems printing, check "Include PostScript error handler" in the Print Options dialog box and carefully note the error codes and messages you receive. This is valuable information for Tech Support to help you through your problem.

If:	Then follow these steps:	Shortcuts ▾ Notes ▾ Hints

22.48 You get an error message saying your publication is damaged and won't open	There's not much you can do except try to rescue as much of the information as you can.
	■ Copy the damaged document and try opening the copy at the Finder.
	  □ If it opens, save it with a different name (18.29) and then do a diagnostic recompose (21.28).
	■ Try importing the file into a new PageMaker publication (17.42).
	■ Open the file in Word and copy usable text into a new PageMaker publication.
	  □ Open Word.
	  □ In Word 4.0, choose "Open any file" while holding down the Shift key;
	  □ **Or,** in Word 5.0, choose "Open"; select "All Files" from the pop-up menu.
	■ Try using a disk repair or file recovery program such as Norton Utilities or Disk Repair on the file or, if it is on a floppy disk on the disk itself.
		■ You *always* should do a diagnostic recompose whenever a publication begins acting funny.
		■ Excessive use of compression utilities, working without "Save as," and having a publication open during a System crash are reportedly some of the more common causes of damaged files.

22.49 A font name in your menu is followed by another font name in parentheses	■ PageMaker has substituted another font in your publication for one whose screen font is not currently installed in your System. If you use a font utility, you just may have just forgotten to open the suitcase that contains that font.	■ If you print the publication on a printer that has the missing font, the correct font will take the place of the substitution, although the text composition may be incorrect (1.242–1.243).

If:	Then follow these steps:	Shortcuts ▾ Notes ▾ Hints
22.50 PageMaker re-downloads fonts to the printer even though they are resident on the printer's hard drive or you have manually downloaded them	■ To create a PPD that informs PageMaker of additional resident fonts at the printer, see the "Update PPD" Addition, 19.171–19.178. ■ To manually download all the fonts in your publication and prevent PageMaker from downloading any, see 19.132. ■ To create a custom PPD to inform PageMaker of manually downloaded fonts without preventing PageMaker from downloading other fonts, see 21.34.	■ PageMaker no longer talks to the printer each time she prints. She only reads the information in the selected PPD. If the PPD does not list the fonts, PageMaker does not know they are there.
22.51 Your Print dialog box shows duplicate paper sizes in the "Size" menu	■ The PPDs of some printers have included in them information that PageMaker does not recognize. To solve this problem you will need to create a Custom Printer file using "Update PPD" or "PPDShell.ps" to remove any unnecessary comments. Otherwise, you will just have to learn to live with this. ■ If you decide to edit your PPD, look especially at the information in the "Paper Dimension," "PageSize," "Page Region," and "ImageableArea" for each paper size and remove any unnecessary comments that do not apply to your printer (eg., remove info about a 5 MB printer if yours is 8 MB, etc.).	■ According to Aldus, this is especially troublesome for the LaserWriter IIf and LaserWriter IIg printers whose PPDs include the keyword "*Constrain UI." ■ On the other hand, some printers have incomplete paper size names. For instance, with the LaserWriter Select 360, instead of recognizing the "Letter" and "Letter Small" options as two different sizes, PageMaker treats the information as two "Letter" pages and defaults to the "Letter Small" size. ■ If you want to edit your PPD to correct this, contact your Aldus Tech Support or the Aldus forums on-line to obtain the necessary information specific to your kind of printer.

If:	Then follow these steps:	Shortcuts ▾ Notes ▾ Hints
22.52 You can't call up a PostScript printer in the Print dialog box	▪ You haven't done the LaserWrite 8 setup described in 19.20–19.25.	
22.53 You installed PageMaker 5 on more than one computer in a network, but it won't run on all the computers at the same time	▪ PageMaker 5 has a new feature called "Network Copy Detection (NCD). It tells PageMaker if the number of copies of the program in use (either being launched or already in use) exceeds the number licensed to the identification number of that copy of PageMaker. ▪ If PageMaker detects more than the licensed number of copies in use, she prompts the users to save and quit the program.	▪ Besides a serial number, your copy of PageMaker has a unique identification number that is broadcast over a network when the program is launched. ▪ Check out the "About PageMaker…" window (select it under the Apple when PageMaker is running) to see the serial number, identification number, and number of users your copy is licensed for (basically one copy, one user).

Everything is funny as long as it is happening to Somebody Else. —Will Rogers

Being the Last.
In which this valuable tome
is brought to a happy Conclusion.

APPENDICES

Appendix A: Menus and dialog boxes 867

  A1: File menu 868

  A2: Edit menu 870

  A3: Utilities menu 871

  A4: Story menu 872

  A5: Layout menu 873

  A6: Type menu 874

  A7: Element menu 877

  A8: Window menu 879

Appendix B: Tasks 880

          Scenarios 895

Appendix C: Installing PageMaker; the 5.0a patch 896

Appendix D: Entry codes 900

Appendix E: Alternate characters 900

Appendix F: Accent marks 902

Appendix G: Zapf Dingbats 903

Appendix H: Symbols and cursors ... 904

Keyboard shortcuts 905

Appendix I: Control palette 907

Appendix J: Third-party Additions .. 908

Tear-out chart

No, Ted, No! Don't ever make us revise this book again!

A1.1   Whenever you see an ellipsis (…) after a command in a menu, it means that if you choose that item you will see a dialog box. There is always a Cancel button in every dialog box, so it is quite safe to wander around choosing commands with ellipses because you can rest assured that as long as you click "Cancel" you cannot ruin anything.

A1.2   All of these menus and dialog boxes show the defaults that are built into PageMaker. If you need to reset any defaults in your publication or in the PageMaker application, take a look at the original dialog box here.

Remember, you can reset every one of PageMaker's defaults at once by trashing the default file found in the Preferences folder, in the System folder (1.17).

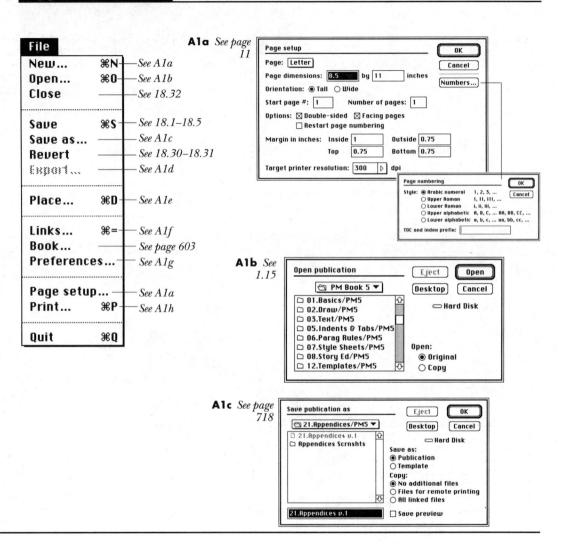

File

New...   ⌘N — *See A1a*
Open...   ⌘O — *See A1b*
Close   — *See 18.32*

Save   ⌘S — *See 18.1–18.5*
Save as...   — *See A1c*
Revert   — *See 18.30–18.31*
Export...   — *See A1d*

Place...   ⌘D — *See A1e*

Links...   ⌘= — *See A1f*
Book...   — *See page 603*
Preferences... — *See A1g*

Page setup... — *See A1a*
Print...   ⌘P — *See A1h*

Quit   ⌘Q

A1a *See page 11*

Page setup
Page: Letter
Page dimensions: 8.5 by 11 inches
Orientation: ● Tall ○ Wide
Start page #: 1   Number of pages: 1
Options: ☒ Double-sided ☒ Facing pages
☐ Restart page numbering
Margin in inches: Inside 1   Outside 0.75
Top 0.75   Bottom 0.75
Target printer resolution: 300 ▷ dpi
[OK] [Cancel] [Numbers...]

Page numbering
Style: ● Arabic numeral   1, 2, 3, ...
○ Upper Roman   I, II, III, ...
○ Lower Roman   i, ii, iii, ...
○ Upper alphabetic   A, B, C, ... AA, BB, CC, ...
○ Lower alphabetic   a, b, c, ... aa, bb, cc, ...
TOC and index prefix:
[OK] [Cancel]

A1b *See 1.15*

Open publication
📁 PM Book 5 ▼
☐ 01.Basics/PM5
☐ 02.Draw/PM5
☐ 03.Text/PM5
☐ 05.Indents & Tabs/PM5
☐ 06.Parag Rules/PM5
☐ 07.Style Sheets/PM5
☐ 08.Story Ed/PM5
☐ 12.Templates/PM5
[Eject] [Open] [Desktop] [Cancel]
▭ Hard Disk
Open:
● Original
○ Copy

A1c *See page 718*

Save publication as
📁 21.Appendices/PM5 ▼
☐ 21.Appendices v.1
☐ Appendices Scrnshts
[Eject] [OK] [Desktop] [Cancel]
▭ Hard Disk
Save as:
● Publication
○ Template
Copy:
● No additional files
○ Files for remote printing
○ All linked files
21.Appendices v.1   ☐ Save preview

A1d *See page 711*

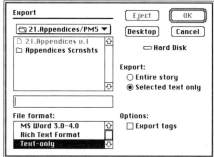

```
Export
[ 21.Appendices/PM5 ▼ ]          [ Eject ]  [ OK ]
                                  [ Desktop ] [ Cancel ]
🗋 21.Appendices v.1                ⬡ Hard Disk
🗀 Appendices Scrnshts

                                  Export:
                                  ○ Entire story
                                  ◉ Selected text only

[                              ]

File format:              Options:
MS Word 3.0-4.0          □ Export tags
Rich Text Format
Text-only
```

A1e *See page 173*

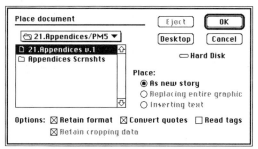

```
Place document
[ 21.Appendices/PM5 ▼ ]          [ Eject ]  [ OK ]
                                  [ Desktop ] [ Cancel ]
🗋 21.Appendices v.1                ⬡ Hard Disk
🗀 Appendices Scrnshts

                        Place:
                        ◉ As new story
                        ○ Replacing entire graphic
                        ○ Inserting text

Options: ⊠ Retain format  ⊠ Convert quotes  □ Read tags
         ⊠ Retain cropping data
```

A1f *See page 536*

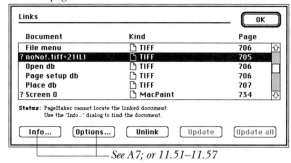

```
Links                              [ OK ]

Document          Kind       Page
File menu         🗋 TIFF      706
? noNo!.tiff+21(L) 🗋 TIFF     705
Open db           🗋 TIFF      706
Page setup db     🗋 TIFF      706
Place db          🗋 TIFF      707
? Screen 0        🗋 MacPaint  734

Status: PageMaker cannot locate the linked document.
Use the 'Info...' dialog to find the document.

[ Info... ] [ Options... ] [ Unlink ] [ Update ] [ Update all ]
```

See A7; or 11.51–11.57

A1g *See page 67*

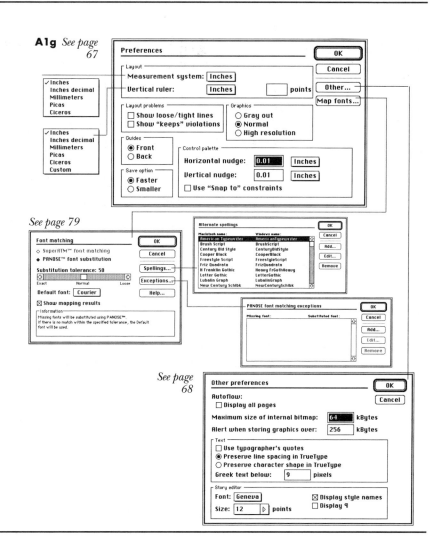

```
Preferences                                      [ OK ]
                                                 [ Cancel ]
Layout
Measurement system: [ Inches ]                   [ Other... ]
Vertical ruler:     [ Inches ]     [    ] points [ Map fonts... ]

Layout problems              Graphics
□ Show loose/tight lines     ○ Gray out
□ Show "keeps" violations    ◉ Normal
                             ○ High resolution
Guides
◉ Front    Control palette
○ Back     Horizontal nudge: [ 0.01 ] [ Inches ]
Save option Vertical nudge:   [ 0.01 ] [ Inches ]
◉ Faster
○ Smaller  □ Use "Snap to" constraints
```

```
✓Inches
 Inches decimal
 Millimeters
 Picas
 Ciceros
```

```
✓Inches
 Inches decimal
 Millimeters
 Picas
 Ciceros
 Custom
```

See page 79

```
Font matching                        [ OK ]
◇ SuperATM™ font matching            [ Cancel ]
◆ PANOSE™ font substitution
Substitution tolerance: 50           [ Spellings... ]
[████████████████]
Exact    Normal      Loose           [ Exceptions... ]
Default font: [ Courier ]            [ Help... ]
⊠ Show mapping results
Information:
Missing fonts will be substituted using PANOSE™.
If there is no match within the specified tolerance, the Default
font will be used.
```

```
Alternate spellings                        [ OK ]
Macintosh name:        Windows name:       [ Cancel ]
American Typewriter    AmericanTypewriter
Brush Script           BrushScript         [ Add... ]
Century Old Style      CenturyOldStyle
Cooper Black           CooperBlack         [ Edit... ]
Freestyle Script       FreestyleScript
Friz Quadrata          FrizQuadrata        [ Remove ]
H Franklin Gothic      Heavy FrGothHeavy
Letter Gothic          LetterGothic
Lubalin Graph          LubalinGraph
New Century Schlbk     NewCenturySchlbk
```

```
PANOSE font matching exceptions            [ OK ]
                                           [ Cancel ]
Missing font:     Substituted font:
                                           [ Add... ]
                                           [ Edit... ]
                                           [ Remove ]
```

See page 68

```
Other preferences                          [ OK ]
Autoflow:                                  [ Cancel ]
□ Display all pages
Maximum size of internal bitmap: [ 64 ] kBytes
Alert when storing graphics over: [ 256 ] kBytes
Text
□ Use typographer's quotes
◉ Preserve line spacing in TrueType
○ Preserve character shape in TrueType
Greek text below: [ 9 ] pixels
Story editor
Font: [ Geneva ]        ⊠ Display style names
Size: [ 12 ] ▷ points   □ Display ¶
```

A1h *See page 734*

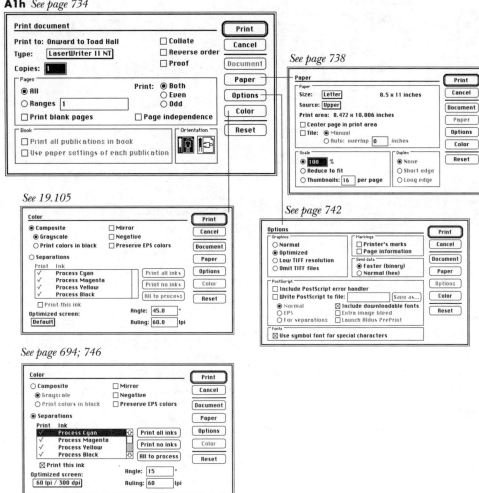

See page 738

See 19.105

See page 742

See page 694; 746

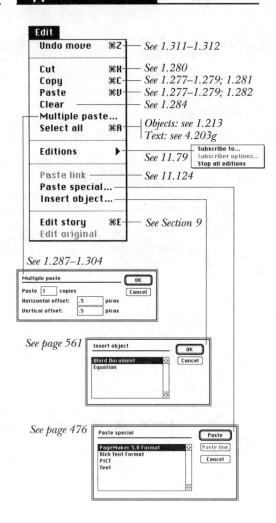

Layout page

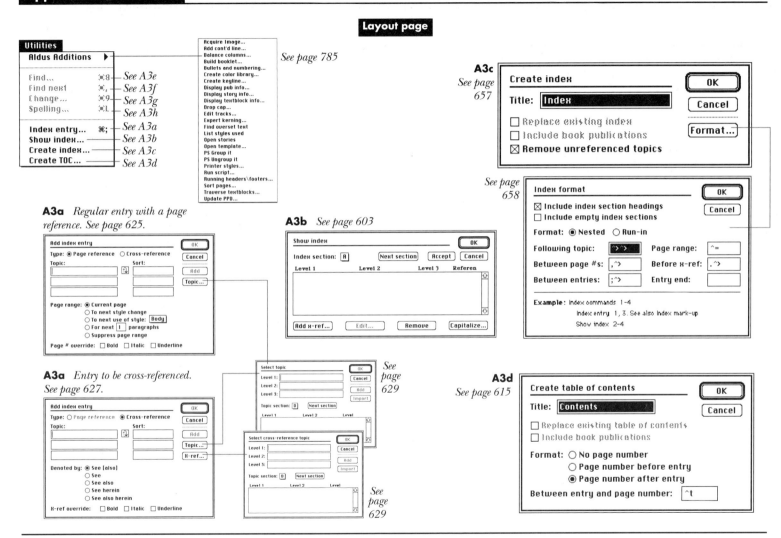

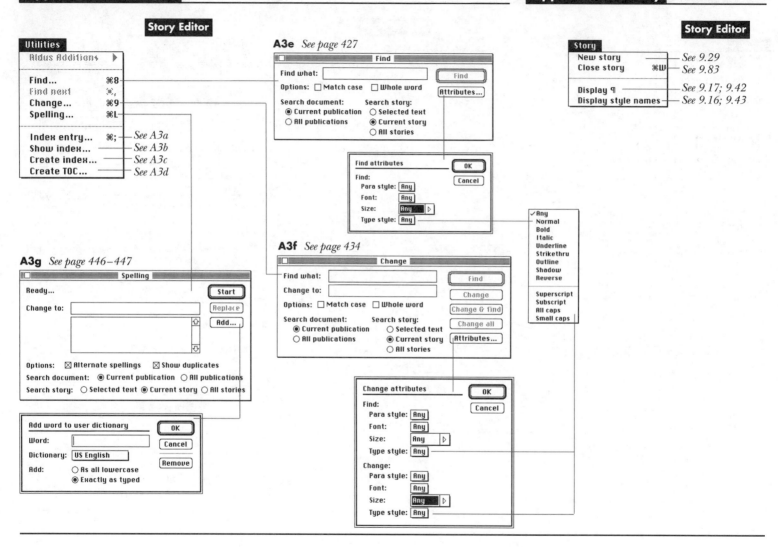

Story Editor

Utilities

Aldus Additions ▷

Find...   ⌘8
Find next   ⌘;
Change...   ⌘9
Spelling...   ⌘L

Index entry...   ⌘;   — *See A3a*
Show index...   — *See A3b*
Create index...   — *See A3c*
Create TOC...   — *See A3d*

A3e *See page 427*

Find

Find what: [   ]   [Find]

Options: ☐ Match case   ☐ Whole word

Search document: Search story:
● Current publication   ○ Selected text
○ All publications   ● Current story
                         ○ All stories

[Attributes...]

Find attributes   [OK]

Find: [Cancel]
  Para style: [Any]
  Font: [Any]
  Size: [Any] ▷
  Type style: [Any]

A3f *See page 434*

Change

Find what: [   ]   [Find]
Change to: [   ]   [Change]

Options: ☐ Match case   ☐ Whole word   [Change & find]

Search document: Search story: [Change all]
● Current publication   ○ Selected text
○ All publications   ● Current story   [Attributes...]
                         ○ All stories

A3g *See page 446–447*

Spelling

Ready...   [Start]

Change to: [   ] [Replace]

[   ]   [Add...]

Options: ☒ Alternate spellings ☒ Show duplicates
Search document: ● Current publication ○ All publications
Search story: ○ Selected text ● Current story ○ All stories

Add word to user dictionary   [OK]

Word: [   ]   [Cancel]
Dictionary: [US English]   [Remove]
Add: ○ As all lowercase
            ● Exactly as typed

Change attributes   [OK]

Find: [Cancel]
  Para style: [Any]
  Font: [Any]
  Size: [Any] ▷
  Type style: [Any]
Change:
  Para style: [Any]
  Font: [Any]
  Size: [Any] ▷
  Type style: [Any]

✓ Any
  Normal
  Bold
  Italic
  Underline
  Strikethru
  Outline
  Shadow
  Reverse

  Superscript
  Subscript
  All caps
  Small caps

Story Editor

Story

New story   ———— *See 9.29*
Close story   ⌘W ———— *See 9.83*

Display ¶   ———— *See 9.17; 9.42*
Display style names ——— *See 9.16; 9.43*

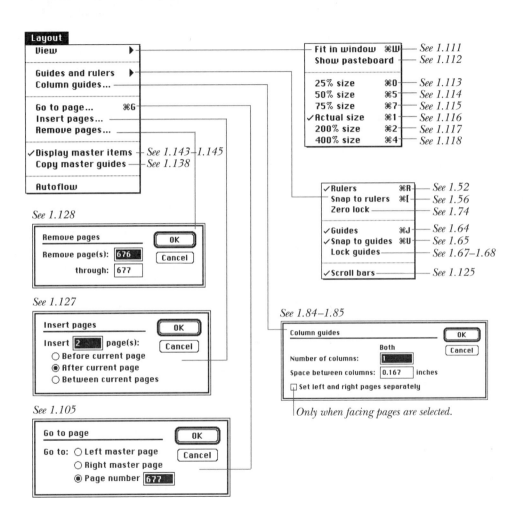

Layout
Uiew ▶
Fit in window   ⌘W — *See 1.111*
Show pasteboard — *See 1.112*

25% size   ⌘0 — *See 1.113*
50% size   ⌘5 — *See 1.114*
75% size   ⌘7 — *See 1.115*
✓Actual size   ⌘1 — *See 1.116*
200% size   ⌘2 — *See 1.117*
400% size   ⌘4 — *See 1.118*

Guides and rulers ▶
Column guides...

Go to page...   ⌘G
Insert pages...
Remove pages...

✓Display master items — *See 1.143–1.145*
Copy master guides — *See 1.138*

Autoflow

✓Rulers   ⌘R — *See 1.52*
Snap to rulers   ⌘I — *See 1.56*
Zero lock — *See 1.74*

✓Guides   ⌘J — *See 1.64*
✓Snap to guides   ⌘U — *See 1.65*
Lock guides — *See 1.67–1.68*

✓Scroll bars — *See 1.125*

See 1.128

Remove pages
             OK
Remove page(s): 676
through: 677   **Cancel**

See 1.127

Insert pages
             OK
Insert 2 page(s):   **Cancel**
○ Before current page
◉ After current page
○ Between current pages

See 1.84–1.85

Column guides
             OK
         Both
Number of columns: 1   **Cancel**
Space between columns: 0.167 inches
☐ Set left and right pages separately

Only when facing pages are selected.

See 1.105

Go to page
             OK
Go to: ○ Left master page   **Cancel**
      ○ Right master page
      ◉ Page number 677

$\mathcal{M}$ore matter is being printed and published today than ever before, and every publisher of an advertisement, pamphlet or book expects his material to be read. Publishers and, even more so, readers want what is important to be clearly laid out. They will not read anything that is troublesome to read, but are pleased with what looks clear and well-arranged, for it will make their task of understanding easier. For this reason, the important part must stand out and the unimportant must be subdued . . .

The technique of modern typography must also adapt itself to the speed of our times. Today, we cannot spend as much time on a letter heading or other piece of jobbing as was possible even in the nineties.

                —Jan Tschichold, 1935

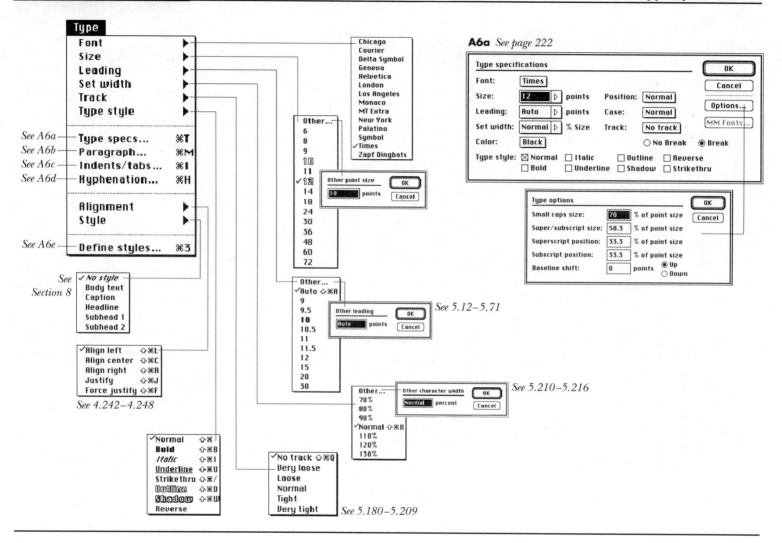

Type

Font ▶
Size ▶
Leading ▶
Set width ▶
Track ▶
Type style ▶

See A6a — Type specs... ⌘T
See A6b — Paragraph... ⌘M
See A6c — Indents/tabs... ⌘I
See A6d — Hyphenation... ⌘H

Alignment ▶
Style ▶

See A6e — Define styles... ⌘3

See Section 8
✓ *No style*
Body text
Caption
Headline
Subhead 1
Subhead 2

Chicago
Courier
Delta Symbol
Geneva
Helvetica
London
Los Angeles
Monaco
MT Extra
New York
Palatino
Symbol
✓ Times
Zapf Dingbats

Other...
6
8
9
10
11
✓ 12
14
18
24
30
36
48
60
72

Other point size
10 points
OK Cancel

A6a *See page 222*

Type specifications

OK
Cancel
Options...
MM Fonts...

Font: Times
Size: 12 ▷ points   Position: Normal
Leading: Auto ▷ points   Case: Normal
Set width: Normal ▷ % Size   Track: No track
Color: Black   ○ No Break ● Break
Type style: ⊠ Normal ☐ Italic ☐ Outline ☐ Reverse
☐ Bold ☐ Underline ☐ Shadow ☐ Strikethru

Type options
OK
Cancel

Small caps size: 70 % of point size
Super/subscript size: 58.3 % of point size
Superscript position: 33.3 % of point size
Subscript position: 33.3 % of point size
Baseline shift: 0 points ● Up ○ Down

Other...
✓ Auto ⇧⌘A
9
9.5
10
10.5
11
11.5
12
15
20
30

Other leading
Auto points
OK Cancel

See 5.12–5.71

✓ Align left ⇧⌘L
Align center ⇧⌘C
Align right ⇧⌘R
Justify ⇧⌘J
Force justify ⇧⌘F

See 4.242–4.248

Other...
70%
80%
90%
✓ Normal ⇧⌘X
110%
120%
130%

Other character width
Normal percent
OK Cancel

See 5.210–5.216

✓ Normal ⇧⌘ |
Bold ⇧⌘B
Italic ⇧⌘I
Underline ⇧⌘U
Strikethru ⇧⌘/
Outline ⇧⌘D
Shadow ⇧⌘W
Reverse

✓ No track ⇧⌘Q
Very loose
Loose
Normal
Tight
Very tight

See 5.180–5.209

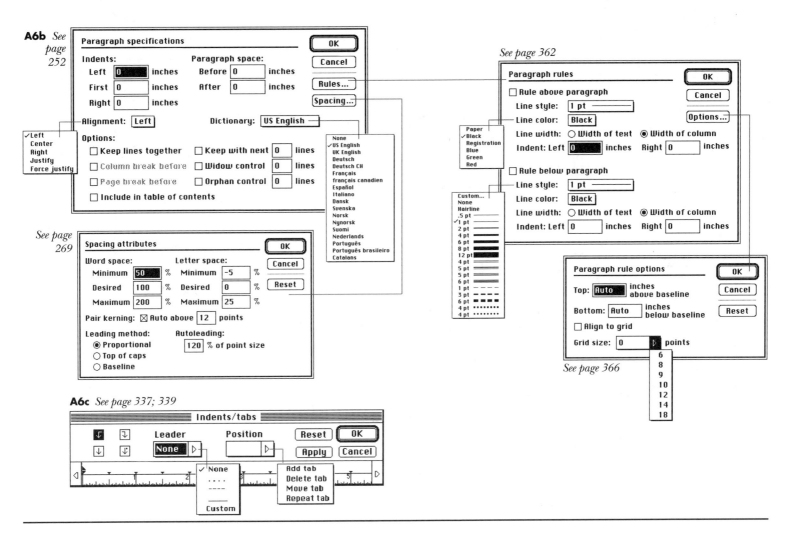

A6b *See page 252*

Paragraph specifications

Indents:
Left [0] inches
First [0] inches
Right [0] inches

Paragraph space:
Before [0] inches
After [0] inches

OK
Cancel
Rules...
Spacing...

Alignment: [Left]   Dictionary: [US English]

Options:
☐ Keep lines together   ☐ Keep with next [0] lines
☐ Column break before   ☐ Widow control [0] lines
☐ Page break before   ☐ Orphan control [0] lines
☐ Include in table of contents

✓Left
Center
Right
Justify
Force justify

None
✓US English
UK English
Deutsch
Deutsch CH
Français
français canadien
Español
Italiano
Dansk
Svenska
Norsk
Nynorsk
Suomi
Nederlands
Português
Português brasileiro
Catalans

See page 269

Spacing attributes

Word space:
Minimum [50] %
Desired [100] %
Maximum [200] %

Letter space:
Minimum [-5] %
Desired [0] %
Maximum [25] %

OK
Cancel
Reset

Pair kerning: ☒ Auto above [12] points

Leading method:
◉ Proportional
○ Top of caps
○ Baseline

Autoleading:
[120] % of point size

A6c *See page 337; 339*

Indents/tabs

Leader [None ▷]   Position [▷]   Reset   OK
Apply   Cancel

✓None
. . . .
_ _ _ _
Custom

Add tab
Delete tab
Move tab
Repeat tab

See page 362

Paragraph rules   OK

☐ Rule above paragraph
Line style: [1 pt]
Line color: [Black]
Line width: ○ Width of text ◉ Width of column
Indent: Left [0] inches   Right [0] inches

☐ Rule below paragraph
Line style: [1 pt]
Line color: [Black]
Line width: ○ Width of text ◉ Width of column
Indent: Left [0] inches   Right [0] inches

Cancel
Options...

Paper
✓Black
Registration
Blue
Green
Red

Custom...
None
Hairline
.5 pt
✓1 pt
2 pt
4 pt
6 pt
8 pt
12 pt
4 pt
5 pt
5 pt
6 pt
1 pt
3 pt
6 pt
4 pt
4 pt

Paragraph rule options   OK

Top: [Auto] inches above baseline
Bottom: [Auto] inches below baseline
☐ Align to grid
Grid size: [0 ▷] points

Cancel
Reset

6
8
9
10
12
14
18

See page 366

A6d *See page 325*

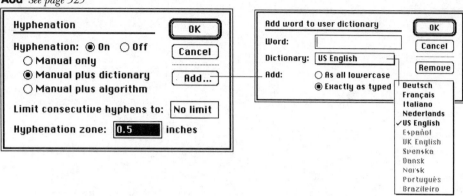

Hyphenation

Hyphenation: ● On   ○ Off
○ Manual only
● Manual plus dictionary
○ Manual plus algorithm

Limit consecutive hyphens to: No limit

Hyphenation zone: 0.5 inches

[OK] [Cancel] [Add...]

Add word to user dictionary

Word:
Dictionary: US English
Add: ○ As all lowercase
      ● Exactly as typed

[OK] [Cancel] [Remove]

Deutsch
Français
Italiano
Nederlands
✓US English
Español
UK English
Svenska
Dansk
Norsk
Português
Brasileiro

A6e *See page 382*

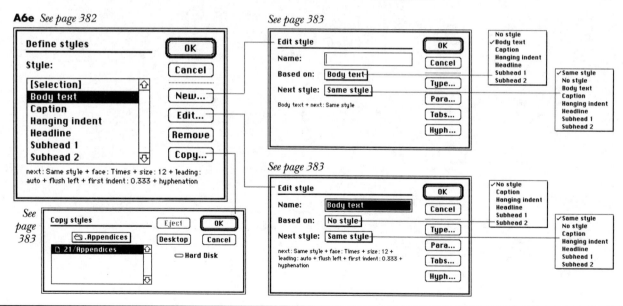

Define styles

Style:

[Selection]
Body text
Caption
Hanging indent
Headline
Subhead 1
Subhead 2

next: Same style + face: Times + size: 12 + leading:
auto + flush left + first indent: 0.333 + hyphenation

[OK] [Cancel] [New...] [Edit...] [Remove] [Copy...]

See page 383

Edit style

Name:
Based on: Body text
Next style: Same style

Body text + next: Same style

[OK] [Cancel] [Type...] [Para...] [Tabs...] [Hyph...]

No style
✓Body text
Caption
Hanging indent
Headline
Subhead 1
Subhead 2

✓Same style
No style
Body text
Caption
Hanging indent
Headline
Subhead 1
Subhead 2

See page 383

Edit style

Name: Body text
Based on: No style
Next style: Same style

next: Same style + face: Times + size: 12 +
leading: auto + flush left + first indent: 0.333 +
hyphenation

[OK] [Cancel] [Type...] [Para...] [Tabs...] [Hyph...]

✓No style
Caption
Hanging indent
Headline
Subhead 1
Subhead 2

✓Same style
No style
Caption
Hanging indent
Headline
Subhead 1
Subhead 2

See page 383

Copy styles

🗁 .Appendices

📄 21/Appendices

[Eject] [OK]
[Desktop] [Cancel]
⊂ Hard Disk

876

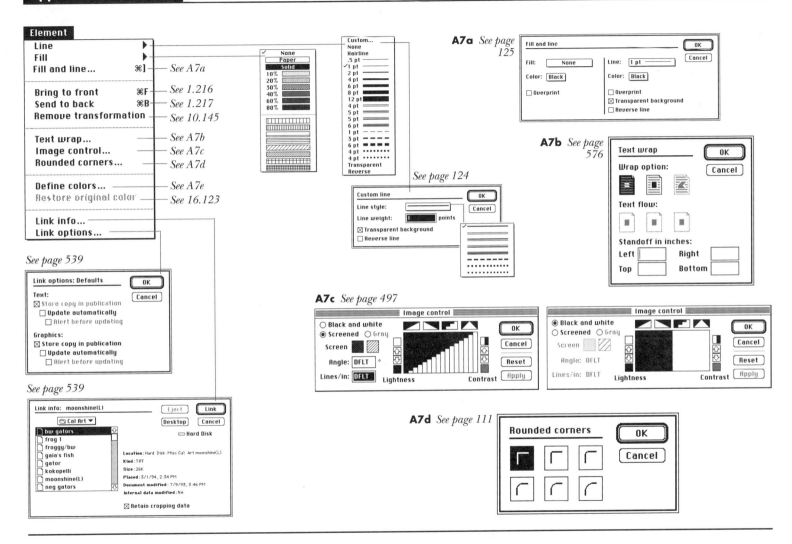

Element

Line	▶	
Fill	▶	
Fill and line...	⌘]	*See A7a*
Bring to front	⌘F	*See 1.216*
Send to back	⌘B	*See 1.217*
Remove transformation		*See 10.145*
Text wrap...		*See A7b*
Image control...		*See A7c*
Rounded corners...		*See A7d*
Define colors...		*See A7e*
Restore original color		*See 16.123*
Link info...		
Link options...		

See page 539

See page 539

See page 124

A7a *See page 125*

A7b *See page 576*

A7c *See page 497*

A7d *See page 111*

(Black is the default color. Blue is selected for the examples here so that the "Edit" option would be available)

A7e *See page 676*

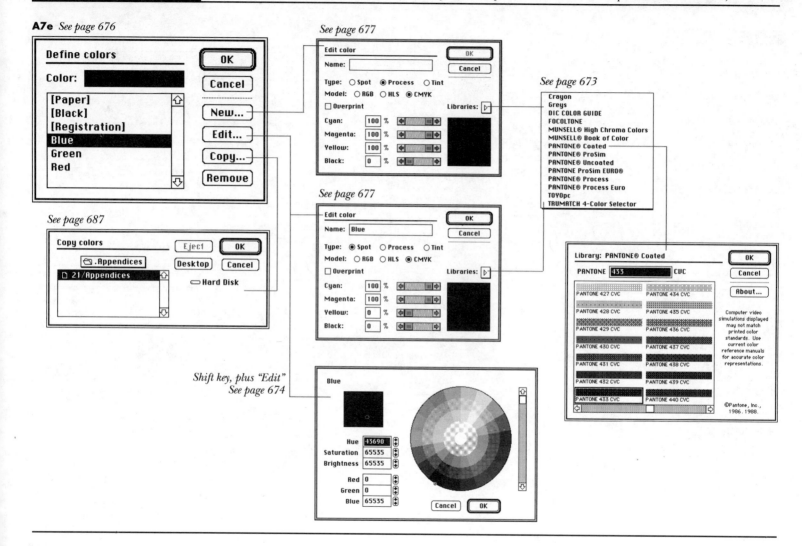

See page 677

See page 673

See page 687

See page 677

Shift key, plus "Edit"
See page 674

Define colors

Color:

[Paper]
[Black]
[Registration]
Blue
Green
Red

OK
Cancel
New...
Edit...
Copy...
Remove

Edit color
Name:
Type: ○ Spot ● Process ○ Tint
Model: ○ RGB ○ HLS ● CMYK
☐ Overprint
Cyan: 100 %
Magenta: 100 %
Yellow: 100 %
Black: 0 %
OK
Cancel
Libraries:

Crayon
Greys
DIC COLOR GUIDE
FOCOLTONE
MUNSELL® High Chroma Colors
MUNSELL® Book of Color
PANTONE® Coated
PANTONE® ProSim
PANTONE® Uncoated
PANTONE ProSim EURO®
PANTONE® Process
PANTONE® Process Euro
TOYOpc
TRUMATCH 4-Color Selector

Copy colors
☐ .Appendices
☐ 21/Appendices
Eject
Desktop
Cancel
OK
☐ Hard Disk

Edit color
Name: Blue
Type: ● Spot ○ Process ○ Tint
Model: ○ RGB ○ HLS ● CMYK
☐ Overprint
Cyan: 100 %
Magenta: 100 %
Yellow: 0 %
Black: 0 %
OK
Cancel
Libraries:

Library: PANTONE® Coated
PANTONE 433 CVC
OK
Cancel
About...

PANTONE 427 CVC | PANTONE 434 CVC
PANTONE 428 CVC | PANTONE 435 CVC
PANTONE 429 CVC | PANTONE 436 CVC
PANTONE 430 CVC | PANTONE 437 CVC
PANTONE 431 CVC | PANTONE 438 CVC
PANTONE 432 CVC | PANTONE 439 CVC
PANTONE 433 CVC | PANTONE 440 CVC

Computer video simulations displayed may not match printed color standards. Use current color reference manuals for accurate color representations.

©Pantone, Inc.,
1986. 1988.

Blue
Hue 43690
Saturation 65535
Brightness 65535
Red 0
Green 0
Blue 65535
Cancel
OK

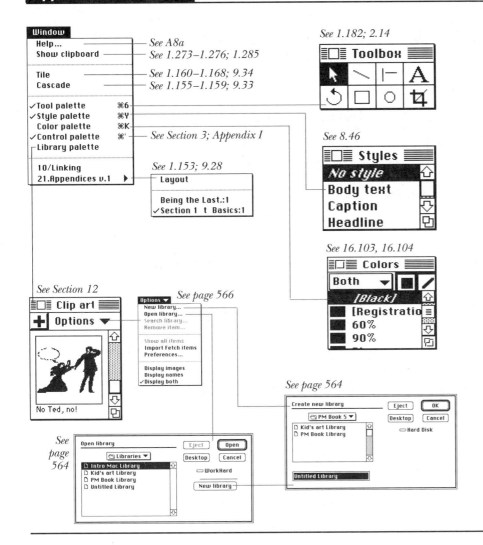

Window

Help... ———— *See A8a*
Show clipboard ———— *See 1.273–1.276; 1.285*

Tile ———— *See 1.160–1.168; 9.34*
Cascade ———— *See 1.155–1.159; 9.33*

✓Tool palette ⌘6
✓Style palette ⌘Y
Color palette ⌘K
✓Control palette ⌘' ———— *See Section 3; Appendix I*
Library palette

10/Linking
21.Appendices v.1 ▶

See 1.153; 9.28

Layout

Being the Last.:1
✓Section 1 t Basics:1

See Section 12

Clip art

✛ Options ▼

No Ted, no!

See page 564

Open library
Libraries ▼
Eject | Open
Desktop | Cancel
□ Intro Mac Library
□ Kid's art Library
□ PM Book Library
□ Untitled Library
WorkHard
New library

Options ▼

New library...
Open library...
Search library...
Remove item...

Show all items
Import Fetch items
Preferences...

Display images
Display names
✓Display both

See page 566

See page 564

Create new library
PM Book 5 ▼
Eject | OK
Desktop | Cancel
□ Kid's art Library
□ PM Book Library
□ Hard Disk

Untitled Library

See 1.182; 2.14

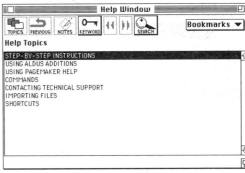

Toolbox

See 8.46

Styles
No style
Body text
Caption
Headline

See 16.103, 16.104

Colors
Both
[Black]
[Registratio
60%
90%

A8a *See 22.3*

Help Window

TOPICS PREVIOUS NOTES KEYWORD ◀◀ ▶▶ SEARCH   Bookmarks ▼

Help Topics

STEP-BY-STEP INSTRUCTIONS
USING ALDUS ADDITIONS
USING PAGEMAKER HELP
COMMANDS
CONTACTING TECHNICAL SUPPORT
IMPORTING FILES
SHORTCUTS

Click on any topic to select it.

Help Window

TOPICS PREVIOUS NOTES KEYWORD ◀◀ ▶▶ SEARCH   Bookmarks ▼

STEP-BY-STEP INSTRUCTIONS

Publication Setup
Text
Graphics and Text Blocks
Indexes, Contents, and Pagination
Color
Importing, Linking and Exporting
Printing

❖

Click on any underlined topic to display more info.

Help Window

TOPICS PREVIOUS NOTES KEYWORD ◀◀ ▶▶ SEARCH   Bookmarks ▼

PUBLICATION SETUP

Publication Setup
Automatic page-numbering
Creating a page with different numbers of columns
Creating multiple columns
Defaults
Nonprinting guides
Opening, naming and saving publications
Working with master pages
Working with templates
Text

SECTION 1 ▾ BASICS

1.12   Launch the Pagemaker application
1.13   Set the application defaults for the entire PageMaker program
1.14   Open a new publication
1.15   Open an existing PageMaker publication
1.16   Set publication defaults for the current open publication
1.17   Revert back to the original PageMaker defaults
1.25   Change the page size
1.26   Create a custom page size
1.27   Change the orientation
1.28   Establish the number of pages
1.29   Add or delete pages
1.30   Start numbering pages with a number other than 1
1.31   Renumber the pages, starting with a different number
1.32   Format the page numbers
1.33   Create a prefix for Index and Table of Contents entries
1.34   Create a single-sided publication
1.35   Create a double-sided publication
1.36   Show facing pages
1.37   Set or change the margin
1.52a Show the rulers
1.52b Hide the rulers
1.53   Change the horizontal ruler measurements
1.54   Change the vertical ruler measurements
1.55   Use a custom measurement in the vertical ruler
1.56   Use "Snap to rulers"
1.58   Add a ruler guide, either on a master page or on any publication page
1.59   Reposition any ruler guide either on a master page or on any publication page

1.60   Delete a ruler guide either on a master page or on any publication page
1.61   Show the master page guide changes on a publication page where they're not showing up
1.62   Delete all ruler guides at once, except the master guides
1.63   Delete all ruler guides on a page or facing pages
1.64a Hide all guides
1.64b Show all guides
1.65a Use "Snap to guides"
1.65b Turn off "Snap to guides"
1.66a Send all guides to the back layer
1.66b Bring all guides to the front layer
1.67a Lock all guides
1.67b Unlock all guides
1.69   Reposition margin guides
1.70   Reposition the zero point, both horizontally and vertically
1.71   Reposition just the horizontal zero point
1.72   Reposition just the vertical zero point
1.73   Reset the zero point to its default position
1.74a Lock the zero point
1.74b Unlock the zero point
1.84   Create equal columns
1.85   Create unequal columns
1.88   Widen or narrow a column
1.87   Widen or narrow the space between columns
1.88   Revert the columns to equal widths
1.89   Change a master page column guide on one publication page
1.90   Revert any customized columns back to the master page columns
1.91   Delete all columns
1.92a Hide the column guides

1.92b Show the column guides
1.93a Send the column guides to the back
1.93b Bring the column guides to the front
1.94a Lock the column guides in place
1.94b Unlock the column guides
1.100 Go to the next page
1.101 Go to the previous page
1.102 Go several pages next
1.103 Go several pages previous
1.104 Go to any page, if there are fewer than about 15 pages (meaning all page icons are visible)
1.105 Go to any page, if there are more than about 15 pages (page icon *scroll arrows* are visible)
1.106 Show the first or last page icon in the publication
1.107 Jump past half-a-dozen page icons
1.108 Pan through all the pages
1.109 From a master page, return to the page you were last working on
1.110 Change the view of the page you are going to into "Fit in Window" size
1.111 View the entire page in the window ("Fit in window")
1.112 View the entire pasteboard ("Show pasteboard")
1.113 View the page at 25%
1.114 View the page at 50%
1.115 View the page at 75%
1.116 View the page at Actual Size
1.117 View the page at 200% (twice Actual Size)
1.118 View the page at 400%
1.119 Change the view of all the pages in the publication
1.120 Toggle between "Actual size" and "Fit in window" view

1.121 Toggle between "Actual size" and "200% size"

1.122 Use the magnifying tool to enlarge the page to the next page view size

1.123 Use the reducing tool to reduce the page to the previous page view size

1.124 Custom enlarge a section of the page using the magnifying tool

1.125 View the pages of a publication without the scroll bars showing

1.126 Move the page in any direction without using scroll bars

1.127 Add or insert pages

1.128 Remove or delete pages

1.129 Replace pages that were deleted

1.136 Go to a master page

1.137 Set up guides on a master page

1.138 Show newly-created master guides on a previously-created or customized publication page

1.139 Place text on a master page

1.140 Place a graphic on a master page

1.141 Set up a graphic to text wrap on a master page

1.142 Modify or delete master page items from the master page

1.143 Remove master page items from any single page in the publication

1.144 Hide just some of the master page objects so they don't appear on the publication page (and thus will not print)

1.145 View (display) the master page items on the publication page (if for some reason they're not visible)

1.147a Automatically number the pages from the master page so every page number will be in the same place

1.147b Automatically number the pages individually

1.148 Format the automatic page numbers, whether on the master page or on individual pages

1.149 Override the automatic page number formatting on pages you have automatically numbered individually

1.150 Quick tip for auto-numbering individual pages

1.169 Open an existing publication

1.170 Open more than one publication

1.171 Create a "New" publication without closing the active publication

1.172 Switch between open publications

1.173 Save changes made in all the open publications in one step

1.174 Close all the open publications in one step

1.175 Cascade all the open publication windows.

1.176 View a different window in the cascade layout.

1.177 Tile all the open publication windows

1.178 Bring one window from the tiled layout forward

1.179 Drag an object from one tiled publication to another

1.180 Drag an object from one tiled publication and place it as an inline graphic in another

1.202 Select a text block

1.203 Select a graphic

1.204 Select a line

1.205 Deselect an object (text blocks, graphics, lines, etc.)

1.206 Deselect all objects

1.207 Select more than one object using the Shift-click method

1.208 Select more than one object using the marquee method

1.209 Add objects to those already selected

1.210 Deselect an object or two from a group of selected objects

1.211 Select an object that is underneath another object

1.212 Select an object that is under a guide

1.213 Select all objects on the screen, no matter what layer they are on

1.214 Select an object that seems to be invisible

1.215 Select an object that is hidden or trapped under another, including a line or border that is under a guide

1.216 Bring an object in front of another

1.217 Send an object behind another

1.218 Select text to modify

1.219 Select text or an object to rotate

1.220 Select an imported graphic to crop

1.221 Switch to the pointer tool without deselecting a newly drawn, cropped, or rotated object

Preferences

1.224 Change the unit of measure on the horizontal ruler and in the dialog boxes

1.225 Change the unit of measure for the vertical ruler

1.226 Customize the measurement of the vertical ruler

1.227 Show loosely-spaced and tightly-spaced lines

1.228 Show lines that violate the "keeps" commands established in the Paragraph dialog box

1.229 Adjust the resolution of detailed, non-PageMaker graphics

1.230 Send the guides to the front or to the back

1.231 See each page of a publication as text is placed using the "Autoflow" command

1.232 Set the maximum amount of memory to be used for graphic image screen display

1.233 Set the maximum file size for imported graphics that are being stored in the publication

1.234 Make the inch and foot marks automatically display and print as true quotation marks and apostrophes.

1.235 Make TrueType stay true to its linespacing or to its character shape

1.236 Change the number of pixels for showing "greek" text

1.237 Change the font displayed in the Story Editor

1.238 Change the font size displayed in the Story Editor

1.239 Automatically display style names and/or non-printing characters in the Story Editor

PANOSE

1.267 Set Panose font matching options

1.268 Disable Panose font substitution

1.269 Choose whether to temporarily or permanently accept the font substitutions PageMaker offers for a particular publication

1.270 Create your own font substitutions

1.271 Select your own substitutions in the "Panose font matching results" dialog box

Miscellaneous

1.280 Cut

1.281 Copy

1.282 Paste

1.283 Power-paste a text block or a graphic into the exact position from which it was cut or copied

1.284 Clear (from the menu or Backspace/ Delete)

1.285 View the contents of the Clipboard

1.286 Choose which format PageMaker uses to paste a Clipboard item

1.305 Multiple paste an object

1.306 Multiple paste objects to the left and above the original

1.307 Multiple paste text

1.308 Multiple paste an object as an inline graphic

1.309 Multiple paste a graphic or text without reopening the dialog box.

1.310 Use Multiple paste to create a quick two-tone grid

1.311 Undo

1.313 Put a graphic into the Scrapbook

1.314 Put text into the Scrapbook

1.315 Delete any image from the Scrapbook

1.316 Paste an object from the Scrapbook onto a page

1.317 Paste text from the Scrapbook onto a page

1.318 Place Scrapbook items as graphics

1.319 Create a bounding box to type into

1.320 Paste text into a bounding box

1.321 Drag-place text into a bounding box

1.322 Drag-place a graphic into a bounding box

1.323 Override the current ruler measurement in any dialog box that asks for measures

1.324 Type numbers with the keypad

1.325 Use the keypad as arrow keys

1.326 Select text with the keypad

1.327 Cut and paste with the keypad

1.328 Use other keyboard shortcuts to move the insertion point

1.329 View the Key Caps keyboard layout

1.330 View all four of the keyboard layouts

1.331 Use alternate characters in your publication (for accent marks, see 1.333)

1.332 Insert an alternate character from another font

1.333 Use accent marks, as in the word piñata

1.334 Use Find File to locate a file while at your Desktop

1.335 On a small screen, open up more space in the window

SECTION 2 ▾ DRAWING TOOLS

2.23 Draw an object

2.24 Select one or more drawn objects

2.25 Delete a drawn object

2.26 Delete lots of objects

2.27 Move one or more objects

2.28 Move one or more objects to another page

2.29 Move a tiny little object

2.30 Move objects in a straight line

2.31 Draw or move objects in perfect alignment with guide lines

2.32 Draw or move objects in perfect alignment with the ruler tick marks

2.33 Stop the cursor or the objects you are moving from jerking around on the screen

2.34 Change a line width or a border

2.35 Change the line width or the border of a group of lines or drawn shapes

2.36 Make a patterned line width or border transparent

2.37 Reverse a line width or border

2.38 Find an invisible or "lost" object

Lines

2.39   Lengthen or shorten a line

2.40   Straighten a crooked line

2.41   Change the direction of a line

Rectangles and Squares

2.42   Draw a perfect square

2.43   Change a rectangle into a perfect square

2.44   Change the corners of one or more rectangles to a different corner

2.45   Re-size a rectangle or square

2.46   Change the fill pattern

Ovals and Circles

2.47   Draw a perfect circle

2.48   Change a drawn oval into a perfect circle

2.49   Change the fill pattern of one or more ovals or circles

2.50   Change the shape of the oval or circle

2.75   Create a custom weight line

2.76   Let the background show through the lines or patterns of double, triple, dashed, or dotted lines

2.77   Select a line or object that is underneath another line or object

2.78   Change the way two objects are layered

2.79   Apply a color to the line and fill of an object

2.80   Make an object print over an object underneath it without knocking out any of the bottom object

2.81   Group lines or objects together so they can be copied, moved or re-sized as one object

2.82   Set defaults for any of the lines, fills, or corners for the current publication

2.83   Set defaults for any of the lines, fills, or corners for the entire PageMaker application

2.84   Set a text wrap default for drawn objects

The Rotating tool

2.94   Select and rotate an object using the rotating tool

2.95   Select and rotate more than one object using the rotating tool

2.96   Keep the rotated object(s) selected while you choose the pointer tool from the Toolbox

2.97   Rotate an object in increments of 45°

2.98   Rotate a group of objects around the center point of the selected items

SECTION 3 ▾ THE CONTROL PALETTE

3.19a   Show the Control palette

3.19b   Hide the Control palette

3.20a   Make the Control palette active

3.20b   Make the Control palette inactive

3.21   Make the Control palette appear everytime you open a new publication (set it as a publication default.)

3.22   Change the unit of measure used for the Control palette

3.23   Change the unit of measure used for just the nudge buttons.

3.24   Change the nudge amount of the Position and Sizing options.

3.25   Constrain objects changed through the Control palette to "Snap to" guides and/or rulers

3.26   Change a selected item by clicking on a button

3.27   Change the value of an option by "nudging" it

3.28   Power-nudge a selected item

3.29   Select a Control palette option from a pop-up menu

3.30   Change an option by typing into the edit box

3.31   Use mathematical formulas to change the value of an option

3.58   Select an active reference point on the Proxy

3.59   Change the reference point from a box to an arrow or vice versa

3.87   Change the position of a selected object

3.88   Change the position of an object on the page by entering new values for its active reference point

3.89   Resize a selected object by entering new values for its active reference point in the Position option edit boxes

3.90   Resize a line

3.91   Reduce or enlarge an object by a given percent

3.92a   Proportionately change an object's width or height

3.92b   Change an object's width or height independently

3.93a   Rotate an object clockwise around a fixed point on the object

3.93b   Rotate an object counterclockwise around a fixed point on the object

3.94   Rotate an object in an arc using the arrow reference point (moving the reference point)

3.95   Skew (tilt) an object to the right or left keeping the object anchored in one place (the active reference point stationary)

3.96   Skew an object to the right or the left, sliding it along the active reference point (moving the active reference point)

3.97   Flip an object horizontally around a stationary reference point

3.98   Flip an object horizontally, flipping (moving) the active reference point with it

3.99 Flip an object vertically around a stationary reference point

3.100 Flip an object vertically, flipping (moving) the active reference point with it

Using the keyboard to operate the Control palette

3.110 Use the keyboard to move from one option to the next in the Control palette

3.111 Use the keyboard to turn a button in the palette on or off

3.112 Apply changes to your document while keeping the palette active and moving to the next option

3.113 Display the last valid entry for a palette option when you enter an invalid value

3.114 Change the measuring system "on the fly" for certain options without going into the Preferences dialog box

3.115 Use key commands to move an object

3.116 Select an active reference point on the Proxy using the arrow keys on the keyboard.

3.117 Select an active reference point on the Proxy using the Numeric keypad.

3.118 Change the type of active reference point from a box to an arrow (or vice versa) using only keyboard commands

3.119 Move the cursor through an edit box without using the mouse

Section 4 ▾ Text

4.25 Type onto the page

4.26 Restrain the size of the text block (create a bounding box to type in so the handles don't run across the whole page)

4.27 Make the insertion point align on the left

4.55 Place text as a new story while retaining the format of the original document

4.56 Place text as a new story without retaining the format of the original document

4.57 Replace an entire story

4.58 Insert placed text into a story that is already on the page

4.59 Replace a portion of an existing story

4.60 Place text and read the tags

4.61 Convert typewriter quotes to real quotes

4.62 Place text into a bounding box to hold it or to override column guides (drag-place)

4.82 Place (import) an entire PageMaker file

4.83 Place selected stories from another PageMaker 5 publication, or a PageMaker 4 publication

4.84 Limit the display of story titles in the list box to just those stories that are greater than a certain number of characters

4.85 View any story

4.86 Drag-and-drop text between PageMaker 5 publications

4.95 Place text from a file, or place the rest of an existing text block, using manual flow

4.96 Use semi-auto text flow

4.97 Use autoflow

4.98 Override autoflow or manual flow

4.99 Stop autoflow

4.100 Cancel the loaded text icon without placing the text

4.114 Select a text block or several text blocks

4.115 Move a text block

4.116 Widen a text block, or make it narrower

4.117 Shorten a text block

4.118 Lengthen a text block

4.119 Delete a text block

4.120 Delete several text blocks

4.121 Delete all the text blocks on the page

4.122 Divide a text block into two or more parts, keeping the separate text blocks threaded

4.123 Remove one or more of several threaded text blocks in a story without deleting the text in them

4.124 Put separate, threaded text blocks back into one text block

4.125 Cut a text block

4.126 Copy a text block

4.127 Delete a text block

4.128 Paste a text block

4.129 Separate a text block into two or more separate, unthreaded stories

Additions for text

4.179 Locate all instances of overset text—text blocks that have text hidden in their windowshade

4.180 Locate text blocks linked to the one currently selected

4.181 View "Story info..." for a particular story

4.182 View the "Text block info..." box about a particular text block

4.183 Add the jump-line "Continued on..." to a threaded text block

4.184 Add the jump-line "Continued from..." to a threaded text block

4.185 Edit the styles of the jump-line stories

4.186 Balance two or more columns of text in a story, aligning the top of each text block, and adding the extra lines starting in the far left column

4.187 Balance two or more columns of text in a story, aligning the bottom of each text block, and adding extra lines starting in the far right column

Selecting and formatting

4.203 Select text using the mouse
    a) one character
    b) one word
    c) one line

d) one sentence
e) one paragraph
f) range of text
g) entire story
h) extend or shorten the selection

4.204 Use the keyboard to move the insertion point and to select text
4.225 Display the character-view Control palette
4.226 Navigate the character-view Control palette using just the keyboard
4.227 Turn the type style, case, and position options on and off using just the keyboard
4.228 Change the font
4.229 Change the type size
4.230 Change the type size from the keyboard
4.231 Change the type style of selected text
4.232 Change the type style of text from the keyboard before you type it
4.233 Change text back to Normal
4.234 Change the leading
4.235 Create reverse text
4.236 Finding lost reverse text
4.237 Prevent reverse text from getting lost
4.238 Expand or condense the type
4.239 Make several type specification changes at once
4.240 Change the type default specifications through the Control palette
4.241 Keep selected text from breaking at the end of a line
4.242 Change the alignment
4.249 Force justify display text with wide letterspacing
4.251 Change the case
4.252 Change the size of the small caps
4.253 Change the position (normal or superscript or subscript)

4.261 Set a default so you can create beautiful fractions easily
4.262 Create a fraction using the "Run script…" Addition
4.263 Shift the baseline of selected text
4.264 Create interesting bullets
4.265 Make the text or rules gray
4.266 Delete text
4.267 Cut text
4.268 Copy text
4.269 Paste text
4.270 Replace existing text with the text that you cut or copied onto the Clipboard
4.280 Rotate text using the rotating tool
4.281 Rotate text using the Control palette
4.282 Unrotate text
4.283 Edit rotated text
4.284 Change the degree of rotation for a single, already-rotated text block
4.285 Resize a rotated text block
4.286 Wrap rotated text around a graphic
4.287 Rotate more than one text block, or text blocks and objects, at the same time
4.321 Indent a paragraph on the left
4.322 Indent a paragraph on the right
4.323 Indent the first line of every paragraph
4.324 Create a hanging indent
4.325 Set a one-em indent for first lines
4.326 Set up paragraph indents before typing the paragraphs
4.327 Change the alignment of a paragraph
4.328 Change the dictionary, or add another one to check from
4.358 Type a special character
4.359 Type accent marks
4.365 Set the default type specifications for the entire PageMaker application

4.366 Set the default type specifications for the current publication

SECTION 5 ▾ TEXT SPACING

5.59 Figure out the actual value of "Auto" leading in a line of text
5.60 Figure out the actual value of "Auto" leading (or any leading) in a line of text using the Control palette
5.61 Figure out the current leading value of the selected text
5.62 Increase or decrease the leading
5.63 Use the proportional leading method
5.64 Use the top of caps leading method
5.65 Use the baseline leading method
5.66 Adjust the leading of a paragraph so it is consistent
5.67 Adjust the leading above the last line of a paragraph of body text
5.68 Change the Auto leading value
5.69 You want to change the leading, but it won't change
5.70 Make the letters reappear after you decrease the leading or when using the Baseline leading method
5.71 Adjust the leading on an inline graphic so it doesn't make the linespace inconsistent
5.93 Add space after a paragraph
5.94 Add space before a paragraph
5.95 Break a line without adding paragraph space
5.96 Remove paragraph space
5.110 Align text to a leading grid
5.111 Align graphics to a leading grid
5.129 Increase the word space
5.130 Decrease the word space
5.131 Reset word space to the original default

5.147 Increase the letter space
5.148 Decrease the letter space
5.149 Reset letter space values to original defaults
5.150 Letterspace a headline
5.166 Turn auto kerning on or off
5.167 Determine the point size of type that will be auto kerned
5.168 Decrease the space between two characters
5.169 Increase the space between two characters
5.170 Decrease or increase the spacing over a range of text
5.171 Remove all kerning from selected text
5.172 Kern text or remove kerning while in the Story Editor
5.178 Use the Expert kerning Addition
5.179 Remove the expert kerning
5.190 Apply tracking to selected text
5.191 Change the tracking
5.192 Remove any tracking
5.204 Copy the "Tracking Values" file before changing the tracking of a font
5.205 Edit the tracking values
5.206 Copy the tracking values from one font to another
5.207 Proof (take a look at in print) your new tracking values
5.208 Print with the font for which you have changed the tracking values
5.209 Reset original Tracking Values
5.215 Apply a set width to selected text, or change the set width of selected text
5.216 Remove any set width
5.223 Create an em space
5.224 Create an en space
5.225 Create a thin space

5.226 Create a fixed space
5.227 Create a non-breaking hyphen
5.228 Create a non-breaking slash
5.249 Enter a discretionary hyphen
5.250 Remove a discretionary hyphen
5.251 Prevent a word from hyphenating
5.252 Change the hyphenation zone
5.253 Add a word to the user dictionary, setting and ranking the hyphenation points
5.254 Remove a word from the user dictionary
5.255 Change the hyphenation points of a word that is already in the dictionary

Section 6 ▾ Indents and Tabs

6.63 Set a new tab, or add a tab
6.64 Set a tab right on top of an indent marker
6.65 Delete a tab
6.66 Move a tab
6.67 Change the alignment of a tab
6.68 Repeat a tab
6.69 Reset the tabs
6.70 Clear all tabs
6.71 Set a tab with leaders
6.72 Create your own custom leaders
6.73 Create fancy custom leaders, where the font of the leaders is different than the font before or after the leaders
6.74 Remove the leaders, not the tab
6.75 Set a tab with leaders that go right over the top of a text-wrapped object
6.76 Use a tab to create text that is both left and right justified
Indents
6.77 Set a first-line indent
6.78 Set a hanging indent
6.79 Delete any first-line or hanging indent
6.80 Indent from the left margin

6.81 Indent from the right margin
6.82 Remove any indents
6.83 Set an indent using the Control palette
Miscellaneous tab and indent info
6.84 Copy the entire tab/indent formatting to other adjacent paragraphs
6.85 Set the default tabs and indents for the current open publication
6.86 Set the default tabs and indents for the entire application
6.87 Reset the tiny triangular pre-set tabs
6.88 Replace spaces (where you spaced more than twice) with tabs
6.89 Deselect a tab in the Indents/tabs ruler

Section 7 ▾ Rules (Lines)

7.41 Set a paragraph rule above, the width of the column or of the text
7.42 Set a paragraph rule above, indenting from the width of the column
7.43 Set a paragraph rule above, extending beyond the width of the column
7.44 Set a paragraph rule above, indenting from the width of the text
7.45 Set a paragraph rule above, extending beyond the width of the text
7.46 Set a paragraph rule below, the width of the column or of the text
7.47 Set a paragraph rule below, indenting from the width of the column
7.48 Set a paragraph rule below, extending beyond the width of the column
7.49 Set a paragraph rule below, indenting from the width of the text
7.50 Set a paragraph rule below, extending beyond the width of the text

7.51 Set paragraph rules above and below
7.52 Create reverse text in a rule
7.53 Remove rules
7.54 Change the rule and/or the position
7.55 Create a Custom rule
7.56 Create a reverse rule
7.57 Change the rule to a color or shade
of gray

SECTION 8 ▾ STYLE SHEETS

8.46 Show or hide the Style palette
8.47 Create a new style from scratch; one
method (also see 8.48, 8.49)
8.48 Create a new style from scratch; a second
method (also see 8.47, 8.49)
8.49 Create a new style from scratch using the
paragraph-view Control palette; a third
method (also see 8.47, 8.48)
8.50 Create a new style based on an existing
style, using the paragraph-view Control
palette; one method (also see 8.51)
8.51 Create a new style based on an existing
style; other methods (also see 8.50)
8.52 Rename a style
8.53 Edit an existing style (change its
definition)
8.54 Replace an existing style
8.55 Remove any style
8.56 Copy styles from another PageMaker
publication
8.57 Import just certain selected styles from
another PageMaker publication
8.58 Copy styles from one publication to
another using the Library palette
8.59 Import styles from a word processing
program
8.60 Fix a "Bad record index"

8.61 Transform one existing style (Style A)
into another existing style (Style B)
8.62 Apply a style to a paragraph
8.63 Change a paragraph's style
8.64 Apply or change a style from the
keyboard
8.65 Override the style sheet
8.66 Preserve temporary overrides when
changing a paragraph's style
8.67 Include overrides as part of a style
8.68 Eliminate all temporary overrides from
tagged paragraphs
8.69 Eliminate permanent overrides
from tagged paragraphs
8.70 Eliminate really permanent overrides
from tagged paragraphs
8.71 View a list of all styles applied in a story.
8.72 Use the Story Editor to find and change
local formatting
8.73 Use local formatting intentionally, then
use the Story Editor to find and change it
8.74 Apply styles to text in the Story Editor
8.75 Create a word processing document so
PageMaker can read the tags
8.76 Place a word processed document
that has been tagged with style names
8.77 Export a story, tagging it with the
style sheet names
8.78 Set a particular style as the publication
default when typing in PageMaker or
when placing text from a word processor

SECTION 9 ▾ STORY EDITOR

9.29 Open the Story Editor to a new, blank
story window
9.30 Open the Story Editor to view a particular
story you want to edit:

9.31 While the Story Editor is active, bring to
the front a story window that is already
open, but is buried under other windows
9.32 While the Story Editor is active, open a
story that is still on the layout page
9.33a While the Story Editor is active, stack the
open story windows of the current pub so
you can see the title of each window
9.33b While the Story Editor is active, stack all
the open story windows of the open pubs
9.34a While the Story Editor is active, tile all the
open stories of the current open pub
9.34a While the Story Editor is active, tile all the
open stories of all the open publications
9.35 Import a story from outside PageMaker
into its own separate window
9.36 Import a story, inserting the text into the
current story, replacing the entire story,
or replacing a portion of the current story
9.37 Import stories from another PageMaker
publication
9.38 Import a graphic into a story, either as a
new inline graphic or to replace an
existing inline graphic
9.39 Export and link a story, either the entire
story, or a selected portion of the story
9.40 Select text in a story
9.41 Edit in a story window
9.42 Display or hide invisible text characters
9.43 Use style sheets in the Story Editor
9.44 Use the Control palette to format text
in the Story Editor
9.45 Move a story window without making it
active (that is, without bringing it to the
top layer)
9.46 Open all the stories in the current pub
using the "Open stories" Addition

9.47   In the story view, close all the open stories in the current publication
9.48   Change the font and/or size text that the Story Editor uses to display text
9.49   Set Story Editor display defaults
Find
9.61   Find text with no particular text attributes
9.62   Find characters with special text attributes
9.63   Find just attributes
9.64   Change all the attributes back to "Any"
9.65   Find invisible or special characters
9.66   To find a wildcard character
Change
9.78   Change characters, regardless of their particular attributes
9.79   Find and change characters with text attributes
9.80   Find and change just text attributes
9.81   Find and eliminate characters or attributes
9.82   Find and change special characters
Closing windows; placing text
9.83   Place a new story (Untitled or imported)
9.84   Discard a new story
9.85   Leave a new story (Untitled or imported) without placing or discarding it
9.86   Return to the layout view
9.87   Return to where you left off in the layout view
9.88   Return to the layout view in the exact spot in the story you are currently editing
9.89   Save a new (untitled, or imported) story without placing or discarding it
Spell Checker
9.117 Check spelling
9.118 Check the spelling of just one word

9.119 Find out why you get the "Error accessing dictionary" or "Cannot open dictionary for this paragraph" message
9.120 Add words to the user dictionary from within PageMaker
9.121 Hyphenate a word you are adding to the user dictionary
9.122 Remove a word from the user dictionary
9.123 Check spelling, using more than one dictionary
9.124 Change dictionaries in a paragraph
9.125 Change the default dictionary
9.126 Copy the user dictionary to give to someone else
Dictionary Editor
9.137 Add, remove or edit words in the user dictionary with the Dictionary Editor
9.138 Specify how a word you are adding to a user dictionary will be hyphenated
9.139 Create another user dictionary
9.140 Import a text-only file to your user dictionary
9.141 Install a user dictionary (switch dictionaries)

Section 10 ▾ Graphics
Independent graphics
10.126 Place a graphic
10.127 Drag-place a graphic
10.128 Replace a graphic
10.129 Paste a graphic from the Scrapbook
10.130 Place a graphic from the Scrapbook
10.131 Place a graphic from the Library palette
10.132 Paste a graphic from the Clipboard
10.133 Cut or copy a graphic
10.134 Copy a graphic by dragging-and-dropping it between PageMaker 5 publications

10.135 Choose a paste format for a clipboard item
10.136 Delete a graphic
10.137 Move a graphic
10.138 Resize a graphic
10.139 Resize a graphic using the Scaling option on the Control palette
10.140 Resize a graphic back into its original proportions
10.141 "Magic-resize" a bi-level graphic
10.142 "Magic-resize" a bi-level graphic using the Printer-resolution option on the Control palette
10.143 Crop a graphic, uncrop a graphic, and pan a graphic
10.144 Crop a graphic using the Cropping option in the Control palette
10.145 Transform graphics (skew, rotate, or reflect) using the Control palette
10.146 Edit the original copy of a graphic from within PageMaker
10.147 Edit the original copy of a graphic from within PageMaker when you do not have the originating graphic program
10.148 Edit the original copy of a graphic from within the Story Editor
10.149 Text wrap a graphic
10.150 Remove text wrapping from a graphic
10.151 Turn text into a graphic
10.152 Compress a TIFF file to save disk space
10.153 Replace a TIFF file on the page with a compressed TIFF file
10.154 Decompress a TIFF file
10.155 Display all graphics as gray boxes for fastest screen display
10.156 Display all graphics as low-resolution screen images
10.157 Display all graphics at high-resolution

10.158 Display a single graphic at high-resolution

10.159 Apply color to a graphic

10.160 Create an EPS file of a PageMaker page

Image control

10.209 Adjust the appearance of a TIFF image

10.210 Lighten a TIFF or paint-type image to a shadow so you can print text over the top of it

10.211 Return a TIFF image to its original specifications

10.212 Lighten a PICT or EPS graphic to a shadow

Inline graphics

10.234 Paste a graphic inline

10.235 Place a graphic inline

10.236 Replace an existing inline graphic with another graphic file

10.237 Replace an existing inline graphic with another graphic from the Clipboard

10.238 Import (place) an inline graphic into the Story Editor

10.239 Resize an inline graphic

10.240 Cut or copy an inline graphic

10.241 Delete an inline graphic

10.242 Delete an inline graphic you can't see because it is too big or it disappeared somewhere or there's so many of them you can't select them all at once

10.243 Adjust the leading and tracking of an inline graphic using the "Inline specifications" dialog box

10.244 Move an inline graphic horizontally

10.245 Step-and-repeat inline graphics

10.246 Adjust the baseline of an inline graphic

10.247 Precisely adjust the space above and below an inline graphic that is in its own paragraph

10.248 Adjust the baseline of an inline graphic using the Control palette

10.249 Perfectly center an inline graphic in a text block

10.250 Use image control on or apply color to an inline graphic

10.251 Set an inline graphic to the side of a paragraph

Additions for graphics

10.284 Group two or more objects

10.285 Ungroup a group

10.286 Make changes to an object within a group, and then group it again

10.287 Add an object, objects, or group of objects to a group

10.288 Disable the "PS Ungroup it" dialog box and set a PMG file default

10.289 Display the "PS Ungroup it" dialog box again

10.290 Manipulate a group

10.291 Take a publication that contains grouped objects to a service bureau for printing

10.306 Create a keyline to mark the position for a halftone or artwork to be dropped in by your printer

10.307 Create a keyline to use as a frame or decorative box

SECTION 11 ▾ LINKING TEXT AND GRAPHICS

11.58 Establish a link to a file that has been placed or imported

11.59 Edit a linked item in its original application

11.60 Set the link options for a file

11.61 Determine the status of a file

11.62 Determine the status of any and all files

11.63 Change a link

11.64 Unlink a file

11.65 Reestablish a broken link

11.66 Update one file immediately

11.67 Update all files immediately

11.68 Update the external version of a text file with the internal version

11.69 Establish a "hotlink"

11.70 Establish an external link to text that was typed directly in PageMaker

11.71 Establish a link to a graphic that came in through the Clipboard

11.72 Copy linked documents when saving a PageMaker file

11.73 Copy the files linked to your publication for remote printing

11.74 Create a template with linked files that will automatically update

11.75 Edit an imported item in an application other than the original one

11.76 Set a default to store large graphic files externally

11.77 Set link option application defaults

11.78 Set link option publication defaults

11.100 Subscribe to an Edition

11.101 Choose "Subscriber options" for a selected subscriber

11.102 Stop all editions from updating

11.122 Embed an OLE object

11.123 Edit an OLE-embedded object

11.124 Paste link an OLE object

11.125 Edit an OLE-linked object

11.132 Use the "Insert object" command to create and embed an object

—continued

Section 12 ▾ The Library Palette

12.51 Open the Library palette for the first time
12.52 Create a new Library palette once the Library palette has been established
12.53 Add text or an object to the Library palette
12.54 Place a library object in your current publication
12.55 Delete an object from a Library palette
12.56 Compress the Library after removing items
12.57 Add information in the "Item information" dialog box each time you add an item to the Library palette
12.58 Add a title, author, date, keywords, or description to an object already in the Library
12.59 Add color or grayscale images to the Library, and view them color or grayscale thumbnails
12.60 See a list of all the objects in the palette
12.61 Open an existing Library
12.62 Add text to the Library
12.73 Search for a specific object in the Library
12.74 Search the Library for a group of related objects
12.75 Have all the items in the Library show again after a search
12.76 Search for an object or group of objects using a search operator
12.77 Add an Aldus Fetch item to your Library

Section 13 ▾ Text Wrap

13.27 Create a standard rectangular text wrap around one or more objects
13.28 Change the text wrap standoff from the dialog box

13.29 Change the text wrap standoff on the object itself
13.30 Customize the text wrap to an odd shape
13.31 Add handles to a text wrap boundary
13.32 Move the handles on a text wrap boundary
13.33 Delete the handles on a text wrap boundary
13.34 Delay the text reflowing until you finish changing the boundary
13.35 Resize the graphic object without affecting the text wrap boundary
13.36 Put text, such as a caption, inside a text-wrapped object
13.37 Set a tabbed leader that goes right over the top of a wrapped object
13.38 Use text wrap on a master page
13.39 Use text wrap to create angled margins
13.40 Text wrap an initial cap
13.41 Wrap text inside a graphic object (also known as an inside-out text wrap)
13.42 Remove all text wrapping from an object or group of objects
13.43 Set text wrapping as a default
13.44 Delete the text wrapping default

Section 14 ▾ Templates

14.13 Open a copy of a template
14.14 Save your PageMaker document as a template
14.15 Open the original template
14.16 Replace a template headline with your headline
14.17 Replace an entire template story with your story
14.18 Replace a selected portion of template text with new text

14.19 Replace a template graphic with another graphic from the Clipboard or from the Scrapbook
14.20 Replace a template graphic with a new graphic file
14.29 Open a PageMaker template

Section 15 ▾ Book Publications

Book List

15.21 Create a Book List
15.22 Add a publication to the Book List
15.23 Remove a publication from the Book List
15.24 Change the order of the publications in the Book List
15.25 Copy the Book List into every other publication in the list
15.26 Print all the publications on the Book List
15.27 Print all the publications on the Book List but keep each publication's "Size" and "Source" settings
15.28 Print selected publications on the Book List
15.29 Automatically and consecutively renumber all the pages in the publications printed from the Book List
15.30 Print a selected range of pages in each of the publications in the Book List
15.31 Print an entire Book to disk as a PostScript file

Table of Contents

15.59 Tag individual paragraphs to be included in a table of contents
15.60 Use a style sheet to tag paragraphs to be included in a table of contents
15.61 Define a prefix for the page numbers in a table of contents (optional)

15.62   Create a table of contents for the current publication, using PageMaker's defaults

15.63   Create a table of contents for an entire Book List, using PageMaker's defaults

15.64   Change the presentation of the page numbers

15.65   Format the space between the entry and the page number

15.66   Update an existing table of contents

15.67   Edit TOC styles to format the table of contents

Index

15.143   Add an index entry: enter an existing, selected word

15.144   Add an index entry: enter your own word that you want referenced to this paragraph

15.145   Enter a list of topics with no page numbers (useful as an outline or used later for topics and cross referencing)

15.146   Add an index entry with no page number reference

15.147   Create a secondary (second-level) entry (one method)

15.148   Create a secondary (second-level) entry (another method)

15.149   Add another secondary entry under the same primary topic

15.150   Create a tertiary (third-level) entry (one method)

15.151   Create a tertiary (third-level) entry (another method)

15.152   Add another tertiary entry under the same secondary topic

15.153   Check the Topic List to see what's available

15.154   Import topics

15.155   Automatically index proper names

15.156   Automatically capitalize index entries

15.157   Index all occurrences of key words

15.158   Customize entries made for keywords

15.159   Index keywords in more than one publication at the same time

15.160   Create secondary entries for keywords indexed in the "Change" dialog box

15.161   See the contents of an index marker

15.162   Move an index entry

15.163   Show all the entries before generating the actual index

15.164   Edit entries

15.165   Undo the latest index additions or deletions

15.166   Remove entries from the index

15.167   Remove all page-referenced entries from the entire index

15.168   Remove all cross-referenced entries from the entire index

15.169   Remove all cross-referenced and page-referenced entries from the entire index (which means eliminating the entire index)

15.170   Sort an entry by characters different than the entry's original characters

15.171   Sort an entry by several different sets of characters

15.172   Cross-reference an entry

15.173   Cross-reference a secondary or tertiary entry as you create the entry

15.174   Choose the type of cross-reference option you want.

15.175   Format the type style in which the cross-reference text or the page numbers appear

15.176   Show all the index entries

15.177   Show the index for the active publication only

15.178   Locate an index entry according to its reference in the "Show index" dialog box

15.179   Get rid of all those useless topics that you don't need anymore in the "Index entry…" Topic and Cross-references Lists

15.201   Create/place the index for the first time (actually put it on the page)

15.202   Update an existing index, replacing the existing one

15.203   Update an existing index without replacing the existing one

15.204   Search the index for an entry

15.205   Define a prefix for the page numbers in the index

15.206   Eliminate the entire index (the internal index, not the index that has been placed on the page)

15.207   Eliminate the index in the current publication (the internal index, not the index that has been placed on the page)

SECTION 16 ▾ COLOR

16.103   Show or hide the Color palette

16.105   Create/define a new color

16.106   Create a tint of any color

16.107   Create a color that sometimes overprints and sometimes doesn't

16.108   Edit (change) a color in the Color palette

16.109   Change the name of a color

16.110   Use the Apple Color Wheel to edit an existing color

16.111   Use a color from one of the color matching systems (one of the Libraries)

16.112   Change the color "Registration"

16.113   Change the color "Black"

16.114 Change the color "Paper"
16.115 Change the color "Paper" back to its original color (white)
16.116 Remove a color from the Color palette
16.117 Change one color into another existing color (rather than remove a color)
16.118 Copy a Color palette from another publication
16.119 Copy just one or two colors from another Color palette
16.120 Apply colors to text
16.121 Apply colors to text through style sheets
16.122 Create a shape with a colored border and a fill of a different color
16.123 Apply colors to an imported graphic
16.124 Edit an imported EPS spot color
16.125 Trap a color
16.126 Print separations of a file that contains an RGB TIFF
16.127 Create and use a custom color library
16.128 Print color separations directly from PageMaker
16.140 Set a default color for graphics
16.141 Set a default color for text

Section 17 ▾ Importing and Exporting

17.28 Check to see which import and export filters are installed
17.29 Install a filter that was not originally installed
17.30 Import a text file into the layout view
17.31 Import a text file into the Story Editor
17.32 Import a graphic
17.33 Import a "Text-only" file
17.34 Import a Microsoft Word file, with control over the Table of Contents entries, index entries, character spacing, and "Page break before" setting

17.35 Import a Microsoft Word (4 or 5) table as a graphic (PICT)
17.36 Import a Microsoft Word table as text (tab-delimited)
17.37 "Place" a Microsoft Excel spreadsheet
17.38 Import an Excel spreadsheet as a PICT
17.39 Import an Excel spreadsheet as an OLE object
17.40 Import a text file from a PC (except from Microsoft Word; see 17.34)
17.41 Import a Microsoft Word text file from a PC
17.42 Import stories from a PageMaker 4 or 5 publication
17.43 Export a PageMaker story as a text document
17.44 Drag-and-drop objects from one PageMaker publication to another
17.45 Import text or graphics through the Library palette

Converting 4.0 Mac or PC to 5.0 Mac

17.46 Convert a Macintosh PageMaker 4.01, or 4.2 publication
17.47 Transfer a PC PageMaker publication to Mac PageMaker 5.0
17.48 Use the tracking information from a previous version of PageMaker

Section 18 ▾ Saving and Reverting

18.20 Save a publication
18.21 Save changes to the publication
18.22 Save changes to the all the open pubs
18.23 Save a template
18.24 Save changes to the template before it has ever been closed
18.25 Open the original template again in order to create and save changes

18.26 Save a copy of the publication or template, with the same name, into a different folder or onto a different disk
18.27 Save a copy (a separate version) of the publication or template, with a different name, into any folder or onto any disk
18.28 Reduce the size of a publication each time you save it
18.29 Reduce the size of a PageMaker publication
18.30 Revert to the last saved version
18.31 Revert to the last mini-save version
18.32 Close the publication or quit PageMaker without saving changes
18.33 Open a publication that was closed due to a power failure or system malfunction
18.34 Copy files for remote printing when saving a PageMaker file
18.35 Copy linked documents when saving a PageMaker file
18.36 Save a screen version of the first page of your publication to catalog it in Aldus Fetch

Section 19 ▾ Printing

19.127 Use Chooser to select a printer
19.128 Print a publication
19.129 Print a variety of page ranges and non-consecutive pages
19.130 Save print specifications without printing the publication
19.131 Print items outside the boundary of the page
19.132 Manually download all the fonts in your publication
19.133 Prepare a publication for do-it-yourself remote printing (printing on a Mac at a copy center, for instance)

19.134 Prepare a publication as a PageMaker file for remote printing at a service bureau (as opposed to preparing it as a PostScript file; 19.147)

19.135 Copy the publication's Tracking Values for remote printing

19.136 Copy only the linked files that are not stored in the publication

19.137 Install another PPD

19.147 Prepare a publication as a PostScript file ("Normal" or "For separations") for remote printing at a service bureau (as opposed to preparing it as a PageMaker file; 19.134)

19.148 Create an EPS file of one or more pages in a publication.

19.149 Print a "Normal" PostScript file yourself

Aldus Additions for printing

19.178 Run the "Update PPD" Addition

19.188 Display the "Pub info…" for your active publication

19.189 Save the information in the "Pub info" dialog box

19.190 Print the pub info

19.217 Create and print a queue of publications

19.218 Remove a publication from the print queue

19.219 Temporarily override the print style assigned to a publication in the queue

19.220 Create a print style

19.221 Edit a print style

19.222 Remove a print style

19.223 Rearrange the order of publications in the print queue

19.224 Print an informational page at the end of every publication

19.225 Save a queue log

19.244 Turn a publication into a booklet ready for printing and binding

19.245 Add blank pages to a publication

19.246 Delete pages of a publication

19.247 Move pages of a publication

19.248 Use "Build booklet" to create a three-paneled brochure

SECTION 20 ▾ ALDUS ADDITIONS

20.7 Install Aldus Additions after you have already installed PageMaker

20.36 Add bullets to paragraphs in a story

20.37 Edit a bullet style

20.38 Consecutively number paragraphs in a story, starting with 1 (or I, i, A, or a)

20.39 Consecutively number paragraphs in a story, starting with a number other than 1 (or I, i, A, or a)

20.40 Change the tab of the text after you've inserted bullets or numbers

20.41 Remove bullets or numbers from a story

20.59 Create a drop cap

20.60 Select only the drop cap

20.61 Remove a drop cap from a paragraph

20.62 Create or remove drop caps in more than one paragraph at the same time

20.63 Change the leading, point size, or font of a paragraph with a drop cap

20.64 Edit the word that has the drop cap

20.76 Run the "Star Wrap" script

20.77 Run a script created in another program

20.78 Trace a script

20.79 Write and run your own script created in PageMaker

20.80 Write and run your own script created in another program and saved as text

20.121 Set a header on every right hand page of a publication, using the first instance of a style

20.122 Set a footer on every page of a publication using the last instance of a style

20.123 Add repeating text to the headers\footers.

20.124 Remove headers\footers

20.145 Rearrange the pages in a publication

20.146 Enlarge or reduce the size of the page icons

20.147 Rearrange the pages without moving any of the elements on the page

20.148 Rearrange the pages so the elements fit within the new margins and guides

20.149 View one or more of the page icons in detail

SECTION 21 ▾ SPECIAL TECHNIQUES

21.3 Custom enlarge the page view

21.4 Make Zapf Dingbat arrows point to the left, up, or down

21.5 Eliminate some master page items from a publication page, but leave others

21.6 Remove a headline from a story and make it span several columns

21.7 Adjust line breaks

21.8 Maintain consistent linespace between two separate text blocks

21.9 Keep linespacing consistent when an inline graphic has been added

21.10 Hang the punctuation

21.11 Start a publication on a left-hand page or on a double-page spread

21.12 Let go of the text or graphics that are in the loaded text icon without placing them on the page.

21.13 Prevent a word from hyphenating

21.14 Proportionally resize a PageMaker-drawn rectangle

21.15 Use Baseline-shift for special effects

21.16 Adjust the height of parentheses, hyphens, quotations marks, etc.

21.17 Use leaders for creating lines that end evenly (when you don't want to, or can't, use paragraph rules)

21.18 Print one PageMaker publication while inside another

21.19 Automatically number the pages, but prevent the front matter (title page, introduction, etc.) from being included in the numbering

21.20 Keep track of certain information about a publication, such as time spent, client comments, etc.

21.21 Arrange text in several sets of columns on one page; e.g., in a three-column format across the top two-thirds of the page and a five-column format on the bottom third

21.22 Create text up to 1300 points

21.23 Create a line of text that is longer than 22.75 inches

21.24 Prevent the last text block from expanding as text is edited

21.25 Delete multiple items as you select them

21.26 Apply the same Image Control settings to several TIFFs

21.27 Recompose all the text in the publication

21.28 Run a diagnostic on the publication, in addition to recomposing all the text

21.29 Create paragraph rules that begin outside the text block

21.30 "Crop" a graphic into an oval or circular shape

21.31 Set text flush left and right so it will adjust if the text block changes width

21.32 Create two separate paragraphs on the same line so you can create columns but still retain each one as a paragraph with style sheets

21.33 Find out what page you're on when there are more than 999 pages in your publication

21.34 Create a custom PPD file that prevents PageMaker from downloading fonts you have already downloaded

SECTION 22 ▾ HELP!

22.3 You want to use PageMaker's on-line Help

22.4 You want to reduce the file size of the publication

22.5 There is not enough room on the disk to "Save as…"

22.6 The OK button is gray when you try to "Save as…"

22.7 A file won't complete the "Save as…" process

22.8 You click the I-beam, but you don't see the insertion point

22.9 You can see the insertion point, but it is not at the left edge where you want it

22.10 You can't see the guides that you are bringing in

22.11 You can't unroll a text block, or the text block "exhibits puzzling behavior"

22.12 You lost a text block—you rolled it up (or maybe it rolled itself up) and now it has disappeared

22.13 You can't tell what page you are on

22.14 You can't align objects exactly where you want because they jump around

22.15 You want to unload the text or graphic that is in the loaded icon, but you don't want to put it on the page

22.16 You type, but no text appears on the screen

22.17 Some reverse text you created is now lost and you want to find it

22.18 Every time you type, the text shows up in a font you don't want

22.19 You draw a line, but it doesn't show up

22.20 You think you created a bunch of reverse lines and you want to get rid of them

22.21 Every time you draw a line or a box, it shows up in a line width or a fill you don't want.

22.22 Everything you draw or paste or place shows up with a text wrap around it (that is, the text jumps away from every graphic you put on the page)

22.23 The last line of a paragraph has too much linespace above it

22.24 You enlarged a character in a paragraph (like an initial cap) or you inserted an inline graphic, and it changed the linespace in a way you don't like

22.25 You changed the master page guides, but they didn't change on your publication page

22.26 You changed the leading and now the tops of the letters have disappeared

22.27 You specified paragraph rules that extend beyond the text block, but they don't show up on the screen

22.28 Paragraph rules show up where you don't want them

22.29 You converted a publication from PageMaker 4.x and the line breaks are not the same as in the original

22.30 When you type, the text squishes up

22.31 You lengthened the text block to lengthen the line, but the line length didn't change

22.32 You want to type numbers with the numeric keypad

22.33 Sometimes the numeric keypad types numbers and sometimes it moves the insertion point

22.34 You pasted or placed a graphic and it is inverted (reversed; black instead of white)

22.35 Everything you place, paste, or draw is automatically tagged with a color

22.36 A dialog box yells at you because it thinks you have inserted incorrect values, but you don't know which values it's talking about

22.37 You entered an invalid value in the Control palette and you want to reinstate the previous value

22.38 You placed or pasted a graphic, but you don't see it anywhere

22.39 You accidentally placed a giant-sized graphic in your text and now your text block won't unroll

22.40 When you try to import or place a graphic or text, PageMaker tells you "Unknown file format"

22.41 You can't change the style sheet specifications; PageMaker tells you there is a bad record index

22.42 In the Story Editor, the "Find" command or the "Change" command is gray

22.43 The Story Editor cannot find something that you know is there

22.44 The cursor is jumpy on screen even when you are making choices in dialog boxes

22.45 You can't find a graphic or text block that you dragged onto the pasteboard

22.46 You receive "Low memory" or "Out of memory" alerts, or PageMaker crashes when running certain Additions

22.47 Your computer randomly crashes, freezes, or otherwise acts weird

22.48 You get an error message saying that your publication is damaged

22.49 A font name in your menu is followed by another font name in parenthesis

22.50 PageMaker re-downloads fonts to the printer even though they are resident on the printer's hard drive or you have manually downloaded them

22.51 Your print dialog box shows duplicate paper sizes in the "Size" box

22.52 You can't call up a PostScript printer in your Print dialog box

22.53 You installed PageMaker 5 on more than one computer in a network, but it won't run on all the computers at the same time

Scenarios

#1 Setting defaults *page* 4
#2 Aligning baselines *page* 22
#3 Using the zero point *page* 28
#4 Using the keyboard to operate the Control palette *page* 164
#5 Using the line-break feature *page* 262
#6 Using Paragraph space "before" and "after" *page* 288
#7 Indents and tabs together— creating numbered paragraphs *page* 343
#8 Examples of nested indents *page* 344
#9 Using style sheets (the "create as you go" method) *page* 410
#10 Using style sheets (the "I know what I want" method) *page* 411
#11 Using "Find…" *page* 428
#12 Finding and changing text *page* 435
#13 Using text wrap on master pages *page* 585
#14 When, why, and how to create your own template *page* 590

The Aldus PageMaker manual does a pretty good job of walking you through the process of installing PageMaker. For those who hate to read manuals, or who perhaps can't find the manual, here is a brief synopsis. First, a few notes.

- You cannot simply copy the files from the floppy disks onto your hard disk; you **must** go through the installation procedure. The application itself is in two parts on separate disks; once the two parts are on the hard disk, the installer program puts them together.

- Make backup copies of your original disks using a disk copy utility like Apple Disk Copy (available free from on-line services, or the disk-to-disk method to copy (drag the icon of the original disk onto the icon of the copy disk; see *The Little Mac Book* if you don't know how to do a disk-to-disk copy with only one floppy drive). Be sure to name the new disks **exactly** the same, spaces and all, as the disks they were copied from!! Then lock your disks.

- You need System version 6.0.7 or later; Finder version 6.1.7 or later.

- You need a minimum of 10.5 megs of hard disk space to allow PageMaker to do the installing. If you install just the application itself with the minimum amount of supporting files, it will need

about 8 megs of hard disk space. If you "Install everything," it will take up about 15 megs of hard disk space.

- You need at least 4 megs of memory (RAM) to run the program; Aldus *recommends* 5–8 megs. See the following page for a few little tricks for making PageMaker function best with minimal RAM.

- The default memory allocation for Page-Maker is 2750k of RAM. But, of course, more is better; see 22.46 to increase the amount of available memory for PageMaker.

- Installing PageMaker 5.0 **does not** replace PageMaker 4.0 or 4.2, although it does replace some of the files in the Aldus folder. The new 5.0 version is installed in a separate folder, and the 5.0 documents in the Aldus folder are compatible with 4.0 and 4.2. If you leave PageMaker 4 on your hard disk, when you double-click on a PageMaker 4 document it will open in PageMaker 4. To open a PageMaker 4 document in 5.0, see 17.46.

- **Before installing** PageMaker 5.0:

- Hold down the Shift key as you restart your Mac to turn all extensions off.

- Check out the "Read me." Better yet, print both the "Read me" and "Read me2" and skim through them while PageMaker is installing.

So, here is a very brief rundown on **how to install PageMaker 5.**

1. Insert Disk 1.

2. The windows will automatically open (if they don't, double-click on the disk icon; then double-click on the folder titled "Utilities"). Double-click on the **Aldus Installer/Utility** icon.

3. You will get a window titled **Aldus Installer Main Window.** You will see some other windows on the screen; read them or ignore them, as you choose.

- In the Main Window you'll see six checkboxes. "Install everything" is selected for you. With this option checked the only choice you make is which PPDs to install.

- Instead you can check "Aldus PageMaker 5.0" and decide which other options you want to install. The "Tutorial" files include an online tutorial and all the files needed to complete the printed tutorial in the "Getting Started" manual. Check the boxes for "Filters" and "Additions" to choose which filters and Additions are installed. To install PPD files other than "General" and "Color General," you must check the box for "Printer description files."

- If you want to install the application with the minimum amount of supporting files, check only the box next to "Aldus PageMaker 5.0."

- Click **Install.**

Depending upon what you chose to install, you will see the following dialog boxes:

4. In the **Aldus filters** dialog box select the filter(s) that you want to install (see 17.8–17.20 for info on filters). I know the list looks intimidating, but it is just a list of word processing programs and graphic file formats. **Import** filters allow you to place files created in that program or format; **export** filters allow you to export PageMaker text into that program.

  - Hold down the Shift key and click on the program names that you may want to *import text from* or *export text to*. Also, be sure to select any RTF filters, ASCII and Smart ASCII filters, the Story Importer filters (for placing stories from other PageMaker publications), and any graphic formats you may be importing.

  - Click OK.

5. The **Printer description files** dialog box asks you to select the PPDs you want to install. A PPD is an PostScript Printer Description file (see 19.11–19.12). Hold

the Shift key down and click on the name of your printer *and the name of any printer you may ever want to print to,* such as the one your service bureau uses.

  - Click OK.

6. In the **Aldus Additions** dialog box all the Additions are selected for you. You can install them all (about 1.5 megs), or shift-click to select just the ones you want.

  - Click OK.

7. Now you will get the **Install files** dialog box, telling you whether there is enough room on this disk to install the program and asking where you want PageMaker to put the new folder that will contain the program. If you want the PageMaker folder right there on the hard disk, just click "Install." If you want the PageMaker folder inside another folder, double-click on the folder name in the list before you click "Install."

8. In a minute you'll get a chance to **personalize your copy of PageMaker 5.0.** Your name and company are optional, but you must enter the serial number. You must type the serial number exactly as it appears on your license agreement, including any hyphens, spaces, and zeros. If you don't enter your name now, you must reinstall the program to do so.

- When you click OK, you will be asked to confirm the data. It had better be right, because you won't be able to change it later.

9. Now the installer will just roll along, putting PageMaker together. When it is finished with Disk 1, the disk will pop out and you will be asked to insert Disk 2. When Disk 2 pops out, insert Disk 3, and so on. A nice little window tells you exactly what is going on while you wait.

When it is all finished, you will have a new folder on your hard disk titled "Aldus PageMaker 5.0." This folder contains the application itself, as well as the tutorial files (if you chose to install them), the Help file for providing online Help, and a couple other goodies. If you experience any trouble at all while installing, hang on to the installer files you see in there; they contain information about the installation. If you call Tech Support, they may want to know what the files say *(don't worry about the filters the Installer couldn't remove. Unless you received an error dialog box during installation everything is just fine).*

There will also be a folder inside your System folder titled "Aldus." That folder contains the Additions, the dictionaries, the filters, and a few other odds and ends. The PPD files, along the Shared code folder for OLE, are stored in the Extensions folder.

Aldus recommends leaving the previous version of PageMaker on your drive until all of your publications are converted to version 5.0. If you don't have enough room on your drive for both PageMaker 4 and 5, or when you are ready to delete PageMaker 4 from your drive, remove these files:

PageMaker 4.0

- Remove the Aldus PageMaker 4.0 folder from your hard drive.

- Remove the PM4 Defaults file from your System folder (System 6.0x) or the Preferences folder (System 7.x).

- Remove the Aldus prep file, the APDs folder, and the PM4 RSRC or PM4.01 RSRC file from the Aldus folder in your System folder.

PageMaker 4.2

- Remove the Aldus PageMaker 4.2 folder from your hard drive.

- Remove the PM4.2 Defaults file from your System folder (System 6.0x) or the Preferences folder (System 7.x).

- Remove the Aldus prep file, and the PM4.2 RSRC file from the Aldus folder in your System folder.

Setting up a PostScript printer for PageMaker:

- Turn on your printer (with some printers this is not necessary).

- From the Apple menu select the Chooser (see 19.127).

- In the left hand side of the window select the "LaserWriter 8" icon.

- Select your printer's name from the list of the available printers on the right.

- Click "Setup…."

- Click "Auto setup."

- Click OK when the process is finished.

- Close the Chooser window.

- If you have added fonts or RAM to your printer, please see the "Update PPD" Addition (19.171–19.178) so you can optimize PageMaker's printing speed.

Running PageMaker on 5 megs of RAM:

- "Save as…" regularly to keep the file size as small as possible (18.1–18.5; 18.29).

- Keep your System as small as possible: install only the fonts you use regularly; eliminate any unnecessary Desk Accessories, CDEVs, and INITs.

- Install the minimum number of filters and PPDs.

- Set the "Detailed graphics" option to either "Normal" or "Gray out" (1.229). Set the "Greek text below" option to a higher value (1.236).

Installing the 5.0a Patcher kit

Since Aldus first released PageMaker 5, they have introduced a "patcher kit" intended to solve a number of annoying problems that came with the original 5.0 version. The kit is available either from the Aldus forums on CompuServe or America Online or as part of the Filter/Driver Pack Plus available from Aldus or an Apple dealer.

The 5.0a patch fixes the following problems:

- TIFFs printing either too dark on certain imagesetters, or as black boxes with some FAX or QuickDraw printer drivers.
- Text in documents with a lot of EPS graphics not printing all the way through.
- EPS graphics converted from PageMaker 3.0 losing their link information and therefore printing either bitmapped or at low resolution.
- Black-and-white bitmapped inline graphics being assigned "Registration" as a default color no matter what you had specified as a default color.

To find out if you already have the patcher installed, select the PageMaker application and resource file icons and choose "Get Info" from the File menu (Command I).

The PageMaker application should be in the PageMaker 5.0 folder on your hard drive (unless you renamed the folder); the "PM5.0 RSRC" resource file should be in the Aldus folder in the System folder (unless you moved it). If either one has already been updated, it will read "Version: Aldus PageMaker 5.0a" in the Get Info dialog box. **Important: If it is already updated, do not run the patcher utilities! Updating either file twice can corrupt it!**

To update your copy of PageMaker 5.0 to PageMaker 5.0a:

- Make backup copies of the original PageMaker application file ("Aldus PageMaker 5.0" in your PageMaker folder) and the original PageMaker resource file (PM5.0 RSRC" in the Aldus folder in your System Folder) by copying the files into another folder on your hard drive.
- Copy the Patcher kit onto your hard drive.
- Quit all applications and restart your computer with all extensions turned off including any virus detection software (hold down the Shift key as you restart your machine).
- Double-click on the icon for the "Aldus PageMaker 5.0 Patch" utility found in the PageMaker 5.0a Patcher folder.

- A box will appear reminding you to make a backup of your original application. If you have not already done so, do it now. Click "Patch."
- Select the original PageMaker 5.0 application in the PageMaker 5.0 folder; click OK.
- Click OK when the patcher is through running the update.
- **Right away,** open the "PM5.0 RSRC Patch" utility.
- Click "Patch" when you see the reminder to back up your original "PM5.0 RSRC" file.
- Select the original "PM5.0 RSRC" file in the Aldus folder inside your System folder; click OK.
- Click OK when the patcher is through running the update.
- Launch and run PageMaker to be sure the updates were correctly installed. If so, you can delete the backup copies and the patcher from your hard drive.

If you get the message "-109 error," either while trying to update PageMaker 5.0, or while launching the updated version of PageMaker, then you must start over from scratch. Reinstall PageMaker completely **from the original disks** and immediately run the update again. This should solve the problem.

The chart below provides the entry codes for **invisible characters.** They are indispensable when using the "Find" or the "Change" dialog boxes, or when formatting with the "Index format" dialog box. *These are not for typing regular text.*

To find, change, or enter this character:

To find, change, or enter this character:	Type this:
	The ^ symbol, a caret, is Shift 6.
Spacebar space	*type a space*
Non-breaking space	Option Spacebar *or* ^S *or* ^s
Non-breaking slash	^/
Non-breaking hyphen	^~
Em space	^M *or* ^m
En space	^>
Thin space	^<
Any kind of blank space	^W *or* ^w
En dash	^=
Em dash	^_ *(Shift-hyphen)*
Return	^P *or* ^p
Line break	^N *or* ^n
Tab	^T *or* ^t
Discretionary hyphen	^ - *(hyphen)*
Automatic page number	^# *or* ^3
Index marker	^ ;
Caret	^^
Inline graphic (in the Story Editor)	Control Q
Wildcard character	^?

These **alternate characters** can be entered directly into your text. In the Story Editor or in a dialog box, many of these characters will appear to be blank boxes. That's okay—if you are using an outline font (which you should be; 19.29–19.32), you will see the actual characters on your screen and they will print.

Character	Type it this way	What is it?
'	Option]	opening single quote
,	Option Shift]	apostrophe; closing single quote
"	Option [	opening double quote
"	Option Shift [	closing double quote
‹	Option Shift 3	opening single French quote (guillemets)
›	Option Shift 4	closing single French quote (guillemets)
«	Option \ *(notice that's a backslash)*	opening double French quote (guillemets)
»	Option Shift \	closing double French quote (guillemets)
-	Command - *(hyphen)*	discretionary hyphen (5.234–5.235; 5.249–5.251)
-	Command Option - *(hyphen)*	non-wordbreaking hyphen
–	Option - *(hyphen)*	en dash
—	Option Shift - *(hyphen)*	em dash
…	Option ;	ellipsis
®	Option r	registration symbol
©	Option g	copyright symbol
TM	Option 2	trademark symbol
•	Option 8	bullet
·	Option Shift 9	raised period (·)
˙	Option h	really raised period (˙), or a dot
°	Option Shift 8	degree symbol
/	Option Shift 1	fraction bar (slash: /; fraction bar: ⁄)
fi	Option Shift 5	ligature for the f-and-i letter combination
fl	Option Shift 6	ligature for the f-and-l letter combination

*The font of these three symbols will usually match the font in which you are typing.***

900

Char.	Type it this way	What is it?
œ	Option q	lowercase oe diphthong, or ligature
Œ	Option Shift q	uppercase OE diphthong, or ligature
æ	Option '	lowercase ae diphthong, or ligature
Æ	Option Shift '	uppercase AE diphthong, or ligature
¶	Option 7	paragraph symbol
§	Option 6	section symbol
†	Option t	dagger
‡	Option Shift 7	double dagger
◊	Option Shift v	diamond, lozenge
¢	Option 4 *(the dollar sign)*	U.S. cent
£	Option 3 *(pound sign: #)*	British pound sterling
¥	Option y *(y for yen)*	Japanese yen
¤	Option Shift 2	general currency symbol
¿	Option Shift / *(question mark)*	inverted question mark
¡	Option 1 *(exclamation point)*	inverted exclamation point
ß	Option s	German double s (ss) *or* Beta
ø	Option o	lowercase letter o with slash
Ø	Option Shift o	uppercase letter o with slash
≠	Option =	does-not-equal sign
≈	Option x	approximately-equals sign
≤	Option < *(above the comma)*	less-than-or-equal-to sign
≥	Option > *(above the period)*	greater-than-or-equal-to sign
±	Option Shift =	plus-or-minus sign
÷	Option /	division sign
√	Option v	radical sign; square root
ƒ	Option f	function symbol *or* freeze

Char.	Type it this way	What is it?
∫	Option b	integral symbol
∞	Option 5	infinity symbol
¬	Option l *(the letter el)*	logical NOT, negation symbol
‰	Option Shift r	salinity symbol
ı	Option Shift b	dotless i
ª	Option 9	feminine ordinal indicator
º	Option 0 *(zero)*	masculine ordinal indicator
Δ	Option j	uppercase delta
Σ	Option w	uppercase sigma; summation
Ω	Option z	uppercase omega
∏	Option Shift p	uppercase pi
π	Option p	lowercase pi
μ	Option m	lowercase mu
∂	Option d	lowercase delta
ˆ	Option Shift i	circumflex*
˜	Option Shift n	tilde*
¯	Option Shift , *(comma)*	macron*
˘	Option Shift . *(period)*	breve*
˙	Option h	dot*
˚	Option k	ring*

* *These accent marks cannot be placed above a letter, as can the accent marks on the next page. If you need to place one of these over a character, you can certainly do it by kerning extensively:* ō *(5.151–5.168).*

***If you need one of these symbols as a serif or a sans serif and you can't get it in your current font, use the font* **Symbol** *and these key combinations:*

serif		sans serif	
®	Option [	®	Option Shift 0 (zero)
©	Option Shift [	©	Option Shift w
™	Option]	™	Option Shift r

These are the five main **accent marks:**

~	tilde
¨	diaeresis (umlaut)
^	circumflex
´	acute
`	grave

Where the accent is just applied above a regular character you apply in two steps. For others, you can press a keyboard combination to get the character with its accent mark attached. The accent marks over capital letters may look a little odd on the screen (sometimes they scrunch the letter and sometimes most of the accent disappears). When you redraw the screen (change view, etc.), the accent marks will re-appear. They print fine.

Tilde	Press	Let go, then press
~	Option n	Spacebar
ã	Option n	a
Ã	Option n	Shift a
ñ	Option n	n
Ñ	Option n	Shift n
õ	Option n	o
Õ	Option n	Shift o

Diaeresis	Press	Let go, then press
¨	Option u	Spacebar
ä	Option u	a
Ä	Option u	Shift a
ë	Option u	e
Ë	Option Shift u	
ï	Option u	i
Ï	Option Shift f	
ö	Option u	o
Ö	Option u	Shift o
ü	Option u	u
Ü	Option u	Shift u
ÿ	Option u	y
Ÿ	Option Shift `	

(` is next to 1, or next to Spacebar; the same key as the regular ~ key)

Circumflex	Press	Let go, then press
^	Option i	Spacebar
â	Option i	a
Â	Option Shift m	
ê	Option i	e
Ê	Option i	Shift e
î	Option i	i
Î	Option Shift d	
ô	Option i	o
Ô	Option Shift j	
û	Option i	u
Û	Option i	Shift u

Acute	Press	Let go, then press
´	Option e	Spacebar
á	Option e	a
Á	Option e *or* Option Shift y	Shift a
é	Option e	e
É	Option e	Shift e
í	Option e	i
Í	Option e *or* Option Shift s	Shift i
ó	Option e	o
Ó	Option e *or* Option Shift h	Shift o
ú	Option e	u
Ú	Option e *or* Option Shift ;	Shift u

Grave	Press	Let go, then press
`	Option `	Spacebar

(` is next to 1, or next to Spacebar; the same key as the regular ~ key)

Grave	Press	Let go, then press
à	Option `	a
À	Option `	Shift a
è	Option `	e
È	Option `	Shift e
ì	Option `	i
Ì	Option `	Shift i
ò	Option `	o
Ò	Option ` *or* Option Shift l (*letter el*)	Shift o
ù	Option `	u
Ù	Option `	Shift u

Miscellaneous:	Press:
å	Option a
Å	Option Shift a
ç	Option c
Ç	Option Shift c

	a	b	c	d	e	f	g	h	i	j	k	l	m	n	o	p	q	r	s	t	u	v	w	x	y	z
Zapf	✺	✹	✻	✼	❄	❅	❆	✤	✣	✥	✦	●	○	■	□	◻	◻	◻	▲	▼	◆	❖	◗	❘	❘	❙
Shift	✡	✚	✜	♣	✠	◆	✧	★	☆	★	☆	★	✭	✮	✯	✰	✱	✲	✳	✴	✵	✶	✷	✸	✹	✺
Option	{	❺	}	❶	♠	⑤	♦	→	✿	⑦	✈	③	⑩	❞	⑩	❹	❻	♣	☙	①	④	❷	⑥	⑨	❽
Opt Shift	)	➵	(	⇨	➤	⇦	⇨	⇨	⇨	⇨		⇨	➧	➚	④	❸	❺	➡	⇨	➡	➡	↕	➢	➤	➧	➻

	`	1	2	3	4	5	6	7	8	9	0	-	=	[	]	\	;	'	,	.	/	spacebar
Zapf	✿	➛	➜	✓	✔	✕	✖	✗	✘	✚	✎	✐	†	✶	✷	✸	✢	❂	✌	✎	✏	
Shift	❞	✄	✄	✄	✄	☎	❀	✆	☛	✈	✉	✿	☞	'	"	'	✚	✄	✢	✝	✞	
Option	→	②	♥	❣	❣	⑤	♥	❦	❧	❻	❼	❼	②	❾	→	⑧	⑩	❾	⑦	⑧	↔	❶
Option Shift	➙	➚	➙	➡	➝	➞	➟	➠	❡	➡	➢	❽	❻	❿	→	⑨	⊃	③	➳	➳	①	❶

Opt Sh /	①	Opt u Spcbar	①	Opt d	❶	Opt Spcbar	❶	n (outline)	□	(and shadow) ◻
Opt 1	②	Opt =	②	Opt w	❷	Opt ` then Sh a	❷	l (outline)	○	(and shadow) ◖
Opt l	③	Opt Sh '	③	Opt Sh p	❸	Opt n then Sh a	❸	t (outline)	▽	(and shadow) ▽
Opt v	④	Opt Sh o	④	Opt p	❹	Opt n then Sh o	❹	s (outline)	△	(and shadow) △
Opt f	⑤	Opt 5	⑤	Opt b	❺	Opt Sh q	❺	u (outline)	◇	(and shadow) ◇
Opt x	⑥	Opt Sh =	⑥	Opt q	❻	Opt q	❻	Opt 6 (outline)	♡	(and shadow) ♡
Opt j	⑦	Opt ,	⑦	Opt 0	❼	Opt -	❼			
Opt \	⑧	Opt .	⑧	Opt z	❽	Opt Sh -	❽			
Opt Sh \	⑨	Opt y	⑨	Opt '	❾	Opt [	❾			
Opt ;	⑩	Opt m	⑩	Opt o	❿	Opt Sh [	❿			

Outline and Shadow Zapf Dingbats will laser print, but not imageset.

You can't make the outline bold.

Sh]	"
Sh `	"
Sh [	'
Sh \	'

☞ ✈ ➠ ✄ Type a dingbat into its own text block; rotate the text (21.4).

Opt *means press the Option key.* Sh *means press the Shift key.* Spcbar *means press the Spacebar.*

From the Toolbox:

ᐳ Pointer tool   1.182; 2.13

Ⅰ Text tool; the I-beam   4.12

+ Lines and shapes;
the crossbar cursor   2.12

⌗ Cropping tool   10.143

⁜ Rotating tool   2.8; 2.87

Loaded text icons:

▤ Manual flow   4.89; 4.90

▥ Autoflow   4.89; 4.92

▦ Semi-autoflow   4.89; 4.91

Loaded graphic icons:

▣ Paint-type   10.15; 10.126

▨ PICT format   10.23; 10.126

▦ TIFF format   10.32; 10.126

▩ EPS format   10.39; 10.126

▦ Scrapbook file   10.126; 10.130

⊠ Library palette item   12.19

Text block windowshade loops:

⨀ Very beginning of story   4.107

⊞ Has more text preceding   4.107

▽ Very end of story   4.108

⊞ Has more text following,
and it is placed on a page   4.109

⊟ Has more text following,
but it has not been placed
anywhere (overset text)   4.109

Stretching and moving text and graphics:

↕ Vertical stretch   2.45; 10.138

↔ Horizontal stretch   2.45; 10.138

⤡ Bi-directional stretch   2.45; 10.138

⤢ Bi-directional stretch   2.45

✛ Moving a text block
or an independent
graphic   2.27; 10.137

⇳ Moving an inline graphic
vertically on its baseline   10.246

Story Editor:

· Space marker   9.42

¶ Paragraph marker   9.42

→ Tab marker   9.42

↵ Line break marker
(Shift-Return)   9.42

⊞ Automatic page number
marker   9.18

⬘ Index marker   9.18

▨ Inline graphic marker   9.18

⬚ End of story   9.18

□ Special character that isn't
in the Story Editor font   9.65

Image control:

◣ Preset setting: Normal   10.205

◥ Preset setting: Reverse   10.206

▰ Preset setting: Posterized   10.207

◢ Preset setting: Solarized   10.208

Links dialog box:

Blank; element is up-to-date
or is not linked   11.42

? Cannot find the linked
element's external file   11.46

◆ Linked external file has
been modified; internal
file will be updated
automatically   11.44

◇ Linked external file has
been modified; internal file
will **not** be updated
automatically   11.43

△ Both the internal and the
external files have been
modified   11.45

> Microsoft Windows link not
completely supported   11.47

¿ Link may not print as
expected   11.48

File compression codes:

(P) Moderate compression of
black-and-white or palette-
color TIFFs   10.152

(L) Maximum compression of
black-and-white or palette-
color TIFFs   10.152

(LD) Moderate compression of
grayscale or color TIFFs   10.152

(LD2) Maximum compression of
grayscale or color TIFFs   10.152

(U) Decompressed TIFF   10.152

Style sheet:

+ Style has an override   8.35

* Style is imported   8.36

Menus:

⇧ Shift key

⌘ Command key

Spacebar (blank, as in
Type Style "Normal")

… Dialog box will appear

▶ Submenu will appear

✓ Command is chosen, or "on"

⌦ Grey items indicate command
cannot be used

Miscellaneous:

𝆑 Grabber hand to move page
or to move cropped graphic
within frame   1.126; 10.143

? Menu-sensitive Help   22.3

⌚ Wait a minute or two

RM Right master page
automatic page number
placeholder   1.147a

LM Left master page
automatic page number
placeholder   1.147a

PB Pasteboard automatic page
number placeholder   1.150

OV Overset text   4.179; 15.178

Gray or yellow bar over text:
line violates the "Keeps" rules
or desired letter/word
spacing   1.227; 4.331

Graphics set to
"Gray out"   10.155

Selection
marquee   1.208; 1.215

Everything on this page is done with the *text tool* chosen and with text selected or an insertion point flashing.

Select text

(4.189–4.203; also see 4.204)

One word	Double-click
One paragraph	Triple-click
A range of text	Press-and-drag
A large range of text	Click at one end, press Shift, click at the other end
Entire story	Click anywhere in the story, press Command A
With the keypad	See **Numeric keypad**
Deselect text	Click anywhere

Text formatting

(4.189–4.249)

Normal	Command Shift Spacebar
Bold	Command Shift B
Italic	Command Shift I
Outline	Command Shift D
Shadow	Command Shift W
Strikethru	Command Shift /
Underline	Command Shift U
All caps	Command Shift K
Small caps	Command Shift H
Superscript	Command Shift +
Subscript	Command Shift - (hyphen)
Remove kerning	Command Option K
Remove tracking	Command Shift Q
Remove set width	Command Shift X
Apply autoleading	Command Shift A

Paragraph alignment

(4.243–4.248)

Align left	Command Shift L
Align right	Command Shift R
Align center	Command Shift C
Justify	Command Shift J
Force justify	Command Shift F

Kern

(5.151–5.172; arrow keys or the Control palette: 5.168–5.169)

Fine kern closer	Option Delete
Fine kern apart	Option Shift Delete
Coarse kern closer	Command Delete
Coarse kern apart	Command Shift Delete
Remove kerning	Command Option K
Remove tracking	Command Shift Q

Change point size

(4.230)

One point smaller	Command Option Shift <
One point larger	Command Option Shift >
One standard size smaller	Command Shift <
One standard size larger	Command Shift >

Text flow

(4.87–4.100)

Temporarily change Auto to Manual	Command
Temporarily change Manual to Auto	Command
Temporarily change to Semi-Auto	Shift
Interrupt Autoflow	Command Period
Unload the text without placing it	Click on the pointer tool, or press Command Spacebar

Numeric keypad

(1.325–1.327; 4.204)

Use the numeric keypad to move the insertion point. Hold the Shift key down to *select* the text as the insertion point moves. Use the text tool, of course.

With Caps Lock down, you will type numbers. Or you can press Clear (num lock) to use the numbers.

Left one character	4, or LeftArrow
Left one word	Command 4
To beginning of line	7
To beginning of sentence	Command 7
Right one character	6, or RightArrow
Right one word	Command 6
To end of line	1
To end of sentence	Command 1
Up one line	8, or UpArrow
Up one paragraph	Command 8
Up a screen	9, or PageUp key
To top of story	Command 9, or Home key
Down one line	2, or DownArrow
Down one paragraph	Command 2
Down a screen	3, or PageDown key
To bottom of story	Command 3, or End key

Non-breaking spaces

(5.217–5.228)

Em space	Command Shift M
En space	Command Shift N
Thin space	Command Shift T
Fixed space	Option Spacebar
Non-breaking hyphen	Command Option -
Non-breaking slash	Command Option /

To next page	Command Tab
To previous page	Command Shift Tab
From master page, return to layout page	Command Tab
Jump six page icons	Press Shift and click on either page icon arrow
Instant scroll to last page icon	Press Command and click on right page icon arrow
Instant scroll to first page icon	Press Command and click on left page icon arrow
Go to page... (number of page)	Command G; enter page number and click Return

Change page view
Use any tool
(1.110–1.119)

To Actual Size	Press Command Option and click on the area to view
To Fit in Window	Command W; or Command Option click
To 200%	Command Option Shift and click on the area you want to view
To 400%	Command 4
To 25%	Command 0 *(zero)*
To 50%	Command 5
To 75%	Command 7
Custom (up to 800%)	Command Spacebar and marquee the area you want to enlarge
View at next size	Command Spacebar and click on the area to view

Miscellaneous

Select entire story	With the **text tool,** click anywhere in story; press Command A
Select all objects (text blocks and graphics)	With the **pointer tool** selected, press Command A
Cancel out of dialog boxes	Press Command Period
Cancel out of nested dialog boxes	Press Command Option Period
OK out of dialog boxes	Return or Enter
OK out of nested dialog boxes	Option Return
View actual fonts	Press-and-hold Option Shift while choosing "Font"
Edit style sheet	Command-click on style name in Style palette
Edit color style sheet	Command-click on color name in Color palette
Index entry	Command Shift ;
Switch to pointer tool	Command Spacebar
Switch to the magnifying tool	Command Spacebar; hold
Switch to the reducing tool	Command Option Spacebar
Recompose text	Press Option while choosing "Hyphenation"
Move publication page	Option; press-and-drag
Menu-sensitive Help	Command ?, or Help key
Cancel Help	Command Period, or click in the Toolbox
Power paste	Command Option V
Print bypassing the PPD	Press Option while choosing "Print..." (File menu)

All the Graphic shortcuts are done with the *pointer tool* chosen.

Graphics
(Section 10)

Select an object under another layer (1.211)	Hold the Command key down; click. Each click will select an object on the next layer deep
Restrain a PageMaker-drawn line to 45° angles, a rectangle to a square, or an oval to a circle	Hold the Shift key down while drawing a line, a rectangle, or an oval
Change a PageMaker-drawn rectangle into a square, or an oval into a circle	Hold the Shift key down. Point to a handle; press and hold
Straighten a crooked PageMaker-drawn line	Hold the Shift key down; press on a handle
Resize a graphic proportionally	Hold the Shift key down while dragging a handle
Resize a bitmapped graphic to fit the resolution of your target printer	Hold the Command key while resizing; (see 10.141)
Restore a graphic to its original proportions	Hold the Shift key down. Point to a handle; press and hold
Temporarily view a grayscale image or color TIFF at high-res	Hold the Control key anytime you redraw the screen (see 10.158)
Compress a TIFF or a MacPaint graphic as you place it (10.152)	When you are about to place the file, press the Command, Option, and Shift keys before you click OK. Hold the keys to the count of two

Some functions have more than one shortcut; for the sake of clarity, only one is printed here. The Delete key is also known as the Backspace key on some keyboards.

© 1994 Robin Williams, *Peachpit's PageMaker 5 Companion*

Palette view

(3.19–3.20; 4.220)

Display or Hide	Command ' *(apostrophe)*
Activate or Deactivate	Command ` *(grave)*
Switch between character-view and paragraph-view	Command Shift `

Keyboard shortcuts

(3.101–3.119)

Move to next option	Tab
Move to previous option	Shift Tab
Move within options	Arrow keys when the option is active
Turn an option on or off or apply options	Spacebar when the option is active
Move the cursor within an edit box	Arrow keys when the option is active
Apply changes and deactivate the palette	Return
Apply changes and keep the palette active	Shift Return
Apply changes and move to the next option	Tab (character-view and paragraph-view only)
Apply changes and move to the previous option	Shift Tab (character- and paragraph-view only)
Display the last valid value for an option	Esc
Select a different unit of measure	Command Option M when the option is active
Type numbers in an edit box	Numbers on the numeric keypad or keyboard

Object-view palette

when Proxy is active (3.116–3.119)

Select a reference point	Arrow keys or Numbers on the numeric keypad
Change the type of reference point	Spacebar
Change reference point to a box	Press M
Change reference point to an arrow	Press S

Object-view palette

when the Control palette is **inactive** (3.115)

Nudge a selected object	Arrow keys
Power-nudge a selected object	Command Arrow keys

Apply button icons

(3.41–3.47)

🖼	Paint-type	10.15; 10.126
📷	PICT format	10.23; 10.126
🖼	TIFF format	10.32; 10.126
🖼	EPS format	10.39; 10.126
🖼	OLE format	11.103–11.132
☐	PageMaker object	Section 2
🖼	Multiple objects	3.45
A	Text block	3.43
🖼	Text tool	3.44; Section 4

Pointer tool selected; 3.60

Text tool selected, character-view; see page 223

Text tool selected, paragraph-view; see page 253

Object selected; see page 142

Line selected; 3.90

Graphic selected; see page 142

Text block selected; see page 142

Multiple objects selected; 3.45

Inline graphic selected; 10.248

These Additions can be purchased either from the independent developer or from the Aldus Developers Cooperative (ADC). The list of Additions available from ADC is frequently updated. For current information (but not technical support!) call 1-800-685-3547.

This is the Spring 1994 listing of Additions available from the Aldus Developers Cooperative. Other Additions are available through independent developers.

ADDWARE S.A.S.

AreaFit – regulate the space used by text.
MemoClip – attach electronic memos to publications.
Plas-L – automatic page layout.
Plas-T – supply ready-formatted files to the layout designer.
TrackSet – convert publications between 4.2 & 5.0 while maintaining the tracking values.

ALDUS CORPORATION

InfoPublisher Database Addition – automate publishing info from a database.
Aldus CheckList – analyze font and printer info to help prevent printing problems.

ARTLAB

PDF NAVigator – add navigational capability to publications viewed with Adobe Acrobat.

AZALEA SOFTWARE

POSTNet Bar-code Additions – create high-quality bar codes.
C39 Tools – make Code 39 symbols for identification, inventory and tracking.
POSTools – create bar-codes for Zip codes.
UPCTools – Type 1 fonts for bar-codes; create codes from any appliation.

COMMON SENSE COMMUNICATIONS

Active Help – CD-ROM plays multimedia Help movies from within PageMaker.

DIAMAR INTERACTIVE CORP

DiAMAR Portfolios – stock photography on CD.

EDCO SERVICES, INC.

PMproKit – text tools for total text control.
PMcopyFit – control over vertical justification.
PMhyphen-perfect hyphenation – hyphenation dictionary that you can customize.

HUMAN SOFTWARE

SpeechWare – replace repetitive keystroke and mouse movements with speech.

INTEGRATED SOFTWARE, INC.

AA Celler – design tool for complex layouts.
AA Nudge – place and move page elements.
AA Shadow – instant drop shadows.

IRIS GRAPHICS LTD.

Iris Designer – create custom borders and designs.

LOGIC ARTS CORPORATION

DesignKit for PageMaker – templates and tips from Chuck Green; includes clip-art.

MANAGING EDITOR SOFTWARE, INC.

AdForce – automated ad dummying system.

MAPSOFT COMPUTER SERVICES LTD.

KeyJuggler – character mapping for any key.
Mapsoft Style Groups Addition – group styles for importing and exporting.
Mapsoft Additions Palette – create a custom floating palette for Additions.

PERSONAL TRAINING SYSTEMS

Personal Training Systems Tutorials – beginning, intermediate, and advanced tutorials.

SHADETREE MARKETING

Fræmz Proportional Borders Libraries – distortion-free, scalable, decorative borders.
Patternz – distortion-free, scalable, fill patterns.

STEP 2

DataShaper – database import filter.

SUNDAE SOFTWARE

Baseline Grid – set baselines from one location.
Galley Oops! – hunt down typographical errors.
Gridzoid – instant designs for forms and grids.
Marksmaker – gang jobs for film.
Pandora – generate unfolded box layouts.
Resizer – expand, reduce, stretch anything to fit.
Safari – guide manager to .001 inch accuracy.

SYNEX

Bar Code Pro – create EPS graphics of bar codes.

TECHPOOL

ArtSPREE – EPS and vector image control.
Transverter Pro – a complete PostScript-equivalent interpreter for translating files across applications and platforms.

VIRGINIA SYSTEMS

Sonar Bookends – automatically generate an index based on word frequency; handle names and numbers.

ZEPHYR DESIGN

Zephyr DisBatch – turn scripts into workhorses, includes seven scripts.
Zephyr CleanSweep – update all your 4.x files to 5.0 and optimize your publications.
Zephyr Grids – create custom grid designs; apply, store and scale them.
Zephyr Palettes – create custom font sets and use a floating palette for font info.
Zephyr SmartAlign 1.2 – alignment accuracy to $\frac{1}{1440}$ of an inch.
Zephyr SuperSnap 2.0 – floating palette for snapping and resizing.

SYMBOLS

"# of pages," 1.23, 1.28
200% page view, 1.117
25% page view, 1.113
400% page view, 1.118
50% page view, 1.114
75% page view, 1.115
800% page view, 1.96, 1.124

A

"About PageMaker," 17.28
Accent marks, 4.359
   using from key caps, 1.333
"Accept" (Index entries), 15.141
Acta Advantage (version 1.0)
   import filter for, 17.10
Actual size page view, 1.116, 1.120-
   1.121
"Add" (Index entries), 15.117, 15.141
"Add cont'd line...," 4.160-4.167,
   4.183-4.184
   editing jump lines, 4.185
"Add index entry" dialog box
   with text selected, 15.79
   without text selected, 15.98
"Add tab," 6.63
"Add word to user dictionary,"
   5.253-5.254
   dialog box, 5.242-5.248, 9.120
Additions. *See* Aldus Additions
Adobe Illustrator, 10.39, 10.42,
   11.80
   "Include preview for," 10.97
   saving files in, 10.97
Adobe Photoshop, 10.16, 10.31,
   11.80
   saving files in, 10.100
Adobe Systems Incorporated, 5.92
Adobe Type Manager (ATM), 19.29,
   19.41
"After," 5.74-5.76, 5.79-5.84, 5.92-5.93
ALDTMP00, ALDTMP01, 18.33

Aldus Additions, pp. 785-812
   "Add cont'd line...," 4.160-4.167,
      4.183-4.184
   Additions for text, 4.130-4.187
   "Balance columns...," 4.168-4.178,
      4.186-4.187
   "Build booklet...," 19.226-19.248
   "Bullets and numbering...," 20.8-20.41
   "Create color library...," 16.128
   "Create keyline...," 10.255, 10.292-
      10.302, 10.306-10.307
   "Display pub info...," 19.179-19.190
   "Display story info...," 4.139-4.150,
      4.181
   "Display textblock info...," 4.151-4.159,
      4.182
   "Drop cap...," 20.42-20.64
   "Edit tracks...," 5.193-5.209
   "Expert kerning...," 5.173-5.179
   "Find overset text," 4.133-4.135, 4.179
   impact in the System folder, 20.3
   installing Aldus Additions, 20.7
   list of, 20.1
   "List styles used," 8.44-8.45
   "Open stories," 9.10, 9.46
   "Open template...," 14.21-14.26 595
   "Printer styles...," 19.191-19.225
   "PS Group it," 10.254, 10.259-10.291
   "PS Ungroup it," 10.267, 10.271-
      10.289
   "Run script...," 4.262, 20.65-20.80
   "Running headers\footers...," 20.81-
      20.124
   see which Additions are installed,
      20.6
   "Sort pages...," 20.125-20.149
   "Traverse textblocks...," 4.136-4.138,
      4.180
   "Update PPD...," 19.171-19.178
Aldus Fetch, 12.38, 12.77
   save file preview for, 18.36
Aldus Freehand, 10.39, 10.42, 11.80
   importing colors from, 16.86

   saving files in, 10.98
   updating files from, 10.98
Aldus Persuasion, 10.109
Aldus PrePrint, 10.109, 16.36, 16.141
Aldus TrapWise, 16.30, 16.127
"Alert before updating," 11.56-11.57
Alert boxes
   about links, 11.27
   "Cannot place this file." 17.13, 22.40
   "Cannot save as. Disk full." 22.5
   "Continue from beginning of story?"
      9.61, 9.78
   "Couldn't add word to dictionary,"
      5.255
   "Couldn't delete word from
      dictionary," 5.254
   "Include complete copy?" 10.104-
      10.105
   "Invalid___...," 22.36, 22.37
   "Low memory," 22.46
   "Out of memory," 22.46
   "Replace existing document," 18.29
   "Revert to last mini-save," 18.31
   "Revert to last-saved version," 18.30
   "Save changes before closing?" 18.32
   "This story has not been placed," 9.83
   "Word removed," 9.122
   "Word was not found in user
      dictionary," 9.122
Algorithm, 5.237
"Align to grid," 5.97-5.111
   with inline graphics, 5.108-5.109
   with "snap to rulers," 5.107
Alignment, 4.243, 4.299, 4.312
   examples of, 4.244-4.248
   of insertion point, 4.27
   of baselines (Scenario), 1.57
   on using the spacebar for, 6.3
   paragraph, 4.242-4.248, 4.293
   changing, 4.327
   "Paragraph specs" dialog box, 4.299
   paragraph-view Control palette
      option, 4.312

   text block
      flush left and right, 20.31
      type, 4.243-4.249, 4.293
      changing, 4.242
"All linked files"
   saving, 18.35
"All to process," 16.138, 19.119
Alternate characters
   "Bullets and numbering..."
      Addition, 20.8
   using from key caps, 1.331-1.332
Andrews, Edward, p. 754
"Angle" (Image control), 10.177-
   10.178, 10.182
   default, 10.178
   examples of, 10.181-10.183
"Angle:" 16.139, 19.110, 19.120-
   19.121
Appendices, pp. 867-908
Apple Color Wheel, 16.38, 16.54-
   16.61
   editing existing colors through,
      16.110
Apple File Exchange utility
   importing text files from PC, 17.40
   transferring PC PageMaker pubs to
      Mac PageMaker pubs, 17.47
Apple LaserWriter, 10.39
   graphic examples from, 10.92-10.93
   halftoning capabilities of, 10.77
Application defaults, 1.7-1.8, 1.10,
   1.13
"Apply" button
   Image control, 10.167
   indents/tabs ruler, 6.29, 6.31, 6.35
"Apply" button (Control palette, 3.41-
   3.47
   applying changes, 3.47
   different button icons, 3.42-3.46
**Arrow button (in "Create index
   entry"),** 15.81, 15.128
Arrow keys
   kerning with, 5.168-5.170

moving cursor through the Control palette edit boxes, 3.110

moving insertion point with, 1.328

selecting an active reference point with, 3.106

selecting text with, 1.326, 1.328

Arrows (Zapf Dingbats)
changing direction of, 21.4

"As all lowercase," 5.248

"As inline graphic," 10.235

"As new story," 4.54-4.56

Ascender," 5.51-5.56

ASCII, 17.11, 17.19. *See also* Smart ASCII
export filter, 17.18,
Smart ASCII sort order, 15.134

Ashford, Ms. Daisy, p. 544

Asterisk (in Style palette), 8.36

ATM. *See* Adobe Type Manager

Attributes
"Attributes" dialog box, 9.58, 9.74
PageMaker can import, 17.16-17.17
paragraph, 4.288
text
changing certain, 9.68
finding certain, 9.51-9.52, 9.62-9.63

Autoflow, 4.92-4.93, 4.97
"Display all pages," 1.231
overriding, 4.98
stopping, 4.99

Auto kerning, 5.5, 5.160-5.162, 5.167
determining point size of type for, 5.167
turning on or off, 5.166

Autoleading, 5.19-5.24
adjusting, 10.243
changing default value of, 5.68
figuring value of, 5.59
inline graphics and, 10.228, 10.232-10.233
using "Control palette," 5.60

"Auto overlap," 19.76

"Auto renumbering," 15.19, 15.29

Awazu, Kiyoshi, p. 170

B

"Background Printing," 19.18, 19.127
causing the cursor to be jumpy, 22.44

Bacon, Francis, p. 834

"Bad record index"
fixing, 8.60
running a global diagnostic, 21.28

"Balance columns..." Addition, 4.168-4.178, 4.186-4.187

"Based on," 8.15, 8.21-8.27, 8.50-8.51
creating new styles using, 8.51
in the paragraph-view Control palette, 8.50

"Baseline" leading, 5.37, 5.45-5.50
examples of, 5.44, 5.58
how to use, 5.65
paragraph rules and, 7.33-7.35

"Baseline-offset" option, 3.86, 10.248

"Baseline-shift" option, 4.205, 4.218
for special effects, 21.15
in the Control palette, 4.218
shifting text, 4.263
using to create bullets, 4.264
using to create two paragraphs on the same line, 21.32

Baselines, 7.20
aligning (Scenario), 1.57
grids and, 5.97-5.111
inline graphics and, 5.108, 10.220, 10.232
adjusting, 10.243, 10.246, 10.248
paragraph rules and, 7.20-7.21

Basics, pp. 1-108

Baskerville, John, p. 288

Beauvoir, Simone de, p. 197

"Before," 5.77-5.80, 5.92, 5.94

"Before x-ref:" 15.197

Behrens, Peter, p. 413

"Between entries:" 15.195

"Between entry and page number:" 15.56, 15.65

"Between page #s:" 15.194

Bi-level bitmap, 10.15, 10.71, 10.168-10.169

Billings, Josh, p. 242

Bitmapped fonts, 19.27-19.28, 19.31

Bitmapped graphics, 10.15, 10.32. *See also* TIFF
examples of, 10.37
image controlling, 10.162-10.211
"magic resizing," 10.141-10.142
paint programs, 10.16
place icon for, 10.126
saving as EPS, 10.40

"Black and white," 10.168-10.170

Black and white graphics, 10.32, 10.168-10.170
angles for halftoning, 10.177
"Brightness" and, 10.60
examples of 10.62, 10.64
"Contrast" and, 10.60, 10.193-10.194
lightening, 10.210
"Lightness" and, 10.189
scanning, 10.58-10.59
"Screened," 10.190

Blank spaces, 5.217-5.228

Blaschek, Gunther, p. 105

"Book," 19.64

Book List, 15.6-15.31
adding a publication to, 15.22
"Book publication list" dialog box, 15.13-15.20
copying into other pubs on list, 15.25
creating, 15.21
lost in files converted from PageMaker 4.x, 15.21
numbering pages of publications in, 15.10
automatically and consecutively, 15.29
printing, 15.26
keeping original "Size" and

"Source," 15.27
selected page ranges, 15.30
selected publications from, 15.28
to disk as a PostScript file, 15.31
with renumbered pages, 15.29
re-ordering publications in, 15.24
removing publications from, 15.23
style sheets in, 15.12
templates in, 15.12

"Book publication list" dialog box, 15.13-15.20

Book Publications, pp. 601-664.
See also Book List; Index; Table of Contents

Bookbinding, the art of, p. 778

Booklet, creating, p. 19.244

Borders
changing, 2.34-2.35
reversing, 2.37
transparent patterned borders, 2.36

"Bottom"
in "Paragraph rule options," 7.24-7.32, 7.46-7.51

Boundary
of inline graphics, 10.220, 10.244

Bounding box, 1.319-1.322
creating to type into, 1.319, 4.26
drag-placing graphics into, 1.322
drag-placing text into, 1.321, 4.26
pasting text into, 1.320

"Break," "No break," 4.205, 4.241

Breaks
keeps
column, 4.335
page, 4.336
paragraph, 4.337
line, 4.348-4.353
paragraph, 4.350
preventing, 4.241

Brewer, Alisandra, p. 423

Bridges (communication), 17.40, 17.47

"Brightness" (Color), 16.61

"Brightness" (Graphics), 10.60

when scanning black & white images, 10.60
    examples of, 10.62, 10.64
"Bring to front," 1.216
    for inline graphics, 10.223
Brochure
    creating a three-paneled, 19.248
Broken links (re-establishing), 11.65
Brown, Mrs., pp. 287, 295
"Build booklet..." Addition, 19.169, 19.226-19.230
    adding blank pages, 19.245
    creating a 3-panel brochure, 19.248
    creep, 19.239, 19.244
    deleting pages, 19.246
    dialog box, 19.231-19.240
    guidelines for using, 19.241
    layout options, 19.242-19.244
    limits of, 19.229-19.230
    master page items, 19.228
    page numbering, 19.237
    rearranging pages, 19.247
    turning a pub into a booklet, 19.244
Bullets, 4.358
    "Bullets & numbering..." Addition, 20.8-20.41
    creating, 4.264
"Bullets & numbering..." Addition, 20.8-20.41
    adding bullets to a story, 20.36
    adjusting tabs in, 20.9, 20.40
    dialog boxes, 20.13-20.22, 20.29-20.35
    editing bullet styles, 20.22
    numbering paragraphs, 20.29, 20.38-20.39
    removing, 20.20, 20.41
Butcher, Janet, p. 764
Byron, Lord, p. 144

C

Caen, Herb, pp. 312, 766
Calendaring, 5.92

Calendar template, 14.29
Calkins, Kent, p. 158
Campbell, Roy, p. 854
Camus, Albert, p. 146
"Cannot open dictionary for this paragraph," 9.119
"Cannot place this file...," 17.13, 22.40
"Cannot save as. Disk full." 22.5
Canvas, 10.23, 10.31, 10.122
    saving files in, 10.95
"Capitalize" index entries, 15.142, 15.156
Caps
    all caps, 4.251
    as an attribute in "Find," and "Change," 9.51, 9.62, 9.79
    "Drop cap..." Addition, 20.42-20.64
    in Spell Checker, 9.92-9.93
    initial
        creating, 21.15
        problems with linespace of, 22.24
        text wrapping, 13.40
    small, 4.205, 4.215, 4.251
        changing, 4.251, 4.252
"Card stock," 19.72
Carroll, Louis, p. 821
"Cascade," 1.154-1.159, 1.175
    in Story Editor, 9.33
    view a different window, 1.176
"Case," 4.205, 4.215
    changing, 4.251
Catt, Serena Pickering, 10.205-10.208
Cella, Richard Thomas, p. 355
Center align, 4.246
"Center page in print area," 19.74
Chan, Augustine, 17.28
"Change," 9.24, 9.67-9.82
    attributes, 9.80
    back to "Any," 9.62, 9.64, 9.78
    by eliminating character attributes, 9.81
    characters with no special attributes, 9.78

characters with special attributes, 9.79
    invisible or special characters, 9.82
    "Options" in, 9.70-9.75
    what to do when gray, 22.42
    window, 9.67-9.76
    choosing, 9.76
Character
    formatting, 4.196-4.199
    invisible
        inputting into "Change" box, 9.82
        inputting into "Find" box, 9.65
    special and alternate, 1.331, 4.264, 4.355-4.359
    wildcard
        finding, 9.66
Character codes, 15.200
Character-view Control palette
    "Baseline-shift," option 4.218
    changing default specs, 4.240
    character-view button, 4.209
    displaying, 4.220, 4.225
    "Font" option, 4.210
        changing the font, 4.228
    "Kerning" option, 4.213
        changing, 5.168-5.171
    "Leading" option, 4.216
        changing the leading, 4.234, 5.60, 5.62
    navigating with the keyboard, 4.226-4.227
        important info about, 4.224
    power nudge, 3.11, 4.222
    "Set width" option, 4.217, 4.238
        changing, 5.215-5.216
    style, case, and position options, 4.215
    turning on and off with the keyboard, 4.227
    toggle with paragraph-view, 4.200
    "Tracking" option, 4.212, 5.190
    "Type size" option, 4.211

changing from the keyboard, 4.230
    changing type size, 4.229
    "Type specs" buttons, 4.215
    ways to use, 4.221-4.224
        buttons, 3.10, 4.223
        edit boxes, 3.13, 4.223
        menus, 3.12, 4.223
        nudge buttons, 3.11, 4.222
Chermayoff, Ivan, p. 65
"Choose editor," 10.147, 11.75
Chooser, 19.127
    Background printing, 19.18, 19.127
    dialog box, 19.21
    LaserWriter 8 setup, 19.20-19.25
    selecting printers from, 19.127
    setting up a PostScript printer, 19.20-19.25
    "Setup" dialog box, 19.21-19.25
    "Printer Info," 19.24
Ciceros, 1.323
Circle. *See also* Fills (graphic)
    changing an oval into a perfect, 2.48
    changing border of, 2.34-2.35
    changing fill pattern of, 2.49
    changing shape of, 2.50
    drawing the perfect, 2.47
    drawing tool for, 2.10
    reversing border of, 2.37
    transparent patterned border, 2.36
ClarisWorks, 10.23
    saving files in, 10.96
"Clear"
    from the Edit menu, 1.284
    from the Keypad, 1.324-1.325
    from the Scrapbook, 1.315
Clipboard, 1.273-1.286
    copying into, 1.281, 10.133
    copying OLE objects, 11.103-11.132
        insufficient memory and, 11.108
    copying text into
        turning text into a graphic, 10.151
        with pointer tool, 1.277-1.278

with text tool, 1.277, 1.279
cutting into, 1.280, 10.133
inline graphics and
    pasting into, 10.234
    replacing, 10.237
limits, 1.274-1.276
linking graphics from, 11.71
multiple paste, 1.287
"Paste special," 10.110-10.119
pasting from, 1.282
power-paste, 1.283
replacing inline graphics with a
    graphics from, 14.19
using text from to replace, 4.270
using with other software programs,
    1.275
using with templates, 14.19
viewing contents of, 1.285
"Close story," 9.25, 9.83
close all open stories, 9.47
Closing
multiple publications, 1.174
without saving changes, 18.32
Codes for compressed TIFFs, 10.152
"Collate," 19.56
Color, pp. 665-696
Apple Color Wheel, 16.38, 16.54-16.61
    editing existing colors through,
        16.110
applying
    to graphics, 10.159, 16.123
    to text, 16.120-16.121
"Black"
    changing, 16.113
"Brightness," 16.61
changing
    in graphics, 16.124
    name of, 16.109
"Commercial Printing Guide," 16.1
create a tint of any color, 16.106
creating/defining new, 16.105
CMYK (process colors), 16.41, 16.47-
    16.48

color libraries of, 16.53
"Edit color," 16.76-16.84
    limitations of colors in, 16.35,
        16.52
defaults, 16.97-16.102
    for graphics, 16.125
    for text, 16.126
    unwanted, 22.35
"Define colors" dialog box, 16.69-
    16.75
drag-and-drop between pubs, 16.119
drawn boxes
    creating two-color, 16.122
"Edit color" dialog box, 16.76-16.84
    CMYK, 16.47-16.48
    HLS, 16.44-16.46
    RGB, 16.42-16.43
    shortcut to, 16.77
editing/changing, 16.108
    through Apple Color Wheel,
        16.110
four-color separation process, 16.31-
    16.36
    dialog box for printing, 16.130-
        16.139
    preparing a file for, 16.140
    reds and metallics in, 16.35
HSB model, 16.38
    "Edit color," 16.44-16.46
"Hue," 16.61
imported EPS colors, 16.85-16.86
    editing spot colors, 16.24
libraries, 16.49-16.53
minimums and maximums, 16.1
models, 16.37-16.61
one-color jobs, 16.6-16.9
palette, 16.85-16.96
    copy from one pub to another,
        16.118
    copy selected colors from, 16.119
    hide, 16.104
    recognizing types of colors in,
        16.91-16.93, 16.9

removing colors from, 16.116
    show, 16.103
"Paper," 16.63
    changing, 16.114-16.115
    color vs. fill, 16.64-16.68
percentage values (tints), 16.7-16.8,
    16.15
    creating and applying, 16.106
"Preserve EPS colors," 16.136
printing, 16.129-16.140, 19.105-
    19.121
"Registration," 16.62
    changing, 16.112
    removing, 16.116
"Restore original color," 16.123
RGB model, 16.38
    "Edit color," 16.42-16.43
"Saturation," 16.61
spot color (multi-color jobs), 16.10-
    16.15
    changing to process colors,
        16.138
    color libraries of, 16.53
    knockouts for, 16.24, 16.27-16.30
    overprinting, 16.24-16.26, 16.107
    separations (overlays) for, 16.16-
        16.22
    tints and (percentage values or
        screens), 16.15
    traps for, 16.29-16.30
style sheets, 16.69, 16.78
    adding to text style sheets, 16.121
    applying color through, 16.120-
        16.121
tagging with, 16.69
tint screens, 16.7-16.8
    creating, 16.106
    overlapping to create colors,
        16.15
"Color"
in Type specs dialog box, 4.205,
    4.265
"Color" (Print), 19.105-19.121

"Composites," 19.115
    dialog box, 16.129-16.139
"Mirror," 19.116
"Negative," 19.116
"Optimized screen:" 16.134, 19.121
    printing composites, 16.129
    printing separations, 16.130-16.139,
        19.105, 19.117-19.121
Color libraries, 16.49-16.53
    creating custom, 16.128
    in "Edit color," dialog box, 16.84
        process color libraries, 16.53
        spot color libraries, 16.53
    selecting a color from, 16.111
Color models, 16.37-16.41
    CMYK, 16.47-16.48
    Color Libraries, 16.49-16.53
    HLS, 16.44-16.46
    RGB, 16.42-16.43
Color palette, 16.85-16.96
    adding colors in EPS files, 16.86, 16.96
    copying from one pub to another,
        16.118
    copying selected colors, 16.119
    hide, 16.104
    in Story Editor, 9.13, 9.16
    recognizing
        EPS colors in, 16.96
        process colors in, 16.91
        spot colors in, 16.92
        tints in, 16.93
    removing colors from, 16.116
    show, 16.103
Color rules
    creating, 7.57
Color separation. *See* Four-color
    separation; Spot color
Color Studio, 10.109
"Column break before," 4.335
Column guides
    bringing to front, 1.93b
    examples of, 1.77
    hiding, 1.92a

locking in place, 1.94a
master page
    changing on pub. page, 1.89
    reverting customized back to,
    1.90
    setting up, 1.137
    showing on customized publica-
    tion page, 1.138
    sending to back, 1.93a
    showing, 1.92b
"Snap to guides," 1.65
unlocking, 1.94b
Columns and column guides, 1.76-
1.94
    "Balance columns...," Addition,
    4.168-4.178
    creating
        different sets on one page, 21.21
        even, 4.186-4.187
        equal, 1.84
        unequal, 1.85
    creating two paragraphs on the same
    line, 21.32
    deleting all, 1.91
    faking two styles in one paragraph,
    21.32
    headlines spanning several, 21.6
    minimums and maximums, 1.76
    reverting to equal widths, 1.88
    space between
        widening or narrowing, 1.87
    widening or narrowing, 1.86
"Commercial Printing Guide," 10.292,
16.1
Communication bridges, 17.40, 17.47
Companion files
    when going to a service bureau,
    19.157
Composing stick, p. 15
"Composite," 19.115
    "Grayscale," 19.115
    "Print colors in black," 19.115
Compressed TIFF codes, 10.152

Compressing
    documents, 18.3-18.5, 18.29
        automatically when saving, 18.5
    graphics, 10.34, 10.152-10.153
        decompressing, 10.154
Conch system, 11.50
Condensing
    documents, 18.3-18.5, 18.29
    graphics, 10.34, 10.152-10.153
        decompressing, 10.154
    type, 4.238
Confucious, p. 829
Consistency
    using a style manual
        custom dictionary as, 9.127
        publication info as, 19.179
    using templates to ensure, 14.6
"Continue from beginning of story?"
9.61, 9.78
"Contrast," 10.162, 10.192-10.195
    examples of various settings for,
    10.196-10.203
    light pixels and, 10.192
    when scanning black & white images,
    10.60
    with black & white images, 10.193-
    10.194
Control bars, 10.162, 10.172, 10.188-
10.195
    examples of settings for, 10.196-10.203
Control palette, pp. 133-164
    "Apply" button, 3.41-3.47
    basics, 3.7-3.14
    buttons, 3.10
    changing unit of measure, 3.22
        for nudges, 3.24
        "on the fly," 3.114
    character-view
        basics, 3.7-3.14, 4.221-4.224
        "Baseline-shift" option, 3.86, 10.248
        changing default specs, 4.240
        displaying, 4.220, 4.225
        "Font" option, 4.210, 4.228

    "Kerning" option, 4.213
    "Leading" option, 4.216, 4.234
        making several changes at once,
        4.239
        navigating with the keyboard,
        4.224, 4.226-4.227
    "Set width" option, 4.217, 4.238
        toggling with paragraph-view,
        4.200
    "Tracking" option, 4.212
    "Type size" option, 4.211, 4.229-
    4.230
    "Type specs" buttons, 4.215, 4.227
    constrain objects to rulers or guides,
    3.25
    edit boxes, 3.13
        using arithmetic in, 3.14
    examples of palettes, 3.6
    graphics and, 10.14
        "Baseline-offset" option, 10.248
        cropping, 10.144
        "magic-resizing," 10.142
        resizing, 10.139
        transforming (skew, rotate,
        reflect), 10.145
        transforming grouped items,
        10.290
    in Story Editor, 9.16, 9.44
    inline graphics
        adjust baseline using, 10.248
    invalid entry, 22.37
    measurement system, 3.15
    menus, 3.12
    more precise than rulers, 3.2
    moving objects, 1.201
    nudge buttons, 3.11
        changing measurement system,
        3.18
        changing nudge amount, 3.17
    object-view Control palette, 3.32-3.40
        "Baseline-offset" option, 10.248
        "Percentage-scaling" option, 3.33
        "Position" option, 3.32

    "Printer-resolution-scaling" option,
    3.75
    "Proportional-scaling" option, 3.34
    "Reflecting" options, 3.38
    "Rotating" option, 3.35, 3.76-3.79
    "Scaling and Cropping" options,
    3.74
    "Sizing" option, 3.36, 3.63-3.69
    "Skewing" option, 3.37, 3.80-3.81
    options overview, 3.1
    paragraph-view Control palette,
    4.300-4.320
        "Align-to-grid" option, 4.315
        alignment buttons, 4.311
        "Cursor-position indicator," 4.304,
        4.318
        "Grid-size" option, 4.307
        Indent options, 4.305, 4.312-4.313
        "Paragraph space after," 4.314
        "Paragraph space before," 4.306
        paragraph-view button, 4.313
        "Style" option, 4.303
    power-nudge, 3.11
    "Preferences" choices, 3.15-3.18
    Proxy, 3.48-3.57
        arrow reference point, 3.54-3.55
        box reference point, 3.52-3.53
        choosing an active reference
        point, 3.50-3.51
        importance of position of an
        active reference point, 3.56
        reference points, 3.49-3.57
        recalling last valid entry, 3.69, 3.113
        set default to always display, 3.21
    setting indents, 6.83
    style sheets
        create new style using, 8.50
        to make active and inactive, 3.20
        to show and to hide, 3.19
    using the keyboard to operate, 3.101-
    3.109
        activate options, 3.102-3.106
        apply changes, 3.107

change the measurement system "on the fly," 3.114
change the type of reference point, 3.118
display last valid entry, 3.113
display the palette, 3.102
move an object, 3.115
move the cursor thru the edit box, 3.119
select an active reference point using Numeric keypad, 3.117
select an an active reference point using the arrow keys, 3.116,
Shift Tab to previous option, 3.105
Tab to next option, 3.103-3.105
turn a button on or off, 3.111
undo mistakes, 3.101
X and Y coordinates, 3.60
Control palettes, pp. 134-135
Converting
earlier PM versions to PM 5.0, 17.46
PC files, 17.21
filters for, 17.40
PC PageMaker pub, 17.47
"Convert quotes," 4.51, 4.61
"Copies," 19.55
Copy centers
preparing pub for printing at, 19.134
as a PostScript file, 19.147
do-it-yourself, 19.133
"Copy" existing styles, 8.13, 8.20, 8.56
Copying
documents, 18.13, 18.26-18.27
with a new name, 18.13, 18.27
graphics
drag-and-drop method, 10.134
into the Clipboard, 10.133
into the Scrapbook, 1.313
using the Library palette, 10.131

inline graphics, 10.240
linked documents
while saving, 18.34-18.35
master guides to publication pages, 1.61, 1.138
objects or characters, 1.281
style sheets
all, 8.20, 8.56
using the Library palette, 8.58
with drag-and-drop text, 8.37, 8.57
text, 4.268
blocks, 4.126
drag-and-drop between pubs, 4.86
from "View" in Story Importer, 4.85
with the pointer tool, 1.277-1.278
with the text tool, 1.277, 1.279
Copy machines
reproducing on, 10.185
Corner styles (for drawing tool) 2.15
changing, 2.44
"Couldn't add word to dictionary," 5.255
"Couldn't delete word from dictionary," 5.254
Crashes, PageMaker
due to fonts, 22.47
due to memory allocation, 22.46
due to old filters, 22.47
freezes or crashes
possible ways around, 22.47
"Network Copy Detection," 22.53
System error, 22.47
when printing particular pubs, 22.47
"Create color library..." Addition, 16.128
"Create index..." command, 15.76
"Create index" dialog box, 15.184
"Create keyline..." Addition, 10.292
as a design feature, 10.292, 10.302
dialog box, 10.293-10.297

"Attributes," 10.297
"Extend," 10.293, 10.300
trapping feature, 10.295
fill and line weight, 10.297, 10.299
with inline graphics, 10.301
"Create table of contents" dialog box, 15.51-15.56
Creep, p. 778
creep value, 19.239, 19.244
Crop marks, 19.96, 19.131
Cropping, 10.143
Control palette "Cropping" option, 10.144
creating reverse circles or ovals for, 21.30
inline graphics, 10.220
scanned images, 10.57
uncropping, 10.143
Cropping tool, 1.187
Cross-reference (X-ref), 15.82, 15.97, 15.106-15.113
"Denoted by" options, 15.106-15.108, 15.174
ways to, 15.109, 15.112, 15.172-15.173
problem with, 15.113
"x-ref override," 15.175
"X-ref override:" 15.104, 15.175
"X-ref..." (Index), 15.103
Cursor. *See also* Appendix H
acting funny on screen, 22.44
"Cursor position indicator," 4.304, 4.318
drawing tool crossbar, 2.12
for placing graphics, 10.19, 10.126
Scrapbook icon, 10.130
four-headed arrow, 2.27, 2.45
loaded text, 3.88-3.89
cancelling, 4.100
PageMaker's online Help, 22.3
rotating tool, 2.87
stop jerking on the screen, 2.33
text tool "I-beam," 4.12

Custom enlarge page view, 1.124, 21.3
Custom headers and footers, 20.81
"Custom" line
and paragraph rules, 7.37
"Custom line" dialog box, 2.51-2.61
Customizing
headers and footers, 20.123
leaders with tabs, 6.72-6.73
text wraps, 13.30
vertical rulers, 1.226
Cutting
graphics
inline, 10.240
into the Clipboard, 10.133
into the Scrapbook, 1.313
objects or characters, 1.280
text, 4.267
text blocks, 4.125
with the keypad, 1.327
CMYK (process colors), 16.41, 16.47.
See also Four-color separation
"Edit color," 16.47-16.48
importance of color proofs, 16.52
limitations of colors in, 16.35
process color libraries, 16.53
reproduction basics, 16.31-16.35

D

Dair, Carl, pp. xviii, 563
Dashed lines. *See also* Patterned lines
point sizes of, 7.40
Dashes (em and en), 4.358
Davis, Bette, p. 527
DCA
DCA/RTF export filter, 17.18
import filter, 17.40
Decimal tabs, 6.13
"Default font," 1.244, 1.262
Defaults, 1.6-1.18, 4.20-4.22, 4.36
application, 1.7-1.8, 1.10, 1.13
for updating links, 11.14a, 11.77
color, 16.97-16.102

for graphics, 16.101, 16.125
for text, 16.99, 16.126
Control palette, to display, 3.21
drawing tool, 2.82-2.84
in style sheets, 8.78
insertion point, 4.20-4.23
leading, 5.64
letter spacing, 5.136
linking, 11.77-11.78
list of what you can set as, 1.18
PPD, 1.13
print
    "Include downloadables," 19.103
    setting publication, 19.66-19.67,
      19.130
    symbol font, 19.104
print specifications, 19.130
printer, 1.16
publication, 1.9-1.11, 1.16
    for updating links, 11.14b, 11.78
    reverting to original PageMaker, 1.17
setting (Scenario), 1.11
Story Editor display, 9.49
text, 4.36, 4.365-4.366
    in insertion point, 4.20-4.24
text wrap
    deleting, 13.44
    setting, 13.43
type specs, 4.20-4.22, 4.365-4.366
word spacing, 5.122-5.123
"Define colors" dialog box, 10.159,
    16.69-16.75
"Define styles," 8.7-8.13
"Delete tab," 6.65
  Deleting. *See also* Clear; Cutting
    as you select, 21.25
    drawn objects, 2.25-2.26
    graphics, 10.136
      inline, 10.241-10.242
    many objects, 2.26
    pages, 1.29, 1.128
    tabs, 6.65
    text, 4.266

text blocks, 4.120-4.121, 4.127
text or graphics from the Scrap-
    book, 1.315
words from user dictionary, 9.122
"Denoted by:" 15.105
Deselecting, 1.186
  all objects, 1.206
  certain objects from a group, 1.210
DeskDraw, 10.23
  saving files in, 10.96
DeskPaint, 10.16
  saving files in, 10.99
Desktop publishing service
    bureaus. *See* Service Bureaus
DeskWriter
  resolution examples, 2.20, 19.8
"Detailed graphics," 1.222
  adjusting resolution of, 1.229,
    10.155-10.158
  set maximum memory, 1.232
Diagnostic
  running on a publication, 21.28
Diagonal line tool, 2.6
Diagonal lines. *See* Lines (drawing)
Dialog boxes
  "Add index entry"
    with text selected, 15.79
    without text selected, 15.98
  "Add word to user dictionary," 5.242-
    5.248
  Apple Color Wheel, 16.54-16.61
  "Book publication list," 15.13-15.20
  "Build booklet," 19.231
  "Bullets and numbering"
    bullet style, 20.13-20.21
    "Edit bullet," 20.22
    numbering style, 20.29-20.35
  "Chooser," 19.21
  Color libraries, 16.49-16.53
    accessing, 16.84
  "Color" print, 16.129-16.139
  "Copy styles," 8.20
  "Create index," 15.184

"Create keyline," 10.293-10.297
"Create table of contents," 15.51-
  15.56
"Custom line," 2.51-2.61
  CMYK "Edit color," 16.47-16.48
"Define colors," 16.69-16.75
"Define styles," 8.8-8.13
"Drop cap," 20.51
"Edit colors," 16.76-16.84
  Libraries, 16.84
"Edit style," 8.18, 8.24
"Export," 9.39
  tagging with style sheets, 8.77
"Fill and line," 2.63-2.74
  finding default values for, 22.36
  HSB "Edit color," 16.44-16.46
"Hyphenation, 5.229
"Image control," 10.162-10.167
"Import to Story Editor," 9.36, 9.38
"Indents/Tabs," 6.18, 6.33-6.48
"Index format," 15.188
"Inline specifications," 10.243
Library palette
  "Create new library," 12.11-12.12
  "Item information," 12.41, 12.46-
    12.49
  "Open library," 12.13-12.15, 12.61
  "Search library," 12.63-12.72
"Library Preferences," 12.44-12.45
"Links," 11.31-11.39
"Microsoft Word 4.0/5.0 import
  filter," 17.34
"Multiple paste," 1.291, 1.300-1.302
"Other preferences," 1.223
"Page numbering," 1.24
"Page setup," 1.23-1.24
"PANOSE font matching" system,
  1.255
  "Show mapping results," 1.264
"Paragraph rules," 7.5-7.12
  "options," 7.5, 7.23-7.32
  "Paragraph specifications," 4.299
  "options," 4.295, 4.329-4.347

"Paste special" 10.114-10.115
"Place document" 4.42-4.54
"Place Excel range:," 17.37
"Preferences,"
  for Story Editor, 9.48
"Preferences," 1.222
"Print document" (to non-PostScript
  printers), 19.122
"Print document," 19.47
  "Color," 19.105
  "Options," 19.86
  "Paper," 19.65
"Printer styles," 19.195-19.205
"PS Ungroup it," 10.278-10.283
Publish and Subscribe
  "Subscribe to," 11.88
  "Subscriber options," 11.93
  RGB "Edit color," 16.42-16.43
"Rules," 7.5
  "options," 7.5
"Run script," 20.68-20.71
  "Trace script," 20.72-20.75
"Running headers\footers," 20.89
  "Create custom content," 20.115
"Save as," 18.6-18.19
"Select cross-reference topic," 15.114
"Select topic," 15.114
"Show index," 15.119
"Sort pages," 20.135-20.140
  "Options," 20.141-20.144
"Spacing attributes, 5.10-5.11
"Text wrap," 13.6-13.9
  icons, 13.10-13.15
"Text-only import filter," 17.21-17.27
"This story has not been placed,"
  9.83, 17.31
"Type specs," 4.205
  "options," 4.205, 4.255-4.260
DictED, 9.132, 9.137
Dictionary, 4.294, 5.242
  changing default for, 9.125
  changing hyphenation of word in,
    5.255

changing or adding, 4.328
check spelling with more than one, 9.123
foreign language, 9.96-9.100
in Story Editor's Spell Checker, 9.95-9.126
installing, 9.100-9.101
legal, 9.96, 9.101-9.103
medical, 9.96, 9.101-9.103
Merriam-Webster, 9.97, 9.120
paragraph specific nature of, 9.96
problems in opening, 9.119
user dictionary, 5.242, 9.97-9.99
    "Add word to user dictionary," 5.229, 5.242-5.248
    adding words to, 9.120
    copying, 9.126
    hyphenating words in, 5.253, 9.121
    in foreign language dictionaries, 9.100
    making a new, 9.126
    removing words from, 5.254, 9.122
    switching, 9.124
"Dictionary Editor" utility, 9.127-9.141
    adding words to existing user dictionary, 9.129, 9.138
    creating user dictionaries, 9.128, 9.139
    DictEd, 9.132, 9.137
    "Export" dictionary words, 9.133
    hyphenation with, 9.130, 9.138
    "Import" a text-only file, 9.132, 9.140
    installing a user dictionary, 9.141
    using "Find," 9.131, 9.137
Digital halftoning, 10.66
Dingbat arrows
    changing direction of, 21.4
Dischy. See Discretionary hyphen
Discretionary hyphens, 5.234-5.235
    entering, 5.249
    removing, 5.250
"Disk full." 22.5
Disks
    unlocking, 22.6

Disk space (conserving)
    compressing graphics, 10.34, 10.152-10.153
    "Save as," 18.3-18.5, 18.29
Displaying
    contents of Clipboard, 1.285
    detailed graphics, 1.229
    different pages, 1.100-1.105, 1.107-1.109
    guides, 1.64b
    palettes
        Color, 16.103
        Control, 3.19
        Library, 12.8
        Style, 8.46
        Tool, 2.5
    pub info, 19.188
    rulers on screen, 1.52a
    Style palette, 8.46a
    styles
        "List styles used" Addition, 8.44-8.45
"Display ¶," 9.17, 9.49
"Display pub info..." Addition, 19.167, 19.179-19.190
    print pub info, 19.190
    saving info, 19.189
"Display story info," 4.139-4.150, 4.181
"Display style names," 9.16, 9.43, 9.49
"Display textblock info...," 4.151-4.159, 4.182
Distorted graphics
    restoring, 10.140
Dividing text blocks, 4.122
Document Content Architecture. See DCA
Dot-screen angle, 10.162
Dots per inch, 10.15, 10.20
    example of, 10.90
    scanning grayscales, 10.90
Dotted lines. See also Patterned lines
    point sizes of, 7.40
Double lines. See also Patterned lines
    point sizes of, 7.40

Double-sided publication
    creating, 1.35
    icons for, 1.35, 1.99, 1.133
Downloadable fonts, 19.33-19.35
    avoiding, 10.28
    creating a custom PPD for, 21.34
    downloading
        automatically, 19.42-19.43
        manually, 19.45, 19.132
        permanently, 19.46, 19.166
    font downloader, 19.44
    organizing in menus, 19.35
    RAM and, 19.40, 19.43, 19.45
    with PICT files, 10.28
DPI, 10.15, 10.20, 10.90
    example of, 10.90
Drag-and-drop between open pubs
    colors, 16.119
    graphics, 10.134
    objects, 1.179
        inline, 1.180
    text, 1.167, 1.179-1.180, 4.86
        copying style sheets, 8.37, 8.57
Drag-placing
    graphics
        from outside PM, 10.127
        graphics into a bounding box, 1.322
    text into a bounding box, 1.321
Draw-type (vector) graphics, 10.23
    place icon for, 10.126
    saving as EPS, 10.40
    saving files in, 10.96
Drawing
    a perfect circle, 2.47
    a perfect square, 2.42
    objects, 2.23
        in perfect alignment with guidelines, 2.31
        in perfect alignment with ruler tick marks, 2.32
        problem defaults with, 22.21
Drawing tools, pp. 109-132
    choosing, 2.5

cropping tool, 2.11
cursor, 2.12
defaults, 2.2, 2.82-2.84
    for application, 2.83
    for publication, 2.82
    for text wrap, 2.84
    problems with, 22.21
diagonal line tool, 2.6
oval/circle tool, 2.10
perpendicular line tool, 2.7
rectangle tool, 2.9
    corner styles available for, 2.15
rotating tool, 2.8
toolbox, 2.14
Drawn boxes
    setting a color default for, 16.101, 16.125
Drivers, 19.13-19.15
Drop caps. See Drop cap Addition, Initial caps
"Drop cap" Addition, 20.42-20.64
    and paragraph alignment, 20.48-20.49
    changing a paragraph's formatting, 20.64
    creating in multiple paragraphs, 20.62
    dialog box, 20.51
    editing a word with a drop cap, 20.60
    removing a drop cap, 20.61
    selecting a drop cap, 20.60
"Duplex," 19.85
    Odd/even as substitute, 19.61
Duplicate words
    finding in Spell Checker, 9.92
Duplicating
    objects with multiple paste, 1.287-1.310
    publications, 18.26-18.27
    style sheets, 8.20, 8.56-8.58
Durant, Will, p. 34
Dwiggins, W.A., pp. 244, 401

E

"Edit colors" dialog box, 16.76-16.84
  shortcut to, 16.77
"Edit layout," 9.23
Edit menu
  in Story Editor, 9.23
"Edit original," 10.108, 10.146, 11.59
  "Choose editor," 10.147, 11.75
  "Excel Worksheet object," 11.123
  from within the Story Editor, 10.148
  "Microsoft Word object," 11.123
"Edit story," 9.23, 9.30
"Edit" styles, 8.11, 8.18, 8.53
"Edit tracks" Addition, 5.193-5.209
  "Tracking Values," 5.204-5.209
    copy, 5.204
    copy from one font to another,
      5.206
    edit, 5.205
    print font, 5.208
    proof tracking values, 5.207
    reset, 5.209
  window, 5.195-5.203
Editing text, 4.10-4.17
  in Story Editor, 9.41
  rotated, 4.274
  in Story Editor, 4.283
Editions
  editing, 11.87, 11.98, 11.101
  link options, 11.84, 11.101
  PageMaker as a subscriber, 11.80,
    11.100
  "Stop all editions," 11.86, 11.102
    overriding, 11.102
  "Subscribe to...," 11.88-11.92
  "Subscriber options...," 11.93-11.99
800% page view, 1.96, 1.124
Einstein, Albert, p. *xx*
Ellipses, 4.357-4.358
Em dashes, 4.358
Em space, 5.217-5.218, 5.222
  creating, 5.223

Embedding objects (OLE), 11.103-
  11.113
  "Insert object," 11.114, 11.126-11.132
Emerson, Ralph Waldo, pp. 696, 833
En dashes, 4.358
En space, 5.217, 5.219, 5.222
  creating, 5.224
Encapsulated PostScript. *See* EPS
  graphics
Enter key, 4.288
"Entry end:" 15.198
Entry, Index. *See* Index (entry)
Entry, Table of Contents. *See* Table of
  Contents (entry)
EPS graphics, 10.5, 10.39-10.46
  bitmapped images saved as, 10.40
  color applied to, 10.159
  examples of, 10.43, 10.45
    without screen version, 10.44
  fonts in, 10.46
  from Adobe Illustrator, 10.97
  from Aldus Freehand, 10.98
  imported EPS colors, 16.86, 16.124
    as shown in color palette, 16.96
    editing spot colors, 16.124
  lighten, 10.212
  place icon for, 10.126
  "Preserve EPS colors," 16.136
  printed on QuickDraw printers, 19.8
  restoring original color, 16.123
  saving PageMaker pages as, 10.40,
    10.160, 19.148
  scanned images saved as, 10.40,
    10.55
  storing in publication, 10.106
EPS Import filter, 17.12
EPS Import Nested DCS filter, 17.12
"EPS" PostScript file, 19.142
  creating, 10.160, 19.148
EPSF code, 10.39, 10.43-10.44
Errors
  PostScript error handler, 19.101
"Even/odd pages," 19.61

"Exactly as typed," 5.248
Excel. *See* Microsoft Excel
"Excel Worksheet object," 11.123
Expanding type, 4.238
"Expert kerning..." Addition, 5.173-
  5.179
  "Design class," 5.176
  "Kern strength," 5.175
  removing, 5.179
  using, 5.178
  when to use, 5.174
"Export," 9.39
  tagging with style sheets, 8.77
Exporting
  filters for, 17.8-17.20
    checking which are installed,
      17.28
    installing, 17.29
  graphics, 17.43
  in Rich Text Format (RTF), 17.19
  in Story Editor, 9.39
  story as text document, 17.43
  tagged stories, 8.77
  what it creates, 17.20
Extensions (filename), 17.40
External files (linked), 11.7, 11.16-
  11.26
  combining with PM revisions, 11.15
  editing from within PM
    "Choose Editor," 10.147, 11.75
    "Edit original," 10.108, 10.146,
      11.59
    editions, 11.87, 11.98
    OLE-linked objects, 11.125
  hotlinks, 10.98, 10.109, 11.69
  lost, 11.12
  updating with PM revisions, 11.68
"Extra image bleed," 19.145

F

Facing pages, 1.36
Fax cover sheet template, 14.36
Feathering, 5.97

Fellini, Federico, p. 164
Fenton, Erfert, p. 731
50% page view, 1.114
File
  external
    determining status of, 11.61-11.62
    linked, 11.7, 11.18-11.30, 11.65
    linking, 11.58
    lost, 11.12
    preventing updates from, 11.19-
      11.22
    setting link options for, 11.60
    "Store copy in pub," 10.103-10.104,
      11.16-11.19, 1
    unlocking, 22.6, 22.7
    updating, 10.14d, 11.66-11.68
  locating, 18.7-18.11
  placing, 3.30
  reducing size of, 18.29, 22.4
  saving, 18.20
  unlocking, 22.7
  won't "Save as," 22.7
Filename extensions, 17.40
Files
  dividing lengthy works into separate,
    15.7
"Files for remote printing"
  saving, 18.34
"Fill and line" dialog box, 2.63-2.74
Fills (graphic), 2.19
  changing, 2.46, 2.49
  examples of, 2.20-2.22
  "Fill and line" dialog box, 2.63-2.74
  problems with defaults of, 20.21
Filters (import and export), 17.8-17.20
  checking which are installed, 17.28
  Help file about, 17.16-17.17
  installing, 17.29
"Find," 9.24, 9.50-9.66
  attributes, 9.63
  characters with no special attributes,
    9.61
  characters with special attributes, 9.62

invisible or special characters, 9.65
"Options" in, 9.53-9.57
problems with, 22.43
using (Scenario), 9.60
what to do when gray, 22.42
wildcard characters, 9.66
window, 9.50-9.59
choosing, 9.59
Find File, 1.334
"Find overset text," 4.133-4.135, 4.179
"First" indent
in Control palette, 4.305
in Paragraph specs dialog box, 4.299
setting, 4.323-4.325
Fisher, Dorothy Canfield, p.326
"Fit in window" page view, 1.4, 1.110-1.111
Fit in world page view ("Show pasteboard"), 1.4, 1.112
Fixed leading, 5.25-5.26
inline graphics and, 10.228-10.229, 10.233
Fixed space, 5.220
creating, 5.226
Folders, 18.10
Folio, p. 778
"Following topic:" 15.193
Font downloader utility, 19.44
Font handler utilities, 19.35
Fonts. *See also* Type
across platforms, 1.241, 1.252
bitmapped, 19.27-19.28, 19.31
bracketed names in font menu, 1.248, 22.49
changing, 4.228
changing size of, 4.229
from the keyboard, 4.230
corrupted, 22.47
creating a custom PPD
for downloaded fonts, 21.34
creating substitution exceptions, 1.253, 1.261
"Default font," 1.244, 1.262

displaying in Story Editor, 9.13
changing 9.15, 9.48
downloadable, 19.33-19.35
avoiding in PICTS, 10.28
in EPS files, 10.46
organizing in menus, 19.35
problems with, 22.50
RAM and, 19.40, 19.43, 19.45
downloading
automatically, 19.42-19.43
manually, 19.45, 19.132
permanently, 19.46, 19.166
"Edit tracks..." Addition, 5.193-5.209
"Expert kerning..." Addition, 5.173-5.179
families of, 19.43
font emulation with SuperATM, 1.244, 1.257
font metrics, 1.242
in the Control palette, 4.210, 4.221
installing, 19.33
installed sizes, 4.229
listed by number, 1.254
manually downloading, 19.45, 19.132
"Map fonts," 1.255
missing, 1.240-1.245
outline size in menu, 4.229,
outline, 19.29-19.31
printer, 19.30-19.33
screen, 19.30-19.31, 19.33, 19.35
"PANOSE font matching", 1.240-1.271
and EPS files, 1.245, 10.46
permanently downloaded, 19.46, 19.166
printing errors and, 22.47
telling PageMaker about new
fonts at the printer, 19.178
resident fonts, 19.34
results of using only, 19.39
TrueType, 19.36-19.38

mixing with PostScript fonts, 19.38
viewing a list of all the
fonts in a pub, 19.180
Footers, 20.122
Force justify, 4.248-4.249
letterspaced heads, 4.248, 5.150
Ford, Henry, p. 489
Foreign language dictionary, 9.100
"Format:" (Index), 15.192
"Format:" (TOC), 15.55
Formatting
characters, 4.196-4.199, 5.123
insertion point, 4.20-4.24, 4.194
options in style sheets, 8.33
paragraphs, 4.200-4.202, 4.350
text, 4.189-4.249
character, 4.196-4.199, 5.123
options in style sheets, 8.33
paragraph, 4.200
Four-color separation, 16.31-16.36
changing spot colors to process, 16.138
files formats PM can separate, 16.36
moire patterns and, 16.34
printing separations, 16.130-16.140
"Angle:" 16.139
dialog box for, 16.130-16.139
"Optimized screen:" 16.134
"Ruling:" (lpi), 16.135
task for, 16.140
reds and metallics in, 16.35
Four-headed arrow, 2.27
400% page view, 1.118
Fractal Painter, 10.95
Fractions
creating beautiful, 4.261
creating with the "Run script..."
Addition, 4.262
Franklin, Ben, p. 756
Frost, Robert, p. 716
Full color. *See* Four-color separation

G

Gans, R. David, p. 460
Garamond, Claude, pp. 496, 519
Ginsberg, Allen, p. 494
Glaser, Milton, p. 235
Global diagnostic, 21.28
Global recomposition, 21.27
Goethe, pp. 71, 230
Gottschall, Edward, p. 344
Grabber hand, 1.126
Graphics. *See also* Objects; Graphics
(from outside PM)
Additions for, 10.258
"Alert when storing graphics over,"
1.233
"Apply button" icons for, 3.42
basics, 10.6-10.14
clearing or deleting, 1.284
color, setting a default for, 16.101, 16.125
copying, 1.281
cropping, 1.187
cutting, 1.280
deleting from Scrapbook, 1.315
detailed
adjusting resolution of, 1.229
drag-and-drop between PM pubs, 10.134
drag-placing into a bounding box, 1.322
examples of Control palettes for, 3.6
file formats PM can color separate, 16.38
inline, 10.9, 10.213-10.251
adjusting leading on, 10.233, 1.243
in Story Editor, 9.18, 9.38
with "align to grid," 5.108
"Maximum size of internal bitmap,"
1.232
multiple pasting, 1.305
pasting, 1.282
placing from Scrapbook, 1.318

placing on a master page, 1.140
placing Scrapbook text as, 1.318
power-pasting, 1.283
putting into Scrapbook, 1.313
"Remove transformations," 10.145
replacing, 14.19
    template graphics, 14.20
Scrapbook
    replacing template graphics with, 14.19
set maximum file size for imported graphics, 1.233
template, replacing, 14.20
text wrapping, 13.2-13.38, 13.41-13.44
wrapping text inside, 13.41

Graphics (from outside PageMaker),
    pp. 461-530
Additions for, 10.258
Adobe Illustrator, 10.39, 10.42, 11.80
    saving files in, 10.97
Aldus Freehand, 10.39, 10.42, 11.80
    hotlinked, 10.109, 11.69
    saving files in, 10.98
Aldus Persuasion, 10.109
Aldus PrePrint, 10.109
"Angle," 10.177-10.178, 10.181-10.183
    default, 10.178
bi-level bitmapped, 10.15, 10.71, 10.168-10.169
bitmapped, 10.15, 10.32, 10.126, 10.162-10.212
black, 22.34
"Black and white," 10.168-10.170
black and white, 10.32, 10.59-10.61, 10.193-10.194
"Brightness," 10.60, 10.62, 10.64
Canvas, 10.23, 10.31, 10.122
    saving files in, 10.95
ClarisWorks, 10.23
Clipboard
    creating links for, 11.71
    Ole-linked objects, 11.115-11.118

replacing template graphics with, 14.19
color
    setting a default for, 16.101, 16.125
    applying, 10.159
    restoring original, 16.123
Color Studio, 10.109
compatible file formats, 10.2
compressing, 10.34, 10.152-10.153
"Contrast," 10.162, 10.192-10.195
    examples of various settings for, 10.196-10.203
    when scanning black & white images, 10.60
control bars (Image control), 10.162
copying, 10.133
cropping, 10.57, 10.143, 10.220, 10.244
cursors, 10.126, 10.130
cutting, 10.133
decompressing, 10.154
"Define color," 10.159
deleting, 10.136
DeskDraw, 10.23
    saving files in, 10.96
DeskPaint, 10.16
    saving files in, 10.99
"Detailed graphics," 10.155-10.158
digital halftoning, 10.66
displaying on screen, 10.155-10.158
    high resolution, 10.36, 10.158
distorted
    restoring, 10.140
    removing transformations, 10.145
dot-screen angle, 10.162
drag-placing, 10.127
draw-type (vector), 10.23, 10.96. See also Pict graphics
"Edit original," 10.108, 10.146, 10.148
editions (P & S), 10.4, 10.12, 11.79-11.102
    updating, 10.107-10.108

Encapsulated PostScript. See EPS
EPS, 10.5, 10.39-10.45
    examples of, 10.43, 10.45
    from Adobe Illustrator, 10.97
    from Aldus Freehand, 10.98
    place icon for, 10.126
    printing on QuickDraw printers, 19.8
    storing in pub, 10.106
EPSF code, 10.39, 10.43
"Gray" (Image control), 10.169, 10.171-10.172, 10.191, 10.195
grayscale, 10.32, 10.55, 10.77
    examples of, 10.38, 10.65
    halftoning through printers, 10.76-10.79, 10.86-1
    image controlling, 10.83-10.85, 10.171-10.175
    scanning, 10.58, 10.61, 10.72-10.93
grouping
    "PS Group it" Addition, 10.254, 10.259-10.291
    "PS Ungroup it" Addition, 10.254, 10.271-10.289
halftoning, 10.66-10.71
    examples of, 10.80-10.88
    through Image Control, 10.162-10.167
    when to, 10.89
hotlinks, 10.98, 10.109, 11.69
icons for, 10.126
"Image," 10.18, 10.164. See also TIFF
"Image controlling," 10.89, 10.162-10.212
    applying the same setting to several Tiffs, 21.36
"Include complete copy?" 10.101-10.106
incompatible file formats, 10.117, 10.122
independent, 10.4, 10.123-10.124, 10.126-10.160

inline, 10.123, 10.125, 10.213-10.251
    applying graphic attributes to, 10.214
    keeping consistent linespace with, 21.9
inverted, 22.34
keyline
    "Create keyline..." Addition, 10.292
Library palette, 10.51, 10.131
lightening
    EPS, 10.212
    PICT, 10.212
    TIFF, 10.209
"Lightness," 10.188-10.191
    examples of various settings for, 10.196-10.203
line art (scanned), 10.55, 10.58-10.59
    examples of, 10.37, 10.63
line frequency, 10.58-10.59, 10.179
    for copy machines, 10.185
line screen of, 10.69-10.72, 10.78-10.79
lines per inch frequency, 10.162
"Lines/in," 10.179-10.187
    default, 10.180, 10.187
linked, 11.12
    editions, 11.79-11.102
    high resolution, 11.12
    lost, 11.12
    OLE objects, 11.103-11.132
    options for, 11.55-11.57
    storing in pub, 11.2, 11.12, 11.17-11.26
    updating, 11.13-11.26
linking, 10.102
    default option, 10.103
MacDraw Pro, 10.23, 10.122
    saving files in, 10.96
MacPaint, 10.5, 10.17, 10.95
    example of, 10.29
"magic-resizing," 10.20-10.22, 10.141-10.142
    files not available to, 10.25

TIFF files, 10.33
minimums and maximums, 10.1
moving, 10.137
object-oriented, 10.18, 10.23, 10.96,
   10.126. *See also* PICT graphics
paint-type, 10.5, 10.15-10.22, 10.95,
   10.126
   examples of, 10.21-10.22
panning, 10.143
PANOSE font matching and, 10.46
pasting, 10.4, 10.129, 10.132
Photo CD images, 10.5, 10.47-10.50
   color with, 10.50
   "PCD," 10.49
   resolution, 10.50
   within a PM publication, 10.48
PhotoShop, 10.16, 10.31
   saving files in, 10.100
PhotoStyler, 10.109
PICT, 10.5, 10.18, 10.23-10.31
   image controlling, 10.163, 10.212
   saving as, 10.55
PICT2, 10.26
placing, 10.4, 10.101-10.106, 10.126-
   10.128, 10.13
   inline, 10.222, 10.224, 10.235
PostScript, 10.39, 10.41, 10.97-10.98
   code for, 10.41-10.43
PostScript print options, 10.160
printed
   commercially, 10.93
   inaccuracy of, 10.92
   to a non-PostScript printer, 10.7
"PS Group it" Addition, 10.254,
   10.259-10.291
"PS Ungroup it" Addition, 10.254,
   10.271-10.289
QuickDraw, 10.39
   saving files in, 10.96
QuickScript, 10.39
"Remove transformations," 10.145
replacing, 10.128
resizing, 10.138-10.140

resolution
   for commercial printing, 10.70
   of TIFF files, 10.99
   on printers, 10.77-10.78
   storing low, 10.103
"Restore original color," 16.123
reversed, 22.34
saving
   copies of, 10.94
   for placement into PM, 10.94-
      10.100
   PM pages as EPS files, 10.40,
      10.160
scanned images, 10.4, 10.40, 10.54-
   10.88
   chart for types of, 10.58
   examples of, 10.37-10.38, 10.62-
      10.65, 10.80-10
   grayscales, 10.91-10.93
scanning, 10.54-10.79
   chart for, 10.58
   examples of, 10.62-10.65
   grayscales, 10.72-10.93
   line art, 10.59-10.61
   line screen and, 10.72
   rules of thumb for, 10.89-10.93
"Screen," 10.176, 10.181-10.183
screen, 10.69-10.88
screen pattern for
   changing, 10.162
screen view
   inaccuracy of, 10.91
"Screened," 10.169, 10.171, 10.173-
   10.175
   "Contrast," 10.195
   "Lightness," 10.191
screened, 10.68
settings (preset Image control),
   10.204-10.208
"Store copy in publication," 10.103-
   10.104
stretching, 10.138
SuperPaint, 10.16, 10.28-10.30

saving files in, 10.95
Tagged Image File Format. *See* TIFF
text turned into, 10.151
text wrapping, 10.149
   removing, 10.150
TIFF, 10.5, 10.18, 10.32-10.38
   compressing, 10.152-10.154
   examples of, 10.37-10.38, 10.65
   grayscaling, 10.32, 10.175-10.176
   image controlling, 10.162-10.211,
      21.26
uncropping, 10.143
updating files of, 10.105
vector, 10.23
video grabs, 10.53
viewing on screen, 10.36
"Write PostScript to disk," 10.160
"Gray" (Image control), 10.169, 10.171-
   10.172
   "Contrast" and, 10.195
   "Lightness" and, 10.191
"Gray out," 10.36, 10.155
Gray rule
   creating, 7.57
"Grayscale"
   as a composite print option, 19.115
Grayscale graphics, 10.32, 10.55
   examples of, 10.38, 10.65
   halftoning through printer, 10.76-
      10.79
      examples of, 10.86-10.88
   image controlling, 10.83-10.85,
      10.171-10.173
      "Screened," 10.175
   lightening, 10.210
   scanning guidelines, 10.89-10.93
   TIFF, 10.32, 10.77
   ways to halftone, 10.76-10.77
Gray text, creating, 4.265
"Greek text below," 1.223
   changing the number of pixels for
      showing, 1.236
Grid, 5.97-5.111, 14.38-14.39

creating with "Multiple paste," 1.310
"Grid size," 5.97
Grimes, John, pp. 857, 863
Guides, 1.193
   drawing or moving objects in
      alignment with, 2.31
   finding lost or invisible, 22.10
   master page guides showing on
      pub pages, 1.61, 1.138, 22.25
   selecting objects under, 1.212
   sending to the back or front, 1.66,
      1.68, 1.230
Guides, column. *See* Column guides
Guides, margin. *See* Margin guides
Guides, ruler. *See* Ruler guides
Gutenberg, Johannes, pp. 56, 100,
   191

H

Halley, Allen, pp. 47, 496
Halftone graphics, 10.66-10.71
   default angle for, 10.178
   digital, 10.66
   examples of, 10.80-10.88
   for commercial printing, 10.93
   scanned, 10.55, 10.58, 10.89, 10.176
   "Screened," 10.195
   through Image control, 10.76,
      10.162-10.167
      examples of, 10.83-10.85
   through PostScript printers, 10.77
   when to, 10.89
Handles, 1.5, 1.190
Hanging
   graphics, 10.231, 10.251
   indents, 4.324, 6.60
      deleting, 6.79
      setting, 6.78
   punctuation, 21.10
Hard returns, 4.348-4.354
Hard spaces, 5.217-5.228
   adjusting line breaks with, 21.7
   with inline graphics, 10.244

with paragraph rules, 7.44
Hawes, Michael, p.144
Hawks, Nelson, pp. 341, 496
Headers/footers
creating on the master page, 1.139
"Running headers\footers," 20.89
Headlines
attached to next paragraph, 4.337
letter spacing, 5.150
reverse, prevent losing, 4.237
spanning several columns, 21.6
with paragraph space, 5.85
Heartbreak House, p. 508
Help, pp. 839-866
"Help" (Story Importer dialog box),
4.78
Help file, 22.2
using 22.3
Henry, V, p. 819
Herodotus, p. 820
Hidden codes, 9.17
"High resolution" display, 10.36,
10.157-10.158
High resolution imagesetters
line frequency for, 10.185-10.186
Hoffman, Hans, p. 839
"Horizontal-reflecting" button, 3.38,
3.82-3.85
Horizontal ruler
changing the unit of measure for,
1.53, 1.224
measurement options for, 1.39
repositioning, 1.70-1.71
Hotlinks, 10.98, 10.109, 11.69
How to Boss Your Fonts Around,
pp. 310, 731
Howe, Norm, p. 840
HSB color model, 16.38
"Edit color," 16.44-16.46
"Hue," 16.61
Huxley, Aldous, p. 428
Hyphen
adjusting height of, 21.16

discretionary, 5.234-5.235
entering, 5.249
removing, 5.250
non-breaking
creating, 5.227
Hyphenating
preventing a word from, 5.251, 21.13
words in user dictionary, 9.121,
9.138
Hyphenation, 5.229-5.255
changing in main dictionary, 5.255
dialog box, 5.229
discretionary, 5.234-5.235
entering, 5.249
removing, 5.250
in user dictionary
adding, 5.245-5.248, 5.253
changing, 5.255
ranking, 5.253
removing, 5.254
limits, 5.238
manual only, 5.232-5.233
manual plus algorithm, 5.237
manual plus dictionary, 5.236
preventing, 5.251
turning off, 5.230
turning on, 5.231
zone, 5.239-5.241
changing, 5.252

I

I-beam, 4.10-4.14, 4.192. *See also*
Insertion point
Icon
LaserWriter 8, 19.21, 19.25
loaded text, 4.88-4.89
cancelling, 4.100, 21.12
PageMaker application, 1.12
place
cancelling, 21.12, 22.15
for graphics, 10.19, 10.126,
10.130
printer, 19.20-19.21

printer font, 19.30, 19.32
screen font, 19.31, 19.35
TrueType font, 19.36
Igarashi, Takenobu, p. 194
"Ignore," 9.114
Illustrator, 10.39, 10.42, 11.80
"Include preview for," 10.97
saving files in, 10.97
"Image," 10.18. *See also* TIFF
"Image control," 10.89, 10.162-10.212
adjusting appearance of a TIFF,
10.209
"Angle," 10.177-10.178
"Apply," 10.167
the same setting to several Tiffs,
21.36
"Black and white," 10.168-10.170
changing line screen through, 10.78
"Contrast," 10.192-10.203
control bars, 10.165, 10.172, 10.188-
10.195
examples of, 10.196-10.203
dialog box, 10.162-10.167
files not available to, 10.25
"Gray," 10.169, 10.171-10.172, 10.195
halftoning through, 10.76, 10.162-
10.167
examples of, 10.83-10.85
inline graphics, 10.217, 10.250
lightening TIFFs through, 10.210
"Lightness," 10.188, 10.191, 10.196-
10.203
"lines/in," 10.179-10.187
default, 10.187
PICT and EPS graphics, 10.212
"Reset," 10.166
returning to original specs, 10.211
"screen," 10.176, 10.181-10.183
"Screened," 10.162, 10.169-10.175,
10.191, 10.195
Settings (preset), 10.204-10.208
Imagesetters, 19.9-19.10
saving paper when printing to, 19.70

"Import" (Index Topics), 15.116, 15.124-
15.126, 15.154
Importing, 4.73-4.83, pp. 697-716. *See
also* Placing
drag-and-drop between pubs, 17.44
filters for, 17.8-17.20
checking which are installed, 17.28
installing, 17.29
format attributes PageMaker supports,
17.16-17.17
graphics, 10.101-10.106, 10.126-10.131,
17.32
import filters, 17.12, 17.40
Index topics, 15.154
inline graphics, 10.235-10.238
into Story Editor
graphics, 9.38
stories, 9.22, 9.35-9.37
methods of, 17.1
Microsoft Excel spreadsheet, 17.37
as an OLE object, 17.39
as PICT, 17.38
Microsoft Word 4.0/5.0, 17.34
table as a graphic, 17.35
table as text (tab-delimited), 17.36
"OLE," 17.1, 17.6
PageMaker files into PM, 4.73-4.86
copying text from Story view, 4.85
drag-and-drop between open pubs,
4.86
limiting display in text box, 4.84
placing entire file, 4.82
placing selected stories, 4.83
viewing any story, 4.85
"Paste," 17.1, 17.3
"Paste special," 17.1, 17.35
"Place," 17.1, 17.4-17.5
"Publish and Subscribe," 17.1, 17.6
Smart ASCII, 17.10-17.11
text-only filter dialog box, 17.21-
17.33
stories from a PM 4 or 5 pub, 17.42
drag-and-drop method, 17.44

styles in style sheets
signs for, 8.36
text (word-processing files), 4.28-
4.62, 17.30
from Microsoft Word 4.0/5.0,
17.34
from PCs, 17.40-17.41
into Story Editor, 17.31
text-only files, 17.33
unloading "place" icon, 21.12, 22.15
using the "Library palette," 17.45
"Import to Story Editor" dialog box
graphic 9.38
text, 9.36
Imposition, p. 778
"Include complete copy?" 10.101-
10.106
"Include empty index section,"
15.191
"Include index section headings,"
15.190
"Include PostScript error handler,"
19.101
"Indent" (Paragraph Rules), 7.5, 7.10
Indents (and Tabs), pp. 333-360
"Apply" button, 6.29, 6.31, 6.35
avoiding, 6.11
copy formatting of, 6.84
dialog box, 6.18
defaults
setting for application, 6.86
setting for current publication,
6.85
examples of, 6.57-6.62
first-line, 6.55
deleting, 6.79
examples of, 6.59
setting, 4.321-4.326
hanging
deleting, 6.79
examples of, 6.60
setting, 4.324

inline graphics and, 10.231, 10.244,
10.251
left margin
example, 6.58
setting, 4.321, 6.80
minimums and maximums, 6.1
nested, 6.62
numbered paragraphs, 6.61
one em
setting, 4.325
removing any, 6.82
right margin
example, 6.57
setting, 4.322, 6.81
ruler for, 6.18-6.22, 6.33-6.48
using, 6.23-6.32
setting, 4.250, 4.321-4.326
before typing a paragraph, 4.326
troubleshooting with, 6.4-6.9
using the Control palette, 6.32, 6.83
Indents (Control palette), 4.291
"First," 4.305
"Left," 4.311
"Right," 4.310
Indents (Paragraphs specs), 4.291
"First," 4.323
"Left," 4.321
"Right," 4.322
Independent Additions, 20.5,
Appendix J
Index, 15.68-15.207
"Accept," 15.141
"Add," 15.141
"Add index entry" dialog box, 15.79
basic process of creating, 15.72-15.78
"Create index" dialog box, 15.184
creating first, 15.201
"Cross-reference:" 15.97, 15.172-15.173
formatting, 15.175
types of ("Denoted by"), 15.174
eliminating, 15.206-15.207
entering proper names automatically,
15.155

entries, 15.143-15.144
by key word, 15.157-15.160
capitalizing automatically, 15.156
cross-referencing, 15.172-15.173
editing, 15.164
removing, 15.166-15.169
secondary, 15.128, 15.147-15.149
showing before creating actual,
15.163, 15.176-15.
sorting, 15.170-15.171
suppressing page numbers of,
15.146
tertiary, 15.128, 15.150-15.152
ultra-zippy shortcut for making,
15.143
example of, 499
formatting, 15.180-15.200
example of, 15.80
"Import," 15.116, 15.124-15.126,
15.154
in Story Editor, 9.18, 9.24
"Include book publications," 15.185
"Index entry…" command, 15.135
"Index format" dialog box, 15.188
character codes for, 15.200
immediately viewing changes in,
15.199
specifications, 15.189-15.198
index markers
moving, 15.162
viewing contents of, 15.161
key word entries, 15.157
creating in multiple pubs, 15.159
creating secondary entries for,
15.160
customizing, 15.158
move-down (arrow) button, 15.81,
15.128
"Page range:" 15.90-15.96
placing, 15.180-15.200
for the first time, 15.201
prefix for page numbers in, 15.127
defining, 1.333, 15.205

proper names automatically, 15.155
"Range:" 15.90-15.96
"Remove unreferenced topics,"
15.187
"Remove:" 15.138-15.140
"Replace existing index," 15.182
searching for an entry in, 15.204
"Select cross-reference topic" dialog
box, 15.114
"Select topic" dialog box, 15.114
separate files for, 15.7
"Show index" dialog boxes, 15.119
list box in, 15.136
using, 15.163, 15.176-15.177
"Show index…" command, 15.135
"Sort," 15.83, 15.129-15.134, 15.170-
15.171
style sheets in, 15.71
time needed to "Create" or "Show,"
15.5
title for, 15.186
topic list
checking, 15.153
deleting, 15.179
entering with no page numbers,
15.145
importing, 15.154
"Topic section," 15.110
topics vs. entries, 15.121-15.123
undoing additions or deletions,
15.165
updating or replacing existing,
15.202-15.203
"Index entry…" command, 15.135
"Index format" dialog box, 15.188
Initial caps
creating, 21.15
creating "Drop caps," 20.59
problems with linespace of, 22.24
text wrapping, 13.40
Inline graphics, 10.123, 10.125,
10.213-10.251
adjusting leading on, 5.71

"align to grid" with, 5.108-5.109
applying graphic attributes to, 10.214
baseline of, 10.221, 10.232
    adjusting, 10.246, 10.248
"Baseline-offset" option, 10.248
between tiled publications, 1.180
boundaries of, 10.220; 10.244
    cropping, 10.143
centering, 10.249
cutting or copying, 10.240
deleting, 10.241-10.242
disappearing, 10.223, 10.242
graphic qualities available to, 10.217
image controlling, 10.250
in own paragraph adjusting space of, 10.247
in Story Editor, 9.18, 10.222
    finding through, 10.222
    importing into, 10.238
    placing or replacing, 9.38
"Inline specifications" dialog box, 10.243
insertion point, 10.224
leading of, 10.228-10.233
    adjusting leading, 10.243
linespace with
    maintaining consistent linespace, 21.9, 22.24
moving, 10.137, 10.232-10.233, 10.246, 10.248
    horizontally, 10.244
pasting, 10.224-10.225, 10.234
    step-and-repeat pattern, 10.245
placing, 10.224-10.225, 10.235
positioning to the side of a text block, 10.231, 10.251
problems with text blocks of, 10.225
replacing, 10.236-10.237
    with graphics from the Clipboard or Scrapbook, 14.19
resizing, 10.226, 10.239

selecting, 10.214
tabs/indents with, 10.231, 10.244, 10.251
text attributes of, 10.215
    applying, 10.214
    those not available, 10.216, 10.218
    tracking, 10.243
    what to expect from, 10.227-10.233
"Insert object," 11.126-11.132
"Inserting text," 4.54, 4.58
Insertion point, 4.14-4.24, 4.194
    aligning on the left, 4.27, 22.9
    finding lost, 22.8
    formatting and loading, 4.20-4.24, 4.232
    moving and selecting text with, 4.204
    moving with keyboard shortcuts, 1.328
    moving with keypad shortcuts, 1.328
    using to copy and paste, 1.279
    with inline graphics, 10.224
Inside-out text wrap, 13.41
Installed fonts, 4.228-4.229, 10.28
Installing PageMaker 5, Appendix C
Internal file, 11.7
"Invalid___ ...," 22.36, 22.37
Invisible characters
    in Story Editor
        finding, 9.65
        hiding, 9.42
        showing, 9.17, 9.25, 9.42
Italic type, history of, p. 215
ITC Baskerville, 5.92
Itten, Johannes, p. 686

J

James, William, p. 724
Jannon, Jean, p. 519
Jerome, Jerome K., p. 68
Jones, Keasley, p. 820
Jump-lines, 4.160-4.167

adding to a story, 4.183-4.185
Justifying text, 4.247
    force, 4.248-4.249
    letter spacing with, 5.137, 5.140
    word spacing with, 5.121

K

Kazantzakis, p. 374
"Keep lines together," 4.334, 4.347
"Keep with next__ lines," 4.337
"Keeps," controls 4.329-4.347
    removing all, 4.333
    violations of, 1.228, 4.331
"Keeps violations," 1.228, 4.331
Keller, Helen, p. 546
Kerning, 5.151-5.172
    auto kerning
        pairs, 5.160-5.162
        turning on or off, 5.166
    decreasing, 5.168
    "Expert kerning" Addition, 5.157, 5.173-5.179
    hanging punctuation, 21.10
    in Story Editor, 5.172
    increasing, 5.169
    initial caps, 21.15
    manual kerning, 5.163-5.165
    over a range of text, 5.170
    removing, 5.171
    with the Control palette, 5.168-5.169
Kerr, Jean, p. 769
Key Caps, 1.329-1.333
    using accent marks from, 1.333
    using alternate characters from, 1.331-1.332
    viewing all four keyboards of, 1.330
    viewing keyboard layout of, 1.329
Keyboard, 1.3
    changing styles using, 8.64
    changing type styles with, 4.232
    selecting text with, 4.204
    shortcuts for moving insertion point with, 1.328

using the character-view Control palette with, 4.226-4.227, 3.120
using to operate the Control palette, 3.101-3.109
    applying changes to your document, 3.112
    changing the measurement system "on the fly," 3.114
    changing the type of active reference point, 3.108
    display last valid entry, 3.113
    selecting an active reference point, 3.107
    to move an object, 3.105
    to move between palette options, 3.110
    turning a button on or off, 3.111
Keypad (numeric), 1.3, 1.324, 1.328
    cutting and pasting with, 1.327
    moving the insertion point with, 1.328, 22.33
    selecting an active reference point on the Proxy with, 3.117
    selecting text with, 1.326
    typing numbers with, 1.324, 22.32
    using as arrow keys, 1.325
Key word index entries, 15.157
    creating in multiple pubs, 15.159
    creating secondary entries for, 15.160
    customizing, 15.158
"Kind" (in Link info), p. 11.49
Kissinger, Henry, p. 705
Knockouts, 16.24, 16.27
    by default, 16.24
    creating with "Paper" color or fill, 16.66-16.67
    problems with, 16.28-16.29
    trapping, 16.28-16.30
Kvern, Olav Martin, pp. 193, 397, 508, 516

L

Label, 18.7-18.9
Lagercrantz, Olaf, p. 817
Lamartine, Alphonse de, p. 726
Laser printers, 19.6
  energy consumption of, 19.4
  "Printer Info," 19.24
  ROM in, 19.40
  troubleshooting, 19.162-19.164
LaserWriter
  lines/in default for, 10.180
  paper sizes available to, 19.55
  printing from
    resulting screen angle, 10.182-
      10.183
  proofs
    appearance of, 10.93, 10.196
  resolution, 10.77, 10.90
    examples of, 2.21
  screen default for, 10.175
LaserWriter 8, 19.13-19.15
  "Auto Setup," 19.22
  icon in Chooser, 19.21, 19.25
  keeping previous version of driver,
    19.15
  linking to your printer, 19.20-19.25
  PSPrinter 8, 19.13
  selecting from Chooser, 19.21
  upgrades, 19.14
"Launch Aldus PrePrint," 19.143
Lauper, Cyndi, p. 786
Layering, 1.189-1.195
Layers, 1.181, 4.102
  invisible, 1.192
  selecting objects hidden under, 1.215
Layout view
  in Preferences dialog box, 1.53-1.54,
    1.222
  in Story Editor, 9.6
  returning to from Story Editor, 9.87-
    9.88
Leaders
  creating custom, 6.72-6.73

  making even-ending lines with,
    21.17
  over text-wrapped objects, 6.75
  removing, 6.74
  setting with tabs, 6.34, 6.71
Leading, 5.12-5.71
  auto, 5.19-5.24
    changing default values of, 5.68
    figuring value of, 5.59-5.60
  baselines and, 5.37, 5.39-5.41, 5.45-
    5.50
  changing, 4.234
  comparison of leading examples,
    5.58
  decreasing, 5.62
  default, 5.63
  definition, 5.5
  disappearing fragmented letters
    from, 22.26
  fixed, 5.25-5.26
    adjusting linespace with, 22.24
  increasing, 5.62
  inline graphics and, 10.228-10.233
    adjusting, 10.243
  making consistent, 5.66-5.67
  measure of, 5.14-5.18
  methods, 5.35-5.58
    baseline, 5.37, 5.45-5.50, 5.58,
      5.65
    proportional, 5.25, 5.38, 5.39-
      5.44, 5.58, 5.63
    top of caps, 5.36, 5.51-5.57, 5.58,
      5.64
  paragraph rules and, 7.17, 7.21
  on inline graphics
    adjusting, 5.71, 10.228-10.233,
      22.24
  selecting text to change, 5.27-5.31
  slugs and, 5.32
  standard value for, 5.19
  submenu, 5.33-5.34
  troubleshooting for, 5.69-5.70
  value of, 5.61

"Leading"
  in the Control palette, 4.216, 4.234
  in Type specs dialog box, 4.205, 4.234
Lee, Donald K., p. 756
Lee, Stanislaw J, p. 321
Left align, 4.244
"Left" indent
  in the Control palette, 4.312, 4.321
  in the Paragraph dialog box, 4.299,
    4.321
Lennon, John, p. 30
Letter space, 5.5, 5.132-5.150
  changing value of, 5.143
  decreasing, 5.148
  desired, 5.136-1.138
  examples of, 5.146
  for a headline, 5.150
  increasing, 5.1147
  maximum, 5.142-5.143
  minimum, 5.141, 5.143
  resetting, 5.149
Libraries, color, 16.49-16.53
  creating custom, 16.128
  list of, 16.53
  selecting a color from, 16.111
Library palette, pp. 563-574
  add an item, 12.16, 12.53
  "Add" button, 12.32
  add multiple items, 12.20
  add text, 12.62
    threaded text blocks, 12.23
  basics, 12.8-12.24
  compressing, 12.56
  create new, 12.9, 12.36, 12.51-12.52
  display options, 12.35, 12.60
  importing text or graphics, 17.45
  "Item information," 12.40-12.49
    add color or grayscale images,
      12.44, 12.59
    add information, 12.57-12.58
  keywords, 12.49-12.50, 12.65 567
  "Library preferences," 12.40, 12.44-
    12.45

  linking information, 12.21-12.22
  minimums and maximums, 12.1
  open existing, 12.9, 12.13, 12.33, 12.61
  "Options" menu, 12.32, 12.39
  place items into publication, 12.19,
    12.54
  "Preferences," 12.39
  "Remove item," 12.33, 12.55
    compressing after, 12.56
  "Search library," 12.63-12.76
  search operators, 12.68-12.69, 12.76
    572
  "Show all items," 12.34, 12.75
  styles sheets
    transferring through, 8.57-8.58,
      12.24
  using "Aldus Fetch," 12.38, 12.77
  window, 12.25-12.39
    "Options" menu, 12.29, 12.33-12.39
  with graphics, 10.51, 10.131
Ligatures, 4.385
  find and change, 9.77
Lightening
  EPS and Picts, 10.212
  TIFF graphics, 10.210
Lightness ("Brightness"), 16.61
"Lightness," 10.188-10.191
  black and white images and, 10.189
  dark pixels and, 10.188
  examples of various settings for,
    10.196-10.203
"Limit consecutive hyphens to," 5.229,
  5.238
Line art
  scanned, 10.55, 10.58-10.59
    examples of, 10.37, 10.63
Line breaks, 4.348-4.354, 6.11
  adjusting, 21.7
  maintaining in converted
    PM4.x publications, 19.48
  preventing line breaks, 4.241
  to avoid "next style" in Style sheet,
    8.32, 8.79

without adding paragraph space, 5.95
"Line color," 7.5, 7.8
Line frequency, 10.17-10.187
Line pattern, 10.176
Line screen, 10.69
"Line style," 7.5, 7.7, 7.36-7.40
  examples of, 7.40
"Line width," 7.5, 7.9
Lines (drawing). *See also* Drawing tools
  applying color or gray to, 4.265
  applying widths and styles to, 2.17-2.18
  changing, 2.34-2.35
  changing the direction of, 2.41
  create custom, 2.75
  "Custom line" dialog box, 2.51-2.61
  diagonal drawing tool for, 2.6
  examples of, 2.20-2.22
  "Fill and line" dialog box, 2.63-2.74
  leaders for even-ending, 21.17
  lengthening or shortening, 2.39
  perpendicular drawing tool, 2.7
  point sizes of, 7.40
  problems with
    not showing, 22.19
    width of, 22.21
  resize using the Control palette, 3.90
  reversing, 2.37
    getting rid of, 22.20
  straightening, 2.40
  transparent and reverse, 2.53
    examples, 2.62, 2.76
  transparent patterned lines, 2.36
Lines (text)
  creating longer than 22.75", 21.23
  lengthening or shortening, 4.116
    problems with, 22.31
  preventing line breaks, 4.241
  showing "keeps" violations, 1.228
  showing loose/tight, 1.227
Lines per inch (screen), 10.69

Lines per inch frequency, 10.162, 10.179
"Lines/in," 10.179-10.187
  default, 10.187
Linespace, 5.18
  maintaining consistent
    between two text blocks, 21.8
    with inline graphics, 21.9, 22.24
  removing
    above last paragraph line, 22.23
"Link," 11.53
"Link info," 11.33, 11.51-11.54
"Link options," 11.34, 11.55-11.57
  setting, 11.60
    application defaults, 11.77
    publication defaults, 11.78
Link status indicators, 11.40-11.49
  kind indicators, 11.49
  page location, 11.49
  status chart, 11.40
Linked documents
  copying while saving
    "all linked documents," 18.35
    "files for remote printing," 18.34,
    only files not stored in pub, 19.136
Linking Text and Graphics, pp. 531-562
  automatically, 11.7, 11.58
  benefits of, 11.3
  changing links, 11.10, 11.63
  copying linked files, 11.72
    for remote printing, 11.73
  defaults for, 11.57
    application, 11.14a, 11.77
    editions, 11.85
    OLE objects, 11.111, 11.116
    publication, 11.14b, 11.78
  determining status of linked files, 11.61-11.62
  dialog boxes
    "Link info," 11.51-11.54
    "Link options," 11.55-11.57

"Links," 11.31-11.39
  graphics, 10.101-10.102
    default option for, 10.103
    "Include complete copy?" 10.104-10.105
  linking through the Library palette, 12.21-12.22
  managing links, 11.13-1.15, 11.50
  methods of, 11.1, 11.5-11.6
  missing linked documents, 11.24-11.28
  OLE objects, 11.103-11.125
  "Paste link," 11.115, 11.124
  printing linked documents, 11.27-11.30
  Publish and Subscribe, 11.79-11.102
  stories
    in Story Editor, 9.39
    typed in PM, 11.11, 11.70
  storing graphics externally automatically, 10.104-10.105, 11.76
  storing in publication, 11.16-11.22
  "Unlink," 11.22, 11.35, 11.64
  updating, 11.16-11.26, 11.66
    choosing not to, 11.20-11.23
    choosing to, 11.14d, 11.24-11.25, 11.66
    graphic files, 10.107
    "Include complete copy?" 10.104-10.105
    instantly, 11.14d, 11.66, 11.67
    preventing, 11.20-11.23
    separate files, 11.14c, 11.60
Links
  changing, 11.63
  creating for Clipboard graphics, 11.71
  defaults for, 11.57
    application, 11.14a, 11.77
    editions, 11.85
    OLE objects, 11.111, 11.116
    publication, 11.14b, 11.78
  dialog box, 11.31-11.39

hotlinks, 11.58
re-establishing broken links, 11.65
viewing a list of all the
  links in a pub, 19.179
Linotronic printer, 10.39, 10.92
  examples from, 10.92-10.93, 10.198-10.208
  lines/inch default for, 10.180
  resolution of, 10.78
    examples of, 2.22
Linotype machine, p. 191
List box, 4.46, 18.9
"List only stories over," 4.80, 4.84
"List styles used" Addition, 8.44-8.45
The Little Mac Book, pp. 97, 414, 685, 896
LM, 1.147a, 15.178
Loaded text icon, 4.88-4.89
Locked files or disks
  unlocking, 22.6, 22.7
"Loose/tight lines," 1.222, 1.227
Lord Byron, p. 144
Lost files. *See* Find file
Lost objects, 1.207-1.208
  finding, 1.214-1.215
Loupe, 16.33
"Low memory," 22.46
Low resolution versions of graphics, 10.41
  printing, 11.29
    from QuickDraw printers, 19.8
Lowercase
  changing text into, 4.251
Lubalin, Herb, pp. 227, 380, 575

M

The Mac is not a typewriter, p. 411, 414, 435, 591
MacBeth, p. 74
MacDraw Pro, 10.23, 10.122, 11.80
  saving files in, 10.96
The Macintosh Font Book, p. 731
MacPaint, 10.5, 10.17, 10.95

example of, 10.29
MacWrite II
export filter for, 17.18
exporting to, 17.43
import filter for, 17.10
MacWrite Pro, 17.10
"Magic-resizing," 10.20-10.22, 10.141-10.142
files not available to, 10.25
TIFF files, 10.33
Magnifying tool, 1.122, 1.124, 20.3
Mailing address templates, 11.74
Malfunctions
"mini-save" for, 18.2, 18.33
Management systems for linking, 11.14
avoiding trouble in workgroups, 11.50
Manual flow, 4.90, 4.95
overriding, 4.98
Manual kerning, 5.5, 5.163-5.165
"Manual only," 5.232-5.233
"Manual plus algorithm," 5.237
"Manual plus dictionary," 5.236
"Manual" tile, 19.77-19.78
Manutius, Aldus, pp. 1, 215, 519
"Map fonts," 1.255
Margin guides, 1.50
on master pages
setting up, 1.137
showing on customized pub. pages, 1.138
repositioning, 1.69
setting or changing, 1.37
"Margin in inches," 1.23, 1.37
Margins, setting or changing, 1.37
Marquee method of selecting, 1.208, 1.215, 2.24
deleting at the same time, 21.25
Martin, Noel, p. 177
Martin, Steve, p. 741
Marx, Groucho, p. 292
Master Juggler, 19.35

Master pages, 1.130-1.142
changing or deleting items on, 1.142
column guides on
changing on a publication page, 1.89
reverting customized, 1.90
displaying master page items on publication pages, 1.145
going to, 1.136
graphics on
placing, 1.140
text wrapping, 1.141
guides on
adding, 1.58
deleting, 1.60, 1.63
repositioning, 1.59
setting up, 1.137
showing on publication page, 1.61, 1.138
hiding master page items on publication pages, 1.144
icons for, 1.133
LM (left master), 1.147a
numbering pages on, 1.146, 1.147a
placing text on, 1.139
printing, 1.134-1.135
removing master page items from publication pages, 1.143
while leaving others, 21.5
RM (right master), 1.147a
selecting objects on, 1.188
setting up separately, 1.136
showing master page guides on pub page, 1.61, 1.138, 22.25
"Match case"
in "Change," 9.70-9.73
in "Find," 9.53, 9.56
Measurement system. *See also* Preferences
changing, 1.224, 5.8-5.9
horizontal ruler, 1.53, 1.224
"on the fly" for Control palette options, 3.114

paragraph rules, 7.25
vertical ruler, 1.54, 1.225
customizing vertical ruler, 1.226
options, 1.39-1.40
overriding, 1.323
for paragraph rules, 7.25
Melville, Herman, p. 57, 495, 503
Memory allocation
changing, 22.46
"Low memory," "Out of memory," 22.46
Menu
font names in brackets, 22.49
Menu bar
in Story Editor, 9.21
Mergenthaler, Otto, p. 191
Merriam-Webster dictionary, 9.97, 9.120
Microsoft Excel
as a Publisher, 11.80
creating objects "on the fly" in, 11.127-11.132
import filter for, 17.10
importing from
as a PICT, 17.38
as an OLE object, 11.103-11.132, 17.39
placing a spreadsheet from, 17.37
Microsoft Word
as a Publisher, 11.80
creating objects "on the fly" in, 11.127-11.132
dialog box, 17.34
export filter for, 17.18
import filter for, 17.10
importing, 17.34
OLE objects from, 11.103-11.132, 17.35
tables from, 17.35-17.36
"Microsoft Word 4.0/5.0 import filter"
dialog box, 17.34
Microsoft Works 1.0 and 2.0

import filters for, 17.10
"Mini-save," 18.2-18.3, 18.31
automatic deleting of, 18.5
Mini-view page view, 1.112
Minimums and maximums (Ranges)
Color, 16.1
Columns and column guides, 1.76
Graphics, 10.1
Indents and Tabs, 6.1
Index entry, 15.1
Letter space, 5.141-5.143
Library Palette, 12.1
Page setup, 1.19-1.20
Paragraph rules, 7.1
Printing, 19.1
Rulers and ruler guides, 1.38
Story Editor, 9.1
Table of contents entry, 15.1
Text, 4.1
Text spacing, 5.1
Text wrap, 13.1
Word space, 5.122-5.124
Missing links, 11.24-11.28 531
Mistakes. *See* Undo
Moby Dick, pp. 57, 495, 503
Modems
using with a service bureau, 19.161
Moiré, 10.20-10.21
resulting from screen percentages, 16.15
Molière, 5.186-5.189
"Monospace, import as Courier," 17.26, 17.33
Monotype Corporation, p. 288
Morison, Stanley, p. 407
Morrison, Sean, p. 737
Move-down button, 15.81, 15.128
"Move tab," 6.66
Moving
graphics, 10.137
inline, 10.137, 10.232-10.233, 10.246, 10.248
objects, 1.196-1.201, 2.27

drag-and-drop between open
pubs, 1.179-1.180
fast move, 1.197
in a straight line, 2.30
in perfect alignment with guide
lines, 2.31
in perfect alignment with ruler
tick marks, 2.32
slow move, 1.198
to another page, 2.28
undoing, 1.200
very small, 2.29
with the Control palette, 1.201,
3.87-3.88
text, 4.115
text blocks, 4.115
drag-and-drop between open
pubs, 1.167, 1.179-1.180
"Multiple paste," 1.287-1.310
bypassing the dialog box, 1.309
creating a grid, 1.310
dialog box, 1.291, 1.300-1.302
horizontal offset, 1.301
vertical offset, 1.302
inline graphics and, 10.245
negative values, 1.304, 1.306
number of copies, 1.291, 1.300
objects, 1.305
objects as inline graphics, 1.308
positive values, 1.303, 1.306
step-and-repeat patterns, 1.287
text, 1.307
to cancel pasting sequence, 1.297
Multiple publications, 1.151-1.180
"Cascade" view, 1.154-1.159, 1.175
view a different window, 1.176
close all open publications, 1.174
creating a print queue, 19.217
in Story Editor
"Cascade" story windows, 9.33
closing windows, 9.20, 9.47
list of open windows, 9.9, 9.28
"Search," 9.61, 9.78

spell-checking, 9.110, 9.117
"Tile" story windows, 9.34
new publication without closing active,
1.171
open existing publication, 1.169
opening more than one, 1.170
"Printer styles" Addition, 19.168,
19.191-19.194
save all, 1.173, 18.22
selecting from Window menu, 1.153
switch between, 1.172
"Tile" view, 1.160-1.168, 1.177-1.180
drag-and-drop objects between
pubs, 1.167, 1.179-1.180
Mutiny on the Bounty, p.370

N

Name box, 18.11, 18.20
Nash, Ogden, p. 808
National Velvet, pp. 287, 295
NCD. *See* "Network Copy Detection"
Nelson, Christian, p. 265
"Network Copy Detection" (NCD),
22.53
"New...," 1.14, 1.171
"New Story," 9.25, 9.29
"New" styles, 8.10, 8.14-8.17
creating, 8.47-8.51
using the paragraph-view Control
palette, 8.49-8.50
Newsletter template, 14.37
"Next section," 15.111, 15.118
"Next style," 8.16, 8.28-8.32
example of using, 8.82
"No conversion, import as is," 17.27
Non-breaking spaces, 5.217-5.228
"Normal" (Image control), 10.205
"Normal" screen resolution, 10.36,
10.156
Nudge buttons, 3.11
changing measurement system, 3.18
changing nudge amount, 3.17
"# of pages," 1.23, 1.28

Numbering pages, 1.146-1.147
automatically, 1.146-1.147a
overriding format for, 1.149
tip for using on individual pages,
1.150
without front matter, 21.19
in Index
defining prefix for, 15.205
individually, 1.146, 1.147b, 1.150
of publications in Book List, 15.10
automatically and consecutively,
15.29
manually, 1.146
Numbering paragraphs
"Bullets and numbering...," 20.8
using indents and tabs, 6.61
Numbers
typing with the keypad, 1.324, 22.32
problems with, 22.33
"Numbers...," 1.23, 1.24, 1.32
Numeric keypad. *See* Keypad

O

Object-oriented graphics, 10.18,
10.23. *See also* PICT graphics
place icon for, 10.126
saving as EPS files, 10.40
saving files as, 10.96
Object-view Control palette, 3.32-
3.40
"Percentage-scaling" option, 3.33,
3.70-3.72
"Position" option, 3.32, 3.60-3.62
"Proportional-scaling" option, 3.34,
3.73
"Reflecting" options, 3.38, 3.82-3.85
"Rotating" option, 3.35, 3.76-3.79
"Scaling and Cropping" options, 3.74
"Sizing" option, 3.36, 3.63-3.69
"Skewing" option, 3.37, 3.80-3.81
Objects, 1.181-1.185. *See also* Graphics
bringing to the front, 1.216
clearing, 1.284

copying 1.281
cutting, 1.280
deleting, 2.25-2.26
as you select, 21.25
deselecting, 1.205-1.206, 1.210
drag-and-drop, 1.179-1.180
drawing, 2.23
finding invisible or "lost," 1.207-1.208,
1.211, 2.38
flipping, 3.97-3.100
grouping with "PS Group it," 2.81
layering, 1.189-1.195
losing, 1.191
moving, 1.196-1.201, 2.27
four-headed arrow cursor, 2.27
in a straight line, 2.30
in perfect alignment, 2.31-2.32
to another page, 2.28
to another publication, 1.179-1.180
using the Control palette, 3.87-3.88
very small, 2.29
multiple paste, 1.305
as inline graphic, 1.308
pasting, 1.282, 1.316
placing from Scrapbook, 1.318
reduce or enlarge by percentage, 3.91
resize using the Control palette, 3.89
proportionately, 3.92
resizing or modifying, 2.45
proportionally, 3.73
rotating, 2.85-2.93
using the "Rotating" option, 3.76-
3.79
using the rotating tool, 2.94-2.98
selecting, 1.182-1.188, 1.203-1.215,
2.24
all, 1.213
graphic, 1.203
hidden or trapped, 1.215
invisible, 1.214
line, 1.204
using marquee method, 1.208
using shift-click method, 1.207

selecting and deleting simultaneously, 21.25
sending to the back (or behind), 1.217
skewing, 3.95-3.96
stop jerking on the screen, 2.33, 22.14
Octavo, p. 778
"Odd/even," 19.61
OK button (in "Save as..." dialog box)
what to do when gray, 22.6
OLE, object linking and embedding, 11.103-11.132
"Apply button" icon for (Control palette), 11.123
cross-platform capabilities, 11.106
editing
embedded objects, 11.123
linked objects, 11.125
Excel spreadsheet, 17.39
"Insert object," 11.126-11.132
link info, 11.107, 11.109-11.110
maximum size of imported objects, 11.104
Microsoft Word table, 17.35
OLE-embedded, 11.111-11.114
"Insert object," 11.126
OLE-linked, 11.115-11.118
"Paste link," 11.115, 11.122
"Paste special," 11.122, 11.124
dialog box, 10.114-10.115
reliability of, 11.119-11.121
One color jobs, 16.6-16.9
Online Help file, 22.2
using, 20.3
"Open...," 1.14-1.15, 1.169-1.171
Opening
a new story in Story Editor, 9.25, 9.29
existing publications, 1.15, 1.169
more than one publication, 1.170
new publications, 1.14, 1.171
PageMaker application, 1.12
templates, 14.15
"Open stories" Addition, 9.10, 9.46

"Open template" Addition, 14.21-14.26
"Optimized screen:" 16.134, 19.121
"Options"
in Page setup, 1.23, 1.35-1.36
in "Place document" dialog box
"Convert quotes," 4.51
"Read tags," 4.52
"Retain cropping data," 4.50
"Retain format," 4.49
paragraph, 4.295, 4.329-4.347
"keeps" controls in, 4.329-4.347
removing "keeps" controls in, 4.333
violations of "keeps," 4.331
widows and orphans in, 4.340-4.347
"Options..."
in "Sort pages" dialog box, 20.139
"Paragraph rule options," dialog box, 7.5
"Type options" dialog box, 4.205
"Options" (Print), 19.86-19.104
graphics, 19.88-19.91
"Low TIFF resolution," 19.90
"Normal," 19.88
"Omit TIFF files," 19.91
"Optimized," 19.89
markings, 19.94-19.100
"Color-control strip," 19.96
"Crop marks," 19.96
"Density-control bars," 19.96
"Page information," 19.100
"Printer's marks," 19.95
"Registration marks," 19.97
PostScript, 19.101-19.104
"Include downloadable fonts," 19.103
"Include PostScript error handling," 19.101
"Use Symbol font for special characters," 19.104

"Write PostScript to file," 19.102, 19.138-19.149
send data, 19.92-19.93
"Faster (binary)," 19.92
"Normal (hex)," 19.93
"Orientation," 1.23, 1.26-1.27, 19.63
"Orphan control___lines," 4.344
Orphans, 4.340, 4.342-4.344, 4.347
Orwell, George, p. 155
"Other preferences" dialog box, 1.223
"Out of memory," 22.46
Outline fonts, 19.29-19.31
organizing, 19.35
printer, 19.30-19.33
installing, 19.33
screen, 19.30-19.31
installing, 19.31
"OV," 15.178
Ovals
changing borders of, 2.34-2.35
changing fill pattern of, 2.49
changing into a perfect circle, 2.48
changing shape of, 2.50
cropping with reversed, 21.30
drawing tool for, 2.10
reversing borders of, 2.37
transparent patterned border, 2.36
Overlays, 16.16-16.22
printing separate for spot color, 16.130
Overprinting, 16.24-16.26
colors
creating, 16.107
"Overprint" option, 16.80
examples of, 2.74, 16.26
fills, 2.65-2.66, 2.70
lines, 2.65-2.66, 2.71
Overrides
of measurement systems, 1.323
for paragraph rules, 7.25
style sheets, 8.3, 8.34-8.43
finding and changing, 8.72-8.73

including as part of a style, 8.67
permanent, 8.41-8.43, 8.69-8.70
removing, 8.68-8.70
sign for, 8.35
temporary, 8.38-8.40, 8.66, 8.68
Overset text
finding, 4.179
"OV," 15.178

P

"Page:" (from "Page setup"), 1.23, 1.25-1.26
"Page break before," 4.336
"Page dimensions," 1.23, 1.25-1.26
printing outside of, 19.131
vs. paper size, 19.69
Page icons, 1.95, 1.99
scrolling, 1.107
showing, 1.106
thumbnail view of publication pages, 20.125
"Page independence," 19.62
"Page information," 19.100
PageMaker 5.0 Script Language Guide, 20.78
PageMaker documents
converting earlier versions to PM 5.0, 17.46
converting PC Pagemaker pubs, 17.47
exporting
graphics, 17.43
text, 17.43
maintaining PM 4.x line breaks, 17.48
saving as templates, 14.8, 14.14
PageMaker files (Importing into PM), 4.63-4.86
copying text from Story view, 4.85
drag-and-drop between open pubs, 1.179, 4.86
inline, 1.180, 4.86
limiting display in list box, 4.84
placing
entire file, 4.82

selected stories, 4.83
"Story importer" dialog box, 4.73-4.81
viewing any story, 4.85
"Page # override:" 15.87, 15.175
"Page numbering" dialog box, 1.24
Page numbers. *See also* Numbering
pages
finding out in documents over 999,
21.33
formatting, 1.32, 1.146-1.149
identifying in publication, 21.33
Index, defining a prefix for, 1.33,
15.205
marked placeholders for, 1.146-
1.147a
in Story Editor, 9.18
Table of Contents
changing presentation of, 15.64
defining a prefix for, 15.61
formatting space before, 15.65
"Page range,"
"Add index entry," 15.90-15.96
"Index format," 15.196
Page "Ranges," 19.59
Pages
adding, 1.29, 1.127
deleting, 1.29, 1.128
establishing number of, 1.28, 1.98
finding out which page you are on,
22.13
limits, 1.95
moving among, 1.100-1.105, 1.107-
1.109
moving on screen, 1.126
numbering, 1.30-1.31, 1.32, 1.146-
1.149
rearranging with the "Sort pages"
Addition, 20.125
replacing, 1.129
starting publication with
double-page spread, 21.11
left-hand page, 21.11
viewing as thumbnails, 20.125, 20.144

Pages, Master. *See* Master pages
Page setup, 1.19-1.37
dialog box, 1.23-1.24
double-sided publications in, 1.35
margins in
setting or changing, 1.37
minimums and maximums, 1.19
page sizes, 1.20
changing, 1.25
changing orientation, 1.27
customizing, 1.26
pages in
adding or deleting, 1.29
establishing number of, 1.28
numbering, 1.30-1.32
starting on double-page spread,
21.11
starting on left-hand, 21.11
show facing pages in, 1.36
single-sided publication in, 1.34
"Target printer resolution," 10.20,
10.22
magic-resizing, 10.141, 10.142
Page views, 1.96
changing
all publication, 1.119
to 200%, 1.117, 1.121
to 25%, 1.113
to 400%, 1.118
to 50%, 1.114
to 75%, 1.115
to actual size, 1.16, 1.120—1.121
to "Fit in Window," 1.110-1.111,
1.120
to "Show pasteboard" (mini-view;
fit in world), 1.112
toggle "Actual size" and "200%,"
1.121
toggle "Actual size" and "Fit in
window," 1.120
using magnifying tool, 1.122
using reducing tool, 1.123
custom enlarge, 1.124, 21.3

moving, 1.126
using magnifying tool, 1.122, 21.3
viewing pub as thumbnails, 20.125
without scroll bars, 1.125
Paint-type graphics, 10.5, 10.15-10.22
as PICT, 10.28
examples of
"magic-resized," 10.22
normally resized, 10.21
pasted from Scrapbook, 10.24
placing, 10.126
icons for, 10.19, 10.126
saving, 10.17, 10.95
"Pair kerning," 5.10, 5.156, 5.160-5.162
point size of type for, 5.167
turning on or off, 5.166
Palettes
Color, 16.85-16.96, 16.103
in Story Editor, 9.16, 9.27
Library, 12.25-12.39, 12.51
Style, 8.46
Tool, 2.14
Panning graphics, 10.143
"PANOSE font matching" system,
1.240-1.271
and EPS graphics, 1.245
creating substitutions, 1.270-1.271
current status of, 1.263
"Default font," 1.262
dialog box, 1.255-1.266
disabling substitution, 1.268
EPS files and, 1.245, 10.46
"Exceptions," 1.253, 1.261
permanent substitutions, 1.250, 1.266
setting PANOSE options, 1.267
"Show mapping results," 1.264-1.266
"Spellings," 1.252, 1.260
"Substitution tolerance," 1.247, 1.258
"SuperATM™ font matching," 1.257
temporary substitutions, 1.250, 1.266,
1.269
turning on and off, 1.256
using with SuperATM, 1.244

"Paper," 16.63
changing, 16.114
color and fill, 16.64-16.68
"Paper" (Print), 19.65-19.85
"Auto overlap," 19.76
"Card stock," 19.72
"Center page in print area," 19.74
"Duplex," 19.85
"Manual tile," 19.77
"Print area," 19.73
"Reduce to Fit," 19.83
"Scale," 19.79-19.80
"Size," 19.69
"Source," 19.71
"Tall," 19.70
"Thumbnails," 19.84
"Tile," 19.75
Paragraph, 4.288-4.347
adding bullets to, 20.8-20.21
alignment, 4.242-4.248, 4.293
changing, 4.327
in Control palette, 4.311
break, 4.350
creating a drop cap in, 20.42-20.50
dialog box, 4.288-4.299
dictionary, 4.294
changing or adding, 4.328
formatting, 4.200-4.202, 4.288-4.289,
4.350
Control palette options, 4.300-
4.320
"Paragraph" dialog box options,
4.288-4.347
indents, 4.250, 4.291, 4.321-4.326
in Control palette, 4.305, 4.312-
4.313
inline graphic in its own, 10.247
numbering automatically, 20.8,
20.29-20.35
"Options," 4.295, 4.329-4.347
"keeps" controls, 4.330-4.339
widows and orphans in, 4.340-
4.347

paragraph-view Control palette, 4.300-4.320
returns
  when importing ASCII files, 17.22-17.24
rules, 4.296, 4.299
selecting, 4.289-4.290
space
  "After," 5.74-5.76, 5.79-5.84, 5.92-5.93
  "Before," 5.77-5.80, 5.92, 5.94
  cumulative nature of, 5.81-5.85
  eliminating too much space above last line, 22.23
  headlines, 5.85
  Scenario, 5.92
spacing, 4.297
two separate paragraphs on the same line, 21.32
"Paragraph rule options," 7.5
  "align to grid," 5.97-5.111
Paragraph rules
above and below, 7.51
above text, 7.41-7.45
baselines and, 7.20-7.21
baseline leading and, 7.33-7.35
below text, 7.46-7.50
"bottom," 7.24-7.32, 7.46-7.50
changing
  color or shade of, 7.57
  position of, 7.54
creating reverse, 7.56
"Custom," 7.37-7.40
dialog box, 7.5-7.12
  "indent," 7.5, 7.10
  "line color," 7.5, 7.8
  "line styles," 7.5, 7.7, 7.36-7.40
  "line width," 7.5, 7.9, 7.11-7.12
  "paragraph rule options," 7.5, 7.23-7.32
examples of, 7.30-7.32, 7.59
extending beyond the text block, 7.12

problems with not showing on screen, 22.27
hard spaces and, 7.44
in style sheets, 8.82
leading and, 7.17
notes about, 7.13
outside of the text block, 21.29
points and picas in relation to, 7.14
remove rules, 7.53
size of patterned, 7.39-7.40
slugs in relation to, 7.15-7.21, 7.35
style sheets and, 8.82
"top," 7.24-7.32, 7.41-7.45
unwanted, 22.28
with reverse type
  creating over a rule, 7.52
"Paragraph space," 4.292, 5.5, 5.72-5.96
"After," 5.74-5.76, 5.79-5.84, 5.92
  adding, 5.93
"Before," 5.77-5.80, 5.92
  adding, 5.94
cumulative nature of, 5.81-5.85
headlines, 5.85
in the Control palette, 4.306, 4.314
removing, 5.96
Scenario, 5.92
subheads, 5.85, 5.92
"Paragraph specifications," 4.288-4.299
in the Control palette, 4.300-4.320
Paragraph-view Control palette, 4.300-4.320
"Align-to-grid" option, 4.315, 5.110
"Alignment" buttons, 4.311
"Cursor-position indicator," 4.304, 4.318
"First-line indent," 4.305
"Grid-size" option, 4.307
"Left indent," 4.312
"Paragraph space after," 4.314
"Paragraph space before," 4.306
"Paragraph-view" button, 4.313

"Right indent," 4.313
"Style" option, 4.303, 4.319
toggling with character-view Control palette, 4.316
Parentheses
adjusting height of, 21.16
Pasteboard, 1.4, 1.150
finding objects lost on, 22.45
identifying page numbers, 21.33
stashing text on, 4.101
"Paste link," 10.117-10.120, 11.115, 11.124
"Paste special," 1.286, 10.110-10.119, 17.1
dialog box, 10.114-10.115
OLE, 10.11, 10.106, 10.117-10.120
  OLE-embedding, 11.122
  OLE-linking, 11.124
"Paste link," 10.118-10.120, 11.115, 11.124
text wrap an inital cap, 13.40
Pasting, 1.273, 1.282
from the Scrapbook, 1.316-1.317, 10.129
graphics
  from the Clipboard, 10.4, 10.131
  into the Scrapbook, 1.313
inline graphics, 10.224-10.225, 10.234
step-and-repeat, 10.245
linking and, 11.8-11.9
"Multiple paste," 1.287-1.310
"Paste special," 1.286, 10.110-10.119
power-, 1.283
problems with, 22.38
text, 4.269
text blocks, 4.128
text into a bounding box, 1.320
text into the Scrapbook, 1.314
with pointer tool, 1.278
with text tool, 1.279
with the keypad, 1.327
Patterned lines

custom weight, 2.52, 2.75
examples of, 2.20-2.22, 2.76
line styles, 2.61
reverse and transparent, 2.53, 2.59-2.60
examples, 2.62, 2.76
Patterned rules, 7.39-7.40
Patterns (screen), 10.176
PB, 1.150, 15.178, 21.33
PCs
converting PM files from, 17.47
importing files from, 17.40
  Microsoft Word, 17.41
Percentage values (tints), 16.7-16.8, 16.15
creating and applying, 16.106
with multi-color, 16.15
Perfect bound, p. 778
"2-up perfect bound," 19.244
Perpendicular lines. *See* Lines (drawing)
Perpendicular-line tool, 2.7
Pham, Tuan, pp. 466, 728
Photo CD images, 10.5, 10.47-10.50
color with, 10.50
filter for, 17.12
"PCD," 10.49
resolution, 10.50
within PageMaker publication, 10.48
PhotoShop, 10.16, 10.31, 11.80
saving files in, 10.100
PhotoStyler, 10.109
Picas, 5.6-5.7
development of system of, 496
interesting information about, 6.53
paragraph rules and, 7.14, 7.25
PICT graphics, 10.5, 10.18, 10.23-10.31
color applied to, 10.159
downloadable fonts with, 10.28
examples of, 10.30
image controlling, 10.163, 10.212
lightening, 10.212

paint-type graphics turned into, 10.24
saving
  paint images as (don't!), 10.55
  scanned images as, 10.55
turn into an EPS or TIFF file, 10.31
unpredictability of, 10.27
PICT 2, 10.26
Pixels, 10.15, 10.18
brightness of
  dark, 10.188
  light, 10.192
"Place"
in "Place document" dialog box, 4.54
in Story Editor
  inline graphic, 9.38
  placing a story on a publication page, 9.83
  text, 9.22, 9.35-9.37
"Place document" dialog box, 4.42-4.54
"Place Excel range:" dialog box, 17.37
Place icons
for graphics, 10.126
for text, 3.89
Placeholders
as text and graphics in templates, 14.3
for page numbers, 1.147
Placing. *See also* Importing
graphics, 10.4, 10.126-10.128, 17.32
  from the Scrapbook, 10.130
  icons for, 10.19, 10.126, 10.130
  "Include complete copy," 10.101-10.106
  independent, 10.4, 10.126-10.128
  inline, 10.224-10.225, 10.235
  problems with, 22.38-22.40
Library palette items, 12.19-12.20, 12.54
PageMaker pages as EPS files, 10.160

spreadsheets, 17.37
text, 4.28-4.83, 17.30
  as a new story, 4.55-4.56
  cancelling, 4.100
  from Story Editor to publication page, 9.83
  from the Scrapbook as a graphic, 1.318, 1.321
  in a bounding box (drag-placing), 1.321, 4.62
  in Story Editor, 9.22, 9.35-9.37, 9.83, 17.31
  PageMaker files into PM, 4.63-4.83
  text-only files, 17.33
  using autoflow, 4.92-4.93, 4.97
  using manual flow, 4.90, 4.95
  using semi-auto flow, 4.91, 4.96
  while ignoring the format, 4.35, 4.56
  while reading tags, 4.38-4.41, 4.60
  while retaining format, 4.34, 4.55
  with PageMaker reading tags, 4.60
Plus sign (in Style Palette), 8.35
PMG files, 10.260, 10.268-10.274
deleting, 10.278
Pointer tool, 1.182-1.190, 1.277-1.278
copying and pasting with, 1.277-1.278
switch to without deselecting object, 1.221
with graphics, 2.13
with inline graphics, 10.214
Points, 5.6-5.7
changing measurement system to, 5.9
development of system of, 496
interesting information about, 6.53
overriding measurement system with, 5.86-5.91
paragraph rules and, 7.14, 7.25
size of patterned rules, 7.40

PopChar, 1.331
"Position"
for super and subscript, 4.205, 4.215
changing, 4.253, 4.257-4.260
for tabs, 6.45, 6.63, 6.65-6.66
Posterized settings (Image control), 10.207
example, 10.210
PostScript, 10.39, 10.41, 10.97-10.98, 19.6
code, 10.41-10.43, 19.29
printers, 10.39
  example from, 10.45
  halftoning capabilities of, 10.77
  lines/inch default for, 10.180
  "Print document" dialog boxes for, 19.47-19.121
PostScript error handler, 19.101
PostScript laser printers. *See* Laser printers
PostScript print options, 19.102, 19.138-19.149
"EPS," 10.160, 19.146, 19.148
"Extra image bleed," 19.145
for a service bureau, 19.157-19.158
"For separations," 10.143, 19.147
  "Launch Aldus PrePrint," 19.143
  "Include downloadable fonts," 19.144
  "Normal," 19.139-19.141, 19.147
  printing hard copies yourself, 19.149
PostScript Printer Description. *See* PPD
Power failure
"mini-save" for, 18.2, 18.33
Power-nudge, 3.11
Power-paste, 1.283
PPD, 19.11-19.12, 19.21-19.23
as an application default, 19.20-19.25
"Auto Setup," 19.22
creating a custom PPD for downloaded fonts, 21.34

installing, 19.137
linking with LaserWriter 8, 19.20-19.25
"Select PPD," 19.23
"Update PPD" Addition, 19.166, 19.171-19.178
Preferences, 1.222-1.239
changing, 5.8-5.9
dialog box, 1.222
  for Story Editor, 9.48
  nudge button options, 3.15-3.18
  for Library palette, 12.39-12.41, 12.44-12.45
"Other preferences," 1.223
"Preserve EPS colors," 16.136
Preset settings (Image control), 10.204
normal, 10.205
posterized, 10.207
reverse, 10.170, 10.206
solarized, 10.208
Press, 1.1
Press-and-drag, 1.2
"Print" (odd or even pages), 19.61
"Print area," 19.73
"Print blank pages," 19.60
"Print colors in black," 19.115
"Print" dialog box, 19.47-19.121
"Color," 19.105-19.121. *See also* Color (Print)
  "Composites," 19.115
  "Mirror," 19.116
  "Negative," 19.116
  "Preserve EPS color," 19.111
  "Separations," 19.114, 19.117-19.121
"Document," 19.47-19.64. *See also* "Print document"
non-PostScript printers, 19.122-19.126
"Options," 19.86-19.104 *See also* "Options" (Print)
  "Graphics," 19.88-19.91

"Markings," 19.95-100
"PostScript," 19.101-19.104
  pre-press specifications, 19.87
"Send data," 19.92-19.93
"Paper," 19.65-19.85. *See also* "Paper"
  (Print)
"Duplex," 19.85
"Paper," 19.69-19.78
"Scale," 19.79-19.84
"Print document," 19.47-19.64
"Book," 19.64
"Collate," 19.56
"Copies," 19.55
"Orientation," 19.63
"Page independence," 19.62
"Pages," 19.59
"Print," 19.61
"Print blank pages," 19.60
"Print to," 19.53
"Proof print," 19.58
"Reverse order," 19.57
"Type" (printer), 19.54
"Print Monitor," 19.18
Print spoolers, 19.16-19.19
"Print to," 19.53
Print to disk, 19.138-19.149
Printer fonts, 19.30, 19.32
icons for 19.32, 19.35
  storing, 19.33
Printers
Apple LaserWriter, 10.39
  examples from, 10.92-10.93
  halftoning capabilities of, 10.77
Chooser, 19.20-19.25
  selecting from, 19.127
color, 16.38
  printing color comps on, 16.129
driver for, 19.13-19.15
high resolution imagesetters
  line frequency for, 10.185-10.186
Imagesetters, 19.9-19.10
  saving paper when printing to,
  19.70

Laser, 19.6
energy consumption of, 19.4
ROM in, 19.40
troubleshooting, 19.162-19.164
LaserWriter
appearance of proofs from, 10.92,
  10.196
lines/in default for, 10.180
paper sizes available to, 19.55
resolution of, 10.90
screen angle for, 10.181-10.183
screen default for, 10.175
Linotronic, 10.39, 10.92
examples from, 10.92-10.93, 10.198-
  10.208
lines/in default for, 10.180
paper sizes available to, 19.55
resolution, 10.78
PostScript, 10.39
examples from, 10.45
font downloading and, 19.41
halftoning capabilities of, 10.77
lines/in default for, 10.180
"Print" dialog box, 19.47-19.121
PPDs for, 19.11-19.12, 19.21-19.23
installing, 19.137
"Update PPD" Addition, 19.166
QuickDraw printers, 19.7-19.8
print dialog boxes for, 19.122-
  19.126
resizing graphics to fit the resolution
  of, 10.141
resolution of
  HP DeskWriter, 2.20
  LaserWriter 600 dpi, 2.21
  Linotronic 1270 dpi, 2.22
spoolers for, 19.16-19.19
"Printer styles" Addition, 19.168,
  19.191-19.194
copying print styles
  creating based on styles, 19.213,
  19.220
  to another computer, 19.208

creating a queue, 19.217
creating a print style, 19.220
"Define print styles," 19.206-19.213
  creating a print style, 19.220
  editing a print style, 19.221
  removing a print style, 19.222
dialog box, 19.195-19.205
"Job slugs" and "Queue logs," 19.214-
  19.216
  print info page, 19.224
  save a queue log, 19.225
"Preferences," 19.214-19.216
rearranging the order of a print
  queue, 19.223
removing a pub from queue, 19.218
temporarily overriding a print style,
  19.219
"Printer's marks," 19.95
Printing, pp. 727-784.
"Background printing," 19.18, 19.127
Book List, 15.26
  keeping original "Size" and
  "Source," 15.27
  selected page ranges, 15.30
  selected pubs in, 15.28
  to disk as a Postscript file, 15.31
  with auto renumbering, 15.29
"Build booklet..." Addition, 19.226-
  19.243
  booklet example, 19.244
  brochure example, 19.248
card stock, 19.72
Color, 16.129-16.139
  "Angle:" 16.139
  basics of color reproduction,
  16.10-16.15
  composites, 19.115
  four-color process basics, 16.31-
  16.36
  knockouts and traps, 16.23-16.30
  "Optimized screen:" 16.134
  overprinting, 16.24-16.26
  "Ruling:" (lpi), 16.135

separations, 16.16-16.22
  task for, 16.140
"Composite," 19.115
dialog boxes for, 19.47-19.121
enlarged pages, 19.80-19.82
envelopes, 19.72
error messages, 19.101
film, 19.116
from Story Editor, 9.10
graphics
  commercially, 10.93
  inaccuracy of, 10.92
higher resolution, 19.82
"Include PostScript error handler,"
  19.101
LaserWriter 8 driver, 19.20-19.25
linked documents, 11.27-11.30
multiple publications, 19.191, 19.217
non-consecutive pages, 19.129
number of copies, 19.1
outside page boundary, 19.131
page ranges, 19.129
portions of pages, 19.81
PostScript files yourself, 19.149
preparing pub for remote, 11.73,
  19.133-19.134
  do-it-yourself, 19.133
"Print Monitor," 19.18
"Printer styles" Addition, 19.191-19.216
printing to disk, 19.138-19.149
publications, 19.128
reduced pages, 19.79, 19.83
saving print specifications, 19.66
  without printing, 19.67, 19.130
scaling, 19.1, 19.79-19.82
"Reduce to fit," 19.83
"Separations," 19.106-19.121
service bureau for, 19.150-19.151
  tips, 19.152-19.161
"Setup," for PostScript printers, 19.20-
  19.25
three-paneled brochure, 19.248
thumbnails, 19.1, 19.84

transparencies, 19.72
troubleshooting, 19.162-19.164
using "Printer styles," 19.195-19.205
with a custom PPD for downloaded
   fonts, 21.34
Process colors (CMYK), 16.41,
   16.47. *See also* Four-color
   separation; CMYK
   as shown in color palette, 16.91
   "Edit color," 16.47-16.48
   libraries of, 16.53
"Proof print," 19.58
Proportional leading, 5.25, 5.38, 5.39-
   5.44
   baseline of, 5.39-5.44, 7.21
   examples of, 5.44, 5.58
   how to use, 5.63
Proportional type, 6.2
Proximity folder, 9.95, 9.100, 9.126
Proxy, 3.48-3.57
   arrow reference point, 3.54-3.55
   box reference point, 3.52-3.53
   changing the type of reference point,
      3.59
   importance of position of an active
      reference point, 3.56
   selecting an active point, 3.50-3.51,
      3.58
      using the keyboard, 3.116
      using the Numeric keypad, 3.117
P's and Q's (minding), p. 15
"PS Group it," 10.254, 10.259-10.291
   adding object(s) to a group, 10.287
   changing an object within a group,
      10.286
   grouping two or more objects, 10.284
   PMG files 10.260, 10.268-10.274
   taking a pub with a grouped object to
      a service bureau, 10.291
PSTYLES folder, 19.207
"PS Ungroup it," 10.267, 10.271-10.289
   changing an object within a group,
      10.286

deleting PMG file, 10.278
dialog box, 10.283
   disabling, 10.288
   displaying, 10.289
setting PMG file default, 10.288
ungrouping, 10.285
Publication
   Book List, 15.8-15.9
   charting professional info, 21.20
   closing multiple pubs, 1.174
   closing or quitting
      without making changes, 18.32
   compressing, 18.3-18.5, 18.28-18.29,
      22.4
   compressing, 18.3-18.5, 18.28-18.29
   dividing lengthy work into separate,
      15.7
   information about
      "Display pub info," 19.179
      job slugs and queue logs, 19.214-
         19.215
   missing link alert, 11.27
   multiple pubs, 1.151-1.180
   opening
      after power failure or malfunction,
         18.2; 18.33
      existing, 1.15, 1.169
      multiple, 1.170
      new 1.14, 1.171
   printing, 19.128
      one from inside another, 19.217,
         21.18
   recomposing text in, 21.27
   reducing size of, 18.28-18.29, 22.4
   running a diagnostic on, 21.28
   saving, 18.20
      changes to, 18.21
      copies of, 18.26-18.27
   sorting pages of, 20.125-20.149
   starting
      on a double-page spread, 21.11
      on left-hand page, 21.11
   templates for

making your own, 14.2, 14.7-
   14.12
   premade, 14.1, 14.29, 14.35-14.37
viewing as thumbnails, 20.125
Publication defaults, 1.9-1.11, 1.16
   changing through the character-view
      Control palette, 4.240
Publication page
   vs. master page, 1.131
   vs. story view, 9.6
Publish and Subscribe, 11.79-11.102
   defaults, 11.85, 11.100
   editing the original edition, 10.108,
      11.87, 11.98
   graphic formats supported, 11.82
   importing a text edition as a PICT,
      11.100
   link options, 11.84, 11.101
   PM as a "Subscriber," 11.80
   preventing updates, 11.86, 11.102
   preview window, 11.82, 11.90
   "Subscribe to," dialog box 11.88-11.92
   "Subscriber options," 11.93-11.99
   updating editions, 10.107, 11.97,
      11.101
Punctuation
   adjusting height of, 21.16
   hanging, 21.10

Q

Quatro, p. 778
QuickDraw, 10.39
   saving files in, 10.96
QuickDraw display language, 19.7,
   19.28
QuickDraw printers, 19.7-19.8
   print dialog boxes for, 19.123-19.126
QuickScript, 10.39
Quitting
   without saving changes, 18.32
Quote marks
   adjusting height of, 21.16
   converting typewriter to real, 4.61

R

RAM
   downloadable fonts and, 19.40, 19.45,
      22.50
   changing the memory allocated to
      PageMaker, 22.46
Rand, Paul, p. 579
"Range:"
   in "Bullets and Numbering..."
      Addition, 20.15-20.21
Ranges. *See also* Minimums and
   maximums
   printing page ranges, 19.129
"Read tags," 4.52, 4.60
Real World PageMaker, pp. 193, 397
Rearranging publication pages,
   20.125
Recomposing text, 1.242, 21.27
Rectangle tool, 2.9
Rectangles. *See also* Fills (graphic)
   changing borders of, 2.34-2.37
   changing corner styles of, 2.44
   changing fill pattern of, 2.46
   changing into a perfect square, 2.43
   creating two-color, 16.122
   drawing tool, 2.9
   resizing, 2.45
      proportionally, 3.73, 21.14
   reversing borders of, 2.37
   rounded corner styles, 2.15
   transparent patterned border, 2.36
Redraw the screen, 5.70
"Reduce to Fit," 19.83
Reducing the size of a publication,
   18.3-18.4, 18.12, 18.29
Reducing tool, 1.123
Reference points
   on the Proxy, 3.48-3.57
"Reflecting" option, 3.38, 3.82-3.85
"Registration," 16.62
   changing, 16.112
Registration marks, 19.97, 19.131
"Relist," 4.81

Remote printing
copying
only linked files not stored in pub, 19.136
Tracking Values for, 19.135
preparing pub for, 11.73, 18.34, 19.134
do-it-yourself, 19.133
PostScript file, 19.147
"Remove"
bullets or numbers, 20.20
Index entry, 15.138-15.140
styles, 8.12, 8.19, 8.55
"Remove extra carriage returns:," 17.22-17.24
"Remove transformations," 10.145
"Remove unreferenced topics," 15.187
"Repeat tab," 6.68
"Replace"
in "Spelling" window, 9.115
"Replace___ blank or more spaces with a tab," 17.25
"Replace existing index," 15.182
"Replace existing table of contents," 15.53, 15.66
Replacing
files, 18.12, 18.29
graphics
back to original proportions, 10.140
from outside PM, 10.128
inline, 10.236-10.237
with compressed version, 10.153
in "Save as" dialog box, 18.12, 18.21
text
a portion of a story, 4.59
an entire story, 4.57
between open pubs, 1.180
from the Clipboard, 4.270
in Story Editor, 9.36
with drag-and-drop text, 4.86
"Replacing entire story," 4.54, 4.57
in templates, 14.17

"Replacing selected text," 4.59
in templates, 14.18
Reproducing
graphics
on a copy machine, 10.185
"Reset tabs," 6.69
Resetting
spacing attributes, 5.11
Resident fonts, 19.34
results of using only, 19.39
Resizing
graphics
back to original proportions, 10.140
"magic," 10.22, 10.25, 10.33, 10.141-10.142
with the Control palette, 10.139
independent graphics, 10.138-10.139
inline graphics, 10.226, 10.239
"Proportional-scaling" option, 3.73
rectangles proportionally, 21.14
rotated text, 4.285
Resolution (graphic)
adjusting
detailed, nonPageMaker, 1.229
for commercial printing, 10.70
on a Linotronic printer, 10.78
on an Apple LaserWriter, 10.77
on TIFF files, 10.99
storing low, 10.103
Resolution (printing)
achieving higher, 19.82
"Restore original color," 16.123
"Retain format," 4.49, 4.55
Retrieving
documents "lost" to a power failure, 18.2, 18.33
Return (hard), 4.348-4.354
adjusting line breaks with, 21.7
Return key, 4.288, 6.5-6.12
paragraphs breaks and, 4.350

"Reverse" (Image control), 10.170, 10.206
"Reverse order," 19.57
Reversed
lines, getting rid of, 22.20
rule, 7.56
type, 4.235
finding lost, 4.236
preventing from getting lost, 4.237
setting over a paragraph rule, 7.52
"Revert to last mini-save," 18.31
"Revert to last-saved version," 18.30
RGB color model, 16.38
"Edit color," 16.42-16.43
Rich text format. *See* RTF
Right align, 4.245
"Right" indent
in the Control palette, 4.313, 4.322
in the "Paragraph specs" dialog box, 4.299, 4.322
Right reading emulsion up/down, 19.116
RM, 1.147a, 15.178
Rogers, Will, pp. 705, 866
ROM
resident fonts and, 19.34, 19.40
Rotating
an object, 2.85-2.98
in 45° increments, 2.92, 2.97
keeping objects selected after rotation, 2.93
multiple objects, 2.91, 2.95, 2.98
using the "Rotating" option, 3.76-3.79
using the rotating tool, 2.94-2.98
multiple text blocks, 4.277, 4.287
text, 4.271-4.287
changing, 4.277, 4.284
editing, 4.274, 4.283
how it affects text flow, 4.276
inline text or graphics, 4.278

text-wrapping and, 4.286
unrotating, 4.282
using the rotating tool, 4.272, 4.280
using the "Rotating" option, 4.273, 4.281
"Rotating" option, 3.35, 3.76-3.79
Rotating tool, 2.85-2.98
fixed point, 2.86
center point as, 2.91, 2.98
rotation lever, 2.90
selecting with, 1.187, 1.219
Roth, Steve, p. 397
Rousseau, p. 374
RTF
export filter for, 17.18
import filter for, 17.10-17.11
from PCs, 17.40
Rubinstein, Arthur, p. 16
"Rule above paragraph," 7.5, 7.41-7.45
"Rule below paragraph," 7.5, 7.46-7.50
Ruler guides, 1.38-1.75
adding, 1.58
deleting, 1.60, 1.62-1.63
hiding, 1.64a
locking, 1.67a, 1.68
minimums and maximums, 1.38
on layers
bringing to the front, 1.66b
sending to the back, 1.66a, 1.68
on master pages
setting, 1.137
showing changes, 1.61
showing changes on publication page, 1.38
repositioning, 1.59
showing, 1.61, 1.64b
"snap to guides"
turning off, 1.65b
using, 1.65a
tips on using, 1.43

unlocking, 1.67b
Ruler tick marks
drawing or moving objects
in perfect alignment with, 2.32
Rulers, 1.38-1.75
hiding, 1.52b
horizontal, 1.46
customizing, 1.53
how to use, 1.75
measurement options, 1.39-1.40
repositioning, 1.70-1.71
zero default for, 1.48
zero point, 1.44-1.45
"Indents/Tabs," 6.18, 6.33
minimums and maximums, 1.38
overriding measurements of, 1.323
showing, 1.52
"snap to," 1.56
tips on using, 1.43
vertical, 1.49
custom measurement, 1.55
customizing, 1.54
how to use, 1.75
measurement options, 1.40
repositioning, 1.70-1.72
zero default for, 1.48
zero point, 1.47-1.48
zero point
locking, 1.74a
repositioning, 1.70
resetting, 1.73
unlocking, 1.74b
using (Scenario), 1.75
Rules (lines). *See* Paragraph rules
"Ruling:" (lpi), 16.135, 19.109, 19.120-
19.121
"Run script..." Addition, 20.65-20.80
creating beautiful fractions, 4.262,
20.66
dialog box, 20.68-20.71
PageMaker 5.0 Script Language
Guide, 20.78

running a script
created in another program,
20.80
created in PM, 20.79
"File," 20.68
"Selection," 20.69
"Script language," 20.65
"Star Wrap," 20.76
trace a script, 20.78
"Running headers\footers..."
Addition, 20.81-20.124
"Create custom content" dialog box,
20.115
creating custom headers/footers,
20.123
creating footers, 20.122
creating headers, 20.121
dialog box, 20.89
if it won't run, 20.87
removing headers/footers, 20.124
with repeating text, 20.123

S
Saddle-stitch, p. 778
"2-up saddle stitch," 19.244
Saroyan, William, p. 271
"Saturation," 16.61
Save and Revert, pp. 717-726
"Save as...," 18.1-18.4
dialog box, 18.6-18.19
"All linked files," 18.17, 18.35
desktop, 18.18
eject, 18.19
"Files for remote printing, 18.17,
18.34
folders, 18.10
labels, 18.7-18.9
list box, 18.9
name box, 18.11, 18.20
generating templates from, 14.8,
14.14
to reduce size of documents, 18.3-
18.4, 18.29

when a file won't complete
the process, 22.5-22.7
when the OK button is gray, 22.6
when there's no room, 22.5
"Save changes before closing," 18.32
"Save option:" 18.5
"Save publication as." *See* "Save as..."
Saving
a publication, 18.20
changes to, 18.21
copies of, 18.26-18.28
changes in all open publications,
1.173
"faster," 18.5
for remote printing, 18.34
graphics
copies of, 10.94
draw-type, 10.96
files as MacPaint, 10.95
for placement into PM, 10.94-
10.100
from Adobe Illustrator, 10.97
from Aldus Freehand, 10.98
paint-type, 10.17, 10.95-10.96
PM pages as EPS, 10.40, 10.160
importance of doing so frequently,
18.1
linked files, 18.35
"mini-save," 18.2, 18.31
multiple publications, 18.22
"smaller," 18.5, 18.28
templates, 18.23
changes to, 18.24
copies of, 18.26-18.27
while copying linked documents,
18.34-18.35
Sayers, Dorothy L., p. 586
"Scale," 19.79-19.82
enlarge a portion, 19.80-19.81
enlarge the page, 19.80
reduce, 19.79
"Reduce to fit," 19.83
to increase resolution, 19.82

Scanned graphics, 10.4, 10.54-10.88
as EPS, 10.40, 10.55
as PICT, 10.55
as TIFFs, 10.32-10.33
examples of, 10.37-10.38
chart for, 10.58
examples of, 10.37-10.38, 10.62-
10.65, 10.80-10.88
grayscales, 10.58, 10.83-10.88
examples of, 10.83-10.93
halftones, 10.58, 10.66-10.71, 10.74
examples of, 10.80-10.88
line art, 10.58
examples of, 10.37
Scenarios
baselines, aligning, p. 22
defaults, setting, p. 4
"Find," using, p. 428
"Finding and changing text," p. 435
nested indents, examples of, p. 344
numbered paragraphs, creating with
tabs and indent, p. 343
paragraph space "before" and
"after," p. 288
style sheets, using
"Create as you go," p. 410
"I know what I want," p. 411
WOW p. 412
templates, when, where, why, and
how to create, p. 590
text wrap on master pages, p. 585
using the keyboard to operate the
Control palette, p. 164
zero point, using, p. 28
Schiller, Friedrich, p. 3
Scrapbook, 1.313-1.318
deleting images from, 1.315
image controlling graphics from,
10.163
pasting graphics from, 1.316, 10.129
pasting graphics into, 1.313
pasting text from, 1.317
pasting text into, 1.313-1.314

place icon for, 10.130
placing
  graphics from 10.130
  text from as graphics, 1.318
using with templates, 14.19
Screen, 10.69
defaults, 10.79
for grayscales, 10.72-10.79
  examples of, 10.83-10.88
for halftones, 10.70-10.71
  examples of, 10.80-10.82
in Linotronic, 10.78
in PostScript printers, 10.77
"Screen," 10.176, 10.181-10.183
Screen fonts, 19.30-19.31, 19.33
improving look of, 19.41
installing, 19.31
Screen patterns, 10.162, 10.176
Screen percentages (tints), 16.7-16.8
creating and applying, 16.106
with multi-color, 16.15
Screen redraw, 1.97
Screen version of graphic files,
  10.41
printing, 11.29
from QuickDraw printers, 19.8
Screen view
inaccuracy of, 10.91
interruptible screen redraw, 1.97
"Screened," 10.162, 10.169, 10.171,
  10.173-10.175
"Contrast" and, 10.195
"Lightness" and, 10.191
Screened graphics, 10.68
Scripts, 20.65-20.80
fraction scripts, 4.262, 20.66
from other programs, 20.67, 20.80
PageMaker 5.0 Script Language
  Guide, 20.78
ready-made scripts, 20.65-20.76
running a script on the pasteboard,
  20.71, 20.79
trace a script, 20.72-20.75, 20.78

"Scrollbars"
view page without, 1.125
Seagull, Nathan, p. 813
"Search," 9.57, 9.75
Index, 15.204
"Search library," 12.63-12.76
"Select all"
from Edit menu, 1.213
in Story Importer dialog box, 4.74,
  4.82
"Select cross-reference topic" dialog
  box, 15.114
"Select topic" dialog box, 15.114
Selecting, 1.181-1.188, 1.202-
  1.221. *See also* Deselecting
deleting at the same time, 21.25
graphics, 1.203
imported graphics to crop, 1.220
inline graphics, 10.214
lines, 1.204
lines and shapes, 2.16
marquee method of, 1.208, 1.215,
  2.24
more than one object
  using the marquee method, 1.208
  using the shift-click method,
    1.207
objects
  additional, 1.209
  all, 1.213
  hidden or trapped, 1.215
  invisible, 1.214
  one or more, 2.24
  to rotate, 1.219
  under a guide, 1.212
  underneath another object, 1.211
paragraphs, 4.290
shift-click method of, 1.207
text
  to change leading, 5.27-5.31
  to modify, 1.218
  to rotate, 1.219
  while in Story Editor, 9.40

with keyboard, 1.328
with keypad, 1.326
text blocks, 1.202
with text tool, 1.277-1.279
with the pointer tool, 1.277-1.278
Semi-autoflow, 4.91, 4.96
"Send to back," 1.217
Separations, 16.16-16.30. *See also*
  Four-color separation; Spot color
knockouts, 16.24, 16.28-16.30
  traps, 16.29-16.30
overprinting, 16.24-16.26
printing, 16.12, 16.130-16.140
  "Angle:" 16.139
  "Optimized screen" 16.134
  "Ruling:" (lpi), 16.135
  selecting inks to print, 16.131-
    16.133, 16.137
  spot colors as process colors,
    16.138
  task for, 16.140
  with "Print blank pages," 16.133
when you don't need them, 16.13,
  16.22
when you need them, 16.14
Serianni, Tom, p. 652
Service bureaus, 19.10, 19.150-19.161
preparing publication for, 19.134
  do-it-yourself, 19.133
  PostScript file, 19.147
tips
  on driving them nuts 764
  on using appropriately, 19.152-
    19.161
"Set width," 4.205, 5.210-5.216
applying, 5.215
changing, 4.238
removing, 5.216
Settings (preset Image control)
normal, 10.205
posterized, 10.207
reverse, 10.170, 10.206
solarized, 10.208

75% page view, 1.115
Shakespeare, William, pp. 74, 236,
  361, 508, 751
Shaw, George Bernard, pp. 508,
  520, 835
Shift-click
method of selecting, 1.207
Shift-Return
in style sheets (Scenario), 8.79
indents/tabs and, 6.10-6.12
line breaks, 4.348-4.354
without adding paragraph space,
  5.95
"Show index" dialog box, 15.119
list box in, 15.136
"Show index..." command, 15.135
"Show layout problems," 1.222
"keeps" violations, 1.228, 4.331
"loose/tight lines," 1.227
"Show pasteboard," 1.112
Signatures and impositions, p. 778
Sikora, Gaia, p. 645
Sikora, John, p. 715
Single-sided publication
creating, 1.34
icon for, 1.34, 1.99, 1.133
"Size," 19.69
"Size" of font, 4.205, 4.229-4.230
in Control palette, 4.211
Size of publication
reducing, 18.29, 22.4
Slash (non-breaking)
creating, 5.228
Slide recorder, 16.38
Sloan, Jr., Alfred P., p. 515
Slugs, 5.32
paragraph rules and, 7.15-7.22, 7.35
Small caps, 4.205
as an attribute in "Find," and
  "Change," 9.51, 9.62, 9.79
changing sizes, 4.252
in Control palette, 4.215

Smart ASCII
export filter for, 17.18-17.19
import filter, 17.10-17.11
for files from PCs, 17.40
import text-only files using, 17.33
"Text-only import filter" dialog
box, 17.21-17.27

"Snap to guides"
nudge buttons and "Snap to"
constraints, 3.16
turning off, 1.65b
using, 1.65a

"Snap to rulers"
nudge buttons and "Snap to"
constraints, 3.16
using, 1.56
with "Align to grid," 5.107

Solarized setting (Image control),
10.208

Sontag, Susan, p. 409

"Sort" (Index entry), 15.83, 15.129-
15.134

"Sort pages..." Addition, 20.125-
20.149
dialog box, 20.135-10.140
if it won't run, 20.145
rearranging publication pages,
20.147
moving elements to fit new
margins, 20.148
reduce or enlarge the page icons,
20.146
viewing a pub as detailed thumbnails, 20.144, 20.1

"Source," 19.71

"Space after," 7.18

"Space before," 7.18

Spacebar
on using to align text (don't!), 6.3

Spaces
blank, non-breaking, 5.217-5.228
adjusting line breaks with, 21.7
with inline graphics, 10.244

with paragraph rules, 7.44
em, 5.217-5.218, 5.221-5.222
creating, 5.223
en, 5.217, 5.219, 5.221-5.222
creating, 5.224
thin, 5.217, 5.219, 5.221-5.222
creating, 5.225

"Spacing," 4.297, 4.299
attributes dialog box, 5.10-5.11
in the Control palette, 4.306, 4.314

Spacing, text. *See* Text spacing

Special characters, 1.331, 4.264,
4.355-4.359
inputting into "Find" box, 9.65

Special effects
creating a star-shaped text wrap,
20.76
creating drop caps for, 20.59
creating initial caps for, 13.40

Special Techniques, pp. 813-838
list of throughout the book, 21.2

Specifications (type), 4.205-4.235
character-view Control palette,
4.206-4.218
making several at once, 4.239
"Type specs" dialog box, 4.205

"Spelling," 9.24

Spelling checker, 9.90-9.120
adding words to, 9.120
dictionaries, in 9.95-9.103
user, 9.97-9.99, 9.120-9.126
limitations of, 9.91
using, 9.117
for one word, 9.118
in multiple publications, 9.110,
9.117
window, 9.104-9.116

Spinoza, p. 34

Spoolers, 19.16-19.19

Spot color, 16.10-16.15
as shown in color palette, 16.92
changing to process color, 16.138
knockouts, 16.24, 16.27-16.28

with traps, 16.29-16.30, 16.127
libraries of, 16.53
overprinting, 16.24-16.26
percentage values (tints) with, 16.15
separations for, 16.16-16.22
printing, 16.130-16.140
tints, 16.7-16.8, 16.15, 16.106
trapping, 16.29-16.30, 16.127

Spreadsheet
importing
as a PICT, 17.38
as an OLE object, 17.39
placing, 17.37

Square. *See also* Fills (graphic)
changing
a rectangle into, 2.43
borders of, 2.34-2.37
corner styles of, 2.44
fill pattern of, 2.46
creating a two-color, 16.122
drawing a perfect, 2.42
resizing, 2.45
reversing borders of, 2.37
rounded corner styles, 2.15
transparent patterned border, 2.36

Standard, Paul, p. 9

"Standoff in inches," 13.9, 13.16-13.20

"Start page #:" 1.23, 1.30

"Status," 11.38
determining, 11.61-11.62

Status indicators, 11.40-11.49
kind indicators, 11.49
page location, 11.49
status chart, 11.40

Stevenson, Robert Louis, pp.
262, 357, 378

"Stop all editions," 11.86, 11.102
overriding, 11.102

"Store copy in pub...," 10.103-10.104,
11.16-11.17, 11.19, 11.55, 11.57

Story, 4.31, 4.113
"Add cont'd line...," 4.160-4.167
tasks for, 4.183, 4.185

adding bullets to paragraphs within,
20.36
"Display story info...," 4.139-4.150,
4.181
drag and drop between pubs, 1.179,
4.86
inline, 1.180, 4.86
"Find overset text," 4.133-4.135, 4.179
inserting placed text into, 4.58
numbering paragraphs in, 20.38-
20.39
placing
from another PM file, 4.82-4.83
new, 4.56
with tags read, 4.60
replacing
entire, 4.57
portions, 4.59
with drag-and-drop text, 4.86
"Traverse text blocks...," 4.136-4.138,
4.180
viewing from other PageMaker files,
4.85

Story Editor, pp. 413-460
accessing layout page while in, 9.31,
9.87-9.88
applying styles to text in, 8.74, 9.43
"Change," 9.24, 9.67-9.82
attributes, 9.62-9.64, 9.80
"Attributes" dialog box, 9.58, 9.74
characters with no special
attributes, 9.78
characters with special attributes,
9.79
eliminating characters or text
attributes, 9.81
invisible or special characters,
9.82
"Options" in, 9.70-9.75
text attributes, 9.80
what to do when gray (not
available), 22.42
window, 9.67, 9.76

"Close," 9.11, 9.22
closing
  all stories in, 9.20, 9.47
  "Close story" 9.25, 9.83
  with close box, 9.83, 9.89
color palette in, 9.13, 9.16
Control palette in, 9.16, 9.44
discarding stories, 9.84
"Display ¶," 9.17, 9.42, 9.49
"Display style names," 9.16, 9.43, 9.49
editing text while in, 9.41
exporting story while in, 9.39
"Find," 9.24, 9.50-9.66
  attributes, 9.63
  characters with no special
    attributes, 9.61
  characters with special attributes,
    9.62
  invisible or special characters,
    9.65
  "Options" in, 9.53-9.57
  problems with, 22.43
  using (Scenario), 9.60
  what to do when gray (not
    available), 22.42
  wildcard characters, 9.66
  window, 9.50, 9.59
font displayed in
  changing, 1.237
  changing size of, 1.238
font displayed in, 9.13
  changing, 9.15, 9.48
important note about stories in, 9.19
importing
  graphics into, 9.38
  inline graphics into, 9.38, 10.238,
    17.32
  outside story into, 9.35-9.36
  PageMaker story into, 9.37
  text, 17.31
Index entries in, 9.18, 9.24
index markers
  moving, 15.162

viewing contents of, 15.161
indexing by keyword, 15.157
  adding secondary entries, 15.160
  customizing entries, 15.158
  in more than one pub, 15.159
inline graphics in, 9.18, 10.222
  finding, 10.225
  placing or replacing, 9.38, 17.32
invisible characters in, 9.17, 9.25
  displaying or hiding, 9.42
kerning while in, 5.172
layout view in, 9.6
leave a story in without placing, 9.85
linking story while in, 9.39
menu bar in, 9.21
minimums and maximums, 9.1
"New story," 9.25, 9.29
opening
  existing story in, 9.30
  new story in, 9.25, 9.29
  stories from multiple publica-
    tions, 9.9
page-number markers in, 9.18
"Place," 9.22, 9.35-9.38
  placing text onto pub page, 9.83
"Preferences" in, 9.48
printing from, 9.10
returning to layout page from, 9.32
  where you were in Story Editor,
    9.88
  where you were originally, 9.87
saving a story while in, 9.89
"Search," 9.57, 9.75
  for an index entry, 15.204
selecting text while in, 9.40
set defaults, 1.239
spelling checker, 9.90-9.120
  adding words to, 9.120
  dictionaries, in 9.97-9.103
  limitations of, 9.91
  using, 9.117-9.126
  window, 9.104-9.116
"Spelling" function in, 9.24

story view, 9.6
style palette in, 9.16
style sheets in, 8.74, 9.43
Table of Contents in, 9.24
  creating, 15.44
title bar
  numbers in, 9.8
Toolbox in, 9.7
type specs while in, 9.13, 9.26, 9.44
unplaced stories in, 9.11-9.12, 9.85
using with style sheets
  to find and change, 8.72-8.73
window menus in, 9.27-9.28
windows in
  bringing to the front a buried,
    9.31
  cascading, 9.33
  moving without making active,
    9.45
  numbers in title bar, 9.8
  open all story windows of active
    pub, 9.10, 9.46
  resizing, 9.5
  sending to back, 9.9
  tiling, 9.34
Story importer, 4.63-4.71
  dialog box, 4.73-4.81
  on-line Help, 4.70
  Story Importer Filter, 4.71-4.72
Story Importers 4 and 5, 17.11
  importing PM 4.x and 5.0 stories
    with, 17.42
"Story view," 1.222, 9.15
  changing font displayed in, 1.237,
    9.48
  changing size of font displayed in,
    1.238, 9.48
Strunk, William, Jr., pp. 382, 406
"Style" (in "Page numbering" dialog
  box), 1.24, 1.32
Style manual
  custom dictionary as, 9.127
  publication info as, 19.179

Style names
  typing in tags, 4.39
Style of type, 4.205
  changing, 4.231-4.232
  in the Control palette, 4.206-4.218
Style palette
  asterisk in, 8.36
  hiding, 8.46b
  plus sign in, 8.35
  showing, 8.46a
Style Sheets, pp. 381-412
  applying color, 16.121
  overriding color, 16.100
  applying, 8.62
    from the keyboard, 8.64
    to text in Story Editor, 8.74
  "bad record index"
    fixing, 8.60, 21.28
  "based on," 8.15, 8.21-8.27, 8.50-8.51
    creating through the Control
      palette, 8.51
  Book Lists and, 15.12
  changing, 8.63
    using keyboard, 8.64
  color style sheets, 16.69, 16.78
    adding color to text Style Sheets,
      16.97
    applying color, 16.120-16.121
    editing, 16.69
  copying, 8.5, 8.13, 8.20
    all styles from another pub, 8.56
    drag-and-drop text, 8.57
    through the Library palette, 8.58,
      12.24
  creating new styles for, 8.10, 8.14-
    8.17, 8.47-8.
    using the Control palette, 8.49-
      8.50
  dialog box, 8.7-8.13
  editing, 8.11, 8.18, 8.53
  examples for how to use
    (Scenarios), 8.79-8.82
  exporting a tagged story with, 8.77

for printing, 19.192
formatting options in, 8.33
importing styles into, 8.36, 8.59
in Story Editor, 9.25, 9.43
in Table of Contents, 15.35-15.36
    created by, 15.42-15.43
    editing, 15.45
    title, 15.48
    using, 15.60
including "keeps" controls in, 4.295
modifying copied, 8.3, 8.11, 8.18,
    8.53
names of styles in, 8.8
"next style" in, 8.16
overriding, 8.3, 8.35, 8.38-8.43, 8.65
    finding and changing, 8.72-8.73
    include as part of style, 8.67
    permanent, 8.41-8.43, 8.69-8.70
    preserving, 8.66
    removing, 8.68-8.70
    sign for, 8.35
    temporary, 8.38-8.40, 8.66, 8.68
palette, 8.46
paragraph rules used with, 8.82
removing styles from, 8.12, 8.19,
    8.26-8.27, 8.55
renaming style in, 8.52
replacing styles in, 8.54
saving, 8.5
Scenarios, 8.79-8.82
setting defaults for, 8.78
Shift-Return used with, 8.79
specifications for, 8.9
tagging, 8.2, 8.4
    word processing documents, 8.75-
    8.76
text formatting in, 8.2, 8.33
transforming one style to another,
    8.61
two styles in one ¶ (faking it), 21.32
using Control palette, 8.49-8.50
using "Find" for, 9.60
using the Library palette, 8.58

viewing styles, 8.71
    "List styles used" Addition, 8.44-
    8.45
    styles, fonts and links in a pub,
    19.179

Subheads
    with "paragraph space," 5.85, 5.92
"Subscribe to...," 11.88-11.92
"Subscriber options...," 11.93-11.99
Subscript, 4.205, 4.215
    as an attribute in "Find," and
    "Change," 9.51, 9.62, 9.79
    changing size and placement of,
    4.253-4.261
Suitcase II, 19.35
"SuperATM," 1.244, 1.257
SuperPaint, 10.16
    examples from, 10.29-10.30
    saving files in, 10.95
Superscript, 4.205, 4.215
    as an attribute in "Find" and
    "Change," 9.51, 9.62, 9.79
    changing size and placement of,
    4.253-4.261
"Suppress page range," 15.96
Swanson, Chip, p. 822

T
Table of Contents, 15.4, 15.32-15.67
    "Create table of contents" dialog box,
    15.51-15.56
    creating
        for Book List, 15.63
        for current publication, 15.62
        in Story Editor, 15.44
        on publication page, 15.44
    default style for, 15.43, 15.63
        example of 15.57
    entry
        formatting space after, 15.65
        tagging, 15.59
    examples of, 15.57-15.58
    formatting, 15.67

in Story Editor, 9.24
page numbers
    changing presentation of, 15.64
    defining prefix for, 1.33, 15.61
    formatting space before, 15.65
paragraphs in
    selecting, 15.34
    use of, 15.33
placing in publication, 15.49-15.50
replacing or updating existing, 15.66
separate files for, 15.7
style sheets in, 15.35-15.36
    created by placing, 15.42-15.43
    editing, 15.45, 15.67
    example of customized, 15.58
    using, 15.60
tagging material for, 15.59
time needed to "Create" or "Show,"
    15.5
title, 15.47
    style assigned to, 15.48
Tabs (and Indents), pp. 333-360
    adding or setting new, 4.250, 6.63
    changing alignment of, 6.67
    clearing, 6.70
    copying formatting of, 6.84
    defaults
        application, 6.18, 6.86
        publication, 6.18, 6.85
    deleting, 6.65
    deselecting in ruler, 6.89
    examples of alignment for, 6.13
    frustrations of, 6.1
    how they work, 6.14-6.52
    inline graphics with, 10.231, 10.244,
    10.251
    internal, pre-set, 6.18
    leaders with, 6.71
        creating custom, 6.72-6.73
        over text-wrapped objects, 6.75
        removing, 6.74
    measurement system of, 6.22
    minimums and maximums 6.1

moving, 6.66
numbered paragraphs, 6.61
on top of indent markers, 6.64
paragraph specific, 6.10-6.12, 6.18,
    6.63
"Position" of, 6.45, 6.63, 6.65-6.66
repeating, 6.68
replacing spaces with, 6.88
resetting, 6.69
ruler for, 6.18-6.22
    using, 6.23-6.48
    to justify text left and right, 6.76,
    20.31
troubleshooting for, 6.4-6.9
Tagged Image File Format. *See* TIFF
Tags
    creating
        Scenario, 8.81
    exporting, 17.43
    in style sheets, 8.2, 8.4
    placing text with, 4.38-4.41, 4.60,
    8.76
    with autoflow, 4.93
Taming of the Shrew, p. 380
"Target printer resolution," 10.20,
    10.22
    magic-resizing, 10.141
    using the Control palette, 10.142
Templates, pp. 589-600
    advantages of using, 14.5-14.6
    Book Lists and, 15.12
    copies of, 14.4
    creating with links, 11.74
    grid, 14.38-14.39
    making your own, 14.3
        when, why, and how, 14.7-14.12
    opening
        copies of, 14.4, 14.13
        original, 14.15, 18.25
    premade
        calendar template, 14.29
        envelope template, 14.35
        fax cover sheet, 14.36

how to use, 14.30-14.34
list of, 14.1
newsletter template, 14.37
placeholders in, 14.3
replacing graphics from
    with a graphic file, 14.20
    with Clipboard or Scrapbook
        graphics, 14.19
replacing text from premade
    entire stories, 14.17
    headlines, 14.16
    selected portions, 14.18
saving, 14.14, 18.23-18.24
    copies of, 18.26-18.27
Style sheets and, 8.5

Text, pp. 165-266. *See also* Text blocks,
    Type
adding bullets to, 20.36-20.39
Aldus Additions for, 4.130
aligning, 4.243-4.248
changing
    alignment, 4.242
    case, 4.251
    default specs through the
        Control palette, 4.240, 4.239
    font, 4.228
    leading, 4.234
    position, 4.253
    several specs at once, 4.239
    shifting the baseline, 4.263
    size of small caps, 4.252
    superscript and subscript, 4.254-
        4.261
    type size, 4.229-4.230
    type style, 4.231-4.233, 4.235
    with key commands in the
        Control palette, 4.227
clearing, 1.284, 4.266-4.267
color, setting a default for, 16.126
columns of. *See also* Columns
    arranging in several sets, 21.21
condensing, 4.238
copying, 1.281, 4.268

creating a bounding box for, 1.319,
    4.26
creating drop caps, 20.59
creating headers/footers for, 20.81-
    20.100
creating in PageMaker, 4.5
    on a master page, 1.139
creating two paragraphs on the same
    line, 21.32
cutting, 1.280, 4.267
default style for, 4.36, 4.365-4.366
    changing through the Control
        palette, 4.240
    setting in insertion point, 4.20-
        4.24
deleting
    from the Scrapbook, 1.315
deleting, 4.266
    from the Scrapbook, 1.315
displaying story info, 4.139-4.150,
    4.181
drag-and-drop between open pubs,
    1.179, 4.86
drag-placing into a bounding box,
    4.62
editing, 4.10-4.17
    prevent text block from
        expanding while, 21.24
expanding, 4.238
    prevent text block from, 21.24
finding text hidden in
    windowshades, 4.133-4.135,
formatting, 4.189-4.249
    in style sheets, 8.2, 8.33
gray shading for, 4.265
inserting into a story, 4.58
lines of
    creating longer than 22.75
        inches, 21.23
    lengthening or shortening, 4.116
    maintaining PageMaker 4.x line
        breaks, 17.48
linking, pp. 531-562

automatically, 11.2, 11.12, 11.16-
    11.22
"Link options for," 11.55-11.57
when typed in PM, 11.11, 11.70
lost
    finding, 4.236
    preventing, 4.237
minimums and maximums, 4.1
multiple paste, 1.307
numbering paragraphs, 20.38-20.39
pasting, 1.282, 4.269-4.270
    from the Scrapbook, 1.317
    into a bounding box, 1.320
    into the Scrapbook, 1.314
placing, 4.28-4.62, 17.30, 17.33
    as a new story, 4.55
    dialog box for, 4.42-4.54
    from the Scrapbook, 1.318
    in a bounding box (drag-
        placing), 4.62
    into Story Editor, 9.22, 9.35-9.37,
        17.31
    PageMaker files into PageMaker,
        4.63-4.86
    with PM reading the tags, 4.60
placing while
    ignoring the format, 4.35
    reading the tags, 4.38-4.41
    retaining the format, 4.33-4.34
power-pasting, 1.283
problems with
    always showing up in the wrong
        font, 22.18
    "puzzling behavior," 4.332, 22.11
    refusing to appear when you type,
        22.16
    squishing up, 22.30
recomposing, 21.27
replacing
    a portion of a story, 4.59
    an entire story, 4.57
    from the Clipboard, 4.270
    with drag-and-drop text, 4.86

reverse
    finding lost, 4.236
    preventing from getting lost,
        4.237
    setting over a paragraph rule,
        7.52
rotated, 4.271-4.287
    changing degree of, 4.284
    editing, 4.274, 4.283
    multiple text blocks, 4.287
    resizing, 4.285
    to unrotate, 4.282
    using the "Rotating" option in
        the Control palette, 4.281, 4.28
    using the rotating tool, 4.280
    with inline graphics, 4.278
    wrapping around a graphic, 4.286
selecting
    to change leading, 5.27-5.31
    with the keypad, 1.326
selecting, 1.181-1.215, 4.191, 4.195-
    4.203
    to modify, 1.187, 1.218-1.220
    with the keyboard, 4.204
    with the keypad, 1.326
    with the mouse, 4.203
shifting the baseline, 4.263, 21.32
solutions for behavioral problems of,
    4.332
stashing text on the pasteboard,
    4.101
threaded, 4.109-4.112, 4.123-4.124
turning into a graphic, 10.151
wrap around a star-shape, 20.76

Text attributes
of inline graphics
    applying, 10.214
    available to, 10.215
    no available to, 10.216, 10.218

Text blocks, 4.4, 4.8-4.9, 4.102-4.129.
    See also Text
aligning flush left and flush right,
    6.76, 21.31

balancing columns of, 4.168-4.178
copying, 4.126
creating longer than 22.75 inches,
    21.23
cutting, 4.125
deleting, 4.119-4.121, 4.127
displaying info about, 4.151-4.159,
    4.182
dividing, 4.122
drag-and-drop between open pubs,
    1.179, 4.86
    placing inline, 1.180, 4.86
finding linked text blocks, 4.136-
    4.138, 4.180
finding lost or rolled up, 22.12
finding overset text, 4.133-4.135,
    4.179
handles of, 4.104-4.109
inline graphics and
    centering, 10.249
    problems with, 10.225
linespace between two
    maintaining consistent, 21.8
moving, 4.115
narrowing, 4.116
on the pasteboard, 4.101
    lost, 22.45
pasting, 4.128
power pasting, 1.283
preventing from expanding, 21.24
puzzling behavior of, 4.332, 22.11,
    22.39. See also Text, problems
    with
re-uniting threaded, 4.124
    finding adjacent text blocks,
        4.180
removing threaded, 4.123
replacing, 4.128
restraining size of, 4.26
rotated, 4.275-4.277
selecting, 4.114
separating, 4.129
shortening, 4.117

threaded, 4.107-4.109, 4.122-4.124
    adding jump-lines to, 4.183-4.184
    finding adjacent text blocks,
        4.180
unrolling stubborn, 22.11, 22.39
widening, 4.116
windowshade loops belonging to,
    4.106-4.109, 4.111
Text flow, 4.32, 4.87-4.100
    autoflow, 4.92-4.93, 4.97
        overriding, 4.98
        stopping, 4.99
    icons for, 4.88
    keyboard shortcuts for, 4.98
    manual, 4.90, 4.95
        overriding, 4.98
    semi-autoflow, 4.91, 4.96
"Text flow," 13.8, 13.13-13.15
Text icon (loaded), 4.88-4.89
    cancelling, 4.100
"Text only," 17.11, 17.19
    importing files, 17.33
"Text-only import filter" dialog box,
    17.21-17.27
Text spacing
    "align to grid," 5.97-5.111
    blank spaces, 5.217-5.228
    hard spaces (non-breaking), 5.217-
        5.228
    hyphenation, 5.229-5.255
    kerning, 5.151-5.172
        "Expert kerning..." Addition,
            5.173-5.179
    leading, 5.12-5.71
    letter spacing, 5.132-5.150. See also
        Letter space
    minimums and maximums, 5.1
    paragraph spacing, 5.72-5.96
    set width, 5.210-5.216
    tracking, 5.180-5.192
        "Expert tracks..." Addition, 5.193-
            5.209

word spacing, 5.112-5.131. See also
    Word spacing
Text tool, 4.10-4.11, 4.191-4.192
    copying and pasting with, 1.277
    with inline graphics, 10.214
Text tool cursor, 4.12, 4.193
Text wrap, pp. 575-588
    adding handles to, 13.31
    changing, 13.29
    "Column break," 13.13
    creating a standard, 13.27
    customizing, 13.30
    default, 2.84
        deleting, 13.44
        problems with, 22.22
        setting, 13.43
    delaying redrawing objects with,
        13.34
    deleting handles from, 13.33
    dialog box, 13.6-13.9
        icons in, 13.10-13.15
        "standoff in inches," 13.9, 13.16-
            13.20
    examples of, 13.1, 13.18-13.26
    graphics, 10.149
    initial caps, 13.40
    inside a graphic, 13.41
    "jump over," 13.14
    minimums and maximums, 13.1
    moving handles on boundaries of,
        13.32
    on master pages, 13.38
    problems with, 22.22
    putting text inside objects with,
        13.36
    removing, 10.150, 13.42
    resizing graphics without affecting,
        13.35
    rotated text, 4.286
    script for a custom star-shape, 20.76
    "standoff in inches," 13.9
    tabbing leaders over objects with,
        13.37

"text flow," 13.8
    using to create angled margins,
        13.39
"wrap all sides," 13.15
"wrap options," 13.7
Thin space, 4.217, 5.219, 5.221-5.222
    creating, 5.225
"This story has not been placed,"
    9.83, 17.31
Thoreau, Henry David, p. 562, 860
Threaded text blocks, 4.106-4.112,
    4.122-4.123
    creating headers/footers for, 20.81-
        20.100
    creating jump lines for, 4.183-4.184
    finding, 4.180
    re-uniting, 4.124
"Thumbnails," 19.84
    viewing a publication as, 20.125
    in detail, 20.144
TIFF, 10.5, 10.18, 10.32-10.38
    adjusting for commercial printing,
        10.93
    as scanned images, 10.55-10.65
    black and white, 10.32, 10.174
        example of, 10.37
        lightening, 10.210
    color applied to, 10.159
    compressing, 10.152-10.154
        codes for, 10.152
    converting PICT or EPS files into,
        10.31
    decompressing, 10.154
    examples of, 10.29, 10.37-10.38,
        10.62-10.65
    grayscaling, 10.32, 10.175-10.176
        examples of, 10.38, 10.65
        lightening, 10.210
    image controlling, 10.162-10.212
        adjusting appearance of, 10.209
        applying the same settings to
            several, 21.26
        as inline graphics, 10.217

lightening to a shadow through, 10.210
returning to original specs, 10.211
"magic-resizing," 10.20-10.22, 10.141-10.142
"Omit TIFF files," 19.91
palette color, 10.32
place icon for, 10.126
printing resolution options, 19.88-19.89
omitting when printing, 19.91
replacing with compressed, 10.153
saving files as, 10.95, 10.99-10.100
viewing at high resolution, 10.36, 10.157-158
"Tile"
in Story Editor, 9.34
multiple publications, 1.160-1.168, 1.177
drag-and-drop text, 1.167, 1.180, 4.86
dragging objects between, 1.179
"Tile," (Print) 19.75-19.78
"Auto overlap __ inches," 19.76
"Manual," 19.77-19.78
maximum overlap, 19.1
Tints, 16.7-16.8
as shown in color palette, 16.93
creating a tint of any color, 16.106
using to create more colors, 16.15
"Title" (Table of Contents), 15.52
"TOC and index prefix," 1.24, 1.33
in Index, 15.127
in Table of Contents, 15.61
Toolbox, 1.182
in Story Editor, 9.7
"Top" (paragraph rule), 7.24-7.32, 7.41-7.45
"Top of caps" leading, 5.36, 5.51-5.57
examples of, 5.55, 5.58
how to use, 5.64
sole advantage of using, 5.57

Topic lists
checking, 15.153
deleting, 15.179
entering with no page numbers, 15.145
importing, 15.154
"Topic section:" 15.110
"Topic:" (Index), 15.89
"Topic..." (Index), 15.86, 15.102
"Track," 4.205, 5.180
in the Control palette, 4.212
Track kerning, 5.180-5.185
Tracking, 5.5, 5.180-5.192
applying to selected text, 5.190
changing, 5.191
copying "Tracking Values" for remote printing, 19.135
"Edit tracks" Addition, 5.193-5.209
examples of, 5.187-5.189
inline graphics, 10.243, 10.244
removing, 5.192
using PM 4.x track values, 17.48
"Tracking Values"
copying for remote printing, 19.135
using previous version settings, 17.48
Transferring
PC PageMaker pubs to Pac PM, 17.47
Transparent
background (in lines), 2.59
lines, 2.53, 2.59
examples of, 2.62, 2.75
patterned lines and borders, 2.36
Trapping, 16.29-16.30
using online "Help," 16.127
"Traverse textblocks" Addition, 4.136-4.138, 4.180
Triple lines. *See also* Patterned lines
point sizes of, 7.40
Troubleshooting
running a diagnostic, 21.28
TrueType, 19.36-19.38
icon for, 19.36

preserve character shape, 1.235b
preserve line spacing, 1.235a
what to avoid, 19.38
when to use, 19.37
Tschihold, Jan, p. 873
TWAIN, 10.303-10.304
Image Importer, 17.12
Twain, Mark, pp. 118, 376, 658, 819
25% page view, 1.113
200% page view, 1.117
Type
alignment, 4.243-4.248
changing, 4.242
baseline-shift of, 4.205, 4.218
changing, 4.263
font, 4.205, 4.210
changing, 4.228
condensing, 4.238
defaults, 4.360-4.366
changing through the Control palette, 4.240
determining point size of for auto kerning, 5.167
expanding, 4.238
force justifying, 4.248-4.249
line breaks, preventing, 4.241
leading, 4.205, 4.216
changing, 4.234
lowercase, changing, 4.251
menu
font names in brackets, 22.49
position, changing, 4.253
reversing, 4.235-4.237
over a paragraph rule, 7.52
size, 4.205, 4.211
changing, 4.229-4.230
creating up to 1300 points, 21.22
relation to proportional leading, 7.20-7.21
specifications
changing, 4.219-4.235
in the Control palette, 4.206-4.218

in the Type specs dialog box, 4.205
making several changes at once, 4.239
while in Story Editor, 9.13, 9.26, 9.44
style, 4.205, 4.215
changing, 4.231-4.232
uppercase, changing, 4.251
"Type" (printer), 19.54
"Type options," 4.252, 4.255-4.261
dialog box, 4.205
Type Spec defaults, 4.360-4.366
setting for application, 4.365
setting for publication, 4.366
through the Control palette, 4.240
"Type Specs" dialog box, 4.205
"Type Style," 4.205, 4.215, 4.231-4.232
Typeface. *See* Fonts
Typewriter quotation marks
converting to real, 4.61
Typing
on a page, 4.25
problems
no text appearing on the screen, 22.16
text squishing up, 22.30
the wrong font continually showing up, 22.18
text into a bounding box, 1.319
Typographer's quotes
using, 1.234

U

Undo, 1.311
what you can, 1.312a
what you cannot, 1.312b
"Unknown file format." 22.40
"Unlink," 11.22, 11.35, 11.64
"Update," 11.36
OLE-embedded objects, 11.129
"Update all," 11.37

"Update automatically," 11.55, 11.57
"Update PPD" Addition, 19.166,
  19.171-19.178
  manually downloaded fonts and,
    19.176
  reasons to run, 19.171
  running, 19.178
  setting the updated PPD as
    an application default, 19.175
Updating
  choosing not to, 11.20-11.22
  choosing to, 11.17, 11.66
  graphic files, 10.105
  immediately, 11.66-11.67
  "Include complete copy?," 10.104-
    10.105 11.124
  preventing, 11.20-11.22
  setting options for, 11.77-11.78
Updike, John, p. 61
Uppercase
  changing, 4.251
**"Use Symbol font for special charac-
  ters,"** 19.104
"User dictionary," 5.242
  "Add word to user dictionary," 5.229,
    5.242-5.248
  adding words to, 9.120
  copying, 9.126
  Dictionary Editor and, 9.127-9.141
  hyphenating words in, 5.253, 9.121
  in foreign language dictionaries,
    9.100
  making a new, 9.126, 9.139
  removing words from, 5.254, 9.122
  switching, 9.124
Utilities menu
  in Story Editor, 9.24

V

Vector graphics, 10.23. *See also* Draw-
  type graphic
"Vertical-reflecting" button, 3.38, 3.82-
  3.8

Vertical ruler
  changing the unit of measure for,
    1.54, 1.225
  changing to picas, 5.9
  customizing, 1.55, 1.226
  measurement options, 1.40
  repositioning, 1.70, 1.72
"View" (Story Importer dialog box),
  4.77
  any story, 4.85
  copy text from, 4.85
Voltaire, pp. 374, 705

W

Warde, Beatrice, p. 433, 519
Watson, Thomas, p. 793
"Whole word"
  in "Change," 9.71-9.73
  in "Find," 9.54-9.56
"Widow control__ lines," 4.345
Widows, 4.340-4.347
"Width of column," 7.5, 7.11
"Width of text," 7.6, 7.12
Wildcard characters
  finding, 9.66
Williams, Jimmy, pp. 498, 501
Williams, Robin, pp. 235, 465, 472,
  835
Williams, Ryan, p. 473
Williams, Scarlett, p. 519
Wilson, E., p. 486
Window menu
  in Story Editor, 9.27
  submenu, 9.28
  list of open publications, 1.153
Windows
  "Cascade," 1.175
    in Story Editor, 9.33
  "Close all," 1.174
  creating more space within, 1.335
  "Tile," 1.177
    in Story Editor, 9.34

Windowshade loops, 4.106-4.109,
  4.111
Word. *See* Microsoft Word
"Word document object," 11.123
WordPerfect
  import filter for (Mac versions 1.0,
    2.x), 17.10
  import filter for (PC versions 4.2,
    5.0), 17.40
"Word removed," 9.122
"Word space," 5.5, 5.112-5.131
  changing values of, 5.124
  decreasing, 5.130
  desired, 5.116-5.117
  examples of, 5.128
  increasing, 5.129
  justified text with, 5.121, 5.128
  maximum, 5.123-5.124
  minimum, 5.122, 5.124
  resetting, 5.131
Wordsworth, William, p. 517
**"Word was not found in user
  dictionary,"** 9.122
Workgroups
  avoiding trouble in, 11.50
Wrapping text. *See* Text wrap
WriteNow (2.0 and 3.0)
  export filter for, 17.18
  import filter for, 17.10
"Write PostScript to file," 19.102
  creating an EPS file of a PageMaker
    page, 10.160
  "EPS," 10.160, 19.146, 19.148
  "Extra image bleed," 19.145
  for a service bureau, 19.157-19.158
  "For separations," 10.143, 19.147
    "Launch Aldus PrePrint," 19.143
  "Include downloadable fonts," 19.144
  "Normal," 19.139-19.141, 19.147
    printing hard copies yourself,
      19.149

X

X-coordinate, 3.60
"X-ref..." (Index), 15.103
"X-ref override:" 15.104
  formatting, 15.175
XyWrite III (PC)
  export filter for, 17.18
  import filter for, 17.33

Y

Y-coordinate, 3.60

Z

Zapf Dingbats, 1.332, 4.264
  changing direction of, 21.4
Zero point, 1.44-1.45, 1.47-1.48
  horizontal, 1.45
    default for, 1.48
    reposition, 1.71
  locking, 1.74a
  repositioning, 1.70
  reset default position, 1.73
  Scenario, 1.75
  unlocking, 1.74b
  using (Scenario), 1.75
  vertical, 1.47
    default for, 1.48
    reposition, 1.72
Zoom box
  for redrawing the screen, 5.70
  in "Cascade" view, 1.157
  in "Tile" view, 1.165

943

What do I do?

People always ask me what I do and I don't quite know what to say. I've written a few books, but I really wouldn't say I'm a Writer. My background is in graphic design, but I wouldn't call myself a Designer. I do have a particular passion for typography, but no one makes a living being a Typographer. I dance as often as I can, but I'm not really a Dancer. I love to teach, but the college only lets me teach part time so I certainly don't make a living as a Teacher. I suppose I could call myself a Consultant like everyone else, but I do hate to do what everyone else does. I am truly a mother of the three greatest kids in the world, but I've never had the privilege of having Mother as my sole occupation. If I had the option, I would like to study world literature and live theater and languages. I love to overcome obstacles. I work hard. I throw great parties. I sincerely believe that your attitude is your life.

What do I do? Well, I wear a lot of different hats.

And Who Are These Other People?

It was Robin's generosity as a teacher and friend that led me down the Macintosh way. Currently I work at home on a wide variety of desktop publishing projects and at the Santa Rosa Junior College where I get to share my love of typography and the Mac with both adults and kids. I live in the coastal hills of Cazadero, California and enjoy a techno-peasant lifestyle with my husband and daughters.

—Barbara Sikora

I live in the hills of Sonoma County on 14 acres with a creek, redwoods, sun, and views of the wine country below. I share the acreage with two cats, three dogs, miscellaneous wildlife, and a great husband. I have a background in graphic design and journalism and write extensively for various publications throughout Northern California. My passions, other than my husband, are travel, food and wine, hiking, gardening, great music heard in front of the fireplace, and words. I love words—mine or anyone else's!

—Vicki Calkins

Sally Forth ® By Greg Howard and Craig MacIntosh

The first time around this book was created entirely in PageMaker: versions 3.0, 4.0, 4.01. This time it was created entirely in PageMaker 5.0 and 5.0a.

The first half of the first edition of the book was created on an SE with one meg of RAM. The second half was created on a Mac IIcx with lots of RAM. The revised edition was created on a Mac IIci and a Quadra 700. Parts of it were even worked on with a PowerBook 140 with RamDoubler.

Main fonts are ITC Baskerville and Futura, both from Adobe. Lots of other fonts from Bitstream, Emigre, LaserMaster, and Linotype-Hell.

Concept, design, and layout by Robin.

Pampered out of Lino by Janet Butcher, Petaluma Imagesetting, Petaluma, California.

Order Form

Peachpit Press
2414 Sixth Street ▾ Berkeley ▾ California ▾ 94710
phone: 800.283.9444 or **510.548.4393**
fax: 510.548.5991

Everyone's Guide to Successful Publications	$28.00	
How to Boss Your Fonts Around	$12.95	
Jargon: An Informal Dictionary of Computer Terms	$22.00	
The Little Mac Book, 3rd Edition	$16.00	
The Macintosh Bible, 5th Edition	$30.00	
The Macintosh Bible CD-ROM	$25.00	
The Mac is not a typewriter	$ 9.95	
The Non-Designer's Design Book	$14.95	
Real World Scanning and Halftones	$24.95	
Tabs & Indents on the Macintosh	$12.00	
ZAP! How Your Computer Can Hurt …	$12.95	

Shipping .... UPS Ground

First item $4

Each Additional $1

Subtotal	
Add Applicable Sales Tax	
Shipping	
TOTAL	

Name

Company

Address

City

State   Zip

Phone

▽ Check enclosed
▽ Visa
▽ MasterCard

Credit Card Number

Expiration Date

EVERYONE'S GUIDE TO SUCCESSFUL PUBLICATIONS

Elizabeth Adler

Packed with ideas, practical advice, and examples, this reference book discusses planning the printed piece, writing, design, desktop publishing, preparation for printing, and distribution. $28 *(412 pages)*

HOW TO BOSS YOUR FONTS AROUND

Robin Williams

Ever had a power struggle with your fonts? This book will put *you* in control and answer all your Macintosh font questions. Learn about screen fonts, outline fonts, resident fonts, downloadable fonts, ATM, and how to avoid font conflicts and hassles. $12.95 *(120 pages)*

JARGON: AN INFORMAL DICTIONARY OF COMPUTER TERMS

Robin Williams with Steve Cummings

Jargon is a terrific compendium of over 1,200 of the most useful computer terms explained in a way anyone can understand. Covers both the Macintosh and PC worlds. $22 *(688 pages)*

THE LITTLE MAC BOOK, 3RD EDITION

Robin Williams

This concise, beautifully written book covers the basics of Macintosh operation. It provides useful reference information, including charts of typefaces, special characters, and keyboard shortcuts. Totally updated for System 7.1. $16 *(336 pages)*

THE MACINTOSH BIBLE, 5TH EDITION

Edited by Darcy DiNucci

This classic reference book for the Mac is now completely updated. The Fifth Edition is crammed with tips, tricks, and shortcuts to get the most out of your Mac. $30 *(1,100 pages)*

THE MACINTOSH BIBLE CD-ROM

Edited by Jeremy Judson

Here's a collection on CD-ROM of the best shareware and clip media available. You get hundreds of megabytes of valuable software and reference information for your Macintosh! $25 *(CD-ROM)*

THE MAC IS NOT A TYPEWRITER

Robin Williams

This best-selling, elegant guide to typesetting on the Mac has received rave reviews for its clearly presented information, friendly tone, and easy access. Twenty quick and easy chapters cover what you need to know to make your documents look clean and professional. $9.95 *(72 pages)*

THE NON-DESIGNER'S DESIGN BOOK

Robin Williams

Do you have little background in design and typography, but find yourself designing pages? Do you want to make your printed pages look better and learn how to effectively use type? Learn about design and typographic principles that will help you avoid the common pitfalls of most beginners' work. $14.95 *(144 pages)*

REAL WORLD SCANNING AND HALFTONES

David Blatner and Steve Roth

Master the digital halftone process—from scanning images to tweaking them on your computer to imagesetting them. Learn about optical character recognition, gamma control, sharpening, PostScript halftones, Photo CD and image-manipulating applications like Photoshop and PhotoStyler. $24.95 *(296 pages)*

TABS & INDENTS

Robin Williams

Tabs and indents can be confusing. But with help from Robin Williams you will learn how tabs and indents can become powerful tools that will make your documents more attractive and your work more productive. This simple, tutorial-style guide covers a variety of popular software and comes with a companion disk. $12 *(64 pages with disk)*

ZAP! HOW YOUR COMPUTER CAN HURT YOU—AND WHAT YOU CAN DO ABOUT IT

Don Sellers

This book tackles the critical issues of computer-related health. Learn hundreds of remedies and resources to help you work smarter and healthier. $12.95 *(150 pages)*